The **Rough Guide** to

Ecuador

D0169555

written and researched by

Harry Adès and Melissa Graham

ROUGH
GUIDES

NEW YORK • LONDON • DELHI

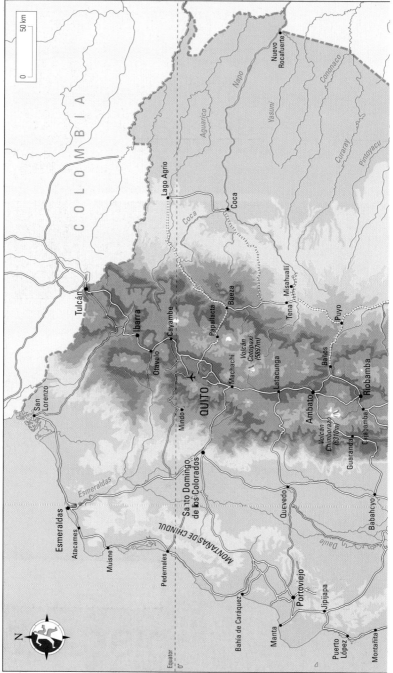

N

COLOMBIA

Esmeraldas
Atacames
Muisne
Pedernales
San Lorenzo
Tulcán
Ibarra
Otavalo
Cayambe
Lago Agrio
Coca
Nuevo Rocafuerte

Bahía de Caráquez
Manta
Portoviejo
Jipijapa
Puerto López
Montañita

Santo Domingo de los Colorados
MONTAÑAS DE CHINDUL

Quevedo
Babahoyo

Mindo
QUITO
Machachi
Volcán Cotopaxi (5897m)
Latacunga
Ambato
Volcán Chimborazo (6310m)
Guaranda
Guabanda
Riobamba

Papallacta
Baeza
Tena
Misahualli
Baños
Puyo

Esmeraldas
Daule
Coca
Aguarico
Napo
Yasuni
Curaray
Cononaco
Pintoyacu

Equator
0°

Galápagos Islands (980km)

0   50 km

ii

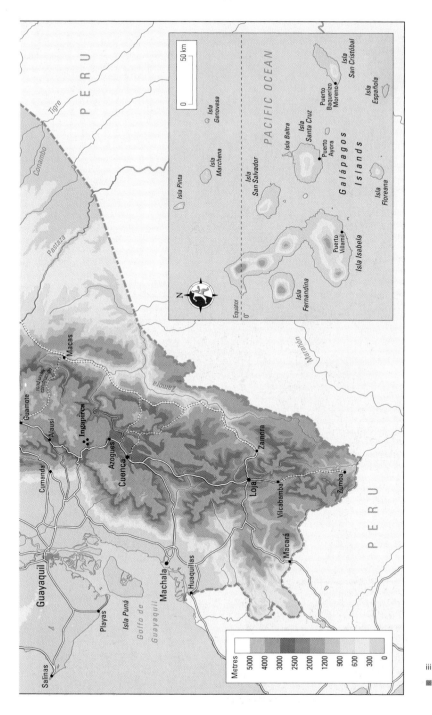

50 km

PACIFIC OCEAN

Isla San Cristóbal
Puerto Baquerizo Moreno
Isla Española

Isla Genovesa

Isla Marchena

Isla Pinta

Isla Baltra
Isla Santa Cruz
Puerto Ayora

Isla San Salvador

Galápagos Islands

Isla Floreana

Isla Fernandina

Puerto Villamil
Isla Isabela

N

Equator 0°

PERU

Tigre

Conambo

Pastaza

Marañón

Zamora

Macas

road under construction

Guamote

Alausí

Ingapirca

Azogues

Cuenca

Zamora

Cumanda

Loja

Vilcabamba

Zumba

Macará

Huaquillas

Machala

Guayaquil

Salinas

Playas

Isla Puná

Golfo de Guayaquil

PERU

Metres
5000
4000
3000
2500
2000
1200
900
600
300
0

iii

Introduction to

Ecuador

"Ecuador, so tiny on the map of the world, has always possessed the grandeur of a great country to those who know her well."

Albert B. Franklin, *Ecuador: Portrait of a People*

Sitting on the equator between Colombia and Peru, Ecuador is the smallest of the Andean nations, covering an area no bigger than Nevada. For all its diminutive size, however, the country is packed with startling contrasts of scenery, from steaming tropical rainforests and windswept highlands to ice-capped volcanoes and palm-fringed beaches, all within easy reach of the capital, Quito. In this land of bold contours and bright colours, you can find yourself beneath a canopy of dripping vegetation amongst clouds of neon-coloured butterflies one day, and in a highland market mixing with scarlet-ponchoed *indígenas* the next.

The country also features astounding biodiversity, boasting some 1600 species of bird (more per square kilometre than any other South American country), 4500 butterflies and more than 3500 orchids, and a considerable historic and cultural legacy, with stunning colonial architecture and a diverse array of indigenous groups. Not surprisingly, many travellers regard Ecuador as a microcosm of South America, offering a pocket-sized version of almost everything one could hope to find on this bewitching continent. Perhaps Ecuador's greatest attractions, though, are its Galápagos Islands, whose extraordinary wildlife played a pivotal role in shaping Charles Darwin's theories on evolution.

v

Fact file

- In **area** Ecuador is around 285,000 square kilometres – roughly equivalent to the US state of Arizona, or the United Kingdom combined with Belgium.

- Spanish is the official **language** of Ecuador, but there are more than twenty other native tongues, including several dialects of Quichua, the language of the Inca Empire.

- The majority of Ecuador's fourteen million **people** are *mestizos*, a quarter are indigenous peoples from more than a dozen native groups, and the remaining ten percent are divided between black descendants of slaves and whites of Spanish extraction.

- The Spanish first established the rough boundaries of what is now Ecuador in 1563, and the country became an **independent republic** in 1830, when it was officially named for the equator running through it. Voting is compulsory for any literate person aged between 18 and 65, and optional for other eligible citizens.

- Ecuador's **main exports** are petroleum products, bananas, coffee, cacao, cut flowers and shrimp. Despite its large oil reserves and rich farmland, the economy is often severely affected by fluctuation in world commodity prices. The country's external debt is $19 billion, and more than seventy percent of its people live in poverty.

Ecuador's mainland divides neatly into three distinct regions running the length of the country in parallel strips. In the middle is the **sierra**, formed by the eastern and western chains of the Andes and punctuated by more than thirty volcanoes. Joined by a series of high plateaux at around 2800m above sea level, the two chains are separated by gentle transverse ridges, or *nudos* ("knots" of hills), which make up the agricultural and indigenous heartland of Ecuador, a region of patchwork fields on the mountainsides, stately haciendas and dozens of remote communities. The sierra is also home to many of the country's oldest and most important cities, including Quito. East of the sierra is the **Oriente**, a large, sparsely populated area extending into the upper Amazon basin, much of it covered by dense tropical rainforest – an exhilarating, exotic region, though under increasing threat from the oil industry and colonization. West of the sierra, a fertile alluvial plain forms the **coastal region**, the site of tropical croplands for bananas, sugar, coffee and cacao, bordered on its Pacific seaboard by a string of beaches, mangrove swamps, shrimp farms and ports. Almost a thousand kilometres of ocean separate the coast-

Volcanoes

Ecuador lies on the "Ring of Fire", part of a highly seismic zone that encircles the Pacific. It's one of the most volcanically active areas on the continent, and the two cordilleras of the Ecuadorian Andes here are studded with snow-crested cones looming into the sky either side of a broad central valley, which the explorer Alexander von Humboldt grandly called the "avenue of the volcanoes". While many of the country's 55 volcanic peaks are extinct, eight remain active, while another nine have erupted in the last few thousand years and are classified as "potentially active". Anyone who stays for a few months is likely to feel a small earth tremor or see puffs of

volcanic ash curling into the air from a summit on the horizon. Every now and then volcanoes overshadowing population centres, such as Guagua Pichincha above Quito or Tungurahua by Baños, rumble into life triggering civil safety precautions. Nevertheless, Ecuador's volcanoes – which include the furthest point from the centre of the Earth (Chimborazo), the highest point on the equator (Cayambe), and one of the highest active peaks in the world (Cotopaxi) – are spectacular fixtures, attracting mountaineers from across the globe and admiration from all who see them.

line from the **Galápagos** archipelago (annexed by Ecuador in 1832), which offers a wondrous display of endemic birds, mammals, reptiles and plants.

Ecuador's regions provide a home to some fourteen million people, the majority of whom live on the coast and in the sierra. For the most part, they are descendants of the various **indigenous groups** who first inhabited Ecuador's territory twelve thousand years ago, **Incas** who colonized the land in the late fifteenth century, **Spaniards** who conquered the Incas in the 1530s and **African slaves** brought by Spanish colonists. Although the mixing of blood over the centuries has resulted in a largely **mestizo** (mixed) population, the indigenous element remains very strong, particularly among the Quichua-speaking communities of the rural sierra, and the various ethnic groups of the Oriente such as the Shuar, Achuar, Huaorani and Secoya, while on the north coast there's a significant black population. As in many parts of Latin America, **social and economic divisions** between *indígenas*, blacks, *mestizos* and an elite class of whites remain deeply entrenched, exacerbated by a slew of recurrent economic and political crises. And yet, even though the national currency has been replaced by the US dollar, poverty and unemployment continue to worsen, and political leaders repeatedly fail to tackle the country's problems, the overwhelming majority of Ecuadorians remain resilient, remarkably cheerful, and very courteous and welcoming towards visitors.

Where to go

Thanks to its compact size, travelling around Ecuador is easy and relatively fast, with few places more than a day's bus ride from the capital. Unlike the attractions found in larger South American countries such as Brazil, Argentina and Chile, Ecuador's contrasting regions and highlights are within easy reach of each other, allowing for a more flexible approach to route-planning.

Many travellers regard Ecuador as a microcosm of South America

The majority of visitors fly in to **Quito**, whose glorious if chaotic colonial centre – a maze of narrow streets and exquisite monasteries and churches – demands at least a couple of days to explore. Its modern **new town** is packed with hotels, restaurants and services that make it a convenient base for excursions. Striking north from Quito, the **northern sierra's** green valleys are dappled with glistening lakes and crested by volcanic peaks, and the area is famed for its **artesanías**, centres of native craftwork, leather goods and woodcarving all within a short bus ride of each other. Of these, **Otavalo** is undoubtedly the biggest attraction, thanks to its enormous Saturday market – one of the continent's most renowned – and flourishing weaving industry. The region also offers plenty of scope for walkers and horse-riding enthusiasts, who should consider splashing out on a stay in any of several beautiful converted **haciendas**. The attractive regional capital, **Ibarra**, is dominated by elegant nineteenth-century architecture and is far less touristy than nearby Otavalo. South of Quito, the **central sierra** is home to the most spectacular of the country's volcanoes, including the snow-capped cone of **Cotopaxi**, and **Chimborazo**, Ecuador's highest peak at 6310m. Also in this rural region are some of the more exciting **markets** in the sierra, such as those of the villages of Saquisilí and Zumbahua, and the small town of Guamote. Rewarding off-the-beaten-track destinations include the dazzling crater lake of **Laguna Quilotoa**, with its remote páramo setting, while more established attractions include the busy little spa town of **Baños**, framed by soaring green peaks, and the **train** ride down the **Nariz del Diablo** ("the Devil's Nose") from **Riobamba**, the most fetching of the central sierra's cities. In the **southern sierra** lies the captivating colonial city of

Handicrafts

For many of Ecuador's indigenous people, artistic expression finds its outlet in the production of handicrafts, highly localized artisanal traditions that have passed down the generations and in some cases predate the Spanish conquest. The most notable of them is weaving, a skill that was exploited ruthlessly by the conquistadors in hacienda workshops, particularly in the Otavalo region where traditional techniques are still used alongside modern looms to supply one of the largest craft markets on the continent. Nowadays, whether it be at a classy Quito boutique or seductive highland market, there's a fantastic array of Ecuadorian crafts to be had, often at very good prices, ranging from wall hangings, baskets, clothes and traditional garments to wood carvings, leatherwork, naïve paintings, musical instruments, and carved gourds and tagua nuts. As if this wasn't enough, Ecuador's best known craft export is the world-famous but sadly misnamed Panama hat (see p.402), which is still woven by hand in family homes and workshops on the coast and around Cuenca. For more details on Ecuador's varied handicrafts see "Basics" p.49.

Cuenca, recently declared a UNESCO World Heritage Site and a convenient base for visiting **Ingapirca** – the country's only major Inca ruins – and **Parque Nacional El Cajas**, a starkly beautiful wilderness. Further south, the charming city of **Loja** is a jumping-off point for visits to the **Parque Nacional Podocarpus**, whose humid lower reaches are particularly sumptuous, and the easy-going mountain village of **Vilcabamba**, a popular gringo hangout.

The **Oriente** embodies one of Ecuador's greatest wildernesses, a thick carpet of **tropical rainforest** unfurling for almost 300km, which was home only to isolated indigenous groups and the odd Christian mission until the discovery of oil here in the late 1960s. Since then, the region's infrastructure has developed at pace, allowing easier access to the **Amazonian jungle** than any other Andean country. Two of the country's largest wild areas – the **Reserva Faunística Cuyabeno** and the **Parque Nacional Yasuní** – and a number of private reserves protect substantial forests that have survived the incursions of the oil industry and colonists. Jungle lodges, many of them a canoe ride down the **Río Napo**, make for the most comfortable way of experiencing the thrill of this diverse and exciting habitat, while guided tours are often inexpensive and straightforward to arrange. You can't do better, though, than staying with an indigenous community for a glimpse of the jungle's resident peoples. In the north, **Tena** and **Misahuallí** are the best towns from which to organize a jungle trip, though the bigger and grittier oil centres of **Lago Agrio** and **Coca** are the gateways to the most remote forests and reserves. Tourism is considerably less developed in the southern Oriente, though the towns of **Puyo** and **Macas** offer possibilities for ecotourism through local indigenous groups, even as many of the more isolated destinations can be reached only by light aircraft.

A few hours' drive from Quito on the

x

■

Wildlife and nature

Unmatched by any country of its size, Ecuador's considerable biodiversity includes more than 25,000 plant species, or ten percent of the world total, compared to around 17,000 for all of North America. Its 1600 types of birds are about twice as many as all of Europe and half the total for South America, and it also holds more varieties of mammals and amphibians per square metre than any other country on Earth.

This extraordinary concentration of wildlife is largely due to Ecuador's unique geography, its position on the equator and the geologically recent appearance of Andean cordilleras, which divide the coastal and Amazonian basins and provide an array of habitats and isolated areas for the evolution of new species. The country's highly varied terrain encompasses Andean mountains, parched semi-desert scrub, chilly high-altitude grasslands, subtropical cloudforests, tropical rainforests, dry forests, mangrove forests, warm Pacific beaches and the unique environment of the Galápagos Islands.

way to the coast, a number of private **reserves** showcase the country's beautiful **cloudforests** – otherworldly gardens of gnarled and tangled vegetation, wrapped in mosses and vines, and drenched daily in mist – and provide accommodation and guides for exploring or bird watching, with some of the best sites on the western slopes of the Andes. The village of **Mindo**, enveloped in richly forested hills brimming with endemic species, is the birding capital of the country. Continuing westward, Ecuador's varied coastline begins at the Colombian border in a profusion of **mangrove** swamps, protected by the **Reserva Ecológica Manglares Cayapas-Mataje** and best visited by canoe from **San Lorenzo**, a down-at-heel town rich in Afro-Ecuadorian culture. The surrounding **north coast** is best known, however, for its **beaches**. The boisterous resort at **Atacames** is one of the most popular, though there are quieter places to enjoy the warm Pacific waters, including **Súa**, **Same**, **Muisne** and **Canoa**. Among the chief attractions of the **southern coast** is **Parque Nacional Machalilla**, with its dry and humid forests, superb beaches and impressive birdlife on its offshore island, **Isla de la Plata**. Further down the coast, **Montañita** is rapidly gaining popularity with surfers and backpackers, while **Salinas** is perhaps the country's most prestigious seaside resort. **Guayaquil**, the region's main port and the largest city in Ecuador, is a frenetic and humid spot that's slowly emerging as a tourist destination, while quieter attractions include the mangrove forests of the **Reserva**

Ecológica Manglares Churute, the warm, picturesque hill village of **Zaruma** and the petrified forest of **Puyango**.

Finally, the **Galápagos Islands** are for many visitors the initial lure to the country, and arguably the most compelling natural spot in the world. Almost 170 years since Darwin dropped anchor there, the forbidding volcanic islands and their motley assortment of creatures still provide enchantment to anyone who sees them.

When to go

There's no real summer and winter in Ecuador, and its **weather** generally varies by regional geography, with temperatures determined more by altitude than by season or latitude. The warmest and driest months in the sierra are June to September, though this is complicated by various microclimates found in some areas. Outside these months, typical **sierra** weather offers sunny, clear mornings and cloudy, often wet, afternoons. In the **Oriente**, you can expect it to be warm, humid and rainy throughout the year, though there are often short breaks from the daily

Average temperatures (°C) and rainfall (mm)

	Jan	Feb	Mar	Apr	May	Jun	Jul	Aug	Sep	Oct	Nov	Dec
Quito (sierra)												
Max	19	19	19	19	19	19	19	19	20	19	19	19
Min	10	10	10	11	11	9	9	9	9	9	9	10
Rainfall	114	130	152	175	124	48	20	25	79	127	109	104
Guayaquil (coast)												
Max	31	31	32	32	31	29	29	29	30	29	30	31
Min	23	24	24	24	23	22	21	21	21	22	23	23
Rainfall	224	279	287	180	53	18	3	0	3	3	3	30
Puyo (Oriente)												
Av daily	21	20	21	21	21	20	19	20	20	21	21	21
Rainfall	302	297	429	465	409	457	389	345	366	381	363	333
Nuevo Rocafuerte (Oriente)												
Av daily	26	25	25	25	25	24	23	24	25	25	25	26
Rainfall	160	188	206	284	356	320	295	224	241	229	198	152
Puerto Ayora (Galápagos)												
Max	28	30	31	30	28	26	25	24	24	25	26	27
Min	23	23	23	23	22	21	20	19	19	20	20	21
Rainfall	44	56	80	73	70	49	25	8	10	11	11	41

rains from August to September and December to February. In the **lowlands** it can get particularly hot on clear days, with temperatures easily topping 30°C. The **coast** has the most clearly defined wet and dry seasons, and the best time to visit is from December to April, featuring frequent showers alternating with clear blue skies and warm weather. From May to November the **southern coast**, in particular, is often overcast and relatively cool, with less chance of rainfall. The **Galápagos** climate sees hot, sunny days interspersed with the odd heavy shower from January to June, and dry and overcast weather for the rest of the year, when the *garúa* mists are prevalent. **El Niño** years (see pp.522 & 538) can bring enormous fluctuations in weather patterns on the coast and at the Galápagos archipelago, when levels of rainfall can be many times the norm.

23
things not to miss

It's not possible to see everything that Ecuador has to offer in one trip — and we don't suggest you try. What follows is a selective and subjective taste of the country's highlights: fun festivals, outstanding beaches, spectacular wildlife and extraordinary landscapes. They're arranged in five colour-coded categories, so you can browse through to find the very best things to see, do, buy and experience. All highlights have a page reference to take you straight into the guide, where you can find out more.

01 **Mama Negra Fiesta** Page **194** • One of the country's best-loved festivals features a carnival of dazzling costumes, dancing troupes and marching bands parading through the streets of Latacunga.

02 Museo del Banco Central Page **98** • See the riches of more than five thousand years of Ecuadorian culture at the country's top museum, which includes in its collection some of the oldest ceramics discovered on the continent, exquisite pre-Columbian worked gold, and masterpieces of colonial and modern art.

03 Ingapirca Page **242** • Perched on a hillside overlooking serene pastoral countryside, Ecuador's best-preserved Inca ruins exhibit the fine stonemasonry and trapezoidal doorways that were the hallmarks of their architecture.

04 Termas de Papallacta Page **293** • Fantastic hot springs complex couched in a peaceful páramo valley, the perfect setting for a long, hot, al fresco soak, especially as the sun dips behind the mountain ridges to reveal a dazzling star-filled sky.

05 **Nariz del Diablo train ride** Page **227** • Experience one of the world's great feats of railway engineering from the roof of a train as it descends the Andes over the "Devil's Nose" in a sequence of thrilling switchback turns.

06 **Climbing Cotopaxi** Page **188** • Ecuador is a paradise for experienced climbers, but even complete novices under guidance can have a crack at Cotopaxi, one of the highest active volcanoes in the world.

07
Orchids
Pages **352**, **354** & **357** • A miracle of biodiversity, Ecuador is thought to have more orchid species than any other country on Earth.

08 **Galápagos wildlife** Pages **455** & **538** ● The fearless creatures ekeing out an existence on a few scarred volcanic islands that inspired Darwin, still give an unparalleled insight into the mechanics of nature at work. The Galápagos Islands comprise one of the world's most treasured wildlife destinations; indeed, numerous visitors bypass the rest of Ecuador (save Quito) altogether in favour of a trip here. Below is a very brief sampling of the diversity you'll encounter on the islands – check out Chapter 8 as well as the piece on Galápagos wildlife in the Contexts section for specific locations of where you can see all the various animals.

Giant tortoise

Hammerhead shark

Nesting magnificent frigate birds

Brown pelican

Masked booby

Whale at sunset

Sea lion

Sally lightfoot crab

Marine iguanas

09 **Otavalo market** Page **144** • Even hardened skinflints won't be able to resist bagging a few of the fabulous handicrafts and weavings on offer at one of the largest and most colourful artesanía markets on the continent.

10 **Jungle observation towers** Page **288** • From the rainforest floor it's sometimes difficult to discern wildlife in the treetops, but several jungle lodges feature observation towers that soar above the vegetation to give unbeatable views across the forest canopy.

11 **Quito** Page **72** • A mixture of church spires, tiled roofs and skyscrapers glinting in the sunlight against the brooding backdrop of Volcán Pichincha, the second highest capital in the world is an enthralling blend of urban and traditional indigenous cultures.

12 Contemporary art Pages **101**, **102** & **199** • Ecuador's great modern artists are like the conscience of the nation, influential social commentators whose work, on view at several impressive galleries, shouldn't be ignored.

13 Isla de la Plata Page **450** • A short jaunt by boat from the mainland gives access to large colonies of seabirds, such as blue-footed boobies and waved albatrosses – a flavour of the Galápagos at a fraction of the cost.

14 Pahoehoe lava Page **486** & **497** • You don't have to be a geologist to admire the squiggles, ripples and tongues of this extraordinary lava formation, resembling a petrified lake of rumpled ooze, found at several sites in the Galápagos.

15 **Cerro Santa Ana** Page **429** • It's hard to imagine that only a few years ago the picturesque buildings lining an elegant stairway up to a spectacular viewpoint over downtown Guayaquil were part of a notorious slum.

17 **Baños** Page **209** • Whether it's nibbling on the local specialty, *melcocha* (a sticky toffee made in shop doorways), wallowing in thermal baths, or hiking, biking or rafting in the surrounding countryside, there's plenty to keep you occupied in this charming spa town.

16 **Colonial Cuenca** Page **250** • Pristine colonial architecture, cobbled streets, illustrious churches and flowering plazas give Cuenca a distinguished air and the well-deserved reputation of being the country's most enchanting city.

18 Páramo Page **168** • High-altitude grassland wildernesses rolling uninterrupted for miles between lonely, mist-shrouded lakes in many of the country's highland reserves – the páramo is bleak, cold and wet, but hauntingly beautiful.

20 Good Friday in Quito's old town Page **109** • Staged amongst the majestic buildings of the historic centre, the capital's most important religious procession is a window on Quito's colonial past.

19 La Compañía Page **92** • Quito's centre is packed with magnificent churches, monasteries and convents, but few can match La Compañía's outstanding Baroque facade and sumptuous interior.

xxiii

21 Laguna Quilotoa Page **200** • This glittering green crater lake sits at the heart of a popular scenic diversion through the beguiling landscapes and villages of the rural highlands.

22 Zumbahua market

Page **199** • As the early-morning mists rise from Zumbahua into the hills, the village plaza fills each Saturday with locals huddled up in colourful shawls and ponchos keen to trade their produce and livestock at the quintessential indigenous highland market.

23 Atacames Page **379** • A laid-back seaside resort by day, Atacames pulsates at night to thumping music blaring from dozens of beachfront bars, where revellers show off their salsa skills and sip rum cocktails into the small hours.

Contents

Using this Rough Guide

We've tried to make this Rough Guide a good read and easy to use. The book is divided into six main sections, and you should be able to find whatever you want in one of them.

Colour section

The front colour section offers a quick tour of Ecuador. The **introduction** aims to give you a feel for the place, with suggestions on where to go. We also tell you what the weather is like and include a basic country fact file. Next, our authors round up their favourite aspects of Ecuador in the **things not to miss** section – whether it's great food, amazing sights or a special hotel. Right after this comes a full **contents** list.

Basics

The Basics section covers all the **pre-departure** nitty-gritty to help you plan your trip. This is where to find out which airlines fly to your destination, what paperwork you'll need, what to do about money and insurance, about Internet access, food, security, public transport, car rental – in fact just about every piece of **general practical information** you might need.

Guide

This is the heart of the Rough Guide, divided into user-friendly chapters, each of which covers a specific region. Every chapter starts with a list of **highlights** and an **introduction** that helps you to decide where to go, depending on your time and budget. Likewise, introductions to the various towns and smaller regions within each chapter should help you plan your itinerary. We start most town accounts with information on arrival and accommodation, followed by a tour of the sights, and finally reviews of places to eat and drink, and details of nightlife. Longer accounts also have a directory of practical listings. Each chapter concludes with **public transport** details for that region.

Contexts

Read Contexts to get a deeper understanding of what makes Ecuador tick. We include a brief history and coverage of **wildlife** both on the mainland and in the Galápagos Islands, together with a detailed further reading section that reviews dozens of **books** relating to the country.

Language

The **language** section gives useful guidance for speaking Ecuadorian Spanish and pulls together all the vocabulary you might need on your trip, including a comprehensive **menu reader**. Here you'll also find a **glossary** of words and terms peculiar to the country.

Index + small print

Apart from a **full index**, which includes maps as well as places, this section covers publishing information, credits and acknowledgements, and also has our contact details in case you want to send in updates and corrections to the book – or suggestions as to how we might improve it.

Chapter list and map

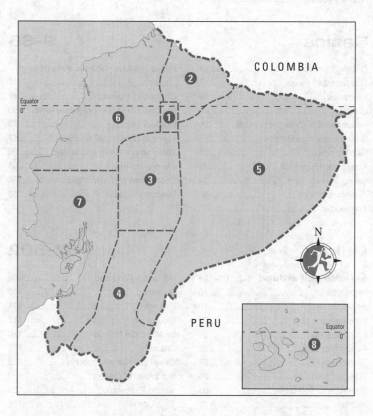

Contents

Contexts

Language

Index and small print

Map symbols

maps are listed in the full index using coloured text

-----	International boundary		〰	Mountain range
—--	Provincial boundary		⌂	Cave
----	Chapter boundary		〽	Rocks
═══	Road		🏄	Waterfall
:::::	Unpaved road		■	Restaurant
——	Track/seasonal road		◉	Accommodation
▥▥▥	Steps		★	Public transport stop
▬▬▬	Pedestrianized street		Ⓣ	Trole stop
------	Path		Ⓔ	Ecovía stop
━┿━	Railway		⊞	Hospital
——	Waterway		ⓒ	Telephone office
——	Wall		ⓘ	Information office
✈	Airport		⊠	Post office
♦	Point of interest		@	Internet access
ⱡ	Church (regional maps)		🅿	Parking
∴	Ruins		⊠—⊠	Gate
♟	Museum		▮	Building
⌂	Lodge		⊞	Church (town maps)
ⵟ	Lighthouse		⬭	Stadium
☉	Statue/monument		▦	Cemetery
⚘	Viewpoint		▨	Parks/reserves
〰	Spring/spa		▨	Beach
⩘	Volcano		▨	Forest
⊛	Crater		▨	Glacier
▲	Mountain peak			

Basics

Basics

Getting there

Outside of Latin America, there are only a handful of airlines and departure points offering direct flights to Ecuador. In the United States, regular services leave from Miami, Houston and New York for Ecuador's two international airports at Quito and Guayaquil, while in Europe direct flights are available from Amsterdam and Madrid. Airlines running these routes, however, have connecting flights from many other destinations, meaning that in most cases you can reach Ecuador with only one change of aircraft. For travellers already in **Latin America**, there are also regular direct services from Bogotá, Caracas, Havana, Lima, Panama City, San José and Santiago, plus connecting flights from many cities.

Airfares always depend on the **season**, with the high season being July to August, early December to mid-January and the weeks surrounding Easter; fares drop during the low season, mid-January to June and September to November. Prices also vary depending on the length of your stay and the flexibility of your ticket. You can often cut costs by going through a **specialist flight agent** – either a consolidator, who buys up blocks of tickets from the airlines and sells them at a discount, or a **discount agent**, who in addition to dealing with discounted flights may also offer special student and youth fares and a range of other travel-related services such as travel insurance and tours.

If Ecuador is only one stop on a longer journey, you might want to consider buying a **Round-the-World** (RTW) ticket. Some travel agents can sell you an "off-the-shelf" RTW ticket that will have you touching down in about half a dozen cities, though Quito doesn't figure particularly regularly on these itineraries. Otherwise, you can get an RTW ticket tailored to your needs, which can be more expensive, typically starting from around £1400/US$2200.

You could also consider an **open-jaw** ticket if you're planning to include Ecuador as part of a South American tour. This lets you make your own way overland between your arrival and departure points, the "jaws" of your flight. Popular combinations are Quito and Lima, or Quito and La Paz, and tickets cost about the same as a normal return ticket. In a similar vein, **stopovers** are often offered at the connection points, if you have any, on your air route to or from the country.

Ecuador is too small to warrant its own **airpass**, but is included in larger networks, such as the All America Airpass (ⓦwww.allairpass.com), which connects hundreds of destinations and 30 airlines across North and South America. While this is good value if you plan on flying between the two continents, you're best off buying individual tickets if you're just making short hops across South America.

Booking flights online

Many airlines and discount travel websites offer you the opportunity to book your tickets online, cutting out the costs of agents and middlemen. Good deals can often be found through discount or auction sites, as well as through the airlines' own websites.

Online booking agents and general travel sites

ⓦ**www.travel.yahoo.com** Incorporates a lot of Rough Guide material in its coverage of destination countries and cities across the world, with information about places to eat and sleep, etc.
ⓦ**www.cheapflights.com** Bookings from the UK and Ireland only (for US, ⓦwww.cheapflight.com; for Canada, ⓦwww.cheapflights.ca; for Australia, ⓦwww.cheapflights.com.au). Flight deals, travel agents, plus links to other travel sites.
ⓦ**www.cheaptickets.com** Discount flight specialists (US only).
ⓦ**www.etn.nl/discount.htm** A hub of

consolidator and discount agent Web links, maintained by the non-profit European Travel Network.

ⓦ **www.expedia.com** Discount airfares, all-airline search engine and daily deals (US only; for the UK, ⓦ www.expedia.co.uk; for Canada, ⓦ www.expedia.ca).

ⓦ **www.flyaow.com** Online air travel info and reservations site.

ⓦ **www.gaytravel.com** Gay online travel agent, offering accommodation, cruises, tours and more.

ⓦ **www.geocities.com/thavery2000** Has an extensive list of airline toll-free numbers (from the US) and websites.

ⓦ **www.hotwire.com** Bookings from the US only. Last-minute savings of up to forty percent on regular published fares. Travellers must be at least 18 and there are no refunds, transfers or changes allowed. Log-in required.

ⓦ **www.priceline.com** Name-your-own-price website that has deals at around forty percent off standard fares. You cannot specify flight times (although you do specify dates) and the tickets are non-refundable, non-transferable and non-changeable (US only; for the UK, ⓦ www.priceline.co.uk).

ⓦ **www.skyauction.com** Bookings from the US only. Auctions tickets and travel packages using a "second bid" scheme. The best strategy is to bid the maximum you're willing to pay, since if you win you'll pay just enough to beat the runner-up regardless of your maximum bid.

ⓦ **www.smilinjack.com/airlines.htm** Lists an up-to-date compilation of airline website addresses.

ⓦ **www.travelocity.com** Destination guides, hot Web fares and best deals for car hire, accommodation and lodging as well as fares. Provides access to the travel agent system SABRE, the most comprehensive central reservations system in the US.

ⓦ **www.travelshop.com.au** Australian website offering discounted flights, packages, insurance and online bookings.

Flights from the UK and Ireland

There are no direct flights to Ecuador from Britain, but there are plenty of indirect flights to both Quito and Guayaquil involving just a single change of plane in either a European or American city. Four airlines – American Airlines, Continental, KLM and Iberia – have flights from Britain via, respectively, Miami, Houston or Newark, Amsterdam (also stop-

ping at Bonaire, in the Dutch Antilles), and Madrid. All offer connections from London, and most can arrange flights from other British airports such as Manchester, Birmingham and Glasgow. Typical journey times are between fifteen and seventeen hours, with Iberia and American Airlines offering marginally faster services. You can expect to pay around £550–700 return including tax in the low season and £650–800 in the high. Note that one of the less expensive airlines, Avianca, flies from Madrid to Quito via Bogotá and is worth looking at if you can find a cheap connection to Madrid.

There's less choice if you're flying **from Ireland**, but you can still get to Ecuador with only one change by flying with Continental (to Quito via Newark from Dublin or Shannon), or you can buy an add-on flight, typically with British Airways, British Midland or Aer Lingus, to connect with the appropriate services departing from Miami, Newark, Amsterdam or Madrid. Another option is to take a separate no-frills flight to a British departure city, most obviously London, and go on from there, which can work out at a better price.

Airlines

Aer Lingus UK ☎ 0845/084 4444, Republic of Ireland ☎ 0818/365 000, ⓦ www.aerlingus.ie
American Airlines UK ☎ 0845/7789 789 or in London ☎ 020/7365 0777, Republic of Ireland ☎ 01/602 0550, ⓦ www.aa.com
Avianca UK ☎ 0870/576 7747, ⓦ www.avianca.com
British Airways UK ☎ 0845/77 333 77, Republic of Ireland ☎ 1800/626 747, ⓦ www.ba.com
British Midland UK ☎ 0870/607 0555, Republic of Ireland ☎ 01/407 3036, ⓦ www.flybmi.com
Continental Airlines UK ☎ 0800/776 464 or 01293/776 464, ⓦ www.continental.com/uk; Republic of Ireland ☎ 1890/925 252, ⓦ www.continental.com/ie
Iberia Airlines UK ☎ 0845/601 2854, Republic of Ireland ☎ 01/407 3017, ⓦ www.iberiaairlines.co.uk
KLM UK ☎ 0870/5074 074, ⓦ www.klmuk.com

Flight and travel agents

Apex Travel Republic of Ireland ☎ 01/241 8000, ⓦ www.apextravel.ie. Specialists in flights to the US.

Bridge the World UK ☎0870/444 7474,
@www.bridgetheworld.com. Specializing in round-the-world tickets, with good deals aimed at the backpacker market.

Flightbookers UK ☎0870/010 7000,
@www.ebookers.com. Low fares on an extensive selection of scheduled flights.

Joe Walsh Tours Republic of Ireland ☎01/676 0991, @www.joewalshtours.ie. General budget fares agent.

Journey Latin America London ☎020/8747 3108, Manchester ☎0161/832 1441,
@www.journeylatinamerica.co.uk. Knowledgeable and helpful staff, good at sorting out stopovers, airpasses and open-jaw flights. Also do package tours (see p.14).

Lee Travel Republic of Ireland ☎021/4277 111, @www.leetravel.ie. Flights and holidays worldwide.

McCarthy's Travel Republic of Ireland ☎021/427 0127, @www.mccarthystravel.ie. General flight agent.

North South Travel UK ☎ & ⊕01245/608 291, @www.northsouthtravel.co.uk. Friendly, competitive travel agency, offering discounted fares worldwide – profits are used to support projects in the developing world, especially the promotion of sustainable tourism.

Premier Travel Northern Ireland ☎028/7126 3333, @www.premiertravel.uk.com. Discount flight specialists.

Rosetta Travel Northern Ireland ☎028/9064 4996, @www.rosettatravel.com. Flight and holiday agent.

Scott Dunn ☎020/8682 5030, @www.scottdunn.com. Good South American specialist, offering low-cost fares and helpful advice.

South American Experience ☎020/7976 5511, @www.southamericanexperience.co.uk. Mainly a discount flight agent but also offers a range of tours.

STA Travel UK ☎0870/1600 599,
@www.statravel.co.uk. Worldwide specialists in low-cost flights and tours for students and under-26s, though other customers welcome.

Top Deck UK ☎020/7244 8000,
@www.topdecktravel.co.uk. Long-established agent dealing in discount flights.

Trailfinders UK ☎020/7628 7628,
@www.trailfinders.co.uk, Republic of Ireland ☎01/677 7888, @www.trailfinders.ie. One of the best-informed and most efficient agents for independent travellers; produce a very useful quarterly magazine worth scrutinising for round-the-world routes.

Travel Cuts UK ☎020/7255 2082 or 7255 1944, @www.travelcuts.co.uk. Canadian company

specializing in budget, student and youth travel and round-the-world tickets.

usit NOW Republic of Ireland ☎01/602 1600,
@www.usitnow.ie, Northern Ireland ☎028/9032 7111, @www.usitnow.com. Student and youth specialists for flights and trains.

Tour operators

Abercrombie & Kent UK ☎0845/0700 610,
@www.abercrombiekent.co.uk. Upmarket tours and Galápagos cruises.

Adrift ☎01488/71152, @www.adrift.co.uk. Specialist rafting company offering trips down the Río Upano in the Southern Oriente and hair-raising runs on the Río Quijos.

Bales Worldwide UK ☎0870/241 3208,
@www.balesworldwide.com. Family-owned company offering mainly Galápagos tours as well as tailor-made itineraries.

Discovery Initiatives ☎01285/643 333,
@www.discoveryinitiatives.com. Conservation-minded outfit that organizes trips to the Galápagos, rainforests, cloudforests and volcanoes.

Encounter ☎01728/862 222, @www.encounteroverland.com. Adventurous small-group overland trips in a special truck including one of nine weeks from Quito to Santiago or Quito to Rio, and a 27-week trip around the entire continent, starting in Quito.

Exodus UK ☎020/8675 5550, Republic of Ireland ☎01/677 1029, @www.exodus.co.uk. Organize adventure tours to highlands, jungle and coast as well as Galápagos cruises.

Explore Worldwide UK ☎01252/760 000,
@www.explore.co.uk. Offers a three-week tour of the country including markets, jungle, volcanoes and the Galápagos.

Footprint Adventures ☎01522/804 929,
@www.footprint-adventures.co.uk. A company with a conservation ethos offering a good choice of small-group tours, including trekking, rafting, birding and climbing holidays.

Galápagos Adventure Tours ☎020/74071478, @www.galapagos.co.uk. Specializes in Galápagos cruises on a variety of yachts, but can combine these with treks and jungle trips.

Guerba Expeditions ☎01373/826611,
@www.guerba.co.uk. Group tours of Ecuador and South America, including a 17-day trek incorporating jungle, volcanoes and markets.

Hayes & Jarvis UK ☎0870/898 9890,
@www.hayes-jarvis.com. Tours to Quito, the highlands and Cuenca, the Amazon and the Galápagos.

Journey Latin America London ☎020/8747 3108, Manchester 0161/8321441, ⓦ www.journeylatinamerica.co.uk. Specialists in flights, packages, adventure tours and tailor-made trips to Latin America.

Kumuka Expeditions ☎0800/068 8855 or 020/7937 8855, ⓦwww.kumuka.com. Independent tour operator specializing in overland expeditions. Ecuador features in multi-week trips combining one or more of Peru, Bolivia and Chile.

Naturetrek ☎01962/733051, ⓦwww.naturetrek.co.uk. Specializes in bird-watching and botanical holidays, with cloudforest tours, and trips to the Oriente and Andean páramo.

Ornitholidays ☎01794/519445, ⓦwww.ornitholidays.co.uk. Specialist birding tours of Ecuador and the Galápagos.

Penelope Kellie ☎01962/779317, ⓦwww.pkworldwide.com. Penelope Kellie is the UK representative for Amerindia, a top-end Quito-based tour company (see p.112), and Quasar Nautica (see p.16), which offers Galápagos cruises on a selection of top-class boats.

Reef and Rainforest ☎01803/866965, ⓦwww.reefrainforest.co.uk. Trips to the Galápagos, plus birding groups in the Amazon basin and cloudforests.

South American Experience ☎020/7976 5511, ⓦwww.southamericanexperience.co.uk. Offers packages to the Galápagos, jungle trips, Otavalo and highlands.

Sunbird ☎01767/682969, ⓦwww.sunbirdtours.co.uk. Specialist bird-watching tours to northern Ecuador, the Oriente, Podocarpus and the Santa Elena peninsula.

Travelbag Adventures ☎01420/541007, ⓦwww.travelbag-adventures.co.uk. Group tours of the highlands, the Amazon and the Galápagos.

Tribes ☎01728/685971, ⓦwww.tribes.co.uk. Environmentally and culturally sensitive operator offering a range of small-group and special-interest tours, such as "Arts and Crafts" or "Spiritual" Ecuador.

Tucan Travel ☎020/8742 8612, ⓦwww.tucantravel.com. A range of overland expeditions passing through Ecuador and a variety of other South American countries.

Wildlife Worldwide ☎020/8667 9158, ⓦwww.wildlifeworldwide.com. Offers an 18-day "Complete Ecuador" package, in which you choose the components such as jungle lodges, cloudforest trips and the Galápagos.

Worldwide Journeys & Expeditions ☎020/7386 4646, ⓦwww.worldwidejourneys .co.uk. Arranges Galápagos cruises with the possibility of combining them with tours of the sierra and Amazon.

Flights from the US and Canada

While departure cities offering direct flights to Quito or Guayaquil are limited in the US to Miami, New York and Houston, it is easy to pick up connecting flights from all major US cities to these three points. There are no direct flights from Canada to Ecuador, so you'll need to catch a flight to the US, typically Miami, where you can connect with a plane to Ecuador.

From the US, direct routes to Quito and Guayaquil are operated by American Airlines twice daily and LanChile daily from Miami, and Continental Airlines daily from Houston and Newark (sometimes stopping once in Panama City and Bogotá respectively). Avianca Airlines, the Colombian carrier, also runs regular flights from Los Angeles, New York (JFK) and Miami changing in Bogotá, as does Lacsa (of Costa Rica), but changing in San José. The Panamanian airline, Copa, offers flights from Los Angeles and Houston via Panama City. Approximate flying times from the US to Quito without stops are: from Miami four hours; from Houston five hours; and from New York six to seven hours. As for fares, expect to pay around US$650 in low season and US$650–750 in high season from New York; $450–550/$500–750 from Miami; $700/$800–900 from Houston and $800/$900–1000 from Los Angeles. It's worth hunting around, however, because prices can vary greatly.

From Canada, American Airlines has connecting services to Miami and Quito from Toronto and Calgary, while Continental flies from Vancouver and Calgary to Ecuador via Houston. Canadian Airlines also offers daily flights from all major Canadian cities to the US departure points, often connecting with other airlines. Fares from Toronto and Vancouver are around the CAN$1400 mark, while Calgary comes in a little dearer. Quito is about seven and a half hours from Toronto, or about ten hours from Calgary and Vancouver.

Airlines

Air Canada ☎1-888/247-2262,
🌐www.aircanada.ca
American Airlines ☎1-800/433-7300,
🌐www.aa.com
Avianca ☎1-800/284-2622,
🌐www.avianca.com
Continental Airlines domestic ☎1-800/523-
3273, international ☎1-800/231-0856,
🌐www.continental.com
Copa Airlines US ☎1-800/FLY-COPA,
🌐www.copaair.com
Lacsa US ☎1-800/225-2272, Canada ☎1-
888/261-3269, 🌐www.taca.com
LanChile US ☎1-800/735-5526, Canada
☎416/862-0807, 🌐www.lanchile.com

Discount travel companies

Air Brokers International ☎1-800/883-3273,
🌐www.airbrokers.com. Consolidator and specialist
in round-the-world and Circle Pacific tickets.
Airtech ☎212/219-7000, 🌐www.airtech.com.
Standby seat broker; also deals in consolidator fares
and courier flights.
Airtreks.com ☎1-877/AIRTREKS or 415/912-
5600, 🌐www.airtreks.com. Round-the-world and
Circle Pacific tickets. The website features an
interactive database that lets you build and price
your own round-the-world itinerary.
Council Travel ☎1-800/2COUNCIL,
🌐www.counciltravel.com. Nationwide organization
that mostly specializes in student/budget travel.
Flights from the US only. Owned by STA Travel.
Educational Travel Center ☎1-800/747-5551
or 608/256-5551, 🌐www.edtrav.com.
Student/youth discount agent.
SkyLink US ☎1-800/AIR-ONLY or 212/573-8980,
Canada ☎1-800/SKY-LINK,
🌐www.skylinkus.com. Consolidator.
STA Travel US ☎1-800/781-4040, Canada ☎1-
888/427-5639, 🌐www.sta-travel.com. Worldwide
specialists in independent travel; also student IDs,
travel insurance, car rental, etc.
TFI Tours ☎1-800/745-8000 or 212/736-1140,
🌐www.lowestairprice.com. Consolidator.
Travac ☎1-800/TRAV-800, 🌐www.thetravelsite
.com. Consolidator and charter broker with offices in
New York City and Orlando.
Travelers Advantage ☎1-877/259-2691,
🌐www.travelersadvantage.com. Discount travel
club; annual membership fee required (currently $1
for 3 months' trial).
Travel Avenue ☎1-800/333-3335,
🌐www.travelavenue.com. Full-service travel agent

that offers discounts in the form of rebates.
Travel Cuts Canada ☎1-800/667-2887, US ☎1-
866/246-9762, 🌐www.travelcuts.com. Canadian
student-travel organization.
Worldtek Travel ☎1-800/243-1723,
🌐www.worldtek.com. Discount travel agency for
worldwide travel.

Tour operators

Abercrombie & Kent ☎1-800/323-7308 or
630/954-2944, 🌐www.abercrombiekent.com.
Upmarket tours of Ecuador and the Galápagos
Islands.
Adventure Center ☎1-800/228-8747 or
510/654-1879, 🌐www.adventurecenter.com.
Hiking and "soft adventure" specialists with a
number of tours to Ecuador and Galápagos.
Adventures Abroad ☎1-800/665-3998 or
360/775-9926, 🌐www.adventures-abroad.com.
Adventure specialists and general tours to Ecuador.
Andean Treks ☎1-800/683-8148 or 617/924-
1974, 🌐www.andeantreks.com. For Ecuador,
Andean Treks offer customized tours including one or
more of four "segments": Amazon, highlands and
haciendas, cities, and the Galápagos Islands.
Backroads ☎1-800/GO-ACTIVE or 510/527-
1555, 🌐www.backroads.com. Cycling, hiking and
multi-sport tours available in Ecuador.
Elderhostel ☎1-877/426-8056,
🌐www.elderhostel.org. Educational programmes
for seniors, such as "Natural History and
Biodiversity", ten nights exploring the culture,
geography and ecology of Ecuador.
Geographic Expeditions ☎1-800/777-8183 or
415/922-0448, 🌐www.geoex.com. Offer
Galápagos cruises.
Mountain Travel Sobek ☎1-888/MTSOBEK or
510/527-8100, 🌐www.mtsobek.com. Good for
hiking tours, visits to several haciendas, rafting on
the Upano, and Galápagos cruises.
Myths and Mountains ☎1-800/670-MYTH or
775/832-5454, 🌐www.mythsandmountains
.com. Socially responsible tours visiting indigenous
communities in the highlands and Oriente, meeting
shamans and exploring local medicine.
Nature Expeditions International ☎1-
800/869-0639, 🌐www.naturexp.com. Tours
combining the Galápagos with highland markets and
horse rides.
Overseas Adventure Travel ☎1-800/955-1925,
🌐www.oattravel.com. Small-group tours of the
jungle and Galápagos, with add-ons to northern
Ecuador, including the little visited Afro-Ecuadorian
communities.

Quasar Nautica ☎ 1-800/247-2925,
ⓦ www.quasarnautica.com. Well respected
Galápagos specialist, owning a range of luxury and
first-class yachts. Also arranges tailor-made land
tours through its sister company, Amerindia.
Wildland Adventures ☎ 1-800/345-4453,
ⓦ www.wildland.com. Responsible conservation-
minded operator offering hacienda tours of the
highlands, jungle treks in the Amazon lowlands, and
Galápagos wildlife and diving packages.

Flights from Australia and New Zealand

There are no direct flights to Ecuador from
Australia or New Zealand, though there are
two main indirect routings, one via Santiago
in Chile, the other via the US. The most
straightforward is the Qantas/LanChile route
from Sydney to Quito and Guayaquil, stopping in Auckland and changing in Santiago.
Travelling to Ecuador by way of the US
means changing in Los Angeles and then
Miami or Houston. There are no real bargains on either routing, and connections can
be complicated.

From Australia, flights to **Santiago** leave
from Sydney, though you can buy an add-on
from other major cities connecting either in
Sydney or Auckland. Qantas have teamed
up with LanChile to provide a thrice-weekly
service to Ecuador via Santiago, taking
almost 27 hours, for around A$2500.
Alternatively, you could fly to **Los Angeles**
with Qantas or Air New Zealand, then take
either American Airlines to Ecuador via
Miami, or Continental Airlines via Houston.
Prices for these US routings start at around
A$2600, and the journey takes around 27
hours, though watch for bad connections
that can push travel times beyond 35 hours.

From New Zealand, you can join the
Qantas/LanChile Sydney–Santiago service
at Auckland, continuing to Ecuador, or take
Air New Zealand to Papeete (Tahiti), connecting with LanChile to Santiago and
Quito/Guayaquil. The fare for either is from
about NZ$2600 and the journey lasts
around 25 hours. Going through the US, you
can fly Air New Zealand or Qantas to Los
Angeles and take American Airlines to
Ecuador via Miami, or Continental via
Houston, from around NZ$2650. The jour-
ney time is usually a little longer than if you'd

gone by Santiago, but, as always, this
depends on connections.

Airlines

Air New Zealand Australia ☎ 13 24 76,
ⓦ www.airnz.com.au, New Zealand ☎ 0800/737
000, ⓦ www.airnz.co.nz
American Airlines Australia ☎ 1300/130 757,
New Zealand ☎ 09/309 9159, ⓦ www.aa.com
Continental Airlines Australia ☎ 1300/361 400,
New Zealand ☎ 09/308 3350,
ⓦ www.flycontinental.com
LanChile Airlines Australia ☎ 1300/361 400 or
02/9244 2333, New Zealand ☎ 09/309 8673,
ⓦ www.lanchile.com
Qantas Australia ☎ 13 13 13,
ⓦ www.qantas.com.au, New Zealand ☎ 0800/808
767, ⓦ www.qantas.co.nz

Travel agents

Flight Centre Australia ☎ 13 31 33 or 02/9235
3522, ⓦ www.flightcentre.com.au, New Zealand
☎ 0800 243 544 or 09/358 4310,
ⓦ www.flightcentre.co.nz
Holiday Shoppe New Zealand ☎ 0800/808 480,
ⓦ www.holidayshoppe.co.nz
New Zealand Destinations Unlimited New
Zealand ☎ 09/414 1685, ⓦ www.holiday.co.nz
Northern Gateway Australia ☎ 1800/813 288 or
08/8941 2167, ⓦ www.northerngateway
.com.au
STA Travel Australia ☎ 1300/733 035,
ⓦ www.statravel.com.au, New Zealand
☎ 0508/782 872, ⓦ www.statravel.co.nz
Student Uni Travel Australia ☎ 02/9232 8444,
ⓦ www.sut.com.au, New Zealand ☎ 09/300 8266,
ⓦ www.sut.co.nz
Trailfinders Australia ☎ 02/9247 7666,
ⓦ www.trailfinders.com.au
travel.com.au and **travel.co.nz** Australia
☎ 1300/130 482 or 02/9249 5444,
ⓦ www.travel.com.au, New Zealand ☎ 0800/468
332, ⓦ www.travel.co.nz. Comprehensive online
travel company.

Tour operators

Abercrombie & Kent Australia ☎ 03/9536 1800
or 1300/851 800, New Zealand ☎ 0800/441 638,
ⓦ www.abercrombiekent.com.au. Upmarket tours
and Galápagos cruises.
Adventure Associates ☎ 02/9389 7466,
ⓦ www.adventureassociates.com. A variety of
mainland tours involving markets, the Devil's Nose

train ride, Amazon lodges, volcanoes, as well as Galápagos cruises.

Adventure World Australia ☎02/8913 0755, ⓦwww.adventureworld.com.au, New Zealand ☎09/524 5118, ⓦwww.adventureworld.co.nz. Agents for a vast array of international adventure travel companies that operate trips to every continent, including tours of Ecuador and the Galápagos Islands.

Austral Tours Australia ☎1800/620 833 or 03/9600 1733, ⓦwww.australtours.com. Central and South American specialist offering trips to Kapawi Lodge (see p.344) and Galápagos cruises.

Birding Worldwide Australia ☎03/9899 9303, ⓦwww.birdingworldwide.com.au. Organizes group trips around the globe. In Ecuador, the tour goes to Tinalandia, the páramo, the eastern Andean flank, La Selva Lodge in the Oriente and the Galápagos Islands.

Classic Safari Company Australia ☎1300/130 218 or 02/9327 0666, ⓦwww.classicsafaricompany .com.au. In partnership with Mountain Travel Sobek (see p.15) to offer hiking and rafting tours of Ecuador.

Kumuka Expeditions Australia ☎1800/804 277 or 02/9279 0491, New Zealand ☎0800/440 499, ⓦwww.kumuka.com.au. Independent tour operator specializing in overland expeditions. Ecuador features

in multi-week trips combining one or more of Peru, Bolivia and Chile.

South America Travel Centre Australia ☎1800/655 051 or 03/9642 5353, ⓦwww.satc.com.au. A 26-day tour including the Galápagos Islands and Otavalo in Ecuador, before heading off for Peru and Chile. "Short tours" of the mainland including Devil's Nose, Ingapirca and Cuenca also available.

Overland from neighbouring countries

Overland entry into Ecuador is possible from Peru and Colombia, its only land neighbours. Details on border crossings are given at the relevant places in the guide text, but briefly, from Peru, there are three main crossing points: Aguas Verdes north of Tumbes to Huaquillas in Ecuador (see p.434); La Tina to Macará, southwest of Loja (see p.279); and Namballe to Zumba, south of Vilcabamba (see p.279). From Colombia, the safest and most important crossing is from Ipiales to Tulcán (see p.176), but you should always check with authorities for the latest security information in this area.

Red tape and visas

Most nationals, including citizens of the EU, and North American and Australasian countries, do not need a visa to enter Ecuador, and only require a passport valid for more than six months, a return ticket and proof of having enough money for the duration of the stay. You'll be issued with a T-3 tourist card on arrival, which you should keep with your passport – it will be collected when you leave the country. The tourist card can allow up to ninety days' stay, though it's up to the official whether you're allocated thirty, sixty or ninety days on arrival.

You can get **extensions** for US$10 at the Jefatura Provincial de Migración in provincial capitals – it's often at the same address as the police headquarters – and in Quito at Isla Seymour N44-174 and Río Coca, Sector Jipijapa (☎02/2247510; Mon–Fri 8am–12.30pm & 3–6.30pm). You can't be granted an extension until the day on which your

tourist card runs out and there's a small fine if you renew it after it's expired. Extensions are given at the discretion of the relevant official in batches of thirty days, up to a maximum of 180 days per twelve months. It's unusual that you'll be refused an extension, but politeness and smart dress certainly won't harm your cause. In some

Ecuadorian embassies around the world

Australia 1st Floor, The Law Society Building, 11 London Circuit, Canberra, ACT 2601 ☎02/6262 5282, ℻6262 5285, ✉embecu@hotkey.et.au
Canada 50 O'Connor St, Office 316, Ottawa, Ontario, K1P 6L2 ☎613/563 8206, ℻235 5776, ✉mecuacan@sprint.ca
Ireland 27 Library Rd, Dun Laoghaire, Dublin ☎01/280 5917, ✉ecucon@iolfree.ie
New Zealand Ferry Building, 2nd Floor, Quay St, Auckland ☎09/309 0229, ℻303 2931
UK Flat 3b, 3 Hans Crescent, London SW1X 0LS ☎020/7584 1367, ℻7823 9701, ✉embajada@ecuador.freeserve.co.uk
US 2535 15th St NW, Washington, DC 20009 ☎202/234-7200 or 234-7166, ℻667-3482, ✉embassy@ecuador.org

cases you'll be asked to prove you have enough money to stay in the country for the length of your extension.

Visas

If you want to work in Ecuador, or simply to **guarantee a stay of over ninety days**, you'll need a **visa**. There is a range of visas available, all of which last from six to twelve months, covering study (12-V), work (12-VI), volunteering (12-VII), cultural exchanges (12-VIII) and long-stay business or tourism (12-IX). Each has its own application procedure – you should contact your consulate before travel for advice well in advance. The **prices** of visas were raised significantly following dollarization. It costs $30 for a visa application form, $100 for a student visa, $200 for a work visa, $150 for volunteers, $50 for cultural exchanges and $200 for long-stay business or tourism.

Once in Ecuador, you have to report to the Dirección de Extranjería at 10 de Agosto and General Murgeon in Quito (☎02/2231022; Mon–Fri 8am–1pm) within thirty days of arrival in order to get a **censo** (identity card). You should bring your passport, *certificado de visación* (given to you at the consulate in your home country), and copies of your

entry stamp, a large envelope (*manila*) and a folder (*carpeta*). Write your name, Quito address and passport number on the envelope containing your passport; it'll be stamped and ready for you to collect the next day. After this, go to the Jefatura de Migración at Isla Seymour N44-174 and Río Coca, Sector Jipijapa (☎02/2247510; Mon–Fri 8am–12.30pm & 3–6.30pm) armed with your passport, three passport photos, photocopies of your passport, entry stamp and *Extranjería* stamp, and a letter from your hotel owner or landlord confirming your address, plus a copy of their identity card (*cédula*). You'll be given a form to sign, asked to stick your photos on various bits of paper, and pay a small fee, after which you'll be presented with your *Certificado de Empadronamiento* (the *censo*), which you can have laminated at a stall outside.

The officials often neglect to tell you this, but you'll also need **permission to leave** the country (*permiso de salida*), which you can buy here for a small fee. You can use it for multiple exits during the course of one year. Please note that visa regulations and procedures change regularly, and can take several days to sort out.

Insurance

It's essential to take out an **insurance policy** before travelling to cover against theft, loss and illness or injury. Before paying for a new policy, however, it's worth checking whether you are already covered: some all-risks home insurance policies may cover your possessions when overseas, and many private medical schemes include cover when abroad. In Canada, provincial health plans usually provide partial cover for medical mishaps overseas, while holders of official student/teacher/youth cards in Canada and the US are entitled to meagre accident coverage and hospital in-patient benefits. Students will often find that their student health coverage extends during the vacations and for one term beyond the date of last enrolment.

After exhausting the possibilities above, you might want to contact a specialist travel insurance company, or consider the travel insurance deal we offer (see box below). A typical policy usually provides cover for the loss of baggage, tickets and – up to a certain limit – cash or cheques, as well as cancellation or curtailment of your journey. Most of them exclude so-called dangerous sports unless an extra premium is paid: in Ecuador this can mean scuba-diving, whitewater rafting, mountaineering and trekking, though probably not kayaking. Many policies can be chopped and changed to exclude coverage you don't need – for example, sickness and accident benefits can often be excluded or included at will. If you do take medical coverage, ascertain whether benefits will be paid as treatment proceeds or only after return home, and whether there is a 24-hour medical emergency number. When securing baggage cover, make sure that the per-article limit – typically under £500 – will cover your most valuable possession. If you need to make a claim, you should keep receipts for medicines and medical treatment, and in the event you have anything stolen, you must obtain an official statement from the police (called a *denuncia*).

Rough Guides travel insurance

Rough Guides offers its own travel insurance, customized for our readers by a leading UK broker and backed by a Lloyd's underwriter. It's available for anyone, of any nationality and any age, travelling anywhere in the world.

There are two main Rough Guide insurance plans: **Essential**, for basic, no-frills cover; and **Premier** – with more generous and extensive benefits. Alternatively, you can take out **annual multi-trip insurance**, which covers you for any number of trips throughout the year (with a maximum of 60 days for any one trip). Unlike many policies, the Rough Guides schemes are calculated by the day, so if you're travelling for 27 days rather than a month, that's all you pay for. If you intend to be away for the whole year, the Adventurer policy will cover you for 365 days. Each plan can be supplemented with a "Hazardous Activities Premium" if you plan to indulge in sports considered dangerous, such as skiing, scuba-diving or trekking.

For a policy quote, call the Rough Guide Insurance Line on UK freefone ☎0800/015 0906; US toll-free ☎1-866/220 5588, or, if you're calling from elsewhere, ☎+44 1243/621 046. Alternatively, get an online quote or buy online at ⓦwww.roughguidesinsurance.com.

✚ Health

Although Ecuador has its fair share of scary-sounding tropical diseases, there's no reason to be paranoid about contracting them. In reality, most are rare and pose much more of a threat to residents – especially poorer communities with limited access to clean water and healthcare – than tourists. The two illnesses you should be especially vigilant against, however, are stomach upsets caused by contaminated food and water, and malaria. You can dramatically cut the risks of getting either through simple practical steps.

Before you go

Consult your doctor or a travel clinic at least **two months before** you leave to discuss whether you need vaccinations or malaria prophylaxis. If you're travelling for more than a few weeks, it's also worth having a dental checkup. Spectacle and contact lens users should bring spare glasses and their prescription.

The only inoculation you are required to have by Ecuadorian law is for yellow fever – but only if you're coming from a tropical African or South American country, when (in theory, at least) you're supposed to show a vaccination certificate. It's a good idea to have the jab anyway if you're planning to visit the Oriente, where the disease is rare but present. The vaccination lasts for ten years. You should also make sure that you're up to date with your vaccinations and boosters for polio, tetanus, hepatitis A and typhoid. Also consider jabs for rabies, diphtheria, tuberculosis and hepatitis B if you anticipate spending a long time in rural areas or with animals, if you're doing work in health care, or if you're planning on lots of long hikes in the wild.

Food and water

The traveller's commonest health complaint is a stomach upset, usually caused by **contaminated food or water**. Tap water is unsafe to drink in Ecuador; bottled water and soft drinks, widely available in all but the remotest places, are safe alternatives, but always check that the seal is intact. Wash your hands before meals and use bottled or boiled water to clean your teeth. You can also pick up stomach upsets from swimming in unclean water; only use chlorinated swimming pools and avoid beaches near large population centres or sewage outlets.

As for food and drink, avoid the following: ice made from tap water; fruit juices with tap water added; raw vegetables and salads; undercooked, partly cooked or reheated fish, crustaceans, meat or eggs; dairy products and ice cream made from unpasteurized milk; and food that's been lying around uncovered where flies can get at it. Food that's freshly prepared and hot, and fruit and vegetables that you can peel yourself rarely cause any harm.

If you plan to visit remote areas, you may have to **purify your water**. Boiling water for at least ten minutes (longer if you're at altitude) is effective, though chemical purification is simpler. Chemical and iodine tablets are small, light and easy to use, and iodine tincture is particularly effective against amoebas and giardia, even if the resulting liquid doesn't taste very pleasant (although neutralizers that improve the flavour are now available). Note that iodine is unsafe for pregnant women, babies and people with thyroid complaints. Portable water purifiers give the most complete treatment but are expensive, fiddly to use and relatively bulky to carry.

A bout of **diarrhoea**, sometimes accompanied by vomiting and stomach cramps, is an annoyance that most travellers have to suffer at one time or another. In most cases it passes within a couple of days and is best remedied by resting and taking plenty of fluids. Avoid milk, alcohol and caffeine-based drinks; still drinks are preferable to fizzy.

Rehydration salts are widely available in Ecuadorian pharmacies and are very helpful in replenishing lost salts. You can make your own solution by adding a generous pinch of salt and three to four tablespoons of sugar to a litre of clean water – aim to drink at least three litres a day if you're unwell, or a couple of glasses for every loose movement. Current medical opinion is that you should continue to eat normally as opposed to fasting, though you'll probably find that you won't feel like eating much, if anything, and even then only the blander foods are palatable. Anti-diarrhoeal drugs, such as Imodium, only suppress symptoms rather than solving the underlying problem, but can be useful when you're on the move and don't know when the next toilet stop might be.

You should **consult a doctor** if symptoms last for longer than five days; there is blood in your stools; you also have a high fever; or if abdominal pain is severe and constant. Most towns have facilities for testing stool samples; tests often only take a matter of hours, cost a few dollars and are invaluable for diagnosis. You'll usually have to buy your own sample pot (*caja de muestra*) from a pharmacy.

Blood and mucus in your diarrhoea may be caused by bacterial dysentery or amoebic dysentery. For **bacterial dysentery**, a course of antibiotics like Ciprofloxacin (available over the counter in most Ecuadorian pharmacies) can be effective, though do get medical advice first. Ciprofloxacin does not work against **amoebic dysentery** (amoebiasis), which can become very serious if it's not treated with metronidazole (Flagyl).

Giardia is a parasitic infection that induces sudden, watery and bad-smelling diarrhoea, bloating, fatigue and excessive rotten-eggs wind. Symptoms wax and wane but can last for weeks if left untreated with a course of metronidazole or tinidazole (Fasigyn). Note that you should avoid alcohol if taking metronidazole or tinidazole.

Cholera – transmitted through contaminated water – occasionally breaks out in rural areas, but tends to be very localized and restricted to poor communities with inadequate sanitation. As a tourist, it's unlikely you'll go anywhere near these places, but if you suspect you're infected (symptoms include profuse watery diarrhoea, explosive vomiting and fever) it's easy to treat, provided you get to a doctor immediately and keep rehydrating by drinking large quantities of bottled or boiled water. There's no point getting a cholera inoculation as the cholera germ has become resistant to the vaccine, which is generally acknowledged to be worthless.

Insect-borne diseases

Heavy rains can trigger a sharp increase in **insect-borne diseases** in Ecuador, particularly malaria and dengue fever in the coastal provinces. By far the best way of avoiding such diseases is not to get bitten in the first place. Straightforward **precautions** include: using insect repellent – those with at least 35 percent DEET in them are most effective, though this is strong stuff and care should be taken in application; covering up as much skin as possible with light-coloured, loose-fitting but tight-cuffed clothing, perhaps with the insides of the shirt ends and trouser cuffs dabbed with DEET; sleeping in screened rooms with a mosquito net, preferably treated with Permethrin insecticide; and spraying your room with insecticide.

The risk of **malaria** should never be taken lightly: tens of thousands of people contract the disease every year in Ecuador, about a quarter of them with the very serious *falciparum* variety. The worst-affected areas are below 1500m, especially in or around population centres and when there's plenty of stagnant water for the mosquitoes to breed in. Above 1500m the risk falls substantially, and above 2500m the malaria mosquito cannot survive. Quito and the Galápagos Islands are free of malaria, and if you're keeping to the highlands, the risk is generally small.

You'll need to consult your doctor if travelling in malarial areas, and follow a course of prophylactic medication. This usually consists of chloroquine (Avloclor or Nivaquine) and proguanil (Paludrine), though if you're travelling in Esmeraldas province mefloquine (Lariam), doxycycline or Malarone are now recommended; Malarone is reportedly the best tolerated of the three drugs. Malarial tablets need to be taken prior to arriving in risk areas and also after leaving them. It should be stressed that these drugs do not completely wipe out the risk of the disease, and you should always take care to avoid being bitten. Note that the malaria mosquito is active from dawn till dusk. Symptoms include fever, diarrhoea, joint pain, shivering and flu-like symptoms; if you suspect you've caught the disease, see a doctor immediately and have a blood test. Remember that symptoms can appear several months after leaving a malarial area.

Dengue fever is a painful and debilitating disease spread by the *Aedes* mosquito, which bites during the day. There's no vaccine against dengue fever and there's not a lot you can do should you contract it except from resting, and taking painkillers (avoid aspirin) and plenty of fluids. Symptoms include headaches, severe joint pain (its other name, "breakbone fever", is indicative) and high fever, though it's usually only fatal if caught repeatedly.

Avoiding insect bites will also provide you with protection against a number of rarer diseases, such as **leishmaniasis**, a parasitic disease spread by the bite of infected sand flies, which produces skin sores and lesions, fever, anaemia and enlargement of the spleen and liver, usually months after infection. The flies are about one-third the size of mosquitoes, so a fine-mesh (18 holes per inch is recommended) mosquito net, preferably treated with insecticide, is advisable for rural tropical and subtropical areas. In parts of Esmeraldas province, **river blindness** (onchocerciasis) is spread by the bite of black flies found around fast-moving water. It can lead to unpleasant inflammation around the eyes, with blindness resulting in a small proportion of cases. People working or living near black fly habitats in endemic regions for long periods are the only ones likely to be at risk. **Chagas disease** (also called American trypanosomiasis) is carried by reduviid bugs found in rural mud, thatch and adobe buildings, and transmitted when the bug's faeces are unwittingly rubbed into its bite wound. The disease can take up to twenty years to show, but can lead to severe heart problems. You're very unlikely to come in contact with the disease – if you have to sleep in these conditions, use a mosquito net.

Altitude and hypothermia

If you've flown to Quito from sea level, you may feel a bit woozy, sleepless and lethargic – normal symptoms of the **acclimatization** process that the body undergoes over a few days as it adjusts to reduced levels of oxygen encountered at altitude. Symptoms, which might also include breathlessness, needing to urinate frequently, fatigue and strange dreams, will abate naturally if you rest and avoid alcohol and sleeping pills.

Altitude sickness, known as *soroche* in Ecuador, and more accurately called **Acute Mountain Sickness** (AMS), occurs when your acclimatization process does not keep pace with your rate of ascent. Your age, sex and fitness have no bearing on whether or not you will develop AMS. It's a debilitating and potentially dangerous condition caused by the reduced oxygen levels and atmospheric pressure that occur at high elevations, and if you're going to go much above 3000m you should be aware of the full risks. Symptoms include headaches, nausea and extreme tiredness, dizziness, insomnia, confusion and a staggering gait. The best way to relieve the condition is also the simplest – lose altitude.

You can minimize the risks of developing AMS by ascending to high elevations slowly and allowing yourself to acclimatize – don't be tempted to whizz straight up the nearest volcano without spending a night or two at altitude first. You should also avoid alcohol and salt, and drink lots of water or try the local remedy for altitude sickness, **coca-leaf tea** (*mate de coca*). A course of acetazolamide (Diamox) speeds up the acclimatization process, but this is a prescription-only drug in most countries, as it can be dangerous for people with heart conditions. It's unlikely you'll need this drug in Ecuador, but if you're planning to go to very high elevations, you might consider it as a precaution.

If you develop AMS, it is essential that you do not ascend any further. Your condition will worsen and may become life-threatening. There are two severe forms of AMS which usually only appear above 4000m. **HAPO** (high altitude pulmonary oedema) is caused by a build-up of liquid in the lungs. Symptoms include fever, an increased pulse rate, and coughing up white fluid; sufferers should descend immediately, whereupon recovery is usually quick and complete. Rarer, but more serious, is **HACO** (high altitude cerebral oedema), which occurs when the brain gets waterlogged with fluid. Symptoms include loss of balance and co-ordination, severe lassitude, weakness or numbness on one side of the body and a confused mental state. If you or a fellow traveller displays any of these symptoms, descend immediately, and get to a doctor; HACO can be fatal within 24 hours.

Decompression sickness is a more oblique problem associated with gaining altitude quickly. If you have been scuba diving in the Galápagos or on the coast, wait at least 24 hours before coming to the highlands or flying.

Another concern for people at altitude is **hypothermia**, an underestimated enemy that's responsible for more deaths among trekkers and climbers than anything else. Brought on by exposure to cold and when the body loses heat faster than it can generate it, hypothermia is greatly accelerated when you're wet, tired and in the wind. Wet clothes lose most of their insulating value – cotton and down are particularly bad; wool and synthetic materials generally retain more heat. Because early symptoms can include an almost euphoric sense of sleepiness and disorientation, your body's core temperature can plummet to danger level before you know what has happened. Symptoms include violent shivering, erratic behaviour, slurred speech, loss of coordination, and drowsiness, and are much easier to spot in other people than yourself. Victims should be given dry clothes, warm drinks (slowly) and wrapped in a dry sleeping bag. Make a fire to warm rocks or canteens – these can be wrapped up and placed where major blood vessels are near the skin (such as under arms and in the crotch) and will help to raise the body's core temperature. In more serious cases, concentrate on keeping the victim awake (falling asleep will reduce body temperature even further). Take off their clothes and yours and jump into a sleeping bag together, or better still with a third stripped person, so the victim can be warmed from both sides – this is one of the best ways of restoring body temperature.

The sun

It's not a good idea to strip off and soak up the rays of the **equatorial sun**. Serious sunburn and sunstroke are real risks, particularly at altitude, when the temperature is not necessarily that high but the thin air amplifies the harm done by the sun's ultraviolet rays. Jungle and coastal boat rides can also be dangerous, as cool river or sea breezes disguise the effects of the sun as it is reflected off the water. Use a high-factor sunscreen (factor fifteen and above) on all exposed skin, reapplying after bathing, and wear a wide-brimmed hat. Well-known brands of high-factor sun creams are available in pharmacies, particularly in large towns and tourist centres, more or less at Western prices; some combine sun block with insect repellent. Drink plenty of water, particularly if you're exercising, and consider taking a rehydration solution or adding more salt to your food to counterbalance the effects of excessive sweating.

Other health hazards

HIV and AIDS (SIDA, in Spanish) are not as widespread in Ecuador as in certain other parts of South America, but they are on the increase, with around 20,000 Ecuadorians having contracted HIV. Unprotected sex is the most common form of transmission. Condoms (*condones* or *preservativos*) are not as widely available as in Western countries – it's a good idea to take your own supply if you're worried about the safety of unfamiliar brands. Not all hospitals screen blood adequately or have enough sterilized disposable needles, so it's also advisable to carry a supply of sterile syringes in your first-aid kit.

At some point you're bound to come across unfriendly **dogs**, especially if you're a hiker, as they're often used in rural communities to deter thieves. Though they may act tough, they seldom attack. If a dog snarls and bares its teeth at you, back off slowly, without turning your back on it, staring at it, or showing any fear. **Rabies**, though only a remote risk, does exist in Ecuador, with a couple of hundred cases a year: if you get bitten or scratched by a dog, cat or most other mammals you should wash the affected area thoroughly with soap and clean water and seek medical attention *immediately*. The disease can be cured, but only through a series of stomach injections administered before the onset of symptoms (which can appear within 24 hours, and include irrational behaviour, aggression, headache, fever and fear of water). There is a vaccine – a course of three injections that has to be started at least a month before departure – but it's expensive and doesn't prevent you from contracting rabies, though it does buy you time to get to hospital.

Stings and bites from other creatures such as scorpions, spiders and snakes are very uncommon but can be terribly painful and, in rare cases, fatal. It's good practice to go through your clothes, socks and shoes before dressing, and to check your bedclothes and under lavatory seats. In the rainforests, watch where you put your feet and hands, and don't lean against trees. Walking around barefoot is not only an invitation to get bitten or stung, but opens the door to hookworm too.

Ecuador does have its share of venomous **snakes**, but most of them are more concerned with getting away from you than attacking. Even if they do strike, there's every chance that they won't inject any venom. In the unlikely event of snakebite, reassure the victim and keep them still. If possible, kill the snake for identification purposes, and get medical help as quickly as possible. In remote rainforest communities, following local knowledge may sometimes be better than spending hours getting to a hospital. Village doctors (*curanderos*) may know effective antidotes, and be able to prepare them quickly.

Hospitals and pharmacies

As a general rule, the larger a city is, the better its **medical care** is likely to be. In Quito and Guayaquil, English-speaking doctors trained overseas are relatively easy to find; your embassy should have a list of recommended practices. Standards deteriorate the further you go from the cities, particularly in remote rural regions. If you have a choice, private hospitals and practices are invariably better staffed and equipped than their state-managed counterparts. Make sure you have adequate health insurance and remember to obtain itemized receipts after treatment so you can recover your costs. Carrying a credit card is a good idea in case you need to make large payments for treatment up front.

You'll find **pharmacies** in almost all Ecuadorian towns. They're invariably stocked with a wide range of familiar drugs and medicines, which can be bought without a prescription; if you're likely to need to buy medication, make a note of its generic name, as brand names may be different. Women taking oral **contraceptives**, however, are better off bringing their own supply from home. For many locals, pharmacists act as no-cost, stand-in doctors, but their advice should be taken with a pinch of salt: there's no substitute for lab tests and a trained practitioner's opinion. If you see a *turno* sign, it means that there's a night shift and the pharmacy is open 24 hours, more common in the large cities.

A traveller's first-aid kit

Among items you might want to carry with you, especially if you're planning to visit remote areas or go trekking, are:

- Antiseptic cream
- Anti-fungal cream
- Hydrocortisone cream (Eurax) is good for insect bites and skin irritations
- Moisturizing cream
- Insect repellent
- Plasters/band aids
- Anti-blister treatment, such as Compeed
- Scissors, lint, sealed bandages and surgical tape

- A course of metronidazole (Flagyl) and Ciprofloxacin
- Imodium or Lomotil for emergency diarrhoea treatment
- Paracetamol or aspirin
- Multivitamin and mineral tablets
- Oral rehydration sachets
- Sunscreen, lip salve, calamine lotion and sunglasses
- Water sterilization tablets or water purifier
- Sterilized syringes and skin wipes

Medical resources for travellers

Websites

ⓦ **www.cdc.gov/travel** Excellent website listing diseases by region, suggesting vaccinations and precautions, and giving warnings on outbreaks, as well as plenty of other travel health information.
ⓦ **www.fitfortravel.scot.nhs.uk** UK NHS website carrying information about travel-related diseases and how to avoid them.
ⓦ **www.health.yahoo.com** Information on specific diseases and conditions, drugs and herbal remedies, as well as advice from health experts.
ⓦ **www.istm.org** The website of the International Society for Travel Medicine, with a full list of clinics specializing in international travel health.
ⓦ **www.tmvc.com.au** Contains a list of all Travellers Medical and Vaccination Centres throughout Australia, New Zealand and Southeast Asia, plus general information on travel health.
ⓦ**www.tripprep.com** Travel Health Online provides an online-only comprehensive database of necessary vaccinations for most countries, as well as destination and medical service provider information.

In the UK and Ireland

British Airways Travel Clinics 213 Piccadilly, London W1 (Mon–Fri 9.30am–6pm, Sat 10am–5pm, no appointment necessary; ☎0845/6002236); 101 Cheapside, London EC2 (Mon–Fri 9am–4.30pm, appointment required; ☎020/7606 2977), ⓦwww.ba.com/travelclinic Vaccinations, tailored advice from an online database and a complete range of travel healthcare products.
Hospital for Tropical Diseases Travel Clinic 2nd floor, Mortimer Market Centre, off Capper St, London WC1E 6AU (Mon–Fri 9am–5pm best by appointment; ☎020/7388 9600; a consultation costs £15 which is waived if you have your injections here). A recorded Health Line (☎0906/133 7733; 50p per min) gives hints on hygiene and illness prevention as well as listing appropriate immunizations.
Infectious Diseases Unit Brownlee Centre, Glasgow G12 0YN ☎0141/211 1062. Travel vaccinations including yellow fever.
Liverpool School of Tropical Medicine Pembroke Place, Liverpool L3 5QA ☎0151/708 9393. Walk-in clinic Mon–Fri 1–4pm; appointment required for yellow fever, but not for other jabs. Travel

health advice line is on ☎0906/708 8807 and costs 50p per min.
MASTA (Medical Advisory Service for Travellers Abroad) 40 regional clinics (call ☎0870/6062782 for the nearest, or consult ⓦwww.masta.org). Also operates a pre-recorded 24-hour Travellers' Health Line (UK ☎0906/822 4100, 60p per min), giving written information tailored to your journey by return of post.
Nomad Pharmacy 40 Bernard St, London WC1N 1LE (Mon–Fri 9.30am–6pm, ☎020/7833 4114 to book vaccination appointment); 3–4 Wellington Terrace, Turnpike Lane, London N8 0PX (☎020/8889 7014); and 43 Queens Road, Clifton, Bristol BS8 1QH (☎0117/922 6567). They give advice free if you go in person, or their telephone helpline is ☎0906/863 3414 (60p per minute). They can give information tailored to your travel needs.
Trailfinders Immunization clinics (no appointments necessary) at 194 Kensington High St, London W8 7RG (Mon–Fri 9am–5pm except Thurs to 6pm, Sat 10am–5.15pm; ☎020/7938 3999). Reduced charges for those that buy travel tickets through the company.
Travel Health Centre Department of International Health and Tropical Medicine, Royal College of Surgeons in Ireland, Mercers Medical Centre, Stephen's St Lower, Dublin 2 ☎01/402 2337. Expert pre-trip advice and inoculations.
Travel Medicine Services PO Box 254, 16 College St, Belfast BT1 6BT ☎028/9031 5220. Offers medical advice before a trip and help afterwards in the event of a tropical disease.
Tropical Medical Bureau ⓦwww.tmb.ie. Four travel clinics in Ireland (two in Dublin, one in Dun Laoghaire and one in Galway), plus five associated clinics across the country. Call ☎1850/487 674 to find your nearest clinic and make an appointment.

In the US and Canada

Canadian Society for International Health 1 Nicholas St, Suite 1105, Ottawa, ON K1N 7B7 ☎613/241-5785, ⓦwww.csih.org. Distributes a free pamphlet, "Health Information for Canadian Travellers", containing an extensive list of travel health centres in Canada.
Centers for Disease Control 1600 Clifton Rd NE, Atlanta, GA 30333 ☎1-800/311-3435 or 404/639-3534, ⓦwww.cdc.gov. Publishes outbreak warnings, suggested inoculations, precautions and other background information for travellers. Useful website plus International Travelers Hotline on ☎1-877/FYI-TRIP.
International Association for Medical Assistance to Travellers (IAMAT) 417 Center

St, Lewiston, NY 14092 ☎716/754-4883, ⓦwww.iamat.org, 40 Regal Rd, Guelph, ON N1K 1B5, Canada ☎519/836-0102, or 1287 St Clair Avenue West, Toronto ☎416/652 0137. A non-profit organization supported by donations, it can provide a list of English-speaking doctors in Ecuador, climate charts and leaflets on various diseases and inoculations.

International SOS Assistance Eight Neshaminy Interplex Suite 207, Trevose, US 19053-6956 ☎1-800/523-8930, ⓦwww.intsos.com. Members receive pre-trip medical referral info, as well as overseas emergency services designed to complement travel insurance coverage.

MEDJET Assistance ☎1-800/9MEDJET, ⓦwww.medjetassistance.com. Annual membership program for travellers ($195 for individuals, $295 for families) that, in the event of illness or injury, will fly members home or to the hospital of their choice in a medically equipped and staffed jet.

Travel Medicine ☎1-800/TRAVMED, ⓦwww.travmed.com. Sells first-aid kits, mosquito netting, water filters, reference books and other health-related travel products, and maintains a directory of travel clinics in the US and Canada.

Travelers' Medical Center 31 Washington Square West, New York, NY 10011 ☎212/982-1600. Consultation service on immunizations and treatment of diseases for people travelling to developing countries.

In Australia and New Zealand

Travellers' Medical and Vaccination Centres A full list of over twenty TMVC clinic locations in Australia and New Zealand is given on ⓦwww.tmvc.com.au. 27–29 Gilbert Place, Adelaide, SA 5000 ☎08/8212 7522. 5th Floor, 247 Adelaide St, Brisbane, Qld 4000 ☎07/3221 9066. Level 5, 8–10 Hobart Place, Canberra, ACT 2600 ☎02/6257 7156. 270 Sandy Bay Rd, Sandy Bay Tas, Hobart 7005 ☎03/6223 7577. Level 2, 393 Little Bourke St, Melbourne, Vic 3000 ☎03/9602 5788. Level 7, Dymocks Bldg, 428 George St, Sydney, NSW 2000 ☎02/9221 7133. Shop 15, Grand Arcade, 14–16 Willis St, Wellington ☎04/473 0991.

Travelvax ☎1300/360 164, ⓦwww.travelvax.com.au. Gives anti-malarial and vaccination advice, has travel clinics in Australia, and sells first-aid kits and travel health accessories.

Worldwise 72 Remura Road, New Market, Auckland ☎9/520 5830, or Level 2, Anglesea Street, Hamilton ☎7/839 7761, ⓦwww.worldwise.co.nz. Travel health clinics. Website has a list of travel doctors and general travel health advice.

Information, websites and maps

Ecuador doesn't have any tourist offices abroad, but you should be able to get glossy tourist bumf and answers to specific questions from the Ecuadorian embassy in your country. Better sources of information are the tour operators who organize trips to the country, and the many websites devoted to Ecuador carrying detailed travel information, from rundowns on the main tourist attractions to hotel directories.

General information

In Ecuador, there's a Ministry of Tourism **information office** in every provincial capital and the main tourist centres. The quality of service varies widely from office to office – some aren't much geared to off-the-street enquiries, while others pull out all the stops to help. The majority of offices won't have an English-speaker on hand, but almost all will have rudimentary maps, lists of hotels and restaurants, leaflets, and probably basic information on any sites of interest in the area. The head office in Quito (see p.79) is friendly and helpful. Many regional centres also have tourist offices run by the municipality, which can be as good or better than their government counterparts.

Another good source of information is **South American Explorers (SAE)**, a non-profit organization that provides the latest information on travel, research and adventure sports in Central and South America. Their Ecuador Information Packet (US$6.50/$4.50 members) and Galápagos Information Packet (US$10/$4.50 members) can be ordered in the US on ☎1-800/274-0568 or ☎607/277-0488, ℻277-6122, and online at ⓦwww.samexplo.org. Membership is $50 per year ($80 per couple), which entitles you to use the clubhouse in Quito (plus two others in Peru at Lima and Cusco) where you can gain access to detailed country information and trip reports on everything from a Galápagos cruise to climbing Cotopaxi, a large range of maps, a lending library, bag storage, book exchange, phone, and files listing volunteer opportunities across the country. You can join at any clubhouse or by contacting their US headquarters at 126 Indian Creek Rd, Ithaca, NY 14850, US (☎607/277 0488, ℻277 6122, ℮explorer@saexplorers.org).

In the UK, The **Latin America Information Centre**, PO Box 24, Manchester M7 4EX (☎0161/708 9240, ℮laic@globalnet.co.uk), is a non-profit organization that seeks to raise awareness of Latin America. They have a free walk-in research facility, stocked with books, journals and reports (ring for an appointment), and send out weekly news updates on countries or regions as desired (around £20–30 for a year's subscription, depending on range of request).

Maps

The widest selection of **maps** covering Ecuador is published by the Instituto Geográfico Militar; outside of Ecuador these are available by mail order from South American Explorers. The best internationally available general map of Ecuador is the 1:1,000,000 International Travel Maps Ecuador map (530 W Broadway, Vancouver, BC V5Z 1E9, Canada, ⓦwww.itmb.com). They also produce a map of the Galápagos Islands and Quito. Quito's best bookshops (see p.111) should stock these along with a series of blue **pocket guides** to Ecuador by Nelson Gómez E. published by Ediguías, which have reasonable fold-out colour maps of the country and major cities. He has also produced guides containing snippets of history, general tourist information, and street plans for Quito, Guayaquil (Spanish only),

Cuenca (Spanish only) and Otavalo, a similar guide for the Galápagos, and a road map of the country. **Road maps** are, however, notoriously unreliable in their representation of unpaved roads – cross-reference between different maps to avoid difficulties.

The **Instituto Geográfico Militar** (IGM) in Quito, up on the hill overlooking the Parque El Ejido at Senierges and Paz y Miño (you'll need to bring your passport or ID along), have maps on a variety of scales, including *Hojas de Ruta*, a selection of the most popular **specific driving routes** (for example, Quito–Esmeraldas and Quito–Tena–Puyo) with tourist information marked on them. The most useful maps for **trekking** are their 1:50,000 series, which show accurate contour markings and geographic features and cover most of the country except for remote corners of the Oriente. Unfortunately, popular maps are often sold out, in which case you'll be supplied with a difficult-to-read black-and-white photocopy. However, they have brought out glossy *"mapas ecoturísticos"* for Volcán Cotopaxi, and Chimborazo and Carihuayrazo. Maps are also available in a 1:250,000 series for the whole country, and a 1:25,000 series for approximately half of it. You may need a supporting letter from a government agency if you require maps of sensitive border areas and the Oriente.

Map outlets

In the UK and Ireland

Blackwell's Map and Travel Shop 50 Broad St, Oxford OX1 3BQ ☎01865/793 550, and eight other outlets listed on ⓦwww.maps.blackwell .co.uk.
Easons Bookshop 40 O'Connell St, Dublin 1 ☎01/858 3881, ⓦwww.eason.ie.
Heffers Map and Travel 20 Trinity St, Cambridge CB2 1TY ☎01223/568 568, ⓦwww.heffers.co.uk.
Hodges Figgis Bookshop 56–58 Dawson St, Dublin 2 ☎01/677 4754.
The Map Shop 30a Belvoir St, Leicester LE1 6QH ☎0116/247 1400, ⓦwww.mapshopleicester.co.uk.
Meridian Map Services 10 Regent Street, Nottingham NG1 5BQ ☎0115/950 3434, ⓦwww.meridianmapservices.co.uk.
Newcastle Map Centre 55 Grey St, Newcastle-upon-Tyne NE1 6EF ☎0191/261 5622.

Stanfords 12–14 Long Acre, London WC2E 9LP
℡ 020/7836 1321, ⓦ www.stanfords.co.uk.
The Travel Bookshop 13–15 Blenheim Crescent,
London W11 2EE ℡ 020/7229 5260,
ⓦ www.thetravelbookshop.co.uk.

In the US and Canada

Adventurous Traveler.com US ℡ 1-800/282-
3963, ⓦ adventuroustraveler.com.
Book Passage 51 Tamal Vista Blvd, Corte
Madera, CA 94925 ℡ 1-800/999-7909,
ⓦ www.bookpassage.com.
Distant Lands 56 S Raymond Ave, Pasadena, CA
91105 ℡ 1-800/310-3220,
ⓦ www.distantlands.com.
Elliot Bay Book Company 101 S Main St,
Seattle, WA 98104 ℡ 1-800/962-5311,
ⓦ www.elliotbaybook.com.
Globe Corner Bookstore 28 Church St,
Cambridge, MA 02138 ℡ 1-800/358-6013,
ⓦ www.globecorner.com.
Map Link 30 S La Patera Lane, Unit 5, Santa
Barbara, CA 93117 ℡ 1-800/962-1394,
ⓦ www.maplink.com.
Rand McNally US ℡ 1-800/333-0136,
ⓦ www.randmcnally.com. Around thirty stores
across the US; dial ext 2111 or check the website
for the nearest location.
The Travel Bug Bookstore 3065 W Broadway,
Vancouver V6K 2G9 ℡ 604/737-1122,
ⓦ www.swifty.com/tbug.
World of Maps 1235 Wellington St, Ottawa,
Ontario K1Y 3A3 ℡ 1-800/214-8524,
ⓦ www.worldofmaps.com.

In Australia and New Zealand

The Map Shop 6–10 Peel St, Adelaide, SA 5000
℡ 08/8231 2033, ⓦ www.mapshop.net.au.
Specialty Maps 46 Albert St, Auckland 1001
℡ 09/307 2217, ⓦ www.specialtymaps.co.nz.
Mapland 372 Little Bourke St, Melbourne, Victoria
3000 ℡ 03/9670 4383, ⓦ www.mapland.com.au.
MapWorld 173 Gloucester St, Christchurch
℡ 0800/627 967 or 03/374 5399,
ⓦ www.mapworld.co.nz.
Perth Map Centre 900 Hay St, Perth, WA 6000
℡ 08/9322 5733.

Useful websites

Travel

Budgettravel.com ⓦ www.budgettravel.com.
Long list of Ecuador links to cover traveller
enquiries.

Ecuador Explorer ⓦ www.ecuadorexplorer.com.
Website for most of the country's better hotels and
tour operators, plus a lot of useful travel
information.
Ecuador Travel.info ⓦ www.ecuador-travel.info.
Good general information site with articles on art and
culture as well as travel.

Government websites

British Embassy in Quito
ⓦ www.britembquito.org.ec. Latest information and
travel advice for Ecuador.
British Foreign & Commonwealth Office
ⓦ www.fco.gov.uk. Constantly updated advice for
travellers on circumstances affecting safety in over
130 countries.
Embassy of Ecuador in Washington
ⓦ www.ecuador.org. Packed with nitty-gritty facts
about visiting Ecuador.
Quito ⓦ www.quito.gov.ec. Informative municipal
website in English and Spanish, covering most
aspects of life in the capital.
Ministerio de Turismo ⓦ www.vivecuador.com.
Ecuadorian ministry of tourism site with information
in English and Spanish.

Nature and outdoor pursuits

Climbing ⓦ www.ecuador-rock-climbing.org. A
dedicated climbing site with general information on
the country's most popular climbs.
The Galápagos Islands
ⓦ www.darwinfoundation.org. Website of the
Charles Darwin Research Station on Santa Cruz
island, including Galápagos conservation news and
links.
El Niño ⓦ www.cpc.ncep.noaa.gov. With links to
the definitive El Niño page, maintained by the US
Climate Prediction Center.
Volcanoes ⓦ www.volcano.si.edu. Lists volcanoes
from around the world, including a comprehensive
section on Ecuador's, with photos, info and the latest
updates. Also try the Spanish-language
ⓦ www.igepn.edu.ec for information directly from
Ecuador.

Daily newspapers

The day's news and articles from Ecuador's most
important papers, in Spanish only:
El Comercio ⓦ www.elcomercio.com
Hoy ⓦ www.hoy.com.ec
El Universo ⓦ www.eluniverso.com

Costs, money and banks

In the year 2000, the US dollar became the official currency of Ecuador, replacing the sucre, which had been in use for over a century but steadily declining in value. The dollar bills are those issued from US banks and the coinage is a mixture of familiar US-minted cent pieces and Ecuadorian-minted coins that cannot be used outside the country. Cents are called *centavos* in Ecuador.

Bills come in denominations of $1, $5, $10, $20, $50 and $100. There is also a $2 bill, but it's uncommon. Coins come in 1, 5, 10, 25 and 50 cent pieces, plus there are $1 coins only minted in the US. Be warned that $100 and $50 bills are rarely accepted at most shops and restaurants, and small change is often in short supply, so bring plenty of low-denomination bills from your home country if possible.

Costs

It was widely expected that dollarization would end Ecuador's reign as one of South America's cheapest countries. There's no denying that prices have risen under the dollar, but as far as travellers are concerned, Ecuador is still a great-value destination. Those on a tight budget should be able to get by on $15–20 (£10–13) per day, with the occasional treat. Spending $30–40 (£20-£27) daily will get you accommodation in more comfortable hotels, better food and the occasional guided tour. Those paying over $100 (£65) a day (travelling independently) are likely to find themselves in the country's best hotels and restaurants.

Accommodation prices are usually around the $7–15 mark for a standard bottom-end double room with private bath, falling to as little as $3–5 at the really basic places. Above $15 and you're into mid-range territory, while anything over $40 a double is likely to be pretty smart. The price of **food** is also low, with an à la carte main course in a standard restaurant costing $2–4, and a set lunch or dinner around only $1–2 for up to three courses. Expect to pay a dollar or two more in the restaurants of the smart La Mariscal district of Quito. If you want to cut food costs, local markets are a

superb source of provisions. **Public transport** also offers excellent value for money. Broadly speaking, an hour's worth of bus travel will set you back 75 cents to $1.50 – the 472-kilometre ride from Quito to Cuenca taking around eleven hours costs $10, for example. You very much get what you pay for on **guided tours**, but count on $30 a day for a standard package (including transport, lunch and accommodation if applicable), rising to about $55 for smarter agencies. Prices go down the larger the group and the longer the tour.

The most widespread **hidden cost** in Ecuador is **IVA** (*Impuesto al Valor Agregado*), a tax of 12 percent which is added to most goods and services. In lower-end restaurants and hotels it's taken for granted that IVA is included in the quoted price. Other places will whack it on to the end of the bill, often in tandem with a further 10 percent service charge, making the final total 22 percent more than you might have bargained for. Car rental is almost always quoted without IVA. If in doubt, always clarify whether prices for anything from souvenirs to room rates include IVA.

Another unexpected cost is the **airport departure tax**, payable in cash when you fly out of Ecuador: $25 from Quito and $10 from Guayaquil.

It's also worth noting that the practice of charging foreigners much higher prices than Ecuadorian residents is becoming increasingly common for tourist attractions, museums, national parks and domestic flights. Some hotels and tour operators are also adopting this policy. It's not intended as a rip-off "gringo tax" so much as a way of neutralizing the inordinate spending power of foreigners, allowing nationals the chance of affording their country's attractions. If you have a *censo* (see p.18), officials are often satisfied that you're entitled to pay the lower rate. Note that this two-tier system is not in operation for taxis and buses; you should be paying the same as anyone else. Ask around about typical taxi fares (or use the metre in Quito), and check bus ticket prices at the ticket office or with other passengers if you think you're being overcharged by the conductor.

Youth and student discounts

Full-time students should consider getting the International Student ID Card, better known as an "ISIC card" (ⓦ www.istc.org), which in Ecuador is the only widely recognized student identification that entitles the bearer to discounts at museums, some attractions, and occasionally at hotels, airlines and tour agencies. In some cases, only Ecuadorian students are eligible for the discounts. A 24-hour hotline to call in the event of a medical, legal or financial emergency is available for card holders of several countries, and for Americans there's also travel insurance, providing up to $3000 in emergency medical coverage and $100 a day for 60 days in the hospital. The card costs $22 in the US; Can$16 in Canada; AUS$16.50 in Australia; NZ$21 in New Zealand; £7 in the UK; and €12.70 in the Republic of Ireland.

ISIC cards are available in the US from Council Travel, STA, Travel CUTS and, in Canada, Hostelling International in Australia and New Zealand from STA or Campus Travel; and in the UK from STA.

Money, credit cards and getting cash

The key to carrying money when you travel is not to have all your eggs in one basket. Taking funds in a mixture of traveller's cheques, cash, and by credit/debit card will keep you covered should any problems arise with any one of them.

ATMs are becoming increasingly widespread in Ecuador, and offer a convenient way to get cash. Visa cards and those using the Plus system are accepted at many ATMs in branches of Banco del Austro and Banco de Guayaquil; MasterCard and Cirrus or Maestro-related cards can be used at the machines owned by Banco del Pacífico and some branches of the Banco de Guayaquil and Produbanco. A smaller number of machines also accept American Express and Diners Club cards. Usually, you won't be able to withdraw more than $200 from an ATM in a day, and a **handling charge** of around 1–2 percent will be deducted from your account. Don't rely solely on your plastic, however – apart from the risk of losing your card or getting it stolen, Ecuador's electronic banking systems go down with inconvenient regularity. Moreover, you won't find that many ATMs outside of medium-sized towns anyway.

Some affiliated banks offer a **cash advance** facility on your card, which usually enables you to withdraw more than you could by ATM. This is usually a relatively painless process, though you may find yourself at the mercy of long queues, short opening hours and administrative delays. Remember that all cash advances are treated as loans, with interest accruing daily from the date of withdrawal; there may be a transaction fee on top of this. However, you can make withdrawals from ATMs in Ecuador using your debit card, which is not liable to interest payments, and the flat transaction fee is usually quite small – your bank will be able to advise on this.

Besides being useful for getting cash, credit cards are also helpful for emergencies, surprise costs, deposits on car rental and splurging in a high-end hotel or restaurant. Visa and MasterCard are the most widely accepted (note that in the Galápagos, MasterCard is just about the only option), followed by Diners Club and American Express. You may have to pay a surcharge of around 10 percent on purchases in some places. Standard hotels, restaurants and shops are unlikely to accept credit cards even when they have stickers on the door; check first. Keep a written record of your card numbers and the numbers to call if your card is lost or stolen.

Take a reasonable proportion of your money in **traveller's cheques** for security, even though they're not as convenient as cash or plastic. Get US dollars cheques – other currencies are rarely exchanged –

preferably American Express, which is currently the most widely accepted brand. You can change them at some branches of Banco de Guayaquil, Produbanco, Banco del Pichincha, which each charge 1–2 percent commission, and Banco del Pacífico, which charges a flat fee of $5 per transaction ($200 limit). It can be a time-consuming and bureaucratic process, and banking hours end at 1pm Monday to Friday. Casas de cambio (exchange bureaus) offer longer opening hours and swifter service, but have all but disappeared since dollarization. Most tour agencies and better hotels will take traveller's cheques in payment, usually with a surcharge. Bear in mind that changing facilities can be hard to find outside of cities and tourist centres. If you expect to be away from either for any length of time change an adequate amount of money first. Make sure to keep the purchase agreement and a record of cheque serial numbers safe and separate from the cheques themselves.

Cash is obviously very convenient, but it's also the riskiest way of carrying your funds. Bring only US dollars cash to Ecuador; other currencies are rarely exchanged. It's also a good idea always to have a bit of cash stashed away in case of an emergency.

Wiring money

If you need emergency cash in a hurry, you can have it **wired** to you ready for collection at one of hundreds of agents within twenty minutes using one of the companies listed below, though it's an expensive thing to do and really only suitable as a last resort.

Money-wiring companies

Travelers Express MoneyGram
US ☏1-800/955-7777, Canada ☏1-800/933-3278, UK ☏0800/018 0104, Republic of Ireland ☏00800/8668 8002, Australia ☏0011800/8668 8002, New Zealand ☏00800/8668 8002, Ecuador ☏1800/999119 or ☏1800/5925755, ⓦwww.moneygram.com.
Western Union US and Canada ☏1-800/325-6000, Australia ☏1800/501 500, New Zealand ☏0800/005 253, UK ☏0800/833 833, Republic of Ireland ☏1800/395 395, Ecuador ☏1800/989898, ⓦwww.westernunion.com.

 # Getting around

Ecuador's inexpensive and generally reliable buses are the country's most useful and preferred form of public transport, trundling along just about everywhere there's a road. By contrast, the train network covers only a small fraction of the country.

The **road network** is limited by North American and European standards, but expanding and improving all the time thanks to recent investments in the country's infrastructure, supported by the introduction of road tolls. Less than 20 percent of the highways, however, are paved so expect a bumpy ride if you're going on any but the most important routes. The **Panamericana** (Pan American Highway) forms the backbone of the country's road network, linking all the major highland towns and cities from Tulcán to Loja. A handful of other good roads spill down the Andes to important coastal cities such as Guayaquil, Manta and Esmeraldas, while in the Oriente the road system is the least developed and exists almost entirely to serve the needs of the local oil industry. The network's biggest problem has always been the **weather**, with floods and landslides both common. But even in fine conditions, rough terrain means that travelling in the country's highland and mountainous regions is often much slower than you might expect: going the length of the country by bus from the Colombian border to Peru, a distance of 818km on mostly paved roads, takes around 18 hours – an average speed of 45km/h.

By bus

Ecuador's comprehensive **bus** service makes getting around simple. Hundreds of bus companies ply the country's roads, often with dozens competing on the most popular routes, transporting people at little cost to all but the remotest regions. Levels of comfort can vary widely between companies: some have fleets of air-conditioned buses with TV, toilet and on-board snacks, while others run beaten-up old monsters with cracked windows, growling gears and belching exhausts. As a general rule, **luxury buses** (ask for an *autobús de lujo*) travel the most popular long-distance routes, leaving regularly all day and night, and require passengers to have a pre-booked ticket. They won't allow standing passengers on board, and only stop at scheduled destinations, reducing journey times.

The further into the backwaters you go, the more the standards of comfort are likely to drop. **Standard buses** will stop anywhere for anyone who wants to get on until every available crack of space has been filled – you're likely to end up sharing the aisle with a bag of clucking chickens and a fat sackful of corn. Obviously, the remoter the area, the less frequent the buses will be and most local and provincial services won't run much after nightfall. At the margins of the bus network, pick-up trucks (**camionetas**), minibuses (**busetas**) and open-sided trucks converted to hold wooden benches (**rancheras**) often fill the vacuum. If you're unsure of the area you're travelling to, note that most drivers know their routes well and are happy for you to ask them to stop at your destination – they'll let you know when you've arrived. For reasons of safety (see p.58), **avoid travelling at night** on buses, when hold-ups are more likely.

Larger towns usually have a main **bus terminal** (*terminal terrestre*), where all the long-distance bus companies are based. In smaller towns, company offices and departure points may be scattered around, though they're usually never very far from the central square or main thoroughfare. Out of town, it's easy to hail non-luxury class buses if you stand in a place where they have plenty of time to spot you; the standard gesture to flag one down is an apathetic point to the ground in the middle of the road next to you.

You can buy your **fare** from the conductor (*ayudante*) on board, who will come and collect it. Overcharging is uncommon, but keep an eye on what others are paying. To get off, make for the door and say "*bajo*" or "*gracias*". Alternatively, if you can, it's a good idea to buy your ticket at the company office in advance to guarantee yourself a seat, something you can do on all long-distance buses whether luxury class or not – seats towards the front are less prone to bumping and lurching. There's never much of a difference in price between companies unless it's a luxury bus, in which case fares will naturally be a little more expensive, but look around the terminal to see what sort of condition the different companies' buses are in – you'll soon get an idea who the best outfits are in any given area. Buses can be noisy what with on-board TVs and blaring music, so earplugs come in handy.

If you can, bring your **luggage** inside the bus with you and keep it in sight. Otherwise, the conductor might put your bag in a locked hold beneath the vehicle. It's pretty safe here, but keep an eye on what's going on down there at each stop and before the bus departs. Smarter buses may give you a special luggage ticket which you have to match with your bag at your destination. Don't panic if your gear is put on the roof because it'll usually be covered in a tarpaulin to keep both the weather and light fingers at bay; don't feel shy about climbing up and checking it's secure. Fortunately, bus drivers are increasingly unwilling to let people ride on the roof, where they can get at your stuff.

Local **city buses** in the larger towns generally carry a board in the window showing their route, with a list of street names and key landmarks. There's normally a flat fare (currently around $0.20), which you pay as you enter. Local buses often stop to pick up and put down anywhere on request, though in some city centres proper **bus stops**, marked "*parada*", are respected.

By train

The old traveller's adage, that all the fun is in the getting there, is never truer than with Ecuador's **trains**. If you're in a hurry this is not the way to go; landslides, delays and problems are frequent and services are regularly suspended. The situation changes all the time, so check the current state of affairs first – South American Explorers (see p.80) is a good place to ask. When everything works, however, a train ride is a real treat; you can sit on the roof enjoying the scenery, while the train slowly rattles down the track.

The rail system once stretched from Guayaquil and Cuenca in the south to San Lorenzo near the Colombian coast in the north, but lack of funding, the rise of road-building, and a string of disruptions caused by landslides and El Niño events has effectively finished it off as a means of public transport, and relegated it to a tourist curiosity. Three main routes remain: Riobamba to Durán, Quito to Riobamba, and Ibarra to San Lorenzo. At the time of writing, all of these services were in operation, albeit in greatly restricted form. The first of these, the spectacular descent of the Andes from Riobamba to Durán, down the Nariz del Diablo (see p.227), is currently running only three times weekly as far as Sibambe. The Quito–Riobamba route is now a truncated tourist service from Quito to El Boliche (by the Cotopaxi national park), departing every Saturday and Sunday (see p.118). The ride down from Ibarra in the northern sierra to San Lorenzo on the coast was badly disrupted by the 1997–98 El Niño and now only operates for 45km from Ibarra to Primer Paso (see p.160), and 25km from San Lorenzo to communities inland (see p.367).

By air

Flying within Ecuador is a quick, convenient and relatively inexpensive way of getting around. Those short on time can cut an all-day bus journey down to a 30-minute hop – and if the weather's clear, enjoy wonderful aerial views of volcanoes and rainforests in the process. There are two main domestic carriers, Tame (ⓦ www.tame.com.ec) and Icaro (ⓦ www.icaro.com.ec), plus a number of small-scale and local charter companies, particularly on the coast and in the Oriente.

Tame offers the most extensive service, flying to most of the country's major centres, with ticket prices between $30 and $60 one-way, apart from flights to the Galápagos Islands, which are disproportionately expensive (see the Galápagos chapter on p.468 for full details). Busier routes should be booked days, if not weeks, in advance and it's important to reconfirm, as overbooking is not uncommon. The weather can be a problem, particularly in Quito and the Oriente, resulting in fairly frequent delays, cancellations or diversions. Note that the baggage allowance is considerably less than on international flights, being about 15–20kg per person; a charge is payable on the excess. Details of the various airline offices and information are given in the relevant chapters.

By car

Given that so much of Ecuador is covered by regional and local buses, few travellers find it necessary to **rent a car** to get around. However, if you intend to zoom around the country in a short space of time, or want to get to really off-the-beaten-track destinations, renting your own vehicle is a worthwhile option. You will need to be at least 25 years old and have a major credit card for the deposit. Theoretically, you only need your national licence to rent a vehicle, but you're strongly advised to bring an **international licence** as well – the Ecuadorian police, who frequently stop drivers to check their documents, are often suspicious of unfamiliar foreign licences and much happier when dealing with international ones. The national **speed limit** is 100km per hour on highways (or less if indicated), and usually around 50km per hour in towns or urban areas. Note that there are some draconian penalties for minor motoring offences, such as not wearing your seat belt; driving the wrong way down a one-way street is supposedly punishable by a fourteen-day mandatory jail sentence.

Rental outlets, costs and vehicles

For convenience's sake, you might want to arrange your car rental in advance through your nearest branch of an international rental company (see p.35), but it nearly always works out cheaper to sort it out when you get there. The only cities offering a large choice of car rental outlets, including well-known international operators like Budget and Hertz, are Quito and Guayaquil. In both cities, the easiest way to compare prices is to head out to the airport, where all the main outfits have branches right next to each other. It's well worth shopping around, as at any given time there's usually one company or another offering a special deal or promotional rate. **Costs** are reasonable compared to Europe or North America: in general, expect to pay around $35 a day or $230 a week for a small hatchback, and from around $60 a day or $450 a week for a mid-sized 4WD, including insurance and IVA (see p.29) – always make sure you're clear whether a price quoted includes **insurance** (generally around $5 a day), IVA and unlimited mileage. Check, too, what the excess is on the insurance (that is, the amount up to which you are liable in the event of an insurance claim). This is known as *el deducible*, or *la franquicia*, and is usually frighteningly high – around $1000 in the case of damage to the vehicle, and around $3000 for theft or "total destruction", as the rental companies alarmingly put it. These figures will be even higher for large or luxurious vehicles.

When choosing which type of vehicle to rent, bear in mind that only a small portion of the country's roads are paved, and those that are surfaced can be in an atrocious state of disrepair. Thankfully, much of the Panamerican Highway and the main coastal highway are currently in excellent condition, freshly resurfaced and maintained. Even so, roads are always at the mercy of the weather and easily damaged, so you'll be better off with a vehicle having high clearance and sturdy tyres unless you know you're sticking to the busy highways. Four-wheel-drive definitely comes in handy on unpaved roads, especially in the rainy season, but isn't necessary for the busier and better-maintained parts of the road network. Air conditioning is another consideration for long journeys in the lowlands and Oriente.

It's essential to **examine the vehicle** very carefully **before** you sign any documentation or hand over any money. Even reputable firms may try to pass you off with an old and not particularly roadworthy vehicle. Check the locks, lights, wipers, tyres, wheel nuts, oil, water, windows and mirrors. Ask to give the car a test drive and check the brakes, steering and listen out for any unhealthy noises. Complain if something looks or feels amiss and if they can't fix it there and then insist on a better car. To some extent, rental companies expect you to do this, so don't be shy about holding out for a replacement. When you are satisfied, go over the vehicle carefully for scratches and dents and make sure all are marked on the damage sheet. Also, get the staff to show you where the jack (*gato*) and lever (*palanca*) are, how to open the bonnet/hood, and how to release the spare tyre (*rueda de repuesto*) as some need to be unlocked or winched down; if the spare is on the car's exterior, check it has a lock. Make sure, too, you know how to use the 4WD function if your car's got one – on most vehicles, you need to get out and turn the wheels to the "lock" position every time you use 4WD. It's a good idea to carry a tow rope with you as well, and a spade to dig the car out of a rut if you get stuck.

On the road

Ecuadorian drivers tend to be very undisciplined and often downright dangerous, with bus and lorry drivers usually being the worst offenders; aggressive overtaking is particularly common, as is abruptly veering over to the wrong side of the road to avoid potholes. As long as you drive defensively and keep your wits about you, however, it's perfectly possible to cover thousands of kilometres without running into problems. **Never drive at night** if you can avoid it, as this is when most accidents occur, in part due to the absence of decent road markings and the lack of signs alerting drivers to hazards. In addition, although **ambushes** against drivers are extremely rare, when they do happen it's invariably at night. As for **petrol/gasoline** (*gasolina*), filling stations are located at adequate intervals down most major roads, and even when travelling into very rural areas you can usually get away without carrying spare petrol in jerry cans – though it's a wise precaution, to avoid being caught out. Fuel prices were recently increased by over 30 percent, but are still cheap by European standards. It comes in two grades: "Extra" (around $1.50 per gallon), which is the more popular and widely available; and the higher-octane "Super" (around $2 per gallon), both of which are unleaded.

Driving in the larger **towns** can be a bewildering experience, with the frenetic traffic and confusing one-way systems. If you get lost (which is pretty much inevitable) a good tip is to flag down a taxi and ask the driver to take you to your hotel or wherever you're trying to get to, while you follow behind him in your car – explain that you will pay him the normal price of a cab ride on arrival. Most towns have plenty of inexpensive **car parks** dotted about, advertised by large *parqueadero* signs by the entrance. They're usually large back yards with a caretaker keeping an eye on the vehicles. Otherwise, during the daytime it's fairly safe to leave your car in busy downtown streets or around the central square, often under the watchful eye of a *guarda-auto*, a young boy who springs out of nowhere as soon as you park and offers to keep an eye on your car in exchange for a tip. Never, ever leave valuables in your car at any time, or your car on the street overnight, as it will almost certainly be broken into; try only to stay in hotels with a garage, or else leave your vehicle overnight in a securely locked *parqueadero*.

Toll gates are now operated by private companies responsible for road maintenance on an increasing number of trunk routes. Light vehicles should head for the *"liviano"* lane; tolls typically cost between $0.50 to $1.50.

Car rental agencies

In the UK

Avis Britain ☎0870/606 0100, Northern Ireland ☎028/9024 0404, ⓦwww.avis.co.uk
Budget ☎08459/606 060, ⓦwww.budget.co.uk
Hertz ☎0870/844 8844, ⓦwww.hertz.co.uk

In Ireland

Avis ☎02/128 1111, ⓦwww.avis.ie
Budget ☎0903/277 11, ⓦwww.budget.ie
Hertz ☎01/676 7476, ⓦwww.hertz.ie

In North America

Avis US ☎1-800/230-4898, Canada ☎1-800/272-5871, ⓦwww.avis.com
Budget US ☎1-800/527-0700, Canada ☎800/268 8900, ⓦwww.budgetrentacar.com
Hertz US ☎1-800/654-3001, Canada ☎1-800/263-0600, ⓦwww.hertz.com

In Australia

Avis ☎136 333 or 02/9353 9000, ⓦwww.avis.com.au
Budget ☎1300/362 848, ⓦwww.budget.com.au
Hertz ☎13 30 39 or 03/9698 2555, ⓦwww.hertz.com.au

In New Zealand

Avis ☎09/526 2847 or 0800/655 111, ⓦwww.avis.co.nz
Budget ☎09/976 2222, or 0800/652 227, ⓦwww.budget.co.nz
Hertz ☎0800/654 321, ⓦwww.hertz.co.nz

Hitchhiking

While **hitching** is not recommended as a safe way of getting about, it's widely practised by Ecuadorians, particularly in rural areas. For backpackers, the bus service is such that you'll only really need to hitch in the remoter places – you're most likely to get a ride in the back of a pick-up truck, the preferred private vehicle in rural Ecuador. As with stopping a bus, face the oncoming vehicle and point vaguely at the road a few yards from your feet. The etiquette is to ask *"¿Cuánto le debo?"* ("How much do I owe you?") at the end of the journey, at which point you may be asked to pay a small amount, rarely more than the bus fare would have been, or let off for free. If you're worried about being overcharged, ask *"¿Cuánto sería?"* ("How much would it be?") before climbing aboard.

By taxi

Most towns in Ecuador have a fleet of yellow **taxis** – in some Oriente towns, white pick-up trucks (*camionetas*) take their place. Only in Quito are you going to find metered taxis (see p.82); everywhere else taxis operate on a fixed-fare system, with a standard short journey typically costing around $1. If you're dropping someone off, the driver will often charge this as an extra journey, even if it's only a few hundred metres from your final destination. For longer distances and in larger towns, such as Guayaquil, the fixed rate doesn't apply, and it's far more difficult to know what the fares should be. Most drivers are honest, but the best way to avoid being ripped off is to ask locals what the standard fares are to various destinations. Always agree the price with the driver beforehand, and don't be afraid to haggle. Tipping isn't necessary, but it's common to round fares up for friendly service.

Taxis are also sometimes the best way of getting to out-of-the-way places such as national parks or mountain refuges, particularly if you're in a group and can share the cost. Hiring a taxi by the day could cost anywhere between $40–60; some taxi drivers will increase the price for bigger groups. Needless to say, there's always room for negotiation.

By boat

Boat travel can make a pleasant change to buses, though your exposure to the elements means that you can get either very cold and wet if it rains or badly sunburnt if it doesn't. Unless you're on a private boat transport to a smart jungle lodge, seats are invariably wooden and thoroughly uncomfortable. Bring something to sit on and keep food and water with you, as the bulk of your luggage will usually be put under wraps at the front of the boat.

The most likely place you'll end up in a boat is in the **Oriente**, where the best of the jungle is often a boat ride away. On the **coast**, the repaired coastal highway now runs the entire length of the Ecuadorian seaboard, meaning you're less likely to need to travel by boat, but it's still fun to tour through the mangroves around San Lorenzo or Muisne. A few communities in the northern Pacific lowlands are still only reachable by river boat.

A **chartered boat** (*flete*) is always much more expensive than going on a public one, though you can reduce costs by gathering a group; the fare is usually fixed for the journey regardless of the number of passengers. Travel around the Galápagos Islands is almost exclusively by boat; refer to that chapter for details.

By bicycle

Even if Ecuador's chaotic roads don't always make the ideal cycleways, **cycling** can offer unrivalled closeness to the land and its people. Bike rental outlets are thin on the ground outside the main tourist centres and aren't usually equipped with bikes suitable for extended rides. For proper **cycle touring**, you're best off bringing your own bike and equipment from home; airlines usually don't have a problem transporting them if packed in bike boxes with the pedals removed. You're unlikely to want to stay solely on the busy paved roads, so a mountain bike is almost certainly better than a conventional touring bike. A range of low gear ratios will make the long highland climbs more tolerable when loaded up, and the wider, knobbly tyres will aid you on poor surfaces. Bicycle repair shops (*talleres de bicicletas*) are far more widespread than bike shops, but will only have parts for rudimentary repairs – bring a comprehensive tool kit and a selection of essential spares. When **planning your route**, don't forget that at altitude you won't be able to cover anywhere near the distances per day that you do at home: reckon on about half.

In the UK, the CTC (Cyclists' Touring Club), 69 Meadrow, Godalming, Surrey GU7 3HS (℡01483/417217, ⓦwww.ctc.org.uk), is an excellent source of information for cycle tourists, and has factsheets on a range of subjects including recommended itineraries for touring in Ecuador, Peru and Bolivia.

Accommodation

Ecuador's plentiful supply of accommodation encompasses everything from international luxury hotels charging $200 a night to the most meagre kinds of shelter going for less than a couple of dollars. You can get good value for money across the spectrum: at the high end, you'll find beautiful haciendas rich in history which have lost none of their period charm. In the mid-range there are hotels as good as any in North America or Europe, but for a fraction of the cost. Travellers on a tight budget won't be disappointed either, as just about every town in Ecuador has a hotel offering clean double rooms, often with a private bathroom, for $5–10.

Supply is such that it's unlikely you'll have any trouble getting a cheap room, though coastal resorts can get very crowded during holidays, while city accommodation tends to fill for major fiestas. Except for the Galápagos Islands, the top jungle lodges, and the most popular seaside resorts like Atacames, there's not much of a price difference between **seasons**, but broadly speaking the high season is mid-June to August and December to January, and at beach resorts during national holidays. Choices at the top end are always going to be fewer, so if you're on a higher budget, it's a good idea to phone ahead and book at the smarter hotels, especially if you're set on a particular one. Outside high season it's worth trying to negotiate a **discount**, wherever you are. A simple "*¿Tiene algo un poco más barato?*" ("Do you have anything a little cheaper?") or "*¿Me puede dar un discuento?*" ("Could you give me a discount?") will often get you a lower price on the spot. The more expensive hotels are likely to charge 22 percent on to your bill for IVA and service (see p.29), which we have included in the price where relevant.

Hotels masquerade under a variety of names in Ecuador; generally, in increasing order of comfort they are: *pensión*, *residencial*, *hostal*, *hotel* and *hostería* – terms that will often help give you some idea what to expect of the place. Beware of anything calling itself a *motel*, which in Ecuador indicates the sort of place that charges guests by the hour. Some *hoteles* are as bad as the worst *pensiones*, however, and there's no substitute for having a good look round the rooms yourself before you sign in. Within any establishment, you'll often find wide variation in the quality of the rooms even though they may be priced the same: for example, you might be suffering in a dank, windowless room while across the corridor is something bright and clean with a balcony and views. You won't necessarily be given the best room, so if you're not happy, say something.

Accommodation price codes

Unless otherwise indicated, **accommodation** in this book is coded according to the categories below, based on the price of a **double room in high season**, including tax and service if appropriate. Seasonal differences, usually found in tourist centres and coastal resorts, when prices can rise or fall by as much as fifty percent, are signalled in the text. In lodgings at the lower end of the scale, **single travellers** usually pay half rate, but more expensive hotels often charge close to or the same as the full double rate.

❶ $5 and under	❹ $16–25	❼ $61–85
❷ $6–10	❺ $26–40	❽ $86–120
❸ $11–15	❻ $41–60	❾ over $120

Note that there are differences between the highlands and lowlands too. In the highlands, you can hope for **hot water** in all but the cheapest places, but in the lowlands, where people largely consider it unnecessary, only the more exclusive hotels will offer such a luxury. Conversely, **air conditioning** and fans are more common at a cheaper level in the lowlands than in the highlands. **Mosquito nets** are usually – but not always – only in evidence on the coast and in jungle lodges; consider bringing one from home if you plan to spend time in remote lowland areas. Across the country in almost all hotels, you'll rarely find a bathtub. A shower, sink and lavatory makes up the standard **bathroom**.

Pensiones and residenciales

The humblest type of accommodation is the **pensión**, usually a simple family home around a small courtyard with a couple of basic rooms and a cold-water shared bathroom. At $5 and under for a double, this is about as cheap as you can go without being in a tent. At these prices *pensiones* tend to be either great value or uninhabitable. In some cases they won't even supply lavatory paper. **Residenciales** are larger, slightly more comfortable versions of the *pensión*, on the whole offering simple, modestly furnished rooms, often arranged around a courtyard or patio. They usually contain little more than a bed (or up to four single beds), and a bedside table, though some provide more furniture (perhaps a writing desk, chair and lamp), and a few more comforts, like towels and soap. Most, but not all, have shared baths – not necessarily with hot water (and sometimes it's only on for an hour or two a day), even in the highlands. Where places differ is in the upkeep or "freshness" of the rooms: some of the really cheap rooms are dank and damp, with peeling paint and saggy beds, while others, though still very simple, have good bed linen, walls that are painted every summer, and a clean, swept feel to them.

Hostales and hoteles

Hostales form a linking category between the *residencial* and the *hotel*, being anything from attractive nineteenth-century family houses with waxed wooden floorboards, floor-to-ceiling windows and courtyards draped with flowers, to the generic and uninspiring hotel block. Facilities, on the whole, are better than in a *residencial*, with more likelihood of private bathrooms, hot water, clean towels, soap and now and again perhaps even a TV. They'll typically cost anywhere between $5 and $25 a double. **Hoteles** are supposed to cover one of the top categories, but in fact encompass wide variations in quality. Many are more or less identical to *hostales* including in price, and a few are considerably worse, but all usually occupy purpose-built buildings. When you pay $25 a double and beyond, you should really start to notice the difference in comfort. Rooms should be well kept, clean and fresh, have good mattresses, all-day hot water powered by a *califón* (water heater) rather than an electric shower (touching the pipes can give you a mild shock when it's on), air conditioning in the lowlands, minibar, phone and cable TV. At this level the hotel often has its own restaurant and bar, and perhaps a laundry service. Some people feel it's well worth paying a few dollars more to get such facilities, and even budget travellers occasionally loosen their belts to take advantage of prices so low by Western standards. It should be said, though, that more expensive does not necessarily mean better. There are quite a few ugly hotels built in the 1960s or 70s for local business executives, which charge inflated prices to tourists. The best luxury hotels, however, have all you'd expect of such anywhere in the world, excellent facilities and service, and charge at North American or European prices.

Haciendas and lodges

Among the treats of accommodation in highland Ecuador are the **haciendas**, grand farming-estates of colonial times converted into magnificent, out-of-the-way hotels. Many are truly luxurious, with all the period details, such as open fires in each room, and augmented by modern comforts and conveniences, like plush carpets and thundering hot-water showers. In some cases, they're still working farms, making their own produce, and keeping stables and horses both for farm work and for guests. They're sometimes called **hosterías**, which signifies a large country hotel, but this category also includes the far less charming out-of-town tourist complexes with concrete rooms and a large swimming pool.

Lodges, most normally found in the country's forested regions and often made from natural materials, serve as bases for exploring the surrounding environment. Top-end lodges have all the modern comforts allowed by their isolated locations; dining rooms and sitting rooms, libraries and lookout towers for bird watching, and live-in naturalist guides to lead forest tours. Most won't have electricity, and some are lodges only in name, perhaps little more than open-sided shelters with raised platforms, mattresses and mosquito nets. Lodges usually consist of a collection of **cabañas**, simple cabins with thatched roofs and wooden walls and floors. These are also popular on the coast, particularly at beach resorts.

Camping and youth hostels

With so few designated campsites in the country and budget accommodation being so cheap, not many people bother with camping, unless they're out exploring Ecuador's wildernesses. Generally, you'll be allowed to pitch a tent inside most parks and reserves, where you can sometimes use the facilities of a nearby guardpost or refuge, but on the whole you'll have to be entirely self-sufficient. On private land, you should seek permission from the owner, but bear in mind that camping near towns is uncommon and not regarded as particularly safe; most people eschew the canvas for four walls and a door. A few hotels mentioned in the Guide allow you to pitch a tent on their grounds and use their facilities at cheap rates. See the relevant "Listings" sections for individual cities and towns for advice on where to find **camping equipment**.

Ecuador has a handful of **youth hostels** accredited with Hostelling International (HI). They're often quite comfortable, with dorms as well as double rooms, and non-members are welcome to stay. Discounts of a few dollars are available to HI members, but if you're on a budget, there's no great advantage of being one in this country, since many hostels charge around $10–15 per person – substantially more than perfectly adequate non-hostel accommodation.

Eating and drinking

Ecuador is a land of plenty when it comes to food, and it's easy to eat well for little. As a fertile country comprising three distinct geographical regions, it can produce a startling array of foods, including dozens of exotic fruits, and three different regional styles of cooking.

That said, there's surprisingly little variation between restaurant menus in these areas, with either fish (usually *trucha* or *corvina*, trout or sea bass), chicken or beef served with rice, chips or *patacones* (fried plantain), topped off with a smidgen of salad. Though the fish or chicken may be fried, boiled or breaded, it's easy to get tired with the overall monotony of the cuisine, meaning you'll want to be on the lookout for the more exciting **comidas típicas**, the traditional food of each region, cropping up on menus. Less adventurous souls can also find recourse in Western **fast-food** outlets, such as *Burger King* and *KFC* in the cities, or the **pizza and pasta** parlours which are springing up in many Ecuadorian towns.

Eating out

Ecuador's restaurants range from those charging Western prices for top-class international cuisine to the grimiest roadside eatery serving chicken, rice and little else besides. The majority of **restaurants**, however, are clean but modest, and offer decent food at low prices. Most of them simply call themselves **restaurantes**, but others you might encounter are **cevicherías** (for *ceviche*), **asaderos** (usually roast chicken), **pizzerías** (pizzas), **marisquerías** (seafood), **picanterías** (cheap snacks and sometimes spicy food), **parrilladas** (grillhouses) and **paradores** (roadside stophouses). The Chinese restaurant, or **chifa**, is to Ecuador as the curry house is to Britain; chifas are found in just about every town in the country, dishing out tasty, inexpensive food to a loyal local following. The typical chifa dishes are *chaulafán* (fried rice) and *tallarines* (noodles), both mixed with meat and vegetables and served in large helpings.

Vegetarians are likely to become well-acquainted with chifas for their *tallarines con verduras* (noodles and veg), one of the few hot veggie meals available across the country. There's no shortage of vegetarian food in the main tourist centres, but away from those, the cry of "*soy vegeteriano*" ("*vegeteriana*" for a woman), "I'm a vegetarian", will sometimes be met with offers of fish or chicken. A quick discussion with the staff usually ends with them finding something appropriate for you, even if it's just egg, chips and rice – and even the blandest food can be enlivened by *ají*, the chilli sauce found on most restaurant dining tables. It's one of the few spicy-hot elements of Ecuadorian cooking, but the degree of spiciness depends on the establishment.

Many **restaurants** open early in the morning and serve **breakfast** (*desayuno*) in either the *continental* or *americano* varieties, the former being bread (*pan*), butter (*mantequilla*) and jam (*mermelada*), accompanied by coffee (*café*) and juice (*jugo*); add *huevos revueltos* or *fritos* (scrambled or fried eggs) to this and you've got an *americano*. In the Oriente, you'll come across the *petrolero* (oil man), which is all this plus a chunk of meat or some similar manly accessory. Fruit salad, granola and yogurt also make appearances on breakfast tables in tourist centres.

Eating out can cost less than $2 per head if you stick to set menus; at **lunch** this is called *almuerzo* and at **dinner** *merienda*, which consists of two or three courses and a drink. À la carte and individual **main courses** (*platos fuertes*) are typically $2–5 – you're probably in a smart place if it's much more than $7. A real blowout in a nice restaurant shouldn't go much over $15 a head. Bear in mind that the better places will add 12 percent **tax** (IVA) and 10 percent service to your bill.

Markets are among the cheapest sources of food, not only because of the range of nutritious fruits and produce on offer, but also from the makeshift restaurants and **stalls** that dole out fried meats, potatoes and other snacks. Although some stallholders may not be overly scrupulous on the hygiene front, sizzling-hot food prepared and cooked in front of you should be fine. **Street vendors** also supply **snacks** such as corn-on-the-cob or *salchipapas*, a popular fast food comprising a bag of chips propping up a sausage, all doused in ketchup. Vendors often carry their wares onto buses and parade the aisles to tempt passengers; as you haven't seen how or where these have been prepared, you should probably resist their advances.

Comidas típicas

In the **highlands**, a typical meal might start off with a *locro*, a delicious **soup** of potato, cheese and corn with half an avocado tossed in for good measure. This is great for vegetarians, who'll want to steer well clear of its relative, *yaguarlocro*, which swaps the avocado for a sausage of sheep's blood, tripe and giblets. Other soups might be *caldo de patas*, cattle hoof soup; *caldo de gallina*, chicken soup; or even *caldo de manguera*, which literally means "hose pipe soup", a polite name for bull's penis soup. A number of different grains, such as *morocho*, similar to rice, and *quinoa*, a small circular grain, are also thrown into soups, along with whatever meat and vegetables are available. Other possible **starters**, or snacks in their own right, include *empanadas*, corn pasties filled with vegetables, cheese or meat.

For a main course you might go for *llapingachos*, cheesy potato cakes – cheese, corn and potatoes are big in the highlands – often served with *chorizo* (sausage), *lomo* (steak) or *pollo* (chicken) and fried eggs. The famous *cuy*, guinea pig roasted whole, has remained for centuries a speciality of the indigenous highlanders, and is rather good, if a bit expensive. Another traditional dish is *seco de chivo*, a stew usually made out of mutton in the highlands, and goat on the coast, as the name would suggest. The unappetizing-looking *guatita*, tripe smothered in peanut sauce, is actually much better than it sounds.

Mote, a hard corn that is peeled with calcium carbonate solution, and then boiled in salt water, is frequently served as accompaniment to main courses, particularly *fritada*, seasoned pork deep-fried in lard, and *hornado*, pork slow-roasted in the oven. *Motepillo* is a Cuenca speciality, in which the mote is mixed with eggs to make corn-filled scrambled eggs. Another common side dish is *tostado*, toasted maize, or *canguil*, popcorn that often comes with soups and *ceviches*.

If you still have space left then there's *morocho de leche*, similar to rice pudding flavoured with cinnamon and often served cold; *quesadillas*, baked cheese doughballs brushed with sweet syrup; *humitas*, ground corn mixed with cheese, sugar, butter and vanilla, wrapped in banana leaves and steamed, or *quimbolitos*, which are similar but more spongy. *Higos con queso*, figs with cheese, is another common highland dessert.

Coastal delicacies, unsurprisingly, centre on **seafood**. The classic *ceviche* is prepared by marinating raw seafood in lime juice and chilli, and serving with raw onion. It can be dangerous to eat uncooked seafood, so it's worth knowing that shrimps (*camarones*) and king prawns (*langostinos*) are usually boiled for ten minutes before they're marinated. If a *cevichería* (*ceviche* restaurant) looks unhygienic, you should probably give it a miss. On the north coast, *encocados* are fantastic fish dishes with a Caribbean flavour, cooked in a sauce of coconut milk, tomato and garlic and often served with a huge mound of rice. Bananas and plantain often replace the potato, appearing in many different forms on the side of your plate. *Patacones* are thick-cut plantains fried up in oil and served with plenty of salt, while *chifles* are thinly cut plantains cooked the same way. *Bolón de verde* is a rather stodgy ball of mashed baked plantain, cheese and coriander traditionally served as a snack with coffee.

The **Oriente**, being originally composed of many disparate indigenous groups, has rather less well-defined specialities, but you can count on *yuca* (a manioc similar to yam) making an appearance, alongside rice, bananas, and fish (including the scrawny piranha) caught in the rivers. As a guest of a forest community, you may eat game such as wild pig or *guanta*, a large rodent not that different to *cuy*.

Drinks

Bottled **fizzy drinks** (*colas* or *gaseosas*) can be obtained all over Ecuador, particularly Coca-Cola, Sprite, Fanta and 7-Up (which is called "*eseven*"). Note that if you want to take your pop away with you, you'll have to pay a deposit on the glass bottle; a more common solution is to get it put *en bolsa*, in a small plastic bag with a straw. Plastic bottles and cans are becoming more common, but they are more expensive. Bottled **mineral water** can be bought throughout the country in still (*sin gas*) or sparkling (*con gas*) varieties. Home brands, such as Güitig from the mineral springs at Machachi, are facing stiff competition against new arrivals from the Coca-Cola corporation, plastic-bottled "mineralized water", such as Bonaqua, which seem to have the upper hand in distribution.

Ecuador has more types of fruit than you can imagine, certainly far more than there are English names for, and just about all of them are made into mouthwatering **juices** (*jugos*). The most common fruit juices are made from *maracuyá* (passion fruit), *tomate de arbol* (also known in the West as tamarillo, it's orange and more fruity than a tomato), *naranjilla* (native to Ecuador, sweet and tart at the same time), *piña* (pineapple), *naranja* (orange), *guanábana* (a very sweet white fruit), *taxo* (another kind of passion fruit), *mora* (blackberry) and *babaco* (indigenous relative of the papaya, juicy and slightly acidic), but there are many others. Juices can come pure (*puro*) or mixed with water – make sure it's purified water. When they're mixed with milk they're called *batidos*.

Considering that Ecuador is a major **coffee** producing country, it's a shame there's not more of the real stuff about. Most cafés and restaurants will have a jar of Nescafé on the table, though a few places have *esencia de café*, a liquid coffee distillate. You'll get a cup of hot milk if you ask for *café con leche*, and hot water for black coffee if you specify *café negro*. There's often a pot of chocolate powder lying around as well, for **hot chocolate** or for mixing the two together for mocha. **Tea** (*té*) is served without milk and usually with a slice of lemon. Asking for *té con leche* is likely to get you a cup of hot milk and a teabag. For just a dash of milk, it's best not to say anything until your (milkless) tea arrives, and then ask for a little milk. **Herbal teas** (*aromáticas* or *mates*) come in a variety of flavours, some of which are familiar, while others are made from native plants.

Beer essentially comes in three forms: Pilsener is the people's beer, weak and light and in big bottles; Club is a bit stronger, a bit more expensive and comes in small bottles or cans; and Biela, from the slang word short for "*bien helada*" ("well chilled"), which one beer critic described as "not horrible but not worth trying once". Foreign brands are available in some city bars, but you'll have to pay for the privilege. Ecuadorian **wine** isn't common, but you'll find good Chilean and Argentinian vintages in the better restaurants for less than you'd pay at home.

The local tipple, especially in the sierra, is **chicha**, a fermented corn drink of which there are many varieties. Buckets – literally – of the stuff do the rounds at all highland fiestas. In the Oriente, the *chicha* is made from *yuca*, which is chewed up, spat in a pot and allowed to ferment. *Aguardiente* (also called *caña* or *punta*) is a sugarcane **spirit**, sharper than rum (*ron*), that will take off the roof of your mouth. In fiestas they might mix it with fruit juices, or in the sierra drink it as *canelazo*, adding sugar, cinnamon (*canela*) and hot water to make a traditional highland warmer. On the coast it stars in many cocktails, the most ubiquitous being *caipiriña*, in which it (or rum) is combined with lime juice, sugar and ice.

Communications

Even small towns in Ecuador have post and telephone offices, which generally offer reliable domestic and international services, making it fairly straightforward to keep in touch with home. The dire economic problems of recent years triggered a mass emigration from the country, which in turn has stimulated the development of Ecuador's international communications. Most significantly, Internet, net phone and email access – by far the cheapest and easiest way to send and receive news – has grown dramatically, with Internet cafés and new servers springing up all over the country. The price of international calls has also fallen greatly as the state telephone companies begin to modernize and deregulate. The same benefits have not yet spread to the postal system, however, which is becoming increasingly expensive without noticeable improvements in service.

Mail

Letters and postcards **sent from Ecuador** can take anything from five days to a month to reach their destination, though they're often faster to North America than anywhere else. The economic problems of a few years ago seemed to have had a bad effect on the postal service, which has simultaneously become less reliable and more expensive. If you need to send something of value, you're probably better off using a courier (DHL, for example, has offices throughout the country; refer to "Listings" p.115 for contact details in Quito).

Postcards and letters up to 20g sent by airmail (*por avión*) cost $0.90 to America, or $1.05 to the rest of the world; add $0.95 if you want it registered (*con certificación internacional*). Prices rise steeply for personal mail that weighs more (around $4.45 for America, $6.55 for the rest of the world for a letter of 101g), though you might get away with sending a chunky letter in a big, brown envelope and calling it *impresos* (printed matter), for which you'll pay at substantially reduced rates (101g is roughly $2.40 for the Americas and $4.90 for everywhere else). When buying stamps it pays to check the clerk's arithmetic and to get your mail franked in front of you. Note that many envelopes (*sobres*) in Ecuador don't have a sticky back; you should find a pot of glue somewhere in the post office.

For **parcels** sent airmail, it costs $14.55 for 1kg to the Americas with each additional kg costing $4.45 to a maximum of 31.5kg. For the rest of the world this is marked up to $23.90 for the first 1kg, and $12.85 for each extra kilo. Surface Air Lifted mail (SAL/APR) is about 10 percent cheaper but much slower. Sending **large packages** means getting a box from a supermarket or a sack from a market, and turning up at the Correo Marítimo Aduana on Ulloa 273 and Ramírez Dávalos in Quito, near the Santa Clara market. Take it unsealed but bring string or tape to seal it after it's been inspected by customs. Again you may find it easier to go through a private courier, or a cargo company. The SAE (see p.26) keeps up-to-date information on the best ways to send heavy parcels home.

You can receive **poste restante** at just about any post office in the country. Have it sent to "Lista de Correos, the town concerned, Ecuador", and make sure that your surname is written as obviously as possible, as it will be filed under whatever the clerk thinks it is; you'll need to have photo ID to pick it up. If there's a return address on it, it will be sent back if you don't manage to pick it up. In Quito, Lista de Correos mail usually ends up at the main office on Espejo and Guayaquil in the old town; if marked "Correo Central", it could well go to the head office on Eloy Alfaro 354 and Avenida 9 de Octubre. The most convenient post office for people staying in the new town is usually the Surcursal #7, at Torres de Almargo on Reina Victoria and Avenida Colón, which also has a poste restante service.

American Express card holders can make use of AmEx offices for mail services, and some **embassies** also do poste restante. The **SAE** will take mail, phone messages (during club hours) and fax messages for members.

Telephones

The nationalized telephone service, which has been periodically offered up for international tender – so far without much success – is currently split between three state-run arms: **Andinatel**, serving the sierra and the Oriente; **Pacifictel** for the coast and Galápagos; and **Etapa** for Cuenca. The system is slowly modernizing, with more phone offices opening, and far cheaper prices for international calls, though the service can still be erratic in rural areas. Cities, towns and some villages have at least one **telephone office** (daily 8am–10pm, except in remoter places), which are generally the cheapest and most straightforward places for conventional calls. In the phone office, you'll normally be given a plastic token from the counter with your cabin number on it. In some older offices you have to tell the clerk the number you want, and wait in the cabin for your phone to ring, which shows a connection has been made. In others you'll be able to dial the number directly yourself. When you've finished, you hand back the token at the counter and pay for the calls you've made. Note that calling from hotels, while convenient, usually involves a big surcharge; always check before using a hotel phone.

There's a three-tiered tariff system for **domestic calls**: local calls cost around $0.11 per minute, regional calls $0.16, and national calls $0.22. Calls to cellular phones (prefixed ☏09) are charged at $0.37 a minute. The phone companies are also beginning to install **public phone boxes**, but more prevalent at the moment are the cellular public phones maintained by Porta and Bell South, which use prepaid phone cards specific to each company, usually sold at a nearby shop or kiosk (look for a sign). Being cellular, these are a bit more expensive than landlines (unless calling cell phones), but you can also receive calls on them.

Telephone codes and useful numbers

International codes from Ecuador

Dial the international access code (00) + country code + area code (omitting the zero if there is one) + phone number.

Australia ☎00/61   **Ireland** ☎00/353   **UK** ☎00/44
Canada ☎00/1   **New Zealand** ☎00/64   **USA** ☎00/1

Ecuador area codes

Only use the prefix when calling from outside the area. Drop the zero if calling from outside Ecuador. ☎02 (Quito and Pichincha), ☎04 (Guayaquil and Guayas) and ☎09 (cellular phones) phone numbers now have seven digits, the old six-digit number prefixed by 2 for Quito and Guayaquil, and by 9 for mobiles. There are plans to extend seven-digit numbers to other areas also.

Quito and Pichincha province ☎02
Bolívar, Chimborazo, Cotopaxi, Tungurahua and Pastaza provinces ☎03
Guayaquil and Guayas province ☎04
Manabí, Los Ríos and Galápagos provinces ☎05

Carchi, Imbabura, Esmeraldas, Sucumbíos, Napo and Orellana provinces ☎06
Cuenca and Azuay, Cañar, El Oro, Loja, Morona-Santiago and Zamora-Chinchipe provinces ☎07
Mobile phones ☎09
Ecuador country code ☎593

Collect-call and calling-card access numbers

Canada Direct ☎999175
UK BT ☎999178
USA AT&T Andinatel ☎999119
Pacífictel ☎1800/225528

USA MCI Andinatel ☎999170
Pacifictel ☎1800/999170
USA Sprint Andinatel ☎999171
Pacífictel ☎1800/877800

Useful phone numbers in Ecuador

Police ☎101
Fire ☎102

National operator ☎105
International operator ☎116 & 117

International calls are now a fraction of their cost a few years ago. Calling North America costs $0.47 a minute, Europe $0.58 and the rest of the world $0.73 (except South American countries). Many offices will now let you dial direct without questions, but a few places may still want to know how long you wish to speak for, or ask for a deposit, and cut you off if you overstep either.

Collect calls and charge cards

One of the most convenient ways of phoning home from abroad is via a **telephone charge card** from your phone company back home. Using a PIN number, you can make calls from most hotel, public and private phones (non-cellular only) that will be charged to your account. Since most major charge cards are free to obtain, it's certainly worth getting one at least for emergencies; enquire first though whether Ecuador is covered by your operator,

as only a handful currently have agreements with the state phone service (see box above), and bear in mind that rates are likely to be more than from a public phone, sometimes substantially so. The codes listed can also be used to make **collect calls** home.

In theory, you shouldn't have to pay anything in phone offices for using this service, but only a few of them seem to recognize this. It's not worth bursting a blood vessel arguing your case if you're charged – you won't win and it'll usually not be more than local rate anyway.

Cellular phones

Before even thinking about bringing your cellular phone abroad, check with your service provider to see if it will work in Ecuador and if so what the cost of calls will be. Bear in mind that you're likely to be charged extra for incoming calls and messages when abroad, as the people calling you will be paying the usual rate. In many cases it's probably cheaper to buy or rent a cell phone in Ecuador from one of the two mobile phone companies, Porta and Bell South.

The Internet

A large Ecuadorian migration to far-flung places in recent years has spurred the rapid expansion of **Internet** facilities across the country, enabling families to stay in touch regularly at low cost. Where Internet cafés only catered to travellers in the main tourist hotspots, you can now get Internet access in small towns, villages and even some remote backwaters. The pace of change has been startlingly fast, and where the country had only three servers a few years ago, it now has over thirty, ensuring lower prices and better access outside the big cities. Quito is the national centre of Internet activity, with a huge number of cafés, mostly focused in the Mariscal area, and fierce competition which keeps prices as low as $0.50–0.70 for an hour online. Even in areas further afield where national phone rates are needed to link to a server, it's rare to be charged more than $2–3 per hour.

In light of such low prices, **email** and net phone services represent by far the cheapest ways to stay in touch with people back home. You can get free email accounts from a number of different providers, Hotmail (ⓦwww.hotmail.com) and Yahoo Mail (ⓦwww.mail.yahoo.com) being among the most popular. They only take a moment to set up and are accessible from any computer linked to the Net. Many places now offer a **Net phone** service, which allows you to make international telephone calls via the Internet at little over the price it takes to be online (domestic rates). The quality of the calls isn't yet as good as being on a proper phone, but the technology is constantly improving and many "cafés" (often a bare room with a couple of machines linked up) have installed cabins for better privacy.

It's generally not worth bringing your own **laptop** for Internet access, unless you're going to rent your own place. Relatively few hotels allow direct dialling from rooms, making logging on difficult. Make sure you have a surge protector (*supresor de picos/regulador de corriente*) before you plug in to the power supply; without one your hard disk can be badly damaged (see also "Directory" p.65, for electricity and telephone jack requirements). You can get them at home or in Quito for around $10–20. Check out ⓦwww.kropla.com for useful details on how to plug your laptop in when abroad and general information on electrical systems and appliances in different countries.

 # The media

The media in Ecuador are torn between its great cities, with ownership of the main nationals and television station based in Quito and Guayaquil. Even on the televised nightly news, coverage is split equally between newsdesks based in each city.

Newspapers run the gamut from national broadsheets offering in-depth reporting to tabloids spilling over with lurid tittle-tattle. **Television**, on the whole, has a smattering of quality news and documentary programmes, but is dominated by imports, soaps and game shows. Ecuador has many local **radio** stations, which are considered the glue that binds remote communities together.

Newspapers

Ecuador produces several high-quality daily newspapers. Leader of the pack is the Quito-based *El Comercio*, a traditional **broadsheet** that has good coverage of home and international news, and comes with supplement sections on sport and business. The more progressive *Hoy*, again from Quito, also enjoys a high standard of writing, particularly in its robust editorials. The Guayaquil broadsheets, *El Universo* and *El Telégrafo*, are solid publications, the latter printing a news summary in English. There are a number of **regional newspapers** too, such as *El Mercurio* in Cuenca. Just about all of these major dailies have their own websites, which hold a selection of the day's articles and headlines (see p.28).

The gravity of the broadsheets is counterbalanced by a racy **tabloid** press, such as *La Segunda* and *La Tercera* in Quito, which try to find the lighter side of the most grisly news stories, sometimes in questionable taste; following a fatal blast at an arsenal in Riobamba, one headline was "Riobooooumba!!" *Últimas Noticias*, Quito's afternoon tabloid, isn't as flippant, but Guayaquil's *Extra*, available across the country, manages to plumb the depths of tabloid journalism with an unsavoury mix of sex and violence; the front-page picture is invariably a bloody murder scene alongside a photo of a semi-nude woman.

A few **English-language** pocket-sized city guides are published in Quito, which have tourist information and the odd article in English and Spanish, such as *The Explorer*. Imported news magazines – *Newsweek*, *Time* and *The Economist* – are usually only found in the tourist centres, where you're also likely to get copies of the *International Herald Tribune*, and the overseas edition of the *Miami Herald* newspaper.

Television

Ecuador has five main **national television** stations, and several other **regional channels**. Of the nationals, Ecuavisa and Teleamazonas are the most highbrow, with the best news bulletins and the occasional quality imported documentary. At the other end of the spectrum, there's Gamavision, based in Quito, which has a penchant for screening soaps (*telenovelas*) of the big hair, shaking sets, rags-to-riches-and-back-to-rags variety; and Telesistema, from Guayaquil, which favours epic-length game shows, over-dubbed US imports and home-grown comedy. Telecentro holds the middle ground with a balance of popular programming interspersed with news and sport.

Cable TV is making big inroads in Ecuador, and even some cheaper hotels are beginning to get it installed in their rooms. The number of channels you'll get depends on how much the hotel owner has paid in subscription, but if it's installed you'll almost always have an English-language film channel and a music channel. Only the top-end places are likely to have Direct TV, a satellite setup with dozens of familiar channels in English and Spanish.

Radio

Radio is an important part of community life in Ecuador, particularly in the rural regions where **local stations** are used to pass news and messages between villages. There are hundreds of such stations across the country, the majority broadcasting on AM, with a significant minority on shortwave frequencies. **Religious broadcasting** from evangelical Christians is also widespread and can be picked up across the country; the best known station, **HCJB** (⊛ www.vozandes.org), features programmes and **news** in English and Spanish. With a shortwave radio, you'll also be able to pick up **BBC World Service** (⊛ www.bbc.co.uk/worldservice), **Voice of America** (⊛ www.voa.gov) and **Radio Canada International** (⊛ www.rcinet.ca).

Public holidays, festivals and opening hours

Ecuador has a long tradition of **festivals** and fiestas, dating from well before the arrival of the Spanish. Many of the indigenous festivals, celebrating, for example, the sun, the movements of the stars or the harvests, became incorporated into the Christian tradition, resulting in a syncretism of Catholic religious imagery and older indigenous beliefs. Most **national holidays**, however, mark famous events in post-conquest history and the standard festivals of the Catholic Church. Whether public holiday or fiesta, Ecuadorians love a party and often go to much trouble and expense to ensure everyone enjoys a great spectacle lubricated with plenty of food and drink. For most Ecuadorians the big fiestas mark the year's highlights, the community-wide events that define local and national identity. If you get the chance, you should get to a fiesta at some point during your stay; these are among the most memorable and colourful expressions of Ecuadorian culture – not to mention good plain fun.

Carnaval is one of the more boisterous national festivals, climaxing in an orgy of water fights before Lent. No one is safe as children fill streets and balconies, hurling water balloons, squirting water pistols and chucking buckets of the stuff at open bus windows. **Local fiestas** can also be fairly rowdy, and are reasonably frequent with even small places having two or three a year. Most towns and villages have a foundation day or a saint-day festival, and then maybe another for being the capital of the canton (each province is divided into several cantons). Provincial capitals enjoy similar festivals. You can expect anything at these celebrations: music, dance, food, plenty of drink, gaudy parades, beauty pageants, bullfights, marching bands, tournaments and markets. In the remoter highland communities, they can be very local, almost private affairs, yet they'll usually always welcome the odd outsider who stumbles in with a few swigs from the chicha bucket. They'll be much more wary of ogling, snap-happy intruders, who help themselves to food and drink – sensitivity is the key.

National holidays and major festivals

Note that on public holidays, just about all shops and facilities are closed all day.
January 1 New Year's Day (*Año Nuevo*). Public holiday.

January 6 Epiphany (*Reyes Magos*). Celebrated mainly in the central highlands, but also in Montecristi on the coast.
February/March Carnival (*Carnaval*). The week before Lent is marked by nationwide high jinks, partying and water-throwing. Beach resorts can get packed to the gills. In Ambato, it's celebrated by the grand Fiesta de las Frutas y las Flores, with parades, dancing, bullfights and sporting events (see p.204) – water-throwing is banned here. Two days' public holiday.
March/April Holy Week (*Semana Santa*). Religious parades take place across the country during Holy Week, when many shops and services close and lots of people head to the beach. The big processions in Quito are on Good Friday. Public holidays for Maundy Thursday and Good Friday.
May 1 Labour Day (*Día del Trabajo*). Public holiday.
May 24 Battle of Pichincha (*La Battala del Pinchincha*). Public holiday commemorating the famous battle in 1822.
June Corpus Christi. A moveable festival sometime in mid-June, on the first Thursday after Trinity Sunday, celebrated in the central sierra, particularly Salasaca (see p.208) and Pujilí (see p.198) with danzantes (masked dancers), wonderful costumes and in the latter town 5–10m poles that people climb to get prizes at the top.
June 21 and onwards *Inti Raymi* ("Festival of the Sun"). A pre-conquest festival celebrated on the solstice at important ancient sites such as Cochasquí. Also subsumed into the Catholic festivals of San Juan, and San Pedro and San Pablo (see p.48), collectively known as "Los San Juanes" in the

Otavalo and Cayambe regions.

June 24 San Juan. For John the Baptist's saint day, celebrated particularly heartily in the Otavalo region, beginning with ritual bathing in Peguche and ending with tinku – ritual fighting – in San Juan on the outskirts of Otavalo (now discouraged). These two activities should be avoided by outsiders, but there is plenty of music, drinking and dancing that you can take part in.

June 28–29 San Pedro and San Pablo. Celebrated across the country, though particularly in Cayambe and the northern sierra.

Last Friday in June Bank holiday.

July 24 Birthday of Simón Bolívar. Countrywide celebration of the birth of El Libertador. Public holiday.

July 25 Foundation of Guayaquil. The festivities often blur with the previous day in Guayaquil.

August 10 Independence Day (*Día de la independencia*). Public holiday commemorating the nation's first independence uprising in Quito in 1809, which was thwarted.

September Yamor Festival. A big shindig in Otavalo for the first two weeks of September (see p.145).

September 24 Mama Negra de la Merced. The religious one of two important fiestas in Latacunga, marked with processions and focusing on the Virgen de la Merced (see p.194).

October 9 Independence of Guayaquil. Big celebrations in Guayaquil. Public holiday.

October 12 Columbus Day (Día de la Raza). Marks the discovery of the New World. Public holiday.

November 1 All Saints' Day (*Todos Los Santos*).

November 2 All Souls' Day or Day of the Dead (*Día de los Muertos*). Highland communities go to cemeteries to pay their respects with flowers, offerings of food and drink, and incantations. Public holiday.

November 3 Independence of Cuenca. The city's largest celebration, which merges into the preceding holidays. Public holiday.

Early November Mama Negra. Famous fiesta in Latacunga (see p.194) with colourful parades and extravagant costumes, centred around the Mama Negra – a blacked-up man in woman's clothing – thought to be related to the town's first encounter with black slaves. Usually held on the first Saturday of the month, but recently moved to Friday to inhibit drunkenness. Events continue up to November 11 celebrating the Independence of Latacunga.

November 21 Festival of the Virgen of El Quinche. Pilgrims celebrate at the famous church outside Quito (see p.123).

December 6 Foundation of Quito. Festivities across the capital, with parades, dances and sporting events. Public holiday.

December 25 Christmas Day (*Navidad*). Public holiday.

December 31 New Year's Eve (*Nochevieja*). *Años viejos*, large effigies of topical figures representing the old years are burnt at midnight.

Opening hours

Most **shops** are open Monday to Saturday from 9am to 6pm. Many occupy the family home and, outside the biggest cities, open every day for as long as someone is up. Opening hours of **public offices** are generally from 9am to 5 or 6pm Monday to Friday, with an hour or so for lunch. In rural areas, the working day often starts earlier, say at 8am, and a longer lunch of a couple of hours is taken.

Banks do business from 8am or 9am to 1.30pm, Monday to Friday, sometimes closing at 1pm on Saturdays. Some banks extend business to 6pm during the week, though with reduced services – usually this means you can't change traveller's cheques after 1.30pm. **Post offices** are open Mondays to Fridays from 8am to 7pm, closing at noon on Saturdays, and **telephone offices** are open daily from 8am to 10pm; in rural regions and smaller towns, expect hours to be shorter for both services. **Museums** are usually closed on Mondays.

Crafts and markets

The rich tradition of craftwork (artesanía) in Ecuador was ingrained in the indigenous culture long before the arrival of the Spanish. Weavings, ceramics, leatherware, paintings and woodwork form the core of the handicraft scene, but use of new materials, such as tagua nuts (vegetable ivory), shows a willingness to adapt to the times. Nevertheless, many of the skills and techniques employed have changed little in centuries and often it's the same families and communities that have kept the traditions alive.

Markets are among the best places to pick up finely crafted pieces at good prices, and even if you can't find a bargain, all the bustle and business makes a true window on life in rural Ecuador.

Artesanías

A walk down Avenida Amazonas in Quito will quickly give you an idea of the wealth of handicrafts being made in Ecuador; you'll also see, in some of the classy boutiques, that the work can be of a very high quality. For the best deals, however, for both you and the artist, go to the source, where you'll also get a chance to watch pieces being made. Some local markets, most notably Otavalo, feature a range of crafts from many surrounding communities. In other cases, you can go to the workshops themselves, chat to the experts and buy from them directly.

Perhaps Ecuador's best-known craft is **weaving** (see p.138), in part due to the popularity of the Otavalo weaving market. A good deal of textiles, certainly those of the highest quality, are still made by traditional means, using backstrap looms, for example. Although you'll see plenty of chunky woollen hats, gloves and sweaters, hammocks and wall hangings woven en masse on electric looms, not everything is made with an eye for the tourist dollar; home-woven belts, blouses, hair wraps, shawls, ponchos and hats are as much a part of indigenous traditional dress as ever.

Weaving is not confined to the Otavalo area, and you can pick up fine textiles and tapestries across the sierra. Salasaca (see p.208), near Ambato, is famous for its colourful **tapestries**, while other villages in the area produce **shigras**, knotless net bags made from woven fibres. Further south, around Cuenca, you'll find the beautiful ikat **ponchos**, made by the time-consuming process of weaving previously tie-dyed threads. On the coast in villages in Guayas and Manabí provinces, most famously in Montecristi (see p.401) near Manta, weavers work in dimly lit workshops to produce **Panama hats**, the world's worst-named piece of headgear, considering it originated and is just about exclusively made in Ecuador.

Woodcarving is also a strong tradition, with San Antonio de Ibarra (see p.163) in the northern sierra enjoying a reputation for some of the best carvings on the continent. Far removed from the graceful lines and intricate chiselling of San Antonio's workshops, in the Andean foothills of the Oriente, brightly coloured balsa parrots and toucans are made, from the smallest keyrings to carvings you'd have trouble hauling through the front door. Further into the Oriente, the distinction between craft and function becomes more blurred. Blowpipes, bows and arrows, and knitted fibre bags are as much tools of the trade as handicrafts, though necklaces and ceremonial headdresses are often available too (avoid those made from birds' feathers; it's illegal to take them out of the country for obvious reasons). **Tagua nuts**, also known as vegetable ivory, are the sustainable alternative to the real thing, and are carved into exquisite miniatures of animals and birds, while in Calderón (see p.122), outside Quito, **bread dough** is the material of choice for making colourful figures and gewgaws.

Cotacachi (see p.151), near Otavalo, is the country's centre for **leatherware**, having countless boutiques brimming with belts, bags and jackets. In other highland towns, such as La Esperanza (see p.163) outside Ibarra, you can have bespoke riding gear made, including saddles and boots. Charming naïve **paintings** of sierra life and legends can be bought in all the tourist centres, but the style developed in the community of Tigua in Cotopaxi province, where there is a dedicated gallery (see p.199).

Markets

Apart from some notable exceptions, such as the famous **market** at Otavalo (see p.144), you won't necessarily find much in the way of artesanías at most standard highland markets. After all, these are places where locals primarily come to do their week's shopping, meet friends, catch up on news, and sell their own produce. A local weekly market is often regarded as the linchpin that holds many dozens of remote communities together;

there's always a hint of fiesta at these weekly gatherings, even if an undercurrent of tough negotiation flows beneath the cheer. While you might not find much more to buy than some exotic-looking fruits and vegetables, half-a-dozen chickens or a new pair of nail clippers, the real thrill of traditional highland markets is to be present at the week's most important social occasion.

Making a purchase at a market is a skilful art that's second nature to locals, who can make their customers think they've got a bargain no matter how much they've paid. In craft markets, you should generally expect to find lower prices than in shops, but only if you haggle. Offering to pay far less than asking price, looking both uninterested and extremely knowledgeable, and threatening to walk away are tried and tested techniques for getting the price down, but it kills the fun to argue endlessly over a few cents near the close of a deal. Everyone should have a smile on their face when the transaction is completed.

National parks and protected areas

Some seventeen percent of Ecuador's mainland territory is protected within 26 state-run national parks and biological, wildlife and woodland reserves, in addition to 97 percent of the Galápagos Islands' land mass and a marine reserve surrounding them – the world's second largest. Encompassing mangrove swamps, dry and wet tropical coastal forests, cloud and montane forests, páramo and volcanoes in the sierra, and tropical rainforests in the Oriente, the protected areas represent a cross-section of the country's most outstanding natural attractions. Some are so important that they have earned international recognition – such as Sangay, a World Natural Heritage Site; Yasuní, a World Biosphere Reserve; and the Galápagos Islands, which are both. The principal aim is to protect native flora and fauna from ever-increasing external pressures; few protected areas have the resources beyond this to invest in tourist facilities. Some parks might have a rudimentary refuge and a few trails, but for the most part these are pure wildernesses – areas that are primarily protected by virtue of their remoteness and inaccessibility – and exploring them is only possible with a guide and the logistical help of a tour operator.

The job of managing the protected land falls to the **Ministerio del Ambiente** – formerly known as, and sometimes still referred to, as both **INEFAN** (Instituto Ecuatoriano Forestal

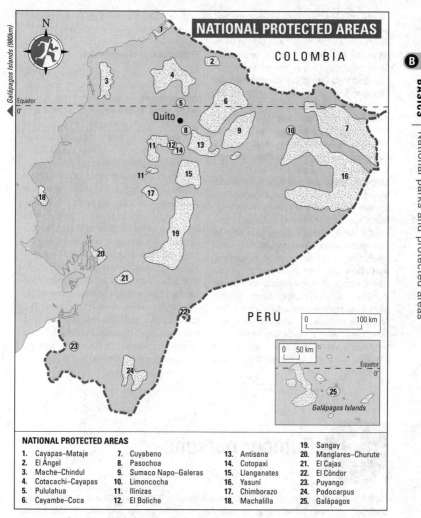

Galápagos Islands (980km)

NATIONAL PROTECTED AREAS

COLOMBIA

Equator
0°

Quito

PERU

| 0 | 100 km |

| 0 | 50 km |

Equator
0°

Galápagos Islands

NATIONAL PROTECTED AREAS

1.	Cayapas–Mataje	7.	Cuyabeno	13.	Antisana
2.	El Ángel	8.	Pasochoa	14.	Cotopaxi
3.	Mache–Chindul	9.	Sumaco Napo–Galeras	15.	Llanganates
4.	Cotacachi–Cayapas	10.	Limoncocha	16.	Yasuní
5.	Pululahua	11.	Ilinizas	17.	Chimborazo
6.	Cayambe–Coca	12.	El Boliche	18.	Machalilla

19.	Sangay
20.	Manglares–Churute
21.	El Cajas
22.	El Cóndor
23.	Puyango
24.	Podocarpus
25.	Galápagos

de Areas Naturales y Vida Silvestre) and the Ministerio de Medio Ambiente – whose key concerns are to conserve the biodiversity of the parks; stop poachers; and to prevent incursions from big business, most notably the oil, timber and African-palm-oil industries. The tourist potential of these areas remains largely undeveloped (with the notable exception of the Galápagos), but with the help of a guide or organized tour, a good map and camping equipment you can immerse yourself in some stunning and little-explored country.

Visiting national parks

No **permit** is needed to visit any of Ecuador's national parks; you simply turn up and pay your **entrance fee** if there's a warden (*guardaparque*) at the guardpost (*guardería*) to collect it. Protected areas are divided into two price categories: A ($10) and B ($5), roughly according to visitor numbers, except for Cuyabeno ($20), Machalilla ($12–20), and the Galápagos Islands ($100). Ecuadorian nationals, and foreigners holding a *censo* (see p.18), pay substantially reduced rates in all cases.

Ease of **access** differs wildly from one park to the next, but most are reached via rough, bumpy dirt roads, and getting there often involves renting a vehicle or booking transport through a local tour company.

Invariably, the *guardaparques* are the best people to speak to if you want **information**; they can also put you in touch with a good local guide, if not offer their own services. Alternatively, try the Ministerio del Ambiente office in the nearest town, which should have small leaflets (*trípticos*) about the park and basic maps. Finally, there's the head office in Quito (on the 8th floor of the Ministerio de Agricultura y Ganadería on Avenida Amazonas and Avenida Eloy Alfaro), which keeps information on all the parks and runs a library, though it can take time to track down what you want there.

Very few parks have provision for **accommodation**. Wardens are happy to let you **camp**, but there's rarely a designated camping area or camping facilities. Some reserves have a basic **refuge** (*refugio*) – most of the volcanoes popular with climbers (see below) have these within a day's climb of the summit, usually a hut with a couple of rooms full of bunks, some simple cooking facilities and running water. They cost $5–20 a night and you should bring your own sleeping bag.

Private reserves

In addition to the state-managed parks, there is a growing number of small-scale **private reserves** set up for conservation, scientific research or ecotourism projects and managed by philanthropists or ecological foundations. Generally these places are much better geared to receiving tourists than the national parks and many have a purpose-built lodge or accommodation within the main research station. They will often also have clear trails, equipment to borrow such as rubber boots, binoculars, guides and information such as bird lists. All this convenience comes at a price, however – anything from $20 to over $100 a night, including meals, unless you're a volunteer (see p.60), but it's well worth the extra cash for the chance to experience some of the most exciting ecosystems on the planet. The most obvious examples are the cloudforest reserves of northwestern Ecuador (see "Northern Lowlands" in Chapter 6) and the jungle lodges in the Oriente (see Chapter 5).

Outdoor pursuits

Having so much untamed wilderness within easy striking distance of major population centres, Ecuador is a superb destination for outdoor enthusiasts. Traditionally it's been a target for climbers, boasting ten volcanoes over 5000m, including the beautifully symmetrical Cotopaxi, and the point furthest from the centre of the Earth, the summit of Chimborazo. In recent years, Ecuador has been making a name for itself in international rafting and kayaking circles too, with a broad range of exciting runs packed into a small area, but opportunities also exist for hiking, mountain biking, surfing, diving, fishing and horse riding. Amongst less strenuous activities, bird watching is one of the biggest draws, with Ecuador's extraordinary biodiversity supporting more than 1550 bird species, almost a fifth of the world's total.

Climbing

Ecuador's "avenue of the volcanoes", formed by the twin range of the Andes running the length of the country, offers numerous **climbing** opportunities, from relatively easy day-trips for strong hill-walkers to challenging technical peaks for experienced climbers. The most popular **snow peaks**, requiring full mountaineering equipment, include **Cotopaxi** (5897m), **Chimborazo** (6310m), **Cayambe** (5790m) and **Iliniza Sur** (5263m). Lower, less demanding climbs, not requiring special equipment and suitable for acclimatizing or simply enjoying them in their own right, include **Guagua Pichincha** (4794m), **Imbabura** (4609m) and **Pasochoa** (4200m).

Not all of the higher peaks require previous mountaineering **experience**: many beginners make it up Cotopaxi, for instance, which demands physical fitness, stamina and sheer determination rather than technical expertise. Others, such as **El Altar** (5319m), are technically difficult and should only be attempted by climbers with experience behind them. It is, of course, essential that an experienced and utterly dependable **guide**, whose first concern is safety, accompany climbers with limited mountaineering experience. Ecuador's best-trained mountain guides are those certified by an organization called ASEGUIM (Asociación Ecuatoriana de Guías de Montaña), whose members have to pass exams and take courses spread over a three-year period before receiving the Diploma de Guía. It's always worth paying the extra for an ASEGUIM guide (usually in the region of $250 in total per person, per climb) – remember that even relatively straightforward, non-technical climbs carry an inherent risk, and your life may depend on your guide. More experienced climbers should also seriously consider ascending with a guide, whose intimate knowledge of the route options, weather patterns, avalanche risks, glaciers and crevasses can make all the difference to the safety and success of an expedition. For a list of recommended guides, see p.114 and p.224.

Practical considerations

December and January are generally regarded as the **best months** to climb, followed by the dry summer months of June to August. March, April and May are considered the worst months, but because of the topography and microclimates of the land, several mountains, such as Cotopaxi, are more or less climbable throughout the year. It's important to emphasize that the **weather** is highly changeable, as are snow and glacier conditions. Unlike their alpine counterparts, Ecuadorian glaciers do not follow normal patterns of ablation and accumulation in summer and winter months respectively. Instead, glacier conditions can change from day to day, meaning that the technical difficulty is also constantly changing; all the more reason to employ a properly trained guide who knows the mountain and its variable conditions well. All your **equipment** will be provided by the guiding company if you're going with one, or can be **rented** from the listed companies or from specialist mountaineering outlets in Quito if you're not (see p.115). Check the equipment over very carefully before deciding which company to sign up with. Guides also provide all **food** on the climb, but you should take your own chocolate and nibbles, to keep your energy levels up, as well as your own water bottle. **Accommodation** is usually in mountain refuges, which serve as the starting point of the climbs. Note that you will typically only get three or four hours' sleep before a big climb, as it's common to set off around midnight or 1am, so as to ascend and descend before the sun starts to melt the snow.

One point that cannot be stressed forcefully enough is the importance of **acclimatizing** before attempting the higher peaks. This should involve spending a few days at the altitude of Quito (2800m), taking in a combination of rest and moderate exercise, followed by at least four or five days around 3500–3800m, ideally including some trekking at this altitude and hill-walking up to around 4200m and then a little higher. If you ignore this warning and try to shoot up Cotopaxi after a couple of days' hill-climbing around Quito, you may well find yourself vomiting every half-hour or so as you try to ascend, or simply too dizzy and nauseous to carry on climbing. See p.22 for more on the risks of **altitude sickness**. A couple of good bases for acclimatizing include the walker's refuge at La Urbina (3620m; see p.229) near Riobamba, and the tiny village of Salinas (3500m; see p.221), near Guaranda. As well as taking time to acclimatize, another measure that helps combat the effects of altitude is drinking enormous quantities of **water** as you ascend.

Remember also that several popular climbs are on **active volcanoes** – particularly Guagua Pichincha, Reventador, Sangay, Cotopaxi and Tungurahua – and you should be fully aware of the current situation before you ascend. You can check the latest volcanic activity news on ⓦ www.igepn.edu.ec, or contact the SAE (see p.80) for up-to-date climbing conditions.

Hiking

Ecuador's great wilderness areas and striking landscapes offer fantastic opportunities for **hiking**, though a general absence of well-marked trails and decent trekking maps does mean a little effort is required to tap into the potential.

The widest choice of hikes is found in the sierra, where numerous mule paths lead into the mountains and up to the páramo, providing access to stunning views and exhilarating, wide-open spaces. The country's best-known long-distance hike is in the southern sierra: the **Inca Trail to Ingapirca** (see p.244), a three-day hike ending up at Ecuador's most important Inca ruins. Also down in the south, **Parque Nacional El Cajas** (see p.258) provides some of the best hiking in the country, in a landscape strongly reminiscent of the Scottish highlands, while **Parque Nacional Podocarpus** offers a fabulous two-day hike across the páramo to the Lagunas del Compadre (see p.271).

Elsewhere in the sierra, rewarding possibilities include day-hikes in the area around **Laguna Quilotoa** and the nearby village of **Sigchos** (see p.196), and a wonderful two-day hike to El Placer hot springs in **Parque Nacional Sangay** (see p.231). There are few options for hiking in the Oriente, owing to dense forest cover – one notable exception is the two- to four-day **Reventador** trail, described on p.298. **Cotopaxi** (see p.188) and **Machalilla** (see p.448) national parks also present good hiking possibilities, as do many areas of open country throughout the highlands. These suggestions are far from exhaustive, but provide a starting point for ideas should you want to plan your trip around a few hikes.

Hiking equipment

If you're thinking of going long-distance hiking without a guide, you should be competent at route finding and map reading, and equip yourself with the necessary IGM **topographical maps** before you leave Quito (see p.116). You will also need a **compass** and – for multi-day hikes – a waterproof **tent**, a warm **sleeping bag** (which needs to be good for -5°C in the sierra), a reliable **stove**, **candles** and waterproof **matches**. Other **equipment** essential for hiking in the sierra – whether you're on a day-hike or long-distance hike, and with or without a guide – includes: strong, water-resistant hiking boots; thermal underwear; warm layers such as a fleece or down jacket; waterproof jacket and gaiters; hat and gloves; water purification tablets; sunglasses; sun screen; lipsalve; spare boot laces; medical kit. You might also consider taking high **rubber boots** – widely available at market stalls in most towns – for wading through the deep mud that commonly blights mountain paths after rainfall. Bear in mind that, as a general rule, weather conditions in the sierra are driest from June to September and wettest from February to April.

Guided hikes

One way of getting around logistical difficulties is by **hiring a guide**, usually through a local tour operator. This solves the problem of arranging transport to the trailhead, and ensures there's far less danger of getting lost while hiking. A good guide can also enhance your enjoyment of the hike by sharing his or her knowledge of local flora and fauna with you, or of the history, legends and customs associated with the places you're hiking through. On the downside, if you're lumbered with a guide you don't get on with, or who wants to walk at a different pace from your own, this can really sour the whole experience. When booking a tour, it's always a good idea to ask to meet the person who will be guiding you before parting with your money, and it's essential to make clear what level of difficulty you're willing to tackle, and what pace you want to go at.

Typical **rates** for guided hikes are $20–40 per person per day, often with a minimum of three to four people per group. A good Quito-based company offering a number of hiking programmes is Safari Tours at Calama 380 and Juan León Mera (℡02/2552505); a selection of additional Quito companies is on p.112, while provincial guides and tour operators are detailed throughout the Guide.

Rafting and kayaking

White-water rafting combines the thrill of riding rapids with the chance to reach some spectacular landscapes that simply can't be visited by other means. The rafts are heavy-duty inflatable dinghies that take six to eight people plus a guide. Rapids are categorized according to a **grading system**: beginners can happily handle waters of Class II and III rating, which usually involve substantial sections of quiet paddling between rougher and more exciting rapids; Class V runs, on the other hand, are very difficult, sometimes dangerous, and can be terrifying for the non-expert.

A small number of rafting and **kayaking** companies, mainly based in Quito, Tena and Baños, organize trips to dozens of rivers. Not far from Quito, on the way to Santo Domingo, the **Ríos Blanco and Toachi** offer a selection of popular runs suitable for beginners and old hands alike. A high density of rivers around Tena has brought the town to the fore as a centre for the sport in Ecuador. Among the most popular is the **Upper Napo**, a typical beginner's run, while the nearby **Río Misahuallí** is suitable for more advanced paddlers, weaving through a stunning canyon in a remote section of rainforest, described as the best rafting trip in the country. Other options from Tena include the **Río Hollín**, **Río Anzu**, and the **Río Quijos** and tributaries, all of which give up a range of possibilities. In the southern Oriente, the **Río Upano** is one of the most talked about runs, involving a trip of several days which has the spectacular Namangosa Gorge on the itinerary.

Safety is the prime consideration before you choose to go white-water rafting or kayaking. Rainfall can have a dramatic effect on a river, and an easy Class II in the dry months can turn into a swollen torrent too dangerous to run in the rainy season. Obviously, a good rafting company will be on top of the situation and will not attempt to run unsafe water. A few shoddy outfits with untrained guides and inappropriate equipment do exist; only go rafting with a reputable company, those that have fully trained guides who know first-aid, can supply good-quality life jackets and helmets, and employ a safety kayak to accompany the raft on the run. Check too that your guide is accredited with AGAR (Asociación de Guías de Aguas Rápidas). For rafting companies operating out of Tena, refer to p.321; for runs around Quito, try Yacu Amu rafting (see p.114). Note that rafting companies in Baños are not as highly regarded as those listed in Tena and Quito.

Bird watching

With roughly as many species as North America and Europe combined crammed into a country that's smaller than Nevada, Ecuador arguably has the best birding in the world. There are hundreds of endemic species, and even some recent discoveries, such as the Jocotoco Antpitta found near Vilcabamba in 1997. The greatest diversity is to be found in transition zone habitats and montane forests, most famously on the **western flank** of the Andes, which forms part of the Chocó bioregion. The village of Mindo, west of Quito, is internationally recognized as an Important Bird Area, and there are several fine private reserves in the area renowned for their birdlife (see Chapter 6).

On the **eastern slopes of the Andes** (covered in Chapters 4 and 5) the Cosanga and Baeza areas are recommended, and in the south, Podocarpus national park and the areas around Loja, Zamora and Vilcabamba. The most convenient way to bird-watch in the **Oriente** is at one of the lodges, such as La Selva (see p.315), Sacha (see p.314) or Kapawi (see p.344), where ornithologist guides and bird lists, some recording well over 500 species, are provided. The best **highland and páramo** habitats are usually found in the national parks, for example El Ángel and Cajas, and the highland sections of Cotacachi-Cayapas and Cayambe-Coca reserves.

It's always worth getting a local **guide** to go bird watching with you. They tend to know where to look and have a knack for picking out birds amidst the undergrowth and greenery. Most of the better lodges and private reserves will have in-house guides, often trained ornithologists, or be able to get hold of one for you.

Binoculars are an invaluable piece of equipment for spotting birds up in the forest canopy, and you may find a field guide handy (see "Contexts", p.554, for recommended ones), though many private reserves supply their own bird lists.

Mountain biking

Mountain biking is more widespread in the sierra than in the lowlands, and a handful of rental companies in the main tourist centres can sort you out with wheels at fairly cheap rates per day or half day; always check the bike's in good working order before you leave. Several specialist biking operators, mainly based in Quito (see p.113), also arrange single- or multi-day mountain biking tours of diverse parts of the sierra, such as Cotopaxi National Park, the Papallacta area, or the Otavalo region. Itineraries are carefully chosen so that there's plenty of descent, which usually means driving up to a high spot and cycling on from there. Even so, being at altitude some trips can be hard work, but a reasonable level of fitness is generally all that's required. The better operators will be able to provide helmets.

Horse riding

Ecuador's sierra region offers numerous opportunities for **horse riding**, particularly at the many haciendas that have been converted into country inns, where riding has been a way of life for centuries. Riding up to the region's sweeping páramos framed by snowcapped volcanoes is undoubtedly a memorable experience, especially if you get an early start to catch the clear morning light and avoid the characteristic afternoon highland showers. Ecuadorian **horses** are a very tough breed, capable of climbing steep slopes and trotting and cantering at high altitudes.

Most haciendas and reputable tour companies provide healthy, well looked-after horses, but it's not unusual for cheaper outfits to take tourists out on neglected, overworked animals. If you sign up to a riding tour and your horse looks lame or ill, refuse to ride it and ask for another one. Also, be sure to check that the saddle is securely fitted, with the girth pulled tight, and take time to adjust your stirrups to the right length – they should be level with your ankles if you let your legs hang freely. Be warned that Ecuadorian riding outfits hardly ever provide protective hats.

Two highly recommended dedicated riding operators are: the Green Horse Ranch, north of Quito (☎02/2374847, ⓦwww.horseranch.de), which offers one- to nine-day rides throughout the Sierra; and Ride Andes (☎09/9738221, ⓦwww.rideandes.com), run by a British woman who organizes riding holidays throughout Ecuador. Other outfits and guides are detailed throughout the text, including: *Hacienda Guachalá* (see p.135); *Hacienda Cusín* (see p.143); *Hacienda Pinsaquí* (see p.143); *Hacienda Zuleta* (see see p.143); *Hacienda Yamahurco* (see p.191); and *Hostería La Cienega* (see p.191).

Diving and snorkelling

Ecuador's top **scuba-diving** spots are in the Galápagos (see p.472), where there are good chances to see large sea fish as well as a number of spectacular endemic reef fish. Most people arrange diving tours before arrival, but there are several operators on the islands who can arrange trips for you there and then. Note that the Galápagos is not the easiest place for novices to learn to dive – mainly due to strong currents and cold temperatures – but it is possible. **Snorkelling** is likely to be an important part of a Galápagos cruise: bring your own gear if you have it; even though most boats can provide it, there may not be enough to go around and what there is may not fit. A **wet suit** is recommended between July and December. On the mainland, there's not a lot of scuba or snorkelling, apart from tours arranged in Puerto López (see p.447) for dives around the Isla de la Plata.

Surfing

The coasts of Manabí and Guayas provinces are the country's most popular places for surfing, and laid-back Montañita in Guayas province has the reputation of being the leading surf centre, though quieter Canoa and Ayampe to the north also have a loyal, less hippy-ish following. There are some keen surfers on the Galápagos Islands too, particularly at Puerto Baquerizo Moreno on San Cristóbal island, where you'll find several places to hire a board and even get a lesson. You won't need to take a wet suit if you're surfing on the mainland, but the water in the Galápagos can get cold in the dry season. The surf **season** is at its height from December to February, when the waves are usually at their fiercest. Canoa Surf Explorer (ⓦ www.canoasurfexplorer.com) is a good specialist agency to talk to, if you're thinking about a surf tour.

Fishing

Fishing (*pesca deportiva*) for trout (*trucha*) in the lakes of the **sierra** is quite a widespread local hobby. A couple of the national reserves are well-known fishing spots, namely El Ángel in the north and El Cajas in the south. Few tours to the **Oriente** forgo the chance of fishing for what is reputedly the world's most ferocious fish, the piranha (*piraña*), with nothing more sophisticated than a line, hook and bait. Take care when de-hooking Oriente fish: some have poisonous spines discreetly tucked into their fins. **Deep-sea fishing**, a sport for the coast's wealthier people, is, as such, less widespread, with Salinas and Manta as the main centres for hooking marlin, tuna, dorado and others.

Crime and personal safety

Ecuador has long enjoyed a reputation for being one of the safest Latin American countries. In recent years, however, crime levels have been on the rise, fuelled in part by a string of national economic crises, to an extent that Ecuador can no longer really justify its old reputation. There's no need to be paranoid, but by using a bit of common sense and taking some simple precautions, as you would in any unfamiliar environment, you can greatly reduce the likelihood of being a victim, and help ensure that you join the overwhelming majority of people who leave the country without being involved in any trouble at all.

Theft

Comparatively wealthy foreign visitors are naturally targets for thieves, though it's worth remembering that the vast majority of crime against tourists is non-violent **opportunistic theft**, which more often than not comes as the result of carelessness. The first rule is, if you really don't want to lose something, don't bring it along in the first place – for example, jewellery, expensive watches, flashy sunglasses and so on. Take out adequate **insurance** (see p.19), check the terms of the policy and its requirements in the event of a theft; most will need a police report. **Make notes** of ticket numbers, emergency credit-card phone numbers, traveller's cheques numbers (always keeping the receipt separately), and insurance numbers, and copy the important pages of your passport and other travel documents. Consider registering with your embassy especially if you plan on a long stay in Ecuador – this will greatly speed up the process of replacement should your passport be lost or stolen.

There are many other basic **precautions** you can take besides. **When you go out**, take as little money as you think you'll need, and keep small notes and change that you'll regularly be using apart from the bulk of your cash – you don't want to reveal how much you're carrying, nor its location, to anyone that might be watching. Wallets, especially those poking out of a back pocket, are easy prey for pickpockets, as are bumbags or fannypacks. Wearing a **money belt** is a good way to carry cash, cards and important documents if you have to take them onto the street with you, though thieves are aware that travellers use them. Make sure the pouch and belt are entirely hidden from view, keeping the pouch tucked well beneath your trousers, even in your underpants. Try not to get money out of it in public – this is your secret stash. Other hiding places might be pockets sewn into the lining of your clothes, trouser belts with zip pockets, or leg pouches that you strap to your calf, sold by the SAE (see p.80). Splitting valuables between more than one hiding place is better than keeping everything together. Avoid anything that is easy to see beneath your clothing.

If you plan on returning to Quito in between trips to various parts of the country, you can leave unneeded valuables and luggage at the SAE or a trustworthy hotel, and travel light using a small commonplace bag that most Ecuadorians would use, found in most markets. Leaving your rucksack and the bulk of your belongings behind will make you feel far less conspicuous, more confident and help you act assuredly when you go about your business, greatly diminishing your chances of being singled out by thieves.

In **hotel rooms**, never leave cameras lying about, or money and traveller's cheques in a drawer. Many hotels have a safe (*caja fuerte*) at reception for storage of valuables; make sure you get an itemized receipt for everything that is stored. Alternatively, lock valuables in your bag, secure it to something (many people take a light chain and some small padlocks) and hide it away (for example, under the bed). In some places, you may be able to use your own lock on the door. In dormitories or rooms that you share with people you don't know, be just as cautious: other travellers can be thieves too.

Pickpockets and thieves favour **crowded places**, typically bus stations, markets, city centres, public transport, crowded beaches, fiestas and anywhere that lots of people congregate to give them cover. Carry daypacks on your front, and swap camera bags for normal holdalls. If seated, loop bag straps around your leg. Busy **bus stations** are particularly bad places, as you tend to be loaded up with all your gear and are more concerned about getting a good seat or finding a hotel; reason enough to avoid arriving at night if you can help it. Take a taxi between your hotel and the station (and vice versa), especially early in the morning and after dark.

When boarding a **bus**, avoid leaving one bag on the ground while you stick another on the roof: keep a hand or a firm foot on everything. If you can, take your bags into the bus with you, and sit where you can see them. Most of your valuables can be transferred to a small pack (beforehand at your hotel) that you can keep with you on your lap during the journey. Buying a sack or tailor-made covers for your rucksack helps to deter light fingers and razor bladers, and some people go to the lengths of lining them with chicken wire. You can always buy a seat for your bag so it's with you throughout your journey. On crowded buses this may seem a bit antisocial, but one excuse is to claim you have a very fragile cargo. **Travelling at night**, whether in your own vehicle or on public transport, is a bad idea whatever part of the country you're in, but especially in Guayas, where hold-ups have been an ongoing problem, as well as Esmeraldas province and the border regions with Colombia.

In the big cities, especially Quito, always **take a taxi at night** rather than wandering the streets; staff at restaurants and hotels will be happy to call you one. Also take a taxi whenever you're weighed down with all your gear, no matter what time of day it is. Do bear in mind, however, that while the vast majority of cabbies are helpful, and taxis safer than walking, you should still not drop your guard. Don't get into taxis already carrying someone; don't use the front seat if on your own; if the cabbie's at the wheel, avoid having luggage in the car while you are outside it – don't put your bags in before you, don't pay until your gear is safely out, and let the driver get out first to open the boot/trunk for you.

Sometimes thieves work in teams and look to set up **distractions** while their colleagues take off with your belongings. Such **con**

tricks include: spraying you with ketchup, mustard or any generic goo and trying to wipe it off; telling you you've dropped some money; asking you to translate a letter; pointing at your shoes as if you've stepped in something; even spitting in your face to shock you – anything to stop you thinking about your possessions. Note too that often the people involved are smartly dressed and seem implausible thieves. Walk briskly away with firm hold of your gear, and ignore them entirely. Fraudsters also like to impersonate policemen; if you're stopped by a policeman who asks to see anything more than your ID, be very suspicious, scrutinize their ID and make a note of all the details. Offering to walk with them to the nearest police station or calling for an officer on ☎101 can stop them in their tracks. Don't ever get into unmarked cars or taxis with anyone, don't take anyone to your hotel room and never show anyone your money.

Armed robbery is unusual, but does happen – sadly with increasing frequency in the Mariscal hotel district in Quito. Other danger spots are parts of the old town, the walk up to El Panecillo (always take a cab), Rucu Pichincha and Cruz Loma volcanoes, and Parque Carolina. You shouldn't go into any city park outside of full daylight hours. Security in Guayaquil is improving, but nevertheless you should be extra vigilant in the downtown areas, the dock and the airport. If you see a shifty-looking gang or sense someone is acting suspiciously up ahead, keep your distance; they can do you no harm if they can't get near you. Unless you are utterly confident you know what you're doing, you should never resist an armed robber – these are desperate people.

Even less likely to happen – but something you should be aware of – is **drugging**. This problem is better known in Colombia, but a few cases have been reported in Ecuador. Extract from the datura plant is slipped into food, drinks or cigarettes, incapacitating the victim, who generally wakes up a day or two later minus money, luggage and any recollection of what has happened. Never accept food, drink or cigarettes from strangers, especially on public transport, no matter how benign they appear. In bars, you can lessen risks by watching your bottle being uncapped and by keeping an eye on your drink. South American Explorers (see p.80) has all the latest on crime hotspots and scams, and keeps a file of travel warnings and advice, available in a concise form online.

Identification

By law you are required to carry "**proper identification**" at all times – for foreigners this means a passport. Visa holders will also need to carry their *censo* and any other relevant documentation. Most of the time photocopies of the stamps and important pages are sufficient, so that you can keep the original in a safe place. In the Oriente and border areas, however, only the originals will do. If you're stopped by the authorities and can't produce identification you can be detained.

The police

All being well, the only contact you're likely to have with the **police** (*policía*) are at road **checkpoints** at various places around the country, mentioned in the guide text. Often you will be waved through, but sometimes you'll be asked to register by writing your name and passport number. In some cases you may also have your bags searched. Watch as they search, and even better get a witness to watch with you; it's very rare, but corrupt officials have planted drugs in bags with the end of extracting a large "fine" from the terrified tourist. The **possession of drugs**, regardless of whether it's for personal use or not, is a very serious offence in Ecuador, one that can end in fifteen years in jail. People who've been charged may have to contend with the country's dilapidated and overcrowded prisons for more than a year before they're even brought to trial. Don't take any chances with drugs or drug dealers – set-ups have happened – as it's simply not worth the consequences. If offered drugs in the street, walk quickly away.

You will need to go to the police as soon as possible **if you are robbed**, in order to make a report (*denuncia*). The report should include an itemized list of everything that was taken and is a vital document if you want to claim on your insurance. Beyond this, there's not a lot they can do, but they may go back to the scene of the crime with you for a look around – a gesture of sympathy more than anything else.

Other risks

There are certain areas in Ecuador that, should you plan to visit, you'll need to check the latest information on safety with your embassy (or see p.28 for useful travel advice websites). Drug smuggling and Colombian guerrilla activity in the northern border areas have made certain parts of Sucumbíos (capital Lago Agrio), Carchi (capital Tulcán) and Esmeraldas (capital Esmeraldas) provinces unsafe. On the southern border, the Cordillera del Cóndor, southeast of Zamora, a region long involved in a border dispute with Peru, still contains unmarked **minefields** and should be avoided altogether.

From time to time, certain of Ecuador's **active volcanoes** threaten to erupt. Occasionally they do belch clouds of ash over the surrounding countryside; Guagua Pichincha and Reventador were the most memorable culprits in recent years. In 1999 Tungurahua reached orange alert (the scale runs from white to yellow to orange then red), and whole towns were evacuated. These are not the only active volcanoes in the country; you can keep abreast of the level of volcanic activity at Ecuador's Instituto Geofísico website (ⓦ www.igepn.edu.ec), or through local press and your embassy.

The mood of the public can also periodically erupt in Ecuador, especially in times of economic uncertainty. **Demonstrations** (*manifestaciones*) and strikes (*paros* or *huelgas*) form a common and normal part of political expression in the country. Violence is rare, and the climax is often little more than the odd burning tyre in the middle of the road, though it can be a frightening experience. Occasionally trouble can break out, when the police move in with tear gas and water cannon – reason enough to steer clear. When there's widespread discontent, roadblocks, particularly on the Panamericana, are common, so make allowances for delays in your itinerary.

Work, volunteering and study

There's plenty of scope for spending fruitful time in Ecuador other than travelling. A huge number of possibilities exist for prospective volunteers, with a growing number of foundations and NGOs seeking outside help to keep running. Finding placements is straightforward, and vacancies exist from periods of only a week up to a year or more. It's even easier to enrol at one of the country's many language schools. Indeed, Ecuador is one of the top choices on the continent for learning Spanish: lessons are good value, and the language spoken in the sierra is clear and crisp.

Volunteering

Many opportunities exist for **volunteers**, though most require you to pay your own way for food and accommodation and to stay for at least a month, with a donation of around $200–250 going towards food and lodging. Reasonable Spanish skills will usually be needed for any kind of volunteer work with communities, and a background in science for research work. Someone without these skills should still be able to find places with no trouble, especially in some areas of conservation work demanding a degree of hard toil, such as reforestation or trail clearing in a reserve. In fact, short-term, unskilled volunteering has evolved into a kind of ecotourism in its own right in Ecuador. You can arrange to volunteer either from home – probably better for more formal, long-term posts – or on arrival in Ecuador, which is simpler and more convenient. The SAE in Quito (see p.80) keeps files on dozens of organizations looking for volunteers. We've listed below a few popular ones based in

Ecuador, plus useful organizations based abroad.

Volunteer contacts in Ecuador

AmaZOOnico ℱ06/887304, ⓦwww.amazoonico.org. Volunteers (no experience necessary) needed to help tend to rescued forest animals and show guests around a jungle rehabilitation centre on a tributary of the Río Napo (see p.334).

Bosque Nublado Santa Lucía ℡02/2866695, ⓦwww.santa-lucia.org. A community-based organization (see p.353) based in the cloudforests of northwestern Ecuador, which seeks to protect community-owned cloudforest, establish sustainable sources of income and educate local people. Volunteers required to help with agroforestry, trail clearing, teaching local guides English, and many other worthwhile projects.

Centro de Investigaciones de los Bosques Tropicales (CIBT) ℡02/2231768, ⓦwww.reservaloscedros.org. Postal address: Apt 17-7-8726, Quito. This organization manages the remote Los Cedros reserve (see p.354) and needs volunteers to ensure the reserve's survival. Expect to work on such things as reforestation, trail maintenance and general upkeep of facilities.

Centro de la Niña Trabajadora (CENIT) Huacho 150 and José Peralta, Quito, ℡ & ℱ02/2654260, ⓦwww.cenitecuador.org. Helping children and families, especially working girls and women, overcome extreme poverty in Quito. Volunteers help in primary and high schools, a medical centre, production workshop or with outreach projects.

Ecotrackers Amazonas N21-217 and Roca, 2nd floor, ℡02/2564840, ⓦwww.ecotrackers.com. Organize mainly short-term placements to villages across Ecuador, for any work currently required by that community.

Fundación Jatún Sacha Eugenio de Santillán N34-248 and Maurian, Quito ℡02/2432240 or 2250976, ⓦwww.jatunsacha.org. Postal address: Casilla 17-12-867, Quito. The foundation manages several reserves around the country – Bilsa (see p.363), Guandera (see p.172), a biological station on the Río Napo (see p.331), at Congal near Muisne (see p.384) and a station at Jama (see p.389) – all of which require volunteers for conservation, education, maintenance, research and sustainable agriculture projects.

Fundación Maquipucuna Baquerizo 238 and Tamayo, Quito ℡02/2507200 or 2507202, ⓦwww.maqui.org. Researchers and volunteers are welcome at the Maquipucuna reserve and nearby Yunguilla community in the western flank cloudforests (see p.352), to volunteer on conservation, maintenance or education projects.

Fundación Sobrevivencia Cofán Domingo Rengifo N74-96, Quito ℡ & ℱ02/2470946, ⓦwww.cofan.org. Volunteers needed at a Cofán community at Zábalo on the Río Aguarico (see p.288) deep in the Oriente for help on a number of ongoing projects.

Río Muchacho Organic Farm ⓦwww.riomuchacho.com, Guacamayo bahíatours in Bahía de Caráquez, Bolívar 902 and Arenas ℡05/691107, ℡ & ℱ 691412. Volunteers are needed to work on this ecological farm near the coast in Manabí province for reforestation, education in the local school, and general helping out (see p.389).

Overseas volunteer organizations

In the UK and Ireland

Earthwatch ℡01865/318838, ℱ311383, ⓦwww.earthwatch.org. A non-profit organization undertaking conservation field research worldwide. In Ecuador it runs key projects on birds and endangered frogs. Typical work might be bird identification, making recordings of birdsong, and general fieldwork and data collection. Participants from all backgrounds are welcome as paying volunteers.

i to i International Projects ℡0870/333 2332, ⓦwww.i-to-i.com. TEFL training provider operating voluntary teaching, conservation, reforestation, health internships and work with children in Ecuador.

Quest Overseas ℡020/8673 3313, ℱ8673 7623, ⓦwww.questoverseas.com. Organizes volunteer work for gap-year students in three phases lasting a total of thirteen weeks. First is an intensive Spanish course in Quito, then four weeks' volunteering in Santa Lucía (see p.353) or Yachana (see p.333), ending with a six-week "Andean Expedition" through Bolivia, Chile and Peru.

Year Out Group ⓦwww.yearoutgroup.org. Full of useful information for students thinking of taking a gap year.

World Challenge Expeditions ℡020/8728 7200, ⓦwww.world-challenge.co.uk. Company providing placements for gap-year students in Ecuador, as well as training for potential leaders.

In North America

AFS Intercultural Programs 10016 ℡1-800/876-2377 or 212/299 9000, ⓦusa.afs.org. Runs summer experiential programmes in Ecuador aimed at fostering international understanding for teenagers.

Earthwatch Institute ☎1-800/776-0188 or 978/461-0081, ⓦwww.earthwatch.org. International non-profit organization with projects in Ecuador requiring volunteers to work in the field with research scientists.

Experiment in International Living ☎1-800/345-2929 or 802/257-7751, ⓦwww.usexperiment.org. Summer programmes in Ecuador for high-school students.

Global Exchange ☎415/255-7296, ⓦwww.globalexchange.org. A non-profit organization that leads "reality tours" to Ecuador, giving participants the chance to learn about the country while seeing it.

Peace Corps ☎1-800/424-8580, ⓦwww.peacecorps.gov. Places people with specialist qualifications or skills on two-year postings in Ecuador, to help local communities with agriculture, animal production, healthcare, natural resources and youth development.

Volunteers for Peace ☎802/259-2759, ⓦwww.vfp.org. Non-profit organization with links to "workcamps" in Ecuador, two- to four-week programmes that bring volunteers together from many countries to carry out needed community projects. Annual membership including directory costs $20.

World Learning ☎1-800/257-7751 or 802/257-7751, ⓦwww.worldlearning.org. World Learning's School for International Training (☎1-800/336-1616, ⓦwww.sit.edu) runs accredited college semesters abroad, comprising language and cultural studies, homestay and other academic work in Ecuador.

Worldteach ☎1-800/483-2240 or 617/495-5527, ⓦwww.worldteach.org. A non-profit organization placing volunteers as teachers in impoverished communities throughout the world. The Ecuador programme consists of about 75 volunteers a year who teach English, mostly at the university or mature student level.

In Australia and New Zealand

Earthwatch ☎03/9682 6828, ⓦwww.earthwatch.org. Organizes volunteer work overseas on scientific and cultural projects. See Earthwatch in the UK on p.61 for more information.

Language schools

One-to-one **Spanish lessons** arranged in Ecuador on average cost $5 an hour, offering tremendous value for money to prospective learners. Most language schools are based in Quito (see p.78), with a few others

in Cuenca and the main tourist centres. You'll normally have lessons for the morning or afternoon (or both if you have the stamina), and there are often social activities arranged in the evenings and at weekends. To immerse yourself totally in the language, **homestays** arranged through language schools are a good idea, sometimes costing as little as $10 a day for accommodation and meals. You can arrange Spanish courses in Ecuador from home, but it's unlikely to be as cheap as doing it when you get there. For arranging lessons and stays in advance, try **Amerispan**, PO Box 58129, Philadelphia, PA 19102-8129 in the US (US ☎215/751-1100, US and Canada ☎1-800/879-6640, ℻215/751-1986, ⓦwww.amerispan.com), or **CESA Languages Abroad**, CESA House, Pennance Road, Lanner, Cornwall TR16 5TQ (☎01209/211800, ℻211830, ⓦwww.cesalanguages.com).

More adventurous linguists could also have a stab at an indigenous language, such as **Quichua**, which a few schools offer on the side. The reaction you'll get off native speakers, even with some elementary knowledge, is well worth the effort.

Work

Unless you have something arranged in advance with an international company or organization, you're unlikely to find much paid work up for offer in Ecuador. Being an English speaker, the only type of job you can expect to get with relative ease is as an **English-language teacher**. It's usually stipulated that English should be your native tongue for these posts, but completely fluent non-native speakers shouldn't have much difficulty. Don't expect to be paid very much, unless you have a TEFL (Teaching English as a Foreign Language) or similar qualification, which will give you greater bargaining power. It's best to find work before arrival, as you'll have to have a work visa which costs $200 (see p.18) – enough to put most people off in the first place. If you have any training in ecology, biology, ornithology and the like, you could do worse than to hunt around the jungle lodge operators (see p.290) asking if they need a **guide**. Fluent English speakers with such qualifications are often in demand.

Women travellers

Travelling as a lone woman in Ecuador presents no major obstacles: plenty of women do it, and the well-trodden gringo trail down the country makes it very easy to hook up with other travellers if you choose to do so. That said, there are a number of irritations you may have to put up with – as in any country – and certain precautions you should take.

The main nuisance faced by solo women travellers is the habit, prevalent among groups of young men, of whistling or making hissing or kissing noises at unaccompanied young women as they walk past. Fair-haired women, or those who obviously look like a *gringa*, are likely to be subjected to these brainless displays of machismo more than others, but even Ecuadorian women aren't let off the hook. The accepted wisdom is to pointedly ignore the perpetrators, or perhaps give them a withering stare – shouting abuse back at them will only be greeted with hilarity and convince them you're *loca* (mad). Note that these situations rarely represent a real threat and are more about a group of guys flexing their muscles in front of each other. And, thankfully, you'll encounter them far less frequently – and maybe not at all – outside the larger cities.

The more annoying problem of **unwanted attention** tends, on the whole, to be more of an issue in large cities and areas with a lot of tourists, such as Baños, where you may find yourself being stared at insistently and engaged in conversation by men who enquire about your love life or make suggestive innuendoes. This stems partly from the fact that many Ecuadorian men perceive Western women to be "easy" and "loose" – an image to some extent exacerbated by Western women's more liberal attitudes to the way they dress and socialize, for example. The ex-head of South American Explorers in Quito – a Canadian woman who's spent many years in Ecuador – advises women travellers to "be respectful of where they are, what impression they are leaving behind, what message they are sending out" in order to avoid reinforcing cultural misconceptions, and to minimize the amount of unwanted attention they receive.

Sexual assault and rape are not common in Ecuador, but there have been a number of incidents reported by female travellers. It is important to note that these are by no means carried out exclusively by Ecuadorians, with several foreign men reported as having assaulted women travellers. Beach resorts such as Atacames, Playas and Montañita are known to have a higher incidence of reported assaults – under no circumstances walk on any beach alone or even in a group at night. Other sensible precautions include avoiding walking alone after dark in towns, and avoiding lone hiking – hook up with a couple of companions or sign up to a guided hike rather than take a risk, however low. If you are unfortunate enough to be the victim of rape or sexual assault, report the incident immediately to the local police and get in touch with your embassy in Quito as soon as possible for advice and support.

Despite the tone of warning, it must be stressed that most Ecuadorians are friendly and respectful of solo female travellers, and most women experience no major problems while travelling through the country. As for practical concerns, note that **sanitary protection** comes almost exclusively in the form of towels, with tampons very difficult to get hold of.

Ecotourism and responsible travel

Tourism may soon become the world's largest industry. Although it often provides a significant portion of a country's foreign revenue, bringing many benefits, there are also some irreversible and detrimental effects on communities and cultures when tourism is allowed to expand unchecked.

In Ecuador, tourism is the fourth largest source of foreign income. Not being a "mainstream" destination, Ecuador so far has largely escaped the worst excesses brought about by an irresponsible tourist industry, witnessed in some parts of the world. Moreover, Ecuador is fortunate enough to have developed an important "ecotourism" sector, which, when working, strives to protect the environment, while contributing positively to the community.

Even so, Ecuador is a remarkably ecologically and culturally **sensitive** country, one of the most biodiverse countries on Earth, home to pristine rainforests and cloudforests and hundreds of species of flora and fauna found nowhere else on the planet. It has many indigenous peoples, whose cultures and territories are under constant pressure from external influences; indeed, some groups have stated they wish to have no further contact with the world outside. With this in mind, we should apply even higher standards of responsibility when we travel in Ecuador than perhaps we are used to.

Ecotourism is now so big in Ecuador, that almost every hotelier, tour operator and travel agent is cashing in on its appeal, slapping the "eco" prefix about, often without any real thought to its meaning. There's no official system in place to ensure that ecotourism operations are really acting in a socially and environmentally responsible way; some hoteliers for example consider their property *ecológico* if it doesn't have a TV.

Travellers can play an important role in making sure that the concept of ecotourism does not get degraded to little more than a cheap marketing ploy. Check that people offering "eco" products are members of ASEC (Asociación Ecuatoriana de Ecoturismo, ⒺＥasec@accessinter.net). Look to see how your visit to protected areas is really helping the conservation effort. Ask how your eco-hotel or operator manages its impact and waste; does it recycle, does it conserve water and energy or use ecological waste systems such as composting toilets or "grey water" systems (waste laundry and shower water used again). Is the place sustainable – the buildings constructed from local materials by local people, the food grown nearby in organic gardens? Ask how the community benefits from your presence: do they have a stake in the property; are locals employed in non-menial tasks; how are they profiting from the resources that they are sharing with you, the visitor? By choosing hoteliers and operators who can satisfy such questions, pressure can be exerted on those that don't, so moving ecotourism towards a national or international standard.

You can **travel responsibly** in small ways on a daily basis too: by buying locally made products rather than imports; by using local rather than foreign-owned services which send profits out of the country; and by avoiding souvenirs and goods made from local fauna, unless you can be sure it came from sustainable suppliers and is not protected by the Convention on International Trade in Endangered Species (CITES, Ⓦwww.cites.org). On a cultural level, learning a little of the language will let you engage better with local life, increase cultural exchange and better mutual understanding. Treat people with courtesy by using everyday greetings and pleasantries. Always respect people's privacy and **never take someone's photograph without asking first**; usually they will be flattered and sometimes ask for a small fee. The cumulative effect of tens of thousands of visitors enjoying a beautiful country by travelling responsibly will help ensure that tourism continues to be a benefit and not a burden to Ecuador and its people.

Contacts

Campaign for Environmentally Responsible Tourism (CERT) ⓦwww.c-e-r-t.org. Lobbies to educate tour operators and tourists in a sensitive approach to travel, focusing on immediate practical ways in which the environment can be protected.
Partners in Responsible Tourism (PIRT)

ⓦwww.pirt.org. An organization of individuals and travel companies promoting responsible tourism to minimize harm to the environment and local cultures. Their website features a "Traveler's Code for Traveling Responsibly".
Tourism Concern ☎020/7753 3330, ⓦwww.tourismconcern.org.uk. Campaigns for the rights of local people to be consulted in tourism developments affecting their lives, and produces a quarterly magazine of news and articles. Also publishes the *Good Alternative Travel Guide*.

Directory

Addresses Written addresses appear as a street and a number (Sucre 353), a street and the nearest intersecting street (Sucre y Olmedo) or all three (Sucre 353 y Olmedo). The number is often hyphenated – such as Sucre 3-53 – so that there's no confusion between the first digits (the block number) and the last digits (the house number). Post is kept in boxes and not delivered to the door in Ecuador, so many people understandably have no idea what their number is, or don't have one at all (written *s/n* for *sin número*). Quito has adopted a new system of numbering (see p.83). Note that the ground floor (US first floor) is known as the *planta baja*, while the first floor (US second floor) would be the *primer piso*.
Disabled travellers There's very little provision for disabled people in Ecuador. Public transport and public places such as museums are seldom equipped with ramps, widened doorways or disabled toilets. Pavements are often narrow and full of obstructions. Some of the smarter

hotels do cater for disabled guests though, and Quito's *trole* system affords full access too, but is often too crowded to be usable.
Electricity 110V/60Hz is the standard supply, and sockets are for two flat prongs. Fluctuations in the supply are common so you need to use a surge protector if you're plugging in expensive equipment (see p.45).
Gay and lesbian travellers Ecuador has recently taken a leap forward in gay and lesbian rights by decriminalizing homosexuality. It's still a very macho society, however, and public attitude has a fair bit of catching up to do. A tentative gay scene is establishing itself in Quito, but in public places overt displays of affection are likely to be met with stern disapproval, even abuse.
Laundry Most large towns and tourist centres will have an inexpensive laundry (*lavandería*) that charges by the kilo, where the washing and drying is done for you and your clothes are neatly folded

Metric equivalent weights and measures

1km = 0.62 miles	1 foot = 0.3m
1m = 1.09 yards	1 inch = 2.54cm
1cm = 0.39 inches	1lb = 454g
1kg = 2.2lbs	1 gallon (imperial) = 4.55 litres
1 litre = 1.76 pints (UK)	1 gallon (US) = 3.79 litres
1 litre = 2.1 pints (US)	°C = 0.56 x (°F-32)
1 mile = 1.61km	°F = (1.8 x °C) + 32
1 yard = 0.91m	

ready for collection – a wonderful service for travellers. In other areas, dry cleaners or laundries that charge by the item, which work out to be expensive, are more common. Many hotels offer a laundry service, or failing that are happy to let you use their laundry basin and clothes lines.

Metric system Ecuador uses a metric system for weights and measures. See box on p.65.

Telephone jacks Ecuador uses international standard telephone jacks (US-style), compatible with standard email and fax connections.

Time Ecuador is 5 hours behind GMT (the same as US Eastern Standard Time), and the Galápagos Islands are 6 hours behind GMT (or one hour behind US EST).

Tipping In smarter places, ten percent service charge will automatically be added to your bill, and tipping above this is only warranted for exceptional service. Cheaper eateries will not usually expect you to leave a tip, though of course it's very welcome if you do. Airport and hotel porters should be tipped, as should the people who watch your car for you if you've parked in a street. Taxi drivers don't normally get a tip, but will often round up the fare if there's only a few small coins in it. Guides are tipped depending on the length of your stay or trip, from a couple of dollars to over ten. Tour crews in the Galápagos also receive tips (see p.470).

Toilets The bin next to the toilet is for your toilet paper – the plumbing can't cope with paper being flushed. Public toilets are most common at bus terminals, where you'll see them signposted as *baños* or *SS HH* (the abbreviation for *servicios higiénicos*); women are *damas* or *mujeres* and men *caballeros* or *hombres*. Often there's an attendant who sells toilet paper at the door. Most restaurants will let you use their facilities if you're not a customer so long as you ask politely, though at cheap places they're usually in pretty bad shape. It's a good idea to carry some paper (*papel higiénico*), wherever you are.

Guide

Guide

Quito and around

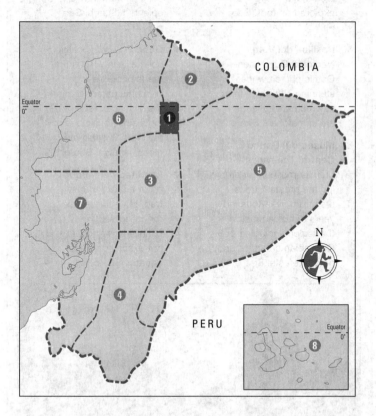

CHAPTER 1 # Highlights

* **Colonial Quito** Quito's magnificent historic quarter, holding some of the continent's best-preserved, most beautiful Spanish Colonial architecture, all in a compact area that's easily explored on foot. **See p.87**

* **Basílica del Voto Nacional** Quirky neo-Gothic church whose stunning city views from its breathtaking ledges are unmatched. **See p.96**

* **Museo del Banco Central** The nation's premier museum, featuring the greatest treasures from five thousand years of human history in the region, including pre-Columbian ceramics and gold artefacts. **See p.98**

* **Guápulo** Just a short taxi ride from the city centre, but a world away from its noise and bustle, a peaceful haven of steep cobbled streets and whitewashed houses, overlooked by a splendid church. **See p.102**

* **Good Friday** Evocative spectacle in which hundreds of purple-robed penitents parade through the historic core, providing a striking glimpse of the city's Spanish religious heritage. **See p.109**

* **La Mitad del Mundo** A bit of a tacky tourist trap, but still essential for giving you the chance to stand near – if not exactly on – the equator. **See p.120**

Quito and around

H igh in the Andes, Ecuador's capital, **Quito**, unfurls in an implausibly long north–south ribbon, more than 30km long and just 5km wide. To the west, the city is dramatically hemmed in by the steep green walls of **Volcán Pichincha**, the benign-looking volcano which periodically sends clouds of ash billowing into the sky and over the streets. Eastwards, Quito abruptly drops away to a wide valley known as the **Valle de los Chillos**, marking the beginning of the descent towards the Amazon basin. It's a superb setting, but outside of July and August it can be bone-chillingly cold, with its much-vaunted "spring-like climate" all too often giving way to grey, washed-out skies that somewhat undermine the beauty of the surroundings.

Central Quito divides into two distinct parts. The compact historical quarter known as the **old town** is the city's undisputed highlight, a jumble of narrow streets and wide, cobbled plazas lined with churches, monasteries, mansions and colourful balconied houses. Declared a UNESCO World Heritage Site in 1978, the old town contains some of the most beautiful Spanish Colonial architecture on the continent, and the frenetic crowds of *indígenas* and *mestizos* that throng its streets give the place a tremendous energy. However, beset by poverty and crime, it can be a dangerous place after dark and few tourists actually stay here, choosing instead the adjacent bland, modern **new town** as their base. Although there's nothing very distinctive about it, the new town's concentration of banks, hotels, restaurants, tour operators and Internet cafés is undeniably convenient, and even here the main shopping districts are enlivened by numerous *Otavaleño* street traders, whose colourful wares are enticingly spread out over the pavement.

As a major crossroads with 1.2 million residents, Quito is a busy **transit hub** to which travellers usually return between forays to the jungle, the coast, the Galápagos Islands and the northern and southern sierra. Featuring dozens of language schools, it's also a good place to learn Spanish, and many visitors spend several weeks or longer here mastering their *castellano*. And for all its inevitable pollution and screeching horns, Quito is an easy city to spend time in, with a great choice of restaurants and the lively presence of backpackers and foreign visitors.

The most popular **day-trip** is to the **Mitad del Mundo** (Middle of the World) on the equator, marked by a massive monument and several museums, a trip often combined with a visit to the giant volcanic crater of **Pululahua**. Other attractions in the area include the market at **Sangolquí**, the house of Eduardo Kingman in nearby **San Rafael**, and the **Pasochoa** forest reserve to the south, which offers great bird watching and hiking just half an hour from the city. Lesser-known attractions can be found northeast of Quito, such as the religious sanctuary of **El Quinche**, the little town of **Calderón**, where curious dough figurines are made, and the well-designed zoo at **Guayllabamba**, featuring a host of native species.

If this is your entry point into the country, be aware that Quito's **altitude** (2800m) can leave you feeling breathless and woozy when you first arrive – most visitors adjust in a couple of days, often by resting, drinking plenty of water and avoiding alcohol.

Quito

Although second to Guayaquil in population and economic clout, **QUITO** is the political and cultural hub of highly centralized Ecuador, where power is wielded by an elite class of politicians, bankers and company directors, often from old, moneyed families. Far more conspicuous than these sharp-suited executives, though, are the city's eye-catching *indígenas*, who make up a large part of its population. Whereas most other Latin American capitals have been stamped with the faceless imprint of imported US culture, Quito is still a place where Quichua-speaking women queue for buses in traditional clothing with metres of beads strung tightly around their necks, and where it's not uncommon to see children carried on their mothers' backs in securely wrapped blankets, as they are in the rural sierra. All this makes for a somewhat exotic introduction to the country, though the proliferation of ragged shoeshine boys and desperate hawkers selling miracle products is a sobering reminder of the levels of poverty in the city, and its considerable social inequalities.

The key to **orientation** in Quito is to see the city as a long, narrow strip. At the southern end is the **old town**, focused on three large squares: the **Plaza de la Independencia** (also known as the Plaza Grande), **Plaza San Francisco** and **Plaza Santo Domingo**. The street grid around these squares comprises a small, compact urban core dominated to the south by the hill of **El Panecillo** (the Little Bread Roll), crowned by a large statue of the **Virgin of Quito**. Fanning north from old Quito towards the new town is a transitional stretch around **Parque La Alameda**, while the **new town** proper begins a few blocks further north at **Parque El Ejido**. Known by Quiteños simply as **El Norte**, the new town stretches all the way north to the airport, but the only parts you're likely to visit are the central areas of **La Mariscal**, just north of Parque El Ejido, where most accommodation and tourist facilities are located, and the business district further north, around **Parque La Carolina**.

Some history

Very little is known about the indigenous people who until the fifteenth century inhabited the terrain now occupied by Quito. Until recent decades, it was widely believed that the area had been the capital of a large and powerful kingdom known as **El Reino de Quito**, an idea asserted in the 1789 *Historia Moderna del Reino de Quito* by Padre Juan de Velasco. Modern archeologists,

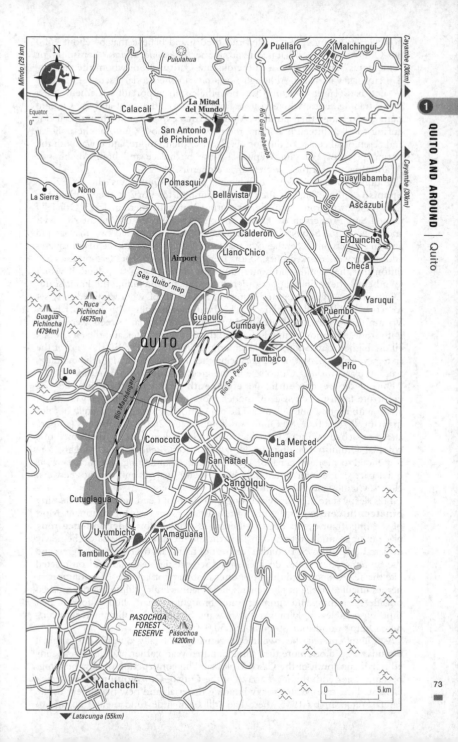

however, have largely discredited this theory and believe that by about 1500 the Quito basin was inhabited by a number of *señoríos étnicos* ("lordships" or "chiefdoms"), including that of the obscure **Quitus**, from whom the present-day city takes its name. Although not a city in the modern sense – as Padre Velasco had claimed – Quito was nonetheless an important settlement and a major trading centre where visitors from the sierra, the coast and the Oriente came to exchange their produce. After the **Inca** expansion north into Ecuador during the late fifteenth century, the new rulers chose Quito as the political and ceremonial centre of the northern part of their empire, and it was both the resting place of **Huayna Capac** and the birthplace and home of his son **Atahualpa**, two of the last great Inca emperors.

Doubtless because of its considerable prestige, Quito was chosen by the **Spanish** as the capital of their newly acquired territory, as they pushed the Conquest north from Peru after executing Atahualpa there in 1533. Officially named **San Francisco de Quito**, the city was founded on August 28, 1534, and its governor **Sebastián de Benalcázar** soon appointed two mayors and a town council on December 6 of that year. With great speed, the major squares and streets were marked out and lots were granted to 204 settlers, on the condition that they build solid houses on them or risk losing their land. It wasn't long before the main religious orders moved in, too, including the Franciscans, Dominicans, Augustinians and Sisters of Mercy, all of whom immediately set to work building their own churches and monasteries with Indian labour. Within thirty years, the **Cathedral** was finished, the main streets were paved with stone, irrigation channels supplied the city with water, and the city council established regulations for slaughterhouses and markets. By the end of the sixteenth century, most of the great churches, monasteries and public buildings were in place, making Quito one of the great cities of Latin America.

During the **seventeenth** and **eighteenth centuries**, there was no real departure from the city's early model: more houses and churches were built, along with modest public works. The population increased moderately, but not dramatically, and by 1780 Quito was home to just 25,000 inhabitants (a figure already reached by Lima, Peru, in 1610). Indeed, despite being the capital of a colonial administrative division (known as a *Real Audiencia*) that roughly corresponded to modern Ecuador, Quito remained something of a backwater, its quiet pace of life interrupted only by the petty quarrels and rivalries between clerics, Creoles and public officials.

This sleepy state of affairs was brought to an abrupt end, however, in the early **nineteenth century** as the tide of revolution swept over the continent. Most of the important events marking Ecuador's struggle for **independence** took place in or around Quito, and in 1830 the city became the capital of the newly declared **Republic of Ecuador**, the seat of national government, congress and the supreme court. Later decades would see prestigious buildings constructed like the Teatro Sucre and the astronomical observatory, statues of revolutionary heroes installed in the public squares, new bridges built, additional streets paved outside the centre, and running water brought to many houses for the first time. Nonetheless, growth was still slow and by the end of the nineteenth century, Quito's population stood at just 50,000.

As Quito entered the **twentieth century** it finally outgrew its original boundaries, laid out more than three hundred years earlier, and slowly expanded north and south of the Casco Colonial. The construction of new buildings became easier with the 1909 arrival of the **Quito–Guayaquil railway**, which facilitated the transport of heavy building materials and new machinery to the capital. Yet even by 1945, there had still been little fundamental change to

Quito's long-standing physical and social landscape: the wealthy still lived in the colonial centre, the working class occupied a barrio near the railway station to the south, and the city was still mostly surrounded by farms and countryside.

All this changed dramatically in the **postwar** years, fuelled initially by the **banana boom** of the 1940s, which turned Ecuador into an important exporting country and gave it the resources to pay for new infrastructure in its capital, such as hospitals, schools, universities, prisons and an airport. When the city's wealthy moved out to the fashionable new barrio of Mariscal Sucre, Quito's social geography underwent a fundamental change as well. Further transformations came following the **petrol boom** of the 1970s, which funded the construction of high-rise offices, new residential districts, and public buildings such as ministries, courts and the Palacio Legislativo. Accordingly, the population exploded and passed the **one-million** mark in 1990 – due in part to the migration of workers from the countryside to the capital. Since then, Quito's boundaries have been spreading further outwards, literally stretching the city's resources to their limits, and the population boom shows no signs of fading, putting an ever-greater strain on housing, employment, transport and even sanitation and water supplies.

Arrival

However you get here, **arrival** in Quito can be a little unnerving, with huge, excited crowds pressing around the exit gate at the airport and a confusing layout and menacing atmosphere at the bus terminal. Still, as the focus of Ecuador's national transport network, Quito offers **bus** access to just about every corner of the country, along with regular intercity **flights** – though the ever-declining **train** service is now limited to just one short route. Once you do arrive, the best thing to do is jump in a **taxi** and get to your hotel, where you can unwind and settle in. (For details of air, bus and train services leaving the city, see "Moving on from Quito", p.117.)

By air

The city's **airport**, Aeropuerto Internacional Mariscal Sucre (information on ☏02/2430555 or 2440080), serves both national and international flights, and is located in the northern part of the new town, 6km from the hotel district of La Mariscal. While it's not particularly modern or attractive, the airport does offer reasonable facilities: inside the international terminal there's a **tourist information desk** (daily 6am–midnight) and a **casa de cambio**, while throughout the complex you'll find several **ATMs**.

A block outside the airport, you can catch a **bus** to the city centre (30min; $0.50), but by far the easiest and safest option is take one of the many yellow **taxis** lined up outside the arrivals gate, which charge $2–3 for a daytime trip to the new town, about a dollar more to the old town, and a dollar extra for a night-time trip to either destination. Check the going rate to the city centre at the tourist information desk on your way out of the airport, and confirm the price with your driver before you set off. You can also pay a **fixed fare** of $4 at the dedicated taxi desk in the airport (just beyond customs), the best guarantee you won't be ripped off outside. If you've already booked your accommodation, many hotels now offer a **pick-up service** with prior reservation. In light traffic, your driver should be able to get you to your hotel in less than twenty minutes.

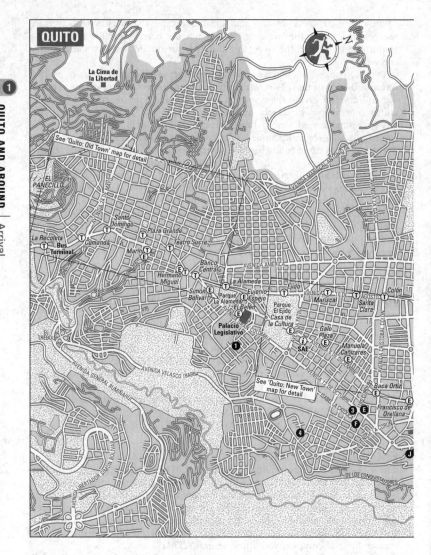

By bus

Quito's main **bus terminal**, the Terminal Terrestre de Cumandá, at Avenida Maldonado 3077 on the southern edge of the old town, is a horrible multi-storey concrete pile that makes for a rather dismal point of entry, especially at night. As with the airport, however, there's an **information desk** near the pedestrian entrance (Mon–Fri 8.30am–5.30pm; ☎02/22289047 or 2289049), an **ATM** and, adjacent to the place where buses arrive, a long line of **taxis** – which you should take if you're arriving late at night, early in the morning or if you have luggage. Establish a price with the driver before you get in, as most

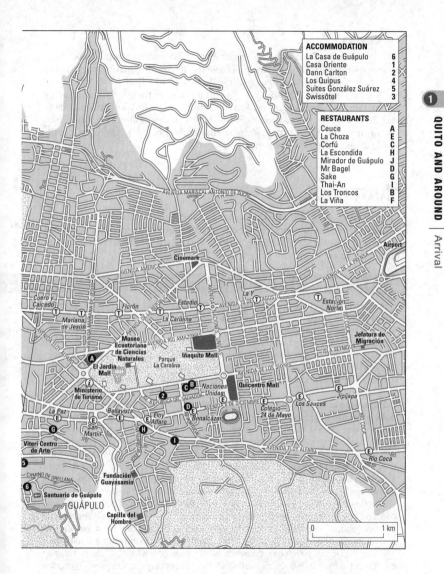

will refuse to use the meter from the bus station. You shouldn't have to pay more than a few dollars to get to the hotel district of the new town, though a bit of firm bargaining may be called for.

Alternatively, the bus terminal is a short distance from the stop for the Cumandá **trolley** (see "City Transport", p.80), but beware of encountering pickpockets in the few minutes it takes to walk there, not to mention petty thieves on the crowded trolley buses themselves. A small number of bus companies also have their own separate terminals in the new town (for details, see p.118).

By train

With hardly any railway services still operating, it's unlikely you'll make your first entrance into Quito by **train**. However, if you do manage to take the tourist train from the Area Nacional de Recreación El Boliche to the capital (see "Moving on from Quito", p.117), you'll arrive at the gracefully decaying train station, La Estación de Ferrocarril Chimbacalle, off Avenida Maldonado about 2km south of the old town. From there you can easily catch a **taxi** into town or, if you're free of luggage, take the **Trole** (see p.81) from the north-bound Chimbacalle stop opposite.

Information

As key sources of tourist **information** in Quito, the Ministerio de Turismo and Ministerio del Ambiente are large, monolithic government offices only just waking up to the needs of walk-in visitors. Better bets are the US-based South American Explorers and the private CAPTUR offices.

Learning Spanish in Quito

Home to more than sixty **language schools**, Quito is the most popular place in South America to learn Spanish, partly because rates are so cheap – $4–8 per hour for one-to-one classes – and partly because Spanish is spoken much more clearly here than in many other countries, making it easier for beginners to pick up. Unlike Chileans or Argentinians, for example, or even people from Guayaquil and the coast, Ecuadorian *serranos* (highlanders) tend to speak slowly and pronounce all the letters in each word (elsewhere, consonants are frequently dropped), making them easy to understand.

Choosing a school may seem like a daunting task, given the city's many choices. To book lessons in advance, you can check websites or email or fax a few of those listed below to request brochures or ask questions, but if you're sorting them out after your arrival, the best thing to do is visit a few schools, look at their classrooms and enquire about their facilities and methods – or even ask to sit in on a lesson. Nearly all schools offer **one-to-one lessons** or classes in small groups, but not all use books or visual aids. It's a good idea to ask if you can rotate your teachers, as this keeps the lessons fresher and allows you to compare techniques and decide what suits you best.

Some schools will encourage you to sign up for seven hours a day, but most students find it exhausting trying to concentrate for this length of time – four hours a day is about the most people can cope with comfortably, whether studying for just a few days or several weeks. The majority of schools offer the option of **staying with a family** (usually $10–15 per day, with meals included), while others now offer daily classes as part of full tours to the jungle or coast. **Activities** such as cookery classes, dancing lessons or day and weekend trips are also offered by many schools – all good ways to meet other students. The following institutions are established and reputable; South American Explorers (see p.80) and many embassies also supply lists of language schools.

Language schools

Academía Latinoamericana de Español José Queri 2 and Eloy Alfaro ⓣ02/2452824, ⓕ2433820, ⓦwww.latinoschools.com. Well-structured courses, complete with homework and testing, with most teaching in small groups of four students or fewer, though one-to-one lessons are also offered. More expensive than most.

Ministerio de Turismo

In the north end of town at Avenida Eloy Alfaro N32-300, the **Ministerio de Turismo** (Mon–Fri 8.30am–5pm, with an irregular lunch break; T02/2507555, F2507565, Wwww.vivecuador.com) is located opposite Parque La Carolina. To arrive by public transport, take any bus north along Amazonas and get off at Eloy Alfaro, then walk east down the avenue for about 400m, or hop on another bus. Once there, you'll find a number of glossy **brochures** and fold-out **maps** of Quito as well as general information on the rest of Ecuador. The staff are very friendly and willing to help, but not all of them speak English. The ministry has also initiated a new 24hr **information service**, which it claims you can access from any Ecuadorian phone by calling T1800/004887.

Ministerio del Ambiente

The **Ministerio del Ambiente** is located in a big building marked by a large iron sculpture of a bull, at Amazonas and Eloy Alfaro (Mon–Fri 8.30am–4.30pm; T02/2529845, Wwww.ambiente.gov.ec). Up on the building's seventh and

Amazonas Jorge Washington 718 and Amazonas, Edificio Rocafuerte, second floor T & F02/2504654, Wwww.eduamazonas.com. Large, long-established school with a branch in the Oriente as well. Students are offered use of pool, sauna and Jacuzzi at the *Hilton Colón* (see p.84).

Bipo & Toni's Carrión 300 and Leonidas Plaza T & F02/2556614, Ebipo@pi.pro.ec. Excellent school with great teachers, plus a lovely garden with barbecue facilities, video room, library and café. Regularly donates a portion of its profits to environmental projects.

Galápagos Amazonas 258 and Jorge Washington, second floor T & F02/256 5213, Wwww.galapagos.edu.ec. As well as ordinary language lessons, offers courses in literary analysis and business-oriented Spanish. Has a large reference library and arranges weekly activities.

Instituto Superior de Español Darquea Terán 1650 and 10 de Agosto T02/222 3242, F2221628, Wwww.instituto-superior.net. Well-regarded school in a renovated Spanish Colonial house, with an on-site gym and garden, just north of La Mariscal.

La Lengua Colón 1001 and Juan León Mera, Edificio Ave María, eighth floor T02/2543521, F2501271, Wwww.la-lengua.com. Friendly, centrally located school with a range of good-value, flexible programmes, including some on Latin American history, economics, politics, literature and culture.

Ruta del Sol Avenida Tarqui 243 and Vacas Galindo T02/2553914, Wwww.rutasolacademy.com. Courses include cultural lessons, literature discussions and museum visits, with diplomas offered for some classes upon completion. South of Parque El Ejido.

Simón Bolívar Leonidas Plaza 353 and Roca T & F02/236688, Wwww.simon-bolivar.com. Dynamic young school in a quiet corner of the new town, making for a peaceful environment in which to study. Offers daily classes and a wide range of activities and tours, including six-day trips to the jungle or coast.

South American Spanish Institute Amazonas N26–59 and Santa María T02/2544715, F2226348, Wwww.southamerican.edu.ec. Long-established school with a good reputation and facilities. Popular with Ecuadorians for English lessons, making for a pleasant intercultural exchange.

eighth floors, the ministry governs all of Ecuador's **national parks and reserves**, but often makes it frustratingly difficult to get hold of any information about them. If you're persistent, though, you should be able to track down the person with the key to the drawer containing the information leaflets on all the parks and reserves. Available for sale are several **books** and even **CD-ROMs** on Ecuador's flora, fauna and protected areas.

South American Explorers

At Jorge Washington 311 and Leonidas Plaza, **South American Explorers** (Mon–Fri 9.30am–5pm & Sat 9am–noon, Thurs closes 8pm; ⓣ & ⓕ 02/2225228, ⓔ quitoclub@saexplorers.org, ⓦ www.saexplorers.org) is a rich source of information on Quito and the whole of the country, and is run with formidable efficiency. Non-members can pick up numerous **information sheets** on subjects as diverse as accommodation, restaurants, Internet access, climbing guides, outdoor-equipment suppliers, banks, embassies and doctors. Along with this, members have full run of the clubhouse and access to a size-able reference library, a vast number of **trip reports** (mainly recommendations or warnings) filed by other members, one-to-one trip-planning advice, and the **"Explorers' Volunteer Resource"**, possibly Ecuador's most comprehensive list of non-governmental organizations and community-based projects seeking volunteers. For a small cover charge, non-members are welcome to the organization's Thursday-evening **lectures**, covering anything from travel safety to Amazonian frogs, and to the "Walkabout Club", which meets for weekend hikes and other activities. For more on the South American Explorers, including membership requirements, see p.26.

CAPTUR

CAPTUR (Cámara Provincial de Turismo de Pichincha) is an association of more than a thousand companies involved in the tourism industry in and around Quito – mainly hotels, restaurants, travel agencies and tour operators – with several **information offices**: in the new town at Parque Gabriela Mistral, wedged between Luis Cordero, Diego de Almagro and Baquerizo Moreno (Mon–Fri 9am–6pm; ⓣ 02/2551566, ⓔ promocion@captur.com, ⓦ www. captur.com); inside the Museo del Banco Central, Avenida Patria and 6 de Diciembre (Mon–Fri 9am–5pm, Sat & Sun 10am–4pm); in the old town at Venezuela and Chile (Mon–Fri 9am–5pm; ⓣ 02/2954044); and in the airport at international arrivals (daily 7.30am–2.30pm & 5.30pm–midnight; ⓣ 02/2462977). These are essentially places for association members to promote themselves, but the friendly, English-speaking staff also stock files of practical information such as museum opening hours, and can answer most questions about the city.

City transport

Since most visitors stay in the new town and do their sightseeing in the old town, you'll probably end up using **public transport** as a means of shuttling between the two (the alternative is a 45-minute walk of some 3km). Despite the frenetic volume of traffic on Quito's streets, taking mass transit is much easier than you might think, especially if you use the superb **El Trole** and **Ecovía** systems. Ordinary **buses** are a bit more daunting, but once you get the hang of them, they turn out to be quite straightforward. Finally, **taxis** are so cheap compared to those in Europe or North America that you may well end up using them alone to get around the city. At night, or if you are carrying valuables or luggage, you should use nothing else.

El Trole and Ecovía

Quito's modern, eco-friendly **trolley-bus** system, known as **El Trole** (Mon–Fri 6am–midnight, Sat & Sun 6am–10pm), comes as quite a surprise amidst the general chaos, noise and pollution of the capital. Identified by a green-metal and glass structure on a raised platform, each stop offers clean seating areas and a TV, and the buses themselves provide automatic wheelchair access and a quiet, smooth and fast ride. Not surprisingly, the system is extremely popular, so you'll likely have to ride it squashed between dozens of other passengers. The flat **fare** is $0.20, which you put into the machine by the metal barrier at the entrance to the platform; change is available at the kiosk alongside, where you can also buy books of tickets at slightly discounted rates. Once you've paid, the barrier opens and you can walk through to the platform.

The basic **route** runs through the city for 11km on a segregated north–south axis, mainly along the **Avenida 10 de Agosto**, with the northern terminus at Terminal La Y, out towards the airport, and the southern at El Recreo, south of the old town. A further five-kilometre extension leads south to an "integration point" at Morán Valverde, and from this station and the two other terminals, city buses branch off in a series of feeder routes (*rutas alimentadoras*) to the suburbs. Not every trolley bus serves the entire line, with different route numbers and colour codes indicating where they begin and end, but unless you're travelling outside the central areas – including the old town and hotel district – it makes no difference which number you take. One thing to be aware of, though, is the **one-way system** through the old town: southbound buses go along Guayaquil, while those returning north use Flores and Montúfar. In short, going to the old town, you can get off at Teatro Sucre, Plaza Grande or Santo Domingo; coming back, the most central stops are Santo Domingo and La Marín.

The **Ecovía** (Mon–Fri 6am–midnight, Sat & Sun 6am–10pm; $0.20) runs for 9km, mainly along the Avenida 6 de Diciembre, and operates in much the same manner as the Trole, though without the overhead electric cables. In place of trolley buses, the Ecovía uses a state-of-the-art fleet of deep crimson "**buses ecológicos**", low-emission vehicles that service the segregated lanes between La Marín in the old town and the Río Coca transfer station in the north, every ten to fifteen minutes. A new Ecovía route is planned for early 2004 along the Avenida América, linking the Carcelén district in the north to the old town.

Buses

In stark contrast to the Trole and Ecovía systems, Quito's plain old **buses** are for the most part ancient, decrepit affairs, hurtling noisily through the city streets at top speed, belching fumes into the air and screeching to a halt whenever anyone wants to get on or off. There's no route map available, but since most of Quito is laid out in a grid and most buses ply the main arterials like 12 de Octubre, Amazonas, 10 de Agosto and Colón, it's not difficult to get where you want to go. Main stops and final destinations are marked on the front window, and if you're not sure where to get off, ask the driver ("*¿me puede avisar cuando lleguemos a…?*") and you'll doubtless find half the bus keeping an eye out for you as well.

Buses charge a flat **fare**, though the exact cost varies by the type of bus you use, with more modern vehicles that are supposedly sitting-only (marked with "*ejecutivo*" or "*selectivo*" on the sides) charging a little more ($0.25) than the older ones, labelled "*popular*" ($0.18). Use coins or small-denomination notes to pay; the smarter buses have well-manicured, short-skirted attendants sitting by the door to collect your fare as you get on, while the older ones pack everyone in first, then send boys scurrying down the aisle to get your money and give you a ticket.

Although there are designated **bus stops**, it's normally possible to flag down a bus wherever you are, and to get off at any street corner (shout "*en la esquina, por favor*" to the driver). Pink "**interparroquial**" buses service the outlying suburbs and districts such as Calderón and La Mitad del Mundo, and many city buses pass through Plaza Marín (known simply as "La Marín"), a chaotic bus station at the east end of Chile in the old town.

Taxis

Quito swarms with thousands of yellow **taxis**, from the immaculately cared-for to those hanging together by a piece of string, but regardless of quality, you can usually flag one down in seconds wherever you are. Make sure you pick one with a four-digit code plastered on its doors and windscreen, which signifies a legal, registered taxi and identifies the vehicle to authorities if you have any complaints. Quito is the only city in Ecuador where taxis use a meter (*taxímetro*), and fares normally work out to be very cheap. Check that your driver resets the meter when you get in; it should flash "LIBRE" and display the **starting fare**, currently $0.30, and then increase by a cent every three seconds or so. If he doesn't turn it on, a polite "*ponga su taxímetro, por favor*" should jolt his memory; if he claims it's broken, either set a price immediately or get out and take another cab.

The minimum **fixed fare** is $0.80, but check the current rate with locals to avoid being overcharged. Note that even though they're legally required to do so until 10pm, most taxi drivers don't use their meters at night, when fares can be as much as double the daytime rate – so agree on a price before you set off. Try also to carry small notes and coins to pay the fare exactly, as *taxistas* have an uncanny knack for running out of change when you need it the most.

If you want to **book** a taxi, try any of the following 24hr radio taxi companies: Central Radio Taxis (☎02/2500600), City Taxi (☎02/2633333), Cooperativa Colón 10 (☎02/2543621) and Teletaxi (☎02/2222222). Booking a taxi for the day costs $50–70, something your hotel can easily arrange for you.

Accommodation

Nearly all visitors to Quito stay in the **new town**, where there's a huge choice of **accommodation** in all price ranges. The area is also lively after dark, and convenient for changing money, booking tours, sorting out laundry and the like. Be warned that many streets are very noisy, so it's always worth asking for a back room.

Staying in the **old town** is not as unthinkable as you might assume – just choose your hotel carefully and accept that you can't wander around freely after dark. Wherever you stay, if you're arriving at night, make sure to book ahead and take a taxi there. The following accommodation is marked on the maps on pp.76–77, p.88 (old town) and p.97 (new town).

Quito addresses

Quito is currently caught between two contradictory **street-numbering** systems. A few years ago, an attempt was made to phase out the old system and modernize **addresses**, whereby north–south streets would be prefixed by the letter N (for *norte*) if north of the old town, while addresses on east–west streets would be prefixed by E (*este* – east) or O (*oeste* – west) to indicate their orientation to Avenida 10 de Agosto. The numbers following these letters were meant to represent the block number and then the house number, separated by a dash. Unfortunately the impetus to complete the project began to falter when planners were confronted with the irregular, non-grid areas of the city. Many individuals and businesses have also resisted the new address system, so throughout the chapter we provide the form of address used by the establishments themselves.

The new town

Most **new town** accommodation is in the downtown zone of **La Mariscal**, with the biggest concentration on the streets around José Calama, where new *hostales* keep springing up all the time. There are lots of restaurants and Internet cafés around here as well, not to mention a steady stream of backpackers.

Alcalá Luis Cordero E5-48 and Reina Victoria ☎02/2227369, ⓦwww.alcalahostal.com. Newer, more spruced-up version of its sister hostel, *Posada del Maple*, offering dorms and doubles at the same prices, along with breakfast, unlimited tea, coffee and hot chocolate. Rooms upstairs are fresher and brighter. Dorms $6.70, doubles ❹

Amazonas Inn Joaquín Pinto E4-325 ☎02/2225723. Modern hotel with a pleasant street-level café. Some rooms are small, but all are spotless and have private baths, cable TVs and decent carpets. ❹

Ambassador 9 de Octubre 1052 and Av Colón ☎02/2561777, ⓕ2503712. Rather like a Scottish country inn with its nooks and crannies and stags' heads on the walls. Rooms are comfortable if drab, but the bar and lounge are quite cosy. ❺

Antinéa Juan Rodgríguez 175 ☎02/2506838, ⓕ2504404, wwww.hotelantinea.com. Elegant French-run villa containing a mix of en-suite rooms, suites and mini-apartments, all tastefully furnished and equipped to a high standard. Also has a very pretty interior patio with lots of flowers and includes a sizeable French breakfast. ❻–❽

Bask Lizardo García E7-56 ☎02/2503456. Hospitable place with a mix of small dorms and private rooms painted in cheery pink tones throughout. Guests have access to a kitchen and lounge with a huge cable TV. ❶–❷

Bavaria Ulpiano Páez 232 ☎02/2509401. Cosy hotel with flowers around the door, chintzy decor and almost every inch of wall space taken up by the owner's bright paintings. The rooms – all en-suite – are good value, and the interior garden makes a peaceful retreat from Quito's noise. ❹

Books & Coffee Juan León Mera 1227 and Calama ☎02/252879. Three comfortable en-suite rooms decorated with dramatic landscape murals are located upstairs at this café. Overall a good value place that includes a fine breakfast and use of all facilities, including cable TV, video, a huge range of board games, library and table football. ❹

Café Cultura Robles 513 and Reina Victoria ☎ & ⓕ02/2224271, ⓦwww.cafecultura.com. Exuberantly decorated old house with high ceilings, big stone fireplaces and bright walls with frescos of parrots, flowers, dolphins and cherubs. Rooms on the ground and first floors are best, along with the three suites, each with a Victorian cast-iron bath. ❼

El Cafecito Luis Cordero E6-43 and Reina Victoria ⓦwww.cafecito.net. Nice clean dorms for four to five people, with spacious bunks and swept wooden floors, plus a single and a double room. The disadvantage of the late-night noise from the café below is offset by a ten percent discount on food and drink. Dorms $6, double ❸

Calama José Calama E7-49 ☎02/2237510. Popular budget hotel offering neat, square rooms with white walls, clean floors and private baths. Not much character, but functional and good value. ❸

La Cartuja Leonidas Plaza 180 ☎02/2523577, ⓕ2226391. Excellent little hotel with stylish rooms offering TVs, safes, parquet floors and beautiful ceramic tiles in the bathrooms. Best of all is the interior garden with deck chairs and parasols – a real oasis of tranquillity. ❻

La Casa de Guápulo Leonidas Plaza Lasso 257, Guápulo ☎02/2220473, ⓔguapulo@mailexcite .com. Sited in the picturesque district of Guápulo (see p.102), a charming hotel clinging to the hillside above the Sanctuario and offering a fine escape from the city bustle. Rooms are unfussy but tastefully decorated, with optional private baths. Breakfast and free transfer from any point in the city are included. ❹

La Casa Sol Calama 127 ☎02/2230798, f2223383, ⓦwww.lacasasol.com. Lovely guesthouse with comfortable, neatly decorated en-suite rooms set around a pretty little courtyard; run by cheerful staff, mainly from the Otavalo region, who are unfailingly polite and helpful. Features a sitting room with fireplace, luggage storage, laundry, tour services and lounge with cable TV, plus a tasty breakfast. SAE and long-stay discounts. ❻

Cayman Juan Rodríguez 270 and Reina Victoria ☎ & ℻02/2567616, ℮hcayman@uio.satnet.net. Beautifully renovated old house with polished floors, attractive decor and a huge chimney in the sitting room, plus wooden shutters and firm orthopedic mattresses in all the rooms. ❺

Centro del Mundo Lizardo García 569 y Reina Victoria ☎02/25229050, ℮centrodelmundo @hotmail.com. Characterful old house with a permanent array of long-limbed backpackers sprawled out in the sitting room. Most accommodation is in 8- to 12-bed dorms, all with lockable trunks; also offers free breakfast, laundry facilities, use of a kitchen and stacks of information on local activities. Dorms $3–5, doubles ❷–❹

Crossroads Foch E5-23 ☎02/2234735, ⓦwww .crossroadshostal.com. Popular American-run hostel with a range of dorm and private rooms (some en suite) in a handsome old house, with a small café, TV room with VCR, and kitchen and storage facilities. Dorms $5–6, doubles ❹

Dann Carlton Av República de El Salvador 513 ☎02/2249008, ℻2448807. Part of a Colombian chain, a new hotel that's one of Quito's best, with a sumptuous marble lobby and good-quality rooms, complete with electronic safe, huge TV with cable and immaculate furnishings. Some rooms have great views of the Volcán Pichincha hills, and there are substantial discounts for stays over five days. ❾

Euro Amazonas 553 and Roca ☎02/2555075. Simple but well-kept rooms with whitewashed walls, wooden floors and small bedside tables. The back rooms are surprisingly quiet, and the shared and private bathrooms and toilets are spotless – a definite plus at this price range. ❷–❸

Florencia Reina Victoria N21-248 ☎02/2230489. One of the few hotels in La Mariscal mostly patronized by Colombians and Ecuadorians, with clean, cheap and simple rooms and a quiet but central location. ❷–❸

Florencia 2 9 de Octubre 237 ☎02/2224332. Clean, no-frills hotel that's good value if you don't mind sharing a bathroom. En-suite rooms, on the other hand, are not worth the extra cost. ❷–❹

Fuente de Piedra Juan León Mera 721 and Baquedano ☎02/2900323. New, well-located hotel given an Old World feel by means of sombre ochre colours and wooden beams, offering comfortable rooms with private baths and cable TVs. Breakfast included. ❺

La Galería Calama 233 y Diego de Almagro ☎02/2500307, ℮hostallagaleria@hotmail.com. Friendly hotel with a range of different en-suite rooms, one with a log fire. Some are a bit dog-eared and the hot water is not always reliable, but it's still decent value. ❷

Hostal del Gnomo Luis Cordero E4-148 and Foch ☎02/2528298, ℻02/2562178, ℮hostaldel-gnomo@andinanet.net. Set in a peaceful location amid pleasant gardens, a very clean hostel featuring lots of polished wood and comfortable shared sitting room with fireplace. Breakfast included. ❹

Hilton Colón Amazonas 110 and Av Patria ☎02/2560666, ℻2563903, ⓦwww.quito.hilton .com. Luxurious international hotel boasting stylish modern decor, well-appointed rooms and a great fitness centre, including pool, gym and sauna. ❾

HotHello Amazonas N-20-20 ☎ & ℻02/2565835, ⓦwww.cometoecuador.com. Small European-style hotel with immaculate en-suite rooms, all with floor-to-ceiling windows, cable TVs and plug-in heating. Full breakfast included and served in bed on huge wicker trays, if you wish. An excellent choice for this price range. ❺

JW Marriott Orellana 1172 and Amazonas ☎02/2972000, ℻2972050, ⓦwww.marriott.com. Unmistakeable ziggurat of cream stone and green glass, Quito's plushest and best-appointed luxury hotel, boasting all the facilities you would expect. Discounted rates at weekends. Non-guests can use the gym and spa complex for $15. ❾

El Kapulí Robles 625 ☎02/2221872. Big old house with high ceilings, a hint of shabbiness and a handful of airy rooms, each with one to four beds and mostly with shared baths. ❸–❹

Lafayette Baquedano 358 ☎02/2224529. Not very stylish with its faded red carpets and dark ceilings, but the en-suite rooms are neat, comfortable and good value, and those on the top floor have balconies and nice views. Sited above *Le Arcate*, Quito's best pizzeria (see p.105). ❷–❸

Magic Bean Foch E5-08 ☎02/2566181. A handful of rooms above the popular café, some with bunks and shared baths, others with a double beds and en-suite baths. All are spotlessly clean, light and airy, and come with free luggage storage and breakfast. Dorms $7, doubles ❺

Long-term accommodation

The best place to look for **long-term accommodation** is in the classified section of the daily newspapers *El Comercio*, especially on Sundays, and *Hoy*, both of which post classifieds on their websites (Ⓦwww.elcomercio.com, Ⓦwww.hoy.com.ec). You might also try the notice boards of the South American Explorers (see p.80), drop in on various Internet cafés such as *Papaya Net* (see p.107) and *El Maple* (see p.105), or simply walk around a neighbourhood that appeals to you, as some landlords prefer to place signs outside their properties rather than pay to advertise. **Rates** average $150 to $250 per month for a two-bedroom apartment in the new town, but prices tend to shoot up if the landlord senses you're a foreigner; try to get a local friend to come along to negotiate the price, as he or she will probably know the going rate.

Other good options, particularly for medium-term stays, are **"apart-hotels"**, which are a bit more expensive than renting your own apartment, but are comfortable, furnished and straightforward to arrange. *Antinéa* (see p.83) offers several luxurious apartments and duplexes for up to six people ($60–120 per night), while the more economic *Los Quipus*, Lérida E14-55 and Lugo in the Floresta district (Ⓣ02/2224037, Ⓦwww.aquipus.com; $35 double occupancy), also offers discounts for longer stays. One convenient option is *Casa Oriente*, Yaguachi 824 and Llona, near the Parque La Alameda (Ⓣ02/2546157), a block of eighteen apartments whose one- or two-bedroom units have private bathrooms and small kitchens (doubles $120, two-bedroom apartments $130–150). Those on the higher floors also have great views, and the rooftop terrace has laundry facilities. It's popular, so book as far in advance as possible.

Mansión del Angel Wilson E5-29 Ⓣ02/2557721, Ⓕ2237819. Superb old mansion lavishly decorated with crystal chandeliers, gilt cornices, chaises longues and dark oil paintings. Most beds are four-posters, adding to the sense of luxury. Great place for a splurge. ❽–❾

Mercure Alameda Roca 653 Ⓣ02/2562345, Ⓕ2565759. Large American-style hotel with great views from the higher floors. Feels a little dated, with its low ceilings and coffee-coloured furnishings, but offers all the facilities you'd expect, including cable TVs, direct-dial phones, a gym and fluffy white towels in the bathrooms. ❽

Posada del Maple Juan Rodríguez E8-49 Ⓣ02/2544507, Ⓦwww.posadadelmaple.com. Relaxed and friendly house offering rooms of varying shapes and sizes for a wide range of budgets. Use of kitchen, plus tea, coffee and breakfast included. Dorms $6.70, doubles ❹

La Quinta Luis Cordero 1951 Ⓣ02/2551269, Ⓕ2558857, Ⓔcame@uio.satnet.net. Distinctive yellow-and-white house with a brightly painted glass corridor around it, offering dorm beds or large, slightly tired rooms with shared baths, secure luggage storage and private parking. A little out of the way, though. Dorms $6.50, doubles ❸

Hostal de la Rábida La Rábida 227 and Santa María Ⓣ02/2221720, Ⓦwww.hostalrabida.com. Charming Italian-owned hotel on a quiet residential street, providing the feel of a converted period house with its wooden floors, crackling fire and elegant rooms. Excellent service and good food in its cosy restaurant. ❼

San Jorge 4km west of Avenida Occidental on the Nono road Ⓣ02/2494002, Ⓕ2565964, Ⓦwww.hostsanjorge.com.ec. Only ten minutes from the new town on the foothills of Volcán Pichincha, a country hacienda featuring comfortable rooms with stone fireplaces, plus a swimming pool, sauna and Jacuzzi, and a private nature reserve ideal for hiking, horse riding and bird watching. ❼–❽

Suites González Suárez San Ignacio 2750 and Av González Suárez Ⓣ02/2224417, Ⓕ2231399, Ⓦwww.sgshotel.com. In a quiet district east of town, a comfortable mid-range hotel whose standard rooms offer cable TVs, spacious bathrooms and sofas. Pricier options include Jacuzzis and balcony views over Guápulo. Buffet breakfast and airport transfers included. ❻

Swissôtel 12 de Octubre 1820 and Luis Cordero Ⓣ02/2567600, Ⓕ2568080, Ⓦwww.swissotel.com. Deluxe five-star hotel boasting five top-class restaurants, plush rooms, a wonderful spa and gym complex and all the facilities you would expect for the price. Buffet breakfast included. ❾

El Taxo Foch 909 Ⓣ02/2225593, Ⓕ2554551, Ⓦwww.hostaleltaxo.com. Bohemian hostel featuring dorms and private rooms with shared baths, a sitting room with big wood fire and musical instruments, and a bamboo-roofed patio with "holistic sound stage" for musical performances. Kitchen

85

facilities and Internet, laundry and tattoo services available, and buffet breakfast included. ❷–❸
Tortuga Verde Juan León Mera and Joaquin Pinto ⓣ02/2556829 ⓔtortuga_verde@hotmail.com. Good little spot offering a few small dorms with four to six bunks and secure lockers, and doubles with shared baths. Also has a sitting room with cable TV and a fireplace. Noisy location, however. Dorms $5, doubles ❸
Villa Nancy B&B Carrión E8-158 and 6 de Diciembre ⓣ02/2563084, ⓕ2549657,

ⓔvilla_nancy@yahoo.com. Quiet and agreeable B&B with seven rooms, all with shared baths. Two of the rooms have fireplaces, and there's a garden. Free pick-up from the airport with advance booking. ❹
Villantigua Jorge Washington E9-48 and Tamayo ⓣ02/2528564, ⓕ2545663, ⓔalariv@uio.satnet .net. Family-run hotel in an attractive house in a quiet part of town, offering en-suite rooms with colonial-reproduction furniture. Some rooms have balconies and fireplaces, and interconnecting sets are popular with families. Breakfast included. ❻

The old town

Accommodation is generally cheaper in the **old town** than in the new town, though a lot of places are quite unsavoury. The reward of staying in old Quito is waking up in the very heart of things, and the feeling that you're not surrounded by hundreds of gringos.

Huasi Continental Flores 332 ⓣ02/2957327. Doesn't look like much from the outside, but the rooms are surprisingly nice, all with plenty of light and little noise, and some with polished parquet floors and clean en-suite baths. ❷–❸
Internacional Plaza del Teatro Guayaquil N8-75 ⓣ02/2959462, ⓕ2519462. Distinctive green-and-white building with its own parking. Rooms are a little dowdy, but large, clean and comfort-able, and all have private baths. Room 202 has an enticing balcony with views of El Panecillo. ❸
La Posada Colonial Paredes 188 and Rocafuerte ⓣ02/2282859, ⓕ2505240. Not located in a great area, but still a secure and friendly hotel with clean and spacious rooms, offering two to six beds in each. Has an attached language school. ❷–❸
Residencial Sucre Bolívar 615, Plaza San Francisco ⓣ02/2954025. Very basic and faintly

squalid hotel on the corner of the plaza; rooms are just about passable, though, and those directly on the corner have fantastic views over the square. ❶
San Francisco de Quito Sucre 217 and Guayaquil ⓣ02/2287758, ⓕ2951241, ⓔhsfquito@ andinanet.net. An absolute bargain and the best choice in the old town, located in a beautiful colo-nial building, with modest but clean en-suite rooms around a charming, geranium-filled courtyard with a fountain. Breakfast and use of sauna and steam room included. ❹
Viena Hotel Internacional Flores 600 and Chile ⓣ02/2954860, ⓕ2954633, ⓔvienaint@interactive .net.ec. Colonial-style building with rooms around a patio filled with potted ferns and a shrine to the Virgin. Slightly faded but still clean, with comfortable beds. ❹

Quito tours

Tours of Quito are offered by numerous operators, including most of those listed in the "Tours from Quito" box on p.112. **Standard tours** ($25–35) last about three hours and usually include a mix of riding in a vehicle and walking around the old town, vis-iting a few churches and museums, and then taking a trip to the top of El Panecillo hill for its great views of the city. Many operators also make tours of the old town **by night**, when the churches and monuments are illuminated to stunning effect. Others feature **special-interest** tours, such as the contemporary-art tour offered by *Enchanted Expeditions*, Foch 769 and Amazonas (ⓣ02/2569960), which looks at the works of Oswaldo Guayasamín and other modern Ecuadorian artists. **Transport** on most city tours is in small minivans, but Klein Tours, Eloy Alfaro N34-151 and Catalina Aldaz (ⓣ02/2267000), drives its clients around in a splendid 1950s wooden bus.

One recommended and less expensive alternative to these private tours is to take a municipal **walking tour** (Tues–Sun 10am, 11am & 2pm; $10), organized by the metropolitan police and led by English-speaking guides, which leaves from the tourist information office in the Palacio Arzobispal (Local no. 3; ⓣ02/2586591; see p.89). Two circular walking tours are given, which together cover most of the old-town sights.

The old town

For general sightseeing, Quito's chief attraction is the **old town** and its dazzling array of churches, monasteries and convents dating from the early days of the colony. Known to Quiteños as **el Centro Histórico**, the old town falls into a fairly small area that can be comfortably covered on foot in a day. However, trying to take in old Quito's thirty-odd churches and assorted museums will quickly leave you feeling swamped and exhausted, so try to single out a few highlights. These should definitely include the three main squares – **Plaza de la Independencia**, **Plaza Santo Domingo** and **Plaza San Francisco** – as well as the charming little **Plaza del Teatro**. Of the city's churches (most daily 8–11am & 3–6pm), the most impressive are **San Francisco**, **La Compañía** and **La Merced**, along with **El Sagrario** and **San Agustín**.

The old town's most rewarding museum is the excellent **Museo de la Ciudad**, while the **Museo Nacional de Arte Colonial**, with its important collection of religious art, and the newly opened **Museo Alberto Mena Caamaño** and **Museo Numismático** are also worth a visit. For a glimpse inside a traditional old-town house, head for the **Casa de María Augusta Urrutia** or the **Casa de Sucre**, while for sweeping views of the city, a short taxi-ride up to the summit of **El Panecillo** is highly recommended – though the panoramas from the precipitous ledges on the spires of the **Basílica del Voto Nacional** can hardly be bettered.

Orientation in the old town can sometimes be confusing, as many streets have two completely different **street names**: the official name on green plaques, and the historical one painted on ceramic tiles – Calle Sucre, for instance, is also signed as Calle de Algodón (Cotton Street). Only the official names appear on the maps and in the text of this guide; for information on how to read precise street addresses, see box on p.83.

Plaza de la Independencia and around

The **Plaza de la Independencia**, also known as the **Plaza Grande**, was first laid out with a string and ruler in 1534, and still preserves its original dimensions almost five hundred years later. Surrounded by the city's most important civic and religious buildings – the Cathedral, Government Palace, Archbishop's Palace and City Hall – the plaza has always been the city's focus. On Sundays, when traffic is prohibited from the surrounding streets (9am–4pm), the square is at its best, offering a great place for **people-watching**, especially the permanent array of dapper old men out for a stroll in their Sunday best, and the school kids, grandmothers and sweethearts sitting on benches amid the spindly palm trees and flowerbeds.

The Cathedral and Palacio de Gobierno

The south side of the square is dominated by the sturdy horizontal outline of the **Cathedral**, with its gleaming white walls, grey-stone portals and terracotta-tiled roof. Constructed in 1678 and restored in 1806, the cathedral's interior is not especially impressive, though it does contain the remains of Ecuador's most famous historical figure, Field Marshal Sucre (see p.512). More interesting, though, are the details of the sensational murder that took place here when the Bishop of Quito was poisoned by strychnine dissolved in the holy wine during the Good Friday Mass of 1877.

Perpendicular to the Cathedral on the west side of the square, the **Palacio de Gobierno** (Government Palace) was the site of another dramatic murder

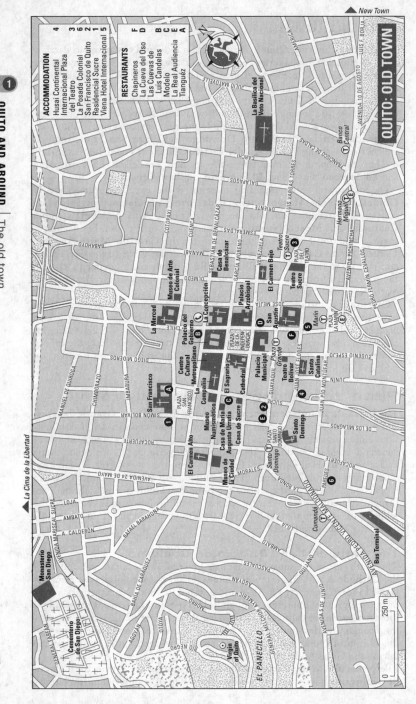

ACCOMMODATION

Husai Continental 4
Internacional Plaza
del Teatro 3
La Posada Colonial 6
San Francisco de Quito 2
Residencial Sucre 1
Viena Hotel Internacional 5

RESTAURANTS

Chapineros F
La Cueva del Oso D
Las Cuevas de
Luis Candelas B
Modelo C
La Real Audiencia E
Tiangüez A

when President García Moreno was macheted to death in the outer corridor of the palace in 1875 (see "History", p.512). This white-stuccoed, perfectly symmetrical building – fronted by a long row of columns supporting an upper balcony – is both the seat of government and the presidential palace, and is guarded by a couple of ineffectual-looking soldiers decked out in antiquated gold-and-blue uniforms. Entrance is not allowed.

Hotel Majestic, Palacio Arzobispal and Palacio Municipal

On the north side of the Plaza is a bright apricot-coloured building embellished with fancy white pillars and plaster mouldings – the former **Hotel Majestic**, now the city planning offices. Next door to it is the grand and dazzlingly white **Palacio Arzobispal** (Archbishop's Palace), a two-storey Neoclassical building, part of which is being converted into a shopping centre, that acts as the starting point for municipal walking tours (see p.86). Finally, the east side of the square is taken up by the 1970s concrete **Palacio Municipal** (City Hall), which blends in surprisingly well with the neighbouring colonial buildings, thanks to its low, horizontal design and white-painted walls.

Centro Cultural Metropolitano and El Sagrario

The recently renovated **Centro Cultural Metropolitano** (℡02/2950272), on the southwest corner overlooking the plaza, is the new focus of cultural life in the old town, housing gallery space for temporary exhibitions, lecture rooms, the municipal library and a museum, as well as elegant, glass-covered courtyards and a café.

The centre occupies a site rich in **history**, supposedly the location of one of Atahualpa's palaces before becoming a Jesuit university in the early colonial period, then a military barracks, and once more a university – which in 1830 hosted the signing of the Act of Constitution of the Independent State, bringing the Republic of Ecuador into being. Its most infamous moment came in 1810, when a group of revolutionaries was executed in a cell inside the building, an event commemorated by a display of waxwork figures in situ, a *museo de cera* that forms the best-known part of the newly refurbished **Museo Alberto Mena Caamaño** (Tues–Sun 9am–5pm; $1). Home to a collection of colonial, republican and contemporary art, the museum also features an interesting permanent exhibit, "**De Quito al Ecuador**", which sheds light on the murky period in the nation's history between 1700 and 1830, from Pedro Vicente Maldonado's work on La Condamine's expedition measuring the shape of the earth, to the rise of the new independent republic.

Opposite the Centro Cultural Metropolitano, just off the plaza and adjoining the cathedral, is **El Sagrario**, a seventeenth-century church topped by a pale-blue dome, whose colourful interior features turquoise walls embellished with bright geometric designs and stone pillars painted dark coral. The underside of the main dome, too, is covered with swirling multicoloured frescos, while the altar is often festooned with dozens of fresh white lilies.

La Concepción and around

On the north side of the Plaza de la Independencia, the street of Chile runs westward uphill and soon becomes congested with street vendors selling cheap bags, baby clothes, wooden kitchen utensils, Shakira posters and nylon underwear, climaxing in the frenetic **Feria de Ipiales** market a few blocks further up, where you'll find just about every imaginable item for sale, including your stolen wallet or camera. Towering over the melee, cater-cornered to the Plaza on the northwest, are the thick, impregnable-looking walls of **La Concepción**, Quito's oldest convent, dating from 1577 and off-limits to visitors.

Iglesia de la Merced

Continuing a couple of blocks west from La Concepción on Chile, the **Iglesia de La Merced** features a wonderfully over-the-top Baroque interior that's one of the old town's highlights. Its ceilings and walls offer a confection of white, lace-like plaster relief against a sugary pink background, looking like icing on a cake, with the side walls further adorned by dozens of oil paintings set in immense gilt frames. The main altar and two side altars are resplendent with gold leaf, while the choir, on a raised gallery at the back of the church, is ablaze with yet more gilding. You can also visit the adjoining **convent** (Mon–Sat 7am–noon & 1–6pm), built around a huge central patio enclosed within beautiful arched cloisters.

Colonial religious art and the Quito School

Once the conquistadors had carried out the brutal work of seizing huge tracts of South America, the Spanish Crown was faced with the task of colonizing its new territories and subsuming their indigenous population into its empire. From the beginning, Catholicism was a fundamental element of the process, and conversion became one of the most powerful tools used to consolidate the Conquest. Accordingly, **religious art and architecture** took on an enormous importance very early on: splendid monasteries and cathedrals were built partly to dazzle the natives and give them a sense of awe and devotion, while paintings and sculpture were used both for visual religious instruction and to provide icons of worship that would replace their former idols.

In the early days, religious art was imported from Spain, but the need to disperse large quantities of it around the continent prompted the growth of homegrown **artists' workshops** and **guilds** in the colonial centres, where Spanish teachers trained Indians and *mestizos*. This resulted in a unique blend of indigenous and European elements: carvings of biblical characters were frequently clothed in typical native dress, for instance, and sometimes given indigenous traits and colouring; Andean plant life and animals cropped up in traditional religious paintings; and symbols of pre-Hispanic worship, such as sun motifs, were incorporated into altars and church decoration.

The main production centres of religious art were Quito, Bogotá and Cuzco, each developing its own style. Over time, Quito artists became known for their mastery of **polychromy** (decorative colouring), particularly in their carvings of Mary, Christ and numerous saints, made out of cedar or red oak. Characterized by bold colours and exuberant decoration, the style found its greatest expression between 1660 and 1765, when the proliferation of high-quality Quiteño artists gave rise to the **Quito School** of art.

Led by **Miguel de Santiago** and **Bernardo de Legarda** in the early eighteenth century, and later by Manuel Chili, known as **Caspicara**, the Quito School's most delicate and beautiful creations were its polychrome carvings, often of the Virgin, covered in sumptuous attire and exposing only the head, face, hands and feet. One of the most peculiar aspects of the style was an excessive take on **realism**, using human hair and false eyelashes, nails and glass eyes. The School's paintings were characterized by vivid shades of red against darker, duller tones.

The movement began to wane towards the end of the eighteenth century, when secular subjects such as landscapes, portraits and town scenes began to replace religious ones. It finally died out after Ecuador's independence from Spain in 1822, when the type of religious art produced by the School was rejected for its associations with the old regime.

Museo Nacional de Arte Colonial

Directly behind La Merced, at Cuenca and Mejía, is the **Museo Nacional de Arte Colonial** (Tues–Fri 10am–6pm, Sat 10am–2pm; ☎02/2282297; $1), inside a handsomely restored sixteenth-century colonial house built around a colonnaded courtyard with a fountain. Note that with the museum closed for refurbishment until 2004, its collection has been moved temporarily to the Casa de la Cultura (see p.98).

Dedicated almost exclusively to **religious art**, particularly oil paintings and carved, polychrome statuary, the museum contains some impressive work by Quito School artists (see box opposite). The first two rooms are devoted to the art of the sixteenth and seventeenth centuries, but the bulk of the collection, filling three rooms, is made up of eighteenth-century works. One of the most compelling of these is a strikingly naturalistic carving by the famous indigenous artist Caspicara of the **Virgen Dolorosa** (Virgin of Sorrows) clad in a sumptuously brocaded dress, her sad eyes cast down as a knife pierces her heart.

Standing out as one of the few non-devotional pieces amidst the Virgins, saints and bleeding Christs is a large canvas depicting a tribunal of the **Spanish Inquisition**, wherein a menacing inquisitor stands over a kneeling, frightened crowd while two victims are tortured in the background. Other highlights include the richly ornamental *bargueños*, carved wooden chests with many small drawers, often inlaid with bone or ivory in intricate geometric designs.

Casa de Benalcázar

If the prospect of all the Baroque religious imagery in the colonial art museum seems overwhelming, head two blocks northeast to the **Casa de Benalcázar**, Sebastián de Benalcázar and Olmedo (Mon–Fri 9am–1pm & 2–5.30pm; ☎02/2288102; free), for a bite-sized chunk of the same thing. A splendid colonial mansion with a gorgeous courtyard, holding a small collection of religious paintings and statues in one room on the ground floor, the house is also the site of occasional free lunchtime concerts.

Iglesia San Agustín and around

Leading east downhill from the Plaza de la Independencia, the busy, pedestrianized stretch of **Chile** - whose lower portion features an informal street market peddling bric-a-brac – is well worth a look for its beautifully renovated nineteenth- and early twentieth-century buildings, painted in rich colours set off by elaborate cornices and white-plaster window mouldings.

One block east of the plaza, at Chile and Guayaquil, the imposing **Iglesia San Agustín** dates from the sixteenth century but was substantially rebuilt in 1880 after an earthquake, and features a massive 37-metre bell tower crowned by a statue of St Augustine. Its dark, neo-Gothic interior contains a series of enormous paintings by the distinguished seventeenth-century artist, Miguel de Santiago, depicting the life of St Augustine. The adjoining **Convento de San Agustín** has survived intact since its completion in 1627, and contains a fine cloister with two levels of thick stone columns. It was in the convent's chapter house (*sala capitular*) where fledgling patriots signed the Act of Independence on August 10, 1809, and the great hall also boasts an intricately painted, highly ornate ceiling and glittering gold-leaf altar. On the second floor of the convent, a **museum** (Mon–Fri 9am–noon & 3–5.30pm, Sat 9am–noon; $2) houses a large, dusty collection of religious paintings attributed to artists of the Quito School (see box opposite).

Teatro Bolívar and Monasterio Santa Catalina

A block south of San Agustín, on Calle Eugenio Espejo, the flamboyant Moorish **Teatro Bolívar** was lavishly restored in 1997 but gutted by a fire two years later, which started in a neighbouring pizza joint. Peek through the iron grille across the doorway for a glimpse of what's left of the grand pillars and galleries. Sadly, there are still no funds available for its reconstruction. Half a block down from the theatre, at Espejo and Juan José Flores, the **Monasterio Santa Catalina** is Quito's most colourful religious building, sporting bright coral-coloured walls trimmed with white-plaster relief.

Plaza del Teatro, Teatro Sucre and Iglesia del Carmen Bajo

Two blocks north of San Agustín, on Juan José Flores, one of the most charming squares in the city, the intimate **Plaza del Teatro**, sits surrounded by meticulously restored nineteenth-century buildings. Chief among these is the white, temple-like **Teatro Sucre**, whose glorious facade features six Corinthian columns and bas-reliefs of human figures representing music, drama and poetry. The theatre is being restored but should be open by 2004. A block west of the theatre, at Olmedo and Venezuela, stands the lovely stone **Iglesia del Carmen Bajo**, whose main entrance features two enormous wooden doors dating from 1745, elaborately carved with heraldic motifs.

La Compañía and around

On the west side of the Plaza de la Independencia, Calle García Moreno runs south towards El Panecillo past a string of churches and other points of interest. The most opulent of these is **La Compañía**, Garcia Moreno and Sucre, half a block from the Plaza (outside of church services, Mon–Fri 10am–1pm & 2–5pm, Sat 10am–1pm; $2 with guide), built by Jesuits between 1605 and 1765 and completed just two years before Spain expelled the order from the continent. Boasting an extraordinary Baroque facade of carved volcanic stone, the church is piled high with twisted columns, sacred hearts, cherubs, angels and saints. Inside, any thoughts of restraint vanish amidst the wild extravagance of gold leaf gone mad, with a reputed seven tonnes of the stuff covering the altars, galleries and pulpit.

Museo Numismático

For even more displays of colonial wealth, the new **Museo Numismático**, across the street from La Compañía (Tues–Fri 9am–1pm & 2–5pm, Sat & Sun 10am–1pm & 2–4pm; $1, free on Sun), outlines the history of the country's various forms of money, currency and coinage. Starting off with *spondylus* shells, which were effectively used as money along the Pacific coast, the museum explores pre-Columbian commerce in salt, coca leaves, obsidian, axe heads, cloves and cinnamon, before passing on to the elegant gold and sliver *reales* of the nascent Spanish colony. The post-independence section shows how the earliest examples of the sucre, Ecuador's first decimalized currency (created in 1868 and in use until 2000), turn out to have been minted in Birmingham, England. A fascinating inflation chart accompanies the displays throughout, and reveals that in the seventeenth century one peso could buy almost 4kg of cacao, while at the end of the twentieth, one sucre (the sucre replaced the peso one-for-one) wouldn't be enough for a tenth of a gram.

Casa de María Augusta Urrutia and Casa de Sucre

Diagonally opposite the Museo Numismático is the **Casa de María Augusta Urrutia** (Tues–Sun 9am–5pm; $2.50), a fine nineteenth-century mansion built around three inner patios. Guided **tours** are offered around the house where Doña María – widowed at an early age – lived alone with her 24 servants until her death in 1987. Many of the rooms have been left virtually untouched, and provide a fascinating glimpse of the tastes of Quito's upper classes in the twentieth century. Tours take in the bathroom, with its beautiful hand-painted glass and fittings imported from England; the kitchen, sporting a huge old German range and lots of copper pots; the dining room, crammed with crystal chandeliers, French china, silver tea services and other family heirlooms; and the grand drawing room, with fancy gilded furniture imported from Europe. The house is now owned by the charity founded by Doña María in the 1930s (Fundación Mariana de Jesús), which aims to alleviate poverty in Quito by building low-price housing.

Further down the block to the east, at Venezuela and Sucre, the nineteenth-century **Casa de Sucre** (Tues–Fri 8.30am–4.30pm, Sat & Sun 10am–3pm; $1) was once the property of Ecuador's liberator Field Marshal Sucre. Unless you're into military history, though, the battle plans, weapons, uniforms, standards and portraits of generals exhibited in the rooms around the courtyard are not that exciting, though the building itself is a beautiful example of a late-period Spanish Colonial house.

Arco de la Reina and Monasterio del Carmen Alto

Three blocks south of La Compañía is the **Arco de la Reina**, a thick-walled, plum-coloured arch spanning the street at the corner with Rocafuerte, built in the eighteenth century to provide shelter from the rain to local Mass-goers. Just beyond the arch is the eighteenth-century **Monasterio del Carmen Alto**, where Carmelite nuns still live in complete isolation. They do, however, manage to sell honey, herbs and wine through a revolving wooden contraption that allows them to remain hidden from view; to buy something, go through the iron gates, then through the small door next to the main entrance, and tap on the wooden screen in the wall (Mon–Fri 9–11am & 3–5pm; alternatively, the on-site shop is open Mon–Fri 9am–5pm).

Museo de la Ciudad

Directly opposite the Carmen Alto monastery, taking up the whole block, is the old Hospital San Juan de Dios, which functioned as such from 1565 until 1974, but now houses the dynamic **Museo de la Ciudad** (Tues–Sun 9.30am–5.30pm; $3, $4 with guide), perhaps the best museum in the old town, whose mission is to present Quito's social history in an accessible and engaging way. There are no original works of art, archeological relics or other typical museum showpieces here – instead, replicas, scale models, mannequins, friezes and sound effects are innovatively used to illustrate the city's development through time.

Some of the most notable exhibits include a scale model of the construction of the Iglesia San Francisco, with hundreds of miniature workers toiling away, and a reconstruction of the inside of a sixteenth-century house, with corn laid out to dry and sacks of potatoes lying around. Other engaging displays include life-size mannequins in religious processions, the reconstruction of a Quito School artist's workshop, depictions of candle- and furniture-making, and assorted antique clothes, harps, trunks and carriages.

Plaza San Francisco and around

Several blocks northwest of the Museo de la Ciudad is the vast, cobbled **Plaza San Francisco**, perhaps Quito's most beautiful square. In contrast to the Plaza de la Independencia, the square's grey colour and sweeping proportions are accentuated by its total absence of trees and benches, giving it an empty, slightly melancholy air.

Iglesia y Monasterio de San Francisco

Stretching across the plaza's western side is the monumental **Iglesia y Monasterio de San Francisco**, whose horizontal whitewashed walls are dominated by the twin bell towers and carved-stone portal of the church's entrance. Hidden behind this facade are the extensive buildings and seven courtyards that make San Francisco the largest religious complex in South America.

From the square, a broad flight of stone steps leads up to the front entrance of the **church**, whose construction began in 1536 shortly after the founding of Quito. It's rather dark and gloomy inside, but once your eyes become accustomed to the shadows you'll notice that the walls, altars, pillars and pulpit are encrusted with gilt, almost rivalling the theatricality of La Compañía. The main altar fills a large, domed area and is adorned by Bernardo de Legarda's famous winged carving of the **Virgin of Quito**, which served as a model for the giant statue on El Panecillo (see opposite).

On each side are two lateral chapels, resplendent with gold leaf, and more gilt can be found in the adjoining **Capilla de Cantuña** (Cantuña Chapel), entered through a door to the left of the entrance to the Iglesia de San Francisco. Inside are a splendid altar and many paintings and carvings produced by the Quito School (see box on p.90). According to legend, the chapel was built by an Indian named **Cantuña**, whom the Devil assisted to complete the work. When the time came to hand over his soul, however, Cantuña was saved on discovering that a single stone was missing from the structure.

Museo de San Francisco

On the other side of the church entrance is the door to the **Museo de San Francisco** (Mon–Sat 9am–6pm, Sun 9am–noon; $2.50), displaying an impressive collection of religious sculpture, paintings and furniture in a gallery off the monastery's main cloister. If you take advantage of the free guide service (small tip expected) available at the entrance, you'll also be led to the otherwise locked **coro** (choir) of the church, housed in a raised gallery overlooking the central nave, which features a spectacular carved *mudéjar* (Moorish-style) ceiling and a row of 36 painted wooden carvings of Franciscan martyrs on the walls, above the choir stalls. Just outside there's a so-called "**whispering corridor**", where two people speaking into diagonally opposite corners can hear each other's voices.

Plaza Santo Domingo and around

From the Plaza San Francisco, a three-block walk east along Simón Bolívar leads to Quito's third major square, the **Plaza Santo Domingo**, frequently used as a venue for outdoor concerts and festivals. Fronting its eastern side is the graceful **Iglesia Santo Domingo**, built by Dominican friars during the sixteenth century. Unfortunately, an ill-conceived interior remodelling took place in the nineteenth century, leaving the church with an altar that looks more like a miniature Gothic castle, surrounded by dozens of flickering candles. An adjoining monastery houses the **Museo Fray Pedro Bedón** (daily 9am–1pm & 2–4pm; $2), which contains a large collection of Dominican religious art from the sixteenth to eighteenth centuries, including remarkable life-size sculptures of various saints with moving arms and hands, as well as gold and silver ornaments and beautiful furniture delicately inlaid with bone and marble.

Not far from the square, branching downhill from Guayaquil, the narrow, pedestrianized section of Calle Morales is still known by its original name of **La Ronda**. Lined with thick-walled, whitewashed houses with tiny windows and brightly painted balconies, this picturesque alley is one of Quito's oldest streets, and one of the few remaining stretches of eighteenth-century working-class housing. It's also, however, notorious for its pickpockets and thieves – though the government is now trying to make the area a bit safer – so be alert and only come during daylight hours.

El Panecillo and the Virgin of Quito

Rising over the southern edge of the old town is the hill known as **El Panecillo** (the little bread loaf), featuring exhilarating views of the city enclosed by green hills and spread out in a blanket of pearl-white miniature houses, and crowned by a magnificent, thirty-metre high statue of the **Virgin of Quito**. A long flight of steps leads to the summit (a 40min walk) from the end of García Moreno, but violent muggings are common along the way, so make sure to take a taxi ($3 round trip, $7 from the new town). It's perfectly safe at the top, though, with teams of uniformed security guards patrolling the place (9am–7pm).

Compared to the striking city vistas, a dizzying contrast in scale is provided by the close-up view of the colossal winged Virgin, standing on an orb with a serpent curled around her feet and chained to her arm, as she gazes serenely down to the city. You can climb the fifty-odd steps up the small tower on which she's standing to a **viewing platform** (daily 9am–5pm; $1). At weekends a **bus** service (45min; $0.75) runs every fifteen minutes between El Panecillo and the country's other famous landmark, La Mitad del Mundo (see p.120).

La Cima de la Libertad and Monasterio San Diego

Sweeping hilltop views are also available from **La Cima de la Libertad** (Tues–Fri 8.30am–4.30pm, Sat 10am–3pm; $1), a military museum on a neighbouring foothill of Volcán Pichincha, marking the site of the victorious **Battle of Pichincha** that sealed Ecuador's independence from Spain on May 24, 1822. The museum houses a large collection of nineteenth-century uniforms, weapons and other military paraphernalia, enlivened by some massive **murals** depicting the history of Quito from pre-Columbian times to the creation of the modern Ecuadorian state, and one by Eduardo Kingman covering 200 square metres, which explores the historical roots of the nation. You'll need to take a **taxi** up here, which shouldn't cost more than $5 for the return ride, including waiting time at the top.

Between the two hills, just northwest of El Panecillo, the fascinating **Monasterio San Diego**, Calicuchima 117 and General Farfán (daily 9.30am–1pm & 2.30–5.30pm; $2), is a beautiful early-colonial Franciscan monastery of quiet cloistered courtyards, a refectory with a painting of Christ sitting down to eat *cuy* at the Last Supper, simple whitewashed walls and the fragments of some recently restored murals. Informative guided **tours** explore nearly the whole complex, offering a taste of both colonial and contemporary monastery life, disclosing secret doors and old pit tombs, and reaching the top of the bell tower for views over the old town; only the modest living quarters of the monastery's current denizens remain out of bounds. The church features an exquisite **pulpit** thought to be the second-oldest in South America – carved by an *indígena*, Juan Bautista Menacho – and a small **museum** offering a modest collection of colonial religious art.

Basílica del Voto Nacional

Perched on a small hill on Calle Venezuela, eight blocks north of the Plaza de la Independencia, the **Basílica del Voto Nacional** (towers daily 9am–5pm; $2; church Mon–Fri 7–9am & 6–7pm, Sat 6am–6.30pm; free) is the tallest church in Ecuador, thanks to its two imposing, 115-metre towers plainly visible throughout the city. Built in a flamboyant neo-Gothic style, it's a wild concoction of spires, flying buttresses, turrets, parapets, arches, gables and elaborate stained-glass windows. Even more striking, the church is built largely in concrete, begun in 1892 and still not entirely completed. A nice contemporary touch are the **gargoyles**, which instead of representing mythical creatures are carved with images of actual Ecuadorian fauna like monkeys and jaguars.

Don't miss the fantastic **views** from two church vistas accessed by lift and steep metal ladders: an unnerving buckling roof on the northern steeple, and a higher spot way up on the east tower. Stairs and ladders continue beyond the third-floor café, past the clock machinery and then up above the belfry to an artificial floor made only of wide steel grille. From here, those with a head for heights can squeeze out onto tiny **ledges** on the spire's exterior for a genuine thrill – and electrifying views.

The new town

Quito's **new town** sprang up in the 1940s, when the city's elite abandoned their old-town mansions and moved north. The heart of the area, officially called **Mariscal Sucre** but known locally as **La Mariscal**, is roughly bound by avenidas Patria in the south, Orellana in the north, 12 de Octubre in the east and 10 de Agosto in the west, and the main commercial artery is **Avenida Amazonas**, lined with banks, tour operators, restaurants and souvenir shops. With its peculiar mix of colonial-style town houses, Art Deco villas and functional 1970s blocks, La Mariscal no longer looks particularly fresh or new, nor is it particularly attractive, but it is where the vast majority of visitors to Quito base themselves, thanks to its many convenient facilities.

With the exception of the first-rate **Museo del Banco Central** and the captivating **Casa-Museo de Viteri** and **Museo Fundación Guayasamín**, there are no outstanding attractions here, though the **Museo Amazónica**, **Parque La Carolina** and **Vivarium** can be fun to visit.

Parque La Alameda to Parque El Ejido

North of the old colonial centre lies a transitional area between the old and the new towns, the main landmark of which is the triangular **Parque La**

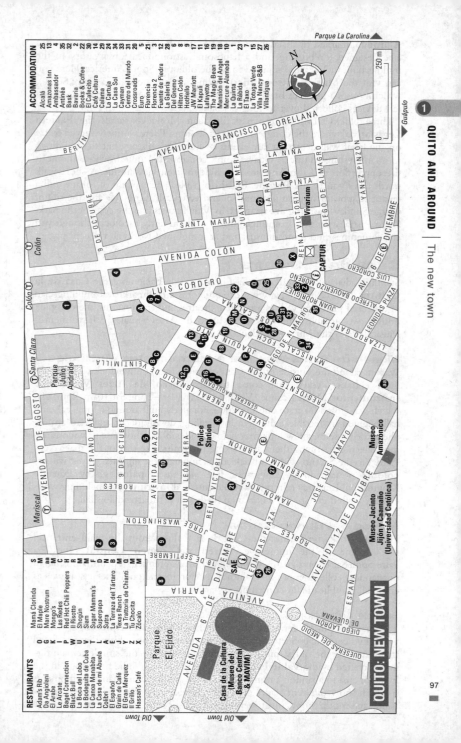

RESTAURANTS

Adam's Rib	S
Da Angioliani	M
El Arabe	aa
Le Arcate	C
Bagel Connection	I
Black Bull	P
La Boca del Lobo	W
La Bodeguita de Cuba	U
La Canoa Manabita	V
La Casa de mi Abuela	T
Colibrí	M
El Español	F
Grain de Café	D
El Gran Marquez	N
Il Grillo	B
Hassan's Café	M
Mamá Clorinda	O
El Maple	G
Mare Nostrum	K
Mongo's	I
Las Redes	R
Red Hot Chili Peppers	P
Il Risotto	W
Shogún	M
Siam	M
Sugar Mamma's	F
Superpapa	D
Sutra	B
La Terraza del Tártaro	E
Texas Ranch	J
La Trattoria de Chianti	Q
Tu Chocita	Z
Zócalo	M

ACCOMMODATION

Alcalá	25
Amazonas Inn	13
Ambassador	4
Antinéa	35
Bask	32
Bavaria	2
Books & Coffee	22
El Cafecito	30
Café Cultura	14
Calama	29
La Cartuja	24
La Casa Sol	34
Cayman	33
Centro del Mundo	31
Crossroads	20
Euro	5
Florencia	21
Florencia 2	3
Fuente de Piedra	12
La Galería	28
Del Gnomo	6
Hilton Colón	8
HotHello	9
JW Marriott	17
El Kapulí	11
Lafayette	16
The Magic Bean	19
Mansión del Angel	18
Mercure Alameda	10
La Quinta	1
La Rábida	23
El Taxo	7
La Totuga Verde	15
Villa Nancy B&B	27
Villantigua	26

QUITO: NEW TOWN

0   250 m

Alameda, marked by a stately statue of Simón Bolívar at its southern end, a lake designed for boating, and a handsome astronomical observatory in the middle, built in 1873 and reputed to be the oldest in South America. Here you can visit the **Museo Astronómico** (Mon–Fri 9am–noon & 3–5pm; $0.20), which houses a glorious brass telescope and an assortment of other astronomical devices collected over its long history.

Three blocks north of the park on Juan Montalvo stands the **Palacio Legislativo**, where the congress holds its sessions. There's a finely carved frieze on the front wall depicting key events of Ecuador's history, but the building's most interesting feature – Guayasamín's controversial mural, whose theme is the oppression of Latin America – is hidden from view inside. A short walk north takes you to the **Parque El Ejido**, a pleasant expanse of foliage and a favourite spot for impromptu football and volleyball games. It's also the site of a large Sunday-morning **art market**, in which artists line the edge of the park, along Patria, with their paintings – most of them fairly mediocre, though you can sometimes find more unusual and accomplished works at a decent price.

Casa de la Cultura

Standing adjacent to the Parque El Ejido, on 6 de Diciembre, the **Casa de la Cultura** (℡02/2902262, Ⓦwww.cce.org.ec) is a landmark oval building clad in mirrored plates. As well as a cinema, theatres and auditoriums, the complex houses two notable museums, the Museo de Artes Visuales e Instrumentos Musicales and the Museo del Banco Central.

Museo de Artes Visuales e Instrumentos Musicales

Walking along the outside of the Casa de la Cultura counterclockwise from its main entrance, you'll first come to the **Museo de Artes Visuales e Instrumentos Musicales** (MAVIM; Tues–Fri 10am–5pm, Sat 10am–2pm; $1), which was closed for restoration in 2003. Formerly built around a long, echoing hall blighted by terrible lighting, a low ceiling, dowdy decor and zero atmosphere, the museum's new look may help considerably to showcase its wide-ranging collections. Among them are striking **portraits**, like that of the malevolent Padre Vicente Solano, with his black robes, hooked nose and steely eyes; **watercolours** of Ecuadorian landscapes; fine *indigenismo* **paintings** by Eduardo Kingman; and an array of three thousand **musical instruments**, including wonderfully crafted guitars and a charango made out of an armadillo shell.

Museo del Banco Central

Heading clockwise around the Casa de la Cultura from the main entrance, you'll come to the impressive **Museo del Banco Central** (Tues–Fri 9am–5pm, Sat & Sun 10am–4pm; $2), Ecuador's premier museum, housing an outstanding collection of pre-Columbian ceramics and gold artefacts, as well as colonial, republican and contemporary art.

Sala de Arqueología

The first hall off the central lobby is the huge **Sala de Arqueología**, where you'll find ceramic collections grouped according to the culture that produced them. Among the oldest pieces, near the entrance, are the simple female figurines crafted by the **Valdivia** culture (3500–1500 BC) – the first group in the Ecuador area to abandon a nomadic existence and form permanent settlements – which show different stages of female development, such as puberty, pregnancy and motherhood, in a touching, naturalistic style. Close by are many fine examples of **Chorrera** ceramics (900–300 BC), most famously the "**whistle-bottles**" in the form of various creatures, which expressively mimic animal noises when water is poured into them. Look out for the monkey scratching its head, and the quizzical-looking duck.

Perhaps the most striking pieces in this room, though, are the large seated humans known as the **Gigantes de Bahía**, the work of the hierarchical **Bahía** culture (500 BC–650 AD), which range from 50–100cm in height and show men and women sitting with their legs crossed or outstretched, wearing many fine ornaments and elaborate headdresses. Also eye-catching are the pots and figurines of the northern coast's **La Tolita** culture (600 BC–400 AD), comprising fantastical images like fanged felines with long, unfurling tongues, or realistic representations of decapitated "trophy heads".

Among the few non-ceramic works in the room are the **stone seats** supported by human figures on their hands and knees – the work of the **Manteño–Huancavilca** culture (500–1532 AD) – probably thrones used by high-ranking authorities during religious ceremonies.

Sala de Oro

At the far end of the Sala de Arqueología, a ramp leads down to the darkened **Sala de Oro**, where dozens of pieces of pre-Hispanic gold are displayed to stunning effect, their brilliance enhanced by black backgrounds and dramatic lighting.

Ecuadorian metallurgy goes back some two thousand years, when the emergence of large ceremonial centres spurred the production of decorative arts and crafts for votive offerings. The most finely crafted **ceremonial offerings** were produced by the culture of La Tolita, whose work forms the bulk of the museum's gold collection and is characterized by beautiful filigrees and extremely fine detail worked on tiny objects. The masks, breastplates, headdresses, earrings, nose rings, necklaces, pendants and ceremonial bowls displayed here are both exquisite and exotic, with recurring motifs of cats, serpents and birds of prey. Highlights include the sun-like image of a mythical face sprouting dozens of twisted rays tipped by monkeys and snakes, and the feline mask adorned by an elaborate, removable headdress, from which two eyes hang suspended, their irises and pupils marked by green and black stones.

Sala de Arte Colonial

Back in the Sala de Arqueología, steps lead up to the **Sala de Arte Colonial**, where you are greeted by a massive, eighteenth-century Baroque altar. Since religious themes were the only acceptable subjects for paintings and sculpture during much of the colonial period, this room is packed with numerous images of the Virgin, Christ, and angels and saints. Among them are works by the most outstanding artists of the Quito School (see p.90), including Caspicara and Bernardo de Legarda. Although these **paintings** and **polychrome carvings** are brilliantly executed and wonderfully expressive, the most striking aspect is the gory and macabre nature of Hispanic colonial religious art: countless images of lacerated Christs dying in agony on the cross, a decapitated San Dionisio standing with his head in his hands, and several paintings of Christ dragging his cross through the streets, showing blood spurting in thick jets from his wounds.

Other museum rooms

The adjacent **Sala de Arte de la República** shows how religious themes were gradually replaced by more humanist, secular ones during the nineteenth century, starting with portraits of revolutionary heroes and moving through landscapes and images of fruit-sellers, workers and festival dancers. There are also some compelling, occasionally fanciful paintings of volcanoes and high-sierra and jungle scenes, but the room's most appealing works are those produced in the 1930s and 1940s, when artists like Eduardo Kingman, Diógenes Paredes and Oswaldo Guayasamín turned their attention to *indígenas* and the need for social change.

This trend – known as *indigenismo* – continues in the **Sala de Arte Contemporáneo**, upstairs on the third floor, but quickly gives way to more diverse subjects and abstract styles. The quality in this room is rather uneven, but several exhibits really stand out, including Camilo Egas' *Subway*, and Oswaldo Guayasamín's *Angustia*. Finally, the museum's collection is topped off with the small **Sala del Mueble** on the third-floor landing, displaying a number of wooden chests exquisitely inlaid with shell, bone, ivory and ebony in geometric motifs.

Museo Jacinto Jijón y Caamaño and Museo Amazónico

A five-minute walk up Avenida 12 de Octubre from the Museo del Banco Central, on the corner with Roca, the **Museo Jacinto Jijón y Caamaño** (Mon–Fri 8am–4pm; $0.60) is located inside the library of the Universidad Católica and offers a small-scaled version of the Museo del Banco Central, with some well-presented pre-Hispanic ceramics, seventeenth-century religious art and beautiful inlaid colonial furniture.

For something a little different, continue three blocks up 12 de Octubre to the Abya Yala building, whose first floor houses the **Museo Amazónico** (Mon–Fri 8.30am–5pm, Sat & Sun 9am–1pm; $1), dedicated to the indigenous peoples of the Oriente. It's not a big-budget museum, but the exhibits – among them vibrantly coloured feather headdresses, a long dugout canoe, musical instruments and fabulous beaded skirts and belts – are absorbing and well displayed. There are also a few evocative old black-and-white **photographs** of Shuar *indígenas* standing with a Catholic missionary, and modern photos showing the devastating effects of the oil industry on the rainforest. The only downside is the lack of information on the different Amazonian groups, but this you can find in the excellent **bookshop** on the ground floor, packed with volumes on the native peoples of the continent.

The Vivarium

At the northern end of La Mariscal, at Reina Victoria 1576 and Santa María, is one of Quito's most unusual attractions, the **Vivarium** (Tues–Sat 9am–12.45pm & 2.30–5.45pm, Sun 11am–5.45pm; $2), part of a non-profit organization that promotes public education on Ecuador's native fauna and tries to improve conditions in the nation's zoos. It consists, basically, of two rooms full of snakes and other **reptiles** and **amphibians** kept in large glass cabinets, and offers well-designed information panels explaining which snakes are poisonous and where they're found in Ecuador - though it's unlikely you'll remember any of this when faced with one in the jungle. Showpieces here include an **Equis** (the Spanish for "x"), one of the country's deadliest snakes, and a five-metre cobra; if you're feeling up to it, the staff will obligingly place a boa around your neck while you have your photo taken – many such photos of nervously grinning tourists are stuck on the wall.

Viteri Centro de Arte and Casa-Museo de Viteri

About 1.5km east of the Vivarium, at Orellana 473 and Whymper, the **Viteri Centro de Arte** (Mon–Fri 10am–1.30pm & 3–7.15pm, Sat 10am–1pm; ☎02/2561548, ⊛www.viteri.com.ec; free) is the gallery of Ecuador's greatest living contemporary artist, **Oswaldo Viteri**, whose boldness and versatility are shown in striking portraits like *Autorretrato con Amigos* (*Self-portrait with Friends*), confident virtuoso sketches, and brooding oil paintings like *Quito Gris II* (*Grey Quito II*), depicting a vast swirl of gloom squeezing the tiny images of city life to the margins of the canvas.

He is perhaps best known, however, for his **assemblages**, such as the astounding *Ojo de Luz* (*Eye of Light*) and *Y Surgiran de la Sombra y la Tierra* (*And They Shall Rise from the Shadow and the Earth*), mixed-media works combining colourful dolls made by Ecuador's indigenous communities with material such as sackcloth or pieces of ornate Catholic livery. The idea is to explore notions of *mestizaje*, which defines much of Latin America's cultural identity, in which the modern "mixed" society is both born of and reacting against its colonial past.

If you enjoy Viteri's work, the staff at the Viteri Centro de Arte may be able to arrange a visit to the artist's house, what he calls the **Casa-Museo de Viteri**, an extraordinary spot in the wooded hills overlooking the northern fringes of the city ($4–5 by taxi). He or his wife, Marta, will guide you around their formidable **art collection**, spanning from the pre-Columbian to the colonial and republican eras, ingeniously displayed to emphasize *mestizaje* and the rich diversity of Ecuador's cultural heritage. Among the many treasures are a model of the Santa María, one of Columbus's three ships, sailing on a sea of pre-Columbian axe-heads; an exquisite eighteenth-century representation of the Virgin of Quito with real hair and a silk dress; Amazonian-made Shuar violins, a striking example of Ecuadorian syncretism; and Spanish engravings by Goya and Picasso, jostling with ancient Jama ceramics. The creative centerpiece, though, is Viteri's **studio** itself, filled with paints and brushes, works in progress, finished portraits, artistic paraphernalia, antique tomes and the sharp smell of oils and white-spirit solvent.

Parque La Carolina and Museo Ecuatoriana de Ciencias Naturales

A kilometre north of La Mariscal is the southern tip of the large and leafy **Parque La Carolina**, which stretches north for another 1.5km, the most popular green space in the city and always buzzing with football games, joggers, hyperactive kids and strolling families, particularly on weekends. It's located in quite a swank part of town, flanked by a wealthy barrio full of smart condos to the east, and brilliant views of the Pichinchas to the west, rising above the canopy of trees.

In the middle of the park, at Rumipamba 341 and Los Shyris, the **Museo Ecuatoriana de Ciencias Naturales** (Mon–Fri 8.30am–1pm & 1.45–4.30pm, Sat 10am–1pm, Sun 9am–2pm; $2, weekends free) clearly suffers from a lack of cash, but does boast some fascinating bits and pieces, including the seven-metre skeleton of an anaconda, gigantic cranium of a blue whale, parts of the skeleton of a mylodon (prehistoric giant sloth), shells of giant tortoises and a chilling display of enormous spiders.

Museo Fundación Guayasamín

East of Parque La Carolina, in the hilltop barrio of Bellavista Alto at Bosmediano 543 (best reached by taxi), the **Museo Fundación Guayasamín** (Mon–Fri 9am–1.30pm & 3–6.15pm; $2) houses one of Quito's most compelling collections of art, divided into three sections. The **Sala de Arqueología** offers a beautiful array of more than 1500 pre-Columbian works from all the region's major aboriginal cultures; the **Sala de Arte Colonial** has representative Quito School carvings and paintings (see box p.90), which include pieces by Caspicara and Miguel de Santiago; and the main attraction, the **Sala de Arte Contemporáneo**, features a permanent exhibit of the work of the late **Oswaldo Guayasamín**, Ecuador's most renowned contemporary artist.

Displayed in the first room, Guayasamín's early work from the 1940s deals mainly with "the struggle of the Indian" in paintings such as *El Paro* (*The Strike*), showing a prone *indígena* with blood spilling out of his mouth while a policeman lurks in the background, and *Los Niños Muertos* (*The Dead Children*), whose subjects lie in a heaping, naked pile. By contrast, the second room is devoted to his series *La Edad de la Ternura* (*The Age of Tenderness*), with his famous moon-faced, round-eyed women and children shown in close, tender embraces, and painted in glowing yellows, golds and reds. Guayasamín's great triumph is, however, his disturbing **Edad de la Ira** (*Age of Anger*) series, displayed in the final room, where massive canvases tower over you with repetitive images of giant clenched hands, faces screaming in agony, skeletal figures that look utterly defeated and bodies in positions of torture.

Capilla del Hombre

A ten-minute walk around the corner from the Museo Guayasamín at Mariano Calvache and Lorenzo Chávez, on a hillside overlooking the capital, the **Capilla del Hombre** (The Chapel of Man; Tues–Sun 10am–5pm; $3) is Oswaldo Guayasamín's pet project, a must-see collection of disturbing and poignant works, begun in 1995 but only completed in 2002 – three years after the artist's death.

An ardent pacifist, Guayasamín wanted a secular "chapel" dedicated not to any god, but to humanity itself. The two-storey gallery is therefore both a memorial to the suffering of the oppressed and victims of war and torture, and a celebration of Latin American identity and the positive aspects of human nature. Some of the most notable works include an image of the execution of Tupac Amaru, the last Inca; a domed mural depicting the agonies of workers in the silver mines of Potosí, Bolivia, where nine million people perished over three centuries; and modern triptychs like **Ríos de Sangre** (*Rivers of Blood*), regarding the infernal acts of Chilean dictator Augusto Pinochet. More affirmative pieces include paintings of motherhood and the family, a wonderful self-portrait, and the lively and lighthearted *Bull and the Condor*, representing the tensions between Andean traditions and Spanish influences. On the lower floor, an **eternal flame** flickers for the cause of human rights – though it was initially broken on the gallery's inaugural night when a child dropped a cola bottle on it.

The outdoor terrace of the Fundación Guayasamín affords great views down to the picturesque village of **GUÁPULO**, perched on the steep slopes flanking the east side of town, whose narrow, cobbled streets and terracotta-roofed, whitewashed houses have the look of a Mediterranean village, and feel far removed from the hurly burly of the capital. Still, Guápulo is less than two kilometres from the new town, and shouldn't cost more than $2–3 to reach by taxi.

Besides the town's idyllic streets, charming houses, and relaxed atmosphere, the principal attraction is its magnificent **Santuario de Guápulo**, a beautiful church and monastery built in the latter half of the seventeenth-century, housing an impressive collection of colonial art and a masterful pulpit carved by Juan Bautista Menacho, one of the continent's finest sculptors. A fine new museum inside, the **Museo Franciscano Fray Antonio Rodríguez** (daily 9am–6pm; $2), named after the church's architect, displays some of the best pieces from the collection, such as Quito School paintings by Miguel de Santiago and elegantly carved ecclesiastical furniture. Guided tours (included in ticket price) are available in Spanish outside the hours of Mass.

Restaurants and cafés

Quito boasts by far the best and most varied choice of **restaurants and cafés** in the country, from humble canteens to classy outfits offering a wide range of **world cuisines** – including Thai, Italian, Mexican and Lebanese – along with tasty **seafood** restaurants and typical **Ecuadorian and Latin American** eateries. In Quito, *comidas típicas* generally comprise hearty fare based around a fatty meat dish, such as roasted or fried pork (*hornado* or *fritada*), delicious cheesy potato cakes (*llapingachos*) and a range of soups (*caldos* or *locros*) and stews (*secos*); see "Basics" on p.39 for more details. Eateries here are markedly more expensive than those outside the capital, but even the priciest are far cheaper than their equivalents in Europe or North America. Set-menu meals, *almuerzos* at lunch and *meriendas* at dinner, are even better value, sometimes consisting of two or three courses for a dollar or two.

Some restaurants, particularly inexpensive and informal cafés, are open all day (usually 8am–10pm), while more traditional establishments just serve lunch and dinner (often noon–3pm & 6–10pm), and most eateries close on Sunday afternoons around 3pm. Otherwise, only those restaurants with unusual opening hours are noted in the listings, and phone numbers are included for those where advance **reservations** are advisable. Restaurants are marked on the maps on pp.76–77, p.88 (old town) and p.97 (new town).

The new town

The great majority of restaurants are in the **new town**, particularly around Juan León Mera and José Calama, and many of these are specifically geared towards foreigners. Some of the best restaurants, which cater to Quito's middle class, are outside the main tourist zone, though well worth the taxi ride.

Cafés

Bagel Connection Reina Victoria and Pinto. Simple spot specializing in toasted bagels with a number of spreads, as well as breakfasts. Fine for a quick snack. Closes Sat & Sun 1.30pm.

Books & Coffee Juan León Mera 1227, same as the hotel (see p.83). Peaceful café offering good coffee and a range of cakes and snacks. Upstairs there are comfy armchairs, English magazines, a book exchange, table football and dozens of board games and chess sets. A great place to hang out and relax.

El Cafecito Luis Cordero 1124, same location as the hotel (see p.83). Lovely, laid-back spot with a big open fire, smoke-stained walls, creaky wooden floors and a large choice of coffees and home-made cakes. Also offers bargain vegetarian lunches, light evening meals and breakfast specials that come with unlimited coffee.

Ceuce El Jardín mall, third floor. Classy café with enormous windows looking down to Parque La Carolina and the Quito skyline. Excellent national and international food, and fairly reasonably priced.

Colibri Pinto E4-170 and Luis Cordero. Pleasant German-owned café, with a tree-shaded patio on a quiet street, offering good breakfasts ($3–4), crêpes and sandwiches, as well as central European specialities such as rösti, leberknödel-suppe, goulash and German sausages. Mon–Fri 8.30am–6.30pm, Sat & Sun 8am–5pm.

Corfú Portugal and Los Shyris, east of Parque Carolina. A café that, according to locals, serves up the best lattes and cappuccinos in Quito. Mouth-watering ice cream and pastries, made at the associated bakery next door, *Cyrano*, make the perfect accompaniments.

Cultura Robles 21. Quiet, relaxed café on the ground floor of the eponymous hotel (see p.83), featuring the same arty decor and colourful frescos. Not cheap, but the breakfasts, cream teas, cakes, soups, crêpes and other snacks are delicious, and it's one of the few places in town to serve Earl Grey tea. Closes 7pm.

El Español Juan León Mera and Veintimilla. Fantastic but pricey Spanish deli chain specializing in huge baguette sandwiches crammed with imported serrano or parma ham. Mainly takeout, but with a sit-down area.

Grain de Café General Baquedano 332. Cheerful little café-restaurant serving fresh and tasty food and excellent-value set lunches, always with a vegetarian option, plus à la carte dishes like quiches, croques monsieur, Caesar salads, home-made cheesecakes and much more. Closed Sun.

HotHello Amazonas N20-20, in the eponymous hotel (see p.84). French-owned pavement café selling excellent, moderately priced pastries, cheesecakes, quiches, salads and sandwiches. Covered by transparent plastic screens when it rains and, unlike other such places, warmed by gas heaters.

Magic Bean Foch E5-08, same location as the hotel (see p.84). Hugely popular café-restaurant with a little garden warmed by hot coals, where you can sit out until late. Great for its moderately priced breakfasts, brownies, strudels, pancakes, toasted sandwiches, organically grown salads and other backpacker-friendly fare.

Mr Bagel Portugal and 6 de Diciembre, east of Parque La Carolina. American-owned café selling Quito's best bagels, as well as offering English-language newspapers and a book exchange.

Sugar Mamma's Juan León Mera N24-19 and Wilson. Great little snack and juice bar, with a wide range of speciality juices on offer, including "healers", "energizers" and even "aphrodisiacs". Also does good set lunches and dinners for less than $3. Student and SAE discounts. Closes Sat 1pm & Sun all day.

Superpapa Juan León Mera 741. Popular and fairly cheap gringo-oriented eatery, serving baked potatoes topped with fillings like chili con carne, tuna and mayonnaise, and chicken curry. Offers a good breakfast and has a full notice board.

Ecuadorian and Latin American cuisine

La Bodeguita de Cuba Reina Victoria N26-105 ☎02/2542476. Well-made mid-priced Cuban food, including delicious *ropa vieja* (shredded beef cooked in wine and tomato sauce), served in a rustic dining room covered in graffiti written by previous guests. Live Cuban music on Thursday nights (reservations essential), when it gets packed with locals eating, drinking and dancing until 2am. Closed Mon.

La Casa de Mi Abuela Juan León Mera 1649 and La Niña. Really does feel like a granny's house, with its brown carpet and dark old chairs. A tiny menu – steak, chorizo, roast chicken and ravioli – but the quality is good, and the service very friendly. Quite expensive. Mon–Sat 11am–2.30pm & 7–10pm, Sun 11am–2.30pm.

La Choza 12 de Octubre and Luis Cordero. Excellent, moderately priced *comidas típicas*, efficiently served in a space reminiscent of an elegant hacienda's dining room. Where Ecuadorians go to eat top-shelf home cuisine. Closes 4pm Sat & Sun.

El Gran Marquez Calama 153. Locally popular lunchtime vegetarian restaurant nearly hidden by trees and a facade draped in ivy. Interior is gloomy and cavernous, but the set lunches are cheap (around $2) and excellent. Mon–Sat noon–4pm.

Mamá Clorinda Reina Victoria 1144. Friendly local restaurant serving tasty and good-value Ecuadorian dishes like *llapingacho* (mashed potato patties with fried egg and chorizo) and *caldo de gallina* (chicken soup). Regularly features live music. Closes Mon & Sun 5pm.

Mirador de Guápulo behind *Quito* hotel, Rafael León Larrea and Pasaje Stubel. Intimate and attractively decorated restaurant-bar serving delicious *comida típica*, perched on the hill above Guápulo and commanding spectacular views over the church and eastern cordillera. Live Latin music Thursday to Saturday nights. A short taxi ride from the centre.

Los Troncos Avenida de Los Shyris 1280 and Portugal ☎02/2437377. Moderately priced Argentinian steak house with a huge charcoal grill sizzling up prime cuts of every type of meat. A popular place, so reservations are advised in the evenings.

Tu Chocita Calama E5-10 and Juan León Mera, upstairs. Traditional Ecuadorian restaurant sporting furniture decorated with local fabrics. Popular for its good, cheap lunches (less than $2) as well as national specialities such as *yaguarlocro* and *churrasco*. Closed Sun.

La Viña Isabel La Católica and Cordero ☎02/2566033. Eatery with a large dining room that can feel a bit impersonal, though the food is among the finest (and most expensive) in town, highlighted by prawns cooked in wine with artichokes, and steak with wild mushrooms and asparagus. Closes Sun 4pm.

Seafood

La Canoa Manabita Calama 247 and Reina Victoria. Authentic, no-nonsense seafood restaurant like any on Ecuador's coast, serving inexpensive but good fish meals and set-lunches, all accompanied with *chifles*. Usually only open for lunch, but variable.

Mare Nostrum Mariscal Foch and Tamayo ☎02/2528686. Excellent but expensive fish and seafood served up in a dark, Gothic interior complete with huge candlesticks, wooden chandeliers and windows painted with medieval tableaus.

Las Redes Amazonas 845. Cosy little restaurant decked out with fishing nets (*redes*) on the ceiling, serving moderate-to-expensive fish and seafood, highlighted by the excellent *Gran Mariscada* – mixed seafood pan-fried in butter, garlic and herbs. Mon–Sat 10am–4.30pm.

World cuisines

Adam's Rib Calama and Reina Victoria. Busy, informal mid-range restaurant serving up huge portions of steak and ribs against a backdrop of American football on satellite TV. Predictably popular with US expats.

El Arabe Reina Victoria 627 and Carrión. Inexpensive Middle Eastern restaurant serving delicious hummus, falafel, kebabs and shawarmas to take away or eat in.

Le Arcate Baquedano 358. Quito's best pizzeria, offering no less than 59 pizzas (the strangest, *alla russa*, is made with brie, bressaola, vodka and lemon) cooked in a huge wood-fired oven. Snappy service, smart decor and reasonable prices. Closed Mon.

Black Bull Reina Victoria and La Niña. Striking purple, English-owned restaurant with slightly pricey but interesting dishes like steak flambéed in brandy with pepper sauce, chicken in sherry and amaretto sauce, plus traditional fare such as beer-battered fish and chips with tartare sauce.

La Boca del Lobo Calama E7-07. Mellow, friendly bar-restaurant in a renovated old house sporting vividly coloured walls and ceiling frescos. Original, moderately priced menu includes novelties like salmon ishpingu (a spice from the Oriente) in white wine sauce, plus a range of appetizing snacks like camembert with pears, honey and nuts. Mon–Sat 6pm–midnight.

Da Angiolani Juan León Mera N23-106. Unpretentious Italian restaurant with some outdoor seating, serving fresh pasta, good cannelloni and a number of vegetarian dishes. Closes Sat 3pm & Sun.

La Escondida General Roca N33-29 and Bosmediano ☎02/2242380. Relaxed, attractive restaurant serving excellent if pricey Californian cuisine – including goat-cheese salad and fresh pasta with smoked salmon and asparagus – prepared by a young American chef. Tucked away at the end of a cul-de-sac near the *Tribunal Supremo*. Closed all day Sat & Sun afternoon.

Hassan's Café Reina Victoria and Colón. Friendly Lebanese restaurant offering inexpensive staples like falafel and shawarma, and grilled beef in a pitta with yoghurt sauce and vegetables.

Il Grillo Baquerizo Moreno 533 ☎02/2234785. Dark wood panelling, starched linen tablecloths, attentive waiters and excellent Italian food, including home-made ravioli and thin, crispy pizzas. The free mineral water is a nice touch, and the steady flow of guests gives the place a good atmosphere. Expensive. Closed Sat lunch & Sun.

Il Risotto Pinto 209 ☎02/2220400. Italian-owned restaurant spread over several small rooms of a colonial-style house. Diners are pampered with complimentary home-made pâté, a huge bread basket and constant mineral-water refills. Trademark risottos are delicious and not too expensive.

El Maple Calama N10-5 and Juan León Mera. Trendy vegetarian restaurant, as popular with the city's businessfolk as it is with tourists, offering a broad menu of international dishes, from curries and pastas to burritos and stir-fries. Breakfast gets you free time on the Internet terminals.

Mongo's Calama E5-10 and Juan León Mera. Somewhat gimmicky themed "Mongolian" restaurant attracting a mainly gringo crowd. The big draw is a huge circular frying area where you take your food to be cooked after dousing it in your chosen sauces. Good value when the "eat as much as you like" deals go for half-price.

Red Hot Chili Peppers Foch 713 and Juan León Mera. Good Tex-Mex restaurant with patrons' graffiti on its walls, serving generous portions of standards like enchiladas smothered with cheese, accompanied by frijoles, sour cream and guacamole for $4–5. Closed Sun.

Sake Paul Rivet N30-166 and Whymper ☎02/2524818. Smart, top-shelf sushi restaurant on a par with anything outside of Japan, boasting a massive menu with eel, octopus, sea urchin and Canadian conch. A bit out of the way, and mainly frequented by city executives and expats, but a taxi ride is less than $1.50 from La Mariscal. Better to book Thurs–Sat.

Shogún Juan León Mera E5-134 and Calama, upstairs. Sushi restaurant with fancy interior designed in minimal white, with glass panels on floor and ceiling. The moderately priced food, although fine, does not quite match up to the awe-inspiring surroundings.

Siam Calama E5-10 and Juan León Mera, upstairs. Overlooking the heart of "gringoland" from a glass-covered balcony and outside terrace, a colourful but fairly pricey spot with tasty, straightforward Thai fare. Closes Sun 4pm.

Sutra Calama 380 and Juan León Mera, upstairs. Good hearty meals of a Middle Eastern bent, such as falafel, pitta and hummus, plus a full drinks menu. Often packed at night with locals and expats, squeezed in around little candlelit tables in rooms overlooking the busiest corner of La Mariscal.

Tanoshii at Swissôtel, 12 de Octubre 18-20 and Carrión ☎02/2566497. Expensive Japanese restaurant with first-rate *teppenyaki*, sushi and sashimi. The elegant white screens, black-lac-quered tables and waiters in red-satin dressing gowns add to the exotic atmosphere.

La Terraza del Tártaro penthouse floor of Edificio Amazonas, Veintimilla and Amazonas. Accessed by a glass elevator, a comfortable, moderately priced restaurant featuring wonderful views of the city. No great surprises on the international menu, but the food and service are good, and the atmosphere very relaxed. Closed Sun.

Texas Ranch Juan León Mera 1140 and Calama. Humble little steakhouse sporting a row of frilly 1970s lampshades, some twee pony posters on the wall and a cosy log fire. More expensive than appearances might suggest, but the meat is of decent quality and well prepared.

Thai-an Av Eloy Alfaro N34-230 and Portugal ☎02/2446639. One of Quito's best restaurants, with a stylish interior and a range of mouthwatering, moderate-to-expensive Thai dishes like crispy duck seasoned in cinnamon, and sea bass fillet with ginger, coconut and chilis. Closed Sun afternoon.

La Trattoria del Chianti Lizardo García 668. Small restaurant with candles on the table, cosy decor and a very welcoming Chilean owner. Serves reasonably priced if unexceptional pastas, pizzas and beef dishes.

Zócalo Calama 469, entrance on Juan León Mera. Trendy bar-restaurant featuring a bright, modern interior and an outside terrace, with overpriced but satisfying breakfasts, sandwiches, pastas and other such meals.

The old town

Places to eat in the **old town** are much thinner on the ground than those in the new, and tend to be busy during the day but closed or almost empty at night.

Chapineros Chile 916 and Flores. Tiny place with a handful of tables, leatherette booths and an old wooden counter, serving tasty *humitas*, bargain sandwiches and little else.

La Cueva del Oso Chile 1046 ☎02/2583826. Elegant dining room in a covered courtyard surrounded by pillars and arches, steps from the Plaza de la Independencia. Moderately priced food is traditional Ecuadorian, including delicacies such as *caldo de patas* (cow-hoof broth) and *seco de chivo* (goat stew) alongside less challenging dishes. Closed Sun afternoon.

Las Cuevas de Luis Candelas Benalcázar 713. Dark, cavernous restaurant owned by a friendly bullfighting fanatic, with pictures of famous toreadors on the walls and a stuffed bull's head in the corner of the room. The Spanish menu is quite appetizing, though the rather expensive food doesn't always live up to its promise.

Hotel La Real Audiencia Bolívar 220 ☎02/2950590. Despite the small portions and uninspiring food, an eatery whose superb views over the Plaza Santo Domingo make it one of the most memorable places to dine in town, especially at night when the church is floodlit. Worth phoning in advance to book a window seat. Only open for breakfast on Sundays.

Modelo Sucre 391. Going since 1950, the oldest café in Quito. Customers are shoehorned into the small room and tiny mezzanine to take their coffees, beers, sandwiches, *empanadas*, ice creams and pastries. Good for a cheap lunch or snack.

Tianguéz west side of Plaza San Francisco. Lovely little café-restaurant under the stone platform on which the Iglesia de San Francisco stands. The food (snacks and entrées) is a bit pricey, but the outside tables and chairs on the plaza can't be beaten for atmosphere. Also has an excellent crafts shop attached. Daily 9am–6pm.

Quito's cybercafés

Quito has embraced the Internet with great enthusiasm and is reputed to have among the highest number of **cybercafés** per square kilometre of any of the world's cities. In the past, the concentration of cafés in the Mariscal area, particularly around the intersection of Juan León Mera and Calama, mainly catered to the needs of backpackers, but after a recent surge in Ecuadorian emigration, the need for cheap communication with family overseas has given the Internet broad local appeal and stimulated a surge of new cybercafés. Prices in Quito are among the lowest in the country, with the average **cost** only $0.50 to $1 per hour, usually with sliding-scale rates for fractions of an hour.

Although most places offer at least coffee and packaged muffins or biscuits, not all are literally "cafés": some are small, bare rooms with a few desks and terminals, while others are quite stylishly decorated, play funky music and serve many different drinks and snacks. Many cafés also offer cheap telephone calls via the Internet (see p.45), as well as fax, scannzing and printing services.

Café Web Amazonas 333 and Jorge Washington. One of several such cafés at the southern end of Amazonas near Parque El Ejido. Discounts for students.

Choclo Net Juan León Mera N26-153 and La Niña. Cabins for phone calls, consistently cheap Internet rates and headphones for personal music.

Ciber Net Café Reina Victoria and Colón, under the post office. A functional assortment of desks and terminals, but also features a self-service washing machine and dryer.

Papaya Net Calama and Juan León Mera. Many terminals, but always packed with gringos, so there's often a waiting list.

Pizza Net Calama 354. Usually room here when other cafés are full. Also serves pizza by the slice.

Pool Net Calama 233 and Diego de Almagro. As the name suggests, a café with pool tables.

La Sala Reina Victoria 1137 and Calama. Fast, popular and reliable, with a smart adjoining bar offering pool tables.

Tomato Net Juan León Mera and Calama. Quick access, plus pizza and snacks.

Z@mbo Net Juan León Mera 932 and Pinto. Fast computers and open into the small hours if there's enough business.

Nightlife

Quito's **nightlife** is, on the whole, a bit parochial, with only a small number of really good **bars** and **clubs**, and a smattering of **live music**, mostly salsa or Cuban, with jazz here and there. Inevitably La Mariscal is a focus of clubs and bars, particularly the streets north of Colón between Juan León Mera and Diego de Almagro – mainly crammed with small, steamy **disco-bars** pumping out loud techno music. Many better-off Quiteños, however, prefer to spend their evenings in more exclusive places in smarter districts outside the Mariscal crush.

Most places tend to be fairly quiet through the week, totally packed Thursday to Saturday, and closed on Sundays. In general, bars are usually **open** 8pm to 2am, while clubs stay open from around 8pm or 9pm until around 4am or longer, but often only from Thursday to Saturday. Although **cover charges** are usually minimal, some disco-bars and clubs have a small cover (Thurs–Sat; $4–10), which sometimes includes your first drink, while others may have a *consumo mínimo*, meaning you have to spend a specified amount at the bar, usually the price of one or two drinks. Remember to take a **taxi** when getting about Quito at night.

Bars

Bogarín Reina Victoria and Lizardo García. Stylish bar hosting excellent live music and serving drinks and snacks. Popular with a slightly older crowd. Closed Sun & Mon.

El Cafecito Luís Cordero 1124. Cosy café (see p.103) that also serves as a relaxing place for an evening drink, with a background of soothing recorded jazz from the likes of Billie Holiday and Stan Getz. Closes 10pm Mon–Thurs and midnight Fri & Sat.

King's Cross Underground Bar Reina Victoria 1781 and La Niña. Snug little bar, popular with older visitors, serving a decent range of imported beers, and with a large and smoky outdoor BBQ every night except Sun.

Naranjilla Mecánica Tamayo and Veintimilla. A bit cramped but a unique place to enjoy a drink and a chat with friends. Frequented by Quito's arty crowd, its decor is imaginatively done, with off-the-wall artwork everywhere and low tables to enhance the cosiness.

El Pobre Diablo Isabel La Católica and Galavis, not far from *Swissôtel*. One of Quito's most appealing bars, a large but softly lit venue with exposed brickwork, and a favourite among young artists and writers. Expect good music (often live acts Thurs & Sat), a mellow atmosphere and tasty, reasonably priced food and drinks. Closed Sun.

La Reina Victoria, Reina Victoria 530 and Roca. Surprisingly authentic British-style pub popular with expats, with a roaring log fire, decent pub food (with BBQ nights on Sat) and beers, bitters and darts. Closed Sun.

Sutra Calama 380 and Juan León Mera, upstairs. Popular drinking hole with a huge cocktail list, and a good place to have a meal or snack (see p.106). Always buzzing in the evenings.

Trilce Baquedano 340 and Reina Victoria. Small lounge-bar that's a favourite of locals in the know, who come to chat more than dance, and enjoy excellent *canelazos*. Often has live music acts, with $3 cover charge. Wed–Sat 5pm–1am.

Turtle's Head La Niña E4-57 and Juan León Mera. Bawdy Scottish-owned pub featuring its own microbrewery, which produces excellent draught beer including bitters and Guinness-style creamy stout. Also serves British staples such as fish and chips and curry. Lots of fun.

Disco-bars and clubs

Acústica Eloy Alfaro and Portugal. The city's most exclusive, expensive and sought-after techno and dance-music club, regarded as *the* place to be seen by Quito's top trendies, but reportedly difficult to get into if your group is all male or you're poorly attired. $7 cover.

Cerebro 6 de Diciembre and Los Shyris. Expansive dance floors and slick ultramodern styling have made this club, which plays anything from techno to hip-hop, a favourite of twenty-somethings.

Manta Ray Av González Suárez and Rafael León Larrea. Techno and rave music are on offer at this huge dance floor packed with a young, enthusiastic crowd fuelled from several bars. $4 cover.

No Bar José Calama 360 and Juan León Mera. Extremely popular with gringos and locals alike, with a reasonably sized dance floor and loud pop and rock. Thursday is the big night, when it's not uncommon to have women dancing on the bar.

Quiteño Libre Av González Suárez and Rafael León Larrea, next to *Quito* hotel. One of the hippest clubs of the moment, a great place to dance to a range of Latin music with a young energetic crowd. $4 cover.

Live music and salsatecas

La Bodeguita de Cuba Reina Victoria 1721 ☎02/2542476. Actually a restaurant (see p.104), but on Thursday nights offers a spirited atmosphere, with people of all ages dancing to live Cuban music.

Cafelibro Almagro 1550 and Pradera ☎02/2526827. Arty café with live jazz on Saturday nights, and on other evenings a variety of song and dance, music, poetry readings and sometimes even theatre. Daily until midnight.

Mirador de Guápulo behind *Quito* hotel on Rafael León Larrea and Pasaje Stubel. Live Latin music from Thursday to Saturday nights in this restaurant-bar boasting spectacular views (see also p.104). A short taxi ride from the centre.

Seseribó Edificio El Girón, Veintimilla and 12 de Octubre. A salsateca that's a Quito institution on Thursday nights, with a good mix of students in jeans and gyrating devotees. Features occasional live acts.

Varadero Reina Victoria 1751 and La Pinta. Unpretentious bar-restaurant with live Cuban music (Wed, Fri & Sat), a great atmosphere and knockout *mojito cubano*, a potent cocktail of mint with rum and soda. Closed Sun.

Verde Pintón y Maduro Whymper 394 and Coruña. Compact and expensive bar with a small dance floor and stage, hosting good live music ranging from cover bands to original local talent. Open Wed–Sat. $5 cover.

Fiestas in Quito

Aside from the national public holidays and mischief of Carnaval (for details, see p.47), Quito features several of its own colourful **fiestas** that are well worth a look if you're in town. The city's most prominent religious festival is **Good Friday**, when hundreds of barefooted penitents solemnly cross through the old town in mourning, many dressed in purple robes with pointed hoods, others dragging huge crucifixes and a few even wearing crowns of thorns. Another major event comes on **May 24**, honouring the 1822 day when the colony finally threw off the Spanish yoke at the Battle of Pichincha, when Quito erupts in a spectacle of booming cannons and military parades. The biggest fiesta of the year, however, kicks off at the beginning of December and lasts for a week until **December 6**, marking the city's foundation. The celebrations include street parties, music and dancing, processions, bullfights at the Plaza de Toros, the election of the *Reina de Quito* (beauty queen) and general high spirits. December is generally regarded by Quiteños as a party month, topped off on **New Year's Eve** with a street parade of *años viejos* – effigies, often of current political figures, which are burnt at midnight.

Performing arts and film

As the national centre for the **performing arts**, the **Casa de la Cultura**, 6 de Diciembre N16-224 and Patria (℡02/2902262, 🅦www.cce.org.ec; see p.98 for more details), is one of the best venues for theatre, dance and classical music, attracting international performers as well as national artists. Other sites include the renowned **Teatro Malayerba**, Luis Sodiro E2-65 and 6 de Diciembre, near the Parque Alameda (℡02/2235463), which puts on exciting new works in its small theatre, and **El Patio de Comedias**, 18 de Septiembre and 9 de Octubre (performances Thurs–Sun 8pm; ℡02/2561902), presenting new shows every month. By the end of 2003, the elegant, nineteenth-century **Teatro Sucre**, on the Plaza del Teatro (℡02/2281644; see p.92), will have undergone an extensive restoration, and is likely to reward a visit regardless of what's playing.

Folk ballets

Regular **folk ballets**, with costumed dancers representing different Ecuadorian cultural groups, are performed by **Jacchigua** at the Teatro del Aeropuerto, opposite the airport on Avenida Paz (Wed & Fri 7pm; bookings through Metropolitan Touring on ℡02/2464780), and by **Humanizarte**, Leonidas Plaza N24-226 and Lizardo García, entrance on the tiny street of Xaura off Lizardo García (Wed 7.30pm, ℡02/2226116), which stages innovative and excellent experimental theatre and dance productions, usually on Wednesday evenings. The best way to find out what's on is to check the "Chévere" section of Friday's *El Comercio*; most performances take place Thursdays through Saturdays.

Film

Cinema is very popular in Quito, with English-language **films** almost always shown in their original versions with Spanish subtitles. Several excellent multiplexes offer plenty of screens and first-rate sound systems: **Cinemark**, Plaza de las Américas at avenidas América and República (℡02/2262026, 🅦www.cinemark.com.ec), has huge screens, comfortable armchair-type seating and several adjacent eateries; and **Multicines**, in the basement of the CC Iñaquito mall at Amazonas and Naciones Unidas, and at the CC El Recreo on Avenida Maldonado (℡1800/352463, ⓦwww.multicines.com.ec), provides similar facilities. Both show American new releases, with the odd European or independent film thrown in. Movie **tickets** cost around $4, or $3.50 before 4pm, with special rates of $2.60 at Cinemark (Mon–Wed only).

There are a number of other cinemas dotted around town, but most are hopelessly antiquated with poor sound systems that spoil enjoyment. The exception is the Casa de la Cultura (see p.109), which regularly screens art-house films. Details of film programmes are available at the cinemas' websites and in the daily listings of *El Comercio*.

Shopping

Among Quito's **shopping** districts, the tourist zone of **La Mariscal** is well stocked with artesanías from the sierra, selling items such as brightly painted balsawood parrots and fish, shigra bags, Otavalo tapestries, chunky woollen sweaters, baggy trousers, leather goods and tagua-nut carvings. For cheap clothes and bags, wander up **Calle Chile** or around the **Feria de Ipiales** in the old town, while for cheap food and produce, try the bustling **Mercado Santa Clara** in the new town to the west of the Santa Clara Trole stop, Versalles and Marchena. Good-quality clothes, shoes, electronic items and other goods are sold in several modern **shopping malls**; those listed below are open daily.

Handicrafts, leather goods and souvenirs

There are countless shops for **handicrafts** and **leather goods** along **Amazonas**, as well as items laid out by sierra *indígenas* on the pavement, and **Juan León Mera** also has a lot of **souvenir** shops. The following stand out from the competition.

La Bodega Exportadora Juan León Mera N22-24 and Carrión. Attractive, quality handicrafts, most fairly reasonably priced.
Comisariato del Cuero Olmeda OE3-12 and Guayaquil, old town. Huge choice of leather bags and jackets, and much better value than the leather shops on Amazonas.
Folklore Olga Fisch Colón E10-53 and Caamaño. Boutique of the late Olga Fisch, a renowned artesanía collector. The quality of the pieces on show is a notch above the rest, as are the prices.
Fundación Sinchi Sacha Reina Victoria 1780 and La Niña. Non-profit organization aimed at promoting fair trade and providing indigenous people, particularly from the Oriente, with a venue for their products. Stocks a wide variety of good-quality handicrafts at reasonable prices and has temporary exhibitions of individual artists' or artisans' work. Also a branch at Tianguéz on the Plaza San

Francisco in the old town.
Galería Latina Juan León Mera N23-69 and Veintimilla. Upmarket and expensive, but stocks one of the best selections of handicrafts and fine knitwear in Quito.
Hilana 6 de Diciembre 1921 and Baquerizo Moreno. Sells wool and alpaca blankets woven with typical pre-Hispanic motifs – very attractive and not too expensive.
Homero Ortega & Hijos Isabel La Católica N24-100 and Madrid ⓦ www.homeroortega.com. Very good Panama-hat shop run by a family that's been in the business for five generations.
Mercado Artesanal La Mariscal Jorge Washington and Juan León Mera. Huge artesanía market housing many of the vendors who used to clutter the streets of La Mariscal. Worth a look, though the quality is not always of the highest level.

Books, magazines and music

English-language **books** and non-Ecuadorian **newspapers** and **magazines** are not particularly easy to get hold of outside of La Mariscal and the better-stocked shopping malls. **Music**, on the other hand, is widely available on cheap CDs and cassettes at the dozens of informal stalls cluttering the city's streets. These are pirate copies, of course – the real thing costs up to ten times the price and is available at only a handful of upmarket outlets.

Confederate Books Calama 410 and Juan León Mera. Excellent secondhand bookshop with a large and well-ordered English section.

Libri Mundi Juan León Mera N23-83 and Veintimilla, Ⓦ www.librimundi.com. Quito's best bookshop, with a good selection of English novels, guidebooks and Spanish-language books. The staff are very helpful and will go out of their way to get hold of a particular title for you.

Libroexpress Amazonas 816 and Veintimilla. Impressive choice of English-language magazines, including both mainstream and obscure titles.

Mr Books El Jardín mall, third floor. Large bookshop with a good choice of both English- and Spanish-language books.

South American Explorers Jorge Washington 311. New and secondhand guidebooks in English, also with an excellent book exchange, whose titles are colour-coded according to literary quality. For more information on this organization, see p.80.

Tower Records Quicentro Mall (see below). Huge, modern store selling a vast range of international and Latin CDs.

Shopping malls

Most of Quito's **shopping malls** are as polished and characterless as anything you would find at home. They are undeniably convenient, though, and usually feature a **Supermaxi**, the country's best-stocked supermarket chain. Note that you may often see the following names preceded by "CC", for "*Centro Comercial*".

Iñaquito Amazonas N36-152 and Av Naciones Unidas. Often called CCI, a large mall on the north side of the Parque La Carolina, with a multiplex cinema.

El Jardín Amazonas and República. Modern, attractive mall, conveniently located by Parque La Carolina. Many Amazonas buses go past it.

Quicentro Av Naciones Unidas and 6 de Diciembre. Quito's swankiest mall, boasting lots of designer stores, including DKNY and Liz Claiborne, plus a Tower Records.

El Recreo Av Maldonado 14-205. Large, busy mall in the south of the city, by the southern terminus of the trolley line. Not as smart as the others.

Listings

Airlines Aerogal, Amazonas 7797 and Juan Holguín ☎ 02/2441950; Air France, Tower A, World Trade Centre, 12 de Octubre N24-562 and Luis Cordero ☎ 02/2524201; Alitalia, Eloy Alfaro N32-541 and Los Shyris, Edificio Nuevola ☎ 02/2272802; American, Amazonas and Av Naciones Unidas, Edificio Puerto del Sol, also at *Colón* hotel, Amazonas and Robles ☎ 02/2260900; Austro Aéreo, Amazonas and río Curaray ☎ 02/2271536; Avensa, Portugal E10-29 and República de El Salvador ☎ 02/2253043; Avianca, Twin Towers bldg, República de El Salvador 780 and Portugal ☎ 02/2264392; Continental, World Trade Centre, Tower B, 12 de Octubre and Luis

Cordero ☎ 02/2557170; Copa, República de El Salvador 361 and Moscú ☎ 02/2273082; Iberia, Amazonas 239 and Jorge Washington ☎ 02/2566009; Icaro, Palora 124 and Amazonas ☎ 02/2448626; KLM, 12 de Octubre N26-97 and A Lincoln, Torre 1492 ☎ 02/2986828; LanChile, Pasaje Río Guayas E3-131 and Amazonas ☎ 1800/526328; Lufthansa, 18 de Septiembre N20-705 and Reina Victoria ☎ 02/2508396; Tame, Amazonas 1354 and Colón ☎ 02/2509375; Varig, Porto Lisboa bldg, Portugal 794 and República de El Salvador ☎ 02/2250126.

There's no shortage of **tour operators** in Quito, with many of them located in La Mariscal, particularly along Amazonas, Juan León Mera and their adjoining streets. Almost all can book trips to the Oriente and Galápagos, but it's usually better to book directly with the service provider – refer to our list of Quito-based specialist operators for the **Oriente**, pp.288–290, and the **Galápagos**, p.470.

It's difficult to generalize about **prices**, as these can vary wildly between operators, though most tours get cheaper the larger your group is; prices here are quoted per person based on two people sharing. Cheapest are half-day trips to the Mitad del Mundo ($20–40), with day-trips to Cotopaxi, indigenous markets and nearby cloud-forests ranging from $30 to $100. The difference is partly based on the type of **lunch** offered, with some tours including three-course gourmet meals in haciendas, and others simply providing a packed lunch (in Ecuador, *un boxlunch*). Biking, rafting and trekking tours ($45–70) are a bit cheaper than other day-trips, while **multi-day** trips vary in price by the type of accommodation offered, ranging from bare-bones camping to comfortable *hosterías*. When comparing prices, always make sure to check what is included, particularly equipment, food, accommodation and the availability of English-speaking **guides**. For multi-day trips, try to meet your guide beforehand – a good, personable tour leader can make a world of difference.

General operators

Standard day-trips from Quito offered by **general operators** include trips to the Mitad del Mundo monument (see p.120), indigenous markets of Otavalo (see p.144), Saquisilí (see p.195), Zumbahua (see p.199) and Parque Nacional Cotopaxi (see p.188). Many also offer birding tours to cloudforest reserves close to the capital, as well as multi-day packages, often based around accommodation in luxurious haciendas. The larger companies can put together complete **customized packages** for you, including hotel bookings and transfers.

An increasing number of operators now offer activity-focused **adventure tours**, such as one-day **white-water rafting** down the Toachi and Blanco rivers west of Quito (grade III–IV rapids); **mountain biking** on nearby volcanoes such as Cotopaxi, with vehicle transport to the site; **horse riding** in the surrounding countryside; and **hiking** through the sierra or the subtropical cloudforests west of Quito.

Amerindia Brasil 293 and Granda Centeno, Edificio IACA, second floor ☏02/2446996, ℻2259305, ⓦwww .quasarnauticausa.com. Part of the Quasar Nautica group, a top-end operator providing customized tours of the whole country, often using luxury accommodation.

Eco Adventour Pasaje Cordova N23-26 and Wilson ☏02/2223720, ℻2544073, ⓦwww.ecoadventour.com. Adventure-tour specialists, including kayaking, mountain biking, and white-water rafting, with packages that combine several activities.

Ecuadorian Tours Amazonas 329 and Jorge Washington ☏02/2560488, ℻25 01067, ⓦwww.ecuadoriantours.com. Experienced and reliable operator providing the usual sierra tours, plus a wide choice of programmes in other parts of the country, such as the southern coast.

EcuadorVerde Roca 736 and Amazonas, Pasaje Chantilly ☏02/ 22906021, ⓦwww.ecuadorverde.com. A cooperative network of some of Ecuador's best ecotourism ventures that demonstrate ecologically sound principles as well as social responsibility, offering direct links to lodges, retreats and community tourism projects in the Andes, cloudforest, Oriente and coast.

Enchanted Expeditions Foch 726 and Amazonas ☏02/2569960, ℻2569956, ⓦwww.enchantedexpeditions.com. Professional operator with an enormous number of touring options throughout Ecuador, including trekking, birding and archeological tours. Also offers customized packages.

Explorandes Presidente Wilson 537 and Diego de Almagro ⓣ02/2222699, ⓕ2556938, ⓔexploreandes@ ecuadorexplore.com. Wide range of pricey tours out of Quito, Cuenca and Guayaquil, including many adventure-focused options such as cloudforest treks and white-water rafting. Established for more than twenty-five years in Peru, ten in Ecuador.

Islazul Tours La Isla N266-46 and Mosquera Narváez ⓣ & ⓕ02/2224393, ⓦwww.ecuador-travel.net. Personalized and good-value hiking, climbing and other adventure tours in the sierra and subtropical cloudforests. All tours guided by the Austro-Canadian owner.

Klein Tours Eloy Alfaro N34-151 and Catalina Aldaz ⓣ02/2267000, ⓕ2243302, ⓦwww.kleintours.com. One of Quito's most established and polished operators, offering all the standard tours as well as custom packages.

Metropolitan Touring Republica de El Salvador N36-84 and Naciones Unidas ⓣ02/2464780, ⓦwww .metropolitan-touring.com. Sizeable travel agent and operator, with branches all over Ecuador and a wealth of resources, offering tours and packages throughout the country.

Native Life Foch E4-167 and Amazonas ⓣ & ⓕ02/2550836, ⓔnatlife1@natlife .com.ec. Various day-trips from Quito, including biking and rafting excursions, plus a choice of trekking and climbing programmes. Also Oriente specialists (see p.289).

Nomadtrek Amazonas N22-29 and Carrión, second floor ⓣ02/2547275, ⓕ254 6376, ⓦwww.nomadtrek.com. German-run company specializing in trekking, biking, birding, climbing and cultural tours, plus a two-day introduction to kayaking ($140) and jungle journeys (see p.289).

Nuevo Mundo Av Coruña N26-207 and Orellana ⓣ02/2564448, ⓕ2565261, ⓦwww.nuevomundotravel.com. Wide choice of tours and tailor-made packages, taking in horse riding, the Devil's Nose train ride, cloudforest treks and indigenous markets.

Positiv Turismo Voz Andes N41-81 and Mariano Echeverría ⓣ02/2440604, ⓕ2257883, ⓦwww.positivturismo.com. Friendly Swiss-Austrian company providing excellent-value, one- and two-day tours in the sierra. Tours are in small groups and some include light hiking.

Safari Tours Calama 380 and Juan León Mera ⓣ02/2552505, ⓕ2223381, ⓦwww.safari.com.ec. British-Ecuadorian-run operator with climbing tours (see p.114), as well as a wide choice of adventure or expedition day-tours from Quito, with custom trekking or jeep tours available. Also offers women-only tours, with female drivers and guides.

Surtrek Amazonas 897 and Wilson ⓣ02/2231534, ⓕ2561132, ⓦwww .surtrek.com. Offers various adventure tours, including light treks and expeditions, biking, mountain climbing, rafting, diving, jungle trips and cruises.

Tropic Ecological Adventures Edificio Taurus 1-A, República E7-320 and Diego de Almagro ⓣ02/2225907, ⓕ2560756, ⓦwww.tropiceco.com. Ecologically focused Oriente specialist (see p.289) offering upmarket one- to five-day tours in the sierra and western cloudforests.

Specialist operators

A few **specialist operators** incorporate a number of singular pursuits, including adventures oriented around the likes of **bird watching**, **biking**, **rafting** and **kayaking**.

Biking Dutchman Foch 714 and Juan León Mera ⓣ02/2568323, ⓕ2567008, ⓦwww.biking-dutchman.com. The original bike-tour operator in Ecuador, appropriately run by a pedalling Dutchman, with a wide range of mainly downhill biking tours from one to twelve days, always with a support vehicle.

Mindo Bird Tours ⓣ02/2454304 or 09/9042210, ⓔjlyons@pi.pro.ec, ⓦwww

.mindobirds.com.ec. Offers tours of all the best bird-watching areas in Ecuador, with special emphasis on the Chocó bioregion forests of northwestern Ecuador. Run by Jane Lyons, one-time head of BirdLife International for the Americas, and Vinicio Pérez, a highly respected ornithologist and Mindo native with a fantastic memory for bird calls.

World Bike Pinto E4-350 and Av Amazonas ⊤02/2352769 or 2231123, ⓦwww.andesworldbike.com. Good-value mountain-biking day-trips down volcanoes and hills near Quito, or week-long trips combining day rides in various locations across the country. Also provide trekking, climbing and high-altitude training services.

Yacu Amu Foch 746 and Juan León Mera ⊤02/2904054, ⓦwww.yacuamu.com. Largest and longest-established white-water rafting and kayaking specialist in Ecuador, offering runs down the Toachi, Blanco and Upano rivers, among others. Also has a sister office in Tena (see p.321).

Climbing operators

Other specialized operators guide **climbers** up the sierra's volcanoes and rent equipment to solo climbers. Regardless of cost, make sure to have a good **guide** – while many of the climbs near Quito are not technically difficult, the potential hazards are very serious. Check that your operator uses only guides trained by ASEGUIM (Asociación Ecuatoriana de Guías de Montaña), and take a close look at its equipment before signing up. Ideally, the company should provide one guide for every two climbers. For more on climbing, see p.52; for a selection of Riobamba-based guides and operators, see p.224.

Alta Montaña upstairs at Books & Coffee, Juan León Mera 1227 and Calama ⊤02/2528769. Quito office of the respected Riobamba-based climbing operator, which owns the *Posada La Urbina* acclimatization centre on Chimborazo (see p.229).

Compañía de Guías de Montaña Jorge Washington 425 and 6 de Diciembre ⊤ & ⓕ02/2504773, ⓦwww.companiadeguias.com. Very reliable outfit run by a group of Ecuadorian and Swiss mountain guides, taking climbers up all the main snow peaks, plus several lower ones.

Ecuadorian Alpine Institute Ramírez Dávalos 136 and Amazonas, office 102 ⊤02/2565465, ⓦwww.volcanoclimbing.com. As well as guiding up all the main peaks, offers a climbing school teaching basic mountaineering skills to beginners.

Moggely Tours Joaquín Pinto E4-255 and Amazonas ⊤ & ⓕ02/2554984, ⓦwww.moggely.com. Friendly, accommodating Swedish-run climbing operator providing thrice-weekly climbs of Cotopaxi, as well as regular expeditions to other popular mountains. Also runs trekking and riding tours.

Safari Tours Calama 380 and Juan León Mera ⊤02/2552505, ⓕ2223381, ⓦwww.safari.com.ec. Long-established and highly regarded British–Ecuadorian outfit offering a wide range of climbing tours.

Sierra Nevada Joaquín Pinto E4-150 and Luis Cordero ⊤02/2553658, ⓕ255 4936, ⓦwww.hotelsierranevada.com. Small, dependable climbing operator offering rafting and biking, as well as accommodation in Quito.

American Express Represented by Ecuadorean Tours, Amazonas 329 and Jorge Washington (⊤02/2560488); does not exchange traveller's cheques but replaces lost cards and sells cheques to Amex card users.
Banks and exchange Most facilities are in the new town and generally open Mon–Fri 8.30am–

4pm or 5pm, and Sat mornings. Exchange and cash-advance facilities usually Mon–Fri 8.30am–2pm or 3pm. Banco del Austro, Amazonas and Santa María, offers Visa ATM and Visa cash advance; Banco de Guayaquil, Reina Victoria and Colón, changes traveller's cheques and provides Visa cash advances, maximum $400 (Visa,

MasterCard, Cirrus, Maestro, Plus ATM for withdrawals up to $100), also located at the corner of Amazonas and Veintimilla (same facilities but no cash advances); Banco del Pacífico, Amazonas N22-94 and Veintimilla, changes Amex cheques up to $200 (MasterCard, Cirrus, Maestro ATM, $5 commission per transaction), with other facilities at Av Naciones Unidas E7-95 and Los Shyris, Benalcázar 619 and Chile in the old town, and many other locations, including at El Jardín shopping mall and the *Colón* hotel; Produbanco, Amazonas 3575 and Japón, provides cash and cheque exchange and MasterCard cash advance, also at Amazonas 350 and Robles at the airport, and Benalcázar 842 and Olmedo in the old town. Outside of the airport, *casas de cambio* have largely disappeared following dollarization, but a survivor is Vazcambios, Amazonas and Roca (Mon–Fri 8.45am–5.45pm & Sat 9am–1pm), which changes cash and cheques in several currencies.

Camera equipment and film Numerous film shops and processing labs on Amazonas include Difoto, Amazonas 893 and Wilson, with a multilingual staff and good service; Ecuador Laboratorios Fotográficos, Amazonas 888 and Wilson, for Kodak film, which it can develop and print in an hour; Fujifilm, Amazonas 1429 and Colón, with a good choice of Fuji slide film; and Kis Color, Amazonas 1238 and Calama, which does passport photos and sells cameras, tripods and other equipment. Also Fotogermana, 12 de Octubre and Lincoln, and Fotomania, Av 6 de Diciembre N21-163 and Roca.

Camera repairs Luis Méndez at International Color, Amazonas 503 and Roca (ⓔaranhac@usa.net), for manual cameras; Foto Imagen, Av Mariana de Jesús E5-11 and Italia, for general repairs.

Car rental Major car rental companies have offices just outside the international terminal of the airport – the best place to compare prices – though some also have downtown offices. Companies include Avis, at the airport ⓣ02/2440270; Budget, Colón and Amazonas ⓣ02/2237026, ⓕ2562705, and at the airport ⓣ02/2459052; Ecuacars, Colón 1280 and Amazonas ⓣ02/2529781, and at the airport ⓣ02/2247298; Expo, Av América 2166 and Bolivia ⓣ02/2228688, and at the airport ⓣ02/2433127; Hertz, Luis Cordero 433 and Av 12 de Octubre ⓣ02/2569130, and at the airport ⓣ02/2254258; Localiza, Veintimilla E8-124 and 6 de Diciembre, and at the airport, both ⓣ1800/562254. Budget and Localiza are the most well regarded; Expo is less expensive, but check the car very carefully before signing anything. For more on renting a vehicle in Ecuador, including typical prices, see "Basics" on p.33.

Climbing and trekking gear Los Alpes, Reina Victoria 2345 and Baquedano ⓣ02/2232362, sales and rentals; Altamontaña, Jorge Washington 425 and 6 de Diciembre ⓣ02/2558380, ⓔaltamont@netzone.com.ec, climbing equipment, sales and rentals; Andísimo, 9 de Octubre 479 and Roca ⓣ02/2223030, sales and rentals; Camping Cotopaxi, Colón 942 and Reina Victoria ⓣ02/2521626, camping gear; Equipos Cotopaxi, 6 de Diciembre N20-36 and Jorge Washington ⓣ02/2250038, camping and climbing gear; Explorer, Reina Victoria 928 and Joaquín Pinto, ⓣ02/2550911, sales and rentals; Moggeley, Joaquín Pinto E4-255 and Amazonas ⓣ & ⓕ02/2554984, sales, rentals, white gas and kerosene. Most of the above outlets stock butane and propane gas canisters; for rubber boots, mosquito nets, machetes, ponchos, white gas and kerosene try the hardware store Kywi, 10 de Agosto 2273 and Cordero ⓣ02/2221832.

Courier services DHL, many branches including Colón 1333 and Foch ⓣ02/2556118, and Eloy Alfaro and de Los Juncos ⓣ02/2485100; EMS, run by the Ecuadorian postal service, Eloy Alfaro and 9 de Octubre ⓣ02/2561962; Fedex, Amazonas 517 and Santa María ⓣ02/2909201; UPS, Iñaquito 35-155 and Ignacio Santa María (10 de Agosto and Naciones Unidas) ⓣ02/2256790.

Dancing lessons Salsa, merengue and cumbia lessons available for around $5 an hour at Son Latino Dancing School, Reina Victoria 1225 and Lizardo García ⓣ02/2234340. Also lessons at Cuba Son, Calama E6-05 and Juan León Mera ⓣ02/2228151; Ritmo Tropical, Edificio Santa Rosa, office 108, 10 de Agosto 1792 and Jorge Washington ⓣ02/2227051; and Tropical Dancing School, Foch E4-256 and Amazonas ⓣ02/2224713.

Dentists Reliable English-speaking dentists include Alfonso Arcos Barona, second floor, Edificio Rosanía, República de El Salvador 525 ⓣ02/2457268; and Victor Peñaherrera, Amazonas 44-30 and Vilalengua ⓣ02/2255934.

Doctors Recommended English-speaking physicians include Martín Domski Zumárraga, Complejo Médico La Salud, República 754 and Eloy Alfaro ⓣ02/2553206, home ⓣ02/2871187; Alvaro Dávalos Pérez, La Colina 202 and San Ignacio ⓣ02/2500268, home ⓣ09/9739694; John Rosenberg, Foch 476 and Diego de Almagro, first floor ⓣ02/2521104 or 09/9739734; and sport-injury and back-pain specialists Ramiro Velasco and nurse Karin Behnert, Reumototal, Acuña 107 and Inglaterra ⓣ02/2224084 and 09/9470896.

Embassies and consulates Argentina, Amazonas 477 and Robles, Edifico Río Amazonas

☎02/2562292; Belgium, República de El Salvador 1082 and Naciones Unidas, Edificio Mansión Blanca, Torre Paris ☎02/2467851; Bolivia, Eloy Alfaro 2432 and Fernando Ayarza ☎02/2244830; Brazil, Amazonas 1429 and Colón, Edificio España ☎02/2563086; Canada, 6 de Diciembre 2816 and Paul Rivet, Edificio Josueth González ☎02/2232114; Chile, Juan Pablo Sanz 3617 and Amazonas ☎02/2249403; Colombia, Colón 1133 and Amazonas, Edificio Arist ☎02/2228926; France, Leonidas Plaza 107 and Patria ☎02/2560789; Germany, Naciones Unidas and República de El Salvador, Edificio Citiplaza ☎02/2970820; Italy, La Isla 111 and Humberto Albornoz ☎02/2561077; Ireland, Antonio de Ulloa 2651 and Rumipamba ☎02/2451577; Netherlands, 12 de Octubre 1942 and Cordero, World Trade Centre, Torre 1 ☎02/2229229; Peru, República de El Salvador 495 and Irlanda ☎02/2468389; Sweden, Alonso Jerves 134 and Orellana ☎02/2509514; Switzerland, Amazonas 3617 and Sanz, Edificio Xerox ☎02/2434948; UK, Naciones Unidas and República de El Salvador, Edificio Citiplaza, 14th floor ☎02/2970800, ⊛www.britembquito.org.ec; US, 12 de Octubre and Patria ☎02/2562890, ⊛www.usembassy.org.ec; Venezuela, Cabildo 115 and Quito Tenis ☎02/2268635.

Emergencies ☎911, police ☎101, fire ☎102, ambulance ☎131.

Festivals see box on p.109.

Health clubs New Gym, Amazonas 11114 and Pinto (☎02/2550462), is inexpensive, while Gimnasio González Suárez, González Suárez 718 and Gonnessiat (☎02/2561600), offers good value. More luxurious hotel facilities include *Hilton Colón* (see p.84), $50 per month for use of gym, pool, sauna and steam room; *JW Marriott* (see p.84), $15 per daily use of pool, gym and spa; and *Swissôtel* (see p.85), with excellent facilities for $30 daily.

Hospitals Best is Hospital Metropolitano, Av Mariana de Jesús and Av Occidental (☎02/2261520, emergency and ambulance ☎02/2265020). Also recommended are Clínica Pichincha, Veintimilla E3-30 and Páez (☎02/2562408), and Hospital Voz Andes, Villalengua Oe2-37 and 10 de Agosto (☎02/2262142), which is less expensive. All have laboratories for samples and testing.

Internet facilities see box on p.107.

Laundry Plenty of good laundries in La Mariscal, with a particular focus on Foch between Reina Victoria and Amazonas. Typical rates around $0.80 per kg for wash; dried and folded clothes ready same or next day. Lavanderías Industriales, San Javier N26-155 and Orellana (☎02/2527551), and Super Lavado, Pinto E6-32 and Reina Victoria

(☎02/2502987), both offer free pick-up from and delivery to your hotel. Vicmar, Calama E7-49 and Reina Victoria, is also a reliable option.

Maps Topographic maps (from 1:25,000 to 1:250,000) produced by the Instituto Geográfico Militar and sold at its headquarters at Senierges and Paz y Miño, up on the hill overlooking the Parque El Ejido. Bring your passport or other form of photographic identity, which will be held at the entrance.

Opticians Opticum Katz, 6 de Diciembre 4455 and Av Portugal ☎02/2443408; Albert A. Lagomarsini, CC Iñaquito, Amazonas and Naciones Unidas, Local C-102 ☎02/2252514.

Pharmacies The biggest and best-equipped chain is Fybeca, with 35 stores in Quito. Call ☎1800/392322 to find your nearest branch and for 24hr locations. Fybeca at Amazonas N42-72 and Tomás de Berlanga is always open 24hr. Other central branches at 10 de Agosto N15-37 and Ríofrio and the El Jardín shopping centre. The smaller chain Pharmacy's has ten Quito stores (☎1800/909090), while independent stores in La Mariscal include Farmacia Doral, Amazonas 244 and Jorge Washington, and Farmacia Amazonas, Amazonas and Foch.

Police Dirección Nacional de la Policía Judicial, Roca 582 and Juan León Mera ☎02/2503945, open daily 24hr.

Post offices Main office at Eloy Alfaro 354 and 9 de Octubre, but many other branches as well. The most convenient for La Mariscal is at Reina Victoria and Colón, in Edificio Torres de Almagro; old-town branch at Guayaquil 935 and Espejo (branch hours Mon–Fri 8am–7pm, Sat & Sun 8am–noon). Large packages are best sent from the office at Ulloa and Ramírez Dávalos. See "Basics" p.42 for more on postal services.

Telephones Andinatel is in the process of privatizing, and phone offices are appearing all over Quito. In the new town, offices at Colón E4-284 and Amazonas, Amazonas and Washington (concessional office), Reina Victoria 1225 and Lizardo García (concessional office, collect calls not allowed), and Eloy Alfaro and 9 de Octubre, among others. In the old town, head to Benalcázar and Mejía. General hours Mon–Fri 8am–10.30pm, Sat & Sun 8am–9.30pm, though concessional offices may have somewhat shorter hours. Porta and Bell South phonecards available from shops displaying their signs; many Internet cafés (see box, p.107) offer cheap online phone calls as well. See p.43 in "Basics" for more information.

Travel agents IATA-registered travel agents include Delgado Travel, Amazonas 1226 and Foch ☎02/2520229; Ecuadorian Tours, Amazonas 329 and Jorge Washington ☎02/2560488; Polimundo,

Amazonas 2374 and Eloy Alfaro ☎02/2509619; and Turismundial, Amazonas 657 and Ramírez Dávalos ☎02/2506050. For tour operators offering programmes within Ecuador, see p.112.

Visas and passports To register your visa on arrival in Ecuador, go to the Dirección General de Extranjería on 10 de Agosto and General Murgeon (Mon–Fri 8am–1pm; ☎02/2231022), Trole stop at Cuero y Caicedo. To validate it and receive your *censo*, go to the Jefatura de Migración at Isla Seymour N44-174 and Río Coca, Sector Jipijapa

(Mon–Fri 8am–12.30pm & 3–6.30pm; ☎02/224 7510); taxi drivers will know it by name rather than address. None of this is necessary for tourists receiving a T-3 tourist card on arrival in Ecuador, who can extend their cards at the Jefatura de Migración (as above); full details given on p.18. Many places on Amazonas, including Novedades Ebenezer at Amazonas 523 and Roca, can make laminated copies of your passport should you prefer to leave the original in your hotel safe – look for signs reading "*plastificacción*".

Moving on from Quito

As well as the nucleus of the country's tourism industry, Quito is a major transport hub, so it's quite common to return here before **moving on** to another destination in Ecuador. Many travellers periodically come back to pick up and drop off luggage between trips to the different regions, or just to rest and enjoy city life before planning their next move. Further transport details are listed at the end of the chapter on p.126.

By air

All flights from Quito leave from the airport, **Aeropuerto Mariscal Sucre** (☎02/2430555 or 2440080), on Amazonas about 6km north of the Mariscal hotel district. Buses regularly ply the route up Amazonas, but take a cab ($3–4) if you're travelling with luggage or late at night. The domestic and international terminals are next to each other, and facilities such as ATMs are located in between them. Note that when you leave Ecuador by air from Quito, you are required to pay $25 **departure tax** in cash at check-in.

Bypassing the country's serpentine and often crude road network, **internal flights** can be a boon for anyone short on time, often cutting down a ten-hour bus journey to a 30-minute air hop. The widest choice of domestic flights is provided by Tame (☎02/2509375), but the up-and-coming Icaro (☎02/2448626) is steadily increasing its coverage and has a reputation for better service, and Austro Aéreo (☎02/2271536) offers the most regular flights to Cuenca. For further details of domestic and international airlines, see "Listings" on p.111; for domestic flight destinations and frequencies, refer to "Travel Details" on p.127.

By bus

Most regional and long-distance journeys from Quito are likely to be by **bus**, almost all of which leave from the **Terminal Terrestre Cumandá**, a short distance south of the old town on Avenida Maldonado 3077, next to the Cumandá Trole stop. It's an unsightly, badly designed bus station with plenty of gloomy corners, and is certainly not a place to linger, especially after dark.

If travelling with your luggage, take a **taxi** here and insist on being taken to the main drop-off point *inside* the station complex. Drivers are often reluctant to do this as it costs them $0.25 to enter, so paying the fee for them should settle the argument. Ticket offices are downstairs on the lower-ground level of the terminal, where it shouldn't take long to find the right bus, as destinations are frenetically called out by rival conductors. The buses are reached via a turnstile (about $0.10), but once through, you can't re-enter the main hall. For **information** on bus schedules, refer to "Travel Details" on p.126 or call the station office (Mon–Fri 8.30am–5.30pm; ☎02/2289047 or 2289049).

A few bus companies also have offices in the **new town**, and can be more convenient than the Terminal Terrestre: Flota Imbabura, Manuel Larrea 1211 and Portoviejo (☎02/2572657), for Cuenca, Guayaquil, Manta, Ibarra and Tulcán; Flor del Valle, Manuel Larrea and Asunción (☎02/2527495), for Mindo and Cayambe; Panamericana Internacional, Colón 852 and Reina Victoria (☎02/2559427), for Huaquillas, Machala, Loja, Guayaquil, Manta and Esmeraldas; and Transportes Ecuador, Juan León Mera 330 and Jorge Washington (☎02/2225315), for Guayaquil, Ambato and Riobamba.

International buses to other South American countries are operated by Panamericana Internacional (see above) for Caracas (its only direct service), Pasto, Cali, Bogotá, Medellín, Lima, Arica, Santiago, La Paz and Buenos Aires; and Expreso Internacional Ormeño, Avenida Los Shyris 11–68 (☎02/2460029), for Lima (its only direct line), Cali, Bogotá, Caracas, La Paz, Santiago and Buenos Aires. Check waiting times and layovers between connections on these services, as they can be considerable. It's actually less expensive to take regular **interprovincial buses** to the border and change on the other side, allowing you to cover large distances at your own pace.

By train

Sadly, the formidable **train** network that was once the infrastructural backbone of the country, linking the highlands to the coast, is now only a shadow of its former self. All that remains is the **tourist train** (Sat & Sun 8am; $2.30 one-way, $4.60 return) running to the Area Nacional de Recreación El Boliche, adjoining the Parque Nacional Cotopaxi (see p.191), which leaves from La Estación de Ferrocarril Chimbacalle, just off Avenida Maldonado 2km south of the old town. It's a beautiful ride (2hr 30min), taking you through sweeping agricultural landscapes towards Volcán Cotopaxi, which on clear days can be seen as you pull out of Quito.

Buy **tickets** beforehand from the office at Bolívar 443, between García Moreno and Benalcázar (Mon–Fri 8am–4.30pm, ☎02/2582927), and bring along your passport (or a copy). The train arrives back in Quito around 4.30–5pm. Foreigners have to pay $10 to enter El Boliche; if you want to catch a bus onwards from El Boliche rather than return to Quito, it's 3km or a 30-minute walk from the park entrance to the Panamericana, where buses pass frequently.

Around Quito

Of those attractions **around Quito**, the most dramatic may be the looming outline of the potentially explosive **Volcán Pichincha**, but the most famous, busiest and most developed is **La Mitad del Mundo**, almost directly north, a

△ Iglesia San Francisco, Quito's ols town

complex celebrating – and almost positioned on – the equator, with a monument, museum, exhibition spaces and the famous line itself, marked in the pavement. Nearby, and often included on trips to the Mitad del Mundo, is the huge volcanic crater **Pululahua**, whose foothills are home to thousands of acres of rich, cultivated farmland supported by a benevolent microclimate.

Northeast of Quito are the towns of **Calderón** and **Guayllabamba**, which have little intrinsic appeal, but are notable respectively for distinctive dough figurines, produced for fiestas, and the capital's zoo, aimed more at Quito urbanites than international tourists. Southeast of Guayllabamba, the village of **El Quinche**, an important religious centre with an impressive church, pulls in more visitors than La Mitad del Mundo during its November festival, when pilgrims crowd in to venerate the miraculous statue of the Virgin.

Heading southeast of the capital, the thriving town of **Sangolquí** is home to the most interesting market in the immediate Quito environs, and the wonderful Museo de la Casa de Kingman is located in nearby **San Rafael** – both of them easy to reach in a single outing. A little further on, another volcanic crater awaits at **Pasochoa**, a woodland refuge where trails pass through abundant native forests rich in birdlife.

Other excursions and attractions within a short distance of the capital (but discussed in other places) include the bird-watching mecca of **Mindo** (see p.356), the **cloudforest reserves** a few hours northwest of the capital, such as Bellavista, Tandayapa, Maquipucuna and Santa Lucía (pp.352–355), the fabulous hot springs at **Papallacta** (p.293), the huge artesanía market at **Otavalo** (p.144), the ruined pyramids of **Cochasquí** (p.136) and the **train ride** to El Boliche (p.118), next to **Cotopaxi** national park (p.188).

La Mitad del Mundo

Twenty kilometres north of Quito, at 2483m, lies the colonial-styled complex of whitewashed buildings, gift shops, snack bars and museums known as **LA MITAD DEL MUNDO** (The Middle of the World), straddling the line that divides the earth's northern and southern hemispheres and gives the country its name – the **equator** (latitude of 0° 0' 0"). Its exact demarcation was first ascertained by **Charles-Marie de la Condamine** and his Geodesic Mission in 1736–44, and a monument to this achievement was raised across the line in 1936. Perhaps deemed not grand enough, however, it was replaced in 1979 with the current one. Modern GPS readings have revealed, however, that even the new monument is seven seconds of a degree off the true equator, roughly 250m adrift, but the finding has done little to dent the popularity of the attraction – local crowds flock to the site, particularly on Sundays and holidays, when music and dance performances are put on in the afternoons.

Practicalities

To get to the complex from Quito, catch one of the pink-and-white "Mitad del Mundo" **buses** (40min; $0.35) that run every few minutes along Avenida América; its intersection with Colón is probably the most convenient place to pick one up from the Mariscal hotel district. At weekends a special bus service (45min; $0.75) runs every fifteen minutes between the complex and El Panecillo in the old town (see p.95). A **taxi** from the new town will cost around $15 one-way, or $20 return including waiting time. Most **tour** operators in Quito arrange trips here, to Pululahua and to the various archeological sites around the area.

The monument

From the entrance to the site (Mon–Thurs 9am–6pm, Fri–Sun 9am–7pm; $0.50, plus $1 if using car park), a cobbled street, lined with busts of la Condamine's expedition members, leads up at a dramatic angle to the plaza Círculo de la Paz, the centrepiece of which is the thirty-metre-tall **La Mitad del Mundo monument**, a giant concrete monolith replete with large metal globe. From its base, a line representing the equator extends outwards – even running down the middle of the aisle (and altar) of the church within the complex. Inside the monument is the **Ethnographic Museum** ($3), accessed via lift. Once at the top, you descend by stairs through the museum, which displays region-by-region exhibits on Ecuador's indigenous populations and their customs, with fine exhibits of native dress and artefacts.

National pavilions and the Museo Quitsa To

Unsurprisingly, much of what else there is to see is equatorially themed. Among the other sites in the complex are various **national pavilions**, including that of **Spain**, exhibiting contemporary art; **France**, giving a rundown on the work of the French-led expedition; and **Ecuador**, bizarrely showing international stamps depicting trains, bikes and monkeys, among other themes.

By far the best of these exhibits, however, is the **Museo Quitsa To**, which brilliantly shows how the pre-Columbian understanding of astronomy was far better than previously imagined. With the aid of computer demonstrations, it claims that the great churches of Quito were built atop ancient monuments perfectly aligned with the earth's axis, and video footage even reveals that certain altarpieces are flooded with sunshine only on the summer solstices. The museum also runs tours to nearby astronomically important ruins, such as **Rumicucho**, **Pambamarca**, **Cochasquí** (see p.136) and the recently discovered **Catequilla**, which it maintains lies exactly on the equator, unlike the modern monument.

The rest of the complex

Other notable sights here include a **planetarium** (closed Mon; $1) that offers rather unimpressive hourly shows, and the nearby **Fundación Quito Colonial** (daily 9am–5pm; $1), containing richly detailed miniature models of Guayaquil, Cuenca and Quito – the latter featuring its own artificial sunrise and sunset. Also on the square is a **post office** selling appropriately decorated postcards and stamps, a rather expensive restaurant, a few small snack bars, several gift shops and a bank. There are even a few weighing scales here, demonstrating that you do, in fact, lose a little weight while on the equator – thanks to the bulge in the earth's crust at its widest point, you're further from the centre of the planet's gravity than you would normally be.

Finally, leaving the complex, turn left as you go and walk a few hundred metres uphill, and turn left again to reach the enjoyable **Museo Inti Ñan** (daily 9am–6pm; $2), housing an idiosyncratic collection of equator-related experiments and curios, including a fascinating nineteenth-century solar chronometer.

Pululahua

A visit to the Mitad del Mundo is commonly combined with a trip up to the rim of the extinct volcano of **Pululahua**, whose 34-square-kilometre **crater** – one of the continent's largest – has been protected since 1966 as a **geobotanical reserve**, its unusual topography and associated microclimates not only supporting rich cultivated land on the valley floor, but also lush cloudforests, 260 types of plants and a large variety of orchids. Outlooks on the rim afford **views** over bucolic scenery within the crater, beautiful networks of fields, and small settlements squeezed around the two volcanic cones of Pondoña and Chivo, all cradled by the thickly forested and deeply gullied crater walls. It's best to get up here early in the morning as thick clouds engulf the crater later in the day.

Practicalities

There are two points of **access**: the first, 4km from the equator monument along the Calacalí highway, is a paved road that climbs to a car park at **Ventanillas** viewpoint, from where a steep **trail** leads down to the crater settlements below (30min down, 1hr back up); the second branches off about 3km further along the highway, and leads up to the **Moraspungo** guard post and viewpoint, where you may be asked to pay the $5 reserve entrance fee, especially if you plan to continue into the reserve on the eight-kilometre dirt track that leads down to the crater floor. Near the guard post are cheap, basic **cabins** and **camping** facilities. If on foot, your quickest journey is to catch a **bus** heading to Calacalí and get off at the Ventanillas turn-off, from where it's a 30-minute uphill walk, though at weekends you've a good chance of getting a lift or a camioneta. A **taxi** will take you from the Mitad del Mundo to the viewpoint and back for about $5. Calimatours (℡02/2394796) have an office inside the equator complex, and arrange tours to the crater for around $4.

Calderón

An easy half-day trip from Quito, 9km northeast of the capital, is **CALDERÓN**, a small town renowned for its brightly coloured **dough figures** (*masapán*). The tradition, thought to be pre-Hispanic but subsumed into Catholicism under All Saints' Day and the Day of the Dead (Nov 1 and 2), involves simple bread figures being taken to the cemetery and placed on top of the graves as an offering to departed souls. Nowadays this has become a very colourful affair, and its popularity has spawned a thriving figurine-making industry. You can't eat them, but then again you wouldn't want to – many feature intricate detailing, such as clowns with extravagant mock-filigree ruffs and fibrous hair.

In town there are a number of good **artesanía shops** on the main street, Carapungo, which leads uphill from the main square. Most have a workshop at the back where you can see the figures being made with an unpalatable mixture of flour, water, colourings, paint and varnish. They're all open on weekdays and occasional Saturdays, and one of the best is **Artesanía Carapungo**, halfway up the street, which exports its striking pieces to Europe.

To visit Calderón, pink-and-white *interparroquial* **buses** leave old-town Quito from the Plaza La Marín (40min) every few minutes. If you're in the new town, pick them up at Avenida América and Colón.

Guayllabamba and around

Just after Calderón, the Panamericana begins to climb, finally sweeping over a pass to reveal astounding views on your right of the dry **Guayllabamba gorge**. Lower and warmer than Quito, the gorge provides ideal conditions for horticulture, with colourful bursts of flowering trees and orchards.

Guayllabamba and the zoo

About 32km from Quito, **GUAYLLABAMBA** lies in a vibrant oasis of green, with vendors lining the main road, their stalls laden with outsized avocados and exotic fruits. Off the Panamericana 1km before the town, the **Zoológico Guayllabamba** (Tues–Sun 10am–5pm; $3, guides free, English spoken) is a well-designed zoo that strongly emphasizes native fauna, with a good range of animals from the sierra and Oriente, such as pumas, ocelots, sloths, monkeys and condors. The only gesture to the outside world is the presence of four African lions.

Practicalities

Buses from Quito, leaving from the Terminal Terrestre, heading to Cayambe usually stop at Guayllabamba (45min–1hr); Flota Pichincha buses leave from the new town at Avenida América and Colón. From Guayllabamba it's a 30-minute walk up a cobblestone road to the zoo, though at weekends a free bus service regularly ferries visitors to the zoo from the turn-off, and you can also take a **camioneta** ($0.50). You're unlikely to want to stay here, but **accommodation** and a **restaurant** are available nearby at the *Guayllabamba* hostería (T02/2368670; ❸), a five-minute walk from the zoo; turn right at the T-junction.

El Quinche

The village of **EL QUINCHE**, 7km southeast of Guayllabamba, is famous for its outsized **church**, as large as the monasteries and cathedrals of colonial Quito. Grand as the building is, for pilgrims its most important feature is the wooden image of **El Virgen del Quinche**, carved at the end of the sixteenth century by artist and architect **Diego de Robles**, who was saved from tumbling hundreds of feet into the Río Oyacachi by a thorn snagging on his clothes.

Ever since Robles cheated death, the Virgin has been credited with countless other miracles, depicted by paintings inside the church and plaques on the walls. Visitors make their way from across the country to venerate her, especially during the **festival** in the third week of November, climaxing on November 21, and throngs of people receive blessings all year round for everything from newborn babies to a newly bought taxi. There are regular *interparroquial* **buses** to El Quinche from Quito via Pifo (leaving from 6 de Diciembre and Av Interoceánica) and others from Guayllabamba.

Southeast of Quito

A fast highway runs **southeast** from the Trébol junction 1km outside old-town Quito into the **Valle de los Chillos**, a fertile agricultural valley with a warm and pleasant climate.

Sangolquí

The most important town in this region, **SANGOLQUÍ**, 15km from the capital, has an impressive **church** with an imposing facade and grand bell tower, but is much better known for its **market**, which runs all week, but on Sundays (and to a lesser extent, Thursdays) expands from its three dedicated market squares to fill much of the town. It's a hard-edged and busy affair, perhaps lacking the charm of a highland-village market, but the energy of the local commerce is compelling, and being so close to Quito, it makes an easy option for those with limited time.

Practicalities

Buses leave every five to ten minutes from Plaza Marín in the old town (25min), and **taxis** cost about $12. There are several good **places to stay** close to Sangolquí, but not much for those on a tight budget. The best is *La Carriona*, km 2.5 via Sangolquí–Amaguaña (℡02/2332004, ℻2332005, ⓦwww.lacarriona.com; ❼, including breakfast), an attractive converted hacienda from the early 1800s with a grand cobbled courtyard, colourful gardens, swimming pool and spa, well-appointed rooms and delicious food. The staff can organize tours to Pasochoa with horses and guides, and trips to a dairy farm near Papallacta. The German-owned *Sommergarten*, Chimborazo 248 and Riofrío (℡ & ℻02/2330315, ⓦwww.ecuador-sommer.com; ❼, with breakfast), also has comfortable rooms, pleasant gardens and a swimming pool.

San Rafael and the Museo de la Casa de Kingman

Just twenty minutes from Quito or five minutes by bus from Sangolquí, and easily combined with a trip to its market, the unassuming town of **SAN RAFAEL** has little of inherent interest, except for the excellent **Museo de la Casa de Kingman** (Thurs–Fri 10am–4pm, Sat & Sun 10am–5pm; ℡02/2861065; $1.50), a block from the central square at Portoviejo and Dávila. Occupying a peaceful spot high on the banks of the Río San Pedro (he named it *Soledad*, or "solitude"), this was the house of **Eduardo Kingman**, one of Ecuador's greatest twentieth-century artists. Kingman is best known for depicting the privation suffered by Ecuador's indigenous peoples, often capturing their plight in the expression of their hands – a technique he taught to Oswaldo Guayasamín, who also used it to great effect. There are some wonderful pieces exhibited here, as well as a diverse range of other paintings, drawings and sculptures that support Kingman's considerable reputation.

Groups of more than ten people can arrange to visit the house outside of normal opening hours. **Buses** to Sangolquí pass right by San Rafael's park, from where the museum is just a short walk away: from the main road, head for the park's upper, right-hand corner and continue to the end of the road. A **taxi** from Quito costs around $10.

Refugio de Vida Silvestre Pasochoa

Thirty kilometres southeast of Quito, the luxuriant **Refugio de Vida Silvestre Pasochoa** (℡09/9787621; $7) is a dense forest spread over the blown-out crater of **Cerro Pasochoa**, an extinct volcano whose western side collapsed in an eruption more than 100,000 years ago. Because of the irregularity and inaccessibility of the terrain, hemmed in by the remaining walls of the crater, the forest has been left largely undisturbed and is now one of the sierra's last tracts of native forest that hasn't been cleared to make way for agriculture, or taken over by foreign species such as eucalyptus and pine.

Since 1982 the forest has been managed as a **reserve** by the Quito-based Fundación Natura, which has installed visitor facilities including a basic refuge ($3), **campsites** ($0.75), a kitchen and six marked **trails**, though you'll have to bring your own sleeping bag and food as needed. Five of the trails, which range from an easy thirty-minute walk to a strenuous four-hour hike, take you through the forest itself, where you can admire the rich variety of beautiful native **trees** and **plants** – including laurels, Andean cedars, podocarpus (Ecuador's only native conifer), ferns, orchids and bromeliads – as well as a vast array of **birds**, with turtledoves, tanagers and many varieties of hummingbirds among the reserve's 123 recorded species (a bird guide for sale at the entrance lists them all).

The sixth trail rises out of the forest and heads up across the páramo, following the outer slopes of the crater rim. You can walk just part of the way up for great views down to the forest and across the patchwork fields of the neighbouring valleys, or do the whole six- to eight-hour hike up to the **summit** of Cerro Pasochoa (4200m) – a challenging 1400-metre gain in altitude from the reserve entrance. **Guides** cost $5 for shorter hikes, $7 for longer ones and $10 for the summit journey.

Practicalities

The Pasochoa forest reserve is easy to reach from Quito: from Plaza La Marín in the old town, get on one of the frequent **buses** to the small town of Amaguaña (25min), then take a **camioneta** ($5–6; arrange pick-up for the return journey, or take a Bell South card for the cell phone at the refuge) from the plaza to the reserve entrance, reached along a seven-kilometre cobbled access road leading south from town. Alternatively, you can walk from Amaguaña in less than two hours, though you will have to keep asking directions as it's badly signposted.

Although the reserve makes a good day-trip, you might want to spend a night here for the best birding opportunities (early morning or late afternoon), or to make an early start on the hike up Cerro Pasochoa. To ensure **accommodation**, make an advance reservation with Fundación Natura, in Quito at Avenida República 481 and Diego de Almagro (T02/2503385 or 2503394, Enatura @fnatura.org.ec).

Volcán Pichincha

Rising over the west side of Quito, the broad-based, emerald-sloped **Volcán Pichincha** has two peaks: the slightly lower, serene-looking **Rucu Pichincha** (4675m) soars directly over Quito's new town, crowned by a cluster of aerials and transmitters, but suffers from a serious crime problem; by contrast, **Guagua Pichincha** (4794m), 10km west of the city centre, is often climbed by visiting hikers, despite being an active volcano.

Guagua Pichincha

While Quito is bordered to the west by a chain of attractive hills, only **Guagua Pichincha** is safe to climb – and only when the volcano isn't seismically active. Southwest of Quito, you can reach Guagua through the village of Lloa, from where a signposted dirt track leads up to a **refuge** just below the summit. The refuge is pretty basic, and you'll need to bring your own food and blankets if you plan to spend the night ($5), though this is only necessary if you've walked in from Lloa – an all-day hike.

The **summit** itself is only a short but strenuous push from the refuge, not requiring any special climbing equipment or technical skill, but well worth the effort for its fantastic views; just make sure to avoid the enticing, though dangerous, walk from the volcano's rim down into the crater. Most **climbing operators** in Quito (see box, p.114) offer the Guagua climb as a day tour, including four-wheel-drive transport to or near the refuge.

Note that the neighbouring Rucu Pichincha and Cruz Loma appear to be easy prospects from Quito, but are extremely dangerous due to the frequent assaults and robberies on their slopes, and should be avoided even if you're walking in a large group; check with South American Explorers (see p.80) for the latest security conditions.

Precautions

Although Rucu's collapsed crater has long been extinct, Guagua has experienced renewed **volcanic activity** in the last five years, after more than three centuries of inactivity. The volcano is currently on **yellow alert**, warning of ongoing seismic activity and the possibility of an eruption. Should such an event occur, Quito would likely escape the lava flow, though not the dispersion of ash. Indeed, the volcano's last eruption, in 1660, left the city covered by a thirty-centimetre layer of the volcanic dust, and more recently, on October 5, 1999, a smaller explosion produced an eighteen-kilometre-high column of ash and vapour that loomed over the city in a mushroom cloud. Despite this formidable display, though, experts don't consider Quito to be in any imminent danger, and it's unknown if or when another major eruption will take place.

For adequate precaution, city residents are advised to keep a week's supply of food and drinking water in their homes, along with plenty of candles and matches – you may want to check that your hotel has enough provisions for all its guests, or even equip yourself with a **dust mask**, sold by many street vendors and at local stores. The volcano's activities are closely monitored by the Instituto Geofísico, with results prominently displayed in all newspapers; for up-to-the-minute **news**, check out the institute's website at Ⓦ www.igepn.edu.ec, try Ⓦ www.volcano.si.edu for reports in English, or simply call your embassy.

Travel details

Trains

Quito to: El Boliche, Parque Nacional Cotopaxi (1 daily Sat & Sun; 2hr 30min).

Buses

Quito to: Alausí (3 daily; 5hr); Ambato (every 5min; 2hr 30min); Atacames (5 daily; 6hr 30min); Baeza (22 daily; 3hr); Bahía de Caráquez (3 daily; 8hr); Baños (every 20–40min; 3hr 15min); Coca (20 daily; 10hr); Cotacachi (4 daily; 2hr 20min); Cuenca (40 daily; 11–12hr); El Angel (19 daily; 4hr); Esmeraldas (every 20–30min; 6hr); Guaranda (every 30min; 4hr 30min); Guayaquil (every 15–20min; 8hr); Huaquillas (16 daily; 12hr); Ibarra (every 15–20min; 2hr 30min); Lago Agrio (28 daily; 8hr); Latacunga (every 10min; 2hr); Loja (22 daily; 14hr sierra route, 16hr coast route); Macará (4 daily; 15hr); Macas (5–8 daily; 13hr); Machala (21 daily; 10hr); Manta (31 daily; 8hr 30min); Mindo (1–2 daily; 2hr 30min); Nanegalito (10 daily; 1hr 45min); Otavalo (every 10min; 2hr); Pedernales (12 daily; 5hr); Pujilí (every 30min; 2hr); Puyo (25 daily; 5hr); Quevedo (23 daily; 4hr 30min); Riobamba (every 10–15min; 4hr); Salinas (7 daily; 10hr); San

Gabriel (17 daily; 4hr 15min); San Lorenzo (2 daily; 7hr); San Vicente (3 daily; 8hr); Santo Domingo (every 10–15min; 3hr); Saquisilí (13 daily, Thurs every 30min; 1hr 30min); Sigchos (2 daily; 5hr); Tena (21 daily; 5hr); Tulcán (every 10–20min; 5hr).

Flights

Quito to: Baltra (2 daily; 3hr 15min); Coca (2–3 Mon–Sat; 30min); Cuenca (7 Mon–Fri, 2 Sat, 4 Sun; 45min); Esmeraldas (5 weekly; 30min); Guayaquil (15 Mon–Fri, 7 Sat, 5 Sun; 45min); Lago Agrio (2–3 Mon–Fri, 1 Sat; 30min); Loja (2–3 daily; 50min–1hr); Macas (1 Mon & Thurs; 30min); Machala (1 Mon & Fri; 1hr 30min); Manta (1 daily; 45min); Portoviejo (1 Mon, Wed & Fri; 45min); San Cristóbal (1 Mon, Wed & Sat; 3hr 15min); Tulcán (1 Mon, Wed & Fri; 30min).

The northern sierra

CHAPTER 2

Highlights

* **Haciendas** A handsome collection of old and distinguished estates are clustered around Otavalo and Cayambe, several of which are still working farms. **See pp.135 & p.143**

* **Cochasquí** The country's most important pre-Inca ruins, fifteen grassy pyramids on a lonely hillside commanding views of a half-dozen volcanoes. **See p.136**

* **Oyacachi** Amid forested hills high in the Reserva Cayambe-Coca, a sleepy village famed for its hot springs – a picturesque, peaceful place for a long, hot soak. **See p.137**

* **Otavalo Saturday market** One of the most intense, colourful and enjoyable shopping experiences in Ecuador, where you can find everything from dolls and tapestries to a brood of chickens. **See p.144**

* **Helados de paila** Delicious fruity sorbet made in huge copper pans or *pailas*, a speciality of the relaxed and attractive provincial capital of Ibarra. **See p.161**

* **Autoferro de Ibarra** A curious bus on rails clattering over the old rail line towards the coast, including the long, precarious bridge over the Ambi gorge. **See p.160**

* **Cementerio de Tulcán** The extraordinary topiary gardens are an unexpected delight in an otherwise drab border town. **See p.175**

The northern sierra

A magnificent sequence of volcanoes, sparkling crater lakes and patchwork scenery, the **NORTHERN SIERRA** extends northeast from Quito for 140 kilometres to the Colombian border. When travelling across the region's rugged terrain, however, the actual distance is far greater, as the main transport artery, the **Panamericana**, wends its way for 250km between cloud-piercing mountain peaks, windblown hilltop passes, warm valleys bursting with fruit orchards and flower plantations and two key ecological reserves. This stunning landscape is also home to several commercially successful indigenous groups, whose vibrant **markets** have long made this one of the most popular tourist destinations in Ecuador. Although buses regularly ply the Panamericana, putting the northern sierra within easy reach of Quito, the surrounding territory is much more obscure and little visited by tourists.

Leaving the capital, the first town of any significant size is **Cayambe**, a good base from which to explore the outlying area, set in rich pastureland at the foot of **Volcán Cayambe** – the country's third-highest volcano. Close by are the pre-Inca ruins of **Cochasquí** and **Quitoloma** and the hot springs of **Oyacachi**, an idyllic village nestled in the high forests of the **Reserva Ecológica Cayambe-Coca**. The main attraction of the region, however, just forty minutes from Cayambe and two hours from the capital, is the colourful splendour of **Otavalo**'s Saturday market – one of the continent's most famous agoras – bursting with an irresistible array of weavings, garments, carvings, ceramics, jewellery and many assorted knick-knacks. Since the weaving tradition in the Otavalo Valley predates even the Incas, virtually all of its towns specialize in a particular area of craftwork, from embroidery and woven belts to bulky knitted socks; the nearby towns of **Cotacachi** and **San Antonio de Ibarra**, for example, are the respective national centres of leatherware and woodcarving. Beyond Otavalo, the surrounding terrain is well worth exploring on foot or horseback, while excursions to **Laguna Cuicocha**, tucked in the southernmost corner of the striking **Cotacachi-Cayapas reserve**, and the cloudforests of the **Intag region**, are also popular.

Thirty kilometres north of Otavalo, **Ibarra**, the largest city in the northern sierra, charms with its relaxed atmosphere and elegant, whitewashed buildings. Once the point of departure for a famously hair-raising train ride to the coast at San Lorenzo, Ibarra now sits at the head of a new road providing the country's fastest highway link between the sierra and the sea, descending through dramatic scenery from highlands to cloudforests to the tropical lowlands. A few kilometres north of Ibarra, the old road to the Colombian border branches off from the Panamericana and slowly climbs past **Mira**, a village with stunning

views over the valleys, to **El Ángel**, the 3000-metre-high access point to the remote **Reserva Ecológica El Ángel**, where undulating páramo grasslands are speckled with rare *frailejones* flowers. Meanwhile, the Panamericana ascends the dry and dusty **Chota Valley**, one of the few spots where African and Andean traditions have blended, before passing green farmlands and the peaceful villages of **Bolívar** and **La Paz**, the latter renowned for its huge grotto shrine, and **San Gabriel**, entry point to the **Reserva Guandera**, one of the last pockets of high-altitude cloudforest in the region. **Tulcán**, the last stop on the Panamericana before Colombia, is a frontier town that unexpectedly features some remarkable topiary gardens, and is close to several thermal springs – oases of warmth in the chilly páramo surrounding them.

Cayambe and around

Located on the Panamericana and overshadowed by the eponymous volcano, **CAYAMBE** compares unfavourably with Otavalo due to its lack of artesanía traditions, but is still worth a visit for its renowned home-made **cheese** and

bizcochos – buttery biscuits that locals carry around by the bagful. It's also a regional centre for Ecuador's **flower industry** (its fourth-largest export), visible in a sea of plastic-sheeted greenhouses shimmering across the valley. For much of the year it's a quiet provincial town that most travellers skip on their way from Quito to Otavalo, but during the **fiestas** of late June, things really get busy when *indígenas* descend from the surrounding villages for singing, dancing, parades and bullfights. The celebration kicks off with **Inti Raymi** (Quichua for "sun festival"), which heralds the summer solstice and continues for several days until it merges with the **fiesta of San Pedro** on June 29, honouring the town's patron saint.

Apart from this, there are few things to see in Cayambe other than the archeological site of **Puntiachil** and a small museum displaying local finds. Even so, the town makes a good base for exploring the area, as does the **Hacienda Guachalá**, one of the oldest in Ecuador, a short distance away. To the southeast lie vast tracts of untamed land, including páramo wilderness, spectacular **cloudforests** and the soaring **Volcán Cayambe**, all protected by the **Reserva Ecológica Cayambe-Coca**. Within the reserve, the isolated village of **Oyacachi** offers splendid **hot springs**, while in the surrounding area, the

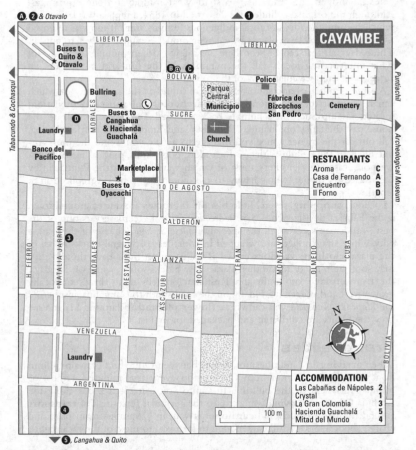

ruins of **Cochasquí** and the pre-Inca fort of **Quitoloma** command superb views.

The Town

Mostly in use during the town's fiestas, the **bullring** is Cayambe's most prominent landmark and marks the point where the main road turns northwest towards Otavalo, while four blocks east, the centre of town is the leafy **Parque Central**. At the plaza's northern end, a fleet of underused taxis waits by the town's grandest building, formerly home to one of Cayambe's wealthiest families but now owned by the *municipio*, which plans to convert it into a museum, exhibiting pieces recovered from an archeological site two blocks east of the plaza.

Known as the **Puntiachil**, this old ceremonial site of the **Cara** people is also owned by the *municipio*, which hopes someday to turn it into an archeological park. Located next to the town cemetery, behind gates decorated with symbols of the sun and moon, the Puntiachil is usually open to the public; if not, ask at the house next to the gates. The centre of the site was once a large upright **cylinder** made of packed earth, which measured celestial movements and cast no shadow at midday on the equinoxes. Although the original cylinder was destroyed in 1834, a replica was later made which became the focus of local indigenous festivals, until it too was removed a few years ago to be replaced by a larger model – which has yet to appear. These days, all that can be seen here are a few earthen mounds, remnants of what enterprising locals call the pyramids of the sun and moon, and an agreeable if unspectacular **view** of the town.

A large number of ancient artefacts were found at the site, many of which can be seen at the exceptional private **archeological museum** (donation) located east up Sucre in a humble backyard shed. To get there, walk to the house past the fancy one named "Bellavista" and, ignoring the unfriendly dog, call out for the owner. Once you manage to get in, you'll find the museum-hut filled to the ceiling with pre-Inca idols, pots, skulls, musical instruments, weapons, vases and jewellery, most of which were found at the Puntiachil by the museum's owner, who's happy to talk about his impressive collection at length.

For local **shopping**, several little **biscuit factories** are dotted around town – the Fábrica de Bizcochos San Pedro, opposite the cemetery, is one of the best – and many stores sell the speciality *queso de hoja* (cheese of the leaf), a salty, white affair boiled and wrapped in *achira* leaves. Several blocks north of the plaza, **clothing vendors** crowd Rocafuerte on most days, though they may soon be moving to another plaza a few blocks south, while on Sundays, the **marketplace** on Junín and Restauración sells many kinds of locally grown fruit and vegetables. Finally, on the road south to Cangahua, just before the *Hacienda Guachalá*, you can visit a **flower plantation** (around $1) and see how the plants are cultivated and packaged for export.

Practicalities

When **arriving** in Cayambe, most **buses** between Quito and Otavalo (40min from Otavalo, 1hr 20min from Quito) stop every few minutes at the two roundabouts next to the bullring. In Quito you can catch a bus along the Avenida Occidental, saving you a trip to the Terminal Terrestre. For **transport** around the region, **taxis** and **camionetas** wait in Cayambe's main plaza and charge about $45 for a full day, enough to take you to most of the local sights, including Quitoloma and Oyacachi, while buses to Tabacundo pass the turn-off for the Cochasquí ruins and head west out of town on Bolívar near the bullring.

The Banco del Pacífico, Jarrín and Junín, changes traveller's cheques and has a MasterCard **ATM**, while **Internet** access and phone service are available in the building between the two cafés on Bolívar.

Accommodation

During the June fiestas it can be hard to find a **place to stay** in Cayambe, so make sure to reserve well in advance.

Las Cabañas de Nápoles Panamericana, 2km north of town ☎02/361388. Comfortable wooden cabins with baths and TVs, plus a decent on-site restaurant and deli specializing in cheeses. Easily reached by a $1 taxi ride. ❺

Crystal 9 de Octubre and Teran, four blocks north of the plaza ☎02/2361460. The cheapest decent accommodation in town, providing clean rooms with en-suite baths and TVs, though the nearby disco can get noisy on Friday and Saturday nights. ❷

La Gran Colombia Natalia Jarrin and Calderon ☎02/2361238, ⓕ2362421. Smart, business-oriented accommodation, offering cable TV and a restaurant. ❸

Mitad del Mundo Natalia Jarrín and Argentina ☎02/2361607. Cheap but adequate rooms with private bathrooms, plus an indoor heated pool, sauna and steam room (Sat & Sun; $2.50 for both guests and residents). ❷

Restaurants

Cheese and *bizcochos* are Cayambe's specialities, but the town also has a few decent **restaurants**.

Aroma Bolívar and Rocafuerte. Popular spot serving traditional dishes, plus vegetarian meals on request. Closes Thurs–Tues 8pm & all day Wed.

Casa de Fernando 50m south of *Las Cabañas de Nápoles*. Local favourite for its fair-priced *platos típicos*.

Encuentro Bolívar and Ascázubi. Pleasant little café offering cured ham, good sandwiches and ice cream. Closed Mon.

Il Forno Sucre and Jarrín. Tiny and inexpensive pizzeria serving good set meals of pizza and soda for $1.50. Closed Mon.

Hacienda Guachalá

Five kilometres south of Cayambe, the distinguished **Hacienda Guachalá** (☎02/2363042, ⓕ2362426, ⓦwww.haciendaguachala.com; ❻), built in 1580, is one of Ecuador's oldest and most affordable haciendas, and one of the most charming places to stay in the northern sierra. Beyond a screen of rustling eucalyptus trees, the main building has comfortable, unpretentious rooms with fireplaces, private bathrooms and hot showers around a large cloistered and cobbled courtyard. The grounds are dotted with agapanthus and alpacas, horses graze the fields and can be hired for $5 per hour, and other attractions include a covered pool, games room, lounge, library and small photograph museum in one of the two chapels. The **restaurant** serves hearty and affordable meals all day to both guests and visitors, including delicious *locro*, cheese and potato soup topped with avocado.

Buses from Cayambe to the hacienda leave from the corner of Restauración and Sucre every twenty minutes (15–20min trip; last bus 7.30pm), and a taxi ride costs just a few dollars. If coming from Quito on a bus to Cayambe, ask to be dropped at the unmarked turn-off to Cangahua, then wait for the bus there or walk for about a kilometre up the tree-lined road towards Cangahua. The hacienda organizes horse riding in the surrounding countryside and camioneta or taxi **tours** to Oyacachi and Quitoloma (around $30).

Cochasquí

Seventy kilometres north of Quito are the ruins of **Cochasquí** (daily 8.30am–4.30pm; $3), the largest archeological site near Cayambe and one of the country's most significant pre-Inca excavations. Built at 3100m by the Cara people around 900 AD, the site's fifteen flat-topped pyramids were constructed from blocks of compressed volcanic soil (*cangahua*), now coated in grass, at the base of Mount Fuya Fuya. Long ramps lead up to most of the pyramids, which were levelled off to accommodate wooden structures that have long since rotted away.

One theory holds that Cochasquí was a **fortress**, and the pyramids do occupy an important strategic position, with Quito and the volcanoes Cotopaxi and the Pichinchas visible in the distance. Perhaps more compelling, though, is the idea that the site was a kind of **observatory** – excavations have revealed the remnants of circular platforms, thought to be calendars of the sun and moon. Holes drilled nearby probably held pillars that would have cast shadows over the calendars during the equinoxes and solstices, and the site is also perfectly aligned with the summit of Cayambe volcano, over 30km away, and the Puntiachil site (see p.134), another ancient monument used for gauging celestial movements. Even today, shamans still congregate at the site around the solstices and equinoxes to perform spiritual rites. Although excavation here is still in its early stages, and some pyramids are little more than large overgrown mounds, the eerie atmosphere and striking **views** alone merit a visit.

Tucked away behind the ruins are two reconstructions of ancient **Cara houses**, circular structures with thatched-grass roofs built around a living tree – almost identical to those in which a few *indígenas* still live. As well as the houses there's a **medicinal plant garden**, plus a small **museum** exhibiting artefacts recovered from the site. A few local Spanish-speaking **guides**, one of whom also speaks English, can meet you at the entrance and show you around the site for free (though tips are always appreciated).

Practicalities

There are no direct **buses** to Cochasquí. Instead, take a service between Quito and Ibarra going via the small village of Tabacundo, 8km west of Cayambe (from Cayambe proper you can pick up a local bus for Tabacundo on Bolívar), and ask the driver to let you off at the junction for Cochasquí, 4km southwest of Tabacundo. From here, you're faced with an 8km uphill **walk** (3hr), so take adequate water and food, though you might be able to pick up a **camioneta** for a few dollars from the village of Tocachi after 2.5km. Note that the alternative turn-off at the Cochasquí tollgate is also 8km from the ruins and does not pass the village. The other option is to take a **taxi** from Tabacundo or Cayambe ($8–10 return trip, including waiting time), or go with one of the many **tour operators** in Quito (see p.112) that include Cochasquí in day-trips through the region.

Quitoloma

The road to *Hacienda Guachalá* heads east from the Panamericana about 5km south of Cayambe, and leads on to the unremarkable village of Cangahua before rising up to a complex of pre-Inca **hilltop forts**, or *pucarás*. Sited on the slopes overlooking a pass between Quito and the Oriente, the forts' strategic value made them a prime target for the Incas, who seized them and reinforced them with stone, though the defences have since tumbled into the thick tussocks of páramo grass. The biggest fortification in the complex is

QUITOLOMA, which at 3765m stands high above the capital and the pass, and from which you can see the other ruins on the neighbouring hilltops of Hambimachi and Francisyurco. There is no public transport to the ruins, but you can rent a **camioneta** or **taxi** from the plaza in Cayambe ($30–40 per day), perhaps also using it for a trip to the Oyacachi hot springs (see p.138), or hire **horses** from the *Hacienda Guachalá* (see p.135).

Reserva Ecológica Cayambe-Coca

Heading southeast of Cangahua past the turn-off for Quitoloma, the dirt road climbs through onion fields and páramo grasslands for an hour's drive until it passes the Las Puntas hills, site of the entrance checkpoint to the **Reserva Ecológica Cayambe-Coca** (7am–6pm; $10, though this is often overlooked; ID required), founded in 1970 and protecting over 4000 square kilometres of land, from 5790m high to just 600m above sea level. On the eastern side of the hills, the moister air supports beautiful high-altitude cloudforest that forms the western edge of this enormous reserve, whose ten ecological zones harbour a vast number of plant and animal species, including nine hundred birds, such as the condor, mountain toucan and Andean cock-of-the-rock, and rare mammals such as the spectacled bear and dwarf deer. Also living within the reserve are **Quichua** language speakers, possibly descendants of the ancient Cara people, at **Oyacachi**, a village renowned for its hot springs (a few kilometres beyond the checkpoint), and the **Cofán** people, in the far northeast of the reserve at **Sinangüé**, who offer family-based **accommodation** for $30–40 per person per day (arrange through the Fundación Sobrevivencia Cofán; ☏02/2470946, Ⓦwww.cofan.org).

The reserve's highest point is the summit of **Volcán Cayambe** (5790m), Ecuador's third-highest mountain, while just south of the summit is the **highest point** on the equator, reputed to be the only place on the planet where the latitude and average temperature are both zero degrees. The volcano has a **refuge** ($17) at about 4700m, reached by a 25-kilometre dirt track leading southeast from Cayambe, with bunks, kitchen facilities, electricity and running water, but bring your own sleeping bag. The ascent from the refuge to the summit is a rather perilous **climb**, with crevasses and icefall hazards, though many agencies in Quito (see p.114) can arrange guides, equipment and transport.

There are several other points of **access** to the Cayambe-Coca reserve, mostly in the Oriente. The road from Papallacta to Baeza and Lago Agrio borders the easily accessed southern and eastern edges of the reserve, and the most common points of entry along this road are from Papallacta (see p.293), El Chaco (see p.296) and Lumbaquí, 70km west of Lago Agrio, and at the other end of the hike from Oyacachi.

Oyacachi

Beyond the Las Puntas checkpoint, the entry road descends into soft cloudforest and ends at **OYACACHI**, nestled at 3200m in the crook of a valley. Probable descendants of the Cara people, the village residents live by the reserve's environmental regulations, which prevent them from developing or cultivating the surrounding terrain, but do grant them generous plots of communal and individual land nearby. A hydroelectric dam provides their energy, and a number of enterprises such as **woodcarving** bolster the local economy. On the main street opposite the school is a **communal store** that many local families supply, where you can buy anything from a simple *batea* (tray) to elaborate animal carvings.

Before the founding of the reserve, Oyacachi was a town literally split down the middle by missionary activity. The main street divides Protestants on the right from Catholics on the left, and former conflicts between the two occasionally escalated into violence. However, the village's integration into the reserve has united its people, who collectively own a trout farm, small cheese factory and an excellent thermal springs, **Fuentes Termales** (closed Tues, $1), offering several steaming pools with fantastic views of the wooded hills and a **restaurant** serving fresh trout from the farm.

Oyacachi receives few tourists, but there is a **bus** service from Cayambe (daily leaves 2pm, returns 7am; also Sun leaves 7.30am, returns 2–3pm), meaning you'll probably have to **stay** the night here. While there are no hotels, the house next to the artesanía puts people up for a nominal fee, **campers** can pitch their tents near the springs for a few dollars, and you can sleep in the schoolhouse if you can find someone to open it for you. A **taxi** or **camioneta** from Cayambe costs around $20 one way (1hr), or $30 for a full day if you bargain hard enough.

From Oyacachi to the Oriente

A pleasant 45-minute stroll east from Oyacachi, the cemetery of **Nuacallacta** occupies the pre-Inca ruins of an ancient village, while further east, a centuries-old paved **trail** follows the Río Oyacachi down to El Chaco in the Oriente (see p.296), a stunning three- to four-day hike traversing the cloudforest of the Cayambe-Coca Reserve. Keep in mind, though, that the trail's sometimes dense undergrowth can make the journey pretty tough going, not to mention the difficulty of crossing rivers by cable alone, thanks to a 1987 earthquake that destroyed the bridges. The safest method is to use a harness-and-pulley you can disassemble, though locals sometimes slide across on scraps of wire attached to their belts – definitely not recommended.

Although the odd empty hut along the way can provide you with free overnight **lodging**, such accommodation is rather infrequent, so you'll need a **tent**. Also make sure to bring insect repellent and a machete to hack through the difficult terrain. Overall, you're better off finding a **guide** in Oyacachi ($10–15 per day) or asking around in Cayambe's *parque central* for Héctor Parión, in charge of tourism for Oyacachi. He can also provide equipment for a half-day hike from Oyacachi that includes a thrilling rappel down a 30-metre rockface.

Otavalo

A two-hour bus ride north of the capital, **OTAVALO** is one of Ecuador's top attractions, thanks largely to its world-renowned **Saturday market**. For hundreds of years, *indígenas* from some seventy surrounding villages have brought their crafts and produce down from the hills for a day of frenzied sale and barter. Nowadays, it draws producers from across Ecuador and Colombia as well, along with hundreds of overseas travellers who flood the town's streets every weekend and fill its disproportionate number of hotels. Although much of the business is still local, substantial sections of the market are devoted to tourists, with a boggling range of carvings, clothing, craftwork, musical instruments, ceramics and souvenirs. It's most famous, though, for its **weavings**, sold mainly at the **Plaza de Ponchos** in the heart of the tourist zone, a dizzying labyrinth of colour whose winding, makeshift passageways are lined with countless hanging tapestries and garments. Luckily, the town's produce and animal markets help prevent the Saturday market from descending into a tourist circus. During the week, Otavalo has a quiet provincial air, but **walks** to the nearby lakes, mountains or weaving villages are more than enough to keep you busy for days.

Some history

Otavaleños have been accomplished weavers since pre-colonial times, when they traded textiles for *achiote* (a red dye) and cotton with peoples from the Oriente. When the **Incas** finally took control of the region in 1495, so began almost five hundred years of exploitation of the Otavaleños' skills. The Incas brought llamas and alpacas with them for wool, which was easier to weave and dye than cotton, and extracted tribute from the weavers. The locals, meanwhile, adopted Inca clothing, a form of which can still be seen in the traditional dress of native women, which resembles the old look more closely than that of any other indigenous people of the Andes.

The Incas, however, only ruled for forty years before the **Spanish** swept in, dividing the country into **encomiendas**, in which the conquistadors exploited the people's labour and land and forced them to convert to Christianity. The ruthless *encomenderos* in charge founded the infamous **obrajes**, forced-labour sweatshops in which men, women and children were put to work for endless hours in atrocious conditions. With the introduction of silk, the spinning wheel and the treadle loom, Otavaleños began producing large quantities of quality textiles, supplying Spanish aristocrats all over the colonies.

At the start of the eighteenth century, the *encomienda* was phased out, only to be replaced by the equally pernicious **huasipungo**, a form of debt servitude that condemned *indígenas* to work in the large haciendas, often the very same *obrajes*, without any prospect of owning land or breaking free. In return for their labour, they were given a tiny plot of land, from which they had to provide all their own food.

In the middle of the nineteenth century, the industrial revolution in Europe allowed the mass production of textiles, sending the *obrajes* into decline, though the Otavalo weavers continued to work on a small scale in the traditional styles – often using old techniques, such as the backstrap loom – to satisfy local demand. This changed in 1917 with the adaptation of techniques used to make Scottish tweeds. The new fabrics, known as *casimires*, proved hugely popular in Ecuador and rekindled the industry, but it wasn't until the **Agrarian Reform Law** of 1964 that the oppressive *huasipungo* system was finally made illegal,

Traditional clothing in Otavalo

With the business acumen of Otavalo weavers as honed as their weaving skills, the demand for their craft has allowed them to travel abroad; many thousands of Otavaleños have set up outlets across the world, but prosperity hasn't tainted their cultural identity. For the most part, Otavaleños still wear **traditional garments** even as they own gleaming pick-up trucks, electric looms and modern hotel blocks. Women can often be seen in embroidered white blouses (*camisas*), shawls (*rebozos*), black-wrap skirts (*anakus*), gold-coloured bead necklaces (*walkas*) and red-bead bracelets (*maki watana*), with their hair wrapped up in strips of woven cloth (*cintas*). Men sport dapper blue ponchos (*ruwanas*) and mid-calf-length white trousers (*calzones*), with their hair braided (*shimba*) beneath felt hats (*sombreros*). Both wear *alpargatas*, sandals made from the fibre of the *penko* cactus.

breaking up the great estates and giving *indígenas* their own five-hectare plots of land. More importantly, the weavers could at last profit from their talents by setting up their own home businesses, and the rise of regional tourism opened up the Otavalo valley to the outside world and spread the word of its marvellous textiles.

Thanks to the success of the weaving industry, the Otavaleños are now one of the most prosperous indigenous groups in South America. If their **commercial success** is now well established, though, it has been slow to translate into real political power, as indifferent or resentful Ecuadorean elites have done little to improve the lot of the average citizen. The election of the town's first indigenous mayor in 2000, however, was a landmark event for the country's under-represented peoples, ensuring that Otavalo's markets will continue to flourish.

Arrival, city transport and information

In an effort to keep **buses** out of the centre, a terminal has been built on Atahualpa and Neptali Ordoñez at the northeastern edge of the town, serviced by Trans Otavalo and Trans Los Lagos from Quito (passing by Avenida Occidental). If riding on other bus lines, you'll probably be dropped off at the Panamericana, at the far southern end of Atahualpa, from where it's at least a six-block walk north to the nearest accommodation – an unsafe journey at night.

From the bus terminal, the Plaza de Ponchos is a five-minute walk to the southwest, and most hotels are located between the Plaza de Ponchos and the Parque Central. **Taxis** are available around the terminal, but are found in the greatest numbers at the Parque Central, and charge about $1 for a local trip. Still, Otavalo is easy to navigate on foot and **walking** across the town centre (roughly Plaza de Ponchos to the central park) only takes five minutes. Mountain **bikes** are available from La Tierra, Salinas 5-03 and Sucre ($7 per day; ☎06/923611), which also offers "emergency kits" for basic repairs and riding maps; and from the hotels *Jatún Pacha*, no. 19, 31 de Octubre ($3 per hour, $10 for 5 hours, $12 per day; ☎06/922223), and *Valle del Almanecer*, Quiroga and Roca ($5 per half-day, $8 per day; ☎06/920990). Always check bicycles are in good working order before you leave.

The train station is just behind the Plaza Copacabana, south of the bus terminal, but local rail lines have long been defunct. For **information** and **maps**, try the Ministerio de Turismo office in the Edificio Unaimco above the post office, Sucre and Salinas (Mon–Fri 8.30am–12.30pm & 2–5.30pm; ☎06/920460, ◎www.otavalo-web.com, ◎www.otavalo.com).

Accommodation

Otavalo probably has more **hotels** per capita than any other town in Ecuador, despite most of them being virtually empty during the week. Even so, things can get busy on Friday nights, so arrive early and reserve in advance during high season.

Ali Shungu Quito and Quiroga, Casilla no. 34 ☎06/920750, ◎www.alishungu.com. The best place to stay in Otavalo, run by an hospitable American couple and a helpful and dedicated local staff. Lavishly decorated with plants and fine weavings, and featuring comfortable rooms over-

looking a colourful garden towards Volcán Imbabura, plus excellent service, powerful hot showers, maps and information, a superb restaurant (see p.145) and no check-out time. Two luxury family apartments also available, from $80 to $120 depending on size of unit. ⑤

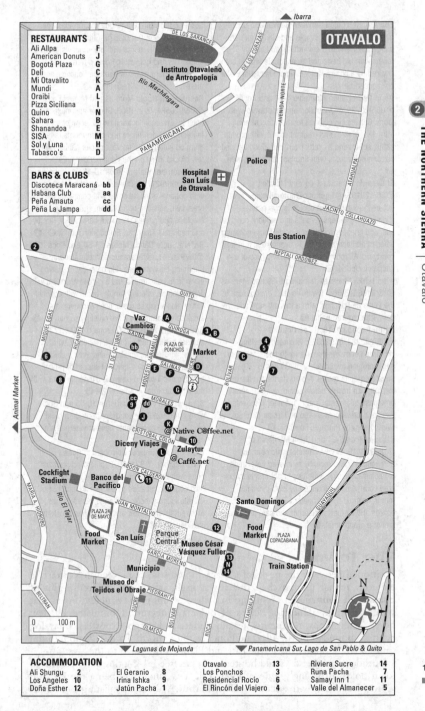

RESTAURANTS

Ali Allpa	F
American Donuts	J
Bogotá Plaza	G
Deli	C
Mi Otavalito	K
Mundi	A
Oraibi	L
Pizza Siciliana	I
Quino	N
Sahara	B
Shanandoa	E
SISA	M
Sol y Luna	H
Tabasco's	D

BARS & CLUBS

Discoteca Maracaná	bb
Habana Club	aa
Peña Amauta	cc
Peña La Jampa	dd

OTAVALO

THE NORTHERN SIERRA | Otavalo

Ibarra

DE LOS SARANCES

DE LOS COMAS

Instituto Otavaleño
de Antropología

Río Machángara

AVENIDA NORTE

PANAMERICANA

Police

Hospital
San Luís
de Otavalo

ATAHUALPA

JACINTO COLLAHUAZO

Bus Station

NEPTALÍ ORDÓÑEZ

Quito

MIGUEL EGAS

Vaz
Cambios

QUIROGA

SALINAS

PLAZA DE
PONCHOS

Market

3

B

4
5

C

7

31 DE OCTUBRE

MODESTO JARAMILLO

RICAURTE

SUCRE

BOLÍVAR

ROCA

E F

D

G

MORALES

9

cc dd

J

I

K

CRISTÓBAL COLÓN

@ Native C@ffee.net

10

Diceny Viajes

Zulaytur

L

@ Caffé.net

Cockfight
Stadium

Banco del
Pacífico

ABDÓN CALDERÓN

11

M

GUAYAQUIL

MARÍA A. HIDROBO

Río El Tejar

JUAN MONTALVO

Santo Domingo

PLAZA 24
DE MAYO

Food
Market

San Luís

Parque
Central

12

Museo César
Vásquez Fuller

Food
Market

PLAZA
COPACABANA

GARCÍA MORENO

13

Municipio

N

14

Train Station

Museo de
Tejidos el Obraje

SUCRE

PIEDRAHITA

A. BELTRÁN

BOLÍVAR

ROCA

ATAHUALPA

OLMEDO

Animal Market

0   100 m

N

Lagunas de Mojanda

Panamericana Sur, Lago de San Pablo & Quito

Los Ángeles Colón between Bolívar and Sucre ☎06/920058. Clean, simple and cheap, an ultra-budget choice with a colourful patio lined by rooms with big beds and an adequate shared bath, and run by a chatty, welcoming old lady. Hot water on request. ❶

Doña Esther Juan Montalvo 4-44 and Roca ☎06/920739, ⊛www.donaesther.otavalo-web .com. Convincing colonial reproduction offering attractive, well-lit and fragrant rooms with private baths, set around a pretty courtyard. Good bar and pizzeria downstairs with fireplace and giant oven. ❺

El Geranio Ricaurte 1-01 and Morales ☎06/920185, ⓔhgeranio@hotmail.com. Quiet, out-of-the-way budget choice in two parts – slightly more expensive units in a modern concrete pile, and cheaper rooms in a rickety but endearing wooden addition at the back, overlooking a breezy courtyard. All rooms are en suite, with use of a kitchen included. ❷

Irina Ishka Modesto Jaramillo 5-69 and Morales ☎ & ⓕ06/920684. Clean, no-frills option close to the Plaza de Ponchos, with a friendly staff and cosy little covered patio. ❷

Jatún Pacha no. 19, 31 de Octubre ☎06/922223, ⓕ922871, ⓔchalethostelling @hotmail.com. Welcoming youth hostel with garden (camping available), spotless dorms ($8) and private en-suite rooms. A bit distant from the centre, but with freshly baked bread, complimentary breakfast, bike rental and HI member discounts. Weekend breakfasts served at *Terraza Café Sol*, overlooking the Plaza de Ponchos. ❹

Otavalo Roca 5-04 and Juan Montalvo ☎ & ⓕ06/920416, ⊛www.hotelotavalo.com.ec. Distinguished and recently renovated hotel in an old colonial building, with two bright and leafy covered courtyards surrounded by high-ceilinged rooms warmed by gas heaters. Polished floorboards and a smart restaurant and café add to the feel of a grand hotel. ❹

Los Ponchos Sucre and Quiroga, on Plaza de Ponchos ☎ & ⓕ06/923575. Glitzy white-tiled floor and decent rooms with big windows, private baths, TVs and hot water. Rooftop terrace café offers excellent views of Plaza de Ponchos, and there's also a decent restaurant. ❷

Residencial Rocío Morales and Miguel Egas ☎06/920584, ⓕ921806. Simple and inexpensive hotel in a tranquil location on the edge of town, featuring wooden floors and clean rooms (a few of them en suite), with smarter, pricier cabins (❸) a few blocks away on the Panamericana. ❷

El Rincón del Viajero Roca 10-17 and Quiroga ☎ & ⓕ06/921741. Clean, safe and quiet rooms with optional en-suite baths and complimentary breakfast, plus use of a kitchen, sitting room with fireplace and games area with hammocks. Run by an hospitable American-Ecuadorian family. ❸–❹

Riviera Sucre García Moreno 3-80 and Roca ☎06/920241, ⓔrivierasucre@hotmail.com. Charming old hotel featuring greenery cascading down from balustrades and a garden abundant with bright blooms, offering simple rooms with optional baths, plus a games room, book exchange and small café warmed by a fire on chilly nights. ❸–❹

Runa Pacha Roca and Quiroga ☎06/921730. Modern hotel kitted out like a hacienda, with wagon wheels strewn about and even a stuffed calf on the stairway. Choice of shared or private baths, cable TVs and balconies, though rooms with the latter tend to be noisier. ❷–❸

Samay Inn 1 Abdón Calderón 10-05 and Sucre ☎ & ⓕ06/922871. Nondescript modern hotel whose inexpensive rooms have private baths and cable TVs. ❷

Valle del Almanecer Quiroga and Roca ☎06/920990, ⓕ921159. Popular backpackers' hotel with bamboo-thatched rooms around a cobbled courtyard shaded by palms and hammocks. On-site laundry, book exchange, board games, bike rentals, hot water and restaurant. Breakfast included. ❸–❹

The Town

Positioned between the peaks of Cotacachi and Imbabura, Otavalo's attractive environs are far prettier than **the town** itself, which has suffered a glut of unchecked construction, resulting in a slew of unsightly concrete boxes that swamp the few remaining scraps of older architecture. Dominated by new hotels, craft shops, restaurants, textile outlets and cargo exporters, Otavalo's centre is bounded by the Plaza de Ponchos to the north, Parque Central to the south, Plaza Copacabana to the east and Plaza 24 de Mayo to the west.

Outside of market days and boisterous fiestas (see p.145), this quiet provincial town holds surprisingly little of interest, its few landmarks being the **Parque Central**, adorned with a statue of **Rumiñahui**, Atahualpa's valiant general who

Haciendas and country hotels around Otavalo

There are several fine **haciendas** in the Otavalo region, originally built to oversee local *obrajes* (see "Some history", p.139), which generally cost more than in-town accommodation, but are well worth it for their historical character, colonial architecture, beautiful grounds, sumptuous furnishings and well-appointed rooms. Most also provide horse riding or hiking expeditions into the surrounding countryside. As well as those listed below, a few comfortable country hotels in **Cotacachi** (see p.151) and near the **Lagunas de Mojanda** (see p.150) provide upmarket accommodation outside town, but close enough for you to get an early start at the Saturday market. **Campers** should contact *El Rincón del Viajero* in Otavalo (see opposite), which runs a campsite ($3) by its farm about 1km out of town.

Hostería Cusín 9km southeast of Otavalo, on the edge of San Pablo del Lago ⊤06/918013, Ⓕ918003, Ⓦwww.haciendacusin.com. Beautiful early seventeenth-century hacienda, set amid peaceful gardens with little cobbled courtyards connected together and bursting with flowers. Rooms feature en-suite baths and striking views of the estate and its environs, and some have fireplaces and beamed ceilings. The complex includes a converted monastery, garden cottage, library, games room and an excellent restaurant. Many activities offered, not least horse riding ($13 per hour). Reservations required, with a two-night minimum stay. ❾

Hacienda Pinsaquí Panamericana Norte, km 5 ⊤ & Ⓕ06/946116 or 946117, Ⓦwww.pinsaqui.com. Historic hacienda built in 1790, which hosted Simón Bolívar and signatories of the 1863 Treaty of Pinsaquí between Colombia and Ecuador. Stately drawing and dining rooms with huge fireplaces, courtyards with trickling fountains, and luxurious but simple rooms pervaded by the faint aroma of furniture polish and wood smoke evoke a bygone age. Equine-related trappings and trophies abound, particularly in the snug bar, hung with stirrups and show-jumping memorabilia. All rooms cost the same, though some are far larger than others, and breakfast is included. Guided horse rides $30 for three hours. ❽

Hostería Puertolago Panamericana Sur, km 5.5 ⊤06/920920, Ⓕ921901. Purpose-built hotel on the shore of Lago de San Pablo opposite Volcán Imbabura, with smart and clean rooms equipped with cable TVs, fireplaces, alarm clocks and phones, plus use of sailboats, windsurfers and *pedalos*. Hotel ferry with on-site bar cruises the lake several times daily ($4) from the hotel dock, offering live *folklórica* (Fri–Sun 8.45pm; minimum ten people required). ❼

Hacienda Zuleta 12km east of Lago de San Pablo ⊤02/262580, Ⓦwww.zuleta.com. A working dairy farm and hacienda dating from 1690 and former home of Ecuadorian president Galo Plaza Lasso, set in beautiful bucolic countryside near the village of Zuleta, famed for its embroidery. Nine comfortable guestrooms with garden views accommodate visitors, who are treated as guests of the family. The farm produces delicious organic fruit, vegetables, trout and dairy products, and activities include horse riding (multi-day programmes available), embroidery trips and visits to condor repopulation projects. Reservations and minimum two-night stay required. ❾

led a fierce resistance against the Spanish, and the main church of **San Luis**, on the park's western side. The other major church, **Santo Domingo**, two blocks east at Calderón and Roca, is more striking with its large red bricks.

Just off the Panamericana on the northern edge of town ($1 by taxi, or 10min walk from the Plaza de Ponchos), the **Instituto Otavaleño de Antropología** (Mon–Fri 8.30am–12pm & 2.30–6pm; free) has exhibits on archeology, ethnography and musical instruments, scale models of the town's fiestas and a small academic library. Much more fun, however, is the eccentric

Museo César Vásquez Fuller, above the *Residencial Los Andes* on Juan Montalvo and Roca (Mon–Sat irregular hours; $2 donation), which squeezes more than ten thousand Inca and pre-Inca artefacts into a cramped room, including axe-heads, masks, ceramics, jade frogs and necklaces encrusted with precious stones – a bewildering collection, clarified somewhat by the owner's spirited commentary. Another worthwhile attraction, the wonderful **Museo de Tejidos el Obraje**, Sucre 6-08 and Piedrahíta (Mon–Sat 9am–1pm & 3–5pm; $2), presents lifelong weavers Don Luis Maldonado and his wife, Luzmaría, demonstrating traditional methods of local textile production, from cleaning and carding wool to spinning, drying and weaving it on pedal and backstrap looms.

If you're around on a Sunday afternoon (about 3–4pm) head to the north side of the Plaza de Ponchos to view a brisk game of **pelota de mano**, in which two opposing teams hit a tiny, hard black leather ball high into the air across the square with their bare hands.

Town markets

Every Friday afternoon, Otavalo comes to life as pick-up trucks laden with merchandise and vendors bent double under great blocks of textiles stream into town from the surrounding countryside, preparing for the fabulous **Saturday market**, which includes one of the largest and most colourful artesanía markets on the continent. The **Plaza de Ponchos** is the centre of the activity, where *indígenas* dressed in all their finery offer a wide choice of clothes, textiles, hammocks and weavings, as well as jewellery, ceramics, dolls and many other craftworks. Artisan stalls spill off the square in all directions, especially up Sucre, recently improved with wide pavements and gaudy lampposts, all the way to the Parque Central. By 7am on Saturday morning, the market is already buzzing, so arrive early for the widest choice and lowest prices, before the tour groups roll in from Quito from 9 to 10am.

Although the Otavaleño sales patter is not at all aggressive, you will be expected to **haggle**, which should result in significant discounts, often by as much as 25 percent or more; a good time for reductions is towards the end of the day, when some vendors look to unload their remaining wares before sundown. The Saturday craft market has become such big business that most of the town's weaving and artesanía shops stay open throughout the week, and you'll find stalls on the Plaza de Ponchos every day, particularly during the busy **Wednesday market** – not a bad substitute for the real thing.

To get a better idea of the Saturday market's importance beyond tourism, go to the north side of the Plaza de Ponchos, site of the **vegetable** and **grain sellers** and a row of makeshift street restaurants. From here head south up Modesto Jaramillo to the hardware and everyday-clothing sections and the town's best **food market**, at the Plaza 24 de Mayo (with another at the Plaza Copacabana). This covered square has all the bustle of an eastern bazaar, where simple eateries carve up hog roasts and sizzle scraps of meat and potatoes for shoppers at long refectory tables. You can't help wondering if the victuals have come straight from the **animal market** (5–10am), a packed field of farm animals bellowing through the early morning mists, tugging hard on their busily negotiating owners. To reach it, go to the west end of Calderón, cross the bridge, and then follow the crowds going up S. J. Castro to the Panamericana and the market ground on the other side.

Behind the produce market, on 31 de Octubre, when the traders are packing up between 5 and 6pm and the smell of discarded mangoes is halfway between sweetness and decay, locals head to the **cockfight stadium** (*gallera municipal*) for a flutter. It will set you back $1 to sit around a blood-smeared circle watching two roosters try to peck each other to death.

Finally, Otavalo's markets can get very crowded at times, providing perfect cover for **pickpockets** and **bag slashers**. Look after your belongings and keep valuables hidden from view as much as possible. If you're going back to Quito by bus on Saturday evening, be aware that a bag stuffed full of goods is an inviting target.

Festivals

Otavalo hosts several major **festivals**, including **San Juan** on June 24, which is celebrated with bonfires and fireworks as *indígenas* from the surrounding villages parade in costumes and masks, dancing and singing their way to the Church of San Juan, west of town. The festivities last for several days, blending with those for **San Pedro** on June 29, and are thought to be Christianized versions of the ancient **Inti Raymi** celebration of the solstice. The San Juan fiesta once involved a kind of ritual fighting (*tinku*) between rival villages, but these days the ceremonies are largely confined to ritual bathing in the Peguche waterfall, followed by shindigs in the outlying communities; foreigners should only attend these events if they have an invitation to do so from a local, and should show sensitivity at all times.

Another big event, the **Fiesta del Yamor**, during the first two weeks of September, sees bullfights, music, dancing and traditional food and drink, including *yamor* itself, a chicha made from seven types of corn and prepared over twelve hours. Among the smaller events are **Mojanda Arriba** (Oct 30–31), a two-day walk from Quito to Otavalo, stopping at Malchinguí over the Mojanda hills, marking the foundation of the town, and **Diciembre Mágico**, a minor arts festival in the weeks leading up to Christmas.

Restaurants and cafés

Otavalo's **restaurants** cater to a broad clientele and feature a wide choice of cuisines, with pizza parlours in particular abundance. Most establishments are open daily from breakfast to 9pm or 10pm, often later if there are enough customers. **Prices** are a bit higher than at other Ecuadorian restaurants, but are still quite affordable, at $2.50–$5 for the typical main course. The best place to stock up on cheap fresh fruit and vegetables is naturally the Saturday produce market (see opposite), where the vendors also offer high-cholesterol meals of *chicharrón* and *llapingachos* for not much more than $1. As with most things in Otavalo, restaurants become more colourful at the end of the week, when many offer live Andean **folk music** (*folklórica*), often of a high standard.

Restaurants

Ali Allpa Salinas 5-09. Reliable restaurant on the Plaza de Ponchos with a predictable, if inexpensive, menu of meat, fish, chicken, pasta and a few vegetarian options thrown in. The *almuerzos* are great value.

Ali Shungu Quito and Quiroga ℗06/920750. Otavalo's best restaurant, in the eponymous hotel (see p.140), where the excellent meals are made with local organic produce and include plenty of vegetarian dishes. While costing a little extra, it's all good value considering the choice ingredients,

such as the heavenly tomatoes in the lasagne. Try to reserve on Fridays, when there's live music (8–9pm). Last orders Sat–Thurs 8.30pm, Fri 9.30–10pm.

Il de Roma Juan Montalvo 4-44, at the *Doña Esther* (see p.142). Attractive and atmospheric pizzeria, featuring a large clay oven and good pizzas.

Mi Otavalito Sucre 11-13 and Morales. Reasonably priced traditional food, including inexpensive set-menu options, such as $3 for a hearty four-course *menu del día*, and good à la carte fried fish. Closes Sun–Thurs 4pm.

Pizza Siciliana Morales and Sucre. The town's most popular pizzeria, notable for its excellent live music on Fridays and Saturdays and occasionally during the week, too. Pizzas range from $4 to $14, depending on size and toppings, which include vegetarian options.

Quino Roca and García Moreno. Colourful restaurant specializing in seafood dishes, including fish stew, trout and shrimp, for around $4–6 per entrée.

SISA Abdón Calderón 4-09 and Sucre, upstairs. Classy but moderately priced restaurant serving tasty meals of trout and large salads. Live music Friday and Saturday. Part of an arts complex that includes a bookshop, gallery, café and art workshop.

Tabasco's Sucre and Salinas. Moderately priced Mexican restaurant in a great location, with a terrace overlooking the Plaza de Ponchos, though the view is somewhat marred by copious telegraph cables.

Cafés

American Donuts Modesto Jaramillo 5-36 and Colón. One of the town's best bakeries, offering breakfasts, coffee, croissants, rolls, loaves, cakes and donuts.

Bogotá Plaza Sucre and Morales. Coffee house serving real Colombian brews, plus snacks, burgers, cheap set meals and pies whose recipes seem to have been "borrowed" from *Shanandoa*.

Deli Quiroga and Bolívar. Friendly little place offering breakfasts and a range of inexpensive international fare such as enchiladas, quesadillas, pasta and pizzas. Wed–Thurs 8am–6pm, Fri–Sun 8am–9pm.

Mundi Quiroga and Modesto Jaramillo. Well-sited café on the Plaza de Ponchos, good for taking a break and a bite to eat in comfortable low-slung chairs on market days. Crêpes, salads, sandwiches and snacks for $2–3.

Oraibi Sucre and Colón. Serves good vegetarian food, such as quinoa soup and quiche, and stages live music on Saturday nights in its pleasant little courtyard. Wed 11am–9.30pm, Thurs–Sun 7am–9.30pm.

Sahara Quiroga between Bolívar and Sucre. Lounge on cushions at floor level and enjoy Middle Eastern food served on low tables – or order a hookah pipe filled with fruit-flavoured tobacco.

Shanandoa Salinas and Modesto Jaramillo. Also known as *The Pie Shop*, a good spot for juices, milkshakes, sandwiches and, above all, tasty home-baked pies with several fruity fillings. A Plaza de Ponchos stalwart, in business for a quarter-century.

Sol y Luna Bolívar and Morales. Popular, brightly painted café and art gallery with a shaded patio set back from the street, serving sandwiches, organic salads, veggie burgers, breakfast and bar snacks. Closed Mon & Tues.

Nightlife

The energy and excitement generated by the market find their outlet on Friday and Saturday nights at Otavalo's **peñas**, several of which feature **live music** at some point in the evening. Usually this is **folklórica**, traditional Andean folk songs accompanied by *rondador* (small panpipes), *quena* (wooden flute), *charango* (a lute, sometimes made from armadillo shell) and guitars, though salsa and tropical music is also performed on occasion.

Discoteca Maracaná Salinas and 31 de Octubre. Conventional club experience in a dark, three-floor venue strafed by ultraviolet lights and laser beams, pumping out hot merengue, salsa, techno and rock hits into the small hours. Fri & Sat 9pm–3am; $1.50, one drink included.

Habana Club Quito and 31 de Octubre. Popular hangout for Otavalo youths, who play pool, boogie to Latin pop and dance, or croon away in the karaoke bar downstairs. Fri & Sat 9pm–3am; $1.50.

Peña Amauta Jaramillo and Morales, across from *Peña La Jampa*. Friendly spot with good, established *folklórica* groups, sometimes followed by less expert new bands. Also worth sampling are the *guayusa* cocktails, hot infusions of the eponymous leaves from the Oriente topped off with a healthy slug of sugarcane spirit. Food also available at the upstairs restaurant. Fri & Sat 8pm–2am, live music from 10pm; $2.

Peña La Jampa Jaramillo and Morales. The most popular venue of the moment, a covered courtyard with a bar, stage, and plenty of chairs, tables and dancing space. Features good live Andean *folklórica*, but also occasionally puts on other types of music, from Cuban outfits to mariachi bands. Fri & Sat 8pm–3am, live music 9.30pm; $2–3.

Tour operators in Otavalo

Otavalo hosts a number of **tour operators** providing worthwhile treks into the surrounding area.

Diceny Viajes Sucre 10-14 and Colón ☎ & ℱ 06/921217. Friendly outfit operated by *indígenas*, offering information and excellent tours of weaving villages in English, French, Spanish and Quichua ($20 including lunch), plus mountain hiking ($20), horse riding ($35 per day) and visits to a remote jungle community.

Fundación Cordillera Colón and Sucre ☎ 06/923633 or 648133. Organizes one- or multi-day trips to Chachimbiro hot springs (see p.165) in a ranchera ($5 return), and biking and horse riding in the surrounding area.

Runa Tupari Sucre and Quiroga on the Plaza de Ponchos ☎ & ℱ 06/925985, ⓦ www.runatupari.com. Offers intercultural exchange with local indigenous communities, with accommodation in "rural lodges" ($15 including breakfast and dinner), as well as standard tours of the area ($20) and one- to four-day treks ($30–50 per day) led by an indigenous guide.

La Tierra Salinas 5-03 and Sucre ☎ 06/923611. Has mountain bikes and horse riding ($20 per 5hr, $30 full day including meal).

Zulaytur across from Diceny Viajes on the second floor ☎ 06/921176, ℱ 922969. Organizes village tours in easy Spanish ($16) and horse-riding trips ($5 per hour).

Listings

Banks and exchange Banco del Pacífico, Jaramillo and Calderón, has a MasterCard ATM. To change traveller's cheques try Banco del Pichincha, Bolívar and García Moreno; Fax Cambios, Sucre 11-05 and Colón (closed Sun); or Vaz Cambios, Saona and Jaramillo (closes Mon 1pm, Tues–Fri 2.30pm, Sat 3pm & Sun all day).

Buses All services, local and interprovincial, leave from the terminal on Athualpa and Neptali Ordoñez.

Hospitals and doctors Centro Medico Quirurgico "El Jordan", Quiroga and Roca (daily 8am–7pm, ☎ 06/921159), has several doctors and 24hr emergency service, where doctors Patricio and Rubén Buitron speak some English. Hospital San Luis de Otavalo is on Sucre, 500m north of Plaza de Ponchos (☎ 06/920444).

Internet access Numerous options in the town centre, most around $1.20 per hour and offering netphone services as well as drinks and snacks:

Caffé.net, Sucre and Morales; Call.Center, Sucre and Colón; Ishka, Sucre 10-09 and Colón; Native c@ffee.net, Sucre and Colón; Santa Fe Café Net, Roca and García Moreno.

Language schools Instituto Superior de Español, Sucre 11-10 and Morales ☎ 06/922414; Mundo Andino, Salinas 4-04 and Bolívar ☎ 06/921864; Otavalo Spanish Institute, 31 de Octubre and Salinas, third floor ☎ 06/921404.

Laundries Lavandería Asianshop, Colón 5-14 and Sucre; New Laundry, Roca 9-42 and Calderón.

Police station Av Norte, north of Bolívar ☎ 06/920101.

Post office Salinas and Sucre.

Telephone The Andinatel office, Calderón and Sucre (daily 8am–7.45pm), can be inexplicably hostile about collect and charge-card calls. You're better off making international calls from an Internet café.

Around Otavalo

A trip to Otavalo doesn't have to end when the market vendors pack up shop, as the **region** offers a number of attractions, especially the many **weaving villages** in the Otavalo valley, most within a few kilometres of town. Local tour agencies (see box, above) combine visits to several villages, giving you a cross-section of the different techniques and traditions employed by each. **Peguche**, within walking distance northeast of town, has a cooperative that features

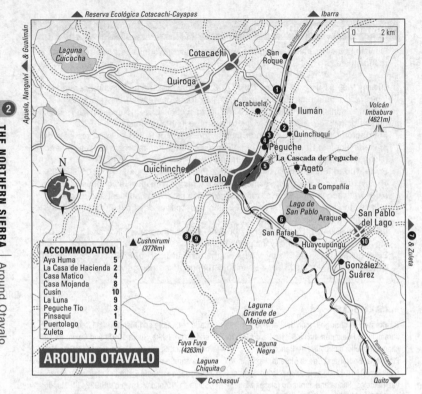

Apuela, Nangulví & Gualimán

▲ *Reserva Ecológica Cotacachi-Cayapas* ▲ *Ibarra*

0   2 km

Laguna Cuicocha

Cotacachi   San Roque

Quiroga

Carabuela   ● Ilumán   *Volcán Imbabura (4621m)*

❷ ● Quinchuquí

❸ **❷**
❹ Peguche
   ■ La Cascada de Peguche
   ❺ ● Agato

Quichinche   Otavalo

    ● La Compañía

N

Lago de San Pablo   Araque   San Pablo del Lago

❻   San Rafael   **❼** & *Zuleta*

▲ *Cushnirumi (3776m)*   **❽** **❾**   Huaycupungu **❿**

ACCOMMODATION
Aya Huma	5
La Casa de Hacienda	2
Casa Matico	4
Casa Mojanda	8
Cusín	10
La Luna	9
Peguche Tío	3
Pinsaquí	1
Puertolago	6
Zuleta	7

González Suárez

Laguna Grande de Mojanda

▲ *Fuya Fuya (4263m)*   *Laguna Negra*

AROUND OTAVALO

Laguna Chiquita

▼ *Cochasquí*   *Quito* ▼

weaving demonstrations and a secluded waterfall nearby, while the villages huddled around the reed shores of **Lago de San Pablo**, 3km southeast of Peguche, are also home to many weavers, and celebrate colourful **fiestas** such as the banner-waving processions of Los Pendoneros (Oct 15). On the lake's southern shore, **San Rafael** hosts the costume ritual of El Coraza (Aug 19), in which one of the village's wealthiest men appears in a feathered hat hung with so much gold chain and jewellery that his face is concealed. If you turn up at any of these fiestas, try to be discreet (or better yet, invited), as they can be rather private affairs.

The **Lagunas de Mojanda**, three lakes surrounded by brooding, cloud-hung peaks south of town, are set in ideal country for hiking and horse riding and command breathtaking views, while another popular excursion is to **Laguna Cuicocha**, on the edge of the huge **Cotacachi-Cayapas reserve**, extending from the páramo down to tropical forests in the coastal Esmeraldas province. The lake is best reached from **Cotacachi**, 11km north of Otavalo, a smart little town famous for its market, leather goods and boutiques. Your best bet for leaving the crowds behind, though, is by taking a bus west to the remote **Intag region**, where small villages such as **Apuela** nestle in richly forested hills, close to thermal springs at **Nangulví** and pre-Inca ruins at **Gualimán**.

Unfortunately, some of these areas around Otavalo can be unsafe. Over recent years armed robberies, rape and violent assaults have been reported in the Mojanda lakes and Laguna Cuicocha areas and occasionally on trails to the Peguche waterfall and Lago de San Pablo. Trouble is uncommon, but ask locally about **safety** before hiking around Mojanda or Laguna Cuicocha in particular, and bear in mind that large groups are less vulnerable to attack than small ones.

Peguche and La Cascada de Peguche

Three kilometres northeast of town, **PEGUCHE** is one of the nearest weaving villages to Otavalo, a quiet community comprising a central square and a few unmarked streets lined with simple, whitewashed houses, where almost all the families are involved with the textile business, though many of them now use electric looms. The best place to see the town's traditional **weaving demonstrations** is at the workshop of **José Cotacachi**. The village is also known for producing **musical instruments** like the *rondadores*, Ecuadorian panpipes, and for the talented *folklórica* musicians who play them (regularly performing in Otavalo *peñas* on weekend nights; see p.146).

From the main terminal in Otavalo, Co-op Imbaburapac and Transportes 8 de Septiembre, **buses** make the short hop to Peguche every twenty to thirty minutes, while **taxis** from Plaza de Ponchos take five to ten minutes and cost a couple of dollars.

Set in a eucalyptus grove about a kilometre southeast of the village, the sacred waterfall of **La Cascada de Peguche** – a modest cascade whose spray shimmers in the dappled sunlight – is the site of private ceremonial bathing during the San Juan fiesta (see p.145), but for the rest of the year is a popular weekend picnic spot. To get there, head south from Peguche along the main street for about fifteen minutes until you reach some whitewashed arches and a low, barn-shaped building marking the entrance. You can also walk there in less than an hour from Otavalo by heading east out of town towards the railway tracks, then turning left onto a cobbled road running parallel to them. Keep with the road where it leaves the tracks to go up the hill, and follow it around to the south to the entrance. A few slippery logs laid across the stream at the foot of the falls lead to a trail up to the top of the waterfall.

Accommodation

Aya Huma by the railway tracks up from the waterfall ℡06/922633, ℻922664, ⓦwww.ayahuma.com. Provides pleasant, simple rooms with hot water in shared or private baths next to a garden with hammocks; offers tourist information and maps, a book exchange and small library, and a good restaurant with live music on Saturdays. ❸–❹

La Casa de Hacienda on the road to Ilumán, turn-off at Panamericana km 3 ℡06/923105 or 946336, ⓔhosteriacasadehacienda @hotmail.com. Swiss-owned establishment featuring mini chalet-style cabañas at the foot of Imbabura, each with rocking chairs on the porch and views of Otavalo. ❻

Casa Matico Peguche ℡06/922789, or contact **Casa Sol** in Quito (see p.84). Local family providing affordable bed-and-breakfast accommodation and offering lessons in cooking corn humitas and fire-roasted tortillas, plus guided hikes around Imbabura and assistance in haggling at the Otavalo market (extra services $20 per person, $35 per two for day-trips). ❸

Peguche Tío just off the Panamericana at the north end of the village ℡ & ℻06/922411, ⓦwww.joinme.net/peguchetio. Distinctive, circular wooden building with a lookout tower, offering modest rooms with private baths and fireplaces, plus a stage and dance floor for monthly live music, and a library and craft shop. ❸

Other weaving villages

Other well-known **weaving villages** outside Otavalo include Agato, Ilumán and Carabuela, all with workshops that you can drop into during the day. Dozens of other villages in the valley have their own specialities, such as tapestries (*tapices*) or embroidery (*bordado*), but often without open workshops, making it much harder to see their weavers at work.

Miguel Andrango, perhaps Ecuador's most famous weaver, is based in **Agato**, 1km east of Peguche, where he demonstrates use of the backstrap loom. Just east of the Panamericana in **Ilumán**, 6km north of Otavalo, similar demonstrations are given at the **Inti Chumbi Co-op** on the plaza, though hat-making is also an important local industry. However, the village is better known in Ecuador for its *curanderos* (healers) and *brujos* (sorcerers), and there are around thirty of them practising their art, involving a curious mixture of pagan and Christian rituals and herbal medicine to drive out illnesses or evil spirits. If you visit one, be prepared to walk away coated in spit; it's all part of the cure.

Further along, **Carabuela** has a few open workshops, the most interesting of which is that of Don José Carlos, who demonstrates his production technique in all its stages, from the sheep to the loom, including a double-ended spinning wheel. Each of his **ponchos** takes about three months to create, making the $200 price tag good value. Other villages worth a look are **La Compañía**, on the northern shore of Lago de San Pablo, which produces sashes (*fajas*) and hair wraps (*cintas*), and **Huaycupungu**, at its southern shore, 7km south of Otavalo, for *totora*-reed mats (*esteras*).

Practicalities

The easiest way to visit these weaving villages is by picking up a **tour** in Otavalo (see box, p.147), which may combine visits to several and ensure that the weavers are expecting you; by contrast, if you're going independently, you won't have this luxury, though it is the cheaper option. **Buses** to most villages cost about $0.20 and leave the main terminal regularly during the day, and **bikes** are also available for rent in Otavalo (see "Arrival, city transport and information", p.140).

Lagunas de Mojanda

The three dark lakes of the **Lagunas de Mojanda** are clutched by grassy hills 16km south of and 1200m above Otavalo. The dramatic scenery has made the area a favourite for hikers, horse riders and other visitors, who can visit independently or on tours from Otavalo (see box, p.147), or stay at one of the nearby hotels that arranges excursions.

A dirt track winds from the southwest corner of Otavalo up to the **Laguna Grande de Mojanda**, by far the largest of the three, more than 2km wide. On the other side of the lake to the southeast, brooding **Laguna Negra** and glassy **Laguna Chiquita**, 1km further south, are surrounded by a ring of ragged peaks topping 4000m. These smaller lakes are linked to the Laguna Grande de Mojanda by a **trail** along its west side, which reaches a fork at its southernmost shore: turn left and continue round the lake for Laguna Negra, or head south to Chiquita by bearing right.

Arrival and information

You can take a **taxi** from Otavalo to the lakes ($10 one-way, $6 per hour waiting time for return trip), and then walk back down to town (3hr 30min) to enjoy the spectacular views. Be aware, though, that while the Mojanda area is safer in recent years with the introduction of security patrols funded by donation, it's also had an unfortunate history of **robberies** and **violent assaults**, so make sure to ask about safety before heading off.

The best resources for independent hikers are the IGM **maps** for Mojanda and Otavalo (1:50,000), possibly with the aid of maps for San Pablo del Lago and Cayambe, for the widest picture of the area.

Accommodation

The best **accommodation** near the lakes – and one of the most peaceful hotels in the region – is *Casa Mojanda*, 3.5km up Mojanda road from Otavalo (℡ & ℻09/9731737, ℡09/9703843, in Quito ℡02/2465745, ⓦwww.casamojanda.com; ❾), a collection of beautiful whitewashed cottages poised on a hillside, with stunning views of the Imbabura, Cotacachi and the Cushnimuri mountains. Run by an American-Ecuadorean couple, the hotel features an organic garden that supplies delicious produce for its largely vegetarian restaurant, and a portion of the profits goes to the Mojanda Foundation, supporting progressive educational and environmental initiatives. Many of the comfortable rooms have their own fireplaces, and other perks include an outdoor Japanese-style hot tub, games room, piano and library, plus guided horse tours ($25 per two hours) and hiking expeditions. Its nearby hostel, fitted with a kitchen and bathroom, sleeps ten and costs $40 per person. The price for a hotel room also includes breakfast, afternoon tea and dinner, with discounts for children, students and SAE members.

A little further up towards the lakes, the Argentinian-owned *La Luna* (℡ & ℻09/9737415 or 9816145; ❸–❹) is a good choice if you're on a budget but desire a relaxed and attractive hotel outside Otavalo. It features a few clean and simple cabins with dorms ($4), a **campground** ($2) and rooms with optional private baths and fireplaces. Reservations are advised for weekend stays, and the hotel offers free pick-up from Otavalo if you ring before 6pm. Otherwise, a **taxi** from Otavalo costs about $3.

Cotacachi

Five kilometres from Otavalo on the road to Ibarra is the turn-off to **COTACACHI**, a small town on the other side of the Río Ambi at the foot of Volcán Cotacachi, where a grandiose, flag-lined boulevard welcomes you – a reflection of the locals' belief that they live in an upmarket town. As well as being a self-proclaimed "eco-city" which has successfully cut down on waste and pollution, Cotacachi is a prosperous community thanks to its flourishing **leather industry**. Dozens of smart boutiques selling every conceivable form of leatherware line 10 de Agosto, the main street running north–south up to the simple Parque San Francisco, where the **Sunday leather market** is held, the best place to pick up a bargain-priced bag or jacket.

To escape all the tanned hides, try the **Museo de las Culturas**, García Moreno 13-41 (Mon–Fri 9am–noon & 2–5pm, Sat 2–5pm, Sun 10am–1pm; $1, including guided tour in Spanish), set in a cloistered colonial building and showcasing Cotacachi traditions through costumed mannequins and exhibits on craftwork and fiestas. The building lies in the shadow of the white-domed **La Matriz** church, which stands on the grand and leafy **Parque La Matriz**.

Practicalities

Buses for Cotacachi leave from the Otavalo terminal every ten to fifteen minutes (6am–6pm), and return to Otavalo from the station at 10 de Agosto and Salinas, at the north end of Cotacachi (you can also hail them on Peñaherrera as they leave town). The town is also good for accessing Laguna Cuicocha in the Cotacachi-Cayapas reserve (see p.152); to visit, pick up a **taxi**

or **camioneta** from around the bus station ($7 return trip, including 1hr waiting time).

Outside of the fancier **hotels** (see below), good choices for **dining** include the cheerful *Inti Huasi*, Bolívar and 10 de Agosto, and the slightly more expensive *El Leñador*, Sucre and Juan Montalvo, both of which offer varied menus and good trout dishes, while *Swiss Coffee*, Bolívar 3-08 and Parque de la Interculturalidad, is a solid **Internet café**. The Banco del Pichincha, on the Parque San Francisco at the south end of town, **exchanges** traveller's cheques. The **post office**, on Peñaherrera, is next to the church on the main square, and the **phone office** is on Sucre opposite it.

Hotels

Bachita Sucre 16-74 and Modesto Peñaherrera ☎06/915063. Cheap hotel providing decent rooms, but no hot water in those with shared bathrooms. ❷–❸

El Mesón de Flores García Moreno 13-67 and Sucre ☎06/916009 or 915264, ☏915828. Higher-end option set in a charming colonial house with creaky floorboards and en-suite rooms set around a pretty courtyard decked in flowers. It also has a good restaurant. ❺

La Mirage 500m north of town on 10 de Agosto ☎06/915237 or 961561, ☏915065, ⍟www .mirage.com.ec. A "contemporary hacienda" and one of the most expensive hotels in the country, featuring peacock-filled gardens, palatial rooms with fireplaces, four-poster beds with a scattering of fresh rose petals, swimming pool, tennis court and excellent restaurant. On-site spa offers such luxurious treatments as "Cleopatra's Bath", a thirty-minute soak in a milk-and-oil bath, followed by a wrap in a thermal blanket and a massage in the special "Egyptian Room". Price includes breakfast and dinner. ❾

Plaza Bolívar Bolívar and 10 de Agosto ☎06/915327, ☏915755. Comfortable and friendly budget choice with hot water, complimentary breakfast, use of a kitchen and Internet access. ❸

Sumac Huasi Juan Montalvo 10-09 and Pedro Moncayo ☎ & ☏06/915873. Clean, modern and comfortable new hotel featuring rooms with cable TVs, private baths and hot water. Breakfast is included. ❺

Reserva Ecológica Cotacachi-Cayapas

Thirteen kilometres west of Cotacachi is the entrance to the **Reserva Ecológica Cotacachi-Cayapas** ($5), established in 1968 and covering more than two thousand square kilometres of the western Andes, ranging from the summit of Volcán Cotacachi (4944m) to the coastal lowlands (300m), and protecting ecological habitats from páramo grasslands in the east to the dense rainforests of Esmeraldas province. The reserve is part of the **Chocó** bioregion, which extends into southern Colombia, where high levels of rainfall support one of the earth's most diverse ecosystems. Twenty percent of Ecuador's endemic plants are found here, as well as thousands of mammals, birds and insects, including Andean spectacled bears, ocelots, jaguars and river otters.

From Cotacachi and Otavalo, it's simple to get to the centre of the highland section, **Laguna Cuicocha** ("Guinea Pig Lake" in Quichua), a spectacular crater lake at 3060m, located at the foot of the dormant Volcán Cotacachi in the southeastern tip of the reserve ($1 entrance to lake only). The two islands in the middle of the lake, **Isla Wolf** and **Isla Yerovi**, are a pair of old volcanic cones that grew up from the floor of a collapsed crater 200m below, and according to legend were used by the Incas as a prison. Nowadays they're off-limits due to on-site research, but the lake itself is still a popular destination, and you can take a jaunt across it on a **motorboat** ($2 per person, $10 for a group of six), or learn more about it in the **visitor centre** (Tues–Sat 9am–5pm, with lunch break). Better still, you can walk around the rim of the crater on a well-kept, circular **trail**. The ten-kilometre hike (best walked counterclockwise) takes about five to six hours to complete, though your effort is well rewarded by wonderful views of Cayambe and Cotopaxi, not to mention orchids and giant hummingbirds, and even condors if you are lucky. The trailhead is behind the guard post at the reserve entrance.

Practicalities

To get to Laguna Cuicocha, take a **bus** (every 10–15min) from the Otavalo terminal to Cotacachi or Quiroga, a village about five minutes beyond Cotacachi. From either stop, take a **taxi** or **camioneta** to the lake ($3–4 one-way, $7 return trip with waiting time); from Otavalo a taxi is about $8 one-way. If you fancy **walking** back from the lake through beautiful scenery on the old road to Quiroga (9km, 3–4hr), turn left off the main road at the junction with the old road, and continue east where the new road turns west, about 2km below the guard post.

The lowland **forests** are best accessed by boat from Borbón (see p.371), up the *ríos* Cayapas (see p.372) and Santiago (see p.373), but such a journey is best attempted outside the dry season (July–Dec), when water levels can be too low to go very far. You can also reach **cloudforest** areas from the Los Cedros reserve (see p.354), which borders Cotacachi-Cayapas to the south.

The two **restaurants** at the lake are *Muelle*, on the shore, with a moderately priced menu, and *El Mirador*, on the hill directly behind it, offering cheap fish specials and good views.

Check with the guards at the reserve entrance for the current **security precautions**, and note also that the succulent-looking blue berries growing in abundance by the shore are poisonous.

The Intag region

West of the entrance to Laguna Cuicocha, the dirt road skirts the boundary of the Reserva Ecológica Cotacachi-Cayapas to join the main road – still a bumpy track – from Otavalo to the **Intag region**, a remote area in the western Andes cradling a few isolated highland settlements amid its richly forested hills. The road climbs to 3300m before descending into cloudforest, where mosses and epiphytic plants dangle from the trees, and wonderful views then appear of the forests and valleys below. A good place to see these forests is at the private **Intag Cloudforest Reserve**, five square kilometres of primary and secondary forest ranging from 1800 to 2800m in altitude, where high rainfall (2500mm annually) and humidity nurture countless plants and animals, including more than twenty types of hummingbirds.

Accommodation at the simple lodge here costs $98 per person (minimum two-night stay) for groups of eight or more, including food, lodging and transport from **Santa Rosa**, the nearest village to the reserve, on the road to Apuela. Reservations must be made well in advance by post to Intag Cloudforest Reserve (PO Box 18, Otavalo, Imbabura, Ecuador). The owners also helped found DECOIN (ⓦ www.decoin.org), a local environmental organization that works on regional ecotourism projects and provides information on all the latest developments, including Santa Rosa's new community-run reserve.

A two-hour walk from Santa Rosa, the **Siempre Verde Reserve** (ⓦ www.siempreverde.org) protects about two square kilometres of cloudforest contiguous with the Reserva Ecológica Cotacachi-Cayapas, and provides simple accommodation and excellent opportunities for hiking and bird watching. Another community-run reserve, set up to counter powerful and destructive local mining interests, can be visited at Junín (see p.156).

Apuela

Eleven kilometres from Santa Rosa, and 45km along the winding road west of Cotacachi, **APUELA** is a small village at the confluence of *ríos* Apuela and Azabi, enveloped by thickly forested hills. A remote highland settlement, the town has two simple streets, shops selling little more than biscuits, cola and tuna, a battered church and lethargic men sitting around the volleyball court on the main square. While there's not much of interest here, hiking **trails** festoon the surrounding hills, and Nangulví and Gualimán provide worthwhile nearby excursions. Another option is to contact the local coffee-producing association AACRI, whose office is located in the village (☎06/648489, ⓔ aacri@andinanet.net), and enquire about their agro-tourism projects, which can involve trips to nearby coffee farms.

Transportes Otavalo **buses** leave for Apuela from the Otavalo terminal (8am, 10am & 2pm; buy your ticket early). Apuela's few **hotels** are simple and inexpensive, the best option being *La Estancia Residencial*, above the grocery store opposite the church (☎06/648552; ❶), which doesn't have a sign but does have clean rooms and shared bath and laundry facilities.

Nangulví

NANGULVÍ, less a village than a sparse array of roadside homesteads west of Apuela, has better accommodation than its neighbour and features the appealing **Piscinas de Nangulví** (daily 6am–9pm; $0.50), set in a gorgeous location in a steep-walled valley, with four thermal pools and a larger plunge pool of diverted river water – which during the week you'll have all to yourself.

Buses from Otavalo to García Moreno pass through Nangulví; otherwise, it's an hour's **walk** if you follow the road down from Apuela and, at the second bridge, turn left and keep going till you reach Nangulví. **Accommodation** is available just before the pools at *Cabañas Rio Grande* (☎06/920171; ❸), a collection of clean, flower-draped wooden cabins with hot water and private baths set in pleasant riverside gardens, which also has a **restaurant** with meals for around $2. If these cabins are full, there are also some boxy brick cabins (❷) with baths, but no hot water, at the thermal pools.

Gualimán

In the hills above Nangulví, a spectacular three-kilometre-long **plateau**, in places barely wider than the path that crosses it, affords breathtaking views over the Intag region and hosts **GUALIMÁN**, a complex of more than forty overgrown burial mounds, including a handful of pre-Inca pyramids. Despite the plateau's apparent isolation, tucked away at its far end is a basic, friendly **hotel** (☎06/648588; $20 including full board; reserve in advance), offering simple rooms with shared baths and cold showers, and a little **museum** displaying ancient ceramics found at the site. Accommodation includes a guided tour of the plateau and the ruins and some cold restorative pools behind the hotel.

To get here by **bus**, Transportes Otavalo leaves the Otavalo terminal at 1pm and passes Apuela at around 3.30pm, arriving at the Gualimán trailhead around 45 minutes later (ask the driver to drop you off); the Co-op 6 de Julio leaves at 3pm and reaches Apuela at 5.30pm and Gualimán around 6.15pm. You can **walk** to Gualimán from Apuela (2–3hr) by following the main road down to the right from the village, then turning right at the second bridge up a steep, meandering road; near the top there's a sign directing you to a dirt path leading to the plateau. To walk there from Nangulví (3hr), head back to Apuela but continue straight when you reach the bridge, instead of turning right.

△ No hunting sign, Reserva Ecol gica Cayambe-Coca

Junín

Northwest of García Moreno, a dirt track leads up to the remote community of **JUNÍN**, the site of a dramatic 1997 demonstration in which hundreds of villagers descended on a Mitsubishi-owned mining camp, removed its equipment and burnt it to the ground – due largely to the company and government officials ignoring local concerns that contaminated mining waste and camp latrines were discharging straight into the Río Junín, the only water supply for hundreds of families. After this abrupt – but, doubtless temporary – end for local mining, the village set up its own **lodge** and twenty square-kilometre **cloudforest reserve** in the middle of one of the world's 25 "biodiversity hotspots", according to the organization Conservation International. The lodge has room for sixteen people and costs around $30 per day, including guide (reservations at Ⓔecojunin@yahoo.es, Ⓦwww .decoin.org).

The only vehicular **access** is a 90-minute trip by four-wheel drive from García Moreno, though in the wet season, the road can be impassable except to horses (4hr). For further information on the lodge contact the British group Rainforest Concern (Ⓦwww.rainforestconcern.org).

Ibarra and around

Some 125km north of Quito, the Panamericana passes around the base of Volcán Imbabura and into a broad, sunny valley to reveal **IBARRA**, known as the *ciudad blanca* (white city), its low, whitewashed and tiled buildings gleaming with stately confidence, interrupted only by the occasional church spire. Founded in 1606 to oversee the region's forced-labour textile workshops, only a few of Ibarra's original colonial buildings survived the great earthquake of 1868, from which the town eventually recovered to become the commercial and transport hub of Imbabura province. By far the largest highland city north of Quito, Ibarra's population of more than 100,000 comprises an unusual blend of *mestizos*, *indígenas* and Afro-Ecuadorians from the Chota valley and Esmeraldas province, and the city boasts an enjoyably slow pace and easy-going charm.

Ibarra is worth visiting for its good cafés and bars, friendly residents and pleasant climate, and it makes a good base for hikes into the surrounding countryside, the setting for the peaceful highland villages of **La Esperanza** and **Urcuquí**. Also worthwhile are excursions to the woodcarving town of **San Antonio de Ibarra**, picturesque **Laguna Yahuarcocha** and the excellent hot springs at **Chachimbiro**.

Among the most important local **festivals** are the **Fiesta del Retorno**, on April 28, commemorating the return of the town's citizens after the 1868 earthquake; **independence day** on July 17, marking Simón Bolívar's triumph over the Spanish at the Battle of Ibarra in 1823; and the biggest of all, the **Fiesta de los Lagos**, on the last weekend in September, celebrating the city's foundation (Sept 28) with parades and decorated floats rolling through town and motorcar races held at Laguna Yahuarcocha (see p.164).

Arrival, information and getting around

Buses from different regional destinations arrive at no fewer than seven different terminals in Ibarra (see box on p.162), all downtown west of the obelisk and within a few blocks of the major hotels. Note that a new, centralized bus terminal is planned for a site on Avenida Galindo and Avenida Espejo. Most of the hotels and restaurants are north of the obelisk but south of the three main parks of **Pedro Moncayo**, **La Merced** and **Calderón**, roughly as far as Calle Pedro Moncayo. Further south, the nineteenth-century whitewashed blocks give way to the newer but more dilapidated buildings of the **downtown** area, where the bustle intensifies around the **market** near the train station, southwest of the obelisk. For personal **safety**, stay alert at the station if you're carrying all your gear, and at night take a taxi to your hotel from downtown, which is unsafe after dark.

The well-staffed Ministerio de Turismo **tourist office**, García Moreno on Parque La Merced (Mon–Fri 8.30am–1pm & 2–5pm; ☏06/955711,

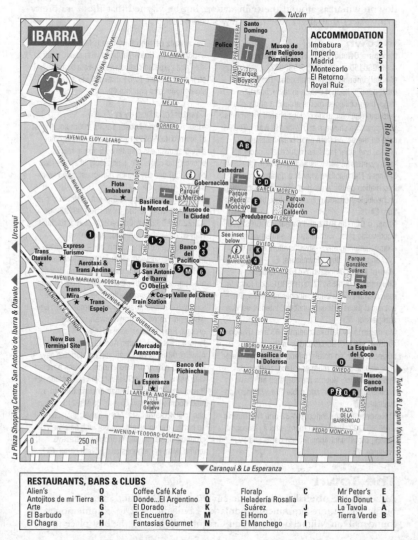

ACCOMMODATION	
Imbabura	2
Imperio	3
Madrid	5
Montecarlo	1
El Retorno	4
Royal Ruiz	6

RESTAURANTS, BARS & CLUBS

Alien's	O	Coffee Café Kafe	D	Floralp	C	Mr Peter's	E
Antojitos de mi Tierra	R	Donde...El Argentino	Q	Heladería Rosalía		Rico Donut	L
Arte	G	El Dorado	K	Suárez	J	La Tavola	A
El Barbudo	P	El Encuentro	M	El Horno	F	Tierra Verde	B
El Chagra	H	Fantasías Gourmet	N	El Manchego	I		

ⓕ958759), provides free **maps** and general **information**, and the municipal tourist office on Plaza de la Ibarreñidad (Mon–Fri 8am–noon & 2.30–5pm; ⓣ06/955051) may also be able to answer your questions.

Local buses leave from the obelisk and service the main thoroughfares such as Avenida Mariano Acosta and Oviedo, or depart from Bolívar and Mosquera and head south to Caranqui ($0.20). **Taxis** gather around the main parks, bus stations and downtown streets, and cost about $1 for a local ride.

Accommodation

Ibarra has a wide selection of good-value **hotels** and just about all of them have hot water. Several rock-bottom budget joints are located in the rougher downtown areas around the train station, but be warned that these are pretty grim places that aren't worth the few saved cents.

In town

Imbabura Oviedo 9-33 and Chica Narváez ⓣ06/950155 or 958522, ⓕ958877, ⓔhotel_imbabura@hotmail.com. The best and most popular budget choice in town, boasting large, high-ceilinged rooms around a pretty courtyard and fountain, and spotless shared bathrooms with powerful showers and 24hr hot water. The café on the patio offers good breakfasts and drinks, and other facilities include left-luggage, laundry, Internet services and tours of the Reserva El Ángel. The helpful owner is a great source of information on the area: don't miss his fascinating archeological museum and miniature bottle collection. ❷

Imperio Olmedo 8-62 and Oviedo ⓣ06/952929. Good-value place with simple, clean en-suite rooms, featuring office-style furniture and cable TVs, and a free disco downstairs. ❷

Madrid Pedro Moncayo 7-41 and Sánchez y Cifuentes ⓣ06/956177, ⓕ955301. Comfortable rooms with private baths, phones and cable TVs – but avoid those without windows. Internet service and parking. ❸

Montecarlo Av J. Rivadeneira 5-63 and Oviedo ⓣ06/958182, ⓕ958266. One of the smarter business-oriented hotels, offering an indoor heated pool, sauna, steam room and Jacuzzi (open Sat, Sun & holidays). Rooms are carpeted and have phones, private baths and cable TVs, with parking available. ❺

El Retorno Pedro Moncayo 4-32 and Rocafuerte ⓣ06/957722. Nice clean rooms and a restaurant serving meals until 4pm. Private baths and TVs available. ❷

Royal Ruiz Olmedo 9-40 and P. Moncayo ⓣ & ⓕ06/641999. Upmarket hotel with clean, comfortable and carpeted rooms with private baths, phones and cable TVs. Extras include a sauna, steam room and parking. ❹

Outside town

Ajaví Av Mariano Acosta 16-38, 200m southwest of town ⓣ06/955221, ⓕ955640. Smart hotel aimed at business clients, with ample rooms, phones and cable TVs, plus plenty of sports facilities ($3.50 per day fee for non-guests) and weekend live music. ❻

Chorlaví Panamericana Sur km 4, down a cobblestoned drive to the west ⓣ06/932222 or 932223, ⓕ932224. Converted colonial hacienda with whitewashed buildings and an old monastery – now a cocktail bar – set in palm-fringed gardens with various sports and leisure facilities, including a cockfighting arena. Rooms are comfortable with period furnishings, phones, cable TVs and private baths. The restaurant is locally renowned (main courses around $5), and weekend live music draws swarms of tour groups. Reservations advised. ❺

Palma Real Av Mariano Acosta, opposite the Ajaví ⓣ06/642416. Clean and comfortable new hotel with glitzy mirrored exterior. Rooms have private baths and cable TVs, with private parking. ❹

Rancho de Carolina Panamericana Sur km 4, next door to Chorlaví ⓣ & ⓕ06/932215, ⓔrancho_c@uio.satnet.net. Many similar facilities to its better-known neighbour, but with smaller grounds, newer buildings and less attractive rooms, with TVs, phones and private baths. ❺

The Town

Although the **obelisk** at the traffic circle at Chica Narváez and Velasco is one of the city's more prominent landmarks – built in 1952 to commemorate its founders Don Miguel de Ibarra and Cristóbal de Troya – the best place to start exploring is Ibarra's focal point, the **Parque Pedro Moncayo**, featuring a statue of the eponymous nineteenth-century journalist. The neatly clipped lawns and lofty palms of this grand square are flanked to the north by the **cathedral**, adorned with a golden altar and displaying portraits of the disciples by **Rafael Troya**, born here in 1845 and one of Ecuador's greatest artists. Along the west side of the park, the seat of the province's government, the **gobernación**, is a colonial-style building painted in white and butterscotch, which looks ravishing under evening floodlights.

A block to the west, tall flowering trees fill the quieter Parque Victor M. Peñaherrera, better known as the **Parque La Merced** after the **Basílica de La Merced**, an imposing grey-stone church crowned with a weighty statue of the Virgin and housing a towering red-and-gold altarpiece. Opposite the basilica, on the eastern side of the park, the old **infantry barracks** gives the square a distinctly Mediterranean flavour with its impressive Moorish castellations and arches, under which **street vendors** in their sunshaded stalls sell sweet Ibarra specialities like *nogadas* and *arrope de mora* (see p.160). As the planned **Museo de la Ciudad**, the building will soon showcase local traditions and culture and house temporary art exhibits.

A block south of the Parque Pedro Moncayo, the paved **Plazoleta Francisco Calderón**, more recently called the **Plaza de la Ibarreñidad**, was the city marketplace until the 1960s, but is now its cultural focus with occasional shows, concerts, dance performances and readings held on the corner stage. Along its northern side a new development – with a bar, artesanía, *heladería* and several restaurants – provides a good spot to sit in the sun and enjoy a beer, an inexpensive meal or ice cream. Nearby at Sucre and Oviedo, a lonely coconut tree, known as **La Esquina del Coco**, is a rather unlikely emblem of city pride, supposedly the reference point used by President García Moreno for the layout of the new Ibarra after the old one was destroyed in the 1868 earthquake.

Four blocks south is the modern **Basílica de la Dolorosa**, Sucre and Avenida Pérez Guerrero, which suffered earthquake damage in 1987, but despite its later reconstruction, offers little to see beyond its fresh white-and-cyan interior. Heading west down Avenida Pérez Guerrero, the teeming **Mercado Amazonas** is open daily and provides clothes and produce in the heart of downtown.

At the northern end of Bolívar, the **Museo de Arte Religioso Dominicano** (daily 8am–noon & 2–6pm; $0.50) holds a small collection of interesting eighteenth- and nineteenth-century canvases by fine Ecuadorian artists like Troya, Reyes and Salas, along with Quito School carvings, church silver, an old harmonium and assorted stuffed animals like condors. Next to the museum is the **Iglesia Santo Domingo**, which itself features some flamboyant paintings inside.

Museo Banco Central

Just off the Plaza de la Ibarreñidad, the engaging **Museo Banco Central**, Sucre and Oviedo (Mon–Fri 8.30am–1.30pm & 2.30–4.30pm; $0.50), is divided into two sections, with displays labelled in English and Spanish. The first room covers Ecuadorian archeology from prehistory to the Inca era and features some superb ceramics, including the mythological beast of the **Jama-Coaque** culture (1600 BC onward), with its penetrating eyes, tusked teeth and fish mouth. The second room concentrates on northern highlands history and presents **gold pieces** from the nearby Pimampiro area, including a funeral mask, and a grisly diorama of the bloody war between the Incas and the

Caranqui at Laguna Yahuarcocha (see p.164). On the other side of the court-yard is a **library** and small bookshop selling subsidized books in Spanish.

Caranqui

Two kilometres south of the centre along Bolívar (which becomes Av Atahualpa), the **Museo Atahualpa de Caranqui**, Atahualpa and Cory Cory, is located at Plaza Atahualpa in the barrio of **Caranqui**, for which **buses** leave from outside the Banco de Pichincha, on Bolívar and Mosquera in Ibarra. Distinguished by a replica of an Inca pyramid of the sun, the museum is quite eye-catching, but is currently closed and shows no signs of reopening any time soon.

Thought to be the birthplace of Atahualpa, the last king of the Incas, the sur-rounding area is dotted with the remains of ancient temples, both of the Incas and their Cara predecessors, along with the remnants of an old Inca **fortress wall**, southeast of the museum on Calle La Huaca.

On Sundays, there's a small **craftwork market** on Plaza Atahualpa, specializ-ing in embroidered shirts and blouses and featuring many of the same tradition-al, flowery designs as in the Otavalo region. About a block to the west are the twin yellow-and-green spires of the **Iglesia Señor del Amor**, which features such novelties as spray-painted scenes from the life of Christ and a terrifying **mural** of Hell depicting a blasphemer with his tongue torn out by a snake, and an insanely envious man biting into the scalp of another lost soul. In the transept, an unusual artificial **cave-shrine** stretches up to the roof with a painted back-drop of a local landscape and an altarpiece illuminated by garish neon lights. The church may have been built on the site of a **Cara palace**, and recent excavations have uncovered a network of subterranean tunnels that might have been employed as wartime defences, though are presently only open to researchers.

The tourist train

Once extending to San Lorenzo down on the coast (see p.367), Ibarra's rail-way now runs from the train station only as far as Primer Paso, a 45-kilome-tre journey serviced by a **tourist train** known as an *autoferro*, actually a con-verted bus on rails (1hr 40min trip; Mon–Fri 7am, Sat–Sun 8am; $3.80 one-way, $7.60 return; ticket office daily 7am–noon & 2–6.30pm, ☎06/950390). The train only departs if there are at least fifteen passengers or $50 worth of ticket sales – though you can always pay the difference if there aren't enough people. The ride itself, though truncated, is still a fun experience, and you can sit on the roof while the train skirts vertiginous drops, clatters over the rick-ety 120-metre **Ambi bridge**, and disappears into the gloom of a dozen tun-nels, one with its own waterfall. At the end of the route, the train pulls in at the *Tulquizán* hostería (☎06/641989; ❸), where you can get lunch, swim in the pool for a few dollars, and stay in rustic cabins. From here you can take a **bus** back to Ibarra (30min) or along the greatly improved highway to San Lorenzo (3hr).

Eating, drinking and nightlife

Most of Ibarra's **restaurants** are south of the main squares up to Calle Velasco, though there are countless budget options where you can get perfectly good *almuerzos* and *meriendas* for a dollar or two, with other cheap meals available from the cluster of **chifas** along Olmedo between Flores and Velasco, serving Chinese food at the same low prices and offering takeaways as well. For **sweets and snacks**, the stalls around the Museo de la Ciudad (see p.159) sell *nogadas* – nougat-style treats made from sugar, milk, egg whites and walnuts, sometimes flavoured with cinnamon, aniseed or vanilla – and *arrope de mora*, a sticky blackberry syrup, usually diluted with water or spirits. Ibarra's other speciality is its wonderfully smooth and flavoursome **helados de paila**, a sorbet prepared in great copper pans (*pailas*) kept cool on a bed of straw and salted ice, into which fruit, sugar and water are stirred – found at a number of excellent *heladerías* throughout town.

Restaurants

El Alpargate in the eponymous barrio east of town (ask for directions or get a taxi). Good and inexpensive *platos típicos*, such as *empanadas* and *mote* (boiled maize). Very popular with locals, and often full at weekends.

Antojitos de mi Tierra Plaza de la Ibarreñidad. Excellent, friendly little place specializing in Ecuadorian dishes, such as delicious *humitas*, *bonitísimas* and *quimbolitos*, which make the perfect accompaniment to a coffee served al fresco. Good set-lunches for about $2. Daily noon to 10pm.

Los Ceviches de la Rumiñahui La Plaza Shopping Centre, Av Mariana Acosta. Good, clean and efficient place serving seafood and *ceviche* for $2–3. Popular meeting place for Ibarreños doing their weekend shopping.

El Chagra Olmedo 7-48 and Flores. Intimate eatery doling out inexpensive *platos típicos* and trout under the not-so-romantic glow of a large-screen TV.

Donde...El Argentino Plaza de la Ibarreñidad. Friendly Argentinian steak and grill house with outdoor seating, offering affordable meals that are best devoured with a jar of Argentinian wine ($5). Closed Mon.

El Dorado Oviedo 5-47 and Rocafuerte. Smart restaurant in the eponymous hotel, staffed by waiters in bow ties and offering good *platos típicos* such as *carne colorada*, *empanadas*, *bonitísimas* and chicken in cider, for $4–6 per main course.

Fantasías Gourmet Bolívar 10-90 and Av Pérez Guerrero. Swanky seafood restaurant with pretensions of being Ibarra's classiest. Moderately priced *ceviche* and oysters.

El Horno Rocafuerte and Flores. Excellent pizzas (from $2.50) cooked in a big clay oven that dominates the restaurant. Vegetarian options and wine available. Tues–Sun 6pm–midnight.

El Manchego Oviedo and Chica Narváez. Ecuadorean food with sizeable trout dishes for $3, in a restaurant where wagon wheels and a stuffed bull's head decorate the walls. Closes Mon–Sat 4pm & all Sun.

Mr Peter's Sucre and García Moreno. Wide-ranging, inexpensive but mostly meat-based menu of traditional dishes, tacos and Italian cuisine. A popular Ibarra institution often buzzing during weekday lunchtimes, offering good *almuerzos* for $1.50 ($3 at weekends).

La Távola Sucre 3-37 and Grijalva. Attractively decorated pizzeria just off the courtyard of *Tierra Verde*, offering four sizes of pizza in the usual flavours at reasonable prices. Live music two Fridays per month. Another branch on the Plaza de la Ibarreñidad. Opens 4pm.

Tierra Verde Sucre 3-37. Inexpensive *ceviches* and *encocados* at this typical coastal-seafood restaurant set in a pleasant courtyard. Daily 8.30am–4pm.

Cafés

Arte Salinas 5-43 and Oviedo. Artist-owned café-cum-art gallery with a classy wooden interior and outside sculpture garden. Intellectual flourishes abound, from the mock triptych menu to the Frida Kahlo cocktail. Mon–Sat from 4pm. Concerts Fri or Sat.

Coffee Café Kafe G. Moreno 4-04 and Rocafuerte. Coffee bar with a cool, fresh interior lit by incandescent and ultraviolet lights, serving great coffee and home-made cocktails like the Rojo de Yahuarcocha. Mon–Thurs 4–10pm, Fri 4pm–midnight, Sat 6pm–midnight.

Floralp García Moreno 2-42 and Rocafuerte. Smart Swiss-owned operation that runs its own dairy in Caranqui and offers fantastic cheeses, yogurts, milkshakes and ice creams – plus great fondue and raclette ($3.50–5). A little more expensive than other cafés, but well worth it. Mon–Sat 8am–10pm, Sun 3–9pm.

Heladería Rosalía Suárez Oviedo and Olmedo. The oldest and most renowned place to devour tasty *helados de paila* ice creams, and also watch them being made.

Rico Donut Chica Narváez 8-41 and Pedro Moncayo. Good bakery serving coffee and donuts. Also at Av Pérez Guerrero and Sánchez y Cifuentes.

Clubs and bars

The presence of a large university on the outskirts of Ibarra means that at weekends hundreds of students are out on the prowl, looking for noisy fun at the town's various **bars** and **discos**. The younger crowd often ensures a fizzing atmosphere, even if the town's size makes the action feel more dispersed than in, say, Otavalo.

Alien's Oviedo and Sucre. Popular with students for its pumping techno and Latin dance music, with a clientele prone to dancing on the bar and tables. Pool tables and free table football entertain the less footloose. Thurs–Sat 9pm–2am; $1.50 cover, including one drink.

El Barbudo on Plaza de la Ibarreñidad, Pedro Moncayo and Sucre. Easy-going bar with comfortable seating, gentle lighting and pictures of world pop-culture greats upstairs, and beer on tap downstairs. Also a good chillout zone by day, with outside chairs and tables. Wed–Sat 4pm–late, Sun 10am–4pm.

El Encuentro Olmedo 9-59 and Velasco. Friendly and popular bar for students and Ibarreños alike, with a mellow atmosphere and occasional live music. Daily 5pm–2am.

Listings

Banks and exchange Banco del Austro, Colón and Bolívar, has a Visa ATM and offers cash advances; Banco del Pacífico, P. Moncayo and Olmedo, changes up to $200 Amex traveller's cheques ($5 commission) and has a MasterCard ATM; Banco del Pichincha, Mosquera and Bolívar, changes traveller's cheques and has an ATM for Visa, MasterCard and Diners Club; Produbanco, Sucre and Flores, has a MasterCard ATM.

Internet facilities Click Net, Oviedo 11-80 and Rivadeneira, good service, netphone, $1 per hour; Compu Store, Sucre 6-40, netphone, closes Sun 1pm; Cr@zy-ciber.net, $1 per hour, closed Sun; Ibanet, Oviedo and Olmedo, netphone, $1 per hour; Ingedata, Grijalva and Bolívar, $1 per hour, closed Sun; Internet, Sucre and Oviedo, netphone.

Bus terminals and operators in Ibarra

Aerotaxi runs the most frequent **buses** to Quito, though Expreso Turismo is also good, and Transportes Otavalo has the most efficient services to Otavalo. A new bus terminal housing all the various companies is planned for a site southeast of the train station, on Avenida Galindo and Espejo. Even so, the old **bus station** addresses are listed below.

Terminal location	Operators
Flores and Luis C. Borja	Flota Imbabura, for Quito, Guayaquil, Cuenca, Manta and Tulcán.
Luis C. Borja and Av Mariano Acosta	Aerotaxi, for Quito, Guayaquil and Esmeraldas. Flota Anteña, for Atuntaqui and Chaltura. Transportes Andina, for Quito and Santo Domingo.
Pedro Moncayo and Flores	Co-op Buenos Aires, for Chachimbiro. Expreso Turismo, for Quito and Tulcán. Transportes Oriental, for Pimampiro, Chota and Salinas. Transportes Urcuquí, for Urcuquí.
Av F.V. Galindo and Mariano Acosta	Transportes Otavalo, for Otavalo and Quito.
Av Espejo and Velasco	Co-op Valle del Chota, for Chota and San Lorenzo. Transportes Cotacachi, for Cotacachi and Otavalo. Transportes Los Lagos, for Otavalo, San Pablo and Quito.
Av Guerrero (by the petrol station)	Transportes Espejo, for San Lorenzo and El Ángel. Transportes Mira, for Mira.
R. Larrea Andrade, on Parque Grijalva	Transportes La Esperanza, for La Esperanza and Zuleta. Transportes Olmedo, for Olmedo.

Laundry Lavafacil, Sucre and Grijalva.
Medical services Instituto Médico de Especialidades, Jacinto Egas 1-83 and T. Gómez (℡06/955612 or 956043), is the best medical facility in town, with 24hr emergency service; Clínica Médica del Norte, Oviedo and Olmedo (℡06/955099), has 24hr emergency service; and the Hospital San Vicente de Paúl, Vargas Torres 11-56 (℡06/957272), is also open 24hr.
Police and immigration Av J. Roldos and Av V.M. Peñaherrera, at the north end of town ℡06/950444.

Post office Main office at Salinas and Oviedo; a more centrally located sub-office at Parque P. Moncayo, Flores 6-31.
Spanish classes Blanca Vaca Rosero, Condominio El Recreo, Casa 5 (℡06/641408), is recommended.
Telephone Andinatel, Sucre and García Moreno. Daily 8am–10pm.
Tour agencies Metropolitan Touring, Flores and Sucre, contact in Quito on ℡02/2464780; Recotur, Olmedo 5-79 and García Moreno ℡06/957795.

San Antonio de Ibarra

Just off the Panamericana, 6km west of Ibarra, **SAN ANTONIO DE IBAR-RA** is not much more than a handful of streets and a little square, but has nevertheless chiselled its way to fame as a major centre for **woodcarving**, where the shops and galleries are crammed with a huge array of subjects and styles mostly carved in cedar, from religious imagery to chess sets to life-size carvings of Don Quixote. San Antonio's best-known artist is **Luís Potosí**, whose gallery on the main square has several rooms, and features many sculptures of nude mothers nursing their newborns. Most of the town's **showrooms** are located on the main square and Avenida 27 de Noviembre, which leads down from the square towards the Panamericana. **Prices** range from $1500 for large pieces down to $1 for a key ring.

Buses to San Antonio leave the obelisk in Ibarra every twenty minutes (10min), though you can also **walk** (1hr 30min–2hr) from Ibarra along an older road that bypasses the busy Panamericana. Its entrance isn't well marked, so ask for directions at La Plaza Shopping Centre, close by on Avenida Mariano Acosta.

La Esperanza and around

Along the road from Caranqui at the foot of Volcán Imbabura, **LA ESPER-ANZA** is a tranquil village where Simón Bolívar planned the defeat of General Agualongo and his Spanish forces holding Ibarra, 7km to the north. On July 17, 1823, Bolívar's troops swept down from this hillside into Ibarra, winning its independence by trapping the Spanish with a pincer movement. Forty-five years later, when it was flattened by the 1868 earthquake, Ibarra again looked to La Esperanza for assistance, its survivors taking refuge here for four years while their city was rebuilt. A century on, La Esperanza briefly became a hippie enclave as its soil nurtured fields of magic mushrooms, but these days most visitors come for the restful atmosphere and the excellent mountain **walks** nearby.

There's a discreet but flourishing **artesanía** scene in the village, seen in several houses a few hundred metres down the road from La Esperanza's two hotels. Eugenio Obando's **leather** workshop (℡06/641998) produces high-quality custom saddles, bags, boots, chaps and hats. A little further on are workshops where beautiful marquetry (*taracea*) is inlaid onto guitars, and exquisite embroidery (*bordado*), as seen on the blouses of Otavaleña *indígenas*, is produced for sale at the Otavalo market. For fine embroidered tablecloths (*manteles*) and napkins, Guadalupe (Lupita) Gómez de Arroyo (℡06/641951) will stitch custom designs.

Practicalities

Buses to La Esperanza (every 20min, 30min trip; last bus 7.30pm) leave Ibarra from the Parque Grijalva, a few blocks south of the obelisk. Tell the driver you want a **hotel**, otherwise you'll be taken to the end of the village about fifteen minutes away from them. *Casa Aída* (⊕06/642020; ❷) is the best, with simple and pleasant rooms, a two-floor thatched cabin with connecting ladder, and clean shared bathrooms and hot showers. The **restaurant** offers meat and vegetarian dishes and a good breakfast, and can make sandwiches for a packed lunch. A few doors further down the street, *Hospedaje María* (⊕06/641973; ❶) is more basic, where the clean rooms have micro-thin walls and only one shared bath (with hot water), though a pretty garden can be found out back.

Volcán Imbabura and Cubilche

La Esperanza makes an excellent base for climbing **Volcán Imbabura** and **Cubilche** to the west, and trails for both begin to the right by the bridge up from the *Casa Aída* hostel. The IGM San Pablo del Lago **map** (1:50,000 scale) is a good resource, but both of the town's *hostales* provide information as well, and can also provide a **guide** ($7–10 per day). Hiking to the summit of Volcán Imbabura (4621m) is straightforward, except for some loose rock at the top, and takes about ten hours round trip. Get an early start and don't forget food, water and warm clothing. Other options include taking a **camioneta** up as far as the water tank, about three hours' walk from the summit (around $5, ask at *Casa Aída*; see above), or just spending a day walking through the pastureland around the mountain's base.

Compared to Imbabura, the summit of **Cubilche** (3826m) is an easier proposition (3hr trip), offering great views of the lake and Ibarra. Indeed, on the mountain's lower slope, at the hamlet of **El Abra**, Bolívar surveyed the Spanish enemy in preparation for his successful attack.

Laguna Yahuarcocha

On the northern outskirts of Ibarra and flanked to the east by misty hills, **LAGUNA YAHUARCOCHA** ("lake of blood" in Quichua) was the site of the decisive 1495 defeat of the indigenous Cara people. Led by **Huayna Capac**, the Inca victory marked the gory climax of a seventeen-year campaign, ending in the massacre of twenty to fifty thousand Cara, whose bleeding bodies turned the waters crimson. The survivors, however, became so respected for their fighting skills that Inca royalty subsequently employed them as bodyguards in Cusco. Nowadays, herons swoop in and out of the dense reedbanks here, while *campesinos* gather bundles of the *totora* reeds and dry them on the shore to make mats – a potentially picturesque setting marred by the strangling tarmac of a race track, the venue for competitions during Ibarra's September fiestas.

To visit, take a **bus** (every 15min; 10min) in Ibarra from the obelisk, or on Oviedo at the corner of Sánchez y Cifuentes, or simply **walk** there (1–2hr) by one of two routes: the busier path heads east down Oviedo, crossing the bridge and continuing along the Panamericana to the lake, while the far more pleasant trail to the hilltop *mirador*, with its excellent **views** of the lake and Ibarra, is reached by turning right after the bridge and heading east towards the Universidad Católica. At the end of the road is a dirt path leading left (north) uphill to the viewpoint, after which you can descend to the lake on the other side.

Urcuquí

URCUQUÍ, 22km by winding road northwest of Ibarra, is little more than a pretty rural village with a pleasant tree-filled square, brilliant-white church and simple hotel. Few people stop here, save hikers on a four-day trek to the **Piñán lakes** around Yana Urcu de Piñán mountain (4535m), an outing best arranged through a Quito-based operator (see p.112). **Buses** to Urcuquí (every 30min, 30min trip) leave Ibarra from the terminal on Pedro Moncayo and Flores.

Chachimbiro

Sixteen bumpy kilometres beyond Urcuquí, along a flower-lined cobbled road that weaves through charming countryside, **CHACHIMBIRO** lies in a tight valley in the foothills of Yana Urcu de Piñán, and is most notable for its popular **thermal springs** (Mon–Thurs 7am–5pm & 6–8pm, Fri–Sun 6am–10pm; $1–2.50), a selection of hot mineral baths and swimming pools managed by the Fundación Cordillera, which seeks to foster sustainable development in the area. The spa facilities include one scorching pool (55°C), and the volcanic waters are rich in sulphur, chlorides, iron, copper and manganese – widely believed to provide relief from neuralgia, arthritis and rheumatism. Extras include self-guided nature trails, organic gardens and environmental lectures and education.

Practicalities

From the terminal on Pedro Moncayo and Flores in Ibarra, one daily **bus** goes to Chachimbiro (leaves 7.30am, returns 12.15pm; 1hr 15min trip; $1; arrive early on weekends). You can also book a **tour** with the Fundación Cordillera in Otavalo (see box, p.147) and take their *ranchera* to the site ($5 return trip). Comfortable **rooms** and cabins are available inside the spa complex (❸–❹), or you can rent a mattress and sleeping bag in *La Choza* ("the hut") for $5 at the site. The downmarket *Chachimbiro* hostel, at the entrance (no phone; ❶), has musty rooms that look like they haven't seen a guest in a while, with optional private baths, while the pricier *San Francisco* hostería, on the via Chachimbiro km 19 (☎06/934161; ❺), is an attractive, isolated hacienda with its own heated pool, set amid rolling countryside.

From Ibarra to the coast

Less than a decade ago, the train to San Lorenzo from Ibarra was the only way to get to the remote northern coast without spending days hacking through thick forests with a machete and getting very sore feet. Today, a newly paved **road** speeds from Ibarra down the parched Chota valley, slicing through crumbling cliffs prone to falling rocks, and descends into the warmer, moister climes of the green coastal lowlands. As Ecuador's fastest road between the highlands and the Pacific (3hr 30min), the new highway, in combination with El Niño damage in the late 1990s, largely put an end to the train service, once an epic eight-hour journey in which rockfalls, farm animals, fallen trees and landslides constantly delayed progress, and thrill-seeking tourists sat on the roof dodging low-slung branches. What remains now is a truncated 45-kilometre **tourist service** from Ibarra to Primer Paso in an old bus bolted onto a set of bogeys (see p.160 for details). It's still worth the ride, even if it is just a fraction of the original 200-kilometre journey.

Two **bus** companies in Ibarra service the highway to San Lorenzo: Transportes Espejo (6 daily; $4) and Co-op Valle del Chota (3 daily; $4), which also runs four buses that pass El Limonal and Guallupe and continue on to **Lita** (2 hr; $1.85), roughly the halfway point, where you'll need to show your passport at a **police checkpoint**. For details of bus departure points, see box on p.162.

El Limonal

Some 39km beyond the junction at Salinas, where the San Lorenzo road branches from the Panamericana, the settlement of **EL LIMONAL** lies east of the Río Guallupe and Guallupe sits to the river's west, but on some maps both are marked as **La Carolina** – which is actually the name of the administrative district.

At 900m the climate is warm enough for fruit farming, and local *serranos* fleeing the highland chill drop in for comfortable **accommodation** at places like the hosterías *El Limonal* (☎06/956523; ❸), with its swimming pool, and *Marthy Zu* (☎06/906606; ❸), which also has a pool, but is slightly less appealing. El Limonal is also the location of a couple of **ecotourism** ventures, such as the *Finca Forestal Bospas*, 800m uphill from the main square (no phone, ℮bospas@gardener.com, ⓦwww.ecuativer.com/bospas; $8, including breakfast), an organic fruit farm with simple rooms commanding splendid views over the valley. The hospitable Belgian environmentalist owner leads treks and horse rides in the area ($10 per day, including lunch), and his Ecuadorian wife gives salsa lessons. **Volunteers** are welcome to work on the farm, for a minimum of one month ($150 contribution).

Guallupe and the Cerro Golondrinas Cloudforest Reserve

Guallupe, a sleepy village downhill from El Limonal, is the access point for the **Cerro Golondrinas Cloudforest Reserve** 15km to the northeast (ⓦwww.ecuadorexplorer.com/golondrinas), a 14-square-kilometre reserve around Cerro Golondrinas peak (3120m) that makes a fine spot for birdwatching, with more than two hundred recorded species, including tanagers, toucans, hummingbirds and even condors.

Closer views of the local flora and fauna are available at two **lodges** at different elevations inside the reserve (both $25 per person), or another lodge at 3000m in the páramo, operated by the community of Morán ($10, plus $2 access fee), or at the hostel in Guallupe (☎06/648679; $15). One highlight is the four-day **trek** from El Ángel in the highlands (see opposite), down from the páramo through the Golondrinas cloudforests to the village ($220–250 per person, depending on group size). For information about visiting the reserve and **volunteering** ($280 per month contribution), contact *La Casa de Eliza*, in Quito at Avenida Isabel La Católica 1559 (☎02/226602, ℮manteca@uio.satnet.net). Note, however, that the ownership and administration of the reserve are under legal dispute; contact the *Finca Forestal Bospas* (see above) for more details.

The old road to Colombia

From Laguna Yahuarcocha, the Panamericana follows the Río Ambi on the eastern edge of the fertile El Olivo plain, and at the Río Chota the highway swings sharply east and slowly climbs up its dry and dusty valley. The road forks 33km from Ibarra at the village of **Mascarilla**, where there is a **checkpoint** (have your passport ready). To the left is the **old road** to Colombia via **Mira**, which is paved as far as **El Ángel**, but for the final 48km to Tulcán is in poor shape and rarely used; to the right, the busy Panamericana carries buses and cars past Chota, Bolívar, La Paz and San Gabriel up to Tulcán and the Colombian border.

Mira

The old road climbs sharply out of the dusty Chota valley after Mascarilla, and then up the fifteen-kilometre ascent to **MIRA**, a hillside town whose striking views of the countryside have earned it the title "balcony of the Andes" – according to its signposts, at least. The town is also known for its excellent **woollen goods**, sold both in Otavalo and locally at places like **Artesanías Ana Guerrero**, opposite the bus stop on the main road, with its colourful jumpers and ponchos, and **Co-operativa Artesanía Mira**, further up the hill, with similar woollens for sale.

Mira is exceedingly quiet, and even the Sunday produce **market** is pretty low-key. Its **fiestas**, however, are much more exciting, when fireworks shoot off the hillside and buckets of *tardón* – a delicious mixture of sugar, lemon, orange and *naranjilla* juice fortified with a liberal dose of *aguardiente* – help to lubricate the shenanigans. The most important event is the **Fiesta de la Virgen de la Caridad**, on February 2 with festivities over the weekend, but the **cantonization** of Mira in mid-August comes a close second.

Practicalities

Buses run hourly from Ibarra to Mira until 6pm (1hr), and the last returning bus departs at 3pm; buses leave hourly from Mira to Tulcán until 9pm (2hr). The only **place to stay** is *Residencial Mira*, left off the main square at González Suárez 8-01 and Chonta Huasi (⊕06/280228; ❷), with simple rooms and a shared electric shower. The owner will cook for you for a little extra, a useful service considering the dearth of local restaurants, though you can always try the *Bar Restaurant*, by the obelisk on the Panamericana.

El Ángel and around

From Mira the road continues to climb for the next 25km until at 3000m it reaches **EL ÁNGEL**, a friendly highland town whose most famous resident was topiarist **José Franco Guerrero**, responsible for the fantastic gardens in Tulcán (see p.175) and the pleasant **Parque Libertad**, the sketchpad for his more advanced later work, which is still maintained seventy years after being snipped into shape.

Peaceful for most of the week, El Ángel gets busy during its **Monday market**, held on the streets running downhill from the Parque Libertad, largely selling clothes, produce and fresh fish caught from the nearby mountain lakes. Down from Parque Libertad on Calle Bolívar, the **public swimming pool** was built in the 1930s in irresistible Italian style, surrounded by terracotta-and-cream balustrades and little red-brick changing rooms. In recent years it has been shut, but in case it reopens, don't expect Mediterranean temperatures, as it's fed by icy páramo streams.

Beyond visiting the market, most people use the town as a base for seeing the nearby Reserva Ecológica El Ángel (see p.168) further north, though the pleasant **La Calera hot springs** (daily 7am–6pm; $0.50) are 11km southwest of town, at the bottom of a winding cobbled road in the crook of a forested valley. The site is pretty well deserted during the week, when you'll have its naturally heated pool and cooler, larger swimming pool all to yourself – though the latter is emptied three times a week for cleaning (Mon, Wed & Fri after 1pm). At weekends, **jeeps** leave for the springs when full from the Parque Libertad ($1), but at other times you'll have to rent a **camioneta** (25min; $5 one-way, $8 return).

Practicalities

Transportes Espejo **buses** from Quito (15 daily, 4hr) travel via Mira (45min) and Ibarra (1hr 30min) to the Parque Libertad. When leaving El Ángel, Transportes Mira buses depart from the larger Parque Calderón in front of the church, and go hourly to Mira, Ibarra and Tulcán (last bus to Tulcán at 1.30pm; 1hr 15min). **Taxis** ply the attractive route between El Ángel and Bolívar on the Panamericana, usually leaving when full from around the Parque Libertad. The **phone office** is on the Parque Calderón, the **post office** is on Grijalva between the two parks, and **Internet** facilities are available at World Computer, on Bolívar north of the Parque Libertad.

El Ángel has only a few **places to stay**, the best of which is the *El Ángel* hostería, Panamericana Norte and Av Espejo 1302, by the roundabout on the south edge of town, a ten-minute downhill walk from the centre (T & F06/977584; ❺, including breakfast), which has clean, comfortable rooms with baths and hot water. The hotel offers one- or two-day **tours** of the region and the reserve by car, on foot or on horseback (around $10 a day), as well as guided hikes up Volcán Chiles ($15), and can arrange trips to the community-run cabañas in the páramo at Morán. The *Los Faroles* hostel, on the corner of Parque Libertad (T06/977144; ❷), has a few simple rooms in a family home, mostly with bunks and a shared shower, plus a communal sitting room. The hostel has a **restaurant** that serves good, inexpensive fish and chicken dishes, and the town's other eateries, as well as two **bakeries** at the corners of the parks, are mostly on José Grijalva and serve up much the same unsurprising fare.

Reserva Ecológica El Ángel

Established in 1992, the **Reserva Ecológica El Ángel**, 15km north of the town of El Ángel ($10), is home to some of Ecuador's most interesting páramo, ranging in altitude from 3644m to 4768m, and is most famous for its **fraile-jones**, peculiar furry-leaved plants endemic to the northern Andes, which grow on dark stems up to seven metres in height and cover 85 percent of the reserve's 160 square kilometres. The reserve's **wildlife** includes foxes, deer and condors, as the páramo is about the closest thing you'll find to moorlands in Ecuador, a windblown wilderness of rolling grassland hills and several lakes and streams teeming with rainbow trout – **fishing** is allowed, with permission from the Ministerio del Ambiente office in El Ángel town.

The year-round average **temperature** is 11°C, and the spongy soil and high levels of rainfall (1500mm per year) help supply water for most of the province, but the reserve is too sodden for much human habitation. In a few of its sheltered pockets, montane forest supplants the grasses, and dense thickets of trees such as the **polylepis** – draped with mosses, orchids and bromeliads – make the best places to spot hummingbirds and armadillos.

The most heavily visited parts of the reserve are predictably the most accessible. At the southwest edge, the **Cañón El Colorado** is a popular spot for trout fishing, while at the southeast corner, the **Lagunas El Voladero** are set in a glacial valley dotted with tall *frailejones*, with three glittering lakes that offer decent angling. Legend has it that rather than surrender to the Spanish invaders, an old Carchi chieftain fled to the lakes before diving into the crystal waters, disappearing forever.

Arrival and transport

There are three **routes** to the reserve, the **first** of which follows the old road from El Ángel to Tulcán for 15km until reaching the parking space at the edge of the reserve. From the guard post, a well-defined one-kilometre trail leads to the Lagunas El Voladero, while another trail leads from El Voladero north to Laguna de Potrerillos, a two-hour walk away. Both El Voladero and Potrerillos are popular fishing spots, well stocked with trout. The **second route** heads northwest from El Ángel, through the villages of La Libertad and Jesús del Gran Poder, to the reserve guard post at El Salado, from which a dirt road leads up past the Cañón El Colorado to a viewpoint on Cerro Socabones. The **third route** runs along the road heading west out of Tufiño (see p.177) to Maldonado, bordering the northern part of the reserve, from which you can see the green waters of the Lagunas Verdes. Although a number of **trails** run across the reserve, the only one clearly marked is to the Voladero lakes from the main road, so if you plan on hiking, take the IGM **maps** for Tufiño and La Carolina (1:50,000 scale).

From the town of El Ángel, you can take a **camioneta** or **taxi** to the reserve ($12 one-way, $25–30 for full day), or get a ride on the **milk truck** that leaves the Parque Libertad around 8am for the hamlet of Morán, beyond the Cerro Socabones, and returns around 10–11am. You can reach Fernando Calderón, the driver, at ☎06/977274, or check for details with locals.

Information and accommodation

The *El Ángel* hostería offers **tours** into the reserve ($10 per day; see opposite), and a few **places to stay** have recently opened within it, offering an up-close view of the stunning windswept scenery – and penetrating chill. One of them, *Paz y Montaña* hostería, 22km from El Ángel and a few kilometres beyond the El Salado checkpoint ($50 per person, including board and transport from Quito), has simple but comfortable rooms next to a trout farm, offering hikes and horse rides in the reserve from $10. For more information, contact the Mundo Valle tour agency in Quito, Av Colón 13-10 and Amazonas (☎02/2542884 or 09/9073758).

The Ministerio del Ambiente office in El Ángel, Salinas and Esmeraldas, second floor of the Sindicato de Choferes building (☎06/977597), can provide **information** about visiting the reserve and put you in touch with local **guides** ($10–15 per day).

The Chota valley to Tulcán

Where the old road to Colombia heads north at Mascarilla, the busy Panamericana continues east, beginning its climb up the **Chota valley**. Soon after, the hills become barren, turkey vultures circle in the sky, sand blows across the road driven by the warm winds, and the only greenery lines the banks of the Río Chota. As the one part of the Ecuadorian highlands with a significant black population, descendants from slaves brought to work on Spanish plantations, the area's biggest settlement is the dusty, ramshackle town of **Chota**, sitting on the banks of the Río Chota. Growing fruit in the fertile river margins, the community has developed a unique culture, an exotic mix of African and Andean traditions best experienced at a cultural performance (check the local press or ask at the tourist office in Ibarra). Their distinctive **Bomba music**, for one, features percussion, guitars and impromptu instruments, such as those made from leaves, while local **dances** involve such feats as balancing a bottle on the head, thought to represent the traditional African way of carrying objects. The valley is also home to many of Ecuador's best professional footballers, including several of the World Cup team, despite a lack of grass pitches or stadiums.

A few kilometres further on, the Panamericana straightens out as it climbs the warm and dry **Quebrada de Ambuquí** (Ambuquí Gorge), where local **resort-hotels** draw weekend crowds of affluent Colombians and Ecuadorians. The best of these is the *Oasis*, at km 39 (T & F 06/941200 or 941192; $36 per person Fri–Sun, $30 Mon–Thurs), which hosts a live Afro-Ecuadorian music show at weekends and features "mini cabañas" set around three pools, one with a wave machine and a large double-helix waterslide (weekends only).

Pimampiro and around

Several kilometres away, **El Juncal** is a small settlement of around two thousand people, famed for its prodigious number of professional footballers, probably more per capita than any other place in the world. From here a turn-off southeast leads from the Panamericana to the dusty hillside town of **PIMAMPIRO**, where you're greeted by a plaza decorated by trees, a statue of country folk trading tomatoes, and a plain white church. A five-minute walk up to the top of the hill, a larger paved square is the departure and arrival point for **buses** and **camionetas**.

Located 20km north of the Reserva Cayambe-Coca (see p.137), Pimampiro is best used as a base for treks to the páramo and cloudforests to the south, with a notable two-day **hike** heading to the **Laguna de Puruhanta**, a trout lake in the páramo best accessed via the village of Mariano Acosta (daily camionetas from Pimampiro; 1hr; $0.50). The lake is a six-to-seven-hour walk from the settlement, and the relevant IGM **maps** are those for Mariano Acosta and Nevado Cayambe (1:50,000 scale); you can also ask for a **guide** ($10–15 per day) at the basic, nameless **pensión** at Olmedo and Flores (no phone; ❶). Near the pension, several **restaurants** like *El Florastero* on Flores offer decent inexpensive fare, while *El Vecino* on Espejo has good fried chicken. **Buses** to Pimampiro (every 15min; 1hr 15min) leave from Ibarra's terminal on P. Moncayo and Flores.

Bolívar

Northeast of El Juncal, the Panamericana continues its climb up to Tulcán and the Colombian border, emerging from the sandy Ambuquí Gorge and crossing the Río Chota into Carchi province, where the familiar sierra landscape of rugged green hills and mosaic-like tilled fields returns. Just off the main road, 20km north of El Juncal, **BOLÍVAR** is a little hillside town with attractive pastoral views, where painted tubs of flowers sit on the roadside, and the pastel houses are painted peach and sky blue, with pink doors and window frames.

Aside from the nearby Gruta de La Paz, there's not much to do here, though the road running northwest from Bolívar to El Ángel gives astounding views on clear days all the way to snow-topped Volcán Cayambe, almost 60km distant, dwarfing the green hilltops around it. The town's only **accommodation** is *Residencial Santa Elena*, on Julio Andrade, just off the plaza (T 06/287212; ❶), whose rooms have shared baths and electric showers. The best **restaurant**, *Los Sauces*, on the Panamericana where the buses stop at the turn-off to town, has agreeable fresh produce, great yogurt drinks and main courses for $2–3. During the day, **taxis** wait at this junction and leave when full.

Gruta de La Paz

The next stop just off the Panamericana, 6km north of Bolívar, is **La Paz**, a well-tended village spruced up with colourful flowerbeds, from where a cobblestoned road leads down into a gorge threaded with high waterfalls to the major shrine of **GRUTA DE LA PAZ**. This important pilgrimage centre has spawned its own "village", with monastery and chapel, sizeable basilica, telephone office, store peddling religious souvenirs, volleyball court and several restaurants and hotels – all perched on the cliff above the grotto.

The **grotto** itself is so big that its true size isn't clear until you're a few steps into it, shielded from the sunlight. At about 40m deep, there's even room for another small **chapel**, this one dedicated to La Virgen de La Paz. The grotto's dank interior is impressive but not exactly heavenly, with hundreds of slimy stalactites crowding the ceiling and bats flitting around its darkest recesses. Water from the heart of the grotto is piped down to **bathing pools** about 100m away (Tues–Sun; $0.50, showers $0.40; tickets from Almacen Santa Clara shop by the convent), which are actually rather tepid, though the setting is still quite picturesque, with a waterfall cascading down the high valley wall above.

Practicalities

The grotto gets very crowded at weekends and religious holidays and on the first weekend of July, during the **festival** for the Virgen de La Paz. At weekends, **jeeps** (*patroles*) ferry visitors to the grotto from the main squares in Bolívar and San Gabriel ($0.50), and on Saturdays a **bus** leaves the cathedral in Tulcán at 8am, returning about 3pm ($2 each way). During the week the grotto is much quieter and you'll have to **rent a jeep** to get there ($3 from La Paz, $5 from Bolívar, $8 from San Gabriel), or you can **walk** 6km from La Paz to the grotto – a two-hour hike, longer on the way back – but make sure to take water, as there are no facilities on the way.

The **places to stay** are mostly used by pilgrims and include the *Rumichaca* hotel, at the top end of the "village" above the grotto (no phone; ❶), a big coffee-coloured building with simple rooms of diminishing price for each ascending floor, down to a mere dollar per bed; trails behind the hotel lead up the valley for pleasant walks. The *Casa del Peregrino* (no phone; ❶), in the white building above the basilica, has hot water and decent views.

San Gabriel and around

The farming centre of **SAN GABRIEL**, 22km north of Bolívar, is the busiest town between Ibarra and Tulcán – it even has traffic lights – and features a thriving **Saturday market** and narrow, busy streets cluttered with advertising slogans and shop signs. In the grand **Parque Principal** is a golden **statue** of a nude man clutching a pickaxe, claimed to represent the hard work of San Gabrieleños on local roads and waterways. The only other notable sight is the impressive thirty-metre-high **Cascada de Paluz**, 4km west of town, which makes for a pleasant hour's walk, though you'll need to ask for directions as there are no signs.

Buses between Quito and Tulcán stop at San Gabriel on request. You're unlikely to need **accommodation** here, but in case of emergency, *Residencial*

Ideal, one block up from the Parque Principal on Montúfar and Sucre (☎06/290265; ❶), has undulating beds and little else, while *Residencial Montúfar*, on the Parque Principal (☎06/290163; ❶), is a marginally better bet, with a red-and-chocolate balustraded courtyard and some rooms with private baths. The best **restaurants** are also on Parque Principal; *Asadero Piko Riko*, for one, has decent grilled chicken.

From San Gabriel, as the rugged terrain gives way to rolling pastures, cycle signs appear along the road and bike workshops (*talleres*) crop up in all but the smallest villages – **cycling** is a favourite pastime in Carchi province, and at weekends Ecuadorian racers stream up and down the Panamericana. About 20km from San Gabriel – halfway to Tulcán – the small town of **Julio Andrade** marks the junction with the route east, passing remote villages on the Colombian border such as Santa Bárbara, before heading south to Lumbaquí on the Baeza–Lago Agrio road in the Oriente. Do not attempt to travel on this road without making relevant enquiries about **safety** beforehand – the area has been destabilized by Colombian guerrilla activity and can be dangerous.

Reserva Guandera

Ten kilometres east of San Gabriel, the hamlet of **Mariscal Sucre** is the point of access for the **RESERVA GUANDERA**, protecting over ten square kilometres of rare high-altitude cloudforest and páramo grassland along the ridge of Loma del Corazón. The **cloudforest** (3100–3600m) is the last significant tract of its type in northern Ecuador and, considering its altitude, is extraordinarily diverse in plants and wildlife, with more than 150 recorded **bird** species (a world record for this altitude) that include the newly discovered chestnut-bellied cotinga and the swallow-tailed nightjar, with its unmistakeable metre-long tail. Andean spectacled bears can occasionally be seen around the páramo, pumas roam the entire reserve and occasionally come close to the research station, and the dominant tree, the **Guandera**, towers up to 30m and casts out its roots from the top, creating a thick forest canopy rich in mosses, bromeliads and orchids. The reserve, managed by the Fundación Jatún Sacha, also works closely with the community in Mariscal Sucre to encourage sustainable agriculture practices.

Practicalities

Access to the reserve is through Mariscal Sucre, easily reached from San Gabriel. The park guard, José Cando Rosero, or his wife can lead you up to the reserve station, a 90-minute walk from the village, but make arrangements with Jatún Sacha before turning up. The reserve's adobe research station, at 3330m on the edge of the forest ($25 per person including board), has several cosy dorms with shared baths, hot water and 24hr electricity, and **volunteers** are also welcome ($300 donation per month or $75 per week, plus $30 application fee). If you just want to visit for the day, entrance to the reserve is free. Give notice of your arrival in advance to the Fundación Jatún Sacha in Quito, Eugenio de Santillán N34-248 and Maurián, Urbanización Rumipamba Casilla 17-12-867 (☎02/432240 or 432173, ⓕ453583, ⓦwww.jatunsacha.org).

Tulcán and around

As the provincial capital of Carchi, **TULCÁN** is a skittish frontier town, shifting people with ruthless efficiency across the Ecuadorian-Colombian border, 7km away. The main bus terminal has dozens of services primed for Quito, and every other car seems to be a taxi or camioneta. Commerce thrives here with **markets** on Thursdays and Sundays, and shops crammed with merchandise crowd the narrow streets. Since dollarization in 2000, however, and the concomitant rise in domestic prices, business has not been so brisk. Where Colombians used to trawl the town looking for bargains, Ecuadorians are now the ones making the quick trip over the border in search of cheaper goods.

Most travellers don't linger in Tulcán, but if you've got time between buses, make sure to see the splendid **topiary gardens** in the town cemetery, or for longer layovers, you could visit the isolated **thermal springs**, set high in

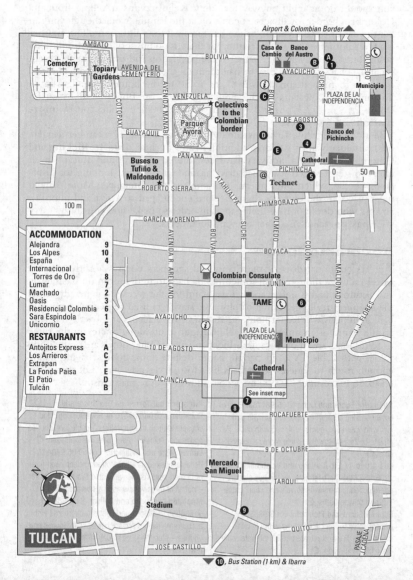

ACCOMMODATION
Alejandra	9
Los Alpes	10
España	4
Internacional Torres de Oro	8
Lumar	7
Machado	2
Oasis	3
Residencial Colombia	6
Sara Espindola	1
Unicornio	5

RESTAURANTS
Antojitos Express	A
Los Arrieros	C
Extrapan	F
La Fonda Paisa	E
El Patio	D
Tulcán	B

TULCÁN

Bus Station (1 km) & Ibarra

beautiful páramo near **Tufiño** to the west. The town's two spirited **fiestas** occur on April 11, for the cantonization of Tulcán, and November 19, to mark the day Carchi became a province.

Arrival and information

Buses from within Ecuador deposit you at the large terminal on Bolívar, from where it's a twenty-minute walk (1.5km) uphill northeast to the city centre and most of the hotels. Local buses run from here up to the centre, but can get very crowded, so you may want to take a taxi instead (about $1) – something you should do at night anyway for safety. Regular **vans** travelling from the Colombian border usually drop people off at the Parque Ayora, though you can ask the driver to take you on to the bus terminal for a little extra. The **airport** is a few kilometres east of the centre, but there is no bus service there and **taxis** cost about $3 each way; they gather at the bus station and around the two main squares, but it's relatively easy to hail them on the central streets, too. The cost of a trip to most destinations is $1, or $3.50 to the border. The Cámara de Turismo office, upstairs in the Edificio Muñoz on Bolívar and Ayacucho (Mon–Fri 9am–12.30pm & 2.30–6pm; ℡06/986606), provides tourist **information** and brochures.

Be aware that while Tulcán is safe during the day, at night it can get dangerous, particularly after 10pm. In addition to street crime, **drug trafficking** and Colombian **guerrilla activity** have destabilized areas around Tulcán. In an effort to step up security, police drive around late at night looking for suspicious people, which often means Colombians and foreigners. More than in most places in the country, the police are encouraged to arrest and imprison anyone who does not have their papers in order, so make sure you always carry your **passport** and any other relevant documents.

Accommodation

Tulcán's continual flow of merchants and shoppers ensures a fairly buoyant **hotel** industry, though it can sometimes be hard to find a room on Wednesday and Saturday nights before market days, and for the weekend generally, when the shoppers really get down to business. Travellers used to peeling paint and bare lightbulbs will feel at home in Tulcán, as most places are strictly no-frills, with a string of cheap, unremarkable **budget** joints along Sucre, on the three or four blocks south of Plaza de la Independencia. Other hotels are pretty good value, with cable TVs and private baths, despite some rooms having barely enough room to squeeze your bags in. Most places now have hot water, but check to make sure – at 3000m, a cold shower is pure masochism.

Alejandra Sucre and Quito ℡06/981784. Popular hotel boasting a smart exterior and private parking, with well-kept rooms equipped with cable TVs, private baths and towels. Single rooms also available. ❷

Los Alpes Av J.R. Arellano and Veintimilla ℡06/982235. The best hotel by the bus station, offering clean rooms with towels and soap, cable TVs and private baths. ❷

España Sucre and Pichincha ℡06/983860. Decent value for its clean rooms with big windows, cable TVs and private baths. Hot water only available 6am–noon. ❷

Internacional Torres de Oro Sucre and Rocafuerte ℡06/984670 or 980296. Upgraded cheapie with all the trimmings – cable TVs, phones and laundry service – and breakfast included. ❹

Lumar Sucre and Pichincha ℡ & ℻ 06/980402. Reliable, businesslike hotel offering clean, well-furnished en-suite rooms with cable TVs and hot water – not all of them with windows, however. ❸–❹

Machado Ayacucho and Bolívar ℡06/984221, ℻980099. Spacious and comfortable rooms with accoutrements like private baths, soap, towels and phones – plus the largest (cable) televisions in town. ❸

Oasis 10 de Agosto and Sucre ☎ 06/980342. A bit dog-eared and draughty, with flickering fluorescent lights that are almost too dim to read by, but a decent choice of budget rooms en suite or with shared baths. ❶

Residencial Colombia Colón and Ayacucho ☎ 06/982761. Very cheap hotel on a quiet street, with simple, clean rooms with shared baths. Rooms are a little more private upstairs away from the lobby. ❶

Sara Espindola Sucre and Ayacucho ☎ & ⓕ 06/986209 or 985925. Smartest, most comfortable place in town, with light and airy en-suite rooms with cable TVs and phones. Added bonuses are its sauna, steam room, disco and laundry service. Breakfast included. ❺

Unicornio Sucre and Pichincha ☎ & ⓕ 06/980638. Wall-to-wall carpets, a paint job and general facelift have elevated this old standard to a higher bracket. Fair-value rooms come with private baths and cable TVs, and the hotel is well positioned above one of the town's better restaurants. ❸

The Town

Although an express route now bypasses its centre, Tulcán is a town that grew up along the road to Colombia, stretching lengthways for several kilometres, while barely topping one kilometre in width. The central district is similarly elongated, arrayed along two central streets, **Bolívar** and **Sucre**, which are home to most of the hotels, restaurants and shops. The **Plaza de la Independencia** marks the centre of town, and the larger **Parque Ayora**, about six blocks north down Bolívar, is a popular open space. However, with the great exception of the fabulous topiary gardens (the only other green space in town), Tulcán comes across as a cold and bleak town, where at 3000m the early-morning sun struggles to warm the grey-concrete buildings and dusty streets.

Lifting Tulcán from its drabness, the Thursday and Sunday **markets** are well worth a look, when Sucre is draped in billowy white textiles, and clothes are sold along Tarqui, with fruits and vegetables around the corner on Olmedo. At the entrance to the covered meat market of **Mercado San Miguel**, Sucre and Tarqui, you can find huge blocks of ice – used for cold medicinal drinks that allegedly benefit the kidneys – wrapped in highland grasses and furry *frailejón* leaves for insulation, brought down from the upper slopes of Volcán Cumbal (4764m), just inside Colombia.

Topiary gardens

Its one undeniable highlight, Tulcán's glorious **topiary gardens**, at the cemetery on Cotopaxi and Avenida del Cementerio (daily 8am–5.30pm; free, with a planned charge for foreigners), are a fifteen-minute walk northeast of the centre, or a short taxi ride from the bus station ($1). Fragrant cypresses have been snipped with meticulous care into more than a hundred different figures and patterns, including Arabian palms, Egyptian columns, trapezoidal shapes and Inca faces, along with heads from stone figures found in San Augustín in Colombia, and images from the ancient Valdivian culture of coastal Ecuador.

Some avenues of greenery are based on formal French styles, while others are decorated with Galápagos turtles and even an Antarctic Emperor penguin, and the lines of white-walled **columbaria** (where cinerary urns are stored) framing the gardens stand in remarkable contrast to the organic shapes of the topiary. Known as *escultura en verde* (sculpture in green), the gardens were created by José Franco Guerrero, who began working on them in 1936, and since his death, his son, Benigno Franco, has continued to expand them.

Eating

Although many local **restaurants** feature the usual fried-chicken fare, several good **Colombian** restaurants have opened to save homesick nationals from the imagined perils of Ecuadorian cooking. Try a *bandeja paisa*, which comes in big portions piled high with vegetables, or the tasty *pollo sudado*, less appetizingly translated as "sweaty chicken".

Los Arrieros Bolívar and 10 de Agosto. Very good Colombian restaurant decorated in thatch and bamboo.

Chifa Pack Choy Sucre and Pichincha, ground floor of Unicornio hotel (℡06/982713 or 980638). Very popular Chinese place with big portions at low prices. Open late.

Extrapan Bolívar and Boyaca. The best bakery in town, boasting a tempting range of inexpensive buns and pastries, but also with full meals like chicken and rice at its restaurant and bar. Open until midnight, a good choice to get a late-night bite.

La Fonda Paisa Bolívar and Pichincha. Informal restaurant enlivened by a mock colonial facade on one of its walls, with inexpensive Colombian dishes.

El Patio Bolívar and Pichincha. Excellent Colombian fare in a restaurant with an identity crisis – interior thatched awning and bamboo-and-reed walls versus gaucho saddlebags, wagon wheels and swinging doors. Main courses for $2–3.

Tulcán Sucre and Ayacucho. Unremarkable café, but a possibility if you're stuck for breakfast, with a $1 cheese roll, juice, coffee and eggs combo.

Listings

Airlines TAME, Sucre and Junín (℡06/980675 or ℡987281), or at the airport (℡06/982850), has flights to Cali (11am Mon, Wed & Fri; $78) and Quito (2.15pm Mon, Wed & Fri; $32); the office staff move to the airport branch around flight-departure times.

Banks and exchange Banco del Austro, Ayacucho and Bolívar, has a Visa ATM and offers Visa cash advances; Banco del Pichincha, on Plaza de la Independencia, has an ATM for Visa and Diners Club; and Casa de Cambio, Ayacucho and Bolívar, provides fair rates for changing Colombian pesos. Official money changers carry IDs and hang around the Plaza de la Independencia, but make sure to check their calculations, count what they give you and put it away before handing anything over. Changing traveller's cheques can be a problem in Tulcán, so until new facilities appear, try one of the smarter hotels like *Lumar* or *Sara Espíndola*,

though commissions can run up to 10 percent.

Cinema Cine Activo, Sucre and 9 de Octubre, planned opening in 2003.

Consulate Colombia, Bolívar and Junín (Mon–Fri 8am–1pm & 2–3pm; ℡06/980559).

Internet facilities Antojitos Express, Sucre and Ayacucho, has fast food and is open daily ($0.06 per min); Café Net, near the bus station at Ecuador and Bolívar (closed Sun; $2 per hr); Technet, Bolívar and Pichincha ($2 per hr).

Medical services Clínica del Volante, Bolívar 48-056 and Rocafuerte (℡06/981889, ℡980361), has 24hr emergency service, and Dr Winston Revelo there speaks a little English; the town hospital is at 10 de Agosto 9-17 (℡06/980315).

Police Av Manabí and Guatemala ℡06/980622.

Post office Bolívar and Junín.

Telephone office Andinatel, Olmedo and Junín, and at the bus station.

The Colombian border

Seven kilometres east of Tulcán, the **Rumichaca** bridge marks the busy **Colombian border**, while a little upstream you can see the old crossing, a tiny bridge fronted by two small and stately buildings, relics of a time when only a handful of people crossed over each day. Now, customs controls on both sides are modern, efficient facilities (daily 6am–10pm, planned 24hr if border security improves), and there's even a **telephone office** and **restaurant** in the vicinity.

To cross the border, you'll need an **exit stamp** from Ecuadorian customs, in the building marked *Migración*, and an **entry stamp** from the Colombians on the other side of the bridge (both stamps free). The Colombians will give you up to ninety days on entry, but ask to make sure you get the full amount if you need it, and note that stamps are always required, even if only visiting Ipiales for the day. If you're arriving from Colombia, the Ecuadorians will also give you up to ninety days and a tourist card, which you should retain until you leave the country (see "Basics", p.17, for more on Ecuadorian entry requirements).

Colectivos to the border leave when full from the corner of Venezuela and Bolívar, on the Parque Ayora (10min; $0.70), while a **taxi** costs about $3.50 from there, or $4 from the bus station. From the border *colectivos* to **Ipiales**, a town with plenty of hotels 3km inside Colombia, cost about $0.40, while taxis are around $1.50; add a few hundred pesos (dimes) if you're heading straight for the Ipiales bus terminal. *Colectivos* to **Tulcán** ($0.70) from the frontier usually stop at the Parque Ayora, though if you're in a hurry to get to the bus station, the driver will usually take you there for a little extra. Official **money changers** throng the border on both sides, offering acceptable rates for cash dollars and pesos, but always check the calculations and money you receive before handing anything over.

West of Tulcán

The remote and haunting páramo grasslands **west of Tulcán** are easier to access than the nearby El Ángel reserve (see p.168), and make as good a place as any to see the páramo, its unusual *frailejón* flowers and, with luck, even condors wheeling high above. Geothermal activity deep below **Volcán Chiles** heats numerous thermal springs that bubble along the Colombian border around the village of **Tufiño** to its east, while further west of town, the road begins to descend off the páramo into the remote cloudforests around **Maldonado** and **El Chical**. As with any area on the Colombian frontier, make sure to check the current **security** conditions before exploring – at present, a rather dangerous state of affairs.

Tufiño

Eighteen kilometres west of Tulcán, **TUFIÑO** is a highland farming village on the border where the men return from the fields late in the day with bundles of wood strapped to their horses, while youngsters play volleyball and ride bikes across the main square. Tufiño itself has very little to offer visitors, but there are many **thermal springs** nearby, along with an informal **border crossing**, uphill and to the right of the main square, marked only by a swinging barrier. Unlike the one at Rumichaca (see opposite), however, this checkpoint is rarely manned and has no facilities to issue entrance and exit stamps, so don't attempt to enter Colombia from this point, unless you just want to amble across for the day and walk downhill to the village of Chiles, or to the **Juan Chiles** thermal springs, about thirty minutes beyond it.

Buses to Tufiño (11 daily, 45min trip; $0.80) leave Tulcán from opposite the Instituto Tecnico Superior, R. Sierra and Avenida R. Arellana, near the Parque Ayora; the last bus back is at 5pm. Bring your passport, as there's a military **checkpoint** just before the village. There is nowhere to stay in Tufiño and only a few basic **restaurants**.

Aguas Hediondas

Set at 3500m at the head of an isolated valley split between Ecuador and Colombia, 6km west of Tufiño, **AGUAS HEDIONDAS** (stinking waters) is a hot-springs complex ($1) of three baths, including one steaming open-air pool, that are rich in **sulphur**. The fumes of the source pools further up the hill are strong enough to be overpowering, and have been walled off for safety, but the others aren't dangerous at all and are reputed to be highly curative – you'll leave from a long soak feeling fresh and revitalized, but smelling of egg. The pools are much busier at weekends than during the week, when you can freely wallow in the steam and enjoy the eerie scenery. A **restaurant** here provides drinks and simple meals.

To get here from Tufiño, follow the signposted **dirt road** uphill from the square, and after a thirty-minute walk you'll come to a marked turn-off to the right for the springs, located another 4km away (1hr on foot). The road passes through a beguiling landscape, where fields of human-sized *frailejones* on burnt-matchstick stems seem to watch you from the hillsides, while closer to the valley head, rocky cliff faces and the gnarled fingers of altitude-stunted trees poke through the mist. The sole purpose of the lonely line of telegraph poles along the way becomes clear as you arrive – to power the ghetto blaster piping pop music out of the changing rooms.

At 8am every Sunday, a **bus** from Tulcán departs from outside the cathedral on Sucre and goes direct to the springs, returning around 3pm. At other times, ask the drivers of buses to Maldonado (see below) to drop you at the marked turn-off for the walk to the springs.

Volcán Chiles and around

Fifteen kilometres west of Tufiño, the dirt road to Maldonado rises above 4000m as it skirts **VOLCÁN CHILES** (4723m), which straddles the Colombian border to the north. The highest point along the road is known as **El Azuay**, 3km south of the summit of the volcano, from which it takes about three hours to ascend the mountain, three more to descend, and another three to walk back to Tufiño. The climbing is straightforward enough, but it can be foggy or even snow, so it's best to dress for the worst and hire a **guide** in Tufiño ($10–15). The IGM **map** of Tufiño (1:50,000 scale) is also useful for the area.

Just before El Azuay, the road borders the northern edge of the Reserva Ecológica El Ángel (see p.168), and offers views of the **Lagunas Verdes**, curative lakes that take their murky green hue from algae and a high sulphur content. The village of **Maldonado**, 52km further west and 1500m lower down, is much warmer and definitely off the beaten track for gringos, though there are a couple of **hotels** here, catering primarily to Ecuadorian and Colombian tourists. Descending 12km further into the forest, the road ends at **El Chical**, which rarely gets visitors and has no accommodation.

Check with your embassy before you travel to the area, as remote Colombian border regions have been prone to guerrilla activity and can be dangerous. Daily **buses** leave midday, with an extra service at 1pm on Mondays, Thursdays and Sundays, and go to Maldonado (5hr; $2.50) and Chical (5hr 15min; $3), leaving Tulcán opposite the Instituto Tecnico Superior, R. Sierra and Avenida R. Arellana, and returning early the next morning.

Travel details

Buses

Ibarra to: Chachimbiro (1 daily; 1hr 15min); Cotacachi (every 30min; 30min); Cuenca (7 daily; 11–12hr); El Ángel (every 30min; 1hr 30min); Esmeraldas (hourly; 8hr 30min); Guayaquil (16 daily; 10hr); Guallupe (13 daily; 1hr 30min); La Esperanza (every 20min; 30min); Lita (13 daily; 2hr); Manta (4 daily; 11–12hr); Mira (hourly; 1hr); Otavalo (every 5min; 30min); Pimampiro (every

15min; 1hr 15min); Quito (every 15min; 2hr 30min); San Antonio de Ibarra (every 20min; 10min); San Lorenzo (9 daily; 3hr 30min); San Miguel de Yahuarcocha (every 20min; 15min); Santo Domingo (every 45min; 5hr 30min); Tulcán (hourly; 2hr 30min); Urcuquí (every 30min; 30min); Zuleta (hourly; 50min).

Otavalo to: Apuela (5 daily; 2hr 30min); Cayambe (every 10min; 45min); Cotacachi (every 10min; 20min); Cuellaje (2 daily; 3hr 30min); García Moreno (3 daily; 4hr); Ibarra (every 5min; 30min); Peguche (every 20min; 15min); Quito (every 10min; 2hr); San Pablo del Lago (every 15min; 20min).

Tulcán to: El Chical (1–2 daily; 5hr 45min); Huaquillas (1 daily; 18hr); Ibarra (every 5–10min; 2hr 30min); Maldonado (1–2 daily; 5hr); Quito (every 5–10min; 4hr 30min–5hr); Tufiño (11 daily; 45min).

Flights

Tulcán to: Cali, Colombia (3 weekly; 40min); Quito (3 weekly; 30min).

The central sierra

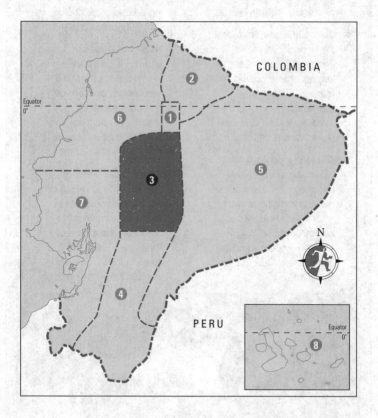

CHAPTER 3

Highlights

❊ **Parque Nacional Cotopaxi** The flawless cone of Cotopaxi, one of the highest active volcanoes in the world and an enticing prospect for visiting climbers, dominates the country's favourite highland park. **See p.188**

❊ **Saquisilí** Every Thursday the unassuming town is engulfed by one of the largest of all highland markets, with every imaginable kind of produce, hardware and livestock. **See p.195**

❊ **Quilotoa loop** A grand tour of the sierra's most beguiling rural landscapes, passing vertiginous patchwork fields, windswept páramo, isolated indigenous communities and the crater lake at Quilotoa. **See p.196**

❊ **Baños** The ultimate spa resort town blessed with a warm sunny climate, delightful hotels and restaurants, and plenty to do in the lush hills and valleys that surround it – not to mention the rejuvenating powers of its fabulous hot springs. **See p.209**

❊ **Nariz del Diablo** Ecuador's definitive train journey, a breathtaking switchback descent of an 800-metre rock face, is justly proclaimed "the most difficult railway in the world". **See p.227**

❊ **Chimborazo** To reach just the second refuge of the highest mountain in the world – when measured from the centre of the Earth – will leave you gasping for air, and choking with pride. **See p.229**

The central sierra

South of Quito, the two parallel chains of the Andes running the length of Ecuador rise to their most dramatic and spectacular in the **central sierra**, forming a double row of snowcapped peaks that the nineteenth-century German explorer, Alexander von Humboldt, memorably christened "the avenue of the volcanoes". Eight of the country's ten highest summits are found here, including **Chimborazo** (6310m), **Cotopaxi** (5897m) and **El Altar** (5320m), towering over a series of inter-montane basins that separate the two ranges. Sitting in these basins, at an altitude of around 2800m, are the region's principal towns – **Latacunga**, **Ambato** and **Riobamba** – strung north to south along the Panamericana. On a very clear day, the drive south from Quito through this parade of mountains facing each other across the highway ranks among the world's great road journeys. Frustratingly, however, the highest peaks are often lost in the low, grey clouds so typical of the region, and it's quite possible to travel right through the central sierra without spotting a single summit.

Even with these pinnacles hidden from view, the landscape is utterly beautiful. Almost every mountain is covered by a dense patchwork of fields stretching up the slopes to extraordinary heights. Alternating strips of maize, barley, potatoes and *quinoa* (a cereal grown only in the Andes) form streaks of intense greens and muted yellows, oranges and limes, splashed with the occasional scarlet poncho of the *indígenas* tending the crops. In fact, this deeply rural region is the **indigenous heartland** of Ecuador, a place still littered with Quichua-speaking communities whose lifestyles and work patterns have remained virtually unchanged for centuries. The economic and social focus of these communities, and the best place to get a feel for traditional Andean life, are the weekly **markets** held throughout the region. One of the largest and most exciting is at the small town of **Saquisilí**, near Latacunga, where hundreds of red- and pink-shawled *indígenas* fill the streets, examining mountains of fresh produce or stalls selling anything from rope to soap. Other notable markets include those at the village of **Zumbahua**, also near Latacunga, and the town of **Guamote**, south of Riobamba.

Most tourists stick to the more obvious destinations like **Parque Nacional Cotopaxi**, dominated by the perfect cone of the eponymous volcano, and the little town of **Baños**, whose warm climate, spectacular setting and thermal springs have made it a magnet for Ecuadorians and foreigners alike – despite the renewed activity of nearby Volcán Tungurahua. Another favourite with gringos is the famous **train ride from Riobamba**: it no longer runs all the way to Guayaquil, on the coast, but the hundred-kilometre stretch as far as the dramatic incline known as the **Nariz del Diablo** ("Devil's Nose") is

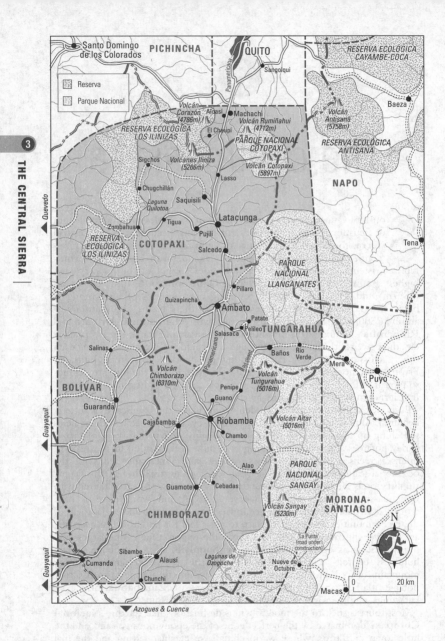

maintained as a tourist service, offering fanatastic views and a thrilling ride. To get the most out of the central sierra, though, it's worth straying off the beaten track, into the more remote areas east and west of the Panamericana. Rewarding outings include a trip to the stunning crater lake of **Quilotoa**, approached from Latacunga via some of the most gorgeous scenery in

Ecuador; a trip from Ambato to the isolated town of **Guaranda**, then on to the lovely, lost-in-the-hills village of **Salinas**; or an exploration of the valleys, lakes and peaks of **Parque Nacional Sangay**, a sprawling wilderness area east of Riobamba, approached from various access points scattered around the western cordillera.

Most of the region's highlights can be reached by local **buses**, which make their way along the most potholed and precarious dirt roads to dozens of highland villages. Otherwise, many towns on the Panamericana have camioneta co-operatives which you can hire to take you to and from outlying points. As for the **weather**, expect regular afternoon rainfall and plenty of cloud cover from September to May, with June to September significantly sunnier and drier. At this altitude it can be bitterly cold at any time of year, though when the sun comes out for long spells it's often warm enough for just a T-shirt.

Machachi, the Ilinizas and around

Heading south from Quito, the jolting, potholed Panamericana winds its way past a trail of dusty satellite towns, soon emerging into open, cultivated pastures flanked by the eastern and western cordilleras. If you're lucky with the weather, you'll be treated to superb views of Volcán Cotopaxi, its fat, white cone dominating the region. A handful of lesser peaks punctuate the surrounding landscape, including Volcán Corazón, opposite the small town of **Machachi**, and, a little further south, the two **Ilinizas**, popular with climbers wanting to acclimatize before tackling Cotopaxi.

Machachi

About 35km south of Quito along the Panamericana, a side road shoots east for a kilometre or so to **MACHACHI**. There's nothing special about the town itself, but its setting – within a ring of hills and volcanoes – is magnificent, and it's a popular jumping-off point for visiting the **Ilinizas** (see p.186). There's little else to do in Machachi, save wander around its **central square**, dominated by the handsome old **Teatro Municipal** (now disused) and the white-walled **church**, whose interior is embellished by swirling, brightly coloured Baroque designs, and a gilded altar proclaiming "Fear of God". If you've time to kill while you're here, you could visit the nearby **Güitig plant**, where Ecuador's most famous mineral water is bottled. The plant sits in extensive, manicured gardens 4km northeast of the town ($2 by taxi from main square), and has a couple of fairly large swimming pools (daily 7.30am–3.30pm; $0.70) filled with cold, crystal-clear mineral water. On or around July 23, the town celebrates "**El Chagra**", the Andean version of the cowboy, with rodeos and parades.

Arriving in Machachi on one of the frequent Transporte Mejía buses from near the Villaflora trolley stop in Quito, you'll be dropped on the main street, Avenida Amazonas, leading down towards the square; any interprovincial bus heading south of Quito can drop you at the town entrance. The best **place to stay** is *La Estancia Real* (℡02/2315760; ❷), two blocks south of Amazonas at Luis Cordero and Panzaleo; the rooms are clean and spacious with private bathrooms, and there are great views of the surrounding peaks from the roof terrace. Of the town's limited choice of **restaurants**, the best is probably the *Pedregal* on the main square, serving bargain staples like fried chicken. As for **moving on**, there are frequent bus connections from Avenida Amazonas to the nearby villages of Aloasí and El Chaupi (see below), as well as to Quito and Latacunga. Several **camioneta** cooperatives provide a faster alternative; pick one up on Amazonas, or call Cooperativa Luis Cordero (℡02/2314625) to collect you from an outlying base. **Internet** facilities can be found on Colón just off the main square.

Aloasí and El Chaupi

Just south of the turnoff to Machachi another side road branches west to the village of **ALOASÍ**, about 1km back from the highway. Apart from its beautiful, rural setting, Aloasí's main interest is as a base for climbing **El Corazón**, an extinct volcano sitting immediately west of the village. Its 4788-metre summit can be reached in about five hours on a strenuous but straightforward hike, following the track branching west from the train station, 1.5km west of the village square. While here, a very appealing place to **stay** is the delightful *La Estación* (℡ & ℻02/2309246; ❹), a nineteenth-century farmhouse right next door to the train station, with comfortable rooms, polished wooden balconies, open fires and great views of El Corazón. You can practically step off the Quito–El Boliche train service (see p.118) into the *hostal*; otherwise, take a **camioneta** direct from Machachi ($2), or a **bus** to Aloasí's central square from Machachi (every 30min) followed by a half-hour walk up the cobbled road leading to the train station.

Continuing south down the Panamericana, you come to the signposted turning to the village of **EL CHAUPI**, sitting at the end of a seven-kilometre cobbled road, a thirty-minute **bus** ride from Machachi (every 30min). This rural, isolated village enjoys a privileged setting, with stunning views onto the Ilinizas to the west and Cerro Rumiñahui to the east. As the closest community to the Ilinizas it's a popular base for climbers, and 50m back from the church *Hostal Llovizna* (℡09/9699068, ✉iliniza_blady@yahoo.com; ❹) provides the best in-village **accommodation**, offering simple rooms with bunks around a large seating area heated by two central fires. You can arrange **climbs** of Iliniza Norte (around $80 per person), Iliniza Sur ($160) and horse rides from here. About 3km south (follow the road straight through the main square), the *Hacienda San José* (℡02/2891547 or 09/9737985; ❹) is a working cattle farm with a few simple but cosy rooms and a very friendly owner. Even if you don't plan to climb the Ilinizas, this is a great base for **walking** in the lovely surrounding countryside, or **riding** on one of the owners' horses, guided by a farmhand ($10 per half-day). Note that breakfast is available but you need to cook your own supper, so bring food. It takes about forty-five minutes to walk here from the village, but it's usually possible to hitch a lift (or take a camioneta from Machachi for $7; see p.185). If there's no one in the house, ask in the white house next door or the barn behind.

Reserva Ecológica Los Ilinizas

Looming over the west side of the Panamericana is the sharp, jagged outline of the twin-peaked **Ilinizas**, two massive pyramids of rock about a kilometre apart joined by a wide saddle, which are the namesakes of an **ecological reserve** (entrance $5) set up in 1996 to protect just under 1500 square kilometres of rugged hilly terrain, páramo, lakes and cloudforest of the western cordillera. The horseshoe-shaped reserve curves from the Ilinizas and El Corazón around the northern half of the Quilotoa loop to Zumbahua and beyond (see p.196), encompassing picturesque countryside also favoured for hikes. In its eastern region, the reserve is most easily **accessed** from El Chaupi (see opposite), from where expeditions to climb the two Ilinizas most commonly depart. The larger **Iliniza Sur** (5248m), pronounced by Baron von Humboldt, the famous nineteenth-century German naturalist and explorer, to be "one of the most picturesque and majestic of the many peaks that surround Quito", dominates the view from the Panamericana; it is an exciting technical climb that should be attempted only by experienced mountaineers. **Iliniza Norte** (5126m), on the other hand, can be managed by strong, confident hill walkers, though there is a demanding scramble near the summit and the altitude can be really debilitating if you're not sufficiently acclimatized. The basics of climbing the Ilinizas are outlined below, but be warned that the route on both peaks is difficult to follow in bad weather, when use of a guide is strongly advised (for recommended **climbing guides** in Quito see p.114).

Both Norte and Sur are approached from a mountain **refuge** sitting at 4765m, just below the saddle between the two peaks. It has bunks for 25 people (bringing a sleeping bag is essential), cooking facilities, gas lighting and running water. It costs $10 per person to sleep here, payable to the warden either at his office in El Chaupi (about 200m from the bus stop, past the church on the road towards the Ilinizas), or at La Virgen parking area (see below) or at the refuge itself.

Climbing the Ilinizas

The easiest way of getting to the refuge is to take a 4WD **camioneta** to the parking lot known as **La Virgen**, marked by a shrine to the Virgin Mary, near the base of the Ilinizas, 9km from El Chaupi. There are sometimes a couple of camionetas hanging around El Chaupi's main square (about $10), or you could take one from Machachi for about $15 (see p.185). From La Virgen, you continue on foot along a clearly marked trail to the refuge (2–3hr). To get to the refuge entirely **on foot** takes around five hours from El Chaupi, or about four hours from *Hacienda San José*, whose owner will draw you a map showing a short cut. Coming back, allow about three hours to get from the refuge down to El Chaupi.

From the refuge count on needing two to three hours to reach the summit of **Iliniza Norte**. The route is easy to follow, though very steep in parts. The bulk of it involves crossing a rocky ridge – via the unnervingly named Paso de Muerte (Death Pass), which requires great care in high winds and snow. The final climb to the summit, marked by an iron cross, involves some scrambling, and needs a bit of a head for heights. Coming down is quite fast if you follow the scree slopes below the ridge (1hr 30min).

Climbing **Iliniza Sur** involves crossing glaciers and crevasses and is becoming increasingly complicated with the recent retreat of snow ramps and collapse of a snow bridge. You'll need plenty of experience and full mountaineering equipment, including rope and harness, crampons, ice axe and ice screws. You should also wear a helmet to provide protection from falling rocks. It takes three to five hours to reach the summit depending on conditions, after an early start from the refuge; the SAE in Quito can give you the latest news on both peaks (see p.80).

Parque Nacional Cotopaxi

Cotopaxi's shape is the most beautiful and regular of all the colossal peaks in the high Andes. It is a perfect cone covered by a thick blanket of snow which shines so brilliantly at sunset it seems detached from the azure of the sky.

Alexander von Humboldt, 1802

Almost opposite the Ilinizas, the snowcapped, perfectly symmetrical **Volcán Cotopaxi** (5897m) forms the centrepiece of Ecuador's most-visited mainland national park, **Parque Nacional Cotopaxi** (daily 8am–5pm, last entrance 3pm; $10), covering 330 square kilometres of the eastern cordillera. With its broad, green base and graceful slopes tapering to the lip of its crater, Cotopaxi is the most photogenic of the country's thirty or so volcanoes, and on a clear day makes a dizzying backdrop to the stretch of highway between Quito and Latacunga. One of the highest active volcanoes in the world, it's also one of Ecuador's most destructive, with at least ten major eruptions since 1742 responsible for repeatedly destroying the nearby town of Latacunga. It's been fairly quiet since its last burst of activity in 1904, and today Cotopaxi is the most popular climb in Ecuador. Although the volcano dominates everything around it, and the aim of most visitors is simply to get a close-up view of its dazzling form before turning home, a number of other attractions make a visit to the park very rewarding. Not least is the wild and starkly beautiful **páramo** setting, with its rolling moorland streaked by wispy clouds and pockets of mist. At an altitude of some 3500–4500m, the air up here is thin and crisp, and the tundra-like vegetation is made up principally of cropped *pajonales* (straw-like grass) and shrubs, lichens and flowers adapted to harsh climates. Over ninety species of **birds** inhabit the park, including the tury hummingbird, Andean hillstar and Andean lapwing, while **mammals** include white-tailed deer, rabbits, Andean foxes and pumas.

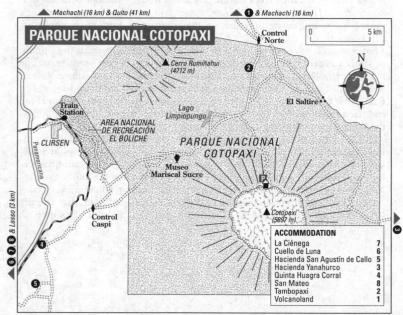

PARQUE NACIONAL COTOPAXI

Machachi (16 km) & Quito (41 km)

& Machachi (16 km)

Control Norte

0   5 km

N

▲ Cerro Rumiñahui
(4712 m)

El Saltire

Train Station

Lago
Limpiopungo

AREA NACIONAL
DE RECREACIÓN
EL BOLICHE

CLIRSEN

PARQUE NACIONAL
COTOPAXI

Panamericana

Museo
Mariscal Sucre

P

▲ Cotopaxi
(5897 m)

& Lasso (3 km)

Control
Caspi

ACCOMMODATION

La Ciénega	7
Cuello de Luna	6
Hacienda San Agustín de Callo	5
Hacienda Yanahurco	3
Quinta Huagra Corral	4
San Mateo	8
Tambopaxi	2
Volcanoland	1

A rather uninspiring collection of stuffed animals, however, and a three-dimensional scale model of the park are on display at the **Centro de Información Mariscal Sucre** (daily 8am–noon & 1–5pm), 10km from the main entrance checkpoint and often the first stop on a Cotopaxi tour. Outside the centre there's also a short self-guided trail to introduce you to the páramo, but a more satisfying way to explore this habitat is on the one-hour footpath around the **Lago Limpiopungo** around 5km further up the road – a long, shallow lake lying at 3800m, surrounded by boggy reeds that provide a habitat for numerous birds. When the clouds part, its waters present a striking reflection of the 4712-metre peak of **Cerro Rumiñahui**, looming over it to the northwest, whose lower slopes can be reached by a path branching off the north shore of the lake. Located right next to the access road into the park, the lake is easy to reach and a convenient place for a break, with a few picnic tables by its shore. Most visitors get back in their taxi or car and head south from the junction up the road for a further 13km as far as the **parking area**, known as the Parqueador del Refugio, sitting at 4600m on the slopes of Cotopaxi. From here, a footpath leads steeply up a scree slope to the **José F. Ribas refuge** (4800m), a popular target for day visitors. It looks tantalizingly close, and entire families on Sunday outings from Ambato or Riobamba seem to have no trouble zooming up in 30 minutes, but if you're not acclimatized it can be a real struggle; count on taking 45 minutes to an hour to reach it. Once there, you can warm yourself with hot tea and snacks.

From a junction near the lake, another track skirts northeast around Cotopaxi passing by several archeological sites, most notably **El Saltire**, the remains of an Inca *pucará* or fortress used to control access down to the Amazon basin. Apart from the atmospheric scenery, there's not a great deal to see here, though you can see some of the pieces recovered from the sites at the Centro de Información.

Visiting the park

There are three points of **access** to the park, but the most often used is off the Panamericana about 25km south of Machachi and 7km before the little village of Lasso. At this access point, a signposted turn heads east for 6km to the **Control Caspi** guard post, situated 3km before the park boundary proper. Unless you're on a **guided tour** (provided by many of the Quito operators listed on p.112, and outfits in Latacunga listed on p.192) you'll have to sort out your own **transport**. The easiest way to get here is to take a **bus** down the Panamericana to the village of **Lasso** and hire one of the white Cooperativa de Camionetas de Lasso **pick-up trucks** (☎03/719493) from outside the train station. They charge about $25 per group to go up to the parking area below the refuge, and $40 for the round trip, including waiting time of a couple of hours. These trucks can also be booked to pick you up from nearby hotels, or to collect you from the parking area at a prearranged time. If staying in a hotel near the park (see overleaf), the staff should be able to arrange transport for you, but if you want to go all the way up to the refuge parking area make sure they've got a 4WD vehicle as other cars can't make it up the final stretch of road. Often, there are also pick-ups waiting on the Panamericana by the main entrance waiting to ferry people around the park for similar prices ($25 one-way; $40 return). Note that it takes about 40 minutes to get from the Panamericana to Laguna Limpiopungo, and a little over an hour to get to the parking area below the refuge.

The other accesses are via the entrance to the Area Nacional de Recreación

Climbing Cotopaxi

It's possible to **climb Cotopaxi** with little or no technical mountaineering experience, but you'll need to be fit, strong, fully acclimatized and have a good, reliable **guide**, preferably certified by ASEGUIM (Asociación Ecuatoriana de Guías de Montaña). Many climbing and tour companies in Quito offer guided climbs up Cotopaxi, and can rent equipment to solo climbers – see p.114 for a list of recommended companies. Typical **costs** are around $200 to $250 per person, including all equipment, transport and food. If you're on a guided climb, you'll arrive at the **refuge** on Cotopaxi the afternoon before climbing (see p.189), and will probably be taken to practise crampon and ice-axe techniques at a nearby glacier. You then try to get a few hours' sleep before being woken at around midnight. Most groups set off at 1am. The ascent takes, on average, six to eight strenuous hours, and involves negotiating several crevasses and climbing on snow and ice. From the top, you're treated to exhilarating views onto all of Ecuador's major peaks, just after sunrise, and down to the wide crater, steaming with sulphurous fumes. The descent normally takes three to four hours. If you plan to do this climb, the importance of **acclimatizing** properly beforehand cannot be stressed enough; staying in and around the park for a few days (see p.188) and going for plenty of hikes in the area will greatly aid your summit attempt while reducing the risk of developing altitude sickness. Note that if you're walking up to the refuge from the Panamericana it's a thirty-kilometre-plus muscle-sapping slog that will tire you out before the climb proper; break the hike into manageable pieces over a few days, rest and acclimatize. Cotopaxi can be climbed all year round, but December and January are regarded as the **best months**, with February to April a close second. The late summer (Aug–Sept) can also be good, but is likely to be windy.

El Boliche (see opposite) and the **Control Norte** at the north end of the park, reached by an eighteen-kilometre track (mostly cobbled) from Machachi (or a 30km dirt road from Sangolquí).

Staying in and around the park

There are a few accommodation options for those looking to **stay inside the park**. The Cotopaxi refuge (reserve 2–3 days beforehand on ☏02/2222240, ℻02/2265530; $17 per person) has bunks and mattresses (bring your own sleeping bag), cold running water, electricity and basic cooking facilities but you'll need to take your own food; it's mainly used for climbers the night before they ascend. A much better choice for park visitors and those wishing to acclimatize is *Tambopaxi* (☏09/9448223 or ☏02/2224241 in Quito, ⓦwww.tambopaxi.com; $17 for a dorm mattress) at an altitude of 3750m some 2km from the Control Norte. Modelled on a comfortable Alpine refuge but built from local materials, the rooms here are well-insulated and feature warm duvets. The restaurant serves good food (lunch and dinner are around $10 each, and breakfast is $6.50) including some Swiss specialities, such as fondue, and has stunning views of Cotopaxi. Staff at *Tambopaxi* can also arrange guided hikes, horse rides, transport to and from the park, and offer **camping** facilities ($6 per person) that are far better than the park's own two official camping areas. The first of the park-run campsites, the only one with running water, is midway between the information centre and Laguna Limpiopungo: take the first left after the information centre and head for the concrete outbuilding. The second, with no facilities, is another 2–3km up the road towards Cotopaxi, this time signed to the right of the road. El Boliche also offers a few rudimentary places to stay (see p.192).

There's a far greater choice of hotels and haciendas just **outside** the park, most of which can be reached by camioneta from Lasso for a few dollars. Besides the following, there are many inexpensive alternatives in the town of Latacunga (see p.193).

Hacienda La Ciénega ☎03/719093, ⓔhcienega@uio.satnet.net. Just south of Lasso, reached along a 1km side road branching west from the highway and at the end of a grand avenue of tall eucalyptus planted by García Moreno, is a magnificent seventeenth-century hacienda with an exquisite private chapel and beautifully manicured gardens. The rooms in the main building (especially rooms 7 and 8) have bags of character but can be cold, while those in the modern annexe have cosy log fires. Despite not being a tremendously sumptuous conversion like other more expensive haciendas, this is still a wonderful place to stay. ⑥

Cuello de Luna ☎09/9700330 or 02/2242744, ⓌWwww.cuellodeluna.com. Just south of the sign on the Panamericana announcing the main turn-off to the park, a signed 2km track leads west to this lovely, informal hotel, colourfully decorated with a choice of spacious cabins with private bathrooms and open fireplaces, or semi-private mattresses in the loft ($21 per person). ⑤

Quinta Huagra Corral ☎09/9801122. A friendly *hostal* located a few hundred metres from the Panamericana on the Control Caspi track, offering accommodation in a few simple double rooms, one with private bath. There's an on-site restaurant and breakfast is included in the rate. ④

Hacienda San Agustín de Callo 5km south of the park's main entrance ☎03/719160 or ☎ & ⓕ02/2906157 (in Quito), ⓌWwww.incahacienda.com. This glorious colonial hacienda is built on the site of Inca ruins (excavations are ongoing) and incorporates some of the stonework into its structure, including the "Inca

Chapel" complete with original trapezoidal windows and walls built with expertly carved volcanic rock. The accommodation is very luxurious and beautifully designed, with fireplaces in all the rooms and even in some bathrooms. Biking, trekking, horse riding, and market visits are offered. Rates include some meals and a day tour. ⑨

San Mateo a few kilometres south of Lasso at km 75 on the Panamericana ☎03/719015, ⓌWwww.hosteriasanmateo.com. An attractive and compact country hotel offering rooms or four-person cabañas with mountain views, private baths and hot water, and a restaurant serving organic home-grown produce. Activities on offer include riding, climbing, hiking and milking cows on a neighbouring farm. ⑥

Hacienda Yanahurco 10km east of the park, on its main access road ☎02/2226360, ⓌWwww.haciendayanahurco.com. A huge working cattle ranch at 3600m in an isolated valley location with some 260 square kilometres of private land. The ranch has seven rooms, each equipped with private bath, hot water and fireplace or heater, and offers riding excursions on special highland horses, fly fishing for trout, and hiking trips to nearby lakes and waterfalls. All-inclusive tours start from $590 per person for two days. ⑨

Volcanoland on the road to the Control Norte ☎02/2231806, ⓌWwww.volcanoland.com. An adobe lodge with gorgeous views of Cotopaxi offering comfortable accommodation, good traditional food and plenty of activities including biking, hiking, riding, fishing and excursions to a nearby hacienda. Rates are $90 per person per day including board, lodging, transportation, tour and guide, with reductions for groups. ⑧

Area Nacional de Recreación El Boliche

Adjoining the northwest border of Parque Nacional Cotopaxi, the small 200-hectare **Area Nacional de Recreación El Boliche** (daily 7am–4.30pm; $10 ticket interchangeable with Cotopaxi's) mainly caters to family groups and Quito weekenders. Here you'll find picnic tables, restaurant, barbecue spots and short self-guided **hiking trails** up towards Cerro Rumiñahui (see p.189) or through its forests, largely composed of pines from California planted as part of a refor-estation project dating back to 1928. El Boliche also has a **train station**, the last stop for the weekend tourist service from Quito before it returns to the capital in the early afternoon (see p.118), and two "**interpretation centres**" (*centros de interpretación*), one by the entrance covering the history of the recreation area, and another a five-minute walk up the hill past a field of llamas and alpacas, having more engaging displays on Ecuador's protected areas and habitats.

The **access** to El Boliche (which also serves Parque Nacional Cotopaxi) is on the Panamericana some 17km south of Machachi, marked by a huge sign for "CLIRSEN", a satellite-tracking station set up by NASA in 1960. From the turning it's 3km or a 30-minute walk to the Boliche entrance post. You can **stay the night** at El Boliche at some simple *cabañas* (❷) which have showers but no bedding (bring a sleeping bag), or at various campsites, two of which have hot showers ($5 per tent).

Latacunga and around

Some 20km south of the turn-off to Cotopaxi, **LATACUNGA** is a charming, mid-sized market town of narrow, cobbled streets and whitewashed, clay-roofed houses, huddled on the east bank of the Río Cutuchi. Its centre looks distinctly colonial, but most buildings date only from the early twentieth century – a fact owed to Cotopaxi's repeated and devastating eruptions, which have seen the town destroyed and rebuilt five times since its foundation in 1534, most recently in 1877. Despite its troubled history, Latacunga is a cheerful, easy-going place, full of activity in the day though something of a ghost town at night. It gets very busy, however, during its two famous and colourful **Mama Negra** fiestas, the original religious celebration of which is held on September 24, and the newer secular festival, involving local colleges and civic institutions, falling on the first weekend of November.

At other times of year, there's little to occupy you in town after a couple of hours' wander. Close at hand, though, is the **Parque Nacional Cotopaxi** as well as the sprawling, hectic indigenous market at the town of **Saquisilí**. The sparkling crater lake of Quilotoa can also be visited on a long day-trip, or as part of a circuit – often called the **Quilotoa loop** – taking in the remote villages of Zumbahua and Chugchilán.

Arrival and information

The Panamericana and the rail tracks run parallel to each other on the opposite side of the Río Cutuchi from the town. **Buses** coming into town will drop you at or near the large bus station on the Panamericana from where you can catch a **taxi** to the centre ($1 max), or walk there in about ten minutes over the 5 de Junio bridge. **Camionetas** (☎03/802625) line up just off the square at the corner of Valencia and Antonio Vela, outside *Residencial Jacqueline*; they charge around $30 one-way or $40 for a return trip to Cotopaxi, including waiting time, and around $40 to Laguna Quilotoa and back.

Save for a small municipal office with limited material at the bus station, there's no tourist **information** office in Latacunga, but there are several **tour operators** happy to answer most questions about the town and its surroundings. Among them are: Neiges, at Guayaquil 5-19 and Belisario Quevedo (☎03/811199), a friendly company offering climbing and walking trips to Cotopaxi and the Ilinizas, horseback trekking, fishing trips, and day-trips to Laguna Quilotoa; Tobar Expeditions on Guayaquil and Quito (☎03/811333), who mainly specialize in climbing and are run by an ASEGUIM guide; and Expediciones Volcanroute on Quito and Padre Salcedo (☎03/812452), who plan treks around Cotopaxi, Quilotoa and the Ilinizas. In addition, several hotels offer guided **day-trips** up to Cotopaxi (around $20 per person, including lunch) and to Laguna Quilotoa ($30), including the *Estambul*, *Central* and *Cotopaxi* (see opposite). If you're looking for a **bank**, try either the Banco del

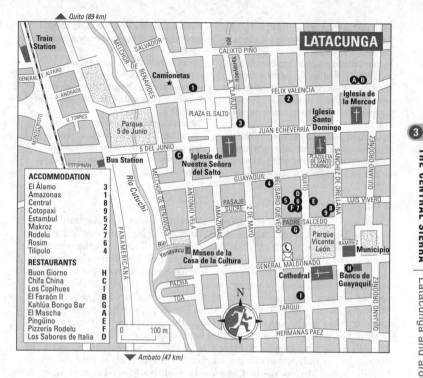

Map labels:

Train Station
SALVADOR
MELCHOR DE BENAVIDES
Río Yanayacu
CALIXTO PIÑO
LATACUNGA
GENERAL F. ALFARO
J. ANDRADE
Camionetas ★ **1**
FÉLIX VALENCIA **2**
A. CLAVIJO
A B
Iglesia de la Merced
V. TORRES
PLAZA EL SALTO **3**
Iglesia Santo Domingo
Parque 5 de Junio
JUAN ECHEVERRÍA
MONTECRISTO
5 DEL JUNIO
ESTUPIÑÁN
C Iglesia de Nuestra Señora del Salto
Bus Station
PLAZOLETA DE SANTO DOMINGO
SÁNCHEZ DE ORELLANA
QUIJANO ORDÓÑEZ
GUAYAQUIL **4**
Río Cutuchi
MELCHOR DE BENAVIDES
ANTONIO VELA
AMAZONAS
PASAJE SUCRE
2 DE MAYO
BELISARIO QUEVEDO
QUITO
D 6 **E** **8** LUIS VIVERO
5 **7** PADRE SALCEDO **G**
Parque Vicente León
RAMÍREZ
Municipio
PANAMERICANA
Río Yanayacu
Museo de la Casa de la Cultura
GENERAL MALDONADO
Cathedral ✝ **Cathedral**
PACHA
TOA
N
TARQUI
HERMANAS PAEZ
Banco de Guayaquil **H**
I
QUIJANO ORDÓÑEZ
0   100 m

ACCOMMODATION
El Álamo   3
Amazonas   1
Central   8
Cotopaxi   9
Estambul   5
Makroz   2
Rodelu   7
Rosim   6
Tilipulo   4

RESTAURANTS
Buon Giorno   H
Chifa China   C
Los Copihues   I
El Faraón II   B
Kahlúa Bongo Bar   G
El Mascha   A
Pingüino   E
Pizzería Rodelu   F
Los Sabores de Italia   D

Austro (Visa), on the corner of Quito and Guayaquil, and Banco de Guayaquil (Visa and MasterCard; changes traveller's cheques), on General Maldonado and Sánchez de Orellana. The **post office** is on the corner of Belisario Quevedo and General Maldonado, and the Andinatel office is next door. There are also several **Internet cafés** around town costing around $1 per hour, including *Giovany's Net* on the corner of 2 de Mayo and Padre Salcedo and *Net One* on the Plaza El Salto.

Accommodation

There's a cluster of **hotels** on the Panamericana, around the intersection of 5 de Junio, but you're better off continuing into the centre. Here you'll find a choice of decent budget and mid-range places, but no real upmarket options. Several offer **laundry** services, but Lavatex on Gallindo and Amazonas will wash clothes by the kilo.

El Álamo 2 de Mayo and Echeverría ☏03/812043. Offers light, comfortable rooms with flowery curtains, TVs and decent en-suite bathrooms and has a restaurant open all day from breakfast. **4**

Residencial Amazonas Félix Valencia 4-67, Plaza El Salto ☏03/812673. Best of a grubby bunch of bottom-dollar hotels around the noisy market square. **2**

Central Sánchez de Orellana y Padre Salcedo ☏03/802912. Established hotel with clean, spa-

cious, carpeted rooms with private bath and TV, run by a friendly owner. Has its own parking as well. **3**

Cotopaxi Padre Salcedo 5-61 on Parque Vicente León ☏03/801310. Welcoming hotel with pleasant views onto the square from the front rooms, which have en-suite baths. The wallpaper's old and gloomy though, and some beds sag a bit. **3**

Estambul Belisario Quevedo 6-44 ☏03/800354. Spotless little hotel with polished wooden floors, good hot showers (private or shared) and quiet rooms around a courtyard. Also has laundry facilities and a cafeteria. ③–④

Makroz Félix Valencia 8-56 and Quito ☎ & ☎03/800907, ✉hotelmakroz@latinmail.com. Well-turned out, modern hotel, currently the most comfortable in town, boasting cable TV, carpets, laundry service, games room, parking and restaurant. ④

Rodelu Quito 16-31 ☎03/800956, ☎812341, ✉rodelu@uio.telconet.net. Comfortable, well-run hotel with neatly kept rooms, good bed linen and curtains, en-suite bathrooms, phone and TV in

rooms and private parking. The rooms on the upper floors are cheaper and less well appointed. ③–④

Rosim Quito 16-49 and Padre Salcedo ☎03/802172, ☎800853. Spacious, clean rooms with firm, comfortable beds and large en-suite bathrooms. Those at the back of the hotel are very quiet. ④

Tilipulo Guayaquil and Belisario Quevedo ☎03/810611. Bright, tidy rooms with wooden floors, warm bedding and tiny bathrooms. The hotel's corner rooms are noisy as all cars honk when passing. ③

The Town

Latacunga's focal point is the **Parque Vicente León**, a wide, leafy square enclosed by iron railings that are locked after dark. The south side is dominated by a **cathedral**, featuring plain, whitewashed walls on both the inside and outside, while the east side is flanked by the austere **Municipio**. A couple of blocks north, the large, twin-towered **Iglesia Santo Domingo** is the most impressive of the town's churches, with its Grecian pillars and extravagantly painted interior covered with swirling blue, green and gold designs. Right in front of it, on the little Plazoleta de Santo Domingo, you'll find a small **artesanía market** selling knitwear, *shigras* and other souvenirs (daily except Thurs & Sun). The town's daily **main market** is a huge, outdoor affair spreading over Plaza El Salto (also known as Plaza Chile), off Avenida Amazonas and at its liveliest on Saturdays. Just off the market, on the corner of Vela and Padre Salcedo, is the **Museo de la Casa de la Cultura** (Tues–Fri 8am–noon & 2–6pm; $0.50), where you'll find a collection of effigies that are paraded through the streets in local festivals, as well as some textiles and ceramics.

Mama Negra fiestas

A highlight of the Latacunga year is its renowned **Mama Negra fiestas**, commemorated twice in religious and secular festivals within a couple of weeks of each other. The fiesta is thought to have derived from the expulsion of the Moors from Spain or the astonishment of the local *indígenas* on seeing black people for the first time, the slaves that the Spanish had brought here to work in nearby mines. The colourful **religious celebration** (also called the *Santísima Tragedia*) is held on September 24, with brightly costumed paraders and various mischief-making characters such as the white-robed *huacos*, and the whip-wielding *camisonas*, and the belle of the ball, a blacked-up man gaudily dressed as a woman – the Mama Negra. In the midst of this, the focus is supposedly the Virgin of the **Iglesia de la Merced** (known as Our Lady of the Volcano because she is believed to have saved the city many times from Cotopaxi's eruptions), who is paraded through the town and up to **El Calvario**, the concrete monument on the hill to the east of town. The flamboyant **secular Mama Negra festival** usually begins on the first weekend in November, though the big parades have been scheduled for the Friday in recent years to discourage excessive drinking, with the same cheerful costumes and characters, marching bands and street dancing. The festive mood continues until November 11, on which day the town's **independence** is celebrated.

Eating and drinking

There's not a great deal of choice when it comes to **eating** in Latacunga, whose residents seem to have a marked preference for pizzerias. In addition to the places listed below, a number of out-of-the-centre restaurants (generally humble affairs) specialize in the town's traditional dish of *chugchucaras* (pork crackling and fried potatoes), including *Chugchúcaras Aqui Son* at Av Unidad Nacional 5468 and *Chugchúcaras Don Pancho* at Ordoñez 66-36 and Quijano. For **drinking and nightlife**, try the *Kahlúa Bongo Bar* on Padre Salcedo and Quito (Tues–Sat), or *Galaxy* (Fri & Sat), Latacunga's best club, on a hill at the fringes of the town at Barrio El Mirador, with music pumping out over several dance floors.

Buon Giorno cnr of Sánchez de Orellana and General Maldonado, Parque Vicente León. Long-established pizzeria in a good location; pleasant enough dining room and large portions. Closed Sun pm.

Chifa China Antonio Vela and 5 de Junio 76-85. Clean and cheap Chinese restaurant, serving a mixture of Ecuadorian and vaguely Chinese dishes. Usually open when everywhere else has closed for the night.

Los Copihues Quito 70-83. Large restaurant with faded carpets and colourful weavings on the wall, serving decent steaks, chops and mixed grills. Closed Sun.

El Faraón II Félix Valencia and Sánchez de Orellana. Neat place with simple pine furniture, which is particularly popular for *almuerzos*. Closes 6pm.

El Mascha Félix Valencia 1067. Simple, friendly canteen specializing in roast chicken.

Pingüino Quito 73-102 and Guayaquil. A good stop for snacks, coffee, milkshakes and ice creams.

Pizzeria Rodelu Quito 16-31. Tasty pizzas cooked in a wood-fired oven in the dining room of *Hotel Rodelu*. Also a good place for breakfast. Popular with travellers. Closed Sun.

Los Sabores de Italia Quito and Guayaquil. Relocated from Baños when the town was evacuated in 1999, this simple restaurant serves the best pizzas in Latacunga, as well as delicious hot sandwiches made of pizza dough with locally produced cheese, olive oil and black pepper.

Saquisilí

A twenty-minute bus ride northwest of Latacunga, **SAQUISILÍ** is a quiet, slightly ramshackle little town that explodes into life with its **market** every Thursday morning – one of the biggest in the highlands. It fills seven plazas, each one specializing in different types of goods. There's an extraordinary breadth of merchandise for sale, supplying just about every consumer need of the hundreds of *indígenas* who journey here from all over the central sierra. Lining the pavements are mountains of vegetables balanced on wooden crates, sacks full of grain, mounds of fluorescent yarns used for weaving shawls, kitchen utensils, finely woven baskets and curiosities like stuffed animals from the Oriente. Also on Thursday, about a ten-minute walk north of the centre, dozens of sheep, cows, pigs and the odd llama exchange hands in the **animal market** (before dawn to around 10am), dotted with women clutching tangled cords attached to black, squealing piglets.

Moving on from Latacunga

The **bus station**, the other side of the river over the 5 de Junio bridge, is well connected for most local and many interprovincial locations. A few major destinations such as Riobamba and Cuenca, however, do not have services that stop at the terminal; you can hail these buses as they pass on the Panamericana nearby. Alternatively, you could take one of the regular buses to Ambato and change there. On Thursdays, the day of the Saquisilí market, many local destinations are diverted to that town and leave from there rather than Latacunga. Details about transport around the Quilotoa loop are in the box on p.197.

If you need a break from the tumult of the market, pop in to have a look at the **church** on the main square. Its original facade has been preserved, but everything behind it was replaced in the 1970s – the interior is quite striking, with its brightly painted windows, blue-and-white metal roof and minimalist altar. Otherwise, there's little else to do in Saquisilí, and certainly nothing to draw you here outside market day.

Practicalities

It's easy to come in for the morning from Latacunga, with **buses** leaving every five minutes (every 10min Fri–Wed) from the bus station. All the same, checking into a **place to stay** on Wednesday night allows you to catch all the market action early. Right on the attractive *parque central*, about the only square that's not part of the market, the *San Carlos* on Simón Bolívar and Sucre (T03/721057; ❷) offers bright, clean rooms with private bath, electric shower and attractive views of the church and hills behind. A couple of blocks south at the corner of Simón Bolívar and Pichincha, *Salón Pichincha* (T03/721247; ❶) has small, very basic rooms with chamber pots under the beds and a toilet and cold shower one floor down from the rooms, as well as an inexpensive restaurant. A ten-minute walk from the centre, off the south end of González Suárez, German-owned *Hostería Rancho Muller* (T03/722282, F722051; ❺, including breakfast) offers simple but comfortable rooms with private bathrooms, and a decent but pricey restaurant; they also organize tours of nearby attractions and the country as a whole. One of the very few other restaurants in town is the *Cevichería Paty*, next to the bakery a few doors down from the *San Carlos*, which only irregularly has seafood despite its name. Otherwise, try your luck at the unnamed corner canteens or countless pavement food stalls.

The Quilotoa loop

Some 90km west of Latacunga and the Panamericana, in one of the most beautiful parts of the Andes, the remote and isolated **Laguna Quilotoa** is a spectacular crater lake filled with emerald waters. It's most directly approached along the road from Latacunga to Quevedo (see Chapter 6, p.364), via the villages of **Pujilí**, **Tigua** and **Zumbahua**. Once there, you can take a different route back, heading north to the villages of **Chugchilán** and **Sigchos**, then southeast to rejoin the Panamericana near the market village of Saquisilí. This route, often referred to as **the Quilotoa loop** or the Quilotoa circuit, can just as easily be done in the opposite direction to that described above. If you can, try to time your stay in Zumbahua with the Saturday-morning **market**, one of the most fascinating in the sierra, while a tour of the loop coinciding with any of the major Catholic religious **festivals** – especially Epiphany, Carnaval, Semana Santa, Corpus Christi and Día de los Muertos/Finados; refer to p.47 for dates – will give you the chance to experience some wonderful spectacles that give these sleepy villages an entirely new complexion.

You'll find **accommodation** in Tigua, Zumbahua, Laguna Quilotoa, Chugchilán and Sigchos, but it's pretty basic for the most part. If you want to sleep in the cabañas by the lake, a **sleeping bag** is a must; elsewhere it's a welcome bonus as it gets very cold at night. Count on spending a very minimum of two days to do this route; it's much better to take three or more nights if you want to do it at a more relaxing pace, which will also give you time to explore this magnificent countryside with hikes or horse rides. The most convenient overnight stops are in Zumbahua, at Quilotoa next to the lake, which is for hardy travellers only, and at Chugchilán, where the most comfort is on offer.

When planning **bus** transport around the loop, it's the section between Zumbahua and Sigchos that is the most infrequently serviced and needs most attention; bear in mind that timetables do change, so make enquiries beforehand if travelling on a tight itinerary. Buses on the loop are often very full with locals, especially on market days; get there early and be prepared for a squeeze. An alternative to buses is to arrange transport to your first overnight stop with a **camioneta** in Latacunga (see p.193), and lifts for other parts of the loop with local pick-up owners in Zumbahua (see p.199) and Sigchos (see p.203). There's also an early-morning **milk truck** running between Sigchos and Chugchilán that you can ride on, offering another transport option over this remote stretch. If time's short, consider renting a vehicle or going with a Quito-based **tour company** such as Positiv-Turismo (see p.113), which offers a two-day jeep trip around the circuit for $125 per person, with an overnight stop in Chugchilán.

Buses: clockwise

Latacunga to: Zumbahua (2hr). One daily Transportes La Iliniza bus at noon; buy a ticket early. In addition, hourly buses to Quevedo can drop you at the turn-off to Zumbahua, a ten-minute walk from the village. Quilotoa (2hr 30min) and Chugchilán (3hr 45min). Daily at noon (the Transportes La Iliniza bus).

Zumbahua to: Quilotoa (30min) and Chugchilán (1hr 15min). One daily at 2pm. Services leave from the central square.

Chugchilán to: Sigchos (1hr). Daily at 3am, plus Thursday at 2pm, Saturday late morning, and Sunday at noon. Latacunga (3hr 45min). Daily at 3am.

Sigchos to: Latacunga (2hr 15min). Seven daily. The last bus leaves at 2.30pm.

Buses: anticlockwise

Latacunga to: Sigchos (2hr 15min). Seven buses daily. Chugchilán (3hr 45min). A Trans La Iliniza bus leaves daily at 11.30am (buy tickets early), with additional Saturday services (10.30am & 2–3pm). On Thursday this bus leaves from Saquisilí at 11.30am (buses leave every 5–10min from Latacunga to Saquisilí).

Sigchos to: Chugchilán (1hr), Quilotoa (2hr) and Zumbahua (2hr 45min). Daily at 4am, plus Friday 5am.

Chugchilán to: Quilotoa (1hr) and Zumbahua (1hr 45min). Daily at 5am, plus Friday 6am. Latacunga (3hr 45min). Daily at 4am, plus Sundays at 6am, 9.30am and 9.45am.

Zumbahua to: Latacunga (2hr): Hourly buses from the main Quevedo–Latacunga road, plus buses from Chugchilán, via Quilotoa which leave Zumbahua's plaza at around 6am daily, and Sundays at around 8am, 11.30am and 11.45am.

Milk truck

Ask about the *lechero* at local hotels in these villages.

Sigchos to: Chugchilán (1hr). Daily at 6am.

Chugchilán to: Sigchos (1hr). Returns to Sigchos anytime between 9–10.30am.

Camionetas

Latacunga to: Laguna Quilotoa (around $40) and Chugchilán (around $45), from the corner of Valencia and Antonio Vela, Plaza El Salto.

Zumbahua to: Laguna Quilotoa (from $5) and Chugchilán (from $15), from the main square, or ask in any of the hotels around the square.

Chugchilán to: Laguna Quilotoa (from $15), Zumbahua (from $20) and Sigchos (from $15), from the main square.

Sigchos to: Chugchilán (from $15) and Laguna Quilotoa (from $20), from the main square.

◀ Quevedo (100 km)

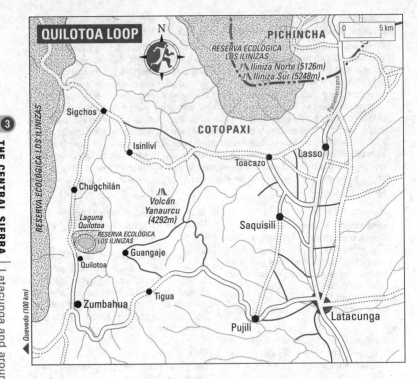

Pujilí

Heading west from Latacunga for 12km leads to the pretty little market town of **PUJILÍ**, whose centre is marked by a beautifully tended **plaza**, dotted with flowers, lawns and palm trees. At one end of the square is the **church**, with an unpainted stone facade, bell towers, and an intricately carved wooden door. It's usually open, though an iron grille often blocks entrance to the nave – you can peer through it to get a look at the wonderful vaulted brick ceiling and bare stone walls, dotted with carvings of saints in various postures of misery. It's worth a closer look and to do so ask for the *padre* at the adjoining church office. Stretching across another side of the square is the single-storey, white-stuccoed **Municipio**, with a clock tower in the middle – clearly a fine public building in its day, but now abandoned, with broken windows and graffiti on the walls. The rest of the square is overlooked by handsome colonial-style houses with whitewashed walls, clay-tiled roofs and brightly painted balconies.

Pujilí has a large Sunday **market** and a smaller one on Wednesday, held on Plaza Sucre, two or three blocks from the main square. You'll find everything from vast quantities of plastic containers to the characteristic mountains of fresh produce, laid out in front of indigenous and *mestizo* women sitting cross-legged on the ground. While you're here, try a bit of *panela*, enormous "loaves" of coarse brown sugar, sold at several stalls. If you're lucky enough to be in the area around Corpus Christi (a moveable feast in June, on the first Thursday after Trinity Sunday), don't miss the town's celebrations of this **festival**, involving fabulous costumes and masked dancers (*danzantes*), as well as competitions to climb up wavering poles many metres high to retrieve prizes tied to their tops.

Practicalities

Most visitors only pass through Pujilí, anxious to push on to the Laguna Quilotoa, but if you want to stay you'll find basic but adequate **rooms** at *Residencial Pujilí* at Vicente Rocafuerte 5-17 (℡03/723649; ❷), a couple of blocks from the plaza, towards the market. It's above a roast-chicken **restaurant**, one of a number of basic places serving food around town. There are **buses** between Pujilí and Latacunga every ten minutes, plus hourly services to Quevedo to get to Zumbahua.

Tigua

From Pujilí, the road skirts the wall of a broad valley, all the while climbing higher and higher, giving stunning views down to the valley floor. Even more striking is the patchwork of cultivation covering the surrounding hills with fields of potatoes, onions, barley and broad beans. As you ascend the temperature begins to drop noticeably, and soon you're in wild, starkly beautiful countryside. After crossing a pass, the road levels out on the páramo, dotted with igloo-shaped thatched shelters known as *chozas*, a dwelling hut characteristic of the rural sierra.

About 35km west of Pujilí is the village of **TIGUA** (more accurately Tigua Chimbacucho, as Tigua is the name of the whole canton), whose modern, tiled-roof houses contrast sharply with the rough thatched huts elsewhere. The most impressive of the village's buildings, perched on the hillside above the road, is an **art gallery** cooperative, devoted to the naive art, painted on sheep hide, for which Tigua is famous throughout Ecuador. The gallery sells the works of around thirty-five local artists, painted in the characteristic Tigua style, showing scenes of daily life, legends and village fiestas against a background of brightly coloured peaks and fields. In addition, there are decorated festival masks representing characters that feature in local folklore, such as wolves, lions, dogs, monkeys and tigers, as well as basketwork and painted boxes. The prices, though higher than those charged by vendors next to Laguna Quilotoa, reflect the quality of the paintings: expect to pay around $30 for a mid-size painting by the more established artists like Alfredo Toaquiza, whose father was the first person to begin painting in this style in 1973.

Practicalities

There are a couple of **places to stay** in the community. The *Hostería Samana Huasi* (❹) near the art gallery is run by a local cooperative, and offers simple rooms and meals in a building overlooking the valley. A more romantic option is the charming *Hacienda Tigua Chimbacucho* (by reservation in Latacunga on ℡03/813682 or 800459; ❸), a working dairy farm at 3450m, tucked nearer the valley floor 3km before Tigua village, down a winding signposted 800-metre track. The small farmhouse, which is warmed on cold nights by an old wood stove by the front door, has four rustic rooms sleeping thirteen guests in total and one bathroom that the entire household shares. Meals are good and inexpensive, and are accompanied by delicious home-made cheese and *dulce de leche*. You can also hire horses here to ride to Quilotoa in a couple of hours, or hike there in twice the time. Bus drivers know the farm and can drop you at the turning.

Zumbahua

About 30km beyond Tigua, a sideroad leads downhill to **ZUMBAHUA**, a small village set about half a kilometre north of the Latacunga–Quevedo road; if your bus is continuing to Quevedo, get off here and walk for ten minutes or so down to the village. It's a poor place, with muddy, potholed streets, tin-roofed houses and dust blowing about in the wind, but the setting is spectacular thanks to the backdrop of sharp peaks covered with chequered, tawny fields. Zumbahua's large **central square** looks desolate and empty through the week, but on Saturdays is crammed with traders, buyers and produce to make it one of the most enjoyable and dazzlingly colourful **markets** in the sierra. Among the piles of potatoes and beans, you can also see freshly chopped sheep's heads along with various other parts of their anatomy, used to make soup that's often prepared at the makeshift stalls. Other curiosities include a row of barbers, and a cluster of tailors who briskly mend clothes at their old-fashioned sewing machines.

Practicalities

Zumbahua makes a convenient overnight stop before visiting Laguna Quilotoa, and a number of **hostales** have sprung up over the last few years. The best is the *Cóndor Matzi* (**❷**), a whitewashed building on the square fronted by a carved wooden balcony. Owned by a village cooperative, it's got a hot-water shower and small, tidy rooms with bunks and clean linen, but has a slightly abandoned feel to it. There are kitchen facilities and meals can be provided. If no one's there to let you in, ask around in the village for the key. Just round the corner, the ambitiously named *Oro Verde* (**❷**) has simple rooms with basic en-suite bath (though with unreliable hot water), tiled floors and yellow walls decorated by a few festival masks, and a simple restaurant. A few doors along, *Richard* (**❷**) has basic dorm rooms and one double with concrete floors, and decent hot showers inside and out back. Apart from the hotels mentioned above, there are a couple of very basic **restaurants** just off the square. The Andinatel **phone office** is near the church.

Besides the daily 2pm **bus** to Quilotoa, several locals will take you there by **truck** for about $5–8 – just ask around on the square, or in your hotel. Alternatively, it's a fabulous four-hour, ten-kilometre **hike** to the lake, gently downhill for the first three hours, but then quite steeply uphill for the last forty-five minutes; **guides** are available from *Cóndor Matzi* for this and other páramo hikes.

Laguna Quilotoa

Laguna Quilotoa is a breathtaking glass-green lake lying in the crater of an extinct volcano, surrounded by steep slopes and jagged cliffs. Arriving by bus, you're dropped at a fork in the road from where it's a straightforward five- or ten-minute walk up to the lake, which remains hidden from view until you're practically on top of it. On the way up you'll pass an **entrance kiosk** where you pay a $0.50 visitor's fee, used to aid the local community of Quilotoa, whose meagre shacks huddle by the side of the track up to the lake. Local artists gather around the crater, near the parking area, trying to sell their Tigua paintings, while children flock around, hoping to prise a sweet or a few cents out of you. It's possible to **walk down to the lake** from the crater's edge in about half an hour, following the path that starts at a muddy chasm just left of the parking area as you face the lake. It's steep, and not to be undertaken lightly, but the solitude and views at the bottom are highly rewarding. Getting back up involves either a stiff one-hour climb, or a 45-minute **mule ride** (around $4), which you can organize in the parking area before you start walking down to the lake.

△ Descending Volcán Cotopaxi

Practicalities

There are a couple of simple **hotels** in Quilotoa, and several houses in the hamlet also rent beds to tourists: they're all very basic, and at around 3800m you'll need a warm sleeping bag. By far the largest and most patronized is *Cabañas Quilotoa* ($3 per person), which has a leaky roof, but the rooms come with wood-burning stoves, which provide smoky but welcome warmth, and shared hot-water showers; a newer annexe is better protected from the elements but is without fireplaces. *Hostal Sunrise* (ⓔjose_guamangate@ latinmail.com; ❷) has a few beds and a large fireplace, and extra rooms with private fires with an outside hot-water shower are being built; the toilet is unattractive. The owner takes on **volunteers** to teach English (and learn Quichua) for $35 a week. The nearby friendly *Refugio de Jorge Latacunga* ($2 per person) is more basic, but Jorge takes tourists on **guided walks** around the crater rim (6hr; $10) and rents mules ($4) to carry them back up from the lake. The owners of *Cabañas Quilotoa* arrange **mule treks** to and around the lake, as well as a day-trip to the Chichucaucho hot springs ($15) or to the Cueva de los Incas in local cloudforest (5hr; $12). Each of these places to stay can provide simple **meals**.

Chugchilán

North of Quilotoa, a hair-raising 22-kilometre drive along a narrow dirt road skirting a cliff edge takes you through dramatically beautiful scenery to **CHUGCHILÁN**, a tiny settlement in a remote rural setting that's home to little more than a dozen families. Although one of the poorest villages in the region, it's the location of some of the most comfortable places to stay on the whole loop, including the famous *Black Sheep Inn*, as well as an excellent base for hiking, mountain biking and horse riding. Ask in the village for Humberto Ortega (or contact him at the inn if staying there – see below), who offers four-hour horse rides ($10), usually to a small, isolated cheese factory up on the páramo, where you can buy delicious cheeses, and then on to a tract of cloudforest. This route can also be done as a five-hour round-trip walk; this and other **hiking routes** are described in detail on hand-outs given to guests at the *Black Sheep Inn*. One of the most popular trips involves catching the early-morning bus to Laguna Quilotoa and hiking back from the crater via the scenic **Toachi canyon** (5–6hr), part of the Reserva Ecológica Los Ilinizas (see p.186); hire a **guide** at Quilotoa (about $3) for the first hour or so of the walk to avoid getting lost on the confusing paths, and note that the last hour is quite hard going.

Practicalities

Half a kilometre east of Chugchilán's main square, on the road towards Sigchos, a steep path leads up to the *Black Sheep Inn* (☎03/814587, ⓦwww. blacksheepinn.com; ❻, including two meals, with discounts for students, SAE members, children and during the low season). This lovely **guesthouse**, perched on a hillside, offers rooms in thatched adobe huts, most with wood-burning stoves, or a bunkhouse dorm for those on a tighter budget ($20 per person). It's run by a couple of North Americans committed to sustainable, eco-friendly agriculture, with schemes such as composting toilets, water recycling systems, organic gardens and reforestation programmes. For visitors, the *Inn* offers treats such as tasty vegetarian cooking, home-made brownies with free tea and coffee, a lounge with plenty of books and fantastic views, a 100-metre zipline cable ride down the hillside and a sauna to keep the highland chill at bay. It's very popular so reservations are advised. Down on the main road, closer towards the village centre, is *Mama Hilda's* (☎03/814814, ✉mama_ilda@hotmail.com; ❹ including breakfast and dinner), offering clean and tidy rooms – the newer ones have split-levels and fireplaces – and shared bathrooms with hot-water showers. As the enthusiastic recommendations in the guest book attest, the owner is very welcoming and a great cook (she can do vegetarian meals on request). Next door downhill, the *Hostal Cloudforest* (☎03/814808; ❷ including dinner) has pleasant rooms with shared hot-water bathrooms, and a restaurant. Horse rides and hikes can be arranged from all three hotels.

Sigchos

Twenty-four kilometres east of Chugchilán, the road passes through the busy little town of **SIGCHOS**. With its paved streets, modern school and conspicuous absence of ponchos around town, you get the distinct impression you've left the rural sierra behind. It's more of a place to pass through than to base yourself, but if you get stuck you'll find comfortable en-suite **rooms** at the orange-painted *La Posada* (☎03/714224; ❷) on the Plaza 24 de Mayo (the square with the covered basketball court), which also has the town's best **restaurant**, serving the standard menu of chicken, meat or fish and rice. Other hotel choices include the modest and noisy *Residencial Sigchos* (☎03/714107; ❶) on Calle Carlos Hugo Páez, the main thoroughfare running through town; or the *Pensión Tungurahua* (☎03/714114; ❶) on Tungurahua and Iliniza, offering simple rooms with or without en-suite bathrooms. Continuing east, you're quickly in wild, remote countryside again, winding down countless hairpins into a spectacular canyon, though having climbed out of it again, the landscape becomes tamer and less striking as you head back towards the Panamericana.

Salcedo

Back on the Panamericana, some 10km south of Latacunga, you pass through the little town of **SALCEDO** (officially San Miguel de Salcedo). There's nothing particularly exciting about it, though it does boast a very beautiful **central square**, where tall, stately palms and immaculately tended lawns take precedence. Overlooking the square is a gorgeous whitewashed, colonial **church** (usually locked) and a rather grand **Palacio Municipal** of pink-hued stone. Wrapping up the town's attractions is the lively **Sunday market**, held round the corner from the square, though it feels more urban and less colourful than other sierra markets.

Otherwise, there's little to detain you in town, and with plenty of **buses** whizzing up and down the Panamericana, getting stuck here is unlikely to be a problem. If you do need a **place to stay** for the night, though, you'll find *La Casona* (☎03/728224; ❹) at Bolívar 6-34, a stately hotel on the main square with fresh en-suite rooms and a sauna set around a pleasant courtyard, or cheaper, clean little rooms with private bath at the *Residencial Central* (☎03/726099; ❶), on the same street just off the square. For more luxury, head for the *Hostería Rumipamba* (☎03/726128, ℻727103; ❻) on the Panamericana, about 1km north of town. Built in the style of an old hacienda, it offers upmarket, comfortable rooms, some with log fires, a good restaurant, handsome grounds and a large pool. It's good value for a couple of days' pampering, despite the proximity of the highway ruining the illusion of a country setting. Back in Salcedo proper, the best **restaurant** is *La Casa del Marquez*, on García Moreno and Quito at the north exit of the town, which offers good, inexpensive food in a plush dining room.

Ambato and around

Continuing south down the Panamericana from Salcedo, the next town you reach is **Ambato**, sitting in a fertile agricultural zone some 47km south of Latacunga. Although an important commercial centre with a bustling downtown core, there's little here to hold your interest for more than an afternoon or so, and many travellers choose to whiz straight through on their way to Baños or Riobamba. It's handy, however, as a jumping-off point for a couple of neighbouring low-key attractions, including **Quizapincha**, a major producer of leather goods, **Salasaca**, famous for its weavings, **Patate**, a small village set in a fruit-growing valley, and, for the more adventurous, the **Parque Nacional Llanganates**, one of Ecuador's least-explored wildernesses.

Ambato

San Juan de Ambato – known simply as **AMBATO** – was founded in 1570, but very little remains of its colonial character due to a catastrophic **earthquake** that virtually razed the city to the ground in 1949. The modern buildings that sprang up in its wake are for the most part bland and unattractive, making Ambato a less appealing place for a stopover than Latacunga or Riobamba, the two other main central sierra towns on the Panamericana. That said, the town is the provincial capital of Tungurahua province, and has a couple of enjoyable museums, plenty of banks and some great-value hotels and decent restaurants. If you're passing around Carnaval time (just before Lent, in February or early March), don't miss the **Fiesta de las Flores y las Frutas**. Celebrated since 1951, the festival is held over several days with big parades, beauty pageants, bullfights, music and plenty of fruit and flowers; you'll need to book a room in advance when it's on. Unlike the rest of the country, water fights are banned in Ambato during Carnaval.

Arrival and information

Ambato's **bus terminal** and **train station** (currently disused) are right next to each other a couple of kilometres northeast of the centre; taxis to the centre ($1 max) line up outside, or you can walk up to Avenida de las Americas, directly behind the bus terminal (turn right and right again) and catch a local bus to the downtown Parque Cevallos. **Taxis** in town rank around Parque Cevallos and the central Parque Montalvo; if you want to book one, call Cooperativa de Taxis Bolívar (☎03/821190).

For **tourist information** head for the helpful Ministerio de Turismo office (Mon–Fri 8.30am–5pm; ☎ & ℻03/821800) at Guayaquil and Rocafuerte, next door to the *Ambato* hotel. The Ministerio del Ambiente (☎03/848452), a short taxi ride ($1) from the town centre at Alfredo Baquerizo 603 and Avenida los Chasquis, can give you information on Parque Nacional Llanganates (see p.208).

Accommodation

While mid-range **accommodations** are spread about town, Ambato's cheapest hotels are on or near the Parque 12 de Diciembre. It's a slightly run-down area of town but it is central, busy and reasonably safe during the day.

Ambato Guayaquil 01-08 ☎03/412005, ℻412003, ✉hambato@hotmail.com. Ambato's top hotel, offering quiet, spacious rooms with good-quality though slightly dated furnishings and decor, and big picture windows looking down to the Ambato river valley. Also has private parking, a decent restaurant (breakfast included) and a pleasant outdoor terrace. ❻

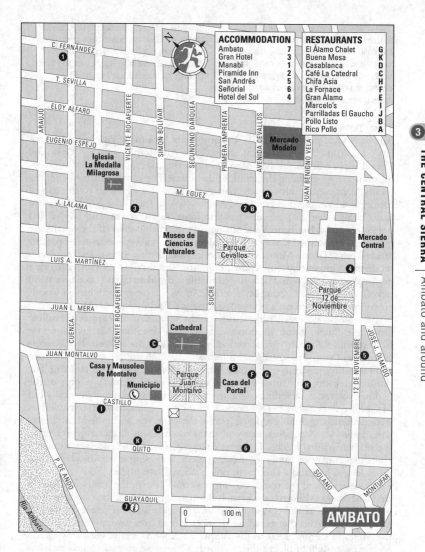

ACCOMMODATION

Ambato	7
Gran Hotel	3
Manabí	1
Piramide Inn	2
San Andrés	5
Señorial	6
Hotel del Sol	4

RESTAURANTS

El Álamo Chalet	G
Buena Mesa	K
Casablanca	D
Café La Catedral	C
Chifa Asia	H
La Fornace	F
Gran Álamo	E
Marcelo's	I
Parrilladas El Gaucho	J
Pollo Listo	B
Rico Pollo	A

Gran Hotel Lalama 05-11 ☎ & ℻ 03/825915.
Friendly hotel overlooking a pretty church, with a
café and private garage. Most rooms are large,
with en-suite bath, carpets and cable TV, though
some are looking a little worn. ❹
Residencial Manabí Cuenca and Fernandez
☎ 03/826693. Quiet, family-owned *residencial* a
few blocks from the centre with basic but
adequate little rooms with shared bath. A couple of
rooms at the front have balconies. ❷

Piramide Inn Cevallos and Mariano Eguez
☎ 03/842092. Well-run hotel offering comfortable
rooms with spotless en-suite bathrooms and cable
TV, and windows that seem to do a better job at
keeping out the noise than most places. Breakfast
included. ❹
Residencial San Andrés 12 de Noviembre and
Montalvo ☎ 03/821604. Spotless budget rooms
with tiled floors, green or salmon-pink painted
walls and private bathrooms. They all give on to a

small internal patio, so are a bit dark. **②**
Señorial cnr of Cevallos and Quito ☏ 03/825124,
Ⓕ 829536. Best mid-range choice in town, with
bright, cared-for rooms (ignore the awful plastic
headboards), gleaming en-suite bathrooms, good
showers and cable TV. A few are on the small side,
so ask to see a room first. **④**

Hotel del Sol Luis A. Martínez ☏ 03/825258.
Modest but clean and cheerful rooms with private
bath in a bright-green building on the corner of
Parque 12 de Noviembre. Run by a friendly family.
Good for the price, but can be noisy. **③**

The Town

Ambato's focal point is the leafy **Parque Juan Montalvo**, overlooked by the city's brash, modern **cathedral**, monolithic **Municipio** and the **Casa del Portal** – a handsome survivor of the 1949 earthquake, sporting a row of graceful stone arches spanning the width of the square. The square is named after the locally born nineteenth-century writer, the most distinguished of the trio of former residents that has prompted Ambato to call itself "the city of the three Juans": the other two are the novelist **Juan León Mera**, and lawyer and polemicist **Juan Benigno Vela**. Sitting on the north corner of the square, the humble, whitewashed **Casa de Montalvo** (Mon–Fri 9am–noon & 2–6pm, Sat 10am–1pm; $1) was Montalvo's birthplace and former home, and displays a moderately interesting collection of photos, manuscripts, clothes and other personal effects. Adjoining it is the **Mausoleo de Montalvo** (same hours and ticket), an elaborate Grecian-style temple in which the writer's carved wooden coffin is displayed on a platform, forming a kind of morbid altar.

Three blocks northeast is the city's second major square, **Parque Cevallos**. On Calle Sucre, lining its northwest side, the Instituto Técnico Superior Bolívar houses Ambato's most compelling attraction, the **Museo de Ciencias Naturales** (Mon–Fri 8.30am–12.30pm & 2.30–6.30pm; $1), an old-fashioned natural history museum spread over five halls of a Victorian-style building. The displays kick off with some evocative early twentieth-century photos of the region's volcanoes, including one showing fumaroles spouting dramatically out of Cotopaxi's crater in 1911. The bulk of the collection, though, is formed by stuffed animals, including a jaguar, puma, elephant, boa, spectacled bears, iguanas, monkeys and condors, many of them mounted in dioramas representing the animals' natural habitat. These are followed, towards the end, by a stomach-churning display of preserved freak animals, including a two-headed calf, a three-legged hen and a lamb with one head and two bodies.

A wander around the rest of downtown could take in the handsome **Iglesia de la Medalla Milagrosa**, a French Romanesque-style church built of lovely golden stone, at the corner of Rocafuerte and Egüez. If you're around on Monday, check out the sprawling **market** spread over several sites, including the Mercado Central, next to the Parque 12 de Noviembre, and the Mercado Modelo, a couple of blocks further north. Otherwise, jump in a taxi or a bus from Parque Cevallos and head out to the **Quinta de Mera** (Wed–Sun 8.30am–4pm; $1), a couple of kilometres north of the centre in the suburb of Atocha. The former home of Juan León Mera, it's a grand nineteenth-century adobe house with an overhanging clay-tiled roof supported with thick wooden pillars. There are some original furniture and paintings inside, but what makes a trip here worthwhile are the lush gardens and woods that fill the extensive grounds. Paths lead through them down to the river, and half a kilometre east to the neighbouring **Quinta de Liria**, once a fine house but now dilapidated and empty. Across the main road from the Quinta de Liria, the **Centro Cultural La Liria** (same hours and ticket as Quinta de Mera) displays changing exhibitions of photography, sculpture and paintings.

Eating and nightlife

Ambato offers a very respectable choice of places to **eat**, from budget to fine dining. It's particularly strong on cheap **spit-roasted-chicken** joints such as *Rico Pollo* and *Pollo Listo*, opposite each other on the corner of Cevallos and Egüez, and *Casablanca*, at Vela 622. **Nightlife** is very quiet through the week, but livens up on Fridays and Saturdays: popular **bar-nightclubs** include *Ilusiones*, at Quisquis 1717 and Madrid, which has a restaurant on the ground floor and a disco upstairs, and *Imperio Club*, at Pacha and Saraguro.

El Álamo Chalet Cevallos and Montalvo. Classic, mid-priced *comidas típicas*, including humitas, quimbolitos and seco de chivo (goat stew), as well as international food in a comfortable restaurant.

Buena Mesa Quito 924. Very 1960s in style, with polystyrene ceiling tiles and piped music, but the expensive French-based menu – including seafood crêpe, coq au vin and trout meunier – is appealing, and the food is well prepared. Closed Sun.

Café La Catedral Bolívar 17-50 in the CC La Catedral. A presentable café offering snacks, drinks and inexpensive *almuerzos*. Closed Sun.

Chifa Asia Vela 5-58. Clean, cosy restaurant run by a Beijing family, serving a mixture of Ecuadorian and Chinese dishes. Good choice for a budget meal.

La Fornace Av Cevallos 17-28. Intimate, relaxed and very popular place, serving delicious, inexpensive Italian food; pizzas are cooked in a large clay oven in the dining room.

Gran Álamo Montalvo and Sucre. Civilized if slightly subdued restaurant serving good, moderately-priced *comidas típicas* such as *locro criollo*, crêpes and all the standards. Closed Sun.

Marcelo's Castillo and Rocafuerte. Spick-and-span, cheerful café serving snacks, sandwiches, burgers, hot dogs and the great Chilean classic *el Barros Luco* (griddle-fried beef with melted cheese), as well as 24 flavours of ice cream. Closes Sun 6pm.

Parrilladas El Gaucho Bolívar and Quinto. Tasty, charcoal-grilled parrilladas served in a dimly-lit basement dining room with neon lights on the wall. Popular with local families and good value. Closed Sun.

Listings

Banks and exchange Banco del Pacífico (MasterCard and Cirrus ATM), Lalama and Cevallos; Banco de Guayaquil (Visa, MasterCard and Cirrus ATM), corner of Sucre and Juan Léon Mera; Produbanco, Montalvo 5-30 and Sucre, and cnr of 5 de Junio and Cevallos (MasterCard and Cirrus ATM, changes TCs); Banco del Austro, cnr of Castillo and Sucre (Visa ATM).
Car rental Localiza, cnr of Juan Cajas and Av 12 de Noviembre (℡03/420415).
Hospital Hospital Regional de Ambato, Av Pasteur and Unidad Nacional ℡03/821059.
Internet facilities Many places, including: Jeb Systems.Net, Sucre and Juan León Mera; El Portal, Vela 08-23 and Montalvo; Café Internet, Castillo between Parque Montalvo and Cevallos.
Laundry Fast Clean, Rocafuerte 16-21 and Quito.
Police Atahualpa 568 (℡03/840101).
Post office Parque Juan Montalvo, at the corner of Castillo and Bolívar.
Telephone office Andinatel, Castillo and Rocafuerte.
Travel agents General travel agents for flights and so on include: Clantour, Cevallos 536 and Castillo (℡03/828014); Ecuadorian Tours, Cevallos 428 (℡03/844420); Metropolitan Touring, Rocafuerte 1401 and Montalvo (℡03/824084).

Quizapincha

Up in the hills, just 10km west of Ambato, **QUIZAPINCHA** is something of a surprise, a small, dusty village crammed full of family-run "factories" and shops selling **leather goods**, most of which are bulk-bought by wholesalers and distributed around the country. The quality is generally high and the prices low: you can pick up a fitted leather jacket for around $30 and a well-stitched shoulder bag for around $12. Moreover, as it's less well-known than Cotacachi (see p.151), the leather-manufacturing town near Otavalo, it attracts fewer tourists, keeping prices down.

Buses to Quizapincha leave every half-hour from Ambato's Plaza Rodó, six blocks north up Martínez from Plaza Cevallos. It's a lovely ride, crossing the river and climbing high onto the opposite wall of the valley, giving striking views down to Ambato. Ask to be dropped at the *tiendas de cuero* (leather shops), most of which are clustered near the entrance to the village. If you come back to Ambato at nightfall, you'll be treated to dazzling views of the city lights spread out below you on the valley floor.

Píllaro and Parque Nacional Llanganates

Just north of Ambato, a side road shoots east from the Panamericana for 20km to **Píllaro**, an agricultural village known for its **bullfights** and fine hand-crafted guitars. The time to be here is August 10, the **festival** of San Lorenzo, when bulls are released to charge through the streets, chased on foot by exuberant crowds.

Otherwise, Píllaro's main interest is as a gateway to the **PARQUE NACIONAL LLANGANATES**, created in 1996 to protect the Llanganates mountain range, a spur of the eastern Andes. A wild, little-visited territory of forbidding mountains, bleak páramo, unnamed lakes and impenetrable forest, the mountains have gone down in Ecuadorian mythology as the hiding place of vast quantities of **gold** that was on its way to Peru to pay for Atahualpa's ransom (see p.508), buried here by the general Rumiñahui on hearing that the Inca had been murdered by the conquistadors. The legend gained even greater currency in the late sixteenth century when a Spanish soldier named Valverde – once the sweetheart of the daughter of Píllaro's chief – dictated a map to the treasure on his deathbed, known as *el Derrotero de Valverde*. Since then, countless expeditions have set off to unearth the mythical stash of gold. As you might imagine, none has found it.

One reason given for these many failures is the appalling weather conditions that plague the Llanganates, with continual heavy rain and thick, freezing fog thwarting expeditions. One early twentieth-century explorer concluded that the Llanganates should be marked on maps as "Forever Uninhabitable", and described the region as "dreadful and hostile". The same reasons keep most tourists out of the park, which has no real infrastructure or marked trails. An easy enough **day-trip** is possible by following the road from Píllaro for around 20km east to the Embalse Pisayambo, a reservoir surrounded by many smaller lakes. For the authentic Llanganates experience, however, you'll need to branch south of here into the wilderness – if you're keen, your best bet is one of the **tour operators** in Baños (see p.218) who offer treks in the park, or you could ask around in Píllaro for a local **guide** and **mules** a couple of days before you want to set off (around $10 per day). You'll need to come fully equipped and self-sufficient (you will also need to provide shelter for the guide). The driest time of year here is December and January.

Salasaca, Pelileo and Patate

Southwest of Ambato, some 14km down the road to Baños, **SALASACA** is a small, ramshackle village named after the Salasaca *indígenas* who live here and in the surrounding area. Originally from Bolivia, the Salasacas were relocated to this region by the Incas as part of the *mitimae* system, a practice intended to help colonize new areas and undermine local resistance. Today, the Salasacas still have a very distinct identity, and in some places still buy and sell land according to the original divisions, or *mitmakuna*, granted to their ancestors when they settled here. They are famous for their custom of dressing in black – in mourning, it is said, for the Inca Atahualpa – and for their elaborate woollen

weavings, mostly rugs or wall hangings showing images of stylized human forms or geometric animal motifs. The best time to come and buy is on Sundays, when the town square, right by the main road, hosts a busy **handicrafts market**; on other days, visit the workshops dotted on and around the square, including the Cooperativa Artesenal near the church.

A further 5km down the road, **PELILEO** is to jeans what Quizapincha is to leather, with dozens of small shops selling nothing but. They look a bit tacky but the quality isn't bad and it's certainly a cheap place to stock up on a pair or two. Otherwise, there's little going for this rather charmless town, which was erected from scratch after the dreadful 1949 earthquake completely demolished the original Pelileo, 2km from its present site. Just east of town, a fork branches 5km north from the main road to the little farming village of **PATATE**, reached by climbing into the hills and then making a breathtaking descent into a lush cultivated valley, styled as the "Valley of Eternal Spring". Patate's warm and sunny climate is evidenced by its central square filled with bright flowering trees, and, a couple of blocks to the east, a Complejo Turístico ($1), offering two outdoor pools with great views, a sauna, steam room and restaurant. Between the square and the pools, the *Jardin del Valle Hospedaje* (☎03/870208; ❸) is the place to stay in town, offering reasonable rooms and a decent breakfast. For something a little classier, take a camioneta from the square ($3) 12km north to the impeccably managed *Hacienda Mantieles* (☎03/870123; ❼), a rustic farmhouse offering fabulous views down the valley. It's pretty expensive, particularly when meals are added on ($7 for breakfast, $14 for lunch or dinner), but it makes a seductive place to get away from it all. The hosts also offer horse-riding treks through the valley and hikes up to a nearby cloudforest. If you want to phone for a camioneta to take you back to Patate, book one on ☎03/870193. A couple of kilometres downhill from Patate on the old cobbled road to Baños is *Hostería Viña del Río* (☎03/870143; ❻), a country hotel basking on the valley floor with swimming pools, tennis courts, sauna and steam room that's popular with middle-class *serranos* at weekends.

Patate is also a launchpad for **excursions** to a nearby hilltop aerial station known as Las Antenas, used as an observation point for watching the nightly fireworks produced by **Volcán Tungurahua** (see overleaf), when the sky's clear. Camionetas will take you there from Patate for about $5, including an hour's wait at the top. Note that Salasaca, Pelileo and Patate are all served by Transportes Patate **buses**, which leave every twenty minutes from Plaza La Dolorosa in Ambato.

Baños and around

Continuing east from Salasaca and Pelileo, the Ambato–Puyo road drops sharply in altitude, threading its way down the narrow Río Pastaza gorge before arriving at the small mountain town of **BAÑOS**, 44km southeast of Ambato. A good 1000m lower than most sierra towns, at 1820m above sea level, Baños enjoys a warm, subtropical climate and a spectacular location, nestled among soaring green hills streaked with waterfalls. Add to this the **thermal baths** that give the town its name and the presence of a major **religious shrine** and it becomes clear why Baños has developed into one of the most popular tourist destinations in the country, attracting Ecuadorians and foreigners alike, despite the unpredictable condition of Tungurahua volcano towering above the town to the south (see box overleaf). Visitors to Baños will find a great

Volcán Tungurahua

On September 15, 1999, Ecuador's Instituto Geofísico declared **Volcán Tungurahua** – the 5016-metre-high volcano immediately south of Baños – to be in a state of yellow alert, following a sudden increase in volcanic activity. Within a month, magma had risen towards the crater's surface and the volcano's status was upgraded to **orange alert**, indicating the likelihood of an eruption within days or weeks. On October 16, the inhabitants of Baños and neighbouring villages were forcibly evacuated, leaving some 20,000 people homeless and with no means to support themselves. Roads to the town were sealed off and guarded by the military to prevent people from returning, and rumour began to circulate that some homes were being looted by rogue soldiers. When no large-scale eruption materialized, the people of Baños began to question the need to stay away from their homes, and on January 5, 2000, some 5000 townspeople fought their way through the military blockade, armed with shovels and rocks. The authorities subsequently agreed to re-open the town, but made it clear that those who returned were doing so at their own risk, against official advice. The most serious risk, although only a small one, is of part of the cone collapsing, which would cause potentially lethal mudflows to hurtle down the side of the volcano.

At the time of writing, volcanic activity is ongoing at a low level (yellow alert) with the occasional belch of ash or explosions from the crater. The road up to the mountain refuge is closed, and the volcano supposedly out of bounds to climbers, though a few operators have been ill-advisedly attempting the summit by a reverse route. The highway between the town and Riobamba remains damaged and closed, meaning those travelling to and from the south have to go via Ambato. Nonetheless, as far as tourism is concerned, Baños has completely recovered and the town is filled with hotels, restaurants, travel agencies and visitors. Most hotels have evacuation instructions stuck on the walls, and large yellow arrows and dotted lines on the streets point the way to a designated safety zone on the eastern side of town, in the Santa Ana area. Before you decide to visit Baños, however, you should get **news** on Tungurahua's current state from the daily reports in all the national newspapers, from the SAE in Quito (see p.80) or from the Instituto Geofísico's (Spanish) website Ⓦwww.igepn.edu.ec.

In the meantime, watching Tungurahua has developed into a popular tourist attraction; unless obscured by cloud cover, the most sensational views are to be had at night when the spitting lava and igneous rocks light up the sky like fireworks. From Baños, a *chiva* (wooden bus) takes tourists up to the Bellavista **observation point** every night at 9pm; tickets cost $3, and the bus leaves from Eloy Alfaro, opposite the *Hard Rock Café*, coming back around 11pm (advance tickets can be bought from *Café La Abuela*, on Ambato and Eloy Alfaro, or Córdova Tours at the corner of Maldonado and Espejo). Tungurahua can also be viewed from several other points, including near the village of Patate (see p.209).

choice of good-value hotels and restaurants, as well as excellent opportunities for **outdoor activities** like hiking, cycling, horse riding and rafting.

East of Baños, **the road to Puyo**, in the Oriente, offers one of Ecuador's most scenic approaches to the Amazon basin, taking you past a string of diaphanous waterfalls along the way. Some hang right over the road, while others are approached along short trails, including the thundering **Pailón del Diablo** close to the village of **Río Verde**, about 20km down the road. The **best months** to visit Baños are between September and April; from May to August it can be cloudy and rainy.

Arrival and information

Buses, including those from Quito, Ambato and Puyo, drop passengers inside or right next to the **bus terminal**, three blocks north of the central square, just off the main Ambato–Puyo road. While here you can pick up maps, brochures and other tourist information at the municipal **tourist office** (Mon–Fri 8am–12.30pm and 2–5.30pm, ☎03/740483), on the upper level of the bus terminal. It's an easy walk to most hotels from the terminal, but if you want to take a **taxi** you'll find them parked just outside on the corner of the main road with Maldonado. Local buses run every fifteen minutes during daylight hours between Agoyán east of town to El Salado to the west, stopping in the centre behind the market on Rocafuerte.

Accommodation

Baños has a huge choice of **places to stay**, especially at the middle and lower end of the scale, often offering comfortable accommodation at a very reasonable price. Availability is unlikely to be a problem during the week, but if you've got somewhere particular in mind, it's always worth booking ahead for

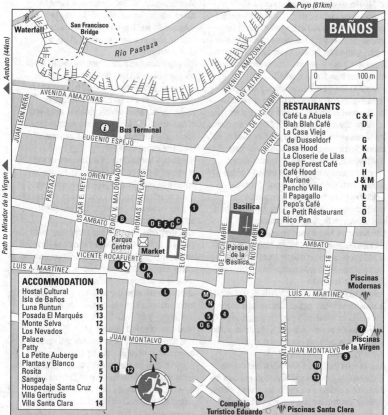

▲ Puyo (61km)

BAÑOS

Waterfall San Francisco Bridge

Río Pastaza

Ambato (44km) ◀

0   100 m

RESTAURANTS

Café La Abuela	C & F
Blah Blah Café	D
La Casa Vieja de Dusseldorf	G
Casa Hood	K
La Closerie de Lilas	A
Deep Forest Café	I
Café Hood	H
Mariane	J & M
Pancho Villa	N
Il Papagallo	L
Pepo's Café	E O
Le Petit Réstaurant	B
Rico Pan	

AVENIDA AMAZONAS

AVENIDA AMAZONAS

AVENIDA AMAZONAS

ELOY ALFARO

16 DE DICIEMBRE

ORIENTE

i Bus Terminal

EUGENIO ESPEJO

JUAN LEÓN MERA

PASTAZA

OSCAR E. REYES

ORIENTE

AMBATO

PEDRO V. MALDONADO

THOMAS HALFLANTS

ELOY ALFARO

16 DE DICIEMBRE

12 DE NOVIEMBRE

A

Basílica

Parque de la Basílica

Path to Mirador de la Virgen ◀

Parque Central

Market

VICENTE ROCAFUERTE

LUÍS A. MARTÍNEZ

AMBATO

CALLE 16

Piscinas Modernas

LUÍS A. MARTÍNEZ

SANTA CLARA

Piscinas de la Virgen

JUAN MONTALVO

JUAN MONTALVO

N

ACCOMMODATION

Hostal Cultural	10
Isla de Baños	11
Luna Runtun	15
Posada El Marqués	13
Monte Selva	12
Los Nevados	2
Palace	9
Patty	1
La Petite Auberge	6
Plantas y Blanco	3
Rosita	5
Sangay	7
Hospedaje Santa Cruz	4
Villa Gertrudis	8
Villa Santa Clara	14

Complejo Turístico Eduardo

Piscinas Santa Clara

▼ Hiking path to ⑮ & Bellvista (starts at end of Maldonado)

weekends and during holidays such as Carnaval and Semana Santa, when you'll probably be charged a little extra.

Hostal Cultural Pasaje Velasco Ibarra and Montalvo ⊕& ⓕ 03/740083. A lovely house in a pretty spot on the edge of town, with comfy sitting room and huge TV showing films in English. The en-suite rooms feature polished wooden floors and firm mattresses and the pricier ones have open fires. A great restaurant with a vegetarian emphasis is attached. Breakfast included. ❹–❺

Isla de Baños Thomas Halflants 1-31 ⊕ & ⓕ 03/740609, ⓔ islabanos@andinanet.net. Appealing German-run hostel, set in an attractive landscaped garden with riotous greenery around a pond, offering comfortable rooms with scrubbed wooden floors and spotless en-suite bathrooms. Also has a café, restaurant, book exchange, library, and can arrange horse and jeep tours. ❸–❹

Hostería Luna Runtun on hill east of town, 8km by road, turning 2km east of Baños ⊕03/740882, ⓕ 740376, ⓦ www.lunaruntun.com. Swiss-run luxury retreat perched on spur affording spectacular views of Baños and of Tungurahua, with landscaped gardens and a spa centre offering massages, mud baths, facials, steam baths and sauna. A fantastic place to unwind. Includes breakfast and dinner. Taxi from Baños is $6. ❾

Posada El Marqués Pasaje Velasco Ibarra and Montalvo ⊕ & ⓕ 03/740053. Good-value, comfortable hotel in a gorgeous spot, right by a waterfall splashing down the mountain. Splendid views from the upstairs rooms (all en suite) and the balcony. ❸

Monte Selva south end of Thomas Halflants ⊕03740566, ⓔ hmonteselva@andinanet.net. Pleasant cabins with sofas and cable TV dotted around pretty gardens on a hillside. Facilities include spa and sauna (only open weekends unless there are plenty of guests), swimming pool and billiards room. Breakfast included. ❺

Los Nevados Ambato and Pasaje Hermano Enrique Mideros ⊕ 03/740673. Modern, functional and spotlessly clean budget *hostal* with a covered rooftop bar-café. All rooms (one to four beds) have private bath. ❷

Palace Montalvo 20-03 ⊕03/740470, ⓕ 740291. A favourite with tour groups, this old-time upper-end hotel offers well-furnished en-suite rooms with cable TV, as well as indoor and outdoor pools, sauna, steam bath and Jacuzzi and a games room ($4 entry for non-residents). ❺

Residencial Patty Eloy Alfaro 556 and Oriente ⊕03/740202. Bargain rooms with shared bath on three floors around a courtyard, and use of kitchen facilities. Pretty basic, but it's kept clean and is a backpackers' institution. ❶

La Petite Auberge 16 de Deciembre and Montalvo ⊕03/740936. Delightful French-run hotel set back from the road in its own peaceful garden, with a pleasant open-sided sitting area and a choice of en-suite rooms and split-level suites, all attractively furnished, many with fireplaces and patios. Breakfast included at its good restaurant *Le Petit Réstaurant* (see p.215). ❹–❺

Plantas y Blanco Martínez and 12 de Noviembre ⊕03/740044. Charming French-owned *hostal* offering spanking clean rooms with private and shared bath and lots of services including laundry, luggage storage and movie rental. Added highlights are the great breakfasts served on the rooftop terrace and the morning steam bath (you sit in a steam-filled wooden box with your head sticking out, and then throw cold water over yourself). ❸

Residencial Rosita 16 de Deciembre and Luis A. Martínez ⊕03/740396. Reasonable lower-end option, offering rooms with one to three beds with shared bath, and four two-bed apartments with a kitchen. All a bit basic and worn, but airy and clean enough. ❷

Sangay Plaza Ayora and Montalvo ⊕03/740490. Long-established hotel offering suites, cabañas, and rooms in the older "colonial" building which have the feel of a faded central European spa resort. There's good service, however, and plenty of facilities ($3.50 for non-guests), such as pool, spa, tennis and squash courts, and a masseur. Breakfast included. ❺–❻

Hospedaje Santa Cruz 16 de Deciembre and Montalvo ⊕03/740648. Great-value French-run hostel with clean and tidy en-suite rooms around gardens. Large range of videos for hire, and excellent breakfast menu including rösti and sweet-potato hash browns. ❷

Villa Gertrudis Montalvo and Eloy Alfaro ⊕03/740441, ⓕ 740442. An elegant and clean old house with a pretty garden offering simple yet comfortable rooms that haven't changed much in the three decades or so the place has been open; some have bathtubs and feather duvets. It has the best swimming pool in Baños for lengths – covered, heated and usually quiet (7am–1pm & 2–6pm; $1.50 non-residents). Breakfast included. ❺

Villa Santa Clara 12 de Noviembre and Velasco Ibarra ⊕03/740349, ⓕ740240. The rooms with shared bath in the main building of this *hostal* are pretty basic, but those with private bath are fantastic value, particularly the neat wooden cabins around the garden. Lovely location, and rate includes use of kitchen and laundry facilities. ❷–❸

The Town

Founded by the Dominicans in 1553 as a staging post between the sierra and the Oriente, and a base from which to evangelize the Amazonian *indígenas*, Baños has evolved into a tidy, prosperous little town built around a luxuriantly landscaped *parque central*. Enclosed as it is by such dramatic, verdant scenery, there's little to catch your eye in the town itself, with the exception of the massive **Basílica de Nuestra Señora del Rosario de Agua Santa** on Calle Ambato, dominated by a pair of 58-metre spires. This "moderated Gothic" basilica, designed by the Belgian Dominican Thomas Halflants, with a later injection of Gothic styling from Cologne-born Padre Pedro Bruning, is the latest incarnation of the town's church, which has been threatened by lava or razed by earthquakes at least half-a-dozen times in its history. It attracts thousands of pilgrims each year, who come to worship **Nuestra Señora de Agua Santa**, a supposedly miraculous icon credited with rescuing Baños and its citizens from countless calamities over the years, many of them – including volcanic eruptions, fires and collapsing bridges – vividly depicted in a series of paintings inside the church. Faith in the Virgin's powers to intervene in the face of disaster still runs very strong in the community, as was demonstrated in September 1999, when the icon was paraded through the town in a procession attended by thousands of people in an attempt to invoke protection from Tungurahua. Upstairs from the cloisters, a **museum** (daily 8am–5pm; $0.50) houses a fascinating and quite bizarre assortment of objects including a shrunken head from the Oriente, pickled snakes in jars, priests' robes, the processional wardrobe of the Nuestra Señora and a collection of stuffed Ecuadorian wildlife put together by someone with a very poor grasp of anatomy.

Beyond the church, sights around town are limited to visiting the baths and to a lesser extent the local zoo and minor attractions near it. One of the most rewarding things to do in Baños then is to explore the surrounding hills, suggestions for which are detailed beginning on p.216.

The baths

Once you've visited the basilica and museum there's nothing to detain you from taking a plunge in one of the town's six **thermal baths**, four of which are in the centre and two on the outskirts. They're all a little institutional-looking, fashioned into rectangular concrete pools with no-frills changing facilities, but wallowing in their yellow-brown waters heated by Tungurahua makes for an irresistible treat. There's no better time for a soak than an hour or so before sunrise – few gringos manage to drag themselves out of bed at this hour, and you'll be sharing the waters with local Ecuadorian families. It's all very friendly and atmospheric, especially in the thin dawn drizzle.

Probably the most appealing set of thermal baths is the **Piscinas de la Virgen** at the eastern extreme of Avenida Martínez, sitting at the foot of a waterfall which tumbles down a rocky cliff; at night it's floodlit to spectacular effect. There are three daytime pools (4.30am–5pm; $2), plus a couple of separate pools downstairs only open at night (6–10pm; $2), all of which are touted as being good for stomach and liver ailments; note that the biggest pool is closed at night. About half a block north, the **Piscinas Modernas** (Fri–Sun 8am–5pm; $2) consist of a large wiggly-shaped pool filled with cold mineral water and a smaller, warmer one (26°C). There are plans to combine these pools with those at la Virgen to make one huge complex. A couple of blocks southwest on Rafael Vieira, the **Piscina Santa Clara**, also known as the Piscina del Cangrejo (Fri–Sun 8am–5pm; $2), is more of a classic swimming pool for doing lengths, and is filled with 23°C mineral water; it's a little run-down but earmarked for a makeover. You can also swim lengths in the three-lane pool next door at **Complejo Turístico Eduardo** (daily 9am–6pm; $2.50) or wallow in their sauna and spa complex. About 2km east of town (a 30min walk, or take any bus to Puyo) off the right-hand side of the road, the **Complejo Santa Ana** (Fri–Sun 8am–5pm; $2) has a big cold pool, and a cou-ple of smaller, warmer ones – they're a bit shabby but in a nice enough spot, set back from the road and banked by green hills. In the opposite direction, 1.5km west of the centre, the popular **Piscinas El Salado** (daily 4.30am–5pm; $2) offers six small pools at various temperatures, each heavily mineralized and reputedly highly curative, plus an ice-cold river for a cool dip. Unfortunately, the baths lie in a danger zone right in the crook of a ravine leading up to the volcano – a gorgeous spot, but, if the volcano is looking active, one of the last places you want to be. Because of its precarious location, by law no public money can be allocated for its improvement, of which it is in increasing need; a few of its most secluded pools have been washed away and cannot now be restored. El Salado can be reached by local **buses** that leave every fifteen min-utes (6am–5pm) from Vicente Rocafuerte and Eloy Alfaro, behind the market, or on foot in about 25 minutes (turn left up a prominently signed fork off the road to Ambato).

The Zoológico San Martín and around
A little further west along the road to Ambato, a couple of hundred metres beyond the turn-off to El Salado, a second turn-off heads north across the dizzying San Martín bridge to the **Zoológico San Martín** (daily 8am–6pm; $1), located in a narrow valley. It's quite a well-managed zoo, with fairly spa-cious enclosures for its occupants, including fenced-off natural areas for the larger mammals. Opposite is the **Acuario y Serpentario San Martín** (same hours; $0.50) housing a decent representation of reptiles and fish from the coastal and eastern rainforests, including the much-feared and highly poison-ous *equis* (fer-de-lance). From the zoo, continue a further 50m down the road and you'll reach a signed path on the right leading through tangled under-growth to the **Cascada Inés María** – a low waterfall and not the most strik-ing in the area, but attractive nonetheless. The zoo is 3km from the centre of Baños and can be reached by **buses** (every 15–30min) from the corner of Vicente Rocafuerte and Eloy Alfaro; alternatively, it's about a 40-minute walk.

Eating and nightlife
As you might expect from a town with so many foreign tourists, Baños boasts a great spread of international **restaurants** offering everything from crêpes to curries, as well as traditional Ecuadorian food and the ubiquitous pizza. Most places are inexpensive, with main courses typically costing around $2–4, and tend to open at around 8am for breakfast and close around 10pm; you'll find a cluster of decent eateries on Ambato between Thomas Halflants and Eloy Alfaro. Baños' most famous **speciality** is a type of toffee made from sugarcane, called *melcocha*, which is hung from the wall and stretched into long, pale-gold strips before being sold in small plastic packets on the street. As for **nightlife**, there are plenty of bars serving cheap cocktails and beers, and several places to dance, often to live *folklórica* music (when a small cover charge might be levied), particularly the stretch of Eloy Alfaro between Ambato and Espejo. Most open daily around 8pm, but usually only the ones that pull in a crowd will still be open in the small hours.

Restaurants and cafés

Café La Abuela Ambato and Eloy Alfaro, also around the corner on Eloy Alfaro. Small, cosy café with warm lighting, lots of natural wood, and an agreeable choice of breakfasts, salads, snacks, pancakes and ice cream. Also has a well-stocked bar, with decent cocktails and five types of rum. Closes 11pm.

Blah Blah Café Ambato, opposite the market. Small, cheap and cheerful café serving breakfasts, salads, sandwiches, omelettes and fruit juices, among other snacks and light meals. Closed Wed.

La Casa Vieja de Düsseldorf Ambato and Eloy Alfaro. Full service eatery with attentive service and a friendly atmosphere, with a decent choice of fish and seafood – including seabass and trout – enlivening the more predictable chicken, pizza and pasta choices. They also offer the "*oreja de elefante*" (elephant's ear), a massive but thin piece of steak that will fill much of your plate.

Casa Hood Martínez and Thomas Halflants. Attractive and popular restaurant with huge range of international (mostly vegetarian) cuisine, including Indian, Chinese, Indonesian, Thai and Mexican. Also has a book exchange and a choice of videos to play ($1). Closed Tues.

La Closerie de Lilas Alfaro 620 and Oriente. Simple, good-quality and reasonably priced French food, including tasty steak and trout. The atmosphere can be a bit subdued, but is occasionally perked up by live folk music.

Deep Forest Café Rocafuerte and Halflants. Decorated with rainforest murals and abstract splashes, this café offers inexpensive food with plenty of veggie dishes, including Greek salad, falafel and tabouleh.

Café Hood Maldonado and Ambato. Good food and a menu oriented towards Tex-Mex are on offer at this little restaurant enjoying a nice location overlooking the square. Closed Wed.

Restaurante Mariane Rocafuerte and Halflants, plus Martínez and 16 de Diciembre. Wonderfully indulgent French food including *steak à la crème, poivre et cognac* (peppered steak in a brandy cream sauce) and *crepe au chocolat*. The original restaurant at Rocafuerte has a dining room featuring a huge old gramophone, among other oddities. The branch on Martínez is only open after 4pm.

Pancho Villa 16 de Diciembre and Martínez. Cheerful, thronging Mexican restaurant serving delicious, inexpensive food in a room covered in postcards from around the world, largely sent by satisfied customers. Good margaritas too. Closed Sun.

Il Papagallo Martínez and Eloy Alfaro. Appealing Italian restaurant offering a range of fresh pasta dishes made by an internationally trained Ecuadorian chef. The *Cannelloni alla Florentina* (spinach cannelloni) is very good. Closed Tues lunch.

Pepo's Café Ambato and Eloy Alfaro. Quiet place on a busy thoroughfare, offering a range of inexpensive Ecuadorian and international dishes.

Le Petit Réstaurant attached to *La Petite Auberge* hotel on 16 de Deciembre and Montalvo. Warm, cosy French-run bistro serving excellent crepes, steaks and trout, as well as their speciality meat and cheese fondues.

Rico Pan cnr of Ambato and Maldonado. Popular bakery and café, serving sandwiches in delicious wholemeal bread and a range of snacks, salads and light meals. Plenty of newspapers to read and a book exchange. Closed Sun pm.

Bars and discos

Peña Ananitay 16 de Diciembre and Espejo. One of the best places to hear live *folklórica*, even though it's an intimate space with only a small dance floor. A popular place with a good atmosphere and great music. Opens at 9.30pm.

Bamboos Eloy Alfaro and Espejo. Funky, lively place, playing a decent mixture of salsa and dance in a small venue decorated with murals of Celia Cruz and Che Guevara, and a big, spangly mirror ball.

Peña Canela y Clavo Rocafuerte and Maldonado, on the *parque central*. Relaxed establishment with plenty of upholstered seating and tables, but little space to dance, featuring live music each night (usually *folklórica*).

Coco Bongo Montalvo and 16 de Diciembre. Large karaoke and pool bar that's frequently more miss than hit, but occasionally packed. There are a couple of pages of English songs to pick, from artists such as the "Roline Stobe" and "Jhon Lebon".

Hard Rock Café Eloy Alfaro, just north of Ambato. Not a member of the international chain, but a cross between a pub and a school disco, with a bar, table football and seating area in one room and an adjoining room for dancing. Plays mainly North American music, but is popular despite the soft rock.

Kasbah Eloy Alfaro and Espejo. Two-floor bar with drinks downstairs and a pool table upstairs, playing dance and Latin music. Closed Sun.

Pipas Bar 16 de Diciembre between Ambato and Oriente. Colourful bar, decorated with surreal murals on the walls and a pool table downstairs. Excellent piña coladas.

Volcán Eloy Alfaro and Espejo. Friendly, rustic little bar with a band which plays Andean folk music most nights. Try their *volcán* cocktail, a concoction of hard spirits that goes down like molten lava.

Listings

Banks and exchange Banco del Pacífico, cnr of Halflants and Rocafuerte (Visa, MasterCard, Cirrus ATM), changes TCs for $5 commission; Banco MM Jaramillo Arteaga on Ambato and Halflants, changes TCs; Comercial Torres, cnr Ambato and Halflants, and Comercial Don Pedro next door also change TCs; Le Petit Breton, Oriente and Eloy Alfaro, changes TCs and euros.

Camping equipment Voraxi, Maldonado and Oriente, repairs rucksacks and sells others of reasonable quality, many of which are made on site.

Dancing lessons Ritmo Son, below Casa Hood (T03/740359). Daily classes for $5 an hour.

Internet facilities Typical rates are around $2 per hour. Access is available at many places around town, including venues on Ambato between Halflants and the Basílica; on Martínez between Alfaro and 16 de Diciembre; and on 16 de Diciembre between Montalvo and Marínez.

Language schools Baños Spanish Center, Oriente 8-20 and Julio Cañar (T03/740632); Mayra's Spanish Lessons, at Oscar Reyes 3-30 and Martínez (T03/740331); International Spanish School, 16 de Diciembre and Espejo (T03/740612); Instituto de Español Alternativo (IdEA), cnr of Alfaro and Montalvo (T03/740799); Raices Spanish School, 16 de Diciembre and Pablo A Suárez (T & F03/740090, Eracefor @hotmail.com).

Laundry Cheap wet-wash laundries charging by the kilo include: La Vieja Molienda, Thomas Halflants and Martínez; Le Petit Breton, Oriente and Eloy Alfaro; Lavandería La Herradura, Luis A. Martínez and Eloy Alfaro; and Lavandería Nicole, 16 de Diciembre, between Luis A. Martínez and Montalvo.

Massage From around $20 per hour. Stay in Touch Therapeutic Massage, Martínez and Alfaro, also offers aromatherapy; Joana Massage, cnr of Martínez and Alfaro, Thai and Swedish.

Police and immigration Casa de Gobierno, Thomas Halflants between Ambato and Vicente Rocafuerte (T03/740122).

Post office On Thomas Halflants, between Ambato and Vicente Rocafuerte.

Shopping A small crafts market on Pasaje Ermita de la Virgen, off Ambato, sells balsawood and leather goods, but is nothing special. There are many shops in town offering a range of handicrafts including: Artesanías Las Orquídeas, cnr of Ambato and Maldonado, also Montalvo and Halflants; Taller en Tigua, Maldonado and Espejo, specializing in jewellery and objects carved from tigua, "vegetable ivory"; the Centro Cultural Huillacuna, on the corner of Montalvo and Santa Clara, exhibits and sells an excellent range of contemporary Ecuadorian art.

Telephone office The Andinatel office is on the corner of Vicente Rocafuerte and Thomas Halflants.

Activities and tours around Baños

Few visitors come to Baños without wanting to strike out into the surrounding countryside to explore its hills, ravines, rivers and waterfalls. There are a number of highly rewarding **hikes**, many of them giving superb views onto town or Volcán Tungurahua when the weather's clear. **Cycling** is another great way to explore independently, especially along the descending road to Puyo. In addition, several **tour operators** offer a wide range of guided excursions, including: **horse riding** in the hills around Baños; **white-water rafting** on the Río Pastaza (class III rapids), or other rivers such as the Patate (II–III), Palora (III–IV) and Anzu (III); **canyoning**, which involves rappelling down river ravines; and **jungle trips**, which usually mean a bus or jeep ride to Puyo, followed by an hour or two's drive to a base in the rainforest. Several companies also offer **climbing tours** – they traditionally focused on Tungurahua, but since it became active, attention has moved to other peaks like Cotopaxi and Iliniza. If you're considering booking a climbing tour, however, bear in mind that Baños, at just 1820m above sea level, is not the ideal base from which to embark on a high-altitude trek or climb. A few agents also offer **bridge jumps** from the Río Blanco bridge, 8km east of town, a risky activity at best, which is least hazardous and stressful to the rope if you swing off gently rather than leap headfirst.

It's worth keeping in mind that sports such as rafting, canyoning and climbing are potentially **dangerous** when led by untrained people using substandard equipment. Make sure your guide is properly qualified where possible (AGAR for rafting; ASEGUIM for climbing), and your gear is in good condition.

Hiking

There are several interconnecting **footpaths** leading up the mountainside over the south side of town, all clearly marked on the large colour map of Baños available at the tourist office and many local shops. Starting at the south end of Maldonado, a path heads up for around forty-five minutes to a large white cross marking a spot called **Bellavista**; the views at the top are breathtaking. From here, you can continue uphill for another kilometre or so to the *Hostería Luna Runtun*, where you can loop west on a downhill path that takes you to the **Mirador del Virgen**, from where it's an easy downhill walk back to Baños (the round-trip takes around four hours). The *mirador*, marked by a statue of the Virgin, can be reached directly from Baños in about thirty minutes on the path starting at the end of Juan León Mera. On the opposite side of the town, follow the path starting at the corner of Reyes and Amazonas, behind the bus terminal, for about ten minutes down to the **San Francisco bridge** spanning the beautiful Río Pastaza gorge. Across the river, several paths lead steeply up the hillside, as well as east and west along the bank of the gorge, linking up with several other bridges across the river. Another enjoyable walk west is to the **zoo** and waterfall nearby (see p.214); continuing on from both leads up to the village of Lligua, from where a trail leads to hilltops with fine views. On the whole, the paths around Baños are perfectly safe, but it should be pointed out that, though few in number, some **robberies** and **assaults** have been reported on them.

Cycling

Countless establishments in Baños rent **mountain bikes** for around $4–5 per day; the quality is improving, and most machines now come with front suspension to help you with the bumpy roads. That said, you should shop around for the best bikes, and test the brakes, gears and tyres before committing yourself; consider also asking for a helmet, pump and basic toolkit. The most popular **cycling route** is east along the road to Puyo (for more details, see p.218) – mostly downhill, but with uphill stretches appearing fairly regularly – returning to Baños on one of the half-hourly buses that trundle along the road (you can store your bike on the roof; last bus around 6pm). Most people are happy to limit themselves to the first fifteen kilometres to the village of Río Verde, near the Paillón del Diablo falls, reached in about two hours from Baños; the scenery is dramatically beautiful, but beware of narrow sections and sheer drops. Note too that there are a couple of pitch-black tunnels on the ride: the first (at km 6) is 100m long and can be cycled with care; the second (km 7) is almost a kilometre in length and prohibited to cyclists – use the old road to the side. Some people complete the whole 61km to Puyo (7–8hr with breaks), which is quite a challenging ride, with some very stiff uphill stretches along the second half of the journey. The road is unpaved with lots of potholes and gravel between Baños and Río Negro (27km), a stretch that can turn into a muddy quagmire after heavy rainfall, but paved from Río Negro to Puyo. Several agencies rent out **motorbikes** and scooters for around $10 per hour, though the latter are unsuitable for the uneven road surfaces on this route.

Canyoning

Canyoning is a sport that beginners with a good head for heights can have a go at, provided, of course, they have an experienced guide who knows the route well. The best canyoning area is around the Río Negro (27km east of town), though the San Jorge waterfall (11km east) is a popular, if less spectacular alternative. Although several agencies offer canyoning trips, Franco de Antoni (☏09/9819756), the owner of *Pequeño Paraíso* at Río Verde (see opposite), is the best person to speak to. He introduced the sport to the region and leads trips for $35 per person.

Tour operators

Adventurandes Eloy Alfaro 554 ☏ 03/740202. Offers two- to four-day jungle trips, as well as a range of trekking programmes around the central sierra volcanoes. Most tours are around $35 per day.

Aventura Travel Agency Montalvo and Thomas Halflants ☏ 03/740566. A range of horse and bike rides around Baños from four to eight hours, from $16 to $22. Also rents mountain bikes.

Caballos Con Christián at the Hostal Isla de Baños, Thomas Halflants 1-31 ☏ & ☏ 03/740609. Two one-day horse treks for experienced and novice riders at $22–25 in the foothills of Tungurahua or outside the Baños area, including jeep transport, lunch and horses in good health.

Córdova Tours cnr of Maldonado and Espejo ☏ 03/740923. Runs a *chiva* (wooden, open-sided bus) to the waterfalls on the road to Puyo including the Pailón del Diablo (9.30am–2.30pm; $8); around the town (4–6pm; $5); and to watch the volcano by night (9–11pm; $3).

Deep Forest Adventure Rocafuerte and Thomas Halflants ☏ 03/741815. Eloy Torres speaks English, German and Greek and leads trekking

trips to Sangay and Llanganates national parks, jungle tours to a Shuar community in the southern Oriente, as well as a three-week adventure trip down the Bobonazo to Iquitos, Peru.

Expediciones Amazónicas Oriente 11-62 and Thomas Halflants ☏ 03/740506, also Ambato and Eloy Alfaro. Offers a three-day "Shaman tour" which includes participation in a shaman ritual, and a go at using a *cervátana* (blowgun), as well as hikes through the rainforest.

Geotours Ambato and Halflants ☏ 03/741344. Offers a range of half- to two-day rafting trips on the ríos Patate, Pastaza, Palora and Jatun Yacu for around $60–100 per day.

Rain Forestur Ambato 8000 and Maldonado ☏ & ☏ 03/740743. Jungle-tour specialist with experienced guides and a good reputation. Most tours (from $25 per day) are around Puyupungo, an hour's drive south of Puyo.

Río Loco Maldonado and Luis A. Martínez ☏ 03/740929. Swiss–Ecuadorian company, offering rafting down the Río Pastaza ($30 for half-day, $60 full day) plus guided horse and bike rides around Baños. Also rents bikes.

East to Puyo: Río Verde

East of Baños, the road to Puyo begins its descent towards the Oriente, carving its way through the Pastaza Valley, high above the river. It's 61km to Puyo, but even if you're not heading there you should take a bus (or bicycle) along the first 20km to the village of **RÍO VERDE**, for the spectacular scenery along the way. The lush walls of the valley are sprinkled with waterfalls, some of them falling right overhead from overhanging rocks. The vegetation, too, is exuberant and exotic, with numerous wild orchids peppering the hillsides. Some 12km down the road you pass a sign advertising "**the longest cable car in Ecuador**" ($1) where – if you dare – you can step into a flimsy-looking box with sides that only come up to your waist and take a gut-churning cable ride across the gorge and back. A further 3km down the road you get to Río Verde, a collection of modest houses, stores and truckers' stops. From here, a well-maintained one-kilometre path leads down to the **Pailón del Diablo** ("Devil's Cauldron"), a thundering waterfall formed by the Río Verde as it hurtles down the gorge to join the Río Pastaza. You can buy refreshments at a small café by the falls, which asks visitors for contributions to conserve the trails and viewing areas.

A short walk past the waterfall, a wobbly bridge leads across the river to *El Otro Lado* ("the other side"), a group of romantic and secluded **cabañas** with hot water and electricity surrounded by a relatively small patch of forest that you can explore on several trails (☎03/884193 or contact *Hostal Cultural* in Baños; ❻ including two meals). A couple of kilometres east of Río Verde, the Swiss-run *Pequeño Paraíso* (☎099819756, ⓦwww.geocities.com/pequeno_paraiso; ❺ including breakfast and dinner) is another peaceful place to stay, with pleasant en-suite cabins with hot water, a climbing wall, a pool, volleyball court and access to hikes through bird-filled forests (home to the Andean cock-of-the-rock). The owner also leads canyoning and climbing expeditions in the area and can provide equipment. **Camping** is also possible here for $3 per person.

Río Negro to Puyo

About 13km from Río Verde is the little hamlet of **RÍO NEGRO**. Here there is a turning 3km up to the *Vrindavan Jardin Ecológico* (☎02/2491563 in Quito, ⓦwww.vrindavan.org; ❹ including breakfast), a spiritual retreat offering "alternative relaxation" by means of yoga, tai chi, African drumming, kung fu and ayurveda classes, as well as walks into the forests and horse rides. The simple cabins have shared bath (hot water is planned), and inexpensive vegetarian meals ($2.50 for three courses) are available in the dining room. Heading east from Río Negro, the road is paved, and as you enter Pastaza province, the scenery opens out revealing broad views of the valley, now hot and humid with Oriente air. **MERA** is 17km further, and 44km from Baños, which has a church, a phone office, a basic hotel, and a **police checkpoint** at which you will probably be asked to show your passport. Some 7km down the road, there's a greater military presence at **SHELL**, more hotels (but no reason to stop) and an airstrip which is used by several light-aircraft charter companies that service remote communities in the Oriente, most of which you'd need permission to visit. A couple also fly to cities such as Quito, Lago Agrio and Coca, but these are not generally regarded as tourist services. **Puyo** (see p.336), lying at the end of the descent 10km to the east, is the capital of Pastaza province, from where other roads head north to Tena and south to Macas. **Buses** run from Baños to Puyo every 30 minutes.

Guaranda and Salinas

From Ambato, most tourists head either east to Baños or south to Riobamba, with few opting for the route west to Guayaquil. This is a shame, because the road makes for one of the most scenic bus rides in the sierra: even if you don't plan to go all the way to the coast, it's worth doing the first 99km to **Guaranda**. The paved, though somewhat potholed, road snakes first through low, round, intensively cultivated hills – if you look right, about half an hour into the journey, you'll see some of the most vertiginous fields imaginable, running in near-vertical strips up the hillsides. Presently, you leave these behind as you climb up to the highest stretch of paved road in Ecuador (4300m) to head across the bleak, cold páramo. To the left, you're treated to dizzying views onto 6310-metre-high Chimborazo, unless it's hidden by the thick blankets of fog that so often roll across the high moorland.

The town itself, although boasting a beautiful location and some handsome, colonial-style architecture, has little to keep you interested for more than a couple of hours. Nearby **Salinas**, however, is one of the prettiest and most rewarding villages in the whole sierra, particularly if you enjoy departing from the beaten track and getting to know the local community.

Guaranda

About two hours after leaving Ambato, you wind your way down to **GUARANDA**, which sits in a shallow basin surrounded by hills. It's hard to believe this is the provincial capital of Bolívar, what with its physical isolation and sleepy, small-town air. The centre of town is marked by the charming **Parque Bolívar**, lined with old adobe houses with painted wooden balconies and sloping, red-tiled roofs flecked with lichen. The square also houses a grand, twin-towered **church**, a striking mixture of bare stone and white stucco, and the gleaming, white-walled **Municipio**, looming over the mature palms that give this place a more tropical look than its climate warrants.

Elsewhere, the town's narrow, cobbled streets see relatively little traffic, and it's not unusual to spot someone leading his horse down the road, or a couple of hens clucking around the pavement. After you've nosed around the square, the only real "sight" to head for is the towering stone statue of "**El Indio Guaranga**", the sixteenth-century indigenous chief after whom the town is said to have been named. It's up on one of the nearby hills ($1 by taxi), with sweeping views down to the town and across to Chimborazo, and a modest museum (variable hours; free) alongside it, offering displays on Guaranda's history. Otherwise, check out the colourful Saturday **market** on the Plaza 15 de Mayo, where you'll see *campesinos* from local villages trading wheat, barley and maize for fruit brought up from the coast.

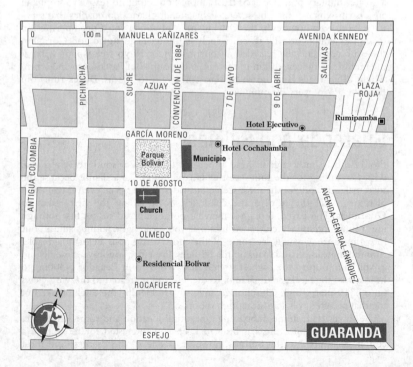

Practicalities

The **bus station**, on the outskirts of the town centre about ten blocks east of Parque Bolívar, is served by a few taxis. In town, you'll find **taxis** hanging around Plaza Roja, where **local buses** pull in and out. The fanciest **place to stay** in Guaranda is *La Colina* (☎ & ℱ 03/980666; ❺), a hotel perched up on a hill overlooking the town ($0.80 by taxi), with comfortable, cosy rooms, some of which have balconies with fantastic views. There's also a reasonable restaurant and a small indoor pool and sauna. Down in the centre, the best choice is the *Ejecutivo*, at García Moreno 803 (☎ & ℱ 03/982044; ❸), with clean white walls, firm beds and parquet flooring. Stand-bys include the large, echoing *Cochabamba*, at García Moreno and 7 de Mayo (☎03/981958; ❹), whose rooms are en suite and fairly comfortable though showing their age, and the cheerful *Residencial Bolívar* at Sucre 704 (☎03/980547; ❸), with uninspired rooms around a little courtyard full of potted plants.

There are no particularly good **restaurants** in Guaranda: the one at *Cochabamba* hotel is decent, but only opens when they've got guests. Otherwise, try *Rumipamba* on Plaza Roja, a basic place with fake red roses on the table and paintings of the specialities on the wall (spaghetti, chops and fried chicken). For the best albeit priciest food in the area, reserve a table at *La Colina* and take a taxi there and back.

Salinas

The final bend in the dirt road branching north from Guaranda for 30km reveals, quite suddenly, **SALINAS** at its most dramatic: a collection of flashing white houses huddled together near the foot of a vertical wall of rock, surrounded by rolling fields and plains. This isolated village, sitting high in the sierra at 3500m, is named after the abundant supplies of salt that have been exploited here since pre-Hispanic times. These days, Salinas is a fascinating example of a flourishing cooperative-based economy, founded on a multitude of local industries.

It was the arrival in Salinas in 1971 of the Salesian missionary, Father Antonio Polo, that turned the village's fortunes around. With the help of various Christian and international aid agencies, Father Antonio established the **FUNORSAL** foundation (Fundación de Organizaciones de Salinas) to encourage locals to set up a number of cooperatives, providing them with training, materials, technical support, bank loans and accounting assistance. Before long, the villagers' lives were transformed: sheep owners, for instance, who had previously sold raw wool to middlemen for a pittance, began to spin their own yarn and supply directly to manufacturers, for a decent profit, while dairy farmers, with the help of Swiss technicians, set up several highly productive milk and cheese factories in the area, supplying retailers at a national level. Today, FUNORSAL represents 26 cooperatives from Salinas and the surrounding area, whose activities range from mushroom growing to honey production. Visiting the village's cooperatives, particularly the **cheese factory**, **wool workshop** and **chocolate workshop**, makes for an enjoyable and enlightening few hours, especially if you take a local guide to show you round, which you can arrange for a couple of dollars at *El Refugio*. This pleasant, rustic **hotel** – run, of course, by a cooperative – offers private rooms (☎03/981266; ❸) and cheaper dorms, along with an inexpensive **restaurant**, Spanish lessons and a small archeology museum on the ground floor. You can also arrange guided **hikes** or **horse treks** (around $10 per day) from the hotel into the surrounding hills; for something less energetic, take a short walk up the hillside to the village cemetery for memorable views down the valley. Local **buses** to Salinas leave from Guaranda's Plaza Roja at around 6.15am and 1pm, returning at 1pm and 3pm; the journey takes around one hour.

Riobamba and around

From Guaranda, a serpentine dirt road leads 61km east to **Riobamba**, the liveliest and most attractive city in the central sierra, sitting on the Panamericana 52km south of Ambato. With an appealing blend of fast-paced buzz and old colonial charm, Riobamba easily merits a visit in its own right, but can also be combined with worthwhile excursions. Most famously, it's the start of the **Devil's Nose train ride**, and is also a popular base for visiting **Volcán Chimborazo**, while nearby **Guano** is a less demanding, if somewhat duller, target. East of Riobamba, the northern stretch of **Parque Nacional Sangay** offers some great trekking opportunities, in particular to the volcanic crater of **El Altar** which is approached from the community of **Candelaria**, and to **El Placer hot springs** and **Volcán Sangay**, both reached from the village of **Alao**.

Riobamba

The self-proclaimed "Sultan of the Andes", **RIOBAMBA** is a handsome city made up of stately squares, flaking, pastel-coloured buildings, cobbled streets and sprawling markets. Though its location has moved several times, it's been an important centre since the earliest days of Spanish rule, when it was founded as the colony's first city as Santiago de Quito in 1534. It remained so, however, for less than two weeks before the Spanish decided to relocate to the Pichincha foothills where the capital was refounded as San Francisco de Quito, but even so, Riobamba, as it was now called – a castilianization of the Quichua word for the area – soon grew into a flourishing town. The place was dealt an abrupt and catastrophic blow, however, when a massive earthquake left it in ruins in 1797, though it was quickly rebuilt where it stands today, 20km north of its original site. Located as it is in the centre of the Ecuadorian sierra, Riobamba is a major trading nucleus, with part of its appeal stemming from the lively mix of suited city dwellers and large numbers of indigenous traders from the countryside. The main **market day** is Saturday, when the city overflows with energy and colour. Another draw is the wonderful views (if you're lucky with the weather) across the city to Volcán Chimborazo; most hotels have flat roofs, so if you wake up on a clear morning – the earlier the clearer, generally speaking – ask to go up to the roof patio.

Arrival and information

Riobamba's main **bus terminal** (☎03/962005) is a couple of kilometres from the centre, at the intersection of avenidas Daniel León Borja and De La Prensa; cabs into the centre cost $0.80, or you can take a bus down Daniel León Borja as far as the train station. If you're arriving from Baños or the Oriente, you'll pull in at the smaller **Terminal Oriental** (☎03/960766) on the corner of Espejo and Luz Elisa Borja, about 1km northeast of the centre and served by plenty of taxis and city buses. A third bus station, the **Terminal La Dolorosa** on Puruhá and 10 de Agosto, eight blocks southeast of the Parque de la Libertad, services the small provincial communities to the south on the road to Macas including Alao and Atillo. The **train station** (☎03/961909) is very central at Avenida

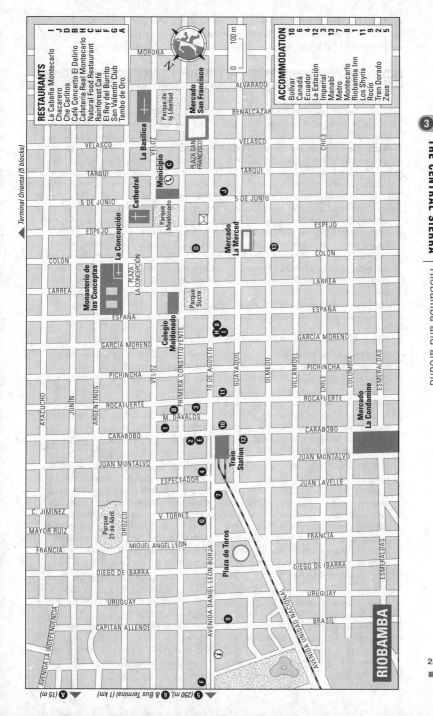

RESTAURANTS

La Cabaña Montecarlo	I
Chacarero	J
Che Carlitos	D
Café Concerto El Delirio	B
Cafetería Real Montecarlo	H
Natural Food Restaurant	C
Rainforest Café	E
El Rey del Burrito	F
San Valentín Club	G
Tambo de Oro	A

ACCOMMODATION

Bolívar	10
Canadá	6
Ecuador	4
La Estación	12
Imperial	3
Manabí	13
Metro	7
Montecarlo	8
Riobamba Inn	1
Los Shyris	11
Rocío	9
Tren Dorado	2
Zeus	5

MORONA

ALVARADO

BENALCÁZAR

VELASCO

TARQUI

5 DE JUNIO

ESPEJO

COLÓN

LARREA

ESPAÑA

GARCÍA MORENO

PICHINCHA

ROCAFUERTE

CARABOBO

JUAN MONTALVO

JUAN LAVELLE

FRANCIA

DIEGO DE IBARRA

URUGUAY

BRASIL

CHILE

ESMERALDAS

COLOMBIA

VILLARROEL

OLMEDO

GUAYAQUIL

10 DE AGOSTO

PRIMERA CONSTITUYENTE

VELOZ

Mercado San Francisco

Parque de la Libertad

VELASCO

La Basílica

La Cathedral

Municipio

PLAZA SAN FRANCISCO

Cathedral

La Concepción

Parque Maldonado

Mercado La Merced

Monasterio de las Conceptas

PLAZA LA CONCEPCIÓN

Parque Sucre

Colegio Maldonado

Mercado La Condamine

Train Station

Plaza de Toros

Parque 21 de Abril

AYACUCHO

JUNÍN

ARGENTINOS

M. DÁVALOS

ESPECTADOR

V. TORRES

OROZCO

MIGUEL ANGEL LEÓN

C. JIMÍNEZ

MAYOR RUÍZ

FRANCIA

DIEGO DE IBARRA

URUGUAY

CAPITÁN ALLENDE

AVENIDA LA INDEPENDENCIA

AVENIDA DANIEL LEÓN BORJA

AVENIDA UNIDAD NACIONAL

RIOBAMBA

Terminal Oriental (5 blocks)

▲ 5 (250 m), 6 & Bus Terminal (1 km)

▲ (A) (15 m)

0 100 m

Daniel León Borja and Carabobo. In town, you'll find plenty of **taxis** hanging around Parque Maldonado, Parque Sucre and Parque Libertad. If you need to call one, try one of the cooperatives (☎03/960088, 961646 or 966011).

Guided tours and climbs around Riobamba

A number of outfits and independent guides offer a range of **tours around Riobamba**. For day visitors, the most popular target is the refuge at 4800m on the slopes of Volcán Chimborazo, from where you can take a strenuous half-hour to hour walk up to the second refuge (5000m); see p.229 for details. Several hotels in Riobamba offer good-value **day-trips** here, including the *Tren Dorado*, Carabobo 22-35 (☎03/964890) and the *Imperial*, Rocafuerte 22-15 (☎03/960429), though these aren't recommended for any serious mountaineering. Dedicated **climbing companies and guides** (see below) concentrate on guided ascents of Chimborazo (6310m), the highest peak in Ecuador and the most popular volcano climb after Cotopaxi; most also offer climbs up neighbouring Carihuairazo (see p.229) and other central sierra volcanoes. Some also do multi-day **hiking** programmes around the sierra, providing tents, sleeping bags, food and transport. All prices quoted below are per person for a group of two people, including a guide and equipment rental.

Riobamba is the only place outside Quito for top-quality specialist **mountain-bike tours**, organized by Pro Bici, Primera Constituyente 23-51 and Larrea (☎03/941880, ℱ961923, ⓦwww.probici.com); if there's no one there, ask in the fabric shop opposite. Itineraries range from riding down the slopes of Chimborazo and gentler outings around rural villages to multi-day tours of the Atillo or Ozogoche lakes; good bikes, protective equipment and a support vehicle are provided.

Climbing companies and guides

Alta Montaña Av Daniel León Borja 35-17 and Diego Ibarra ☎03/950601, ℱ942215, ℮aventurag@laserinter.net. Well-respected company offering ascents up Chimborazo and Cotopaxi for around $180, plus two- to five-day hikes in the sierra for $90–350. Owns the *Posada La Urbina*, a walkers' hostel and acclimatization centre near Chimborazo (see p.229).

Andes Trek Colón 22-25 and 10 de Agosto ☎03/940964, ℱ940963, ⓦwww .andes-trek.com. Run by established guide Marcelo Puruncajas, who's been climbing Chimborazo since 1968. Offers guided ascents up all the sierra peaks, including Chimborazo ($180), and hiking programmes around Cotopaxi, Chimborazo and El Altar from $70 per day.

Expediciones Andinas Km 3.5 along the road to Guano ☎03/940820, ℱ940819, ⓦwww.expediciones-andinas.com. A polished full-service outfit run by the respected mountaineer Marco Cruz, offering everything from single ascents up Chimborazo ($210) to multi-climb packages ($1820 for a sixteen-day tour including 5 peaks). Uses its own mountain hut at 4000m, the *Estrella del Chimborazo*, as base camp for Chimborazo and also owns the *Albergue Abraspungu*, an upmarket lodge near Riobamba.

Julio Verne 5 de Junio 21-46 and 10 de Agosto, ☎ & ℱ03/963436, ⓦwww .julioverne-travel.com. Reputable Dutch-Ecuadorian operator specializing in adventure tours such as mountaineering, cycling, white-water rafting, jungle trips and multi-day treks – for example, the Inca trail from Alausí to Ingapirca ($200); 5 days in the páramo around the El Placer hot springs ($375); and around the spectacular El Altar peak ($190).

Veloz Coronado Expediciones Chile 33-21 and Francia ☎ & ℱ03/960916, ℮ivoveloz@yahoo.com. Run by Ivo Veloz, an ASEGUIM qualified guide, who comes from a strong mountaineering family – his father has climbed Chimborazo 230 times in forty years. Chimborazo ascents start at $200 per person.

The very helpful **Ministerio de Turismo** (Mon–Fri 8.30am–1pm & 2.30–6pm; ☎ & ⓕ03/941213) is in the Centro de Arte y Cultura on Avenida Daniel León Borja and Brasil. For basic information on Volcán Chimborazo or Parque Nacional Sangay, take a taxi to the **Ministerio del Ambiente** (Mon–Fri 8.30am–4.30pm; ☎03/963779) at 9 de Octubre, near Calle Duchicela, or to the **Fundación Natura** office, at Segundo Rosero and Saint Amound Montriu (☎03/943192) in the Barrio Los Álamos.

Accommodation

There are some good budget-to-mid-price **accommodation** options in Riobamba, but nowhere really smart in the town centre. If you're after luxury, you'll need to take a bus or taxi to the *Albergue Abraspungu* (see below), 3.5km along the road to Guano, or head to the *Hostería La Andaluza* (☎03/949370, ⓦwww.hosteria_andaluza.com; ❼), a converted hacienda exactly 16km north up the Panamericana, some fifteen minutes by taxi ($4). If arriving in Riobamba the night before the "Devil's Nose" train departs, it's worth phoning ahead to book a room, as the most popular places fill very quickly. Most of the very cheap hotels are clustered around the train station.

Albergue Abraspungu Km 3.5 along the road to Guano ☎03/940820, ⓕ940819, wwww.hosteria-abraspungu.com. Upmarket, tastefully designed lodge owned by Expediciones Andinas, offering a rustic, hacienda-style look with plenty of modern comforts. Can be reached by taxi ($1.50) or the bus to Guano (see p.228). ❻

Bolívar Carabobo and Guayaquil ☎03/968294. Basic bottom-dollar hotel with dark old rooms, shared bathrooms and uninviting beds, redeemed by the swept, waxed wooden floors, cheery colour scheme and attractive, colonial-style courtyard. Ask in the bag shop next door if there's no one there. ❷

Canadá Av de la Prensa 23-31 ☎ & ⓕ03/946676. Modern hotel with English-speaking owners diagonally opposite the bus terminal, offering simple, spotless rooms with private bath and cable TV. ❹

Ecuador Espectador 22-32 ☎03/940800. One of many basic old hotels in town, with ancient beds, very high ceilings, tall windows and the reassuring smell of cleaning products in the air. ❷

La Estación Av Unidad Nacional 29-15 and Carabobo ☎03/951541. Well-presented new hotel by the station, offering tidy rooms with private bath and cable TV. The more comfortable suites cost the same, but are on the noisier street side of the building. Breakfast can be served early in its restaurant for those making the train ride. ❹

Imperial Rocafuerte 22-15 ☎03/960429. A notch above the real cheapies, with spacious, reasonably comfortable rooms with and without private bath – popular and good value, though the TV in the central living room can be noisy. Also organizes day-trips to Chimborazo. ❷–❸

Manabí Colon 19-28 ☎03/967967. Old fashioned, rather dated hotel offering light, tidy rooms with wooden floors, cable TV and some with brown en-suite bathrooms. There's an on-site garage as well. ❸–❹

Metro Av Daniel León Borja and Lavalle ☎03/961714. Simple, spick-and-span rooms in a distinctive older hotel with lots of light, en-suite bathrooms and cable TV (in most rooms). Has its own parking. ❷

Montecarlo 10 de Agosto 25-41 ☎03/960557. *Hostal* featuring comfortable, carpeted rooms with private bathrooms and cable TV arranged around a lovely two-storey courtyard, festooned with hanging plants. Very colonial looking. Breakfast included. ❺

Riobamba Inn Carabobo 23-20 ☎03/941311, ⓕ940974. Well-run little hotel with pleasant, cared-for rooms, some with attractive new bedding and curtains, others more dated. All have private bathroom and most have cable TV; has private parking. ❹

Los Shyris cnr of 10 de Agosto y Rocafuerte ☎03/960323. A hotel with low ceilings and dowdy wallpaper, that's kept clean and tidy by the friendly staff. It's popular with backpackers for its central location, computers with Internet access, and huge cable TV in a cosy lounge area. Most rooms have private bath. ❹

Rocío Brasil 21-68 ☎03/971848. Pleasant, tidy, good-value *residencial* on a quiet side street, run by an elderly couple. Rooms are spacious and come with private bath and cable TV. Breakfast not available. ❸

Tren Dorado Carabobo 22-35 ☎ & ⓕ03/964890. Friendly, popular hotel with a choice of newer, quiet rooms at the back (no TV), or slightly older ones at the front (with cable TV), all with private bath. Also offers outside washtubs and clothes lines, early-morning breakfasts before the train ride and tours to Chimborazo. ❸ **Zeus Av Daniel León Borja 41-29** ☎ 03/968036, Ⓔ hotelzeus1@hotmail.com. Large hotel with a flash reception, glass-backed elevator and a lovely restaurant. The standard rooms have cable TV and private bath, but are slightly drab, while executive suites have more ostentatious furnishings and bathtubs. ❺–❻

The City

The best place to start exploring Riobamba is the **Parque Maldonado**, a wide square lined by the city's most impressive nineteenth-century architecture, including the colonnaded, peach-and-white **Municipio**, where Ecuador's first constitution was signed in 1830, and other flamboyant colonial buildings trimmed with elaborate stucco mouldings. On the northeast side of the square, the delicately carved stone facade of the **cathedral** is Riobamba's only survivor of the 1797 earthquake, painstakingly transported and reassembled here when the town was rebuilt. The city's two other major churches are the Neoclassical, pink-domed **Basílica**, three blocks southeast on Parque La Libertad, and the red-brick, neo-Gothic **Iglesia de la Concepción**, a couple of blocks northeast of Parque Maldonado.

Adjoining the Iglesia de la Concepción, the **Monasterio de las Conceptas** houses one of the best museums of religious art outside Quito (entrance on Argentinos, Tues–Fri 9am–noon & 3–6pm, Sat 9am–6pm; $4). A series of small rooms around a leafy patio is devoted to various themes, such as the Nativity, with most pieces dating from the eighteenth century. The bulk of the collection is made up of carvings and paintings, but you'll also find some richly embroidered robes, beautifully carved inlaid chests, and silver lecterns and crowns. The museum's most prized possession is a gold, jewel-encrusted monstrance used to display the consecrated wafer of the Eucharist during Mass, believed to be one of the most valuable in South America.

Riobamba's only other museum is a modest natural history collection (Mon–Fri 8am–1pm; $0.25) in the imposing **Colegio Maldonado**, on **Parque Sucre**. Even if the museum is closed, it's worth taking a look inside the college building to admire its marble staircases and arcaded courtyard. If you're in town on a very clear day, take a wander out to the **Parque 21 de Abril**, a small, landscaped hill about eight blocks north of Parque Sucre, offering fine views over the town and across to Volcán Chimborazo.

Finally, if you're around on a Saturday you can't fail to be impressed by the immense **market** bulging out of the streets bounded by calles España, 5 de Junio, Guayaquil and Argentinos. The range of products for sale is staggering, from squawking chickens to rubber boots; for **artesanías** head to the Plaza La Concepción, in front of the church, where you'll find many *shigra* bags, ponchos, shawls and jewellery. If you're not in town on Saturday you can still catch the smaller-scale Wednesday version, as well as the daily covered **fruit and vegetable market** at La Condamine, or the smaller **flower and fruit market** at La Merced off Colón, between Guayaquil and Olmedo. Something else to look out for is Riobamba's speciality, **tagua nuts** (see p.49) carved into items ranging from massage contraptions to jewellery. You'll find a handful of tagua carving shops on Daniel León Borja between Lavalle and Francia.

Eating and nightlife

Riobamba offers a decent choice of **restaurants**, but very little in the way of **nightlife**. What there is is usually only open from Thursday to Saturday – the city's favourites *La Vieja Guardia*, on Manuel E. Flor and Zambrano, and *Romeo*

& Juliet Bar, on Vargas Torres and Avenida Daniel León Borja, are both fairly small disco-bars playing a mixture of salsa and dance music.

The Devil's Nose train ride

In 1899, after twenty-five years of frustrated plans and abortive attempts, work finally started on Ecuador's first **railway**, which would link the coastal city of Guayaquil with the capital, Quito, in the highlands. The first hundred-kilometre stretch was laid without too much difficulty, but as the tracks advanced eastwards towards the mighty barrier of the Andes it was obvious that a serious challenge lay head. The greatest obstacle, which prompted the line to be dubbed "the most difficult railway in the world", was met 130km east of Guayaquil when the tracks reached a near-vertical wall of rock, known as **El Nariz del Diablo (The Devil's Nose)**. The ingenious solution was to carve a series of tight zigzags out of the rock, which allowed the train to climb at a gradient of 1-in-18, from 1806m to 2607m, by going forwards then backwards up the tracks. Once past Alausí in 1902, progress speeded up and the tracks reached Riobamba in 1905 and Quito in 1908. Considered a triumph of railway engineering, the line continued, however, to face many financial difficulties, and soon acquired a reputation for poor equipment and administration, and frequent delays and derailments.

The service from Guayaquil to Riobamba and Quito continued to run, with interruptions, until 1997, when the tracks were devastated by El Niño. The hundred-kilometre stretch from Riobamba to Sibambe, at the end of the Devil's Nose descent, has since been restored and is now operated by the Empresa Nacional de Ferocarriles del Estado as a **tourist service**; there are no plans to repair the rest of the line. Considered one of the highlights of a trip to Ecuador by many visitors, the ride offers spectacular views of Chimborazo and Carihuairazo, and a thrilling descent down the Devil's Nose itself. The most popular way to travel is on the roof of the train, to the amusement of locals who watch it trundle by, piled high with gringos.

Taking the train

The train leaves Riobamba on Wednesdays, Fridays and Sundays at 7am, taking roughly four hours to get to the town of **Alausí**, from where it's another hour to the little station of **Sibambe**, at the bottom of the Nariz del Diablo. After a twenty-minute pause, the train heads back up the Nariz del Diablo and stops at Alausí at around 1.30pm (for more on Alausí, see p.236), where it pauses again for over an hour, prompting many passengers to travel the last stretch by bus (2hr), cutting several hours off the return journey. The train finally gets back to Riobamba at about 6–7pm. **Tickets** cost $11 for the standard Riobamba–Sibambe–Alausí route, and a further $3.40 for the slow haul back from Alausí to Riobamba, and are available at the city's train station (daily 8am–noon & 2–6pm, also in the morning before departure from 6am; ☎03/961909). It's a good idea to get your ticket the day before travelling to avoid the long queues. An alternative is to join the train at Alausí (arrive before 11am), for the Nariz del Diablo alone (Alausí–Sibambe–Alausí), a ticket for which costs $7 and can be bought in Riobamba or at the station in Alausí.

If you plan to **ride on the roof**, dress in layers as the weather is freezing at the beginning of the journey but warms up considerably after a couple of hours. It's also a good idea to take your sleeping bag to sit on, if you've got one, or to buy one of the inexpensive cushions on sale by the tracks, as the tin roof offers little comfort. **Refreshments** are available at many short stops along the way, when vendors climb onto the roof to sell drinks, fried bananas and other snacks. The traditional train is regularly replaced by two smaller and less nostalgic **autoferros**, bus chassis attached to rail undercarriages, especially during the week when there aren't so many passengers. The service is subject to unpredictable changes, so call the station office ahead for all the latest news.

La Cabaña Montecarlo García Moreno 21-40. Slightly formal restaurant with a wide-ranging menu and a large, TV-free dining room that can feel really empty when not busy. The mid-priced food is cooked with more enthusiasm than flair, but does the job. Closed Mon.

Chacarero 5 de Junio 21-46. Small, family-run restaurant serving the best pizzas in Riobamba; very popular with locals. Open 3–10pm; closed Sun.

Che Carlitos Colón 22-44. Down-to-earth Argentinian steakhouse offering almost every imaginable part of a cow's anatomy cooked over a blazing, charcoal-fired grill. Stick to the steak and you'll have no regrets. Often has live music on Friday and Saturday nights. Closed Sun.

Café Concerto El Delirio Primera Constituyente 28-16 ☎03/960029. Beautiful colonial house, once the home of Simón Bolívar, with a flower-filled patio and a cosy indoor dining room with a crackling log fire. Its elaborate meat and fish dishes (often swimming in sauces) are pricier than average ($5–9 a main course), but there's a great atmosphere and live *folklórica* music if there are enough people.

Luigi's Condorazo and Unidad Nacional ☎03/962397. This warehouse of a restaurant is a little cold and out-of-the-way but more than makes up for its lack of ambience with some of the best food in town (around $7–8 a main course). Menu items include warm chicken salad in balsamic vinegar dressing, fresh pasta with roasted vegetables, prawns fried in olive oil, garlic and parsley, and a fabulous chocolate mousse with fresh raspberry sauce. A short taxi ride. Closed Sun & Mon evenings.

Cafetería Real Montecarlo 10 de Agosto 25-41. Good-value snacks, sandwiches and some main meals served in intimate wooden booths. Soft lighting and soothing music make it more of an evening place.

Natural Food Restaurant Tarqui and Veloz. Inexpensive vegetarian meals along with standard meat dishes. The two-course veggie *almuerzo* is only $1.20 and filling. Closed evenings and all Sun.

Rainforest Café next to *Tren Dorado* on Carabobo and 10 de Agosto. An option for early breakfasts before train departures, this jungly café done up with tiger-print tablecloths also serves up crêpes, hot drinks and snacks. Closed Mon.

El Rey del Burrito Av Daniel León Borja and Costales. Inexpensive Mexican restaurant on the ground floor of a large old house decorated with sombreros and textiles, serving reliable enchiladas, burritos and all the other standards.

San Valentín Club Av Daniel León Borja 22-19. Lively, diner-style café-bar that's best for evening fare, serving pizzas, burgers, tacos and burritos, best washed down with plenty of beer. Fills with a young and cheerful local crowd. Tues–Sat 5pm–midnight.

Tambo de Oro Carlos Zambrano and Junín, five blocks west of the Parque 21 de Abril ☎03/962668. Not very central, but the delicious home-made soups, such as the prawn bisque, and well-prepared meat and fish dishes make the five-minute taxi ride worthwhile. Closed evenings.

Listings

Banks Banco del Pacífico, on the corner of Veloz and Av Miguel Ángel León, has a MasterCard and Cirrus ATM and changes TCs for $5 commission; and Banco de Guayaquil on Primera Constituyente, between Moreno and Pichincha, has a Visa, MasterCard and Cirrus ATM.

Buses See "Arrival and information" on p.222 about the location of Riobamba's three bus terminals. Local city buses regularly go to the Terminal Terrestre along Orozco, returning down Av D L Borja. For the Terminal Oriente, they leave from the train station. A few local destinations are serviced from other parts of the city: buses to Guano depart from Mercado Dávalos on Rocafuerte and Nueva York.

Festivals The biggest are *Las Fiestas Abrileñas*, leading up to April 21, which commemorates the victory over the Spanish at the Battle of Tapi in 1822, and November 11 for the Independence of Riobamba.

Hospital Best hospital in town is the private Policlínico on Olmedo and Cuba (☎03/965725).

Internet facilities Several around the centre offering access for around $0.80 per hour, including *Los Shyris*, cnr of 10 de Agosto and Rocafuerte; Compu Net, Juan de Lavelle and Daniel León Borja; Le Monde, Primera Constituyente and Carabobo; LM Internet, 5 de Junio and 10 de Agosto.

Laundry *Café Ashoka*, on Carabobo and 10 de Agosto (☎03/942567), is cheap and charges by the kilo; phone for free collection and delivery.

Police Calle Policía (☎03/969300).

Post office 10 de Agosto 21-72 and Espejo.

Telephone office Andinatel is in the big, grey concrete building at Tarqui and Veloz; also at the Plaza de Toros on Av Unidad Nacional and Francia.

Travel agents Most general travel agents, for booking or changing flights, are strung along the main artery formed by Daniel León Borja and 10 de Agosto. Reliable agents include Metropolitan Touring, Daniel León Borja 3764 and Miguel Ángel León (☎03/969 600); and Viajes Quálitas, 10 de Agosto and Colón (☎03/960081). For climbing, trekking and biking tour operators and guides, refer to the box on p.224.

Volcán Chimborazo and around

At 6310m, **Volcán Chimborazo** is the highest peak in Ecuador. A giant of a mountain thought to have last erupted some 10,000 years ago, its base spans approximately 20km and its upper elevations are permanently covered in snow and ice. The summit was once imagined to be the highest in the world, and still enjoys the distinction of being the furthest point from the centre of the earth, thanks to the bulge around the equator.

With a good access road and two mountain refuges perched on its lower slopes, Chimborazo can easily be visited on a **day-trip** from Riobamba. While going for the summit is a challenging undertaking only to be attempted by climbers with plenty of mountaineering experience, day-visitors can make it as far as the second of its two refuges. If you don't fancy basing yourself in town, another good place in which to acclimatize and from which to hike to Chimborazo lies some 26km north of Riobamba on the Panamericana; follow the signs west to "La Urbina" for a couple of kilometres to *Posada La Estación* (☎03/963694; ❹), a former railway station sitting on high moorland. Now an attractive walkers' *hostal*, at 3620m this is the highest point on the Quito–Riobamba train line (currently disused); the owners, the Alta Montaña tour company in Riobamba (see box, p.224), can arrange guided hikes and horse treks.

Just north of Chimborazo, **Cerro Carihuairazo**, although an interesting and enjoyable climb and, at 4900m, a very respectable mountain in its own right, is generally overlooked by climbers in favour of its higher neighbour. It's usually approached from a scenic camping area at 4200m, and takes about seven to eight hours to get up and down, including some basic ice climbing. Most of the guides and climbing companies listed on p.224 offer programmes to Carihuairazo; Andes Trek is highly recommended for this trip.

Note that Chimborazo and the area around it – including Carihuairazo – is part of the **Reserva Faunística Chimborazo** and subject to a $10 **entrance fee**, which is usually collected at the guard post near the *cruce del arenal*. On the way up, look out for **wild vicuña**, which now number eight hundred in the páramo around Chimborazo, following a reintroduction programme underway since 1987 – vicuñas disappeared from Ecuador around the time of the Conquest.

Visiting Volcán Chimborazo

The **first refuge** sits at 4800m and can be reached in about ninety minutes along a mostly paved road from Riobamba; most day-trippers either take a camioneta from near the train station (about $15 per person) or arrange transport with their hotel. On the way up, about 12km short of the refuge, you'll pass the tiny community of **San Pablo** (3730m), composed of a few thatched huts and a basic walkers' **hostal**, the *Casa Cóndor* ($2.50 per person) – if you're planning on climbimg the summit, you may want to spend a night here acclimatizing. The refuge can also be reached by a dirt road branching south from the Ambato–Guaranda road; if you want to **hike** up, this is the shortest approach: take a Guaranda bus from Ambato and ask to be dropped at the crossroads ("*el cruce del arenal*") from where it's a four- to five-hour walk. Once there, you can buy hot tea and basic foodstuffs; there are also cooking facilities, running water, electricity and bunkbeds ($10).

A popular target for day-visitors is the walk (30min–1hr) from the first refuge up to the **second refuge**, referred to as the Whymper refuge after Edward Whymper, the British climber who made the first ascent of Chimborazo in 1880. At an altitude of 5000m, there's only 200m to climb to the refuge here, but it can be totally exhausting if you're not acclimatized. With any luck, the views will more than repay the effort, but it's possible that everything will be hidden by clouds. In any event, take plenty of sunscreen, water and very warm gear. This is the larger and marginally more comfortable of the two refuges, also with cooking facilities, running water, electricity and also costing $10 for the night. If you're sleeping at either refuge, bring a warm sleeping bag; there are lockers to store your gear while you're climbing, but you'll need to bring a lock. For information on either refuge contact Alta Montaña (details on p.224).

Although not Ecuador's most technically difficult ascent, the rest of the **climb** requires large amounts of stamina, previous climbing experience and complete ease with full mountaineering equipment. Adequate **acclimatization** is essential, and climbing several other peaks in advance, such as Iliniza Norte or Cotopaxi, is common preparation. Also, consider spending a couple of nights at the refuge before the climb. There are several **routes to the summit** and, since the choice of which one to take is helped by an understanding of the local climate and conditions, you are strongly advised to go with a **guide** who knows the mountain well (see box on p.224). Most climbers set off at around midnight, taking eight to ten hours to reach the summit and about three to four to descend. The way up is relentlessly steep, and a long, hard slog. Along with all the standard mountaineering equipment, be sure to take sun block, sun goggles and plenty of water; it's also a good idea to take your own snacks in addition to the food brought by your guide. The best months for climbing Chimborazo tend to be November to May, with December often being particularly good; between June and October it can be windy.

Guano and Santa Teresita

The sleepy little village of **GUANO**, 10km north of Riobamba, can seem a little dull in comparison to world-famous train rides and ice-capped mountains. That said, it's set in a picturesque valley, with hills all around, and boasts a lovely, flower-filled square and a couple of handsome old churches. Guano is best known as a rug-manufacturing centre, and you'll find lots of small workshops dotted about the square making and selling rugs of somewhat questionable taste. Most are made from sisal, which you can see growing and being cut down by children in the fields surrounding the village. Guano is very quick and easy to reach from Riobamba, with **buses** leaving every ten minutes from the Mercado Dávalos at Rocafuerte and Nueva York, three blocks north of Ayacucho.

From Guano, frequent buses shuttle to the neighbouring village of **SANTA TERESITA**. From the village's church, where they drop and pick up passengers, it's a twenty- to thirty-minute downhill walk to the **Balneario Los Helenes**, a spa complex with three spring-fed pools (Mon–Fri 9am–6pm; $1). The setting is outstanding, with fabulous views onto Tungurahua, and thanks to a local microclimate the weather is often warm and sunny. The water, however, is quite cold, and usually has dead insects and leaves floating on the surface, and the changing rooms and administration building have something of a derelict look.

El Altar

Twenty-five kilometres east of Riobamba, **EL ALTAR** is an extinct, heavily-eroded volcano rising to the south of Volcán Tungurahua, inside **Parque Nacional Sangay**. Named Cupac Urcu, or "sublime mountain", in Quichua, El Altar boasts a breathtaking crater set within an amphitheatre of jagged, ice-

The **Parque Nacional Sangay** is a vast, sprawling wilderness area covering more than 5000 square kilometres of the central sierra's eastern cordillera, with its eastern edge spilling down into the Amazon basin (see p.343). The park's stunning Andean scenery takes in three volcanoes (Tungurahua, El Altar and Sangay), over three hundred lakes, pristine páramo and native cloudforest, providing a habitat for spectacled bears, Andean condors, pumas and deer, among other mammals, while jaguars, monkeys and ocelots inhabit the lower, tropical areas. There's very little infrastructure for tourists, and no marked trail system. Apart from the soon-to-be-completed **Guamote–Macas road** slicing through the park from the sierra to the Oriente (see p.234), access to Parque Nacional Sangay is via a number of remote, potholed dirt roads leading to the various *guarderías*, or **ranger stations**, serving the different areas of the park, often situated near local communities that can be reached by bus. Below are the park's main attractions, from north to south, and their access points. The **entrance fee** for foreigners is $10.

Volcán Tungurahua. A snowcapped, 5016-metre-high volcano, normally approached via the Guardería Pondoa, south of Baños, but currently off-limits due to renewed volcanic activity. See box, p.210.

El Altar. A spectacular volcano with a crater lake, reached on an eight-hour hike from the Guardería Candelaria, connected to the Riobamba–Baños road from the village of Penipe. See opposite.

El Placer hot springs and **Volcán Sangay.** Rustic thermal springs and a remote, difficult-to-reach volcano, both approached from the Guardería Alao, in the village of Alao, reachable by bus from Riobamba. See overleaf.

Lagunas de Atillo. Beautiful páramo lakes near the Guardería Atillo, right next to the road to Macas, served by buses from Riobamba. See p.234.

Lagunas de Ozogoche. Another collection of páramo lakes set in rugged scenery, reached via a dirt road branching east of the Panamericana for 36km, midway between the towns of Guamote and Alausí. See p.235.

capped peaks studded with hanging glaciers that are constantly rumbling and cracking. Lying in the bottom of the crater at an altitude of 4300m is **Laguna Amarilla**, whose yellow-green waters are dotted with blocks of ice that have calved off the glaciers above. A wide gap in the west side of the crater opens onto a flat plain known as the **Valle de Collanes**, which provides easy access down to the lake. El Altar can be reached on a highly rewarding three-day round-trip **hike**, for which you'll need to carry full camping equipment and all food. The starting point is the tiny village of **Candelaria**, a fifteen-kilometre drive down a dirt track southeast from the village of **Penipe**, which sits 22km northeast of Riobamba on the road to Baños. You can get to Penipe on any of the frequent Riobamba–Baños buses, and once there it's possible to hire a truck from the square (about $8–10, ask around) to take you to the Candelaria **ranger station**, where you pay the $10 entrance fee; be sure to arrange to be picked up again. From the ranger station, it's a five- to six-hour **hike** along a well-trodden, easy-to-follow **path** up to the **Valle de Collanes**, where most people pitch their tent for the first night. From here, it's only a couple of hours up to the gap in the crater rim, from where you can scramble down to the edge of the lake in about half an hour. There are areas where you can camp around the lake, which makes a fabulous place to catch sunset and sunrise. Heading back, count on taking about an hour to get back up to the plain, and then another three hours back to the ranger station. Note that some stretches of the path get extremely muddy after rainfall, so consider taking gaiters or rubber boots.

Alao, El Placer and Volcán Sangay

Southwest of Riobamba, a spectacular rough dirt road with bird's-eye views of the valley floor follows the Alao valley down to the small community of **ALAO**, gateway to **El Placer hot springs** and **Volcán Sangay**, both within the Parque Nacional Sangay. The ranger station for the park, at the end of the road running through the village, is where you pay the **park entrance fee** of $10; hang on to the ticket, as it's valid in all the park's other sectors (see box, p.231) for a two-week period. They also have a few **beds** with use of a kitchen and bathroom that you can use for a few dollars. If there's no one in the station when you get there, the chances are they'll be back within a few hours; if no one turns up, ask in the village for the *guardaparques* or for *alojamiento*, and someone will point you in the direction of someone who can offer a bed for the night as well, usually for around $3–5.

There are a few small stores in Alao where you can buy basic foodstuffs, but you should bring all fresh **food** in from Riobamba. It takes about two and a half hours to get to Alao from Riobamba: **buses** leave from the Terminal La Dolorosa (see "Arrival and information", p.222) according to an irregular timetable (Mon–Fri 6.25am; Mon, Wed, Fri & Sat noon & 6pm; Tues & Thurs 2pm, 4pm & 6pm); it may also be possible to arrange a lift in with the park staff from the Ministerio del Ambiente office. As well as returning buses, a daily milk truck sets off from the centre of Alao every day at 7–8am for Riobamba. The **best months** to hike in this part of Sangay are November to February, when the weather is at its driest and sunniest, though downpours can still spring on you at any moment, so come prepared. Outside these months the area is prone to cold, wet, windy and sometimes foggy conditions.

El Placer

About 25km east of Alao, **El Placer** (which appropriately translates as "pleasure") is a fabulous natural pool filled with deliciously hot thermal water. A few years ago US Peace Corps volunteers installed a small changing area near the pool and a timber **refuge** with bunks, cooking facilities and a toilet. As it's inaccessible by vehicle, you'll almost certainly have it to yourself – it's hard to imagine a more rewarding and exotic end to the hike here.

The well-marked **trail** to El Placer (in fact an abandoned road) heads east from Alao and takes in some glorious scenery, including wild páramo, alpine forest and humid cloudforest. If you have your own transport, or have come in from Riobamba by camioneta, note that it's possible to do the first 15km in a sturdy **4WD**, bringing you to within 4km of pretty **Laguna Negra** from where it's about a four-hour hike to El Placer. Another alternative is to hire **horses or mules** for about $10 (ask in the village the day before), which can take you to within a two-hour hike of the springs.

If you intend to do it all **on foot**, expect the hike to take approximately nine to eleven hours in total – it's possible to cram these into a single day if you set off early, but it's more comfortable to camp en route and spread it over two days. The terrain is not too difficult, with only a couple of hours' steep uphill walking there, though it's a bit tougher walking back. This hike is definitely best done in dry, warm weather; even so, you might still want to carry rubber boots with you to negotiate a few extremely muddy areas.

Volcán Sangay

Exquisitely symmetrical **Volcán Sangay** (5230m) is one of the most active volcanoes on the continent, making any attempt to climb it a seriously risky undertaking due to frequent rock and ash explosions out of its three craters. Add to this the sheer inaccessibility of the mountain and it becomes clear why Sangay is one of the lesser-climbed peaks in Ecuador. That said, significant numbers of undeterred, adrenaline-hungry climbers pass through Alao on their way to Sangay, determined to have a go – enough, in fact, to have prompted locals to organize a guide association, the Asociación de Porteadores y Guías de Turistas.

Several climbing agencies in Riobamba (see p.224) offer this climb, which can be logistically tricky to arrange independently. Hiring a **guide** ($8–10 per day, minimum of 5 days), and **porters** if you want help carrying your equipment, is absolutely essential for the two- to three-day hike to the base camp of La Playa, which requires an intimate knowledge of the local area and its confusing maze of cattle trails; note that you will have to supply all your guide's and porters' **food**. The best-known guides are Roberto and Carlos Cas, Casimiro Leme and Casimiro Quirray – ask the park rangers in Alao to put you in touch with them, or ask around in the village. You might be able to turn up and sort a guide out the day before you plan to set off, but it could easily take longer. Most will refuse to accompany you up the summit – they justifiably consider it too dangerous – but can take you to a spot near the base of the mountain called La Ventana, where they can show you the route up. Make sure everyone is clear as to what is included in the price: in particular, ask to be taken not just to base camp, but beyond it to La Ventana.

It's possible to get away without camping on the hike from Alao to the volcano, as there's a thatched **hut** you can sleep in on the way, and a ten-person **refuge** at La Playa, but bring a **tent** nonetheless. You will also need to bring a stove, plenty of fuel, good waterproofs and a pair of rubber boots for wading through the atrocious mud on the way to base camp. As for the ascent, although not strictly a technical climb, there can be a lot of snow and ice near the top so you will need crampons and an ice axe, and you'll need to be confident at self-arresting on steep slopes. It is crucial, too, to take a **helmet** to guard against falling rocks. It usually takes about three to five hours to ascend, and two to descend. Do not underestimate the risks involved in doing this climb, and get proper advice from the SAE in Quito (see p.80) and the Ministerio del Ambiente office in Riobamba (see p.225) before embarking on the trip.

South to Alausí

Almost 20km southwest of Riobamba, the Panamericana trails past the dusty, unremarkable town of **CAJABAMBA**, standing on the site occupied by Riobamba until it was destroyed by an earthquake in 1797 – look out for the large gash in the hill above the town, still showing signs of the massive landslide caused by the earthquake. A little further south, sitting right by the highway, is the **Iglesia de Balbanera**, said to be the first chapel in Ecuador raised by the conquistadors and founded on September 15, 1534. Though considerably altered since then, it still preserves an early-colonial stone facade around the entrance, embellished with gargoyles and carvings of angels, and topped by a traditional Andean bell tower. If you're lucky enough to pass on a cloud-free day, the little chapel presents an impressive photo opportunity, standing right in front of the dramatic, snowcapped cone of Volcán Chimborazo. South of the church, both the highway and the rail tracks skirt the wide **Laguna de Colta**, its grey waters backed by pale-green hills dotted with fields. Its shores are lined by tall reeds, gathered by local *indígenas* to be woven into mats and other articles – you'll find many for sale in Cajabamba's Sunday-morning market, lining each side of the highway.

South of the lake, the Panamericana carves its way through increasingly wild and less cultivated country as it approaches the small town of **Guamote**, the site of one of the most enjoyable indigenous markets in the sierra. Rewarding sideroads off this stretch of the highway head east to **Laguna Atillo** and **Laguna Ozogoche**, high on the páramo in **Parque Nacional Sangay**. The Panamericana, meanwhile, heads down to **Alausí**, the final town on the central sierra.

Guamote

Fifty kilometres south of Riobamba, set 1km back from the highway, **GUAMOTE** is an attractive town, if slightly down-at-heel, sporting a few handsome timber buildings from the railway era in the early twentieth century, with their characteristic balconies leaning on thick wooden pillars. Although the train from Riobamba still chugs through the middle of town it's no longer a vital commercial artery, and these days Guamote's *raison d'être* is its massive Thursday-morning **market** that almost rivals that of Saquisilí with its size and vigour. Hundreds of *campesinos* inch their way through the streets, with the largest swell of crowds between 10am and noon. Not to be missed is the chaotic **animal market** up in the field behind the Iglesia de San Vicente, where ducks, chickens, sheep, piglets and guinea pigs (ranked among the most delicious in the country) change hands, while, all around, loudspeakers compete in volume to advertise the latest miracle cures.

Practicalities

Buses to Guamote leave Riobamba every ten minutes on Thursdays from Avenida Unidad Nacional and Avenida de La Prensa close to the Terminal Terrestre. **Trains** from Riobamba chug through town on Wednesdays, Fridays and Sundays at around 10am (see p.227); the train station is in the middle of town, on the Calle Principal. The best **place to stay** in town is at the revamped *Ramada* on Vela and Riobamba (℡03/916242; ❸), with neat parquet floors, tiled bathrooms and a pleasant **restaurant**. Otherwise, *Residencial Turismo* (℡03/916173; ❶–❷) offers modest but clean little rooms in an old wooden building directly opposite the railway station; ask in the pharmacy next door if no one's in.

Lagunas de Atillo and the road to Macas

About 500m south of the turn-off to Guamote on the Panamericana, a couple of large signs point east to Macas and the Lagunas de Atillo, marking the start of the controversial **new Guamote-Macas road** slicing through the **Parque Nacional Sangay** to the Oriente. Though due to be completed several years ago, at the time of writing there were still a couple of kilometres to go, which were proving very difficult to finish off. The environmental impact of the road construction has been enormous, prompting UNESCO to declare Sangay one of the world's endangered parks. The end of the road, known as "**La Punta**" – an ever-shifting "point" moving eastwards – is currently about 90km east of Guamote, with an ever-decreasing gap separating it from the end of the road from **Macas.** In the meantime, it's possible to combine bus or truck rides with hiking to cover the whole stretch in a long day – a rewarding trip, taking in high, wild páramo, lakes, waterfalls and virgin cloudforest.

About 48km southeast of Guamote, the new road passes a network of lakes known as the **Lagunas de Atillo**, in whose icy waters the Puruháe people are said to have drowned their most reviled criminals in pre-Hispanic times. The most beautiful is **Laguna Magdalena**, dramatically framed by jagged, spiky peaks, and the best views are to be had looking back from the east, a few minutes after driving past it – bus drivers are usually happy to stop for a couple of minutes at the **mirador** looking down to it, while people take photos. Just beyond, the road climbs to a pass through the eastern cordillera, flanked by a small lake filled with black, sinister-looking water. A few kilometres east, you come to the park ranger station known as the **Guardería Atillo**, where you pay your entry fee ($10) for Sangay park.

East of here the road gradually leaves the windswept páramo behind as it descends towards the Amazon basin, flanked by steep slopes covered by dense cloudforest. As you get lower, the climate gradually becomes warmer and moister, feeling almost tropical by the time you reach the tiny community of **Zuñac**, 15km on from the ranger station. Five kilometres east of here is the park's second ranger station, the Guardería Purshi; followed, a further 5km east, by the hamlet of **San Vicente de Playas**. The next proper village, about 28km east, is **Nueve de Octubre**, with another ranger station, the Guardería Nueve de Octubre, and several daily buses to Macas. At some point in-between San Vicente and 9 de Octubre you'll come upon La Punta, marked by massive machinery ripping out trees and carving the road eastwards, inch by inch. Hiking around the building works can be quite a challenge, but once you've got beyond the bulldozers you should find yourself on a well-defined footpath (which may all be road by the time you read this), used for centuries as a mule trail connecting the Oriente with the sierra. For more information on **Macas**, see p.340.

Practicalities

The **latest information** on the new road and buses servicing it is available from the Ministerio del Ambiente or Fundación Natura office in Riobamba (see p.225), or ask around locally. You can get to La Punta in about four hours by **camioneta** from Riobamba or Guamote for about $30–40. Otherwise, irregular **buses** leave from the Terminal La Dolorosa in Riobamba but timetables are likely to improve when the new road is completed. **Places to stay** on the route tend to be informal and impromptu, so you're best off bringing a tent, sleeping bag, stove and sufficient food if you plan to explore this region. The Guardería Atillo has floor space and allows the use of the kitchen, but from here it's a four- to five-hour, mostly downhill fifteen-kilometre hike to Zuñac, where you can sleep (with permission from the villagers) in the *casa comunal* and buy some basic foodstuffs, or continue for 5km to the Guardería Purshi where floor space is available for sleeping. From here, expect it to take eight to nine hours, with a couple of rests, to hike to Nueve de Octubre, where you can sleep in the third ranger station or catch the bus to Macas.

Lagunas de Ozogoche

Back on the Panamericana, 20km south of Guamote, a rough 36-kilometre dirt road branches east from the village of Palmira to the **Lagunas de Ozogoche**, a cluster of beautiful lakes sitting high on the páramo. Though beautifully set, the lakes are best known as the site of a curious phenomenon that no one has been able to explain: periodically, usually in September, hundreds of birds quite suddenly plunge deep into the icy waters of the lakes and kill themselves. Interestingly, the spur of mountain overlooking the lakes is known as

Ayapungo, which is Quechua for "door of death". If you're happy to overlook these morbid details, the area makes for great wild **camping**, though you'll need either your own transport or a **camioneta** from Guamote to get here (around $15–20).

Alausí

Some 43km south of Guamote, lying far below the highway in a round valley enclosed by hills, **ALAUSÍ** is an atmospheric little railway town made up of crumbling adobe houses leaning over the pavements on thick wooden pillars. Every Wednesday, Friday and Sunday crowds gather around the rail tracks at 11am to watch the train from Riobamba glide right through the middle of town, where it pauses for a short stop while vendors clamber onto the roof to sell fried bananas to gringos. About two and a half hours later, the train reappears on the way back from the Devil's Nose ascent (see box, p.227), at which point most people get off to take a bus (saving a few hours), before it trundles along the track on to Riobamba.

Practicalities

It's very easy to catch a **bus** straight out of town to Riobamba (2hr trip), Quito (5hr trip) or Cuenca (4hr 30min trip); services leave from the corner of the main street, 5 de Junio, with 9 de Octubre, a few blocks from the **train station**, at the north end of 5 de Junio. If you want to stay, however, you'll find plenty of **hotels** to choose from, though none is particularly appealing. The *Americano*, García Moreno 151 (☏03/930159; ❷), offers neat, modest rooms with swept wooden floors, comfortable beds and clean bathrooms, though the service can be a little brusque. The *Panamericano*, at the corner of 5 de Junio and 9 de Octubre (☏03/930278; ❷–❸) and the *Hotel Gampala* (☏03/930138; ❸) opposite, have similar rooms, with reasonable **restaurants** attached. Close by, on 5 de Junio and Esteban Orozo, opposite the grotty *Europa* (currently being renovated, however), the friendly Señora Luz Vinueso offers pleasant rooms in her house with TV and private bath (☏03/930089; ❷); if there's no one there, ask for her in the *Europa* hotel. You can cash **traveller's cheques** at the Banco de Guayaquil at 5 de Junio 143, but it doesn't have an ATM.

All buses from Alausí to Cuenca pass **El Tambo**, 93km to the south, an otherwise unremarkable village that is an access point to the **Ingapirca** ruins, Ecuador's most important Inca archeological site (see Chapter 4, p.242).

Travel details

Buses

Alausí to: Cuenca (6 daily; 4hr 30min); Quito (3 daily; 5hr); Riobamba (every 30min; 2hr).
Ambato to: Baños (every 10min; 50min); Cuenca (2 daily; 8hr); Guaranda (12 daily; 2hr); Guayaquil (every hour; 6hr 30min); Latacunga (every 15min; 1hr); Loja (2 daily; 12hr); Patate (every 20min; 45min); Pelileo (every 30min; 30min); Píllaro (every 30min; 35min); Puyo (every hour; 3hr); Quito (every 5min; 2hr 20min); Quizapincha (every 30min; 20min); Riobamba (every 30min; 1hr);

Salasaca (every 30min; 20min); Tena (2 daily; 6hr).
Baños to: Ambato (every 10min; 50min); Coca (2 daily; 10hr); Guayaquil (2 daily; 6hr) Puyo (every 30min; 2hr); Quito (every 30min; 3hr 30min); Riobamba (every 30min; 2hr); Río Verde (every 30min; 30min); Tena (hourly; 5hr 30min).
Guaranda to: Ambato (12 daily; 2hr); Guayaquil (12 daily; 3hr 30min); Latacunga (hourly; 3hr); Riobamba (10 daily; 2hr); Salinas (2 daily; 1hr).
Latacunga to: Ambato (every 15min; 1hr); Baños (every 15min; 2hr); Chugchilán (1 daily; 3hr 45min); Pujilí (every 10min; 20min); Quilotoa (1

daily; 3hr); Quito (every 10min; 2hr); Quevedo (hourly; 4hr); Salecedo (every 10–15min; 15min); Saquisilí (every 10min; 20min); Sigchos (7 daily; 2hr 15min); Zumbahua (every hour; 2hr).
Machachi to: Aloasí (every 30min; 10min); El Chaupí (every 30min; 30min); Quito (hourly; 1hr).
Riobamba to: Alao (3–4 daily Mon–Fri, 2 daily Sat; 2hr 30min); Alausí (every 30min; 2hr); Ambato (every 15min; 1hr); Baños (hourly; 2hr); Cuenca (7 daily; 6hr); Guano (every 10min; 15min); Guaranda (6 daily; 2hr); Guayaquil (every 30min; 4hr 30min); Huaquillas (2 daily; 10hr); Latacunga (every 15min; 2hr); Puyo (hourly; 4hr); Quito (every 15min; 3hr 30min); Santo Domingo (hourly; 5hr); Tena (6 daily; 7hr).

Trains

The train ride from **Riobamba to Sibambe**, via the **Nariz del Diablo** (Devil's Nose) descent, leaves Riobamba on Wednesdays, Fridays and Sundays at 7am and costs $11 (Riobamba–Sibambe–Alausí). For more information on this service, see box on p.227. The Quito–Riobamba service has been discontinued, and there are no signs that it will be restored in the near future.

The southern sierra

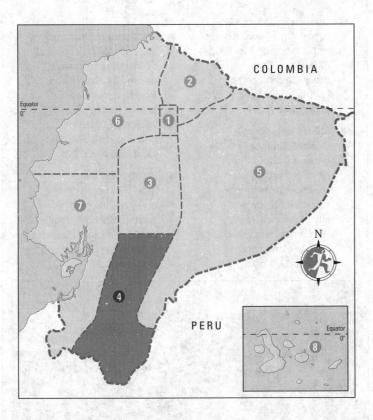

COLOMBIA

Equator
0°

N

PERU

Equator
0°

CHAPTER 4 # Highlights

* **Ingapirca** On a striking hillside perch overlooking bucolic scenery, the best-preserved Inca ruin in the country displays exquisite, trademark stonemasonry. See p.242

* **Cuenca** Ecuador's third largest city is regarded as its most beautiful for its dignified architecture, flower-draped courtyards, cobbled streets and leafy plazas. See p.247

* **Museo del Banco Central, Cuenca** Without a doubt the region's best museum, holding the remains of Tomebamba, the great city of the Inca's northern Empire, alongside various ethnographic exhibits. See p.253

* **El Cajas** A stunning and easily accessed wilderness of sweeping views, sparkling lakes, and exposed crags caressed by whirling mists, laced with worthwhile hikes across lonely páramo. See p.258

* **Podocarpus** This beautiful national park descends from austere páramo into lush cloudforests, a memorable landscape teeming with wildlife and streaked with waterfalls and glinting rivers. See p.271

* **Vilcabamba** The slow pace of this peaceful village – and the great hiking nearby – has rightly made it a fixture for many travelling between Ecuador and Peru. See p.273

4

The southern sierra

A s you head south down the Panamericana from the central highlands, the snowcapped peaks and rumbling volcanoes give way to a softer and gentler landscape of lower elevations and warmer, drier climates. Ecuador's **southern sierra** – made up of the provinces of Cañar, Azuay and Loja – was until recently a very isolated part of the country, left without proper roads to the capital and Guayaquil until the 1960s. Today, the region still has a lonely, faraway feel to it, reinforced by its sparse population, a scarcity of large towns, and long stretches of wild, uninhabited countryside. Its charms, however, are considerable, with some of the most rewarding and beautiful pockets of Ecuador tucked away down here in the south.

The main urban centre – and only large city – of the southern sierra is **Cuenca**, famed for its stunning colonial architecture and graceful churches and monasteries. Easily the country's most captivating city, it was raised on the site of the ruined city of Tomebamba, built by the **Incas** in the late fifteenth century following their conquest of the region, which had been occupied by the **Cañari** people for almost a thousand years (see p.506). Virtually nothing remains of Tomebamba, but you can get an idea of the remarkable stonework the Incas were famous for – executed without iron to carve it or wheels to transport it – at the ruins of **Ingapirca**, Ecuador's only major Inca remains, within easy striking distance of Cuenca. Sitting right on Cuenca's doorstep is an attraction of a very different nature: the starkly beautiful wilderness of **Parque Nacional El Cajas**, which provides some of the best backcountry hiking and trout fishing in the country, if you're willing to put up with a bit of rain and mist.

South of Cuenca, the sense of remoteness and abandonment increases as you drive past mile after mile of largely uncultivated hills and pastures. The few villages and one-horse towns staggered down the highway seem scarcely to have entered the twentieth century, let alone the twenty-first, with their steep cobbled streets, ageing stuccoed houses and grand old churches. The town of **Saraguro**, in particular, feels like a real step back in time, with an indigenous population that maintains a centuries-old tradition of dressing in black. Further south, the small provincial capital of **Loja** is an island of comparative motion and activity, hemmed in by jagged, deep-green hills that soar over the town. It serves as a good jumping-off point for a couple of highly worthwhile excursions: east to **Parque Nacional Podocarpus**, stretching down from the sierra to the tropical cloudforests of the Oriente, close to the old gold-mining town of **Zamora**; and south to the laid-back gringo hangout of **Vilcabamba**, nestled in an idyllic mountain valley. Loja is also the starting point of the only direct bus service to Peru – for more details see p.279.

Ingapirca and beyond

Leaving the central sierra behind at Alausí (see p.236), continue 93km south on the Panamericana and you'll reach the inconsequential village of **El Tambo**. From here, a sideroad branches 8km east from the highway to the southern sierra's first important attraction, **Ingapirca**, Ecuador's only major Inca ruins. Though not as dramatic or well preserved as the Inca remains of Peru, Ingapirca is nonetheless an impressive site that certainly deserves a visit, if only to witness the extraordinary mortarless stonework for which the Incas are so famous. South of here, only a few low-key attractions dot the 79km that separate El Tambo from the city of Cuenca: namely the small market town of **Cañar**, the hilltop sanctuary of **Biblián**, and the sleepy provincial capital of **Azogues**.

Ingapirca

Perched on a breezy hill commanding fine views over the surrounding countryside, **INGAPIRCA** (daily 8am–6pm; $6 including guide), which roughly translates as "Inca wall", was built during the Inca expansion into Ecuador towards the end of the fifteenth century, on a site that had been occupied by the Cañari people for over 500 years. The Incas destroyed most of the Cañari structures (though a burial site remains), replacing them with their own elaborate complex that probably functioned as a place of worship, a fortress, and a *tambo*, or way-station, on the Inca Royal Road connecting Cuzco to Quito.

Since then, many of the Inca buildings have been dismantled, their large stone blocks hauled away by Spanish colonists to be used as foundations for churches and other buildings. The complex's central structure, however – known as the **Temple of the Sun**, or the Adoratorio – remains substantially intact and dominates the whole site. It's composed of an immense oval-shaped platform whose slightly inward-tapering walls are made of exquisitely carved blocks of stone, fitted together with incredible precision. Steps lead up to a trapezoidal doorway – a classic feature of Inca architecture – that gives onto the remains of a rectangular building within the platform. It is the superior quality of the platform's stonework – usually reserved for high-status buildings – that suggests that this was a temple used for ceremonial purposes.

The rest of the site consists mainly of low foundation walls, possibly the remains of storehouses, dwellings and a great plaza, among other things. There's not a great deal left, but the **guides** here (some English spoken), whom you meet near the site entrance, can explain various theories about what once stood where. Guides will also take you on a looping one-kilometre path in and out of the ravine behind the ruins, to the nearby **Cara del Inca** ("Inca's Face"), a huge rockface resembling a human profile with a hooked nose, as well as several other less impressive rock-hewn curiosities such as the **Casa del Sol** with its circular, supposedly astronomical, carvings, or the **Silla del Inca**, a large boulder with a chair cut into it, actually a broken piece of a small Inca bath from the hill above. Count on a guided tour of the site taking two hours. There's also a small but well laid-out **museum** just inside the entrance, displaying some Cañari and Inca pots, tools, jewellery and a skeleton found here, and an attached book and craft shop.

Baño del Inca

There's another obscure but interesting ruin 8km from Ingapirca on the road towards El Tambo, near the little village of **Coyoctor**. The **Baño del Inca**, an

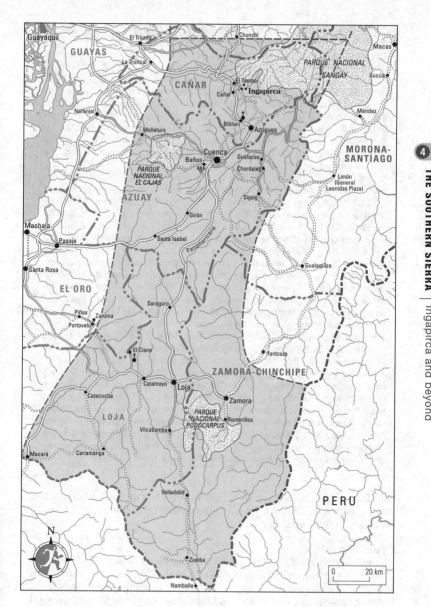

Inca bathing complex chiselled out of an enormous rock with channels and receptacles eventually leading out onto the adjacent field for irrigation. The site hasn't been fully excavated and there's no control or entry fee, though occasionally a guide will be hanging around to show you around for a tip. It's a 30–40-minute walk to Coyoctor from the turn-off on the road to El Tambo

The Inca Trail to Ingapirca

The **Inca trail to Ingapirca** is a three-day hike following a forty-kilometre stretch of the route – and in some parts the original path – of the Inca Royal Road that once linked Cuzco, the Inca capital, with Tomebamba (where Cuenca now stands) and Quito. The hike begins in the tiny village of **Achupallas**, which is an hour's drive along a vertiginous road from the small railway town of **Alausí** (see p.236). Colectivo trucks occasionally leave Alausí for Achupallas, but there are no reliable departure times. Your surest bet is to hire a camioneta to take you there from opposite the *Panamericano* hotel, at the corner of 5 de Junio and 9 de Octubre; if there is none there, just ask around and someone will offer to take you. If you bargain hard, the ride will cost around $10.

Most hikers set off from Alausí at around 5am or 6am. Alternatively, you could turn up in Achupallas the day before you want to start walking – there are no hotels there but Señor Alonso Sea (leave a message for him at the village Andinatel office on ☏03/930642) lets hikers sleep on his floor for a very modest amount: failing that, it's usually possible to sleep in the school if you can find the caretaker. Alonso also leads **guided walks** along the trail for about $7 per day with advance warning.

If you're hiking it independently, as most people do, it's essential to take the IGM **maps** of Alausí, Juncal and Cañar. **Camping equipment** needed includes a compass, decent tent, sleeping bag and stove, warm, waterproof clothing and water purification tablets. Rubber boots or gaiters will also come in handy, as there are some extremely boggy spots to negotiate. Try to take as light a pack as possible, though, as you'll be hiking between some 3100m and 4400m above sea level, which can be quite hard going. The **terrain** you'll cover is mainly wild, open páramo, with some beautiful ridge walks giving fantastic views. Most of it is uninhabited, but the final 8km or so is quite populated with *campesinos*, and you'll probably get a lot of attention from kids asking for sweets or pencils or money.

The hike is commonly divided into the sections you can cover each day. Day one takes you from Achupallas up the Tres Cruces valley to the Laguna Las Tres Cruces (6–8hr), though you may want to cut this hard day short and pitch your tent in the páramo a couple of hours short of the lakes; day two takes you from Laguna Las Tres Cruces to a small collection of Inca ruins known as Paredones, by the shore of Laguna Culebrillas (3–4hr); and day three goes from the Paredones ruins to the Ingapirca ruins (4–5hr). For more information, consult Bradt Publications' *Climbing and Hiking in Ecuador*, or simply follow the IGM maps with a compass.

6km from Ingapirca, followed by a right turn at the crossroads in the village; or a 30-minute walk along a disused railway heading southwest from El Tambo (a camioneta from here costs $2–3).

Practicalities

The two **access roads** for Ingapirca leave the Panamericana at El Tambo and Cañar (7km south), and meet in the middle at the small village – also known as Ingapirca – that overlooks the archeological site, a five-minute walk away. **Getting there** is easy on the buses and camionetas that leave El Tambo around every hour for Ingapirca village. In addition, from Monday to Friday two daily Transportes Cañar buses come directly to the site entrance from Cuenca (a 2hr trip; $2), leaving Cuenca's bus terminal at 9am and 1pm and returning from Ingapirca at 1pm and 4pm; on Saturdays and Sundays there is only one bus in each direction, leaving Cuenca at 9am, and leaving Ingapirca at 1pm. If you're coming in from Cuenca and miss the direct bus, it's easy enough to catch one of the hourly buses to Cañar and then a connection to Ingapirca.

If you want to **stay** overnight, you'll find peaceful, comfortable rooms in *Posada Ingapirca* (℡07/215116; ⑥), a lovely 120-year-old farmhouse with splendid views and a good restaurant, a stone's throw from the ruins. Over in Ingapirca village, *Hinti Huasi* (℡07/215171; ❸) offers basic but reasonably clean rooms with or without private bath and has a simple restaurant, while next door, the *Posada El Turista* (no phone) also has a decent restaurant and plans to offer inexpensive rooms in the near future. Down in El Tambo you'll find basic rooms with shared bath in *Residencial Esthefany* (℡07/233126; ❷) on the main road, near the road sign to Ingapirca. As an alternative, you might want to base yourself at the nearby town of **Cañar** (see below). In addition to the **restaurants** mentioned above, there's a simple canteen at the Ingapirca site itself, and plenty of truckers' stops on the main road through El Tambo.

Cañar

Seven kilometres south of El Tambo, **CAÑAR** is a small town with narrow, twisting streets lined by attractive, colonial-style architecture. It's normally very quiet, but bursts into life on Sunday mornings with its weekly **market**, attended by farmers from all over the region. The market is a good place to admire the beautifully embroidered skirts and blouses the local women are famous for, as well as the finely woven belts worn by the men, embellished with intricate motifs on both sides. You might also see men wearing traditional *samarros*, sheepskin trousers used for horse riding. While Cañar makes a more appealing base for visiting Ingapirca than El Tambo, which is just a ten-minute bus ride away, there's not much **accommodation** to choose from: on the plaza, at the corner of Pichincha and Bolívar, the ageing *Residencial Mónica* (℡07/235486; ❷) has small but relatively clean rooms, and *Ingapirca*, at Sucre 0-11 (℡07/235201; ❷), has faded, musty rooms with private bath and TV. Of the basic bunch of **restaurants**, all offering simple *menus del día*, you could try *Los Maderos* on Calle Pichincha, or the *Reino Cañari* or the *Florida International*, both on 5 de Junio.

Biblián

Some 26km south of Cañar, the extravagantly turreted and spired **Santuario de la Virgen del Rocío** sits on a hillside high above the Panamericana, overlooking the little village of **BIBLIÁN** at its foot. The origins of this neo-Gothic temple go back to 1894, when a terrible drought ravaged crops and cattle. The villagers carried an image of the Virgin Mary up the hillside, where they prayed and sung to her so that she might intervene and save them from starvation. The rains miraculously arrived, and a **church** was built on the site where the image had been placed; it was completed in 1908. You can walk up to it in about twenty minutes from the Panamericana, following a clearly signed flight of steps – it's worth it for the fine views down to the valley in which Biblián sits, and to see the church's interior, set against the bare rock of the hill. The Virgin's feast day is celebrated on September 8, when huge crowds come to venerate the image. Three kilometres south of Biblián, just off the Panamericana, the great-value *Hostería El Camping* (℡07/241928; ❸) offers spacious, comfortable **rooms** with private bath, a pleasant restaurant and an indoor swimming pool with steam baths – a good place to relax for a night or two.

Azogues

Continuing down the Panamericana, around 7km south of Biblián you'll reach **AZOGUES**, a charming town made up of steep, narrow streets and handsome

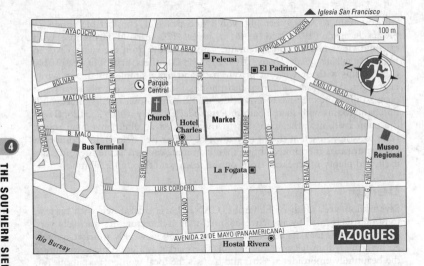

nineteenth-century houses. Many of the buildings in the centre have painted wooden balconies, and a few have the undersides of their eaves painted in intricate designs, as was traditional during colonial times. The chief appeal of visiting Azogues is just strolling around for an hour or two, admiring the architecture and soaking up the atmosphere. You could also visit the monumental, twin-towered **Iglesia San Francisco**, which houses the Virgen de la Nube (Virgin of the Cloud), wrapped in a white cloak and perched on a gold-leaf altar. Standing on a small hill to the southeast of the centre, the church is visible from most parts of town, most strikingly when it's illuminated at night; you can walk there in about thirty minutes, or take a taxi for around $0.80. Azogues also boasts a rather fun **Museo Regional** (Mon–Fri 9am–noon & 3–6pm; free) at the Casa de la Cultura, five blocks south of the square on Bolívar and General Enríquez, with mannequins and dioramas showcasing the crafts and traditions of the region. One of the most important local crafts is weaving Panama hats – most are bundled off to Cuenca to be exported, but you can normally spot a few at the Saturday-morning **market**, a couple of blocks south of the central square.

Practicalities

Azogues' **bus terminal** is just off the Panamericana – called Avenida 24 de Mayo as it runs through the town – about four blocks northwest of the main plaza. A short walk south down 24 de Mayo, at the corner with 10 de Agosto, is the *Rivera* (☏07/248113; ❸), far and away the best **place to stay** in town with its spotless, modern, carpeted rooms, all with private bath and cable TV. A cheaper option is the *Charles*, at Solano and Rivera (☏07/241364; ❶), a budget hotel with grubby walls and old, saggy beds. As for **eating**, *El Padrino*, on Bolívar 6-09 and 10 de Agosto, serves decent roast chicken in a pleasant old dining room, while *La Fogata*, at 3 de Noviembre between Rivera and Luis Cordero, specializes in fish and seafood. A couple of blocks east of the plaza, at the corner of Sucre and Emilio Abad, *Peleusi* is probably the most appealing place in Azogues for a coffee and a snack. The Andinatel **phone office** is on the north side of the square.

Cuenca

Santa Ana de los Cuatro Ríos de Cuenca – otherwise known simply as
CUENCA – is Ecuador's most seductive, and possibly its most beautiful, colonial city. A classic example of a planned Renaissance town in the Americas,
Cuenca shares many architectural features with Old Quito, such as its narrow,
cobbled streets, harmonious, balconied houses with interior courtyards, and
abundance of flashing white churches and monasteries. Here, however, they're
presented without the pollution, noise and overbearing crowds of the capital,
in a relaxed, provincial and altogether more enjoyable atmosphere. Still swollen
with pride from having been declared a UNESCO World Heritage Site in
1999, Cuenca is, moreover, at its gleaming, spruced-up best, further adding to
its appeal.

Founded by the Spaniards on April 12, 1557, Cuenca was not the first dazzling
city to be erected on this site: the city of **Tomebamba** had been founded here
by the Inca Tupac Yupanqui around 1470, and was said to have rivalled Peru's
Cuzco with its splendour. Its glory was short-lived, however, as the city was
destroyed during the Inca civil war that broke out during the second decade of
the sixteenth century, prompted by rival claims to the throne by the brothers
Atahualpa and Huascar. By the time Cieza de León (one of the chroniclers of
the Spanish conquest) passed through in 1547, Tomebamba was in ruins, but
enough remained to evoke its former grandeur: "These famous lodgings of
Tumibamba were among the finest and richest to be found in all Peru . . . The
fronts of many of the buildings are beautiful and highly decorative, some of
them set with precious stones and emeralds . . . Today, all is cast down and in
ruins, but it can still be seen how great they were." These days, Cuenca's Inca
legacy has all but vanished, hinted at only by the foundation stones of some of
its buildings, and some modest ruins excavated in the twentieth century.

Arrival

Cuenca is a popular destination to fly to from Quito, and the **airport** (information on ☎07/862203), named Aeropuerto Mariscal Lamar, is only 5km east
of the centre along Avenida España. The easiest way to get into town is by taxi
(about $2), or you can pick up a Transportes Ricuarte bus on Avenida España
(every 10min) that will take you up Calle Vega Muñoz, on the northern edge
of the city centre. The **bus terminal** is also on Avenida España, close to the
airport; again, the easiest way to get into the centre is by taxi, or you can catch
a bus from Avenida España, as detailed above.

Information and transport

There's a very helpful **Ministerio de Turismo** office on the main square at
Sucre and Benigno Malo (Mon–Fri 9am–1pm & 2.30–5pm; ☎07/839337,
Ⓕ831414, Ⓔmturaustro@ec-gov.net) where you can pick up **maps**, numerous leaflets and a very helpful booklet called *Estar en Cuenca*. General tourist
information in English, including bus, train and flight times as well as advice on
tours, is available at The Travel Center at Hermano Miguel 4-46 and Calle Larga
(closed Sun in low season; ☎07/823782, Ⓕ820085, Ⓦwww.terradiversa.com).
For information on the Parque Nacional El Cajas, head to the Etapa office on
Benigno Malo 7-78 and Sucre (Mon–Fri 8am–1pm & 3–6pm; ☎07/890418
or 846134), a water and telecommunications company that now manages the
park.

The **city centre** is confined to a fairly compact grid sitting on the northern bank of the Río Tomebamba. It's easy enough to get to most sights on foot, but if tired you'll be able to flag down a yellow **taxi** on any main street; rides within the city have a fixed tariff of $0.80, though your hotel will be able to tell you if the going rate has changed. For details of radio taxis, see "Listings", p.257.

Accommodation

Cuenca is blessed with a wealth of **hotels** to suit all budgets, many of them in charming old colonial-style houses built around little courtyards. Despite the great number of places to stay, you'd be wise to book ahead if arriving on a Friday – or any kind of fiesta (see "Listings", p.256) – as Cuenca is a popular weekend destination with Ecuadorians and accommodation can fill quite quickly.

Alli Tiana cnr of Presidente Córdova and Padre Aguirre ☎07/831844, ㊏821788. A modern hotel offering thirty carpeted rooms with firm beds, private bath, cable TV and phone – not luxurious but perfectly fine. The view over the city from the restaurant is one of the best in town. Breakfast included. ❺

El Cafecito Honorato Vásquez 7-36 ☎07/832337, ㊉elcafec@cue.satnet.net. Popular budget rooms with and without private bath, set around an attractive courtyard filled with wooden tables and potted plants. It's also a café-restaurant-bar, and can be noisy on Thursday, Friday and Saturday nights; the quietest rooms face the back. ❷–❸.

Chordeleg Gran Colombia 11-15 and General Torres ☎07/824611, ㊏822536. Lovely old *hostal* featuring lots of highly polished wood and pleasant – if unexceptional – en-suite rooms around a glass-covered courtyard. A few rooms have balconies. ❹

Colonial Gran Colombia 10-13 ☎07/823793, ㊏841644, ㊉hcolonia@cue.satnet.net. Colonial-style building with a very pretty central courtyard (used as the dining area), festooned with hanging plants. The rooms are simple but comfortable, with private bath and cable TV; those at the front look directly onto the Iglesia Santo Domingo. Breakfast included. ❺

Crespo Calle Larga 7-93 ☎07/842571, ㊏839473. Cuenca's most distinguished hotel, operating since 1942 in a handsome 130-year-old building overlooking the river. Lots of dark wood and old-fashioned elegance, along with modern comforts like soundproofed windows and central heating. Specify a room with a river view. Rates include a transfer from the airport or bus terminal and breakfast. ❼

Cuenca Presidente Borrero 10-69 ☎07/833711, ㊏833819. A hotel housed in a distinctive old building with a recently remodelled interior, featuring smart, carpeted rooms with high ceilings, brightly painted walls, cable TV and private bath. Breakfast included. ❺

El Dorado Gran Colombia 7-87 ☎07/831390, ㊏831663, ㊉eldorado@cue.satnet.net. Smart, modern, international-style hotel with a gym, sauna, steam baths and good-quality rooms with large cable TVs; those in the new block ("*de lujo*") are fractionally more expensive than the older rooms, but are immaculately furnished. All guests are offered a cocktail on arrival plus free transfer to the hotel from the airport or bus terminal. Breakfast included. ❽

Inca Real General Torres 8-40 ☎07/823636, ㊏840699, ㊉incareal@cue.satnet.net. The en-suite rooms in this hotel are simple and quite small for the price, but the blue-and-white timber building is splendid, arranged around three glass-covered courtyards. Good service too, and breakfast is included in the nightly rate. ❻

Macondo Tarqui 11-64 ☎07/840697, ㊏833593, ㊉macondo@cedei.org. Quiet, beautiful old house with waxed wooden floors, high ceilings, spotless rooms (shared and private bath) and a delightful garden with chairs and a hammock. Guests can use the kitchen in the afternoon. Highly recommended. ❹

Mansión Alcázar Bolívar 12-55 and Tarqui ☎07/823918, ㊏823554, ㊈www.mansionalcazar.com. Exquisitely renovated colonial building housing one of Cuenca's most luxurious hotels, boasting a grand courtyard converted into a stately drawing room replete with chandelier and fountain. The rooms are equally sumptuous, fragrant from the freshly scattered petals on the beds, some of which are four-posters. Breakfast included. ❽

Milán Presidente Córdova 9-89 ☎ & ㊏07/831104. Friendly, well-run budget hotel offering small, spruce rooms with shared and

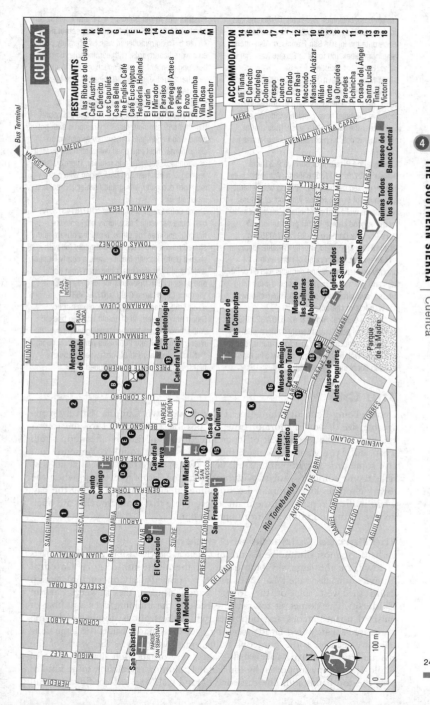

CUENCA

RESTAURANTS

A las Riberas del Guayas	K
Café Austria	16
El Cafecito	J
Los Capulíes	G
Casa Bella	L
The English Café	E
Café Eucalyptus	F
Heladería Holanda	18
El Jardín	14
El Mirador	C
El Paraíso	D
El Pedregal Azteca	B
Los Pibes	6
El Pozo	I
Raymipamba	A
Villa Rosa	M
Wunderbar	

ACCOMMODATION

Alli Tiana	14
El Cafecito	16
Chordeleg	5
Colonial	6
Crespo	17
Cuenca	4
El Dorado	7
Inca Real	12
Macondo	1
Mansión Alcázar	10
Milán	15
Norte	3
La Orquidea	8
Paredes	2
Pichincha	11
Posada del Ángel	9
Santa Lucía	13
Tinku	19
Victoria	18

249

private bath, balconies and cable TV. Rooms can be noisy from the traffic, but some have lovely views onto the Iglesia San Francisco. Also offers laundry facilities and tours to Parque Nacional El Cajas. Breakfast included. ❷–❹

Norte Mariano Cueva 11-63 ☎07/827881. Tidy budget rooms with freshly painted walls, swept floors, decent bedding and firm mattresses. Few rooms in the hotel have outside windows, and those near the TV area are noisy. Note that at night, this is not the most salubrious of areas as well. ❷

La Orquidea Presidente Borrero 9-31 and Bolívar ☎07/824511, ℻835844. Attractive hotel in a renovated old building, offering twelve simply furnished but stylish rooms with lots of natural wood, pale walls and good-quality en-suite bathrooms. A good choice in this price range. ❹

Paredes Luis Cordero 11-29 ☎07/835674, ℻834910. Large, light, mostly en-suite rooms in an extravagantly decorated old mansion with brightly painted pillars and cornices, old oil paintings and gramophones, lots of bric-a-brac lying around, and a resident parrot. A little run-down, but with lots of character. ❷–❸

Pichincha General Torres 8-82 ☎07/823868. Large budget hotel with friendly owners, offering anonymous but clean and spacious rooms (one to four beds) with high ceilings, white walls, bare wooden floors and shared bath. ❷

Posada del Ángel Bolívar 14-11 and Estévez de Toral ☎07/840695, ✉hdaniel@cue.satnet.net. An old building remodelled with two brightly painted covered courtyards, with comfortable rooms boasting plenty of storage space, cable TV and private bath. Breakfast and 30 minutes' free Internet included. ❺

Santa Lucía Presidente Borrero 8-44 ☎ & ℻07/828000. Beautiful hotel in a fine old house, built in 1859 and now tastefully restored with polished wood floors and generously furnished en-suite rooms, most equipped with bathtubs, as well as strongbox, cable TV and minibar. There's also parking, a restaurant and café, along with a drawing room complete with grand fireplace. Breakfast included. ❼

Tinku Calle Larga and Jervés ☎07/814373. An old house reinvented as a funky backpackers' hangout and meeting place, featuring private and shared rooms and a ten-bed dormitory (all with shared bath), kitchen facilities and a comfy lounge with cable TV. It also has a bar open from 6pm, and a good café. Discounts for long stays. ❷

Victoria Calle Larga 6-93 ☎07/845887, ℻832350, ✉santaana@etapaonline.net.ec. Smart new conversion of an old building backed with smoked glass to give stunning views over the river (rooms 207 and 205 being particularly good). The hotel's restaurant, *El Jardín* (see p.254), is highly regarded. Breakfast included. ❻

The City

Despite being Ecuador's third-largest city, **downtown Cuenca** is a very manageable size. If you're short of time, it's possible to get a feel for the town's charms and take in the best of its architecture in a leisurely afternoon stroll. That said, if you want to go inside the churches, visit a couple of museums and save some time for shopping, you'll need two or three days here. If at all possible, try to coincide your stay with a Friday or Saturday evening, when the town's churches are illuminated to stunning effect, or Sunday during the day, when traffic is kept out of the main square. Note that most churches are open between 7am and noon and from 6pm to 8pm.

The Parque Calderón and around

Perhaps the most distinctive feature of Cuenca, clearly visible from most parts of town, are the large, sky-blue domes of the nineteenth-century **Catedral Nueva** (officially called La Catedral de la Inmaculada Concepción), which flanks the west side of the town's central square, the flowery **Parque Calderón**. The domes sit towards the back of the building over a jumble of outsized turrets, arches and buttresses, while the front is dominated by the immense twin-towered facade looming over the square. Inside, the large central nave features some gorgeous stained-glass windows – the work of the Basque artist Guillermo Larrázabal – and a very ornate high altar, made up of a gold-leaf canopy supported by four gilded columns, resembling some kind of over-the-top bandstand. The cathedral's grand scale and self-confidence stand in marked contrast with the modest **Catedral Vieja** (or El Sagrario) facing it across the square. Occupying the site of a mud-and-straw chapel built immediately after the city was founded, the present building dates from the eighteenth century, and is characterized by its low, horizontal outline, simple, whitewashed walls, clay-tiled roof and central bell tower. At the time of writing, it was closed to visitors while being restored, and it's not yet known when it's likely to reopen.

Just off the Parque Calderón, on Calle Sucre, the Plazoleta del Carmen – a tiny square more commonly known as the **Plaza de las Flores** – is home to a daily **flower market**, presided over by *chola* women wearing blue- or pink-checked aprons, long black plaits and Panama hats. Right behind it stands the **Iglesia El Carmen de la Asunción**, a white-walled, eighteenth-century church with a beautiful carved stone portico. One block south of here, on Córdova and Padre Aguirre, you'll find another market square, the **Plaza San Francisco**, this one selling a diverse mix of chunky knitwear, wall hangings and cheap clothes and shoes. It's overlooked by the peach-and-white **Iglesia San Francisco**, rebuilt in the early twentieth century in a neo-colonial style, sporting smooth, stuccoed walls embellished with lots of plaster relief. Inside, the only survivors of the original church, built in the eighteenth century, are the high altar adorned by a carving of the Virgin de la Inmaculada by Bernardo de Legarda (the famous Quito School sculptor; see p.90) and the gold-leaf pulpit. Three blocks north, on Gran Colombia and Padre Aguirre, the grey-blue, twin-towered **Iglesia Santo Domingo** is another early twentieth-century church built in the colonial style. It's worth popping inside to admire the intricate geometric motifs covering every inch of the arches and ceilings, and the series of eighteenth-century paintings on the walls, depicting the Mysteries of the Rosary.

Iglesia San Sebastián and Museo de Arte Moderno

Six blocks west of the Parque Calderón, past the brilliant-white walls of the nineteenth-century **Iglesia del Cenáculo**, the **Iglesia San Sebastián** marks the western limit of Cuenca's *centro histórico*. Built in the seventeenth century, this is one of the city's oldest churches and features a single bell tower over the right-hand side of the entrance, giving the church a slightly lopsided appearance. The quiet little square in front of it was the scene of Cuenca's most scandalous crime of the eighteenth century, when the surgeon of the French Geodisic Mission that was visiting Ecuador to measure the earth's equator (see p.511) was murdered here over his love affair with a Creole woman.

The single-storey whitewashed building with blue windows that spans the southern side of the square was built in 1876 as a Temperance House, in an effort to curb the drinking habits of Cuenca's citizens, and in particular those of its clergy. Since then it's served as a prison, an asylum for beggars and an old people's home, and currently houses the municipal **Museo de Arte Moderno** (Mon–Fri 8.30am–1pm & 3–6.30pm, Sat & Sun 9am–1pm; free). The museum puts on temporary exhibitions of national and Latin American artists, displayed in a series of rooms around a large, beautiful courtyard. It's run by a dynamic team, and the quality of the exhibitions is generally high.

Museo de las Conceptas and the Museo de Esqueletología

A couple of blocks southeast of the Parque Calderón, the **Monasterio de las Conceptas**, founded in 1599, hides behind the thick, white walls that separate its occupants from the outside world. Part of the convent is open to the public as the **Museo de las Conceptas** (Mon–Fri 9am–3.30pm, Sat 10am–1pm; $2.50), with its entrance at Hermano Miguel 6-33. The museum houses a large collection of predominantly religious paintings and sculpture from the seventeenth to nineteenth centuries, displayed in small rooms off a gallery overlooking a lovely interior garden. Setting the collection apart from the usual assembly of saints, Marys and Christs found in other religious museums is a roomful of nineteenth-century toys in room 12, including some small wooden dolls and music boxes. The fact that these were brought here by novices entering the convent makes you realize quite how young some of them were. The museum also contains a small gift shop, where you can buy *quesadillas*, books, postcards and local handicrafts. While you're here, take a look at the attached **Iglesia de las Conceptas**, giving onto Presidente Córdova, which features a flamboyant steeple, some finely carved wooden doors and an impressive gold-leaf altar inside.

For a change of pace, walk two blocks north to Bolívar 6-57 and Presidente Borrero to the little **Museo de Esqueletología** (Mon–Fri 10am–1pm & 4–7pm, Sat 10am–2pm; $1). The collection inside houses an unusual array of skeletons from the tiny frames of a hummingbird and foetus skulls to the rather larger condor, llama and elephant calf; don't miss the sawfish skeleton, a species now on the verge of extinction due to aggressive fishing.

Calle Larga

The southern limit of old Cuenca is marked by **Calle Larga**, which runs parallel with and backs on to the Río Tomebamba. You can't see the river from the street – just a continuous stretch of handsome old houses, including, at no. 7-07, the former home of Dr Remigio Crespo Toral, a nineteenth-century intellectual and diplomat. In 1946 it was turned into Cuenca's first museum: the **Museo Remigio Crespo Toral** (Mon–Fri 8.30am–1pm & 3–6pm, Sat 10am–noon; free), housing a small but noteworthy collection of pre-Hispanic ceramics and tools, documents dating from the city's foundation, religious paintings and sculpture and a *salón* furnished as it was left by Dr Crespo. The house itself has been beautifully restored, and is worth a visit in its own right.

Continuing a block and a half east brings you to the **Museo de las Culturas Aborígenes** at Calle Larga 5-20 and Mariano Cueva (Mon–Fri 8.30am–6pm, Sat & Sun 9am–1pm; $2 including guide book in Spanish, English or French), which exhibits an excellent, wide-ranging and well-presented collection of pre-Columbian ceramics and artefacts, beginning with Stone-Age tools, flints and dinosaur teeth and ending with accomplished Inca earthenware. You can stock up on books, postcards, crafts and replicas in the museum shop and sip a home-roasted coffee in their *Amerindia Café* inside (see p.254).

Along the Río Tomebamba

Between the Museo Remigio Crespo Toral and the Museo de las Culturas Aborígenes, opposite Hermano Miguel, a set of **stone steps** leads down to the **riverside** – "*el barranco*" – giving wonderful views onto the back parts of Calle Larga's grand houses, hanging precipitously over the steep riverbank. At the bottom of the steps, the excellent Centro Interamericano de Artesanías y Artes Populares (CIDAP) has a small but highly enjoyable **Museo de Artes Populares** (Mon–Fri 9.30am–1pm & 2.30–6pm, Sat 10am–1pm; free). The museum brings together arts and crafts from all over Latin America – such as weavings, painted masks, ceramics and papier-mâché sculptures – in exhibitions that change every six months. In addition, every month it exhibits and sells the work of a different Ecuadorian artist or artisan, making the museum a fine place to pick up something original. There's also a shop selling a range of local crafts, such as basketwork.

From here you could walk along the river west, then regain higher ground at Benigno Malo, for the **Centro Faunístico Amaru** (Tues–Sun 9am–1pm & 2.30–6pm; $2). The centre displays a selection of native reptiles, fish and amphibians including the feared piranha, bushmaster and fer-de-lance all kept safely behind glass and often hidden from view amongst leaves and branches; crystallized venom is produced here for antidotes.

Heading east from the steps along the riverbank (or a block from the Museo de las Culturas Aborígenes) you'll come to the white **Iglesia Todos los Santos**, rising impressively over the Río Tomebamba. A church has stood on this site since the earliest days of the colony, and it's thought that the first Catholic Mass in Cuenca took place on this very spot. The current building dates from the late nineteenth century. Half a block east of the church is the **Puente Roto** (Broken Bridge), the remains of an old stone bridge across the Río Tomebamba, used now as a viewpoint onto the river.

Museo del Banco Central and around

About half a kilometre east of the Iglesia Todos los Santos, at the eastern end of Calle Larga, the **Museo del Banco Central** (Mon–Fri 9am–6pm, Sat 9am–1pm, last entry an hour before closing; $1) is Cuenca's most polished and absorbing museum. The ground floor contains a room devoted to the Inca city of Tomebamba, displaying some beautiful **Inca artefacts** including jewellery, fertility symbols and ritualistic objects. Also on the ground floor is a collection of **nineteenth-century art**, dominated by religious paintings and sombre portraits, but with some wonderful *costumbrista* (folk art) pieces showing indigenous people dancing, playing the fiddle, or roasting a hog. The highlight of the museum is the **Sala Etnografía Nacional** on the first floor, which sets out to illustrate the diversity of Ecuador's indigenous cultures using day-to-day objects and reconstructions. Displays include an extraordinary exhibition of Shuar *tsantsas* (shrunken heads) from the southern Oriente; a model of a masked dancer from the southern sierra; a collection of festival costumes; and many musical instruments. At the bottom of the building is the **Museo Numísmatico**, holding coins and notes of the republican and colonial epochs, dating back to the mid-seventeenth century.

Entrance to the Museo del Banco Central also includes access to the **Pumapungo archeological site** (same hours), right behind the museum between Calle Larga and Avenida Huayna Cápac, which is where most of the artefacts displayed in the museum's archeological *sala* were found. Excavations have revealed that this is where the most important religious buildings of Tomebamba were located, though all that's left to see are the foundation walls. The site has been reworked as an archeological park, the so-called **Jardines del Inca**, combining the ruins with botanical displays of important Andean plants and a bird rescue centre. About 300m west along Calle Larga, the **Ruinas de Todos los Santos** (Mon–Fri 8am–4pm; free) has an Inca wall with several trapezoidal niches and an old colonial water mill that was built with Inca stones; it's worth a look-in if you're walking along the river, but not sufficiently impressive to merit a special visit.

Mirador de Turi

The best spot for a panoramic view of the whole city is the **Mirador de Turi**, a lookout point in front of the Iglesia de Turi, perched high on a hill some 4km south of the centre. The **views** are particularly theatrical on Friday and

Saturday evenings when the city could almost be mistaken for a lavish Hollywood film set, with all its church steeples floodlit. A taxi costs about $1.50 each way; during the daytime, you could also take a bus to Turi (approximately every hour) from the corner of 12 de Abril and Avenida Fray Vicente Solano, on the southern bank of the Río Tomebamba, which will drop you at the bottom of the hill from where it's a half-hour walk up to the *mirador*. Plenty of local families drive up here, and it's a safe spot.

Eating, drinking and nightlife

Cuenca offers the best choice of **restaurants** south of Quito, with the usual staple of cheap lunches supplemented by gringo-oriented snacks like crêpes and burritos, as well as fine international cuisines and high-quality *comida típica*. There are a handful of places where you can go for a quiet **drink** through the week, but Cuenca's **nightlife** only really takes off on Thursday, Friday and Saturday nights, when the city's disco-bars and *salsatecas* fill with teenagers and twenty-somethings; bars tend to close around 1am, with disco-bars and nightclubs staying open until 3am.

Restaurants and cafés

A las Riberas del Guayas Bolívar 4-49 and Mariano Cueva. Owned by a Guayaquileño, this traditional restaurant specializes in mid-priced *comidas típicas* such as *guatita* and *seco de chivo*, but especially coastal favourites, including *encocados* and ceviche. Closes Mon–Fri 8pm, Sat 4pm, all Sun.

Amerindia Café *Museo de las Culturas Aborígenes*, Calle Larga 5-20. Quiet café perfect for a breather between museums, most notable for its Ecuadorian coffee, grown on the coast (in Loja and the Galápagos Islands) and roasted on site. They also make their own chocolate. Same hours as the *museo* (see p.252).

Café Austria cnr of Benigno Malo 5-95 and Juan Jaramillo. Excellent cakes, ice creams and specialities such as *Guglhupf* and *Apfelstrudel* in this delightful Austrian-run café, featuring elegant wooden seating, floral cushions and doilies. Closed Mon.

El Cafecito at the hotel of the same name, Honorato Vásquez 7-36. Laid-back café offering reasonably priced cakes, sandwiches, pastas, salads, *quesadillas* and other light meals, inside a covered courtyard. An ever-popular travellers' hangout.

Los Capuliés Presidente Borrero 7-31 t07/832339. Expensive, top-quality *comida típica* – including wonderful *empanadas de queso* – aimed squarely at tourists, served in an attractive courtyard dining room with a gurgling fountain. Has live Andean music at lunchtimes and on Thursday, Friday and Saturday nights. Closed Sun.

Casa Bella Bolívar and Torres. Pretty little restaurant in a bright patio freely garlanded with fronds and cascading plants, serving good Italian cuisine minus the pizzas. Locally popular for its inexpensive *almuerzos*.

The English Café Calle Larga and Presidente Borrero. Relaxed English-owned café offering snacks, sandwiches and a bookshop/exchange, as well as homely dishes such as chips doused in salt and vinegar, or a full English breakfast for $4.50.

Café Eucalyptus Gran Colombia and Benigno Malo. Excellent English-US restaurant in a distinguished building with a large covered courtyard. Offerings from the huge international menu range in scope from Vietnamese *Chaotom* to Jamaican Jerk chicken skewers to English Bakewell tart, all served in good-value tapas portions (most are $1.50–4), so you can try several in a meal. The bar, over which cured hams hang, serves good wines and beers, including bitters from the Turtle's Head brewery in Quito.

Heladería Holanda Benigno Malo 9-55. Scrubbed pine benches, clogs hanging on the wall and posters of windmills and tulips set the scene for the tasty ice cream, yogurts, cakes and sandwiches served in this Dutch-run café.

El Jardín *Hotel Victoria*, Calle Larga 6-93. Smart, well-to-do restaurant with huge smoked-glass windows giving pretty views over the river. The moderate-to-expensive continental cuisine is delicious and particularly strong on seafood.

El Mirador Hotel Allí Tiana, cnr of Presidente Córdova and Padre Aguirre ☎07/821955. Worth putting up with the bland decor and boring, moderately priced, menu of fried chicken and steak for the superb views over the city, especially when it's illuminated on Friday and Saturday nights. Phone to book a window seat to make the most of it.

El Paraíso Tomás Ordóñez 5-84. Modest little canteen with bare cement floors and rickety wooden tables, serving delicious freshly squeezed fruit juices and cheap vegetarian lunches, usually involving noodles or grains.

El Pedregal Azteca Gran Colombia 10-29. Large, lively, mid-priced restaurant in a beautifully restored old house, serving excellent Mexican food like enchiladas, tacos and *quesadillas*. The atmosphere is especially good on Friday nights, when there are live mariachis. Closed Sun.

Los Pibes Gran Colombia and Luis Cordero. Quick service and appetizing, good-value pizzas and lasagnes are the hallmark of this rustic-style restaurant sporting a bamboo roof, log walls and red-checked tablecloths. Attracts a young crowd.

El Pozo Hostal Colonial, Gran Colombia 10-13. Reasonably priced Ecuadorian food served in one of Cuenca's prettiest little courtyards, draped with ferns and flowers.

Raymipamba Benigno Malo and Bolívar, Parque Calderón. *The* classic eating place in Cuenca, both for its unbeatable location under the colonnaded arcade of the Catedral Nueva and for a devoted local following which ensures the place is always packed out. Inexpensive crêpes, pastas, stir-fries, meats and much more are served, typically at a frantic and erratic pace due to the crowds.

Villa Rosa Gran Colombia 12-22 ☎07/837944. Upmarket restaurant favoured by Cuenca's bourgeoisie, set in an attractive covered patio. Offers well-executed but fairly pricey international dishes like *coquilles saint jacques* and wild trout, with some Ecuadorian specialities. Closed Sat and Sun.

Wunderbar Escalinata, off Calle Larga. This German-run café-bar is a great place for lunch on a sunny day, when you can eat in the little garden amongst the trees and flowers. Serves gringo-pleasing snacks and light meals like aubergine and mozzarella sandwiches and Caesar salads. Closed Sat and Sun mornings.

Bars and discos

Aazúcar Pasaje 3 de Noviembre, underneath the Puente Roto. Relaxed disco-bar with bare stone walls, a small dance floor and plenty of tables and chairs. The music – mainly salsa and merengue – is not too loud to rule out conversation.

El Cafecito Honorato Vásquez 7-36. This arty café-bar makes a good place for a quiet drink through the week and gets packed out with locals and gringos at weekends, when the music is turned up a few notches.

Hotel El Dorado Gran Colombia 7-87. Small piano bar on the sixth floor of this upmarket hotel, with great views over the city. A quiet spot for a wind-down cocktail.

Exit Av 12 de Abril and Av Unidad Nacional. Hip, modern nightclub with a large dance floor and lots of dark corners. Plays a mixture of Latin music, techno and rock.

La Mesa Gran Colombia 3-55 and Tomás Ordóñez. Funky *salsateca* with a bright, fun decor, a small dance floor and a great atmosphere.

Prohibido Centro Cultural Cruz del Vado, Condamine 12-102. If your musical tastes include gothic, heavy metal and "doom", then you'll find like-minded folk at this bar, copiously decorated in depictions of skulls, writhing succubi and reproductive organs. Not to everyone's taste, but undeniably different. Mon–Thurs 2–9pm, Fri–Sat 2pm onwards; $0.25.

La Siembra Honorato Vásquez 7-22 and Presidente Borrero. Mellow café-bar taking up several small rooms, with lots of soft lighting, flickering candles, wicker chairs and bluesy music. Best as a place to hang out and chat over a few beers.

Wunderbar Escalinata, off Calle Larga. A café during the day (see above) that turns into a popular bar at night attracting a good mix of foreigners and locals alike with its stylish interior, international bottled beers and occasional live *folklórica* music.

Zoom Calle Larga and Alfonso Jerves. Hip disco spread over several rooms of a beautiful old colonial-style house, playing very loud techno, rock and Latin.

Shopping

Cuenca has a strong tradition of artesanía, making **shopping** a fun and rewarding activity. In particular, it's one of the most important export centres of the **Panama hat** industry (see box, p.402), with some of the finest-quality hats in Ecuador produced here. The best-known factory open to the public is Homero Ortega & Hijos, directly behind the bus terminal at Av Gil Ramírez Dávalos 3-86; visitors are shown the various stages of the hat-making process before ending up at the sales room – prices aren't cheap, with basic Panamas going from around $10 and *superfinos* from $50 upwards, but they still cost a good deal less than they're sold for abroad. Another quality producer is Alberto Pulla at Tarqui 6-91, with similar prices.

The best place for local **artesanía** is the outdoor market at **Plaza Rótary**, some four blocks northeast of the Parque Calderón. Thursday is the main market day, but you'll find stalls here every day of the week, selling vast quantities of ceramic pots and lots of basketwork and carved wooden kitchen utensils. A block to the west, the Mercado 9 de Octubre on and around the Plaza Cívica is a lively produce market that's worth a look, more for the atmosphere than to fill your bags. Local artesanía is also sold on the Plaza San Francisco, and in the covered stalls inside the Casa de la Mujer on the west side of the same square. If you like **ceramics**, be sure to visit Artesa on the corner of Gran Colombia and Luis Cordero – it's one of the country's top manufacturers of fine ceramics, and sells a wide range of bowls, vases, plates and other items, hand-painted in beautiful colours and designs. Finally, you'll find a number of **antique** cum bric-a-brac shops on Presidente Córdova, near the Museo de las Conceptas, selling curiosities like old crucifixes, saints, stirrups, coins, watches and pots.

Listings

Airlines Aerocontinente, Bolívar 12-60 and Tarqui (☏07/840196); American Airlines, Hermano Miguel 8-63 and Bolívar (☏07/841172); Austro Aéreo, Hermano Miguel 6-86 (☏07832677), for Quito, Guayaquil and Macas; Avianca, represented by Importadora Román, Av Huayna Cápac 7111 (☏07/835916); Continental, Padre Aguirre 10-96 and Mariscal Lamar (☏07/847374); Ecuatoriana, Bolívar 820 and Luis Cordero (☏07/832220); Icaro, Av España 11-14 at airport (☏07/802700); Tame, Benigno Malo 5-08 and Calle Larga (☏07/843222).

Banks and exchange Banco de Guayaquil (Visa/MasterCard/Cirrus ATM and changes traveller's cheques), on Sucre, between Hermano Miguel and Presidente Borrero; Banco del Austro (Visa ATM), on Sucre and Presidente Borrero; Banco del Pacífico (MasterCard/Cirrus ATM, changes TCs), Benigno Malo and Gran Colombia; Vazcambios, at Gran Colombia and Luis Cordero, changes TCs and currency.

Camping and fishing equipment Acción Sports, Bolívar 12-70 and Juan Montalvo (☏07/833526), and Bermeo Hermanos, Presidente Borrero 8-35 between Sucre and Bolívar (☏07/831722). Explorador Andino (☏07/847320), at the cnr of Calle Larga and Benigno Malo, manufactures hiking and camping equipment.

Car rental At the airport: Localiza, Av España 1485 and Granada (☏07/863902); and Internacional, Av España 10-50 (☏07/801892).

Cinemas Casa de la Cultura on Sucre just off the main square; Teatro Cuenca, Padre Aguirre and Mariscal Lamar; Multicines, 5-screen multiplex on Plaza Milenio at Cornelio Marchán and José Peralta; Cine 9 de Octubre, Mariscal Lamar and Mariano Cueva.

Consulate US, Centro Abraham Lincoln, Presidente Borrero 5-18 (☏07/823898).

Festivals April 12 for the city's foundation and November 3 for its independence; these are big events spread over several days. Religious festivals such as Corpus Christi (see p.47) and Christmas Eve are also celebrated with parades or fireworks and are well worth seeing.

Hospitals Good private hospitals include: Hospital Santa Inés, Av Daniel Córdova Toral 2-113 (☏07/817888); Hospital Monte Sinai, Miguel Cordero 6-111 and Av Solana (☏07/885595). State-run options include: Hospital Vicente Corral Moscoso, Av El Paraíso (☏07/822100); Clínica Santa Ana, Av Manuel J Calle (☏07/814068).

Internet facilities Located across the centre of town, averaging $0.80–1 per hour. Choices include: Cuenc@net, cnr of Calle Larga and Hermano Miguel; Cybercom, cnr of Presidente Córdova and Presidente Borrero; Cafénet Iguananet, Estevez de Toral and Bolívar; several on Benigno Malo south of the main square to Calle Larga, such as Maxnet; and others on Honorato Vásquez between Presidente Borrero and Hermano Miguel. International calls are typically $0.15-0.20 per minute.

Language schools FCEDEI, Gran Colombia and General Torres (☏07/839003, ⓦwww.cedei.org); Sí Centro, Hermano Miguel 6-86 and Presidente Córdova (☏07/946932, ⓦwww .sicentrospanishschool.com); Amauta Fundación, Presidente Córdova 5-58 and Hermano Miguel (☏07/846206, ⓦwww.amauta.edu.ec); Sampere, Calle Larga and Hermano Miguel (☏ & ☏07/841986).

Laundry Cheap, friendly wet-wash laundry service at Lavahora, Honorato Vásquez 7-72 and Luis Cordero, close to *El Cafecito*; La Química Automática, Presidente Borrero 7-34 and Sucre, is also efficient.

Police and immigration Luis Cordero, between Presidente Córdova and Juan Jaramillo (☎07/831020).

Post office The main post office is at Presidente Borrero and Gran Colombia. The gift shops opposite sell cardboard boxes for packaging.

Taxis Radio taxis include: Atenas (☎07/826464); Paisa (☎07/863774); and Transvista (☎07/818182).

Telephone office Etapa is at Benigno Malo and Presidente Córdova, and Pacífictel is more or less opposite. You can make cheap international calls at most Internet cafés (see opposite).

Travel agents For tour operators offering trips around Cuenca, see the box on p.258. There are numerous travel agents around town for booking or changing flights, and the like; the following are all IATA-registered: Austrotur, Luis Cordero 5-14 and Vásquez (☎07/831927); Delgado Travel, Gran Colombia 5-21 (☎07/835667); Metropolitan Touring, Sucre 6-62 (☎07/831185); The Travel Center, Hermano Miguel 4-46 and Calle Larga (☎07/823782).

Around Cuenca

There are a number of very rewarding excursions you can make in the area around Cuenca, using the city as a base for day-trips. A short, fifteen-minute hop away, the thermal baths of **Baños** are supremely relaxing, particularly after a spot of hiking or fishing in **Parque Nacional El Cajas**, forty minutes west of the city, packed with trout-filled lakes, brooding mountains and swirling mists. Heading east, you can visit the rural communities of **Gualaceo**, **Chordeleg** and **Sigsig** on a scenic bus ride through the hills, and find out more about the crafts produced there. Southwest of Cuenca, on the road to Machala, the small town of **Girón** makes a worthwhile excursion for its nearby waterfall surrounded by lush, humid vegetation.

Baños

Eight kilometres west of Cuenca, **BAÑOS** – not to be confused with the major spa town of the same name in the central sierra (see p.209) – is a small, pretty village perched on the side of a hill, dominated by a beautiful twin-towered church that is often illuminated at night. The place is famous for its volcanic **thermal springs**, whose 75°C waters have been channelled into four commercial bath complexes – they can get very crowded on sunny weekends, but are usually quiet and blissfully relaxing through the week. By far the smartest and most attractive – made up of whitewashed, Spanish-looking buildings with terracota roofs – is the **Balneario Durán** (daily 7.30am–8pm, Wed & Sun closes 4pm), managed by the *Hostería Durán* on Avenida Ricardo Durán, just off the main road as it enters the village. The *balneario's* four thermal pools and two sets of Turkish baths cost $2.60. Further up the road through the village, the **Balneario Rodas** (Wed–Sun 6.30am–9pm) has a less appealing concrete outdoor pool (around $1), but its "*termas exclusivas*" (around $1.50) – a small, very hot indoor pool (45°C) with a cold-water pool for cooling off – are deliciously invigorating.

Once you're done with soaking in the waters, there's little else to do here other than wander up to the church, from where you get bird's-eye views down to the valley below. You could also follow the stream just up from the church for a gentle half-hour stroll through a fragrant eucalyptus grove, or branch out into the hills above the village for something more energetic.

Practicalities

If you want to stay in Baños you'll find comfortable **accommodation** at the *Hostería Durán* (☎07/892485, ⓦwww.hosteriaduran.com; ⑥) and inexpensive

Tours around Cuenca

Cuenca's **tour operator** scene is still pretty low-key, with relatively few companies competing for your business. A great place to get tour information – not only around Cuenca, but the whole of Ecuador and Peru – is at The Travel Center (see "Information and transport" on p.247 for details), who have brochures, maps, storage lockers, a copying service, multilingual assistants and offer a wide range of tours through their partners. As well as inexpensive trips to El Cajas and Ingapirca, other possibilities include exploring the countryside around Cuenca on a **horse-riding trek** with Swiss–Ecuadorian outfit Monta Runa (ⓦwww.montaruna.ch) from $50 per person, or by **mountain bike**, with Biketa who offer programmes around El Cajas, to Ingapirca or descents towards the lowlands and rainforest. Other popular destinations are the hill villages of **Gualaceo**, **Chordeleg** and **Sigsig**, east of Cuenca; Expediciones Apullacta offer an enjoyable and enlightening "**crafts tour**" that takes you to local workshops in these villages where you can see weavings being dyed, Panama hats being woven, and talk to the artisans; prices are around $35 per person. Similarly, the Mama Kinua cultural centre on Juan Jaramillo 6-35 and Hermano Miguel (no phone) offers the "Kushiwaira" ethnotourism project, a chance to visit local **indigenous communities** around Cuenca, learn how to make traditional Andean meals, and go for walks or horse rides in the surrounding hills.

Most tour operators in Cuenca also offer day-trips to **Parque Nacional El Cajas** (see below), where you'll be taken on a three- to five-hour **hike** accompanied by a guide who will point out the páramo flora and birds to you; transport and lunch are provided, but you'll need to have your own hiking gear, including waterproof boots and jacket, and plenty of warm layers. Expediciones Apullacta, at Gran Colombia 11-02 and General Torres (ⓣ07/837815, ⓦwww.apullacta.cedei.org), and Río Arriba Expeditions, Hermano Miguel 7-14 (ⓣ07/830116, ⓔnegro@az.pro.ec), are both recommended for day-trips to El Cajas, and charge around $35 per person, including a bilingual guide. On request, they can also arrange two- to four-day hikes through the park for around $40–45 per day, providing all camping gear and food.

rooms at one of several simple hotels, such as the *Copacabana* (ⓣ07/892456; ❷), a *hostal* just behind. However, most people just come in for the day from Cuenca, which is only a fifteen-minute bus ride away – catch a **bus** (every 10min) from Calle Vega Muñoz or the bus terminal. While you're here, the best **place to eat** in the village is at the *Hostería Durán*, which has a reasonably priced café for snacks, a restaurant serving *comida típica*, and a more expensive restaurant serving international food.

Parque Nacional El Cajas

Only 35km northwest of Cuenca, **PARQUE NACIONAL EL CAJAS** is one of the most beautiful wilderness areas in Ecuador: a wild, primeval landscape of craggy hills and glacier-scoured valleys studded with a breathtaking quantity of lakes, glinting like jewels against the mottled earth and rock surrounding them. Spread over 290 square kilometres of high páramo (3000–4500m), the park offers superb **hiking** and **trout fishing** opportunities and – despite sitting on the doorstep of a major city – a tremendous sense of solitude, with visitors kept at bay by the rain and fog that so frequently plague the area. This inhospitable environment harbours more **flora** and **fauna** than first impressions might suggest: native *quinua* trees, with their gnarled and twisted branches, grow alongside the rivers that thread through the park, and many species of shrubs and flowers adapted to harsh climates – such as the orange-flowered *chuqiragua* – survive on the moorland. There's also a tract of dense, humid cloudforest, peppered with orchids and bromeliads, on the eastern edge of the park. As for animals, the park is home to wildcats, pumas, deer and some spectacled bears, though you're far more likely to see ducks, rabbits and perhaps some recently reintroduced llamas. El Cajas is also rich in birdlife, including woodpeckers, hummingbirds, mountain toucans and Andean condors. Human relics include a scattering of pre-Hispanic **ruins**, probably of former shelters for those travelling between the sierra and the coast, as well as a four-kilometre restored section of the Ingañan, an old **Inca road**, conserving much of its original paving.

The best place to start exploring Parque Nacional El Cajas is at the **Information Centre** (daily 7am–5pm) on the edge of the shimmering **Laguna Toreadora**, easily reached from Cuenca along the paved highway that runs through the park on its way to the coast (see "Practicalities", overleaf). This is where you register your visit, pay your $10 **entrance fee** and pick up a free **map** of the park.

Hiking in Parque Nacional El Cajas

When at the Information Centre, you can also ask the wardens to point out hiking trails to suit the level of difficulty you're after and amount of time you have. The most popular **day-hike** (5–6hr) takes you north and east past Laguna Toreadora, through a *quinua* forest and down past **Laguna Totoras** and **Laguna Patoquinuas**. The hike ends back at the highway some 8km east of the refuge, near a roadside restaurant where you can warm yourself up before catching the bus back to Cuenca; get the warden to show you the path, which is straightforward to follow and quite easy-going.

Another good day-hike (also 5–6hr) starts 4km further west along the highway from the Information Centre, at the Tres Cruces hill on the left-hand (south) side of the road. At 4103m, the hill straddles the continental divide between waters draining west into the Pacific and east into the Amazon basin – you can scramble up it in about fifteen minutes, for great views over the park. The trail (signed "Tres Cruces, Larga, Tagllacocha") takes you down past a string of three lakes – Negra, Larga and Tagllacocha – bringing you close to the Ingañan (paved Inca road) by Laguna Luspa, before heading right (west) back towards the highway.

There are numerous possibilities for **multi-day hikes**, but note that the map handed out at the ranger station is totally inadequate for this purpose, meaning it's essential to take the IGM **maps** covering the area (Cuenca, Chaucha, San Felipe de Molleturo and Chiquintad). One very enjoyable three-day hike starts about 1km east of the ranger station at a trail branching south of the highway, signed "Lagunas Burín, Osohuayco, Mamamag". From here it takes about three to five hours to reach **Laguna Osohuayco**, which makes a good place to camp. The following day, you need to pick up the trail leading east to Laguna Mamamag (another 3–4hr), where most people camp for their second night. The final day (6–7hr) involves some tricky pathfinding and a very challenging but exhilarating descent through a fabulous, orchid-filled **cloudforest** to **Laguna Llaviuco**, from where it's a straightforward walk through the valley to the Llaviuco ranger station and back to the highway.

For any kind of hiking in El Cajas, it's crucial to come properly prepared. With the possibility of thick fog obscuring visibility, and a tendency for paths to peter out into nowhere, it's essential to take a compass, emergency food and ideally a survival blanket even on short day-hikes, in case you get lost. Although it's often hot enough to hike in a T-shirt when the sun's out (usually in the morning), the temperature can quickly drop below freezing in bad weather, and is perishing at night, so take plenty of layers and warm gear, including a hat and gloves. You'll also need waterproof clothing and sturdy, waterproof boots, preferably with gaiters; if you're camping make sure your tent is well sealed or you'll have a wet and miserable time. It's driest between June and August, but it might rain, hail or snow at any time of the year.

Practicalities

Getting to the Parque Nacional El Cajas couldn't be easier, as it's conveniently bisected by the paved highway connecting Cuenca with Molleturo and Guayaquil. Catch any bus from Cuenca's terminal terrestre heading towards Guayaquil via Molleturo, and ask to be dropped at the Centro de Informaciones at Laguna Toreadora, about a forty-minute drive from Cuenca. There's a basic **refugio** attached to the Information Centre with bunks, cooking facilities and a chimney but no firewood; you'll need to bring a warm sleeping bag and food. There's also a simple **restaurant** alongside, which has erratic opening hours limited mainly to weekends. Eight kilometres back towards Cuenca, just past the eastern limit of the park, *Restaurant Guevara* is a cheap and cheerful roadside canteen serving hot drinks and fresh trout. A further 6km east, just off the highway, the beautifully located *Dos Chorreras* (℡07/853924; ❺) has a more upmarket (but still reasonably priced) restaurant with a blazing log fire and a daily changing menu. The *hostería* also has comfortable, heated **rooms** and offers **horse treks** through the park. For details of Cuenca-based operators offering **tours** to El Cajas, see the box on p.258.

Gualaceo, Chordeleg and Sigsig

In contrast to the forbidding, rugged scenery of El Cajas, the landscape east of Cuenca is gentle and pastoral, characterized by rippling hills and fertile orchards and fields. From Cuenca, a very scenic paved road leads through these hills to the small market town of **Gualaceo**, continuing to the villages of **Chordeleg** and **Sigsig**, known for their handicrafts. Gualaceo and Chordeleg both have enjoyable Sunday-morning **markets**, while Sigsig – which also has a small Sunday market – is best visited during the week when its Panama-hat factory-shop is open. **Buses** to Gualaceo (a 1hr trip), Chordeleg (1hr 15min) and Sigsig (1hr 40min) leave every half-hour from Cuenca's bus terminal.

Gualaceo

Beautifully set on the banks of the Río Gualaceo, 36km east of Cuenca, **GUALACEO** is known as the Jardín del Azuay (Garden of Azuay) for its rich agricultural land and mild climate. It's one of the most important fruit-growing centres in the region, and every March celebrates the Fiesta del Durazno (Peach Festival) with street parties and peach-tastings. The town's **central plaza**, dominated by a large stone-and-concrete church with colourful stained-glass windows, is the site of a very lively **Sunday-morning market**, packed with stalls piled high with apples, peaches, chirimoyas and cherries, among other fresh produce. There's always a great atmosphere, but there are few craft items or souvenirs to pick up – for these, head for the main avenue, Avenida Roldós, near the bus terminal (a couple of blocks southeast of the plaza, towards the river), where you'll find chunky handmade sweaters, a few weavings, and baskets.

Most people are happy to make a passing visit to Gualaceo, but if you want to **stay** try *Residencial Gualaceo* (℡07/255006; ❷) at Gran Colombia 3-02 (a couple of blocks northwest of the plaza) for reasonable budget rooms, or the *Parador Turístico* (☎07/255110; ❺), about 1km south of the centre on Gran Colombia, for upmarket rooms with a pool, sauna and good restaurant, in a beautiful, rural setting. The best **place to eat** in the centre is *Don Q*, a few doors down from *Residencial Gualaceo*, where basic but well-prepared staples are served in a pleasant indoor courtyard.

Chordeleg

From Gualaceo, the road from Cuenca continues 6km east to the neighbouring village of **CHORDELEG**. Smaller and quainter than Gualaceo, Chordeleg presents a very pretty picture as you approach it along the main road that climbs steeply uphill towards the centre, lined by lovely old terraced houses with sloping terracotta roofs. Look right as you head up this road (Calle Juan Bautista Cobos) and you'll see a number of shops selling **ceramics**, one of the craft traditions the village is noted for – the largest selection is available at the prominently signed Centro de Artesanías, about halfway up. Chordeleg is also famous as a centre of gold and metalwork, particularly delicately worked filigree **jewellery**, an art that's been practised here since pre-Hispanic times. Numerous shops keep the tradition alive in the village, but a lot of it is made from low-grade gold, so beware of parting with large sums of money. These and other local crafts such as embroidery and hat production are the subject of information panels and displays in the **Museo de Comunidad** (Mon–Sat 8am–6pm & Sun 8am–4pm; free) on the plaza, illustrated with some eye-catching examples. You'll also find lots of Panama hats and colourful textiles at the village's Sunday-morning **market**. There is nowhere to stay in Chordeleg, but you can pick up a filling *campesino* meal at a number of simple **restaurants** on the main square, across from the church.

Sigsig

A further 18km along the still-paved road, **SIGSIG** is a remote agricultural village sitting in gorgeous, hilly countryside near the banks of the Río Santa Barbara, from whose swaying reeds (*sigses*) it takes its name. Surprisingly – for such a small, out-of-the-way place – it's one of the most important centres of **Panama hat** production in the province. A good place to buy one at a reasonable price is at the Asociación de Toquilleras María Auxiliadora, in the old hospital next to the river, whose courtyard is permanently overflowing with hats of various colours and stages of completion (note that this part of the building is usually closed to visitors). Few tourists make it to Sigsig let alone **stay** here, but if you need a bed for the night you'll find basic, airy rooms at *Residencial Lupita* (☎07/266257; ❷) on the main road running through the centre of the village. *Restaurant Turismo*, opposite the covered market building, serves cheap soups, fried meats and other staples. A road descends from Sigsig down to Gualaquiza in the southern Oriente (see p.345).

Girón and El Chorro

Forty-five kilometres southeast of Cuenca, the small hill town of **GIRÓN** is built around a pretty central square overlooked by once-grand old houses with clay-tiled roofs and wooden balconies, and a rather avant-garde concrete church with an enormous blue cross towering over the entrance. Girón's single claim to fame is that an important treaty was signed here in 1829 by generals of Gran Colombia and Peru, after the Battle of Tarqui in which the Peruvians were defeated (see p.512). The colonial mansion where the treaty was signed has been splendidly restored by the army and turned into a museum – the **Museo Casa de los Tratados** (daily 8am–5pm; $1) – displaying nineteenth-century uniforms, weapons, flags, battle standards, portraits and a reconstruction of the table where the signing took place.

If this isn't your thing, head out of town to **El Chorro**, a long, slender water-fall tumbling down a steep cliff between a tangle of lush vegetation. It's reached by a two-hour uphill hike from Girón along 5km of dirt road: ask for direc-tions from the traffic lights on the main road running through town. There's a dollar charge to visit the **mirador** overlooking the fall, or you can hike up the stiff two-hour trail to a viewpoint onto a second, higher waterfall, out of sight from below – the walk is a bit hairy in parts, and involves clinging onto some cords attached to the rock. There's a very pleasant **refuge** (℡07/840031; ❷) right next to the waterfall, owned by the Río Arriba tour operator in Cuenca (see box, p.258), offering hearty, inexpensive **meals** and beds; it's not always open during weekdays, so phone in advance if you want to stay. This is a love-ly, remote spot, and makes a great base for off-the-beaten-track hiking through the hills and nearby cloudforest.

South of Cuenca: Saraguro

South of Cuenca, the Panamericana winds its way through increasingly remote and isolated countryside, passing only a handful of villages on its way to the city of Loja. By far the most interesting stop en-route is the small agricultural town of **SARAGURO** ("land of corn" in Quichua), some 140km south of Cuenca and 64km north of Loja. As you approach from the north, a large sign proudly announces your arrival in "*Saraguro, Tierra de Maíz, centro indígena más importante de América*" – the centre of one of the most distinct highland groups of Ecuador, the **Saraguro indígenas**. Their forebears, originally from the alti-plano region of Lake Titicaca in Bolivia, were relocated here by the Incas dur-ing their expansion into Ecuador, as part of the *mitimae* system used to consol-idate colonization. More than 500 years on, the Saraguros are still set apart by their particularly pure form of Quichua and very distinctive clothing. The men wear black ponchos and black knee-length shorts, often over black wellington boots used for their farm work, while the women wear pleated black skirts and hand-woven black shawls, fastened by elaborate silver or nickel brooches called *tupus*. Saraguros have also maintained very traditional forms of celebrating reli-gious festivals. Their Easter celebrations, in particular, follow a strict pattern of processions, re-enactments and symbolic rituals, all marked by their great solemnity. On the day after Palm Sunday, for example, two separate processions – one carrying an image of the Virgin of Sorrows, the other an image of Christ – meet on a nearby mountain known as El Calvario (Calvary), where sad, haunting songs are sung in Quichua. Then, the following Thursday, special watchmen ride into town on horseback, dressed in white, to stay in the church day and night, guarding the image of Christ until Easter Sunday. Other impor-tant Saraguro festivals include Tres Reyes (January 6), Corpus Christi (early or mid-June) and Christmas.

Most Saraguro *indígenas* live as cattle herders in rural farming communities, but just about all of them come into town for the Sunday-morning **market** for fresh produce, cattle and household goods, and Sunday Mass, held in the handsome, honey-stone church on the main plaza.

Practicalities

There's little to do here other than soak up the atmosphere, and most visitors are happy to pass through for a morning or so. If you want to stay, you'll find simple, acceptable **accommodation** with shared bath at the friendly *Residencial Saraguro* (℡07/200286; **❷**), set around the compact flower-filled courtyard on Calle Loja and Antonio Castro. Another budget option is the *Ñuncanchik Sara Allpa* (℡07/200272; **❷**), in a modern building around the corner on Castro, offering basic rooms with shared or private bath. The most comfortable place is the *Samana Wasi* (℡07/200140; **❸/❹**), near the Panamericana on 10 de Marzo, which has spacious, clean rooms with or without private bath and TV; the interior rooms here aren't so nice. The best **places to eat** are the *Reina del Cisne* and the somewhat cleaner *Mama Cuchara* on the plaza, which serve uncomplicated but tasty Ecuadorian food at reasonable prices. **Buses** from Cuenca and Loja pass through town every hour or so.

Loja and around

Marooned at the bottom of the country, far from Quito and several hours' drive from any other major town, **LOJA** is a remote but thriving little provincial capital. Thanks to its isolation, it has long been good at taking care of its own affairs, even dabbling with self-government in 1857 – not to mention its distinction of being the first city in the country to generate electricity, in 1897. With a progressive emphasis on learning and culture, the city boasts two universities, a law school and a major music conservatory, which give the place a youthful, vibrant atmosphere. Spread over a fertile valley at 2100m above sea level, Loja is about 500m lower than most sierra cities, and noticeably warmer (usually 16–21°C) as well.

Loja's most exciting **fiesta** kicks off on August 20 when the icon of the Virgen del Cisne arrives in the Cathedral for a two-month "visit", having been carried on foot from El Cisne (see p.269), accompanied by hundreds of pilgrims. The festivities which follow, including processions and musical events, culminate on September 8 with the Feria de Integración Fronteriza, a huge craft and trade fair established in 1824 by none other than Simón Bolívar, in an effort to promote cross-border relations. The fair is still attended by many northern Peruvians today.

The town sits on the doorstep of the western edge of **Parque Nacional Podocarpus**, a pristine tract of páramo and cloudforest, and is the best place get information on the park or arrange a visit (see p.271). The eastern part of the park, over the sierra and down towards the Oriente, is approached from the hot, dusty town of **Zamora**, easily reached by bus from Loja. Loja is also the gateway to **Peru** via two border crossings (see box p.279 for full details). The first is a smooth and efficient one located at Macará, 190km southwest, which continues onto Piura in Peru. The second, more difficult, crossing is at Zumba, 145km due south of Loja, beyond the easy-going village of **Vilcabamba**, which has become an obligatory stop for many backpackers before leaving the country.

Arrival

Flights from Quito and Guayaquil land at the **Aeropuerto La Toma**, just outside the small town of **Catamayo**, 33km west of Loja. There are always plenty of shared taxis waiting to meet incoming planes, charging a fixed price of around $3 per person into Loja (you can call for one on ☎07/581769); otherwise a private taxi costs $10–12. Loja's **bus terminal** is 2km north of the centre on Avenida Cuxibamba; from here it's about a twenty-five-minute walk into town, or you can pick up any local bus heading south towards the centre, or one of the taxis that hang around the terminal.

Information and transport

For **tourist information**, head to the excellent municipal office on the central square, at J.A. Eguiguren and Bolívar (Mon–Fri 9–11am and 3–7pm, Sat & Sun 9am–5pm; ☎07/584018). The helpful staff here can supply you with glossy brochures and maps, and should be able to answer most of your questions about Loja and its surroundings. The Ministerio de Turismo office, in the Edificio Banco de Fomento on the corner of J.A. Eguiguren and Sucre (Mon–Fri 8.30am–1pm and 3–5.30pm; ☎07/572964, ☎570485), is similarly helpful. You can pick up maps and information on Parque Nacional Podocarpus at the **Ministerio del Ambiente** office, in the INDA building, at Sucre between Imbabura and Quito (☎07/585421); if you intend to go hiking in Sector Romerillos (see p.272), you should definitely try to get hold of a map while you're here, in case they've run out in Zamora. Several other organizations in Loja have information on Podocarpus, and for details of these refer to the park account beginning on p.271.

Taxis charge around $1 for journeys within the city, and can usually be flagged down on the main avenues or around the Parque Central.

Accommodation

Loja offers a decent spread of generally good-value **hotels**, from the budget to the very comfortable. Unless you're arriving during the festival of the Virgen del Cisne (Aug 20–Sept 8), there's unlikely to be a shortage of beds, so there's no need to book ahead.

Acapulco Sucre 07-61 ☎07/570651, ☎571103. Clean and tidy rooms with nylon bedspreads and dated furnishings, most with private bath. The majority look onto an internal courtyard. There's parking available as well. Breakfast included. ❸

Aguilera Internacional Sucre 01-08 ☎07/584660, ☎572894. Quiet, unremarkable rooms with cable TV and private bath, a short walk from the centre. The main reason you might want to come to this hotel is for the attached steam baths (free to guests), perfumed with eucalyptus leaves, and for the sauna and gym. Breakfast included. ❹–❺

Internacional 10 de Agosto 15-30 ☎07/578486. Old-fashioned house with nicely painted woodwork and adequate rooms with private bath around an internal patio. Fine for the price. ❸

Libertador Colón 14-30 ☎07/560779, ☎572119. Loja's best hotel, offering smart, well-furnished rooms with cable TV, direct-dial phone and good bathrooms. Also has a decent restaurant, a small pool, a sauna and steam bath. Ask for a room in the new block. Buffet breakfast included. ❻

Londres Sucre 07-51 ☎07/561936. Well-maintained old house owned by a friendly young couple, offering spacious rooms with high ceilings, wooden floors and bare white walls. Clean, shared bathrooms and lots of plants and flowers around. The best budget choice in town. ❷

Podocarpus José A. Eguiguren 16-15 ☎ & ☎07/581428, ehotelpod@hotmail.com. Comfortable, modern rooms with spotless en-suite bath, good-quality bedding and cable TV in every room. The hotel's back rooms are quietest. Breakfast included. ❺

The Town

Loja's **centre** – wedged between the Malacatos and Zamora rivers – is a curious mix of the concrete and the colonial. While it lacks the uniform architectural harmony of Cuenca, it preserves enough handsome old eighteenth- and

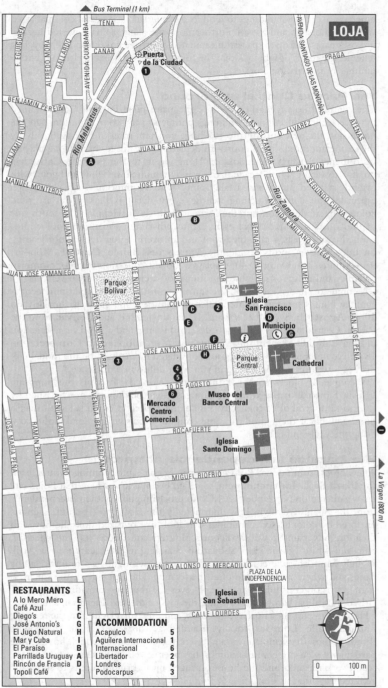

Bus Terminal (1 km)

LOJA

TENA

CANAR

Puerta
de la Ciudad
1

F. EGUIGUREN
ALFREDO MORA
GALLARDO
AVENIDA CUXIBAMBA

PRAGA

AVENIDA SANTIAGO DE LAS MONTANAS

AVENIDA ORILLAS DEL ZAMORA

ATENAS

BENJAMÍN PEREIRA

D. ALVAREZ

Río Malacatus

BENJAMÍN RUÍZ

G. CAMPIÓN

JUAN DE SALINAS

A

SEGUNDO CUEVA CELI

MANUEL MONTEROS

JOSÉ FÉLIX VALDIVIESO

Río Zamora

AVENIDA EMILIANO ORTEGA

SAN JUAN DE DIOS

QUITO

B

JUAN JOSÉ SAMANIEGO

IMBABURA

BERNARDO VALDIVIESO

18 DE NOVIEMBRE

Parque
Bolívar

SUCRE

BOLÍVAR

OLMEDO

JUAN JOSÉ PEÑA

PLAZA

Iglesia
San Francisco

COLÓN

C **2**

D

Municipio

G

AVENIDA UNIVERSITARIA

E

i

F

JOSÉ ANTONIO EGUIGUREN

H

Parque
Central

Cathedral

3

4
5

10 DE AGOSTO

6

Mercado
Centro
Comercial

Museo del
Banco Central

AVENIDA LAURO GUERRERO
AVENIDA IBEROAMÉRICANA

ROCAFUERTE

JOSÉ MARÍA PEÑA
RAMÓN PINTO

Iglesia
Santo Domingo

MIGUEL RIOFRÍO

J

I

La Virgen (800 m)

AZUAY

AVENIDA ALONSO DE MERCADILLO

PLAZA DE LA
INDEPENDENCIA

N

RESTAURANTS
A lo Mero Mero   **E**
Café Azul   **F**
Diego's   **C**
José Antonio's   **G**
El Jugo Natural   **H**
Mar y Cuba   **I**
El Paraíso   **B**
Parrillada Uruguay **A**
Rincón de Francia   **D**
Topoli Café   **J**

ACCOMMODATION
Acapulco   **5**
Aguilera Internacional **1**
Internacional   **6**
Libertador   **4**
Londres   **2**
Podocarpus   **3**

Iglesia
San Sebastián

CALLE LOURDES

0   100 m

4

THE SOUTHERN SIERRA | Loja and around

265

Parque La Argelia (4 km)

nineteenth-century buildings to lend its *centro histórico* a graceful colonial look, with much charm and appeal. Furthermore, the *municipio* has invested heavily in Loja's parks and open spaces, and initiated a garbage collection and recycling scheme, the result of which is that the town has recently been garnered with a number of international prizes.

The Parque Central and around

The centre of Loja is marked by the large, palm-filled **Parque Central**, lined by an eclectic collection of buildings competing for your attention. On the north side, the new **municipio** is a huge concrete monstrosity, saved only by the exuberant murals in its courtyard depicting folk images of *indígenas* playing instruments, dancing and cooking. Alongside it, to the east, the **Cathedral** boasts a towering white facade flamboyantly trimmed in yellow and gold, with brightly painted pillars and a tall, pointy spire. Its interior is equally ornate, especially the coffered ceiling, whose every detail is picked out in vivid colours. In subdued contrast, the former **Casa de Justicia**, on the south side of the square, is a traditional early eighteenth-century mansion with white-washed adobe walls, a clay-tiled roof and an overhanging upper floor leaning on thick wooden posts. Inside, the **Museo del Banco Central** (Mon–Fri 9am–1pm & 2–4.30pm; $0.40) displays a modest collection of pre-Columbian ceramics and religious sculptures in rooms off a creaking wooden veranda.

A couple of streets leading off the square are dotted with elegant nineteenth-century houses sporting painted balconies, shutters and eaves, particularly on **10 de Agosto**, between Bolívar and 18 de Noviembre, and **Bolívar**, from the Parque Central towards Calle Lourdes. In this area, and a good representation of Loja's tidy and efficient spirit, is the busy **Mercado Centro Comercial** on 18 de Noviembre and 10 de Agosto, considered by many to be the model city market – well managed, clean, and run with unfussy competence.

A couple of blocks south of the market along Bolívar sits the imposing **Iglesia Santo Domingo**, whose immense twin bell towers are cherished by Lojanos as a symbol of their city. Inside, the church is crammed with over a hundred biblical-themed oil paintings hanging amid swirling floral motifs covering the walls and ceilings.

The Plaza de la Independencia and around

A few blocks south down Bolívar from the Iglesia Santo Domingo you'll reach the **Plaza de la Independencia**, so called because it was here that Loja's citizens gathered on November 18, 1820 to proclaim publicly their independence from the Spanish Crown. It is undoubtedly the city's most beautiful square, enclosed by colonial-style buildings that look like outsized dolls' houses with their brightly painted walls, balconies, shutters and doors, and the cheerful, blue-and-white **Iglesia San Sebastián**. Standing in the square is a very tall, vaguely Moorish-style clock tower, a decorative wrought-iron fountain, and a bandstand where concerts are often performed. The east side of the square is framed by gorgeous hills rising steeply over the rooftops, providing a particularly beautiful backdrop as they catch the rays of the late afternoon sun.

Head south past the church for a block, and then turn right into the recently restored **Calle Lourdes**, locally regarded as the jewel of all the town's thoroughfares. Between Bolívar and Sucre, the entire street, which boasts some particularly well-preserved buildings, has been given an extensive facelift, the woodwork repaired, and the houses spruced up in bright colours to show the architecture off at its best.

Loja's outskirts

Loja has several worthwhile sights on the outskirts of town. The new **Puerta de la Ciudad**, a mock early-colonial gatehouse complete with tower, crenellations and portcullis, marks the northern entrance to town at the confluence of the two rivers and contains temporary art exhibitions (daily 8am–10pm; free), and a pleasant café on the second floor. You can climb up the tower for attractive views of the town and its environs. About 1km north of this, the **Plaza de El Valle** is a good-looking paved square surrounded by pretty, rustic-style buildings and a lovely old colonnaded church. Continuing three blocks north to reach the **Parque de Recreación Jipiro**, a large, landscaped park with an ornamental lake and a children's playground featuring models of buildings from around the world, such as the Eiffel Tower, an Arabic mosque and a truly bizarre replica of Moscow's St Basil's Cathedral replete with slides. Jipiro is a very popular open space for Lojanos, who also come to enjoy the lovely heated swimming pool here (Tues–Sun 8am–6pm; $1), equipped with retractable glass roof, or the little planetarium in the dome of the "mosque" which has regular 30-minute shows at weekends ($0.25). The Plaza and the park can be reached on foot in about twenty minutes, or on buses marked "El Valle" or "Jipiro" from the centre.

At the opposite end of town, about 4.5km south along Avenida de los Conquistadores, the University-run **Parque La Argelia** (daily 8.30am–5.30pm; $0.50) is a mini slice of wilderness on the edge of the city, with excellent trails running through hills, forests and streams. A part of the park (with a separate entrance, across the highway) is the **Jardín Botánico Reynaldo Espinosa** (daily 9am–noon & 2.30–4pm; $0.60), home to a great variety of native and introduced plant species, including many orchids. Parque La Argelia is on the road to Vilcabamba, so can be reached on any bus from Loja to Vilcabamba from the Terminal; alternatively, take a taxi there for about $1.50.

The whole of Loja can be taken in with sweeping, panoramic **views** from a lookout point at the foot of the statue of the **Virgen de Fátima** (El Churo), perched on a hillside east of the city. To get there, walk east up Riofrío, cross the river, and follow the path up the hillside.

Eating, drinking and nightlife

Loja offers some very inviting, good-value **restaurants** that tend to be packed at lunchtime and very quiet later on, with most winding down around 9pm. Despite being a university town, the town's **nightlife** is tranquil as well. For a quiet, inexpensive cocktail amidst red-carpeted, red-walled and decidedly kitsch surroundings, head for *Unicornio*, on the west side of the Parque Central, opposite the Cathedral – it claims to be a piano bar but rarely has a pianist. A little more up-to-date, with a young, mellow crowd and soothing music, is *Bar La Siembra*, on 24 de Mayo and Segundo Cueva Celi, just across the Río Zamora, which also serves beer on tap, grilled food and chips. Just up the road to the north, *Enigma* is the town's best disco with gorgeous views over Loja from inside, even if the music is recorded and nothing special. For **live acts** – Loja is renowned for producing some of the country's finest musicians – try the lively *Casa Tinku*, an old house on the Plaza de la Independencia, which usually has good live music on Friday and Saturday night. A good back-up choice is *El Viejo Minero* on Sucre and Riofrío, a small and cosy bar, filled with mining memorabilia, which regularly features impromptu live music.

Restaurants and cafés

A lo Mero Mero Sucre and Colón. Simple little restaurant giving onto a busy street, with wooden benches and tables, and sombreros on the wall, serving inexpensive Mexican food. Closed Sun.

Café Azúl José A. Eguiguren, between Bolívar and Sucre. Attractive blue-painted café with changing displays of local artwork on the walls, and an inviting menu including wholemeal sandwiches with fresh fillings, vegetarian crêpes, lots of salads and good cakes. Curious opening hours have it open for breakfast, closed for lunch, and then reopening mid-afternoon. Closed Sat till 3pm & Sun.

Diego's upstairs, Colón 14-66 and Sucre. Housed in a distinguished old house with a leafy courtyard and a grand dining room complete with fancy wallpaper and sheeny drapes, *Diego's* features inexpensive breakfasts and *almuerzos*, as well as hearty mid-priced à la carte dishes, like steak in red-wine sauce. It's also popular for its local specialities, including *cecinas* – chargrilled pork strips – served with *mote pillo* (maize prepared with eggs) and yuca. Closes Sun 4pm.

José Antonio's upstairs, J.A. Eguiguren 12-24 and Olmedo. Excellent, imaginatively prepared food is served in this unpretentious, great-value restaurant. The fish and seafood are especially good – try the *corvina alcaparras con camarón* (sea bass with capers and prawns) or *mariscos al vino en coco* (shellfish with wine and coconut).

El Jugo Natural J.A. Eguiguren and Bolívar. Good place to pick up a freshly squeezed juice, some breakfast and a traditional snack like *quimbolitos*.

Mar y Cuba Rocafuerte 9-00 and 24 de Mayo. For tasty, authentic Cuban food you'll not do any better than this restaurant, which is particularly accomplished with its seafood dishes.

El Paraíso Quito between Sucre and Bolívar. Modest bargain canteen, serving unadventurous set vegetarian meals revolving around rice, noodles or tofu.

Parrillada Uruguay Juan de Salinas and Avenida Universitaria. Friendly, family-run restaurant serving delicious, succulent meat cooked over charcoal on a traditional cast iron *parrilla* (grill). If you're not up to their huge portions, try the steak baguette for a light meal. Evenings only.

Rincón de Francia Valdivieso and J.A. Eguiguren. An intimate restaurant set around a little courtyard, offering a versatile international menu and good, reasonably-priced food.

Topoli Café Riofrío and Bolívar. Great for coffee, snacks, sandwiches, yogurt and breakfasts.

Listings

Airlines Icaro, J.A. Eguiguren and Olmedo (☎07/585956), for Quito; Tame, 24 de Mayo and Emiliano Ortega (☎07/570248), for Quito and Guayaquil.

Banks and exchange Banco del Austro (Visa ATM and cash advance), cnr of J.A. Eguiguren and Bolívar; Banco de Guayaquil, J.A. Eguiguren and Valdivieso (Visa, MasterCard ATM, changes Amex TCs, cash advance).

Buses leave from the bus terminal 2km from the centre; there are regular city buses here or taxis cost $1. For Vilcabamba, there are hourly buses plus Vilcabambaturis minibuses which leave every 15min, or you can get a (less comfortable) *taxi ruta* (shared taxi) from the southern end of Av Iberoamérica for about $1. Cooperativa Loja Internacional sends three buses daily from the terminal to Piura, Peru via Macará at 7am, 1pm and 10.30pm. See box p.279 for more details.

Car rental Arricar at the *Hotel Libertador* (☎07/5588014, @vilcatour@impsat.net.ec).

Consulate Peru, Sucre 10-56 and Azuay (☎07/571668).

Hospitals Hospital Militar, Colón and Bernardo Valdivieso (☎07/578332); Clínica San Agustín, 18 de Noviembre and Azuay (☎07/570314); Clínica

Santa María, Cuxibamba and Latacunga (☎07/581077).

Internet facilities Several places for $1.20–1.50 per hour, including: World Net, Colón and Sucre; Jungle Net, Riofrío 13-64 and Bolívar; Macro Soft, Sucre and Azuay; and Cybertren at the Parque Jipiro.

Laundry Maxilim Lavandería on the corner of 10 de Agosto and 24 de Mayo is the cheapest option in town if you ask for a wet wash ("*lavado en agua*") rather than dry cleaning.

Police and immigration Av Argentina, Tebaida Alta (☎07/573600).

Post office Sucre 05-85 and Colón.

Telephone office The central Pacífictel office is on José A. Eguiguren and Bernardo Valdivieso, but there are other offices around town.

Travel agents and tour operators Reliable travel agents for booking or changing flights include Vilcatur at the *Hotel Libertador*, Colón 14-30 (☎07/588014). Tour operators offering local, city, Podocarpus and Vilcabamba tours include Biotours, Colón 14-96 and Sucre (☎07/578398); Frankhitur, cnr of Bolívar and Azuay (☎07/573620); Quillis Tour, Miguel Riofrío 14-78 and Sucre (☎07/561960); and Aratinga Aventuras

Birdwatchers, especially for birdwatching tours, at Lourdes 14–80 and Sucre (℡07/582434, ✉jatavent@cue.satnet.net). Ask any of these operators or tourist offices about the state of the *ruta ecológica*, a hiking and riding route between Loja and Vilcabamba that is currently being developed.

West to El Cisne

West of Loja, the road to Machala meanders through parched, rippling hills on its way down to the coast. Some 43km out of town, at the small community of **San Pedro**, a paved road branches north and climbs steeply uphill for 22km. A striking sight awaits you at the top, as the road twists around the hill and dips down to reveal a carpet of rustic, terracotta roofs clustered around a huge, white, neo-Gothic basilica, whose pinnacles and spires dwarf everything around it. This is the tiny village of **EL CISNE** and its famous **Santuario**, home to a sixteenth-century painted cedar carving of the Virgin Mary. This icon, known as the **Virgen del Cisne**, is the subject of a fervent cult of devotion, attracting pilgrims year-round from southern Ecuador and northern Peru. This devotion reaches its apogee during the **Fiesta del Virgen**, which begins on August 15. The following day, thousands of pilgrims begin a seventy-kilometre trek to Loja, carrying the Virgin on their shoulders. The image arrives on August 20, where she is deposited in Loja's cathedral, while the partying continues in the city.

You begin to get an idea of the faith that is invested in this icon at the **museum** attached to the basilica (Tues–Sun 8am–noon & 1–5pm; $0.30; if closed, ask in the bookshop at the base of the clock tower, opposite), crammed with hundreds of gifts brought to thank the Virgin for her favours, from exam certificates and medals to jewellery and vases. There's also a large collection of tiny model buses and trucks, left by drivers in return for her protection. Tucked away in a hushed, softly lit side room next door, you'll find a collection of eighteenth-century religious paintings and carvings, along with some richly embroidered garments and silver lecterns. Once you've admired the basilica and its Virgin, and visited the museum, there's nothing else to do in El Cisne, but if you get caught out you'll find clean, budget **rooms** at *Hostal Medina* (no phone; ❷) on Calle Machachi, the road leading down to the church. There are a couple of basic **places to eat** on the plaza in front of the basilica.

East to Zamora

A newly paved road heading east connects Loja with the small town of **ZAMORA**, sitting 55km away at the foot of the Andes on the edge of the Oriente. It's worth going for the bus ride alone, as the road snakes its way down from the sierra past numerous waterfalls, giving occasional views onto mile after mile of densely forested hills. As you get lower, the air becomes warmer and moister, and the vegetation becomes increasingly lush, with giant ferns hanging over the road. By the time you get to Zamora, 970m above sea level, you're in a beautifully warm, subtropical climate, with an average temperature of 21°C. Zamora has a lovely setting at the confluence of the Zamora and Bombuscaro rivers, with a backdrop of steep, emerald-green hills rising over its rooftops. The town itself, however, is not attractive, with sprawling grid-laid streets and functional, cement-built houses, some of them still waiting to be completed. This is still, at heart, a modern, rough-and-ready pioneer town, despite having been founded by the Spaniards back in 1549.

That first settlement – intended to be used as a base for **gold mining** – was quickly destroyed by indigenous groups, but after a second, successful attempt was made to re-found it ten years later, Zamora became a busy mining town for seventy years. When the mines were abandoned, the town all but disappeared until renewed interest in mining led to Zamora's third foundation in 1800. By the time Zamora was named capital of the isolated Zamora-Chinchipe province in 1952, it had gone back to being a marginal outpost, little more than a village, and still accessible only by mule. It wasn't until a road was built from Loja in 1962 that growth began to take off, fuelled by new mining activity in nearby Nambija in the 1980s. Today, Zamora has a growing population of 10,000; its economy is based partly on servicing the local mining industries and partly on agriculture. For most visitors Zamora's main use is as a base for visiting the lower section of Parque Nacional Podocarpus (see opposite).

Practicalities

Many daily **buses** make the two-hour journey from Loja to Zamora, arriving at the terminal at the eastern end of the town centre, which is within easy walking distance of all **hotels**. There's not a great deal to choose from: one of the best is the *Gimifa Internacional*, at Diego de Vaca and Pio Jaramillo (☎07/606103; ❸), whose rooms have clean white walls, swish red carpets, decent bathrooms and cable TV. It also has great views from its roof terrace, and private parking. Another decent hotel is *Macuna* (☎07/605113; ❸–❹) on Diego de Vaca, a couple of blocks west of the square. Its rooms, all with private bath and cable TV, are spacious and airy, especially the back room with the balcony. The most acceptable budget option is *Syma* at 24 de Mayo and Amazonas (☎07/605583; ❷) which, although basic and spartan, is fairly clean and swept; showers are shared and cold-water only.

As for **restaurants**, *King Burger*, on the north side of the square, does surprisingly tasty burgers and grilled-chicken sandwiches, while *El Legendario Pacar*, Diego de Vaca and Pio Jaramillo, offers hearty set meals in a colourful dining room with local artesanía pinned to the walls. *Pepe Junior*, on Avenida del Maestro, next to the bus terminal, is popular with locals for soups, fried meat and the like.

Zamora's **post office** is on Sevilla de Oro, just off the square, while Pacifictel's **telephone office** is on Amazonas and José Luis Tamayo, one block north of the square. You can get a map of the Parque Nacional Podocarpus as

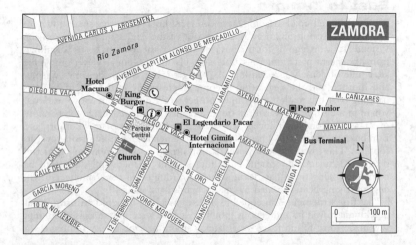

well as **information** about it at the Ministerio del Ambiente office (☎07/606606), just out of town on the road to Loja. General tourist information is available from the municipal tourist office on the main square (Mon–Fri 8am–12.30pm and 2–5pm; ☎07/605996). **Taxis** – part of the Cooperativa Río Zamora (☎07/605065) – are stationed behind the bus terminal from 5am until 10pm; they charge around $3 to go to the Bombuscaro park entrance and $10–15 to go to the Romerillos entrance (see overleaf).

Parque Nacional Podocarpus

Spilling down the eastern flanks of the Andes towards the tropical valleys of the Oriente, **PARQUE NACIONAL PODOCARPUS** presents a spectacular landscape of high páramo, dense, dripping cloudforest, rushing waterfalls and crystalline rivers. Its wide-ranging altitudes (900–3600m), climates and habitats harbour a staggering diversity of flora and fauna, including an estimated 3000 to 4000 plant species, over 500 recorded bird species and important populations of mammals such as mountain tapirs, giant armadillos, pudu (dwarf deer), spectacled bears and pumas. The park was created in 1982, partly to protect some of the country's last major stands of podocarpus trees (Ecuador's only native conifer, also known as *romerillo*), whose numbers had been drastically reduced by commercial logging. Other notable trees here include the cinchona (known locally as *cascarilla*), whose bark is the source of **quinine**, first discovered in this very region. The almost fantastical number of bird species in the park include many varieties of hummingbirds, toucans, tanagers and parrots.

There are two principal **entrances** to the park, corresponding to its geographical divisions: one is the **Sector Cajanuma** in the Zona Alta (upper section), near Loja; the other is the **Sector Bombuscaro** in the Zona Baja (lower section), reached from Zamora. Also in the Zona Baja is a third, little-visited entry post at **Sector Romerillos**, which is the gateway to a very rugged, long-distance hike. The southwestern reaches of the park are often visited on guided hikes and horse treks from the small village of Vilcabamba (for more details see p.278); although there's currently no entry post, there are plans to introduce one here. **Tickets**, available at the entrance posts, cost $10 and are valid in all sectors for up to one week.

Sector Cajanuma

Spread over the northern part of the Zona Alta, the **Sector Cajanuma** is characterized by steep ridges covered with cloudforest, and high, lake-studded páramo. With average elevations of over 3000m, daytime temperatures usually hover around 12°C, though it can get much colder when the wind whips up and the rains start to fall. Rain, unfortunately, is very common between March and September, leaving the park's trails very muddy; the driest months are usually October to December. The Cajanuma **entrance post** is 15km south of Loja, on the road to Vilcabamba. Any bus to Vilcabamba (see p.273) will drop you here, but you're left with an eight-kilometre uphill slog (2–3hr) to the main **ranger station** and park entrance proper, at an altitude of 2750m. The only way to get there directly is by taxi from Loja, for about $6, or $10 for the round-trip (arrange to be picked up).

From the ranger station – which offers floor space and a few **beds** (bring a sleeping bag; $4) for overnight visitors, plus kitchen facilities – there are some well-defined **trails** striking into the park. The **Sendero al Mirador** (3.5km) leads steeply uphill through lush, temperate forest to a lookout point, high on a ridge, giving stunning views across the deep-green mountainsides poking up through the clouds. This makes a very rewarding half-day hike, and is good for spotting **birds** like the bearded guan, grey-breasted mountain toucan, rainbow starfrontlet, chestnut-bearded coronet and red-hooded tanager (all these can also be spotted around the access road close to the ranger station).

Sendero Las Lagunas is a much more demanding hike, leading for 14km through cloudforest and high páramo to the eerily beautiful **Lagunas del Compadre**, a network of fourteen lakes at 3200m above sea level, surrounded by bare granite and sharp, rocky peaks. It takes around six to eight hours to reach the lakes from the ranger station, with some strenuous uphill hiking along the way. There are good **camping** spots around the lakes – you'll need to bring a tent, stove and food, a warm sleeping bag, good waterproof boots and jacket and plenty of layers. The lakes have been stocked with rainbow trout, so if you bring a fishing rod you may be able to catch your supper. With luck, you may also be able to spot mountain tapirs, which are quite common in this area.

Sector Bombuscaro

Down in the Zona Baja, at the foot of the Cordillera Oriental, Sector Bombuscaro is a sensory extravaganza of riotous vegetation, hot, sticky air, squawking birds, mossy smells, fluorescent butterflies, gurgling waterfalls and ice-cold rivers. At just under 1000m above sea level, daytime temperatures rarely fall below a very pleasant 18°C, and even during the rainy season (generally May to Oct) the weather is unlikely to spoil your fun so long as you don't mind walking through muddy trails.

The **entrance** is easily reached from the town of Zamora, either on foot (a 1hr 30min walk) along the road branching south for 6km from behind the bus terminal, following the Río Bombuscaro, or by taxi for around $3. From the parking area at the end of the road, marked by a park entrance sign and a usually empty wooden kiosk, it's a further twenty minutes on foot up to the **ranger station**, where you can chat to the ranger about hiking through the park and bird spotting. Close by, there are a couple of very short, signed paths to some **waterfalls**, and a wooden sign pointing to an "*area de nadar*" (swimming area) – a gorgeous bit of river where you can swim (though not after heavy rains), with hundreds of butterflies hovering around the rocks on the river banks.

There are several **trails** through the park, and one of the best is the **Sendero Higuerones**, which follows the Río Bombuscaro for about 8km through secondary and primary forest, taking about three hours each way. As you walk, you're likely to see an extraordinary number of birds such as ruddy-quail doves, umbrellabirds, copper-chested jacamars, paradise tanagers and orange-eared tanagers, among many others. There are also many biting insects, so be sure to take plenty of **insect repellent** with you. If you plan to stay overnight in the park, you can **camp** by the ranger station or sleep in one of the basic wooden huts nearby (bring a sleeping bag), and use the cooking facilities in the station.

Sector Romerillos

Twenty-five kilometres south of Zamora, the tiny village of Romerillos has a third **entrance** to the national park, which is the starting point for an adventurous but demanding three- to four-day circular hike through lush, dense cloudforest, with a fair amount of uphill climbing. The first half of the loop, to the area known as **San Luis**, follows a very distinct track built by a gold mining company given licence to survey in the 1990s; it covers a distance of some

38km, and takes you past a couple of abandoned wooden shelters and the camp formerly used by the miners. From here onwards, however, it becomes very hard going, with thigh-deep mud in parts, and an increasingly indistinct trail. The reward, though, is the chance to walk through truly stunning virgin cloudforest, peppered with breathtaking views down to a dense canopy of greenery. If you plan to do this hike, be sure to get hold of the **map** available from the Ministerio del Ambiente office in Zamora (see p.271), and to talk to the ranger at Romerillos before you set off, partly for **information** about the route, partly so someone can start looking for you if you're unlucky enough to get lost. You can get to Romerillos on a twice-daily **bus** (6am and 2pm) from Zamora's terminal, or by **taxi** for about $15–20; the journey takes around ninety minutes.

Park practicalities

You can pick up a rudimentary **map** of the park at the Ministerio del Ambiente offices in Loja (see p.264) and Zamora (see p.271). In Loja, the conservationist organization Fundación Arco Iris, at Segundo Cueva Celi 03-15 and Clodoveo Carrión (☏07/577449, ⓦwww.arcoiris.org.ec), is an excellent source of **information** on Podocarpus, with useful **field guides** to the park's birds and trees. They also manage an Interpretation Centre and **hostel** in the San Francisco sector at the northeast end of the park with dorm bunks ($5 if you have your own sleeping bag; $8 to rent one) and two furnished private rooms ($10), along with several interesting nearby trails, most of which you can walk without a guide. Also in Loja, Nature and Culture International (☏07/573691 or 573623, ⓦwww.natureandculture.org), at Mercadillo 18-10 and J.M. Peña, run a **research station** in a private cloudforest reserve adjacent to the park to the north where you can stay for $10 a night. Both organizations and the Ministerio del Ambiente should be able to find a **guide** for you costing around $10 per day. Another option is to visit the park with Loja-based operators offering **tours** into the park, such as Biotours or Aratinga Aventuras Birdwatchers (see "Listings", p.268).

Vilcabamba

Just over 40km south of Loja, sitting in a beautiful valley enfolded by crumpled, sunburnt hills, **VILCABAMBA** is a small agricultural village that's become something of a tourist magnet over the last decade or so. It first caught the attention of the outside world back in 1955, when *Reader's Digest* published an article claiming that Vilcabambans enjoyed a considerably higher than average life expectancy, with a very low incidence of cardiovascular health problems. Soon Vilcabamba was being touted as "the valley of eternal youth" and the "valley of longevity", as international investigators unearthed a string of sprightly old people claiming to be up to 120 or 130 years old. More rigorous studies revealed these claims to be wildly exaggerated, and to date no hard evidence has been produced to support theories of an abnormally long-living population in Vilcabamba – though scientists acknowledge that villagers in their seventies and eighties tend to be extremely fit and healthy for their age.

These days Vilcabamba feels like a place not quite grounded in reality – partly because of the myths associated with it, partly because of the high proportion of resident gringos who've come here in search of the simple life (and, inevitably, have ended up competing vigorously with each other for business), and partly because of the conspicuous presence of foreign tourists. People head here for a variety of reasons. Some come for the hallucinogenic cactus juice, San Pedro, that the village has become famous for, even though this is illegal and heavily frowned upon by locals. Others come for the hiking and birding in the nearby hills of Parque Nacional Podocarpus, but most come just to relax, enjoy the warm climate and nice views, or maybe take a horse ride or indulge in a massage or steam bath. Vilcabamba is not about seeing a slice of traditional Andean life or interacting with locals, but about pampering yourself and re-charging your batteries, enjoying your home-made granola breakfasts and hanging out with other travellers. The best months to be here are June to September, while October to May can often be rainy. Daytime temperatures usually fluctuate between 18°C and 28°C.

Arrival and information

Buses and minibuses from Loja's bus terminal drop passengers off at the **bus terminal** every fifteen minutes on the main road running into town, the Avenida de la Eterna Juventud, a couple of blocks from the central square.

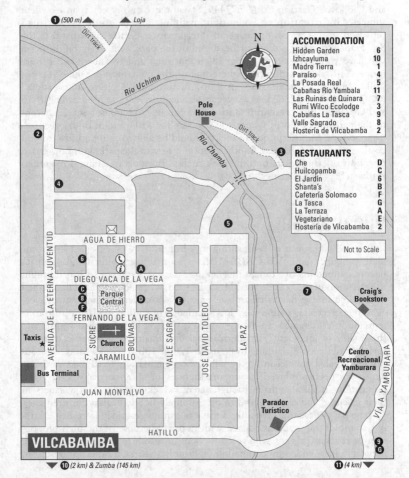

ACCOMMODATION
Hidden Garden   6
Izhcayluma   10
Madre Tierra   1
Paraíso   4
La Posada Real   5
Cabañas Río Yambala 11
Las Ruinas de Quinara 7
Rumi Wilco Ecolodge 3
Cabañas La Tasca   9
Valle Sagrado   8
Hostería de Vilcabamba 2

RESTAURANTS
Che   D
Huilcopamba   C
El Jardín   6
Shanta's   B
Cafetería Solomaco   F
La Tasca   G
La Terraza   A
Vegetariano   E
Hostería de Vilcabamba 2

Not to Scale

VILCABAMBA

Many of the hotels are in the centre of the village, easily reached on foot from the bus terminal, but some are a good fifteen- or twenty-minute walk away – if carrying a heavy pack you might want to hop in one of the pick-up trucks hanging around the bus terminal that act as **taxis**, charging about $1 per ride.

The municipal **tourist office** (daily except Tues & Fri 8am–noon & 2–6pm; ☏07/580890) is opposite the church on the Parque Central; they hand out **maps** and booklets (which enthusiastically promote the longevity theory, with many black-and-white photos of centenarians as evidence) and can give advice on accommodation, restaurants, transport and tour operators. You can get pre-trip information and make online bookings at the English-language **website** ⓦwww.vilcabamba.org. Tourist information and a wide range of **books** (to buy or exchange) in English and other European languages are available at Craig's Bookstore, 1km out of town on the road to Yamburara. Ask about **Spanish lessons** here, at your hotel, or try the New Horizons Spanish School on Valle Sagrado and Diego Vaca de la Vega. **Internet** facilities and international calls are available at Vilc@net opposite *Hidden Garden*, for about $3 per hour.

Accommodation

There's an enormous amount of **accommodation** to choose from for such a small place, most of it very reasonably priced. Where you stay can make a big difference to your experience of Vilcabamba, so consider whether you want to mingle with lots of other travellers or if you want somewhere quiet with a local feel to it, or just somewhere private, where you can enjoy the countryside. Traditionally, travellers have never been hassled for their custom when they arrive at the bus terminal. Lately, however, one or two of the newer places have started doing just that, using taxi drivers to assist them, but check out a few places for yourself before making any decisions.

Hidden Garden Sucre, just north of Parque Central ☏07/580281. Simple rooms with or without en-suite bathroom, some a little dark – though the hotel is being refurbished by its new Mexican owner – around a beautiful walled garden with a pool and hammocks. It has an excellent Mexican restaurant, *El Jardín* (see p.278), plus kitchen and laundry facilities. Breakfast included. ❷–❸

Izhcayluma 2km south of the centre on the road to Zumba, no phone, ⓔinfo@izhcayluma.com, ⓦwww.izhcayluma.com. Popular German-owned hostel set in pretty gardens overlooking the Vilcabamba valley. The rooms and cheaper dorms come with porch, hammock and private bath, and there's a gorgeous pool, giant chess set and a good restaurant that encompasses specialities such as goulash and Käsespatzen. Breakfast, water and mountain bikes to coast to town down a steep hill are included. The taxi ride is $1–1.50. ❹

Madre Tierra 2km before town, a short uphill walk west of the main road from Loja; ask your bus driver to drop you off at the turning; ☏07/580269, ⓦwww.madretierra1.com/infirst. A choice of shared budget rooms and dorms ($5 per person), more comfortable mid-price rooms (some with private bath) and very stylish suites with fabulous views, in a picturesque spot on the

edge of the village. Serves tasty international cuisine, always with a vegetarian option, in its patio restaurant, and has a small, pretty pool, and a spa centre offering a range of treatments (see p.278) that are half price for guests. Fantastic value as it includes breakfast and dinner, and use of the pool, sauna and hot tub. Always popular, so book ahead if you're set on staying here. ❹–❻

Paraíso Av Eterna Juventud ☏07/580266, ⓕ575429. Comfortable tiled cabañas in a pretty garden with a wonderful pool and an outdoor whirlpool. Also offers spotless steam baths and sauna, a rustic bamboo-covered restaurant and a peculiar pyramid for meditating in. Relaxing and welcoming, with relatively few gringos. ❸

La Posada Real Agua del Hierro ☏07/580904. Eccentric red-roofed house featuring bright-yellow railings and balconies. Offers simple, quiet, high-ceilinged rooms with shared or private bath, and swept wooden floors. ❸–❹

Cabañas Río Yambala (also known as Charlie's Cabins) 5km east along the road to Yamburara ⓦwww.vilcabamba.cwc.net (no phone). Five thatched wooden cabañas in a scenic, secluded location overlooking the Río Yambala. Cabaña #2 has the best views and its own kitchen; meals are also available in a rustic (but pricey) all-day restaurant. There are marked trails to cloudforest and waterfalls, and up to a refuge, *Las Palmas* (see p.280), on the edge of Parque Nacional Podocarpus. Taxis between cabañas and village cost about $4. ❷–❹

Las Ruinas de Quinara across the bridge on the road to Yamburara ☎ & ℻ 07/580314, eruinasqui@hotmail.com. Very slick operation offering shared rooms (with 4 beds) with cable TV and shared or private hot shower. Facilities include an attractive pool with slide, steam baths, hot tub, volleyball court, table tennis, pool table and evening movies on a giant TV. Great value but feels rather like a college campus. Breakfast and dinner included. ❹

Rumi Wilco Ecolodge a 15min walk northeast of the centre ☎07/673186, ℮ ofalcoecolodge@ yahoo.com, ⓦ koberpress.home.mindspring.com/ vilcabamba. This ecolodge consists of three different accommodations set well apart in the Rumi-Wilko Nature Reserve, 100 acres of private land being reforested with native trees. Each is quiet and secluded, and all come with cooking facilities of some sort, making them ideal places to escape for a few days. The *Pole House*, a wooden cabin on stilts by the Río Chambo sleeping up to 4 people ($16–20 for the cabin), comes equipped with kitchen and a porch with hammock. The *Upper House* is on an 80-metre-high spur with fantastic views of Vilcabamba and Cerro Mandango, and has four double rooms, gas-heated shower and wood-burning oven. And the *Adobe Shared Houses* are three simple adobe buildings with double rooms, fireplaces, herb garden and cooking facilities. Check availability and directions in the Primavera craft shop on the Parque Central, opposite the church. Discounts available for long stays, or credits for volunteer work reforesting or teaching English. ❷

Cabañas La Tasca about 2km along the road to Yamburara (no phone). Small adobe bungalows with porches and hammocks, perched on a hillside amongst eucalyptus trees. Rustic and simple but very pleasant, with friendly owners. Great French food served in the restaurant, or you can use the kitchen facilities. ❷

Valle Sagrado Calle Sucre, Parque Central t07/580686. Slightly worn but fine budget rooms offering use of kitchen facilities and a pretty garden with hammocks and table tennis. There's an alternative entrance on Fernando de la Vega. ❷

Hostería de Vilcabamba Av Eterna Juventud, as it enters the village ☎07/580271, ℻580273. Upmarket, well-furnished rooms with cool marble floors, mirror wardrobes and comfortable beds. Has a pool, sauna, steam baths and whirlpool, and an attractive restaurant and bar. Breakfast included. ❺

The village and around

For a place that attracts so many visitors, there's not a great deal to do in the village itself. The focal point is the leafy **Parque Central**, surrounded by the main cornerstones of village life: the church, the *municipio* and the telephone office. The **church** is quite a grand affair, with its large, white Neoclassical facade sporting a row of apricot-coloured pillars. Its interior, by contrast, is very modern and quite modest: bare timber walls and arches and a large wooden cross serving as the altar. If you happen to be up early, it's worth wandering down to the square around 6am or 7am – you'll catch lots of beautiful, colourful birds hopping around, and the early-morning light is gorgeous. A short walk southeast of town down Calle Diego de Vaca de la Vega for 1.5km will bring you to the **Centro Recreacional Yamburara** (daily 8am–5pm; $0.30), the site of a swimming pool ($0.50), a small zoo (in which the animals have a reasonable amount of space) and an impressive orchid garden (closed at lunchtime).

Striking a little further afield, you could hike up **Cerro Mandango** for fabulous, panoramic views over the valley. The hill, which is justifiably said to resemble a person lying down – with the forehead, nose and chin quite distinct from certain angles – rises over the southeast side of the village. The tourist office can give you a map with instructions on finding the path, which can be tricky. In brief, you follow the Avenida de la Eterna Juventud south out of town for about 1km before coming to a tall gate on the right with no fence either side. Go around the gate to get onto the path up to the hilltop. About an hour's hike will bring you to the cross marking the first summit, followed by another hour of more strenuous walking to get to the second summit, also

△ Doorway of colonial house, Cuenca

marked by a cross. It's best to set out before 7am to avoid walking in the hottest part of the day; take plenty of sun screen and water with you. For excursions to Parque Nacional Podocarpus, see p.271.

Spa treatments

A number of people in the village offer **massages** and **spa treatments**. Fanny's Massage (which doubles up as the *Cheers Bar* at night), on the corner of Valle Sagrado and Diego Vaca de la Vega, offers inexpensive foot massages, facials, pedicures and cellular body massages using somewhat surprising substances like egg, honey, corn and olive oil. At *Madre Tierra* (see p.275) you can experience full-blown spa treatments in a beautifully designed building offering a range of luxurious treatments, from facials and "hot clay baths", to Swedish reflexology and colonic irrigation. For a selection, try the "Special Well-Being" package for $29, which lasts for almost four hours. You can also pop in just to use the steam baths ($5.50 for 25min) or hot tub ($2 for 20min).

Eating and drinking

Most hotels offer food as well as rooms, sometimes as a package with the room rate. In common with other gringo haunts like Baños and Otavalo, Vilcabamba offers an appealing choice of good-value Western-style dishes alongside the more usual *comida típica*. Most places are very quiet in the evening, and wind down by 9pm. There are several other simple places around the square.

Che Bolívar, on the park. Little Argentinian-owned restaurant with outdoor seating on the square, offering an international menu, but especially good on its substantial steak dishes.

Restaurant Huilcopamba cnr of Diego Vaca de la Vega and Sucre, on Parque Central. Hearty and appetizing meats, pastas, noodles and home-made soups in a nice location on the corner of the square, with outside tables and chairs.

El Jardín The Hidden Garden, Sucre. Very good Mexican restaurant in the garden of the hotel, serving authentic, home-made cooking using plenty of organic and home-grown produce, including yogurt and cheese. Excellent vegetarian dishes.

Shanta's over the bridge heading east on Diego Vaca de la Vega. Good and inexpensive restaurant with items ranging from fish and pasta to pizzas and crêpes in chocolate sauce. It also has a late bar fronted by saddle-topped stools, and a plentiful cocktail list.

Cafetería Solomaco Sucre, on the park. For home baking, this café is hard to beat with its excellent cakes, pastries, donuts and wholemeal bread. A good place for breakfast or a snack and a coffee while watching village life on the square. Closed Tues.

La Tasca about 2km along the road east to Yamburara. Tiny place run by a French woman, offering home-made bread and great food, such as sea bass in white wine, and *beouf bourgignon*. Also does freshly ground coffee served in cafetières.

La Terraza cnr of Diego Vaca de la Vega and Bolívar, on Parque Central. Very popular restaurant with colourful decor and a nice atmosphere, serving well-prepared Mexican, Thai and Italian dishes (always with vegetarian choices). Closed Mon.

Restaurant Vegetariano Diego Vaca de la Vega and Valle Sagrado. Well-presented and imaginative salads, soups, pastas and crêpes are served in this vegetarian restaurant.

Hostería de Vilcabamba Av Eterna Juventud, as it enters the village. Tasty and reasonably priced Ecuadorian food served in an attractive dining room flooded with sunlight from a glass atrium. The starched linen tablecloths give this place an upmarket feel.

Tours and hikes around Vilcabamba

Vilcabamba offers great hiking and birding opportunities up to the cloudforests around Parque Nacional Podocarpus (see p.271), and several outfits and guides offering **tours** of the area. One of the best is Orlando Falco, an outstanding **naturalist guide** who speaks English and offers full-day tours into the tropical cloudforests of Parque Nacional Podocarpus. You're taken to the trailheads in an ancient Land Rover before setting off on foot on your chosen route,

There are two ways to get to Peru from the southern sierra, as well as the frenetic crossing at Huaquillas on the coast (see p.433). By far the most convenient **border crossing into Peru** from the southern sierra is via a paved road from Loja to the small, nondescript frontier town of **MACARÁ**, 190km to the southwest. The route has been serviced since the end of the Peruvian-Ecuadorian border dispute by direct **buses** from Loja all the way to Piura in Peru (see "Listings" p.268), operated by Cooperativa Loja Internacional (⊤07/579014), which has offices at the bus terminal and at 10 de Agosto and Avenida Lauro Guerrero in Loja, and close to the bus terminal and taxi rank in Vilcabamba (note that these buses do not pass through Vilcabamba). **Tickets** cost $8, and should ideally be bought the day before travelling, either directly from the bus company or from one of the *hostales* in Vilcabamba that act as ticket agents, including *Madre Tierra* and *Las Ruinas de Quinará* (see p.275). There are daily **departures** from Loja's bus terminal at 7am, 1pm and 10.30pm, and the journey takes around eight hours. When you arrive at the border (5hr), the bus drops you off to get your **exit stamp** at the Migración office, which is open 24hr. You then walk across the bridge over the Río Macará – which forms the border between Ecuador and Peru in this area – and get your **entry stamp** on the other side, before hopping back on the bus. It's all extremely simple and hassle-free. Should you be delayed in Macará, the *Espiga de Oro* (❸), on Antonio Ante and 10 de Agosto by the market, is a suitable hotel with private baths but only cold water; there are plenty of other hotels besides. Once in **PIURA**, you'll find plenty of inexpensive places to stay, including the friendly, well-managed *Oriental*, at Callao 446 (⊤074/328891; ❷), and the popular *California*, at Junín 835 (⊤074/328789; ❷). Exchange facilities are available at the Banco Continental, on the Plaza de Armas, and at several *cambistas* on the corner of Avenida Arquipa and Avenida Grau. A busy transport hub, Piura also offers plenty of bus connections to most major onward destinations, including Chiclayo, Trujillo and Lima.

There's another less used and less convenient border crossing near **ZUMBA** over 145km due south of Vilcabamba, on a bumpy road through remote and beautiful country that is serviced by ten daily buses from Vilcabamba (5–6hr) and Loja (6–7hr). From Zumba, where there are a few simple hotels, catch a ranchera (Mon–Fri 8am & 2.30pm, Sat–Sun 8am, 10am & 2pm) or hire a private camioneta to the crossing at **La Balsa**, about 1 hour 30 minutes away on a potholed road. The border control itself is far more primitive than Macará's and involves crossing the Río Canchis on an oil-drum raft; a bridge is currently under construction. Once in Peru, busetas ferry you to Namballe (20min), from where there is transport to San Ignacio (around 3hr), then Jaén (3–4hr), a city of reasonable size with hotels, money-changing facilities, and transport connections to major centres, including Chachapoyas and Chiclayo.

pausing frequently while he points out features of the flora and fauna; contact him at the Primavera craft shop on the plaza, opposite the church (✉ofalcoecolodge@yahoo.com). Caballos Gavilán at Sucre and Diego Vaca de la Vega (enquiries on ⊤07/580281, ✉gavilanhorse@yahoo.com, or at the *Restaurant Huilcopamba* on Parque Central), run by New Zealander Gavin Moore, offer great three-day combined **hiking and horse-riding** tours up to the cloudforest from $90 per person, including food and a night in a cabin on the edge of the park, or day rides from $30. Monta-Tours, on Sucre, just north of Parque Central (⊤ & ℻07/673186, ✉solomaco@hotmail.com), operated by a friendly English-speaking French couple, arrange one- to three-day horse treks up to the mountains and the park, with a night spent in a timber cabin on its edge. Fantastic French cooking around the campfire is one of the highlights. Meanwhile, Avetur, with offices in the *Valle Sagrado* on Parque Central

(☎07/580686, ✆avetur@impsat.net.ec), is an association of local people involved in tourism, but dedicated to bettering the social and environmental condition of the area. They offer guided day-treks and horse rides towards Podocarpus ($25), two-day outings ($60) including staying overnight in the *Refugio Las Palmas* (see p.276), three-day excursions ($80–90) that include a hike from the refuge up to the Laguna Rabadilla de Vaca, or multi-day trips along the *ruta ecológica* linking Vilcabamba to Loja, which may be ready by the time you read this. They also have plans to build their own refuge inside the park, and are likely to manage the sector if an entry post is built here.

If you're keen to go **hiking** independently, your best bet is to stay at *Cabañas Río Yambala* (see p.275) and take advantage of the colour-coded trail system from the cabañas up the Yamburara valley towards Parque Nacional Podocarpus. The "red route" is especially rewarding, involving a five-hour trek up to their *Refugio Las Palmas*, a rustic cabin with beds and kitchen facilities on the edge of a cloudforest. You can continue the following day through the forest up to the stunning Laguna Rabadilla de Vaca high in the páramo, spending a second night in the refuge before returning to the *Cabañas Río Yambala*. The owners can also provide horses and arrange for a local **guide** to accompany you too.

Travel details

Buses

Cuenca to: Azogues (every 5min; 30min); Cañar (every 15min; 1hr 30min); Chordeleg (every 30min; 1hr 15min); El Tambo (every 15min; 1hr 40min); Girón (served by buses to Machala every 15min; 40min); Gualaceo (every 30min; 1hr); Guayaquil (every 10–30min; 4hr); Huaquillas (13 daily; 5hr); Ingapirca (2 daily Mon–Fri, 1 daily Sun; 2hr); Loja (20 daily; 5hr); Macas (13 daily; 9hr); Machala (every 15min; 4hr); Quito (every 30–60min; 10hr); Riobamba (12 daily; 6hr); Sigsig (every 30min; 1hr 40min).

Loja to: Cuenca (16 daily; 5hr); Gualaquiza (8 daily; 8hr); Guayaquil (9 daily; 8hr); Macará (7 daily; 5hr); Machala (12 daily; 6hr); Piura, Peru (3 daily; 8hr); Quito (15 daily; 14hr); Saraguro (hourly; 2hr); Vilcabamba (every 15min; 1hr 15min); Zamora (10 daily; 2hr); Zumba (10 daily; 6–7hr).

Zamora to: Gualaquiza (7 daily; 6hr); Loja (15 daily; 2hr).

Flights

Cuenca to: Guayaquil (2 daily Mon–Fri, 1 Sat; 30min); Macas (1 Mon & Fri; 25min); Quito (1–2 daily; 45min).

Loja to: Guayaquil (1 daily Tues & Thurs; 30min); Quito (1–2 daily; 50min–1hr).

The Oriente

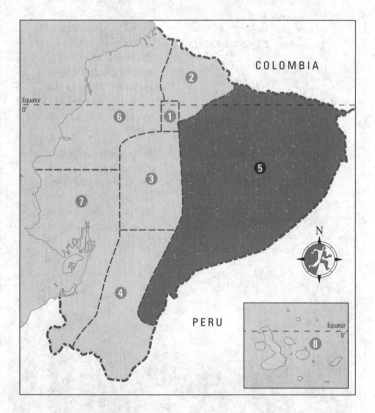

CHAPTER 5 # Highlights

✳ **Jungle lodges** The most comfortable way to see the rainforest. **See p.288**

✳ **Staying with an indigenous community** Ecuador has one of the fastest-growing "ethnotourism" scenes, allowing you to experience "real life" in the rainforest. **See p.290**

✳ **Añangu parrot licks** Extravaganzas of sound and colour made when hundreds of parrots descend on clay banks – called clay licks, salt licks or salados – and chew off mineral-rich chunks to aid the digestion of acidic fruits. **See p.315**

✳ **Parque Nacional Yasuní** A World Biosphere Reserve and the country's largest national park, harbouring the majority of Ecuador's mammals, over a third of all Amazonian bird species, and more tree species for its size any place on Earth. **See p.316**

✳ **Río Napo to Peru** Navigating the muddy Río Napo from Coca to Iquitos past remote Quichua villages and isolated jungle outposts makes for the most daring and little-travelled way to reach Peru. **See p.318**

✳ **White-water rafting around Tena** The country's prime destination for rafting and kayaking, with dozens of rivers and runs of all standards to choose from. **See p.320**

5

The Oriente

The **Oriente**, Ecuador's slice of the Amazonian basin, occupies almost half of the country, but is home to less than five percent of the population, around 480,000 people. Consisting of six provinces – Sucumbíos, Napo and Orellana in the **northern Oriente**, Pastaza, Morona-Santiago and Zamora-Chinchipe in the **southern Oriente** – and nine nature reserves including the two largest mainland protected areas, **Parque Nacional Yasuní** and the **Reserva Faunística Cuyabeno**, the Oriente drops from the highest peaks of the eastern Andean flank at well over 5000m down to the sweltering lowland rainforests at around 300m that in places stretch for more than 250km to the borders of Colombia and Peru. The huge range in elevation and temperature allows for a bewildering diversity of **flora and fauna** within the region. Descending from the *alto* (high) *Oriente*, the windswept páramo – above 3000m and resembling the sodden Scottish moors – gives way to dripping montane forests, swathed in mist and draped with mosses and epiphytes. Waterfalls plunge into broadening valleys and eventually the mountain ridges taper away into the *bajo* (low) *Oriente* like talons sinking into the deep velvet of a vast emerald wilderness, forming Ecuador's **Amazonian jungle**, one of the country's most thrilling destinations. No other Ecuadorian habitat overwhelms the senses like the tropical rainforest, with its cacophonous soundtrack of birds and insects, the rich smell of steaming foliage and teeming soil, the glimmer of fluorescent birds and butterflies in the understorey, or the startling clamour of a troop of monkeys clattering through the canopy above.

Jungle tours – the only practical way of experiencing the rainforest's glories – are the reason most travellers come to the Oriente. Tours range from simple day-trips into pockets of forest close to a town, to staying with a rainforest community or at a jungle lodge, to rugged multi-day camping treks into the remotest tracts of primary jungle in the far-eastern reserves. Nearly every tour will involve guided hikes through lush forests and navigating coiling rivers and lagoons in dugout canoes, often done at night to see the red eyes of caiman and hear the deafening chorus of nocturnal creatures. The most pristine areas, namely the **Reserva Faunística Cuyabeno** and the **Parque Nacional Yasuní**, are best reached from the pioneer oil towns **Lago Agrio** and **Coca** respectively, and demand at least four or five days to enjoy properly. Closer to Quito, and favoured by those with limited time on their hands, **Tena**, **Puyo** and **Misahuallí** are near smaller, more accessible patches of forest. Visits to or stays with **indigenous communities** are also likely to figure in tours from Tena and Puyo. Generally speaking, the tourism infrastructure is much less

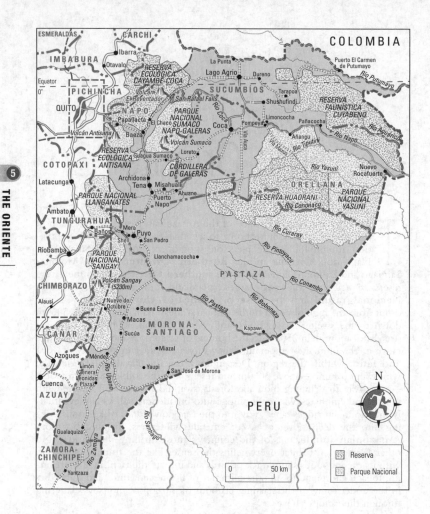

developed in the far southern Oriente, though **Macas** is home to a handful of operators and projects.

The oil **infrastructure** has made the Ecuadorian Amazon one of the most easily accessed rainforest areas in the continent, with its centres of jungle tourism all within a day's bus journey of Quito. There are two main **routes to the Oriente**. The first leaves the capital and descends into the Amazon basin from the Papallacta pass, splitting at Baeza, north to Lago Agrio (and then Coca), and south to Tena and the faster way to Coca. The second drops from Ambato through Baños to Puyo, where it meets the road between Tena and Macas. Two poor roads also descend from Cuenca and Loja to Gualaquiza in the southern Oriente. Finally, a paved road is also being built between Guamote (south of Riobamba) directly to Macas, though at the time of writing, it was not complete; see p.234 for more on this newest route.

The Oriente **climate** is as you'd expect from a rainforest – hot and humid, with plenty of rain. The wettest months are April to July, but you can expect cloudbursts most days throughout the year, usually in the early afternoon. Typical average daytime temperatures are around 25°C, though daily highs can be over 32°C. With such consistent conditions, the Oriente doesn't have a high tourist season as such when everyone flocks to the forests, and hotels and lodges charge much the same all year long. However, at slow times of year when there are few tourists in the country as a whole (Feb–mid-June & Sept–Nov), it's worth asking for discounts on tours.

Note also that the region is militarily sensitive and you'll be required to produce your **passport** at regular checkpoints. More so than at other places in the country, it's important that you have the original document to hand rather than copies. Also note that the areas adjacent to the Colombian border are currently unsafe due to infiltration of guerrilla and paramilitary units and should be avoided (see box on p.304).

Some background

The **jungle** – *la selva* – has taken a curious place in the national psyche ever since the time of the **conquistadors**. The early explorers were drawn here by rumours of it as *el pais de canela* ("the land of cinnamon"), a place of abundant fruits and spices, and the legend of El Dorado, the "Golden Man", that suggested to them a land of staggering natural riches (see also box on p.306). But the first Europeans to venture here soon found that this fabled earthly paradise

---

Jungle essentials

Many organized tours will supply essential items such as mosquito nets, rubber boots, toilet paper, bedding, food and clean water, but always check before you go to confirm what you'll be expected to bring yourself. They are not called rainforests without reason, so put all your belongings in **waterproof bags**, especially valuables and important documents, and carry a rain jacket or poncho. **Banking facilities** are poor in the Oriente, and you should take as much cash as you need for the whole excursion. You will also need:

Binoculars Desirable for spotting birds and animals in the canopy; your guide should carry a pair, but you will increase your enjoyment if you have your own.

Camera Fast film (400 ASA and above) works best for the dark conditions.

Clothing Along with waterproof gear, bring a long-sleeved shirt, lightweight trousers and swimwear for cooling off in rivers. Also bring a hat to block the sun on boat trips.

Emergency supplies As with any hiking trip, bring along a first-aid kit (see p.24), compass and whistle.

Insect repellent Lots of it, preferably containing DEET.

Light sources Bring a torch (flashlight) and extra batteries; electricity is not

always available and you'll need one for getting about the lodge or campsite (or spotting caiman) at night. Candles and waterproof matches or a gas lighter, for evenings in a lodge or cabaña without power, are also a good idea.

Malaria pills A course of which should be started in advance as prescribed by your doctor. You should also have had an inoculation against **yellow fever** (see "Health", p.20).

Passport You'll need one to enter the Oriente; note that it must be the original, as opposed to a copy.

Sun cream Particularly needed during river journeys.

Water purifier and bottes For camping and basic tours.

had a nightmarish underside; their parties were plunged into an impenetrable green hell (the *infierno verde*), teeming with poisonous snakes and biting insects. A string of catastrophic expeditions in the early colonial period quickly discouraged the Spanish from colonizing the Oriente at all. Even until the 1960s, most people, save for a sprinkling of missionaries and pioneers, kept away, leaving the forests and its inhabitants well alone.

This all changed in the late 1960s following the discovery of large **oil and gas reserves** (see also box p.300), now the country's most important source of wealth. The Oriente was divided into 200-square-kilometre *bloques* (blocks) and distributed between the companies, who proceeded to drill and blast in search of black gold. Roads were laid, towns sprouted virtually overnight, and large areas of rainforest were cleared. The Oriente was transformed into a "productive" region, and colonists streamed in on the new roads, looking for jobs and levelling still more land for farms. The speed of the destruction was dramatic, and the Ecuadorian government, under widespread international pressure, began setting aside large tracts of forest as **national parks and reserves**; the largest three – **Sangay** (mainly in the Oriente, but most easily accessed from the highlands; see Chapter 3, p.231), **Cuyabeno** and **Yasuní**, a UNESCO World Biosphere Reserve – were created in 1979, and another three medium-sized parks – **Antisana**, **Sumaco** and **Llanganates** – came in the mid-1990s.

Even though there are more than 25,000 square kilometres of protected land in the Oriente – well over half of which is pristine Amazonian rainforest – conservationists are worried that the cash-strapped Ecuadorian government is unable (or unwilling) to make sure it stays that way. The task of balancing the needs of a faltering economy against the obligation to protect some of the most important forests on the planet has been among Ecuador's central problems for the past few decades. Meanwhile, oil activity is ongoing in several crucial protected areas, including Yasuní.

While most people would concede that the oil industry has been very much a mixed blessing for the country, the **indigenous peoples** of the region – which include the Siona, Huaorani, Secoya, Achuar, Shuar, lowland Quichua, Cofán and Záparo – have had the most to lose. Many groups, rejecting the Western way of life, have been driven into ever smaller, remoter territories where it becomes increasingly hard to support themselves by traditional means. Their rivers and soil already polluted from industrial waste, most of the communities are under mounting pressure to sell out to the oil industry, both culturally and territorially. In recent years, **ecotourism** has emerged as a great hope for some groups seeking to adapt to a life in which external influences are inevitable, bringing in badly needed income, strengthening the case for the conservation of the forests within an economic framework, and reasserting cultural identities.

Visiting the jungle

There are three ways to visit the jungle: on a **guided tour**; at a **jungle lodge**; or by staying with an **indigenous community**. Getting into the wilderness and being immersed in the sights and sounds of the rainforest is the whole point of a tour, and modern luxuries, such as 24-hour electricity, (hot) running water and completely insect-free buildings are absent in all but the most comfortable jungle lodges. **Unguided travel** in the lower Oriente is frowned upon by Ecuadorian authorities, conservation groups and indigenous communities, and is not recommended for your own safety. Off the main rivers, trails are few and difficult to follow, and it's all too easy to get lost in a potentially dangerous

△ San Rafael falls

There are dozens of **jungle tour operators** in Ecuador competing for your attention, including many local agencies working directly out of the main centres of the Oriente, namely Lago Agrio, Coca, Tena, Misahuallí, Puyo and Macas, which are covered at the appropriate places in this chapter. The greatest concentration of jungle tour operators, however, is found in the Mariscal area of **Quito**, giving you the luxury of having your tour fully organized before you set out for the Oriente. A selection of recommended operators is listed below, but it's always worthwhile shopping around to find the price, guide and itinerary that suits you. Note that transport to the starting point of the tour, usually an Oriente town, is rarely included in the price.

Ecuador Amazing Amazonas 1123 and Pinto ☏02/2553750, ⓦwww .ecuadoramazing.com. Owner of the *Selva Rica Cuyabeno Camp* on the Laguna Grande in the Cuyabeno reserve, with 4-, 5- or 8-day trips that include bilingual guides. Around $40 per day.

Emerald Forest Expeditions Joaquín Pinto E4-244 and Amazonas ☏ & ⓕ02/2541543, ⓦwww.emeraldexpeditions .com. Runs 4-, 5- and 7-day tours to their lodge on the Pañayacu river in the Bosque Protector Pañacocha, off the Río Napo. One of their best guides, Luis García, speaks excellent English and is based in Coca. Around $60 per person per day, with discounts for SAE members.

Fundación Sobrevivencia Cofán Domingo Rengifo N74-96, Carcelén Alto ☏ & ⓕ02/2470946, ⓔrandy@cofan.org, ⓦwww.cofan.org. Randy Borman, the son of American missionaries, grew up in Dureno, married a Cofán, and established a new community at Zábalo, where he's a leader, running this well-organized foundation and ecotourist project. Located on the Río Aguarico, in the pristine heart of the Cuyabeno reserve, Zábalo has comfortable cabañas and offers programmes, typically lasting six days, though there is flexibility and special options for those keen on trekking, camping and canoeing. $65 per day with Cofán guide, $100 for an English-speaking naturalist guide. He has also been instrumental in setting up ecotourism projects for other Cofán communities in Sucumbíos, and can put you in touch with those at the Comuna Dureno east of Lago Agrio (see p.303) and Sinangüé in the Cayambe-Coca reserve (see p.137)

Kem Pery Tours Pinto 539 and Amazonas ☏02/2226583, or ☏ & ⓕ226715, ⓦwww.kempery.com. Offers trips to the Huaorani reserve where they have the *Bataburo Lodge* under a special agreement with the Huaorani. About three hours by motorized canoe down the Río Tigüino from the Vía Auca, the lodge has wood-and-thatch cabins with mosquito nets, an observation tower and limited electricity. A four-day tour costs $225, plus there's a $20 donation per tourist to the Huaorani. Trips also available to the Huaorani community of Conanaco near the Peruvian border,

environment. Furthermore, stumbling on indigenous groups, such as the Tagaeri, a branch of the Huaorani who don't take kindly to intruding strangers, can also lead to problems, and around the Colombian border, in northern Sucumbíos province, kidnappings attributed to Colombian guerrilla groups have also occurred.

Jungle lodges

Staying in a **jungle lodge** offers the most comfortable (and most expensive) way to experience the rainforest. Stays usually last from three to five days and all logistical problems are taken care of for you, including river transport, food, any necessary permits and guides. Most lodges consist of cabañas and a com-

and Siona and Secoya communities in the Cuyabeno area.

Magic River Tours of Lago Agrio represented in Quito by Positiv Turismo, Voz Andes N41-81 and Mariano Echeverría ⊕02/2440698, ⓦwww.magicrivertours .com. Specialize in non-motorized kayaking trips down the quiet tributaries of the Cuyabeno reserve; a 5-day package to the Cuyabeno lakes runs at $275, and an 8-day package to the remote Lagartococha lakes costs $480.

Native Life Foch E4 and Amazonas ⊕02/2505158, c550836 or 2236320, ⓕ2229077, ⓔnatlife1@natlife.com.ec. Owners of the *Nativo Lodge* on the Río Aguarico and campsites deeper in the reserve, Native Life uses bilingual and indigenous guides. Discounts are offered to ISIC holders and SAE members. Around $40–50 per day.

Neotropic Turis Pinto E4-340 and Amazonas ⊕02/2521212, ⓕ2554902, ⓦwww.neotropicturis.com. Operators of the *Cuyabeno Lodge* on the Laguna Grande, constructed from hardwoods brought into the reserve. It's still rather simple, but has hot showers, a small library and research facilities. They use bilingual nature specialists accompanied by Siona guides.

Nomadtrek Amazonas N22-29 and Carrión, 2nd floor ⊕02/2547275, ⓕ2546376, ⓦwww.nomadtrek.com. Nomadtrek built the comfortable *Tapir Lodge* in the Cuyabeno lakes area in partnership with some Siona, consisting of a bungalow with shared and private bathrooms and a fifteen-metre tower housing suites. Rainforest walks are lead by multilingual naturalist guides. Stays of 2, 4 or 6 nights available, starting from $300 per person.

Nuevo Mundo Av Coruña N26-207 and Orellana ⊕02/2564448, ⓕ2565261, ⓦwww.nuevomundotravel.com. Operates the new Manatee Amazon Explorer, a luxurious river cruiser, equipped with air-conditioned cabins for 30 people, that navigates the lower Napo on regular four- or five-nightly excursions, including visits to the Yasuní reserve, an observation tower and a parrot lick. From $460 per person in a double cabin.

Siecopai Tours Alme Bompland 177 and Av Velasco Ibarra (also known as Av Oriental) ⊕02/2228894. A Secoya agency offering five- and eight-day tours to their ancestral lands in a remote area of southeastern Sucumbíos around the Río Aguarico and the Lagartococha lakes in the Cuyabeno reserve.

Tropic Ecological Adventures Av República 307 and Almagro, Edificio Taurus ⊕02/225907 or 2234594, ⓕ2560756, ⓦwww.tropiceco.com. Award-winning ecologically minded agency that works alongside community-based ecotourism projects throughout the Oriente. The best people to talk to if you plan on an indigenous community stay. They also offer jungle kayaking tours down the Shiripuno river with Huaorani guides.

munal dining and relaxing area, constructed in wood and thatch, close to primary forest and often a lengthy ride by motor canoe from the nearest town. The cabañas themselves range from a bed and four plank walls to handsomely adorned rooms with ceiling fans, private bath, hot water and electricity, though the nature of their location will mean that even the most well-appointed lodge falls short of luxury.

Days are clearly structured, with guided hikes or canoe trips, and guides are generally of a high standard. In the most expensive places they'll be English-speaking naturalists and ornithologists working with a local guide who'll know the forest intimately. The more upmarket lodges also tend to be environmentally minded and often have mutually rewarding relationships with

The following is a list of all the **jungle lodges** covered in this chapter, with a page reference to the relevant account in the guide text. Most lodges have contact offices in Quito, and visits must be booked prior to arrival, though generally only the higher-end lodges, such as *Sacha*, *Kapawi* and *La Selva*, recommend that reservations be made weeks or even months in advance. Meals, guided forest walks and activities, and river transport to the lodge (where appropriate) are generally included in the price of a stay, but travel to the nearest Oriente town is usually separate; most lodges can help you arrange this if necessary. See "Jungle lodges" on p.288 for more details.

local communities. Some are foreign owned, and most tours are booked before arrival in Ecuador through international agencies (see "Basics", pp.13–17) though most have offices in Quito or Internet booking facilities; preparations have to be made in advance for incoming guests – drop-ins are not usually allowed.

Indigenous-community stays

A growing number of **indigenous communities** in the Oriente have started ecotourism projects, giving visitors a glimpse of village life in the rainforest by staying with a family or in simple cabañas just next to a community. The income raised from guests is intended to provide a sustainable alternative to more destructive means of subsistence, such as logging or farming the poor rainforest soil. The economic success of a project also demonstrates the value of conserving the surrounding forests – the other big attraction of a stay – to government agencies under strong pressure from commercial interests to make forest areas more financially productive, as opposed to "unproductive" community territory.

A few projects set up a decade ago now run reasonably slick operations often in tandem with an outside partner, but the majority are starting out and remain pretty unsophisticated, so you may have to bring your own equipment (rubber boots, mosquito nets and so on – see the box on p.285). Most use simple wooden **cabañas** with beds and mattresses, clean sheets, and sometimes mosquito netting, while bathrooms range from basic latrines to flushing toilets, with most having facilities shared between guests. **Forest walks** are a particular highlight, as your hosts often make excellent guides, and the majority are qualified "native" guides, though you'll need to speak some Spanish to get the most from their extensive knowledge. A common emphasis is on **intercultural understanding**, and you're likely to be treated to singing, dancing and folkloric presentations – and you may be asked to perform likewise about your own society.

The main centres for organizing visits to an indigenous community are **Tena**, **Puyo** and **Lago Agrio**. Allow several days to organize a stay, as the communities need time to make arrangements, and it can be difficult to establish contact in the first place. A good book, combining a discussion of the virtues of indigenous ecotourism with a guide to some of the projects on offer, is *Defending our Rainforest: A Guide to Community-Based Ecotourism in the Ecuadorian Amazon* by Rolf Wesche and Andy Drumm. You should find it in Quito's better bookshops or at the SAE.

Guided tours

Taking a **guided tour** is the cheapest way to visit the jungle, usually costing from $25 to $50 per person per day. The more people you can get together, the cheaper the tour, but the optimum number is between four and six per guide so that everyone has a chance of hearing the guide and of having the wildlife pointed out to them individually before it disappears. **Discounts** are best negotiated in the low season, broadly speaking from February to mid-June and September to November. The best places to meet people looking to share a jungle tour, in roughly descending order, are Quito, Baños, Tena, Misahuallí, Puyo and Macas. Lago Agrio and Coca are home to a growing number of guides and agencies, but groups heading into the jungle from these towns are often made in Quito. It's hard to find people to form a group in these towns in the low season, but you may be able to supplant yourself onto a trip.

All tours should provide **accommodation** – anything from modest cabañas to *campamentos*, open-sided camping platforms, to standard tents (*carpas*) – and adequate **food and equipment**, including water, rubber boots and mosquito nets if necessary. Always check what you're getting before you hand over money. It's also crucial to get a **guide** who has the knowledge and enthusiasm to illustrate the jungle as a vivid living world; meeting them yourself in advance is the best way to find out if they're any good and check the standard of their English (where necessary). All guides should be able to produce a licence from the Ministry of Tourism though this is no guarantee of quality. You can report guides to the ministry or SAE (see p.80) if they behave inappropriately, by hunting for food, leaving litter, or visiting indigenous communities without making a contribution or seeking permission. It's worth noting that while some agencies use an accredited guide alongside a "native guide" for the same group – combining biological and scientific information with indigenous myths and local plantlore – the term "native" may not be synonymous with "indigenous", often referring to anyone that lives in the Oriente.

If your tour includes a visit to an indigenous community, it's crucial that your guide or operator has their **permission** – ask to see the written *convenio* (agreement) between the community and the operator when booking, which apart from anything else emphasizes that this is a priority with tourists, and encourages the operator to follow good practices.

The northern Oriente

The **northern Oriente**'s wealth of natural beauty and wildlife, its indigenous communities and a hard-boiled frontier spirit have all helped make it one of the country's most exciting destinations. Within the provinces of Sucumbíos, Napo and Orellana that make up the region, six major nature reserves and a proliferation of private reserves and protected areas make for excellent opportunities to experience the Amazonian jungle. The two most important are the **Reserva Faunística Cuyabeno** and the **Parque Nacional Yasuní**, in the east, defending over 15,000 square kilometres of pristine rainforest stretching to the Peruvian border. The reserves are reached by bus or canoe from the tough oil towns of **Lago Agrio** and **Coca**, the administrative and infrastructural centres of the industry. **Tena**, the third main town of the northern Oriente, isn't as close to such extensive forest areas, and wildlife populations are likely to be lower, but it's the most pleasant of the three for its fresher climate, friendly atmosphere and proximity to a host of Quichua communities offering ecotourism programmes. Tena is also rapidly becoming a centre for **whitewater rafting**, and at only six hours from Quito is growing into the Oriente's most popular tourist destination. The jungle traveller's traditional favourite, **Misahuallí**, a river port close to Tena, gives access to the many cabañas and lodges of the upper Río Napo and boasts a number of local jungle-tour agencies and guides.

In the west of the region, three more ample reserves, **Reserva Ecológica Cayambe-Coca** (covered in Chapter Two), **Reserva Ecológica Antisana** and **Parque Nacional Sumaco Napo-Galeras** hold dense cloudforests and montane forests, sometimes impenetrably thick, where hiking is a challenge for the adventurous. The little colonial town of **Baeza** sits between the three reserves, making it the most convenient base for such expeditions. In the broadening transitional valleys below Baeza, most notably the **Quijos Valley**, waterfalls streak the landscape, and the **San Rafael falls** here (145m), Ecuador's biggest, are watched over by **Volcán El Reventador**, a smouldering green-black cone towering over the forest canopy. On the uppermost reaches of the Amazon basin, **Papallacta** is perched in the hilly fringes of the Cayambe-Coca reserve, couched by inhospitable páramo, but the hot springs here provide a good antidote to the crisp mountain air.

Two main roads service the northern Oriente. From Quito, the quickest crosses the Andes at the Papallacta pass before hurtling downwards to Baeza, where it splits. The northern branch skirts the immense Cayambe-Coca reserve on its way to Lago Agrio, before turning south to Coca, a full day's bus ride away. The southern branch goes to Tena, passing the faster road to Coca via Loreto. Catching a plane from Quito to Lago Agrio or Coca distils a bus journey of eight to ten hours into a thirty-minute hop. The other main road is no less visually impressive, careering down from Ambato via Baños into forested hills before emerging at Puyo to join the main road going north to Tena and Baeza or south to Macas and the southern Oriente.

The road to Baeza

The fastest and most direct route from Quito to the northern Oriente is the road to Lago Agrio and Tena via Baeza, built in 1972 as a service road for the Trans-Ecuador Oil Pipeline. Giant oil trucks and supply lorries shudder up and down the eastern flank of the Andes, but despite the traffic it's an attractive route, traversing a range of habitats as it plunges over 2km in vertical height across 40km. Heading east from Quito through Cumbayá, an exclusive residential district, the road crosses the Río Chiche at a bridge favoured by bungee jumpers for its dizzying drop. From here buses and lorries inch their way up to the **Papallacta Pass** at 4064m. At its highest point, named La Virgen after the simple shrine on the roadside, a track heads north up to some radio masts, the access point for the beautiful **Páramo de Papallacta** grasslands at the southwestern corner of the Reserva Ecológica Cayambe-Coca.

Crossing the Papallacta Pass takes you over the continental divide, and as the road deteriorates, the bare, lake-studded hills are eclipsed by the four glacier-tipped peaks of **Volcán Antisana** (5758m) looming through the clouds to the south. As the highway descends beyond Papallacta, the temperature and humidity rise and the páramo grasses transform into dripping fronds and broad, waxy leaves. Nearing **Baeza**, rolling pastoral landscapes take over, banked by steep hillsides coated in the thick, green mantle of cloudforest.

Papallacta

At about 60km from Quito, the winding road reaches the quiet highland town of **PAPALLACTA**. Water is the town's greatest resource, with the hydroelectric plant here providing power to the region, while the pure waters from the páramo and nearby lakes is piped by gravity to Quito. Above all it's famous for its **hot springs**, highly ferrous pools reputed to relieve numerous ailments from kidney trouble to ganglions, and Quiteños pack themselves into its steaming pools each weekend. The town itself isn't of much interest, a string of buildings huddling the Baeza road, but lying in a green valley at 3200m, the surrounding scenery is stunning.

The best spring is **Las Termas de Papallacta**, a one-kilometre, twenty-minute uphill slog from town in the crook of a steep valley. Buses running between Lago Agrio and Tena via Baeza should drop you off at La Y de Papallacta (ask the driver), the junction at the head of the village, from where you walk up the signposted track. There are two **bathing complexes** here run by the same company – which also owns on-site restaurants and accommodation (see p.294) – and both are beautifully designed, well managed and quite possibly the best hot springs in Ecuador. On the left (daily 6am–10pm; $5) the nine thermal pools, ranging in temperature between 36°C and 42°C, and four cold pools have been built in gentle terracotta curves and natural rock, while the heart-stoppingly cold Río Papallacta itself offers a serious cool-off. Don't miss the three secluded little pools up the hill to the left of the restaurant: the top one is over 40°C and is perfect for supine gazing at the mountain ridges. On the other side of the road, the **spa** (same hours; $15) is more exclusive, with four large pools shaped for specific purposes, such as a "flying saucer" sculpted with bed-like hollows, and each with water jets or bubble massagers. Aromatherapy massages and other treatments are also on offer at the spa.

At the lower end of the town proper, downhill from the main road, the large municipal **Coturpa** baths (Mon–Fri 7am–5pm, Sat & Sun 6am–6pm; $2) get particularly crowded at weekends, and have four hot pools and one cold one, including a proper swimming pool, and a sauna.

Walks around Papallacta

There's plenty of **walking** to be had in the hills around Papallacta, but take a **compass** and the IGM 1:50,000 **map** for Papallacta as it's notoriously easy to get lost in the featureless páramo, which is often wet, cold, and, between June and August, snowy. The best time to come is from October to February, but you'll need warm clothes and waterproofs all year round. The **Fundación Terra** at the head of the valley above *Las Termas de Papallacta* manages three short and easy trails nearby ranging from one to four hours in length, including their self-guided Sendero de la Isla (Island Trail; $1) along the Río Papallacta, and offers horse rides at weekends. For more serious hikes and treks in the Reserva Ecológica Cayambe-Coca to the north of town, talk to the **Fundación Ecológica Rumicocha** (℡06/2320637, ℮ferumico@pi.pro.ec, or in Quito ℡02/2905747), who have an office on Papallacta's Calle Principal and are responsible for managing this part of the reserve. They offer **hiking tours** using either tents or their two refuges, which are small but comfortable and heated by open fires, and can provide guides for $15 a day.

One of the longer walks begins by heading up the main road toward Quito for 2km to the slender **Laguna Papallacta**, which is disfigured at its eastern end by a promontory of lava. This is the northern tip of a six-kilometre **lava flow** running all the way up the Río Tumiguina valley, the remnants of Volcán Antisana's eruption of 1773. A moderate to strenuous trail traverses the flow, passing some small lakes before ending at the larger Laguna Tuminguina, a full day's hike from town. Another day-walk is over the water-logged **páramo** of the Reserva Ecológica Cayambe-Coca from the Papallacta Pass down to the thermal springs, giving you the best of this bleak landscape: undulating hills, windswept grasses, and silent, mist-laden lakes, with perhaps the occasional glimpse of such creatures as the South American fox, the white-tailed deer, the carunculated caracara, the plumbeous sierra finch, and the endemic Ecuadorian hillstar, a high-altitude hummingbird which draws nectar from the páramo's flowering *puya* plants.

Practicalities

Buses from Quito to Lago Agrio, and Tena via Baeza, pass through town about every forty minutes and stop at La Y on request. The journey takes around two hours. If you want to avoid the steep uphill walk to the Termas de Papallacta complex, you can hire a **camioneta** from the Viveres Mathilde store on the Calle Principal (or ring Sr Cesar Hidalgo on ℡06/320638) up there for $3.

Broadly speaking, the standard and price of **accommodation** drops the further you go from *Las Termas de Papallacta* (℡06/320620, Quito office at Foch E6-12 and Reina Victoria ℡02/2557850, ℗www.termaspapallacta.com), which offers comfortable rooms with private bath (❼) or hot tub (❽), along with fancy two-storey cabins, sleeping up to six and fitted with kitchen, sunken bath and private outdoor hot tub ($125 for the cabin); access to the pools is included in the price. Just outside the *Termas* complex, the modern *Antisana* (℡06/320626; ❸) has clean, unremarkable rooms, but no hot water; prices will rise when it's installed in the near future. The friendly *Hostería La Pampa de Papallacta* (℡06/320624; ❹), halfway down the road to the village, provides home-made bunk beds in compact rooms, most of which have fireplaces, and naturally heated water in private bathrooms, or attractive family cabins sleeping five for $60 (all rates negotiable out of season). They also have a nice indoor pool, a large sitting room with table tennis and a fire, and a trout pond at the back where you can catch your own supper (they'll do the cooking). Down in the village there are two budget hotels on the Calle Principal: *El Viajero* (no phone; ❷), at the top end of town; and the better *Quito* (℡06/320628; ❷), just before the police checkpoint halfway down the street, with shared bath, clean, simple rooms, naturally heated water, a pool and a roof terrace. **Camping** is possible at the *Termas de Papallacta* for $6 per person.

Eating in Papallacta is bound to involve fresh trout from the nearby fish farms and lakes. The best and most expensive **restaurant** is at the *Termas de Papallacta*, which has a dining room in the bathing complex and in the main hotel, and serves excellent trout. For a cheaper feed, the *Hostería Pampa de Papallacta* and the *La Quiteñita* restaurant at the *Quito* hotel are both fine, while the popular *Choza de Don Wilson* at La Y de Papallacta has good views of the valley.

Baeza

From Papallacta the road follows the steep descent of the Papallacta and Quijos rivers for 37km before reaching **BAEZA** at 1850m, the largest town between Quito and Lago Agrio. Before the arrival of the conquistadors, the Baeza region was populated by the Quijos people, but in 1559, Captain Gil Ramírez Dávalos was sent here to bring the 50,000 *indígenas* under control, and he founded Baeza with an eye to its strategic position. Nowadays, there's not a lot to do in town itself, but its location in attractive pastoral hills between three large, richly forested reserves – the Cayambe-Coca reserve is directly to the north, Sumaco Napo-Galeras to the east (see p.328), and Antisana to the southwest (see p.328) – makes it a convenient base for local hikes as well as expeditions into the remoter depths of these protected areas. For **information** on all three reserves, call in at the Centro de Comunicación Ambiental (☎06/320605), in Baeza Colonial on the corner of Ramírez Dávalos and Rey Felipe II, where there's also a small **museum** showing ceramics, and displays on history and tourism in the region (Mon–Fri 9am–5pm; free).

Baeza is split into three small and distinct parts. **La Y de Baeza**, a collection of road-side *comedores*, a couple of basic hotels and a filling station, marks the junction of two highways, one heading northeast to Lago Agrio, the other south to Tena. From La Y, you can see the rusting corrugated-iron roofs of **Baeza Colonial** about 1500m up the hill on the Tena road, the original village which still shows the trappings of its history, with little wooden houses lining a pair of steep, cobbled streets up to a church. Across the Río Machángara,

---

Hikes around Baeza

There are several relatively straightforward half-day **hikes around Baeza** – all with good birding potential – that let you make the most of its hillside location. The IGM 1:50,000 Baeza **map** is a good resource, as are rubber boots if it's been raining as trails can get very muddy. To access some of the best local trails, start from the right-hand side of the church in the old town and take the road heading up through the pastureland. About 700m on, you'll reach a bridge at a fork in the path. If you continue right without crossing the bridge, you follow the **Río Machángara** up an increasingly thickly forested hill to the southwest. The left fork over the bridge takes you up to the mountain ridge overlooking Baeza. Roughly 1km later, this latter track splits again. The steep, muddy branch to the right leads up through lush forest to some **antennas** on top of the hill, affording spectacular views of Baeza and the Quijos valley. The other branch continues along the **mountain ridge**, also with great views, but further along the forest gets very dense and the trail hard to find, so if you attempt this route it's worthwhile seeking out a **guide**, which will cost around $15 a day; the *San Rafael* hotel (see overleaf) is a good place to ask. You can loop down from the mountain ridge round on a trail leading back to Andalucía.

about 800m further along this road, the new town, **Andalucía**, has grown steadily since it was founded in 1987 after an earthquake hit the area. Built along the quiet dual carriageway to Tena, it is now substantially larger than its older neighbour and has all the town's services, the hospital, post office and Andinatel office.

Practicalities

Buses to Lago Agrio stop at La Y, from where occasional camionetas ferry people up to Baeza Colonial and Andalucía, while buses to Tena pass all three parts of town. Both services run several times daily. There are a handful of **places to stay**, but when the pipelines need servicing all the rooms in town can be taken up by oil workers. In Colonial, *El Nogal de Jumandy* (℡06/320208; ❷) is a rickety wooden structure on stilts. The shared living room has comfy sofas and views down the valley, while some rooms have less inspiring views through the floorboards to the grass below. In Andalucía, *Samay* (℡06/320170; ❷) has sprightly wooden rooms and shared bathrooms, and further down the main road, Avenida de los Quijos, *Bambú's* (℡06/320615; ❸) boasts cable TV, private baths and a courtyard with a pool table and ping pong. Further down the hill, *San Rafael* (℡06/320114; ❷–❸) has comfortable rooms with private baths and large TVs for a little extra outlay. It's also a good source for information on the many possible walks around the Baeza area. In addition to the town's hotels, there are a couple of good places to stay in the lush hills south of Baeza on the road to Tena, excellent bases for hiking and bird watching (see p.328).

The best **restaurant** is *Gina*, on the east side of the square in the old village, and tour groups often stop here for its ample trout, meat or vegetarian dishes costing around $2. Other restaurants can be found at the *San Rafael* hotel, and *El Viejo* nearby. The restaurant at *El Oro Negro* hotel, at La Y, decorated with a water feature and posters from the owner's bullfighting days, is a few cuts above its musty accommodation next door.

The Quijos valley

From Baeza, the road to Lago Agrio courses through the broad **Quijos valley** for almost 70km, passing only a handful of settlements on the way. On your left the vast Cayambe-Coca reserve stretches off high into the northern sierra, while on your right you'll see the Río Quijos, its rocky shores banked by grazing land and fruit farms. The Trans-Ecuador Oil Pipeline hedges the road like a hard shoulder much of the way to Lago Agrio.

After 8km you'll pass the nondescript village of San Francisco de Borja, and 10km further on is **EL CHACO**, the largest town before Lago Agrio, known for producing cheese and naranjilla. From El Chaco a dirt road and footpaths access the lowland section of the Cayambe-Coca reserve, allowing **hikes** up the Río Oyacachi. The river is reputed to be rich in gold, though while panning for the stuff is a reasonably common pastime for jungle tours out of Tena, you won't get anything more than a few specks of fine gold dust; walking along, however, is far more rewarding, with great views of the valley before it enters dense primary forest. The trail eventually leads up to the highland village of Oyacachi, but this three-day uphill hike is best attempted with a guide coming downstream – and downhill – from Oyacachi (see p.137). El Chaco only has a pair of very basic *pensiones* at the truck stop, where there's also a reasonable **restaurant**, and a couple of decent cabin complexes at the north edge of town, which are a better bet if you get stuck here.

For the next 60km or so, the road traverses increasingly remote territory. Colonization here came to an abrupt end in March 1987, when a major earthquake, measuring 7.0 on the Richter scale, rocked the area and sent cascades of mud and debris down the hillsides, engulfing scores of hamlets and homesteads, and killing over a thousand people. The damage was so bad that the road wasn't fully repaired for months.

Some 48km beyond El Chaco, the two biggest natural attractions of the area – **La Cascada de San Rafael**, Ecuador's largest waterfall, and **Volcán El Reventador**, a brooding active volcano part-clothed in forest – stand either side of the road 9km apart.

La Cascada de San Rafael

The Río Quijos incises a gash between some tree-fringed cliffs before crashing down a drop of 145m – **La Cascada de San Rafael** – sending great clouds of spray wafting up from its base. Some 61km from Baeza, the **entrance** is marked by a concrete bus shelter on the right of the road (ask the bus driver for the stop). Behind the shelter take the dirt road a few hundred metres down to the guardhouse, where, if anyone's around, they'll charge you $1 for entrance. Beyond the guardhouse, you'll see some simple prefabs, built by INECEL, the state electricity company, but now available as general **accommodation**. Each pastel cabin has a sitting room, two bedrooms and a bathroom, but the sparse decoration does little to disguise their utilitarian past. It's difficult to book ahead and you'll have to negotiate a price with whoever is caretaking the premises after arriving; you'll also have to bring all your own **food** and water, though there is a basic, nameless *salón* with grimy walls and a dirt floor (closes at 7pm), on the right just over the Río Reventador bridge, about ten minutes' walk uphill from the bus stop. About 50m before the *salón*, on the left, the Agua Azul **swimming pool** ($0.50) is fed by the streams from the slopes of the Volcán El Reventador, rising to the west.

Trails to the falls

The two trails to the falls give you quite different views. The easy **first trail** leads to a viewpoint opposite the falls (1hr 30min to the viewpoint and back), and begins at the arrows to the left behind the cabins, heading into forest rich in birdlife, most notably the startling Andean cock-of-the-rock: the males are unmistakeable for the bright-red pompom crest on the front of their heads. After about 25 minutes, you'll hear the low roar of the falls in the distance. A few breaks in the vegetation to the right offer the first glimpses, but mind the edge – a nearby cross commemorates a Canadian photographer who lost his footing. A clearing on the ridgetop affords fine views and is also a suitable place for **camping**, though you'll need to bring all your food and water. Keep going a little farther to a bench at the best **viewpoint**, where the vegetation has been cut far enough back for you to see the pool at the bottom and the entire column of spray. Beyond this, you can continue down a treacherously steep rockface to the foot of the falls (1hr), but this should not be attempted if wet. The guards at the entrance can tell you if it's safe to go down.

The **second trail** to the head of the falls (2hr 15min there and back) involves a bit of scrambling over rock at the end, which can also be tricky in the wet. Check with the guards before you try this trail, as the river is at times prohibitively high; they will **guide** you for a few dollars if they have time. For the trailhead, turn right before the cabins and take the path snaking down the left side of the pipeline. Before the second drop, look for a path on the left heading into thick forest. This crosses a stream and eventually comes out of the forest on the left bank of the Río Quijos. Walk downstream, and about halfway to the rocky outcrop you'll come across another stream. Follow it a little way upstream to a log bridge where you can cross – this can sometimes be hard to spot in the vegetation. Continue on to the outcrop, then hop up the rocks to rejoin the trail. There's a short clamber through the undergrowth, where you have to climb a small muddy cliff using shrubs and tree roots for grip, but you'll come out to breathtaking **views** from the top of the falls. You can also climb even further up on to the rock on your left, from where you can peer into the swirling cauldron on the upper part of the waterfall.

Volcán El Reventador

On the rare occasions when the cloud lifts you can see **Volcán El Reventador** (3562m) poke its triangular mass through the greenery, 9km to the west of the San Rafael falls. El Reventador means "the burster", an apt name as the volcano's been popping away since the first record of its activity was made in 1541. Its 3.5-kilometre crater is evidence that at some time a colossal eruption took place, ripping the volcano apart and leaving it a fraction of its former size.

Its latest outburst was in November 2002, when El Reventador spewed more than 200 million cubic tons of ash and rock – the country's largest **eruption** since Tungurahua's in 1886 – over 15km into the sky. The cloud drifted westwards, smothering the highway and nearby villages, and quickly reached Quito 90km away, where inches of ash fell, closing schools and the airport for days. Lava flows spilled down from the breached crater, burning wide streaks through its forested slopes, and a new cone was reportedly formed on the eastern slopes of the volcano, 600m below the summit. The eruption also moved the oil pipeline twenty metres in places, thankfully without breaking it.

Before the eruption, there was a popular hike to the summit taking two to four days of strenuous, but non-technical climbing. Given the current circumstances, however, it's impossible to give hiking directions. If you are interested, it's essential that you **check the current condition** of the volcano before attempting any climb; ask at the SAE (see p.80) and also check the Instituto Geofísico website (ⓦwww.igepn.edu.ec). Trails are likely to have been obliterated, and the terrain may have changed significantly from that recorded on the IGM 1:50,000 *Volcán El Reventador* map and aerial photo (also available from the IGM). If you decide to hike the volcano, ask locally for a guide and bring a compass, a machete, food and plenty of water along with all other necessary supplies.

Lago Agrio and the Reserva Faunística Cuyabeno

LAGO AGRIO is the capital of Sucumbíos, the country's second youngest province, and was originally founded only a few decades ago by Lojanos looking for a new life in the Oriente (its official name is Nueva Loja). In the late 1960s it was used by Texaco as a base for oil exploration, and soon after took its widely used nickname from Sour Lake in Texas, the company's original headquarters.

Lago, as it is often called by its 30,000 or so locals, has a hot and bustling centre along its main street, **Avenida Quito**, where its high-fronted buildings seem a little grandiose for a hard-edged frontier town. A couple of blocks to the north, Lago's park, fronted by a simple church, is about the only gesture to greenery you'll find. At 250km from Quito, and only 21km from the Colombian border, the town is not the jungle outpost it once was, however. Colonization and oil exploitation in the area have been rapid, and only scraps of forest remain for many miles around, particularly to the south, where oil pipelines crisscross the landscape down to Coca and beyond.

Around 15,000 **Cofán** lived in this area when Texaco arrived, but they were among the worst-hit by the industry, disease and displacement, and now number only a few hundred, squeezed into five small communities, three of them in the forests on the Río Aguarico. At Lago's Sunday **market**, between Avenida Quito and Avenida Amazonas, some Cofán come wearing traditional dress – a long tunic and sometimes a headdress for the men, and colourful blouses, skirts and jewellery for the women – to trade their produce and craftwork, including hammocks, bags and occasionally necklaces made from animal teeth, iridescent insects or birds' beaks. Artesanías Huarmi Huankurina ("United Women"), 12 de Febrero 267 and 10 de Agosto (Tues–Sun), also sells crafts from the region's indigenous communities, including hammocks, bags, ceramics and blowpipes.

Oil has been mined in Ecuador since 1917, but it wasn't until Texaco struck rich with sites around Lago Agrio sixty years later that the Oriente really figured in the industry. During the 1970s, multinational companies swooped into the region, building roads, airstrips and settlements, unlocking the Ecuadorian Amazon to colonization on a scale that hadn't been envisaged since the time of the Conquest. Towns such as Coca and Lago Agrio sprang from the forests as oil output grew by around ten percent a year, and by the late 1990s 400,000 barrels per day were being pumped from the ground. With the completion of the controversial second pipeline that traverses the Mindo-Nambillo protected forest, internationally recognized as an Important Bird Area (see p.356), the country will be able to increase its oil output to 700,000 barrels per day.

Oil accounts for over forty percent of Ecuador's export income, dominating the country's economy, but making it vulnerable to fluctuations in global oil prices. When its value fell in the 1980s, for example, the government signed away larger and larger areas of the Oriente to oil production to make up for the loss in revenue; today virtually all of the Ecuadorian Amazon is available to oil extraction, even indigenous territories and protected areas. As the law has it, no matter what the land's designation is, the oil and minerals below belong to the state, who can grant concessions for their extraction as they see fit. Unsurprisingly, the economy's thirst for oil has been satisfied at considerable cost to the environment.

The damage begins with the **prospecting**; in a typical search for oil, over a thousand helicopter sites are cleared, while hundreds of seismic tests – explosions – destroy thousands of hectares of forest. During **drilling**, waste oil products are collected in *piscinas* ("swimming pools"), filthy pits laced with toxic metals that contaminate surrounding river systems; when work is finished they're covered under a thin layer of earth and left to continue polluting. **Roads** are built to drill sites, unlocking the forest to colonizers who deforest large areas of unsuitable land for farming which quickly becomes degraded. Oil **transportation** is also hazardous, and breaks in Ecuador's pipelines have resulted in around seventeen million gallons of oil pouring into the environment – fifty percent more than the *Exxon Valdez* oil-tanker disaster in Alaska.

The toll on **local populations** has been horrific as well, with many commentators talking of "cultural genocide". In the north, the Cofán, Siona and Secoya have been amongst the worst hit as their rivers were polluted beyond use, forcing them to overhunt the forests and move to the cities to find work in unskilled and poorly paid jobs, sometimes, ironically, in dangerous oil clean-up work. Other indigenous groups have been victim to aggressive tactics used by some companies, who seek to divide

Oil remains Lago Agrio's *raison d'être*, but the basic infrastructure of hotels, paved roads and transport links that arrived with the industry have given tourism a foothold here as well, though the town itself is of very little interest. Nevertheless, just 40km west of the **Reserva Faunística Cuyabeno**, Lago Agrio has become the main access point to vast expanses of forest, encouraging new tour agencies to open every year. However, in recent years the town has been affected by the conflict in Colombia from armed units that are believed to have infiltrated the region. Although this has so far had little impact on tourists, **shootings** have occurred in the town and there have been **kidnappings** in the border areas. It is important that you make enquiries with the authorities before travelling here, and check postings on your embassy websites.

Arrival, information and getting around

The town's centre runs along **Avenida Quito**, the main road connecting Coca and Quito to Lago Agrio, which is also where you'll find most of the communities, corrupt leaders or bribe villages with small entreaties of cash and promises to build schools and medical centres (while offering neighbouring and similarly affected settlements nothing) to obtain permission for oil exploration. In 2003 the leaders of a Quichua community opposed to oil activity were allegedly seized by the Ecuadorian army and handed over to a company security firm, who tortured them; the Inter-American Commission on Human Rights had to intervene and ordered emergency protection measures.

Toxic discharges have also been linked to dramatic increases in rates of cancer, miscarriages, skin complaints and birth defects. A Harvard medical team found unusually high incidences of eight types of **cancer** in areas affected by oil activity, while another study in one village discovered that the local river, used as drinking water, had concentrations of carcinogenic hydrocarbons 144 times higher than is permitted in EU drinking water – the risk of males in the same village developing cancer of the larynx was thirty times the norm.

Slowly, **indigenous opposition** to the oil companies has become better organized. In 1993 a lawsuit was filed against Texaco on behalf of 30,000 indigenous people who claim their land or health has been affected by the company allegedly dumping toxic waste-water into Oriente river systems for twenty years instead of reinjecting them into the ground, but it was recently rejected from US courts before being heard, on the grounds that Ecuador was a more convenient location to hear the case. In May 2003 a new lawsuit was filed in Lago Agrio suing Texaco for clean-up costs that could exceed $1 billion. Some indigenous groups, frustrated by such slow progress, are opting for **direct action**, with large-scale marches to oil headquarters and drilling sites. In December 2002 an Achuar community in Pastaza province seized eight oil workers from an Argentine company, which was exploring the area, in what the community believed was breach of their ancestral land rights; they were released when the relevant oil firms agreed to suspend activities until a proper dialogue is established beween indigenous representatives.

Radical tactics or not, it's an uphill battle for indigenous peoples to protect their forestland, made more difficult by the enormous economic pressures on the country. Ecuador is thought to lose as much as 3000 square kilometres of forest every year, proportionally the highest rate on the continent. The country's current oil reserves will be exhausted in under eleven years according to government figures (the US government puts it at just six years), and if the destruction continues at the present rate, as it's likely to do in the search for new supplies, conservationists predict that the Ecuadorian Amazon will be completely deforested within thirty years.

hotels and restaurants. If your **bus** doesn't drop you on it, you usually won't be more than a block away. There's a **bus station** 2km northwest of the centre on Calle del Chofer, but most buses still pass along Avenida Quito anyway, where you can also jump on. The **airport** is 4km east of the centre, and Tame and Icaro fly here from Quito. A taxi there from the centre will cost a few dollars.

You can get tourist **information** at the Cámara de Turismo, Avenida Quito and Avenida Colombia (☎06/832502), and the Ministerio del Ambiente office, Eloy Alfaro and Av Colombia (Mon–Fri 8am–12.30pm & 1.30–5pm; ☎06/830139), can provide information on the Cuyabeno reserve and some ecotourism projects. The various tourist agencies (see box, p.288) have limited general information. **Taxis** – white and yellow pick-up trucks – cost $1.25–1.50 between any two points in town, and there are plenty of them on Avenida Quito, particularly around the market area.

Accommodation

As far as **accommodation** is concerned, a little extra cash goes a long way in Lago Agrio. The plentiful rock-bottom choices are mostly unattractive and noisy, typically with musty rooms, peeling paint and rotting plaster. For a few dollars more, you can trade in the squalor for a bright, clean room with air conditioning, cable TV and fridge. Only the more expensive rooms will have hot water.

Araza Hotel Av Quito 610 and Narváez
⊤06/830223, ⑰831247. The most comfortable place in town, used mainly by businessmen. It has big, soulless rooms with all the accoutrements, such as a/c, cable TV, private baths and hot water, and an outdoor pool. Breakfast included. **⑥**

D'Mario Av Quito ⊤06/830172, ⑰830456. Popular hotel, and while the downstairs rooms are a bit musty, those on the middle floor are fresher, with a/c, cable TV, fridge and phone, and the top floor has all this with bigger rooms with hot water. The comfortable communal area has a pool table, plus there's a pool, sauna and weights room. **④–⑤**

Ecuador ⊤06/830183 Av Quito and Pasaje Gonzanamá. A decent hotel popular with Ecuadorians, with fans, TV and private baths. There's also a restaurant and parking facilities. **③**

Gran Colombia Av Quito ⊤06/830601. Announced by a sparkling, black-and-white-tiled frontage with flowers hanging over the balustrades, rooms inside the *Gran Colombia* are bright pink-and-white with fan or a/c, fridge and cable TV (those with hot water cost more). The hotel has table tennis, a pool table and chess for guests, but caged birds and a roaming monkey leave a nasty taste. **③–④**

Gran Hostal de Lago Av Quito, 1km west of the centre ⊤ & ⑰06/832415. Comfortable and furnished concrete cabins with a/c and cable TV, located in a large lot with a pool, sauna and steam room and surrounded by pleasant gardens. Breakfast included. **⑥**

Los Guacamayos Av Quito ⊤06/830601. Under the same ownership as the *Gran Colombia*, this is one of the better budget hotels and is popular with Ecuadorians. Small rooms strung down long open-sided corridors may have private bath, fan, a/c and TV. Prices drop the more facilities you forgo. **③–④**

Lago Imperial Av Colombia and Av Quito
⊤06/830453. Pleasant rooms with fan or a/c and private bath. A restaurant and swimming pool are also being constructed. **④–⑤**

Eating and drinking

The best **restaurants** in Lago Agrio belong to the smarter hotels. Two of the most popular are next-door rivals owned by the *D'Mario* and *Gran Colombia*, offering fairly standard menus as well as pizza. Both have low cane chairs with giant cushions, and tables spilling out on to the pavement, oddly evoking the air of a Paris bistro in the heart of the Oriente. Opposite, on the corner of Avenida Quito and Pasaje Gonzanamá, *Oroaz* dishes up ample portions of Colombian specialities at low prices, but is closed by 8.30pm Mondays to Saturdays and by 3pm on Sundays. If you're particularly hungry, try the *Bandeja Paisa*, a huge plate of rice, beans, egg, fried beef, chorizo, *patacones*, avocado and bread. Another good Colombian joint is *Pedacito de Colombia* on Avenida Quito. You won't find better seafood in Lago Agrio than at *El Delfín* on Añasco and Pasaje Gonzanamá, which is kitted out in coastal style and prides itself on its *encebollados*.

There's no shortage of **bars** and **clubs** in town, mostly catering to legions of macho oil workers. Some places can be a bit rough, so exercise discretion and ask around for the classier establishments of the moment.

Listings

Airlines Icaro, at the airport (⊤06/832370); Tame, Francisco de Orellana and 9 de Octubre (⊤06/830113), and at the airport (⊤06/830500).
Banks and exchange Banco de Guayaquil, 12 de Febrero and Av Quito (Visa ATM); Produbanco, at the airport (MasterCard ATM). The *D'Mario* hotel may be able to change TCs.
Buses Buses to the Colombian border depart from Av Colombia and Añasco. *Rancheras* and scrappy oil-company buses for Coca, Shushufindi and other

Community stays and jungle tours from Lago Agrio

From Lago Agrio, most jungle excursions go to the beautiful forests of the Reserva Faunística Cuyabeno (see overleaf). There are several possibilities for people wishing to arrange **indigenous-community stays** in or near the reserve, with the Cofán, Siona or Secoya people. A good place to go for further information is **La Dirección Bilingüe de Sucumbíos** on Av Quito and 20 de Junio (℡06/832681), near the *Gran Hostal de Lago*, an institution responsible for the bilingual education of indigenous people. You can also visit the reserve with a couple of more conventional **tour operators** also based in Lago.

Indigenous-community stays

Comuna Cofán Dureno contact Emire Hildo Criollo through the FEINCE office on the third floor of La Dirección Bilingüe de Sucumbíos on Av Quito and 20 de Junio ℡06/832681, or through ⊛www.cofan.org. This 300-strong community stands near a small pocket of primary forest on the south bank of the Río Aguarico, opposite the colonist village of Dureno some 25km east of Lago Agrio. During your stay in their simple cabins, you're likely to go on forest walks, fish on the river, and learn about medicinal plants and craft techniques. $30–40 per day.

Siona Tours 12 de Febrero 277 and 10 de Agosto, Lago Agrio ℡06/831875, ℻830425. The agency is run by Sionas, who will take you to their communities of Orahuëayá on the Río Shushufindi, Biaña on the banks of the Río Aguarico, or Puerto Bolívar in the Cuyabeno reserve. The office keeps erratic hours, but the FEPP office upstairs (℡06/830232) may also be able to put you in touch with them. $40–60 per day, depending on group size.

Lago tour operators

Magic River Tours 18 de Noviembre and Guayaquil ℡ & ℻06/831003, ⊛www.magicrivertours.com. A German-owned company specializing in non-motorized canoe trips, paddling or drifting down small tributaries in the Cuyabeno reserve (5 days $275), accompanied by an English or German speaker and an expert indigenous guide.

Pioneer Tours no address, but on a dirt road off Av Amazonas to the south in Barrio Colinas Petroleras ℡ & ℻06/831845. Run by Galo Sevilla, who has 18 years' guiding experience; tours typically head to a basic campsite by the Laguna de Cuyabeno with local Siona and Secoya guides. $35–40 per person per day.

---

more local destinations leave from around the market and from the stadium a block to the west on Av Amazonas. Other destinations are serviced from the new bus terminal 2km northeast of the centre ($1.25 taxi ride), though most of these buses (including the smarter buses to Coca) pass by Av Quito as they leave town, where you can pick them up. See "Travel details" on p.345 for further information. **Consulate** Colombia, Av Quito and Av Colombia

(℡06/830084). Look for the flag in an upstairs window.
Police and immigration Av Quito and Manabí (℡06/830101). Daily 8am–noon & 3–6pm.
Post office Vicente Rocafuerte and 12 de Febrero.
Taxis Cooperativo Terminal Terrestre (℡06/831043).
Telephone office Andinatel, cnr of Francisco de Orellana and 18 de Noviembre.

East of Lago Agrio

Although the region around Lago Agrio is one of the worst affected by oil and settler colonization, to the east lies one of the remotest and most beautiful sections of the Oriente, dominated by the huge Reserva Faunística Cuyabeno. Many indigenous people live here, including Quichua, Cofán, Secoya, Siona and Shuar communities, who are struggling to defend their cultures and territory against encroachment from oil companies, settlers and unscrupulous tour operators. Some are turning to indigenous ecotourism programmes for economic and cultural survival.

Travel warning: the Colombian border

Colombia is only 21km north of Lago Agrio, but this is **not a safe place** to enter the country, especially since the US-led "Plan Colombia" has effectively encouraged the displacement of Colombian **guerrilla** and **paramilitary** units into Ecuadorian territory, who are making their presence felt. You should **avoid all border areas** in Sucumbíos; if you're heading to Colombia, cross at Tulcán in the northern sierra (see p.176). Should the situation dramatically change for the better on the Ecuadorian side – and you should check thoroughly with authorities in Quito and Lago Agrio before heading up this way – bear in mind that the nine-hour journey to Mocoa, the nearest place in Colombia to get your entry stamp, traverses important coca-producing country and may well still be **very dangerous**. You will need an **exit stamp** from the migration police, and ask the Colombian consulate if they need to stamp your passport too. **Buses** to **La Punta** (every 15min, a 40min trip), on the Ecuadorian side of the Río San Miguel, leave from Av Colombia and Añasco, and bring you to a new bridge over the river to Puerto Colón in Colombia. Have your **passport** to hand as there are checkpoints along the way.

The main road east of Lago Agrio follows the Río Aguarico to the settler village of **Dureno** skirting Cofán territory, before reaching **Chiritza**, from where some tour agencies take canoes into the southern section of the Cuyabeno reserve. The oil town of **Tarapoa**, over 70km from Lago, is where the road turns north and then west to the Colombian border at **Puerto El Carmen de Putumayo**, over 110km away. You cannot cross into Colombia here, but exploring this remote area is not recommended anyway, due to **guerrilla activity** (see "Travel warning" above).

Reserva Faunística Cuyabeno

One of Ecuador's largest reserves, the **Reserva Faunística Cuyabeno** (full name, Reserva de Producción de Fauna Cuyabeno) encompasses over 6000 square kilometres of rainforest, holding the Río Cuyabeno basin and much of the watershed of the lower Río Aguarico as far as the Peruvian border. Protecting areas with species that survived the last ice age, Cuyabeno harbours abundant birdlife with 494 recorded species, a number that continues to grow, and a staggering 228 tree species per hectare; for the same area in a British forest, you'd be struggling to count ten. The reserve also contains a huge network of lakes and lagoons, including fourteen major interconnected bodies of water and large areas of inundated forest. There are two main black-water lake systems: the **Cuyabeno Lakes**, which include the Laguna Cuyabeno and Laguna Grande, and **Lagartococha**, at the eastern end of the reserve bordering Peru. Black-water rivers typically form where there is little soil sediment and generally originate in the Amazon basin itself; the water takes on a dark tea-like colour from the vegetable humus that falls into it, which also makes it very acidic and rich in tannins. Some people come to the reserve specifically to see its **aquatic wildlife**, such as pink freshwater dolphins, turtles, black caiman, anaconda, manatee, giant otters, countless colourful frogs and toads and 450 species of fish.

The boundaries of the reserve have changed since its creation in 1979, particularly following major incursions by oil companies and settlers into the western areas around Tarapoa, Cuyabeno town and Sansahuari. The governments of the time largely ignored this destruction, but in 1991, after considerable pressure from international agencies and CONAIE (Confederation of Indigenous Nationalities of Ecuador), a vast tract of land on the eastern side was added, almost tripling the size of the reserve. And while the reserve is now less accessible to colonizers and far better protected by politically active indigenous communities, oil extraction is still causing problems through toxic waste and spills that have drained into the Cuyabeno basin; for more on the effects of the oil industry in the Oriente, see the box on p.300.

Visiting the reserve

There are two main **access points** to the reserve, the first where the road crosses the Río Cuyabeno, beyond Tarapoa, from where the river can be navigated down to the Laguna Cuyabeno and the other main lakes. The second is by canoe on the Río Aguarico, which can be navigated from Lago Agrio to the lowest parts of the reserve, but is more commonly joined at Chiritza, about 50km east by road. Visiting the reserve independently is not recommended, but agencies in Quito and Lago Agrio offer a range of **guided tours** (see boxes on p.288 & p.303 for details). Shorter tours are usually based around the lakes, while longer ones tend to go to the eastern reaches around the Río Aguarico or Río Lagartococha. **Indigenous-community stays** are becoming a growing force in the region as well, details of which are also listed in the box on p.303. Note that **transport** to Lago Agrio from Quito, and the reserve **entrance fee** ($20), aren't always included in the price of a tour.

South of Lago Agrio: the road to Coca

The 93-kilometre road running between Lago Agrio and Coca was built to facilitate access between the burgeoning oil towns in the late 1970s. Steamrollered through the forest, the road opened up the area to a flood of colonists to whom the government promised all the land they could clear in an effort to bring economic productivity to the Oriente. The rainforest was speedily hacked down for farming, and the soil, too poor to support long-term agriculture, became degraded pastureland within a few years. Meanwhile, oil companies scoured the region, and a giant latticework of **pipelines** now spreads out from the road; at night the flicker of the refinery fires dyes the sky an unearthly orange. The landscape is not totally unappealing, but feels miserably squandered, with livestock and white-trunked trees dotting tired fields backed by the odd patch of forest in the distance. Simple homesteads lie at the roadside, and some of the successful ones guard defiant gardens and orchards from the surrounding grassland. Along this road, too, is evidence of the new commercial interests in the Oriente – vast plantations lining the horizon with sterile rows of African oil palms.

About halfway to Coca, an army of fruit, sweet and juice sellers ambushes buses pausing in **Proyecto**, where an eastbound road leaves the main Coca highway. This road is the only land access for **Limoncocha** and **Pompeya** (see p.313 for details on both towns), and is serviced by regular buses as far as **Shushufindi**, 25km away, an unsightly town of refineries, compounds and gas-storage tanks, with the occasional *comedor* and "24-hour nightclub" providing the human touch. Beyond, the dirt road turns south, accompanied by several smaller pipelines, which shoot off to suck oil from 2000-square-kilometre *bloques* of land and pump it back to Lago Agrio. A further hour's drive will take you to Limoncocha and then Pompeya on the Río Napo some thirty minutes later.

From Proyecto, the Coca road reaches **La Joya de los Sachas**, where there are a couple of simple hotels, but no reason to stop. Some 39km later, just outside Coca, you'll have to show your passport at the checkpoint at Payamino. Keep an eye on your bus – they are sometimes impatient to leave and not always aware that you aren't on board.

Francisco de Orellana and the discovery of the Amazon

When a band of 200 Spaniards, 4000 *indígenas* and thousands of assorted horses, dogs and pigs set out from Quito, in February 1541, to explore new lands to the east rumoured to be rich in gold and spices, they little expected that some of them would end up making the first recorded descent of the Amazon, a journey of over 6000km down part of the largest river system in the world. They were led by Gonzalo Pizarro, younger brother of the ruthless Francisco – the conqueror of the Incas – who had heard of forests of cinnamon to the east, and El Dorado, "the Golden Man", who painted his body in gold dust for clothes, and washed it off in a lake everyday. As soon as Captain **Francisco de Orellana** heard about the expedition he raced from Guayaquil to catch up. He had won honour as a young man – and lost an eye – in the battles of Lima and Cusco, and at thirty years old was still hungry for adventure.

Even before the expedition had left the mountains, hundreds of *indígenas* had died in the freezing passes, and as they descended into the uncharted forests, they were running desperately low on food. By Christmas the group had travelled around 400km from Quito, when they stumbled across the Río Coca. Having eaten all their pigs and most of their dogs, they decided that their only choice was to build a boat and send a vanguard led by Orellana downstream in search of food. Orellana never made it back to his leader and the waiting men – a failure for which he was branded a traitor for centuries afterwards.

The captain had a group of sixty men, some weapons and a few supplies, but within a couple of weeks they were "eating hides, straps and the soles of their shoes cooked with certain herbs" and forest roots which poisoned them "to the point of death". Worse still, the river (now the Napo) had become so fast-moving that they knew they wouldn't be able to go back upstream, and they were carried down into territory where war drums raged on either side of the river. However, Orellana was a great diplomat as well as soldier, and unlike most conquistadors, he was well versed in indigenous languages and picked new ones up with prodigious speed, an ability that saved his life many times on his journey. Here, instead of fighting, he embraced

Coca

COCA has enjoyed such a boom from oil that in 1998 it was deemed important enough to become the capital of its own province, **Orellana**. Wresting power from the old provincial capital of Tena, the country's youngest province took up the territory of the lower half of the old Napo province, extending from Coca to Peru. Coca's official name is Puerto Francisco de Orellana, after the first Spaniard to navigate the length of the Amazon (see box above), but its nickname – more commonly used – probably derives from local trade in the coca leaf during colonial times.

The settlement first appeared on maps at the end of the eighteenth century, and until even the 1970s Coca remained a forgotten outpost in the midst of virgin jungle, cut off from the rest of the world except by boat or plane. When the whiff of black gold came its way, the sleepy village mutated into an urban nightmare, the result of a speedy influx of oilers and colonists. Until recently its chaotic and filthy potholed streets lined with ramshackle houses made sure that visitors left town in a hurry, taking canoes to lodges further down the **Río Napo**. Lately, however, concerted efforts by its authorities have succeeded in neatening up sections of the waterfront and in paving some of its main roads. There's no main park in town, a symptom of its explosive growth, as if no one had time to plan one, and the town sprawls outwards from the north bank of a local chief and gave him European clothes, receiving an abundance of partridges, turkeys and fish in return.

Before long, they were over 1000km from Pizarro's camp and had no more thought for going back as they did for finding El Dorado – they were just trying to keep alive as they continued their voyage. On the Río Marañón they met four tall white men, decked in gold with flowing hair to their waists (a mystery to this day), and in Machipara territory were set upon by thousands of fierce warriors, whom they managed to keep at bay even though their gunpowder was damp and they had only four or five crossbows. By June 1542 they reached the Río Negro (near what is now Manaus), naming it after its deep-black waters. News of their presence spread before them, and they came across empty villages with decapitated heads nailed to posts in warning. Soon they were set upon by a fierce tribe of warrior-women, whom they named **Amazons**, after the women of Greek legend who each removed a breast to improve their archery skills. The chronicler of the journey, Friar Gaspar de Carvajal, claimed that this jungle tribe could fire arrows with as much force as ten men, and described how the Spanish boats looked like "porcupines" after the shots rained down; the friar himself lost an eye in the exchange. On August 26, 1542, they finally came to the mouth of the world's greatest river and named it Orellana though it soon became known as Amazonas after the tribe. Although these women were never spotted again, it has been hypothesized that they were in fact male warriors from the Yagua tribe, who sport pale yellow, grass-style skirts and headgear.

When Orellana returned to Spain in May 1543, he started making arrangements to return to the river, but didn't get the backing that he needed from the King. When he did finally set out around Christmas in 1545, he was woefully ill-equipped for another expedition and lost a ship and more than 220 men before he even reached South America. As they entered the Amazon estuary, they'd already run out of food and the remaining ships became separated on the rough tidal waters. The river that had brought Orellana fame finally defeated him, and he died from illness and grief there in November 1546.

the Río Napo. Its central streets, Napo and Amazonas, run north–south and are busiest in the few blocks around the river, though the town's produce **market**, *municipio* and bus station are a dozen blocks to the north. Napo even looks quite respectable now, but you only have to peek down the parallel roads to the east to see the town's shabbier side. Most hotels, restaurants and bus companies are along the southern end of Napo or around the waterfront. A block east of Amazonas, the main road from Lago Agrio leads into the town centre before continuing south to a large metal bridge over the river, the start of the **Vía Auca**, a newly colonized oil road tearing south through the jungle to the ríos Tiputini and Shiripuno.

With fewer tourist facilities than Lago Agrio or Tena, and with nothing to see or do, Coca is still a town you'll not want to linger in. After all, its only real attraction as the last major town on the Río Napo is as a gateway to the primary rainforest downstream or south along the Vía Auca. Coca is an ideal jumping-off point for **tours** (see box overleaf) to some of the remotest parts of the Ecuadorian Amazon and offers the best access to the vast **Parque Nacional Yasuní** (see p.316) and the neighbouring **Huaorani Reserve**. It takes the best part of a day on the river to reach the remoter areas, so consider a tour of over three days to allow for more than one full day in the jungle. Some of Ecuador's best **jungle lodges** (see p.290) are also found on this stretch of the Río Napo, though if planning to stay at one you should book before

Tours from Coca

A growing number of local **guides** and **tour agencies** operate out of Coca. For the most part, however, their standard of guiding is only middling (with the exception of those mentioned below), and very few speak English. Always make it clear what you expect from your tour and whether or not essential equipment (see p.285) and transport is included. Touring out of Coca without a guide is not recommended.

Tour operators and guides

Emerald Forest Expeditions Napo and Espejo ☎06/882285. Their tours to Pañacocha are usually arranged in Quito (for details, see box, p.288), but you may be able to graft yourself onto a trip through here.

Expediciones Jarrín Padre Camilo Torrano, opposite *Oasis* ☎06/880860. A simple lodge on the Río Pañayacu in the Pañacocha area with 7 square kilometres of private forest. Meet your guide before your trip – they can be a bit hit or miss. Around $45 per person per day.

River Dolphin Expeditions Napo 432 and García Moreno ☎06/881563 or 880489. Led by Randy Smith, a Canadian author (see "Books" p.556) with ten years' experience of rainforest ecotourism and conservation in Ecuador. He gives tailor-made trips into any part of the Oriente, typically of 5 to 12 days, including trips to Pañacocha, Huaorani communities and the Río Shiripuno. His colleague is Ramiro Viteri, a Quichua from the Pastaza forests, who's also an experienced guide and professional chef. From $70 to $200 per person per day, depending on itinerary.

Wimper Torres ☎06/880336 or 881196, or contact through Mady Duarte in Quito on ☎02/2659311. Enthusiastic guide offering tours of various lengths to the ríos Tiputini and Shiripuno south of Coca, and the Pañacocha area off the Río Napo. Spanish speaking only. Around $40 per person per day.

Indigenous-community stays

Amasanga ask at the FCUNAE headquarters (Federación de Comunas Unión de Nativos de la Amazonia Ecuatoriana) opposite *La Misión* hotel. An enterprise owned and operated by the Quichua community of San Luis de La Armenia, 13km west of Coca. Tours are offered to other Quichua communities down the Río Napo, south to the Río Tiputini and the Yasuní reserve, or west up the Río Payamino to the Sumaco park. $35–40 per person per day.

arriving in Coca. The Vía Auca is the fastest way to get to Huaorani communities ("auca" means "savages" in Quichua), but make sure your guide has full permission from the communities to visit.

Following Ecuador's improved relations with **Peru** since 1999, Coca is also emerging as the departure point for Iquitos in the Peruvian Amazon via the newly opened border crossing at **Nuevo Rocafuerte**. The river journey takes at least five relatively uncomfortable – but exciting – days, and at the moment is not particularly well established for tourists. Before you attempt this route, you must check border conditions and requirements with the Jefetura Provincial de Migración (on Napo opposite *El Auca*), where you also need to get your exit stamp. For more information on getting to Peru see "Boats" in "Listings" on p.310 and refer to Nuevo Rocafuerte on p.318.

Arrival, information and getting around

Coca's **bus terminal** is on Napo and Sergio Saenz, twelve blocks north of the waterfront, but the major bus companies also arrive and depart from offices on

ACCOMMODATION
El Auca	2
Hostería Amazonas Coca	3
La Misión	4
Oasis	5
Puerto Orellana	1

RESTAURANTS
Emerald Forest Blues Bar	E
Medianoche	B
Ocaso	D
Parrilladas Argentinas	A
Rock Café	C

Bus Terminal (5 blocks)

Airport entrance, ❶ (2 km) & Lago Agrio

JUAN MONTALVO

Airport

BOLÍVAR

Trans Zacaray ★   ★ Trans Baños

Ministerio (i)
del Ambiente

CUENCA

Trans Esmeraldas ★   ★ Flota Loja

Ⓐ

ROCAFUERTE

Ⓑ ■ TAME
❷

Flota Pelileo ★

GARCÍA MORENO   GARCÍA MORENO

Ⓒ ■ River Dolphin
Expeditions

ELOY ALFARO

Ⓓ

Ⓔ

ESPEJO

Capitanía

PADRE CAMILO TORRANO

❹

❸

Dock (i)

❺

0   100 m

Río Napo

COCA

Via Auca

or near Napo, a few blocks from the river (see "Listings" overleaf, for details). The main road from Lago Agrio comes in from the northeast, passing the airport, and some buses may drop you on this road at the fringes of the town centre. You can walk in, but white pick-up trucks – the town's **taxis** – usually patrol the main routes and can take you to any destination in town for $1. The entrance to the **airport** is about 1km down the Lago Agrio road from the town centre. **Boat** arrivals come in at the municipal dock between Napo and Amazonas, but some of the smarter tour companies use the dock at *La Misión* hotel.

The **Ministerio del Ambiente** on Amazonas and Bolívar (Mon–Fri 8am–12pm & 2–6pm; ☎06/880171) can answer questions about the Parque Nacional Yasuní, nearby reserves and any new ecotourism initiatives. At the time of writing, they were also setting up the **Centro de Interpretación Ambiental y Turística** on the waterfront opposite the Capitanía, which may be able to provide general information. Most of the local tour agencies (see opposite), who can provide additional information, are within a few blocks of the southern end of Napo on the waterfront.

Accommodation

Coca has a number of very cheap **places to stay** geared to oil workers, but most fail to pass muster. The result is that there are few good budget choices in town, but if you're willing to fork out a little extra then you'll be well catered for.

El Auca Napo and García Moreno ℡06/880127, ℗880600. Located a block or so away from most of the bus offices, this is the most popular hotel and your best bet if hoping to hook up with a tour group, even though its prices have recently gone up. Its large garden makes a peaceful haven from Coca's bustle, fronted by wooden cabins that are clean and compact, with fans, private bath and electric showers. More expensive rooms come with a/c and cable TV, while cheaper, smaller rooms without hot water are also offered. ❺.

La Hostería Amazonas Coca corner of Espejo and 12 de Febrero ℡06/880444. A good option for its bright fresh rooms (some with river views) with fans or a/c, private bath, hot water and cable TV. The hotel also has a bar, restaurant and Internet service, and camping is possible in the grounds outside for free. ❺

La Misión Padre Camilo Torano ℡06/880544, ℗880547, ✉hlamision@hotmail.com. One of Coca's better long-established hotels, offering slightly dated but comfortable rooms, furnished with mocha carpets, cable TV, phone, fridge and a/c for a little extra. It's in a quiet location over-looking the Río Napo, and guests can cool off in the pool. ❺–❻

Oasis Parde Camilo Toranno, east of the bridge ℡06/880206. The town's cheapest passable place, the *Oasis*' scraggy exterior is compensated for with decent rooms that have private bathrooms and battered fans. For a few dollars extra, rooms with hot water and a TV are also available. ❸–❹

Puerto Orellana 2km from the centre on the Lago Agrio road, near the Texaco station ℡06/880970. Coca's newest and plushest hotel is still under construction, but what is finished fea-tures comfortable rooms all with a/c, private bath, hot water, cable TV and phones. ❻

Eating and drinking

There's no shortage of cheap and unattractive **restaurants** dishing up fried chicken and beer to oil-workers in Coca, but few to be excited about. *El Auca* (see above) has a good air-conditioned restaurant patronized by tourists and better-off locals, and a jar of their delicious lemonade is a good antidote to the heat. Next door, on the other side of reception, you can buy ice cream too. Late-night meals are available from *Medianoche* on Napo opposite *El Auca*, which is open from 6pm to 2am. *La Misión*'s restaurant is pricier than its rivals, but the food and service are good. *Ocaso*, on Eloy Alfaro and Napo, is very pop-ular with locals and serves up hearty portions at a decent price. *Parrilladas Argentinas* on Cuenca and Inés is best for chargrilled steaks, chicken and chops.

The *Emerald Forest Blues Bar*, on Espejo and Napo, is a good place to meet travellers, check your email and have a drink, while the *Rock Café*, on García Moreno and Napo, is bright and clean, and also popular for a glass or two.

Listings

Airlines Icaro is represented at *La Misión* ℡06/880546, ℗880997. Tame, cnr of Napo and Rocafuerte (℡06/881078, ℗880768), has had no service since 1998 when their planes were ruled unsuitable for the airport; they await reinstate-ment. Flights are busy so book well in advance and reconfirm regularly. For frequencies see "Travel details" p.345.

Boats Boats (motorized canoes) to jungle lodges are always prearranged for travellers as part of their tour. A regular public service downstream to Nuevo Rocafuerte ($15 for Ecuadorians, usually around $25 for foreigners; a 13hr trip, often broken for the night en route) leaves early (5–7am) Monday and Thursday, returning early on Thursday and Sunday. It stops at requested villages on the way. There's not much regular public traffic apart

from this, but ask at the Capitanía for boat departure schedules as you can often negotiate a ride. For example, Peruvian cargo boats returning to Peru (usually in the third week of the month) are generally willing to take passengers. There is no regular service upstream to Misahuallí, as most people now go there by the Coca–Tena road. Boat charters are available at Coop de Transportes Fluvial Orellana, Napo and Espejo (℡06/880223; very irregular hours), but are likely to be pricey. Note that you must register at the Capitanía before you leave Coca by boat; if going to Peru, you must also get your passport stamped at Migración.

Buses Trans Esmeraldas and Trans Baños run the best services to Quito, and you should buy tickets in advance. Note that it's faster to go via Loreto than Lago Agrio, a route that's also regarded as

safer at night. Trans Esmeraldas has two nightly
buses for Quito; Trans Baños has four buses daily
to Quito via Lago Agrio and three nightly via Loreto,
and other buses to Ambato, Tena, Baños,
Riobamba, Puyo and Guayaquil; Flota Loja runs two
nightly buses to Quito and one evening bus to
Santo Domingo, Machala and Loja; Flota Pelileo
has a bus to Ambato, Tena and Puyo; Trans
Jumandy, at the terminal, has a regular service to
Tena and Puyo. Buses and *rancheras* to local
destinations, including Lago Agrio and south down
the oil road to the ríos Tiputini and Shiripuno, leave
from the bus terminal.
Capitanía Amazonas, opposite the dock

☎06/880231.
Exchange No banks in Coca exchange currency.
El Auca (see "Accommodation", opposite) changes
traveller's cheques.
Internet facilities Several on and around Napo,
including *Emerald Forest Blues Bar* on Espejo and
Napo.
Migration police upstairs on Napo and
Rocafuerte, over the street from *El Auca*.
Telephone office Andinatel, cnr of Eloy Alfaro and
6 de Diciembre. Long-distance calls are notorious-
ly unreliable from Coca. Mon–Fri 8am–4pm &
5–9pm, Sat & Sun 8–11am & 5–8pm.

Coca to Tena by road

If you've come into Coca from Lago Agrio in the north, there are two other
ways you can leave town: by **river to the east** (see below), or by **road to the
west**, all the way to Tena. Though it's also possible to head west by boat up the
Río Napo, there's no public service and the six-hour bus ride is far faster and
more convenient (for more transport information see "Listings" opposite).
Cutting across wild country, the journey is roughly split in half between traversing a substantial tract of lowlands and winding through the Andean piedmont. A new bridge over the Río Payamino and a freshly surfaced road have
made the ride more comfortable than it once was, but on hot days bus drivers
seek what little shade the roadside offers over the road's first stretch, even if it
means driving on the wrong side for miles on end. The only town of any
importance on the road is **LORETO** about 57km from Coca. Should you take
the unusual step of alighting here, you'll find a basic hotel, an Andinatel office,
a police station and little else. Shortly afterwards, the road begins coiling up
into the foothills and at around 30km beyond Loreto you'll pass the guard station for the **Sumaco Napo-Galeras** national park (see p.328) at the hamlet
of **Guagua Sumaco**, its best access point. As you snake up into the hills, ford-
ing streams and overcoming the rubble of old landslides, you get some
astounding views of the plush carpet of the Napo basin unfurling to the horizon. Some 135km from Coca, you reach Narupa, a tiny hamlet that marks the
junction with the Baeza–Tena highway. From here, it's about 35km south to
Tena, or 40km north to Baeza.

East of Coca

From Coca, the muddy waters of the lower Río Napo flow in broad curves for
over 200km to **Nuevo Rocafuerte** on the Peruvian border. Long, motorized
canoes ply the shallow river, searching for the deepest channels between large
and slowly shifting sandbanks, while half-submerged logs wag vigorously in the
currents. The region is only sparsely populated, and you'll pass just the odd
Quichua homestead linked to the riverbank by steep dirt footpaths. The Río
Napo is the region's motorway, and its network of tributaries and backwaters
forms the basic infrastructure to remote indigenous communities deep within
the remaining tracts of pristine rainforest. In the forests to the south, between

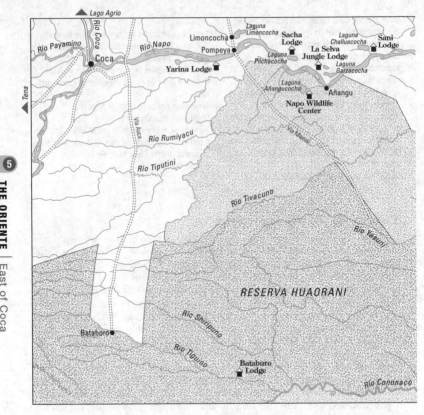

the ríos Napo and Curaray, lies the **Huaorani Reserve**, home to about 2000 people. Their territory acts as a buffer zone to the **Parque Nacional Yasuní**, Ecuador's largest national park, protecting a number of habitats and an extraordinary wealth of flora and fauna.

Since Coca became more accessible in the 1970s, this wild part of the eastern Oriente has been one of the country's top natural attractions, and also the location of several of the best **jungle lodges** (see box, p.314), which provide the most comfortable way of experiencing the rainforest here. Many of them have an observation tower – a high vantage point to see life in the jungle canopy that's all but invisible from the ground – and own private reserves close to much larger national parks. A number of less expensive jungle-**tour operators** (see boxes on p.288 & p.308) also run trips down the Río Napo from Coca, some using their own basic accommodation, others making do with tents and campsites. If your tour is going into Huaorani territory, it's important that the operator has full permission from the community concerned to do so and is making a satisfactory contribution to it. **Añangu**, three hours from Coca, on the edge of the Parque Nacional Yasuní, is one of the few indigenous communities along the lower Napo that has developed an ecotourism programme.

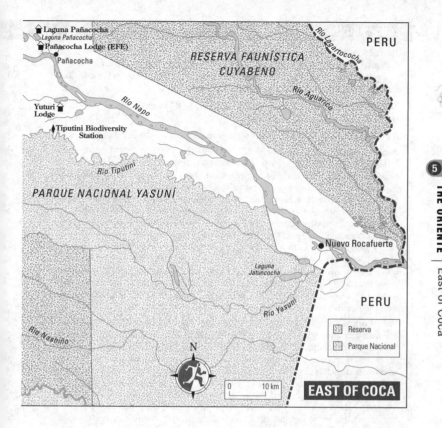

Laguna Pañacocha
Laguna Pañacocha
Pañacocha Lodge (EFE)
Pañacocha

RESERVA FAUNÍSTICA CUYABENO

PERU

Río Lagartococha

Río Napo

Río Aguarico

Yuturi Lodge

Tiputini Biodiversity Station

Río Tiputini

PARQUE NACIONAL YASUNÍ

Nuevo Rocafuerte

Laguna Jatuncocha

Río Yasuní

PERU

Río Nasbiño

N

Reserva
Parque Nacional

0   10 km

EAST OF COCA

Pompeya and Limoncocha

Taking a motorized canoe about 1 hour 30 minutes downstream from Coca will bring you to **POMPEYA**, 33km away. The houses of this tiny settlement on the north bank of the Napo are barely visible from the river, but a heap of unsightly, rusting containers left by the oil industry announces a human presence. At the eastern edge of the settlement are the sparkling whitewashed buildings of the Misión Capuchina, where there's a good collection of ceramics and pre-Columbian objects from the Oriente in their **Museo de Cicame**. It doesn't get many visitors, so if you want to see it ask your tour guide for a quick stop there on your way to or from your destination. Walking west from the mission brings you to Pompeya's **market** area, active on Saturday mornings, when communities from along the Napo bring their home produce up for sale. It's an intimate affair, with traders' first names daubed onto their stalls.

About a thirty-minute drive north on the bumpy road from Pompeya is the pleasant village of **LIMONCOCHA**, where neat cabins are set at regular intervals, some bordered by trimmed hedges and carefully tended lawns. Just a short walk from the village is the **Reserva Biológica Limoncocha**, conserving 46 square kilometres of rainforest and swamps around the light-green waters of **Laguna Limoncocha**. The lake used to be a good place for spotting caiman,

Lodges on the lower Río Napo

These **lodges on the lower Río Napo** are reached by a motor-canoe ride from Coca (included in the price), and are usually visited in stays of four or five days, by prior reservation from home or Quito, where most have an office. Note that prices quoted do not include bus or air transport to and from Coca.

Fundación Pañacocha Lodge see "Pañacocha" p.316.

Napo Wildlife Center see "Añangu" p.315.

Pañacocha Lodge operated by Emerald Forest Expeditions. See box on p.288.

Sacha Lodge Julio Zaldumbide 375 and Toledo, PO Box 17-21-1608, Quito ⓣ02/2566090, 2509504 or 2509115, ⓕ2236521, ⓦwww.sachalodge.com. One of Ecuador's most luxurious jungle lodges, 80km from Coca on the marshy fringes of Pilchacocha, *Sacha* is surrounded by 13 square kilometres of its own primary forest. Cabins have screened windows and sealed ceilings (mosquito nets are unnecessary), private bath, ceiling fans and verandas with hammocks, and are connected to a dining room and observation deck. There's 24-hour hot water and electricity from a generator, plus laundry facilities. Activities include well-marked trails of varying difficulty, plus a canoe trip to a 43-metre observation tower soaring over the canopy – 565 bird species have been seen. There are also tours of its butterfly farm. Each tour group gets its own English-speaking naturalist and Quichua guide. You can combine stays here with trips to *La Casa del Suizo* (see p.332), owned by the same group, and at *Las Termas de Papallacta* (see p.294). Discounts are available for children and SAE members. $1190 a double for four days, $1500 for five days.

Sani Lodge Pasaje Chantilly, Roca 736 and Amazonas, Quito ⓣ02/2558881, ⓦwww.sanilodge.com. About 18km downstream of Añangu and four hours' canoe ride from Coca, on the remote Laguna Challuacocha, the *Sani Lodge* is set in 40,000 acres of community-owned forests, an excellent place to spot some 550 bird species and wildlife such as the manatee and large black caiman that inhabit the lake. It's a small and comfortable lodge, built by the Sani Isla Quichua community with the help of experienced lodge managers, comprising eight screened and thatched cabins, each with private bathroom and solar-power hot showers, and a bar and dining room overlooking Challuacocha. A thirty-metre observation tower

but when Occidental Petroleum developed five oil fields near here in 1992, the blasting and drilling within spitting distance badly disturbed wildlife populations. Pressure from local groups, particularly the Secoya, has tempered oil exploitation here, allowing a formidable diversity of bird species to re-establish themselves – over 460 species have been recorded, including several endemics such as the Martín kingfisher. The reserve's other lake, the black-water **Laguna Yanacocha**, lying to the east and enveloped in vegetation, is steeped in local myth and is rumoured to be home to especially large anacondas.

Many local families happily accept visitors into their homes and there are some old community-owned tourist cabañas in the reserve that may soon be rehabilitated; either way, for a **place to stay**, drop-ins should be accommodated. Several **buses** and **rancheras** service Limoncocha from Shushufindi about 1 hour 30 minutes away (see p.305), which itself is easily accessible from either Lago Agrio or Coca. Only three *rancheras* continue on to Pompeya, returning immediately, roughly corresponding to the working day at 6am, noon and 4pm, though timetables are liable to change. From Coca it's much faster to get to Pompeya by motorized canoe, but availability can be a problem.

provides a better view of the canopy, and there are a number of trails that give access to different lacustrine ecosystems, which you can visit with a local expert as well as a multilingual naturalist. It's a new lodge, and at the time of writing rates were very good value at an introductory rate of $285 per person for three nights. Profits are reinvested in community projects.

La Selva Jungle Lodge 6 de Diciembre 2816 and Paul Rivet, Quito ℡02/2550995 or 2554686, Ⓕ2567297, Ⓦwww.laselvajunglelodge.com. About 10km past *Sacha Lodge*, by picturesque Laguna Garzacocha, is the award-winning *La Selva*. Cabins are simple, with kerosene lamps, mosquito nets, private bath and cold water. Food is excellent, drawing on French, North American and Ecuadorian disciplines. The area has a good reputation for wildlife and they can provide you with Quichua ornithologist guides. Excursions include night walks, caiman-watching, canoe journeys, trips to a forty-metre observation tower, plus the "Amazon Light Brigade", a week of both demanding and easy hiking, ending each day at a pre-prepared campsite where cocktails and dinner await. Its butterfly farm produces specimens for export, plus the Neotropical Field Biology Institute here means there are working scientists *in situ*. $1152 a double for four days, $1380 for five days.

Yarina Lodge Amazonas N24-236 and Colón, Quito ℡ & Ⓕ02/2503225 or 2504037, Ⓦwww.yuturi.com. Only an hour from Coca, on the south bank of the Napo, so you're less likely to spot the variety of wildlife other lodges boast. Nearby is *tierra firme*, seasonally flooded and secondary forest to tour with Quichua guides. $50 per person per day.

Yuturi Lodge Amazonas N24-236 and Colón, Quito ℡ & Ⓕ02/2503225 or 2504037, Ⓦwww.yuturi.com. At 180km (5hr) from Coca, these simple cabins (mosquito nets are a necessity) are on a small hill surrounded by a lake on one of the Napo's tributaries. The surrounding forest is on loan from local Quichua, who help with guiding. English-speaking guides are available, but having some Spanish makes tours more rewarding. Possible excursions include trips to Huarmi Yuturi, canoe expeditions to Manduro Lagoon, and visits to Quichua families. Four days cost around $280 per person, five days $330.

Añangu

The Quichua community of **AÑANGU**, on the south shore of the Napo, about 66km downstream of Coca between *Sacha* and *La Selva* lodges, has access to two stunning natural resources. First, inside the northern reaches of the Parque Nacional Yasuní (see overleaf) and only an hour's walk west from the community, is **Añangucocha**, one of the largest lakes in the region. It's bordered by dense forest, where peccaries and pumas forage and the waters twitch with caimans, piranhas and *paiche*, a fish that reputedly nudges the 200-pound mark (though there are rumours that some weigh twice as much). Secondly, the area is also excellent for bird watchers, holding 560 species and two **parrot licks** (an exposed clay bank) near the community, which provide an extraordinary spectacle as thousands of parrots squabble over the best perches to peck at the clay, gulping the stuff down for its mineral-rich content and to improve digestion of the harsh acidic fruits they usually eat.

In 2002, the community built its own **lodge**, the *Napo Wildlife Center* (reservations in advance in Quito on ℡02/2894525, Ⓔecotours@uio.satnet.net, Ⓦwww.ecoecuador.org), composed of ten beautiful and spacious cabins on

Añangucocha, with private bathrooms, hot water, electric lights, and hammocks on porches overlooking the lake. Next to the dining room, a fifteen-metre observation tower constructed on top of a hill allows you to rake over the forest canopy with binoculars for monkeys and bird species. Highlights of a stay here include possible sightings of giant otters; walks down the "manakin trail" where six species of manakin can be spotted; and visits to the parrot licks, where hides have been built for better observation of the blue-headed and orange-cheeked parrots, cobalt-winged parakeets, scarlet-fronted parrotlets and scarlet macaws, to name just a few, that feed there in a frenzy of sound and colour. Jungle walks and canoe rides are led by expert and extremely knowledgeable local guides who also work as Yasuní park rangers, backed up by bilingual naturalists. A three-night package costs $595, and four nights is $795 per person in a double, including boat transport from Coca.

Pañacocha

Roughly 100km, or five hours, downstream of Coca, and then doubling back for a few more kilometres northwest and upstream along the Pañayacu, brings you to the brooding waters of **PAÑACOCHA** ("piranha lake" in Quichua), the centrepiece of a 560-square-kilometre protected forest created in 1994, connecting the enormous Yasuní and Cuyabeno reserves on either side. From the lake, several coiling waterways retreat into thick primary rainforest, where ocelots, jaguars, nine species of monkey and over five hundred bird species can be seen. As well as the eponymous **piranha** – which are unnervingly easy to catch in the murky waters – the rivers are home to beautiful freshwater dolphins, rosy-pink mammals that locate their prey using sonar. Although the area has remained relatively untouched from outside interference, the new protected forest has no government resources or management plan, leaving it vulnerable to exploitation and damage. There are reports that an oil company has built illegal seismic exploration lines within the protected area.

Standing at the edge of the lake is an old **lodge**, basically a collection of rustic wood-and-thatch cabins with private bathrooms, which was recently bought by the **Fundación Pañacocha**, a conservation organization which is primarily concerned with establishing a forest corridor through Pañacocha between the Cuyabeno and Yasuní protected areas. Money raised from tours here will go towards this end and to protect the core of the Pañacocha reserve from oil activity, and if successful will then be used for full renovation work on the lodge to establish it as a scientific research station, and ecotourism projects with the local Quichua community. Prices are a competitive $50 per day per person, and **volunteers** are also welcome for general maintenance work and other related projects at greatly reduced rates. For more **information** on staying here, contact Maritza Cienfuentes in Quito on ℡02/2231768 or ℡09/7614706, or try the Centro de Investigaciones de los Bosques Tropicales (CIBT), PO Box 17-7-8726, Quito (℡02/2231768 or 2865176).

Emerald Forest Expeditions (see box on p.288) run tours to their **lodge** on the Pañayacu, a little downstream of Pañacocha, for around $60 per person per day.

Parque Nacional Yasuní

By far Ecuador's largest national park, **Yasuní** ($10) encompasses just under 10,000 square kilometres of tropical rainforest around the basins of the ríos Tiputini, Yasuní, Nashiño and Curaray. The gap at the western end, in the shape of a giant horseshoe, was made into a reserve in 1990 (**Reserva Huaorani**) for the 21 Huaorani communities living here, a 6000-square-kilometre buffer zone preventing colonization and oil exploitation from the west.

The Yasuní reserve is part of the "Napo Pleistocene refuge", an area of rainforest thought to have survived the ravages of the ice age, allowing species here to thrive and diversify, generating scores of endemic species. It's theorized that this long period of development is why the Amazon rainforest is much more biodiverse than its African and Asian counterparts, which were affected by the ice age. In fact, Yasuní claims almost sixty percent of Ecuador's **mammal species**, including 81 species of bat, as well as larger animals such as jaguars, ocelots, tapirs, twelve primate species, and aquatic mammals like pink freshwater dolphins, manatee and giant otters. Over 520 **bird species** have been recorded, including harpy eagles and sunbitterns, and one recent botanical study found 473 **tree species** in only one hectare, which is thought to be a world record. Most of the reserve consists of dry upland humid tropical forest (*tierra firme*), but other life zones include **seasonally flooded forest** (*várzea*) and permanently flooded *igapó* **swamp forest**. Even today, scientists believe they've only scratched the surface of identifying all life here, with hundreds of species yet to be discovered.

Because of Yasuní's importance, UNESCO was quick to declare it an International Biosphere Reserve in 1979, two months before the park's official creation, to strengthen its position as protected land before **oil companies** could start prospecting. Despite this, the park is under attack from several of them, and roads have already been built into the protected areas. At Pompeya (see p.313), barges ferry oil vehicles across the Río Napo to a gravel road, known as the **Vía Maxus** after the oil company that built it, which cuts right through the northern arm of the park for 150km. Even though entrance to the park here is monitored to allow in only oil-workers and indigenous groups – three small **Huaorani communities** live inside Yasuní – in order to prevent settlers from colonizing the forest, the road destroyed fifty salt pans, centres of animal activity, and was built of contaminated waste material. Nor is this the only source of concern: as many as four oil companies are operating inside the park, one of them routinely dumping 400–500 barrels per day of waste drilling water. The **damage** hasn't only been environmental, as the Huaorani living in and around the reserve have suffered from interference from oil companies, who have exploited community divisions, spoiled hunting grounds and polluted water supplies.

Visiting the park

Yasuní may be Ecuador's largest national park, but it's an inaccessible tract of rainforest that remains relatively unexplored. Visiting independently is not recommended, being costly and possibly unwittingly damaging to the communities that live there. Three Huaorani groups, the **Tagaeri**, **Taromenane** and **Oñamenane**, have rejected all contact with the outside world, and are understandably hostile to the uninvited. Several tour operators arrange adventure tours into the park (see boxes on p.288 & p.308), but if they are visiting Huaorani villages, be sure that they have permission. Day-trips are sometimes offered from nearby *Sacha* or *La Selva* jungle lodges (see box, p.314), and it is also possible to **stay inside the park** at the *Napo Wildlife Center* near Añangu (see p.315), in its northwestern reaches, or at the *Bataburo Lodge* on the Río Tigüino, inside the Reserva Huaorani, operated by Kem Pery Tours (see p.288) in partnership with the Huaorani communities. You might also try the **Tiputini Biodiversity Station** (in the US ☎ & ☎512/263-0830, ✉tiputini@aol.com or ✉tbs@mail .usfq.edu.ec), built primarily for research, education and conservation by Quito's

San Francisco University and Boston University, which is on the Río Tiputini at the northern fringes of the park. It's reputed to be one of the best places in the Oriente to see wildlife, as the area has largely escaped interference. Facilities for visitors include rooms with cold showers and flushing toilets, and there's electricity for several hours a day. Rainforest education programmes are offered, as well as tailor-made sessions for specific groups according to their interests. From Coca, you'll be taken to the Vía Maxus, where you'll need to show a **valid yellow-fever vaccination certificate** and your **passport** to be permitted to travel down it. After a ninety-minute drive, you'll be transferred to a boat and then it's a further two hours down the Río Tiputini. A typical week-long workshop costs around $1500 per person.

Nuevo Rocafuerte and crossing to Peru

Thirteen hours downstream of Coca, **NUEVO ROCAFUERTE** is about as far as you can go along the Río Napo before the Peruvian border. It's a small town of limited resources with a clear police and military presence. Nuevo Rocafuerte has one simple **hotel** (❷), back from the river a few blocks past the military checkpoint, with clean rooms but unreliable electricity and water, and a couple of basic restaurants. The only reason you're likely to come here is if you're travelling between Ecuador and **Peru**, a crossing made possible by improved relations between the countries since 1999. International traffic is still light, but tourist services are likely to pick up over the coming years as the crossing becomes more established – there is even talk of a boat being built to travel between Coca and Santa Rosa on the Peruvian border with Brazil. Note that border formalities can change swiftly and dramatically; keep yourself informed and check with the authorities in Coca about current conditions before coming here.

From Nuevo Rocafuerte, **boats** go over the border to **Pantoja** in Peru (2hr–2hr 30min; $6, likely to be more for foreigners), where you get an **entry stamp**. There are a couple of very cheap, basic hotels here. From Pantoja, boats leave for Iquitos. Deck space is cramped and often shared with animals; you'll be sleeping in a hammock that you may need to purchase beforehand. The journey takes four or five days: it's a four-day journey (around $20) if you get off at **Mazán**, and take a moto-taxi short cut across a huge river bend, followed by another two-hour boat trip (around $3) to **Iquitos**; staying on the Pantoja boat and navigating the bend will add thirteen hours (effectively another day) to your journey. Iquitos is a major Amazon town, with plenty of hotels, restaurants and tourist facilities, as well as onward transport by boat or air. Those coming **into Ecuador** at Nuevo Rocafuerte can pick up the boat returning to **Coca** on Thursday and Sunday mornings (departs around 5am, 15hr, usually broken en route for the night). For boat information on how to get to Nuevo Rocafuerte from Coca, see "Listings" on p.310.

Tena

When the Spanish founded Archidona in 1560, they shared out the surrounding land, displacing the indigenous Quichua population. Forced down towards the jungle, the Quichua settled on the riverbanks at the confluence of the ríos Tena and Pano, though it wasn't long before the Jesuit missionaries tracked them down, built a church and gave the settlement a name: San Juan de los Dos Ríos de Tena. The name has since shrunk, but the city has continued to grow

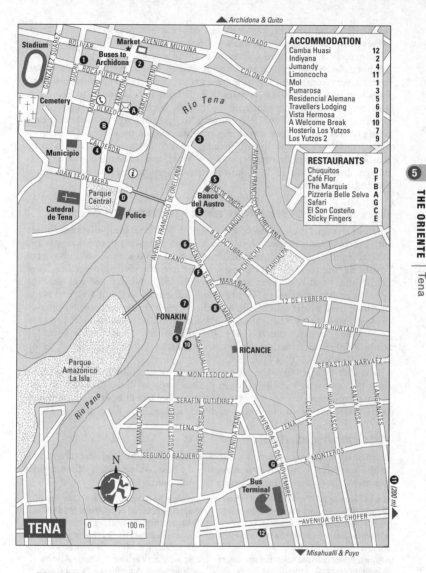

ACCOMMODATION

Camba Huasi	12
Indiyana	2
Jumandy	4
Limoncocha	11
Mol	1
Pumarosa	3
Residencial Alemana	5
Travellers Lodging	6
Vista Hermosa	8
A Welcome Break	10
Hostería Los Yutzos	7
Los Yutzos 2	9

RESTAURANTS

Chuquitos	D
Café Flor	F
The Marquis	B
Pizzería Belle Selva	A
Safari	G
El Son Costeño	C
Sticky Fingers	E

TENA

0   100 m

and **TENA** has been the Oriente's most important town for the best part of the last hundred years. It was the capital of Napo-Pastaza province from 1920, and subsequently of Napo province, which was created in 1959. The birth of the oil industry in the Oriente has seen the gradual erosion of the city's power, and it has lost a huge portion of provincial territory to the new oil capitals, Lago Agrio and Coca. But from a tourist's point of view, Tena is by far the most agreeable of the three big towns in the northern Oriente. The town has made the most of its popularity with visitors and **ecotourism** now makes a signifi-cant part of the local economy. This is one of the best centres in the Oriente to arrange a stay with a Quichua group, mostly in communities that are easily reached by road or river. Don't expect to see much wildlife on these trips, however, especially larger mammals – although small pockets of primary forest remain, most land has been colonized or overhunted.

A huge number of tributaries converge around Tena at the head of the Napo basin. River rapids, waterfalls, mountain streams, sand and pebble beaches allow for a host of water-based **activities**. A tour from Tena is bound to involve at least one of swimming, climbing up brooks, bathing in waterfalls, tubing, kayaking or rafting. Word is beginning to spread across the international **white-water rafting** and **kayaking** grapevines about the scores of runs, from Class I to Class V, all within easy striking distance of town. It's a hot tip to be a major white-water destination in a few years, and a sizeable kayaking contingent already comes to Tena during the northern hemisphere's off season in December and January.

Arrival, information and getting around

The bus terminal, 1km south of the centre, is where all **long-distance buses** stop except those from Archidona, which arrive at the corner of Amazonas and Bolívar in the northern part of town. **Local buses**, such as those from Misahuallí, use part of the terminal fronting Avenida 15 de Noviembre. Most of the hotels and restaurants are on Avenida 15 de Noviembre and near the river on both sides of town. For **maps** and **information** about Tena and Napo province, head to the tourist office on the western riverfront between the two bridges (Mon–Fri 8.30am–5pm). For information on trips to local Quichua communities contact the RICANCIE office on Av 15 de Noviembre 774 (☎06/887953, ✉ricancie@ecuanex.net.ec), or try the FONAKIN offices on Agusto Rueda 242 (☎06/886288).

Tena isn't a large town and it's easy enough to get around on foot: walking from the central park in the north to the bus terminal in the far south should-n't take more than twenty minutes. White pick-up trucks operate as the town's **taxis**, and will take you to any in-town destination for a fixed price of $1.

Accommodation

Tena offers a far greater choice of decent **places to stay** than any other town in the northern Oriente, with a number of good-value hotels offering such luxuries as hot water, cable TV and air conditioning.

Camba Huasi Av del Chofer and Ruben Lerzón ☎06/887429. An imposing concrete hotel next to the bus terminal with clean, no-nonsense rooms with private bath and fan. Fine for a cheap night if you're on the move. ❷

Indiyana Bolívar between Amazonas and García Moreno ☎06/886334. A friendly and well-presented, family-run hotel offering a handful of big, light rooms with polished wooden floors, cable TV, private bath and hot water, and a laundry service. Good value, with breakfast included. ❸

Jumandy Calderón 309 and Amazonas ☎06/886419. *Residencial* featuring a pretty communal balcony and potted plants that go a long way towards making up for the grubby walls, cramped rooms and thin mattresses. Passably clean, however, and very cheap. ❶

Limoncocha Sangay 533, about 300m east of the bus terminal, off Av del Chofer ☎06/887583, ✉limoncocha@andinanet.net. Good-value German-Ecuadorian family hostel on a hillrise with a pleasant prospect over town, even if it is a little out of the way. There's a range of rooms, with the best having fan, cable TV and electric shower. Amenities include kitchen and Internet facilities, and jungle and rafting tours are also on offer. ❷

Mol Sucre 432 and Bolívar ☎06/886215 or 886808. A bit grimy on the outside even though it's actually one of Tena's more exclusive and pricier hotels. Some of the flowery, pink rooms come with balconies and a/c, but all have hot water from a solar-powered heater. ❺

Pumarosa Francisco de Orellana ☎06/886320. A complex on the river with a volleyball court, bar, restaurant, gardens, games room and disco (it can be noisy Fri & Sat). The hotel rooms vary in size and some have a/c so keep asking until you're satisfied. ❸–❹

Residencial Alemana Av 15 de Noviembre 210 and Diaz de Pineda ☎06/886409. Deck chairs and chirping insects line a plant-filled courtyard. The owners are friendly, and although rooms are on the dark side each has private bath and are regularly sprayed for bugs; those with electric showers, cable TV and fan cost double but are still inexpensive. Go for a room away from the road. ❷–❸

Travellers Lodging Av 15 de Noviembre 438 and 9 de Octubre ☎06/886372. A good meeting place, this hotel has everything the gringo needs – a tour agency, a restaurant and a pizzeria next door, a laundry service, and rooms with private bath and

Tena tour operators

If you don't have time to make the necessary arrangements to stay with an indigenous community (see box overleaf), you might consider a **jungle tour** with an operator who can organize a trip relatively swiftly. Several Tena operators are also run by local Quichua, and might include visits to local communities on their itineraries. Many of these tour operators offer **rafting trips** too, but be sure to check safety standards first; there should be a kayaker to accompany you, and the guide should have accreditation, ideally from AGAR.

Agency Limoncocha see hotel *Limoncocha* opposite. For rafting and jungle tours. Around $30–40 per day.

Amarongachi Jungle Trips contact through *Travellers Lodging* (see above). Consistently good operator offering nights in a cabaña on a cliff 100m above the Río Anzu or another on the Jatunyacu, plus stays with a Quichua community in primary forest on the Río Jatunyacu. Around $40 per day.

Runa Ñambi Av 15 de Noviembre 7-23, also at Av Orellana and Pano ☎06886301 or 886318. Jungle, rafting and kayaking trips, and jungle tours to the Runa Huasi community or the *Sinchi Sacha* lodge. $35–40 per person.

Sacharicsina Tour Montesdeoca 110 and Pano ☎06/886839, @sacharicsinatour @yahoo.com. Run by a Quichua family who have some rustic cabañas on the Río Illoculín, southwest of Tena. Rafting, horse riding, waterfalls and jungle walks are on the agenda for $30–40 per day.

Sacha Ursay Jungle Tour cnr of Tena and Agusto Rueda ☎06/886143, @sachaursay @yahoo.com. Tours led by a Quichua guide who can speak some English to cabins on the Achiyacu river, not far from the Parque Nacional Llanganates. Hikes in the park, visits to local Quichua families, walks to local petroglyphs and waterfalls are all on offer. $30 per day.

White-water rafting specialists

Ríos Ecuador opposite the *Travellers Lodging*, on Av 15 de Noviembre ☎06/887438, @info@riosecuador.com; or contact Yacu Amu Rafting in Quito (see p.114). Part of the well-established Yacu Amu Rafting stable, offering rafting and kayaking trips on the Jatunyacu, Misahuallí and Anzu rivers. Expect to pay $50–65 per day.

River People Av 15 de Noviembre and 9 Octubre, opposite the footbridge ☎06/887887 or 888349, @garypdent@hotmail.com. Professional English-run outfit with good guides, offering a range of river-based tours including 1–14-day kayak trips; rafting on the Jatunyacu, Blanco, Toachi and Quijos rivers ($50 including good picnic lunch); kayaking schools; and a combined rafting and jungle tour to their cabins at the confluence of the Jatunyacu and Illoculín rivers near the Parque Nacional Llanganates.

hot water. The top floors are best (and more expensive), not least for their reinforced anti-earthquake joists, cable TV and city views. ❸–❹

Vista Hermosa Av 15 de Noviembre 622 and 12 de Febrero ☎06/886521. As the name suggests, this *hostal* has fine views over the river from each of its open-air patios. All rooms come with fans and

cable TV, but the best to be had are at the top. ❸

A Welcome Break Agusto Rueda and 12 de Febrero ☎06/886301. Five simple, lime-green rooms with little cane lamps and desks and shared bath. Cheap, considering use of a kitchen is thrown in. ❷

Los Yutzos 2 Agusto Rueda and 12 de Febrero

Indigenous-community stays around Tena

As well as several conventional operators offering activities from jungle tours to white-water rafting (see box on p.321), Tena has a burgeoning number of **community ecotourism projects**, coordinated by RICANCIE and the Unión Huacamayos and driven largely by the region's politically active and environmentally aware Quichua population. In most cases, the whole community is involved, from the building of simple tourist cabañas near the villages to the training of their guides. Some projects have been around for a while and have well-honed programmes, while others, though no less interesting, have only received a few dozen visitors in their short histories and are rougher around the edges. Tours typically include guided forest hikes, cultural exchanges through music, dance and narration, participation in a *minga* (shared community work), panning for gold, blowpipe competitions, swimming, tubing and canoeing, discussions on the use of medicinal plants, and craftwork demonstrations.

Unión Huacamayos

The **Unión Huacamayos** consists of eleven Quichua communities. At this time, the union has one successful ecotourism project up and running, AACLLAC (Asociación Antonio Cerda de Llaucana Cocha), only fifteen minutes from Tena and the nerve centre for other union projects. The AACLLAC community, on the shores of the Río Tena, offers a mixture of excursions and cultural activities, including explanations of medicinal plants, hikes to the Cordillera de los Huacamayos, and canoeing and tubing. It's not as rough as you might thingk, as the cabañas are equipped with electricity and mosquito nets, and the food served is good. From AACLLAC you can arrange visits to the other Huacamayos communities, such as Shamato-Sardinas with its network of caves, waterfalls and cloudforests, or Santa Rita, where you can take part in their pottery workshop and examine nearby petroglyphs. Contact AACLLAC through Benito Nantipa in the mornings at FONAKIN, Agusto Rueda 242, Casilla Postal 217 (☎06/886288) or afternoons at the Museo Mundos Amazónicos in Archidona (☎06/889324). You can also ring the cabaña direct (☎06/888608). Ideally, arrangements should be made several days in advance, though drop-ins can usually be accommodated. Tours cost around $45 per person per day, all included.

RICANCIE programmes

Red Indígena del Alto Napo para la Convencia Intercultural y el Ecoturismo, or **RICANCIE**, Av 15 de Noviembre 774 (☎ & ℱ06/887953, ℮ricancie@ecuanex.net.ec), coordinate nine community-based ecotourism enterprises based in the upper Napo region around Misahuallí and Ahuano. Accommodation for the most part is in fairly rustic cabañas, usually equipped with shared showers and occasionally flushing toilets, but a few are still without running water. Circuits are available whereby you visit a series of neighbouring communities as part of one package, and prices depend on group size but are usually around $30–40 per person per day including food, lodging, transport, guides and excursions. In most cases, drop-ins cannot be accommodated and arrangements should be made a few days in advance.

Capirona on the Río Puni about 3km south of Misahuallí. One of the world's first community-based ecotourism projects, with well-marked trails through colourful

06/886717 or 886769. Budget end of the *Yutzos* operation, offering simple rooms with bunks, crisp clean sheets, private bath and hot water in a quiet part of town. Rooms at the back of the *hostal* overlook the river, as does the bar-terrace strung with hammocks. Internet and laundry facilities also available, adding up to an overall good value. ❷

Hostería Los Yutzos Agusto Rueda 190 and Av 15 de Noviembre ☎06/886717 or 886769, ⓦ www.geocities.com/losyutzos. Tena's best hotel, with a pretty, peaceful little garden overlooking the river. The rooms are smart and comfortable with hot water, cable TV, minibar, fans or a/c. Get a balcony if you can. ❺

capirona trees to a salt-lick cavern that is great for seeing nocturnal creatures. Every tour is treated to excellent cultural presentations of song, dance and the making of traditional crafts. Reservations are essential and should be made well in advance during high season.

Chuva Urcu south of Ahuano on the Río Gusano. The community has built pleasant cabañas overlooking the river, and lead strenuous two-day hikes (bring a water purifier) to the top of the Chuva Urcu mountain ridge, where fantastic views await. Other activities include gold panning, basket weaving, and spear fishing for catfish.

Cuya Loma Twenty minutes east of Tena on the Misahuallí road. Easily accessed community offering programmes strongly based on presentations of Quichua culture and traditions, and shamanic demonstrations of medicinal plant healing. One of the families has created an archeological museum displaying traditional clothes, kitchenware and hunting tools. Half- to three-day visits are possible, and drop-ins are welcome.

Huasila Talag about 12km southwest of Tena on the Río Talag. Located in the Andean foothills, this community offers mountain hikes in the nearby Cordillera de Huasila, excellent for bird watching, butterflies and orchids, and walks along the Jatunyacu. Explanations of medicinal plants are given, and in the evening villagers demonstrate how to make chicha.

Las Galeras on the Río Guambuno beyond the Río Blanco community. The community offers moderate to difficult hikes in and around the forested hills of Sumaco Napo-Galeras reserve to spectacular mountain viewpoints, along with lessons in shamanism, Quichua cooking and medicinal plants. A moving traditional farewell ceremony is enacted on the final night.

Machacuyacu 15km east of Tena, north of the Río Napo. Set in a scenic location on elevated ground dotted with viewpoints over the Napo valley, the Machacuyacu community members lead hikes throughout the picturesque landscape as well as to caves steeped in myth, and demonstrate the use of a blowgun in addition to hunting and fishing techniques.

Río Blanco north of the Río Napo and Ahuano, reached by a two-hour uphill hike. Well-established enterprise offering attractive cabañas in a peaceful setting twenty minutes' walk from the community. The typical four-day programme here includes guided hikes in the beautiful Cordillera Galeras and cultural presentations, but a highlight is the medicinal plant garden tended by an expert shaman, who can explain the uses of over four hundred species.

Runa Huasi on the Río Arajuno, near Ahuano. Easily reached from Tena, this community has prettily decorated cabañas a ten-minute walk from AmaZOOnico (see p.334), an excellent animal rehabilitation centre, which is visited during a stay. Hikes are also offered in local primary forest to a fossil lake, and lessons are given on medicinal plants.

Salazar Aitaca a 1hr drive east of Tena then a one-hour hike over steep, muddy trails. Few tourists have visited this community deep in primary forest, but after the exertions of getting there (pack light) you can enjoy beautiful waterfalls, a lagoon, petroglyphs and the best chance of spotting wildlife in the area. One for the independent, fit and adventurous.

The Town

Within sight of the Andean foothills and cooled off by its two rivers, Tena enjoys a slightly fresher climate than its oil-town rivals, Coca and Lago Agrio, and its longer, calmer history lends it a more established and civilized atmosphere. The northern half of Tena is the oldest part, with narrow streets, a modest cathedral fronting the central park, and the post and phone offices. It's the quieter half too, as most of the traffic is routed around it and over a single-lane bridge to the main thoroughfare, Avenida 15 de Noviembre that divides the more sprawling southern half of the town. The bus terminal stands at the less attractive southern fringes of the town, so don't be put off by first impressions.

Locals, a mixture of *mestizos* and Quichuas, can often be found relaxing on the city's **river beaches** – strips of sand or pebbles at the water's edge – or ambling around the pleasant **Parque Amazónico La Isla** (daily 8.30am–5pm; $2), reached by a wooden footbridge over the Río Pano about 200m south of the main pedestrian bridge. It's not actually an island but the wooded tip of a patch of land at the confluence of the rivers. A high observation tower overlooks the treetops and town, and paths meander through the greenery past caged animals recovering from injury and abuse, to swimming spots along the river.

Eating and nightlife

Inexpensive **restaurants** are two-a-penny in Tena, serving up the usual fried chicken or fish dishes for $2 to $4 a main course. Many have good-value *almuerzo* or *merienda* options, including *El Son Costeño*, inside a shopping arcade on Amazonas and Juan León Mera, which is popular with locals. It's not easy to find anything more exciting, but the more expensive hotels are the first places to start looking. Most restaurants are open every day from breakfast to 9 or 10pm at night. Tena's favourite disco is *La Gallera* at *Hotel Pumarosa* (Fri & Sat), which blasts out Latin dance hits into the small hours on its dry-iced dance floors. Otherwise head down to the waterfront, where a string of little bars have music and dance if the mood is right.

Pizzería Bella Selva Olmedo and García Moreno. A good pizza parlour housed in an open-sided thatch-roofed building. A family-size pizza packed with ham, bacon, salami, mushrooms and an egg goes for a little over $5, though you could try an exotic smaller one, topped with bananas, for $4.

Café Flor cnr of 15 de Noviembre and Agusto Rueda, upstairs. Delicious cakes, pizza, chocolate and hand-roasted coffee served in a friendly US–Ecuadorian run café.

Chuquitos García Moreno near the footbridge. A popular choice for its excellent riverside position. The meals are a bit hit and miss, but there's a huge menu ranging from *guatita* to frogs' legs to kidneys, plus all the usual staples. Closes at 9pm Mon–Fri, 4pm on Sat, and all day Sun.

Cositas Ricas Av 15 de Noviembre and 9 de Octubre. Part of *Travellers Lodging*, so it caters to the international crowd, with several vegetarian dishes on top of the usual beef, chicken, pasta and fish *platos*.

The Marquis Amazonas and Olmedo. The classiest restaurant in town by some margin, for its wine glasses and starched table linen and napkins. It's run by a professional Colombian chef who specializes in Latin American food, particularly steaks and *parrilladas* (typical main courses go for $6–10), though vegetarian dishes can be cooked on request. French and Chilean wines are also available. Closed Sun evenings.

Safari Av 15 de Noviembre and F. Montero near the bus terminal. Locally popular and straightforward eatery, serving up generous portions of the national standards (chicken, beef or fish with rice) in quick time.

Sticky Fingers Av 15 de Noviembre and 9 de Octubre. Coffee shop in the River People agency office, offering real coffee, cakes, muesli and yogurt breakfasts along with crumbles, meat pies and other treats not normally found in jungle towns.

Listings

Airlines There's no regular domestic service though a new airport is slated for this purpose, to be built in the near future. Very irregular military flights go to various Oriente towns from a runway at the north of town.

Bank Banco del Austro, cnr of Av 15 de Noviembre and Dias de Pineda, has a 24hr Visa ATM and changes traveller's cheques.

Festivals February 12 for provincialization and November 15 for the town's foundation, both of which involve drinking, dancing, the odd parade and partying.

Internet facilities For around $4–5 an hour at several places including Piraña Net, Av Orellana and Pano; sn@lme.net, Amazonas and Rocafuerte, with international calls; Selva Selva, Av 15 de Noviembre and Av Pano (open Sun).

Post office Olmedo and García Moreno.

Telephone office Andinatel, on the cnr of Olmedo and Juan Montalvo. Daily 8am–10pm.

Around Tena

Although Tena is most commonly used as a launching pad for jungle tours in the upper Napo region, there are a few places nearby that you can visit independently. To the north of Tena, a trip to the nearby colonial town of **Archidona** can be combined with a visit to the **Cuevas de Jumandy**, the most developed and easily accessed of many caves in the area, or to a local forest reserve. Beyond here, the scenery en route to Baeza (see p.295) concertinas into a range of forested gullies and ridges as you pass between two remote protected areas, the **Parque Nacional Sumaco Napo-Galeras** and the **Reserva Ecológica Antisana**.

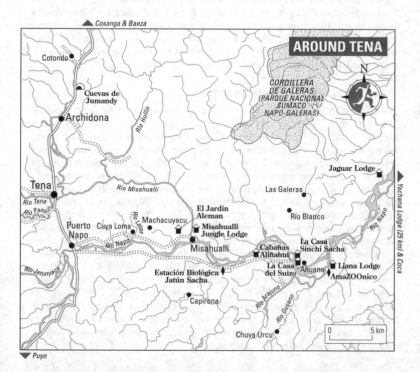

Caves and petroglyphs around Tena

While famed for the Cuevas de Jumandy (see opposite), the Tena region has many other less-visited **caves**, the majority of which are on private property meaning you'll need the owner's permission to visit them. If interested, pick up the *Ecotourist's Guide to the Ecuadorian Amazon* by Rolf Wesche, published by CEPEIGE (the Panamerican Center for Geographical Studies and Research) and available in Quito bookshops like Libri Mundi or at the IGM (see p.111), which has a list of the accessible caves in the area and the relevant land owners to speak with. The area is also littered with **petroglyphs**, rough but lyrical etchings of shapes, creatures and faces onto rocks and boulders, dating from several thousand years ago up until the sixteenth century. No one is exactly sure of their significance, but they are often found near waterways or on high ground, places of strategic and habitational importance. One of the best groupings, including the Piedra Indimama, deemed among the most interesting petroglyphs in the region, is on the hillside north of **Cotundo**, itself about 10km north of Archidona. Ask around in Cotundo for directions; again, the *Ecotourist's Guide to the Ecuadorian Amazon* has a useful account of local petroglyphs and where to find them.

Heading 7km south of Tena brings you to the road bridge at **Puerto Napo**, the last road crossing over the river for 100km before Coca over six hours downstream. Two dirt roads branch off the main highway to the east at this point, servicing either side of the upper Río Napo. Along the northern bank, one runs for 17km as far as the port of **Misahuallí**, the long-established embarkation point for tours of this region. On the southern shore, the other road passes several tourist cabañas and the **Estación Biológica Jatún Sacha** before hitting the water at La Punta 28km down the line. You'll cross the river by canoe here, where the road continues, dribbling on for a couple of kilometres as far as **Ahuano**. On the opposite bank of the river, **AmaZOOnico** is a pioneering animal sanctuary set inside its own private reserve.

Archidona and around

ARCHIDONA, a well-kept town that sits in cultivated fields in the hills 10km north of Tena, was the first capital of the Oriente until 1920, when control shifted to Tena with the formation of the new (and now defunct) Napo-Pastaza province. Since its foundation in 1560, missionaries have ensured the place has stayed shipshape and the **church** is a case in point, its rude concrete blocks painted layer by layer in brown, white and yellow like a Lego building. Apart from gawping at the church and wandering around the pleasant central square crammed with shrubs and flowers, Archidona won't keep you occupied for very long. Not far from the town, however, are a number of caves and petroglyphs including the Cuevas de Jumandy and the **Museo Mundos Amazónicos** (daily 8.30am–5pm; $2.50), signposted on the main road near the Virgen at the southern end of Archidona, and about 250m down a dirt track. Built by the Unión Huacamayos (see box, p.322), the museum's pride exhibit is a huge sacred stone carved with over eighty petroglyphs and thought to be over two thousand years old. Inside the museum, a modest but wide-ranging collection of artefacts with accompanying text gives a good survey of all the Oriente's indigenous peoples; there's also a simple **restaurant** serving typical jungle game, such as *guanta* and *guatusa*, and a small crafts shop.

Cuevas de Jumandy

About 4km north of Archidona are the **Cuevas de Jumandy** (daily 9am–5pm; $2), the region's best-known system of caves. Named after the indigenous general who was supposed to have hidden here before leading an uprising against the Spanish in 1578, the caves have long been venerated by local Quichua communities, but modernity has recently overcome tradition in the form of a *complejo turístico* (tourist complex) bolted onto the entrance. A swimming pool, garish plastic waterslides, a few caged animals, a restaurant and **cabins** (☎06/889185; ❸) make it altogether less of a spiritual experience. Even so, the caves themselves are worth a look, as their dripping walls hanging with bats extend for several kilometres underground. Near the entrance vandals have chipped off stalactites and stalagmites, and daubed the place with graffiti, but guides from the reception area can lead you on a twenty-minute tour into the dark recesses across pools of chilly water (for which you'll need your swimming gear) to deep plunge holes. The guide will have a torch (give a tip to cover the cost of batteries), though it's a good idea to take your own, so long as you can master swimming and holding it at the same time. Take care as you walk, as the rock is very slippery. It's a simple matter to get here; from the top of the main street in Archidona, where it intersects with Jondachi, take a **bus** towards Cotundo and ask the driver to drop you at the caves; a **taxi** from Archidona costs $1–2.

Reserva Ecológica Monteverde and Reserva El Para

Archidona is also close to a pair of small private reserves, which are relatively inexpensive and easily accessed options for those short on time and money. The **Reserva Ecológica Monteverde**, 8km up the San Pablo road to the southeast of town, is a 60-acre reserve containing primary forest, hiking trails and places to swim and fish on the river. There are simple cabins ($25 per person per day) with cold showers overlooking the Río Hollín, to sleep forty people. For information contact the *Residencial Regina* (☎06/889144) on Rocafuerte about 150m north of the plaza in Archidona, or call ☎02/2891041 in Quito. Around 7km further along the same road, the **Reserva El Para** ($30 per person) is a slightly larger reserve, which has good birding, and is apparently the only home of the striated antbird in Ecuador, spotted here in 1999. Accommodation is available at a farmhouse in the reserve, and can be arranged through *Hostería Paraíso Las Orquídeas* 1.5km north of Archidona (☎06/889232).

Practicalities

Buses to Tena from Baeza or Coca usually pass through Archidona along the main road, though there is a bypass, so tell the driver if you want to be dropped off in town. Local buses from Tena to Archidona leave from the corner of Amazonas and Bolívar, stopping at the north end of this main street.

Most people stay in nearby Tena, which is far better geared to tourism, but there are a couple of decent **hotels** in Archidona should you want to make a base there. The new *Palmar del Río Gran Hotel* on Napo and Transversal 13, south of the plaza (☎06/889274; ❸) is a good-value choice for its clean tiled rooms, private bath, hot water and cable television, while a few kilometres south of Archidona, off the main road by the Río Inchillaquí, the European-run *Hacienda Hakuna Matata* (☎09/8020518, ⓦwww.hakunamat.com; ❹ including breakfast) is set on a generous parcel of private land containing petroglyphs, sandy river beaches, swimming spots, comfortable screened cabins and a good restaurant. Horse riding, hiking and trekking in nearby jungle are also offered and the owners will pick you up for free from Archidona or Tena.

North of Archidona to Baeza

In the 65km from Archidona to Baeza, the paved road snakes its way up through a stunning landscape of increasingly compressed and precipitous hill-crests choked with dripping vegetation and dappled with rising wisps of steam. It's a remote and sparsely populated region, dominated by two large and little-visited protected areas, the **Parque Sumaco Napo-Galeras** and the **Reserva Ecológica Antisana**. Having traversed the luxuriant Cordillera de los Huacamayos, an outlying arm of the Antisana reserve, the road descends from its highest point to the village of **Cosanga**, 47km from Archidona, sitting between the two reserves at the head of the green, cloudy Río Cosanga valley. Despite its pretty location, there's not much to the village, though the area as a whole is rich in birdlife, and bird watchers may want to spend a few days at the *Cabañas San Isidro* (T & F02/2228902 or 2547403, E birdecua@hoy.net, W www.ecuadorexplorer.com/sanisidro; $160 for a double room including full board), a **lodge** set in forested hills at around 2000m, reached on a track head-ing west from the Tena–Baeza road, a few kilometres north of Cosanga. Among the 290 bird species spotted here are such rarities as the white-rimmed brush-finch, the greater scythebill and the black-billed mountain-toucan; there's also a cock-of-the-rock lek on the grounds. The comfortable single ($92 including board) and double rooms come with private bath, hot water and electricity, and about a quarter of the proceeds contribute to forest purchase and its protection here. They also offer accommodation at *Guango Lodge* at a higher elevation nearer Papallacta. A less expensive alternative is the British-run *Magic Roundabout* (no phone, W www.themagicroundabout.org; O, dorm beds $5), a group of cabañas on a hillside 150m back from the road set in 30 hectares of cloudforest, 12km short of Baeza. It's a good base for hikes and bird watching in the various protected forests that are nearby, or for independent kayakers looking to paddle in the Río Cosanga.

Parque Nacional Sumaco Napo-Galeras

To the east of the Tena–Baeza road, the **Parque Nacional Sumaco Napo-Galeras**, one of Ecuador's newest and wildest parks, harbours over 2000 square kilometres of pristine Pleistocene areas, where there are incredible amounts of undiscovered species; the few scientific forays into its reaches have revealed a staggering forty percent of the plant samples taken to be new species. On clear days you'll see the cleft peak of Volcán Sumaco (3732m) soaring upwards from the wooded hills, marking the centre of the park. Dense forests and vertiginous ravines have so far kept human influence at bay, and access is difficult; one **entrance** ($5) is at Guagua Sumaco (see p.311), on the Loreto road, which meets the Tena–Baeza road, about 30km north of Tena. A poor trail from the control point north of the village leads past the glassy Laguna de Pacto **Sumaco**, eventually to arrive at the summit of the mist-shrouded Volcán Sumaco. Because of the difficulty of the terrain and frequent fogs, you should allow two days for the climb with the help of a knowledgeable **guide** (whom you should also seek if you plan to explore any part of the park), best found in Guagua Sumaco or one of the other villages along the Loreto road. The RICANCIE community of Las Galeras (see box on p.323) is located near the southern portion of the park, and offers several hikes inside it.

Reserva Ecológica Antisana

Before reaching Cosanga, the Tena–Baeza road winds in and out of the low section of the beautiful **Reserva Ecológica Antisana** ($5). The reserve spreads out for 1200 square kilometres to the west, its knife-edge ridges, with strips of brown marking fresh landslides through their tangled vegetation, rising steadily to prop up the unseen Andean peaks in the far distance – the ice-capped summit of Volcán Antisana (5758m) among them. The road traverses the mist-draped, forested hills and gullies of the verdant **Cordillera de los Huacamayos**, an outlying arm of the reserve which is best accessed on the **Sendero de Jumandy**, once the footpath between Archidona and Baeza, but now the only trail into this remote area. Leaving from the antennas at km 50, the stone path, only rehabilitated for 3km, ends at an oil duct, but the birding is excellent and scenery breathtaking. The hike there and back will take around two hours at a fast pace. You can get a guide and more information at the ranger station at km 38; the best times are before and after work (6–8am & 4–5pm).

The Papallacta–Baeza road parallels the northern edge of the reserve, but the main road access into the **highland section** of Antisana – one of the best places in the country to see condors – is in on its western side, via the village of Píntag about 30km southeast of Quito. This is also the route taken by mountaineers attempting to climb **Volcán Antisana**, not a technically difficult climb but complicated and dangerous for frequent bad weather, lack of shelter, and the series of crevasses on the approach. Needless to say, you'll need to be fully equipped and have an experienced mountaineering guide.

Misahuallí

For many years **MISAHUALLÍ** was *the* place in the Oriente in which to organize a jungle tour. A bustling little port at the confluence of the ríos Misahuallí and Napo, it was the perfect starting point for an adventure. Wooden houses with corrugated-iron roofs clinging to the riverbanks, local Quichua communities, and tracts of rainforest accessible by a quick boat ride gave Misahuallí all the excitement and remoteness of a frontier outpost. However, the road linking Tena to Coca, completed in the late 1980s, slashed the port's commercial trade, while its surrounding forests were cleared or severely disturbed by settlers and oil prospecting. What primary forest remains in the upper Napo has shrunk to such an extent that larger animals, particularly mammals, have all but disappeared from the region. Meanwhile the oil industry has probed ever deeper into the east, opening up far remoter regions to visitors, where the big reserves protect thousands of acres of pristine rainforest and all its wildlife.

Luckily for Misahuallí, its lingering reputation as a good meeting point for arranging jungle trips at the drop of a hat has kept the port in business. With its constant trickle of tourists, almost every hotel, restaurant, craft shop and racketeer offers forays into the jungle, and the section of the Napo around here has more tourist **lodges** and cabañas than any other part of the river (see box on p.332). Competition is fierce, keeping prices consistently low – another of the port's attractions for budget travellers – and the large number of **tour operators** (see box overleaf) offer similar activities and facilities, such as guided jungle hikes, swimming under waterfalls, gold panning and canoeing down rivers, with accommodation either at campsites or in simple cabins. English-speaking **guides** are pretty thin on the ground, so meeting them before you set out is always a good idea. Check too that they have a guiding licence issued by the Ministerio de Turismo and that they can produce written authorization from the community concerned if they plan to visit the Huaorani. Tours to the remoter Cuyabeno or Yasuní reserves, the Río Tiputini or more distant rivers

Misahuallí tour operators

Prices for **tours** below are per person per day, but always make sure you know exactly what you're getting for your money (see also "Guided tours", p.291). Also, it's worth noting that the quality of the guides can vary enormously within a single outfit.

El Albergue Español at the hotel of the same name. As well as trips to their lodges (see *Jaguar Lodge* and *Cabañas Lodge El Albergue Español* p.332), this agency offers a six-day Francisco de Orellana expedition descending from Quito into the Amazon basin and a fifteen-day expedition to Iquitos in Peru, as well as "jungle, river and indigenous life" tours, the latter of which can involve a shaman ritual using ayahuasca. Tours from $25.

Ecoselva on the north side of the park ℡06/890019. Pepe Tapia González, the owner of this company, speaks good English and leads tours to the Río Arajuno, Cuyabeno and Yasuní, and has a good knowledge of the jungle. Tours from $20.

Fluvial Tour based at the *Hostal Sacha*. Run by Héctor Fiallos, a long-established guide who speaks a little English, French and German and who leads tours of various lengths to the Shiripuno and Nushiño rivers and the Cuyabeno and Yasuní reserves. Get Héctor if you can, as he is the best guide here by far. Tours from $25.

Jungle and River Tours on Juana Arteaga, between *Marena* and *El Albergue Español* hotels ℡06/890084, ⓦwww.jungleguide.org. Polish-Quichua run firm offering short trips to nearby cabins, or longer tours to Quichua communities at Río Bueno and Limoncocha, or to Huaorani villages. They are also building an inexpensive hostel in Misahuallí called *Funky Monkey*. Tours from $25.

Quindy Tour at *Hostal La Posada*, on the east side of the park. Several adventurous tours often involving camping, such as one to San Francisco on the Río Indillama, south of the Río Napo in the Pompeya area. Cheaper tours explore areas closer to Misahuallí. Tours from $25.

are more expensive and need to be at least four or five days long to be worthwhile. Before you leave Misahuallí by canoe you should register your **passport** at the Capitanía (see opposite).

Having chosen your jungle trip, there's not a lot else to keep you busy in Misahuallí itself. You can take a dip in the river, or visit the Jardín de Mariposas, a **butterfly farm** ($2) located a couple of blocks north of the square on Rivadeneira, where you can see over a dozen colourful species in the various stages of the lifecycle. Ask at the Ecoselva office for someone to lead you around the farm. Outside town, there's a good short hike up to some small **waterfalls** and **bathing pools** on the Río Latas, a favourite place for local children. Take a bus from the central square towards Puerto Napo and ask the driver to drop you off for "*las cascadas*", around 7km from Misahuallí. They'll leave you at the trailhead; the biggest falls are about a ninety-minute hike away, but most people settle for the streams and pools along the way. Apart from swimming gear, you'll need shoes or sandals that you won't mind getting wet, and food and water.

Practicalities

Buses from the terminal in Tena arrive at Misahuallí's main square every 30–45 minutes (a 45min trip). If you're coming from Puyo, get off at Puerto Napo and wait at the north side of the bridge to pick up the bus from Tena. Public **boat** services downstream from Misahuallí have been discontinued, but motorized canoes are available for charter down at the beach, though this is expensive unless you are in a group – just going to Ahuano will set you back around $40. If looking to head further east, Jungle and River Tours (see box opposite) operate a boat service to Coca on Monday and Friday (7am), if there are eight people ($25 per person). Have your waterproofs and sun cream to hand, bring something comfortable to sit on and wrap your gear up in plastic bags as the boats are very low in the water and it can be choppy (if it rains, prepare to be soaked). Note that you have to register your passport at the **Capitanía**, beyond the square towards the dock, before embarking. If you want to change **traveller's cheques**, you'll find the odd entrepreneur in shops and tour agencies around the main square offering unfavourable rates, but you're better off going to Tena.

Accommodation in town is aimed squarely at the budget traveller, though there are a few more luxurious places on the outskirts of town, as well as a number of jungle lodges in the vicinity (see box overleaf). All of the hotels below except *Sacha* have decent **restaurants**.

El Albergue Español Juan Arteaga ⊤ & ℉ 06/890004, ⓦ www.albergueespanol.com. The downstairs rooms are of the nondescript, concrete-box mould, with private bath, hot water and fan, but those upstairs share an attractive wooden balcony and sitting area along with commanding views of the Napo. Tours are offered to their cabañas and the *Jaguar Lodge* (see box on p.332) down the Napo. ❸–❹

France Amazonia 200m before town on the main road ⊤ 06/890009. One of the smarter accommodations available, offering very pleasant rooms with big screened windows and private bath, set around a pretty garden and kidney-bean swimming pool. Rates include breakfast. Reservations preferred. ❹–❺

Marena Inn ⊤ 06/890002. Housed in a tall building facing the river next door to *El Albergue Español*, rooms at this hotel are plain but contain fridges, private bath and hot water. The top-floor

restaurant also has attractive views. ❸

El Paisano one block north of the square ⊤ 06/890027. Simple rooms with mosquito nets, a hammock and private bath and hot water, set around a pretty little cobbled garden with a restaurant, which offers vegetarian dishes and such cross-over curiosities as yuca omelette. ❸

La Posada east side of the square ⊤ 06/890005. Straightforward hotel featuring small, bright rooms with hot water and private bath. The onsite restaurant, with wooden fittings and gnarled balustrades, has vegetarian food and is a nice place to watch the monkeys and vultures scrutinize the park for scraps. ❷

Sacha on a sandbank beyond the Capitanía ⊤ 06/890065. This cheap *hostal* may only offer basic rooms with shared bath, cold water, and pinups stuck on their wood-plank walls, but it does enjoy the best access to the river beach. ❷

Estación Biológica Jatún Sacha

Founded in 1986 with just two square kilometres of territory, the **Estación Biológica Jatún Sacha** ("big forest" in Quichua) has grown into one of Ecuador's leading tropical field stations. Located eight kilometres east of Misahuallí, and on the opposite bank of the river, the reserve is a luxuriant oasis in an area cleared and cultivated by settlers and Quichua people since the 1970s, whose rising population has put pressure on wildlife – mammals, in particular, have suffered badly from overhunting. It protects almost twenty square kilometres, eighty percent of which is undisturbed primary forest boasting an astounding degree of biodiversity. Crammed into its confines are 525 species of bird and 823 species of butterfly, alongside hundreds of different tree species.

Tourists are welcome to drop in for **day-visits** ($6), which should be enough time to walk the forest trails, including a very good **self-guided tour** on a well-labelled trail with detailed descriptions of features of the ecosystem. Occupying a transitional zone between the Andes and the lowlands proper, the terrain is quite hilly, cut up by creeks and streams, so bring sturdy boots. The

Lodges around Misahuallí

The **lodges around Misahuallí** are easier to get to than those on the lower Napo downstream of Coca and generally less expensive too. Many have small pockets of primary forest attached, but in this more populated region there will be nothing like the vast virgin forests of the big reserves in the eastern Oriente. Even so, there are still plenty of birds and butterflies and dripping forest greenery.

Cabañas Aliñahui Pinto 240 and Reina Victoria, Quito ℡02/2564012, ℱ2227095, ®www.ecuadorexplorer.com/alinahui. In an enviable spot overlooking the Río Napo, about halfway between Misahuallí and Ahuano, *Aliñahui* ("beautiful view" in Quichua) is also known as *Butterfly Lodge* in reference to the 750 species that set the place ablaze with colour. Cabins have balconies, solar-powered lighting, private bath and cold water and stand in fruit orchards. Paths around the grounds lead to spectacular lookouts on the cliff edge. Activities include naturalist and birding hikes, canoe trips and visits to Jatún Sacha. $35 per person including meals; tours extra.

La Casa del Suizo Julio Zaldumbide 375 and Toledo, Quito ℡02/256609 or 2509115, ℱ2236521, ®www.casadelsuizo.com. The biggest and most comfortable hotel along the Río Napo, dwarfing the village of Ahuano, offers a less demanding way to experience the jungle and is very popular with families. Cabins have electricity, hot water, ceiling fans, and porches with hammocks; some also have a/c and river views. Covered walkways running through gardens link cabins to a large restaurant, bar and barbecue set around a pool. Excursions include an easy half-day hike at Pangayacu, the "Misacocha Adventure" (a forest walk after which you float back on your own handmade balsa raft), cultural visits to Ahuano, and trips to nearby AmaZOOnico. $59 per person in a double including board and excursions.

La Casa Sinchi Sacha Reina Victoria 1789 and La Niña, Quito ℡02/2230609, ®www.sinchisacha.org. Operated by the Fundación Sinchi Sacha, a Quichua non-profit organization seeking the sustainable development of Quichua communities through ethnotourism, handicraft production and environmental education. The lodge, which can sleep 24 people and has a shared bathroom with hot water, sits on the banks of the Napo, a ten-minute canoe ride downstream of Ahuano. Jungle hikes, canoeing, rafting and visits to the local Río Blanco community are possible activities for visitors. $25 per person per day including board.

Jaguar Lodge and **Cabañas Lodge El Albergue Español** reservations through *El Albergue Español* in Misahuallí. A 1hr 30min bus ride from Puerto Napo, or you can drift down from Misahuallí on a balsa raft for five hours accompanied by a motorized canoe for safety. *Jaguar Lodge* is one of the oldest in this region, but recently renovated to include solar-powered lighting and hot water. It's set in forest on a spur with good views, and treks are possible into primary forest in the hills behind. The *Cabañas Lodge*, from where you can explore lower primary forest, is 20 minutes further downstream by boat, and built in traditional wood and thatch; each room has its own bathroom and running water. Hikes, swimming, gold panning and navigating

steely nerved can slip on a harness and scale the **observation tower**, a metal mast penetrating the canopy, and you can also visit the **Amazon Plant Conservation Centre**, and see the foundation's ongoing work in agroforestry, silviculture and botanical garden programmes. It's possible to **stay** in simple bunks in screened cabins with shared bathrooms ($25 per person including full board); contact Fundación Jatún Sacha well in advance at Eugenio de Santillán N34-248 and Maurian, in Quito (℡02/2432240, ℱ2453583, ®www.jatunsacha.org), near the Universidad Tecnológica Equinoccial (UTE). **Volunteers** ($300 per month) are welcome and can work on the reserve's various programmes, from reforestation and general maintenance, to teaching tributaries on rafts and kayaks are offered from both. Three-night package available for $135 per person.

Jungle Lodge El Jardín Aleman ℡06/890122, ⓦwww.eljardinaleman.com. Set 3km from Misahuallí up a signed turn north from the Tena road, in spacious, colourful grounds close to its private pockets of primary and secondary forest nearby for jungle hikes, this German-run lodge has fresh double rooms with private bathroom, a whirlpool, games room and satellite TV. Jungle tours include guided walks, canoe trips, and visits to a nearby Quichua community for cultural presentations. Three-day packages start from $270 a double, including meals and tours with a Spanish-speaking guide.

Liana Lodge part of AmaZOOnico, see p.334; ℡06/887304, ⓦwww.amazoonico.org. Beautifully crafted cabins on the east shore of the Río Arajuno, draped by vines at the fringes of the forest. Each cabin has a balcony, two spacious rooms, large screened windows, private bath and hot water. The dining area and kitchen are constructed using the gnarled wood of the *pindja* tree. Activities include guided walks, birding, visits to a Quichua family and shaman, fishing, and going to AmaZOOnico's animal refuge, which the profits help support. If the lodge is full they can put you in touch with the nearby Quichua community of Runa Huasi (see p.323). Three-night packages from $120 per person including meals and tours.

Misahuallí Jungle Lodge Ramírez Dávalos 251 and Páez, Quito, ℡02/2520043, ℻2504872, ⓦwww.misahuallijungle.com. At the confluence of the Napo and Misahuallí rivers, just across the water from Misahuallí town, this lodge consists of wooden cabins with private bath and hot water, a pool and a restaurant all set in 145 hectares of steaming forest. Guided jungle hikes, including explanation of medicinal plants and forest survival techniques, are offered along with visits to AmaZOOnico and walks to the Latas waterfalls. Rates start at $70 per person per day, including full board and guided excursions.

Yachana Lodge Baquedano 385 and Juan León Mera, Quito ℡02/2566035, ℻2523777, ⓦwww.yachana.com. *Yachana Lodge* sits in eight square kilometres of primary and secondary forest and agricultural land, two hours downstream of Misahuallí in the small Quichua village of Mondaña. The comfortable rooms and family cabins, lit by lanterns and equipped with private bath, porches, hammocks and views of the river, are linked by covered walkways to the library, conference room and dining room. The local community, heavily involved with the running of the lodge, lead guided forest walks, impart their knowledge of blowpipes and flora and fauna, as well as taking visits to the food-processing house, which makes jams from tropical fruits (you may get involved in the fruit harvest) or to families involved in cacao production to make the delicious Yachana Jungle Chocolate. Prices at $225 for a 3-night package in the low season, $300 in the high, with discounts for SAE members and students.

English, conservation and biology. Regular **buses** from Tena via Puerto Napo pass Jatún Sacha on the way to La Punta and Santa Rosa, and the nearest comfortable accommodation is *Cabañas Aliñahui* (see box, above), about thirty minutes' walk to the east of Jatún Sacha (which the buses also pass).

Ahuano

On the north bank of the Napo about forty-five minutes by canoe downstream from Misahuallí, **AHUANO** cowers in the shadow of the gargantuan **Casa del Suizo** (see box, above), looking like a medieval village beneath the towering walls of a castle. Despite appearances, the huge hotel has brought money, jobs and a telephone office to Ahuano and kick-started a fledgling tourist economy in the village itself. At Cerámica Indígena, at the eastern end of town, you can watch a demonstration of Quichua **pottery** skills ($2), and then adjourn to the shop next door where you can buy other local products, including natural medicinal lotions and potions such as *sangre de drago*, good for gastric disorders, and *aceite de hungurahua*, used for shampoo, plus cane and gourd flutes, stuck together with beeswax.

Ahuano can be reached by charter canoe from Misahuallí, but a much cheaper option is to take a bus from Tena or Puerto Napo along the southern bank of the Napo as far as **La Punta**, where canoes wait to ferry you across ($0.20). There may be a camioneta on the other side to take you the 2km to Ahuano ($0.30). La Punta has a couple of restaurants and a basic hotel if you get stuck here.

Aside from the *Casa del Suizo*, with so few independent travellers stopping here, **hotels** and tourist facilities are thin on the ground. *La Casa de Estefano* (☎09/9806603; ❹ including breakfast) is on the main street at the east end of town and offers decent rooms, mostly with shared bath and cold water, and tours of the area and hiking and camping expeditions into the forests ($15 per day). The basic *Hostal Samantha* (❷), a family home above the general store by the river, has clothes lines running from wall to wall and children running beneath them, cheap rooms, a shared bathroom and one electric shower. You can get breakfast, lunch or dinner at the simple **restaurant**, which also has a couple of basic rooms upstairs (❷), on the waterfront under the walls of *La Casa del Suizo*. Next door to the pottery, the village **disco** (Thurs–Sun from 9pm; free) could keep you on your feet in the evenings, when local youngsters huddle in bamboo booths under a strobe light and bop to a selection of Latin and pop hits. A number of locals work as **guides** at *La Casa del Suizo*, and you may be able to hire their services for yourself if you ask around for tours into forested areas downstream ($10–15 per day).

AmaZOOnico

Just beyond Ahuano, the Río Arajuno joins the Río Napo. Nestling among the trees a few hundred metres up the Arajuno, you'll find **AmaZOOnico** ($2.50), an animal refuge and rehabilitation centre created in 1993. If you haven't had any luck seeing the big fauna of the rainforest you can't do much better than to come here, where monkeys of the capuchin, squirrel, spider and woolly varieties, coatis, kinkajous, caiman, turtles, jaguarundi, tapirs, boas, peccaries, ocelots and capybara are all cared for. Despite laws forbidding trade in wild animals or keeping them as pets, smuggling and trafficking of animals is rife, and many animals come to the centre in pretty poor shape. A third are deemed suitable for release back into the wild, within the ten-square-kilometre **Bosque Protector Selva Viva** that envelopes the centre in lush forest, but many of the animals recover enough to roam freely around the zoo. A visit consists of an hour's guided tour of the centre along the muddy trails that link the pens, with commentary in English, Spanish, French, German or Quichua. Between December and June, you've a good chance of seeing newborn coatis, squirrel and capuchin monkeys.

Accommodation is offered at the *Liana Lodge* nearby (see box, p.333) which helps fund the zoo and protected forest. **Volunteers** wanting to help care for the animals are welcome, but should be prepared for hard work and be unflinching when it comes to the less romantic side of looking after animals. They can stay at the refuge for free, but should apply first (☎06/887304,

@www.amazoonico.org) and be able to speak one other language besides English. If you reserve in advance, they can make arrangements to pick you up from nearby settlements, or you can take the Santa Rosa **bus** from Tena (6 daily; 1hr 45min), alighting at km 45 at the Puerto Río Barantilla/Liana Lodge/AmaZOOnico sign. Alternatively, from Misahuallí, get a canoe across the river and walk 1.5km to the road, where the Santa Rosa bus passes (cheaper and faster than travelling back to Tena). It's also possible to charter a **canoe** the whole way there from Misahuallí, but this will work out to be expensive (around $60); there is no regular public service downstream, but if you manage to hitch a ride it may cost around $10. Renting a boat from La Punta or Ahuano will cost $10–15.

The southern Oriente

Ecuador's **southern Oriente** is less developed than its northern counterpart in every way, with fewer roads, fewer towns, fewer tourists, and less oil activity. The region's two main population centres are **Puyo**, the provincial capital of Pastaza, and **Macas**, 129km further south, capital of the province of Morona-Santiago. Settlement by colonists is largely confined to a long, thin strip flanking the road that runs from north to south through the region, in the *selva alta*, parallel with the eastern flank of the Andes. This dusty, potholed track is virtually the only road in the southern Oriente, with access east into the heart of the tropical rainforest possible only by boat along the numerous rivers that coil through the forest, or by chartered light aircraft. Most of this territory is communally owned by **indigenous groups**, principally the Quichua in Pastaza, and the Shuar in Morona-Santiago, with pockets of Achuar in the east.

   Tourism in the southern Oriente is considerably less evolved than in the north – with the exception of the luxurious *Kapawi Ecolodge*, close to the Peruvian border, you'll find none of the fancy lodges and cabañas of the kind scattered up the Río Napo. Instead, what the southern Oriente offers are excellent opportunities for culturally focused **ecotourism**, offered by tour operators based in Puyo and Macas in association with host indigenous groups. In Puyo, the Organización de Pueblos Indígenas de Pastaza has developed a variety of programmes opening up tracts of rainforest and local communities to visitors, while in Macas, which has more tour operators, guides take tourists on multi-day trips to remote Shuar communities, often with an emphasis on learning about their customs, mythology and healing rituals, while exploring the jungle.

   The main **route into the southern Oriente** is the hundred-kilometre road from the *serrano* city of Ambato down to Puyo, from where you can branch south to Macas or north to Tena. A considerably slower, rougher and bumpier alternative is the little-used dirt road across the southern sierra from Cuenca or from Loja, both of which eventually arrive at the small town of Gualaquiza, in the southern part of Morona-Santiago. In addition, at the time of writing a new road to Macas from the town of Guamote, near Riobamba, was nearly finished (see p.234 for details). There are also direct **flights** from Quito and Cuenca to Macas twice a week.

Puyo and around

Seventy-nine kilometres south of Tena, **PUYO** is by far the biggest urban centre in the southern Oriente, with a growing population of some 20,000 inhabitants made up principally of *colonos* from the sierra. True to its name – derived from the Quichua word for "cloudy" – Puyo seems to be permanently suffused with a grey, insipid light that gives the town a gloomy air. Founded in 1899 by Dominican missionaries, very little remains of its traditional timber architecture, and these days most of the city's buildings are modern and concrete. Although not particularly appealing in its own right, Puyo does boast several attractions on its outskirts, most notably the fabulous **Jardín Botánico Las Orquídeas**. It also serves as a convenient launchpad for a range of **jungle tours**, commonly to the **Fundación Ecológica Hola Vida**, a tract of secondary rainforest 27km south of town, and to the site of **Indichuris**, a further 7km south, to meet local Quichua families. Puyo is also the **transport hub** of the southern Oriente, with frequent bus connections north to Tena and Coca, south to Macas and west to Baños and Ambato, in the sierra.

Arrival, information and getting around

Buses pull in at the **bus station**, 1km west of the centre on the road to Baños, from where it's a short taxi ride ($0.80) or fifteen-minute walk into town. For **tourist information**, head for the Oficina de Turismo (Mon–Fri 9am–12.30pm & 2.30–6pm; ☎03/885122) on the first floor of the Municipio, on the corner of 9 de Octubre and Francisco de Orellana. There's not much by way of maps and brochures to take away, but the friendly, helpful staff will let you browse through their copious files detailing attractions throughout the

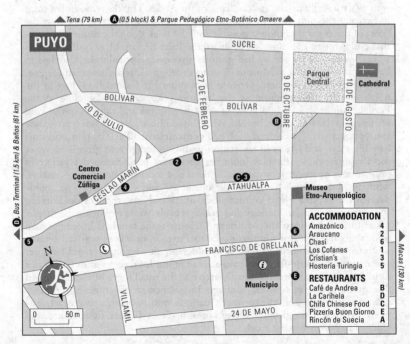

province of Pastaza. Downtown Puyo is compact and entirely manageable on foot, but if you need a **taxi** you'll find plenty of yellow ones and white camionetas lined up on 9 de Octubre and Atahualpa, charging around $0.80 for journeys within the town. **Traveller's cheques** can be cashed at Casa de Cambio Puyo, at Atahualpa and 9 de Octubre, while the Banco del Austro, Atahualpa and 10 de Agosto, has a Visa ATM and offers cash advance. The **telephone office** is on Francisco de Orellana and General Villamil (also at Atahualpa and 10 de Agosto), and the **post office** is on 27 de Febrero and Atahualpa. There are several places around the centre offering **Internet access** for around $2 per hour; try ciber@té opposite *Hostal Araucano*, which also has a netphone. The Lavendería La Mocita on the corner of 27 de Febrero and Bolívar **launders** clothes by the kilo.

Accommodation

The real cheapies in Puyo aren't too nice, leaving a cluster of fairly unremarkable but comfortable enough hotels all pitched at around the same price bracket.

Amazónico Ceslao Marín and Atahualpa ☎03/883094. Clean hotel, decked out in parquet floors smelling of polish, offering decent en-suite rooms with cable TV. Also has a tour agency. ❹

Araucano Ceslao Marín 576 ☎03/883834, ☏885227. Friendly *hostal* popular with backpackers, with a good restaurant and a choice of rooms with shared or private bath (water is only available on request in the dry season), generally decreasing in price the higher up the building you have to go. Also offers tours into the rainforest. ❸–❹

Chasi 9 de Octubre and Francisco de Orellana ☎03/883059. Charmless hotel best used only as a stand-by. The small rooms with private bathroom and TV are functional and clean but the games arcade downstairs ensures a near constant racket. ❷

Los Cofanes 27 de Febrero 629 ☎ & ☏03/885560, ✉loscofanes@yahoo.com. Superior hotel offering immaculate rooms in a modern block, all with cool, tiled floors, freshly painted walls, firm beds, fans and cable TV. ❹

Cristian's 9 de Octubre and Atahualpa ☎ & ☏03/883081. Modern establishment offering spruce, carpeted rooms with en-suite bath, fans, fridges and cable TV. ❹

Hostería Turingia Ceslao Marín 294, ☎03/885180, ☏03/885384. Secure German-owned hotel of long standing featuring modern and older bungalows with private and shared bath respectively, set in pleasant gardens with pool, Jacuzzi and spa complex. ❹

The town and its outskirts

Sitting near the coiling Río Puyo's southern banks, Puyo's focal point is the manicured **Parque Central**, featuring a paved esplanade dotted with flowering trees, ornamental lampposts and a red-roofed bandstand from where you're treated to fine views onto the surrounding countryside. Towering over the east side of the square is the modern, angular **cathedral**, built in 1992, with flashing white walls trimmed in brown. There's little else to grab your attention in town, save the **Museo Etno-Arqueológico** (Mon–Fri noon–6pm; free), located on the third floor of the Casa de la Juventud, at Atahualpa and 9 de Octubre. The displays inside include traditional day-to-day objects used by indigenous communities of the region, such as blowpipes, cane spears, fishing nets and *mucahuas* used to drink chicha out of, along with a modest archeological collection of pre-Hispanic ceramics and tools.

At the north end of 9 de Octubre, a ten-minute walk from the city centre, steps head down to the **Río Puyo**, snaking between dense foliage and crossed by a rickety suspension bridge leading to the **Parque Pedagógico Etno-Botánico Omaere** (daily 8am–6pm; $2). The park offers instant access to a bite-sized chunk of native forest laced with well-maintained paths, along with a nursery where medicinal plants are grown, and several examples of typical indigenous dwellings. A five-minute taxi ride ($1) southeast of the centre in the suburb of Intipungo, the not-to-be-missed **Jardín Botánico Las Orquideas** (daily 8am–6pm; advance reservations essential on ☎03/884855 or 884854; $5) is an outstanding private botanical garden, with over two hundred species of native Amazonian orchids poking out of a lush tangle of vegetation spread over a couple of hills. Visitors are guided through the garden by its enthusiastic owner and creator, Omar Tello, who points out the tiniest and most exquisite flowers hiding under the foliage; at a brisk pace you could get round most of the paths in an hour, but allow at least two to get the most out of it.

Slightly further afield, 6km south of Puyo branching off the road to Macas (about $2 by taxi), **Sacha Huasi** is a smallholding owned by Señor Nelson Santi, a practising shaman who offers healing rituals by night. Dressed in traditional regalia inherited from his father, including a feather headdress and strings of dried seeds, the shaman plays a flute while making his diagnosis, and sends you away with herbal remedies to drink or bathe in; if you're interested, enquire at the Oficina de Turismo to make arrangements. Another attraction in the outskirts of town, 9km north of Puyo on the road to Tena, is the **Centro El Fátima** (daily 8am–6pm; $2), a zoo with a mixture of walk-in enclosures where you can pet some of the smaller animals, and large, fenced-off areas mimicking the larger mammals' natural environment. All the wildlife is from the Oriente, and includes tapirs, caimans, guatusas and many colourful birds. You can get here on any bus to Tena, or else by taxi for about $2.50.

Eating and drinking

There's not a huge choice of places to eat in Puyo, but in addition to those listed below you could also try the restaurants of the *Hostería Turingia* and the *Amazónico* hotel, which are reasonably priced and among the town's better dining establishments.

Café de Andrea 9 de Octubre and Bolívar. For Puyo, this is a smart little café offering breakfasts, proper coffee, cakes and toast.

La Carihuela Av Mons Alberto Zambrano near the bus station. Good restaurant offering tasty, mid-priced pastas, salads, meats and fish, always with vegetarian options as well as inexpensive *almuerzos* and *meriendas*.

Chifa Chinese Food Atahualpa and 27 de Febrero. Presentable, popular chifa, serving big portions in comfortable surrounds, comprising

glitzy floors and burgundy seating.

Pizzeria Buon Giorno Centro Comerical Los Pindos, 9 de Octubre and Francisco de Orellana. Modest but spotless little dining room serving delicious, great-value pizzas cooked by a friendly *señora*.

Rincón de Suecia 9 de Octubre and Sucre. Pleasant Swedish-owned restaurant kitted out in blond-wood tables and benches, offering cheap pasta, pizzas, Swedish goulash and chicken curry. Closes Sun 5pm.

Tours from Puyo

Tourism in the Puyo region is still fairly undeveloped, though a number of opportunities for ecotourism have been opening up in recent years, mainly under the initiative of the Organización de Pueblos Indígenas de Pastaza (**OPIP**), an indigenous organization that controls the bulk of Pastaza's territory. Some of the attractions are open to drop-in visitors, but OPIP prefers tourists to be accompanied by local indigenous **guides**, available at their associated tour agency, Papangu, on 27 de Febrero and Sucre (☎ & ℻03/883875), or other affiliated operators such as Amazonia Touring on Atahualpa (☎03/883219, ℮amazoniatouring@andinanet.net). The **cost** of tours in the Puyo area is normally around $40 per person per day for groups of two, and $35 for three.

Indigenous-community stays from Puyo

For a more costly but truly off-the-beaten-track jungle encounter, there are a number of **far-flung indigenous communities** (Quichua, Záparo, Shuar, Achuar and Huaorani) that have set up ecotourism projects. Many of the villages are reached by light aircraft from Shell (see p.219), lengthy motor canoe rides with a return trip by plane, or – most adventurous of all – several days' paddling in a dugout canoe. You'll need at least four days to make the most of the further communities, even if flying. While facilities are rudimentary, you'll get guided hikes in pristine forests with true experts and be treated to a real insight into authentic rainforest life that few outsiders experience.

Fundación Yawa Jee Ceslao Marín, Edifcio Eva Zúñiga, upstairs ☎03/883782, ✉yawajee@andinanet.net. The foundation manages four protected forests and works with Shuar, Achuar and Quichua communities, several of which are reasonably easy to access from Puyo. At the Quichua community of Cotococha, 25km south of town, you can go on walks, meet a shaman and see ceramics being made. The ecotourism project at Santana, a Shuar village 24km from Puyo on the Palora road, has been operating for over ten years and has accommodation at a biological research station, while Arútam, another Shuar community 56km from Puyo on the Macas road, boasts a larger forest reserve. These three communities can be visited for $35 per person per day, while a tour to Pakintz, a remote Achuar village reached by a 45-minute plane ride, costs $75 per person per day. The latter is deep in the forests of Morona-Santiago province, near a salt-lick, waterfalls and forest trails.

Iari Inti Travel La Y on Ceslao Marín, Centro Comercial Zúñiga, 2nd floor ☎03/886747, ☎09/9716820, ✉zapara@punto.net.ec. Tours to the Záparo communities of Llanchamacocha (35min flight) on the Río Conambo, where you'll be staying in simple en-suite cabins equipped with mosquito nets, and make the two-day canoe journey to the neighbouring community of Jandiayacu. An alternative is to go to Cuyacocha (45min flight), a tiny settlement near the Peruvian border, where you'll be put up by one of just three families that live here. All communities boast fantastically rich forests and lagoons. Canoe rides are also available to nearby salt-licks, swarming with colourful tropical birds. All tours $80 per person including flights.

ONHAE the northern end of Severo Vargas (head west along Ceslao Marín for several blocks and turn right; taking a cab would be easiest) ☎03/886148, 886993 or 884825. This organization offers trips to a Huaorani community at Cononaco, far to the east on the meandering Río Cononaco, close to the frontier with Peru, where there are comfortable cabins with bathrooms and showers. The friendly community immerses visitors in their culture, with stories, songs, rituals, lessons on medicinal plants, and shamanism, as well as guided walks in the forests and lakes by day and night. There are several options on getting here (probably involving an hour's flight, at least to return) which will largely determine the price. They are also planning a tour at Nushiño, on the upper reaches of the Río Nushiño, which is easier to access. ONHAE is also keen to take on volunteers, to teach English to their guides, and to help with permaculture programmes (around $250 per month).

Papangu 27 de Febrero and Sucre ☎ & ☎03/883875. Offers trips to several remote Quichua villages, including Sarayacu (☻www.sarayacu.com/tourism) which requires a canoe journey down the Río Bobonazo to reach and a return by light aircraft ($60 per person per day for a minimum group of four). Tours here are likely to include jungle hikes, river fishing, participation in a minga, drinking chicha and possibly joining in a ceremony using the hallucinogen, ayahuasca. An even more remote option is the community of San José de Curaray ($100 per person), a short plane ride away on the Río Curaray, from where you can paddle a canoe to an enthralling sequence of oxbow lakes abundant with fish, stopping for the night at basic riverside shelters on the way.

The most popular day-tour, usually kicking off with a visit to the Centro El Fátima (see p.338), is to the **Fundación Hola Vida**, a tract of secondary rainforest 27km south of Puyo near the village of Pomona. This can also be visited independently by taxi from Puyo for about $5 each way, with a $1 entrance fee into the forest. On a two- to three-hour hike through the forest, you can visit a stunning thirty-metre waterfall, bathe in crystalline rivers and take in splendid views over the Amazonian plain from a *mirador*. Tours here also include a visit to the nearby **Proyecto Indi Churis**, where you can sample traditional Oriente dishes like *maitos* (meat or fish steamed in palm leaves), take part in a blowgun demonstration or participate in an evening cleansing ritual using medicinal plants. Another option near Puyo is a three-day tour to the **Bosque Protector Chunchu Pamba**, a magnificent primary forest inhabited by five indigenous families, reached by a ninety-minute car ride southeast of Puyo, followed by a two-hour hike. This is an adventurous tour for the physically fit, involving hiking, swimming, fishing and river trips.

Macas and around

South of Puyo, the dusty, potholed road crosses two wobbly suspension bridges over the Río Pastaza – strong enough to take light vehicles, but where buses deposit passengers who cross on foot and pick up a connection waiting at the other side – on its way to **MACAS**, 129km away. Smaller, cleaner and quieter

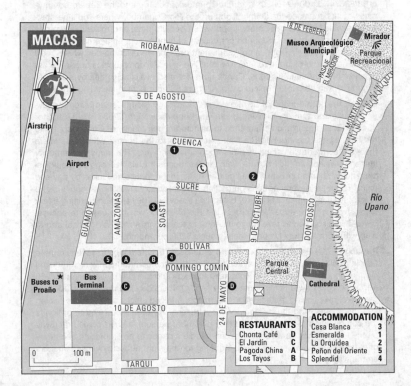

than Puyo, Macas is the most appealing town in the southern Oriente, mainly for its pleasant climate, laid-back atmosphere and beautiful views onto the surrounding countryside. While there is a handful of worthwhile sites in and around town, Macas is best visited as a base for organizing excursions into the hinterlands to the east.

Arrival and information

Arriving in Macas by **bus**, you're dropped at the centrally located bus station on the corner of Avenida Amazonas and 10 de Agosto. Tame **flights** from Quito land on Mondays and Thursdays at the tiny airport on Amazonas and Cuenca, four blocks north of the bus terminal. There's no official **tourist office** in town, but you can pick up a glossy brochure listing attractions and tourist services in Macas at the Municipio on the plaza (☎07/700143).You can cash **traveller's cheques** at Orientravel, on 10 de Agosto and Soasti, and at the Banco del Austro on 24 de Mayo and 10 de Agosto; the Pacífictel **telephone office** is on 24 de Mayo and Sucre, with the **post office** on 9 de Octubre, on the Parque Central, and **Internet facilities** are available at CyberVision opposite *Casa Blanca* ($1.40 per hour) among other places.

Accommodation

Of Macas' dozen or so **hotels**, none could be described as upmarket, but there are plenty of comfortable, good-value options, most offering similar rooms at similar prices. Best is probably the newly-built *Casa Blanca* at Soasti 14-29 (☎07/700195; ❹), offering spacious, clean rooms with tiled floors, private hot-water showers, cable TV and breakfast. Other popular choices include the *Peñon del Oriente*, near the bus terminal on the corner of Domingo Comín and Amazonas (☎07/700124, ☏700450; ❸), with pleasant, though slightly worn, en-suite rooms with cable TV; *La Orquídea*, at Sucre and 9 de Octubre (☎07/700970; ❸), run by a friendly *señora* offering simple but spotless rooms on a quiet street; *Esmeralda* at Cuenca 612 (☎07/700130; ❹), with comfortable beds, clean, white walls, breakfast and cable TV; and the long-established *Splendid* at Soasti and Bolívar (☎07/700120; ❷–❹), with quiet rooms off a courtyard having shared bath, or newer ones with private bath, cable TV and hot water.

The town and around

A good place to take in the lie of the land is on the steps of the modern, concrete **cathedral**, on the Parque Central, giving views across the low roofs of the town onto the eastern flanks of the sierra – on very clear days you can see the smouldering cone of Volcán Sangay, some 40km northwest. Behind the cathedral, the shelf on which Macas is built drops abruptly down to the **Río Upano** whose yellow-brown waters curl around the eastern edge of the town. For the best views eastwards, head five blocks north from the cathedral to the **Parque Recreacional**, a small, pretty park with a *mirador* looking down to the seemingly endless blanket of vegetation, stretching into the horizon in a fuzzy green haze. In the foreground, just across the river, you can see the white-washed buildings of **Sevilla-Don Bosco**, a Salesian mission station with a handsome church, about a forty-five-minute walk from town.While you're up in the Parque Recreacional, take a look inside the **Museo Arqueológico Municipal** (Mon–Fri 8am–noon & 1.30–4.30pm; free), sitting by the entrance. Inside is a poorly presented but fascinating display of Shuar artefacts,

Tours around Macas

Most **tours from Macas** typically take in day- and night-hikes through the forest (often around four hours long), bathing in lakes and waterfalls, river trips in dugout canoes and visits to Shuar communities, occasionally with singing and dancing, or the option of participating in a traditional purification ritual. **Costs** are generally around $35 per person per day, going up to around $50–80 per day for tours including a short flight to the remote areas "East of Macas" (see opposite); bear in mind that much of the final day of the tour may be taken up by a lengthy bus journey returning to town. Expect community facilities to be basic, with **accommodation** in traditional bamboo huts or tents, and an emphasis more on adventure and low-impact cultural exchange than material comforts. Some operators can offer English-speaking **guides**, but few are really fluent – if having an English-speaking guide is a priority, shop around and insist on meeting the guide before booking the tour, always a good idea in any case, to try to ensure you'll get on well with them.

Cabañas Yuquipa contact the Pancesa bakery at Soasti and 10 de Agosto ⊤07/700071. Near the Shuar community of San Vicente, 12km north of town, and an hour's walk from the highway, these rustic cabins with composting toilet are built by the Río Yuquipa near the forest. Packages from around $30 a day include meals and guided jungle walks.

Kujáncham Expeditions 24 de Mayo and Domingo Comín ⊤07/700299, ⓔkujancham_expeditions@yahoo.com. Flexible trips from one to seven days to local Shuar and Quichua communities, involving guided jungle hikes and exposure to indigenous culture at a good price.

Orientravel 10 de Agosto and Soasti ⊤07/700371, ⓔortravel@c.ecua.net.ec. Offers a range of three- to six-day tours, most frequently to their cabins in the Buena Esperanza area, an hour northeast of town. Doubles up as an ordinary travel agent for booking flights, etc.

Winia Sunka the kiosk on Amazonas and Domingo Comín ⊤ & ⓕ07/700088, ⓔwisunka@juvenilemedia.com. Three- to six-day tours, usually to the Buena Vista area, where they have their own cabañas, as well as tours further into the jungle.

including feather adornments, headdresses made of animal heads, blowpipes, basketwork, large clay funerary urns traditionally used to bury dead children, and a replica of a *tsanta* (shrunken skull). You can buy good **artesanías** at Fundación Chunkuap' shop on the corner of Bolívar and Soasti which sells items made by local Achuar communities, such as ceramics, woven baskets and bags, and blowpipes.

Outside of town the **Fundación Rescate Fauna Silvestre Eden** (Mon–Fri 2–5pm, Sat–Sun 9am–5pm; $1) is an animal rescue centre set in grounds full of fruit trees. Among the animals being cared for are tapirs, peccaries, turtles, boas and parrots. It's a short walk north of Proaño, a village which can be reached by a bus ride from Macas (hourly; 15min).

Eating and drinking

When it comes to **restaurants**, best in town by a long shot is the classy *Pagoda China*, on the corner of Amazonas and Domingo Comín, which has large modern windows, bright decor and an extensive Chinese menu, a little pricier than most here but worth it. Otherwise try the *Café-Restaurant El Peñón*, opposite, for light snacks and simple, hearty staples like chicken and rice, as well as pastries from the attached bakery, and decent filter coffee (*café pasado*), or *Los Tayos* on the corner of Soasti and Domingo Comín, an inexpensive and busy eatery featuring a straightforward menu touting all the standards. The *Chonta Café* on 24 de Mayo and Domingo Comín, is a good, clean place for a beer, also serving Mexican and Italian dishes. For Oriente specialities, head for the bargain canteens clustered on Domingo Comín between Soasti and 24 de Mayo, where you'll find *ayampaco* (meat or fish wrapped in palm leaves) and the occasional *guanta* cooking over charcoal grills on the pavement. There's not a great deal to do in the evenings, but if you're looking for **nightlife**, try the underground *Acuario* disco on Sucre and Soasti, or the popular *Ritmo Latino* on Bolívar and 24 de Mayo. The *K Bar*, Soasti and Sucre, is a chirpy little karaoke bar serving snacks and drinks.

Parque Nacional Sangay

Forty-five kilometres northwest of Macas, reached by a ninety-minute bus ride, the small village of **Nueve de Octubre** provides an entry point to **Parque Nacional Sangay** ($10), spread over five thousand square kilometres spilling down from the Andes into the Amazon basin. The lower reaches, composed of dense tropical cloudforest home to jaguars, ocelots, howler monkeys, mountain tapir and numerous birdlife, are a pristine wilderness, for the most part completely undisturbed. **Independent hiking** here is a challenging undertaking, only suitable for fully self-sufficient hikers with an IGM map, a compass and good orienteering skills. An easier and more enjoyable option is to go on one of the guided three- to four-day hiking programmes offered by a couple of the **tour operators** in Macas (see box opposite), led by locals with an intimate knowledge of the paths used by fishermen and hunters. Alternatively, once the Guamote–Macas road has been completed (see p.234), you'll be able to drive through the whole width of the park, from the Oriente to the sierra. For more on the highland regions of Parque Nacional Sangay, see p.231.

East of Macas

So far, the oil giants have been kept at bay from Morona-Santiago by powerful indigenous groups such as the Federación Shuar, and the swaths of primary rainforest in the hinterland east of Macas are among the most pristine in Ecuador. Access is difficult, and many of the Shuar and Achuar communities scattered along the numerous rivers threading through the forest remain relatively cut-off from the outside world. **Independent travel** in the area, besides being discouraged by indigenous groups, is almost impossible to arrange, apart from along the single road branching east just north of Méndez (see p.345) to the little village of **San José de Morona**, a ten-hour bus ride from Macas. The strip along this route, however, has been partially cleared and colonized, so doesn't exactly take you into the heart of the jungle. Instead, the best way to visit the area is on a **guided tour** with an agency working in close cooperation with the indigenous communities it visits or whose territories it travels through.

Tour companies based in Macas (see opposite) visit three main targets east of town. Closest to Macas is the Shuar community of **BUENA ESPERANZA**, reached by a short drive (2hr) northeast from town followed by a one-hour hike. Accommodation here is usually in a traditional open-sided Shuar dwelling, made of palm shoots for the pillars, covered by cane and palm leaves for the roof. The Shuar hosts demonstrate the use the *cervátana* – a long, cane blowpipe used for hunting – and encourage visitors to have a go. Activities around here include hiking through the rainforest, with the possibility of a canoe trip.

Due east of Macas, in one of the most remote tracts of the Ecuadorian rainforest, the **Kapawi Ecolodge** represents a unique model of community-participatory ecotourism. The luxurious jungle lodge, dramatically situated on the edge of a lagoon surrounded by primary rainforest, was created in 1996 by a private operator, Canodros, in close association with the **Achuar** people of eastern Pastaza, represented by the Federación de Nacionalidades Achuares del Ecuador (FINAE). The land occupied by the lodge is leased for a fifteen-year period, at a rent of $2000 per month, and in 2011, when the lease runs out, Kapawi will be handed over in its entirety to the Achuar people. Canodros goes to enormous lengths to minimize the environmental impact of the lodge: most electricity is provided by a photovoltaic system; solar-heated water is used for hot showers; only biodegradable detergents are used; and all non-biodegradable waste is flown out to be properly disposed of.

The complex is composed of twenty waterfront thatched **cabañas** built in the traditional Achuar style, without a single iron nail, along with two central buildings incorporating a bar, lounge and dining room. **Guided hikes** and **canoe trips** in the pristine area around the lodge provide exceptional opportunities for spotting wildlife, including freshwater dolphins, caimans, anacondas and monkeys, as well as over five hundred species of birds. Programmes also include visits to local Achuar communities, where guests are invited to share *chicha*, and to sit and talk with the help of an interpreter. **Prices** start at $600 per person for three nights, going up to $720 for four nights and $1100 for seven nights; to which you need to add $150 for the return flight from Quito or Macas to Kapawi. For more information, contact Canodros at their head office in Guayaquil (☎04/2285711, ℱ2287651, ⓦwww.kapawi.com).

The second (and most popular) destination is to **YAUPI**, another Shuar community, reached on a thirty-five-minute flight from Macas. From here, groups normally set out on a two-hour hike to the beautiful **Lago Kumpak**, where they lodge with Shuar families living on its shores. A canoe ride on the lake by night often features in tours here, to look out for the glowing-red eyes of caiman, as well as by day to spot birds, colourful fish and lizards. Most programmes also include day- and night-hikes through the rainforest, and a canoe trip down the Río Yaupi to visit the **Cueva de los Tayos**, one of several enormous limestone caves in the region, inhabited by *tayos*, nocturnal **oilbirds** that nest in huge colonies in lightless places. At dusk, the birds fly out in a cacophony of shrieks and screams to feed on large fruits that are plucked with their heavy hooked beaks; *tayos* were once considered a delicacy thanks to their exceptionally fatty meat, and a fine butter was extracted from the juveniles. From the cave, tour groups normally continue downstream to join the road from San José de Morona, and catch a bus back to Macas (about 10hr).

The third possibility, though less commonly offered, is to fly from Macas to the community of **MIAZAL**. Programmes here normally involve a seven-hour hike through the forest to a set of remote hot springs, and a canoe ride down the **Río Mangosiza**, sleeping en route with Shuar families, and finally taking the bus back to Macas from Puerto Morona (9hr).

South to Gualaquiza

From Macas, a bumpy dirt road trails down into the southernmost reaches of the Oriente, eventually climbing back up to the highlands at the town of

Zamora, 324km away. The sporadic farming villages and small towns dotted along its length offer little scope for getting into the rainforest further east, and – with the exception of the little town of Gualaquiza, 184km south of Macas – tend to be pretty uninviting places for a stopover.

As you follow the road south from Macas, the first large community you come to is **SUCÚA**, 23km down the road. The town's main interest is that it houses the headquarters of the **Federación Shuar** on Domingo Comín 17-38 (✆ & ℱ07/740108), a large organization representing the interests of the Shuar people, and a good place to enquire about community-based ecotourism programmes in the province. Built around a long, straggly main street, Sucúa has little else to recommend itself, and you're unlikely to want to stay here – if you get caught out, however, you'll find clean **rooms** with parquet floors, shiny wooden furniture and a private bathroom at the *Gyna* on Domingo Comín and Kiruba (✆07/740926; ❸).

A further 48km south is the drab, dusty village of **MÉNDEZ**, where you'll find emergency **accommodation** at the spick-and-span *Los Ceibos*, just off the plaza on Calle Cuenca (✆07/760133; ❷). Continuing south, the next major stop is **LIMÓN** (General Leonidas Plaza on some maps), 43km on from Méndez, with a pleasant climate and tidy streets dotted with trees, but little else. Should you need to stay here, try the *Dreamhouse* on Quito and Bolívar (✆07/770166; ❷) for modest but comfortable **rooms**. Eight kilometres south of Limón, the road forks in two, with the right fork climbing dramatically up into the sierra to Cuenca (see p.247), 100km west, while the left one continues 70km south to **GUALAQUIZA**, sitting at the confluence of the Zamora and Bobonaza rivers, against a backdrop of forested hills. With its quaint, colonial-style church and cobbled streets, Gualaquiza is by far the most attractive little town along the road from Macas, but apart from enjoying the views and taking a stroll by the river, there's nothing much to do here and no compelling reason to stop over. If you do, you'll find spacious, comfortable **rooms** at *Guadelupe* on Pesantez and García Moreno (✆07/780113; ❷), and a couple of basic **places to eat** around the main square. South of Gualaquiza, the road heads into the tiny province of Zamora Chinchipe, through remote gold-mining territory dotted with macho, rough-edged mining settlements like **Yantzaza**, before reaching the hill town of **Zamora**, 120km down the road (see p.269), where it joins the paved highway to **Loja** in the sierra (see p.263).

Travel details

Buses

Coca to: Ambato (3 daily; 12hr); Baños (3 daily; 11hr); Guayaquil (3 daily; 16hr); Lago Agrio (every 15–30min; 3hr); Loja (1 daily; 30hr); Puyo (7 daily; 9hr); Quito (12 daily, mostly at night; 9–11hr); Santo Domingo (3 daily; 11hr); Tena (12 daily; 6hr).
Lago Agrio to: Ambato (6 daily; 10hr); Baeza (every 30min–1hr; 5hr); Coca (every 15–30min; 3hr); Cuenca (1 daily; 16hr); Esmeraldas (1 daily; 14–15hr); Guayaquil (5 daily; 15hr); La Punta (every 15min; 40min); Loja (1 daily; 24hr); Machala (1 daily; 18hr); Puyo (1 daily; 11hr); Quito (every

30min–1hr; 8hr); Santo Domingo (4 daily; 10hr); Shushufindi (every 15min; 3hr); Tena (2 daily; 8hr); Tulcán (2 daily; 13hr).
Macas to: Cuenca (11 daily; 9hr); Gualaquiza (2 daily; 8hr); Guayaquil (2 daily; 13hr); Morona (1 daily; 10hr); Proaño (hourly; 15min); Puyo (20 daily; 5hr); Quito (5 daily; 11hr); Sucúa (hourly; 1hr). Note that frequencies on some routes are likely to change once the road to Guamote is completed.
Puyo to: Ambato (13 daily; 3hr); Baños (13 daily; 2hr); Guayaquil (2 daily; 9hr); Macas (20 daily; 5hr); Quito (7 daily; 6hr); Riobamba (6 daily; 4hr 30min); Tena (17 daily; 3hr).

Tena to: Ahuano (9 daily; 1hr 30min); Ambato (14 daily; 6hr); Archidona (every 20min; 15min); Baeza (26 daily; 2hr 30min); Baños (14 daily; 5hr); Coca (12 daily; 6hr); Lago Agrio (2 daily; 8hr); Misahuallí (every 45min; 45min); Puyo (every 30min–1hr; 3hr); Quito (22 daily; 5–6hr via Baeza, 9hr via Ambato); Riobamba (5 daily; 7hr); Santa Rosa (6 daily; 1hr 45min).

Boats

Coca to: Añangu (2 weekly; 3hr); Nuevo Rocafuerte (2 weekly; 13hr); Pañacocha (2 weekly; 5hr); Pompeya (2 weekly; 1hr 30min).

Flights

Coca to: Quito (3 daily Mon, Fri & Sat, 2 daily Tues–Thurs; 30min).
Lago Agrio to: Quito (3 daily Mon, Thurs & Fri, 2 daily Tues & Wed, 1 daily Sat; 30min).
Macas to: Cuenca (1 Mon & Fri; 25min); Quito (1 Mon & Thurs; 30min).

The northern
lowlands and coast

COLOMBIA

Equator
0°

PERU

N

Equator
0°

CHAPTER 6

Highlights

✳ **Private cloudforest reserves** The most accessible and comfortable places to experience a cloudforest – a misty, half-lit universe of tangled vines, creepers, mosses, orchids, fluorescent butterflies and endemic birds. See pp.352–356

✳ **Mindo** Couched in steep forested hills, a quiet village that has long been a favourite of bird watchers and nature enthusiasts. See p.356

✳ **Cocktails in Atacames** Every night at this seaside resort ends with tasty libations, usually made from fresh fruit juices and fortified with a healthy slug of rum. See p.379

✳ **Beach hideaways** A great way to recharge your batteries and escape the crowds and noise – holing up in a secluded retreat with its own deserted beach. See p.384, p.386 & p.388

✳ **Surfing at Canoa** On a fantastic stretch of beach relentlessly pounded by powerful breakers, the best spot for surfing on the north coast and a great place to unwind. See p.389

✳ **Bahía de Caráquez** Self-proclaimed "eco-city" of white condos rising from a slender peninsula, and the cleanest and greenest resort town on the coast. See p.391

The northern lowlands and coast

U nlike the dry and scrubby shoreline to the south, the **northern lowlands and coast** feature lush vegetation and high levels of rainfall, especially during the wet season (Dec–May) when monthly precipitation averages 300m, but can easily reach 600mm. The main attractions of this lowland zone, lying west of the Andes and north of the road from Manta to Quevedo, are its long sandy **beaches** bathed by a warm ocean and **forests** holding hundreds of unique plants and animals. Also appealing is the fun-loving coastal character of its people, which is more relaxed and uninhibited than that found in the highlands, and is enhanced by a blend of **Afro-Ecuadorian** and indigenous **Chachi** and **Tsáchila** cultures.

Of the several **routes** to the northern lowlands from the sierra, the old road from Quito to the coast, the **Calacalí–La Independencia road**, passes through some of the best bird-watching territory in the country, including the village of **Mindo** in the thickly forested hills, and a handful of excellent private reserves protecting some of the last remaining **cloudforests** in the western Andes. A newer arterial route heads from Quito to **Santo Domingo de los Colorados**, set amid a broad sea of banana and oil-palm plantations, skirting a few tropical wet forests such as the little-explored **Reserva Ecológica Mache-Chindul**, one of the country's newest reserves, protecting coastal hills swathed in impenetrable forests, running parallel to the shore and rising 775m above sea level. From Santo Domingo a network of paved roads connects to the major coastal centres of Esmeraldas, Pedernales, Bahía de Caráquez, Manta, Portoviejo and Guayaquil, via Quevedo.

A jigsaw of knotted mangrove swamps, broad river deltas, low, rugged cliffs and soft, sandy beaches washed by Pacific rollers, the **north coast** can be accessed from the highlands by the fast, paved highway that connects Ibarra with the isolated port of **San Lorenzo** and parallels a famous old railway route, now largely defunct except for two short fragments. A hundred kilometres down the coast from San Lorenzo, and most conveniently reached by paved roads from Quito, the rough oil-refining port of **Esmeraldas** lies just north of the area's best-known **beach resorts**, the biggest and brashest of which is **Atacames**, famous for its bars and nightlife and jam-packed during summer months and holidays with *serranos* seeking sunshine and warm waters. The less-developed beach centres are a bit further afield, including the car-free

sandbar island of **Muisne**, 40km down the coast, and the laid-back surfing zone of **Canoa**, more than 150km south. Between them, many tranquil, deserted beaches and hideaway hotels dot the coastline, while at the southern end of the region, **Bahía de Caráquez** is an elegant resort town and a good base for visiting mangrove and tropical dry forests, and the bustling port of **Manta** is the area's lively economic powerhouse.

The northern lowlands

Rarely found on travel itineraries, major towns in the **northern lowlands** like Santo Domingo and Quevedo tend to be sweaty commercial centres enveloped by acres of agricultural land. However, at higher elevations between the sierra and lowlands, the region holds a number of enchanting **cloud-**

forests, misty worlds of dense, mossy and vine-draped vegetation coloured by orchids, heliconia, birds and neon butterflies, and at lower altitudes harbours a few small fragments of **tropical coastal wet forests** in a handful of reserves. Both types of forests make up part of the **Chocó bioregion** – a stretch of Pacific coastal and montane forests extending into Colombia – which was severed from the Amazon rainforests to the east by the uplift of the Andes mountains one hundred million years ago. Since that time, the western forests have evolved quite differently from their eastern counterparts, resulting in considerable biodiversity and endemism (species found nowhere else). However, with logging, agriculture and human encroachment taking a substantial toll, only seven percent of Ecuador's original Chocó forests remain, and the area has been classified by Conservation International as one of the world's biodiversity "hot spots" – among the planet's most ecologically important and threatened regions.

Serviced by a near-constant stream of buses, the **main route** to the northern lowlands begins south of Quito and starts its descent of the western Andes at Alóag, heading down towards **Santo Domingo de los Colorados** – around which you can see tropical wet forests at **Tinalandia**, **Bosque Protector La Perla** and **Reserva Biológica Bilsa** – and provides access to highways reaching all the major coastal centres. Far more attractive and peaceful, the recently renovated **Calacalí–La Independencia road** is the alternative to the main route, leaving north of Quito, winding through beautiful forests and passing close to some excellent **private cloudforest reserves** and the birding centre of **Mindo** before descending into farmland, where it reaches the main highway between Santo Domingo de los Colorados and Esmeraldas. Keep in mind that only a handful of the less well-known transport companies ply this road, with buses passing every few hours, and these cloudforest reserves are not accessible by public transit alone; contact their offices in Quito before setting out, both to reserve a room and to sort out travel arrangements.

The Calacalí–La Independencia road

Although it's the old route to the northern coast, the **Calacalí–La Independencia road** has recently been resurfaced and is now in excellent condition, providing access to some of the last pristine **cloudforests** in the western Andes, largely protected by private reserves that offer good lodging and excellent **bird watching**. After leaving Quito to the north, the road meets the equator at La Mitad del Mundo (see p.120) before it sweeps west to bypass **Calacalí**, home to its own small equator monument, and begins a dramatic descent from scrubby hillsides (at 2800m) to thickly-matted forests carpeting steep ridges and hills – the rich greenery broken only by curling wisps of clouds. Most of the reserves lie within transitional zones from 1000m to 2500m, where the humid air adds high levels of moisture to the forests.

Sixty kilometres from Quito around the village of Nanegalito are several private reserves, among them **Maquipucuna**, **Yunguilla**, **Santa Lucía** and **Urcu Puyujunda**; beyond them to the northwest, the **Reserva Biológica Los Cedros**; and around the Tandayapa Valley, the **Bellavista Cloud Forest Reserve** and **Tandayapa Lodge**. Some 25km further west from Nanegalito, the road passes the turn-off for **Mindo**, a pleasant village renowned for its birdlife and set in the verdant hills of the **Mindo–Nambillo** protected forest, and winds down from the Andean piedmont into rich agricultural land, passing small farm towns such as **San Miguel de los Bancos** and **Puerto Quito** before meeting the highway that links Santo Domingo to the coast at Esmeraldas.

Pahuma Orchid Reserve

About 22km beyond Calacalí, the **Pahuma Orchid Reserve** protects 6.5 square kilometres of rich cloudforest, from the summit of **El Pahuma** ("flattened peak") down to the highway. Across the road from the car park, a **botanical garden** (daily 8am–4pm; $3) displays three hundred of the five hundred beautiful varieties of orchid found in the reserve, which you can also explore on 6km of hiking trails, including one ancient trail up to the Pahuma peak (guide $1 per person per half-day). For **accommodation** you can either sleep in private double rooms at the **Nature Centre** (④) by the garden, or in dormitory bunks ($8), or hike up to the rustic *Guarida del Oso* cabin (bunks $5), where you'll need your own food, water and sleeping bag. You'll also need to be self-sufficient if you want to **camp** ($3) in a clearing on the summit of El Pahuma. For more **information** contact Fundación Ceiba (℡02/2232240, ℻2432246, ⓦwww.ceiba.org).

Reserva Biológica Maquipucuna

Originally geared for research but now open to the public, eighty percent of the 45 square-kilometre **Reserva Biológica Maquipucuna** ($5) is undisturbed primary **cloudforest**, ranging from 1200m to 2800m across four ecological zones, and bounded by another 140 square kilometres of protected forests. Together the areas are home to a considerable amount of **wildlife**, with two thousand plants, 330 birds and 45 mammals, among them pumas, ocelots, tapirs, agoutis and nineteen types of bats. If you're lucky you may even spot the rare and elusive Andean **spectacled bear** in the southern part of the reserve.

Traversing the northern end of the reserve are five **trails** from fifteen minutes to seven hours long (English-speaking guides available with advance reservation), while near the lodge you'll find an introductory self-guided trail and the cool waters of the **Río Umachaca**, ideal for a quick dip after a long hike. During mealtimes, you can quiz the resident biologist and research scientists based at the nearby laboratory, and the reserve is also dotted with **archeological sites** relating to the **Yumbos** people, who lived in the area before the arrival of the Incas, including fragments of an ancient trail that once connected the sierra to the lowlands, with path-side walls several metres high.

Practicalities

From Quito the reserve is a two-and-a-half-hour journey over sinuous roads that get increasingly bumpy and muddy, and which in the wet season (Jan–May) require a **four-wheel-drive** vehicle for passage over the last stretch. Once through Nanegalito, take the right turn-off to Nanegal and just before you reach that village, the turning for Maquipucuna is signposted to the right. After 2km on a dirt track, pass through the village of Marianitas and proceed a further 4km to the lodge on the fringes of the forest. Alternatively, catch a **bus** towards San Miguel de los Bancos from the main terminal in Quito as far as the turn-off before Nanegal, from where it's a six-kilometre **walk** (75min) to the lodge, by the route described above.

Bedrooms in the attractive wood-and-thatch **lodge** ($50 per person with shared bath, $73 with private bath; meals included) have screens rather than walls, allowing the rich forest soundtrack to waft in. Budget travellers can stay in the less comfortable **research facilities** by the organic garden ($15, including board). **Volunteers** are welcome to clear trails, reforest pastures, tend the garden and help with nearby community projects; to receive further information or make **reservations**, contact the Fundación Maquipucuna in Quito, Baquerizo E9-153 and Tamayo (℡02/2507200 or 2507202, ℉2507201, Ⓦwww.maqui.org).

Yunguilla

On the eastern side of the Maquipucuna reserve, a short camioneta ride from Calacalí, the community of **Yunguilla** runs an ecotourism project and invites visitors to stay at its *Casa Tahuallullo* ($20, including meals), a simple cabin with two rooms and space for eight, or to take residence with local families. Also available are guided walks into the **cloudforest** and along pre-Columbian pathways, long-distance treks for up to five days, and plenty of information on local traditions, culture and legends. For more information and **reservations**, contact Germán Collahuazo (℡09/9580694, Ⓔyunguilla@yahoo.com, Ⓦwww.ecoturismo-ecuador.com/yunguilla) or try the Fundación Maquipucuna (see above).

Bosque Nublado Santa Lucía

On a small plateau affording stunning views of the green-blanketed hills and cloud-filled valleys below, **Santa Lucía Lodge** is run by the local community to fund the conservation of 6.5 square kilometres of communally owned **cloudforest** (*bosque nublado*), eighty percent of which is primary forest harbouring some 330 **bird** species, including dozens of hummingbirds such as the rare violet-tailed sylph, golden and club-winged manakins, and leks (courting display grounds) for the cock-of-the-rock, as well as **mammals** like pumas, ocelots and Andean spectacled bears. A number of forest **trails** traverse various elevations to maximize your sightings of birds and plants, passing by waterfalls and mountain streams that are perfect for bathing. A six-hour hike along a pre-Columbian path links Santa Lucía to neighbouring Yunguilla (guides $10 per day).

Practicalities

Reached by a stiff one- to two-hour **hike** beyond Maquipucuna, on a trail that gets steeper as it coils 700m up a forested ridge, the lodge enjoys a wonderful isolation and tranquillity enhanced by its lack of electricity and, thanks to its 1900m altitude, absence of annoying insects. The lodge offers six double rooms, a dorm with six beds and two large shared bathrooms. The food is delicious and plentiful (much of it grown in the organic garden), and clean hot and cold water flows all day. For less than $40 per person per day, including board and guide on the walk in, this good-value lodge is great for those on a budget. The community is also keen to take on **volunteers** (two-week minimum) at substantially reduced rates to help with projects for reforestation, trail clearance and English teaching; Spanish is not required but certainly useful. Contact the lodge for **reservations** and information (℡02/2866695, Ⓔadministrator@santa-lucia.org, Ⓦwww.santa-lucia.org) or in the UK try Rainforest Concern, 27 Landsdowne Crescent, London W11 2NS (℡020/7229 2093, ℉7221 4094, Ⓦwww.rainforestconcern.org).

Reserva Biológica Los Cedros

As one of the most remote and exciting reserves in the western Andes, the **Reserva Biológica Los Cedros** encompasses 64 square kilometres of pristine rain- and cloudforests and borders the southwestern edge of the Reserva Ecológica Cotacachi-Cayapas (see p.152). Home to hundreds of tropical **birds** inhabiting the misty canopy and howler **monkeys** who bellow across the treetops every morning, the reserve's greenery is a tight weave of vines, lianas, roots, bromeliads and heliconia, and more than two hundred varieties of **orchids** (best seen mid-Jan to end Feb), including three new species that have been discovered here. The network of **trails** across the reserve gets muddy in the rainy season (Jan–Apr), but hiking is possible throughout the year.

Practicalities

Although only 6km northwest of Quito, the reserve is a five-hour **bus** ride followed by a six-hour adventure on foot or by mule. Contact the office for full transport details before leaving; it can provide maps and arrange mules if necessary. The best access is from Nanegalito, where a secondary road goes to Pacto and then Saguangal (two daily Transportes Minas buses leave San Blas in Quito for Saguangal), and from Saguangal a **trail** descends into the Guayllabamba valley and then climbs up the Magdalena river to Magdalena Alto, from which it's another two hours on foot. Another way to reach the reserve is via the Intag region west of Otavalo (see p.153); take a bus from Otavalo to García Moreno (at the end of the road after Apuela and Nangulví), then **hike** to Chontal and Magdalena Alto. It's possible to do the trek in a day, but better to spend the night in Chontal.

The reserve's rustic but comfortable **accommodation** – a wooden lodge where a nearby mountain stream powers the hydroelectric system – comes with hot-water showers and full board ($25 per person). **Volunteers** are welcome for a minimum of one month ($250 per month contribution), and **reservations** should be made at least two days in advance through the Centro de Investigaciones de los Bosques Tropicales (CIBT), PO Box 17-7-8726, Quito (☎02/2865176, ✉loscedros@ecuanex.net.ec, ⊛www.reservaloscedros.org).

Bosque Nublado Urcu Puyujunda

Located near Las Tolas, northwest of Nanegalito, the **Bosque Nublado Urcu Puyujunda** is an ecotourism project perched on a wooded hillside with gorgeous valley views, offering six simple cabins equipped with private cold-water bathrooms ($69 per three-day trip, including lodging, meals, transport and guide). Among its five square kilometres of Chocó forest are found ancient walls, foundations and unexcavated remains of the lost Yumbos culture – easily explored on the reserve's self-guided trails. Other activities include guided hikes, horse riding, fishing, biking and cow milking on community farms partly funded by visitor contributions. **Volunteers** are welcome for reforestation, community education, farm work and biological and archeological research ($140 contribution for three weeks of service). For **information** and reservations, contact the office in Quito, Foch 746 and Amazonas (☎02/2546253 or 2265736, ⊛www.cloudforestecuador.com).

Bellavista Cloud Forest Reserve

The **Bellavista Cloud Forest Reserve** comprises seven square kilometres of knife-edged mountains and deep gorges between 1400m and 2600m, incised by streams and waterfalls and clothed in dense cloudforests, epiphytes, mosses, bromeliads and orchids. Eleven well-marked **trails** provide access to the diverse wildlife of the Tandayapa Valley, including 320 **bird** species like the lyre-tailed nightjar, hoary puffleg and plate-billed mountain toucan, not to mention the countless hummingbirds that hover and zip between the bird feeders, making this a popular choice for bird watchers. The lodge, a four-storey geodesic dome perched high on a mountain ridge, gives astounding views over the valley and effectively doubles up as an observation tower above the forest canopy.

Practicalities

Bellavista is a two-hour **drive** from Quito. Take the Mindo road past Nanegalito to km 32, where a signposted ridge road takes you up to Bellavista, 12km away; small vehicles can continue past Nanegalito to km 58 and take the road doubling back to the left after the sign for the Corps of Engineers. **Buses** to Pacto, Mindo, San Miguel de los Bancos and Puerto Quito leave the Terminal Terrestre in Quito and pass Nanegalito, from where you'll have to hire a **camioneta** ($15).

Double **rooms** in the dome (❼) have balconies and private hot-water bathrooms, with three hearty, usually vegetarian meals included. Above these rooms, and accessed by ladder, are shared sleeping areas ($17 per person), and further accommodation is available in a new two-storey bamboo house with private bath (❼). **Camping** ($5) includes use of the reserve facilities and access to the on-site restaurant (breakfast $6, lunch and dinner $10 each), while self-catering accommodation is available at the nearby research station ($10), though you can't buy food in the vicinity.

A full three-day package, including transport, meals and a guided forest walk, starts at $139 per person. **Volunteers** (around $5 per day) are welcome to work on general maintenance and path clearing, as are visiting researchers to undertake studies. For more **information** and reservations (required) visit the office in Quito, Jorge Washington E7-23 and 6 de Diciembre (☎02/2232313, Ⓦwww.ecuadorexplorer.com/bellavista), or call Bellavista direct (☎02/2116232; the owner-manager is English).

Tandayapa Bird Lodge

Located at 1700m and set on the edge of seven square kilometres of lush cloudforest in the Tandayapa Valley, the British-run **Tandayapa Bird Lodge** (reservations and information on ☎02/2225180 or ☎09/9735536, Ⓦwww.tandayapa.com) is known as one of the best bird-watching spots in Ecuador, where the owners provide advice on the best sites, times of day and weather conditions for seeing any of the more than three hundred **bird** species inhabiting the valley, including 21 endemics found only in the Chocó bioregion, such as the rare **white-faced nunbird**, first discovered nesting nearby. Dozens of colourful hummingbirds flock to the feeders around the lodge, and there are a number of **trails** of varying length and difficulty that crisscross the cloudforest, as well as canopy platforms and balconies that allow close observation of life in the trees. One highlight is the "forest floor species feeding station", a hide that allows you close access to shy ground birds like the **moustached antpitta**, a bird so reclusive that it was first spotted in Ecuador in 1996.

Practicalities

The lodge holds comfortable private double **rooms** ($155, including full board) and cheaper dormitories, plus a library and bar where an ornithologist is always on hand at the end of the day to answer questions over a cocktail. Multi-day packages are also available, including guided walks and transport to and from Quito. By **car**, take the road past Calacalí to km 32 and turn left beyond the *Café Tiepolo* onto a signposted track that continues 6km to the lodge. **Buses** to Nanegalito regularly pass this turn-off, from where you can walk or hitch a ride, or continue to Nanegalito and take a **camioneta** for around $6.

Mindo

Set at 1250m on the forested western slopes of Volcán Pichincha, **MINDO** resembles an Alpine village transplanted to the tropics, with steep-roofed, chalet-like farmhouses punctuating its lush and beautiful landscape, and a pleasant subtropical climate that attracts an increasing number of visitors seeking to spend a few days hiking, horse riding or taking part in "*regatas*" – floating down rivers on inflatable tubes. Most of all, though, the town is renowned as a base for **bird watching** in the surrounding hills, part of the biologically diverse **Chocó Endemic Bird Area**, which BirdLife International has officially designated an "Important Bird Area", the first in South America.

Mindo has been held in high regard amongst **bird watchers** ever since ornithologist Frank M. Chapman described the local avifauna in his seminal 1926 book, *The Distribution of Bird-Life in Ecuador*. One reason for Mindo's prolific biodiversity is its location in a transitional area between higher-altitude temperate zones and the lower humid tropical forests, encompassing several habitats harbouring some 370 bird species, many of them endemic, including the velvet-purple coronet (one of 33 hummingbirds), yellow-collared chlorophonia, orange-breasted fruiteater and the endangered long-wattled umbrella bird – resembling a crow with an unmistakeable, dangling black wattle and a large Elvis quiff for a crest. With a good guide, you may see at least thirty endemic species and many dozens of other birds on a three- to four-day **tour** of Mindo's forests, which also hold several **leks** (courting grounds) for the Andean cock-of-the-rock, boasting a striking crimson pompom crest, and the club-winged manakin, with its unusual twisted feathers.

Threats to the Mindo forests

The most persistent **threats** to the regional ecology have always come from human colonization and the timber industry, which between them can destroy huge areas of pristine natural habitat – untouched for thousands of years – in just a few days, leaving only stumps and, before long, degraded and useless soil. To counter the threat, in 1988 the 192-square-kilometre **Bosque Protector Mindo-Nambillo** was set up to protect the subtropical and montane cloudforest from the hills southeast of Mindo all the way up to the Volcán Pichincha.

Despite their "protected" status, though, Mindo's forests were not saved from the construction in 2002 of a controversial heavy-crude **oil pipeline** that now slices right through the middle of the reserve, after a cheaper alternative running parallel to the existing Trans-Ecuador pipeline was mysteriously rejected by the government. Given the catastrophic threat of pipe ruptures and oil spills, dozens of global and local environmental groups fought against the development of the pipeline to no avail, resulting only in the authorities forcibly breaking up the demonstrations and deporting many of the international activists. Many now fear that it is only a matter of time before this unique area suffers a major ecological disaster.

As well as the birds, there are several hundred types of **butterflies** and a wealth of orchids. The **Caligo Butterfly Farm**, about 2.5km along the sign-posted track from the southwest corner of the town square (daily 9am–6pm; $3), hosts a great number of colourful *lepidoptera* and exports them around the world, while the **Orquideario** ($1), at the west end of the football pitch, cultivates 150 orchid varieties that can grow up to 5m, though many are so small they require a magnifying glass to be seen in any detail.

There are also many good hikes around Mindo in the **private reserves** that adjoin the larger Bosque Protector Mindo-Nambillo (out of bounds to the general public), which usually have **hiking trails** that you can use for a small fee. One of the most popular is to the **Cascada Nambillo** waterfall ($3; 4hr round-trip), tickets for which are available from **Los Amigos de la Naturaleza de Mindo**, which can arrange **guides** from its office two blocks northeast of the main square (☎02/2765463). This local conservation organization also offers stays at **cabins** inside the forest ($9, cheaper if you cook your own food; camping $2) and sets up **volunteer** work ($200 contribution per month). Another good hike is to the **Cascada de Azúcar**, inside the La Isla reserve, which you can rappel down with a guide for $10; for tickets contact the Centro Información Mindo (see below). You can hire **horses** at hotels such as *El Carmelo de Mindo*, *El Monte* and *San Vicente*, though most places in town can arrange guides, hikes and *regatas*.

Arrival and information

Mindo is 6km down a winding road branching south of the Calacalí–La Independencia highway. The town's simple layout features just a few streets lined with wooden houses; the main route, **Avenida Quito**, runs southeast to the quiet **Parque Central** across the Río Canchupi. The first turning right over the bridge takes you to a walled **football pitch**, one of the town's main features.

From its terminal on Manuel Larrea and Asunción in Quito, a few blocks west of the Parque El Ejido, Flor del Valle runs daily **buses** into town (Mon–Fri 8am & 3.30pm, Sat & Sun 8am, 8.30am & 9am; 2hr 30min trip). From Mindo, the buses leave from Avenida Quito (daily 6.30am & 2pm), with some extra afternoon buses at weekends. Seats fill up quickly, so buy your tickets early. From Santo Domingo, Transportes Kennedy offers three daily buses to Mindo, and plenty of other buses pass the turn-off to Mindo on their way down to San Miguel de los Bancos on the Calacalí road. From the turn-off you'll have to wait for a lift into town, or take the ninety-minute **walk** down to Mindo.

Information is available from the excellent Centro Información Mindo, on the corner of the park (daily 7am–7pm), which has up-to-date hotel lists and details on volunteering, tours, hikes, guides, horse riding and *regatas*. The **Internet** can be accessed at the hotels *El Bijao*, *El Descanso* and *La Casa de Cecilia*.

Accommodation

Mindo has more than thirty **hotels**, an almost excessive amount for such a small town, but it does mean that there are plenty of good and inexpensive options as well as a handful of upmarket places, mostly located outside the centre, which can boast their own private reserves.

Arco Iris at the parque central ☎02/2765445. Inexpensive option offering simple rooms down gloomy corridors, with shared or private bathrooms. ❷–❸

Armonía south end of the football pitch (no phone). Has a few modest rooms with shared baths and nicer secluded cabins with their own facilities at the back of the Orquideario. ❸–❹

El Bijao upper end of Av Quito ☎02/2765470. Friendly and helpful place, having simple wooden rooms fitted with screens and repellent coils to ward off mosquitoes, and choice of shared or private bathrooms with hot water. Communal space features hammocks, library and games, and the on-site restaurant is inexpensive, with solid fish, chicken or vegetarian dishes and cheap set menus. ❷

El Carmelo de Mindo 1km south of the football pitch ☎02/224713, ☏2546013. Double rooms, treehouses and cabins for up to six, as well as a pool, forest reserve and campsites ($5 per person). Regular price includes breakfast. Substantial discounts available Sun–Thurs, otherwise ❽

La Casa de Cecilia a few blocks northeast of the main square ☎02/2765453. Occupying a pleasant riverside location, has simple, clean rooms and kitchen facilities, and can arrange excursions and volunteer work. ❷

El Descanso a block from the football pitch at the western corner of town ☎02/2765383, ⒲www.eldescanso.net. An attractive, well-kept wooden house with a garden, offering good rooms and a cheaper shared loft ($12). Breakfast included. ❺

Los Guaduales on the road to *El Carmelo de Mindo* (no phone). Set in pleasant gardens, with clean rooms and optional en-suite bathrooms (❸). At the same site, *Cabañas Los Colibris* (❻) is owned by the same family and is better appointed. Good on-site restaurant, with breakfast included.

Jardín de los Pájaros northwest side of the football pitch ☎02/2765384, Ⓔjlyons@pi.pro.ec. Comfortable and clean lodge featuring good double rooms with private baths and hot water, and a nearby cabin ideal for families. Tasty meals cooked on request. ❹–❺

Mindo Garden 1–2km beyond El Monte ☎02/2252490, ⒲www.mindo-garden.com. Set in a peaceful garden full of flowering plants, featuring plush cabins within the sound of the river, games room and good restaurant. ❼

Mindo Lindo km 79 on the Calacalí road, near the Mindo turn-off ☎09/9244382, ⒺEpuntos_verdes@hotmail.com. Secluded, German-run establishment with attractive rooms and its own small reserve, welcoming volunteers to work for one to three months. Price includes two meals. ❻

El Monte 2km along the road leading southwest from the square ☎02/2765472, ⒲www.ecuadorcloudforest.com. Comfortable lodge a 15min drive from Mindo (transport arranged when you reserve in advance), featuring three two-storey cabins sleeping up to four, with private baths and hot water but no electricity. Price includes board and guided activities and entrance into the forest. ❼

Sachatamia Lodge km 77 on the Calacalí road, east of Mindo turn-off ☎02/2765437. Has smart, comfortable rooms in a polished, well-appointed lodge with a 1.2 square-kilometre private reserve. Breakfast included. ❼

San Vicente five minutes' walk uphill southeast of the square ☎02/236275. Friendly, family-run hacienda renowned for its guava jam, offering simple rooms with shared bath, in a building overlooking a rushing stream. Price includes full board and entrance to its forest. ❻

Séptimo Paraíso signposted 2km down Mindo access road ☎09/9934133, ⒲www.septimoparaiso.com. Large wooden lodge-hotel set in spacious grounds that includes three square kilometres of forest, offering comfortable rooms and a large pool. Breakfast included. ❼–❽

Eating and drinking

Most hotels, particularly the pricier ones, have decent **restaurants**, though there are several well-priced eateries on Avenida Quito, such as *Mi Ormacito* and *El Chef*. On the south side of the football pitch, *El Monte* (open evenings except Sun) cooks up tasty pizzas and also does sandwiches, pancakes, cakes and snacks.

For **drinking**, *Café Canela*, near the bridge, serves cocktails as well as hamburgers, hot dogs and other fast food, while on weekend nights during the high season, you can boogie at *Disco Éxtasis*, opposite the bus office.

West from Mindo

West from the turn-off to Mindo, the old coastal road continues its descent to the coast, leaving the wooded mountain hills and entering open subtropical farmland punctuated by the odd palm tree. This region has long been the domain of cattle ranchers and farmers, who colonized it with *fincas* and homesteads and bought supplies in the three bustling centres along the route: **San**

Miguel de los Bancos, 11km beyond the turn-off, Pedro Vicente Maldonado, 30km further on, and Puerto Quito, 23km west on the banks of the Río Caoni. Inevitably, developers are finally becoming aware of the tourism potential of the area for its warm climate close to the capital, rolling scenery streaked by rivers and hidden waterfalls, and acres of cheap land ripe for exploitation. Regular buses ply the road from the Terminal Terrestre in Quito, and leave Santo Domingo about every twenty minutes for San Miguel de Los Bancos; if you get stuck anywhere en route, each of the three towns along the way provides accommodation.

By the time the old coastal road reaches the main Santo Domingo–Esmeraldas road, 28km on from Puerto Quito, you're very much in the lowlands, where the sun beats down with tropical intensity and huge **African palm** plantations and their oil-extracting factories begin to appear beside **tropical fruit** farms and **banana** plantations. Santo Domingo, the commercial centre of the northern lowlands, is 49km southwest of the junction, while Esmeraldas, the biggest port on the north coast, is 130km north.

Practicalities

The smartest of several **resorts** along the road is **Arashá**, 4km west of Pedro Vicente Maldonado (℡02/2765348 or 2253937, ⓦwww.arasharesortspa .homestead.com; ❾ with breakfast), a collection of luxurious thatched cabins with modern, tiled interiors set amid carefully landscaped gardens and a large springwater pool. The centrepiece of the complex is a spa offering treatments like massages, body wraps, facials, aromatherapy baths and Jacuzzi baths with mineral salts. The resort also arranges excursions into the surrounding countryside to spots like **Laguna Azul**, a fetching lake fed by an impressive thirty-metre waterfall.

By contrast, the **Reserva Río Guaycuyacu** (ⓦwww.ecuadorexplorer.com/ guaycuyacu; reservations required; ❻) is a completely different place to stay near Pedro Vicente Maldonado, a small and isolated forest reserve next to a family-run fruit farm. Activities include swimming in rivers, bathing under waterfalls, hiking and bird watching in the forest, and working on various agricultural projects (one month minimum; $250 contribution).

Two kilometres before Puerto Quito, a minor road on the left at km 140 leads to **Aldea Salamandra** (in Quito, ℡02/2561146; $26 per person with board and excursions), an ecologically minded retreat with composting latrines and simple thatched cabañas and treehouses by the Río Caoni, which offers trips to fruit farms, cacao-picking to make your own chocolate, tubing on the river and bathing in the waters of a small lowland tropical reserve, a ten-minute walk away. **Volunteers** are welcome to help with reforestation, harvesting and maintenance programmes (weekly $65 contribution).

Santo Domingo de los Colorados and around

Getting to and from the major transport hub of **SANTO DOMINGO DE LOS COLORADOS** is far easier than finding anything to do once you're there. The busy arterial route to the northern lowlands and coast leaves the Panamericana south of Quito at Alóag, then trundles down the Andes to Santo Domingo, where it meets a peripheral highway that orbits the congested centre and links a number of other fast radial roads – north to Esmeraldas; west to Pedernales; southwest to Manta, Bahía de Caráquez and Portoviejo; and south to Guayaquil via Quevedo.

When the road from Quito was completed almost forty years ago, the door was unlocked to large tracts of forest, which were rapidly felled to make way for intensive agriculture, notably the enormous banana and oil-palm plantations that contribute a significant chunk to the national economy. Since then, Santo Domingo has grown at a phenomenal rate and is by far the most important commercial centre in the northern coastal interior. Its narrow, crowded and polluted streets hold few attractions to sightseers, though the town does make a serviceable base for seeing nearby forest reserves – the last remaining pockets of coastal tropical wet forest, most of which have accommodation, guides and trails.

Bird watchers on their way to these reserves might consider taking the old road from Quito to Santo Domingo via **Chiriboga**, a little-used dirt track (4WD recommended) that services the Trans-Ecuadorian Oil Pipeline and passes through various transitional forests containing hundreds of bird species, as it plunges from an altitude of 3000m before joining the main road from Alóag near La Unión del Toachi at 1200m. There are few facilities on this road, but you can stay at the rustic **Bosque Protector Río Guajalito** scientific station (ⓔ vlastimilz@mail.usfq.edu.ec; ⑤, reservations required), set amid five square kilometres of forest.

Arrival, information and transport

The **bus** terminal, 1.5km north of the town centre along Avenida de los Tsáchilas, is serviced by dozens of companies with many routes across Ecuador. To reach the centre, either take a **taxi** ($1) or one of the local buses, many of which run along the main street and access the terminal. For **money**, Banco de Guayaquil has a Visa ATM on 3 de Junio and Ibarra, and on Avenida Quito north of town; and Banco del Pacífico has a MasterCard and Cirrus ATM a bit

SANTO DOMINGO DE LOS COLORADOS

ACCOMMODATION
Covi Center 3
Grand Hotel
Santo Domingo 5
Jennefer 4
Sheraton 1
Zaracay 2

RESTAURANTS
Chifa China B
Chifa Vegetariano C
La Siesta A
Stav D

0   100 m

further north, and on the Chone roundabout. Andinatel **telephone** offices are upstairs in the Edificio San Francisco de Assisi, Avenida Quito and Río Toachi, and at the bus terminal, while **Internet facilities** are available around the centre, particularly on Avenida 29 de Mayo.

Accommodation

You'll find a glut of cheap **hotels** around the noisy 29 de Mayo, many of which don't have hot water. Rooms away from the street are usually preferable, unless they lack windows, in which case they're likely to be a bit musty.

Covi Center 29 de Mayo and Cuenca ☎02/2754237. Good value for its clean rooms with private baths, phones and cable TVs, especially its quieter units at the back, though there's no hot water. ②

Grand Hotel Santo Domingo Río Toachi and Galápagos ☎02/2767947, ⓕ2750131. Easily the best place in the centre, an immaculate hotel with smart and comfortable rooms including breakfast, plus Jacuzzi, sauna and pool. ⑥

Jennefer 29 de Mayo and Latacunga ☎02/2750577. Worth paying a bit more to get an electric shower and cable TV in some of the more spacious rooms. Avoid the small, cheap ones at the back. ②

Sheraton opposite the terminal ☎02/751988. The best bet if you're catching an early-morning bus and want to stay close to the terminal, a secure establishment with clean, decent rooms with hot water and a popular restaurant downstairs. ②

Zaracay Avenida Quito km 1.5 ☎02/2750316, ⓕ2754535. On the outskirts of town and set in extensive grounds, with comfortable rooms (some with air conditioning) that include breakfast, plus a pool, tennis court and restaurant. ⑦

The Town

The only thing in town that's really worth a look is the **market** along 3 de Julio, west of the main square of **Parque Zaracay**, which is busiest on Sunday, but bustles all week with locals buying food, clothes and other goods – though the covered section, thronged with butchers, isn't for the squeamish. The streets get even more crowded during the July 3 **fiesta** for Santo Domingo's cantonization, when an agricultural fair packs the *recinto ferial* exhibition hangar opposite the *Zaracay* hotel.

In the 1960s, tourists began coming to Santo Domingo to see the **Tsáchila** people, whom the Spanish labelled "**Los Colorados**", meaning "coloured" or "redheads", due to their bowl haircuts pasted down with bright-red *achiote* dye. Although the city takes part of its name from this Spanish moniker, these days you're unlikely to see any urban Tsáchila wearing traditional dress like short wraparound skirts or sporting their celebrated hairstyles – except for the stereotypes on local billboards and statues. Sadly, the destruction of the forests around Santo Domingo has had a deep effect on the Tsáchila, the majority of whom have been forced to abandon their traditional way of life. A scattering of their villages lines the roads around the city, sometimes marked by roadside signs for **curanderos**, shaman healers who now offer their services to outsiders. You can visit some communities through tour agencies in Santo Domingo, such as Turismo Zaracay, 29 de Mayo and Cocaniguas (☎02/2750546, ⓕ2750873), and at the *Zaracay* hotel (see above), which offers **tours** to Tsáchila communities, along with local forest reserves and an oil-palm plantation.

Eating

The more expensive hotels serve the best **food** in town, notably the *Grand Hotel Santo Domingo*, though the *Zaracay* and the less expensive *La Siesta*, Avenida Quito and Yambo, are also good options. There are also a few reasonable eateries outside the centre on **Avenida Quito**.

Ch' Farina at km 1 ☎02/2763500 or 2750295. Located outside the centre, part of a decent pizza chain that does deliveries.

Chifa China 29 de Mayo and Latacunga. The best of the local *chifas*, tucked in the courtyard of the *Jennefer* hotel.

Chifa Vegetariano inside the shopping arcade on Tulcán. Provides a range of veggie dishes, mostly soya-meat substitutes.

Grand Hotel Santo Domingo Río Toachi and Galápagos. Its superior restaurant has a wide-ranging menu and very good dishes for around $5 per main course, including vegetarian meals, breakfasts and *criollo* specialities at the weekend.

Stav Avenida Quito on the Parque Zaracay. Serves passable fried chicken and *quimbolitos* with efficiency.

Around Santo Domingo

Although a huge amount of lowland forest around Santo Domingo has been flattened for farming, pockets of dense tropical forests remain within striking distance of the city. Pressure to develop "unproductive" land – a euphemism for forests – has been considerable since the late-1950s, as colonists eyed more space for banana, palm and cacao plantations. Under government statute such undeveloped areas were up for grabs to anyone who intended to make them "productive", a policy that led to the destruction of more than ninety percent of Ecuador's northwestern forests. A handful of conservationists, however, were nimble enough to buy forestland and set up their own private reserves, which are now among Ecuador's last stands of **coastal tropical wet forest** in the Chocó bioregion.

Nurturing astounding wildlife diversity, these forest reserves are located in several areas: between Alóag and Santo Domingo; at the **Bosque Protector La Perla**, on the road to Quinindé; at the private **Reserva Biológica Bilsa**, adjoining the little-explored, state-run **Reserva Ecológica Mache-Chindul**, west of Quinindé; and at the **Bosque Protector Río Palenque**, on the Quevedo road.

La Hesperia and the Reserva Otonga

Although the Alóag–Santo Domingo road is one of the busiest routes to the coast, with **buses** passing by every few minutes, there are a few scraps of dense **tropical forest** in secluded parcels off the highway. As you descend from the sierra, the first of these you'll come to is **La Hesperia** (turning at km 58), just a ten-minute drive off the highway, a hacienda with its own seven-square-kilometre **forest reserve**, recently developed for ecotourism and offering comfortable accommodation in three houses: one with private bathrooms and hot water ($80 per person), another with shared bathrooms ($61) and the last a dormitory with a kitchen ($6). The private reserve abuts the larger Bosque Protector Toachi-Pilatón, and there are great opportunities for hiking, bird watching and trout fishing in the Río Pilatón, while back at the hacienda you can rent a horse or get involved in the farming activities. For reservations contact Juan Pablo Jativa in Quito (☎02/2432240, ℗2453583, ⓦwww .la-hesperia.com).

East of Alluriqín, at the small settlement of **La Unión del Toachi**, an access road leads south to the remote **Reserva Otonga**, whose forests are rich in wildlife and thought to contain several endemic species. The site is reached by a two-hour drive in a **camioneta** or ranchera, followed by a two-hour **hike** to the reserve station, which offers simple **accommodation** in a dormitory for thirty people (bring a sleeping bag). For more information, contact the reserve's Italian administrator, Dr Giovanni Onore (🖂gonore@puce.edu.ec, ⓦwww.uscostigliole.net).

Tinalandia

Sixteen kilometres east of Santo Domingo on the Alóag–Santo Domingo road, in the hills above Río Toachi, a signposted driveway leads to **Tinalandia**, a hacienda converted into a hotel in the 1950s, when its nine-hole golf course quickly helped it become one of the best-known lowland country hotels in Ecuador. Today its lush primary forest is renowned for its excellent **bird watching**, in which some 279 species have been spotted around the grounds, including such rarities as the ochre-bellied flycatcher and the scaly-throated foliage-gleaner, and dozens of others at higher elevations nearby. Most of the delicately ageing **rooms** and **cabins** have hot water and are a kilometre uphill from the entrance, and the **restaurant** is known to serve good food. Considering the resort's popularity with birding enthusiasts, try to make advance **reservations**, either directly (☎09/9494727) or through the office in Quito, Urbanización El Bosque, Calle Tercera 98 (☎02/2449028, ⓦwww .tinalandia.net; ❽).

Bosque Protector La Perla

Forty kilometres northwest of Santo Domingo on the road to Quinindé, and a few kilometres short of the unremarkable agricultural centre of La Concordia, the **Bosque Protector La Perla** (☎ & Ⓕ02/2725344; $4, including guide) is a private 2.5 square-kilometre, tropical wet-forest reserve with abundant birdlife set amid African oil-palm and banana plantations. At the reception hut near the signposted entrance off the main road, a Spanish-speaking **guide** (best reserved in advance) can direct you to all the best spots for bird watching along several forested **trails**. You can't stay at the nearby hacienda, but free **camping**, bathroom and shower facilities are available at the site.

Alternatively, the nearest and best accommodation is the large *Athos* hotel, in La Concordia on the Calle Principal (❺), which offers decent rooms with private bathrooms, and some units with air conditioning. Arrive on any **bus** running between Santo Domingo and Quinindé or Esmeraldas, or take a **taxi** from La Concordia for a couple of dollars; they gather around the town's main square.

Reserva Biológica Bilsa

In the Mache hills west of Quinindé, 90km northwest of Santo Domingo on the road to Esmeraldas, is one of the last major tracts of Ecuadorian coastal humid tropical forest, the 30-square-kilometre **Reserva Biológica Bilsa**, which adjoins the enormous Mache-Chindul reserve (see p.364). Founded in 1994, the reserve's forests range from 300m to 750m in altitude, high enough for heavy layers of fog to loom over the upper ridges, saturating the vegetation and allowing for great biodiversity. More than thirty new **plant** species have been discovered here, and it also has some of coastal Ecuador's greatest diversity of **birds** – one of the few places in the country where the rare long-wattled umbrella bird makes frequent appearances. **Mammals** at the reserve include jaguars, ocelots and the diminutive jaguarundi, while substantial numbers of mantled howler monkeys bawl across the canopy. The on-site **Center for the Conservation of Western Forest Plants** produces thirty thousand trees each year for reforestation projects, promotes environmental awareness and teaches land management to local communities.

Accommodation is in simple double or triple rooms with shared baths and latrines ($20 with three daily meals), and **volunteers** are welcome to help with community and reforestation projects (minimum one-month service; $300 contribution). **Reservations** are essential and should be made through the Fundación Jatún Sacha in Quito at Eugenio de Santillán N34-248 and Maurian (☎02/2432240, ⊕www.jatunsacha.org), which can also make arrangements to access the reserve. For this you'll need to take a **bus** to Quinindé, a **camioneta** to the village of La Y de la Laguna, and a four-hour **mule** trek on to the research station.

Reserva Ecológica Mache-Chindul

At the western edge of the Bilsa reserve, 700 square kilometres of coastal trop-ical wet forest are protected as the **Reserva Ecológica Mache-Chindul** (officially $5, but there's no guard post to collect it yet), characterized by extraordinary biodiversity and an unusually high level of endemism – more than ten percent of all its species are thought to be unique, though research is still in its early stages. Covering the northern half of the Mache-Chindul coastal mountains, which reach 800m in altitude, this remote area is one of the least-visited places in the country and has been inhabited for centuries by only a few small groups of **Chachi** and **Afro-Ecuadorian** peoples, who were largely overlooked until a road was built between Santo Domingo and Quinindé in 1948. Since then, colonists have slowly been encroaching on the terrain, chopping down trees and selling Chachi lands illegally to lumber com-panies – hence the creation of this reserve in 1996.

There is no tourist infrastructure within the reserve, so by far the easiest way to **access** it is going through the Reserva Biológica Bilsa (see p.363), whose forests blend into those of Mache-Chindul. All other access points are quite remote and involve making long hikes, hauling food and camping gear, and hiring a guide or possibly even a mule (each $10 per day). Such options are available from the village of Boca de Tazones, 15km south of Atacames; the communities southeast of El Salto, 15km east of Muisne and 23km south of Tonchigüe; and San José de Chamanga, along the new road halfway between Muisne and Pedernales. Further **information** about the reserve is obtainable from the Ministerio del Ambiente office in Quito (see p.79), though you might find it more effective to ask around in the villages nearby.

Bosque Protector Río Palenque

At km 56 on the Quevedo–Santo Domingo road, the **Bosque Protector Río Palenque** ($5) guards a square kilometre of tropical wet forest, ostensibly a small tract of land, though squeezed into its confines are at least twelve hun-dred species of plants (thirty of which are unique), 350 species each of birds and butterflies, and gardens for orchids, bamboo and medicinal plants. The Fundación Wong (☎04/2208670, ⊕www.fundacionwong.org) manages the reserve and encourages visitors to explore the forest on several trails, and to **stay** at the Science Centre (❾), which sleeps fifteen people.

Quevedo

With no other sizeable community within a hundred kilometres, **QUEVE-DO**, south of Santo Domingo, is a major commercial centre amid a sprawling agricultural landscape. After Babahoyo, it's the second town of little Los Ríos province, whose fertile soils are enriched by the regular flooding of its many rivers in the wet season, and support rice fields and a broad swath of banana plantations. At the crossroads with the poor but scenic road from Portoviejo and Latacunga and the heavily used Santo Domingo–Guayaquil roads, it can be a convenient place to break a long journey, but there's little else to detain you and you're unlikely to encounter any other tourists.

A hot and crowded town whose high-fronted buildings lie squeezed between the Río Quevedo and a bank of hills, Quevedo's dust and bustle are relieved only by a few broad avenues studded with ornamental ficus trees. Four main north-south thoroughfares run parallel to the river: **Malecón Eloy Alfaro**, **7 de Octubre**, **Juan Guzman de Cortés** and **Bolívar**, which accesses the fast route south to Guayaquil and passes the busy **parque central**. The numbered streets make the town easy to navigate, with Calle Primera located at the road bridge in the north and Calle Decimcuarta (14th) as the town centre's last street to the south.

On Malecón Eloy Alfaro the daily **riverside market** overflows with fish, fruit and vegetables, and a clothing market displays racks of shoes at Sexta and Juan Guzman de Cortés, a few blocks to the southwest. At nightfall, the streets empty and the shops shut down, until trading kicks off again just before dawn.

Arrival and information

Quevedo doesn't have a central **bus** terminal, only a collection of company offices clustered mostly around the west side of the road bridge. Transportes Ambato stops at Primera and Bolívar with services to Ambato (7hr), Santo Domingo (2hr) and Quito (5hr); Transportes La Maná leaves from Primera and Bolívar for Guayaquil (3hr 30min); Transportes Macuchi departs from Bolívar and Primera for Quito via Santo Domingo (5hr) and Esmeraldas (6hr); Transportes Sucre goes from 7 de Octubre and Cuarta to Santo Domingo (2hr) and Guayaquil (3hr 30min); Transportes Cotopaxi leaves from Séptima and Juan Guzman de Cortés for Latacunga (5hr 30min) and Ambato (6hr 30min); and Reales Tamarindos at Octava and Marco Quintana services Portoviejo (5hr 15min) and Manta (6hr).

The Banco de Guayaquil, on the main square, has a Visa and MasterCard **ATM**, the **post office** is on Bolívar and Decimasegunda in a covered passage, and the **telephone office** is at 7 de Octubre and Decimatercera, though there are private phone stalls all around the centre.

Accommodation and eating

Among a number of no-frills, low-end **hotels** in varying states of disrepair, the *Imperial*, Séptima 104 and Malecón (℡05/751654; **❷**), is an ageing establishment with no curtains, but does provide private bathrooms, a security gate at the entrance and views over the market and river. Away from the river, on Séptima to Marco Quintana, the *Nuevo Hostal Paris* (℡05/760683; **❸**) is cleaner and quieter, offering ample rooms with air conditioning. Quevedo's most luxurious spot, the business-oriented *Olímpico*, a taxi ride south of the centre on Avenida Jaime Roldos and Decimanovena (℡05/750455 or 750210, ℻751314; **❻**), offers spacious rooms with air conditioning, minibars, phones and TVs, plus an enormous ten-lane pool.

The *Olímpico's* **restaurant**, *Rincón Asturiano*, has fine $4–6 main courses. Other good places to eat are the locally popular *Columbus*, 7 de Octubre and Decimasegunda; *Nuevo Chifa Hong Kong*, Cuarta and 7 de Octubre, the best and smartest of Quevedo's chifas; and *Tungurahua*, 7 de Octubre and Séptima, with a cheap, solid breakfast. You'll find other affordable eateries along 7 de Octubre.

The northern coast

Viewed by many Ecuadorians as the nation's playground, the **northern coast** is home to dozens of popular beach resorts lapped by warm Pacific waters, all within a day's drive of the capital. Busloads of *serranos* spill down from the highlands to fill the resorts during weekends and holidays, making the most of the fun-loving and relaxed *costeño* spirit. Despite its popularity, though, the north coast is still relatively undeveloped by international standards, and you'll be able to find peaceful hideaways even at the busiest times. It's not all beaches, bars and discos, though, and the area also holds mangroves, rocky cliffs, tropical wet forests, scrubby tropical dry forests, hidden fishing villages and forgotten ports, as well as some of the least explored parts of Ecuador outside the Oriente.

At the coast's northern tip near Colombia, **San Lorenzo** is a down-at-heel port lost in a maze of mangroves and estuaries, which acts as the launching pad for trips to several little-visited destinations. You can take a bus by an inland road or boat through the mangroves of the **Reserva Ecológica Manglares Cayapas–Mataje** to remote ports such as **Limones**, **La Tola** and **Borbón**. From the latter town, it's possible to head upstream by canoe on the ríos Cayapas or Santiago to **Afro-Ecuadorian** and **Chachi** settlements and community-run lodges such as **San Miguel** and **Playa de Oro**. At the edge of the mangroves, the coast from La Tola down to **Esmeraldas**, a grim industrial port, features long and often deserted beaches. By contrast, on the other side of Esmeraldas, popular resorts like **Atacames** are loaded with beachfront bars, music, cocktails and revellers. Nearby, the smaller villages of **Tonsupa**, **Súa**, **Same** and **Tonchigüe** offer an increasing number of hotels that are slowly taking the place of fishing boats.

Past the rocky **Punta Galera**, the mangroves once again appear around **Muisne**, a less hectic resort on an offshore sandbar, from where a new road goes all the way to **Pedernales** and the closest beach to Quito. Further south, oceanside cliffs and an arid landscape break up the scenery a bit, but the long beaches return at the surfing hangout of **Canoa** and extend all the way to **San Vicente**. Across the Río Chone estuary, **Bahía de Caráquez** is one of Ecuador's smarter resorts, near mangroves and tropical dry forests, while **Manta** is the country's exuberant second port which boasts a few beaches of its own. **Portoviejo** is the staid inland provincial capital of Manabí province, whose locals favour the nearby resorts of **Crucita**, **San Jacinto** and **San Clemente**.

Once the favoured way of **arriving** at the coast, the exhilarating train ride from Ibarra down to San Lorenzo no longer runs in its entirety, so travellers must choose between the **road from Ibarra** that parallels this disused railway, or the **highway** from Quito to Santo Domingo, from where routes lead off to Esmeraldas, Pedernales, Bahía de Caráquez and Manta. Once you're on the coast it's relatively easy to traverse it, especially after a massive, recent road-improvement program, which has made it possible for the first time to travel the full length of the north coast on pavement.

The area has two distinct seasons, but the **climate** changes slightly the further south you go. Temperatures hover around 26°C across the region throughout the year, but greater rainfall and higher humidity are found north of Pedernales, while to the south there's very little rain from June to November. The **wet season** (Dec–May) features clear skies interrupted by torrential afternoon rains that can wash roads out and make travel difficult. **Mosquitoes** tend to be more of a problem at this time, and Esmeraldas province has one of the highest incidences of malaria in the country, so take plenty of insect repellent and check that your hotel provides mosquito nets. During the **dry season** the days are a little cooler and consistently cloudy, without as much rain. The most popular resorts get very crowded during national holidays and the **high season** (mid-June to early Sept & Dec–Jan), when hotel rates can be twice as much as low-season prices and rooms are harder to come by.

San Lorenzo

A small, run-down town at the northwestern tip of the country, surrounded by sea inlets and mangrove swamps, **SAN LORENZO** grew up around the now-closed railway to Ibarra. Its broad central thoroughfare with two parallel streets (Imbabura and Av Camilo Ponce) still has tracks running down it, which once led all the way to the dock at the north end of town and the nearby **main square** – a grassy patch surrounded by stone benches. For years, the train brought a steady stream of tourists to the town, but most quickly fled the local squalor for the beach resorts further south or retreated back into the sierra. The surviving portion of the **railway** now runs only 25km inland to San Javier de Cachaví, and is serviced fairly regularly by a train that leaves when demand is sufficient (1–2 daily; $0.40 for locals, $10 for foreigners). Otherwise, San Lorenzo is well connected with roads linking it to Ibarra and Esmeraldas, via Borbón, as well as the popular coastal resorts.

Unfortunately, **the town** itself has little to offer, with ramshackle houses and a pervasive sense of anarchy and disarray, evident in its dirty, potholed streets strewn with rubbish and periodically turned into muddy soup by the rain. Although there's not much to see, San Lorenzo's considerable number of **Afro-Ecuadorians** provide a distinct cultural flavour, part of what sociologists call the "Pacific lowlands culture area", extending down the coast from Panama to Esmeraldas province in Ecuador. One of its manifestations is the colourful sound of the **marimba**, the wooden xylophone whose driving rhythms are a key feature of music and dance on the north coast. The town has several groups that stage occasional performances, and it hosts an annual international marimba **festival** during the last week of May; enquire for information at the Federación Cultural Afro, on Imbabura opposite the *Continental* hotel.

Some history

San Lorenzo's **history** is murky, but before the Conquest the area was probably occupied by the **Chachi** (or Cayapa) people, who had been pushed down to the coast either by the Incas or the warlike Malaba – whose name in the Chachi language means "the devil". During the colonial era, the area saw an influx of African slaves and labourers migrating from the plantations and mines of Colombia. The first recorded history begins in the mid-nineteenth century with the arrival of **English** and **German companies**, who sought to exploit the region's tagua, balsa, gold, mangrove bark and medicinal herbs, staying here until the 1930s, when the town was still only a tiny port.

Up to 1957, when the **railway** was completed, getting to San Lorenzo involved a long, mosquito-ridden cross-country slog down from the sierra. The train brought an end to the decades of isolation, and its arrival was so momentous that the inhabitants named one of their main streets "26 de Agosto" after its completion, and another after **Camilo Ponce**, the president who oversaw

6

its creation. San Lorenzo's population doubled virtually overnight and the town grew dramatically, but unfortunately the economic miracle predicted with the coming of the railroad never materialized; the train operated at a loss from the day it opened, and it became increasingly difficult to fund the repairs caused by frequent landslides and rockfalls. Damage from El Niño storms finally ended the full service in 1998.

Arrival, information and transport

Buses from Ibarra arrive and depart from the intersection of Imbabura and 26 de Agosto, the site of most of their offices, and often pass by the town square as well. Buses to and from Esmeraldas via Borbón leave from the square opposite the *Carondelet* hotel (5hr; last bus to Esmeraldas at 4pm), and Trans Esmeraldas also runs a daily bus from Quito and Guayaquil, connecting at its office near the train station on 26 de Agosto and Imbabura.

Servicing the rump railway inland, the **train station** is at the southern end of Imbabura, and a ten-minute walk north brings you to the **dock**, the departure point for boats, a block north of the parque central at the end of Imbabura. Transportes Fluvial y Marítimo Pacífico and Transportes San Lorenzo del Pailón, opposite each other at the dock, run three daily **boats** to Limones, and there are also boats for the Colombian border (7am & 2pm), which stop at the San Pedro beach and Palma Real (both $2.50) along the way. Boat travel is exhilarating, but sometimes uncomfortable; have sunblock handy and take something to sit on.

For **information** on visiting nature reserves, try the Ministerio del Ambiente office on the main square (☏06/780184). There's nowhere to cash traveller's cheques in San Lorenzo, but a few of the shops on Imbabura do change Colombian pesos into dollars. The Andinatel **telephone office** is on Avenida Camilo Ponce (east side of main road), opposite the *San Carlos* hotel.

Accommodation and eating

Don't expect much from your **hotel** beyond a simple bed and perhaps a mosquito net. Bring insect repellent and a net, as the **mosquitoes** can get thick in the air at times.

San Lorenzo doesn't offer much in the way of **restaurants**, other than grimy eateries doling out the usual fish dishes. *La Red*, Isidro Ayora and Imbabura, is a lively place in the evenings with good seafood, and the *Carondelet* hotel has passable meals and breakfasts.

Hotels

Carondelet 24 de Mayo and Isidro Ayora, on the main square ⑦06/780202. Friendly place and the cheapest habitable option, with clean, slightly pokey rooms with nets and private baths. ❷

Continental Imbabura and Isidro Ayora ⑦06/780125 or 780304, ⑤78012760. The best place in town, where half the rooms have a/c, private baths and hot water, making it relatively luxurious. Romantic murals on life in San Lorenzo lend a dash of cheer to the place. ❸–❹

San Carlos near the train station on Imbabura ⑦ & ⑤06/780284. Solid choice painted blue and grey, making it resemble an Ecuadorian police station, but inside the decor is a riot of colour. Rooms come with fans and nets (and a few have private baths), but there's no hot water. ❷

Tolita Pampa de Oro Tácito Ortiz and 26 de Agosto ⑦06/780214 or 780263. Comparatively large rooms with nets, fans and TVs, but steer clear of those without baths, as they tend not to have windows. Price increases with optional a/c. ❸

Around San Lorenzo

Apart from checking out the local culture, you're best off using San Lorenzo as a base for a **canoe** excursion into the mangrove swamps of the **Reserva Ecológica Manglares Cayapas-Mataje** (see overleaf), its beaches at **San Pedro** and **Palma Real**, or three archeological sites that include **La Tolita Pampa de Oro**. About 9km outside town towards Ibarra is the **Bosque Protector La Chiquita**, featuring self-guided trails through tropical wet forest. Coopseturi, at the Trans Fluvial y Marítimo Pacífico office on the San Lorenzo dock (⑦ & ⑤06/780161), offers **day-tours** to these places, with boat trips from $20 per person, in groups of four. For independent excursions, charter boats cost around $80 for the day, so you'll save money on a tour if you travel in a group of more than four people.

Beyond town, the new road to Borbón has opened up one of the least explored parts of Ecuador, accessing fantastic rainforests in the lowlands of the **Reserva Ecológica Cotacachi-Cayapas** (see p.152), along with mangrove swamps and the remote black and Chachi settlements on the ríos Santiago and Cayapas.

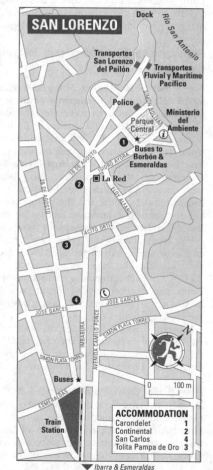

SAN LORENZO

ACCOMMODATION

Carondelet	1
Continental	2
San Carlos	4
Tolita Pampa de Oro	3

▼ *Ibarra & Esmeraldas*

The coast to Esmeraldas

Most travellers rush out of San Lorenzo towards beach resorts further west like Atacames, skipping the poor and largely comfortless **coast to Esmeraldas**, with its rough lumber towns such as **Limones** and **Borbón** and tumbledown fishing villages like **La Tola**. Nevertheless, there are good opportunities here to see the mangroves of the **Reserva Ecológica Manglares Cayapas-Mataje**, and intrepid travellers can also visit the lowland forests of the **Reserva Ecológica Cotacachi-Cayapas** and the fascinating **Chachi** and **Afro-Ecuadorian** communities at the fringes of the reserve. Community eco-tourism projects, such as those in **Playa de Oro** and **San Miguel**, make good bases as well, though there's cheaper and more basic accommodation in some of the river settlements.

There are two **routes** from **San Lorenzo to Esmeraldas**, 110km to the southwest. The fastest by several hours is the new **inland road** to Esmeraldas via Borbón and Maldonado, while the other route involves **taking a boat** via Limones and La Tola and then a **bus** along the coast. Although less comfortable than the first, the second is far more scenic as it passes through the tangled mangrove swamps of the Reserva Ecológica Manglares Cayapas-Mataje.

Reserva Ecológica Manglares Cayapas-Mataje

The **Reserva Ecológica Manglares Cayapas–Mataje** ($5) comprises 513 square kilometres of **mangrove swamps**, a labyrinthine network of natural channels and canals between densely forested islands, stretching from the Colombian border to the estuary at La Tola. The mangroves once provided a sustainable way of life for local residents, who paddled around the latticed trunks on canoes catching small amounts of fish, but since the 1980s huge areas have been destroyed for **shrimp farms** (*cameroneras*). While enriching a few entrepreneurs, these farms have also caused the contamination of the water with noxious chemicals, coastal erosion from the clearance of the mangroves, loss of natural habitat and the disruption of entire ecosystems – along with killing countless seabirds and marine life and triggering a severe crisis for families dependent on the swamps for food and basic materials.

Five types of mangrove grow here, trees uniquely adapted to the salt water and loose sandy soils of the coast, with roots that give them protection from the tides and knit together to provide an anchor during low water levels. Tightly interlaced, they also trap sediments and soils and nurture a wealth of plants, fish, crustaceans and shrimp, while pelicans, frigate birds, egrets and herons nest in their branches, taking advantage of the abundance of food that the reserve provides.

Information about visiting the reserve is available from the Ministerio del Ambiente office in San Lorenzo (see p.368), from where you can head through the mangroves to San Pedro beach by taking a passenger boat, or arrange an organized tour through San Lorenzo's boat companies.

Playa de San Pedro and La Tolita Pampa de Oro

Besides its mangroves, the reserve also features the **Playa de San Pedro**, a twelve-kilometre sandy beach on an island at the northwest of the reserve that links the tiny fishing communities of San Pedro, El Brujo, Palma Real and Cauchal, and presents a quiet place for swimming, sitting under the palms or eating the catch of the day in one of the villages.

Also in the reserve, the several archeological sites of the **La Tolita** people, who inhabited the region from 500 BC to 500 AD, offer little to see beyond a few earthen mounds, though at **La Tolita Pampa de Oro**, at the south end of the reserve on an island near La Tola, gold and platinum ornaments of exquisite craftsmanship have been unearthed, most famously a breathtaking **gold mask**, now the symbol of the Banco Central del Ecuador and housed in its museum in Quito (see p.99). With almost forty mounds distributed on a long east–west axis, the site may have played a major ceremonial or astronomical role, with local groups bringing gold, beads and valuable *spondylus* shells to its religious shrines. A hundred of the region's best warriors once stood guard over its riches, but by the end of the sixteenth century the site had been abandoned. Current archeological work is ongoing, though, and there is a small **museum** that exhibits some of the latest finds. The closest mainland access to La Tolita and the huge mangroves of Majagual is the village of La Tola.

Limones

In the western corner of the reserve, on the wide Boca de Limones estuary, the port of **LIMONES** (officially named Valdez) is accessible only by boat and seldom visited by gringos. The town is a trading centre for timber and bananas floated downriver and for goods moving between Colombia and the provincial coast. Although it's even more dilapidated than San Lorenzo, you'll have to change boats here if you want to get to La Tola, from where buses head down the coast to Esmeraldas. You might also be able to catch a boat from Limones heading upstream to Borbón.

La Tola

Facing the Reserva Ecológica Manglares Cayapas-Mataje across the wide estuary of the Río Cayapas, **LA TOLA** is the fishing village where the boat from Limones drops its passengers for the connecting bus to Esmeraldas, which leaves by the dock (see p.373 for details). While you wait for it, you can grab a bite at the basic eateries that boil up cauldrons of rice to go with the daily catch, or drop by the rather meagre stores stocking biscuits and the bare essentials. Across the river is the site of La Tolita (see above), which you can visit by hiring a launch, and a short bus ride outside town are the **Majagual** mangroves, thought to be the tallest in the world at more than 60m. There are trails through the mangroves here, but take along boots unless you don't mind getting wet.

La Tola has a basic **pensión** (❷) if you get stuck, but it's wiser to push on to Esmeraldas or stay at **Olmedo**, where a women's cooperative runs an ecotourism project with **accommodation** (❸) and clean bathrooms, and a huge veranda strung with hammocks and supported on stilts above the tidal waters. Inexpensive **meals** are available and local **tours** include visits to the mangroves, archeological sites and beaches, plus fishing from a canoe. For reservations contact Luz de Alba (✆06/780239) well in advance of your arrival.

Borbón

Forty kilometres southwest of San Lorenzo, unappealing **BORBÓN** is a rough-and-ready timber town that sits at the confluence of the ríos Cayapas and Santiago. Once a bustling little river port, its population and economy went into a tailspin when the railway opened in San Lorenzo, and nowadays it's mainly known as the hometown of the octogenarian Papa Roncón, Ecuador's greatest marimba player. Borbón is also the embarkation point for the Afro-Ecuadorian and Chachi communities upriver and the tropical forests of the Reserva Ecológica Cotacachi-Cayapas (see p.152).

Buses from San Lorenzo leave every hour or so during daylight and take a little over an hour to arrive; there's also a regular service onwards to Esmeraldas (3hr 15min). Several **boats** depart in the morning for various destinations along the Río Cayapas, but there is no public service up the Río Santiago. Borbón has several simple **hotels**, none particularly appealing, though the *Pampa de Oro*, on the main street (no phone; ❷), has private baths and mosquito nets.

SUBIR, a local organization working around the reserve, combines conservation with sustainable development by setting up ecotourism projects in local communities; to request **information** or arrange a community visit, drop by their local office up the hill on Borbón's main street (no phone), or contact their branch in Quito, Apartado 17-21-190 (☎02/2528696, ℱ2565990, ⓦwww.ns.care.org.ec/subir).

Río Cayapas

On the way to San Miguel from Borbón, the **RÍO CAYAPAS** leaves the pastureland around the estuary and enters dense, lowland tropical forests, where the simple, open-sided stilted homes of the indigenous **Chachi** people occasionally appear at the green fringes of the riverbanks. Also known as the Cayapa, the Chachi have lived on the ríos Cayapas and Santiago at least since the time of the Spanish conquest. Some maintain that the Chachi came from the sierra, fleeing the Incas or Spanish conquistadors, while others claim they were a coastal people forced inland by the descendants of black slaves (see p.374). Whatever their history, some thirty thousand Chachi lived in Esmeraldas province before the Spanish arrived, but the region was so inaccessible that they were spared the worst of the Old World oppression and disease. Even so, only five thousand Chachi remain today, living alongside Afro-Ecuadorians, who both farm small plots of land for plantains, hunt in the forests and fish in the rivers. Since the 1940s and 1950s, however, these communities have been under pressure from the logging industry and more recently from multinational agribusiness, looking to exploit the forests around them. However, **ecotourism** is now emerging as a good alternative means for these communities to receive income and maintain their forests as well.

Boats leave Borbón for various destinations up the river between 10am and 11.30am, but arrive early to get a place. Forty-five minutes upriver, where the river meets the sizeable tributary of the Río Ónzole, *Steve's Lodge* is a comfortable **place to stay**, built by an English-speaking Hungarian and featuring electricity, hot water and cold beer. The lodge is only open for three weeks each year at the beginning of August; accommodation and three meals cost $40 per person, and guided tours of the villages upstream and the Cotacachi-Cayapas reserve are offered, plus waterskiing and canoeing lessons. Make bookings through Steve or Laura Tarjanyi, Casilla 187, Esmeraldas (ⓔstevelodge@earthlink.net).

Punto Venado, Santa María and Zapallo Grande

The next settlement on the river, **Punto Venado**, is unusual for being abandoned for most of the year. As the major Chachi ceremonial centre, it's of special importance during religious occasions such as funerals, Christmas and Easter, when it fills with local people. Further on is **Santa María**, a missionary village inhabited by Chachis and Afro-Ecuadorians, who offer demonstrations of basket- and mat-weaving. The mission has simple accommodation, and there is also a basic hotel, both of which can provide meals or arrange local tours. At **Zapallo Grande**, a well-tended village with a missionary hospital about two hours further upstream, you can buy local **craftworks** such as baskets, textiles, mats and pottery at a local artesanía shop.

San Miguel

Five hours south of Borbón, **SAN MIGUEL** is the last major settlement before the Cotacachi-Cayapas Reserve and lies within reasonable proximity of it. SUBIR (see opposite for information and reservations) and the local communities have developed an ecotourism project based around a large, rudimentary **field station**, providing seven simple but comfortable rooms with shared baths and cold water, and electricity produced by generator. A stay here can include guided **forest walks** and visits to **gold-panning rivers**, but make sure to bring rubber boots. The reserve's guard post offers a basic **refuge** ($4) with small dorms and a kitchen (but no running water or electricity) and space for **camping**. Ask at the guard post about **guides** for the reserve ($10 per day).

Río Santiago

Less travelled than the Río Cayapas, the **Río Santiago** winds through dense forests and provides the only access to the remote northwest section of the Cotacachi-Cayapas Reserve (see p.152). There is no regular boat service up the Río Santiago, though there is a road from Maldonado as far as Selva Alegre. You can ask at the dock in Borbón to charter a **motor canoe** (*flete*), but this can be expensive unless you travel with several people to split the cost (around $80).

As the first settlement upriver of Borbón, **MALDONADO** is a village just off the Borbón–San Lorenzo road, close to the wet forests of the **Bosque Humedal del Yalare**, a good place for bird watching. Beyond Maldonado there's little public river traffic, but a road heads inland as far as Selva Alegre, from where you can get a boat for the 45-minute ride to **PLAYA DE ORO**, a community of fifty Afro-Ecuadorian families who still depend on the shrinking forest for their food. The community has set up a **lodge** providing private bathrooms and electricity for several hours a day, and offers guided excursions further upriver to its **protected forests**. If you plan to stay here, make sure to bring your own food; contact Mauro Caicedo in San Lorenzo for further information (☎06/780787).

La Tola to San Mateo

Back along the north coast, battered buses ply the bumpy coastal road from La Tola 122km west to Esmeraldas (6 daily, 4hr). **Las Peñas** is the first in a succession of small fishing towns scattered along the sandy beaches that line much of this section of coast. It has, however, been earmarked for development as a seaside resort, thanks to the new paved road from Ibarra, which has made it the most easily accessed beach from a large sierra town.

The inland road from Borbón meets the coastal road west of Las Peñas, and on this stretch you'll see plenty of dusty brown pelicans and white cattle egrets in the trees, while frigate birds wheel around overhead. A metal bridge takes you over the **Río Verde** into the eponymous town, the location of Moritz Thomsen's books *Living Poor* and *Farm on the River of Emeralds* (see "Contexts", p.553) and a popular beach resort for Esmeraldas residents – though still well off the beaten track for foreigners.

About 20km further, where the road has been washed away, the bus takes a diversion along the beach, dodging the driftwood and the breakers and making the most of a surface levelled by the tides twice a day. **Camarones**, true to its name, is a quiet shrimping village where there are a few small restaurants and hotels. Ten kilometres west of Camarones is the airport for Esmeraldas, though the city itself is on the other side of the Río Esmeraldas estuary, reached by the crossing at **San Mateo**, 10km upstream. There's a police **checkpoint** here, so have your passport ready.

Esmeraldas

That a city with a name meaning "emeralds" should be so ugly, dirty and depressed comes as a major disappointment. **ESMERALDAS** is the largest industrial port on the north coast, from where bananas, cocoa, citrus fruits and coffee from the lowlands are shipped, while a significant portion of local income comes from an oil refinery at nearby Puerto Balao, which links up to the **Trans-Andean oil pipeline**, snaking 500km from the Oriente. Esmeraldas suffered considerably during the El Niño events of the late 1990s, when mudslides ruptured the pipeline and caused explosions and fatalities, not to mention considerable environmental damage. The water supply was cut off for several weeks, sanitary systems collapsed and disease broke out, prompting a nationwide aid campaign. Esmeraldas' tourism industry, such as it is, is still recovering, but most visitors are Ecuadorian *serranos* and Colombians still drawn by the lively atmosphere and beaches at **Las Palmas**, an upmarket suburb at the north end of town, where the city's bars, discos and the more expensive hotels and restaurants are found.

Be aware that Esmeraldas has a notorious and well-deserved reputation for **crime**, particularly muggings. The definite **areas to avoid** include the Malecón (also called Av Maldonado), location of some of the bus stations, from where you should take a taxi to your hotel, especially after dark; the neighbourhood downhill from the Malecón to the east, which is dangerous at all times; and the main square, regarded as unsafe after about 8pm. The **safest part of town** during daylight hours is the busy centre bordered by Salinas, Eloy Alfaro, Juan Montalvo and Bolívar. Otherwise, don't wander around other areas at any time.

Some history

The town's name derives from the first visits of Spanish conquistadors, who entered coastal villages around here in 1531 and supposedly found **emeralds** the size of "pigeons' eggs"; the moniker stuck, despite years of fruitless expeditions for phantom emerald mines.

Before the conquest, the Esmeraldas coast was so heavily populated with **indigenous tribes** that Bartolomé de Ruiz, who passed through the area on orders from Francisco Pizarro five years earlier, was afraid to land and anchored in the bay instead. Exactly what happened to the native population is a mystery as written records are elusive, but their numbers declined rapidly during the sixteenth century, probably due to the introduction of foreign diseases, Spanish military probes and the arrival of Africans as slaves and soldiers, which dramatically changed the region's ethnic and cultural character.

Some historians contend that the **Afro-Ecuadorians** here are the descendants of escaped slaves from Guinea, who survived a shipwreck off the Esmeraldas coast in 1553 and, led by the *ladino* (an African acculturated in Spanish ways) **Alfonso Illescas**, began marrying local *indígenas*. Others argue that their ancestors were labourers in the Colombian mines to the north or soldiers brought by Pizarro to fight in the conquest. Either way, they had control of much of the region by the early sixteenth century, which hardly bothered the Spanish, who preferred to leave well alone its impenetrable forests and hostile residents. **Pedro Vicente Maldonado**, a precocious *serrano* who became the provincial governor in 1729 at the age of 25, made the most successful exploration of the region in the colonial era, building the first road down from the highlands to the coast as far as Puerto Quito. On a tributary of the Río Esmeraldas, he sailed down to Esmeraldas and the ocean, pacifying the communities on the way.

Little else is known about the region during this period, save for an account by the Irish explorer **William B. Stevenson**, who followed Maldonado's footsteps in 1809 and uncovered the settlement at Esmeraldas, which then comprised 93 houses on stilts. Even then, the legend of the emeralds lived on, as Stevenson wrote that the province derived its name "from a mine of emeralds which is found no great distance from Esmeraldas-town...I never visited it, owing to the superstitious dread of the natives who assured me that it was enchanted and guarded by an enormous dragon".

▲ ❶ & ❷ (3 km), ❸ & ⓘ (1.5 blocks) & Las Palmas

ESMERALDAS

ACCOMMODATION
Apart Hotel Esmeraldas	3
Cayapas	2
Costa Esmeraldas	5
Costa Verde	1
Diana	7
El Galeón	6
Miraflores	4

Museo del Banco Central

ESPEJO

Market

JUAN MONTALVO

★ Trans CITA

ROCAFUERTE

★ Aerotaxi

★ Trans Esmeraldas

Trans La Costeñita

10 DE AGOSTO

Church

Parque Central

9 DE OCTUBRE

★ Trans Occidentales

PIEDRAHITA

★ Trans Zambrano

★ Reina del Camino

Municipio

★ Trans Pacífico

CANIZARES

MEJÍA

★ Panamericana

SALINAS

COLON

OLMEDO

SUCRE

BOLIVAR

MALECÓN (MALDONADO)

N

0   100 m

Río Esmeraldas

RESTAURANTS
Chifa Asiático	D
Las Redes	A
Tía Concha	B
Las Vegas	C

▼ Atacames & Santo Domingo de los Colorados

Despite some short-lived rubber booms, it remained a neglected and isolated area until the mid-twentieth century, when a road was finally built linking it to the highlands. In the 1970s, after the completion of the Trans-Ecuadorian pipeline and the opening of some deepwater docks, the town rapidly developed, becoming the major industrial port it is today.

Arrival and information

Most hotels and shops lie between Salinas and Juan Montalvo on the parallel streets of Bolívar, Sucre and Olmedo. North of Montalvo, Bolívar becomes Avenida Libertad, the main route to Las Palmas. All the **bus stations** are within five blocks of the parque central; if you're coming from outside the province, you'll probably be dropped off at the parque, while provincial companies use the Malecón. You can pick up **taxis** around the central streets and at the parque, which charge less than $1 for most local destinations. **City buses** ply the Avenida Libertad up to Las Palmas ($0.20), while buses to and from San Lorenzo pass the **airport** (served by flights from Quito) across the Río Esmeraldas estuary at Tachina – 25km by road, or a 45-minute taxi ride ($5). The route crosses the river at San Mateo, 10km south of the city. Have your documents ready as there's a police **checkpoint** here, and bag searches are common.

The helpful tourist office, upstairs on the Avenida Libertad opposite the *Apart Hotel Esmeraldas* (Mon–Fri 8.30am–12.30pm & 2.30–5.30pm; ⊕06/711370), provides **information** on Esmeraldas' few attractions.

Accommodation

Finding a cheap **hotel** in Esmeraldas is not a problem, but most are uninspiring, and travellers usually push on to one of the popular beach resorts to the south if possible. A more comfortable option is to stay overnight in Las Palmas, where the better hotels can be found. **Mosquitoes** can be a nuisance during the wet season, and malaria a concern on the north coast, so bring insect repellent and request a mosquito net (*mosquitero* or *toldo*) if necessary. Note that only the top hotels have hot water.

Apart Hotel Esmeraldas Libertad 407 and Ramón Tello ⊕06/728700 or 728701. The best and costliest hotel (and casino) in Esmeraldas proper, frequented mainly by businessmen, offering nice tiled rooms with private hot-water baths and cable TVs. Despite a renovation, the building still feels a bit tired, but the restaurant is good. ⑥

Cayapas Kennedy and Valdez, Las Palmas ⊕06/721318. Rooms come with a/c and hot water, though the ones upstairs enjoy better lighting. Also has a neatly pruned garden and a fine restaurant. ⑤

Costa Esmeraldas Sucre 911 and Piedrahita ⊕06/723912. Despite the thin mattresses, the ample rooms are all decent value, especially considering they come with ceiling fans, private baths, TVs and phones – though a/c is extra. ③–④

Diana Cañizares 224 and Sucre ⊕06/724519. Inexpensive, reliable choice where modest, high-ceilinged rooms with private baths and fans surround an attractive blue courtyard. Owner speaks English. ②

El Galeón Piedrahita and Olmedo ⊕06/723820. Bare, simple rooms offer private baths, ceiling fans and phones, with a/c and cable TV for a dollar more. Avoid the dingy interior rooms. ③–④

Miraflores Bolívar and 9 de Octubre ⊕06/723077. Acceptable rock-bottom choice whose small and simple rooms with shared baths are brightened by scrupulously polished wooden floors and plastic floral arrangements. Located on the main square, so the front rooms are noisy. ②

Suites Costa Verde Luís Tello 809 and Hilda Padilla, Las Palmas ⊕06/728714 or 728717, ⑤728716. Comfortable suites appointed with kitchenettes, minibars, dining spaces, satellite TVs and balconies with flowery window boxes. Use of a sauna, Jacuzzi and small pool are all part of the package, and the restaurant is also very good. ⑥

The City

Dominating the tree-filled but fenced-off **parque central**, a tall and derelict concrete office block leers over Esmeraldas' focal point with gutted black holes like a skeleton's eye sockets. It's a telling symbol of a town that has suffered badly from poverty and neglect, though a dedicated mayor is striving to make changes, implementing rubbish collection and tidying up public spaces. Despite the long-standing privations, the local population of 125,000 are renowned for their fun-loving, if hard-nosed, attitudes, and the spruced-up park bustles with street vendors, shoeshiners and fruit-juice sellers. On the west side of the park, the town **church** built in 1956 seems underwhelming, but is worth a look inside for its unusual, undulating cement arches moulded by bamboo rods that appear to ripple like a hanging curtain.

Heading east, the **Malecón** (Avenida Maldonado) is a busy thoroughfare that's a combination market, bus terminal, taxi rank and sideshow, watched by locals from the balconies of collapsing wooden houses. North along the Malecón to Montalvo, the **market** fills the street with vendor stalls laden with all manner of domestic items, from scrub brushes to Tupperware.

Around the Andinatel office on Montalvo, there are superb views of the river and market below, while a short walk west of the market is the town's only real attraction, the **Museo del Banco Central**, on Espejo between Colón and Olmedo (Mon–Sat 9am–4.30pm; $0.25), a good museum of regional pre-Columbian artefacts, including some wonderfully expressive ceramics and **canasteros** – La Tolita merchants shown bearing huge baskets on their backs. The bank also features a substantial historical **archive** focusing on Afro-Ecuadorians but also covering ethnomusicology, poetry, myths and legends. Next door, the **art gallery** (same hours and ticket) has regularly changing exhibitions of the work of local and national artists.

The city celebrates four main **fiestas**, the biggest of which is the **Independence of Esmeraldas** on August 5, which combines with an agricultural fair. Festivities for the **foundation** of the city are held on September 21, while cantonization is celebrated on July 25 and provincialization on May 7.

Las Palmas

Three kilometres north of the city centre along Avenida Libertad and fronting the Pacific is **Las Palmas**, Esmeraldas' swankiest neighbourhood, where the city's best hotels, restaurants and bars service mostly national tourists and businessmen – though the squalor is never far away and run-down slums fester at its margins. The beach too is litter-strewn and unsafe at night, the sea is polluted and the discos can get rowdy, so Las Palmas doesn't usually figure on the itinerary of most travellers. On the other hand, if you have to stay in Esmeraldas for a few days, this is undoubtedly the best choice.

City **buses** regularly run from Bolívar and Avenida Libertad to Las Palmas (5min trip), dropping off on Avenida Kennedy – an attractive tree-lined boulevard passing most of the hotels and restaurants and leading to the **beach** at its far western end.

Eating, drinking and nightlife

As in the rest of the province, **restaurants** in Esmeraldas serve up tasty seafood blended with delicious tropical flavours drawn from the Afro-Ecuadorian culinary heritage. **Encocados**, fish steeped in spiced coconut milk, is a speciality, and you'll find it at most restaurants and roadside stalls. Although downtown Esmeraldas has a number of cheap eateries with decent food, the best choices are in Las Palmas at the smarter hotels and along Avenida Kennedy, such as *Los Helechos* and *La Cascada*. For **nightlife**, Las Palmas is preferred over the city centre, and its **bars** and **clubs** line the beach blasting music out at ear-splitting levels well into the wee hours. For safety reasons, going in a group is a good idea, as is enquiring about the best and safest places, such as *Chic*, on Avenida Kennedy. Nearer the beach, *Rock Julian's* is Ecuador's version of a warehouse rave, occupying a large structure mimicking an aircraft hangar, while *Keop's*, next door, is fronted with grandiose Greco-Roman decor.

Restaurants

Chifa Asiático Cañizares and Sucre. Boasts a spacious interior with a/c, and doles out cheap and reliable Chinese nosh.

Las Redes on Bolívar at the park. Good little place for its breakfasts and seafood dishes.

Las Vegas Cañizares and Bolívar. Decorated with pictures of European capitals and serves large

portions at low prices: a massive plate of greasy spaghetti goes down for under $2, and fried chicken costs only a little more. Closed Sun.

Tía Concha Piedrahita and Olmedo. Features tasty and inexpensive *mariscos*, and is also popular for its cheap *almuerzos*. Closed Sun night.

Listings

Airline Tame, Bolívar and 9 de Octubre ☎06/726863. All buses heading to San Lorenzo pass by the airport.

Banks Banco de Guayaquil, Bolívar and Montalvo (traveller's cheques, Visa ATM and cash advances); Banco del Austro, Bolívar and Cañizares (Visa ATM); Banco del Pichincha, Bolívar and 9 de Octubre (traveller's cheques, Visa and MasterCard ATM).

Buses Aerotaxi, Sucre and 10 de Agosto, goes to Ibarra via Quito, and to Guayaquil; Panamericana, Colón and Mejía, has a few comfortable buses to Quito; Reina del Camino, Piedrahita and Bolívar, services Santo Domingo, Portoviejo and Manta; Trans CITA, Sucre and Rocafuerte, has the most regular service to Ambato; Trans Esmeraldas, on the parque central at 10 de Agosto, has an efficient service to Quito, Machala and Guayaquil (taking the slower route via Babahoyo); Trans Gilberto Zambrano, Sucre and Piedrahita, operates a fleet of old buses for Santo Domingo, Muisne and Pedernales; Trans Occidentales, 9 de Octubre and

Sucre, goes to Quito, Ambato, Riobamba, Guayaquil and Machala; Trans Pacífico, Malecón and Piedrahita, and Trans La Costeñita, Malecón and 10 de Agosto, send alternate buses regularly to Borbón, San Lorenzo and Muisne via Atacames, Same and Súa, with a handful continuing to Pedernales. La Costeñita also goes to La Tola.

Hospital on Av Libertad, at the north end of town on the way to Las Palmas. Offers 24hr emergency treatment (☎06/710012).

Internet facilities Several options include Coconet, on Bolívar at the park ($1.50 per hour), with netphone service; and Comopunet, Bolívar and Cañizares.

Police and immigration Policía Civil Nacional, in Batallón Montufar Complex, a few kilometres south of the centre on the main road (☎06/724624 or 700739).

Post office Colón, between 10 de Agosto and 9 de Octubre.

Telephone office Andinatel, Juan Montalvo and Malecón, upstairs.

The coast west to Muisne

The expanses of pale sand **west of Esmeraldas** hold some of the country's most popular seaside resorts. During the **high season** (mid-June to Sept & Dec–Jan), a deluge of vacationers descends from the highlands, but the real crush comes during national holidays such as Carnaval, Semana Santa, Christmas and New Year, when hotel rooms are pricey, if there are any left. **Atacames** is the most famous and raucous resort, while others such as **Tonsupa**, **Súa** and **Same** offer a more tranquil atmosphere by the sand and surf, but can be just as busy at peak times. The beaches break around the dry and rocky headland of the **Punta Galera**, whose cliffs and secluded coves provide the quietest and most isolated beaches in the region, giving way to mangrove forests around **Muisne**, one of the remoter seaside resorts of the province. Regular **buses** travel between Muisne and Esmeraldas, allowing easy movement from one place to the next.

Tonsupa

Once a small fishing village, **TONSUPA**, 25km west of Esmeraldas, has developed into a sprawling grid of holiday homes and cabin complexes. **Tricicleros** take you 2km from the bus stop on the main road to the broad beach of **Playa Ancha**, which curves in a soft arc at low tide. At its eastern end, a few tall buildings signal the centre of the village, where you'll find a handful of restaurants, bars and cheap hotels. On the beach, you can watch Tonsupa's dwindling number of fishermen haul in their catches and mend nets on the shore, but spreading back from here, the monotonous white-block holiday cabañas make for a rather sterile and dreary ambience, through it's still classier and more peaceful than its noisy neighbour, Atacames, 5km down the road.

The more expensive **hotels** in Tonsupa typically have a pool, hot water and air conditioning, and you may be able to get substantial discounts during the low season and during the week. *Club del Pacífico*, on the Playa Ancha (℡06/731053; $160 per four-person cabin), is one of the better options, while *Cabañas Turísticas Emerita* (℡06/713226; ❸–❹) provides standard rooms on an undisturbed beach several hundred metres west of the centre.

Atacames

Relaxed by day and brash, noisy and fun at night, **ATACAMES** is one of Ecuador's top beach resorts, always crowded during holidays and at Carnaval, when it's literally standing room only on its dusky beach. The town is divided by the tidal waters of the **Río Atacames**, which parallel the shore for about 1km, resulting in a slender, sandy peninsula connected to the mainland by a footbridge and, further upstream, a road bridge.

Arrival, information and transport

Trans La Costeñita and Trans Pacífico **buses** run between Esmeraldas and Muisne and call every twenty to thirty minutes at the town's central bus stop, marked by a waiting bench and a battered sign proclaiming "*parada*". **Tricicleros** ferry you from here to the beach, though they travel via a road bridge further inland, so it's quicker to **walk**: follow the road diagonally off the main road behind the bus stop, cross the footbridge and turn right onto 21 de Noviembre, which leads to the Malecón. Long-distance buses usually stop at their own respective offices; buy your **ticket** early if you're heading back to Quito (6hr 30min trip). Trans Esmeraldas, at Juan Montalvo and Luis Vargas Torres, has five daily buses to Quito and two to Guayaquil (8hr), while Trans Occidentales, not far from the footbridge, has five to Quito and a night bus to Guayaquil. Aerotaxi and Panamericana have less frequent services to Quito.

Roger Quintero, tourism director at the *municipio*, 1km out of town towards Esmeraldas (Mon–Fri 8am–5pm; ℡06/731395), provides **information**, maps and advice for local trips. For **banks**, Banco del Pichincha, Cervantes and Espejo, changes traveller's cheques and provides Visa and MasterCard cash advance, while Farmacia Su Economía, on the main road near the bus stop, is open late daily. Other facilities include a **laundry**, Zum Tucán, on Vargas Torres, which washes clothes by the kilogram, though

the business was recently up for sale; the Andinatel **telephone** office at Luís Tello and Montalvo; the post office at Espejo and Calderón; and **Internet** access at the stationers on Luís Tello, around the parque central ($2.40 per hour). The **police** are located over the road bridge, first on the right on Avenida Las Acacias.

Accommodation

During high season (July–Sept & holidays), expect to pay up to double the low-season rates for **accommodation**; weekends are also busy, but otherwise hoteliers are happy to bargain. If travelling alone, you may have to pay for all the beds in your room unless you're willing to share. In the wet season, mosquitoes can fill the air, so ask your hotel for a **net**. Unless you're a party animal, get a hotel with a bit of protection from the noise – that is, not overlooking the beach bars on the Malecón. The more expensive cabin complexes are often further from the racket, while the simple budget hotels crowd the centre.

Cabañas Caída del Sol Malecón del Río ☎06/731479. Clean and roomy cabins back from the beach, equipped with private baths, fans, TVs, fridges and kitchen sinks. Good value in the low season, but prices more than double at busy times. ③

Carmita Calle Tagua ☎06/731268. Well-kept little rooms with tiled floors and private baths, decorated in cheerful yellow and dappled blue, though now a bit dwarfed by large hotel blocks. ③
La Casa de Manglar 21 de Noviembre ☎06/731464. Simple rooms, mostly with bunks and

shared baths, set in a peaceful location near the beach and town, where you can put your feet up and watch life on the river. Upstairs a small terrace features hammocks and surprisingly comfortable, gnarled mangrove-wood furniture. ❸

Galería Malecón ☎06/731149. Popular for its central beachfront location and good restaurant, though the rooms are a bit poky. High-season and weekend rates require payment for the whole room, most of which sleep four people. English spoken. ❷

Jennifer Calle Tolita ☎06/731055. Bare and characterless brick bungalows, but good for the price, featuring fans, bathrooms and fridges – and kitchenettes for a little more. ❷–❸

Rincón del Mar towards south end of beach ☎06/731064. Pleasant cabins with fans, mosquito nets and private bathrooms; set well away from the noise but right on the beach. A few units have fridges and kitchenettes. English spoken. ❸–❹

Villas Arco Iris at northern end of Malecón ☎06/731069, ℱ 731437, ⓦ www.villasarcoiris .com. Quiet spot abutting the beach, offering a palm-shaded avenue of attractive cabins with a/c, some with kitchens and fridges, and all with hot water and mosquito nets. Porch-side hammocks and swimming pool also make for good on-site relaxation. English spoken. ❺

The Town

Most of the bars, hotels and restaurants in Atacames are on the peninsula, while the shops and services are on the other side of the water, along the main road from Esmeraldas and around the little **parque central**, a few blocks east of the highway. By the beach, the **Malecón** is the place for night-time action: salsa, merengue, pop and techno pummel the air from rival speakers only metres apart, while revellers dance – or stagger – to the beat and knock back fruity cocktails. On weekdays and during the low season the crowds evaporate, but a smattering of bars stays open to keep international travellers amused.

Be aware that the sea has a strong **undertow** here that has claimed a number of victims, despite the occasional presence of volunteer lifeguards. **Crime** is also an unfortunate element of the quieter beach areas, so stay near the crowds, avoid taking valuables onto the beach and stay off it completely at night. The beachside **market**, mostly stocked with trinkets and sarongs, sometimes has black-coral jewellery for sale – a species under threat and illegal to take out of the country.

Apart from the beach and the bars, there's not much more to Atacames, though the **Museo Acuario Marino**, opposite the *Tahiti* hotel towards the northern end of the Malecón (Mon–Fri 9am–8pm, Sat–Sun 9am–10pm; $0.75), presents starfish, turtles, caiman, seahorses and piranhas in fairly miserable conditions, and some of the exhibits even appear to be dead. Far more uplifting are the **humpback whales** visible off the coast between June and September (boats usually depart from Súa); contact Atacames Ecology Tours at *Le Castell* hotel on the Malecón (☎06/731476 or 731442) or enquire at the *municipio* (☎06/731398). **Diving** trips are also offered by Gina Solórzano, who can be reached through the *Tahiti* hotel or *Villas Arco Iris*.

Eating, drinking and nightlife

The numerous **restaurants** along the Malecón serve up nearly identical fish meals for $3–4, whether they come *apanado* (breaded), *frito* (fried whole), *a la plancha* (filleted and grilled or fried), *al vapor* (steamed) or *encocado* (in coconut sauce). *Marco's*, *Pelicano* and *Galería* are reliable options, but there are many similar choices. The traditional Atacames **breakfast**, reputed to be a great hangover cure, is *ceviche* freshly prepared at the little street stalls on Calle Camarones. The *Restaurant No Name* has tasty pizzas and pasta, served in an attractive site overlooking the Malecón, while *El Viejo Fritz*, a few blocks north, has German and European items like Zeberkäse mit Spiegelei, Kalbsgoulasch and Chateaubriand. *La Estancia*, on the seafront, is pricier than most, but its food is also superior.

Every night most of the town's denizens gravitate towards the Malecón, promenading along its busy central section before making a beeline to any of the dozens of **beach bars** lining the sands, each laden with pyramids of fruit and bottles of rum. Current bar favourites are *Caída del Sol* and *Azul Marina*, but this can change as quickly as a merengue beat. Of the four **discos** on the Malecón, the big black box called *Scala* (closed Sun–Thurs in low season; $1) is the preferred choice, playing energetic dance-music hits.

Súa

From **SÚA**, the exuberance of Atacames, 4km to the east, sparkles in the distance as a tiny mosaic of colour against the scrolling uniformity of the sand. Set in a cosy bay, this once-tiny fishing village can get as crowded as its more renowned neighbour in the high season, when inflatable bananas tear through the waves being dragged by powerboats, and sputtering waterbikes destroy any vestige of the town's tranquillity. Off season, Súa is quiet and friendly, though a bit less idyllic than it used to be.

At the heart of Súa, the **Malecón** offers a small strip of hotels, restaurants and shops overlooking the **beach**, which is diminutive at high tide. Cradled by green hills that protect it from the full force of Pacific rollers, Súa's waters are calmer than those of Atacames. On the west side of the bay, the cliffs plunge 80m into the sea and are known as **Peñón del Suicida** (Suicide Rock), named after a pair of star-crossed lovers, Princess Súa and conquistador Captain de León, who hurled themselves off the edge in a romantic legend of forbidden love and fatal misunderstanding. On moonlit nights, their ghosts are said to drift hand-in-hand along the shore accompanied by the enchanted music of the sea. Your own walks around the Peñón, however, will probably be accompanied by the shrieking and whistling of pelicans, blue-footed boobies and frigate birds nesting on the clifftops, waiting to swoop down on the fishermen's haul. Seasonal boats leave Súa in the morning for **humpback whale-watching** off the coast (June–Sept; $15–20 per person).

Arrival, information and transport

Regular **buses** between Esmeraldas and Muisne deposit passengers on the main road, a five-minute walk from the beach. In the high season, vehicles can be so packed that you might have to cling to the handrails outside the door – it's forbidden to travel on the roof. From the road, **tricicleros** take visitors several hundred metres through the back of the village to the Malecón, where they're dropped off at the east side of the bay, by the *Chagra Ramos* hotel. There are no money-changing facilities in Súa, but for **phones**, go to the Andinatel office near the entrance of *Chagra Ramos*.

Accommodation, eating and drinking

Accommodation in Súa is less expensive and diverse than in Atacames, and it can be difficult finding a room at the height of the holidays. A few reasonable seafood **restaurants**, juice stalls and beach **bars** line the Malecón.

Hotels

Las Buganvillas on the beach ☎06/731008. Friendly budget choice draped in the eponymous flowers. ❸

Cabañas Los Jardines back from the beach ☎06/731181. Clean, family-sized rooms with bunks, double beds and private baths. You'll need to find the owners at Bazar Barcelona on the Malecón to get access to your room. ❷

Chagra Ramos on the hillside at the east end of the bay ☎06/731006 or 731025. Offers large villas that are good value for their private baths and sea-view balconies facing the setting sun, while older cabañas have ceilings that are a bit low and close. Has a popular restaurant, and you can also hire waterbikes and banana boats. ❸

Súa directly on the beach ☎06/731004. Has a good eatery and supplies hot water to its attractive, modest rooms, some with wooden balconies. ❷

Same

The main road leaves the coast beyond Súa to skirt the Cerro Don Juan before swinging back to the beaches at **SAME**, 11km west. Of all the resorts in the Atacames area, Same is the most exclusive and the least prone to overcrowding, where rows of palms shade a beautiful, soft **beach** of clean, grey sand caressed by a warm sea. Developers have long recognized its potential, but strip away their interventions – such as the Jack Nicklaus-designed golf course sitting under the white holiday villas cresting the hills – and Same is just a tiny village with little more than a handful of basic shops.

Practicalities

Buses between Muisne and Esmeraldas can drop you at Same; for the beach, ask the driver for "*el puente de Same*" and he'll stop at a track that leads to Same's bridge, which crosses a little stream over to the more affordable hotels and the beach – otherwise you may be deposited more than 1km from the beach at the golf course and the road up to the luxurious hillside villas of *Club Casablanca* (☎02/2252488, ⓦwww.ccasablanca.com; ❽).

There's very little cheap **accommodation** in town – one reason why it's quieter than Atacames. The most affordable choice is *Azuca*, on the main road at the south end of town (no phone; ❷), offering three large, simple rooms in a pleasant house with a good Colombian restaurant. On the beach to the left, *La Terraza* (☎06/733320; ❹) features attractive seaside cabins under palm trees, furnished with porches, hammocks and private baths, and a restaurant that serves mid-priced pasta and seafood. The *Seaflower*, over the bridge on the left (☎06/733369; ❹), rents four pleasant, arty rooms sleeping two to five, and has an excellent German-run gourmet **restaurant** that's one of the best in the region, offering delicious seafood in enormous portions, accompanied by salads and fresh-baked bread for $8–13 per main course. A few other simple eateries and **bars** on the beach serve up the usual fish dishes and cocktails.

El Acantilado and Tonchigüe

Same's beach stretches 3km down to Tonchigüe, passing expensive *cabañas* and villas, the best of which is the gorgeous German-run **El Acantilado** (☎06/733466; ❺, discounts for *Rough Guide* users), perched on a sandy cliff 1km south of Same. Surrounded by gardens ablaze with flowers, it has a games room, decent restaurant, and cabins for up to eight people and suites for up to four, with hot-water bathrooms, fridges and fans, and some with beautiful ocean vistas. Reservations are advised in high season, particularly for the rooms with views.

Two kilometres further, **TONCHIGÜE** is a fishing village where tourism hasn't yet made a significant dent, and its beach is strewn with blue fishing boats, tangled heaps of netting and fishy detritus. The edge of the village is bounded by the main road, where you'll find the bus stop; walk downhill away from the road past the shaded park, turn right and continue for a few blocks to reach the beach. The cheap, out-of-the-way **accommodation** might be within a walk or bus ride of the more popular beaches, but it's strictly no-frills stuff. The rooms with shared bath above the Tienda Elsa de Pacheco, Luís Córdova and Espejo (☎06/732034; ❷), are the best of a basic bunch, and meals are cooked on request. *Luz y Mar*, on 26 de Noviembre (no phone; ❶), has private baths and temperamental plumbing, while *Tonchigüe*, opposite the beach (☎06/732057; ❶), offers bare rooms with shared baths. A few simple **restaurants** line the main road, and there's an Andinatel **phone** office just off the park.

Punta Galera and Playa Escondida

At El Puente de Tonchigüe, the road splits between the main highway heading south to Muisne and a secondary road going west along the coast to rugged **PUNTA GALERA**, a rocky cape where the coastline bends west to south. Ten kilometres along this bumpy road, the secluded Canadian-run **Playa Escondida** (☎07/733122 or 733106; ❹, typical daily cost $30 per person with meals) is a serene, ecologically minded beach hideaway offering four charming but rustic cabins with shared showers and composting toilets, overlooking a pretty cove – effectively a private beach – backed by a tract of semi-tropical, semi-deciduous forest teeming with birds and wildlife like *guantas* and anteaters. On its tawny beach, marine turtles clamber ashore to lay eggs, and whales are occasionally spotted out at sea. There's good walking at low tide along the craggy shoreline, and you can arrange horse riding in the forest or tours to the mangroves around Muisne.

Transportes Costeñita **buses** for Punta Galera (12.10pm & 4.10pm), sometimes marked for "Estero de Plátano", leave from the Malecón in Esmeraldas and pass all the coastal towns on the way to El Puente de Tonchigüe. River Taviazo also sends **rancheras** from Esmeraldas three times daily, and you can rent a **camioneta** in Tonchigüe for $5.

Muisne

Located some 35km south of the big resorts, luxury seaside villas and condominiums, **MUISNE** lies just beyond the range of most *serrano* vacationers, giving the place a slightly abandoned feel. Nonetheless, the relaxed and friendly air draws a reasonable amount of travellers down to this unusual, rather exotic resort, sitting on a seven-kilometre palm-fringed sand bar amid the **mangrove swamps** just off the mainland, reached only by boat from the small town of **El Relleno**, across the Río Muisne.

Unfortunately, since the 1980s, large numbers of the mangroves surrounding the town have been cut down to create **shrimp farms** – ugly pools resembling sewage treatment facilities – which have dealt a severe blow to the birds, marine life and people who relied on the trees for food and sustenance. A handful of entrepreneurs have become millionaires, but most people have lost their way of life, and many now have to work in the shrimp farms to survive. Government measures to stop the destruction – three to thirty days in jail for felling a mangrove – have largely remained unenforced and ineffective.

The organization **Fundecol**, a block from the plaza (☎06/480167), attempts to protect the trees through security patrols, political activism and education, offering information on this special habitat and running **tours** of the area ($30); local hotels offer similar trips. The Fundación Jatun Sacha manages the **Congal Biological Station** in five square kilometres of primary mangrove forest in two locations near Muisne, developing ecologically sound aquaculture and running reforestation programmes; for **volunteering** work at Congal, contact Jatun Sacha in Quito (☎02/2432240, ⓦ www.jatunsacha.org).

Arrival, information and transport

Buses and **camionetas** connect to El Relleno (also known as Nuevo Muisne), a little town across the Río Muisne, from where boats wait until full before whisking people over the water into town ($0.15). From El Relleno, regular services head to Esmeraldas (2hr 30min), passing the resorts to the north, or travel south via El Salto to Chamanga (45min), from where there's transport to Pedernales (1hr). Long-distance buses depart nightly for Quito (8hr) and Guayaquil (9hr).

The new coastal road has ended public **boat** service to Cojimíes and Mompiche, but expensive charter vessels are still available. It's far cheaper to get a bus down the coast to Daule (on the way to Chamanga) and a canoe over the estuary to Cojimíes. Acting as the island's taxis, armies of rival **cyclists** wait to ferry passengers over the cobbles on yellow vehicles equipped with cushioned seats and parasols, running up and down Isidro Ayora from the dock to the beach.

The **telephone** office (daily 8am–10pm) is on Isidro Ayora, 50m east of the plaza. The **bank** by the plaza doesn't change traveller's cheques, but Marco Velasco's little corner shop does, on the beach north of Isidro Ayora.

Accommodation

The cheapest, most basic **places to stay** in town are around the dock, but are not popular options, being 2km from the sand and sea. Despite the claims of many hotels, water shortages can be a problem in Muisne, as can **mosquitoes** – make sure you get a room with a net.

Calade last hotel on the beach to the south ⓣ06/480279. Features colourful balustrades, swings made out of old tyres, hammocks, a resident parrot, Internet access and decent rooms – some with private baths for a bit more. ❷–❸

Mapara just north of the entrance to the beach ⓣ06/480281, ⓔ mapara@accessinter.net. The most expensive place in Muisne, with electric showers and a swanky wooden interior. Rooms with sea views are the best, fitted with foldable patio doors. ❺

El Oasis 200m back from the beach on Manabí, running parallel north of Isidro Ayora ⓣ06/480186. An English-owned fortress fronted by high walls topped with broken glass, behind which is a pleasant garden lined with sparklingly clean cabins, each with an outside hammock. ❸

Playa Paraíso 150m south of the entrance where Isidro Ayora reaches the beach ⓣ06/480192. Offers bright, fresh rooms kitted out with large mosquito nets and clean shared bathrooms, and has a lounging area with comfy chairs and hammocks. ❷

Sarita on Isidro Ayora, before the square ⓣ06/480118. The most acceptable budget choice of those in town for its private baths, mosquito nets and fans – in flaking rooms. ❶

The Town

As you dock, the initial appearance of **the town** is not promising. The salty breeze, equatorial sun and high humidity bring buildings out in an unsightly rash of peeling paint and mouldy green concrete, giving the place a dilapidated appearance – upkeep and construction are an expensive business on this car-free island, as materials have to be laboriously hauled in from the dock.

The island itself splits into two distinct parts, connected by the double boulevard of **Isidro Ayora**, which runs 2km from the docks to the beach. The town's main shops and services cluster around the dock, where the police, post office and hospital are located, a close distance to the modest **main square** on Isidro Ayora. Muisne's main attractions, though, lie at the boulevard's other end, where the crashing breakers of a broad, flat **beach** are fronted by a handful of inexpensive hotels, restaurants and the odd bar, all shaded by a row of palms.

For **security** reasons, do not take valuables onto the beach, walk on it at night or venture into deserted areas. From time to time you may notice pinprick-like stings when swimming in the ocean; these are caused by tiny **jellyfish** (*aguamala*), whose sting doesn't last much longer than ten minutes. Locals claim a splash of vinegar relieves the pain – ask at a beachside restaurant.

Eating

Among the better **places to eat**, the *Restaurant Suizo-Italiano* on Isidro Ayora, 100m back from the beach, is a friendly spot with delicious pizzas and spaghetti dishes, plus a few board games and a book exchange. The eatery at *Playa Paraíso* dishes up fat breakfasts, including omelettes and fruit salads, as well as vegetarian meals, while the *Calade*'s restaurant *Coral* offers fine seafood and vegetarian dishes. The beachfront is graced with several good **seafood** restaurants around the entrance, *Las Palmeras* and *Santa Martha* being among the most popular.

Muisne to San Vicente

The recent completion of the paved road south of Muisne to Pedernales has made it possible to travel the length of Ecuador's coast by bus or car. The junction for the Pedernales road is at **El Salto**, a collection of grimy roadside stalls, shacks and *comedores*, 11km east of Muisne along the highway to Esmeraldas. From El Salto, the road speeds south for 56km through land dotted with only the odd stilt hut, passing a turn-off to **Mompiche** and then coming within walking distance of **Daule**, where you can get a boat across the broad estuary to **Cojimíes**. Continuing from Daule, the road skirts **Chamanga** (or San José de Chamanga, 2km from the main road), from where there is regular transport to **Pedernales**.

Beyond Chamanga and into **Manabí**, the province of the central seaboard, the climate and scenery soon change from the lush greenery of Esmeraldas to an increasingly dry, scrubby landscape from Pedernales onwards. South of Pedernales is a sparsely populated area of tiny settlements and one town – Jama, 45km away – and a rolling shoreline interspersed with deserted beaches and the occasional secluded hotel. A further 41km away, after turning inland past shrimp farms and through agricultural land, the road rejoins the coast at **Canoa**, an attractive beach resort with good surfing. The beaches continue south from here for almost 20km down to **San Vicente**, a bustling town opposite the high-rises of Bahía de Caráquez, across the Río Chone estuary.

Mompiche

On the sheltered south side of Ensenada de Mompiche, where a beautiful seven-kilometre ribbon of dark sand grows to 100m at low tide, curling around a broad bay and backed by a shock of emerald-green trees, the little fishing village of **MOMPICHE** was once one of the most peaceful spots on the coast, protected from exploitation by its relative isolation. Formerly accessed only by boat or on foot, the town's wooden cabins, fishing boats and simple shops have recently begun to give way to new hotels and a burgeoning tourist industry, ever since the village was linked by road – albeit a poor one that may require a four-wheel-drive vehicle after heavy rains – to the El Salto–Pedernales highway at km 27. River Taviazo runs three **rancheras** a day from Esmeraldas to Mompiche, passing the other beach resorts on the coast. Most hotels (see below) can provide decent **meals**, but there are a couple of inexpensive *comedores* in the village for good seafood, such as *Margarita*.

Accommodation

The village **hotels** are all near the beach on the sheltered side of the bay. *Iruña*, on the other side, gets the brunt of the Pacific and is a good spot for surfing; ask around in the village for a board (*tabla*).

Chao Pescao in the village, just off the road into town (no phone). Cheap and simple, with some of the more basic rooms around. ❷

Gabeal east side of the village ☎09/9696543. Simple cabins of bamboo and concrete with palm-leaf thatched roofs and private bathrooms, with breakfast included. Camping is available ($3), and the owner teaches scuba diving. ❹

Iruña on the far side of the bay ☎09/9472458. Isolated, green-roofed hideaway with clean and spacious cabins painted in fresh pastel colours with porches and hammocks – make sure to reserve in advance. A 45min walk from town, accessible by car at low tide. $36 per person with three good meals.

Mompiche Beach Lodge at the southern end of Mompiche ☎02/2252488 in Quito, ⊛www .mompichebeachlodge.com. Features luxury cabañas sleeping four to six, furnished with kitchens and private baths with hot water, plus a lounge and hammock-strung porch. Provides horses for rides over the hill south of the village, and sea kayaks for trips into the mangroves. ❻

Cojimíes and around

From the El Salto–Pedernales road, you can hike several kilometres to Daule and then take a boat over the wide Cojimíes estuary to the somewhat shabby little town of **COJIMÍES**, squeezed onto the tip of an ever-dwindling tongue of sand, eroded by water on three sides. Over the centuries, the peninsula has given up more than a kilometre of land, and the town has been entirely relocated from its original pre-Hispanic site, where it was known as Quiximíes. Of little inherent interest, the town for most visitors is just a brief hiatus on coastal journeys while swapping between boats and camionetas.

At low tide, locals occasionally boat out to the **sandbanks** in the middle of the estuary and use them as private beaches for parties and barbecues. Ask around at the landing beach north of town about going on a **fishing** trip – many captains will be keen for the extra income ($10–15 per hour). Since disease finished off shrimp farming in the estuary, and the construction of the new inland road has diverted much through-traffic, Cojimíes has been economically suffering. There are a few basic **hotels** here if you get stuck, but you're better off pushing on to *Cocosolo* (see below).

For 30km south from Cojimíes to Pedernales, an idyllic deserted **beach** fronted by coconut groves provides a freshly made surface at low tide for camioneta travel between the two towns – a bracing jaunt – though at high tide the vehicles use a slower road further inland, which adds about 10km to the journey.

Cocosolo

Some 13km south of Cojimíes, a lone hotel, **Cocosolo** (☎09/9215078, or contact Guacamayo Bahía Tours in Bahía de Caráquez, p.394; ❹), has stood for more than twenty years under the coconut fronds, enjoying peaceful isolation during high tide. You can stay either in its eccentric collection of sea-blue cabins, built on long stilts in the grove, or in the main house, which has several spacious rooms and walls painted in pastel swirls, near a garden with a fish pond.

Most accommodation includes private bathrooms, and good meals are served in a large dining room, where you'll find old magazines, a pool table and murals made of marine bric-a-brac. **Camping** ($3) includes use of the hotel's facilities and restaurant, and the owners can arrange fishing **tours** or excursions to the estuary mangroves and forested areas nearby. **Camioneta** drivers know the place and regularly pass through at low tide; at high tide they can drop you on the inland road behind the hotel.

Pedernales

In the mid-1980s, the shrimping industry exploded in **PEDERNALES**, and the town's economy grew rapidly until two viruses (*mancha blanca*, "white spot", and Taura Syndrome) decimated the marine harvest at the end of the decade. Ever since, the town has been at pains to reinvent itself as a holiday destination, but it has a long way to go, despite being one of the nearest beach resorts to Quito. With its crowded, narrow streets and rather grubby beach, Pedernales has remained largely impervious to interest from international travellers, though it is a hub for transport along the coast, and sits at one end of more than 30km of beautiful, palm-shaded sand extending north (see p.387).

The focus of town is the **parque central**, whose centrepiece is a **stone** that La Condamine engraved in Latin during his mission to the equator in 1736 to determine the shape of the Earth. The stone's reverse side was engraved to commemorate the 250th anniversary of the event, listing the names of the expedition's members. The **church** is also worth a look for its colourful stained-glass window and mural overlooking the square, both by José María Peli Romarategui. From the park, the streets fall steeply to the sea for a half-kilometre west to the **beach**, where a few unremarkable hotels, bars and restaurants cater to national tourists. The town's two main **fiestas** are for its cantonization, March 13, and the *fiesta del café*, August 16, honouring the days when coffee was the principal crop.

Practicalities

The **bus terminal** is on Juan Pereira, two blocks northeast of the main square. Every twenty minutes, buses leave for Santo Domingo (3hr), from where there are regular connections to Quito. There are also direct buses to the capital (4 daily; 5–6hr), Guayaquil (2 daily; 9hr), San Vicente (every 40min; 2hr 30min) and Chamanga (every 30min; 1hr). For *Cocosolo* and Cojimíes, **camionetas** and **taxis** leave from the square. The Banco del Pacífico, on García Moreno opposite the *América Internacional* hotel, cashes traveller's cheques and has a MasterCard and Cirrus ATM. The Pacífictel **telephone office** is on Eloy Alfaro, off the square behind the church.

A block east of the bus station at Juan Pereira and Manabí, *Playas* (☎05/681125; ❷–❸) provides good-value **accommodation** with well-kept rooms and private baths and TVs. *América Internacional*, García Moreno and López Castillo (☎05/681321; ❸), is a step up, touting phones, air conditioning and mosquito nets. The hotels along the beach range from smartish *cabaña* complexes to lowly wooden shacks, and the nicest is *Mr John*, Avenida Plaza Acosta and Malecón (☎ & ☎05/681107; ❹), offering bright, fresh rooms, fans, cable TVs and private baths with electric showers.

The local **restaurants** are mostly simple seafood *comedores*; you'll find several on the beach and the south side of the park, including the cheap and popular *Ankris*. Elsewhere, *El Rocío*, on Eloy Alfaro east of the parque, has breakfasts and cheap set menus, while *El Costeñito*, on Garcia Moreno a block and a half east of the park, is also a good choice.

Punta Blanca and Punta Prieta

Some 36km south of Pedernales, the road swings away from the shore to traverse the white cliff of **PUNTA BLANCA**, and the dark one of Punta Prieta, whose colour differences help fishermen navigate. In the 800m between the two cliffs is a cluster of secluded **hideaways** with access to quiet and beautiful stretches of beach. The first is *Punta Blanca Lodge Tent Camp* (☎09/9227559, or in Quito ☎02/2342763, ✉jorgec@interactive.net.ec; ❺), a unique and unusual place with large family tents under a roof, offering seaside views and equipped with double beds, desks, chairs and electric lights – in effect, hotel rooms with tarpaulin walls and zip doors. Set in neatly clipped gardens, the camp has clean shared bathrooms with hot water, and an attractive restaurant and bar with ocean views; more conventional suites have air conditioning and private baths (❻). **Tours** of the inland forests of the Reserva Mache Chindul are available, as well as fishing, diving and canoeing expeditions.

A few hundred metres up the road, *Latitude 7* (☎09/479914; ❷) features a collection of artfully built wooden cabins with composting toilets, located in dry forest a short distance from the beach. A bit run-down and irregularly open, the place nonetheless provides periodic silk-screening and jewellery workshops, plus sailing trips, snorkelling and horse rides along the coast.

A short hop further south at **PUNTA PRIETA**, the *Punta Prieta Guest House* (☎09/9837656, ✉puntaprieta@yahoo.com; ❺) is the most comfortable and private of the three hotels, with attractive cabins and rooms with private baths and hot water, set in fragrant *palo santo* forest on an outcrop with charming views and access to two tranquil beaches. Reasonably priced **meals** are available, and there are **camping** facilities ($3–5).

Don Juan to the Río Muchacho Organic Farm

Further along, the road winds down from low hills to reveal **DON JUAN**, a picturesque village in a cove washed by a pale-green sea, where there are a few basic hotels. From Don Juan a dirt track heads inland for 4km to the **Tito Santos Dry Forest Reserve**, which lies in an important transitional zone protecting rare tropical dry forest habitat, as well as semi-deciduous and wet forest on the highest reaches. Newly set up, the reserve is managed by the Fundación Jatun Sacha, which seeks **volunteers** for on-site projects (☎02/2432240, ⊛www.jatunsacha.org). Passing some huge shrimp farms, after 5km the route reaches the bland market town of **Jama**, the largest settlement between Pedernales and Bahía de Caráquez, and further south turns inland into undulating pastoral lands.

About 30km south of Jama, the highway passes the turn-off to the **Río Muchacho Organic Farm**, reached by a ninety-minute walk in the dry season. In an area damaged by crop-burning and chemical run-off, the farm is an oasis of sustainable agriculture where visitors can milk cows, help with reforestation, and pick, roast and grind coffee, or enjoy more relaxing diversions such as fishing for river shrimp, making tagua jewellery and utensils from gourd, and smearing on local clay for a facial. **Accommodation** is available in a cabin by the river or in the main farmhouse, and costs start at $15 per person. A good way to visit is on a three-day tour ($30 per person per day, including a horse ride to the farm and all meals and activities), though many people come as **volunteers** ($250 per month contribution) for farm work, reforestation or teaching in an environmental primary school; make reservations in advance through Guacamayo Bahíatours in Bahía de Caráquez (see p.394).

Canoa

Sitting at the upper end of a huge beach extending 17km south to San Vicente, **CANOA** has shifted from sleepy fishing village to laid-back beach resort, thanks largely to its fantastic surf and clean sands. With only a single paved street linking its shaded **square** to the sea, the town's low-level hubbub is submerged by the continuous roar of breakers rising and falling on the shore.

Not surprisingly, it's a lovely place to relax, with long, empty expanses of coastline and ample waves for **surfing** (good from Dec–May, best Jan–Feb). Many hotels have boards for hire, and *La Posada de Daniel* is the headquarters of the tour agency Canoa Surf Explorer (ⓦwww.canoasurfexplorer.com), which arranges surfing tours at all the best breaks in Ecuador and the Galápagos. At low tide you can take a **horse ride** or a **walk** to the sandy cliffs rising up through the haze in the north, where there are a pair of **caves** to explore – there used to be nine, but seven collapsed in the 1998 earthquake.

Buses between Pedernales and San Vicente pass through Canoa every thirty minutes and stop at the main square. Pacífictel **telephone** offices are opposite the hotel *Bambú* and a block from the park. You can access the **Internet** and make international calls at *La Posada de Daniel* ($2.50 per hour).

Accommodation, eating and drinking

In addition to Canoa's well-priced **accommodation**, there are also several more expensive, self-contained hotels outside town to the south. Wherever you stay, it's worth asking about discounts during low season.

If you like seafood, you'll enjoy Canoa's **restaurants**. *Torbellino* (closes 5.30pm), down from the square, and *Costa Azul*, on the beach, both dish up cheap and tasty fish and shrimp, while *Jixsy*, opposite the latter, is good but suffers from slow service. The more expensive restaurant at *Bambú* is good and reliable for its lunches and dinners, and does delicious breakfasts of fruit salads and pancakes. For good pizzas, snacks, juices and **cocktails**, try *Arena Bar* on the beachfront, south of the main street.

Hotels

Bambú on the beach at the north end of the village ☏05/616370. The town's best rooms – bright and breezy, with little balconies overlooking a garden and the sea – and less expensive cabins with shared baths. You can sleep in a hammock or camp here for a few dollars with use of the facilities, and longboards ($4 per hour) and bodyboards ($1 per hour) are available for rent. ❷–❹

Canoa 1km out of town to the south ☏05/616380, ⓔecocanoa@mnb.satnet.net. Colourful cabins garlanded with bright bougainvillea and set around a pool, with an on-site sauna and Jacuzzi. Breakfast included. ❻

País Libre several blocks behind *Bambú* ☏05/616387, ⓦwww.paislibre.net. An enormous, four-storey thatched cabaña-cum-hotel popular with *serranos*, offering nice rooms with nets and optional en-suite baths – those on the upper floors have great views – plus a small swimming pool and disco. ❹

La Posada de Daniel by the square, 150m back from the beach ☏05/616373, ⓦwww.posadadaniel.com. Cabins sleeping up to nine people (most are doubles), with private baths, fans, mosquito nets and balconies affording views of the village and shore. Also features a lounge with comfy chairs, bar, restaurant, Internet service and swimming pool. Horse riding is available, and the proprietor, once a junior champion, gives surfing lessons. ❸

Shelmar fifty-metre walk back from the beach, on the main street ☏05/674476 or 09/9842460. Offers simple, clean rooms kitted out with fans and hammocks. ❷

San Vicente

Although on the same magnificent, long beach as Canoa, dusty **SAN VICENTE**, some 17km away, has none of its neighbour's charm, thanks largely to the busy thoroughfare running right next to the beach, jammed with noisy buses and *rancheras*. Even so, there are several holiday hotels, mainly catering to nationals, including a few rather expensive resorts just outside town on the road back to Canoa. The best thing about the place is the **view** across the Río Chone estuary to Bahía de Caráquez, where row upon row of high-rise buildings resemble matchsticks balancing on a finger poking out to sea.

Practicalities

From the dock along the beach, **car ferries** run to Bahía de Caráquez every thirty minutes (15min trip; 6.30am–8.30pm; $2), and foot passengers travel for free. **Pangas** (small boats) cross into the night, and the *panga* dock is closer to the bus offices and town centre. **Buses** regularly leave for Pedernales (every 30–45mins; 2hr 30min), from where you can get connections to Chamanga, the beach resorts to the north, Santo Domingo and Quito. There are less frequent direct services to Guayaquil (7 daily; 5hr 30min), Manta (3 daily; 3hr 15min), Portoviejo (hourly; 2hr 30min) and Quito (3 daily; 8hr), all leaving from bus offices on the Malecón. There is an airport opposite the car-ferry dock, but no scheduled passenger services.

Along the Malecón from the *panga* dock, the *San Vicente* (☏05/674182; ❶–❷) is a basic but adequate **hotel**, while a little further along, opposite the petrol station, the best rooms of the *Vacaciones* (☏05/674116; ❸) are located at the back, as they're quiet and air-conditioned and near the swimming pool. There are several pricier places to stay just outside town, the nicest being *Monte Mar* (☏05/674197; ❹), with plain cabins, a good restaurant and a pool.

Bahía de Caráquez and around

One of Ecuador's most agreeable coastal resort towns, **BAHÍA DE CARÁQUEZ** sits on a slender peninsula of sand extending into the broad mouth of the Río Chone, an upmarket place of spotless, white high-rise apartment blocks, broad tree-lined avenues and leafy parks.

Bahía, as it's known, became one of the most fashionable resorts for moneyed nationals when former president Sixto Durán Ballén spent his holidays here in the early 1990s, but towards the end of the decade unrelenting El Niño rains demolished roads, washed away entire hills and triggered landslides, and a double earthquake demolished more than two hundred buildings. A strong Green movement emerged from the destruction, culminating in the declaration of the town as a *ciudad ecológica*, an **eco-city** with many recycling, reforestation, conservation and environmental-education programmes. These days, even the *tricicleros* paint their vehicles green, adorning them with signs reading "*Bienvenidos Bahía Eco-Ciudad*". The Día del Mangle **fiesta** on February 28 marks the declaration with music and events such as mangrove planting in the estuary.

Arrival, information and transport

Bahía de Caráquez has a straightforward layout, its main avenues running north–south parallel to the estuary on the east side. The **Malecón**, the main road around the edge of the peninsula, is known by several other names at various points: at the southeast entrance to town, it's **Malecón Alberto Santos**; beyond the obelisk and on the west side, **Malecón Virgilio Ratti**; and around the tip of the peninsula, the **Circunvalación**.

Buses to Bahía drop travellers at the obelisk at the junction of Malecón Alberto Santos and Ascázubi, which is close to the cheaper hotels, bus offices and **car ferry** to San Vicente, on Malecón and Ascázubi. **Boats** from San Vicente use docks on Malecón Alberto Santos, not far from the obelisk. The Bahía airport is over the water in San Vicente, but offers no passenger services. There are plenty of **taxis** and **tricicleros** around the obelisk, costing under a dollar for an in-town trip, though the cheaper hotels are within easy walking distance.

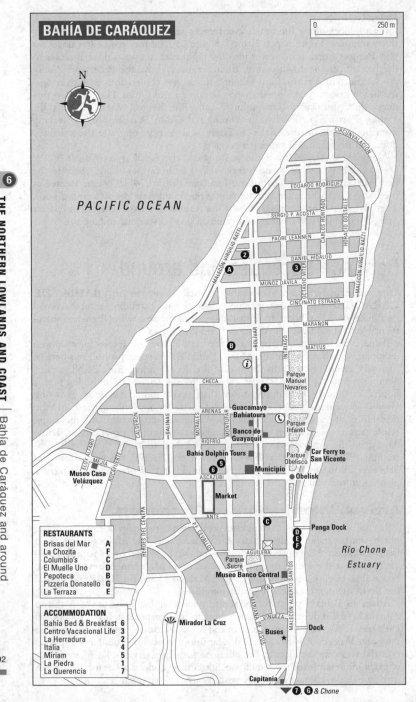

BAHÍA DE CARÁQUEZ

0   250 m

PACIFIC OCEAN

CIRCUNVALACIÓN

EDUARDO RODRÍGUEZ

SERGIO P. ACOSTA

PADRE LEANNEN

CARLOS HURTADO

HORACIO GOSTALLE

MALECÓN VIRGILO RATTI

MALECÓN VIRGILO RATTI

DANIEL HIDALGO

MUNOZ DAVILA

OCTAVIO VITERI

CINCINATO ESTRADA

MARAÑÓN

MATEUS

INTRIAGO

BOLÍVAR

Parque Manuel Nevares

CHECA

Parque Infantil

ARENAS

MORALES

MONTÚFAR

Guacamayo Bahiatours

Banco de Guayaquil

SALINAS

RIOFRÍO

Bahía Dolphin Tours

Parque Obelisco

Car Ferry to San Vicente

CALDERÓN

ASCAZUBI

Municipio

Obelisk

Museo Casa Velázquez

MEJIA

ROCAFUERTE

RÍO ATARO

Market

ANTE

HÉROES DEL CENEPA

P.E. CEVALLOS

Panga Dock

Parque Sucre

AGUILERA

Museo Banco Central

Río Chone Estuary

PEÑA

MARIANA DE JESÚS

VINUEZA

MALECÓN ALBERTO SANTOS

Mirador La Cruz

Buses

Dock

Capitanía

▼ 7, G & Chone

RESTAURANTS

Brisas del Mar	A F
La Chozita	C
Columbio's	D
El Muelle Uno	B
Pepoteca	G
Pizzería Donatello	E
La Terraza	

ACCOMMODATION

Bahía Bed & Breakfast	6
Centro Vacacional Life	3
La Herradura	2
Italia	4
Miriam	5
La Piedra	1
La Querencia	7

Maps and **information** are available at the Ministerio de Turismo, Bolívar and Checa (Mon–Fri 9am–5pm, with lunch break; ☎05/691124), or you can try the tour agencies (see "Listings", overleaf), which often have English-speaking staff on hand.

Accommodation

Most of the smarter **hotels** are found on the northwest side of the peninsula, but wherever you stay, it can be difficult to find a room during the high season and national holidays. One consequence of the earthquakes is that water shortages can be pretty frequent.

Bahía Bed & Breakfast Ascázubi and Morales ☎05/690146. The pricier rooms have private baths and hot water, though some are a little tired, despite nice touches such as candles and dried flowers. Includes breakfast and provides maps and tourist info, but water is by request at off-peak times. ❸–❹

Casa Grande Malecón Virgilio Ratti, reservations through Bahía Dolphin Tours ☎05/692097. Private, chalet-style guesthouse on the oceanfront, set in attractive gardens by a swimming pool. Rooms have hot water, a/c and cable TVs, with breakfast included. ❼

Centro Vacacional Life Octavio Viteri 503 and Muñoz Dávila ☎05/690496. Great value for its large brick cabins housing a bedroom, bathroom, kitchen and dining room, in quiet gardens with table tennis and pool table nearby, but usually fully booked by private groups during high season. ❹

La Herradura Bolívar and Hidalgo ☎05/690446, ℱ690265. Smart seafront hotel evoking the feel of a hacienda by its wrought-iron furnishings, wagon wheels, barrels, horse harnesses and potted plants. Many of the comfortable rooms have

hot water, a/c and TVs. ❻

Italia Bolívar and Checa ☎05/691137, ℱ690449. Rooms are a bit small and not well priced, but they do have hot water, fans, phones, cable TVs and private baths. ❺

Miriam Montúfar and Ascázubi ☎05/690231. Bare rooms and bare bulbs typify this rock-bottom budget spot. Several rooms are without windows, but the place is passably clean and ultra-cheap. ❶

La Piedra Malecón Virgilio Ratti 803 and Bolívar ☎05/690780, ℱ690154, ℰapartec@uio.satnet.net. Clean, comfortable rooms and sun loungers surround an outdoor pool right by a patch of private beach. Spacious bathrooms have proper tubs and hot water, while rooms boast telephones, a/c and cable TVs, with breakfast included. ❼

La Querencia Velasco Ibarra and Eugenio Santos, south of the Capitanía ☎05/690009. Blue-and-white hotel marked by a large palm tree in its front garden, in the house of a friendly family. Some rooms have private baths, though without hot water. Fluffy towels provided and meals cooked on request. ❸

The Town

Bahía is a pleasant town for a stroll – or taking a cruise with a triciclero ($2 per hour) – following the **Malecón** around the peninsula and viewing the busy river estuary on the east side, or the rough rollers coming to shore on the west. Locals swim and surf here, but to avoid the boulders and find more generous expanses of sand, take a taxi to the **beaches** south of town like **Punta Bellaca** (arrange pick-up in advance). A good complement to the seaside promenade is the short push up to **Mirador La Cruz**, on top of the hill at the foot of the peninsula, which affords grand views of the city and bay.

Back in town, the renovated **Museo Banco Central** (Tues–Fri 10am–5pm, Sat–Sun 11am–3pm; $1) houses pre-Columbian artefacts like a Valdivian belt of highly prized *spondylus* (thorny oyster) shells from 3000 BC, plus a replica balsa raft, as well as space for temporary art exhibitions. For a fascinating look at the more recent past, **Museo Casa Velázquez**, Mejía and Eloy Alfaro (Tues–Sun 9am–noon & 3–7pm; $1 low season, $5 high), is a beautiful wood-panelled house from the 1900s filled with antiques and period furniture.

Eating

Along with the superior **restaurants** of the smarter hotels like *La Piedra* and *La Herradura*, there are several very good places to eat, especially on the Malecón around the docks.

Brisas del Mar Hidalgo and Malecón Ratti, on the west side of town. Cheap and simple seafood eatery serving good fish and *ceviche* dishes.

La Chozita Malecón near the dock. A local favourite specializing in *parrilladas*, offering tasty barbecued food.

Columbio's Bolívar and Ante, back from the Malecón. Features large, delicious and affordable Colombian and Ecuadorian dishes and good seafood.

El Muelle Uno Malecón by the dock. Fair-priced restaurant serving generous, savoury fish and bar-

becue lunches and dinners, plus vegetarian options like baked potatoes and cheese.

Pepoteca Montúfar and Mateus. Popular for its cheap set meals, but also offers reliable à la carte dishes.

Pizzería Donatello Malecón south of the Capitanía. Dingy-looking joint, but redeemed by good pizzas packed with toppings. Open evenings only.

La Terraza Malecón near the dock. Decent choice for its inexpensive seafood and grills.

Listings

Banks Banco de Guayaquil, Riofrío and Bolívar, changes traveller's cheques and has a Visa and MasterCard ATM.

Boats and ferries The car ferry leaves the dock on Malecón and Ascázubi for San Vicente (every 30min, 6.30am–8.30pm; $2 cars, foot passengers free), while *panga* boats depart regularly from the municipal docks for San Vicente until late.

Buses Standard services run to Quito (8–9hr) and Guayaquil (5–6hr), and less frequent executive services (2 daily to Quito; 3 daily to Guayaquil) are pricier, more comfortable and don't stop on the road. Coactur has services for Portoviejo (hourly; 2hr), some continuing to Manta (3hr) and Guayaquil (6hr), while Reina del Camino goes to Quito (8hr) and Guayaquil (5hr). These services leave from Malecón Alberto Santos, south of the *Bahía* hotel. Regular buses go to Chone, from where you can catch other buses between Portoviejo and Santo Domingo, and leave opposite the *Bahía* hotel.

Capitanía 3 de Noviembre and Malecón.

Internet facilities $2 per hour. Genesis Net, Malecón 1392 and Ascázubi; Systemcomp, Bolívar and Aguilera.

Post office Aguilera and Bolívar.

Telephone office Pacífictel, Alberto Santos and Arenas.

Tour operators Bahía Dolphin Tours, Bolívar and Riofrío (☎05/692097, ℱ692088, ⓦwww .bahiadolphin.com), owns Chirije and offers various tours around town. Guacamayo Bahíatours, Bolívar 906 and Arenas (☎05/691412 and 691107, ℱ691412, ⓦwww.guacamayotours.com), manages the Río Muchacho Organic Farm and EcoCamaronera Bahía shrimp farm, and runs tours to local environmental projects and paper-recycling, composting and other agro-ecology works. It also provides information on volunteer work at the farm and local schools. Both operators organize whale-watching trips and run tours to tropical dry forests, mangroves, estuaries, beaches, Isla de la Plata and Parque Nacional Machalilla.

Trips from Bahía

Bahía lies near several wonderful natural attractions, including **tropical dry forests**, empty **beaches** and **mangrove islands** teeming with aquatic birds. The vast shrimp farms in the estuary have, however, displaced more than sixty square kilometres of mangrove forest during the 1980s and 1990s, with the obvious exception of the world's first **organic shrimp farm**, a pollution-free enterprise that also helps in reforestation. Two **tour agencies**, which have played a major role in the local Green movement, organize a number of good excursions in the area (see above).

Río Chone estuary and Isla Corazón

Among the touring highlights is a trip around the **Río Chone estuary**, where the network of mangrove islands is home to a **frigate bird** population rivalling that of the Galápagos Islands. Over four thousand of the scissor-tailed birds nest here in the tangled branches of the red mangroves, which also support thirty other species such as petrels, oystercatchers and sandpipers. During the mating season (Aug–Dec, sometimes till Feb), it's possible to see the male frigate birds' characteristic scarlet pouches inflating to woo circling females, and at low tide you can walk around the mangroves to get within a few feet of them, but wear shorts as you may have to wade through thigh-deep mud in places.

Further upriver, the **Isla Corazón** features an "ecological path" through the mangroves, where you can see crabs, shrimp and wetland birds, including the rare roseate spoonbill. One enjoyable element of this trip is taking a **dugout canoe** on the tiny creeks between the trees to view large frigate-bird colonies. **Dolphins** can occasionally be seen in the estuary, and between June and September **whales** can be spotted rolling and diving off the coast.

EcoCamaronera Bahía

Most of the shrimp farms around the Bahía estuary or along the Ecuadorian coast are large, sterile-looking reservoirs resembling water-treatment plants. By contrast, the **EcoCamaronera Bahía** is the world's first and only certified **organic shrimp farm**, whose perimeter bursts with vegetation and complementary crops such as aloe vera, papaya and seed-trees used for shrimp feed. It's also cradled by mangroves that act as both filters and food sources. Tours of the farm are run by Guacamayo Bahíatours (see "Listings", opposite) and include walks through neighbouring wildlife areas, a tasty lunch made of the farm's produce, and visits to a worm farm and local composting centre. The same agency also runs tours to the Río Muchacho Organic Farm, 17km beyond Canoa, a *montuvio* cash-crop enterprise managed on a sustainable, non-polluting basis (see p.389), and to local paper-recycling and reforestation projects.

Jororá, Punta Bellaca and Chirije

On the coast south of Bahía de Caráquez, **Jororá** and **Punta Bellaca** comprise one of the few **tropical dry forests** in the country outside the Parque Nacional Machalilla. Anteaters, sloths and iguanas can be found in this area, which is rich in fragrant palo santo trees, barbasco (a plant whose roots yield a poison used for insecticide) and ceiba trees – easy to identify with their great buttressed trunks. During the rainy season (Jan–May), the forests are luxuriant, but turn dry and brittle in the other months.

About 17km south of town, **Chirije** is an isolated beach couched in tropical dry forest, which once acted as a seaport for the Bahía culture (500 BC–650 AD). Archeologists and volunteers are welcome to help with the ongoing excavations, and artefacts found at the site are exhibited in a small on-site **museum**. You can also stay here in attractive, solar-powered **cabañas** (❺) nestled among beachside greenery, and activities include trekking on forest trails, bird watching and snorkelling. Make reservations through Bahía Dolphin Tours (see opposite).

Saiananda Parque

On the main road 6.5km south of Bahía, **Saiananda Parque** (daily 9am–4 or 5pm; $2) is a real menagerie featuring peacocks, ostriches, ñandu (a small flightless Argentinian bird), macaws, monkeys, deer and sloths, which roam around grounds that include bonsai, cactus and succulent gardens. The park has an excellent waterside vegetarian **restaurant** that looks down the estuary towards the peninsula; call ahead to reserve (☎05/398331). Local **buses** from Bahía pass every ten minutes, or you can hire a **boat** to take you to the park's pier.

San Jacinto and San Clemente

In the 50km or so between Bahía de Caráquez and Manta, the coastline lurches between inaccessible cliffs and lengthy stretches of sandy beach. The **fishing villages** along here have become popular beach resorts with nationals and day-trippers from Portoviejo, and can get quite crowded during holidays and weekends.

Twenty kilometres south of Bahía are two fishing villages connected by 3km of beach and backed by bleak salt pampas. Despite their attractive beach, they seldom receive foreign visitors, but do have a number of inexpensive hotels to satisfy local demand, which can be considerable in July and August. In **SAN CLEMENTE**, the hotel with the most character is *Las Acacias*, 500m north of the village shrine and 300m back from the beach (☎05/615050; ❷), a beautiful old wooden house with spacious verandas and clean and simple rooms with shared or private baths. **SAN JACINTO**, the larger of the two villages, is the site of *Cabañas Ecológicas Casa Mar*, at the town entrance near the Pacífictel office (☎05/615468, ✉manabi1@espoir.org.ec; ❸), a group of pleasant cabins with kitchens, dining rooms and one or two bedrooms. The owner runs local tours, including one to a tropical dry forest.

Both San Clemente and San Jacinto claim several good seafood **restaurants**, and **buses** to Portoviejo leave every twenty minutes, with a less regular service to Bahía de Caráquez. Pick up through buses on the main road.

Crucita

About 14km south of San Jacinto, and 30km northwest of Portoviejo on a fast paved road, the cliffs at the south end of **CRUCITA** fall away to a long **beach**, which is no more than a few metres wide at high tide, but becomes a broad expanse of dark sand when the waters recede. Fronting the beach is the **Malecón**, a shadeless and not very picturesque seafront promenade lined with hotels and restaurants. Still, the rugged cliffs and excellent wind conditions have made the village a minor centre for **airborne activities** such as paragliding and kite surfing; for information, talk to the owners of the *Voladeros* hostel (see below).

The most regular **bus** service to Crucita is from Portoviejo (every 15min; 45min–1hr), but you can also get there from Manta on buses that pass through Portoviejo (12 daily; 1hr 30min); the last bus back to Portoviejo leaves at 7.30pm from the main square. The Pacífictel **telephone office** is on the main road into town, 50m north of the church.

The best **place to stay** in town is *Barandhúa*, central Malecón (☎05/676185, ℻676159; ❺), where the English-speaking owners offer bright, fresh rooms (some of them facing the sea) with electric showers, soap and towels, and an on-site pool, games room and good restaurant. At the northern end of the Malecón, *Rey David* (☎05/676143; ❹) is a reasonable choice, having decent rooms with private baths, and a little pool; other options include *Hipocampo*, south Malecón (☎05/676167; ❸), a friendly hotel whose simple rooms have private baths, though the ones upstairs are brighter and have seaside views, and, at the Malecón's southern end, *Voladeros* (☎05/676200, ⊕www.geocities.com/hostalvoladeros; ❹), a colourful little hostel offering simple rooms with optional en-suite baths and a swimming pool. It's hard to move along the Malecón and find yourself far from a **restaurant**, though most tout the standard list of seafood items.

Manta and around

About 50km south of Bahía de Caráquez, set in a broad bay dotted with freighters, cruise ships and fishing boats, **MANTA** is a city of some 170,000 people and Ecuador's largest port after Guayaquil. Divided by the Río Manta between the throbbing commercial centre to the west, and the poorer residential area **Tarqui** to the east, the city thrives in producing cars, ships, soap, shampoo, oils, butter and candles amongst other things, but it's the **seafood industry** that really drives the economy. Fish and shrimp processors and packers line the roads entering Manta, and the business of netting swordfish, shark and dorado is lucrative enough to draw US and Japanese fishing fleets to these abundant waters.

A more prominent foreign presence in the city is the American military **air base** used for drug surveillance, which Jamil Mahuad granted in one of his last acts as president, a controversial decision criticized by many as unnecessarily drawing Ecuador into the ongoing drug war with Colombia. Its existence, however, has brought capital and a vibrant international flavour – and according to locals, has also made Manta the country's most expensive city.

In addition to being a maritime centre and air base, Manta is known as a lively, popular holiday destination with good hotels and restaurants, and its main **beach**, recently improved with large injections of cash, is relatively clean, regularly patrolled, lined with restaurants and packed at weekends. As a bustling modern port that's more manageable in size and temperament than Guayaquil, Manta is a good place to refuel and make use of the banks, cinemas and services of a busy urban centre. A new road skirting the coast to the southwest also makes Manta a gateway to undeveloped villages and beaches, as well as the more established resorts of the southern coast beyond Puerto Cayo, where the road joins the Ruta del Sol (see p.442).

Some history

Fishing has been important to Manta for many centuries. In the pre-Columbian era the settlement here was known as **Jocay**, or "fish house", and from c.500 AD until the arrival of the Spanish, the region was the home of the **Manta people**, expert fishermen and navigators who tattooed their faces and held sway over the coast from Bahía de Caráquez to Salango, near Puerto López. Above all, the Manta were great traders and sailed on large balsa rafts as far north as Mexico, exchanging goods for their *spondylus* (thorny oyster) shells, which were used by many cultures as ornaments and deemed so valuable that they were as good as money. Shortly after becoming the first European to cross the Pacific equator, Pizarro's sailor **Bartolomé de Ruiz** encountered one of these rafts off the Manabí coast, a craft large enough to carry twenty men and thirty tons of merchandise, including gold, silver and emeralds.

The Manteño culture, though, suffered greatly under the brutal conquistador **Pedro de Alvarado**, who swept through the region in 1534, hanging the chief and putting others to the dogs or burning them alive for failing to supply him with gold, jewels or food. He also put entire communities into irons, and many died from exhaustion or cold in the snowbound passes as Alvarado marched them inland to Quito (see "History", p.509). Jocay, a town of twenty thousand people before the Spanish came, only had fifty inhabitants left when the chronicler Girolamo Benzoni visited in 1546 – typical of Alvarado's devastation of the region. From the 1560s onwards, however, Manta began its long recovery and was soon the preferred **settlement** for colonists, rather than the nearby administrative capital of Portoviejo. Save for a few **pirate raids** in the seventeenth century, which drove some citizens inland to found new towns like Montecristi, Manta's place as the commercial capital of the central coast was assured.

Arrival, information and transport

Excepting the main highways, the city's streets are numbered sequentially from the river – Manta starts at Calle 1, Tarqui at Calle 101 – while avenues running parallel to the seashore use the coast as the starting point. **Buses** enter the city through Tarqui along the main road, Avenida 4 de Noviembre, which crosses the river and continues into Manta as the Malecón. The central bus station, Avenida 8 and Calle 7, is used by all local and long-distance buses except for those from Quito operated by Flota Imbabura, which stop at Malecón and Calle 8, and Panamericana, which use Avenida 4 and Calle 12 (both of these also offer *ejecutivo* services). There are plans to relocate the bus station outside town on a peripheral artery. The **airport** is a few kilometres east of Tarqui, and can be reached by taxi for a few dollars.

Taxis are easy to pick up on the town's main thoroughfares and cost about $1 to anywhere in the city, while **local buses** use the central bus station. If staying in Tarqui, you can easily catch one from Avenida 105 into the city centre – a far more attractive prospect than walking a kilometre over the busy road bridge.

Tourist **information** and maps are available at the helpful municipal tourism office, Avenida 4 and Calle 9 (Mon–Fri 9am–5pm; ℡05/611471, Ⓔmimm@systray.net), or from the Ministerio de Turismo, Paseo José María Egas between calles 10 and 11, near Avenida 3 (Mon–Fri 9am–5pm; ℡05/622944). Open daily at the entrance to Playa Murciélago is the helpful, student-run Centro de Información Turística (℡05/624099).

Accommodation

There are plenty of good choices for **accommodation** in Manta, with most of the more expensive hotels located at the smarter end of town near the beach, and cheaper places around downmarket Tarqui. There are few decent low-budget places, but you can expect fair **discounts** at many hotels in the low season.

Manta

Cabañas Balandra Av 8 and Calle 20 ℡05/ 620316, Ⓕ620545, Ⓦwww.hotelbalandramanta .com. Attractive and commodious cabins sleeping four to five, set amidst garden walkways of fig trees and colourful verbena arches. Similar rooms are also available, and all accommodation features a/c, fridges, phones, cable TVs and private baths with hot water, plus use of a swimming pool. ❽

Lun Fun Av 11 and Calle 2 ℡05/622966 or 622976, Ⓕ610601. Despite its unenviable position in wasteland near the bypass, this plush hotel has it all – cable TV, hot water, a/c, and a fridge and phone in every room. Amiable Chinese–Ecuadorian owners speak English and run a good on-site Chinese restaurant. Breakfast included. ❼

Oro Verde Malecón and Calle 23 ℡05/629200, f629210, Ⓦwww.oroverdehotels.com. Immaculate five-star hotel on Playa Murciélago with supremely comfortable rooms, pool, sports and sauna facilities, casino, delicatessen and an excellent restaurant. Breakfast included. ❾

Tarqui

Boulevard Av 105 and Calle 103 ℡05/625333. Fairly spacious rooms, some with a/c, close to its cheap *comedor* on Tarqui beach. Also has a more luxurious wing over the road, with indoor pool, sauna and restaurant, and rooms with a/c, hot water and cable TVs. Facilities can be used by all residents. ❸–❺

Hostal Miami Av 102 and Calle 107 ℡05/622055. Unlike the nearby *Hotel Miami*, a friendly place abounding with replicas of Manteño-culture artefacts and offering decent, if slightly dog-eared, rooms with private baths around a courtyard. Some have balconies and are the same price as the less impressive interior rooms. One of the town's few passable budget choices. ❷

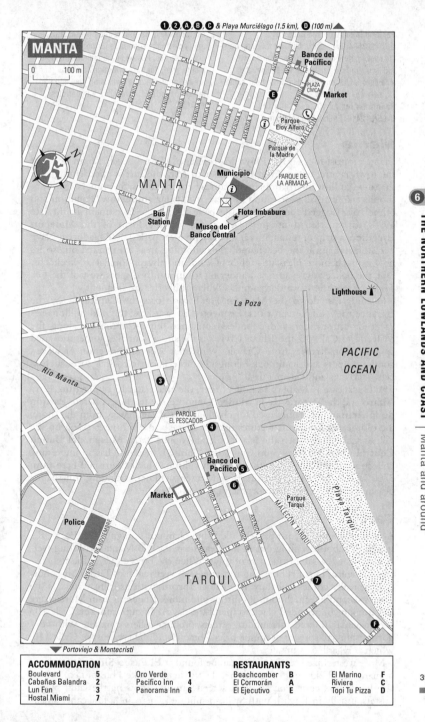

MANTA

0 — 100 m

Banco del Pacífico

PLAZA CÍVICA

Market

MANTA

Parque Eloy Alfaro

Parque de la Madre

Municipio

PARQUE DE LA ARMADA

Bus Station

Museo del Banco Central

Flota Imbabura

Lighthouse

La Poza

PACIFIC OCEAN

Río Manta

PARQUE EL PESCADOR

Banco del Pacífico

Market

Parque Tarqui

Playa Tarqui

Police

MALECÓN TARQUI

TARQUI

▼ *Portoviejo & Montecristi*

❶, ❷, Ⓐ, Ⓑ, Ⓒ & Playa Murciélago (1.5 km), Ⓓ (100 m) ▲

ACCOMMODATION

Boulevard	5	Oro Verde	1
Cabañas Balandra	2	Pacifico Inn	4
Lun Fun	3	Panorama Inn	6
Hostal Miami	7		

RESTAURANTS

Beachcomber	B	El Marino	F
El Cormorán	A	Riviera	C
El Ejecutivo	E	Topi Tu Pizza	D

Pacífico Inn Av 106 and Calle 101 ℡ 05/623584. Unmissable building towering over the stinking river inlet, where the rooms vary widely by traffic-noise levels, smell, light and amenities, which may include private bath, cable TV, hot water or a/c. ❹

Panorama Inn Av 105 and Calle 103 ℡ 05/612416. Friendly hotel where the cheap- est rooms only have fans and private baths, and the pricier units cost more for hot water, a/c and cable TVs. Rooms in the main building are a little tired, but the newer ones over the road are set around a nice swimming pool and perfectly comfortable – though a bit charmless. ❹–❻

Manta

Manta's tourist focus is the **Playa Murciélago**, a broad beach 1.5km north of the town centre, where from December to May the surf is good enough for the town to host international windsurfing competitions. Swimmers, however, should take care all year round as there is a strong **undertow**. Pollution and crime have dogged the beach in the past, but a huge investment in the late 1990s has smartened up the place, mainly in the form of the **Malecón Escénico**, a strip of restaurants and bars with a car park. The Ecuadorian Navy occasionally patrols the beach and safe swimming areas are marked out, so it's now a much more pleasant stretch of sand, and always popular at weekends. Still, the police advise against wandering to undisturbed spots west of the *Oro Verde* towards the Playa Barbasquillo, where robberies are frequent.

Heading east down the Malecón, you'll soon pass the **Capitanía**, by the entrance to Manta's main **port**, frequented by warships, the odd millionaire's yacht or cruise liner, and countless container ships. Continuing along the Malecón to Calle 13, the **Plaza Cívica** is the site of a market sometimes used by indigenous traders from Otavalo, who offer a decent selection of woven goods, jumpers and hammocks alongside more familiar coastal wares such as tagua carvings and Panama hats.

A block east is Manta's leafiest corner, the main square of **Parque Eloy Alfaro** and the **Parque de la Madre**. Opposite, the treeless, concrete **Parque de la Armada** is mainly used for children's pedal carts. Away from the shore, the old heart of the port features narrow streets and old houses rising up the hill. At Calle 7, between the Malecón and Avenida 8, the **Museo del Banco Central** (Tues–Sat 9am–5pm, Sun 10am–3pm; $1, free Sun) has an interesting collection of artefacts from the Valdivian culture, which flourished here from 3500 BC to 1500 BC, and the later Manteño culture, including fish-shaped ocarinas and beautiful zoomorphic jugs and flasks.

Tarqui

As you cross into **Tarqui** past the old fishing harbour known as "La Poza", the stench of rubbish wafting out of the near-stagnant Río Manta is a fitting welcome to the less salubrious part of town. When the breeze carries the stench – reminiscent of burnt rubber and rotten eggs – over much of Tarqui, air conditioning really comes in handy. The **Playa Tarqui**, with its calm waters, is the town's second beach, though it's dirtier and more dangerous than Murciélago, and not a recommended place to spend the day. At Tarqui's **market**, Calle 103 and Avenida 108 and surrounding streets, produce sellers compete with vendors pushing all sorts of domestic bric-a-brac. Avoid the area east of Calle 110, which is regarded as unsafe.

More westernized retail activity can be found at **El Paseo Shopping**, a large upmarket mall 2km out of town on 4 de Noviembre (take a bus or taxi), which also has a food court and an eight-screen **cinema** showing the latest blockbusters, usually in English with Spanish subtitles. There are a few other smaller shopping centres elsewhere in the port, such as the CC Manicentro opposite the *Oro Verde*, with a supermarket, shops and fast-food restaurants.

Eating and drinking

The beaches in Manta and Tarqui are replete with seafood **restaurants** and **bars**. At **Playa Murciélago**, the new Malecón Escénico has a string of near-identical restaurants with concrete walls and blue-and-white canvas awnings. Prices and menus are also virtually the same, and the seafood is generally cheap and good. **Playa Tarqui** is fronted by rustic, thatched-roof bar-restaurants, which dole out a lot of *ceviche* of questionable cleanliness. The town's other good restaurants flirt with various cuisines and styles, from Chinese to Italian. For a **drink**, try the *Cadillac*, Calle M-2 and Avenida 24, a 1950s-America theme bar with outdoor seating and a pool table, done up with pop murals and memorabilia.

Restaurants

Beachcomber Calle 20 and Flavio Reyes. Informal eatery sizzling up fine meat grills and steaks at reasonable prices.

El Cormorán beyond the *Oro Verde* hotel at Av 24 and Calle M-2. Well-presented restaurant regarded as one of the town's better places for fish and *ceviche*.

El Ejecutivo on the eleventh floor of Edificio Banco Pichincha, Av 2 and Calle 12. Has great views of the city and bay and excellent food and service, with $5–6 main courses such as chicken in red-wine sauce with buttered new potatoes, accompanied by artichoke-heart salad. Closed Sat & Sun.

El Marino Malecón Tarqui and Calle 110. Popular spot good for its fish meals, though the menu is limited and the place closes at 5.30pm.

Lun Fun Av 11 and Calle 2 ☎05/622966 or 622976, ℗610601. Upmarket hotel restaurant serving the best Chinese food in town.

Riviera Av 12 and Calle 20. Posh and elegant Italian spot with excellent meals ranging from lobster in saffron sauce to fresh pasta, gnocchi, and risotto ($6–12) and less expensive pizzas.

Topi Tu Pizza Malecón and Calle 15. Popular two-level pizzeria mocked up as a bamboo beach bar.

Listings

Airline Tame, Malecón and Calle 14 (☎05/622006), offers regular flights to Quito and Guayaquil.

Banks Banco del Pacífico, Av 2 and Calle 13, changes traveller's cheques and has a MasterCard and Cirrus ATM, also in Tarqui at Av 107 and Calle 103; Banco del Pichincha, Av 2 and Calle 12, does traveller's cheques and Visa cash advance. There are also ATMs at El Paseo shopping mall.

Buses Flota Imbabura and Panamericana have smart services to Quito; see "Arrival", p.398.

Car rental Budget, Malecón and Calle 15 ☎05/629919; Delgado, Malecón and Calle 2 ☎05/621266; Localiza, Malecón and Calle 16 ☎05/622026.

Internet facilities Around $0.80 per hour. Gerenexa at El Paseo Shopping; Inter@ctive, CC Manicentro; Publi Comp, Av 3 and Calle 12;

Privacy@net, Av 19 and Calle 13.

Police and immigration Av 4 de Noviembre and Calle 104 ☎05/920900; for emergencies ☎101.

Post office Av 4 and Calle 8.

Telephone offices Pacifictel, Malecón and Calle 12 (daily 8am–10pm), with another office next to El Paseo Shopping mall.

Tour operators Blue Marlin Lodge (☎05/626868, ⊛www.bluemarlinmanta.com) runs sports-fishing trips; Delgado Travel, Av 2 and Calle 13 (☎05/624484), does tours of the city and to *Hacienda San Antonio*, on the coast west of Manta; Entorno, in the *Oro Verde* hotel (☎05/629200), offers regional tours; and Metropolitan Touring, Av 4 and Calle 13 (☎05/623090), provides local and national tours. The tourist office at Playa Murciélago offers trips to Parque Nacional Machalilla.

Montecristi

Eleven kilometres inland from Manta, the main road to Portoviejo passes **MONTECRISTI**, a small town nestled at the foot of the green Montecristi hills, founded by beleaguered refugees from Manta after they had lost

Where did you get that hat?

Few injustices are more poignant than having your nation's most famous export attributed to another country, yet this is what Ecuador has suffered with the "**Panama hat**". In the mid-nineteenth century, Panama became associated with the headgear when it was the centre of trade routes between Europe and the east and west coasts of the Americas. Vast quantities of goods were brought to Panama, among them straw hats from Ecuador, which quickly became a favourite with gold prospectors, such as those on their way to San Francisco, and again with labourers on the Panama Canal at the turn of the twentieth century.

Associating the hats with where they were sold rather than where they were made, hat buyers caused the headgear to be misnamed, a mistake that Ecuador is unlikely ever to rectify. Although the indignant words "Genuine Panama Hat Made in Ecuador" are now stamped on hats in an attempt to reclaim sovereignty over the product without upsetting the world-renowned name, this has the unfortunate air of false advertising, as in "Authentic Spanish Champagne".

The first Spanish record of the hats dates from the early seventeenth century and places their origin in Manabí province. In fact, the tradition of **hat-making** probably goes back centuries before that, as the conquistadors had previously written of the broad, wing-like straw hats that the locals wore, calling them **toquillas**, after *toca*, a Spanish word for hat. The Spanish soon began to wear them to stave off the sun's glare, praising their lightness and coolness, and even their ability to carry water, due to the hat's ultra-fine weaving.

The straw, nicknamed **paja toquilla** (or *carludovica palmata*, as labelled by two Spanish botanists at the end of the eighteenth century to honour Carlos IV and his wife Luisa), grows throughout the Neotropics between Panama and Bolivia, but only the conditions in Ecuador's Manabí and Guayas provinces provide a suitable material for hat-making. When the straw reaches about 1.5 metres high, it's cut, boiled, sun-dried and cut into finer strands, and then boiled and dried once more before it's ready to be woven. Weavers get to work early in the morning or late at night, both to avoid the sun, which stiffens the straw prematurely, and so it's not so hot that their hands get sweaty. A *superfino*, the highest grade, has up to 32 fibres per square inch and can take four months to make.

The straw was once exported to the weavers of Venezuela and Peru until Ecuador's hat-makers complained that foreign-made hats were flooding the market, so the government prohibited exports in 1835. At around this time, the hats found a market in the US, where people couldn't believe they were man-made. Attempts to cultivate the straw in the Far East to start a rival industry failed, and Ecuador's position as the world's leading straw-hat producer seemed assured. Thousands of weavers in workshops in the lowlands and Cuenca made the hats to satisfy enormous global demand, even though they were only paid a tiny fraction of what the hats fetched in the boutiques abroad. The tide of fashion turned in the mid-twentieth century, and hat-making has been in sharp decline ever since. Nowadays only a few families produce the immaculately woven **superfinos**, the perfect tropical travel hat that can be rolled up tight enough to pass through a wedding ring, stored in its lightweight balsa box, and unpacked later without even a crease.

everything in the pirate raids of the early seventeenth century. The central street, Avenida 9 de Julio, leads uphill from the highway for almost 1km past a few old colonial houses with the odd skewed balustrade or broken shutter slat, to the main square at the head of the town. There are no hotels in Montecristi, but it's just a short **bus** ride from Manta, so it's not difficult to visit. Buses marked "Montecristi" go right to the main square, while others stop on the main road, from where it's a ten-minute walk uphill.

△ Straw farmer holding palm fronds, Manab province

Montecristi might look quite ramshackle were it not for its beautiful **church**, whose elegant double staircase sweeps up to its stately doors. Overlooking the town's attractive **central square** and set in white against the backdrop of the cloud-draped hills, the church is visible from several kilometres away. A number of miracles have been attributed to the effigy of the Virgin inside – there's a lively **fiesta**, and street markets and processions around November 20 in her honour. The town is also the birthplace of **Eloy Alfaro**, the influential Liberal president at the beginning of the nineteenth century, whose dignified statue adorns the square, and whose house on Eloy Alfaro has been made into a **museum** (Mon–Sat; free), offering a few historical exhibits and a library.

Panama-hat workshops

Montecristi's main claim to fame is as the centre of the **Panama hat** industry. Locals have been weaving the stylish headgear for well over a century (see box, p.402), and while the world's hunger for them has been waning since their heyday in the 1930s and 1940s, a handful of people still produce them. José Chávez Franco is one of the best, and you can see his **workshop** on Rocafuerte 386, between Eloy Alfaro and 10 de Agosto (walk up past the church and turn right), or try Don Resendo Delgado Garay, Rocafuerte 500 and Chimborazo (walk up past the church, turn left and the sign on his house is visible to the right).

Panama hats can cost from a few dollars for a simple model to more than $100 for one that takes three or four months to make, but this is still cheaper than virtually anywhere else in the world. At one time, almost every house in town had its own Panama hat workshop, but many have now turned to more profitable crafts, such as tagua carving and straw-basket weaving, filling the many **craft shops** on Avenida 9 de Julio.

Portoviejo

About 35km east of Manta and connected to it by a fast road, **PORTOVIEJO** sits rather uneasily as the inland capital of coastal Manabí province. Ecuadorians know the province as the relaxed and fun-loving place of beach resorts and peaceful fishing villages, but Portoviejo is seen as its boring overseer, manned by office workers toiling in the heat and dust.

Francisco Pacheco founded Portoviejo on March 12 1535, under the orders of the conquistador **Diego de Almagro**, who wanted to bring order to the region after the destruction wrought by Pedro de Alvarado a year earlier (see p.397). Although founded on the coast, it was relocated "seven leagues inland" later that year, only to suffer a terrible fire in 1541. Nevertheless, the area soon became an important agricultural centre, and in the 1570s even the few nearby indigenous communities that had survived the Conquest were doing well enough to own horses and commercial farms – while still having to pay crushing tribute to their Spanish overlords. During the post-colonial era Portoviejo flourished as a business centre, and while it's now second to Manta in commercial activity, it's still a key administrative centre and the site of an important state university.

Accommodation

Portoviejo has a fair range of **accommodation**, but the cheapest hotels are in the unsafe area around the bus station, from where you should get a taxi to the centre.

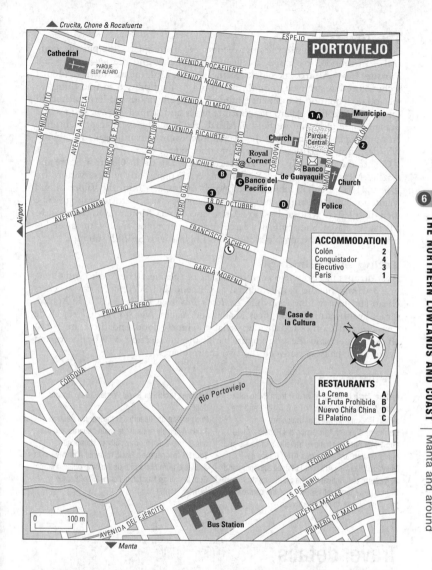

Colón Colón and Olmedo ☎05/634004.
Inexpensive place with a few decent-sized rooms with private baths, and cable TVs and a/c for more money – just make sure to avoid the dank interior rooms. ❸

Conquistador 18 de Octubre and 10 de Agosto ☎05/631678. The best value in town for its private baths, phones, cable TVs and big double beds, though the rooms are showing signs of age. ❹

Ejecutivo 18 de Octubre and 10 de Agosto ☎05/630840 or 630872, ☏630876. An expensive and pretentious spot with its showy lobby and smoked mirror-glass, which is nonetheless Portoviejo's most comfortable hotel, offering smaller interior rooms and larger suites with full amenities. ❻–❼

Paris Sucre and Olmedo ☎05/652727. Offers a real slice of history for its characterful old building and worn floorboards. A little run-down, but one of the best rock-bottom options. ❷

The Town

Portoviejo's central district lies between its two main squares, the **parque central** – surrounded by banks, a few minor churches and the *municipio* – and **Parque Eloy Alfaro**, six blocks further north. Little of the town's colonial architecture has survived, though, and you'll be hard pressed to find things to see and do. The most prominent landmark is the enormous modern **cathedral** on the Parque Eloy Alfaro, its concrete walls and striped brown, yellow and orange dome gleaming in the sun. Murals and stained glass attempt to brighten up the sparse interior, but the overall impression remains bleak as the wind whistles through glassless windows on either side.

One of the town's few other attractions, the **Casa de la Cultura**, Sucre and García Moreno (Mon–Fri 8am–noon & 3–6pm, or by reservation on ℡05/631753; free), exhibits a hotchpotch of artefacts from the Valdivian and Manteño cultures, nineteenth-century paintings and historical documents, including letters written by Eloy Alfaro and García Moreno. On the road to Manta, El Paseo Shopping is a large modern shopping mall with an eight-screen **cinema**, showing blockbusters in English with Spanish subtitles.

Eating and drinking

Restaurants in Portoviejo's centre, such as *El Palatino*, 10 de Agosto and Chile, or *La Crema*, on the parque central at Olmedo and Sucre, feed city workers cheap and hearty lunches, while *La Fruta Prohibida*, Chile and 10 de Agosto, serves healthy fruit salads, juices, shakes and snacks. *Nuevo Chifa China*, 18 de Octubre and Córdova, dishes up reliable Chinese food, and there are fried-chicken diners and the odd yogurt bar at the intersection of Rocafuerte and Pedro Gual, halfway between the two main squares.

Listings

Airline Tame provides a service from Quito (office on Av América and Chile; ℡05/632429), and the airport is 2km northwest of the centre.
Banks and exchange Banco del Pacífico, Chile and 10 de Agosto, changes traveller's cheques and has a MasterCard and Cirrus ATM; Banco de Guayaquil has Visa ATMs at El Paseo Shopping and at Ricaurte and Bolívar, on the parque central.
Buses Local terminal 1km west of the centre, on the other side of the Río Portoviejo.

Internet facilities Royal Corner, 10 de Agosto and Chile.
Post office on Ricaurte, at the parque central.
Taxis Available around the main squares and the bus terminal; $1 for most city destinations.
Tourist information Basic material and city maps available from Ministerio de Turismo office, Pedro Gual and Juan Montalvo, northeast of Espejo (℡05/630877).

Travel details

Buses

Bahía de Caráquez to: Guayaquil (hourly; 6hr); Manta (9 daily; 3hr); Portoviejo (hourly; 2hr); Quito (2 daily; 8hr).
Esmeraldas to: Ambato (3 daily; 8hr); Atacames (every 20min; 1hr); Borbón (hourly; 3hr 15min); Chamanga (every 40min; 3hr); Guayaquil (hourly; 7–8hr); Ibarra (3 daily; 9hr); La Tola (6 daily; 4hr); Machala (3 daily; 12hr); Manta (4 daily; 10hr);

Muisne (every 20min; 2hr 30min); Pedernales (4 daily; 6hr 30min); Quito (hourly; 6hr); Same (every 20min; 1hr 30min); San Lorenzo (hourly; 4hr 30min); Súa (every 20min; 1hr 10min); Tonchigüe (every 20min; 1hr 35min); Tonsupa (every 20min; 50min).
Manta to: Bahía de Caráquez (hourly; 3hr); Crucita (12 daily; 1hr 30min); Esmeraldas (4 daily; 10hr); Guayaquil (every 30min–1hr; 3hr); Jipijapa (every 30min; 1hr); La Libertad (hourly; 6hr); Montecristi

(every 10min; 20min); Pedernales (4 daily; 6hr);
Portoviejo (every 10min; 45min); Puerto López
(hourly; 2hr by coast, 2hr 30min inland); Quevedo
(8 daily; 6hr); Quito (hourly; 9hr); Santo Domingo
(hourly; 6hr).

Pedernales to: Chamanga (every 30min; 1hr);
Guayaquil (2 daily; 8–9hr); Quito (4 daily; 5–6hr);
San Vicente (every 40min; 2hr 30min); Santo
Domingo (every 20min; 3hr).

Portoviejo to: Bahía de Caráquez (hourly; 2hr);
Crucita (every 15min; 45min–1hr); Esmeraldas (4
daily; 10hr); Guayaquil (every 30min–1hr; 4hr);
Manta (every 10min; 45min); Pedernales (9 daily;
5–6hr); Quevedo (every 40min; 5hr 15min); Quito
(hourly; 8hr); Santo Domingo (every 40min; 5hr).

San Lorenzo to: Borbón (hourly; 1hr 15min);
Esmeraldas (hourly; 4hr 30min); Guayaquil (2 daily;
10–13hr); Ibarra (9 daily; 3hr 30min); Quito (1
nightly; 7hr).

Santo Domingo to: Ambato (every 45min; 4hr);
Bahía de Caráquez (2 daily; 5hr); Coca (4 daily;
12hr); Cuenca (3 daily; 8hr); Esmeraldas (every
15min; 3hr); Guayaquil (every 30min; 4hr 30min);
Huaquillas (6 daily; 10hr); Lago Agrio (5 daily;
12hr); Machala (10 daily; 8hr); Manta (every 30min;
6hr); Muisne (4 daily; 6hr); Pedernales (every
30min; 3hr); Portoviejo (hourly; 5hr); Quevedo
(every 15min; 1hr 30min); Quito (every 10min; 3hr);
Salinas (2 daily; 8hr); San Miguel de los Bancos
(every 20min; 3hr); Tulcán (3 daily; 7hr).

Boats

San Lorenzo to: Limones (3 daily; 1hr 30min);
San Pedro (2 daily; 1hr 15min); Palma Real (2
daily; 1hr 30min).

Flights

Esmeraldas to: Guayaquil (4 weekly; 45min);
Quito (1 Sun–Mon & Wed–Fri; 30min).

Manta to: Guayaquil (5 weekly; 30min); Quito (1
daily; 45min).

Portoviejo to: Quito (3 weekly; 45min).

7

Guayaquil and the southern coast

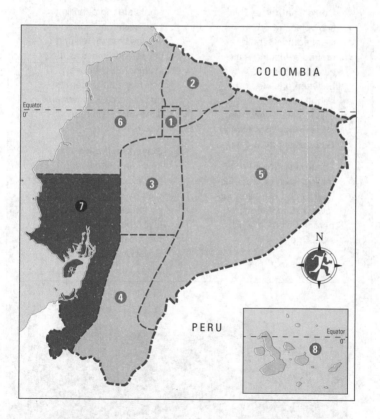

CHAPTER 7

Highlights

* **Malecón 2000** As the centrepiece and symbol of a resurgent Guayaquil, this beautiful tree-lined riverside promenade takes in sumptuous gardens, fountains, cafés, shops and various landmarks. See p.419

* **Cerro Santa Ana** This showpiece of urban regeneration is built around a winding stair-case threading its way between pristine and brightly painted houses to a fabulous viewpoint overlooking downtown Guayaquil. See p.420

* **Zaruma** A remote gold-mining town of graceful wooden houses and narrow twisting streets, perched high on a hill-side. See p.431

* **Surfing at Montañita** Long a surfer's favourite thanks to its attractive beach and celebrated breaks, but now a back-packer magnet, too. See p.444

* **Whale-watching from Puerto López** Few sights are more thrilling than seeing humpback whales breach, roll and call to each other as they swim into Ecuador's warm coastal waters to mate and calve between June and September. See p.447

* **Playa Los Frailes** With its virgin white sands and azure waters cradled by cliffs and backed by forested hills, this idyllic beach is one of the most beautiful on the Ecuadorian coast. See p.449

Guayaquil and the southern coast

Stretching from the Punta de Cayo in southern Manabí down to the border with Peru, Ecuador's **southern coast** sports a mixture of white-sand beaches lapped by cool turquoise waters and burly docks, shrimp farms and mangrove swamps surrounded by the Gulf of Guayaquil, while further inland the dry, brittle scrublands and sprawling banana plantations contrast dramatically with the lush forests found further north. Largely ignored by foreign visitors, the region nonetheless boasts some fine attractions such as deserted beaches, rich natural habitats and the oldest archeological sites in Ecuador. The focus of the southern coast is the port of **Guayaquil**, Ecuador's biggest city and an economic powerhouse that handles most of the country's imports and exports. Traditionally considered loud, frenetic, dirty and dangerous, Guayaquil is in reality much less overwhelming and intimidating than its reputation bears out, and its upbeat urban tempo makes an exciting change of pace from rural Ecuador. Moreover, improvements in public safety and huge investments in regeneration projects, such as the beautiful riverfront promenade **Malecón 2000**, are making Guayaquil a destination in its own right.

South of Guayaquil, the coastal highway slices through the bird-rich **Reserva Ecológica Manglares Churute** – set up to protect one of the last major **mangrove swamps** left on the southern coast – on its way to **Machala**, the provincial capital of **El Oro** province and famous as the nation's "banana capital". Otherwise low on sights and ambience, Machala serves as a useful springboard for outlying attractions such as the scenic hillside village of **Zaruma** and the fascinating petrified forest of **Puyango**, and is also handy as a stop on the way to the border crossing at **Huaquillas**. West of Guayaquil, a succession of long, golden beaches runs up the coast towards Manta and beyond, though apart from the flashy, high-rise town of **Salinas**, most are fairly undeveloped and backed by low-key resorts or down-at-heel fishing villages. Few places see many gringos along here, with the exceptions of laid-back **Montañita**, a grungy surfing hangout, the eco-resort of **Alandaluz**, with its tasteful bamboo cabins and private stretch of beach, and the dusty, tumbledown port of **Puerto López**, a base for summer **whale-watching** and year-round visits to the **Parque Nacional Machalilla**. This park is the southern coast's most compelling attraction, taking in stunning, pristine beaches, dry and humid **tropical**

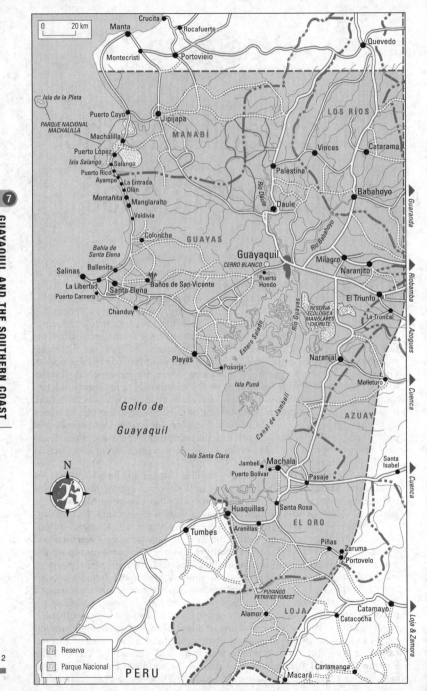

7

0   20 km

Crucita
Manta
Rocafuerte
Quevedo
Montecristi
Portovieio
LOS RÍOS

Isla de la Plata
Puerto Cayo
Jipijapa
MANABÍ
*PARQUE NACIONAL
MACHALILLA*
Machalilla
Vinces
Catarama
Puerto López
Isla Salango   Salango
Palestina
Puerto Rico
Ayampe   La Entrada
Olón
Babahoyo
Montañita   Manglaralto
Daule
Valdivia

Colonche
GUAYAS
Río Daule
Río Babahoyo
*Bahía de
Santa Elena*
Guayaquil
CERRO BLANCO
Milagro
Salinas   Ballenita
Naranjito
La Libertad   Santa Elena
Baños de San Vicente
Puerto
Hondo
El Triunfo
Puerto Carnero
*RESERVA
ECOLÓGICA
MANGLARES
CHURUTE*
La Troncal
Chanduy
Río Guayas

Estero Salado
Playas
Posorja
Naranjal
Isla Puná
Molleturo
AZUAY
*Golfo de
Guayaquil*
Canal de Jambelí

Isla Santa Clara
Jambelí   Machala
Santa
Isabel
Puerto Bolívar
Pasaje

Huaquillas   Santa Rosa
EL ORO
Tumbes   Arenillas
Piñas
Zaruma
Portovelo

*PUYANGO
PETRIFIED FOREST*
LOJA
Catamayo
Alamor   Catacocha
Cariamanga
Macará

N

Reserva
Parque Nacional

PERU

Guaranda
Riobamba
Azogues
Cuenca
Cuenca
Loja & Zamora

forests and, most famously, the **Isla de la Plata**, an inexpensive alternative to the Galápagos for viewing boobies, frigates and albatrosses.

The **best time to visit** the southern coast is between December and April, when bright blue skies and warm weather more than compensate for the frequent showers of the rainy season – the time of year when coastal vegetation comes to life and dry tropical forests become luxuriant and moist. Outside these months, the dry season features warm weather (around 23°C), but often depressingly grey skies. Hotel **prices** during the high season (Dec–April & July–Aug) can be double those of the low. In choosing beaches for your travels, note that not all are safe for swimming and many, like Manglaralto and Montañita, have dangerous currents and riptides that should be approached with great caution. Another consideration is the irregular and unpredictable **El Niño** weather phenomenon (see p.523), when unusually heavy storms can leave the coast severely battered, washing away roads and disrupting communications.

Guayaquil

For years, **GUAYAQUIL** was regarded as one of Ecuador's most dangerous cities, dogged by high crime rates and suffering from a general breakdown in law and order. However, after a recent round of night-time curfews and clean-up campaigns, and following a major redevelopment of key downtown areas, the city has improved beyond measure and is starting to shake off its former notoriety, with the central district now an unthreatening and surprisingly likeable place. Indeed, if you've just come down from the sierra, the city's energy and intensity can seem exhilarating, and its sophisticated shops and restaurants can make for a real treat. But outside the well-to-do areas, and the sparkling and heavily patrolled attractions of the waterfront and city centre, Guayaquil quickly loses its charm – its dynamism turns to chaos, its heat and humidity become oppressive, and its litter-strewn streets seem unsafe to wander.

Away from downtown, Guayaquil's general scruffiness belies the fact that it's the country's wealthiest city – thanks mainly to its massive **port** that handles major national exports like bananas, shrimp, cacao and coffee – and its largest, too, with a population of more than two million people, close to double that of Quito. Although the rivalry between the two cities is deep-seated and taken very seriously, particularly during electoral campaigns, Guayaquil still lags well behind the capital for its historical attractions, with only a smattering of colonial buildings still standing (most of the others having been destroyed in the 1942 earthquake). Nonetheless, Quito has nothing like Guayaquil's gleaming riverside development, the **Malecón 2000**, which incorporates gardens, shopping centres, restaurants, the new **Museo Banco Central** and several of the city's most famous landmarks, and links downtown to the **Cerro Santa Ana**, once a dangerous slum now ingeniously reinvented as a beacon of urban renewal. As well as being huge sources of local pride, these sights symbolize a city transforming itself from a place with a bad reputation, once visited out of necessity rather than choice, to an emerging tourist destination that also serves as a good base for exploring the beaches and protected areas of the southern coast.

Some history

Conquistador Francisco de Orellana founded the city as **Santiago de Guayaquil** on July 25, 1537, its name supposedly honouring the local

Huancavilca chieftain **Guayas** and his wife, **Quil**, who killed themselves rather than be captured by the approaching Spanish hordes. From its earliest years it was the most important entry point into Ecuador (known then as the "Audiencia de Quito") and quickly grew into a flourishing little port. Its fortunes, however, were held back by the repeated attacks of pillaging British, French and Dutch **buccaneers**, regular **fires** engulfing its combustible timber buildings, and the deleterious mix of **tropical climate** and inadequate **sanitation**, which made it a hotbed of smallpox, yellow fever and typhoid. Nevertheless, during the seventeenth and eighteenth centuries Guayaquil gradually took on the shape of a proper city, with new roads, bridges, schools, hospitals and markets, mostly funded by burgeoning exports of **cacao**, **fruit** and **wood**.

On October 9, 1820, it became the first city in Ecuador to declare its **independence** from Spain, and it was from here that **General Sucre** conducted his famous military campaign that culminated in the liberation of Quito on May 24, 1822. Shortly afterwards, Guayaquil went down in history as the site of the legendary meeting between the two liberators of South America, **Simón Bolívar** and **José de San Martín**, whose campaigns from opposite ends of the continent were then drawing together in the middle (see p.511). In the decades following independence, Guayaquil grew rapidly and asserted its considerable role in the new republic – Ecuador's first bank was founded here in 1859, soon followed by a major public library and university. The tide of success, however, turned in 1896, when the worst **fire** in its history wiped out seventy percent of the city in 36 hours.

With characteristic resilience, Guayaquil quickly rebuilt and became prosperous once more in the twentieth century, aided by the dramatic **banana boom** that began in the late 1940s. The city's pivotal role in the country's international trade, and the huge increase in commerce at that time, funded new port facilities - the Puerto Nuevo – in 1963, and the construction of the massive three-kilometre **Puente de Unidad Nacional**, the largest bridge on the Pacific coast of South America. Unfortunately, in the last decade or so numerous **shanty towns** have emerged on the periphery of the city, as thousands of people have migrated from the countryside in search of work, and **crime** levels soared to the point where, in 1998, a state of emergency and nightly curfews were imposed on the city for several months in an attempt to control the lawbreaking. These measures, along with a stronger police presence, seem to have improved security in downtown areas such as the Malecón, but vigilance is still required, as in any city.

Arrival, information and transport

Because of its energy, noise and disorder, **orientation** in Guayaquil takes a little longer than in other Ecuadorian cities. Guard against **petty theft** by staying alert when arriving in town and getting your bearings, don't wander the streets with your valuables, and always take a taxi at night.

Guayaquil's huge, chaotic **bus terminal** is 7km north of the city centre; a Banco del Pacífico ATM near its main exit accepts MasterCard and Cirrus cards. The road that loops around the terminal is used only by streams of **local buses**, several of which will take you into the centre (for example, the #2), though it's a huge challenge trying to work out which bus routes go where. It's far easier and safer to take a **taxi** to your hotel for around $4 – they rank in a large parking area at one end of the terminal (ask anyone to point you in the right direction).

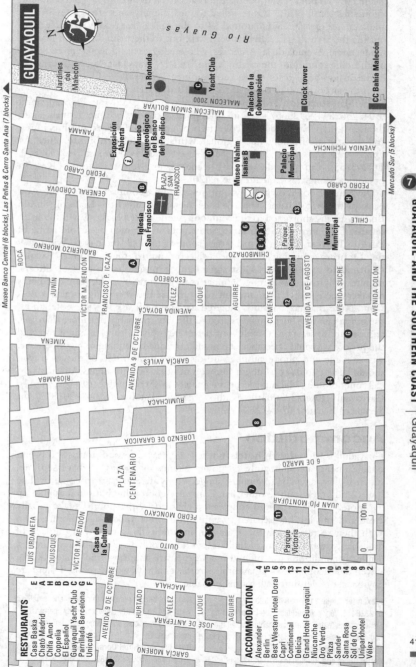

RESTAURANTS

Casa Baska	E
Cható Madrid	A
Chifa Amoi	H
Coppelia	D
El Español	B
Guayaquil Yacht Club	C
Parrillada Barcelona	G
Unicafé	F

ACCOMMODATION

Alexander	4
Berlin	15
Best Western Hotel Doral	6
Capri	3
Continental	13
Delicia	11
Grand Hotel Guayaquil	12
Niucanche	7
Oro Verde	1
Plaza	10
Sander	5
Santa Rosa	14
Sol de Oro	8
Uniparkhotel	9
Vélez	2

415

The busy **airport** – Aeropuerto Internacional Simón Bolívar – is a couple of kilometres south of the bus terminal toward the city, and offers a few ATMs and a *casa de cambio*. **Taxis** (around $4 to the centre) are readily available from outside the arrivals gate; alternatively, walk out to the main avenue in front of the terminal, Avenida de las Américas, where you can flag down a cab or a local bus heading south into the centre (again, try #2). Always take a taxi from within the airport at night or when carrying luggage, however. If leaving Ecuador from the airport, you're required to pay **$10 departure tax** in cash.

The **Ministerio de Turismo** office, Pedro Icaza 203 (Mon–Fri 9am–5pm; ☎04/2562544, ℱ2568774, ℮infotour@telconet.net), is quite a small affair, though it does have a decent collection of up-to-date **maps** and brochures, and the staff are friendly. The regional **Ministerio del Ambiente** office, Av Quito 402 and Padre Solano (Mon–Fri 8.30am–4.30pm; ☎04/2560870, ℱ2293155), can provide you with information on the nearby Reserva Ecológica Manglares Churute (see p.426).

The core of downtown Guayaquil lies within a compact grid on the west bank of the Río Guayas. The riverside avenue is called the Malecón Simón Bolívar, usually shortened to the **Malecón**, while three blocks away is the main square of the **Parque Seminario**, sometimes still known by its old name of **Parque Bolívar**. The principal artery running through the city is **Avenida 9 de Octubre**, running from the Malecón up to the imposing **Parque Centenario** and beyond. Most sights are no more than a ten- or fifteen-minute walk from the Parque Seminario; to get further afield, your best bet is to take a **taxi**, rather than attempt to negotiate the confusing local bus network. Note that taxis are not metered in Guayaquil; ask in your hotel about the going rate for short journeys around the city (probably not more than $1), and be sure to set a price with your driver before you leave. It's safest to avoid the privately owned "freelance" taxis and take one belonging to a cooperative, whose name and phone number are displayed on the side of the car – you should be able to flag one down easily on most city-centre streets. Alternatively, call one of the 24-hour companies such as Aeropuerto (☎04/2294944), Carrousel (☎04/2250610), Radio Taxi El Paraíso (☎04/2201877) or Servitaxis Ecuador (☎04/2301393).

Accommodation

Guayaquil is packed with **hotels**, but few are geared towards tourists. Top-end establishments attract mainly corporate clients and nearly all have separate, much higher, rates for foreigners; single rooms are also hard to come by. The lower-end hotels, on the other hand, are very good value but often double up as "motels" – places where couples are charged by the hour. They're usually clean and safe, but be prepared to bump into a few middle-aged businessmen with their secretaries on the stairs – if in doubt, the giveaway is the lack of available twin beds. Many of the cheaper hotels only have cold-water showers, while air conditioning is offered in all expensive and most mid-priced hotels. Given the cacophony of Guayaquil's streets, it's always worth asking if there are any back, or even internal, rooms available.

Alexander Luque 1107 ☎04/2532000, ℱ2328474. Very polished little hotel with well-furnished rooms featuring a/c and cable TVs. All the doubles are quiet, if dark, interior rooms, while the suites overlook the street. **❺**

Berlin Sucre and Rumichaca ☎04/2524648.

Adequate budget rooms with ceiling fans, small air vents and cold-water showers. Pretty spartan, but clean and spacious, with some rooms giving onto the street. **❷**

Best Western Hotel Doral Chile 402 and Aguirre ☎04/2328490, ℱ2327088, ℮hdoral@

△ Malecón 2000, Guayaquil

gye.satnet.net. Some rooms are a bit gloomy with worn-out furnishings, but the "king-size" rooms have bright decor, huge beds, big cable TVs, a/c and heavily lined curtains to keep out the light. Breakfast included. ⑥

Capri Luque 1221 ☎04/2530093. Small, good-value hotel with parking, offering neat rooms with cool floor tiles and whitewashed walls. All rooms have cable TVs, a/c, fridges and private bathrooms – but those on the street are noisy. ④

Continental Chile 510 and 10 de Agosto ☎04/2329270, ⓕ2325454, ⓔinfo@hotelcontinental .com.ec, ⓦwww.hotelcontinental.com.ec. Business-oriented hotel with spacious, comfortable rooms decorated with attractive canvases by local artists. Every room has its own safe, the mattresses are nice and firm, and breakfast is included. Substantial discounts at weekends. ⑧

Delicia Clemente Ballén 1105 ☎04/2324925. Dozens of rather bare, box-like rooms with shared or private baths, and fans or a/c. Modest but very clean, friendly and safe. Popular with backpackers. ②–③

Ecuahogar out of the centre at Avenida Isidro Ayora, Sauces 1 ☎04/2248357, ⓕ2248341, ⓔyouthost@telconet.net. Well-managed youth hostel with dorm beds for $10 (including break-fast) and hot water, security boxes and a café-restaurant, as well as free pick-up service from the airport or bus station. Rooms ⑤

Grand Hotel Guayaquil Boyacá and Clemente Ballén ☎04/2325127, ⓕ2327251. Large, upmarket hotel boasting a gorgeous outdoor pool with a cascading waterfall. Good rooms and furnishings, as well as a roof deck, sauna, massage rooms, steam baths and 24-hour café open to non-guests. Breakfast and 30min Internet use included. ⑧

Niucanche Pío Montúfar 107 ☎04/2512312. Run by the same family as *Delicia* and equally spotless

and friendly; a good budget choice, but no a/c. ②

Oro Verde 9 de Octubre and García Moreno ☎04/2327999, ⓕ2329350, ⓔov_gye @oroverdehotels.com, ⓦwww.oroverdehotels .com. Guayaquil's premier city-centre hotel, a large, modern and impeccably decorated establishment with several restaurants (see p.423), a pleasant out-door pool and stylish, contemporary rooms. ⑨

Plaza Chile 414 and Clemente Ballén ☎04/2327140. All rooms have cable TV, a/c and decent bathrooms, and as the hotel's undergoing renovation, they're likely to be better appointed still when it's reopened. ⑥

Sander Luque 1101 ☎04/2320030. Great-value hotel offering clean, simple rooms with fans or a/c and private bathrooms. Mostly doubles, but also has some twin rooms. ②–③

Santa Rosa Rumichaca 1423 ☎04/2518105. Small bargain hotel with basic but clean rooms with ceiling fans. One of the nicest of the cheapies, though it has doubles only. ②

Sol de Oro Lorenzo de Garaicoa 1243 ☎04/2532067. Friendly hotel offering well-furnished rooms with cable TVs and a/c. Pricier suites on the top floor are huge and boast excellent views over the city. A good mid-price choice with its own garage and complimentary breakfast. ⑤–⑥

Uniparkhotel Clemente Ballén 406, Parque Seminario ☎04/2327100, ⓕ2328352, ⓔuni_gye@oroverdehotels.com. Large, plush hotel with a vast marble lobby, pleasant piano bar and modern, well-appointed rooms. Private parking. ⑨

Vélez Vélez 1021 ☎04/2530356. Simple but impeccably clean singles, doubles and triples with bare, pale-cream walls and floors and en-suite bathrooms with cold water. Some rooms have a/c, others have ceiling fans. Has its own garage. ②–③

The City

For sightseeing, the most impressive part of Guayaquil is the **Malecón 2000** riverside development, which includes the new **Museo Banco Central**, leading towards the rejuvenated district of **Cerro Santa Ana** and its spectacular viewpoint, and the tiny but attractive district of **Las Peñas**, featuring 1900s architecture and a string of art galleries. Other potential sights include the enjoyable **Museo Municipal** and a few private **museums** showcasing a wealth of religious art and pre-Columbian artefacts. All these museums have air conditioning, providing delicious relief from the heat. There are also several good out-of-town excursions to be made, such as to the **Parque Histórico Guayaquil**, an enjoyable exploration of the city's past and its regional environment, the **Jardín Botánico**, with its estimable collection of plants, the **Bosque Protector Cerro Blanco** (see p.435), a dry tropical forest reserve, and the mangroves at **Puerto Hondo** (see p.436) and the **Reserva Ecológica Manglares Churute** (see p.426).

The city's biggest **fiestas** are July 24 for Simón Bolívar's birthday and July 25 for the foundation of the city, celebrated together in a week of events and festivities that includes processions, street dancing and fireworks, known as the **fiestas julianas**. Another important bash comes in October for the city's **independence** on the ninth, combined with the **Día de la Raza** on the twelfth, commemorating Columbus's discovery of the New World. Finally, New Year's Eve is celebrated with the burning of the *años viejos*, large effigies, on the Malecón at midnight.

The Malecón

The riverside **Malecón** – officially called the Malecón Simón Bolívar – skirts the western bank of the wide, yellow-brown Río Guayas, which empties into the Pacific at the Gulf of Guayaquil, 60km downstream. While the Malecón is always heaving with traffic, the long pedestrianized section by the waterfront is by far the most pleasant place to stroll in town – especially after its massive face-lift funded by the multimillion-dollar **Malecón 2000** project, which has transformed it into the most skilfully designed, diligently maintained and beloved public space in the city. The large paved esplanade is filled with trees, botanical gardens, contemporary sculpture and architecture, shopping malls and restaurants, and connects some of Guayaquil's best-known monuments along a promenade regularly patrolled by security guards, enclosed by railings and accessed only at guarded entrance gates – making it one of the safest places to spend a day in Guayaquil.

Its centrepiece is the **Plaza Cívica**, reached by gates at the end of 9 de Octubre or 10 de Agosto. As you enter by the former gate you're faced with **La Rotonda**, an imposing statue of South America's great liberators, José de San Martín and Simón Bolívar, shaking hands against a background of tall marble columns and billowing South American flags. The monument, which looks stunning when illuminated at night, commemorates the famous encounter between the two generals here on July 26 and 27, 1822, ostensibly to discuss the emancipation of Peru, but used by Bolívar as an opportunity to annex Ecuador to his fledgling nation of Gran Colombia (see p.512). The monument is designed in such a way that two people whispering into the two end pillars can hear each other, though the din of the traffic somewhat undermines the effect.

Walking south from La Rotonda, you'll pass four sculptures dedicated to the four elements, with fire and earth doubling up as timber-and-metal **lookout towers** crowned by sail-like awnings. The views from the top are quite striking: on one side the vast urban sprawl stretches to the horizon, while on the other the low, fuzzy vegetation across the river lies completely free of buildings. Looking north, the huge bridge of **Puente de la Unidad Nacional** stretches across to the suburb of Durán, from where the famous Quito–Guayaquil trains used to leave. Beyond the sculptures and past the Yacht Club, the slender, cream-coloured Moorish **clock tower** is decorated with Islamic geometric designs at its base and long, Mozarabic windows around the column. The 23-metre tower marks the southern end of the Plaza Cívica and was originally constructed in 1842, though the present version, following a relocation and several reconstructions, dates to 1931.

South of the clock tower are fast-food joints and a compact subterranean shopping centre, the CC Bahía Malecón, but beyond them is the dignified **Plaza Olmedo**, dedicated to statesman and poet **José Joaquín de Olmedo** (1780–1847), the first mayor of Guayaquil and a key agitator for the city's independence. At the southern end of the promenade, the beautiful **Mercado Sur** (daily 9am–10pm; $1), a splendid construction of glass and wrought iron, is floodlit at night to dazzling effect and houses an art gallery for temporary exhibitions. Some assert that Gustave Eiffel intervened in the design of the building in 1905, but there's no documentary evidence to support this claim. Opposite, indigenous flower sellers surround the elegant **Iglesía San José**, and south of the Mercado Sur lies a small clothes and **artesanía market**, though you'll have to bargain hard to get a good deal.

North of the Plaza Cívica is a magnificent succession of sumptuous **botanical gardens**, fountains, ponds and walkways, in which each garden is themed on a historical period or Ecuadorian habitat, such as the Plaza de las Bromelias, a lavish concoction of trees swathed in mosses and bromeliads in the manner of a cloudforest. At the northern end of the Malecón 2000, the new Museo Banco Central, officially called the **Museo Antropológico y de Arte Contemporáneo** (MAAC), is due to open in December 2003 and to feature an excellent collection of fine pre-Columbian ceramics, golden objects, and ceremonial paraphernalia such as ancient snuff trays and headdresses, as well as a selection of contemporary art.

Las Peñas and Cerro Santa Ana

The Malecón ends in the north at the picturesque barrio of **Las Peñas**, at the foot of Cerro Santa Ana overlooking the river. While there's little more to it than a single dead-end road – Numa Pompilio Llona – that takes about five minutes to walk up and down, the once-grand houses leaning against the hillside and narrow street paved with uneven, century-old cobblestones make it one of the prettiest corners of Guayaquil. When visiting the barrio make sure you take the correct street, as neighbouring alleys have a reputation for being dangerous: Numa Pompilio Llona begins at a tiny square with a couple of cannons pointing towards the river, honouring the city's stalwart resistance to seventeenth-century pirates.

Part of the area's charm derives from its lack of restoration for the tourist trade, as the houses are covered with flaking paint and give the impression of going gently to seed. However, many are occupied by local artists whose workshops and small galleries are open to the public; one to look out for is the **Casa del Artista Plástico** of the Asociación Cultural Las Peñas, which mounts changing exhibitions of a variety of artists' work.

Rising above Las Peñas, the **Cerro Santa Ana** was a very dangerous slum until a recent regeneration project transformed a swath of its ramshackle buildings – constructed of corrugated iron, raw breeze blocks and split cane – into an eye-catching sequence of brightly painted houses, restaurants, bars and shops built around a winding, 456-step staircase to a viewpoint at the top of the hill: the grandly-titled **Plaza de Honores**, home to a new colonial-style chapel and lighthouse modelled after Guayaquil's first, from 1841.

With its discreet balconies, ornate lampposts, and switchback streets leading from intimate plazas, the development does a fair job of evoking the image of a bygone Guayaquil, but it's most impressive when viewed at a distance from the Malecón, from where you can't see its plastic "tiled" roofs, heavy presence of armed guards and large locked gates blocking out the slums at its margins. Even so, the spectacular **views** from the Plaza de Honores and the top of the lighthouse are well worth a visit, particularly after a day on the Malecón as the suns dips on the seething city below. Just below the Plaza de Honores, the **Museo Abierto** holds the foundations of the fortress of **San Carlos**, built in 1629 to defend the city from pirate attacks.

Parque Seminario and around

Three blocks behind the Palacio Municipal, Guayaquil's central square, the **Parque Seminario** (also known as Parque Bolívar) is famous for its impish iguanas, which make occasional appearances out of the trees and shrubs where they live. The west side of the square is dominated by the huge, gleaming-white **cathedral**, a neo-Gothic confection of spires, arches and lancet windows, which dates only from 1948 and is built solidly of concrete – largely due to the original 1547 cathedral and subsequent incarnations being destroyed by fire. The rest of the square is overlooked mostly by hotels and the monolithic Pacifictel building.

One block southwest, on Sucre and Chile, the **Museo Municipal** (Tues–Sat 9am–5pm; free) focuses on the history of the city and region, with well-presented exhibits and good information panels, in Spanish only. In the entrance lobby, one of its most stunning pieces is an enormous six-hundred-year-old tree trunk embellished with dozens of carvings of human figures, produced by the seafaring Manteño–Huancavilca culture who occupied the coast from the Gulf of Guayaquil to Bahía de Caráquez and were the first in what is now Ecuador to have any contact with the Spanish. Other striking pieces include a ten-thousand-year-old mastodon tooth, pre-Columbian pottery, scale models of early Guayaquil and its docks, a diorama of the great fire of 1896, displays on the seventeenth-century English buccaneers who attacked the city, and various antique portraits, weapons and clothes.

Facing the waterfront three blocks east of the Parque Seminario, roughly opposite the clock tower, the large, Neoclassical **Palacio Municipal** is one of the most beautiful buildings in the city, its grey walls set off by dazzling white balconies and stucco mouldings. Running through the middle of the *palacio*, the central arcade is topped by a glass-and-metal vault and lined by admirable Grecian-style marble statues of women just beneath the roof, flooded in natural light. Adjacent to the palace is the **Palacio de la Gobernación**, similar to its neighbour but smaller, plainer and less well-kept, which stands in front of the **Museo Nahim Isaias B**, Clemente Ballén and Pichincha (Mon–Sat 10am–5pm; free), whose collection is displayed in a gallery overlooking the banking hall. It mostly features pre-Columbian ceramics in glass cases, including some gorgeous, elaborately crafted pottery and a few gold items (though it's all a bit too cluttered to do justice to the objects), and a less-compelling selection of colonial religious art upstairs. Note that the museum was closed at the time of writing and had no date for re-opening.

Plaza San Francisco and around

Five blocks north of the Museo Municipal lies the small, tree-filled **Plaza San Francisco**, at Pedro Carbo and Vélez, where the grey-and-white **Iglesia San Francisco** towers over its flowerbeds and benches. Like many others in town, the original church was destroyed in the 1896 fire, and the current building, erected six years later, preserves its colonial look. In contrast to the church's restrained design, across the road is a large, fantastical statue of a fish-cum-hummingbird covered in bright mosaics, a bright and modern design echoed a few blocks away at the **Exposición Abierta**, around the corner on Icaza and Pichincha, a collection of huge, modern, brightly coloured murals on the side of the Banco del Pacífico building. A little further towards the Malecón, the **Museo Arqueológico del Banco del Pacífico**, Icaza 113 (Mon–Fri 9am–5pm; free), houses a modest but beautifully displayed collection of pre-Columbian ceramics.

Plaza Centenario and around

From the Plaza San Francisco, the frenetic Avenida 9 de Octubre leads seven blocks west to the **Plaza Centenario**, an immense square spread over four blocks and landscaped with flowers and trees, but constantly choked with traffic. Its centre is marked by a towering column crowned by the statue *Liberty*, its arms outstretched and images of independence heroes arrayed around its base. On the west side of the square, at the corner with 9 de Octubre, a slightly down-at-heel building houses the **Casa de la Cultura**, which has a museum upstairs (Tues–Fri 10am–5.30pm, Sat 9am–3pm; $1) exhibiting pre-Columbian items in its Sala Arqueológica – poorly presented and not very engaging – and a small but lovely gold collection in its Sala de Oro. Most exhibits were produced by the Milagro-Quevado culture, with a few pieces by the La Tolita culture, including a beautiful mask with silver eyes and a nose ring. The museum used to have more than five hundred pieces until a dramatic theft in 1987 reduced the collection to just 63 items.

A ten-minute walk north from the plaza along Calle Moncayo (near a rough area and safer travelled by taxi) brings you to the city cemetery, also known as the **Ciudad Blanca** (White City) for its many rows of dazzling white tombs and mausoleums housing the remains of the local elite. Taking pride of place at the end of an avenue lined with palms is the tomb of the former president Vicente Rocafuerte, a Guayaquil native. Here and elsewhere in the cemetery, the funerary sculpture is remarkably indulgent, much of it carved of Carrara marble from Italy. Opposite the cemetery near entrance 6, a **flower market** bursts with colourful blooms.

Parque Histórico Guayaquil

Northeast of town at La Puntilla, on the highway to Samborondón, the **Parque Histórico Guayaquil** (Tues–Sun 9am–4.30pm; $3, $3.50 Sun, holidays and special events; ⓦwww.parquehistorico.com) is a well-designed and slickly operated historical park divided into three sections. A **forest-life** zone features walkways through mangroves, spacious enclosures holding native animals such as tapirs, caimans, ocelots, spider monkeys, sloths and a harpy eagle, and an observation tower for bird watching. The **traditions** zone represents coastal culture and the *montuvio* way of life by a traditional farmstead (*granja*) with crops of cacao, banana, coffee, rice, *paja toquilla* and mate, as well as a reconstructed cacao-plantation hacienda dating to 1883, half of which is original. The **urban architecture** zone displays some of the last fragments of Guayaquil's late-nineteenth-century buildings, which have been reassembled and restored and now overlook the "**Malecón 1900**" – the riverside as it might have looked at the turn of the last century. On Sundays, actors in costume promenade along the waterfront, and plans are underway for a paddle steamer to ferry passengers back through time from the Malecón 2000. City **buses** #97 and #4 pass near the park entrance, but it's probably easier to get a **taxi** from downtown ($3–4).

Jardín Botánico de Guayaquil

On a lofty position on top of the Cerro Colorado, beyond the Ciudadela Las Orquídeas on the north side of town, the **Jardín Botánico de Guayaquil** (daily 8am–4pm; $2) has an excellent collection of orchids, as well as several hundred other plants on a peaceful site with great views over the city. At extra cost, guides can take you around the gardens, which also include a butterfly house, koi pond and geology area with rock and mineral exhibits. The #63 **bus** leaves from the Parque Centenario and takes you to within a fifteen-minute walk of the garden; if going by **taxi** (30min; $4–6), it's not a bad idea to arrange a pick-up time.

Eating

Despite its reputation as the "last port on the Caribbean", Guayaquil is no Havana, and its dining scene downtown is less vibrant than you might expect. Many of the **restaurants** in the centre are attached to hotels like the *Oro Verde*, which makes some of them rather impersonal – though the best ones serve fantastic, high-quality food. A more concentrated collection of restaurants, as well as bars and nightclubs, lines the main drag of Estrada in the affluent suburb of **Urdesa**, which can be reached by buses #52 and #54 from the Malecón, #10 from Parque Centenario, or by taxi (20min; $2) – which is fine if you're on for a night on the town, but quite an effort if you just want to wind down your day over a good meal. For something quick and easy, you'll find plenty of **fast-food** outlets at the CC Malecón mall, including several taco and seafood bars, as well as others at the northern end of the promenade. The big shopping centres like Mall del Sol (see "Listings", p.425) feature huge food courts with dozens of familiar international fast-food chains.

Chifa Amoi Sucre and Pedro Carbo. The smartest of three neighbouring Chinese restaurants. Has a clean, pleasant dining room and serves cheap and tasty Chinese and Ecuadorian food.

Casa Baska Clemente Ballén 422, Parque Seminario. Informal Spanish restaurant with bare brick walls and a long list of mouthwatering tapas chalked up on a blackboard – manchego cheese, *serrano* ham, croquettes, sardines in olive oil, seafood broth and lots more. It's all delicious, but quite pricey. Closed Sun.

Cható Madrid Baquerizo Moreno 1118 and 9 de Octubre. Smart but compact restaurant offering fairly expensive but good Spanish food such as manchego cheese, stuffed squid, crab in green sauce and *crema catalán*, as well as a decent international wine list. Closed Sun.

Coppelia 9 de Octubre and Pedro Carbo. Small, bargain café-restaurant overlooking the Plaza San Francisco, serving simple but well-prepared Ecuadorian food like *humitas*, *empanadas* and *ayacas* (chicken tamales).

El Español Pichincha 406 and Luque, also at Estrada 302, Urdesa. For a quick snack or sandwich, this upmarket chain is a decent choice for its tasty hams, salamis and cheeses served in a variety of rolls.

La Fondue *Oro Verde* hotel, 9 de Octubre and García Moreno. Small restaurant mocked up in a Swiss chalet interior, with the help of dangling cowbells and waitresses dressed as Alpine milkmaids. Despite the gimmicks, the fondues and raclettes are pretty good and cost around $8.

Le Gourmet *Oro Verde* hotel, 9 de Octubre and García Moreno. Rather formal, award-winning restaurant with a sophisticated French menu and a Gallic head chef. Expensive, but not a bad place for a blowout.

Guayaquil Yacht Club Malecón and Luque. Very elegant mid-priced seafood eatery with crisp linen tablecloths, lots of polished wood and brass and great views onto the Malecón and the river. Normally a members-only place, but tourists are allowed up with photo ID, though no shorts or sports gear are permitted.

Parrillada Barcelona Sucre and Boyacá. Large, slightly grubby canteen specializing in roast chicken, which you can see on a big rotisserie over hot coals by the door. No frills but very cheap.

Parilladas Columbus Las Lomas 206 and Estrada, Urdesa. One of the best grill houses in Guayaquil, with excellent steaks and cuts in handsome portions.

Pasta Grill *Oro Verde* hotel, 9 de Octubre and García Moreno. Yet another of the hotel's restaurants, worth visiting for its reasonably priced Italian food that features antipasti, fish, meat, pasta and risotto – but no pizzas.

El Patio *Oro Verde* hotel, 9 de Octubre and García Moreno. Modern, stylish café-restaurant with interesting decor, a buzzing atmosphere and good international food – a fun place to eat, though not cheap. Open 24hr.

Riviera Estrada 707 and Ficus, Urdesa. Slick Italian restaurant with snappy service and accomplished dishes and salads, kitted out with folding "director's chairs" in an airy dining room.

Sushibar *Uniparkhotel*, Parque Seminario, Clemente Ballén. Affordable first-rate sushi served in a classy bar-restaurant next to the hotel's front desk. From early evening onwards a pianist tinkles away in the background, adding to the atmosphere.

Unicafé Clemente Ballén 406, Parque Seminario. Large, attractive dining room with blond wood chairs and bright colours. Does an appealing, if expensive, lunch and dinner buffet in addition to its national and international menu. Popular with business types.

Bars and clubs

Surprisingly perhaps, downtown Guayaquil isn't packed with **bars** and **clubs**, and much of the city's nightlife goes on in the more affluent suburbs.

Artur's Café Numa Pompilio Llona 127, Las Peñas. The best place for an evening drink, a tall old house on the riverbank with several little patios where you can sit and chat while romantic balladeers strum guitars. There are fantastic night-time views onto the illuminated Malecón, and you can buy tasty *platos típicos* like *seco de gallina* (chicken stew), *humitas* and *empanadas*.
Iceland Estrada 704 and Ficus, Urdesa. Trendy spot that's a good place for a pilsener *biela* ("*bien*

helada" – ice cold, in Guayaquil slang).
Infinity Estrada 505 and Ebanos. Slightly dated but enduringly popular nightclub playing a mixture of Latin and Western pop to a fairly young crowd.
El Jardín de la Salsa Avenida de las Américas 140, on the way to the airport. Salsa-only venue boasting an enormous dance floor.
Suruba on Avenida Francisco de Orellana, opposite the World Trade Center. One of the current dance favourites, an upmarket club playing techno.

Performing arts and film

For the **performing arts**, Guayaquil has a thriving **theatre** scene, best seen at the modern, well-designed theatre of the **Centro Cívico**, south of the city centre on Avenida 25 de Julio (taxi $2), which also has an excellent concert hall with regular **classical music** performances by the Orquesta Sinfónica de Guayaquil and visiting musicians. Check the local newspapers *El Universo* or *El Telégrafo* for listings.

Guayaquileños love **film** and the city's best cinema is **Cinemark**, at the large, modern Mall del Sol, reached on frequent Alboruta buses leaving from Pedro Carbo, outside the post office, or faster by taxi (15min; $2). Equipped with twelve screens, comfortable seats and an excellent sound system, the complex usually shows North American mainstream releases, in English with Spanish subtitles. There are other multiplexes at several other shopping centres, the most convenient for downtown being the CC 9 de Octubre, on 9 de Octubre and Rumichaca. You've a better chance of seeing independent films at the Casa de Cultura's modest cinema (Mon, Wed & Thurs 7.30pm).

Listings

Airlines Air Canada, represented by Transinversiones, Icaza 407 and Córdova, office 301 ℡04/2564050; Air France, Edificio Torres del Norte, Av Miguel H. Alcívar, Urbanización Kennedy Norte ℡04/2687149; American, Edificio San Francisco 300, Córdova 1021 and 9 de Octubre ℡04/2564111, airport ℡04/2282082; Continental, Edificio Banco La Previsora, 9 de Octubre 100 and Malecón ℡04/2567241, airport ℡04/2287311; Copa, 9 de Octubre and Malecón, Edificio Banco La Previsora ℡04/2303227, airport 2286336; Iberia, 9 de Octubre 101 and Malecón ℡04/2329558, airport ℡04/2284151; Icaro, airport ℡04/2294265; KLM, Galerías Colón, office 10, next to *Hilton Colón* ℡04/2692876, airport ℡04/2691252; Tame, Edificio Gran Pasaje, 9 de

Octubre 424 ℡04/2560776, airport ℡04/2281182; United, Miguel Alcívar, Torres del Norte B ℡ & ℗04/2687600; Varig, Aguirre 116 y Pichincha ℡04/2327082.
Banks and exchange The major banks have branches all over the city. The most convenient options downtown are Banco del Pacífico, Pedro Carbo and Icaza (traveller's cheques, MasterCard and Cirrus ATM); Banco de Guayaquil, Icaza 105 and Pichincha (Amex traveller's cheques, Visa cash advance, Visa and MasterCard ATM); and Banco del Austro, Boyacá and 9 de Octubre (Visa ATM and cash advance). There are also two ATMs near the main exit of the bus terminal (one for MasterCard and Cirrus, the other for Visa and Amex), plus several at the airport and at all the large shopping centres.

Car rental Most car-rental outfits have offices just outside the airport, and some have a downtown branch as well. Avis, Avenida de las Américas, CC Olímpico ℡04/2285498; Budget, at airport ℡04/2288510; Ecuacars, at airport ℡04/2285533; Expo, at airport ℡04/2282467; Hertz, *Oro Verde* hotel, 9 de Octubre and García Moreno ℡04/2327895, and at airport ℡04/2293011; Localiza, Av J Taca Marengo km 2.5, and at airport ℡1800/562254; Sicorent, at airport ℡04/2690633; and Super-Rent, at airport ℡04/2284454.

Consulates Australia, San Roque and Av Francisco de Orellana, Ciudadela Kennedy Norte ℡04/2680823; Canada, Edificio Torres de la Merced, General Córdova 800 ℡04/2563580; UK, General Córdova 623 and Padre Solano ℡04/2560400; US, 9 de Octubre and García Moreno ℡04/2323570.

Hospital The best choice in town is the Clínica Kennedy on Av del Periodista (℡04/2286963).

Internet facilities Cybercafés typically charge around $1 per hour and can be found downtown and in the suburbs and shopping centres; most have international calling facilities. ACC Cyber Café, 9 de Octubre and Baquerizo Moreno; Cyber Café con Leche, Luque 406 and Pichincha; Cyber Planet, 9 de Octubre and Rumichaca; Multicompu, Quisquis and Pedro Moncayo.

Laundry Lavendería Carmita, Boyacá 925 and V. M. Rendón, does same-day wet washes by the kilogram. Lava Express, Carbo and V. M. Rendón, does wet wash and dry-cleaning and is more professional, but you may have to wait.

Police and immigration Av Río Daule, Prolongación de Av de las Américas ℡04/2297004.

Post office Main office on Pedro Carbo and Ballén, just off the Parque Seminario.

Shopping For Western goods, the best option is the huge, modern Mall del Sol near the airport (Buses Alboruta go there from outside the post office). Other good malls are Garzocentro, Av Guillermo Pareja and Agustín Freire; Policentro in the Ciudadela Kennedy; and Riocentro Los Ceibos, km 6.5 on the coast road. The chaotic outdoor market, Las Bahías, is sited on several blocks

within the triangle formed by Colón, Olmedo and Eloy Alfaro, and has cheap clothes, bags, cosmetics, electrical equipment and more; Mercado Artesenal, Baquerizo Moreno and Juan Montalvo, near Las Peñas, has weavings, knitwear and other artesanía stalls; and Ecua-andino (℡04/2326375, ✉info@ecua-andino.com, ⊛www.ecua-andino.com) sells quality Panama hats.

Swimming pool Piscina Olímpica, Vélez and Masote, a few blocks from the Parque Centenario (Mon–Fri 2–6pm, Sat & Sun 10am–6pm), offers two enormous outdoor pools, one for competitions and one for the general public.

Telephone office Pacifictel, off the Parque Seminario, Ballén and Chile.

Tour operators Canodros, Urb Santa Leonor, Mz 5, Solar 10 (℡04/2285711, ℻280164, ⊛www.canodros.com), owns a large Galápagos cruise boat and operates the Kapawi Ecolodge (see p.344); Galasam, Edificio Gran Pasaje, 9 de Octubre 424 (℡04/2304488, ⊛www.galapagos-islands.com), runs low- to middle-budget Galápagos cruises and offers jungle and regional tours; Klein Tours, Miguel Alcívar and Ángel Barreira (℡04/2681700, ⊛www.kleintours.com), has higher-end Galápagos cruises and land tours; and Metropolitan Touring (see p.113), is a long-established agency for cruises and general countrywide tours. Regional and local specialists include Guayatur, Aguirre 108 and Malecón (℡04/2322441, ℻2328661), organizing tours of the Santa Elena peninsula, Ruta del Sol and elsewhere in the region (from $35 per day); and Ecua-andino, Luque 229 between Chile and Carbo, 4th floor (℡04/2326375, ✉info@ecua-andino.com), running sports-fishing trips, tours around the Ruta del Sol, jaunts to local weaving villages making Panama hats and half-day walking tours of Guayaquil ($8).

Travel agents Among the hundreds of local travel agents, some of the largest, and best for booking flights, include Carlson Wagonlit Travel, Edificio El Fortín, Padre Aguirre 104 and Malecón, 4th floor (℡04/2311800); Delgado Travel, Edificio San Francisco, Córdova 1021 and 9 de Octubre, 3rd floor (℡04/2560680); and Metropolitan Touring, José de Anteparra 915 and 9 de Octubre (℡04/2320300, ⊛www.metropolitan-touring.com).

South to Machala and the border

On its way **south to the border** 244km away, the major coastal highway from Guayaquil passes by one of the most important mangrove estuaries on the coast, protected as the **Reserva Ecológica Manglares Churute**, where you can arrange to take boat rides through the swamps or walk in the surrounding forest. Further south, the road slices through endless **banana plantations** as you enter the country's banana-growing heartland. Ecuador didn't start exporting the fruit until 1945, but the boom that followed was so dramatic that the crop became the country's most important agricultural export within two years, and has remained so ever since. Today, banana cultivation occupies some 125 square kilometres, of which a large portion is in the province of El Oro, whose capital **Machala** is the main service centre of the industry – a busy, workaday town that holds little of interest, but does serve as a handy base for trips to the charming hillside town of **Zaruma**, 86km east, and the petrified forest of **Puyango**, 100km south. It's also a convenient stop on the way to Peru, a one-hour bus ride south, with most travellers choosing to spend the night here before crossing the border at the dusty, ramshackle town of **Huaquillas**.

Reserva Ecológica Manglares Churute

Forty-five kilometres southeast of Guayaquil on the road to Machala, you'll pass the prominent visitor centre of the **Reserva Ecológica Manglares Churute** (daily 8am–2pm; $10), which protects 350 square kilometres of **mangrove** swamps. They're best viewed on a boat ride through the labyrinthine estuaries and channels that thread through the mangroves, whose dense tangle of interlocking branches looms out of the water. Recently covering a much larger coastal area, until many were cleared to make way for shrimp farms, the mangroves are part of a unique ecosystem that provides a habitat for many different fish and crustaceans and more than 260 **bird** species including the purple gallinule, muscovy duck, pinnated bittern, glossy ibis, roseate spoonbill and horned screamer, now only found here in western Ecuador. During select months, rare sightings have been made of Chilean flamingos (Jan–Feb), and bottlenose **dolphins** (June–Nov) are frequently seen frolicking around the boats.

From the visitor centre, a rudimentary path leads inland for an hour's walk along the slopes of Cerro El Mate (a low hill with a lookout point) to **Laguna El Canclón**, a wide, grey lake encircled by low-lying hills and rich in birdlife. Another path, **Sendero La Cascada** (2hr), takes you through dense dry forest by some enormous royal palms and up the slopes of a hill covered in lush vegetation, thanks to the frequent mists that settle on it. Both the dry and humid forests are inhabited by snakes, *guantas* and howler monkeys, which you're more likely to spot if you're with a guide. The path can be found at the end of a track branching west from the coastal highway 5km north of the visitor centre; guides can take you there in a jeep.

Practicalities

The **visitor centre** is easy to access from Guayaquil: take any **bus** to Machala or Naranjal from the Terminal Terrestre and ask to be dropped at the Centro de Visitantes de la Reserva Churute – the sign is on the left-hand (east) side of the road, fifty minutes after leaving the city. You're allowed to **camp** outside the visitor centre, though most people visit as a day-trip. **Boat rides** (3–4hr; $35 per boat) need to be booked at least a couple of days in advance through the Ministerio del Ambiente in Guayaquil, Avenida Quito 402 and Padre Solano (℡04/2397730 or 2560870, ℻2293155), where you can also pick up **information** on the reserve and, with a day's notice, request a **guide** ($5; no English spoken).

Machala

South of the Reserva Ecológica Manglares Churute, the coastal highway ploughs through vast swaths of banana plantations on its way to **MACHALA.** Despite being founded in the sixteenth century, it looks like a city that's sprung up haphazardly in the last two or three decades, with wide streets lined by a hotchpotch of shabby concrete buildings covered in flaking white paint. Like Guayaquil, the place is a good deal wealthier than appearances would suggest, and as the centre of Ecuador's **banana** industry it's proud to call itself the "Banana Capital of the World" (see box, p.428). There's plenty of hustle and bustle here, but little in the way of tourist attractions – most visitors are here en route to Peru, one hour south. Therefore, unless you plan to use Machala as a base for visiting outlying attractions, the only time you might want to make a special trip here is during the annual **World Banana Festival**, a huge commercial fair with festivities and events like the World Banana Queen beauty competition, spread over the last ten days of September.

The centre of Machala is marked by the large, leafy **parque central**, surrounded for the most part by banks and other nondescript buildings, though the modern green-and-white **cathedral** on its west side boasts an eye-catching facade with a tall, thin clock tower flanked by two blue domes. A couple of blocks around the corner on Bolívar, the **Casa de la Cultura** contains the city's only museums, as well as permanent and temporary art exhibits of variable quality. On the ground floor, the **Museo Marino** (Tues–Fri 9am–noon & 2–5pm; $0.50) comprises a small roomful of glass cabinets crammed with fish, marine birds, molluscs, shells, corals and whale and dolphin bones, while upstairs the **Museo Arqueológico** (same hours and ticket) displays

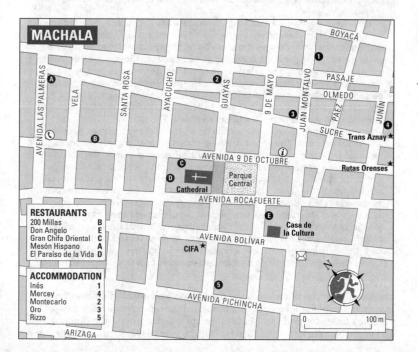

Each year, Ecuador exports more than four million tonnes of **bananas**, contributing around a billion dollars to the national economy and making it the world's biggest producer of its most popular fruit. Stretching over the landscape to the horizon, a series of private, medium-sized **plantations** grows most of Ecuador's bananas. However, a few huge **companies** effectively control their purchase, trade and distribution, including US-owned Dole, Del Monte and Chiquita, as well as Ecuador's own **Noboa**, easily the country's largest exporter, which deals with more than half of the national banana crop and is owned by Alvaro Noboa, the 2002 presidential runner-up. With an 18-kilogram box of fresh-picked plantation bananas selling for just $3–4, the banana trade is a highly profitable business for these companies, not to mention the **supermarkets** back home that sell a single bunch for around $2.

Unfortunately, Ecuador's extraordinary success with this crop is due in large part to the appalling **pay** and **working conditions** of its labourers, who are among the worst-paid in the world. For a full day's labour (12–15hr) in the stifling heat and humidity, the typical banana worker can expect a salary of just a few dollars, perhaps enough to buy two or three bunches of the fruit in a Western supermarket. Such meagre wages also have to cover outlay for the workers' own tools, uniforms, transport to the plantations and drugs should they fall ill or have an on-site accident. Most can't afford **housing** and must share small rooms on the estates with three or four others, or live in squalid, jerry-built shacks.

Only one percent of the country's 250,000-strong workforce is **unionized**, and most workers are effectively denied the right to form unions or bargain collectively, with instant dismissals being common for any involvement. On one Noboa-owned estate, more than a thousand workers went on strike in 2002 to claim legally entitled benefits to clothing and medical care. After a couple of weeks, armed men in hoods broke up the strike, attacked the crowd with rifle butts and opened fire, injuring nineteen people.

Although there are more than three hundred varieties of banana, the most commonly grown is the **Cavendish**, the large, uniform and relatively bland-tasting fruit that is so familiar on supermarket shelves. Since all Cavendish plants come from the same genetic source and are cultivated in close proximity to one another, pests, mould and disease can quickly wipe out a plantation, so the crops must be regularly sprayed with pesticides and other chemicals. Many workers complain of pesticide **poisoning**, and throughout the 1990s Ecuadorian crops were treated with DBCP, a highly toxic chemical thought to cause birth defects, infertility and liver damage, even though it was banned in the US as early as 1977.

Ecuador exports twice as many bananas as the next most productive country, and to compete with it other producers are forced either to degrade conditions for their own workforce or relocate. In other words, Ecuador is winning the race to the bottom. Meanwhile, in their pursuit of the cheapest produce, supermarkets are content to turn a blind eye to workers' low pay, non-existent welfare and even **child labour**, which has been documented on Ecuadorian plantations. **Consumer awareness** in the developed world is one way to counter such corporate actions, as is the use of **alternative products** such as organic and fair-trade bananas, which give banana workers a much better deal. In Machala, **UROCAL** is the organization most involved with such projects, and is happy to show **visitors** around its members' farms, as long as you cover any costs incurred and preferably make a donation for their time. Get in touch on ⓔ urocal@eo.pro.ec or ⓔ urocal@ecuanet.net.ec.

pre-Columbian coastal ceramics, and the **Museo Paleontológico** has an impressive collection of fossils brought over from the Puyango petrified forest (see p.432). There's little else to do in Machala except wander around the outdoor fruit and vegetable **market** – bounded by Boyacá, 9 de Mayo, Sucre and Páez – and marvel at the prodigious quantities of bananas for sale. Finally, if you enter or leave the town by the main artery formed by the extension of 9 de Mayo, look out for the **Monumento Al Bananero**, a towering statue of a workman carrying a mound of bananas.

Arrival and information

Arriving by **bus**, you'll be dropped at your company's depot; most are a few blocks southeast of the central square – mainly on and around Tarqui and Colón, which are parallel to Junín – an easy walk to the city's hotels. **Flights** from Guayaquil arrive at the tiny Aeropuerto General Manuel Serrano, a mere nine blocks from the central square and served by plenty of taxis (around $0.80). There's a very helpful (but unsigned) **Ministerio de Turismo** information office upstairs in the Almacen Galarza, 9 de Octubre and 9 de Mayo (Mon–Fri 8.30am–5pm; ⊕ & ⑤07/932106). The city centre is entirely walkable on foot, but if you need a **taxi** you can flag one down around the central square, or on any of the main arteries such as 9 de Octubre or Vicente Rocafuerte; journeys within the central core cost around $0.80.

Accommodation

Accommodation in Machala is quite pricey for what you get, with not a great choice on offer. That said, there are a couple of decent budget places, and if you're willing to indulge you can treat yourself to the luxurious *Oro Verde*.

Inés Juan Montalvo 1509 ⊕07/932301, ⑤931473. Small and rather old, but with perfectly fine rooms, most offering a/c and cable TVs, in a whitewashed house set back from a busy market area, inside a secure courtyard with private parking. ❹

Mercey Junín, between Sucre and Olmedo ⊕07/920116. Small but clean and tidy rooms around a courtyard, set back from the main road and owned by a friendly elderly couple. Good budget choice, with a/c available. ❷

Montecarlo Guayas and Olmedo ⊕07/931901, ⑤933104. Spacious, light rooms with freshly painted walls, cool stone floors and slightly dated furnishings. All have en-suite baths, a/c and cable TVs, though they can be a bit noisy. ❻

Oro Sucre and Juan Montalvo ⊕07/937569, ⑤933751. Probably the best mid-priced rooms in town, with firm beds, good-quality bedding, new carpets, clean bathrooms, a/c and cable TVs (with more channels than you usually get), and its own garage. ❺

Oro Verde Circunvalación Norte and Calle Vehicular V-7 ⊕07/933140, ⑤933150. Classy hotel resembling an old timber-clad plantation manor, with beautiful gardens and a pool. It's sometimes possible to get a room at the national rate (a third of the foreign rate) if you beg hard enough. A short taxi ride 3km from the centre. ❾

Rizzo Guayas 1923 ⊕07/933651. Showing its age, but the rooms – all with private baths and a/c – are adequate and the pool is very inviting. ❻

Eating, drinking and nightlife

There's not exactly a surplus of restaurants in Machala, but there are a number of inviting places among the more pedestrian options. For the best **fish** and **seafood**, however, nip out to Puerto Bolívar (see p.430), a fifteen-minute bus ride away. There are few decent **bars** in town, but you'll find a large modern **club**, *Twister*, at km 1.5 on the road to Pasaje.

Don Angelo 9 de Mayo and Rocafuerte. Unassuming local canteen that's been going for years, serving cheap and reliable *comida típica* like *locro de papa* and *seco de chivo*, plus staples like spaghetti and fried chicken and fish.

Gran Chifa Oriental 9 de Octubre, between Guayas and Ayacucho. Modest but agreeable Chinese restaurant – a good bet for a cheap, filling meal.

Mesón Hispano Av Las Palmeras and Sucre. Delicious charcoal-grilled meat served on mini-stoves in a bright, attractive dining room, complete with potted ferns and whirring fans. Plenty of non-meat options, too, at this good-value eatery.

Oro Mar at *Oro Verde* hotel, Circunvalación Norte and Calle Vehicular V-7. If you feel like a splurge, this is the place to do it – fairly pricey ($6 or more per main course) but delicious international food served in a dining room overlooking the pool. Reached by taxi for about $1.50.

El Paraíso de la Vida Ayacucho between Rocafuerte and 9 de Octubre. Inexpensive vegetarian restaurant with a pleasant dining room overlooking a little patio. Curiously, most items on the menu are veggie pseudo-meat dishes like "beef steak" and "loin".

200 Millas 9 de Octubre and Santa Rosa. Smart, modern and reasonably priced restaurant with attractive decor and fresh, well-cooked fish and seafood.

Listings

Airline Tame, office at Juan Montalvo and Bolívar (☎07/930139) or at airport (☎07/964865).
Banks and exchange Banco de Guayaquil, on the parque central at Rocafuerte and Guayas, cashes traveller's cheques with MasterCard and Visa ATM; Banco del Austro, across the street, has Visa service; Banco del Pacífico, Rocafuerte and Junín, changes traveller's cheques and has a MasterCard and Cirrus ATM; and another branch of Banco de Guayaquil is nearby at Junín and 9 de Octubre.
Consulate for Peru, Bolívar and Colón (Mon–Fri 8am–1pm; ☎07/920680).
Internet facilities At several places for around $1 per hour, including Aquinet, Sucre and Vela, and others on 9 de Octubre between Santa Rosa and Ayacucho.
Laundry Lavandería Divíño Niño, next door to the Casa de la Cultura on Bolívar.
Post office Juan Montalvo and Bolívar.
Telephone office Pacifictel, Avenida 9 de Octubre and Avenida de Las Palmeras (with several smaller offices around the centre).

Moving on from Machala

With no central bus station, Machala's various **bus** companies operate out of their own mini-terminals, all of which are within a few blocks of the park. Cooperativa CIFA, Guayas and Bolívar, has regular services to the Peruvian border at **Huaquillas** (every 20min; 1hr), while Ecuatoriano Pullman, Colón and 9 de Octubre, offers hourly buses. Ecuatoriano Pullman services **Guayaquil** (every 30min; 3hr), with CIFA and Ruta Orenses, 9 de Octubre and Tarqui, running every hour. Trans Occidental, Buenavista and Olmedo, connects to **Quito** (8 daily; 11hr), while Panamericana, Colón and Bolívar, has a slightly more expensive luxury service (9 daily), one of which continues on to **Tulcán** at the Colombian border. Trans Azuay, Sucre and Junín, goes to **Cuenca** (every 15min, 3hr 30min), and Trans Loja, Tarqui and Bolívar, serves **Loja** (9 daily; 6hr); those going via the village of Alamor can drop you at **Puyango** for the petrified forest (see p.432). For the gold-mining village of **Zaruma** (see opposite), take an hourly bus (3hr) with Cooperativas TAC, on Colón between Rocafuerte and Bolívar, or with Transportes Piñas, on Colón and 9 de Octubre.

Puerto Bolívar and its islands

Just 5km and a fifteen-minute **bus** ride west of Machala (take services marked "Línea 1" from 9 de Octubre and Guayas, on the central square), **PUERTO BOLÍVAR** is a busy international port exporting vast quantities of bananas and shrimp around the world, though it is a little ramshackle and dilapidated, with a long seafront avenue lined by wilting palms, cheap fish diners with bright plastic awnings and the odd children's merry-go-round. Still, the cooling sea breeze and the dozens of wooden fishing boats bobbing in the water make it a pleasant enough place for an afternoon stroll, and it's also a good bet for a fresh seafood lunch or supper: one of the most popular **restaurants** is *Waikiki*, opposite the pier, and the dozen or so *picanterías* (small, simple restaurants) with outside tables and chairs form a strip known as the **Jardín Comedor**, between the church and pier.

A more compelling reason to come here, though, is to take a **boat ride** out to one of the islands close to the shore, run by a couple of operators from the pier, on the Malecón. The Asociación de Ecoturismo Rescate Ecológico offers guided trips in Spanish to the **Isla del Amor** (hourly Fri–Sun 9am–6pm, by reservation Mon–Thurs on ℡07/929474; $2), a small mangrove island just ten minutes away by motorized canoe, where you can get great close-up views of mangroves and their seabird inhabitants, both from the boat and from a raised walkway leading from a docking area through the swamp. Other boat companies provide regular service to this and other further-flung islands; ask around the docks and bargain. There's a small **information centre** by the dock, and a bamboo hut where you can spend the night if you take a sleeping bag and mosquito net.

Motor canoes also leave from the dock for the car-free **Isla Jambelí** (5 daily, 25min; $2), a larger island with a wide, sandy **beach** and a few basic restaurants and hotels, the best of which is *La Casa en la Luna* (℡07/964116; ❷–❸) which has shared bath and no hot water. The beach, one of the few south of Guayaquil, is very tidy, though there's little shade and the seawater is not as clean as it could be. It gets very busy here on summer weekends, but you'll almost certainly have it to yourself through the week.

Zaruma and around

Off the tourist trail, in the scenic back roads that climb into the hills 86km inland from Machala, **ZARUMA** was founded in 1549 and is still one of the prettiest little towns in Ecuador, boasting the country's finest collection of early-twentieth-century timber buildings, which prompted the Ministry of Education and Culture to declare the place a **national monument** in 1970. Conquistadors first established a settlement here to exploit the area's large **gold** deposits, which had previously been mined by indigenous peoples. The new gold mines flourished until the eighteenth century, when they closed down because the seams were thought to be exhausted. Almost a century later, though, a Quito geologist analysing the local rocks discovered a high gold content, and thus in 1880 the gold boom kicked off again with the founding of the Great Zaruma Gold Mining Company in London. Today, mining continues but on a much smaller scale, as the gold deposits are running out and excavation is becoming less productive. The captivating **Museo Municipal**, just off the picturesque main square and opposite the attractive wooden church (Wed–Fri 8am–noon & 2–6pm, Sat 8am–3pm, Sun 8am–noon; free), houses a hotchpotch of curiosities, including artefacts recovered from Ingapirca, whale vertebrae, antique sewing machines, irons, phones, gramophones and mining paraphernalia.

Heading out of town on Honorato Márquez beyond the bus depots, the **Museo Indígena Selva** (daily 8am–noon & 1–6pm; $1) presents a rather unsettling collection of insects, stuffed animals and desiccated snakes in a compact space hung with tangled roots, all apparently meant to emulate the feel of a forest; ask the owner about his other project, the **Museo Montúfar**, up the hill on Damian Meneses.

On warm days, locals flock to the public swimming **pool** in a fantastic location on a hilltop above the town. Excursions from Zaruma include the **Mina Vizcaya-Semo-Miranda**, one of the oldest mines, with tunnels more than 2km deep, and the colourful **Orquideario Gálvez**, a few kilometres out of town on the road to Malvas (℡07/964063), an enjoyable orchid garden with attached accommodation. Apart from these minor attractions, Zaruma's main draw is its collection of steep, narrow streets and admirable wooden houses with brightly painted balconies and balustrades, and its beautiful timber **church** from 1912.

The nearby towns of **Piñas**, 13km west, and **Portovelo**, a few kilometres south of Zaruma, retain less of their historic mining character, though each has at least one good museum. In Piñas the **Museo Mineralógico Magner Turner**, in the Barrio Campamento Americano (☎07/949345), is one of the best mining museums in the country, including a large bunker, 150m of mine-shafts and various mineral and gem exhibits, while at Portovelo the **Museo Ruben Torres** displays a modest array of antiques and pre-Columbian arte-facts. Also in the region are several **reserves** managed by the Fundación Jocotoco (ⓦwww.fjocotoco.org), protecting vital forest habitat harbouring some 630 types of birds, many of which are restricted-range endemic species. The closest reserve to Zaruma is **Buenaventura**, beyond Piñas on the road to Machala; contact Marianna Arcentales for more information (ⓔfjocotoco@andinanet.net).

Practicalities

Zaruma is a three-hour **bus** ride from Machala, and Transportes TAC provides regular service from its depot on Colón, between Rocafuerte and Bolívar, as does Transportes Piñas, nearby on Colón and 9 de Octubre. For onward trav-el, the main depots in Zaruma are on Honorato Márquez, the main road out of town. The first, TAC, runs buses to Guayaquil (5 daily; 6hr) and to Loja (3 daily; 4hr 30min), while the latter is also served by Trans Piñas, a few doors down (3 daily). Both companies, as well as Trans Azuay, run an early-morning bus to Cuenca (6hr). **Internet** access is available at Zarumanet, Colón and 10 de Agosto ($1.50 per hour).

Despite its charms, few tourists make it to Zaruma and there are few options for **accommodation**. On the way into town, the *Roland*, Avenida Alonso de Mercadillo (☎07/972800; ❸), offers comfortable, carpeted en-suite rooms, the best of which have great views down the valley. Up in the centre, the *Aguila Dorada*, at Sucre 156 (☎07/972230; ❸), also has good-value rooms with private baths, electric showers and cable TVs, but no rooms at the back overlooking the valley, while the nearby *Cerro de Oro* (☎07/972505; ❸) has similar facilities for a marginally higher price, as well as family apartments ($40). For **restaurants**, try the *Chifa Chamizal Central*, set in a pretty red house with a terrace on Calle San Francisco off Sucre, for inexpensive Chinese food, international dishes and seafood, or the simple *Cafetería Uno* on Sucre, good for local specialities. **Coffee** is grown around Zaruma, and the rich smell of freshly roasting beans wafts from shops along the high street.

Puyango petrified forest

One hundred kilometres south of Machala, close to the Peruvian border and spread over a dusty, semi-arid river valley, the **Puyango petrified forest** (daily 8am–3.30pm; $5) is the largest such forest in South America, containing dozens of enormous **fossilized tree trunks** up to 120 million years old, many of which you can see from the 8km of marked paths that wend through the min-eralized wood. At the visitor centre, where you pay and register your visit, you can hire a **guide** (usually one of the warden's sons) to show you around the site – while they don't speak English, they will point out many hidden fossils that you'd otherwise miss, such as the imprints of ferns concealed by riverside plants. The most impressive relics are the giant tree trunks lying on their sides – types of **araucaria**, which grew in the region millions of years ago – many of which are in fragments but a few almost whole, the largest being 11m long and 1.6m in diameter. Beyond the stumps, the area is also extremely rich in birdlife, inhab-ited by more than 150 species, including beautiful red-masked parakeets.

Close to the visitor centre, a small **museum** (usually locked; ask the staff for entry) houses a stash of incredible fossils retrieved from the area, including many marine fossils that date from an ancient epoch when much of the region was covered by the sea – now 50km away – before the formation of the western folds of the Andes. The collection also includes fossilized pieces of fruit, including a cherimoya and a custard apple (you can still see the pips), and a ray, small tortoise and octopus with clearly visible eyes. Perhaps the most intriguing pieces are the large, perfectly oval stones that you can hold in your hands – and which the staff believe to be fossils of dinosaur eggs.

Practicalities

The petrified forest is three hours from Machala by **bus**. Take a bus from Machala to Alamor, either with Cooperativa Loja, from Tarqui between Bolívar and Rocafuerte (3 daily), or Cooperativa CIFA, from Bolívar and Guayas (2 daily). Ask to be dropped at the Puente de Puyango, from where a track leads 5km west to the visitor reception area, through a handsome valley with plenty of opportunities for bird watching. There are a few bunk **beds** ($5) for visitors next to the warden's quarters, and a rudimentary **campsite** in a pleasant spot near the river, close to a lovely natural pool for bathing. It officially costs $20 per tent, but this is invariably waived as none of the planned facilities has yet been built, nor shows any sign of materializing. A tiny **shop** near the visitor reception area has basic provisions, but you should bring as much of your food as possible. The nearest village to the site is Puyango, near the bridge where the bus drops you, with little more than a cluster of houses and a few small food stores.

Huaquillas and the Peruvian border

Some 73km southwest of Machala, **HUAQUILLAS** is a chaotic, jerry-built, mosquito-ridden border town that most people try to avoid as much as possible. Its main commercial street is lined by hundreds of hectic market stalls selling cheap clothes, shoes, bags, food, and electrical goods, while enormous shop signs hang over their canopies from the dilapidated buildings either side. Most visitors crossing the border avoid **staying** here by spending the night in Machala, but if you need a place to sleep you'll find clean, modest rooms with private bathrooms, air conditioning and cable TVs at the friendly *Vanessa*, 1 de Mayo 323 and Hualtaco (℡07/907263; ❸), and the *Grand Hotel Hernancor* next door (℡07/995467; ❸), while a cheaper but still passable option is the *Rodey*, Teniente Córdovez and 10 de Agosto (℡07/995581; ❷). There are a number of inexpensive canteens, but good **restaurants** include *La Habana*, T. Córdovez and Santa Rosa, for its affordable seafood, grills, breakfast and *almuerzos*, and *El Flamingo*, Avenida de la República and Costa Rica, for cakes, shakes and ice creams. **Internet** facilities are available at Hot Net, Avenida de la República and Santa Rosa.

If you're just arriving in Ecuador, **buses** from Huaquillas leave from company depots within a few blocks of the international bridge. Coop CIFA, on Santa Rosa and Machala, has the most regular service to the biggest nearby city, **Machala** (every 10–20min; 1hr), with banking facilities and onward transport, and also sends buses to **Guayaquil** (5 daily; 4hr 30min), as do Ecuatoriano Pullman on T. Córdovez, and Rutas Orenses on R. Gómez. Panamericana, on T. Córdovez and Santa Rosa, runs regular buses to **Quito** (7 daily; 12hr), one of which continues to Tulcán (4.30pm; 17hr) on the Colombian border, while Trans Occidentales, on R. Gómez, has five daily buses to Quito. Use Trans Azuay, T. Córdovez and Santa Rosa, for **Cuenca** (8 daily; 5hr).

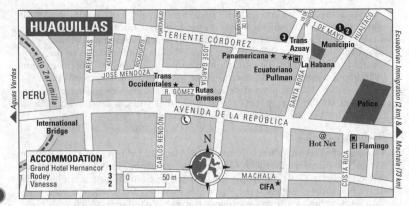

HUAQUILLAS

Ecuadorian Immigration (2 km & ▲ Machala (73 km)

PERU

Aguas Verdes ▲

3 Trans Azuay Municipio
Panamericana ★ ★★■ La Habana
Ecuatoriano
Pullman
Trans
Occidentales ★ ★ Rutas
Orenses

Police

International
Bridge

1 2

Hot Net El Flamingo

MACHALA
CIFA ★

ACCOMMODATION
Grand Hotel Hernancor 1
Rodey 3
Vanessa 2

0   50 m

N

Crossing the border

The Río Zarumilla forms the **border**, hugging the southwestern edge of Huaquillas and crossed by the international bridge leading to the small town of **Aguas Verdes** in Peru. Before crossing it, you'll need to get your **exit stamp** at the **Ecuadorian immigration** office (open 24hr; ☎07/996755), 2km east of Huaquillas on the road from Machala ($1.50 by taxi). If you're coming here straight from Machala, bus drivers will drop you at the office on the way into Huaquillas (remind them as they sometimes forget), but won't wait for you while you get your exit stamp, which is usually a fairly fast and painless process. From here, hop on a bus or take a taxi to the bridge, which you'll have to cross on foot. On the other side Peruvian officials may check your passport, but **entry stamps** are normally obtained at the main **Peruvian immigration office** at **Zarumilla**, a few kilometres away. It can be reached by **mototaxis** for less than a dollar or by various other forms of transport that continue on to **Tumbes**, 27km south: regular **buses**, which won't wait for you while you get your passport stamped; **taxis** ($5–6, including wait at Zarumilla; firm bargaining required); or **colectivos** (about $0.70), though drivers are sometimes reluctant to wait at Zarumilla. Once in Tumbes, it's easy to find a direct **bus** to Piura, Trujillo or Lima.

It's quite a stressful experience, with a bevy of moneychangers, bus touts, bag carriers and taxi drivers jostling for your business, and plenty of thieves around as well – keep your wits about you, and never lose sight of your bags. Change as little **money** as possible, as the rates aren't good unless you bargain hard. Official money changers in Ecuador wear IDs, but always check calculations and cash received before handing anything over.

Playas and the Santa Elena Peninsula

West of Guayaquil, the busy E-40 highway heads to the westernmost tip of the mainland, marked by the **Santa Elena Peninsula**. It's an especially crowded route on Friday evenings when droves of Guayaquileños flee the uncomfortable heat of the city for the cooling westerly breezes of the Pacific. Just fifteen minutes down the road, the highway provides access to a couple of enjoyable attractions that you could take in en route to the coast, or as a day-trip from

Guayaquil, including the **Bosque Protector Cerro Blanco**, a small, well-managed forest reserve, and **Puerto Hondo**, a little village perched by a mangrove swamp that you can explore by boat. A further 45km west, a sideroad branches south to the easy-going, somewhat shabby little town of **Playas**, the closest beach resort to Guayaquil and always heaving with visitors on summer weekends (Dec–April).

Continuing west along the main road, you enter increasingly dry and scrubby terrain as you approach the Santa Elena Peninsula, the site of three small towns – **Santa Elena**, **La Libertad** and **Salinas** – merging into one other almost seamlessly. The peninsula is of great **archeological** interest, as it was originally occupied by the country's most ancient cultures, such as the **Las Vegas**, one of the first in South America to abandon a nomadic hunter-gatherer lifestyle and form semi-permanent agricultural settlements c.6000 BC, and the **Valdivia**, who produced Ecuador's first ceramics from c.3500 BC, among the oldest on the continent. Some of the most important archeological sites have impressive museums attached to them, including the fabulous **Amantes de Sumpa**, near Santa Elena, sporting the tomb of two eight-thousand-year-old skeletons locked in an embrace. However, the peninsula is best known for its **beaches**, the star attraction of which is the glitzy resort of **Salinas**, whose golden sands draw thousands of visitors each summer. A few quieter, calmer alternatives are **Ballenito** and **Punta Carnero**, and the small inland attraction of the thermal baths of **San Vicente**.

Bosque Protector Cerro Blanco

Just 16km out of Guayaquil, the **Bosque Protector Cerro Blanco** ($5) protects around fifty square kilometres of dry coastal forest, owned by the progressive national cement company La Cemento Nacional and administered by the Fundación Pro-Bosque (W www.fundacioneslcn.org.ec), which is also involved in reforestation programmes, fire-prevention campaigns, litter clean-up and recycling initiatives in surrounding areas. The forest provides a vital refuge to **wildlife** such as howler monkeys, collared anteaters, brocket deer, a few jaguars and more than two hundred species of birds, including a group of endangered great green macaw, whose regional numbers had been reduced to a mere eight after the gradual depletion of their habitat. With luck, they can be spotted flying from the coastal mangroves up to the hills of the reserve around 6am, and back to the mangroves around 6pm.

Helpful, enthusiastic guides (see p.436) can accompany you on a choice of three **trails** through the reserve (1hr 30min–4hr). The longest, **Sendero Buena Vista Largo**, is also the best, rising from sea level at the reserve's entrance up to 500m in the hills north of the highway, affording lovely views out to the mangroves opposite the reserve and presenting a greater chance of spotting wildlife. With advance permission, it's possible to camp up in the hills at the far end of the trail, so you can wake up at dawn and catch the birds at their loudest and most visible.

Information on the reserve's flora and fauna is available in the well-designed **Centro de Interpretación**, and nearby there's also a **Centro de Rescate** (animal rescue centre), originally set up to provide a home to abandoned animals before their reintroduction to the wild. However, many of the creatures were bought as pets and have become too tame to survive in the wilderness, so the centre has become something of a zoo, whose occupants include capuchin monkeys, wildcats, caimans and a cageful of great green macaws that have lost their ability to fly.

Entrance to the reserve is a thirty-minute **bus** ride from Guayaquil (every 10min), on any service to Playas, Santa Elena, La Libertad or Salinas from the main bus terminal. Look for the big sign for the Bosque Protector Cerro Blanco on the right-hand (north) side of the highway, where the driver will set you off. From here it's a fifteen-minute walk up a clearly marked track to the information centre. On weekends (8.30am–3.30pm) you can just turn up, but on weekdays you should book ahead through Pro-Bosque's Guayaquil office in the Edificio Promocentro, Eloy Alfaro and Cuenca, office 16 (℗ & ℗04/2416975). The **camping** area is free and has decent facilities, and the site has a small **café-restaurant**. Many of the trail **guides** (free; some speak English) are biology students from Guayaquil University. There are usually several about, but it's worth phoning ahead to book one, particularly if you want to take the Sendero Buena Vista Largo walk.

Puerto Hondo

A kilometre west of the entrance to the Cerro Blanco forest reserve, **PUERTO HONDO** is a dusty, tumbledown little port strung around the head of a narrow saltwater estuary. The village itself is not especially pretty, and the real attraction is the **mangrove swamps** around the estuary, which can be visited on one-hour motorized canoe rides ($7) with members of a guide association set up by the Pro-Bosque foundation (see p.435). Making a far cheaper alternative to the Reserva Ecológica Manglares Churute east of Guayaquil (see p.426), the swamps offer the chance to see the same ecosystem and many wetland birds. In theory you can just turn up and arrange a ride at weekends, only needing to make advance reservations with Pro-Bosque during the week at Edificio Promocentro (see "Practicalities", above), but it's worth phoning ahead anyway. All **buses** passing the Cerro Blanco reserve (see p.435) can drop you at the turn-off to Puerto Hondo, a five-minute walk south of the highway down a potholed street.

Playas

About 45km west of Puerto Hondo along the E-40 highway, you'll pass through the dreary little town of **Progreso** where a major sideroad branches off the highway to the seaside town of **PLAYAS**, a further 30km south. As the closest sandy beach to Guayaquil, Playas (whose official but largely ignored name is General Villamil) bulges with city visitors during the summer months, and has slowly metamorphosed from a sleepy fishing village into a flourishing holiday resort over the last few decades. There's nothing slick about it, though, and despite relying heavily on tourism Playas has a lived-in, unpretentious feel and a slow pace of life, with most traffic in its faintly shabby streets provided by ageing locals on clapped-out bicycles.

The chief attraction is, of course, the long and pleasant **beach**, where you'll still see fishermen hauling in their nets and may be able to spot a couple of traditional, single-sail balsa rafts, which were characteristic of the area for many centuries, though most have now been replaced with motorboats. There's nothing to do in Playas apart from lie on the sands or swim in the sea (sometimes a bit choppy), though if you feel like exploring you can walk 5km northwest along the beach to the **Punta Pelado**, whose usually deserted sands are backed by rugged cliffs.

Arriving by **bus** from Guayaquil, Transportes Villamil will drop you off at the depot behind the town plaza, and Transportes Posorja unloads at the intersec-

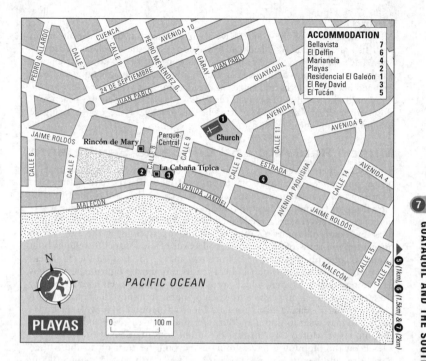

ACCOMMODATION	
Bellavista	7
El Delfín	6
Marianela	4
Playas	2
Residencial El Galeón	1
El Rey David	3
El Tucán	5

PLAYAS

0   100 m

PACIFIC OCEAN

tion of Paquisha and Guayaquil – both points are just three blocks from the seafront. If you need **money**, you can cash traveller's cheques or withdraw cash from the ATM of the Banco de Guayaquil on the main square, opposite the church.

Accommodation

Accommodation in Playas falls into two different areas, with a cluster of lower-end hotels and *residenciales* in the centre, and several upmarket choices dotted up and down the coastal avenue, Avenida Roldos, panning southeast from the centre. The latter places can be reached on the unsigned pick-up trucks that serve as taxis ($0.80) from Avenida Guayaquil, off the main square.

Hostería Bellavista Av Roldos, 2km from the centre ☎04/2760600. Immaculate, efficiently run Swiss-owned operation with a pool and access to a quiet stretch of beach. ⑥

El Delfín Avenida Roldos, 1.5km southeast of the centre ☎04/2761740. Offers charming, wood-panelled rooms a short distance from the sea, and very welcoming owners. ④–⑤

Marianela Avenida Roldos and Paquisha ☎04/2761507. One of the cheapest places to stay in town, where four of the rooms have good sea views, but the rough wooden floors and ancient beds are very basic. ①

Playas Calle 8, just off the seafront ☎04/2760121. Pleasant if tired doubles with private baths, including a few with TVs and a/c. ③

Residencial El Galeón next to the church on the plaza ☎04/2760270. Acceptable budget choice offering electric fans and mosquito nets, though the rooms are a bit cramped. ②

El Rey David Calle 9 and Av Jambeli ☎04/2760024. Smarter than most, with clean rooms and a/c, but overpriced and without sea views. ④

Hostería El Tucán Avenida Roldos, 1km southeast of the centre ☎ & ☞04/2760866. Good-quality rooms with a/c, plus a sauna and large, gorgeous pool. ⑤

Eating

All the hotels out of the centre have their own **restaurants** specializing in fresh fish and seafood, but back in town don't miss the excellent Lebanese-owned *Rincón de Mary*, on Avenida Roldos opposite the Coca Cola deposit, whose owner prepares fabulous falafel, tabbouleh, creamed aubergine and *Kibe* (minced beef with herbs and spices in breadcrumbs) at very reasonable prices. You could also try the attractively rustic *La Cabaña Típica*, on the beachfront close to the *Rincón de Mary*, for its delicious *ceviches*, or the nearby string of *picanterías* selling cheap, fresh fish.

Museo Real Alto and Baños de San Vicente

Seventy kilometres west of Progreso on the E-40 highway, a prominent billboard announces the turn-off to the **Museo Real Alto** (Tues–Sun 10am–5pm; $1), an archeology museum 11km down the road to the tiny fishing village of Chanduy. Marking the site of one of the oldest permanent settlements in South America, established by the **Valdivia** culture c.3000 BC, the museum boasts illuminating displays on the excavations at the site, which uncovered the ruins of an extensive collection of oval-shaped dwellings built around a large, open plaza. The culture was among the first on the continent to produce pottery, and is best known for its tiny female figurines, often representing pregnant women, which were thought to have been used in fertility rites. The museum is impossible to reach by public transport, though, so unless you're willing to take a **taxi** from La Libertad (around $10, with an hour's wait), you may want to skip it and head for the easier-to-reach and more visually impressive Museo Los Amantes de Sumpa in Santa Elena (see below).

Back on the highway, a few kilometres beyond the turn-off to the Museo Real Alto, another well-signed road leads 8km north to the municipal-run **Baños de San Vicente** thermal baths (daily 7am–7pm; $1), comprising two large circular pools (26°C) covered by domes set amid a barren, rocky landscape that give the complex the appearance of a low-budget sci-fi movie set, and a smaller, adults-only pool (41°C). Outside there's a huge pool full of volcanic mud, in which a leisurely wallow allegedly helps cure rheumatic limbs and skin complaints. The complex is very popular but not particularly well maintained, and a little institutional-looking with its cheerless changing rooms and abundance of concrete – though it still makes for an indulgent bit of pampering, not least for its massages ($2.50), sauna ($2) and Jacuzzi ($2).

Buses for the complex leave the market in La Libertad (Mon–Fri 7.10am & 10.10am, with an extra bus Sat–Sun 1.10pm), passing Santa Elena's parque central, or you can arrive by **taxi** from Santa Elena (around $8). Apart from the baths there's nothing much to the rather down-at-heel San Vicente, though a few **hotels** have sprung up around the complex, the best of which is the *Florida*, at the back of the baths (☎04/2535101; ❸), a decent Colombian-owned place offering fair rooms with private baths and meals cooked on request.

Santa Elena and Ballenita

Twelve kilometres beyond the turn-off to Baños de San Vicente, the E-40 hits the little town of **SANTA ELENA**, sited on the eponymous peninsula. Unremarkable in almost every way, the town's sole attraction is the fascinating archeological museum of **Los Amantes de Sumpa** (Tues–Sat 9.30am–4.30pm, Sun 10am–3pm; $1) on the western outskirts of town, signposted from the main road a couple of blocks south of the road to Salinas. The museum is built on the site of one of the oldest burial grounds in South America, established from 6000 BC by the ancient **Las Vegas** culture, one of the first groups on the continent to start shifting from a totally nomadic lifestyle towards semi-permanent settlements. About thirty years ago, some two hundred human skeletons were excavated here, including the remains of "**the lovers of Sumpa**" – the skeletons of a man and woman, about 25 years old when they died, buried facing each other, the woman with her arm raised over her head, the open-mouthed man with an arm on her waist. Their tomb, on display at the museum, makes an unforgettable sight, and the accompanying displays on the Las Vegas and other coastal cultures are excellent, ranging from funerary offerings such as shells, knives and colourful pebbles to a reconstruction of a typical *montuvio* house.

Ten kilometres northwest of Santa Elena, **BALLENITA** is a small village with a long, crescent-shaped beach lapped by calm waters, which chiefly appeals as a quieter alternative to Salinas. There's nothing to do here except swim, sunbathe and clamber around the rock pools looking for shellfish, and there's nowhere to stay in the centre. A kilometre north of the village, however, high on a bluff overlooking the sea, is one of the most delightful **hotels** on the peninsula, *Farallón Dillon* (T04/2953611 or T09/9771746, E ddillon@gu.pro.ec, W www.farallondillon.com.ec; ⑥), whose handful of tastefully decorated rooms have large French windows and fine ocean views. Even if you're not staying here, it's worth eating in the hotel's barn-like restaurant, serving excellent, though quite expensive, freshly caught fish and seafood. The restaurant also houses a fascinating **nautical museum** – put together by the hotel's owner, a retired merchant navy captain – displaying antique sextants and other navigation instruments, a huge nineteenth-century lens from a French lighthouse, gaudy figureheads and the prow of a whaling boat. Outside there's a terrace for spotting **humpback whales**, which swim off this stretch of coast between June and September.

La Libertad and Punta Carnero

West from Santa Elena towards Salinas, a roadside petrol refinery signals your arrival in **LA LIBERTAD**, the largest town on the peninsula and the site of a busy fresh-produce market. With its untidy streets and unattractive beach, there's no compelling reason to stop off here other than to catch a connecting bus north up the coast road (see p.442); the **bus station** is on Avenida 8 and Calle 17, Barrio Eloy Alfaro.

Five kilometres south of La Libertad – but reached by a longer, more circuitous road branching off the highway a few kilometres west of town – is the infinitely more appealing **PUNTA CARNERO**, a lonely, windswept promontory commanding superb views of the fifteen-kilometre stretch of beach flanking it. Pounding waves and strong currents make swimming at the beach a risky exercise, but Punta Carnero still makes a fabulous place to treat yourself to sun and solitude. Among the straggle of houses scattered over the site are a few **hotels**. The first you reach on the road up, and the more modest and less expensive of the two, is *Hostería del Mar* (T042948077, W www .hosteriadelmar.com; ⑤–⑦ by season), with comfortable rooms, a friendly staff and large pool overlooking the ocean. A few hundred metres up the road, the more upmarket *Punta Carnero* (T04/2948477, W www.hotelpuntacarnero .com; ⑤–⑦ by season) has a glass-walled restaurant looking down to the beach, a beautiful swimming pool and air-conditioned rooms with pleasing sea views. You can reach Punta Carnero by **bus** with Buses Libertad from La Libertad (every 20min), and Cooperativas Mar Azul from Salinas (every 15min); ask the driver to drop you off at the road leading up to the promontory.

Salinas

The highway ends its course 5km west of La Libertad and 170km from Guayaquil at **SALINAS**, Ecuador's swankiest beach resort. Arriving at its graceful seafront avenue, the Malecón, feels like stepping into another world: gone are the ramshackle streets characteristic of Ecuador's coastal towns, replaced by a gleaming boulevard lined with glitzy, high-rise condominiums sweeping around a large, beautiful bay. Closer inspection reveals that the streets behind the Malecón are as dusty and potholed as anywhere else, but this doesn't seem to bother anyone – it's the **beach** that counts here, with clean, powdery sand and warm, calm waters that are safe for swimming. The best time to enjoy it is December, early January or March during weekdays. Around Carnaval it gets unbearably packed, along with summer weekends, while from April to November it can be overcast and dreary.

If you tire of the beach, check out the **Museo Salinas Siglo XXI**, on the Malecón and Calle Guayas y Quil (Wed–Sun 9am–1pm & 3–7pm; $2), a well-presented museum divided into two parts: an excellent overview of pre-Columbian cultures on the peninsula, including some beautifully crafted Guayala and Manteño-Huancavilca ceramics; and a section on nautical history displaying a reconstructed balsa raft and original anchor, as well as armaments, naval cannons and anti-aircraft guns. Also on view are items recovered from the galleon *La Capitana*, which hit a submerged reef and sank off the coast near Punta Chanduy in 1654, taking down with it more than two thousand silver bars and two hundred chests of coins.

At the western end of the Malecón near the Yacht Club, the **handicraft market** (daily Jan–March) sells jewellery, leather goods, tagua-nut carvings and sometimes Panama hats, while a taxi ride away, the rocky headland of **La Chocolatera** lies at the westernmost point of the peninsula, battered by powerful, dra-

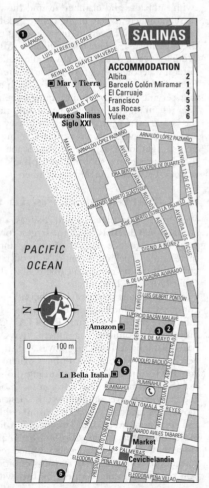

SALINAS

ACCOMMODATION

Albita	2
Barceló Colón Miramar	1
El Carruaje	4
Francisco	5
Las Rocas	3
Yulee	6

matic waves. Note, however, that it also sits within the perimeter of a naval base, and visitors aren't always given access; take your passport along if you want to give it a try.

Deep-sea **sports fishing** is very popular around Salinas, and can be arranged through the very efficient Pesca Tours, on the Malecón near the *El Carruaje* hotel (☎04/2772391, ⓦwww.pescatours.com.ec); the best season is between June and December. For **bird watching**, local ornithologist Ben Haase (☎054/2778329, ⓔbhaase@ecuanet.ec) leads tours to the salt lakes south of town, one of the best places in the country to see the Chilean flamingo as well as more than a hundred other species, including many migratory birds from North America.

Arrival, information and transport

Note that **street names** in Salinas have recently been changed from a straight-forward numbering system to rather unwieldy names, which many locals are still unfamiliar with. CLP **buses** from Guayaquil arrive in Salinas via the Malecón and continue to the avenue's western end; heading out of town, you need to catch one returning along Avenida General Enríquez Gallo.

Banks offering ATMs and able to change traveller's cheques include Banco de Guayaquil (Visa), Malecón and Lupercio Bazan Malave, Calle 23; and Banco del Pacífico (MasterCard and Cirrus), General Enríquez Gallo and Leornado Aviles, Calle 18. The **post office** is by the **police** station on Calle 53 at the east end of town. Places offering **Internet** access include Café Planet, General Enríquez Gallo and Digno A Nuñez, Calle 26; and Cybermar, Malecón and Fidón Tomalá, Calle 19. In the high season, **bicycles** can be rented from a couple of places along the beachfront ($5 per day).

Accommodation

There's no shortage of **accommodation** in Salinas, and though the bulk of it is expensive, there are a few decent budget options around.

Albita on Avenida Aspiazu (Av 6) ☎04/2773211. Offers basic rooms enlivened by potted plants and a balcony with hammocks. ❸–❹

Barceló Colón Miramar Malecón and Galápagos ☎ & ☎04/2771610, www.barcelo.com. Salinas' premier hotel, located in a landmark new building at the east end of the Malecón, with impeccable rooms that all face the ocean. ❾

El Carruaje Malecón 517 ☎ & ☎04/2774282. Upmarket hotel with sea views, whose rooms are smartly furnished and come with cable TVs and a/c. Includes breakfast. ❻

Francisco General Enríquez Gallo and Rumiñahui (Calle 20) ☎04/2774106. Small and

elegant hostel with immaculate, air-conditioned rooms with cable TVs, giving onto a patio with a small pool. ❹–❼ by season.

Las Rocas 24 de Mayo (Calle 22) and General Enríquez Gallo ☎04/2771096. Hostel with basic but clean rooms with optional private baths in a characterless house. ❸

Yulee Eloy Alfaro and Mercedes del Jesús Molina ☎04/2772028. Lovely old house with bright-yellow walls, green shutters and a flower-filled court-yard, offering simple but comfortable rooms with shared or private baths, or smarter ones with a/c and hot-water showers out the back. ❹–❻

Eating

Besides the **restaurants** below, you'll find plenty of fast-food outlets along the Malecón, particularly between Armando Barreto and Rafael de la Cuadra (calles 25 & 28), and a cluster of cheap **cevicherías**, known as "cevichelandia" around the municipal market at General Enríquez Gallo and Las Palmeras (Calle 16).

Amazon Malecón and Lupercio Bazán Malave (Calle 23). Attractive and moderately priced pizzeria and grill, also offering seafood, salads and vegetarian dishes.

Barceló Colón Miramar Malecón and Galápagos. Hotel restaurant that is one of the most stylish and expensive places to eat in town, serving everything from local seafood to national *comida típica* and elaborate international dishes.

La Bella Italia Malecón at Fidón Tomalá Reyes (Calle 19). Serves tasty pizzas and other Italian dishes.

Don Kleber's Cevichelandia at General Enríquez Gallo and Las Palmeras (Calle 16). *Cevichería* that

stands out for quality and good value.

Mar y Tierra Malecón and Reinaldo Chávez (Calle 37). A quality choice for its excellent, if pricey, fish and seafood, served in an informal, open-air dining room that catches the sea breeze.

Ruta del Sol

From La Libertad, a paved road runs 137km up the coast to Punta de Cayo – promoted by the tourist authorities as the **Ruta del Sol** – offering fantastic views of long, empty beaches and passing a string of modest fishing villages, occasionally swinging back from the shore to negotiate the forested hills of the Chongón-Colonche range. At Punta de Cayo, a branch of the highway heads inland to Jipijapa, while a new coastal road continues to Manta. Along the Ruta del Sol, you'll pass the moderately interesting archeological museum at **Valdivia** and the attractive little seaside village of **Manglaralto**, but most foreign visitors give these a miss and head straight for laid-back **Montañita**, popular with surfers and rapidly growing into a backpackers' beach hangout. A little further north, the dry, featureless landscape suddenly gives way to lush vegetation as you enter the **Cordillera Chongón-Colonche**, where the road veers inland from the coast through thickly wooded hills. The next gringo stop is **Alandaluz**, an ecologically focused resort, while further north the dishevelled town of **Puerto López** serves as a base for **whale-watching** trips (June–Sept) and visits to the **Parque Nacional Machalilla**, which takes in a major tract of tropical dry forest, fabulous beaches and the **Isla de la Plata** – favoured by bird lovers as a cheaper alternative to the Galápagos Islands.

From **La Libertad** (2hr 30min from Guayaquil), two **bus** companies – CITM and Transportes Manglaralto – operating out of the bus terminal on Avenida 8 and Calle 17, Barrio Eloy Alfaro, head up the coast road every hour to Montañita (1hr) and Puerto López (2hr), stopping at all the villages en route. From **Manta**, hourly buses follow the coastal road to Puerto López (2hr), while others go via Jipijapa (2hr 15min). From **Jipijapa** (2hr 30min from Guayaquil), hourly Transportes Carlos Alberto Aray buses leave the bus station (20min walk from the central square on the main road out of town) to Puerto López (1hr). From the bus terminal in **Guayaquil**, Transportes CLP runs six daily services directly to Montañita and Olón between January and April, and Cooperativa Jipijapa leaves for Jipijapa every thirty minutes.

Valdivia

North of Santa Elena the road hugs the shore, skirting a string of long, slender beaches backed by a vast expanse of ocean. Brightly painted fishing boats hauled onto the sands add colour to the scene, but the unattractive villages and barren scrubland east of the road aren't too inviting. Forty kilometres up the road you reach the impoverished, litter-strewn village of **VALDIVIA**, whose name was given by archeologists to the **Valdivia culture** that inhabited this region from 3500 BC, one of the earliest in South America to form permanent agricultural settlements and produce ceramics.

Off the main square, the small, cash-starved **Ecomuseo Valdivia** (daily 9am–6pm; $0.60) does its best with a fairly limited collection of ceramics that can't hope to do justice to the rich archeology of the region – you'll find much finer and more abundant examples of Valdivia and other coastal ceramics in the museums of Guayaquil and Quito. The museum does, however, have a souvenir shop selling good replicas of pre-Columbian ceramics, and a **workshop** where you can watch them being made using traditional methods. Valdivia also has a small **aquarium** (daily 9am–6pm; $1) a few blocks west of the village square, with a lacklustre collection of local marine life. You'll probably not want to stay here, and it's easy enough to stop off for an hour two and catch the next **bus** up the coast.

Manglaralto

Twelve kilometres north of Valdivia, the tidy, attractive village of **MANGLARALTO** features a leafy square and a long, very beautiful **beach** – a quiet, remote alternative to the gringo-favoured Montañita and Alandaluz for a couple of days of oceanside relaxation. Note, however, that there are dangerous **riptides** off this part of the coast. Manglaralto has also been the focus of sustainable economic-development programmes by organizations such as **Pro-Pueblo**, a foundation set up by the national cement company La Cemento

Trekking in the Cordillera Chongón-Colonche

Pro-Pueblo, based outside San Antonio south of Manglaralto (℡04/2780230, ✉propueb1@propueblo.org.ec, ⊛www.propueblo.org.ec), has designed four **trekking routes** (detailed below) that lead from coastal villages up into the **Chongón-Colonche** hills, which are luxuriantly forested in parts. A number of locals have been trained to **guide** visitors around, and can provide simple accommodation in their homes. **Costs** are very reasonable (around $4 per day for guide, $10 per day for mule or horse hire, $4 for a bed and meal), and if you turn up at the initial village on the route and ask around for a guide (names given below), you should be able to sort out a hike for the following day. You'll need to take all your own **food and water** and use plenty of **mosquito repellent**. If you carry a **tent**, you can arrange to sleep in the forest overnight. Valdivia, Manglaralto, Olón and La Entrada can be reached by any of the buses serving the coast road.

Ruta Loma Alta An hour's bus or truck ride east of Valdivia, the village of Suspiro is used as a base for visiting a tract of protected cloudforest up on Cerro Loma Alta (6hr one-way), where you can spend the night in a wooden hut. You can also visit the village of Barcelona, where locals boil raw toquilla straw in the first stage of its preparation to be woven into Panama hats. Guides in Suspiro are Celso Tomalá, Felix Tomalá, Eleodoro Rodriguez and Juan Tomalá.

Ruta Dos Mangas The village of Dos Mangas is 4km east of Manglaralto, about an hour on foot or shorter if you arrange a lift with *Hostería Marakayá* (see p.444). From here, you can walk or ride through lush forest to the 600-metre summit of Cerro del Encanto (3hr each way), from where you get fabulous views over the surrounding hills and down to the coast. There are a couple of alternative walks following streams through the forest, ending up at waterfalls. Guides in Dos Mangas are Luis González, Wilson Lino, Félix Trigrero and Colón Nevárez.

Ruta Olón From Olón the route follows the Río Olón into tropical dry forest, speckled with wild orchids in May and December. You can extend the walk by joining the Río Ayampe and following it west to the eponymous village. The trek can take one to three days, depending on how far you want to follow the route. The guide in Olón is Eustacio Salinas.

Ruta La Entrada From La Entrada paths lead to Cerro de la Naranjal (6hr round-trip), where you can see many birds, or through the forest to Vueltas Largas, where it is sometimes possible to spot monkeys and *guantas* (8hr round-trip). Guides in La Entrada are Alcide Merchán, Félix Chilán and Alfonso Asunción.

Nacional in 1992, which runs excellent projects in animal husbandry, organic farming, recycling, family planning, local sanitation and water distribution. It also has a small shop for locally made crafts by the park, and arranges **trekking routes** for guided walks and horse rides in the local hills (see box, p.443).

On the main street, Calle Constitución, the friendly *Marakayá* (℡04/2901294; ❸) has a few pleasant, well-kept **rooms**, which have mosquito-nets and some air conditioning, and a café one block from the beach. Close by, towards the southern end of Constitución, Paquita Jara provides basic accommodation in her home (℡04/2901114; ❷) or in her brother's house (❷) right on the beach, with fantastic views. Roberto Piloso, whose house is opposite the hospital (℡04/2901118 or 2901309; ❷), also offers a place to stay and leads **guided walks** on the Pro-Pueblo hiking trails, as well as coordinating local **volunteer** programs for Ecotrackers in Quito (℡02/2550208).

Montañita

Just 4km north of Manglaralto, **MONTAÑITA** is like nowhere else on the southern coast. Crammed into the centre are straw-roofed, bamboo-walled *hostales* and pizzerias advertised by bright wooden signs, while tanned, chilled-out gringos lounge around in shorts and bikinis, and surfers stride up the streets with boards under arm. The town's transformation from isolated fishing village to backpacker hangout has been brought about by some of the best **surfing** conditions in Ecuador, namely strong, consistent waves ranging from one to three metres in height, and a long right break lying off the northern end of the beach by the rocky promontory of **La Punta**. The best waves fortuitously coincide with the summer months (Jan–April), when the water temperature averages 22–25°C. Every February, surfing fever reaches a peak during the **international surfing competition** held here over Carnaval, which attracts contestants from as far away as the US and Australia.

Surfboards (*tablas*) can be rented for $5 a day at the Tsunami Surf Shop opposite the *Montañita* hotel, and at DMCA on Chiriboga opposite the *Casa Blanca*. Montañita's waves are best suited to experienced surfers, but beginners can get in on the action by taking one-to-one **lessons** at DMCA ($10 per 1hr 30min lesson, plus board hire and wetsuit for the day). Meanwhile, non-surfers are content to laze around the beach or people-watch at the many rustic cafés dotted along the main street, waiting for the sun to go down and Montañita's **nightlife** to heat up, when bars rock to the likes of the Doors and bongo-drummers beat out a frenzied rhythm on the streets, while parties unfold on the beach. There's a certain 1960s, dope-fuelled atmosphere to Montañita that may not appeal to everybody, reaching a height during *la temporada* from January to April. Outside these months, visitors dwindle and the skies cloud over, but the hotels stay open all year catering to the steady stream of surf addicts.

There are no banks in Montañita, so make sure to bring all your **money** before arriving. If you must, the Farmacia San José changes travellers cheques with an eight-percent commission. **Internet access** is at the Montañita Cyber Club ($3 per hour), off Chiriboga walking away from the sea on the street parallel to the river, and they also have a **tour agency**, Montañita Unlimited, offering rappelling, trekking, mountain biking and horse-riding expeditions.

Accommodation

There are two clusters of **accommodation**, one in the village centre and another by **La Punta** in a calmer, quieter location 1km to the north. Note that all prices rise steeply during the high season, sometimes by more than double.

Arena Guadúa La Punta ☎04/2901285.
Argentine-owned surfer hangout with cabins, private baths and hot water, and a sleeping area with multicoloured shower stalls. Boards are for hire and lessons are offered. ❹

Baja Montañita La Punta ☎04/2901219. Resort-hotel in an enclosed complex with all the facilities, including pool and Jacuzzi, and rooms featuring a/c and satellite TVs. A bit of a fish out of water in Montañita, though. ❻

Cabañas Nativa Bambú on the hill behind the village across the main road ⓦwww
.nativabambu.com. Attractive cabins with varnished floors, well-presented shared or private bathrooms, mosquito nets and terraces overlooking the village and sea – not far from the action but away from the noise. Four-person tents are available ($10 with breakfast). Otherwise includes both breakfast and dinner. ❺

Casa Blanca Chiriboga ☎09/9182501. Provides bamboo huts with hammocks, balconies and sea views, and less attractive brick-walled rooms with erratic hot-water showers. ❷

Casa del Sol La Punta ☎04/2901302,
ⓦwww.casasol.com. Hostel whose agreeable rooms have private baths or cheaper dormitory bunks ($8) in a cosy, straw-roofed wooden building with balconies, terraces, hammocks, a TV room and restaurant. ❹

El Centro del Mundo on the beach (no phone). Popular hostel in an unmistakeable tall bamboo house on stilts by the ocean, offering a choice of simple wooden rooms with optional en-suite bathrooms ($3–4), and mattresses in the attic for $2.50.

Montañita next door to *El Centro del Mundo*
☎04/2901296. Imposing modern hotel whose 36 clean, if bare, white-walled rooms have private baths, electric showers, mosquito nets and ceiling fans. Also an on-site swimming pool and terrace overlooking the sea. ❹

Paradise South on the other side of the river bridge from the centre ☎04/2119085. Quiet spot offering spacious grounds, a pleasant lawn and ping pong and pool tables, with clean, compact rooms with optional bathrooms. ❹

Tierra Prometida on Chiriboga (no phone). Israeli-owned establishment with comfortable rooms done up in jazzy colours, with shared and private baths - though it can get a bit stuffy. ❹

Eating

There's a wide choice of **café-restaurants** in the centre, all of them cheap and most offering a fish-based menu supplemented by pizzas, pasta, pancakes and tropical fruit juices. One highlight is *Doña Elena*, on the main street, who serves great sea bass caught by her fisherman husband.

Olón to Ayampe

Three kilometres north of Montañita you pass the neighbouring village of **Olón**, graced by a long white beach, and, 10km beyond, the village of **La Entrada**, so called because it marks the entrance into the **Cordillera Chongón-Colonche**, a range of 800-metre-high hills covered by one of the last remnants of coastal forest in the region, which until the 1950s extended up the whole of Ecuador's coastline north of the Santa Elena peninsula. Aggressive logging of fine native hardwoods such as guayacán, cascol and guasmo has reduced these coastal forests to a tiny fraction of their original area, with the largest remaining tract protected by Parque Nacional Machalilla, a further 30km up the road (see overleaf).

As you enter the forest, the road veers inland into the heart of the Cordillera, and suddenly you're surrounded by dense vegetation dripping with moisture – a dramatic contrast to the dusty landscape further south. Eleven kilometres north of La Entrada, you pass a signed track branching west to the *Atamari* (☎09/9821915 or ☎04/2780430, ⓦwww.hosteriaatamari.com; ❼), perched on a cliff high above the sea, with spectacular views up the coast and access to two beautiful, deserted beaches. This upmarket establishment has private, well-equipped cabañas, a large pool and a lovely restaurant and bar, and any bus serving the coastal route can drop you off at the track leading up to the hotel, a fifteen-minute uphill walk.

Some 3km beyond the *Atamari* turn-off, **AYAMPE** is an unassuming village, home only to a handful of farming families and set back from a huge, empty beach pounded by powerful breakers – a beautiful, little-known spot that has only recently begun to attract visitors to its generally good hotels. On the seafront, *Cabañas La Tortuga* (☎04/2780613; ❹) has airy cabins with spacious bathrooms, electric showers and mosquito nets, while to the south beyond the cemetery, the Swiss-Ecuadorian *Cabañas La Iguana* (☎04/2780605; ❸–❹) has good clean rooms around a pretty garden, with use of a kitchen included. The smartest place is the *Almare* (☎042780611, ⓦwww.hotelalmare.com; ❺–❼), featuring comfortable wooden rooms with private baths and hot water, tiled floors, smoked-glass sliding doors opening onto balconies, and a large terrace with gorgeous views of the sea. The *Finca Punta Ayampe*, 1km south of the village (☎04/2780616, ⓦwww.fincapuntaayampe.com; ❹–❺), is set in fruit orchards and vegetable gardens on a hill with tremendous views. The main building, a tall open-sided wooden structure with a sun deck and open fire, has airy rooms with private baths and hot water; private cabins are also available with similar facilities. The owner offers local tours and can give surf lessons.

Alandaluz to Salango

About 3km beyond Ayampe, the coast road emerges from the Cordillera Chongón-Colonche and passes **Alandaluz**, on the edge of the village of Puerto Rico (☎04/2780686, ☎ & ⒻＩ02/2543042, ⓦwww.alandaluz.com; ❹–❻), a famous ecological resort comprising thirty attractive cabañas scattered around tree-filled grounds, with a magnificent high-roofed dining room, bar and lounge in a central bamboo building; newer accommodation is also available with fireplaces and flush toilets. Everything is designed and run on ecological principles: the cabins are made of local, easily renewable materials like *caña guadúa* bamboo and palm leaves, some units have special compost toilets to produce fertilizer, fruit and vegetables grow in organic gardens, and water is meticulously saved and recycled. It's a lovely, laid-back place to hang out for a few days, whether you want to lounge around on a private beach, use it as a base for visiting Parque Nacional Machalilla up the road (see p.448), or take a tour to the resort's private **Cantalapiedra** nature reserve and stay in a wood-and-thatch tower sleeping thirteen people. Although **camping** is possible ($4 per person), accommodation is expensive by backpacking standards. Nonetheless, *Alandaluz* has poured its profits back into the local community, establishing recycling centres, reforestation projects, and workshops in sustainable farming and building methods, among various other programmes.

A further 7km up the road near **Río Chico**, the *Hostería Piqueros Patas Azules* (☎04/2780279; ❺) has comfortable rooms, a good restaurant and bar, medicinal plunge pool and its own stretch of beach with a scattering of hammocks and deck chairs. Attached to the hotel is a *sala arqueológico*, whose impressive display of artefacts from the Valdivia culture (see p.505) includes fragments of pots and tablets carved with images of animals like a monkey, caiman and pelican, thought to have been used by local chiefs to imprint their own symbolic "signature". Another kilometre up the coast road, the tiny village of **Salango** is the site of a small but well-designed **archeology museum** (daily 9am–noon & 1–5pm; $1), illustrating the area's continuous occupation from the Valdivia culture around 3500 BC to the Manteño culture up to 1550 AD. Especially engaging are the displays on ancient fishing techniques and seafaring practices, including a reconstruction of a single-sail fishing raft like those the Spanish encountered when they first visited this coast in 1526.

Tours from Puerto López

Most of Puerto López' **tour operators** offer the same basic journeys at identical prices, with reductions in the low season. Most popular is the ninety-minute **boat ride to Isla de la Plata** ($30; see p.450), including a guided hike around the island, followed by lunch and snorkelling from the boat. Boats usually set off at 9am and return at 5pm, and the crossing can be rough, so take sea-sickness tablets if you're susceptible. On top of the cost of the tour you'll have to pay for your national park fee (mainland $12, Isla de la Plata $15, combined $20), which is taken care of by the operator. **Whale-watching tours** (June–Sept; $25) are an exciting way of seeing humpback whales, as they travel up the Pacific coast from the Antarctic to give birth to their calves in warmer waters. It's easy to spot the enormous columns of spray they blow out as they re-emerge from the sea, and to hear the loud "singing" noises, and it's usually possible to get quite close-up views of them, too. Both of these trips often require a minimum of four people per boat, and in the low season (for Isla de la Plata) it may take several days to get a group together, with the best chances being at weekends.

Operators generally provide guided tours of the **Parque Nacional Machalilla** ($25; see p.448), including the archeological excavations of **Agua Blanca** and the beach at **Los Frailes**, while two-day hikes up into the forest of **San Sebastián** cost around $40 and include food and camping equipment. **Horse-riding**, **sports-fishing** and **mountain-biking** excursions are other possibilities. Companies can't always provide English-speaking guides, and sometimes make do with asking a member of the tour to translate for everyone else. Recommended operators include Bosque Marino Tours, Malecón and General Córdova (℡05/604606); Cercapez, General Córdova and Juan Montalvo (℡05/604173); Ecuador Amazing, General Córdova and Malecón (℡05/604239); Exploratur, General Córdova and Malecón (℡05/604123, ✉andres@explorerdiving.com); Machalilla, Malecón 119 and Julio Izurieta (℡05/604206); and Mantaraya, Malecón at General Córdova (℡05/604233).

With a few days' advance notice, Exploratur (see above) organizes **scuba-diving** day-tours ($95) with a PADI instructor and two tanks for certified and non-certified divers. Some dives take you down to Ecuador's only coral reef, where you can see many colourful fish as well as octopuses, urchins and sea cucumbers, while other options include a five-day open water course ($350). Machalilla Tours provides **surfing** lessons and excursions as well ($15).

Puerto López

About 5km north of Salango, the coast road cuts across the brow of a hill to provide a sudden, splendid view down to **PUERTO LÓPEZ**, a small fishing town strung along a wide, crescent-shaped bay. Enjoying an undeniably picturesque setting, the town's golden sands are set off by the turquoise waters of the ocean and the green hills rising on either side of the bay. At close quarters, though, Puerto López turns out to be an untidy place with potholed streets, crumbling buildings and a litter-strewn beach. Still, the surge of morning activity of fishermen busying to and from the beach, and the swarm of children playing in the breakers after school, give the place a spirited atmosphere. It's by far the most convenient base for visiting **Parque Nacional Machalilla**, whose headquarters and information centre are based here at García Moreno and Eloy Alfaro, where there's a small **interpretation centre** (see p.448). Indeed, most visitors are here not for the town, but to explore the park's beaches, forests and offshore island, Isla de la Plata, reached by boat from Puerto López on tours offered by several operators based here (see box, above).

Arrival, information and transport

Puerto López is well served by **buses** running along the coast road to La Libertad in the south (every 30min; 3hr) and Manta in the north (hourly; 2hr), as well as inland north to Jipijapa (every 30min; 1hr 30min), where there are connections to Guayaquil. There are direct buses to Quito (5am, 9am & 6.30pm; 10hr), and two daily services from Quito (7am & 10pm). Buses drop passengers on the main road, General Córdova, by the church and the market building. **Tricicleros** ($0.50) will cycle you to your hotel, while **camionetas** linger around the market for longer journeys.

For **money**, the Banco del Pichincha on General Córdova changes traveller's cheques and offers Visa cash advance. The Pacifictel **telephone office** is on the main road, a block north of the church, but you're better off making international calls from an **Internet** café such as Sunset Cyber Café, next to the bank. The **post office** is on the Malecón south of General Córdova, and **laundry** services are offered by several tour operators, including Bosque Marino and Machalilla Tours ($3.50 per load). **Spanish lessons** are given at La Lengua Spanish School, García Moreno and Calderón, near the municipio (ⓔcostamar25 @hotmail.com, ⓦwww.la-lengua.com; $5 per hour), with accommodation also available.

Accommodation

Puerto López offers plenty of choices for **accommodation**, the most notable of which are listed below.

Los Islotes on the seafront, at the corner with General Córdova ℡05/604108 or 604128. Tidy little spot with spacious en-suite rooms. ❷–❹
Hostería Mandála ten-minute walk from the Pacífico, at the far north of the Malecón ℡05/604181. Friendly Swiss- and Italian-owned place with attractively furnished thatched-roof cabins set in lavish botanical gardens with private baths and hot water. Its lovely restaurant overlooks the ocean and serves good international food, including Italian specialities. ❹

Pacífico three blocks north of *Los Islotes* along the Malecón ℡05/604147. Long-established hotel featuring clean, simple rooms with shared bath (❷) set around a swimming pool; some have private baths (❹) and sea views or a/c (❻).
Villa Colombia south of General Córdova on García Moreno ℡05/604105, ⓔhostalvc@uio .satnet.net. The best budget option, a well-managed operation offering bunks ($5) and doubles, with optional private baths, the use of a large kitchen and patios with hammocks. ❸

Eating

In town, the best **place to eat** is *Carmita's*, Malecón and General Córdova, a friendly restaurant run by the same family for thirty years, serving freshly caught fish and seafood at great prices. Especially recommended are the *pescado al vapor* (steamed sea bass in tomato, onion and herb sauce) and *spaghetti con mariscos*. Other decent options include the *Pizzeria Estrella del Mar*, Juan Montalvo, just off General Córdova, and *Rey Hoja* and *Spondylus*, both on the Malecón and specializing in seafood.

Parque Nacional Machalilla

Parque Nacional Machalilla, Ecuador's only coastal national park, was created in 1979 to protect the country's last major tract of tropical dry forest, which since the 1950s has been reduced to a mere one percent of its original size. The forest is especially notable for the remarkable contrast between the vegetation at sea level and that covering the hills rising to 800m above the coastline. The **dry forest**, panning in from the shore, comprises scorched-looking trees and shrubs adapted to scarce water supplies and saline soils, including many different cactuses, gnarled ceibas, barbasco trees and algarrobo (able to photosynthesize through its green bark). Also common are highly fragrant palo santo trees, whose bark is burned as incense in churches. A short hike east into the hills brings you into the wholly different landscape of **coastal cloudforest**, moistened by a rising sea mist that condenses as it hits the hills, where a dense covering of lush vegetation shelters ferns, heliconias, bromeliads, orchids and bamboos, as well as howler monkeys, *guantas*, anteaters and more than 350 species of birds. You can observe the two different habitats on a ten-kilometre trail leading from the community of **Agua Blanca**, north of Puerto López, up to the **San Sebastián** cloudforest area. Agua Blanca sits near one of the most important archeological sites on the coast, the former settlement of **Sangólome**, once an important civic and ceremonial centre of the Manteño culture. Beyond this, the park takes in a number of pristine beaches, of which the most spectacular is **Playa Los Frailes**, whose virgin white sands are framed by dramatic cliffs and forested hills. Offshore areas include the tiny **Isla Salango** and the famous, bird-rich **Isla de la Plata**, the most popular destination in the park.

The park's **visitor centre**, in Puerto López at the brown-and-white thatched building opposite the market, just off the main road through town (daily 8am–noon & 2–6pm; ☎05/604170), is where you pay your **entrance fee**; the three types of tickets, all good for five days, allow access to the mainland ($12) or Isla de la Plata ($15), or provide entrance to both ($20). **Arriving** at the park is easy on any of the buses running north along the coast road (see opposite). The **weather** is typically rainy, hot and sunny in summer (Jan–April), and dry, slightly cooler and overcast the rest of the year, with average year-round temperatures hovering around 23–25°C.

Agua Blanca and San Sebastián

Five kilometres north of Puerto López, at the hamlet of Buenavista, a sideroad leads east to **AGUA BLANCA**, an hour's walk from the main road. This humble village stands near the site of **Sangólome**, a former centre of the Manteño civilization, which occupied southern Manabí from c.500 BC to 1540 AD. A great seafaring and trading people, the Manteños were known for their finely crafted and polished black ceramics, and for their large thrones supported by human or animal figures, several of which were found here. A small **museum** in the village (daily 8am–6pm; $2; park entrance fee not required for museum visits) displays some beautiful ceramics excavated at Sangólome, while the **site** itself is a forty-minute walk away and can be visited with **guides**, either from the village or Puerto López (see box, p.447), where you may be able to find one that speaks English. Unaccompanied visitors, however, are not allowed, in order to prevent the filching of artefacts. There's not a great deal left to see, but the numerous low walls and foundations give you an idea of the size and importance of the city, estimated to have housed around five thousand people.

You can also hire **guides** ($15 per day, plus $15 per horse or mule) in Agua Blanca or Puerto López to take you on beautiful hikes through tropical dry forest, with many colourful birds, up to the lush **San Sebastián cloudforest**, home to black howler monkeys, snakes, *guantas* and anteaters. The route is 10km each way, most comfortably spread over two days while **camping** here, and guides can also provide simple accommodation ($5) and meals.

Playa Los Frailes and Sendero El Rocío

Some 10km north of Puerto López, a signed dirt track branches west from the coast road, just south of the run-down village of Machalilla, to **Playa Los Frailes**, one of the most beautiful beaches on the Ecuadorian coast, enclosed by rocky cliffs at each end and backed by a tangle of forest. Despite its popularity, the beach still feels like a wild, unspoiled place, particularly if you arrive in the early morning, when you're almost guaranteed to have it all to yourself. To get there, hop on any of the **buses** heading north from Puerto López and ask to be dropped at the turn-off to the beach, passed about fifteen minutes out of town. Just off the road at the national park kiosk, show your ticket or buy one if you haven't already paid your entrance fee. From here a footpath leads directly to Los Frailes in thirty minutes (the left fork), or you can follow a four-kilometre circular trail (the right fork) via the tiny black-sand cove known as **La Playita**, followed by **Playa La Tortiguita**, where spiky rocks rise from the turquoise waters. From La Tortiguita continue on the main footpath to Los Frailes, or follow the fork leading through dry forest dotted with fragrant *palo santo* trees up to a wooden **lookout** giving spectacular views of the coast. This longer approach, via La Playita, La Tortiguita and the *mirador*, is by far the more rewarding, and takes several hours to complete.

About 3km north of the turning for Los Frailes, you'll see signs for the **Sendero El Rocío**, an enjoyable two-kilometre trail beginning in the cultivated land of traditional coastal subsistence farms, leading up to a viewpoint and into dry *palo santo* forest, and emerging at an attractive beach. Locals act as guides for visitors; ask at the farmsteads around the trailhead.

Isla de la Plata

Some 37km out to sea from Puerto López, and reached using one of the tour companies there (see box, p.447), **Isla de la Plata** is a small, scrubby island of just eight square kilometres, which was once the ceremonial centre of the La Bahía culture (500 BC–650 AD). Its name comes from the legend of the English explorer, Sir Francis Drake, burying a chestful of silver here in the sixteenth century – still undiscovered – though these days the island is more famous as the "poor man's Galápagos", so called for its abundant population of **marine birds**, which are relatively fearless and allow close observation, attracting many visitors. Notably, though, this is the only place in mainland Ecuador where blue-footed, red-footed and Nazca boobies are all found together.

From the landing point in **Bahía Drake**, two circular **footpaths** lead around the island, each taking three to four hours to travel, including time spent watching the birds and listening to the tour guide's commentary. The most numerous bird on the island is the **blue-footed booby**, though you can also see **frigate birds**, **red-billed tropicbirds** and **waved albatrosses** (breeding season April–Oct; see "Contexts", p.539), as well as sea lions, which are colonizing the island in small numbers. Visits usually include some **snorkelling**, in which you'll see a fabulous array of colourful fish, and you might also spot dolphins and manta rays on the boat ride, as well as **humpback whales** between June and September.

Puerto Cayo to Jipijapa

Heading north of Puerto López along the coast road, the sea is mostly hidden from sight, though at **PUERTO CAYO**, 34km up the road, there are great views onto a lovely broad beach hedged at the south by dramatic sandy cliffs. Although there's accommodation here, the village itself is quite run-down and feels almost abandoned in low season, when unfriendly dogs hold sway over its muddy streets. On the coast road 3km north of Puerto Cayo, a more appealing place for a stopover is the *Luz de Luna* (℡02/2400562; ❺), an hostería with comfortable rooms, small swimming pool, access to a nice stretch of beach and a restaurant serving local *comida típica* cooked in a clay oven.

Just beyond Puerto Cayo, a road branches off the coastal highway (which continues on to Manta) and heads inland for 30km to **JIPIJAPA** (pronounced "hippyhappa"). Disappointingly, this dull town doesn't live up to its delightful name and the only reason to stop here is to change **buses** if you're approaching the coast road from the north, or are moving on from the coast to Guayaquil, Manta or Portoviejo. The terminal is 2km west of the centre, by the main road leading into town. Fortunately, you shouldn't have to wait longer than an hour to catch your connection, but if you're unlucky enough to get stuck here, your best bet for a **place to stay** is the *Jipijapa*, Santiesteban and Eloy Alfaro (℡05/601365; ❹). For **meals** try one of the uninspiring canteens on and around the central square, serving cheap lunches of fried meat or fish.

Travel details

Buses

Guayaquil to: Alausí (3 daily; 5hr); Ambato (hourly; 6hr 30min); Cuenca (every 40min; 4hr); Guaranda (12 daily; 3hr 30min); Jipijapa (every 30min; 2hr 30min); La Libertad (every 20min; 2hr 30min); Loja (16 daily; 9hr); Machala (every 30min; 3hr); Manta (every 30min; 4hr); Playas (every 20min; 2hr); Portoviejo (every 30min; 4hr); Quito (every 20–45min; 8hr); Riobamba (every hour; 4hr 30min); Salinas (every 20min; 2hr 40min); Santo Domingo (every 10min; 6hr); Zaruma (10 daily; 6hr).
Jipijapa to: Guayaquil (every 30min; 2hr 30min); Manta (hourly; 1hr 30min); Puerto López (hourly; 1hr 30min); Quito (2 daily; 9hr).
La Libertad to: Guayaquil (every 20min; 2hr 30min); Manglaralto (hourly; 50min); Montañita (hourly; 1hr); Puerto López (hourly; 2hr); Puerto

Rico/Alandaluz (hourly; 1hr 40min); Punta Carnero (every 20min; 20min); Salinas (every 10min; 10min); Santa Elena (every 10min; 5min); Valdivia (hourly; 40min).
Machala to: Cuenca (every 15–45min; 4hr); Guayaquil (every 30min; 3hr); Huaquillas (every 20min; 1hr); Loja (8 daily; 6hr); Puyango (5 daily; 3hr); Quito (11 daily; 10hr); Zaruma (10 daily; 3hr).

Flights

Guayaquil to: Baltra (2 daily; 1hr 30min); Cuenca (3 Mon–Fri, 2 Sat; 30min); Loja (1 Tues & Thurs; 30min); Machala (1 Mon & Fri, 2 Tues & Thurs; 30min); Quito (around 17 Mon–Fri, around 10 Sat & Sun; 45min); San Cristóbal (1 Mon, Wed & Sat; 1hr 30min).
Machala to: Guayaquil (1 Mon & Fri, 2 Tues & Thurs; 30min).

The Galápagos
Islands

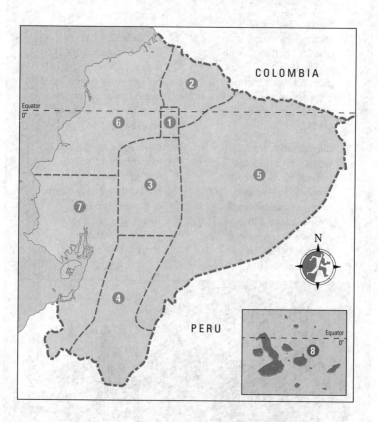

CHAPTER 8

Highlights

✳ **Puerto Ayora** A friendly and bustling little port, home to the islands' best hotels, restaurants and bars, not to mention the Charles Darwin Research Station, the engine of Galápagos study and conservation. See p.475

✳ **Sulivan Bay** Explore a century-old pahoehoe lava flow patterned with petrified ripples, squiggles and swirls that give it the appearance of having only just cooled. See p.486

✳ **Bartolomé** A small island with a spectacular summit vantage point overlooking Pinnacle Rock, a landmark rock poised above a little bay where you can snorkel among Galápagos penguins. See p.487

✳ **Waved albatrosses** After ranging the oceans, the gentle giants of the Galápagos return to Española between April and December, and enact enthralling courtship displays before breeding with their life-long partners. See p.501

✳ **Gardner Bay** One of the finest beaches in the islands, a long streak of brilliant white sand, lapped by azure waters ideal for swimming and snorkelling. See p.501

✳ **Genovesa** An isolated island formed from a half-submerged crater at the northeastern extreme of the archipelago, where you can snorkel with hammerhead sharks. See p.501

The Galápagos Islands

t's quite humbling that a scattering of scarred volcanic islands, flung across 45,000 square kilometres of ocean, 960km adrift from the Ecuadorian mainland and defying permanent human colonization until the twentieth century, should have been so instrumental in changing humanity's perception of itself. Yet, once feared as a bewitched and waterless hell, then the haunt of pirates, and later still an inhospitable pit stop for whaling ships, it was the forbidding **Galápagos Islands** that spurred **Charles Darwin** to formulate his theory of evolution by natural selection, catapulting science into the modern era and colouring the values and attitudes of the Western world ever since.

Three years before Darwin's arrival in 1835, Ecuador had claimed **sovereignty** over the islands. They swiftly took root in the country's consciousness, not as the forsaken land of unearthly creatures and lava wastes that the rest of the world saw, but as a source of great national pride, bolstered still further by Darwin's discoveries. When the islands became desirable to foreign powers as a strategic military base from which to protect the entrance to the Panama Canal, the Ecuadorian government – even after a string of unsuccessful colonization attempts – resisted several enticing offers for territorial rights over them. In fact, it wasn't until World War II, when it became clear that just such a strategic base was necessary, that the US was allowed to establish an airforce base on Baltra. When the war ended, the base was returned to Ecuador and became the principal point of access to the islands for a steadily increasing flow of immigrants and tourists.

Today, the Galápagos Islands' matchless wildlife and natural history pulls in around 70,000 tourists a year to the archipelago – most of which can only be seen on expensive boat tours – financing what is now Ecuador's best-off province. The province's population of 16,000 live in just eight main settlements on four inhabited islands. In the centre of them all lies **Santa Cruz**, site of **Puerto Ayora**, the islands' most developed town and serviced by the airstrip on Baltra, where the majority of tourists begin a visit to the islands. **San Cristóbal**, to the east, holds the provincial capital, **Puerto Baquerizo Moreno**, and while this is less developed than Puerto Ayora, it does possess the archipelago's other major runway and is nurturing a reputation as a surfing centre. Straddling the equator to the west of Santa Cruz is the largest and most volcanically active of all the islands, **Isabela**, whose main settlement, the tiny

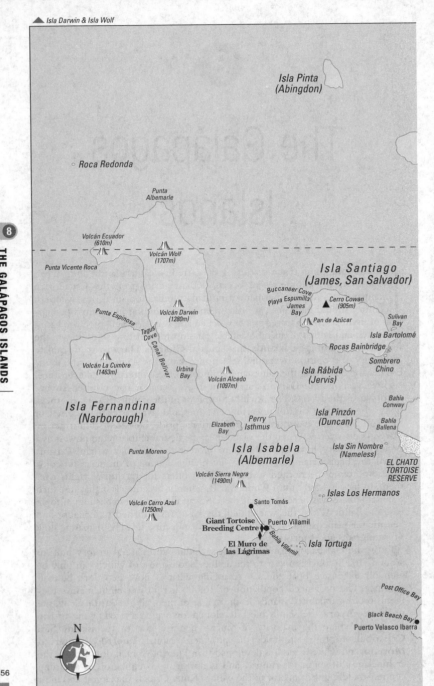

Isla Pinta
(Abingdon)

○ Roca Redonda

Punta
Albemarle

Volcán Ecuador
(610m)

Volcán Wolf
(1707m)

Punta Vicente Roca

Isla Santiago
(James, San Salvador)

Buccaneer Cove
Playa Espumilla
James
Bay

Cerro Cowan
(905m)

Pan de Azúcar

Sulivan
Bay

Punta Espinosa

Volcán Darwin
(1280m)

Tagus
Cove

Canal Bolívar

Isla Bartolomé

Rocas Bainbridge

Volcán La Cumbre
(1463m)

Urbina
Bay

Volcán Alcedo
(1097m)

Sombrero
Chino

Isla Rábida
(Jervis)

Isla Fernandina
(Narborough)

Elizabeth
Bay

Perry
Isthmus

Isla Pinzón
(Duncan)

Bahía
Conway

Bahía
Ballena

Punta Moreno

Isla Isabela
(Albemarle)

Isla Sin Nombre
(Nameless)

EL CHATO
TORTOISE
RESERVE

Volcán Sierra Negra
(1490m)

Islas Los Hermanos

Volcán Cerro Azul
(1250m)

Santo Tomás

Giant Tortoise
Breeding Centre

Puerto Villamil

Bahía Villamil

El Muro de
las Lágrimas

Isla Tortuga

Post Office Bay

Black Beach Bay
Puerto Velasco Ibarra

N

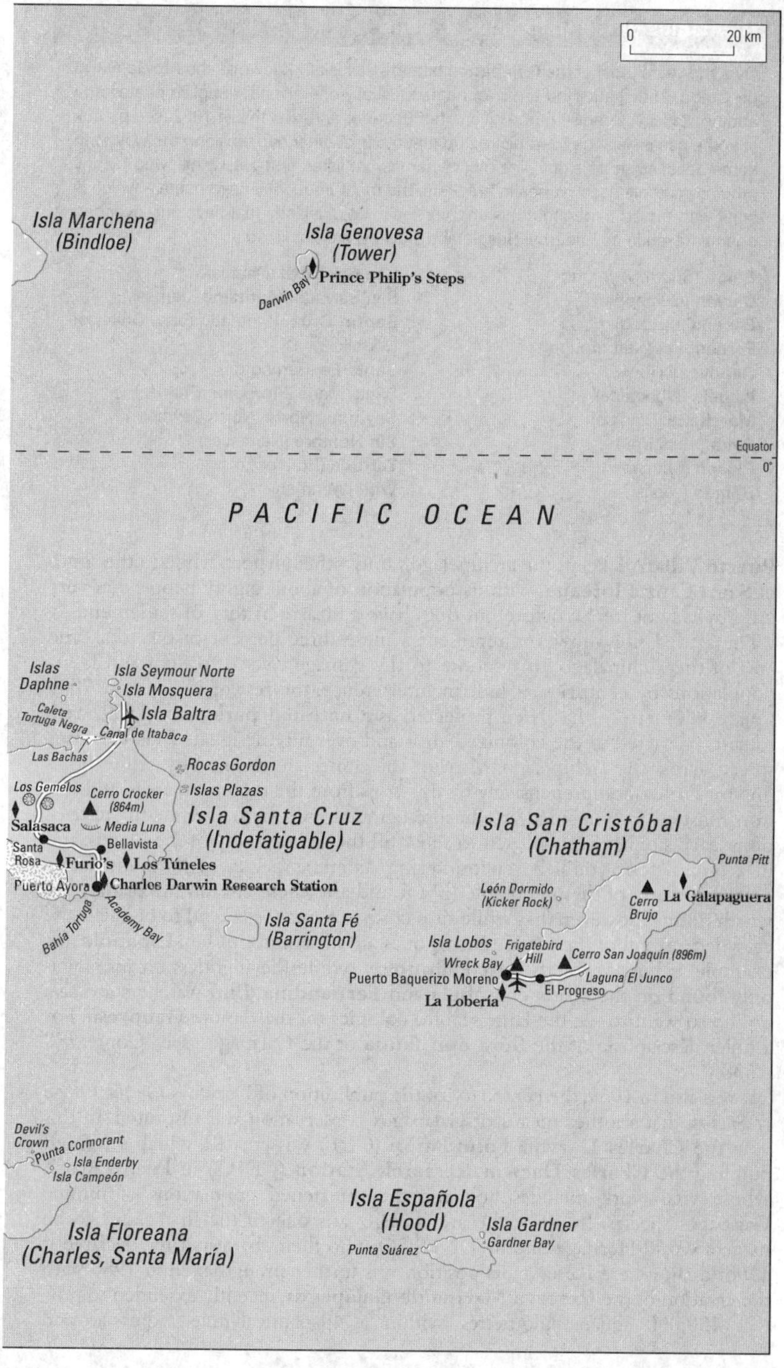
0 20 km
Isla Marchena
(Bindloe)
Isla Genovesa
(Tower)
Darwin Bay
Prince Philip's Steps
Equator
0°
PACIFIC OCEAN
Islas
Daphne
Isla Seymour Norte
Isla Mosquera
Isla Baltra
Caleta
Tortuga Negra
Canal de Itabaca
Las Bachas
Rocas Gordon
Islas Plazas
Los Gemelos
Cerro Crocker
(864m)
Salasaca
Media Luna
Isla Santa Cruz
(Indefatigable)
Bellavista
Santa
Rosa
Furio's
Los Túneles
Puerto Ayora
Charles Darwin Research Station
Bahía Tortuga
Academy Bay
Isla Santa Fé
(Barrington)
Isla San Cristóbal
(Chatham)
Punta Pitt
León Dormido
(Kicker Rock)
Cerro
Brujo
La Galapaguera
Isla Lobos
Frigatebird
Hill
Wreck Bay
Cerro San Joaquín (896m)
Puerto Baquerizo Moreno
Laguna El Junco
El Progreso
La Lobería
Devil's
Crown
Punta Cormorant
Isla Enderby
Isla Campeón
Isla Española
(Hood)
Isla Gardner
Gardner Bay
Punta Suárez
Isla Floreana
(Charles, Santa María)

8

THE GALÁPAGOS ISLANDS

Over the years most of the **Galápagos Islands** – officially known as the **Archipiélago de Colón** – have adopted a pair of names, usually one given by English pirates and another, official, Spanish name given after Ecuador annexed this in 1832 (see p.463). In some cases, islands have picked up a number of other names along the way, with some boasting up to eight. The official names are listed first below, followed by any other commonly used names in brackets: the most frequently used name – which is what we've used throughout this chapter – is in bold. Islands that have only ever had one name, such as Enderby, Beagle and Cowley, are not listed.

Baltra (South Seymour)	**San Cristóbal** (Chatham)
Darwin (Culpepper)	San Salvador (**Santiago**, James)
Española (Hood)	**Santa Cruz** (Indefatigable, Duke of
Fernandina (Narborough)	Norfolk)
Genovesa (Tower)	**Santa Fé** (Barrington)
Isabela (Albemarle)	Santa María (**Floreana**, Charles)
Marchena (Bindloe)	**Seymour Norte** (North Seymour)
Pinta (Abingdon)	**Sin Nombre** (Nameless)
Pinzón (Duncan)	**Tortuga** (Brattle)
Rábida (Jervis)	**Wolf** (Wenman)

Puerto Villamil, keeps the archipelago's only other airport, while to the south of Santa Cruz, **Floreana**, with its population of about eighty people, has very little by way of infrastructure but does have a bizarre history of settlement.

The settled sites, however, represent a mere three percent of the total land area of the archipelago. In response to the damage caused to flora and fauna populations by centuries of human interference, the rest of it – almost 7000 square kilometres – has been protected as a **national park** since 1959, with tourists restricted to the colonized areas and over fifty designated **visitor sites** spread across the archipelago. Most of these sites are reached by cruise boats only, or far less comprehensively by day-trips from the colonized areas, and visitors must be accompanied by a licensed guide to see them. Despite the restrictions, each site has been chosen to show off the full diversity of the islands, and in a typical tour you'll be encountering different species of flora and fauna everyday, many of them endemic (not found anywhere else on the planet). It's worth noting, however, that while sites close to Santa Cruz tend to be the more crowded, several of the most unusual ones are in remoter places: **Española**, for example, is known for its waved albatrosses, while the flightless cormorant is only found on the coasts of **Isabela** and **Fernandina**. Bird watchers are also bound to want to see the large seabird colonies on the remote **Genovesa**. For a fuller description of the **flora and fauna** of the Galápagos, see "Contexts", p.538.

It was also in 1959, the centenary of the publication of Darwin's *On the Origin of Species*, that another means of Galápagos conservation was instituted. In this year, the **Charles Darwin Foundation** (CDF) was created, which set about building the **Charles Darwin Research Station** (CDRS) in Puerto Ayora, whose vital work includes boosting the threatened populations of unique Galápagos species. In 1979, the archipelago was one of the first places to be made a World Heritage Site by UNESCO, who then, six years later, declared it a World Biosphere Reserve. Its position was further strengthened in 1986 with the creation of the **Reserva Marina de Galápagos**, recently extended to protect 130,000 square kilometres within a 40-nautical-mile radius around

Galápagos time

Galápagos time is GMT minus 6 hours, 1 hour behind the Ecuadorian mainland.

the island, and now the second largest marine reserve in the world after the Great Barrier Reef in Australia. It's mainly thanks to the huge conservation effort that the tourists that flock to the islands each year are privy to such incomparable experiences as swimming with hammerhead sharks and turtles, and walking beside the nests of frigate birds and boobies as unique species of finches hop onto their shoes. The animals that have carved out an existence on the dramatic volcanic landscape conjure up visions of life completely devoid of human presence, and their legendary fearlessness only intensifies the other-worldliness of these extraordinary islands.

When to visit

Although wildlife spotting is good throughout the year, the Galápagos Islands' do have a two-season **climate** that's governed by the strong **ocean currents** swirling around them. The **Humboldt current** (or Peru Current) is particularly prevalent in the cool season, helped on by brisk southeast winds. It cools the sea and forms the **garúa mist**, hanging at 300m to 600m where the cool, moist air over the water meets the warm air above that's heated by the sun. The winds blow the mists onto the southeast (windward) sides of the islands, giving consistent precipitation at these altitudes, while the northern (leeward) sides receive very little rain. In the warm season, the winds fall off, allowing warm currents from Panama (the Panama flow) to displace the Humboldt current. Sea temperatures rise, the mist dissipates, and normal rain clouds can form.

The islands are relatively dry all year, but during the **warm-wet season** (Jan–June) sunny skies are broken by short and heavy bursts of rain while temperatures nudge 30°C. You can also expect sea temperatures to be between 20°C and 26°C, reaching perhaps as high as 29°C around the northeastern islands. In the **cool-dry season** (July–Dec), the air temperature drops to around 22°C, the oceans become choppier, and the skies are more consistently overcast, though very little rain falls on the lowlands. Sea temperatures can dip as low as 16°C, especially in August and September, so consider bringing a wet suit if you plan to snorkel. At this time of year, the garúa mists linger over the oceans and bathe the uplands in a near-perpetual fine drizzle, occasionally descending to sea level. The transitional months between seasons can show quite changeable weather combining any of these elements.

In terms of how tour operators and hoteliers divide up the Galápagos year, **high season** begins around mid-June and lasts till August, starting up again in December and carrying on until mid-January. However, exact times vary, usually according to demand, with some operators only counting May to mid-June, and September, as **low season**.

A history of the islands

Until the middle of the twentieth century, the Galápagos Islands were thought to have been out of reach of the prehistoric coastal peoples of the continental mainland. Then, in 1947, explorer and archeologist Thor Heyerdahl proved otherwise with his famous voyage from Peru to Polynesia on a balsa raft, the *Kon-Tiki*. In 1953, his excavations on the islands revealed over 130 shards of **pre-Columbian pottery** from coastal Peru and Ecuador, but no signs of

THE GALÁPAGOS ISLANDS

8

When **Charles Darwin** began his five-year voyage around the world in 1831, he was little more than an enthusiastic amateur naturalist set on a career in the clergy. His formative years had been somewhat direction-less, lacking the stimulation that his mind craved. After an uninspiring stint at boarding school in his home town of Shrewsbury, Darwin was sent to Edinburgh University at the age of 16 to become a doctor, but soon realized he had no taste for the profession. He found the lectures stultifying and even those in geology, a subject that became a passion in later life, he described as "incredibly dull", producing in him "the determination never as long as [he] lived to read a book on Geology, or in any way to study the science". Prompted by his father, he turned to a career in the Church, one of the few respectable options left open to him, and went to Cambridge to study divinity. By his own admission, he spent most of his time there shooting partridge and following country pursuits, and only just scraped through without honours. It was here, however, that he encountered John Henslow, the Professor of Botany, who recognized in the 22-year-old a talented mind with a flair for the science. He was so impressed that he immediately recommended him to Captain FitzRoy, who was seeking a naturalist on a hydrographical expedition to chart the coast of South America, returning across the Pacific. Small reservations from FitzRoy – about the shape of Darwin's nose, which FitzRoy held to indicate a weakness of character – and Darwin's father, were soon overcome, and they set sail on board **HMS Beagle** in December 1831.

Darwin, however, suffered from terrible seasickness and complained bitterly in letters to his family: "I loathe, I abhor the sea and all ships which sail on it". Wherever he could, he stayed on land, and in the entire five-year voyage got away with spending only eighteen months at sea. On September 15, 1835, the *Beagle* arrived at the Galápagos and the desolate landscape startled him. "Nothing could be less inviting," he wrote, "the country is comparable to what one might imagine the cultivated parts of the Infernal regions to be". In the five weeks spent in the archipelago, he feverishly set about collecting samples and was taken aback by the "tameness" of the islands' creatures.

Darwin's own observations were searingly acute, noticing countless things that had passed previous visitors by. Still, it's clear that his experiences on the islands only planted the seeds of ideas that were to blossom on his return to England. Indeed, already exhausted from four years of hard travel, Darwin's normally fastidious sampling was somewhat slapdash in the Galápagos. He failed to label the source islands of his bird collections ("it never occurred to me that, the productions of islands only a few miles apart, and placed under the same physical conditions, would be dissimilar"), and even misidentified the now celebrated **Darwin's finches** (so named in 1936). It wasn't until his return to London, after the taxonomist, John Gould, had examined Darwin's samples and told him about the thirteen closely related species of finch, that the penny dropped. Yet, while he gave acclaimed lectures to London's scientific societies about his geological discoveries, and in 1839 published the cumbersomely titled *Journal of Researches into the Geology and Natural*

permanent settlements, leading him to theorize that the islands were used as a seasonal fishing base. Other early visitors could have included the great Inca **Tupac Yupanqui**, grandfather of Atahualpa, who, according to the early Spanish chronicler, Pedro Sarmiento de Gamboa, may have journeyed to the islands in about 1485 following reports that they held gold, returning almost a year later with "some black men, much gold, a chair made of brass and the skin and jawbone of a horse". This unlikely plunder casts doubts on the story's veracity, handing the prize of first documented visitor to **Tomás de Berlanga**, Bishop of Panama, whose ship ended up here after being swept off

History of the Various Countries Visited by HMS Beagle under the Command of Captain FitzRoy R.N. from 1832 to 1836, better known now as ***Voyage of the Beagle***, he only hinted at the big ideas that were troubling him. For example, about the finches and their beaks, he writes "there is not space in this work, to enter on this curious subject".

Instead, he set about working over his ideas in near secret in his famous **Transmutation Notebooks**, the first of which begins: "Had been greatly struck... on character of South American fossils and species on Galapagos Archipelago. These facts origin (especially latter) of all my views". He saw that the volcanic islands were relatively new and that the life on the islands bore a resemblance to species in South America, but were different in crucial ways. Darwin also came to realize that life had come to the barren islands by air or sea and had adapted to the harsh environment through a process he termed **"natural selection"**. In this, he maintained that at a given time certain members of a species are more suited to their surroundings than others, and are therefore more likely to survive in it, so passing on their advantageous characteristics to their offspring. Over the course of time, an entire population would come to develop those special features, eventually to such a degree that it will have become a new species, what Darwin called "descent with modification", rather than "evolution", which implied progressive movement towards the highest point of development. In his groundbreaking model, change was without direction and could result in a number of new species coming from a single ancestor.

Darwin knew the implications of his theory would upset the public, and the establishment and draw bitter criticism from the Church. A religious man, it was a source of pain to him that his theories came into direct conflict with the creationist dogma of the time, and he grew sick with the stress of it all (though some commentators have since attributed his illness to Chagas' disease, a chronic and withering parasitic infection he may have caught in the tropics). He sat on his theory for nearly twenty years, quietly amassing the information to back it up. It took a letter from **Alfred Russel Wallace**, who had arrived at the idea of natural selection independently of Darwin – though without the latter's intellectual rigour – to jerk him into action. In 1858, they offered a joint paper on their findings to the Linnaean Society in London. Darwin wrote up all his material and in November 1859 published *On the Origin of Species by Means of Natural Selection, or the Preservation of Favoured Races in the Struggle for Life*. It sold out in a single day. Sure enough, ***Origin of the Species*** sent shockwaves throughout the Western world and opened up to science areas that had previously been the province only of philosophers and theologians. Intense debate followed, and by the time of Darwin's death in 1882, the idea of evolution was well established and Darwin was a legend. He was buried in honour at Westminster Abbey next to Sir Isaac Newton. The most important, original and far-seeing part of his theory – the mechanism of natural selection – however, was still highly controversial, and it was only in the 1930s that it received the full recognition it deserved, so forming the basis of modern biology and forever changing humanity's view of itself.

course en route to Peru in 1535. He and his men spent a desperate week on the islands, having to chew cactus pads for their water, before the winds picked up so they could set sail again. Afterwards, he wrote about how water from a well they had dug "came out water saltier than that of the sea" and remarked that the earth was "like dross, worthless" and that the birds were "so silly that they do not know how to flee". He also noted the islands' "many seals, turtles, iguanas, tortoises", references picked up by a Flemish cartographer, **Abraham Ortelius**, who named the islands "Galápagos" (Spanish for "tortoises") on his map of 1574, *Orbis Terrarum*. The islands' other name at that time, Las

Encantadas ("enchanted" or "bewitched"), came from the strong currents and swaths of deep mist that made landing here so difficult, as if the shore itself was being moved by unearthly powers.

Pirates

Their reputation for being haunted made the Galápagos a perfect base for a number of seventeenth- and eighteenth-century **English pirates**, who came to the Pacific to pick off merchant ships as they sailed along the mainland coast. Among the most notorious was **John Cook**, who captured a Danish slave ship and renamed it the *Bachelor's Delight* after sixty slave-girls were found in the hold, before using it to take three merchant ships off the coast of Peru in 1684. He then hid out in the Galápagos, only to discover he had a disappointing booty of thousands of sacks of flour and "eight tons of quince marmalade". Among his crew was **William Dampier**, who wrote the first comprehensive description of the islands in *A New Voyage Round the World* and **William Ambrose Cowley**, the first man to chart the islands, naming them after English notables. In 1709, **Alexander Selkirk**, the inspiration for Daniel Defoe's novel *Robinson Crusoe*, also turned up here after he was rescued from the Juan Fernández Archipelago off the coast of Chile by the English privateer, **Woodes Rogers**. After four years of being a castaway, Selkirk still had enough energy to help Rogers sack Guayaquil before sailing to the Galápagos to make repairs and stock up on tortoises – a prized provision, as they can stay alive for up to a year without food or water, providing a good source of fresh meat during long sea voyages.

Whalers

The buccaneers' secret base became well known, however, after **James Colnett**'s expedition on the HMS *Rattler*, in 1793, revealed the Galápagos to be a convenient base for **whalers** to career their boats and obtain provisions. Sperm whales were then one of the major sources of oil, a growing necessity in early industrial Britain, and the cold currents around the Galápagos guaranteed they would be around in numbers. The whalers not only caused incalculable damage to the whale populations, but also decimated the Galápagos tortoise population as they provisioned their vessels with the creatures. Each ship may have taken as many as 600 of the creatures before setting sail – an estimated total of around 200,000 tortoises were taken during the whaling era, bringing giant tortoise subspecies to extinction on Floreana, Rábida and Santa Fé islands. In the late nineteenth century, almost every whaling ship in the Pacific called at the islands to stock up, and one of them, the *Acushnet*, carried the most famous whaler of them all, **Herman Melville**. He related his experiences in *Las Encantadas*, a book describing the islands as "five-and-twenty heaps of cinders" where "the chief sound of life…is a hiss".

The first settlers

The islands' first documented **settler** was an Irishman, **Patrick Watkins**, who demanded to be put ashore on Floreana in the early nineteenth century after quarrelling with his captain. Despite making a shelter and cultivating vegetables to sell to passing whalers, his ferocious appearance – matted red beard, blistered sunburnt skin and ragged clothes "covered with vermin" – was "so wild and savage . . . that he struck everyone with horror". Sailors assumed he spent all his time drinking rum, but, in truth, he was hatching a plot to get off the islands, as no captain would take him. After two years, he managed to steal a ship, abduct four people to crew it, then sailed to Guayaquil, arriving ominously alone. Mainland life clearly wasn't for him, however, and he was imprisoned in Peru, on suspicion of wanting to steal another boat to take him back to the Galápagos.

Shortly after Ecuador's liberation, **General José Villamil** decided in 1832 to claim the archipelago for the new republic. He gave the islands Spanish names and immediately set about colonizing Floreana with eighty soldiers condemned for mutiny whose death sentences had been commuted for a life of hard labour in the Galápagos. His idea was to start a trade in orchilla moss, used to make a deep-red dye, but the business never took off, and to add to his troubles, the government kept deporting hundreds of unruly criminals and prostitutes to the colony from the mainland. Eventually Villamil gave up and was replaced by the brutal **Colonel José Williams**, who, despite keeping a large pack of ferocious dogs for protection, was chased off the islands after a revolt from the colonists. By 1852 the colony had been abandoned, so setting a long-standing precedent of failure. The infamous **Manuel Cobos** (see p.491) came to a sticky end after a tyrannous rule over a settlement on San Cristóbal, and the entrepreneur, **José de Valdizán**, was murdered in 1878 after a futile eight-year attempt to revive Villamil's colony on Floreana. **Antonio Gil** made a third attempt at the place in 1893, but after four years moved operations to Isabela, founding Puerto Villamil, where he and his group eked out a living ferrying sulphur from a nearby crater to Guayaquil.

Scientists

While colonists were having a hard time of it on the islands, **scientists** were visiting in droves, largely thanks to the enormous publicity that **Charles Darwin**'s 1835 voyage on the HMS *Beagle* had generated (see box on p.460). Over the next century, there were countless other scientific expeditions here from all around the world, though in the race to build up wildlife collections for museums, they often contributed to the damage wreaked by the whalers and settlers. In some instances, expeditions claimed that a species was on the verge of extinction, so justifying the removal of the last few specimens they could find – only for future expeditions to do the same with any survivors. The 1905 voyage of the *Academy*, under **Rollo Beck**, gathered up the largest of all collections, taking over 8500 bird specimens and 266 giant tortoises, including 86 from Isla Pinzón – from where four previous expeditions each believed they had taken the last surviving specimens – and one from Fernandina, the only tortoise ever recorded on this island.

The twentieth century, tourism and immigration

In the early **twentieth century**, European colonists began appearing on the islands, the most extraordinary of whom were three groups of Germans – the Wittmers, the Ritters, and a mad baroness plus lovers, protagonists of the so-called **Galápagos affair**, a mysterious sequence of events ending in several deaths (see box on p.499). During this period, international powers were starting to regard the islands as a place of considerable strategic importance, especially as a base from which to guard the entrance to the **Panama Canal**. When the canal was completed in 1914, a bidding war over the islands had already begun between several interested countries, including the US, Britain and France. However tempting the US's $15 million offer in 1911 for a 99-year lease was, Ecuador stuck firm – by this time the islands were a considerable source of national pride. After the Japanese attack on Pearl Harbor in 1941, however, it was clear that the Panama Canal would need protection, and the Ecuadorian government gave the US permission to use Baltra as an air base. After World

No species has done more to upset the delicately balanced ecosystem of the Galápagos than humans. In one study of thousands of fossil bones, it was found that nearly every extinction of native species began with and followed the arrival of Tomás de Berlanga, the first recorded visitor, in 1535 (see p.460). From that point onwards, the hunting of tortoises, fish, whales, fur seals and other animals through-out the centuries brought populations to the brink of extinction. Although man's depredation of native species within the park has ceased, and fishing in the waters of the marine reserve is now strictly controlled, a human presence on the islands will always require a concerted conservation effort to counter its impact.

The introduction of foreign species

By far the worst human legacy on the islands has been the catastrophic **introduction of alien species**. When settlers arrived they brought with them domestic and farm animals, and plants that soon went wild, overrunning the islands and out-competing native species. **Pigs** trample vegetation, snaffle up land bird hatchlings and young tortoises and devour turtle eggs. Packs of feral **dogs** have attacked land iguanas, killing hundreds at a time on Santa Cruz and Isabela, while **black rats** are thought to be responsible for the extinction of endemic rice rats on four islands, and have killed every tortoise hatchling on Pinzón for most of the twentieth century. Wild **goats**, though, are regarded as the biggest threat, denuding entire islands of vegetation, causing plant species to become extinct as well as depriving native species, particularly tortoises, of food, and encouraging soil erosion. New insects, such as two species of **wasp**, are eating indigenous butterfly and moth larvae, while the introduced **little fire ant**, only 2mm long and easy to unwittingly transport to new islands, is destroying native ant species and attacking tortoise hatchlings as well as being a serious pest to humans. Introduced plants are also a major threat, disrupting the food chain from the bottom up. Agricultural species such as **guava**, **blackberry**, **red quinine** and **elephant grass** are out of control on several islands, squeezing out native plants such as tree ferns, scalesia, guayabillo, cat's claw and others.

The Galápagos National Park Service and the Charles Darwin Research Station have been following a three-pronged approach to the problem of introduced species. In some cases, **eradication programmes** have done enough to allow threatened native species to recover. Feral pigs have been eradicated from Santiago, and goats have been eliminated from five of the islands and islets, while their numbers on Pinta have been brought down from over 40,000 to around a hundred. On Isabela, trained dogs kitted with leather boots to protect their paws from the lava surface are being used to track them down; captured goats – the so-called "Judas goats" – are radio-collared and released, eventually leading hunters back to the herd. The second vital strand of the conservation effort are **repopulation programmes**, such as the giant tortoises gathered, incubated, hatched and raised at the CDRS until large enough to survive predatory attacks, before being repatriated. On Española, where tortoises once numbered just twelve, the thousandth of this unique subspecies was success-fully repatriated in 2000. Land iguanas and rice rats have undergone the same treatment, with similar results. Finally, a **quarantine system** has been set up in relevant ports and airports with inspectors to check incoming cargoes for alien pests and seeds, not to mention the usual stowaway frogs and rats.

Illegal fishing

In recent years, one of the most fiercely fought conservation issues has revolved around **illegal fishing** within the Reserva Marina de Galápagos. In 1998, the **Special Law for the Galápagos** extended the reserve and allowed only tourism and con-trolled "local artisanal fishing" within it, as well as several other important and far-reaching regulations such as curbing immigration to the islands. However, the law did not go down well with the fishing industry and every year the tensions between local fishermen and the park authorities flare up over the harvesting of **sea cucumbers**, a delicacy in the lucrative Asian market. A limited season and quotas have been imposed after years of overfishing, and even though the measures are widely believed to be inadequate to reverse the sharp decline in numbers they have still led to violent protests from local fishermen. Other serious threats to conservation come from unauthorized international fleets fishing in the protected waters, some of them "**long-lining**", a type of indiscriminate fishing responsible for killing large numbers of seabirds as well as unwanted fish. The Ecuadorian Navy and park wardens regularly detain illegal fishing boats, occasionally finding hundreds of **shark fins** (used in shark-fin soup) on board; the non-commercial part of the catch, namely sea lions, turtles, dolphins, pelicans, boobies, and the shark carcasses themselves, are simply dumped at sea.

Tourism

The Galápagos **tourism** industry, which injects over $100 million into the Ecuadorian economy, dwarfs the financial output of both the local agriculture and fishing industries. Even though tourist numbers rise each year, the industry, which has a clear interest in conserving the islands, is very well regulated. Limited visitor sites, defined trails and accredited guides have all kept detrimental impacts to a working minimum.

However, while tourism has generally been a positive influence, it is not entirely above reproach either. The money brought to the islands through the industry means that employment opportunities and salaries are far better than on the mainland, stimulating immigration, which in turn puts pressure on the islands' stretched resources, while the greater influx of goods and people increases the likelihood of introducing more harmful species. The delivery of fuel to cruise boats (as well as to other island services) also raises an ever-present risk, as demonstrated when a small **oil** tanker ran aground in Wreck Bay off San Cristóbal in 2001, spilling many thousands of gallons of diesel and bunker fuel. There could have been a major environmental catastrophe were it not for strong currents which drew much of the oil offshore – though around 15,000 marine iguanas on Santa Fé seem to have died as a result of contamination.

Many tour operators make regular contributions to the conservation effort to offset the detrimental effects of tourism, but even so, the Charles Darwin Foundation claims that only five percent of its entire budget is generated through the industry. In order to achieve its objectives, the foundation claims it needs to double its annual budget of $1.5 million.

Friends of Galápagos

The best thing you can do as a visitor is to join the **Friends of Galápagos**, a network of international conservation organizations based in Europe and the United States. Membership largely consists of previous visitors, who, in return for an annual donation, receive detailed news bulletins about the islands, ongoing conservation work, and information on events and appeals. They provide vital funding for the Charles Darwin Research Station and the Galápagos National Park Service, which are at the centre of island conservation, and encourage the government to safeguard the islands' future. In the UK, contact the Galápagos Conservation Trust, 5 Derby St, London W1J 7AB (℡020/7629 5049, ⓦwww.gct.org); in the US, get in touch with the Charles Darwin Foundation Inc, 407 North Washington St, Suite 105, Falls Church, VA 22046 (℡703/538-6833, ⓦwww.galapagos.org); or in the islands you can join at the CDRS in Puerto Ayora.

War II, the Americans returned the base, and the runway there remains one of the island's main points of access.

When regular flights began in the late 1960s, organized tourism grew at a phenomenal rate to reach annual visitor figures of around 65,000 today. The industry's success also encouraged immigration to the islands: in the 1950s, there were a little over 1000 inhabitants, while now there's a population of over 16,000. The pressure this is putting on already stretched resources led the government to pass a law in 1998 to stem the flow, as further increases in numbers will inevitably lead to compromises in the islands' conservation; see box on p.464 for more on local conservation.

Geography and geology

The thirteen large islands (more than 10 square kilometres in area) and over forty small islands, islets and rocks (many of them unnamed) that make up the **Galápagos Archipelago** cluster around the equator some 960km west of mainland Ecuador. The total land area of the archipelago is 7882 square kilometres, well over half of which is taken up by Isabela, the largest island, consisting of six separate volcanoes joined together by lava. Isabela also has the highest point on the archipelago, Volcán Wolf, at 1707m, bisected exactly by the **equator** line.

The origins of the islands

The archipelago is purely **volcanic** in origin, and remains one of the most volatile such regions on the planet; the most recent eruption was Volcán Cerro Azul on Isabela in 1998. Unlike most of the world's volcanic areas, however, the islands don't lie on the borders of two tectonic plates (slowly moving portions of the Earth's crust floating on a layer of magma), a fact that has puzzled scientists. The **hot spot theory** offers the most plausible explanation for this, whereby a fixed area of extraordinary heat in the magma occasionally bubbles up to form a volcano. The archipelago sits on the **Nazca plate**, which is moving eastwards and downwards to South America at a rate of 3.4cm a year: as the plate shifts, so the volcano comes off the hot spot, becomes extinct, and is eventually eroded by the elements and submerged beneath the sea. Meanwhile, new volcanoes appear over the hot spot. This would explain why the most easterly islands are the oldest and most weathered; San Cristóbal is thought to be between 2.3 and 6.3 million years old. In the west, Isabela and Fernandina are thought to have come into being less than 700,000 years ago, and are the most active and clearly volcanic islands. Two chains of extinct and eroded underwater mountains and volcanoes – the Cocos and Carnegie ridges, which extend for hundreds of kilometres northeast and east respectively of the Galápagos – are evidence that the hot spot has been working for many tens of millions of years.

Volcanic formations

The beautiful **volcanic formations** you'll see on the islands are often quite different from those found on the mainland. This is due to their **basaltic lava**, which, rather than producing high cones, such as Cotopaxi, makes **shield-shaped volcanoes**, such as the one at Fernandina. The broad tops of these can collapse into empty magma chambers below, leaving enormous **calderas**, huge depressions many times the size of the original vents, or **craters**, circular basins rimmed by lava walls at the volcano's summit: the Sierra Negra volcano on Isabela has a crater 10km across, one of the largest in the world. Like steam vents on the volcanoes, sulphur-encrusted **fumaroles** send puffs of gas into the air, as at Volcán Chico on the north side of Sierra Negra.

Much of the Galápagos landmass consists of **lava flows**, and you'll find two particularly interesting types on several islands. **Pahoehoe lava**, from the Hawaiian word meaning "ropy", describes the rippled effect caused when molten lava in contact with the air begins to solidify, but is then ruffled up by molten lava passing beneath it into tongue or rope-like shapes; Sulivan Bay, at Santiago, has excellent examples of this. **Aa lava**, named after the Hawaiian for "hurt", occurs when the surface of the lava flow buckles, breaks and then gets bulldozed by the continuing movement of the flow, resulting in layers of small, sharp rocks that can be very difficult to walk on. It can form a natural barrier to animals, as at the Perry Isthmus on Isabela, and castaways and buccaneers told of how this lava ripped the boots from their feet. If a lava flow hardens on the outside, and then the strength of the flow decreases, **lava tubes** are sometimes formed, and at Santa Cruz there are several large enough to walk down.

Cones of various sizes and types do frequently appear on the islands, from **hornitos** (less than 1m high), resembling burst pimples solidified on a lava bed, to the larger **spatter cones** that give Bartolomé its spectacular lunar landscape, or the impressive **tuff cones**, often made up of stripy layers of rock-hard compacted ash. The **uplift** at Urbina Bay, on Isabela, is one of the more startling products of tectonic activity; in 1954, a five-kilometre stretch of reef was shunted 4m into the air by movements of magma beneath the crust, leaving its marine inhabitants drying in the sun. Islands such as the Plazas and Baltra are entirely the result of uplift.

Visiting the Galápagos

High air fares and a heavy park-entrance tax for foreigners mean that just getting to the Galápagos is a relatively pricey undertaking, and that's before stumping up for a **boat tour** or specialist scuba **diving tour**. Such tours, which last anything from three days up to several weeks and vary greatly in levels of quality and price, are undoubtedly the best way to see the islands. Many people prearrange tours at home – the most expensive but hassle-free way to organize one – but **budget travellers** can cut costs by doing so in Quito and Guayaquil, or even waiting until their arrival in the Galápagos before choosing an operator. The tours sail between **visitor sites** – usually two a day – most having tidy paths bordered by little black-and-white stakes, which you'll be led around by an accredited guide. Most cruises combine a variety of sites, with different endemic animals and plants popping up at each. However, the popularity of the Galápagos does mean that even on longer tours to remoter islands, you'll probably be sharing the sites with several other groups. Where boat tours mostly sail between islands by night, **land-based tours** are also available, in which you sleep ashore and sail to nearby visitor sites in the day.

An alternative to a cruise is **independent travel** around the Galápagos, made possible by using **inter-island flights and ferries**, though these largely restrict you to the colonized areas, and this rather misses the point of a trip here. There are, however, a few visitor sites close to the main settlements that you can reach under your own steam without a licensed guide. In addition to these, you can also strike out on **day-trips** from the larger towns, namely Puerto Ayora and to a lesser extent Puerto Baquerizo Moreno, to a handful of sites around the central islands.

Costs, money and banks: Galápagos prices are higher than on the mainland, and you'll also have to pay at least ten percent extra on credit-card transactions here, so take plenty of cash. Note also that only MasterCard is accepted at the banks and at many hotels.

Clothing: For daytime clothing, you'll be fine in shorts, a T-shirt, a hat and sunglasses; in the evenings, sea breezes make trousers and a long-sleeved top necessary. A lightweight raincoat is adequate for the odd rain shower and garúa drizzle. You'll need sturdy boots or shoes for the jagged lava wastes and sandals for the beaches.

Health supplies: Take plenty of sun screen and a water bottle, and during the wet season or if visiting the highlands, insect repellent. If you wear contact lenses, you may need eye drops as the islands can also be hot, windy and dusty. On board, ear plugs will help block out the engine noise of your tour boat at night, while seasickness tablets, or patches, are a must for sufferers.

Snorkelling and diving: If you're planning on swimming with marine wildlife, your snorkelling gear should include a mask, snorkel and fins, as they may not be supplied by your tour operator or may not fit if they are. You can also rent snorkelling equipment at several places in Puerto Ayora (see p.481). From July to December a wet suit or jacket is a good idea for the cold water. If you're going scuba diving and have your own equipment, bring as much of it along as is practical.

Additional items: Most of the time you'll be watching wildlife from close quarters, but occasionally binoculars are essential. Your camera equipment should include a zoom or telephoto lens and a polarizing filter to prevent colours from being bleached by the fierce sun; remember, too, to bring something to protect your camera from sea spray and rain. A torch (flashlight) comes in handy for visiting lava tunnels, or for the remoter settlements, which don't have 24-hour electricity.

By far the most expensive way to see the islands is to sail in on **your own boat** for which you'll have to pay an extra $200 marine tax on top of the normal park entry fee. Then you'll need to contact the Parque Nacional Galápagos offices in Puerto Ayora to hire your own guide, and once you've agreed on an itinerary with them, they'll charge you $200 per person per day for everyone on board, whether guest, guide, captain or crew. You'll be allowed to stay in the islands for a maximum of twenty days and you need to contact the Capitanía in Puerto Ayora when you arrive.

Getting to the Galápagos

All **flights** to the Galápagos (a 3hr trip in total) depart from Quito and stop over in Guayaquil for around forty minutes, where passengers on board usually have to disembark, then reboard with people picking up the flight at Guayaquil. As seats cannot be reserved, there's usually a scramble for window seats at both embarkation points. Tame fly twice daily to Baltra, a bus ride from Puerto Ayora on Santa Cruz; and on Monday, Wednesday and Saturday to Puerto Baquerizo Moreno on San Cristóbal. Wherever you fly into, **prices** are fixed at $389 return from Quito and $374 from Guayaquil, with low-season and student (with an ISIC card) discounts at $334 from Quito and $294 from Guayaquil. Should you need to, you can switch between Galápagos airports on your ticket for free, though not if you have a discounted ticket. You can also fly from Quito and return to Guayaquil (or vice versa) for $367 in the high season or $317 in the low season. In high season it can be particularly difficult to get a place, so make sure you're not being put on the waiting list. Note that you should reconfirm inward and outward flights two days in advance and that the **luggage allowance** is 20kg. It is prohibited for **cargo boats** from Guayaquil and the mainland to take tourists to the Galápagos.

On arrival in the Galápagos you have to pay a $100 **park entrance fee** in cash at the airport. **Discounts** for foreigners only apply for under-12s ($50), under-2s (no charge), citizens of Andean Community or Mercosur countries ($50), and those holding a visa and *censo* ($25). Your **passport** will be stamped and you'll be given a **receipt**; hold onto it as your boat operator will need it, even if you're just doing day-trips.

Having flown in from the mainland, those with a pre-booked cruise – the majority of tourists on most flights – will be given free transfer to their boat. If arriving in Baltra, your boat will either be waiting at the island's dock nearby, or at Puerto Ayora on Santa Cruz, a short hop by ferry from Baltra over the Canal de Itabaca to a connecting bus on the other side (45min). In Puerto Baquerizo Moreno, San Cristóbal, buses will take you in a few minutes to the harbour. For more information on airport arrival, see p.478 for Baltra and p.488 for Puerto Baquerizo Moreno.

Galápagos cruises

Almost a hundred **boats** currently have licences to tour the Galápagos, divided into several categories of comfort and ranging from converted fishing boats for a handful of people to luxury cruisers for a hundred. The majority carry between ten and twenty passengers, and almost all boats rely on engine power to get them between islands, although several boost their speed with sails.

Boats and costs

Economy boats can cost as little as $60 per person per day in the low season or around $85 in the high season. Many of these boats are poky, and often have tiny bunk-bed cabins, shared bath, uninspiring food, and Class-I guides, who are Galápagos locals with the lowest level of naturalist training and a fair amount of English. If the weather's bad, these are the boats that suffer most from rocking and rolling. **Tourist boats** (around $100 to $150 per person per day) should be a bit more spacious with slightly better facilities and Class-II guides, Ecuadorians with good education, often in related fields, who can speak English, and French or German, fluently. **Tourist-superior boats** (from around $150 to over $300 per day) usually have more comfortable cabins still, sometimes with air conditioning, better food and Class-III guides, the highest level of accreditation, who have degrees in biology, tourism or similar, and can speak fluent Spanish and English plus French or German. Many of the boats in the Galápagos are **first-class**, or **luxury boats**, enjoying the best food, service, comfort and guides, who are always Class-III and invariably very highly qualified naturalists. Cabins typically have beds rather than bunks, private bath with hot water and air conditioning. They also tend to be faster – meaning less time on the move, and often more time on the remoter islands – and a few have stabilizers to lessen the effects of rough seas. While the largest boats tend to have extra facilities, such as a pool, bear in mind that they take longer to disembark, giving you less time on shore. Tours on first-class and luxury boats are most often arranged in your home country (see "Basics", pp.13, 15 & 16 for details of specialist operators); for an eight-day cruise, costs start at around $1500 and can rise to over $3500 excluding flights and entrance fees.

This list is not comprehensive but gives a good selection of boat owners themselves rather than general operators, who can make bookings on boats from a range of companies but will often charge an extra commission. Prices listed are for an eight-day cruise in high season, per person, based on two sharing a cabin, and agencies with offices in the Galápagos are listed under the relevant island. A good general operator is the Galápagos Boat Company, Calama 380 and Juan León Mera in Quito (T02/2552505, F2223381), who can arrange tours on most boats, keep customer reports on good and bad boats, and can give help in finding you a last-minute deal – you will, though, have to pay a $45 commission if you book through them.

Aida Maria Travel Reina Victoria 1439 and Colón T02/2557331, W www .galapagostours.net. One of the less expensive operators, with a fleet of four motor yachts ranging from tourist class to first class. From $680.

Andando Tours Av Coruña N26-311 and Orellana T02/2550952, F2228519, W www.angermeyercruises.com. Andando is owned by a branch of the Angermeyer family, who came to the Galápagos in the 1930s. They have three good-looking first-class sailing yachts (*Sea Cloud*, *Sagitta* and *Heritage*) and also represent the owners of *Samba* and *The Beagle*. From $1500.

Ecoventura Almagro N31-80, Edificio Venecia T02/22906898 or in the US or Canada T1800/6337972, W www.ecoventura.com. Operate three first-class motor yachts, *Eric*, *Flamingo I* and a specialist diving boat, *Sky Dancer*. From $2195.

Enchanted Expeditions Foch 726 and Amazonas T02/2569960, F2569956, W www.enchantedexpeditions.com. A reliable and recommended operator running the luxury *Beluga* motor yacht and the first-class *Cachalote I*, an attractive 96-foot schooner for sixteen people. A good standard of service and guiding is complemented by some excellent cooking. Anna Fitter represents them in the UK (T01243/379953). From $1515.

Galasam cnr of Cordero 1354 and Amazonas, Quito T02/2903851 or 2507080, F2567662, W www.galasam.com; and Edificio Gran Pasaje, Av 9 de Ocutubre 424, Guayaquil T04/2304488, F2311485. Galasam has five boats covering a range of classes. They have a reputation for inexpensive tours, particularly if you book in

Note that if you're travelling alone, you may be asked to pay a hefty **supplement** for your cabin, unless you're prepared to share. Other hidden costs include alcohol, rarely included in the price, and the **tip** at the end of the tour for the guide and crew – this will depend on the service you've received and what you can afford, but as a general rule, an economy guide and crew will each expect around $25 per cabin per week, while luxury boats suggest as much as $100 per person per week for the crew and $40 per person per week for the guide. If you can give the tip directly to the deserving, so much the better, as this avoids the possibility of unfair distribution of a general tip by an unscrupulous captain or guide.

Things to check

Before you plump for a tour, inspect the **itinerary** and make sure it takes in islands with the creatures you want to see; an eight-day tour is long enough for a good overview of the islands. To give you as much time at the sites as possible, don't pick tours that include more than a night in a single port, those that sail during the day, and too many sites that you can visit independently without out a guide anyway. On the lower-end tours in particular, you should check exactly what you're getting: ask about what **food** you can expect (especially if

Puerto Ayora, but quality on the cheaper boats (*Yolita*, *Darwin* and *Antardita*) can vary greatly. From $935 on the mainland.

Kem Pery Joaquín Pinto 539 and Amazonas ℡02/2226583, ℻2226715, ⓦwww.kempery.com. Own *Angelique*, a tourist-superior motor-sailer with capacity for sixteen people, which has a good reputation for inexpensive four-, five- or eight-day cruises. Special deals can be arranged combining a Galápagos trip with a stay at their jungle lodge in the Huaorani reserve (see p.288). From $900.

Klein Tours Av Eloy Alfaro N34-151 and Catalina Aldaz ℡02/2267000, ℻2442389, ⓦwww.kleintours.com. Long-standing operator with two mid-sized first-class boats, *Coral I* and *Coral II*, as well as the luxury ninety-person cruiser, *Galápagos Legend*. From $1750.

Metropolitan Touring Av República de El Salvador N36-84 and Naciones Unidas ℡02/2464780, ℻2464702, ⓦwww.metropolitan-touring.com. One of the pioneers of tourism in the Galápagos, Metropolitan operates two large first-class boats, the ninety-person *Santa Cruz* and the forty-person *Isabela II*. They also offer shore-based tours of the islands from their luxury hotel *Finch Bay* on Santa Cruz. From $2215.

Quasar Nautica Brasil 293 and Granda Centeno, Edificio IACA, 2nd floor ℡02/2446996, ℻2254305, ⓦwww.quasarnautica.com. A well-respected company offering top-level Galápagos tours on six first-class and luxury yachts. Guiding, service and accommodation are excellent, and the boats *Alta*, *Parranda* and *Eclipse* are among the most comfortable in the islands (from $2660). Their less expensive boats, *Mistral* and *Diamante*, are still very well appointed (from $2100), while specialist diving cruises are offered on the exquisite trimaran *Lammer Law* (from $2750). Combined tours of the mainland through their sister company Amerindia (see p.112) are also available. Their UK representative is Penelope Kellie (see "Basics", p.14).

Rolf Wittmer Turismo Galápagos Foch E7-81 and Diego de Almagro ℡02/2563098, ℻2228520, ⓦwww.rwittmer.com. Rolf Wittmer is credited with being the first recorded native of Floreana island, the son of the famous pioneering Wittmer family (see p.499). He owns two first-class motor yachts, *Tip Top II* and *Tip Top III*, each with capacity for sixteen people. From $1680.

you're vegetarian); whether there are **masks and snorkels** for all the passengers; if the **guide** speaks decent English; how much will you see on the first and last days; how many nights will be spent ashore; what the bathrooms and cabins are like; whether you'll have to share with strangers; and whether the boat will sail at night. Some **eight-day tours** are actually a combination of a four- and a five-day tour (with the swap-over day counting twice), which can waste time while new passengers are picked up. Most importantly, make sure that your boat has adequate **safety equipment**, such as life jackets, rafts and fire extinguishers. Following worries about safety standards on tour boats, the Ecuadorian government stipulated in 2000 that boats carrying more than fifteen passengers be required to hold an ISM (International Safety Management) certificate, which should be available for you to inspect on request.

Budget deals

While cruising the Galápagos Islands is not an activity well geared to **budget** travellers, it is possible to minimize costs by getting a **last-minute deal**. Checking out the tour operators based in the Amazonas area in Quito is a good place to start, with the cheapest deals almost always found via companies that own their own boats. You'll get the best prices, however, if you book at

Puerto Ayora in the Galápagos, where you'll be on the spot when the deals come up, and have the advantage of both meeting the guide and checking out the boat in advance; the downside is that you could be waiting for several days for a space, so give yourself plenty of time to sort it out. For a typical eight-day tour on an economy boat count on paying $480–600 in low season, and a couple of hundred dollars more in the high season. Before you pay, ask about unexpected costs that can be associated with economy boats: for example, some don't have a water-maker, and may charge for bottled water, or supply town tap water, which needs purification. Less satisfactory options to cut costs are tours of four or five days, offered by many operators, or doing day-trips (see opposite), but these obviously won't give you the fullest picture of the islands.

The daily routine

Save for the most basic boats, life aboard a ship is relaxed and well organized. After an early breakfast, you'll set out in a dinghy (*panga*) for the visitor site, negotiating either a **wet landing** (wading ashore on a beach) or **dry landing** (on rocks or a dock) on arrival. After three or four hours on the island, you'll return to the boat for lunch and a siesta before another visit in the afternoon; most days, there'll be a chance to have a swim or a snorkel. The boat usually sets sail for the next site after dinner, arriving early next morning: you may find the engine noise and rocking of the boat annoying on the first night, but even those without sea legs tend to get used to it.

Problems

The great majority of tours pass without incident, but occasionally **problems** occur. Generally speaking, economy boats are the worst offenders, and things that can go wrong include overbooking, petty theft, annoying engine noise and smells, food and water supplies running out, changes of itinerary, breakdowns, and sexual harassment from guide or crew. One trick of operators is to swap boats at the last moment, so that your tourist-superior boat has suddenly become a rickety old bucket; your contract should stipulate a refund if the category of boat changes. Even if the operator breaches the contract, getting a reimbursement can be hard work: if you feel wronged, report the operator to the Ministerio de Turismo and Capturgal (see p.478), who may be able to impose a fine on the operator and get you a **reimbursement**, and the Capitanía in Puerto Ayora. You can also tell the SAE in Quito (see p.80), which keeps a file of good and bad operators. In rare cases irresponsible guides have disobeyed park rules, perhaps erring from the path, touching animals, bringing food onto the islands, disturbing nests, or encouraging the crew to fish for food (an illegal activity). This kind of behaviour should be reported to the Galápagos National Park Service.

Scuba diving trips and tours

The Galápagos Islands are one of the best **scuba diving** spots in the world. Marine turtles, schools of hammerhead sharks, sea lions and fur seals, rays and eels, marine iguanas, sailfish, tuna, wahoo, barracudas, dolphins, even boobies are among the creatures you might see. The downside is that diving here isn't easy and at times you'll have to contend with strong currents, surge, low visibility and cold water. With this in mind, the islands are not considered a suitable place to learn to scuba dive from scratch, even though training courses are offered. There is a hyperbaric recompression chamber in Puerto Ayora (see p.482), which is better than any facility on the mainland and is funded by a $35 fee to tourist divers; remember that you should give your body time to adjust between diving and flying back to Quito.

Several companies organize **day-trip dives** from Puerto Ayora to a variety of sites for $80–120, including all equipment and a guide (see p.482 for details). These can be arranged with only a day's notice but are restricted to sites within range of port. There are plenty of such sites to choose from, however, including the reefs around Seymour Norte or Campeón near Floreana to wall dives at Daphne Minor or the Gordon Rocks near the Plazas. Less experienced divers will probably be asked to spend a couple of days diving at Academy Bay, where conditions are easier. **Diving-boat tours** cruise the islands, mixing one to four dives per day with land visits, and you may even get to dive around islands such as Wolf and Darwin, where land visits are prohibited. On such tours, you'll need to be an experienced diver with a certificate, and to bring most of your own equipment, usually with the exception of tanks (and air), weights and weight belts; in the cool season, your wet suit should be 6mm thick. Prices for eight-day diving tours start at around $1300 and rise to $3000 or more, depending on the level of luxury and standard of guiding: reservations should be made well in advance. Quasar Nautica (see box, p.471) is a reputable company with two fully equipped diving yachts, with low-season prices starting at $1785, but several other firms offer diving tours, including operators in Puerto Ayora (see "Listings" p.482).

Day-trips and land-based tours

An inexpensive way to see the islands is to arrange **day-trips**, especially from Puerto Ayora. Costing around $60 per person, these usually include a guide of varying quality, lunch and a visit to one island. They're easy to organize as they're offered by many of the travel agencies in town, though you'll be limited to a handful of islands within striking distance of the port, namely Plaza Sur, Seymour Norte, Santa Fé and Floreana (if the boat leaves from Baltra, you may get to visit Bartolomé also). Some operators also offer **land-based** tours, in which you sleep at night on shore, and sail out to nearby visitor sites during the day – effectively a string of day-trips packaged together as a multi-day Galápagos tour. While this has the advantage of comfortable hotel accommodation and is usually less expensive than a conventional cruise (depending on the level of hotel used), the disadvantages are that sailing in the day makes for less time at the visitor sites and you'll be restricted to the busiest sites nearest to the population centres.

Independent travel between the islands

Independent travel between the islands will confine you to colonized areas and visitor sites close to towns that you can visit without a guide. By far the most efficient means of inter-island travel is by **flying** with EMETEBE (☎ & ℱ 05/526177; see relevant town accounts for details). Their nine-seater light aircraft flies from San Cristóbal to Baltra and then to Isabela, Monday to Saturday, returning by the same route on the same day ($120 one-way, $210 return; each leg around 30min). Planes will fly only if there's sufficient demand, and it's a good idea to buy your ticket at least two days in advance. The luggage allowance is just 13.5kg (30lbs), and the penalty for excess loads is around $0.35 per kg ($0.15 per pound).

If you've got plenty of time, then you could try getting around on the fortnightly **ferry** (one-way $40) operated by the Instituto Nacional Galápagos, or INGALA (☎ 05/526199). The ferry runs from Puerto Ayora (Santa Cruz) to

PuertoVillamil (Isabela) every other Friday, returning on Sunday morning, and continuing in the afternoon to Puerto Baquerizo Moreno (San Cristóbal), from where it returns to Santa Cruz on Monday. If demand is high enough, it makes another run to San Cristóbal on Tuesday, returning on Thursday. Once a month (every other fortnight) on the trip back from Isabela to Santa Cruz (Sun), the ferry stops for a few hours at PuertoVelasco Ibarra (Floreana) before continuing to Santa Cruz. There's also the *Estrella del Mar*, a converted cargo boat fitted out with bus seats, which travels between Santa Cruz and Isabela once a week, but it's currently being renovated; enquire at the Capitanía in Puerto Ayora for the latest.

A more convenient option is to take one of several **fibras** (fibreglass motor-boats) that make daily trips between Puerto Ayora, Puerto Baquerizo Moreno and PuertoVillamil, and far less frequent runs to PuertoVelasco Ibarra (around $30). Piloted by local fishermen, these are faster and more frequent than the INGALA ferry, but the ride can be rough and uncomfortable, and there are no scheduled trips. Ask about outgoing boats at the Capitanía and local travel agents.

Isla Santa Cruz and around

The archipelago's centre and tourist hub, **SANTA CRUZ** is a conical island of just under 1000 square kilometres, whose luxuriant southeastern slopes are cloaked each year in garúa drizzle. Reaching an altitude of 864m, the island supports all the Galápagos vegetation zones (see p.548), from cactus-strewn **deserts** around the coast, to tangled scalesia and miconia **forests** wreathed in cloud in the highlands, and sodden grassy **pampas** at the summit. Many of its endemic plants, however, have become increasingly threatened by a number of introduced species.

Santa Cruz's central location and proximity to the airport on Baltra have conspired to make it the most heavily populated island in the Galápagos. Most of the islanders live in the archipelago's largest town, **Puerto Ayora**, which is also the nerve centre of the conservation programme, headquarters of both the **Charles Darwin Research Station** and the **Parque Nacional Galápagos**. Home to more boats, tour brokers, hotels and restaurants than anywhere else in the islands, Puerto Ayora is also the best place for budget travellers to find last-minute places on cruises. While waiting for an opening, they can make for a selection of nearby visitor sites without a guide, such as **Bahía Tortuga**, the **Chato Tortoise Reserve**, go on half- or full-day trips to highland sights, including several **lava tunnels**, or take day-trips by boat to the nearby islands in this central group, such as **Santa Fé**, **Plaza Sur** and **Seymour Norte**.

On the north side of Santa Cruz, there are a handful of worthwhile sites that can only be visited by boat tours and require guides. Occasionally, day-trips sail there, but more commonly, boats call at these spots having left the harbour at nearby Baltra. A typical first stop is at **Las Bachas** on the north side of Santa Cruz, named for the barges abandoned on the beach here by the US during World War II: their rusting skeletons still poke through the sand. It's a popular place for swimming, but also makes a good introduction to wildlife, with marine iguanas, hermit crabs, black-necked stilts, great blue herons and turtle nests – you may see turtle tracks from November to February – and flamingos tiptoeing around the saltwater lagoon behind the smaller beach. To the west is **Caleta Tortuga Negra**, a cove where Pacific green turtles (despite the cove's name) come to breed at the beginning of the warm-wet season. White-tipped reef sharks and rays can be spotted throughout the year, and the lagoon itself is fringed by mangroves, where herons and pelicans nest. On the northwestern tip of the island, the **Cerro Dragón** site consists of a gravel path winding up from flamingo lagoons to the top of the hill, passing land iguanas and their nests. Most have been repatriated since the extermination of feral dogs here in 1990. Heading further westwards, **Bahía Conway**, where a colony of five hundred land iguanas was killed in an attack by feral dogs in 1976, and **Bahía Ballena**, a one-time whaling post, are seldom visited.

Puerto Ayora and around

Lying around the azure inlets of Academy Bay's rocky shore, **PUERTO AYORA**, on the southern coast of Santa Cruz, was home to fewer than a couple of hundred people until the early 1970s. Now, laden with souvenir shops, travel agents, restaurants and hotels, the town supports a population of around 11,000 people who enjoy a standard of living that's higher than any other

Charles Darwin Research Station & Galápagos National Park Offices

RESTAURANTS & BARS
Capricho	B
La Garrapata	C
Limón y Café	D
Media Luna	A
El Rincón del Alma	G
Salvavidas	H
Tía Juanita	E
William	F

Scuba Iguana ❶

Galápagos Sub-Aqua

Pelican Bay

Moonrise Travel Agency

Banco del Pacífico ❻

La Panga Disco

TAME ❼

Police ❾

Academy Bay

Capitanía

Bus Ticket Office

EMETEBE

Church

★ Buses

Dock

ACCOMMODATION
Los Amigos	8
Castro	10
Estrella de Mar	7
Galápagos	1
Lobo de Mar	9
La Pelegrina	5
Pensión Gloria	4
Red Mangrove Inn	2
Silberstein	3
SolyMar	6

PUERTO AYORA

◀ Highlands & Baltra Airport

◀ Bahía Tortuga

province in the republic, giving the port a distinct aura of well-appreciated privilege. There's a relaxed atmosphere to the place, with tourists meandering down the waterfront in the daytime, browsing through shops stuffed with blue-footed booby T-shirts and carvings of giant tortoises, while fishermen work across the street in little **Pelican Bay**, building boats and sorting through their catches, watched by hungry pelicans. In the evenings locals play five-a-side soccer and volleyball outside the Capitanía, and as it gets darker, the restaurant lights cast a modest glow over the bay and the bars fill with locals, tourists and research scientists, a genial mix that ensures Puerto Ayora has the best **nightlife** of all towns in the Galápagos.

It's easy to find your way around the port. The main thoroughfare is named, predictably, **Avenida Charles Darwin**, and runs along the **waterfront**, from the municipal dock at its southern end to the **Charles Darwin Research Station** at its northern, the latter home to giant tortoise corrals and extensive exhibits on the natural history of the islands. Just about everything you'll need is on Darwin: hotels, restaurants, the bank, travel agents, bars, discos, information, plus a number of less indispensable souvenir shops. The town's other important road is **Avenida Padre Julio Herrera**, running inland from Darwin and the dock to become the main road to the highlands and the link to the airport on Baltra.

If you have some time in the port, there are several worthwhile local excursions, which don't require a guide. For a spot of peace and quiet, you can't do better than one of the local beaches, such as the glorious **Bahía Tortuga**, a short walk southwest of town through a cactus forest, or the **Playa de los Alemanes** and the nearby swimming hole, **Las Grietas**, reached by water taxi. The Santa Cruz highlands (see p.482) also hold a number of natural attractions, including lava tunnels, craters and a tortoise reserve, which can be visited on day tours through many local agencies.

Some history

The first record of human habitation in what is now Puerto Ayora was a group of shipwrecked sailors who had struggled here through cactus forests from the other side of the island. Luckily, they wrecked just a few months before the arrival of the *Academy* (sailing under the auspices of the California Academy of Sciences), which moored in the bay here in 1905, lending its name to it. The castaways kept themselves alive for six months drinking sea-lion blood, chewing unpalatable cactus pads and supping on the brackish water that collected in rock pools by the shore, before being rescued. Puerto Ayora itself was founded in the 1920s by a small group of Norwegians, lured to the Galápagos by ruthless promoters trading on the popularity of William Beebe's 1924 book, *Galápagos, World's End*, an account of his trip there with the New York Zoological Society. They promised the Norwegians – who gave away all their savings to go – a secret Eden where the "soil is so rich that 100,000 people could easily find homes", noting that gold and diamonds were probably around too. Under an agreement with the Ecuadorian government, they landed on Floreana, but within a few months of back-breaking work, some had died and many more given up. In 1926, others went to Academy Bay and built frame houses, a fish cannery and a wharf, so founding the port, and, for a time, things went uncharacteristically well until the cannery blew up, killing two and injuring several others. To rub salt into the wound, the government seized their boat and all their remaining equipment, claiming that they had not built the harbours, roads and schools as laid out in their previous agreement. By 1929, only three Norwegians were left on Santa Cruz, but through sheer guts and hard

△ Waved albatross, Isla Española

work, they built the foundations for the largest and richest city in the Galápagos.

Arrival and information

Flights arrive on the island of Baltra, from where municipal **buses** (no charge) take you either to the dock where your cruise boat will be waiting, or to the Canal de Itabaca, the narrow stretch of water between Baltra and Santa Cruz. Here a passenger **ferry** ($0.70) connects with more buses ($1.50) on the other side taking you over the highlands to Puerto Ayora, ending up on Avenida Charles Darwin. The buses only connect with incoming flights from the mainland, so at other times you'll have to get a **camioneta** or taxi to Puerto Ayora ($8–10). Once in town, **taxis** cost around $1 for most in-town destinations, and about $4 for a trip to Santa Rosa. **Water taxis**, yellow dinghies with blue awnings, are useful for trips across the bay, or for day-and-night runs between the shore and your tour boat ($0.50–1 per person).

In town, you're spoilt for choice as far as **information** goes. The traditional source, the Ministerio de Turismo on Avenida Charles Darwin, stocks simple **maps** of the islands and population centres for free. Next door, Capturgal (Camera Provincial de Turismo de Galápagos) sells large glossy maps of towns and islands for $2; these include the locations of all the boat operators' offices if you're set on seeing the islands by a particular vessel. The Charles Darwin Research Station (see opposite) can furnish you with all the nitty-gritty facts and figures of Galápagos wildlife and natural history, while the Capitanía, near the dock, keeps tabs on boat arrivals and departures.

Accommodation

Like everything in the Galápagos, the price of **accommodation** is higher than on the mainland. The thriftiest backpackers, however, should find something to suit them, and in the low season you may be able to bargain down to the rate nationals pay, though many hotels insist on one price throughout the year. The higher-end hotels can quickly fill up in the high season, so reserve rooms at these well in advance. Hot water is generally only available in such establishments.

Castro Los Colonos ⏻05/526508. Clean and comfortable rooms with private bath, a/c and hot water, along with a pleasant six-person dorm for $13 a head. Reduced rates available in the low season. ❻

Estrella de Mar 12 de Febrero ⏻05/526427. Overlooking the bay, this is a good choice for its attractive rooms (those with bay views cost extra), with private bath and hot water, and blue floors inlaid with red starfish and dotted with "Happy Hanukkah" foot mats. ❸–❹.

Finch Bay Punta Estrada, across the bay and reached by water taxi ⏻05/526297, ⓦwww.finchbayhotel.com. Recently remodelled luxury hotel in a private location surrounded by mangroves with its own large pool, open-air hot tub, beach access and excellent restaurant. The rooms are comfortable and have a/c and unlimited water as the hotel has its own desalinization plant along with garbage processing and recycling programmes. Tours can be arranged to nearby attractions. ❾

Galápagos Av Charles Darwin, near the entrance to the research station ⏻ & Ⓕ05/526330 or 526296, Ⓔhotelgps@pa.ga.pro.ec. A collection of comfortable bungalow cabins set in two hectares of gardens, each having a view of the bay and supplied with hot water. Home-grown, organic food is served in the spacious lounge and dining area, where there's a telescope for gazing out to sea. ❽

Pensión Gloria Av Charles Darwin, down the side street next to *Pizza Media Luna* (no phone). The cheapest place in town and fantastic value if you can get the room with lava walls, fireplace and eccentric cave-like bathroom. Most others are dreary pre-fab affairs, but all have private bath. You can use the kitchen and camp for a dollar or so in the garden too. ❷

Lobo de Mar 12 de Febrero and Av Charles Darwin ⏻05/526188, Ⓕ526569, ⓦwww .lobodemar.com.ec. Remodelled to include a courtyard, swimming pool and a range of rooms, some with gorgeous sea views, some with a/c and all with hot water. Internet and laundry services are available. ④–⑥

La Peregrina Av Charles Darwin and Indefatigable ☎ 05/526323. The price includes a tasty breakfast of fruit salad, bread, juice and coffee, but its four bedrooms, each with private bath (no hot water) and a/c, could do with a good cleaning. ③

Red Mangrove Inn Av Charles Darwin ☎ & ℻ 05/526564 ✉ www.redmangrove.com. At the water's edge amidst mangroves, this secluded bohemian hotel was designed and built by its artist owners and has many idiosyncratic flourishes. Rooms are bright and fresh with bay views and have hot water, and there's a whirlpool on the veranda. Day-trips, windsurfing, kayaking, horse riding and mountain biking can all be arranged. Breakfast included. ⑧–⑨

Residencial Los Amigos Av Charles Darwin and 12 de Febrero ☎ 05/526265. Popular, friendly and inexpensive place, where the cheapest rooms are upstairs, divided by thin plywood and mosquito screening (not the best sound insulators), and have shared bath and tepid water. Rooms downstairs come with private bath and better walls. ②

Royal Palm Km 18 vía Baltra ☎ 05/527409, ℻ 527408, Europe ☎ 0800/414741, US ☎ 1800/5286069, ✉ www.millenniumhotels.com. A luxury hotel set in an exclusive estate in the highlands with gorgeous views over the islands, featuring sumptuous accommodation in villas, studios and suites, all with hot tub, satellite television, Internet access, mini bar, CD and DVD players. Probably the most expensive hotel in the country, with doubles starting from $380 a night. ⑨

Silberstein Av Charles Darwin and Piqueros ☎ & ℻ 05/526277, ✉ hsilbers@interactive.net.ec. Once a well-known backpackers' hangout, the hotel now caters to rather more moneyed guests. The rooms are large and come with hot water (some with a/c), and there's a small swimming pool surrounded by a garden. ⑧

SolyMar Av Charles Darwin ☎ & ℻ 05/526281. The very nicest rooms here have private balconies overlooking the bay, where marine iguanas bask during the day, though all have private bath and hot water. Rooms over the street are smaller, darker and much cheaper. ④–⑥

Charles Darwin Research Station

Even though it is first and foremost a science and conservation facility, just about every tour of the islands sooner or later washes up at the **Charles Darwin Research Station**, twenty minutes' stroll from the town centre at the northern end of Avenida Charles Darwin. Past the **information booth** at the entrance, a path leads between some giant cacti to the **Van Straelen interpretation centre** (daily 7am–5pm; no charge), exhibiting information on geology, climate, conservation and many related aspects of Galápagos nature, including a seismograph that etches the islands' subterranean rumblings. A short video about the CDRS and the islands, introduced by a member of staff, can be seen on request (daily 8am–noon & 2–4pm), and details are available here about joining Galápagos conservation organizations. Walking on from the visitor centre, you'll come to the **tortoise-rearing pens**, where predator-proof enclosures hold batches of miniature giant tortoises divided by age; the creatures are best seen when the covers are off (Mon–Fri 7am–4pm). Since 1965, a programme of tortoise repopulation has been ongoing, with eggs being carefully extracted from the wild and incubated here. After two or three years the hatchlings graduate to larger enclosures with the kind of terrain they might find in the wild, and after four to six years, they are deemed to have grown to an uneatable size as far as predators are concerned, and repatriated to their home islands.

From the pens, a raised boardwalk weaves through the trees, scrub and cacti past the **tortoise corrals**, where you can see fully grown giant tortoises. The most famous resident is **Lonesome George** (*Solitario Jorge*), the last surviving tortoise of the Pinta island subspecies, thought to be around seventy years old with about eighty more years to look forward to. From 1906 until 1971, when George was found, it was thought that the Pinta tortoises were extinct; since then, however, the search has been on to find him a Pinta partner, with a $10,000 reward on offer. At the moment, George is paired up with a couple of females from Volcán Wolf on Isabela, though the unfortunate reptile has shown little interest in love. Recent research has suggested that tortoises from Española – another subspecies from the opposite side of the archipelago – may in fact be George's closest relatives, so he may get on better with them. He's quite a shy animal, and the best time to see him is when he's being fed, on Mondays, Wednesdays and Fridays at 9am.

At the end of the walkway sits an enclosure with half-a-dozen friendly tortoises, mostly former pets donated to the station. This is the best place to get up close and take photos, but be careful not to touch them or walk on their feeding area. Near the exit, you'll pass the CDRS kiosk, selling T-shirts, videos and souvenirs; this is the only place on the islands you can buy CDRS logo clothing, the proceeds of which go straight to the station. Near the exit you'll see a sign for a little **beach**, a hidden spot for lazing about and looking across the bay.

Bahía Tortuga

Three kilometres southwest of town, **Bahía Tortuga** is one of the most beautiful beaches in the islands, a streak of soft, white sand unfurling for almost a kilometre, washed by luminescent blue waters. Although you'll see swimmers here, it's not particularly safe as the currents are very strong and there are no lifeguards around. At the western end of the beach, beyond the rocky outcrop of lava, favoured by the odd marine iguana, an inlet forms a lagoon at low tide, wrapped in mangroves where you may see brown pelicans and even flamingos. To get there, head west out of Puerto Ayora on Charles Binford, which continues as a dirt road to a cliff, at the top of which is a **national park guard house** where you need to sign in. From here a paved trail undulates across a cactus forest to the beach. You can only get to the bay on foot, about forty minutes from town, and as there are no facilities, bring some water. The beach closes at 6pm.

Playa de los Alemanes and Las Grietas

A short water-taxi ride ($0.50) across the bay to the south towards the *Finch Bay Hotel* brings you to two popular swimming spots in an area surrounded by lagoons and saltbush teeming with birdlife. From the dock a path leads to an attractive protected beach ideal for swimming and snorkelling, the **Playa de los Alemanes** named after the early German settlers that made their homes here when the island was first colonized. Beyond the beach, a gravel path leads for fifteen to twenty minutes to **Las Grietas**, inland saltwater grottoes surrounded by high lava walls, which are very popular with locals at weekends for bathing; on weekdays the pools are quiet.

Eating, drinking and nightlife

There are plenty of **restaurants** along Avenida Charles Darwin, including a good proportion of relatively expensive places aimed squarely at tourists, and locally popular eateries such as *El Rincón del Alma* and the downmarket *Frutos del Mar* (closed Mon) on the corner of Naveda nearby, serving bargain *almuerzos* and *meriendas*. To get the best of local **seafood** head to Charles Binford in the evening, where a string of *kioscos* (kiosks) simmer up cauldrons of *encocados* and other *mariscos*, cooked in the style of the mainland coast. Of these, *William* (closed Mon) and *Tía Juanita* (closed Tues) are the best, but anywhere you can see a crowd of satisfied customers washing down their rice and fish with a glass of cold beer is also likely to be good.

A pleasant mix of tourists, locals and resident research scientists brings a healthy international flavour to Puerto Ayora **nightlife**. *Limón y Café*, Avenida Charles Darwin and 12 de Febrero (daily until 1am), is a thatched **bar** with a good atmosphere where you can shoot pool, sip a blue-footed booby cocktail, relax in a hammock and chat to dedicated beer-swilling regulars; food is also served up to 8pm. The disco at *La Panga*, on Avenida Charles Darwin and Tomás de Berlanga (Mon–Thurs 8.30pm–2am, Fri & Sat 8.30pm–3am), tends to fill up quite late in the evening. Here, cheapskates can sink cocktails from "the Titanic Line" – dodgy-label spirits that do the damage at a fraction of the price of better-known brands. Upstairs is the *Bongo Bar*, a rooftop venue offering open-air seating, pool table and a small dance floor. For good live *folklórica* music, ask a taxi driver to take you to *La Taberna del Duende* (Thurs–Sat), in a residential area towards the back of town, a *peña* done up in bamboo and straw matting that's popular with locals.

Restaurants

Angermeyer Point An $0.80 water-taxi ride from the dock. Elegant first-class restaurant serving excellent but pricey international food, including good seafood and fillet steaks, freshly baked bread and great cocktails. It's built on decks over a rocky promontory, home to cormorants and marine iguanas, looking back over Academy Bay. Open for dinner every night except Mon, and Sunday brunch.

Capricho Av Charles Darwin and Floreana. Cheerful restaurant serving fresh bread at breakfast, along with vegetarian dishes during its packed lunches. Also offers a book exchange and souvenirs.

La Garrapata Av Charles Darwin and Tomás de Berlanga. Highly regarded open-air restaurant with candlelit tables and a pleasing ambience, serving delicious seafood and grills. A little costlier than most places, but worth the extra expense.

Media Luna Av Charles Darwin and Los Piqueros. Of all the pizza venues, this is a favourite of locals and tourists alike, offering the best value, the friendliest service and the tastiest food too. Thick-cut sandwiches also available. Closed Tues.

Salvavidas Muelle Municipal. A decent seafood joint overlooking the dock. While you tuck into an ample portion of fish and chips for around $5 or $2 an *almuerzo*, you can watch the herons getting their own nightly feed.

Listings

Airlines Tame is on Av Charles Darwin and 12 de Febrero (☎05/526527) and at Baltra airport (☎05/520111). The EMETEBE office is above the post office, on Avenida Charles Darwin (☎05/526177).

Banks and exchange Banco del Pacífico, on Av Charles Darwin and Charles Binford, has an ATM for MasterCard and Cirrus. Several souvenir shops accept traveller's cheques, including Peer Galápagos, at the traffic triangle on Av Charles Darwin.

Bike and sports rental Galápagos Tour Center, Av Julio Herrera and Av Charles Darwin (☎05/526245), rents out mountain bikes for $2 per hour or $15 per day, surfboards for $16 a day, and snorkelling equipment for $10 a day.

Camera film and repairs Galacolor, opposite TAME, can do minor repairs and sells batteries, disposable cameras and film for just above mainland rates ($10 for slide film). Steer clear of film without a box – it's probably passed its expiry date.

Diving operators Galápagos Sub Aqua on Av Charles Darwin (☎ & ⊕05/526350, ⊛www .galapagos_sub_aqua.com.ec) is a long-established outfit offering introductory dives at Academy Bay, day-trips and longer live-aboard tours, plus PADI and NAUI training courses for beginners and divemasters. Scuba Iguana on Av Charles Darwin near the *Hotel Galápagos* (☎ & ⊕05/526330 or 526296, ⊛www.scubaiguana.com) has a similar range of services, diving at over forty sites on day-trips or live-aboard trips, and can give certified training programmes for beginners, divemasters and instructors. English is spoken at both agencies. Nauti Diving (☎05/526096, ⊛www .nautidiving.com), two doors up from Galápagos Sub Aqua, also offers more or less the same programmes. Rates are fairly standard, with day-trips usually costing around $120 per person (or $80 for introductory dives), while 5-day open-water certification courses start at $400.

Ferries and fibras To buy ferry tickets (see "Independent travel" p.473 for service details), you must visit the INGALA ticket office in person (☎05/526199; Mon–Fri 7am–noon & 1–4pm), a 20min walk from the waterfront, 50m before the petrol station as you head out of town on Av Padre Julio Herrera. A taxi there will cost about $1. Talk to the Capitanía about the *Estrella del Mar* service to Isabela, and for details on departure times for *fibras*; the *Salvavidas* restaurant should also have information on the latter.

Hospitals The public hospital is on Av Padre Julio Herrera and Av Charles Darwin. Dr Pedro Picamunga speaks a little English, as does the dentist here, Dra Digna Pino. In emergencies, call ☏05/526103. A much better-staffed and equipped private clinic is Protesub (☏05/526911, ☏09/9855911) on 18 de Febrero and General Rodríguez Lara, which primarily provides medical services for submarine and aquatic activities, and has a hyperbaric recompression chamber, but also offers general medical attention to the public.

Internet facilities Plenty of places along the main thoroughfares offer connections for around $3 an hour.

Language school Islas Galápagos Spanish Language Center, contact them via their Quito office at Darquea Terán 16-50 and Av 10 de Agosto (☏02/2223242, ☏2221628, ☏www .islas-galapagos.com). From $249 for one week's course, 5hr per day. Dancing and cooking classes, and family stays also available.

Laundry Peregrina, by *El Peregrina*, charges around $1 per kg (Mon–Sat 9am–noon & 3.30–5.30pm). Others are located on Av P.J. Herrera.

Post office Av Charles Darwin, next to the Proinsular Supermarket. Servigalápagos on Av Charles Darwin and Piqueros opposite the

Silberstein (☏05/526041) is a representative for DHL and Western Union couriers.

Telephone office Pacifictel, on Av Padre Julio Herrera and Española, can be chaotic. You'll more than likely have to write your name and number on the list and wait from 15 minutes to an hour for your turn. Calls can also be made from cellular phones operated by Porta and Bell South. Daily 7am–11pm.

Travel agents and tour operators Most of the boats based in Puerto Ayora have a corresponding office somewhere in town; if you're interested in a particular boat ask for the office location at Capturgal (see "Arrival and information", p.478). Moonrise Travel Agency, on Av Charles Darwin, opposite the Banco del Pacífico (☏ & ☏05/526403 or 526402, ☏sdivine@pa.ga.pro .ec), has a reputation for finding last-minute places on the more reliable tour boats quickly, plus they run day-trips to the nearby islands and tours of the highlands, including visits to their farm, Rancho Mariposa, where you can see wild tortoises. Galasam (☏05/526126) on Av Charles Darwin and Av Herrera, offers tours of 4, 5 or 8 days on any of its seven boats, including several budget options. Ensugal, on Binford and Juan Montalvo (☏ & ☏05/526593), runs daily tours on the *Santa Fé II* to Seymour Norte, Plaza Sur, Bartolomé, Floreana and Santa Fé. Aqua Tours (☏05/526632) has a glass-bottomed boat, leaving the dock at 8.30am and 2.30pm for a 4hr tour, subject to demand.

The Santa Cruz highlands

If you're travelling independently, the **highland** sites are relatively easy to get to, though it's better to go with a **guide** (ask any tour operator or at the Parque Nacional Galápagos offices), both to navigate and to spot creatures and plants in the undergrowth. If you're on a **boat tour**, the itinerary may give you a half-day to explore the highlands area, while tour agencies in Puerto Ayora offer **day-trips** to the highlands for around $20–30, often less if you can get a group together. **Buses** going all the way to Santa Rosa, stopping at Bellavista, leave the traffic triangle on Av Charles Darwin in Puerto Ayora (Mon–Sat 6.30am, 12.30pm & 4.30pm), returning immediately. Allow plenty of time to hitch a lift back to town if necessary.

Bellavista, Cerro Crocker and around

The flora and fauna of the **highlands** of Santa Cruz are quite distinct from the parched coastal areas. Leaving Puerto Ayora, the main road over the island ascends from the lowland scrub and cactus fields, and by the time you reach the little cattle village of **BELLAVISTA**, 6km north of the port, introduced elephant grass, plantains, papayas and avocados grow from the fertile red soil. From Bellavista, a trail leads north through farmland, miconia forests and pampa grass for about 8km (a 2hr 30min trek) to the summit of the island, **Cerro Crocker** (864m). When the mists disperse, the panoramic **views** are

Santa Cruz lava tubes

Lava tubes perforate several areas of Santa Cruz, and are all found on private land so you don't need an official guide to visit, though tours can be arranged in Puerto Ayora. The tubes are natural conduits for lava that form beneath a solidified crust, and when the flow stems, the tunnels remain. Large enough to walk through, and extending for several kilometres with high jagged walls disappearing into the gloom and slippery floors strewn with rubble, they are exciting to explore, but bring a torch (flashlight) and sturdy shoes.

One of the easiest to get to is near Bellavista (follow the "*los túneles*" signs from the village), where you can hire a torch ($0.50) to explore a tunnel (admission around $2.50) several hundred metres long. Not far from the main road on the way from Bellavista to Santa Rosa is another set, Furio's ($3.50), which has its own dim lighting in addition to the occasional shaft of sunlight bursting in from small collapses in the ceiling; in places you have to stoop to get through. There's also a restaurant with views over the farmland, beyond the opening at one end, where you can get over-priced drinks; you'll need to contact them in advance (ask at a tour agency) if you plan on a meal. Finally, there are the Salasaca tunnels ($3), 5km northwest of Santa Rosa on the farm of Señor Arias; get in contact with him through one of the agencies to arrange a visit.

---

spectacular. About 5km into the walk you'll reach the crescent-shaped **Media Luna** and nearer the summit **Puntudo**, both old volcanic cones grown over with thick vegetation. The trail can get very muddy and hard to follow in places, so getting a guide is a good idea.

Santa Rosa, the Chato Tortoise Reserve and around

Around 9km further on from Bellavista, the farms of **SANTA ROSA** sit in abundant fruit orchards and cedar trees that dwarf the native vegetation. Close to this unassuming settlement is a **restaurant**, *Narwhal*, offering good three-course lunches and dinners for $16–18 (minimum of four people) in a farm with astounding views from the greenery down to the sea. Ask at *Media Luna* in Puerto Ayora (see p.481) to make reservations.

From Santa Rosa, a track leads through 3km of farmland dotted with white cattle egrets and smooth-billed anis to the edge of the **Chato Tortoise Reserve** on the southwestern corner of the island, among the best places in the Galápagos to see giant tortoises in their natural habitat. Here, the trail forks between a branch heading west through dense endemic scalesia forest up to **Cerro Chato** (about 3km), and east to a small lagoon (2km), where tortoises wallow in the company of white-cheeked pintails. Vermilion and Galápagos flycatchers are common sightings, but you'll need more luck to spot the secretive Galápagos rail. A guide is recommended for visiting the reserve, and you should bring plenty of water, sturdy shoes and wet-weather gear.

A couple of kilometres beyond Santa Rosa on the way to Baltra, the road passes between **Los Gemelos**, a pair of yawning pit-craters, formed when lava collapsed into underlying magma chambers, swathed in emerald scalesia forests. Trails lead from the road to viewpoints overlooking each, and **finches** and **flycatchers** inhabit the surrounding forests.

Islands around Santa Cruz

Among the small islands and islets that surround Santa Cruz, there are five visitor sites, most of which can be reached on day-trips from Puerto Ayora, or being close to **Baltra** are often visited at the beginning or end of a cruise. **Seymour Norte**, **Plaza Sur** and **Santa Fé** are frequently called on by tour boats, but few stop at the tiny lava reef of **Mosquera**, while **Daphne Mayor** is one of the most restricted sites in the archipelago, due to a difficult landing on steep rocks that are prone to erosion.

Baltra and Mosquera

Stunted scrub and cactus growth, dry air and a parched landscape dotted with abandoned buildings isn't much of a welcome to one of the world's natural wonders, but **BALTRA** is most visitors' first taste of the Galápagos Islands, before being whisked off by buses to the dock to join a tour boat or the ferry for Santa Cruz itself. The US Air Force occupied the island during World War II, blasting an airstrip into the rock so planes could swiftly be mobilized to defend the Panama Canal, but today it's controlled by the Ecuadorian Air Force. Except for **pelicans** and **seabirds** around the dock, there's not a lot to see on the island. The population of **land iguanas** was very nearly wiped out during the US occupation, with a few being removed to the safety of Seymour Norte, immediately to the north. Following a repopulation programme by the Charles Darwin Research Station, dozens of the creatures have been repatriated to Baltra.

Lying in the channel between Baltra and Seymour Norte and reached by tour boat, the tiny island of **MOSQUERA** is a shock of coral sand heaving with sea lions. You have free reign to walk about the island, enjoying the company of shore- and seabirds, such as **herons** and **lava gulls**, and you can swim with the sea lions, but keep away from the bull male.

Isla Seymour Norte

Getting around a dozen visitor groups a day, **SEYMOUR NORTE**, directly north of Baltra, a low, flat island, just under two square kilometres in size and created by geological uplift, makes frequent appearances on tour-boat itineraries. *Pangas* put passengers ashore on black lava, where a trail leads past large colonies of **blue-footed boobies**, and both types of **frigate bird** – it's one of the best places in the islands to see this magnificent bird. Along the shore you'll also find barking **sea lions** and **marine iguanas**: take care where you put your feet as they nest here. An endemic variety of the *palo santo* tree borders the inland loop of the trail, smaller than its relative with hairier, greyer leaves, and occasionally **land iguanas** (brought here from Baltra) can be spotted tucked away in the vegetation.

Isla Daphne Mayor

Visible about 10km to the west of Baltra and Seymour, **DAPHNE MAYOR** (the larger of the two Daphnes) is composed of a tuff cone embedded with two craters. Since the early 1970s it's been the focus of research into **Darwin's finches** by two British scientists, Peter and Rosemary Grant, who have weighed, ringed, measured and photographed every finch on the island – about 25,000 altogether – and so documented evolutionary processes at work; Jonathan Weiner's book *The Beak of the Finch* tells the story of their studies (see "Books" p.558). Only small yachts are allowed to call at the islands, and even then only once a month. The dry landing is quite hairy, involving a leap onto a steep rock face, from where a slender trail leads up to the rim of the island; here you can gaze down into the craters. Colonies of **blue-footed boobies** nest in the furnace heat of these natural cauldrons, and **red-billed tropicbirds** tenant the crevices in the cliff walls.

Isla Plaza Sur

Less than a kilometre from the eastern coast of Santa Cruz, the two tiny Plaza islands were formed by seismic uplift, flat islands dramatically tilted to form sheer cliffs on the southern side. Only **PLAZA SUR**, the larger of the two at less than 1.5km long and under 250m at its widest point, is open to visitors. Being within range of the Puerto Ayora day-trippers, the little island can get crowded, so a dock has been built to prevent tourists causing erosion on landing. Vociferous members of the thousand-strong colony of **sea lions** here see this as a territorial boundary, so take care boarding and disembarking; snorkelling and swimming are also better around Plaza Norte, out of the sea lion war zone. A rather more subdued group of elderly bachelors holds a corner of smooth lava (polished by the defeated over the years) up on the cliffs, a tortuous climb over the rocks away from the macho action of the main colony.

The island has striking vegetation, a covering of juicy *Sesuvium* plants that turn crimson in the dry season, punctuated by chunky *Opuntia* cactus trees. When their succulent pads fall to the ground, **land iguanas** wriggle out of their torpor for a bite to eat. Before the park rules were in place, the iguanas were often fed fruit by visitors, and subsequently learned to dash to the dock whenever a party landed. As a hangover from those lax days, you'll often see them lurking around newly arrived groups, trying their luck for a banana or orange.

A trail leads up to sheer cliffs, an excellent vantage point to spot **noddy terns**, **swallow-tailed gulls**, **Audubon's shearwaters** and **red-billed tropicbirds**, as well as the occasional **blue-footed and Nazca boobies**, **frigate birds** and **pelicans**. Looking down into the swell, you may see **yellow-tailed mullet**, **surgeonfish**, **manta rays** and **dolphins**.

Isla Santa Fé

Visitors to **SANTA FÉ**, about 25km southeast of Puerto Ayora, disembark for a wet landing on the northeastern side of the island, at a stunning cove with brilliant-blue water and white sand that's protected by a partly submerged peninsula. The bay is good for swimming – though give the bull sea lions here a wide berth – and snorkelling may yield up **spotted eagle rays** and **stingrays**, **white-tipped reef sharks** and a number of colourful reef fish.

There are two trails on Isla Santa Fé. The first is short and easy, circling through a forest of giant *Opuntia* **cacti** (a variety found only on the island), many reaching 10m in height with trunks 4m in circumference. The second is more strenuous, heading up a steep hill that affords spectacular views of the island. On both, you have a fair chance of seeing a species of **land iguana** unique to Santa Fé, having a paler colour and longer spines on its back than its counterparts on the other islands. You might also be lucky enough to see one of the three surviving endemic species of **rice rat** rustling in the scrub – unlike on Fernandina, the only other island where they are found, this species often appears in the daytime. This is a good island to spot several other endemic species, including the **Galápagos hawk**, **Galápagos dove** and **Galápagos snake**.

Isla Santiago and around

About 25km northwest of Santa Cruz, **SANTIAGO** – officially called San Salvador – is the fourth-largest island in the Galápagos at 585 square kilometres, and the last to have been abandoned by human settlers. In the early nineteenth century, Captain Porter (p.500) is reputed to have set four goats free on the island, which swiftly set about multiplying, within a few decades causing untold damage to the island's native wildlife. Before trained hunters, aided by dogs and satellite tracking systems, could get to work on the island's 100,000 goats, its rampant feral pig population had to be eradicated, a mammoth task that took 28 years and was finally completed in 2001. As well as Santiago's four visitor sites, there are some interesting satellite islands, such as **Rábida**, **Bartolomé** and **Sombrero Chino**, and its proximity to Santa Cruz means that the majority of boat tours stop somewhere in this area. Day-trip boats based in Baltra occasionally call at Bartolomé too.

Puerto Egas

Puerto Egas, in James Bay on the western side of the island, is Santiago's most visited site, good for snorkelling and spotting a healthy cross section of wildlife. A few derelict buildings of the old port litter the bay, the relics of failed salt-mining operations from the 1920s and the 1960s, when Héctor Egas, the namesake of the port, left three men here to look after the property, vowing to return with more money to rekindle his bankrupt industry. One of his employees waited four years in vain for his boss to return, and became a minor attraction for the early tourists in his own right – the vision of a castaway, with shaggy hair and a long, unkempt beard, who scoured the island for food.

A trail leads east from the port area to the old salt mine, a crater where flamingos are occasionally spotted. Along the shore to the west, the bay is an expanse of cracked and weathered black basaltic lava, with enough pools and crevices to sustain a wealth of intertidal wildlife. The **Sally lightfoot crabs**, **urchins**, **anemones**, **eels** and **octopuses** that you'll see make a handsome smorgasbord for a number of shore birds, **herons**, **oystercatchers**, **ruddy turnstones** and **noddy terns** among them. At the far western end of the trail, erosion has formed the **fur seal grottoes**, shimmering turquoise pools and inlets worn into lava tubes by the waves. Natural rock bridges straddle the breaches where **marine iguanas**, **fur seals** and **marine turtles** swim. The sloshing of water in one has earned it the title of "Darwin's Toilet". Behind you, the tuff cone of Pan de Azúcar (Sugarloaf) volcano, at 395m, overshadows scrub and acacia trees often used as perches by **Galápagos hawks**.

Playa Espumilla, Buccaneer Cove and Sulivan Bay

North of Puerto Egas, on the other side of a lava flow, lies **Playa Espumilla**, a tawny beach couched in mangroves, favoured by **marine turtles** as a nesting ground. Feral pigs that dig up and eat turtle eggs have been a serious problem here in the past, but a recovery is expected following the completion of the eradication programme. A trail leads inland from the beach, weaving through the mangroves alongside a salty lagoon into thick vegetation, home to **Darwin's finches** and **flycatchers**.

Many boats cruise by **Buccaneer Cove**, roughly 8km north of Puerto Egas and a favourite hide-out of the seventeenth- and eighteenth-century freebooters looking to careen their boats and stock up on food and water. Fifty-metre tuff cliffs, spattered with guano, taper down to a short, dusky beach and then rise in the north forming pinnacles and spurs. Pre-Columbian pottery shards discovered here led Thor Heyerdahl to suggest that the cove had been used as a campsite by mainland fishermen long before the arrival of the pirates, probably in the wet season when a freshwater stream ran down to the beach.

On the eastern side of Santiago, **Sulivan Bay**, named after Bartholomew

James Sulivan, a lieutenant on the *Beagle*, is one for **lava** fans. A trail leads across a vast, century-old flow of pahoehoe lava, a petrified lake of rumpled ooze, intestinal squiggles and viscous tongues, punctuated by oddities like *hornitos*, solidified pimples made by bursts of gas, and moulds of tree trunks that vaporized in the heat. The lava field is dominated by two large tuff cones, and in the cracks and crevices you'll see the layers of previous flows beneath. In this barren landscape, the pioneering *Mollugo* and the **lava cactus** *Brachycereus* are the only plants that can eke out life.

Isla Bartolomé

BARTOLOMÉ, positioned a few hundred metres off the east coast of Santiago, holds the best-known landmark of the Galápagos, the teetering dagger of **Pinnacle Rock**, a jagged remnant of an old tuff cone overshadowing a streak of pale sand at the southwestern end of the island. The many tours that come here usually combine a hike to the island's summit (114m) and a refreshing swim beneath the Rock, where you'll get some fine snorkelling around the submerged rocks, and perhaps catch a glimpse of **Galápagos penguins** zipping by schools of colourful fish. If you don't see them here, you've a better chance of spotting them on the shaded cliffs each side of the bay from a *panga*.

The **trail to the summit** begins at the man-made dock on Bartolomé's northern point, before crossing a parched landscape relieved only by a scant covering of silvery *Tiquilia* – just about the only plant that can survive such dry, ashy soil – and the infrequent slitherings of a **Galápagos snake**. The trail then loops round to the east and climbs up several hundred wooden steps to reach the top of the hill, to give you the famous view of Pinnacle Rock. On the opposite side a stunning moonscape vista unfolds, with large spatter cones and **lava tunnels** dropping to the southeast to reveal the Daphnes, Baltra, Seymour Norte and Santa Cruz in the distance.

Bartolomé's second trail begins at the beach and leads through the mangroves and dunes across the island's isthmus to a second beach, patrolled by sharks and rays and out of bounds for swimmers. **Marine turtles** nest here at the outset of the warm-wet season.

Isla Sombrero Chino

Barely 100m from the southeastern tip of Santiago, the volcanic cone of tiny **SOMBRERO CHINO** does indeed bear more than a passing resemblance to a Chinese hat. Boats moor in the blazing-blue channel between the islands, a terrific spot for some snorkelling and where **Galápagos penguins** are occasionally seen. A trail on the island follows a white-coral beach, past a **sea lion** colony to a vantage point surrounded by scuttling **Sally lightfoot crabs** and **marine iguanas**, overlooking a cliff battered by the swell. The pockmarked lava is dashed with brighter blotches of **lava cactus**, while around the beach you'll find **saltbush** and colourful **Sesuvium**.

Isla Rábida

RÁBIDA is less than 5km south of Santiago and under five square kilometres in area. A wet landing at the north of the island onto a russet, sea lion-strewn beach brings you to a trail leading through saltbush to a saline lagoon. **Pelicans** sometimes build nests in the saltbush, while **white-cheeked pintails**, bachelor **sea lions** and **stilts** are residents of the lagoon. It's possible to see the odd **flamingo** sifting the murky waters for food here as well. A path rises up through **palo santo** and **Opuntia cacti** to a viewpoint above the carmine cliffs. There's good snorkelling near the cliffs or alternatively at the landing beach and plenty of colourful fish to see, as well as diving **boobies** and **pelicans**.

Isla San Cristóbal and around

Out on the eastern side of the archipelago, and with a shape resembling a "shrivelled appendix" according to the 1940s travel writer Victor von Hagen, **SAN CRISTÓBAL** is the administrative seat of the Galápagos and at 558 square kilometres the fifth largest island in the archipelago. **Wreck Bay**, at its western tip, is the site of the provincial capital, **Puerto Baquerizo Moreno**, a peaceful town that has been slowly awakening to the rustle of tourist dollars since the opening of the airport on the island in 1986, though it's still a way behind Puerto Ayora. In its favour though, you can visit the excellent new **Centro de Interpretación**, which concentrates on the human and natural history of the islands, plus the nearby islets such as **León Dormido** (Kicker Rock) and **Isla Lobos**. On the rest of the island, points of interest include the highland town of **El Progreso**, site of Manuel Cobos's tyrannical regime (see p.491) and the **Laguna El Junco** beyond, or take a boat around to **Punta Pitt**, the far easternmost point of the archipelago.

The southwestern half of the island is dominated by the slopes of the **Cerro San Joaquín** (measurements of its summit range from 730m to 896m), its windward slopes covered in vegetation and farmed by the island's agricultural community. The northeastern area has the characteristic volcanic landscape of the archipelago, a collection of lava flows, spatter cones and other volcanic features, which rise to a couple of hundred metres at **Cerro Pan de Azúcar**.

Puerto Baquerizo Moreno

Founded by the colonist General Villamil in the mid-nineteenth century (see p.463), **PUERTO BAQUERIZO MORENO** was named after the first Ecuadorian president to visit the islands, in 1916. Despite being the capital of the Galápagos, it's a sleepy town, virtually lifeless in the heat of the early afternoon, only coming alive fully when the sun sets over the bay. It may not get as many visitors as Puerto Ayora, but there is a burgeoning industry here: along the waterfront, a glut of travel agents, cafés, restaurants and souvenir shops all show a town keen to cut itself a larger slice of the tourist pie. Puerto Baquerizo Moreno is a bit short of things to do, but there's enough on the island to keep visitors busy for a few days. Just outside the port, the **Centro de Interpretación** has great displays of the archipelago's human and natural history, while spots on the coast nearby, such as **Tongo Reef** west of town, have become the focus of the Galápagos' growing reputation among South Americans as a **surfing** hot spot. The best waves form at the beginning of the warm-wet season (Dec–Feb), when the water is also much warmer.

Arrival, information and transport

From the **airport**, a taxi or truck into the town centre costs $1; it's within walking distance too, only being about 15–20 minutes southwest of the centre along Avenida Alsacio Northía. **Ferries** and **fibras** from Santa Cruz arrive on Friday at the town's dock.

There's an **information** booth by the dock too, identifiable by the giant cement whale on the roof. They can give you **maps**, but opening hours are erratic, so you're better off trying the national park offices for information, north of Alsacio Northía, about a fifteen-minute walk from the town centre.

Pick-up trucks and **taxis** can be caught on the Malecón and charge a minimum fare of $1, and around $2 to El Progreso, $10 to El Junco (return) or about $4 to hire per hour. Island **buses** to El Progreso pick people up on Avenida 12 de Febrero, though the service is irregular so ask locals for details. If you want to go beyond El Progreso, for example to El Junco, catch the bus (Wed & Sat at 2pm) from the market at 12 de Febrero and Juan José Flores. Tell the driver you want the lagoon and check what time it'll be passing back, usually about ninety minutes later.

Accommodation

Puerto Baquerizo Moreno has enough **hotels** to keep its modest flow of tourists sheltered throughout the year. The cheaper, funkier places can fill out with South American surfers during the December to February season, when you'll need to book in advance. The town is equipped with 24-hour electricity, but water shortages and feeble water pressure remain a problem for many of the less expensive hotels. Some locals also rent out **rooms** for short- and long-stay visitors, usually park volunteers, and advertise in the port's bars. **Campers** can get the latest information on permissible sites at the national park offices at the north end of Alsacio Northía.

Los Cactus Quito and J.J. Flores near Pacifictel ℡05/520078. A *hostal* away from the centre, but good value nonetheless for its clean, fresh rooms with private bath and hot water. ❷

Cabañas Don Jorge a 15min walk north of town along Alsacio Northía, near a small beach ℡05/520265, ℮cterana@ga.pro.ec. Four red-roofed cabins with private bath and hot water, slotted between the rocks and cacti in a secluded garden with sea views. One has two floors and kitchen facilities. Reservations advised. ❹

Mar Azul Alsacio Northía and Av Armada Nacional ℡05/520139, ℗520384, ℮seaman1@andinanet .net. Clean and spacious rooms with private bath and electric showers, set around the hotel's two

tranquil, leafy courtyards. ❹

Orca Playa de Oro at the north end of the Malecón ℡ & ℗05/520233, ℮management1 @etnotouronline.com. The most comfortable hotel on the island, but you need to reserve in advance. The hotel offers packages for scuba-diving trips, tours of Isabela, Spanish school and kayaking. ❼

Residencial San Francisco Malecón Charles Darwin and Española ℡05/520304. A quiet, inexpensive place popular with surfers, in a central location offering rooms with private bath, fans and television. Pipes leading all over the cheerfully daubed indoor courtyard reflect the rather erratic plumbing, however. ❷

The Port

Puerto Baquerizo Moreno has three main streets. On the waterfront, the Malecón Charles Darwin is where you'll find several tour agencies, restaurants, souvenir shops and the odd hotel. Running parallel to it, a couple of blocks to the east, is the main thoroughfare, Alsacio Northía, servicing the length of the town, from the national park offices (and interpretation centre) in the north to the airport in the south. Lastly, Avenida 12 de Febrero links the town to the rest of the island, heading east from the centre uphill to the highlands. Although the **church** on Alsacio Northía has a few interesting murals that are made with painted metals, lava and sand, next door is the town centre's only real sight, the **Museo de Historia Natural** (Mon–Fri 8.30–11.30am & 3.30–5pm, Sat 8.30am–noon; $1). Inside you'll witness a woeful and decaying collection of stuffed dolphins, sharks, turtles, boobies, pelicans, penguins, sea lions and frigate birds, not to mention jars of pickled snakes, eels and baby hammerheads – animals that thankfully live in plentiful numbers outside the museum in the archipelago.

The Centro de Interpretación and around

Unlike the sad natural history museum in town, the **Centro de Interpretación**, the Galápagos National Park's exhibition centre located about twenty minutes' walk north of the centre along Alsacio Northía (daily 8am–noon & 1–5pm; donation), is well worth a visit. The displays cover everything from geology, climate and conservation, to attempts at colonization in the 1920s, and have detailed explanations in Spanish and English. Impressive installations include a hold stuffed with overturned giant tortoises as they would have been stored by the pirates and whalers – one beast has its leg cut off for the boiling pot. Keep an eye out as well for details on the worthwhile talks, lectures and concerts that are held regularly in the open-air theatre and audio-visual projection room within the complex.

Behind the last exhibition room at the centre, a path leads up to **Cerro de Las Tijeretas**, or **Frigate-Bird Hill**. It's only twenty minutes' walk through fragrant *palo santo* forests to a viewpoint at the top, where you'll have a fine panorama of the yachts in Wreck Bay, Isla Lobos to the north, and León Dormido to the northeast. Below, a rocky cove echoes with jockeying **sea lions** while **frigate birds** circle in the air above. They nest here in March and April, and are seen less frequently during the cool-dry season. A series of paths networks around the hill, so you can do a circuit; it's relatively easy to stay oriented. One trail leads to the cove where you can snorkel, others go down to the road back to town past the interpretation centre. Heading away from town to the north, you'll come to a secluded beach.

Tongo Reef and La Lobería

At the weekends, crowds of **surfers** make their way to the shoreline west of town to catch the waves. **Tongo Reef** is one of the more popular places, a twenty-minute walk past the Capitanía, but others include Punta Carola and El Cañón. You'll need to leave identification at the entrance, as this is a military area, then cross the runway through the scrub to the rocky shore. Bring sandals that you don't mind getting wet, as the volcanic rocks manage to combine extreme sharpness with extraordinary slipperiness. It's best to be with someone who knows the place as currents can be strong; ask at local travel agents about board hire and guides or instructors.

A good place near town to spot wildlife is **La Lobería**, thirty minutes' walk to the southwest. Here, a trail leads along a rugged coast of pitted black lava buffeted by ocean spray to a small beach, where you'll find sea lions, marine iguanas and many shore birds. Locals take the shortcut to La Lobería, via the airport along to the southern end of the runway and down the steep embankment at the end. Make sure there are no imminent air arrivals if you follow their example. Otherwise continue on from the southern end of Alsacio Northía down a dirt road heading to the shore. Taxis ($2.50) or bikes are alternatives to the walk.

Eating, drinking and nightlife

It's easy to get a cheap feed in town, with a number of **restaurants** and **cafés** offering two-course set-lunch *almuerzos* for around $2. Menus are rather similar, though, concentrating mainly on seafood, with the usual chicken and meat courses as backup. For a good **bakery**, head to the *Panadería Fragata* on Alsacio Northía and Villamil, where you can get your hands on fresh bread, sticky buns, ice creams and yogurts.

The booming teenage population surf in the afternoons and spend their nights enjoying the port's **nightlife**. *Scuba Bar*, on the Malecón and Villamil, is

a popular hangout, while *Neptunus*, above *Casablanca* at the north end of the
Malecón, is a disco with an energetic youthful crowd.

Albacora Av Alsacio Northía and Española.
Popular for its cheap *almuerzos* and *meriendas*,
the decor comprises cane walls, gravel floor and
wicker lights flitting with finches. At night it twin-
kles with fairy lights.
Bambú Villamil and Ignacio de Hernández. In addition to the inexpensive *almuerzo*, you'll also find
pizza and pasta dishes with vegetarian options.
Cabaña Grande Villamil and Malecón Charles
Darwin. Locals come here in the evening to snack,
sip a beer and watch TV. A toasted ham-and-
cheese sandwich plus banana shake can be had
for under $1.

Casablanca Malecón Charles Darwin and Melville.
Offers drinks, light meals, snacks, *ceviche* and
breakfasts, as well as the occasional grill.
Miconia Av Armada Nacional, by the Capitanía.
The best restaurant in town overlooks the bay and
offers a range of à la carte goodies, from tapas to
ceviche.
Rosita cnr of Ignacio de Hernández and Villamil.
Long-standing restaurant, with a patio shaded by a
thatched awning. English names on the menu
betray the place's success with the tourists, so
expect to pay a little more for fish, meat and a
range of *ceviche* dishes.

Listings

Airlines Tame have an office at the airport
(℡ 05/521089), as do EMETEBE (℡ 05/520036).
Bank Banco del Pacífico, on the promenade by
Malecón Charles Darwin, has an ATM for Cirrus
and MasterCard.
Capitanía On the waterfront at the far western
side of the bay.
Ferries and fibras For advance ferry tickets go to
the INGALA office, a 20min walk out of town on
the way to El Progreso (a taxi costs around $1), or
you can buy tickets on board. The ferry departs
every other Mon for Santa Cruz, and again the
Thurs after if demand is high enough. Ask at the
Capitanía for upcoming *fibra* departures.
Hospital Alsacio Northía and Quito (℡ 05/520118
in emergencies). Dr David Vasantes here speaks
some English.
Internet facilities There are a few cafés near the
Malecón charging about $3 an hour.
Laundry Limpio y Seco, Av Alsacio Northía and 12

de Febrero, washes a large basket of laundry for $3.
Police Malecón Charles Darwin and Española
(℡ 05/520101 in emergencies).
Post office Malecón Charles Darwin and Manuel
Cobos.
Telephone office Pacifictel, Av Quito and Juan
José Flores.
Travel agents Chalo Tours, on Malecón Charles
Darwin and Española (℡ & ℗ 05/520953), offers
bay tours to León Dormido and Isla Los Lobos, diving tours, surfing lessons, bike rentals, snorkels
and fins and local excursions; Galparadise, Teodoro
Wolf and Charles Darwin (℡ 05/520618,
℮ galparadise@hotmail.com), runs full-day bay
tours, excursions to the east of the island, trips to
the highlands, bike trips, and diving lessons and
tours; Biological Expeditions, Av Quito and Alsacio
Northía (℡ 05/520933, ℮ bxgalapagos@hotmail
.com), offers bay tours, boat cruises and trips to
other local sites of interest.

San Cristóbal highlands

The road heading east from Puerto Baquerizo Moreno rises swiftly into the
misty highlands. After passing through about 8km of orange groves, you'll reach
EL PROGRESO, a peaceful village of wooden, stilted houses, banana plants
and fruit trees. It was founded in the 1870s by **Manuel Cobos**, an entrepreneur who tried to colonize the place with a hundred convicts. They planted
orchards, sugar cane and vegetable gardens, built a sugar mill, and enjoyed
modest success for a short period – but, just under 1000km away from the gaze
of authority, El Progreso began to slip into brutal tyranny. Cobos paid his
workers in his own invented currency only redeemable in his shop; he owned
the island's only boat too, so in effect, his workers were prisoners and slaves. An
increasingly savage overlord, he regularly beat them, once flogging six to death,
and abandoned a man on Santiago and another on Santa Cruz, leaving them
for dead. The Santa Cruz castaway survived for three years eating iguanas and

cactus pads, and may have been rescued sooner had Cobos not left a sign visible to passing boats but inaccessible to the hapless victim, reading "Do not take this man away. He is twenty times a criminal". The bloody retribution came when Cobos was hacked to pieces by the desperate colonists in 1904, on the spot where he'd recently had five people shot.

Today there's a simple **restaurant** in the village, *La Quinta de Cristi*, and a little further up the road, *La Casa del Ceibo* (℡05/520475 or 520248; ❸), which takes the prize for the most peculiar **hotel** in the archipelago. A precarious bridge of rope and wire takes you 14.5m up into San Cristóbal's tallest tree − a 200-year-old ceibo − to a tree house equipped with sleeping mats, fridge, cooker, bathroom, and a fireman's pole for the shortcut to the ground. Its own restaurant is no less eccentric: the walls are constructed from over 20,000 bottles of beer piled high, while the kitchen and paths are made of plastic crates. There's an irregular **bus** service to the village, but **taxis** can take you for less than $2. It'll take under an hour to get there on a **bike**, though it's uphill all the way.

Laguna El Junco

Ten kilometres beyond El Progreso, **Laguna El Junco** is a caldera lake at about 650m that's often shrouded in mist and surrounded by ferns, miconia, brambles and guava bushes. The quiet is occasionally broken by the squawk of a **moorhen**, or splash of **white-cheeked pintails** and **whimbrels**. Fed by the mists and rain, it's one of the few freshwater lakes in the Galápagos, and as you follow the **trail** around the rim you may see feral mammals come to the banks to drink. When the clouds lift, there are some wonderful views over the island. **Buses** up this far are infrequent (see "Arrival, information and getting around" p.488), but **taxis** will take you there and back for around $10. Ask the bus driver to drop you off at a path on the right, which leads steeply and quickly up to the lagoon, and check when the bus returns so you don't have to walk the 18km back to Puerto Baquerizo Moreno. Bring sturdy shoes as it can be slippery; a waterproof jacket and something warm for the fresher air are also good ideas. Several **travel agencies** make trips to the lagoon (see "Listings" p.491).

Isla Lobos, León Dormido and Cerro Brujo

Thirty-minutes' sail north of Puerto Baquerizo Moreno, **Isla Lobos** is a tiny island of rocky lava shores, covered with *palo santo* and speckled with **candelabra cacti**. It's heaving with **sea lions**, but along the short trail you'll also see **blue-footed boobies** and **frigate birds**. Another hour by boat to the northeast brings you to **León Dormido** (it's said to resemble a sleeping lion), known as **Kicker Rock** in English. Dizzying tuff cliffs rise out of the ocean, cleft at one end by a narrow waterway, wide enough for a dinghy to go down. There's no landing site, but a cruise around the cliffs should reveal plenty of seabirds, including **frigates, red-billed tropicbirds, Nazca and blue-footed boobies**. It's a site that's popular for scuba diving and snorkelling. Visits to León Dormido sometimes return via **Cerro Brujo**, about thirty minutes to the east. On the west coast of San Cristóbal, this cone stands over a white beach alive with **sea lions, pelicans** and **waders**. All the above sites are visitable as part of a **day-trip** arranged through one of the travel agents in Puerto Baquerizo Moreno (see p.491).

Punta Pitt and La Galapaguera

The northeastern extremity of San Cristóbal is rarely visited by tour boats. After a wet landing into a tight sandy cove, a fairly strenuous trail leads between thorny scrub and tuff cones, climbing to a pass with panoramic views. The real treat of **Punta Pitt** is that it's the only place in the Galápagos where all three species of booby are seen together. The **red-footed boobies** cling to muyuyo trees, while the **blue-footed boobies** mark their patches on the ground with a ring of guano. The **Nazca boobies** prefer spots closer to the cliffs, and **frigate bird** nests are also found in the *palo santo*. A trailhead west of Punta Pitt leads to **La Galapaguera** after about ninety minutes' hike, a good place to see **giant tortoises** in the wild. Unless your tour boat is stopping here, the only way to visit Punta Pitt and La Galapaguera is to arrange a **tour and guide** with one of the travel agents in Puerto Baquerizo Moreno (see p.491).

Western islands: Isabela and Fernandina

Straddling the equator, **ISABELA** is the largest island in the Galápagos at 4558 square kilometres, accounting for well over half the total land surface of the archipelago. The island comprises six **volcanoes**, fused together over time: from north to south, Ecuador (610m), Wolf (1707m), Darwin (1280m) and Alcedo (1097m) make up a narrow volcanic chain that tapers into the inaccessible aa lava flow of the Perry Isthmus, on the southwestern side of which Sierra Negra (1490m) and Cerro Azul (1250m) compose the squat base of the island. Several of the volcanoes are still active, the last eruption being in September 1998, when Cerro Azul spurted molten lava into areas populated by two subspecies of giant tortoise, including the endangered *Geochelone elephatopus guntheri*, of which there are fewer than one hundred left. The threatened tortoises were airlifted by helicopter or hauled to safety over the unforgiving terrain by ground crews.

Much of Isabela's huge landmass is impassable, riven by fissures, blocked by jagged lava flows, or clothed in tangled thickets of vegetation. From the air, most of Isabela looks as though it's been cracked and disfigured through overheating, and the rocky shores mean that there are few landing places on the island. Three of the visitor sites – **Urbina Bay**, **Elizabeth Bay** and **Tagus Cove** – are on its far western side, putting them in range only of the longer tours. **Volcán Alcedo**, the only visitor site on the eastern site, is currently closed for the eradication of goats, which are seriously disrupting the largest **giant tortoise** colony in the Galápagos. The upwelling of cold waters off the coast makes for a nutrient-rich zone, supporting such oddities as the **Galápagos penguin** and the **flightless cormorant**, more usually spotted on nearby **Fernandina**. Plentiful stocks of fish also attract **whales**, large schools of **common dolphins** and gregarious **bottle-nosed dolphins** – an unexpected highlight of the western islands.

Puerto Villamil, on the island's southeastern coast, is far less developed than either Puerto Ayora or Puerto Baquerizo Moreno, but makes a quiet retreat away from the tour boats. From the town, you can also visit several interesting sites, as well as take a horse ride through the verdant highlands up to the awesome crater of **Sierra Negra**.

Puerto Villamil and around

PUERTO VILLAMIL, sitting under the cloud-draped slopes of the huge Sierra Negra volcano, was founded at the beginning of the nineteenth century and named after the general who annexed the islands for Ecuador in 1832.

Now home to around a thousand settlers who fish or farm coffee and fruit in the highlands, the quiet port isn't well developed for tourism, and visitors are infrequent enough to stick out here. Just a small town of sandy roads and simple houses with fences of woven branches and cactus, fronted by a beautiful palm-fringed **beach**, it is nevertheless one of the most pleasant off-the-beaten-track places to stay on the islands, boasting several good attractions nearby that can be seen without guides.

Arrival, information and transport

EMETEBE **flights** arrive daily from San Cristóbal via Baltra when there is sufficient demand, and return the same day. Their office is on Conocarpus, opposite the Capitanía (Ⓣ05/529155). The airport is 3km outside town; there's no bus service, and taxis rarely wait here ($2), so try and get a lift with someone. The hour-long walk along the road across the lava wastes is hot and uncomfortable, and best avoided. The INGALA **ferry** arrives from Puerto Ayora every other Friday, and returns from Isabela on Sunday morning; every month, the ferry passes by Floreana on its way back to Santa Cruz. The *Estrella del Mar* public ferry also runs weekly to Puerto Ayora, though it is currently being renovated; enquire at the *municipio*. Check with the Capitanía for the latest *fibra* departures

You can buy **maps** of town in Puerto Ayora, or pick up a thin guide to the island with a fold-out map of the town, by Jacinto Gordillo, in *La Ballena Azul* hotel (see below) for about $5. The **telephone office** is on the corner of Calle Las Escalecias and Calle Los Cactus, a few blocks back from the beach – look for its red-and-white aerial mast. **Internet** facilities are available at *Costa Azul* restaurant, and in the souvenir shop near the *Cormorant Beach House* ($4 an hour). There are no banks, but the *Ballena Azul* will **exchange** a small amount of low-denomination traveller's cheques. Note that there are occasional **water** shortages in town.

Accommodation

Although it's a small town, the **hotels** here are generally of a good standard and cater to a range of budgets. Most of them can provide meals, given some advance notice, and help arrange local tours.

La Ballena Azul Conocarpus, back from *Hostería Isabela de Mar* Ⓣ & Ⓕ05/529030, Ⓦwww.hosteriaisabela.com.ec. A large and attractive Swiss-run house having a few decent budget rooms with shared bath along with a restaurant serving tasty international food (by prior arrangement) in a spacious wooden dining room. ❷–❸

Casa de Marita on the beach, east of town Ⓣ05/529238, Ⓕ529201, Ⓦwww.galapagosisabela.com. A stylish beach house shaded by palms on a gorgeous stretch of sand, offering the best accommodation in town in an array of tasteful colour-coded rooms, all bright, comfortable and spacious, and equipped with a/c, mini-fridge, private bath and hot water. There's a cheaper room in a small building near the house, which is a bit smaller and darker, but still a bargain at $12 per night. Breakfast included and other meals are available by arrangement in an attractive third-floor dining room. Bicycles and snorkelling equipment rented. ❻–❽

Cormorant Beach House on the beach at western end of town Ⓣ05/529192. A colourful two-storey house with four clean and good-value rooms, each with private bath and hot water. Two of the rooms, as well as a simple kitchen/dining area, are found downstairs, while an outdoor staircase leads upstairs to the two other rooms. ❷–❸

Hostería Isabela de Mar Conocarpus, near the beach Ⓣ & Ⓕ05/529030, Ⓦwww.hosteriaisabela.com.ec. A group of cabins, some on the beach, lined by flowery borders, each having large rooms with private bath, hot water and ceiling fans. Meals are available by arrangement at the nearby *Ballena Azul*, which is under the same management. ❹

Tero Real Las Escalecias Ⓣ & Ⓕ529106. Inexpensive accommodation in six cabins equipped with fridge, private bath and hot water, set in a small garden with hammocks. Meals are cooked on request. ❷

The Port and around

A small dusty square, fronted by the *municipio* and a simple church, fixes the centre of town a block back from the waterfront, dock and Capitanía. Heading north of the square takes you out of town towards the airport and highlands. There's not a whole lot going on around the port, but Avenida Antonio Gil, the road heading west out of the port, passes small, secluded lagoons (*pozas*) – where you can spot waders, shore birds and sometimes flamingos – before a signposted track branches off north to the **Giant Tortoise Breeding Center**, about twenty minutes from the town centre. Work is ongoing here to breed the island's five unique tortoise subspecies, each based around the five largest volcanoes. On show are the rearing pens for the tiny hatchlings, and corrals for adult tortoises taken from the wild, including the rescued Cerro Azul tortoises and those saved from a serious forest fire on Sierra Negra in 1994.

The westward road along the coast (ignoring the turn-off to the tortoise centre) continues past several peaceful beaches, including the **Playa de Amor**, where there are some scenic trails perfect for local wildlife spotting. After about two hours' walk, you'll come to **El Muro de las Lágrimas** (The Wall of Tears), a testament to the suffering of three hundred prisoners who toiled here in the 1940s and 1950s. They had the task of building their own prison, using the only material to hand – sharp-edged lava boulders. Driven on by guards, they made a wall some 190m long, 9m high and 6m wide at the base, but many died in the process. The prison colony was closed down after a revolt in 1959, the wall unfinished.

The best place to see marine life in the area is at **Las Islas de los Tiburones** (also known as **Las Tintoreras**), a handful of ragged black-lava grottoes poking out of the sea, a short boat ride from the port ($15–20). From the natural dock a trail leads past scuttling **marine iguanas** up to a lagoon and a narrow channel, where a "viewing gallery" allows you to see the sleek shapes of white-tipped **reef sharks** cruising back and forth. You can swim and snorkel in the lagoon – though don't swim in the channel itself as it's not big enough for both you and the sharks – or back at the landing site. If you're lucky you may see **rays** and **marine turtles**.

Sierra Negra

If you have a day to spare in Puerto Villamil, you can't do much better than go to the summit of **SIERRA NEGRA** (1490m), which reveals a monstrous **crater** some 10km in diameter and 200m deep. It's best reached by horse from **Santo Tomás**, a highland farming community 14km northwest of the port, from where a muddy trail leads uphill over rugged terrain that is frequently cloaked in thick mist during the cool-dry season. Once on the rim, however, the heavy clouds that you've been battling through curl dramatically over the southern lip before evaporating, leaving the gaping black crater stretching out in front of you. On the north side of the rim you can walk to **Volcán Chico**, a collection of hissing volcanic cones that last erupted in 1963 and 1979. It's an utterly barren landscape around Chico: red and black lava coloured by wispy sulphur deposits, and for vegetation, only the odd candelabra cactus and a few hardy shrubs clinging to the walls of the fumaroles to suckle on the volcanic steam. This north side of the volcano is usually in the sun and gives stupendous views of Fernandina and Isabela's four volcanoes beyond the Perry Isthmus.

The **bus** for Santo Tomás (a 1hr 30min trip) leaves on weekdays at 7am and noon, and on weekends at 6am and noon, returning at around 8.30am and 2.30pm. Getting to the crater from there takes about ninety minutes by horse or about three hours on foot, and a further thirty minutes' walk to Volcán

Chico. A **horse** and **guide** cost upwards of $12 for the day, though going in a group can work out cheaper; most hotels in town can arrange things for you. Sheets of rubber and plastic sacks will probably serve for saddles, so you can expect to get pretty sore as you trot up the slopes. Wear long trousers for the horse ride and take a long-sleeved top and rain jacket to keep warm.

Eating and drinking

Being only a small port, there's not a huge choice of **places to eat**, but some of the best food on offer is the international cuisine available at *La Casa de Marita* and *La Ballena Azul*, both of which require arrangement in advance. Other options include *Costa Azul*, on Las Fragatas, offering well-prepared dishes in clean surroundings, and *La Choza*, across the street from the Capitanía, which is fairly pricey but serves tasty meals. Better value is the *Kiosco El Caracol*, between the Capitanía and the police station, which does *almuerzos* for $2 and inexpensive seafood. *El Encanto de Pepa*, on Conocarpus, also does good fish (and more expensive chicken) in a comfortable little restaurant with plenty of character, that has the *Peña La Playita* at the back of it, a small **bar** and disco that only gets going if there are enough people. On the beach near the *Cormorant Beach House*, *Beto's Bar* has lively music and does barbecues when there's a big enough crowd.

Tagus Cove

A secluded cove of tuff cliffs on the Bolívar Channel, at the foot of Volcán Darwin, **TAGUS COVE** is Isabela's most visited site, and a convenient anchorage that has been used for many years, as testified by the dozens of boat names etched and painted onto the cliffs. Many are those of millionaires' yachts that stopped here on grand world cruises in the 1930s, but the oldest is from 1836, only a year after Darwin's visit.

From the landing point, a trail leads steeply up a breach in the cliffs into the scrubby vegetation typical of the dry coastal regions, including **lantana**, **lechoso**, **Galápagos cotton** and an endemic variety of **palo santo**, which provides a good habitat for a number of **Darwin's finches** and **flycatchers**. The path rises around the rim of **Darwin's Lake**, eventually giving wonderful views of its emerald surface: the strange thing about this crater lake is that it has both a higher salinity and water level than the sea, and no one knows how this came about. The trail then leads further up to a tuff cone from where you can see a maroon carpet of **aa lava** extending off to Volcán Wolf and Volcán Ecuador in the distance.

Around the cliffs by Tagus Cove, made stripy by thousands of compacted layers of ash, **blue-footed boobies**, **noddy terns**, **pelicans**, **penguins** and **sea lions** can all be seen. To its north, **marine turtles** make nests on the black-sand beach of **Punta Tortuga**. The beach is backed by mangroves, making it one of the few places to see the endangered **mangrove finch**.

Urbina Bay

Around 25km south of Tagus Cove, **URBINA BAY** shows one of the most dramatic results of tectonic activity. In 1954, a 1.5-square-kilometre section of sea reef was shunted up out of the water, an uplift of almost 4m in places. Skeletons of fish, lobsters and turtles strewn about the rocks told of the violence of the movement; you'll see some sun-bleached brain corals, shells and urchins, several hundred metres from the water's edge.

The trail here forms a long circuit, heading from a wet landing on a black beach inland to where **land iguanas** lurk beneath poison-apple trees, **palo santo**, **Vallesia** and **cordia**. In the rainy season, **giant tortoises** descend from Volcán Alcedo to the lowlands to lay eggs; feral goats have caused damage to the tortoises' habitat in this area. The trail then loops back along the shore, over the twisted black lava, home to **marine iguanas** and a few pairs of **flightless cormorants**.

Elizabeth Bay and Punta Moreno

On the west coast of the Perry Isthmus, it's possible to explore the narrowing inlet crowded by mangroves of **ELIZABETH BAY** by *panga* from your tour boat. This is a great place to spot marine wildlife; **turtles**, **reef sharks**, **sea lions** and **rays** all favour the cold, nutrient-rich waters. **Herons** look on from their perches in the tangled mangroves as **blue-footed boobies** dive-bomb the secluded channels, and **shearwaters** skim the surface of the sea. Tour boats usually anchor at the tiny Mariela islands at the mouth of the bay, a good place to see **Galápagos penguins**.

PUNTA MORENO, around 30km west of Elizabeth Bay, is one of the remotest visitor sites in the islands, and, as such, one of the least seen. An enormous flow of **pahoehoe lava** unfurls into the distance, broken by fissures and peppered with brackish water holes ringed by reeds and buzzing with insects. These are the few sources of life in a virtually sterile landscape, supporting **flamingos**, **herons**, **moorhens** and **white-cheeked pintails**.

Isla Fernandina

FERNANDINA, lying west of Isabela and dominated by the brooding shape of **Volcán La Cumbre** (1463m), is the youngest island in the archipelago, thought to be between 60,000 and 300,000 years old. It's also one of the most volcanically active islands, erupting ten times in the twentieth century alone, most recently in 1995. La Cumbre is crested by a huge caldera, 6km wide and 900m deep, the floor of which exploded in 1968, sending it crashing down by 300m. Happily, Fernandina has so far escaped the introduced species that have been so damaging to the other islands, leading to the claim that it's the world's largest pristine island; take care you're not inadvertently transporting any organisms, such as seeds, on your clothes or the soles of your shoes.

Punta Espinosa, a spiky finger of lava at the northeastern tip of the island, is Fernandina's only visitor site. It's home to a sizeable colony of **marine iguanas**, their ashen bodies crammed head to foot on the black rocks. They lay eggs in the pockets of sand, and you'll see **Galápagos hawks** in the trees nearby waiting to pounce on any stray hatchlings. This is one of the best islands for **flightless cormorants**, which stand at the water's edge after a foray for food underwater, to dry out their useless wings. Another endemic, the **Galápagos penguin**, can also be seen floating around the point, competing for fish with the **sea lions**.

A trail here leads over rippled **pahoehoe lava**, studded with clumps of lava cacti, to a series of tide pools, a great place to spot **crabs**, **octopuses** and a range of shore birds, including **whimbrels**, **herons** and **oystercatchers**. A final trail heads eastwards to an imposing wall of **aa lava**, a jagged barrier to the slopes of Volcán La Cumbre.

Southern islands: Floreana and Española

Floreana and **Española**, in the south of the archipelago, are among the oldest of the Galápagos islands, weather-beaten and eroded over several million years. They are both regularly visited: Floreana, one of the first islands ever to have human settlers – all unsuccessful until the famous **Wittmer** family of the 1930s (see box opposite) – is known for its interesting history, while Española is a favourite for its seabird colonies, most notably of the endemic waved albatross.

Isla Floreana

Arriving at the beginning of the nineteenth century, the deranged Patrick Watkins (see p.462) was the first in a long line of colonists to **FLOREANA**. As the sixth-largest island in the Galápagos (173 square kilometres), and just some 50km south of Santa Cruz, it was favoured as a potential colony for its good supply of both tortoise meat and fresh water up in the hills. General Villamil began Ecuador's first official colony on the islands, the "**Asilo de la Paz**" ("Haven of Peace"), using convict labour in 1832, but he gave up after five years, handing the settlement over to the brutal Colonel José Williams. He kept a pack of vicious dogs to keep his unruly charges at bay, and the Haven of Peace soon acquired the nickname of the "Kingdom of the Dogs", but the hounds weren't protection enough and Williams fled the island for his life after a rebellion in 1841. Almost thirty years later, José de Valdizán sought to rekindle the ill-fated venture, but after eight years his desperate settlers took to arms and fought each other. Valdizán and several others were killed, and the settlement fell apart. All this human interference has not been without effect on Floreana: its tortoise population is extinct, and the **Charles mockingbird** has been so severely decimated by feral cats that it's now only found on the islets Enderby and Campeón off its northeastern shore.

Today, there's a small settlement on the western coast of the island, **PUERTO VELASCO IBARRA**, which is home to fewer than a hundred people. There's just one **place to stay**, the *Pensión Wittmer* (☎05/520150; ❻), run for many years by Margret Wittmer, one of the protagonists of the Galápagos affair (see box opposite), but now taken over by her daughter and grandchildren. As well as providing meals for guests, the Wittmers can give advice on the **hikes** around the island, including back down from the Asilo de la Paz, which is also the site of the island's only water source, having taken a **bus** (truck) to the highlands (2 daily; 30min). Apart from this, it's a very quiet island, with little to see and do, but an unbeatable place to get away from it all. The port is not well connected: the INGALA **boat** passes by for a few hours once every month on its way from Isabela to Santa Cruz. Otherwise, you'll have to arrange a **fibra** which leave from the other ports only infrequently.

Punta Cormorant

At **PUNTA CORMORANT**, on the northernmost tip of Floreana, you'll land by *panga* on a beach made green from deposits of the mineral olivine, a complex silicate of magnesium and iron. If you're expecting to see cormorants here, you'll be disappointed, but a trail to the lagoon behind the mangroves does lead to a variety of wading birds, including **ruddy turnstones, whimbrels, stilts, white-cheeked pintails** and **phalaropes**: above all, though, this

The Galápagos Affair

In the 1930s, a string of deaths and disappearances on Floreana amongst a curious group of European settlers – which became known as the **"Galápagos Affair"** after the book by John Treherne (see "Books" p.557) – made the islands more famous to the contemporary world than even Darwin had done a hundred years earlier. The story began with the arrival of two Germans, **Dr Friedrich Ritter** and his mistress **Dore Strauch**, in 1929. Ritter, a determined, vain and deliberately compassionless man, was pumped up on the ideas of Nietzsche and Lao-tze, and had pretensions to being a great philosopher, rather than breadwinner in a suburban Berlin household. Dore fell under his spell as his patient, and they eventually conspired to run off together, not before setting their abandoned spouses up with each other. Seeing himself as one of Nietzsche's *Übermenschen*, Ritter refused to bring a supply of morphine with him, welcoming the challenge of beating pain "by the power of the will". Not only this, but he had had his and Dore's teeth removed, preferring the reliability of a set of steel dentures – which they shared. He refused to show any love to his mistress, leaving her weeping on the lava when she couldn't carry their supplies, and he wouldn't even clean Dore's burn wounds after she'd knelt in red-hot coals. Towards the end he even beat her, but Dore claimed that her devotion to him never faltered.

The odd couple lived alone on the island until 1932, when the **Wittmer family** – Heinz, Margret and their son Harry – arrived from Cologne. They were a far more practical bunch and stayed out of the way of their strange neighbours as much as they could. A couple of months later, a woman armed with a riding crop and a revolver, calling herself the **Baroness Wagner de Bosquet** and claiming to be an Austrian aristocrat, stormed onto the island with her two German lovers, Rudolf Lorenz and Robert Philippson. Her plan was to build a hotel for millionaires, the *Hacienda Paraíso*, which she set about doing, but before long it became clear to the previous settlers that she was a compulsive liar and a sadistic megalomaniac. She took pleasure in treating Lorenz like a slave and regularly got Philippson to beat him. Soon she was treading on the other settlers' toes, intercepting their mail left at Post Office Bay, stealing supplies left for them by passing yachts, and declaring herself "Empress of Floreana".

Matters came to a head during the long drought of 1934, when the Baroness and Philippson disappeared. According to Margret Wittmer, the Baroness said a friend was taking them to Tahiti, a story backed by Lorenz, who had managed to escape the household shortly before. But Dore claimed she heard a "long-drawn scream" coming from the hacienda and Ritter seemed unusually sure that they had gone for good, even though all the Baroness's belongings were where she'd left them, including her beloved copy of *The Picture of Dorian Gray*. "She won't come back. Take my word for it," he told Margret Wittmer. And he was right – neither the Baroness nor Philippson were ever seen or heard of again.

After their disappearance, Lorenz grew increasingly desperate to leave the island, and persuaded a visiting Norwegian, Nuggerud, to sail him to San Cristóbal. Nuggerud wasn't keen: the sea was rough, he wanted to get back to his wife on Santa Cruz who was about to give birth to their first child, and it was Friday 13th. Nevertheless he relented; four months later, the desiccated bodies of both men were found on Marchena island. Only a few days after this, Ritter fell gravely ill from eating a poisoned chicken cooked by Dore, who said she'd also eaten it, but was only mildly sick. His hatred for his mistress was remorseless and just before he died, he wrote a final message to Dore: "I curse you with my dying breath". Dore returned to Berlin, where she also died, shortly after telling her story in the book, *Satan Came to Eden*. Margret Wittmer, who was the last surviving of the original settlers, died in 2000 aged 95, but the deaths and disappearances on Floreana are no closer to being solved.

is the best place in the islands to see **flamingos**. Around this site are two species of plant found nowhere else in the world, the **cutleaf daisy** (*Leocarpus pinnafitidus*) and a type of **scalesia**.

The trail then passes a viewpoint looking out to a tuff cone, and finishes at **Flour Beach**, so called for its very fine, white sand of ground coral. **Marine turtles** nest here, but it's better known for the schools of **stingrays** that settle in the shallows. You can't swim here, but opposite Punta Cormorant is **Devil's Crown** (also called Isla Onslow), a submerged cone sheltering beautiful coral reefs from the currents outside, which makes for excellent snorkelling and scuba diving. In addition to reef fish such as **surgeonfish**, **angelfish**, **parrotfish** and **wrasse**, you have a chance of meeting **white-tipped reef sharks**, and even **hammerheads**.

Post Office Bay

A few kilometres west of Punta Cormorant is **POST OFFICE BAY**, named such because of a barrel near the beach that has been used for a makeshift mail drop since the end of the eighteenth century. The practice was begun by British whaling ships, who left letters here to be picked up by homeward-bound vessels, and was cleverly exploited during the Anglo-American war of 1812, when the canny US Navy Captain, **David Porter**, intercepted communications here and was able to round up one million tons of shipping in the region's waters.

Over two centuries on and the original **barrel** has long been replaced, but post is still left and delivered free of charge by visitors to the bay. The "post office" is now marked by a shrine of planks, with the names of yachts etched onto them, animal bones, driftwood and many other assorted knick-knacks. Nearby are the remains of a fish canning factory, set up and abandoned by Norwegian colonists in the 1920s, and a trail leading to a lava tube, which you need caving gear to descend. Tour boats and day-trippers from Puerto Ayora regularly call at this site.

Isla Española

In the far southeastern corner of the archipelago, **ESPAÑOLA** is a remote island that features regularly on tour-boat itineraries, a favourite for its seabird colonies and native wildlife. Isolation has led to a number of endemic species. Española's mockingbirds, lava lizards and colourful marine iguanas are found nowhere else in the world, while the waved albatross, the island's star, has only one other home – even then in small numbers – at the Isla de la Plata off the mainland coast. Española's **giant tortoises** were very nearly wiped out – only fourteen were left in the 1970s – but the feral goats causing the problem have since been eradicated from the island, and under a long-term repopulation programme run by the Charles Darwin Research Station, the thousandth Española tortoise reared in captivity was successfully repatriated to the island in March 2000.

Punta Suárez and Gardner Bay

Española's two visitor sites offer very different experiences. At **Punta Suárez**, on the western end of the island, you'll land on a small beach, welcomed by noisy **sea lions**. On the rocks, **marine iguanas** bask in the sun, unusual for rusty colourations that erupt into turquoise and red during the mating season. **Hood mockingbirds**, even more gregarious than their relatives on other islands, will hop to your feet and tug at your shoelaces. From the beach, a long, looped trail heads up to a large plateau covered in **muyuyo**, **croton**, **lycium** and **atriplex** (salt sage), a scrubby costume of plants that bursts into green during the rainy season. The **waved albatross** nests among these bushes from April to December, a giant of a bird that flies alone above the seas for three months, before returning to the island to find its lifelong mate, perform its alluring courtship dance and breed (see also p.541). When it's time to hunt, the adults waddle to the high cliffs at the southern end of the island to launch themselves off, unfurling their 2.5-metre wings. Along the cliffs you'll also find **Nazca boobies**, **swallow-tailed gulls** and **red-billed tropicbirds**; in the west, a blowhole sends a tall jet of spray gushing through a fissure in the lava. The trail then heads back across the plateau, through a field of **blue-footed boobies**, high-stepping and sky-pointing at each other in a cacophony of whistling and honking.

The second visitor site, **Gardner Bay**, on the northeast side of the island, holds one of the most spectacular beaches in the archipelago, a lightly curling strip of soft, white, coral sand, lapped by a dazzling blue sea. Bull **sea lions** energetically patrol the water while their many consorts doze on the sand. As an open site, you can walk the length of the beach without the rest of your group or the guide. It's a good spot for some swimming too, but snorkelling is more fruitful around the offshore islets nearby, most notably **Isla Tortuga**, where **eagle rays**, **white-tipped reef** and **hammerhead sharks** can be seen.

Northern islands: Isla Genovesa

Of the five islands that make up the remote northern group, only **Genovesa** is open to visitors. The tiny islands of **Darwin** and **Wolf**, at the far northwestern reaches of the archipelago, and **Marchena** some 90km north of Santa Cruz, are occasionally visited by scuba divers, but only for offshore exploration, while **Pinta** is out of bounds to all but authorized scientists. Genovesa, lying approximately 95km northeast of Santa Cruz, reached by a night's sailing, is usually only visited by faster boats or as part of longer itineraries. It's well worth the extra effort, however, as it's one of the best bird islands in the Galápagos, and home to the world's largest colony of **red-footed boobies**.

Isla Genovesa

Captains align solar-powered beacons on **GENOVESA** to find the safe route into **Darwin Bay**, formed by a pincer of imposing cliffs rising to 25m over the sea, the remnants of a large, sunken caldera. A wet landing onto a small, coarse-coral beach fringed with saltbush brings you face to face with **Nazca boobies**, **frigate birds**, **swallow-tailed gulls**, **mockingbirds** and **red-footed boobies**. Birds rule the roost here; there are no introduced species, and very few reptiles. The **marine iguanas** on the rocks are among the smallest in the islands, and the absence of land iguanas and giant tortoises means that Genovesa's **prickly pear cacti**, free from their major predators, grow with soft spines. As a trail heads west along the shore past red-footed boobies, you'll also see **great and magnificent frigate birds** nesting in saltbush and red mangroves, with **lava herons** and **Galápagos doves** hopping around the rocks searching for food. **Yellow-crowned night herons** loiter near the tide pools watching for chances to snatch **wrasse**, **blenny** and **damselfish**. Four types of **Darwin's finches** also inhabit the *palo santo* and *croton* scrub. Once you've had your fill of birds, snorkelling in the bay can be thrilling for the schools of **hammerhead sharks** that sometimes congregate at the western arm of the bay.

Amongst the crevices and protrusions at the eastern end of the bay inhabited by **fur seals**, **swallow-tailed gulls** and **red-billed tropicbirds**, is a natural dock and a gully, named **Prince Philip's Steps** after the Duke of Edinburgh's visit in the 1960s. **Nazca boobies** greet you at the top, and another trail takes you through a *palo santo* forest past more red-footed boobies and frigate birds. On the far side you come out of the vegetation to stand above a broad lava flow overlooking the sea. Clouds of **storm petrels** swarm in the sky above their nests hidden in the lava fissures. They're the smallest of the seabirds – small enough, in fact, for the superbly camouflaged **short-eared owls** to prey on them.

Travel details

Ferries

Puerto Ayora to: Puerto Baquerizo Moreno (twice fortnightly; 4hr); Puerto Villamil (fortnightly; 5hr).
Puerto Baquerizo Moreno to: Puerto Ayora (twice fortnightly; 4hr).
Puerto Velasco Ibarra to: Puerto Ayora (monthly; 4hr).
Puerto Villamil to: Puerto Ayora (weekly; 5hr 30min); Puerto Velasco Ibarra (monthly; 4hr).

Flights

Baltra to: Guayaquil (2 daily; 1hr 35min); Puerto Baquerizo Moreno (1 daily Mon–Sat; 25min); Puerto Villamil (1 daily Mon–Sat; 25min); Quito (2 daily; 3hr).
Puerto Baquerizo Moreno to: Baltra (1 daily Mon–Sat; 25min); Guayaquil (1 daily Mon, Wed & Sat; 1hr 35min); Puerto Villamil (1 daily Mon–Sat; 1hr); Quito (1 Mon, Wed & Sat; 3hr).
Puerto Villamil to: Baltra (1 daily Mon–Sat; 25min); Puerto Baquerizo Moreno (1 daily Mon–Sat; 1hr).

Contexts

Contexts

History

Exactly how and when the Americas were populated is still debated, but most authorities accept that humans first migrated from Asia over the Bering land bridge, formed by low sea levels during the last Ice Age, or along the coast aided by prevailing currents, between 40,000 and 12,000 years ago. The earliest evidence of human presence in Ecuador was discovered east of Quito at the El Inga archeological site and dates back to 10,000 BC.

Early cultures

Around this time, small **hunter-gatherer communities** collected seeds, berries, roots, insects and reptile eggs from the valley forests and roamed the high grasslands for bigger game. The set of arrowheads and spear points found here was carved from glassy black obsidian and basalt, materials taken from the huge lava wastes that then scarred the Andes; similar fragments made with hard volcanic materials have been recovered from the Loja and Azuay areas in the southern sierra. On the coast at about this time, other hunter-gatherer groups of the **Las Vegas** culture were emerging around the Santa Elena peninsula, and by 6000 BC they began seasonal cultivation of food crops and cotton – Ecuador's first known **agriculturists**.

Certain characteristics of Las Vegas culture, such as semi-permanent settlements and the fashioning of tools from polished stone, laid the basis for the **Valdivia** culture, which blossomed c.3500 BC and spread across the coast to southern Esmeraldas and El Oro over the next two thousand years, dominating the early **Formative Period** (4000–400 BC). The Valdivia is best known for its ceramics – among the oldest found in South America – especially its "**Venus figurines**", stylized miniatures of women with long, flowing hair and often pregnant, which are believed to have been part of a fertility cult. They lived in oval, wood and thatch houses surrounding a central square, in villages strung along the coast and around river plains, where the soil was fertile enough to grow maize, cotton, cassava, peppers and kidney beans.

In contrast to this, the **Machalilla** culture (1500–800 BC) that followed them preferred rectangular structures on stilts and practised skull deformation as a sign of status. They were more expert than their Valdivia counterparts at fishing and had surplus stores for trading with neighbouring groups. Their ceramic flasks, characterized by circular or "stirrup-shaped" spouts, are similar to those made by the Cotocollao, Cerro Narrío and Upano cultures, suggesting there was contact between them. Based around the Quito area, the **Cotocollao** people traded agricultural produce such as quinoa for coastal cotton, while the **Cerro Narrío** site in the southern sierra was an important trading centre between the coast and the Upano group based around Volcán Sangay in the upper Amazon basin. This communication across the regions seems to have intensified with the **Chorrera** culture (900–300 BC), which flourished on the coast at the close of the Formative Period, a sophisticated people who crafted some of the most beautiful ceramics of that age, distinctive for their iridescent sheen.

The subsequent **Regional Development Period** (300 BC–800 AD) saw a splintering of cultures and the appearance of highly stratified societies. The driving force behind these changes was a burgeoning economy and related interaction between cultures, as each sought goods and resources needed to support an increasingly complex social organization. As trading routes sprang up along the coast, seafaring cultures such as **Bahía** (from south of Bahía de Caráquez, dating to 500 BC–650 AD), **Jama-Coaque** (north of Bahía, from 350 BC to 1540 AD) and **Guangala** (Guayas coast from 100 BC to 800 AD) transported their wares on balsa-wood rafts with cotton sails. The merchants of these cultures took on an elite status alongside their religious orders, in effect acting as diplomats for their group, who ensured a supply of necessary goods from neighbouring tribes. The merchants' most treasured possession, above even gold and platinum, was the deep-crimson **spondylus** (thorny oyster) shell, harvested from a depth of twenty to sixty metres by highly skilled fishermen. Prized ornaments and religious symbols of fertility, the shells were also a kind of universal currency, exchanged for anything from animal furs and armadillo shells to colourful cloths and beeswax. Such was the range of these traders that ceramics representing them – sitting "**basketmen**" figures, often adorned with necklaces, bracelets and earrings, with outsized baskets on their backs – have been found on the Pacific coast from Ecuador to Central America.

Meanwhile, in northern Esmeraldas and stretching into Colombia, the culture of **La Tolita** (500 BC–500 AD) held one of the prime religious and trading centres on the South American coast, thought to have been at the island of La Tolita, in the mangroves near San Lorenzo. Traders, craftsmen and worshippers from different regions swarmed to the site and the intense cross-fertilization of ideas led to the creation of exquisite ceramic styling and, most famously, metalwork, including fine objects of platinum, silver, copper and gold.

The final stage before the arrival of the Incas is known as **Integration** (800–1480 AD), when political leaders and chiefs (*curacas*) of local territories, defined through frequent skirmishes, exacted tribute and levied taxes from their communities. Agricultural productivity surged through improved techniques in irrigation and terracing, and trading continued to boom. On the coast the **Manteño-Huancavilca** culture (500 BC–1540 AD), occupying land from the Gulf of Guayaquil to Bahía de Caráquez, continued the seafaring traditions of their coastal forebears, while also producing distinctive artefacts like ceremonial U-shaped chairs supported by human or animal figures, and black ceramics. To their north, people such as the **Nigua**, **Chachi**, **Campaz**, **Caraque** and **Malaba** continued to live by hunting, fishing and farming small agricultural plots. Inland, to the south, the **Chono** – the ancestors of the Tsáchila (or Colorados) of today, defined archeologically as the **Milagro-Quevedo** culture – were known for fine weavings and gold adornments such as nose rings, headbands and breastplates. They also frequently warred with the fierce **Puná**, who occupied the island of the same name in the Gulf of Guayaquil.

In the highlands at this time, the major population groups occupied the elevated valley basins between the western and eastern cordilleras of the Andes, each basin (*hoya*) separated from the next by mountainous *nudos*, "knots" where the cordilleras tie together. From north to south these were the **Pasto**, occupying southern Colombia and Carchi; the **Cara** (or Caranqui), living around Ibarra, Otavalo and Cayambe, and responsible for enormous ceremonial centres such as the one at Cochasquí; the **Panzaleo** (also called the Quito), who inhabited the Quito valley, Cotopaxi and Tungarahua, and did much trade with the **Quijo** in the Oriente; the **Puruhá**, of the Chimborazo region; the **Cañari**, great gold and copper craftspeople who dominated the southern sierra; and the **Palta**, a tribe whose major centre was Saraguro near Loja and who had strong links with the Amazonian group, the **Shuar**.

The Incas

Around 1200, the **Incas** were an unremarkable sierra people occupying the Cuzco valley in Peru, but when they began large-scale expansion of their territories through victories over neighbouring tribes in the fifteenth century, they grew into one of the most sophisticated civilizations of South America. In about 1460, the Inca **Tupac Yupanqui** set out to conquer present-day Ecuador with a force of 200,000 men. He brushed aside the Palta in the south in a matter of months, but met fierce resistance with the Cañari, and the warring left the whole region devastated. The Cañari had been so impressive in battle that many were eventually recruited into the Inca professional army, but even they weren't as bellicose as the Cara in the north, who managed to keep the invaders at bay for seventeen years before a terrible massacre at Laguna Yahuarcocha in 1495, led by **Huayna Capac**, Tupac Yupanqui's son.

At its height in the early sixteenth century, the Inca Empire, known as **Tahuantinsuyo** ("Land of the Four Quarters", after its administrative division into four regions), extended from Chile and the Argentinian Andes to southern Colombia, a total area of some 980,000 square kilometres, linked by some thirty thousand kilometres of roads. It was a highly organized and efficient society that built great stone palaces, temples, observatories, storehouses and fortresses using masonry techniques of breathtaking ingenuity.

Just as impressive was its administrative system, allowing a relatively small number of people to hold sway over huge areas. **Indirect rule** was imposed on the conquered regions, with the local chief allowed to remain in power as long as he acknowledged the divine sovereignty of the Inca emperor. Lands were divided between the Incas (for the king, nobility and army), religion (for sacrifices, ceremonies and the priesthood) and the local communities, and tribute was paid in the cultivation of the imperial lands. Each year, subjects also had to honour the **mita**, a labour obligation requiring them to spend time working in the army or on public works. A shrewd policy stipulated that the community could not be taxed on its own produce, a measure that did much to ensure contentment and stability in the colonies. Any troublesome subjects were forcefully resettled many hundreds of miles away – and indoctrinated and acculturated colonists were brought in as replacements. Many Palta, for example, were transported to Lake Titicaca in Bolivia, and swapping with communities there that had been under the Inca yoke for decades.

Considering that the Incas were rulers in what is now southern Ecuador for no more than seventy years, and in northern Ecuador for only thirty years, they had an enormous impact on the region. New urban and ceremonial centres were built, such as **Tomebamba** (now buried beneath Cuenca) and **Quito**, with roads connecting them to the rest of the empire, and fortresses were erected at strategic points across the country, as at **Ingapirca**. The language of the Incas, **Quechua**, was imposed on the defeated population and it's still spoken in various forms (as Quichua) by the majority of Ecuador's *indígenas*. The Incas also introduced sweet potatoes, peanuts and oca, and drove large herds of llamas north from Peru for their wool and meat.

By 1525, Huayna Capac was looking to establish a second capital at Quito or Tomebamba. Before he had a chance to act, however, he was struck down by a virulent disease – probably **smallpox**, which had been brought to Central America by the Spanish and had swiftly spread southwards through the continent before them. Not only did he die but so too, among countless other thousands, did his likely heir. In the resulting confusion, two other sons took charge of the Empire: **Huáscar**, who, ruling the south from Cuzco, claimed he was the chosen successor; and **Atahualpa**, who asserted he'd been assigned the north, governed from Quito. Within a few years, friction between the two brothers erupted into a full-blown **civil war**, but Atahualpa had the advantage as the bulk of the imperial army was still in the north after the recent campaigns and under his command. Their forces clashed at Ambato, a pitched battle where more than thirty thousand soldiers from both sides, many of them conscripted locals, were killed. Atahualpa drove his brother south, laying waste to Tomebamba and the Cañari lands in revenge for their support of his enemy. With his superior troops, Atahualpa eventually got the upper hand, but even before he had heard of his generals' final victory over Huáscar in Cuzco, news reached him of a small band of bearded strangers that had landed on the coast nearby, plundering the villages and maltreating the natives.

The Spanish Conquest

C

CONTEXTS | History

In 1526, the Spanish pilot **Bartolomé Ruiz** sailed down the Ecuadorian coast on a reconnaissance mission and, near Salango, captured a large Manta merchant vessel laden with gold, silver and emeralds. His report convinced **Francisco Pizarro** that there were great riches to be had on the continent. After obtaining royal approval, Pizarro set sail from Panama in December 1530 with 180 men and 37 horses, landing at **Tumbes** in northern Peru in May 1532, with a few more troops brought by two other hardy campaigners, Sebastián de Benalcázar and Hernando de Soto. The Inca city, which marked the northernmost limits of the Empire on the coast, lay in ruins from the civil war, and bodies hung from the trees nearby. The Spaniards soon learnt that the civilization had been in the grip of a terrible conflict, and saw that this made the perfect opportunity for conquest.

Pumped up on his victory over Huáscar's army of almost a hundred thousand, Atahualpa didn't regard the Spaniard's straggly band of a few hundred as much of a threat – even the foreigners' fearsome horses, an unknown quantity to the Incas, ate grass and not flesh, as was rumoured. In a fatal miscalculation, the new emperor invited them to a meeting at **Cajamarca**, letting them past countless guard posts and strongholds and over mountainous terrain that would have been too steep for cavalry attacks. A day after his arrival in Cajamarca, Pizarro launched a surprise attack, taking Atahualpa hostage and massacring thousands of Inca soldiers and nobles in just a few hours. Many more were trampled to death in the stampede to escape the Spanish guns, steel armoury and cavalry. Atahualpa, seeing that his captors craved precious metals, offered to fill a room with gold and two huts with silver, in return for which Pizarro promised to restore him to his kingdom at Quito. Within a few months, six metric tons of gold and almost twelve tons of silver had been melted down, making rich men of the conquistadors. Nevertheless, they broke their promise and, fearing a counterattack, swiftly condemned Atahualpa to be burnt alive – a terrifying prospect for someone who believed his body must be preserved for passage into the afterlife – unless he became a Christian. In July 1533, the weeping Inca was baptized and then garrotted.

The Spanish quickly took Cuzco and southern Peru, and then turned their attention to Quito and the northern empire, modern Ecuador – a race was on to find the suspected treasures of its cities. In March 1534, the merciless governor of Guatemala **Pedro de Alvarado** gathered a formidable army, including several thousand Guatemalans, and landed on the Ecuadorian coast in the Manta area. Locals, who entreated him with offerings of food, were either slaughtered or thrown into chains and taken on his campaign. Despite torturing natives to find the best route into the highlands, he ended up going over the highest and most treacherous pass near Chimborazo, and lost many men and horses, as well as the race to Quito.

Sebastián de Benalcázar, meanwhile, had got wind of Alvarado's expedition early on, and swiftly summoned his own forces together, riding across the bleak Peruvian coast onto the Inca highway to Quito. In Tomebamba, where he found beautiful temples encrusted with emeralds and plated in sheets of gold, he forged an alliance with the Cañari, who were bent on exacting revenge for years of subjugation under the Incas. A couple of large Inca armies were still mobilized in the north, and in the cold páramo grasslands at Teocajas above Tomebamba, the tenacious Inca general **Rumiñahui** prepared his fifty thousand troops for attack. They fought bravely, despite a series of devastating cavalry charges, but it was clear that it would take a miracle to beat the Spanish and their horses. He devised a number of ingenious traps, such as pits laid with sharp spikes hidden under the thick grasses, but each time their location was betrayed by informers. Rumiñahui battled with Benalcázar all the way to Quito and before the Spanish could get there he removed the treasures and torched the palaces and food stores. Then, joining forces with another general, **Zopozopagua**, he launched a night attack on the Spanish encamped in the city, but again was thwarted by superior military hardware. Eventually both Rumiñahui and Zopozopagua were caught, tortured and executed. **Quisquis**, the last of Atahualpa's great generals, valiantly fought his way from southern Ecuador to Quito, but when he found the city had already been taken, his army mutinied, hacking him to pieces rather than face death on the battlefields.

In August 1534, the Spaniards founded the city of **San Francisco de Quito** on the charred remains of the Inca capital, and a few months later they had conquered all of the northern part of the Inca empire. The inaccessible north coast and much of the Oriente, however, were deemed too difficult and unproductive to colonize, and stayed out of their control for much of the colonial era. Even so, the Conquest had had a devastating effect on the native populations of Ecuador through war, forced labour and, above all, Old World **diseases**. Smallpox, measles, plague and influenza cut the aboriginal population down from 1.5 million to just 200,000 by the end of the sixteenth century – an overall decline of over eighty-five percent.

The Colonial era

The Spanish were quick to consolidate their victories, with the Crown parcelling out land to the conquistadors in the form of **encomiendas**, grants that entitled the holders, the **encomenderos**, to a substantial tribute in cash, plus produce and labour from the *indígenas* who happened to live there. In return, the *encomenderos* were entrusted with converting their charges to Christianity, a task that was only a partial success; in many cases the *indígenas* merely superimposed Catholic imagery onto their existing beliefs, but eventually the two traditions fused in a syncretism that can still be seen today.

The *encomienda* system grafted easily onto the old Inca order, and the *encomenderos* were soon the elite of the region, which became the **Audiencia de Quito** in 1563. Roughly corresponding to modern-day Ecuador, the *audiencia* had rather vague boundaries, but included a huge swath of the Amazon following Francisco de Orellana's voyage (see p.306). It also enjoyed legal autonomy from Lima and direct links to Madrid, even though it was still a part of the Viceroyalty of Peru. During the early 1600s, there were more than five hundred *encomiendas* in the *audiencia*, run on the labour of about half the region's *indígenas*, who were effectively serfs on these estates, their labour often badly abused despite laws that were supposed to protect them.

Another quarter of the area's *indígenas* deserted the productive *encomienda* lands for the undesirable páramo and lowland forests, but they were rounded up at the end of the century and resettled in purpose-built "Indian towns", or **reducciones**, where colonists could more easily collect tribute and exploit their labour. The Spanish also borrowed – and corrupted – another Inca institution, the *mita*, a system that required these supposedly free *indígenas* to work for a year according to the needs of the colony. These workers, the **mitayos**, received a small wage but it was invariably less than the amount they owed their employers for subsistence purchases. Soon the *mita* system descended into debt slavery, as the *mitayos* worked indefinitely to pay off their unending deficits – which their children would inherit, so trapping them, too. The *audiencia* had such poor mineral resources – the small gold and silver deposits around Cuenca and Loja were exhausted by the end of the sixteenth century – that the *mitayos* were spared the agonies of working in mines: millions of their contemporaries had died in the silver and mercury mines of Peru and Bolivia. Instead, most of the indigenous labourers were involved in agriculture (particularly the farming of introduced wheat, cattle, sheep and chickens) and textiles, an industry that boomed throughout the seventeenth century with the opening of hundreds of sweatshops, known as **obrajes**.

Events of the 1690s, however, saw an abrupt halt to the economic success, as another wave of epidemics wiped out half the native population, droughts destroyed harvests, and severe earthquakes shook the region. This triggered the demise of the *encomiendas*, which were replaced by large private estates, or **haciendas**, but for the *indígenas* the new system of **huasipungo** that the changes entailed brought little relief. In return for their labour on the haciendas, they were entitled to farm tiny plots of land in their spare moments, where they were expected to grow all their own food.

The last quarter of the remaining indigenous population escaped the rule of the Spanish altogether by living in the inaccessible tropical forests of the lowland Oriente or the north coast, the latter area under the control of a **black** and **zambo** (mixed black and indigenous) population, largely the descendants of escaped slaves, brought to work on the coastal plantations or fight in the Spanish army. The south coast had only a tiny workforce available, as more than ninety-five percent of the natives had been wiped out by disease, but even so, **Guayaquil**, founded by Benalcázar in 1535, was developing into an important trade and shipbuilding centre.

In the early 1700s, the Bourbon kings of Spain, who had replaced the Hapsburg dynasty at the beginning of the century, were determined to tighten their grip over their enormous American territories. They embarked on a strategy of economic and administrative reform intended to boost productivity, such as transferring the *audiencia* to the newly established Viceroyalty of Nueva Granada, with its capital at Bogotá, Colombia, in 1717 (an arrangement that lasted three years), and then again in 1739. The expulsion of the Jesuits in

1767 by Charles III, however, only damaged the weak highland economy further. The Jesuits – as well as teaching Christianity to the *indígenas* – had run the best schools and most productive and profitable workshops in the *audiencia*, but their very success had made them unpopular with the Crown. Yet while the highland textile economy suffered severe depression, the **cacao** industry on the coast was flourishing, with the commodity becoming the colony's largest export and plantations springing up all over the countryside north of Guayaquil. Employers were even willing to pay a proper wage for indigenous labourers to work on them, as it was still cheaper than importing slaves.

By the middle of the eighteenth century, a combination of developments brought about a general change of attitude in the Spanish colonies. The **criollos** – Spanish people born in the colonies – were nursing a growing resentment that wasn't helped by the economic situation. High taxes, continual interference from Spain, and the fact that all the best jobs still went to the **peninsulares** – Spanish-born newcomers – only added to the discontent. At the same time, the **Enlightenment** was opening up new lines of political and philosophical thought which filtered down from Europe into the upper-class households of the *audiencia*, fostering ideas that sharply contradicted the semi-feudal organization of the colony. Scientific expeditions, too, were a source of new knowledge, such as **Charles–Marie de La Condamine's** mission (1736–45) to discern the shape of the Earth, which he did by measuring a degree of latitude on the equator north of Quito.

One of the first to articulate the new influences was **Eugenio de Santa Cruz y Espejo**, an exceptional man who, despite being born of *indígena* and mulatto parents in a deeply racist society, obtained a university degree and became an outstanding doctor, lawyer, essayist and satirist. His outspoken views on republicanism and democracy cost him his life – he died in jail in 1795 – but he's still honoured as the progenitor of the country's independence movement.

The birth of the republic

Napoleon's successful invasion of Spain in 1808 sent shockwaves throughout its New World colonies. On August 10, 1809 a short-lived junta in support of the deposed king, **Ferdinand VII**, was established in Quito, but it failed in a matter of weeks when the backing of the rest of the *audiencia* was not forthcoming. Despite assurances of pardons, those involved were rounded up and sentenced to death. In August 1810, an incensed public stormed the prison where the condemned were held, but the guards massacred the junta's leaders before they could be freed. Even so, the disturbances led to a new **junta**, which ambitiously declared the independence of the *audiencia* in 1811, whether the rest of the colony was ready for it or not. With a band of ill-disciplined troops, the new government launched a foolhardy attack against the well-trained Spanish forces and were consequently routed at Ibarra in 1812.

After that defeat, it wasn't until 1820 that the independence movement regained momentum, this time in Guayaquil and led by **José Joaquín de Olmedo**, an intellectual and shrewd politician. Now the timing was right: the city declared its **independence** on October 9, and urgent requests for assistance were immediately sent to the Liberator **Simón Bolívar**, who was marching south from Venezuela, and **José de San Martín**, who was sweeping north from Argentina, crushing the Spanish armies as they went. Bolívar quickly dispatched his best general, the 26-year-old **Antonio José de Sucre**, with a force of seven hundred men. Sucre scored a great victory at Guayaquil, but was thwarted at Ambato, until reinforcements sent by San Martín enabled him to push on to Quito. On May 24, 1822, he won the decisive **Battle of Pichincha**, on the slopes of the volcano above the city, and five days later the old *audiencia* became the **Department of the South** in a new autonomous state, **Gran Colombia**, roughly corresponding to the combined territories of Ecuador, Colombia, Panama and Venezuela today.

The early years of the republic were turbulent, however, and disagreements over the state's border with Peru escalated into armed conflict in 1828. Guayaquil suffered extensive damage during a sea attack, but Sucre and **General Juan José Flores** defeated the Peruvian forces at the Battle of Tarqui in 1829. A year later on May 13, following Venezuela's split from Gran Colombia, Quito representatives also decided to declare their own republic, naming it **Ecuador**, after its position on the equator – other options were "Quito", which wasn't popular with those outside the city, and even "Atahualpia" – and **General Flores**, a Venezuelan by birth who had married into the Quito aristocracy, became the country's first president.

The new nation didn't gel at all well. In the sierra the **Conservative** landowning elites were happy to keep the colonial system in operation, while on the coast the **Liberal** merchant classes, rich on the country's sole export commodity, cacao, wanted free trade, lower taxes and a break with the old order. This dualism between the regions – and their great centres, Quito and Guayaquil – has coloured the politics and history of the country ever since.

Flores soon found his heavy-handed and Quito-oriented administration desperately unpopular on the coast, and cannily arranged for the Guayaquileño politician **Vicente Rocafuerte** to take the second term. Meanwhile Flores lurked in the background, pulling the strings as head of the military, and became president again from 1839 to 1845, when he was ousted by a junta from the coast. For the next fifteen years, the country descended into a political mire, with bitter fighting between the regions and the seat of government moving from Quito to Guayaquil to Riobamba and back to Guayaquil. Eleven presidents and juntas followed each other in power, the most successful being led by the Liberal **General José María Urbina**, who ruled with an iron fist from 1851 to 1856 and managed to **abolish slavery** within a week of the coup that swept him to the presidency. Moreover, he had strongly encouraged his predecessor, **General Francisco Robles**, to axe the tribute that the *indígenas* were still being forced to pay after three centuries of abuse.

The turmoil of the era culminated in 1859 – later known as the **Terrible Year** – when the strain between the regions finally shattered the country: Quito set up a provisional government, Cuenca declared itself autonomous, Loja became a federal district and, worst of all, Guayaquil, led by General Guillermo Franco, signed itself away to Peruvian control. Peru invaded and blockaded the port, while Colombia hungrily eyed the rest of Ecuador for itself.

Conservative rule: 1861–95

Aiming to set the republic right, **Gabriel García Moreno** quashed the various rebellions with the help of Flores and seized power as president in 1861. Although born into a poor family in Guayaquil, García Moreno was educated in Quito and Europe and was both fiercely Conservative and a devout Catholic. He saw the country's salvation in the Church, and set about strengthening its position, establishing it as the state religion, signing control over to the Vatican, founding schools staffed only by Catholics, dedicating the republic to the "Sacred Heart of Jesus" and making **Catholicism** a prerequisite for citizenship. He was also ruthless with his many opponents, crushing them and several coup attempts with savage efficiency – for example, shooting the son of the Liberal rebel Vallejo before his father, then executing Vallejo himself.

His presidency did, however, help foster growth in agriculture and industry, initiating a much-needed programme of road-building and beginning the Quito–Guayaquil railway, as well as creating the first national currency. Nevertheless he was hated by the Liberals for his authoritarianism and for strengthening the Church. One of the loudest critics was **Juan Montalvo**, who vilified his policies from the safety of self-imposed exile. In 1875, just after Moreno had been elected to his third term of office, the president was murdered by an assassin with a machete on the steps of the Palacio de Gobierno; when Montalvo heard, he exclaimed, "My pen has killed him!"

After García Moreno's death, Conservative power waned and an uprising brought military dictator **General Ignacio de Veintimilla** to the presidency, a man who was surprisingly popular, perhaps for his large-scale public works programmes and boisterous public fiestas. From 1884 to 1895 the country returned to constitutional governments, overseen by three progressive Conservative presidents who navigated between radical Conservatism and Liberalism. Yet their success in bridging the divide was limited, and all the while the Liberals were accruing power and influence as the late nineteenth and early twentieth centuries saw phenomenal growth in Ecuador's **exports**. For a time the country was the world's leading producer of cacao, and coffee, tagua nuts and Panama hats were also doing well – products all based on the coast around Guayaquil – and much of the money filled Liberal coffers.

The Liberal era: 1895–1925

A committed revolutionary and Liberal, **Eloy Alfaro** had been involved in guerrilla skirmishes with García Moreno's Conservative forces since his early twenties. He'd already fled the country twice before Liberal cacao lords sought his return and funded a military coup that brought him to power in 1895. Fervently anti-clerical, Alfaro immediately set about undoing García Moreno's work and began measures that would permanently weaken the Catholic Church in Ecuador. In his two terms as president (1897–1901 and 1906–11), Alfaro defined the radical Liberal position, secularizing the state and education, expelling foreign clergy, instituting civil marriage and divorce and cutting links with the Vatican. He ploughed money into public works and saw through the completion of the Quito–Guayaquil railway with the help of US investors.

He was under attack, however, from both Conservatives and Liberal party factions sympathetic to his rival **General Leonidas Plaza** (president from 1901–05 and 1912–16). To fend off the revolts, largely instigated by Conservative rebels with the backing of the Church, Alfaro allocated forty percent of his entire budget to military expenditure. The split within the Liberal camp worsened, and when Alfaro's chosen presidential successor, Emilio Estrada, died suddenly just after his inauguration in 1911, the country fell into a bloody **civil war**. A year later, Plaza's forces defeated Alfaro, and he and his supporters were transported on the new railway to Quito, where they were murdered, dragged through the streets and burnt in the Parque Ejido.

Although the 1918 scrapping of debtor imprisonment ended the system of **debt peonage** against the *indígenas* that had been lingering since colonial times, the civil war had drained the state's cash supply. Power shifted from the cash-strapped government to **la argolla**, a "ring" of wealthy cacao merchants and bankers, underpinned by the private Banco Comercial and Agrícola in Guayaquil. The bank provided loans to a succession of ailing administrations at the expense of rocketing inflation rates, and became so influential that it was said that any politician needed its full backing to be successful.

In the 1920s, Ecuador descended into an **economic crisis**, a symptom of this arrangement, crippling inflation and a severe slump in cacao production. A devastating blight damaged the crop, and cacao prices plunged as the market was swamped by new producers, especially British colonies in Africa. The poor were hit very badly, and uprisings – one in 1922 by workers in Guayaquil and another in 1923 by *indígena* peasants on a highland estate – were suppressed with massacres. The bloodless **Revolución Juliana** of 1925 effectively marked the end of the old Liberal–Conservative tug-of-war and ushered in a disoriented era of coups and overthrows.

The history of a border dispute

Even when the Audiencia de Quito was created in 1563, there was a rumble of discontent from Lima over the position of the **boundary** – the first articulation of a tension that was to dog relations between the two countries for more than four centuries. As a part of the Viceroyalty of Nueva Granada in the early eighteenth century, the territory of the *audiencia* extended well into present-day Peru, far south of Tumbes and at least 200km east of Iquitos. After Independence, bitter fighting between the new states of Peru and Gran Colombia over their border resulted in the **Mosquera-Pedemonte Treaty** of 1830, which established a boundary along the ríos Huancabamba, Marañón and Amazonas all the way to Brazil. During the course of the nineteenth century, the vast eastern areas of rainforest were slowly populated by Peruvian settlers, who began to overwhelm what little Ecuadorian presence there was. The 1890 **García-Herrera Treaty** attempted to address this growing territorial problem, by splitting the region in half, but both Peru and Ecuador threw it out four years later. The king of Spain was called in to arbitrate, but he came up with a solution that left Ecuador even worse off, and the government rejected it outright, leaving the matter undecided. Shortly afterwards, Brazil annexed a chunk of Ecuador's remotest Amazonian lands, and a further sliver was signed away to Colombia in 1916 through the **Muñoz Vernaza-Suárez Treaty** to resolve another border dispute. Six years later, the Colombians traded part of this territory to Peru – much to Ecuador's alarm – for navigation rights on the Amazon. Peru continued to expand into Ecuador's land during the early twentieth century and despite a series of talks and protocols in the 1920s and 1930s, the two countries failed to come to any agreement.

This set the stage for the **Peruvian invasion** in 1941, in which the ill-equipped Ecuadorian army was outnumbered five to one and unable to defend its huge Oriente territory and southern provinces. Lima stated that it would only retreat from El Oro and Loja if Ecuador could come to a final agreement about the border. The result was the 1942 Protocol of Peace, Friendship and Boundaries between Ecuador and Peru, more commonly called the **Rio Protocol**, which gave almost half of Ecuador's territory to Peru.

The Ecuadorian government wasn't happy but had no choice other than to accept these terms, and so they did until 1947, when the US started taking aerial photos of

Political crisis: 1925–47

After two swift juntas, the military handed power to **Isidro Ayora** in 1926, who embarked on a programme of reforms, including the creation of the Banco Central in Quito to smash the influence of *la argolla*. However, the new bank couldn't temper the rate of inflation, and popular discontent forced Ayora's resignation in 1931. Fuelled by the woeful economic condition at home and the Great Depression worldwide, the country's political cohesion finally crumbled away. In the 1930s, a total of fourteen men took the presidency, and from 1925 to 1948, Ecuador had twenty-seven governments.

Out of the turbulence of this era came the first of **José María Velasco Ibarra**'s five presidential terms, which began in 1934 and lasted less than a year, thanks to his removal by the military when he tried to assume dictatorial powers. He went into exile until the 1940s, and chaos reigned.

In 1941, while government troops were tied up in Quito defending the presidency of **Carlos Arroyo del Río**, Peru invaded, quickly seizing much of the Oriente and occupying the provinces of El Oro and Loja in the south. The occupation only ended after the nations signed the **Rio Protocol** of January

the region and found a new river, the **Cenepa**, running between the ríos Santiago and Zamora. Ecuador seized on this discovery to bring the Rio Protocol into question. It stipulated that in the Cordillera del Cóndor the border be drawn at the watershed between the Santiago and Zamora rivers – but now the Cenepa made that division ambiguous. In 1951, President Galo Plaza said that the country did not recognize the border in this area, and in 1960, Velasco Ibarra nullified the entire protocol, severing all diplomatic links with Peru. From then on, Ecuadorian maps showed their territory as it stood before 1920.

During the 1970s, relations thawed somewhat after the foundation of the Andean Common Market (also known as the Andean Pact) in 1969, which joined together Ecuador, Peru, Colombia and Chile as trading partners. But by 1981, the old animosity had returned and fighting broke out along the 78km of disputed border in the Cordillera del Cóndor. Rodrigo Borja did much to heal the wounds when he invited the Peruvian president, Alberto Fujimori, to Quito in 1992, but just three years later an **undeclared war** erupted in the same region. The fighting was the worst seen since the 1941 attack, and for the first time in South American history, air-to-air combat was involved. At one stage, both countries claimed that they had control of a hill region in the midst of it called **Tiwintza**, but Ecuador pulled off a media victory by flying out international reporters to the area equipped with GPS devices to confirm their position and that Ecuador had control of it. After two months of fighting a ceasefire was agreed, and the Ecuadorian president, Durán Ballén, declared that the Rio Protocol was once again in operation, so laying the groundwork for a peace process.

On October 26, 1998, presidents Jamil Mahuad and Alberto Fujimori signed an historic **peace treaty** in Brasilia, setting the boundary over the contested 78-kilometre stretch, and bringing the long-standing dispute to an end. Although the border is little changed from that agreed in 1942, in a gesture of goodwill Peru granted one square kilometre of its territory at Tiwintza to Ecuador as private property under Peruvian sovereignty, and will build a road linking it to the Ecuadorian border. The treaty also provides Ecuador with navigational rights on the Amazon and the establishment of two contiguous national parks on each side of the border. Furthermore, US\$3 billion in international aid has been set aside to regenerate this region, so impoverished by years of dispute.

1942, but 200,000 square kilometres of Ecuador's eastern territory – almost half of the country at the time – were ceded to Peru. Although the land was largely unexplored and uninhabited, the loss was a huge blow to national pride in a country that had identified itself with the Amazon since its navigation by Francisco de Orellana four hundred years earlier.

The exiled Velasco, mouthing promises of "national resurrection" and social justice, forged an unlikely alliance between Conservatives and Socialists, and ousted the disgraced Arroyo in 1944. However, Velasco soon ejected the leftists in his alliance, and his high-minded promises dissolved as he squandered government reserves on various pet projects. By 1947 he lost his support and was deposed. Three presidents soon came and went before Galo Plaza Lasso took the helm in 1948, adding some much-needed stability into the republic.

Prosperity and decline: 1948–72

Galo Plaza Lasso was the son of the former Liberal president Leonidas Plaza, but he also had strong links with the powerful Conservative families in the sierra, and so was well-placed to form a stable government. Committed to democracy, he strove for the freedom of speech and the press, and as a fair and popular president, he was the first since 1924 to complete his term of office.

The stability he had helped foster was due in large part to economic prosperity brought on by the **banana boom**. After World War II, the world demand for bananas went through the roof, and while the traditional exporters in the Caribbean and Central America had trouble with crop diseases, Ecuador had huge parcels of ex-cacao land ready to be given over to bananas – and soon the country became the world's largest exporter, a position that it retains today. Government reserves brimmed over and money was invested in infrastructure to open up more areas of the countryside to banana farms. Large areas around Santo Domingo, for example, were cleared for agriculture and **colonists** flooded to the coast – between 1942 and 1962, the population in the region rose by more than one hundred percent. As the industry was dominated by small and medium-sized farms, the new wealth spread through society far more completely than it had during the cacao boom.

The prosperity and well-being was such that even Velasco managed to complete his third term in office (1952–56), the only one that he did. His successor **Camilo Ponce Enríquez** also saw his term through, but in the late 1950s, as world demand for bananas slumped and export prices fell, **unemployment** began to rise and people took to the streets in protest.

Once again the master-populist Velasco was elected by a large majority, thanks to his oratory and promise of support to the urban poor. Exploiting the popularity of the recent Cuban revolution, he laced his speeches with anti-US attacks, and won the support of the Ecuadorian left. Before long, however, pressure from the US on Latin America to cut ties with Cuba heightened tensions between leftists and anti-Communists. Hopes that the country had at last achieved political maturity were dashed as Velasco's coalition disintegrated under the strain, and rival groups resorted to violence; a gun battle even broke out in Congress between anti-Velasco legislators and pro-government spectators, though no one was hurt. In a desperate search for revenue, Velasco put taxes on consumer items, sparking **strikes** across the country.

As crises loomed and a Cuba-style revolution threatened, the military installed Velasco's vice president, **Carlos Julio Arosemena Monroy**, in 1961, but he soon became unpopular with the establishment for refusing to sever links with Cuba and was branded a Communist. The damage to his credibility had been done by the time he relented in 1962, but by then he was a broken man and had hit the bottle. A year later a **military junta** took power, jailing the opposition and suppressing the left, though it did pass the **1964 Agrarian Reform Law**, which at last brought the *huasipungo* system to an end, even if it didn't achieve a far-reaching redistribution of land. As banana prices plummeted in 1965, the junta ran up against serious cash-flow problems and was forced to step down the following year.

Elections in 1968 brought the 75-year-old Velasco back to power by the slenderest of margins. The economic situation was so serious that Velasco, for once, took the unpopular route, devaluing the sucre and raising import tariffs, but to temper these measures, he seized US fishing boats found inside Ecuador's territorial limits, the so-called "**tuna war**". After two years, and relying heavily on the help of his nephew in the military, he assumed dictatorial powers (as he had done during two of his other terms) and clung to power until his overthrow by the military in 1972, ending his epic political career.

Military control and the oil boom: 1972–79

The military, led by **General Guillermo Rodríguez Lara**, seized control because it was anxious that the flighty populist, **Asaad Bucaram**, former mayor of Guayaquil, would be victorious in the upcoming elections, and because it aimed to be the custodian of the large **oil reserves** found in the Oriente. Texaco's explorations in 1967 had struck rich, locating high-quality oil fields near Lago Agrio, and by 1971 more than twenty international companies had swarmed to the Oriente on the scent of a fortune.

The junta was aggressively nationalist in stance, and determined that the state should get as much from the oil boom as possible. Contracts with foreign companies were renegotiated on more favourable terms, a state-owned petroleum company was set up, and in 1973 Ecuador joined the **Organization of Petroleum Exporting Countries** (OPEC). Money flooded into the public sector, stimulating employment, industrialization, economic growth and urbanization. The Oriente infrastructure was revolutionized, and in 1971 Texaco built a road to Lago Agrio, the first to leave the eastern Andean foothills. To keep Colombia or Peru from getting ideas about the oil-rich lands, colonists such as military conscripts were encouraged into the region by the thousands. The huge **environmental cost** of all the colonization and oil-industry activity, however, is still being felt.

The junta pushed its nationalist stance too far when it declared that the state's stake in Texaco operations should be upped to 51 percent, discouraging further foreign investment and prospecting. Oil production fell by a fifth, but this was offset for the time being by a sharp rise in global prices. Yet even with the huge increases in revenues and booming economy, the government managed to overspend on its nationalization and industrialization schemes, racking up some impressive **debts** along the way. Trying to redress the balance, it slapped sixty-percent duty on luxury imports, upsetting the private sector and sparking a failed coup that claimed 22 lives. Rodríguez Lara's position was weakened enough, though, for a second, bloodless coup in 1976, led by a triumvirate of military commanders, who sought to return government to civilian rule, but on their terms. It took almost three years for them to do so, as they tried to deny the now ardent anti-militarist Bucaram – whom they prohibited from running – and his centre-left coalition from winning.

The return to democracy: 1979–87

No one believed that a begrudging military would hand over power to the new centre-left coalition candidate, **Jaime Roldós Aguilera**, until it actually did so in August 1979, largely thanks to Roldós' landslide election victory three months earlier and heavy pressure from US President Jimmy Carter. Since the oil boom, the **economic landscape** of the country had transformed: per-capita income was five times greater than before 1972, employment was up by ten percent, and a new urban middle class emerged. Despite the new wealth, the position of the rural poor, the *indígenas* and the workers hadn't much changed, and inequality was as entrenched as ever. Roldós' plans for wide-ranging structural reforms fell through as a bitter rivalry had developed between him and his party associate, Bucaram – now the leader of an opposition-dominated Congress – who set about blocking the Roldós agenda.

By 1981, the economic situation again looked precarious. The country had an enormous budget deficit, in large part due to overspending by Bucaram's Congress. Worse still, trouble flared up on the Peruvian border, adding to the financial burden. Then, in May, three months after a ceasefire with Peru, Roldós was killed in an airplane crash near Loja, fuelling conspiracy theories.

His vice president **Osvaldo Hurtado Larrea** stepped in and tried to push on with the reform programme, but the economic situation rapidly deteriorated. Oil prices fell sharply, and gross domestic product shrank by more than three percent; **inflation** rates soared, **unemployment** climbed and the Unitary Workers' Front (*Frente Unitario de Trabajadores*) called four **general strikes**; **El Niño** floods caused US$1 billion of damage, while **blight** ravaged highland potato crops. Still, Hurtado did manage to take unpopular austerity measures to combat a **foreign debt** that had spiralled to US$7 billion, and to secure constitutional elections and the transition of power to a second democratically elected government – the first time in almost 25 years.

The 1984 general election was won by **León Febres Cordero Rivadeneira** and his broad-based centre-right coalition. Inspired by the Reagan and Thatcher administrations, the new government embarked on a "neo-liberal" programme stressing free markets, foreign investment, exports and the roll-back of state power. Yet the government was plagued by allegations of **corruption** and **human rights abuses**, and as the cost of living rose, public disquiet grew. In 1986, shortly after a failed coup attempt by air-force general **Frank Vargas**, Febres Cordero was held hostage by Vargas supporters and threatened with death unless the general was released. The president immediately complied, an act perceived as cowardly by the public. To add to the country's woes, in March 1987 a serious **earthquake** rocked the Oriente, killing hundreds, making tens of thousands homeless, and destroying 40km of the Trans-Andean oil pipeline. The economy was crippled as oil production stopped for six months while the pipeline was repaired, and Febres Cordero was forced to default payment on foreign debts totalling more than US$10 billion.

The close of the twentieth century

The failure of right-wing politics led in 1988 to social democrat **Rodrigo Borja Cevallo** winning a convincing victory with his *Izquierda Democrática* party (Democratic Left). Borja's reform programme, called "**gradualismo**", steered the country away from the policies of Febres Cordero and aimed to protect human rights and press liberties, kick-start the nation's literacy programmes and rejuvenate relations with Peru. However, runaway inflation led to a wave of national strikes, and in 1990 an umbrella organization of the nation's indigenous peoples, **CONAIE** (*Confederación de Nacionalidades Indígenas del Ecuador*), staged an uprising, calling for rights to land and territories, the right to self-government and the creation of a multinational Ecuadorian state. The same year, twelve Huaorani communities received territorial rights to land bordering the Parque Nacional Yasuní in the Oriente.

Desperate to fix the economy, the public switched its support back to the right, voting in the 72-year-old **Sixto Durán Ballén** in 1992. He strove for modernization, privatization and reduction of state bureaucracy, but his administration was dogged by hostility from labour unions and CONAIE, as well as **corruption** scandals, and in 1995 his vice president, Alberto Dahik, fled the country to avoid prosecution over mismanagement of funds.

The 1996 elections brought a shock when outsider **Abdalá Bucaram** – known as "**El Loco**" (the Madman) – the nephew of Asaad Bucaram, won by wooing the masses with an informal populist style, promising increased subsidies and a stronger public sector. His publicity stunts included releasing his own CD ("Madman in Love"), shaving off his Hitler-style moustache (he was an admirer), and offering to pay Diego Maradona $1 million of public money to play a soccer game in Ecuador. Before long, though, Bucaram betrayed his supporters with austerity measures that made utility prices skyrocket, and rumours of large-scale mismanagement of funds and **corruption** involving his family also began to circulate. In just a year, his popularity plummeted and trade unions called a general strike. Congress voted him out of office on grounds of "**mental incapacity**", but Bucaram stubbornly clung to the job, holing up in the presidential palace. For a few days in February 1997, he, his vice president Rosalía Arteaga, and the leader of Congress, Fabián Alarcón, all claimed to be the rightful president. Meanwhile huge crowds gathered around the building, chanting for Bucaram's removal. Ultimately, he fled to Panama, allegedly carrying suitcases stuffed with embezzled cash – according to some reports, he may have robbed the country of nearly a hundred million dollars.

Fabián Alarcón muddled through the commotion as interim president, faced with economic stagnation and corruption allegations, and in 1998 the Harvard-educated mayor of Quito, **Jamil Mahuad**, beat Alvaro Noboa, a wealthy banana baron and candidate of Bucaram's party. But the country's finances were in total disarray and even the government claimed it to be Ecuador's worst **economic crisis** in seventy years. Compounding a zero growth rate in the economy, inflation floated at around fifty percent, oil prices slid and El Niño wreaked $2.6 billion of damage, including the devastation of the banana harvest. By March 1999 rumours circulated that foreign-currency bank accounts would be confiscated to peg the sucre to the dollar. In the confusion, the sucre slumped by 25 percent to an all-time low against the dollar, and Mahuad quickly announced a series of surprise "bank holidays" to prevent panic-stricken investors withdrawing their deposits.

A two-day **general strike** and demonstrations followed, some of them violent. The government declared a state of emergency and deployed more than fifteen thousand soldiers and police to get strikers back to work, but they were left powerless when indigenous groups barricaded the highways, bringing fifteen provinces to a standstill. Even so, Mahuad pushed on with his **austerity measures**, and as the strike ended he announced he was terminating fuel subsidies – hiking the price of a gallon of petrol up from $1 to $1.90, and electricity prices by four hundred percent – increasing sales taxes, cutting state bureaucracy and clamping down on tax evaders. Most controversially, he froze more than $3 billion of bank deposits, preventing people from withdrawing more than a few hundred dollars' savings – measures which didn't save banks from folding or stop the slide of the sucre. His approval rating plummeted instantly to just nine percent and many openly called for his resignation.

In July 1999, another wave of strikes hit, this time from taxi and bus drivers protesting about the rise in fuel prices. Their allies CONAIE helped block the roads and gathered a crowd of twenty thousand to march into the capital, overpowering the military blockades. Mahuad placated them by agreeing to leave prices alone till December, and that September, facing a **foreign debt** of $16 billion, Ecuador defaulted on a Brady-bond interest payment, the first country ever to do so. While bondholders were furious, even Mahuad's opponents praised him for putting the needs of the people above those of foreign creditors. But trouble for the president was by no means over.

Into the 21st century

By January 2000, Ecuador's economy had shrunk by seven percent from the previous year, inflation was running higher than sixty percent and the sucre had devalued by almost three hundred percent in twelve months. In a desperate bid to save his presidency, Mahuad announced the resignation of his entire cabinet and declared his intent to adopt the US dollar as the national currency.

Making up almost half of the country's 12.5 million population, some eighty percent of them living in poverty, Ecuador's indigenous people saw **dollarization** as a nefarious system favouring banks and private interests at the expense of the poor, who would have to meet rising consumer prices with ever-dwindling wages. CONAIE mobilized its supporters, and tens of thousands of *indígenas* filtered into Quito under the noses of troops posted to stop them. After a week of demonstrations, though, even the soldiers started to join in, and on January 21, 2000 the military unit guarding Congress stepped aside, and the indigenous groups stormed the building and announced the removal of Mahuad, the dissolution of Congress and the Supreme Court, and proclaimed the formation of the "**Junta of National Salvation**". The group comprised Antonio Vargas, the leader of CONAIE, Carlos Solórzano, a former Supreme Court chief justice, and Colonel Lucio Gutiérrez, one of the many mid-ranking officers who had joined the rebellion.

Only hours later, however, the junta called for vice president **Gustavo Noboa** to take up the presidency. When members of Congress reconvened, they ruled that Mahuad – still defying calls to resign – had abandoned his office, and voted Noboa in as president, the country's sixth in four years. More than seventy military officers would later be arrested and given prison sentences of just a few days, while a further 113 soldiers were granted amnesty by

Congress. Mahuad went into exile, and he and his finance advisors still face prosecution for abusing their power by freezing private bank deposits during the crisis.

Regarded as honest and unaffected by the grandiose trappings of office, the portly, former university rector Noboa forged ahead with dollarization, implementing it in 2001 with the help of a $2 billion aid package. Though it helped economic stability and averted the threat of hyperinflation, it came at the cost of rising prices and worsening conditions for the ever-increasing poor.

In the 2002 elections another outsider, **Lucio Gutiérrez**, an ex-colonel involved in the 2001 coup, won with the backing of indigenous groups and unions. Pledging to root out corruption – a colossal task in a country rated as the continent's second-most corrupt – Gutiérrez faces a huge national debt and chronic lack of foreign investment, social inequality that has up to eighty percent of the population mired in poverty, and deteriorating security on the Colombian border caused by paramilitaries and guerrillas – problems that will need an exceptional leader to resolve.

Mainland geography and wildlife

I n terms of both wildlife and geography Ecuador is one of the most diverse
countries in the world. No larger than the US state of Nevada, this
diminutive country is home to nearly 1600 species of birds, 230 different
mammals, 680 amphibians and reptiles, twenty thousand flowering plants
and more than a million types of insects.

The mainland comprises three geographical regions and an extraordinary
variety of habitats and ecosystems. In the **sierra**, mountain páramos, snow-
tipped volcanoes and the Andean mountains form the north–south spine of
the country. To the east, they slope down through primeval cloudforests into
the tropical rainforests of the **Oriente** and the Amazon basin, forming an
unassailable wall that prevents moist air from heading west, ensuring the rainforests have high levels of annual precipitation. On the west of the Andes, the
coast (*costa*, or *litoral*) comprises dry and tropical forests, lowland hills and a
shoreline of expansive beaches and mangrove swamps.

The sierra

Around one hundred million years ago, the westward-moving South American
tectonic plate collided with the eastward-moving Nazca plate, which holds the
southern Pacific Ocean, and the **Andes** mountains rose along the edge of the
South American landmass. In Ecuador, they consist of two parallel mountain
chains, or cordilleras, separated by a broad central valley – which the German
explorer, Alexander von Humboldt, named the Avenue of the Volcanoes in
1802. This central valley is itself divided into a series of fertile basins (*hoyas*), cut
off from one another by "knots" (*nudos*) of intermediate hills. The basins have
been populated for hundreds of years – in several cases, thousands of years –
and even today are home to almost half the country's population.

A relatively young mountain range, the sharp, jagged peaks of the Andes,
reaching almost 7000m in places, are not yet rounded by erosion and are still
growing as the two underground giants continue to rumble against each other,
making Ecuador geologically unstable and volatile. Not only are **earthquakes**
and **tremors** common, but Ecuador also has a number of active **volcanoes** –
Cotopaxi, at 5897m, is one of the highest in the world. Ten of Ecuador's volcanoes exceed the snow line (5000m), and the summit of Chimborazo, at
6310m, actually surpasses Everest as the point furthest from the centre of the
Earth, thanks to the planet's bulge around the equator. Major eruptions
occurred as recently as 2002, when Reventador belched out two hundred million cubic tons of ash, much of which settled on and around Quito, while in
1999 Tungurahua spewed out a river of lava, forcing the evacuation of the local
population for several months. Two months later, Guagua Pichincha, bordering
the Quito valley, also exploded and released an eleven-kilometre-high mushroom cloud of ash, vapour and gas into the sky and down onto the city,
although a major evacuation wasn't necessary in this case.

The El Niño effect

Nature's footnote to the end of the last millennium, the 1997–98 **El Niño** wreaked havoc with global climate patterns and brought chaos to much of the world. In Ecuador alone, **floods** and **landslides** killed more than 220 people and made thirty thousand families homeless. The infrastructure, too, was severely damaged as the storms washed away more than 1600km of main roads, 11,000km of secondary roads and over fifty bridges. In the worst affected coastal areas, cases of hepatitis, cholera, malaria and dengue fever escalated. As all the Pacific Rim countries affected by El Niño pick up the pieces, conservative estimates of the cost of reparation is at around US$20 billion.

The phenomenon itself is no new occurrence. Records document such events more than four hundred years ago, but it was only in the 1960s that the Norwegian meteorologist Jacob Bjerknes identified the processes that lead to an event. He saw that the El Niño – meaning "the Little Boy" or "the Christ Child", a name given by Peruvian fishermen to the body of warm water that would arrive around Christmas – was intimately connected to extremes in the so-called **Southern Oscillation**, wherein atmospheric pressures between the eastern equatorial Pacific and the Indo-Australian areas behave as a seesaw, the one rising as the other falls.

In "normal" years, easterly trade winds blow across the Pacific, pushing warm surface water westwards towards Indonesia, Australia and the Philippines, where the water becomes about 8°C warmer and about half a metre higher than on the other side of the ocean. Back in the east, the displacement of this water allows the cold, nutrient-rich water, known as the Humboldt or Peru Current, to swell up from the depths along the coast of South America, providing food for countless marine and bird species.

An **El Niño event**, however, occurs when the trade winds fall off and the layer of warm water in the west laps back across the ocean, warming up the east Pacific and cooling the west. Consequently, air temperatures across the whole of the Pacific begin to even out, tipping the balance of the atmospheric pressure seesaw, which further reduces the strength of the trade winds. Thus the process is enhanced as warm water continues to build up in the eastern Pacific – bringing with it abnormal amounts of rainfall to coastal South America, whilst also completely starving other areas of precipitation. The warm water also forces the cold Humboldt current and its micro organisms to deeper levels, effectively removing a vital link in the marine food chain, killing innumerable fish, sea birds and mammals. Meanwhile, the upset in the Southern Oscillation disturbs weather systems around the world, resulting in severe and unexpected weather.

In the past twenty years, El Niño-Southern Oscillation (**ENSO**) events seem to have become stronger, last longer and occur with greater frequency, leading many to suggest that human activity, such as the warming of the Earth's atmosphere through the greenhouse effect, could well be having an influence. If this is true, failure to cut emissions of greenhouse gases may in the end cost the lives and livelihoods of millions of people across the world.

The **Andean climate** varies widely according to altitude, the time of year, and even the time of day. There are just two seasons: dry (June–Sept) and wet (Oct–May), although even during April, the wettest month, downpours rarely occur every day. Whatever the time of year, daytime temperatures average highs of 20–22°C (68–72°F) and lows of 7–8°C (45–46°F), though there is huge local variation.

Below the snow line of the highest Andean peaks is a slender margin of tundra-like *gelodifitia*, where little more than mosses and lichens can survive the freezing nights and frigid soils. From around 4700m to 3100m, the climate of the **páramo** is less harsh, allowing for a wider range of life. Covering ten percent of Ecuador's total land area, the vegetation is dominated by dense tussocks of *Festuca* or *Calamgrostis* grasses, along with terrestrial bromeliads and ferns. In the wetter páramo, pockets of *Polylepis* forest grow, one of the few trees that can survive at this altitude. Plants tend to have small thick leaves to resist the nightly frosts and waxy skins to reflect the intense ultraviolet radiation during cloudless spells. Páramo soil is sodden, and excess water collects in the hundreds of lakes that spangle the undulating scenery. The first signs of **wildlife** also emerge in the páramo with mammals such as the Andean spectacled bear, South American fox and white-tailed deer, and birds like the Andean condor, Andean snipe, tawny antpitta and various hummingbirds.

Lower than the páramo are the **cloudforests**, masking the sierra in dense vegetation between 1800m and 3500m. Wet, green, vibrant and extraordinarily beautiful, cloudforests feel like the prehistoric habitat of dinosaurs. Streaked by silvery waterfalls, the forests are shrouded in heavy mists for at least part of each day, as moisture from the lowland forests rises, cools and condenses. It's this dampness that creates such lush conditions, giving rise to an abundance of **epiphytes** (from the Greek for "upon plants"), such as **lichens, liverworts, mosses, ferns** and **bromeliads**, which drape over the trees, densely packed together with knotty trunks and dark-coloured bark. They aren't parasites, but simply claim a branch space, set out roots and grow there as independent canopy residents. Many **orchids** are epiphytes, preferring moss-covered branches or exposed bark to normal soil – harbouring more than 3500 species, Ecuador is thought to have more orchids than any other country in the world. In a ten-square-kilometre patch of eastern cloudforest alone, two hundred orchids have been counted, only a little less than Kenya's country-wide total.

Cloudforests are also home to an incredible range of animals such as woolly tapirs, spectacled bears and pumas, and they have an exceptional level of bird endemism – species unique to a place and not found anywhere else. At higher altitudes, the cloudforest is called **elfin forest** because the trees are restricted in growth by the permanent mist that blocks out the sunlight. Elfin forests are an impenetrably dense tangle of short, twisted, gnarled trees barely two metres tall.

The Oriente

The **Oriente** represents Ecuador's own piece of the **Amazon rainforest**, the largest tropical rainforest habitat in the world, with the greatest diversity of plants and animals on the planet – its unidentified varieties of beetles and insects alone are thought to outnumber all of Earth's known animal species. One study has even found that a single hectare of Amazonian forest can contain up to 250 tree species, whereas in Europe and North America only ten different kinds of tree would occupy the same space. Another study has identified more types of ant living on a single tree stump than there are in the whole of the British Isles. The rivers and their banks, too, are home to a fantastic diversity of animals, including nearly two thousand species of fish, plus freshwater dolphins, giant otters, anacondas, caimans and many unique birds.

One reason for this extraordinary diversity is its **climate**, as it never suffers from a lack of heat or water, with high levels of precipitation all year round, particularly from April to July. Annual averages are frequently above 2500mm, while in some areas, rainfall passes above 4000mm. Temperatures are consistent, hovering at around 23–26°C (73–79°F) all year.

Rainforest types

The different types of soil, terrain and rivers of the Amazon basin have allowed various kinds of rainforest to evolve. In the Oriente – and indeed the Amazon as a whole – the majority comprises **tierra firme rainforest** (also known as *terra firme* after the Portuguese term), with well-drained, nutrient-rich soils. Trees typically have huge, flaring buttress roots, tall slender trunks and branches radiating at the top like spokes on a bicycle wheel. Most grow to 25–30m, although some, such as the ceiba or kapok, exceed 50m, with the forest canopy creating a dark, permanently shaded and enclosed space underneath.

Because trees are often interconnected by vines, one falling tree – whether felled by a hurricane, lightning or human activity – can potentially bring all its neighbours down with it. Sunlight floods in, creating a different microclimate to the shadowy world under the canopy. Initially, fast-growing plants that prefer light to shade are favoured, and a dense tangle of competing shrubs, vines and spindly trees proliferates. At this stage, with an undeveloped canopy and few large trees, though with dense ground cover and undergrowth, it is known as **secondary forest**. Over time, it matures into fully developed **primary forest**, as the slower-growing trees out-compete and dwarf the pioneers and the canopy closes over, once again blocking sunlight from the forest floor, allowing only a sparse scattering of low-level plants.

The Oriente also holds large areas of flooded forest around different river systems, providing important alternative habitats for plants and animals. **White-water rivers**, for example – though turbid and muddy would be more accurate descriptions – flow down from the Andes carrying great amounts of suspended sediment, enriching the soil during floods. Over time, accumulated sediment on the riverbanks forms ridges, or levees, which helps prevent regular flooding, meaning the plants that thrive here have to withstand years without a flood. These areas of intermittently flooded forest are known as **várzea**, characterized by a dense understorey, a middle layer of *Cecropia* and a high layer of trees reaching over 35m, such as *Ficus insipida* and *Calycophyllum spruceanum*. Some várzea plants have developed floating seeds to aid their dispersal.

Black-water rivers usually originate within the rainforest area itself, so contain very little suspended sediment, but do have a lot of decomposing organic matter from fallen leaves and dead plants. The result is an acidic, tannin-rich water that looks like strong black tea. The open floodplains around black-water rivers give rise to the haunting **igapó forests**, which you can drift through on a canoe just beneath the canopy. Igapó trees are relatively short and have adapted to floods lasting many months, with roots that can survive underwater for long periods. Many trees here have developed a seed-dispersal strategy that relies on fish: their fruit falls into the water during floods, and their seeds germinate after having passed through the creature's digestive system.

The lush and palm-dominated **moretal** habitat occupies swampy and poorly drained areas near rivers and lakes, which often flood after localized rains. The most striking tree is a palm, *Mauritia flexuosa* (known as *morete* in Spanish, hence *moretal*), which grows to 30m, and the understorey is filled out with thick bursts of *Scheleea brachyclada* and *Croton tessmannii* amongst others.

Rainforest trees and plants

Rainforest trees usually have broad leaves, called drip tips, which thin to a narrow point at the end to facilitate water run-off. **Palm trees**, a good example of this, are extremely common and are used by indigenous peoples not just to make thatch for houses but also for ropes, weavings, hunting bows, fishing lines, hooks, utensils and musical instruments, as well as food and drink.

Many trees are cauliflorous, so their flowers and fruits grow from the trunk, rather than the canopy branches, enabling terrestrial animals – essential to the trees' reproduction – to access their **fruits** containing large seeds, a source of energy for monkeys, tapirs, rodents and peccaries. Other food simply falls to earth: the **brazil nut**, for example, hits the forest floor in large, woody pods, where the agouti, a type of rodent, gnaws through its tough shell. Many palms, too, such as the **coconut palm**, produce large, hard fruits encasing the seeds. Meanwhile, in the canopy, birds like tinamous, guans, curassows, doves, pigeons, trogons, toucans and parrots eat smaller fruits and seeds.

Plants that don't rely on animals and birds for reproduction have developed **protective measures** to counter the attentions of hungry animals, self-defence tactics evident in rainforest leaves blemished by nibble marks. Some plants produce drugs, or **defence compounds**, and many tropical leaves are generously dosed with poisons such as curare, caffeine and cyanide. The **monkey pot tree**, for example, deters foragers by producing rotund "cannonball" fruits, each containing up to fifty long, thin seeds laced with toxic selenium. Other plants grow spines on their trunks to impale voracious caterpillars, while, less vindictively, the sap of the **rubber tree** congeals on exposure to air, so any insects that have gone to the trouble of chewing through the bark are only rewarded with an inedible goo.

Epiphytes flourish on, around and over the vegetation, and sometimes the treetops are so laden with squatters seeking access to the sun that it's hard to define the host under all its house guests. In the competitive world of the cloudforest, even epiphytes can have their own epiphytes. Many bromeliads' leaves arrange themselves in overlapping rosettes, forming a bowl that catches and holds rainwater. Birds bathe in it, monkeys drink from it, and tree frogs, mosquitoes, flatworms, snails, salamanders and crabs can all complete their entire life cycle in these miniature aquatic habitats.

Lianas (a woody vine that roots in the ground) dangle downwards from trees, elaborately draping and entwining around their trunks. A liana may even loop its tendrils through the crowns of several trees, making intricate links in the canopy. **Trunk-climbing vines** start at the bottom of tree trunks and grow upwards, while **strangler vines** start at the top and grow down, encircling the tree and squeezing it tightly enough to choke it: the tree inside dies and decomposes, and the vine claims its place on the forest floor.

The coast

The western slopes of the Andes fall away to the **coastal region**, beginning with a large, fertile lowland river plain that extends for 150km to a range of hills, which rise up to 900m and form a ridge about 20km inland from the sea.

The **coastal lowlands** have a very warm **climate**, with temperatures fluctuating between 25°C and 31°C (77–88°F) throughout the year. Here, the humid rainy season runs from December to May, though the dry season is still fairly muggy. The north of the region is generally much wetter throughout the year than the south coast, which barely receives any rainfall during the dry season. At the coast itself, the climate is heavily influenced by oceanic currents, which from May to December are responsible for keeping temperatures down and skies overcast. From June to August, particularly between the northern Guayas and the southern Manabí provinces, the coast is shrouded in thick mist and illuminated by a grey light that leaches everything else of colour.

The northern coastal region was once thickly forested and included within it the **Chocó bioregion**, an area of extraordinary biodiversity extending up into Colombia. When the Andes were formed, the Chocó region in the west was cut off from the Amazon rainforests to the east. Since then, these highly humid western forests survived Ice Age ravages and followed an evolutionary path that diverged from that of their eastern counterparts, and it's thought that anywhere between one-fifth to a half of the nine thousand estimated plant and animal species here are endemic, such as the glorious scarlet-and-white tanager, the rufous-crowned antpitta and the banded ground cuckoo.

Unfortunately, in Ecuador less than five percent of the Chocó forests (which include coastal mangroves) have survived the twentieth century. Since the 1950s the destruction started apace with new roads leading to unplanned **colonization** and rapid **deforestation**. The region's fertility has given it the dubious honour of being the most intensively farmed area in Ecuador, with banana, rice, cacao, coffee and sugar-cane plantations. The latest threat to the Chocó comes from **oil-palm plantations**, which have felled about a

Mangroves and shrimp farms

As part of the natural ecosystem, **mangroves** act as an effective natural barrier between the land and the ocean, preventing erosion and forming a shield against tidal waves, cyclones and floods. Birds nest in their branches, burrowing animals find homes in their soft, rich, organic soils and many young sea creatures thrive in their shallow waters, which provide an abundance of food and protection from predators.

In the late twentieth century, mangrove forests along the coast of Ecuador began to be systematically cleared to make way for get-rich-quick **shrimp-farming** schemes. Production mushroomed in the early 1980s and shrimp became Ecuador's third most important export after bananas and oil, making the country the second-largest shrimp exporter in the world. To date, as much as seventy percent of the mangrove forests here have been destroyed to make way for breeding ponds. The effects of this clear-cutting have been disastrous, both for the environment and the local human populations, who once relied on the ecosystem for subsistence fishing.

While a few shrimp farmers reaped the benefits, many locals lost their livelihoods. Traditional fishermen, who once waded into the mangroves to collect fish and crustaceans, found little food or were denied access to their fishing grounds altogether. Many private enterprises brought their own people in to work on the shrimp farms, but the number of new jobs created fell far short of the number of people who had once survived off the land. Where a single hectare of mangrove forest provided sustainable food and livelihood for ten families, a typical shrimp farm spread over 110 hectares employed just a handful of people. Moreover, even as the shrimp farms devastated local economies, they contributed little to national coffers – netting around $600 million per year, they collectively payed out as little as $50,000 in tax. The shrimping industry in Ecuador has not even been a reliable source of income for the people involved in it. Farms are often high-risk ventures and the artificially cultured shrimp larvae, like all monoculture crops, are susceptible to outbreaks of disease and require large amounts of **antibiotics** and **pesticides**. These chemicals have further damaged the ocean ecosystem, and local wild marine animals are at risk from exotic diseases to which they have no immunity.

Additionally, the **mancha blanca** (white spot) virus of 1999 wiped out farms up and down the coastline, causing a two-thirds reduction in profits and the cessation of production in more than half the country's shrimp farms. The industry is now stabilizing, but is nothing like it was during the boom years. However, there is evidence that some out-of-business shrimp farmers may have learnt the lesson, turning to sustainable mollusc-farming projects that depend on the survival of the mangrove forests. Ecuador is also home to the world's first fully certified **organic shrimp farm** (see p.395), a model of ecological production that could easily be replicated. In the meantime, it's up to consumers in the developed world to be aware that about a third of the shrimp they eat comes from farms in countries like Ecuador, responsible for mangrove destruction as well as human displacement and untold poverty and suffering.

thousand square kilometres of native forest, much of it primary growth. More than twenty animal species are in danger of extinction in the Chocó.

The southern coastal area forms part of the **Tumbesian bioregion** that continues down into Peru. Originally, much of this distinctive landscape comprised **dry tropical forests** suited to the arid southern climate, but almost all of this habitat has now been cleared for agriculture, save a few pockets such as at the Parque Nacional Machalilla and the Bosque Protector Cerro Blanco. Trees and spiny shrubs, such as acacias and cacti, grow in abundance, as do some otherwise disappearing native trees, such as balsam and *tillo colorado*, long coveted for their fine wood. Plants in the region have adapted to the desert-like environment, and many trees such as the ceiba lose their leaves when water is scarce during the height of the dry season (July–Oct). Fewer birds live here than in the wet forests, but there are a significant number of range-restricted, endangered species endemic to this area, such as the grey-backed hawk, the ochre-bellied dove and the saffron siskin. Mammals include mantled howler monkeys, capuchins, coatimundi, ocelots and pumas.

Long, empty beaches fringe about one-third of Ecuador's 2000km of **coastline**, the rest comprising mangrove swamps, marshes, sandy cliffs, river deltas and estuaries. **Mangrove trees**, growing in shallow salt or brackish waters, are found especially along quiet shorelines and in estuaries. The most common type in Ecuador is the red mangrove, so named because of its reddish wood, and like all mangroves it has a convoluted mass of arching roots, which support it in the unstable sandy shoreline soils and are exposed at low tide. The mangroves build up rich organic soil in the knotted network of their roots and branches, supporting many other plants and wildlife. Frigate birds, boobies and brown pelicans nest amongst the tangled branches and many types of fish, molluscs and crustaceans make homes in the protective shelter of the roots.

Mangroves play an essential role in the ecology of coastal areas, but much of Ecuador's mangrove treasury has been squandered, cut down to make way for the construction of profitable **shrimp farms** – only a few patches have been conserved. Around San Lorenzo near the Colombian border, the **Reserva Ecológica Cayapas-Mataje** harbours the tallest mangrove forest in the world (some over 64m) as well as lovely coconut forests, teeming bird colonies and rare mammals such as the miniature tree sloth. Ecuador's other national mangrove reserve, **Manglares Churute**, south of Guayaquil, is home to flamingos, pelicans and occasionally bottle-nosed dolphins.

Wildlife

Few countries in the world come close to Ecuador for **wildlife**. Blessed with many thousands of colourful **birds** and **animals** crammed into a small area, Ecuador is a naturalist's dream – bird watchers alone can rack up a list of several hundred after only a few days in the forests. To top it all off, a fair number of them are found nowhere else – making Ecuador one of the most biologically important countries on the planet.

Birds

Ecuador is home to just over 1600 different **bird** species, representing a sixth of the planet's total. Because of its small size, the country also has the world's highest **diversity** of birds – even though Brazil is thirty times larger, the two countries are home to about the same number of bird species.

Anhingas

Anhingas are long-necked birds that feed by chasing fish through rainforest waters with sharp, spear-like bills. Unlike many waterbirds, their feathers aren't waterproofed and don't trap air as a buoyancy aid – which is precisely why they're so good at diving. The catch is that they can't fly until their feathers are dry, so they're a common sight perched on sun-warmed branches, holding their wings open to the breeze. Males are black with white markings, while females have a pale head, neck and chest.

Cotingas

The most famous **cotinga** is the fabulous **Andean cock-of-the-rock**, which inhabits lower to mid-montane cloudforest, where several dozen birds gather in **leks** (bird courtship display areas) to reproduce. The chunky males, with spectacular scarlet-orange plumage outlined by black wings and tail and a showy crescent of feathers running over their heads, preen and pose for the females, stroking their wing plumes, turning their heads sideways to display their handsome profiles and catching the females' eyes with their intense gazes. The females spend time looking over the available goods before picking their mate. Relationships are brief, however, lasting for only one or two couplings, after which the male continues to strut his stuff in the search for more mates. The **screaming piha** is another cotinga that lives in the rainforest, but its mating appeals are auditory rather than visual – it may look drab and nondescript but its strident, piercing call is one of the most distinctive sounds of the forest.

Eagles

The **harpy eagle** is the world's largest, at over 1m in height, with sturdy, powerful legs as thick as human wrists and claws the size of human hands. Their wings and back are black and their faces and bellies are grey. Remarkably agile despite their size, harpy eagles twist and turn through the canopy, making swift strikes at monkeys and sloths, plucking them off trees with their legs. They tend not to soar, so they are hard birds to spot, but the best places to see them are the remotest parts of the forest, far from human habitation. **Crested eagles** and three species of **hawk-eagle** are easier to see soaring in high circles over the rainforest canopy.

Hoatzins

Hoatzins are bizarre, almost prehistoric-looking birds. Hopeless fliers, they're usually spotted crashing around in riverside trees and bushes. Their chunky bodies and small heads perched on spindly necks, tattered head feathers and bright blue faces with red eyes are only accentuated by their non-musical guttural vocalizations. Baby hoatzins have claws on their first and second digits, which enable them to clamber through riverside vegetation. Microflora in their stomachs digest the leaves they eat and make the birds smell like cow manure – probably why humans have never been particularly partial to eating them.

Hummingbirds

Hummingbirds' names accurately reflect their beauty: **garnet-throated**, **sparkling-tailed**, **velvet-breasted**, **ruby topaz**, **firecrown** and **mango**, to name but a few. Always highly active, their wings can buzz at eighty beats per second as they dart backwards, forwards and hover on the spot to sip nectar with their bills. They're quite feisty, given their tiny size, and compete aggressively for flowers. Females flirt with dominant males and will mate with them even during the non-breeding season to gain access to the flowers in their territory. Hummingbird habitats range from the jungle to the páramo, with some species such as the sword-billed (which has a bill as long its body) and the booted racquet-tail found in the cloudforests. Cloudforest lodges with hummingbird feeders are the best places to see them up close: sit with the sun to your back to see the iridescent glow of the reds, blues and greens.

Jacanas

Jacanas inhabit swamps, lakes and riversides in the Amazon. The **northern jacana** is the size of a chicken, with a lump of bright-red flesh on its face and dark feathers that expose yellow wing patches when the bird flies. The jacana uses its long, unwebbed toes to walk on floating water plants as it searches out insects and seeds. Female jacanas have reversed the usual sex roles, mating with several males and leaving each with the responsibility for incubating the eggs.

Kingfishers

Kingfishers skim along rainforest rivers and streams and dive into the water in pursuit of fish. The swift **ringed kingfisher** is the largest, with a reddish breast, white neck and blue-grey back. They're extremely common and conspicuous with their distinctive shape and noisy, rattling call. The smallest, the **pygmy kingfisher**, is found only along interior forest streams and can easily be mistaken for a hummingbird as it zooms by.

Oropendolas

Trees favoured by the crow-sized **oropendolas** can be spotted at a distance because they tend to be out in the open, bedecked with their long, pendulous, basket-like nests. The birds pick isolated trees to avoid egg-stealing monkeys, which don't like to traverse open ground. As a further measure oropendolas often locate colonies near nests for wasps and bees, which, with their aggressive nature and territorial tendencies, act as their guard dogs. These birds come in two colour types – one displaying greenish hues, the other mostly black and russet, with yellow on the bill and tail. Males sit prominently on big branches and erupt into noisy burbling song, lurching forwards and downwards.

Parrots and macaws

Most **parrots** are green and well camouflaged in the rainforest, but their harsh, banshee-like screeching makes them easy to locate. Gregarious and sociable, they usually mate for life, and it's possible to pick out the pairs by watching a flock. They crack tough nuts and seeds using formidably strong jaws, while the upper jaw also functions as an extra limb for climbing and manoeuvring.

Macaws are the most spectacular members of the parrot family and their rainbow plumage, ranging from the magnificent **scarlet macaw** to the brilliant **blue-and-yellow macaw**, is easily seen even in the densest forest. About thirty percent of the South American parrots are considered to be at risk of extinction because of habitat loss and the highly profitable trade in exotic pets.

Owls and potoos

Owls are birds of prey that hunt at night. The **spectacled owl**, one of Ecuador's largest, is dark brown with a brown-yellow lower breast and belly and bright yellow eyes ringed by white. The **black-and-white owl** has a horizontally black-and-white striped breast and feeds almost exclusively on bats.

The **common potoo** is another large nocturnal bird and a visual challenge to detect in the daytime – it sits completely still in trees and, with its colouring and artful physical pose, looks exactly like the end of a branch.

Tanagers

These small, gloriously colourful birds feed on fruit, nectar and insects and live in a variety of habitats all the way from the lowland jungle to the highland cloudforest. Montane species include the **golden tanager**, **beryl-spangled tanager** and **blue-winged mountain-tanager**. In the Amazon you can't miss the flocks of exotic **paradise tanagers** with their neon-lime heads, purple throats, crimson lower backs, black upper backs and turquoise rumps.

Toucans

With their flamboyant oversized bills and colour-splashed bodies, **toucans** are easy to spot. The largest is the **white-throated toucan**, which has a black bill with a yellow stripe running down the middle, and baby-blue framed eyes. This species lives in the jungle along with **araçaris**, smaller, more colourful toucans. The highlands are where to find the wonderful **mountain toucans**. All varieties eat by gulping, snipping off bits of ripe fruit and flipping their heads up to toss them back into their throats.

Vultures and condors

Vultures thrive everywhere, from the rainforest to the sierra – wherever other animals die, as they only eat carrion. Their heads and necks are covered with bald skin rather than feathers so that caked blood from carcasses can be easily cleaned off. **Black vultures** are common around urban rubbish dumps, while the **greater yellow-headed vulture** dominates the rainforest niche.

The **Andean condor**, national bird of Ecuador, is the world's heaviest bird of prey, with a wingspan of 3m. Adults are black with a ruff-like white collar and bald pinkish head. Historically condors were a common sight in Ecuadorian skies, but hunting has reduced their population to a maximum of 150 individuals. They live near and above the tree line, with the largest number soaring over the páramo around Volcán Antisana in the northeast.

Mammals

Ecuador is home to 369 species of **mammals**, representing eight percent of the world's total. Many live in the forests and are shy of human presence, making them difficult to spot, though most jungle trips are rewarded with sightings of monkeys skipping through the canopy. The holy grail of the mountain forests is the Andean spectacled bear, but few visitors are lucky enough to see one.

Anteaters

Anteaters eat insects, termites and leaves. **Giant anteaters** can weigh up to 40kg and amble along the rainforest floor looking for ant nests; when they find one, they poke their long tongues inside and trap the ants with gluey saliva. The other three species, such as the tiny **pygmy anteater**, live in trees, where they rip apart the nests of ants, bees and termites and lick up the residents.

Armadillos

Armadillos have bony armour plates shielding their head and body and sometimes their legs and tail. Bands of soft skin separate the plates in the middle so the animal can bend, though they are endowed with a rather comic, waddling gait. They feed on the likes of ants, termites, fruits and plants, and while they have an excellent sense of smell, they also have terrible eyesight – if you see one and remain still, it might well run right over your feet.

Bats

The only mammals that can fly, **bats'** forelimbs are modified into wings, with elongated arm bones enclosed within a tough membrane of flexible skin. All are nocturnal and many are insectivorous, locating prey using **echolocation**, a highly sophisticated sensory system. Most of the sounds bats emit are ultrasonic, outside the human range, but if you've got good hearing you might hear a faint clicking noise as one flies by. **Tent-building bats** live in the rainforest and create homes by selecting a large leaf and nibbling a line down each side so that the leaf flaps droop downwards. Small groups of bats can be seen huddling together in a close-knit scrum underneath their protective tent.

The **common vampire bat** lives in the rainforest and subtropical forests of the Andean slopes up to 1500m, feeding entirely on the blood of mammals and prospering in the presence of domestic cattle and swine. They find their victims at night by sight and smell, scurrying over the ground and climbing onto the sleeping animal. They bite with sharp incisors, rarely waking their victims, and lick up the drops of blood dripping from the wound – vampire-bat saliva contains special anticoagulants so that the blood flows freely without clotting during feeding. They're remarkably cooperative social creatures and will regurgitate blood to sustain group members who have failed to feed – an important survival strategy, since a bat can't go for more than 72 hours without a meal. There are very few cases of bats feeding on humans; it's thought they're only capable of biting through the webbed skin between fingers and toes.

Cats

All **felines** are carnivorous and eat just about anything they can catch using the stealth-and-strike approach. Solitary creatures with large territories, they aren't all that easy to find, but they do scratch logs to proclaim their presence, so look for tell-tale marks. At night, they like to walk down man-made trails, where their bright, reflective eyes identify them in the dark.

Ocelots are small cats with tawny fur and black spots, stripes and rosettes, living on a range of habitats with good cover, from rainforest to desert scrub, sometimes raiding chicken coops in villages. Pale-grey or yellow **pumas** also live in dry areas, while those in the rainforest are yellow-brown to dark red-brown. Sinewy, long-legged cats, they've been known to trail humans down paths out of curiosity.

Jaguars are tawny yellow with black spots. Large and muscular, they're built for power rather than speed and have adapted to a range of habitats, from rainforest to arid scrub, hunting at any time of day for capybaras, deer, turtles, caimans, birds or fish. One of the best places to spot them is from a boat, as they lie on logs over the water, soaking up the rays in the morning sun.

Cat attacks on humans are very rare. If you meet a jaguar or a puma, don't run: stay facing it, make a lot of noise, and wave your arms about.

Dolphins and manatees

Pink river dolphins, or *botos*, hunt for fish, turtles and crabs using their flexible necks to probe for food amongst submerged trunks in flooded forests. Although nearly blind, they navigate and locate prey using a sonar system housed in a large bulge on their foreheads. Curious and intelligent, they'll approach swimmers but won't attack.

Amazonian manatees are highly endangered due to hunting, so you'll be fortunate to encounter one. These large, hairless, cigar-shaped herbivores are docile, browsing on aquatic plants and living under the water, only breaking the surface with their nostrils to breathe.

Monkeys

Ecuadorian **monkeys** live in trees and only hit the ground running to cross open space. Most have long hind limbs and tails that curl up and rest on their backs when walking. **Marmosets** and **tamarins** are the smallest of them and sport flamboyant facial hair, ear tufts, tassels, ruffs, manes and moustaches. They communicate with timid chirps and bird-like whistles, and, being too small for human appetites, they're not always afraid to come into villages and towns.

Howler monkeys are far more often heard than seen. At dawn and dusk they band together for deafening howling sessions – a sound like a croaking hurricane – which carry across the canopy for kilometres. A male usually starts off the clamour with an escalating grunting session, which segues into long, deep roars. Females join in with their higher-pitched voices. **Red howlers** favour tall riverbank trees, so they're most easily spotted from a boat.

Otters

There are two **otters** in Ecuador, the **neotropical river otter** and the **giant otter**, which can grow up to 1.5m in length, not counting its metre-long tail. They have sleek reddish-brown coats, huge, fully-webbed feet and intelligent, canine-type faces (their local name is *lobo del río*, or river wolf). They live in social groups in quiet waters, swimming, diving and feasting on fish, mammals and birds, and reputedly even anacondas. They're among the few carnivores in the world that can single-handedly kill prey much larger than themselves, which they do by means of a single, powerful bite to the victim's head or neck.

Rodents

In Ecuador, **rats** and **mice** thrive in urban environments, **squirrels** leap acrobatically through the trees and **porcupines** root around on the rainforest floor. All rodents have a pair of incisor teeth on each jaw, which never stop growing but are kept in check by attrition through chewing.

The **capybara** is the world's largest rodent, weighing some 55kg, with stocky bodies and thin hind legs – they often sit on their haunches like dogs. Small herds live along Amazonian lakes, rivers and swamps, feeding on water lilies, water hyacinth, leaves and sedges. Humans, caimans, jaguars and anacondas all eat them – that is, if they don't leap into the water and swim away first.

Sloths

Sloths live in the rainforest and hang motionless off branches, using the long curved claws on their two or three toes. They feed on canopy leaves, digesting them in a multichambered stomach. Algae flourishes in tiny grooves on their body hair, turning the sloths an alien green and camouflaging them in the trees. They're hard to see from the ground, but eagles are masters at spotting them and swooping in to pick them off the branches. Once a month, sloths climb down from their trees and dig a hole in the ground in which to defecate. Moths, which live on the sloths and eat the algae, swarm off to lay their eggs in this fertile breeding ground then hurry to catch up with the ascending sloth.

Spectacled bears

Ecuador's only **bear** lives in forested mountain habitats from 1000m to 4000m. They're mostly black or brown, mottled white or cream with distinctive "spectacles" encircling part of each eye. They have massive solid bodies, but by bear standards they're small – the males weigh about 80kg and the females 60kg. Each paw is equipped with short, sharp, powerful claws for climbing or tearing apart trees. Up in the trees they build platforms of branches, on which they rest or feed on fruits and honey. As well, spectacled bears often raid cornfields, enraging farmers and threatening their own survival.

Tapirs

The region's largest terrestrial mammals, **tapirs** have stocky bodies, muscular necks, elongated, overhanging upper lips and short tails. Like all bulky herbivores, they spend about ninety percent of the day eating a calorie-poor leaf diet. Their droopy upper lips are used to reach out and sweep food into their mouths.

The **Brazilian tapir**, the size of a Shetland pony, varies in colour from black to red to tan. They hang out in swamps in the rainforest and in grassy habitats up to 2000m, and if afraid leap into the nearest water and swim away – though if you can imitate their loud whistle, they will answer you. The extremely rare brown, shaggy **mountain tapir** lives in the montane forests and páramo.

Reptiles and amphibians

There are about eight hundred **reptile** and **amphibian** species living in Ecuador. They thrive in the Amazon and also in the Andean foothills, where many are endemic.

Caimans

Crocodilian **caimans** lie motionless along riverbanks waiting for fish and other water-dwelling animals, such as capybaras, snakes and birds, to come within striking distance of their powerful jaws. The best way to see them is from a boat at night. Hold a torch at eye level and scan the riverbank; the caimans are easy to find because their eyes shine red in the beam.

Frogs

Frogs thrive in the Amazon where the hot, damp conditions keep them warm and hydrated. Over seventy-five percent are nocturnal and a deafening chorus wafts each night from ponds, lakes, riverbanks and the depths of flooded forests, as the males compete to attract females with their throaty tones.

The **leaf dweller**, which looks just like a dead leaf, is fairly common but difficult to see, as it's only visible when on the move. Fast-flowing streams are where to look for **glass frogs**, which are completely transparent, revealing their tiny beating hearts and other organs under the skin. The well-known **poison-dart frog** is small and brightly coloured, but is only active during the day.

Lizards and geckoes

Many **lizards** and **geckoes** live in the Amazon, such as the common **iguana**, which, with its heavily scaled head and spiny back, looks like a miniature dinosaur. The **basilisk**, or Jesus lizard, can be seen scurrying across still rivers, but they aren't really walking on water – the hind feet are just under the water's surface and are sprung upwards and onwards by an air bubble trapped beneath the basilisk's webbed foot.

Snakes

Plenty of **snakes**, both harmless and poisonous, slither through Ecuador's forests, but they are encountered only rarely. **Pit vipers** locate prey with heat receptors between their eyes and nostrils that can register changes in temperature of only 0.003°C. The teeth usually lie back horizontally but are erected to strike, bite and inject venom. Tan-coloured with dark diamond patterning, the two-metre-long, highly venomous **fer-de-lance** is the most notorious viper, an aggressive snake with a very painful bite that can kill. The **bushmaster** is the largest viper in the world, at up to 3m in length.

Some snakes kill their prey by squeezing rather than biting, such as the **boa constrictor**, which can reach 4m in length and is found in a variety of habitats from wet lowland forest to arid grassland. Another constrictor, the **anaconda**, is the largest snake in the world, occasionally growing to over 8m and weighing in at more than 200kg. A highly intelligent snake, it lies in wait by rivers for unsuspecting capybara, tapirs, large birds and peccaries, watching their drinking habits for weeks at a time before striking.

Turtles

Aquatic side-necked turtles are frequently seen in the rainforest, sunning themselves on branches sticking out of the water. When defending themselves, they tuck their heads sideways into their shells. Turtles build nests of rotting debris, which incubate their eggs at a constant temperature.

Insects

Insects easily win the global diversity competition – there are more than ten times the number of insect species than all other animals put together. In Ecuador there are at least a million different types, and the rainforest is the best place to find them. At nightfall, they produce the unmistakeable rainforest soundtrack – a cacophony of cheeps, clicks, trills, screeches and wheezes.

Ants

Many rainforest **ants** make their homes on plants, which provide shelter, protection and food via nectar. The relationship between acacia trees and **acacia ants**, for example, is well established: the lodgers pay for their board by defending their tree from unwelcome visitors and will attack beetles, caterpillars and other ants that try to land or climb on it. They also prune back other plants that grow too close or shadow their tree from the sunlight.

Army ant colony members can number over a million. Squadrons run eight to ten abreast along forest trails and cooperate to overpower other invertebrate creatures far larger than themselves. During nomadic phases the worker ants make night-time bivouacs by linking their bodies together, keeping their queen safe inside the living tent. **Leaf-cutter ants** are highly visible as they trudge along forest trails in lengthy columns bearing huge leaf clippings. Up to eight million individuals live in each colony, so their indiscriminate gardening activities can have a dramatic impact on the surrounding vegetation. The leaves are transported back to their vast underground nests, but instead of consuming them the ants chew them into a soft pulp to make a compost on which to grow a special fungus – their favourite food.

One ant to avoid is the **conga** or **giant hunting ant**, a large, aggressive-looking black creature whose sharp sting can cause pain and fever, lasting from a few hours to a few days (its nickname, "bullet ant", gives an idea of the pain).

Beetles

Beetles make up the biggest order of all living things. One of the most common is the **giant ceiba borer**, its outer skeleton gleaming like iridescent metal – the wing covers are popular in the production of earrings. **Hercules, rhinoceros** and **elephant beetles** are hard to miss, as they're the little giants their names suggest. The **headlight** or **cucuyu beetle** is also easily spotted: two round, light-producing organs behind its head give it the appearance of a toy car. The beautiful **tortoise beetle** is worth keeping an eye open for, as it looks as though it's been dipped in liquid gold. If attacked, it pulls in its legs and heads, tortoise-like, and seals itself to the ground.

Butterflies and moths

Ecuador is home to 4500 species of **butterfly**, with the number of known ones growing almost daily. The most striking are the **morphos**, huge tropical visions in electric blue. Their brilliant colour doesn't derive from pigment, but from the way light is reflected and refracted by their complex wing scales. **Owl butterflies** have owl-like eyespots on their wings to direct hungry birds away from crucial body parts. **Clearwings** look like tiny fairies; with completely transparent wings, they're hard to see when motionless. **White-and-sulphur butterflies** are highly visible from rainforest rivers. Droves gather on river-banks to lick salt and other nutrients from the ground. When disturbed by passing boats they swirl up in a confetti cloud of white, yellow and orange.

Many more varieties of moth than butterfly are found in Ecuador, inhabiting all ecosystems from high páramo to lowland tropical forests. Generally dark-coloured and active mainly at night, they are a less visible presence than the country's butterflies, but they often sport very rich and distinctive patterning.

Katydids

Katydids hide themselves out in the open by mimicking bark, twigs, moss and leaves with uncanny accuracy. They usually blend in so well with their background that they're impossible to detect until they move.

Machacas

Also known as the peanut-headed bug, the large, innocuous, sap-feeding **machaca** has an air-filled fake head in front of its real head, which looks exactly like a monkey nut. It has become the foundation of a popular legend in the Amazon that when someone is "bitten" by a machaca they must have sex within 24 hours to avoid certain death. Unsurprisingly, young Don Juans are the most frequent victims – around the time of a first date.

Termites

Termites live in enormous colonies in habitats ranging from rainforest to arid grassland to mangrove. Nests are stuck on tree trunks, sprout from the ground or consist of radiating tunnels beneath the surface. They're the favourite food of many animals, so some species have evolved defence strategies such as forti-fying their nests and apparatus for squirting irritant liquid.

Fish

There are more than eight hundred species of **freshwater fish** in Ecuador, with an incredible diversity in rainforest rivers. The **pirarucu**, possibly the world's largest freshwater fish, lives here – the real giants have all been fished out, but specimens of up to 2m are still caught. Watch for **leaf fishes** bob-bing past your boat, hard to discern from dead leaves on account of their crumpled, blotchy appearance and lower jaw, which mimics a stem.

Forty percent of the fish are either **catfish** or **characins**. Many characins are fruit-eaters and wait for fruit to fall from trees in the flooded forests. The noto-rious **red piranha** is also a characin. Small but ferocious, they are only a dan-ger to human swimmers in large groups when water levels are low and food supplies poor. Far more dangerous is the **electric eel**, which grows up to 1.8m and can produce a jolt of 650 volts.

The catfish to watch out for is the tiny **candiru**, which usually parasitizes other fish but has been known to follow urine currents of human swimmers, entering the urethra on occasion. Once inside, it lodges itself securely with an array of sharp spines and causes unmentionable discomfort. The offending fish is so firmly wedged it has to be surgically removed.

Galápagos wildlife

Compared to the diversity of life found on the mainland, few species have managed to make the 960-kilometre journey to the Galápagos. But it's the islands' small number of lifeforms in isolation that has fascinated generations of scientists. Like a self-contained puzzle, life on the Galápagos can be unravelled in a way impossible for the tangled mass of mainland biological relationships. And as Darwin found, the lessons learnt from the Galápagos microcosm can have implications for the rest of the planet.

The origins of Galápagos life

The Galápagos Islands came into being as barren, lifeless heaps of lava cut off from the rest of the world by vast expanses of ocean. First in making the cross-turn supporting more animals. In fact, it's thought that up to sixty percent of plant species were brought to the islands by **birds**, either as undigested seeds in guano, or regurgitated, or attached to their feet and feathers.

The last route was **by the sea** – several currents converge on the islands, and may have brought species from the Pacific, Central and South American coasts. Swept up in the flow, marine turtles, penguins, seals and sea lions could all have swum to the islands aided by the currents, while giant tortoises – not natural

---

El Niño and the Galápagos

When an **El Niño event** occurs (see box, p.523), the flow of warm water to the Galápagos islands is far more pronounced, leading to dramatic increases in rainfall. The **1982–83** El Niño was among the worst ever recorded, drowning the islands in 3408mm of rain – annual rainfall is commonly between 150mm and 400mm – and pushing sea temperatures up by 10°C. Because the warm waters hold few nutrients, fish stocks were displaced out of the range of many birds, the flightless cormorant population plummeted by 45 percent, and Galápagos penguins fared even worse, losing 78 percent of their numbers. The nesting sites of the waved albatrosses were so overgrown that no chicks were hatched, and marine iguanas died when their seaweed food was killed off by algae. By contrast, plant growth flourished, benefiting many insects and plant-eaters such as tortoises, and finches and mockingbirds did particularly well out of the phenomenon.

In **1997–98**, another severe El Niño event occurred, with levels of rainfall differing from the event fifteen years earlier by less than one millimetre. Again, marine-associated species suffered, with marine iguana and sea lion numbers halving, while penguins fell back to their 1982–83 levels. Unusually though, this time many terrestrial species were also badly hit, in many cases because introduced species, blown on the stronger El Niño winds – particularly aggressive insects – greatly increased in numbers and managed to colonize new areas. Giant tortoises, for example, failed to reproduce in large part because introduced fire ants killed their hatchlings inside their nests. It's thought that the combination of human interference and the extreme weather of increasingly frequent El Niño events is working to increase both the number of introduced species and their populations, which can only threaten the indigenous flora and fauna of the Galápagos.

swimmers – are, however, buoyant and can survive for long periods without
ing were probably the seeds and spores of mosses, lichens and ferns, blown
from the continent by prevailing **winds** and deposited on the islands through
rainfall. Insects, snails and spiders could also have been carried thousands of
kilometres, and when the winds were fierce enough they may also have
blown land birds, such as hawks and finches, and bats to the archipelago.
Many of the seabirds routinely fly long distances and need no vegetation for
nests, making them likely candidates for early pioneers. As the unforgiving
lava broke down into soil patches, many plants would have been able to colonize the island, in
food or water. The only satisfactory explanation for the arrival of other reptiles
and rice rats (the only native land mammal) is on tree trunks and logs, or on
floating rafts made of matted vegetation set adrift from the mainland after
storms. Such a journey would have taken a couple of weeks, too long for most
mammals and amphibians to survive without fresh water under a tropical sun,
but well within the capabilities of reptiles such as iguanas.

The arrival of **humans** in the Galápagos provided a new means for foreign
species to colonize the islands, and creatures such as goats, rats and dogs now
pose one of the greatest threats to the delicate ecology of the islands (see
p.464).

Separated from the rest of their species, the marooned Galápagos denizens
evolved as they adapted to their new environment, often ending up as quite
different species to their mainland counterparts. These new plants and animals, found nowhere else in the world, are termed **endemic** species.
Sometimes a single common ancestor has led to a number of new species –
as with Darwin's finches, a process known as **speciation**. In the Galápagos,
though, the story doesn't end there: not only is the archipelago far from the
continent, but the islands and islets comprising it are distant enough from
each other to bring about their own endemic species. In a few instances, even
the isolated habitats *within* an island can provoke speciation: for example, the
five main volcanoes of Isabela are each populated by their own subspecies of
giant tortoise.

Many Galápagos animals have evolved without the threat of predators, which
accounts for their unusual fearlessness, and some have filled niches that would
have been taken by other species on the mainland. The lack of mammals, for
example, has meant that giant tortoises hold a similar role to mammal browsers,
such as cows and sheep, while small land birds such as mockingbirds occupy
niches similar to mainland mice.

Birds

The Galápagos Islands are a real treat for bird watchers. Despite a relatively
small number of **bird species** for the tropics (there are sixty types of resident birds, and another 81 migratory species visit the islands), about half of
the residents are endemic, and visitors are often able to walk within a metre
of many of them. The naturalist William Beebe, who made two expeditions
to the islands in the 1920s, tells of frantically searching for a flycatcher with
his camera, only to find it perched on the lens "pecking at the brass fittings".
A week's cruise of the islands, taking in a variety of habitats, will enable you
to spot a healthy number of them, but consider the season if you want to see

particular birds or behaviours. **Seabirds** make the most of good fish stocks in the cool-dry season, and migrants are in evidence from around October to February. Most **land birds** breed in the rainy season, when food is more abundant.

Seabirds

Since most **seabirds** are naturally strong long-distance fliers that thrive in island environments, only six out of the nineteen resident species are endemic. Seabirds are also among the most prevalent of Galápagos fauna, having numbers approaching a million.

Boobies

Among the best-known seabirds are the **boobies**, probably named after the Spanish *bobo*, meaning "fool", perhaps for their ungainly waddling walk and relaxed attitude to being caught. In the same family as the gannet (*Sulidae*), the boobies are fantastic fishers; on spying their quarry they tuck their wings behind them and plunge from the sky, entering the water at terrific speed (an air sac in the skull softens the impact).

Of the three species, the **blue-footed booby** is the most widespread but least numerous, occupying small colonies all over the islands, where you'll hear the limp whistle of the males and boisterous honking of the females. Their wonderful courtship display of "skypointing" and "high-stepping", to show off the blueness of their feet, happens throughout the year. The female lays up to three eggs in the "nest" (little more than a ring of guano on a scraped patch of ground) and incubates them with her warm and veiny feet. If food is scarce, the first-born hatchling will tuck in on its less fortunate siblings, a way of guaranteeing that at least one will survive. The world's largest colony of **red-footed boobies** is on Genovesa, and despite numbering around a quarter of a million pairs in the archipelago, the red-foots are the least seen of the boobies, as they tend to inhabit the remoter islands; they're also the only tree-dwelling booby. The **Nazca booby** (formerly called the masked booby, but now considered a separate species) has rather lacklustre feet compared to its relatives, but makes up for it with its dazzling white plumage.

Frigate birds

The two **frigate bird** species in the archipelago, the **great frigate bird** and the **magnificent frigate bird**, are among the most commonly seen seabirds, often spotted manoeuvring in the sky, blotting out the sun with their huge wingspans (up to 2.4m for the slightly larger magnificent frigates), while their twitching scissor tails keep them on course. The two appear similar at first, but are easy to tell apart: male magnificent frigate birds have a purple sheen on their feathers, whereas great frigates have one of green; female magnificent frigate birds have a blue eye-ring, whereas female great frigates have a red eye-ring and a white chest. Once called "**man of war birds**", they have a reputation for aggression, harrying other seabirds to disgorge their catch, which they'll skilfully intercept before it hits the water. Their own fishing technique involves a deft flicking with their long hooked beaks on the surface of the water, whipping out their prey while ensuring that their feathers stay dry (they have lost the ability to oil their plumage, and will drown if they get wet enough). In the mating season, the males inflate their brilliant red "**gular sacs**", or throat pouches, flap their wings and call out to attract the attention of any passing females. At times, dozens of males will be competing for a mate when the colonies, freckled with colour, resound with their wavering calls. You can see the spectacle throughout the year at Seymour Norte or during March and April at Genovesa and San Cristóbal, though you may also be lucky at other times.

Flightless cormorants

Among the endemic seabirds, the **flightless cormorant** is one of the most peculiar-looking on the islands. Forgoing the ability to fly, these blazing-blue-eyed birds have developed large webbed feet and a sturdy lower body better suited to diving for food. Without an oily plumage, the birds hold their useless, bedraggled wings out to dry after each fishing expedition. Their snake-like necks are ideal for reaching into nooks and crannies for eels and octopus, and play a prominent part in their courtship ritual. Their nests are exotic collections of seaweed, twigs, fish bones, starfish and whatever else the male dredges up and offers as gifts to the nest-tending female during the incubation and brooding times. There are only around five hundred pairs of flightless cormorants in the world, all found on Isabela and Fernandina islands, where the fishing is good due to the cold Cromwell Current that comes from the west.

Gulls

The threatened **lava gull** is perhaps the rarest gull in the world, numbering around two hundred pairs. The dusky-coloured bird with white eyelids scavenges the ports, bays and beaches of the population centres, particularly at Puerto Ayora. The other endemic gull, the **swallow-tailed gull**, is far more attractive, having large black eyes set off from its black head by bright red eye-rings. It's one of the world's only nocturnal gulls, flying up to 35km out to sea and picking out phosphorescent shapes of squid in the darkness with its huge eyes, then turning home to locate land by the echo of its strange clacking call.

Waved albatrosses

The **waved albatross** is the emperor of the islands, the largest bird of the archipelago with a wingspan of 2.5m, weighing 4kg and living up to forty years. Save for a few pairs that nest on the Isla de la Plata, the waved albatross is endemic to Española, and each year more than twelve thousand pairs come to nest and breed there from April to December. A favourite of romantics, this bird chooses a mate for life and roams the island after months alone at sea to find its partner. Its beguiling courtship display, a lengthy and eclectic mix of "bill circling", "sky-pointing", "gaping", "clunking" and "sway-walking" amongst other manoeuvres, is thought to cement the marriage bond.

Galápagos penguins

The **Galápagos penguin** is another endemic seabird and always an odd sight in tropical waters, being the only penguin that's found north of the equator. It's related to the Humboldt and Magellan penguins that mostly occupy the Humboldt Current off the coast of Chile, and like its relatives it also prefers the cold water, largely colonizing areas around Isabela and Fernandina islands. Using its small, muscular wings as paddles and its feet as rudders, the Galápagos penguin can propel itself at up to 40kph through the water.

Other seabirds

Other residents of the archipelago include the graceful **red-billed tropicbird**, the widespread **brown pelican**, the **brown noddy** and **sooty tern**, the **Galápagos petrel** (formerly the dark-rumped petrel, and now recognized as endemic), **Audubon's shearwater** and three species of **storm petrel**.

Shore and wetland birds

Rock pools, mangroves, beaches and shallow salty lagoons are common features of the Galápagos coast, providing habitats for as many as fifty bird species, many of them migrants such as the **wandering tattler**, which commutes from the Arctic. Only one of the shore birds is endemic, the **lava heron**, though there are several residents that have shown enough of the slow signs of evolution to have earned endemic subspecies status, such as the **yellow-crowned night heron**. **Striated** and **great blue herons**, which can be taller than a child, are the other resident heron species frequently seen around the coastal waters, gazing into pools with beady eyes. **Greater flamingos** tiptoe about the saltwater lagoons, sifting the silt and surface for water boatmen and shrimp. During the breeding season, care must be taken not to disturb these elegant birds, as they are prone to abandon nests if startled. There are fewer than 250 pairs in the Galápagos.

As well as resident waders such as the **American oystercatcher** and **black-necked stilt**, a number of familiar migrants are in evidence, including **turn-stones**, **sandpipers**, **yellowlegs**, **sanderlings**, **whimbrels**, **phalaropes** and **plovers**. The **white-cheeked pintail duck** is equally at home by the coast or at the freshwater lagoons in the highlands, where the **purple** or **common gallinule** (moorhen) make their home. **Cattle egrets**, nesting in the mangroves, are more usually seen in the highlands in large flocks near livestock. This striking white bird has now managed to colonize much of the world, though it was found only in West Africa till the late nineteenth century.

Land birds

The **land birds** of the Galápagos have been of enormous interest to scientists ever since Darwin's discoveries. Unlike most strong-winged seabirds, which are accustomed to making long journeys, the land birds can only have been brought to the archipelago blown on the winds of freak storms. And yet, of the 29 resident species, a phenomenal 22 are endemic, so such abnormal bird-carrying gales must have occurred no less than fourteen times – quite a feat considering that none strong enough to achieve this has yet been recorded.

Most famous of Galápagos birds are **Darwin's finches**, the thirteen endemic and subtly different finches that proved to be of enormous import to their namesake. These dowdy, sparrow-sized birds are notoriously difficult to tell apart, despite the all-important differences in beak size and feeding habits. Since the finches are so similar, more like each other than any other kind of finch, Darwin suspected that they were all descendants of a common ancestor. No doubt the archipelago's grouping of isolated islands allowed for this remarkable speciation, even though many of them now inhabit the same islands.

The **large ground finch** has the biggest beak and is able to crack open large, hard seeds, while the **warbler finch** probes plants and flowers with its sharp and slender bill and has been called "more warbler than finch". Most of the finches take their food from an array of sources. The **woodpecker finch** and endangered **mangrove finch** are celebrated for their ability to use tools, often fashioning a twig or a cactus spine to wheedle larvae and grubs from tight spots. A subspecies of the **sharp-billed ground finch** on remote Wolf and Darwin islands has earned the moniker **"vampire finch"** for pecking at Nazca boobies and feeding off their blood. The **small ground finch** has better interspecies relations, preening tortoises and iguanas for parasites, which it devours.

The archipelago has four endemic **mockingbirds**: the **Galápagos mockingbird** is fairly widespread, while the **Chatham mockingbird** only inhabits San Cristóbal, the **Hood mockingbird** Española, and the rare **Charles mockingbird** a couple of islets around Floreana. They are among the most confident and inquisitive birds on the islands, having no qualms about hopping around the feet of large groups of tourists.

Galápagos hawks are almost as fearless, having no natural enemies, and are content to let humans get to within a few metres of them. Darwin wrote that "a gun is here almost superfluous; for with the muzzle I pushed a hawk out of the branch of a tree". The Galápagos hawk practises a breeding system whereby the female has as many as four mates, who help her incubate the eggs and tend to the young. With the hawk, the **Galápagos barn owl** and the **short-eared owl** make up the archipelago's birds of prey. The latter is the more commonly seen, particularly on Genovesa, where it swoops on the young of the large seabird colonies. Other endemics include the elegant **Galápagos dove**, the secretive and miniature **Galápagos rail**, the **Galápagos flycatcher** and the **Galápagos martin**, the archipelago's only non-migratory member of the swallow family.

For all their intrinsic interest, the endemics can be a drab bunch, and indeed, the archipelago's two most colourful birds are residents. The **yellow warbler** and the dazzling male **vermilion flycatcher**, boasting a smart red-and-black plumage, are common favourites brightening up the dour scenery.

Reptiles

Above all fauna on the Galápagos, it's the **reptiles** that give the islands their distinctive prehistoric flavour. Until the arrival of humans, its isolation made the archipelago virtually impenetrable to mammal life, allowing the reptiles to take up their ecological niches. Although their appearance is "antediluvian", the Galápagos reptiles have undergone the same evolutionary processes as the islands' other creatures, resulting in a high level of endemism. Of the 22 reptile species, twenty are unique to the Galápagos and several of these are specific to particular islands. Five reptile families are represented on the archipelago: **tortoises**, **marine turtles**, **iguanas** (including lizards), **geckoes** and **snakes**.

Being **ectothermic** animals, reptiles cannot regulate their body temperature through physiology, such as sweating or dilating and constricting blood vessels as humans do. They need to heat their blood up to a certain level before they can become properly active – which is why you'll commonly see iguanas splayed on rocks absorbing the sun's rays for many hours, only moving into the shade if they get too hot. This system also allows them to survive on less food and water than other animals, a characteristic along with tolerance to salt water that made the journey across from the mainland that much easier.

Tortoises

The **giant tortoises** of the Galápagos have come to symbolize the islands – and indeed, they are the origin of their name. The lumbering and hoary beasts weigh up to 250kg and are the largest tortoises in the world. Only one other island on the globe, in the Seychelles and a fraction of the size of Floreana, has a giant-tortoise population. The Galápagos once had fourteen subspecies of giant tortoise, and numbers could have been as high as 250,000. Unchecked slaughter during the height of the whaling era in the nineteenth century brought the population down to 15,000 and made three subspecies extinct. One other is set to be lost too; Lonesome George, kept at the Charles Darwin Research Station on Santa Cruz, is thought to be the last surviving Pinta tortoise. A reward of $10,000 is on offer to anyone that can find him a mate.

Giant tortoises can be identified by two basic types of shell shape, but there's a degree of overlap between the subspecies with other shell shapes that fall somewhere in between. The **dome-shaped tortoise** is found in moister areas with thicker vegetation, while the **saddleback** shape allows a greater reach for the scarcer food on the drier islands.

Giant tortoises are **vegetarians** and enjoy the nourishment of more than fifty plant species. When food is abundant they eat heartily, but it takes as long as three weeks to digest a meal, and even when it finally passes through, it's easy to see what they've been eating. Their somewhat coarse digestion does allow them to gorge on the highly toxic poison apple (even touching it can cause skin irritation to humans) and prickly *Opuntia* cactus pads, despite the spines.

Tortoises are thought to live for more than 150 years, though no one knows for sure as they always outlive the research projects. They only become sexually mature around their 25th birthday. The mating season begins as the warm-wet season nears its end, when males compete for females by extending their necks – the highest head wins. The male mounts the female, fitting perfectly on her back due to the concave shape of his underside, and mates in a cacophony of grunts, wheezes and sighs lasting hours. Females then retreat to coastal areas to lay their billiard-ball-sized eggs, which can take up to eight months to hatch. It's the temperature of the nest that determines the sex of the hatchlings, rather than any specific chromosomal information. Apart from mating, tortoises are virtually silent unless they are alarmed, when they quickly draw their limbs and head into the shell, forcing air out of their nostrils with a sharp hiss.

Marine turtles

Although you may be lucky enough to see the **leatherback**, **hawksbill** or **olive ridley turtles** in Galápagos waters, only the **Pacific green turtle** is a resident, regularly nesting on the islands' beaches. The green turtles weigh up to 150kg and are graceful swimmers, motored by their large front flippers. They've been known to make regular journeys between the islands and the Ecuadorian mainland and can stay submerged for hours on end. Females mate with a succession of males inshore at the surface and dig large holes on sandy beaches to lay clutches of up to a hundred eggs. In less than two months, the hatchlings are ready to make their dash to the sea avoiding mockingbirds, frigate birds, herons, ghost crabs and a host of other hungry predators awaiting a feast. They break out at night simultaneously to keep the number of casualties down to a minimum, but even when they've reached the sea they swim nonstop to avoid sharks and other predators lurking inshore.

Iguanas

The cracked volcanic shores make a fitting home to the demonic-looking colonies of **marine iguana**, the world's only seagoing iguana. Darwin didn't have a kind word to say about them – "it is a hideous-looking creature, of a dirty black colour, stupid and sluggish in its movements" – but he was impressed by their unique adaptation to a difficult habitat.

The marine iguana feeds on small tufts of seaweed or algae in rocky, intertidal areas. The larger males supplement this with the more plentiful supplies found underwater. Using their flattened tails to swim through the waves, they can dive to 12m and stay submerged for up to an hour, while they tear the weeds from the rocks, aided by their broad, blunt mouths. To compensate for such a salty diet, special glands above the eye allow the marine iguana to blow excess salt out of its nose in a fine spray, hence the salt crystals caked to their heads. They'll often "sneeze" at you if you get too close to them. In the mating season, starting in January on most islands, marine iguanas take on a fiery red colouration. On Española they have a blotched black-and-red appearance during the year and burst into bright red and turquoise in the months of breeding.

The larger, orange-yellow **land iguanas** prefer the drier areas of the central and western islands, as they rely on cactus pads and fruits for much of their food, rolling them on the ground first to get rid of the spines before chomping in. Two endemic species inhabit the Galápagos, one of which is confined to Santa Fé island. Introduced species have been very harmful to land-iguana populations: the creatures are now extinct on Santiago and were almost finished off on Baltra during World War II, before they were moved to safety on Seymour Norte. All going well, they can live up to sixty years.

Other reptiles

Seven endemic **lava lizards** dart around the island coasts, hunting for insects and spiders. The males can grow up to 30cm in length and are larger than the females, which are distinguished by the vivid-red colouration on their head or throats. They mark their territories by doing sequences of "press-ups" on their forelegs, and each island has its own unique pattern. The lava lizard is hunted by the three endemic types of **Galápagos snake**, unspectacular non-venomous constrictors about a metre long, which devour **geckoes**, small, wide-eyed nocturnal lizards that can stick to windows with their special toe pads. Five of the six native geckoes are endemic; three others have been recently introduced.

The first amphibian

For millions of years, no amphibian has been able to colonize the Galápagos Islands. Salt water is murderous to them, drying out their delicate skins on contact, making a sea crossing to the islands impossible. Since 1998, however, a two- to three-centimetre **tree frog** (*Scinax quinquefasciata*) has become established on three of the populated islands, and is being found with increasing regularity at Puerto Ayora. It seems the tiny grey-and-black frog, common throughout the coastal mainland, stowed itself away amongst crates of vegetables brought over by boat and air. The abnormally wet 1997–98 **El Niño** event allowed the new arrivals to get a toehold on the islands – probably breeding in small pools of fresh water common around the houses, gardens and leaking pipes of the population centres – as well as the introduction of **kikuyo**, a plant that provides the perfect refuge for frog eggs and tadpoles. It's not clear if this species is a danger to the native wildlife; it must be devouring insects, and if it has poison glands, as many frogs do, it could pose a more serious threat to native predators, wiping out large numbers of them. The Galápagos authorities are still investigating the matter, but are anxious to get the frogs out of the wild and are offering a small reward for each one caught.

Mammals

The travails of making the crossing from the continent have proved too much for most **mammals**, and there is a noticeable absence of them on the islands. Just six native species inhabit the Galápagos, and of them only the **rice rats** made the gruelling sea journey on a vegetation raft (like many of the reptiles, which are far better suited to this kind of transport). Four of the seven rice-rat species are now extinct, wiped out by the introduced black rat, which out-competes them. The remaining three species are found on Santa Fé and Fernandina islands, islands that have so far been spared invasion by the black rat.

The **bats** took the air route: the ancestors of the endemic *Lasiurus brachyotis* were most likely blown over from the mainland like land birds, while the other native species, the **hoary bat**, is a known migrant and widespread throughout North America. There's nothing to stop mammal populations flourishing once they get to the Galápagos, as has been demonstrated by a number of **introduced species**, such as feral goats, cats, dogs and rats, which have been doing terrible damage to native wildlife, all brought to the islands by another late and harmful mammalian arrival, *Homo sapiens*.

Sea lions and fur seals

The archipelago's endemic **sea lions** and **fur seals** may well have swum to the islands, aided by strong currents. A relative of the larger Californian sea lion, the **Galápagos sea lion** never fails to charm visitors to the island. Sometimes boisterous, sometimes lazy, the sea lions' yelping, sneezing, coughing and whooping has an unnerving human quality to it. You'll commonly see sleepy females piled together on the beach, while the large dominant bull, weighing up to 250kg and identifiably male for the pronounced bump on its forehead, aggressively patrols its territory barking loudly above and below the waves. Lesser males have no place at these heavily guarded "harems" and form colonies in less favourable locations, where they build up strength and size to make a successful challenge. The bull spends so much of its time guarding its territory that it doesn't feed, and eventually has to give way to a fitter male. These inquisitive, graceful and friendly animals will often check you out if you're swimming nearby, staring into your mask or tugging at your flippers. The bulls should be given a lot of space, though – they have a nasty bite and don't take kindly to humans who appear to be muscling in on their territory.

Galápagos fur seals are more shy and difficult to see, choosing the shade of craggy cliffs and rocks, where they can find a nook to keep out of the sun's glare. In spite of their name, they are in the same family (Otaridae) as the sea lion, having protruding ears and the ability to "walk" on their front flippers, unlike the Phocidae, the true seals. They're related to the southern fur seals of Antarctica and the southern mainland, and have thick coats like them, though in the heat of the Galápagos they must take care not to overheat. Their large, mournful eyes give them excellent vision for their nightly hunting trips and they avoid expeditions at full moon, when sharks have a better chance of seeing them. In the nineteenth century, their warm, double-layered pelt was highly sought after, and they declined from overhunting. They are now protected and colonies have recovered, numbering around 50,000, like the sea lions.

Whales and dolphins

One of the most thrilling moments during a Galápagos cruise is a sighting of **whales** or **dolphins**. Amiable **bottle-nosed dolphins** frequently surf the bow wave, jockeying for position at the front of the boat and jumping high in synchrony at either side. Huge schools of dark-grey and white **common dolphins** occasionally pass boats, skipping through the waves in long lines, while **striped** and **spinner dolphins** are less frequently seen. Whalers hunted the waters west of Isabela and Fernandina exhaustively during the first half of the nineteenth century, until populations all but disappeared around the 1860s. Today several whale species are found in these areas and the **sperm whale** is known to have breeding grounds in the area. The **humpback whale** is the most easily spotted, sometimes "breaching" – hurling its sixteen-metre body out of the water before crashing down in an avalanche of spray. Other baleen whales, those that sift for plankton and shrimp such as the **sei**, **minke**, **Bryde's** and **finback**, are more usually seen as a fin and a puff of spray in the distance. **Orcas** or **killer whales** feed on dolphins, fur seals, penguins and sea lions.

Fish and marine invertebrates

Bathed in cold upwelling currents and warm tropical waters, the Galápagos enjoys a broad range of 306 **fish** species, with 51 endemics. Plenty of interesting fish can be spotted with a snorkel and mask, but the most thrilling to swim with are the **sharks**. Regularly seen species include **white-tip reef sharks**, **hammerheads** and **black-tip sharks**, none of which is usually dangerous to humans. You'll need to scuba-dive to see the **Galápagos shark**, which prefers deeper waters. There has never been a report of a shark attack in the Galápagos, but follow the advice of your guide. The colossal eighteen-metre **whale shark** is the largest fish in the world and feeds on plankton.

The **rays** include the **stingray**, **golden ray**, the beautiful **spotted eagle ray** and the **manta ray** (which can grow up to 6m across). The larger rays are frequently seen somersaulting out of the water before landing in clouds of spray. Among the more commonly seen bony fishes are the **blue-eyed damselfish**, the stripy **sergeant major**, the **moorish idol**, the **hieroglyphic hawkfish** and the **white-banded angelfish**, as well as several **blennies**, **wrasses** and **parrotfish**. The **four-eyed blenny** is so called because each eye has two facets, allowing it to see both in and out of the water. It can spend two hours flapping about the rocks as it hunts for insects and small crabs.

Many interesting organisms are visible around the shore between the tides. **Octopuses** lurk in rock pools, but can be difficult to see because of their ability to change colour. Among the most visible intertidal animals are the more than one hundred **crab** species scuttling over the rocks and beaches. The brightest is the **Sally lightfoot crab**, whose red casing gleams against the black lava. Its name comes either from a Jamaican dancer or its ability to zip over the water of a tide pool. Young Sally lightfoots are dark to blend in with the background. **Ghost crabs** live in holes dug in sandy beaches, while the soft-bodied **hermit crab** occupies abandoned shells, moving as it grows. **Fiddler crabs** are easy to identify by their outsized claw. **Sea urchins**, **sea cucumbers**, **starfish**, **anemones**, **molluscs** and **sponges** can also be found.

Land invertebrates

There are more than two thousand species of **land invertebrates** – animals without a backbone, such as insects and spiders – in the Galápagos, over half of them endemic. It sounds a huge number, but compared to more than a million species found in mainland Ecuador, it's clear that land invertebrates found the archipelago difficult to reach and colonize.

The arid climate of the islands has meant that many **insects** are nocturnal, escaping the noonday heat in dank and shaded hideouts. For this reason many are drably coloured. **Beetles** account for more than four hundred species, **bugs** eighty or so and **flies** around one hundred, including the bothersome **horsefly** and **midge**. The **carpenter bee** is the only bee in the Galápagos, an important pollinator of native plants. Of the butterflies and moths, the yellow **Galápagos sulphur butterfly** and the **green hawkmoth**, which has a proboscis twice the length of its body, are among the most commonly seen of the two groups. The **Galápagos silver fritillary** has sparkling silvery patches on its wings, but perhaps the most colourful insect outside the eight butterfly species is the **painted locust**, frequently spotted around the coast in black, red and yellow. There are two **scorpions**, both of which can sting but are not dangerous, and more than fifty **spiders**, including a venomous relative of the black widow and the **silver argiope**, which weaves a silky "X" into the centre of its web. A thirty-centimetre, crimson-legged **centipede**, the poisonous endemic *Scolopendra galapagensis*, elicits nightmares thanks to its very painful bite, normally reserved for unlucky insects, lava lizards and small birds.

Ticks and **mites** annoy reptiles rather than humans, and tortoises and iguanas rely on finches to remove them. Of the tiny **land snails**, the *Bulimulus* genus has enjoyed extraordinary speciation with more than sixty known endemics descended from a single ancestor – putting Darwin's finches quite in the shade.

Plants

There are more than six hundred plant species in the Galápagos, around forty percent of which are endemic. Botanists have divided the islands into **vegetation zones**, each of which contains certain groupings of plants. Levels of rainfall play an important part in determining these zones and, generally speaking, the higher the altitude, the more moisture is received, allowing for a greater number of plant species. Usually the southern, windward side of an island receives far more rain than the leeward, which lies in a rain shadow, so in many cases the zones differ from one side of an island to another.

Coastal and arid zones

Going by altitude, the first zone is the **coastal** or **littoral zone** around the shore, dominated by salt-tolerant plants, notably four species of **mangrove** (red, black, white and button), which make important breeding sites for many sea and shore birds. When water is scarce **sea purslane** (*Sesuvium*) turns a deep red, covering shorelines in a crimson carpet, reverting to green in the wet season. **Beach morning glory** is a creeper that helps bind sand dunes together and produces large lilac flowers.

△ Hood mockingbird atop camera, Isla Española (Galápagos Islands)

The **arid zone** is one of the largest zones, and is the most familiar to island visitors for its scrubby and cactus-filled semi-desert landscape. The **candelabra cactus** (*Jasminocereus*), whose distinctive barrel-shaped fingers can grow to 7m, and the **lava cactus** (*Brachycereus*), growing in small yellow clumps on black lava flows, are both endemic genera. The widespread **prickly pear cactus** (*Opuntia*) comes in fourteen endemic types on the islands and forms a major food staple for many birds and reptiles. The most striking of them has developed into tall, broad-trunked trees up to 12m in height, in part an evolutionary response to browsing tortoises. The lower shrubby forms are mostly found on tortoise-free islands, and in the northern islands, where pollinating insects are absent, the spines are softer to allow birds to do the job. The ubiquitous tree of this zone is the **palo santo**, recognizable for its deathly-grey appearance. Its name translates as "holy stick", both because its fragrant resin is burnt as incense in churches (it can also be used as an insect repellent) and because its off-white flowers appear around Christmas. When the rains come, green leaves start sprouting on its branches. Virtually waterless ashy or sandy soils support the low-lying grey *Tiquilia*, as seen scattered around the dry slopes of Bartolomé. The genes of the **Galápagos tomato**, one of the world's only two tomato species, whose seeds germinate best having passed through the giant tortoise's digestive system, have been used to develop drought-resistant tomatoes in other countries. **Lichens** are also common in the arid zone, requiring very little moisture or soil, and grow on trees (such as the grey crustose lichen on the palo santo), rocks and even tortoise shells.

Transition and highland zones

The **transition zone** links the dry zone to the more humid areas of **highland zones**. It's dominated by **pega pega** (meaning "stick stick"), so called for its sticky leaves and fruit, **guayabillo**, an endemic that produces fruits similar to the guava, and **matazarno**, a tall tree used for timber.

The humid area starts at around 200m and is divided into four zones. The **scalesia zone** is lush and densely forested, perpetually soaked in garúa mist during the cool-dry season. It's dominated by **lechoso** (*Scalesia pedunculata*), a fifteen-metre-tall tree with a bushy leafy top, among the tallest members of the daisy and sunflower families, most often seen by visitors in the highlands of Santa Cruz. From one ancestor the *Scalesia* genus has developed into twenty forms according to the various environmental nuances of the islands. Similar to a cloudforest, the trees are covered with **epiphytes**, mainly **mosses**, **liverworts** and **ferns**, but also a few **orchids**, and one **bromeliad** (*Tillandsia*). At the higher end of this zone, the smaller **cat's claw** tree begins to take over, also hung heavy in epiphytes, which appear brown in the dry season, so giving it the name the **brown zone**. On Santa Cruz and San Cristóbal islands, the **miconia zone** is made up of a belt of **cacaotillo** (*Miconia robinsoniana*), an endemic shrub growing to about 5m, producing dark blue berries and resembling the cacao. Beginning at about 700m, the **pampa zone** is the highest and wettest zone, made up mainly of **grasses**, **sedges** and other plants adapted to boggy environments. The **tree fern**, reaching a height of 3m, is by far the tallest plant growing in this zone.

Books

With the possible exception of the Galápagos Islands, foreign writers have paid less attention to Ecuador than to its South American neighbours, and few Ecuadorian works are ever translated into English. That said, there's a reasonable choice of books available in English, covering subjects as diverse as archeology, exploration, travel and cookery, though not all are easy to find. One of the best places to find English-language books is Quito, particularly at the excellent Libri Mundi bookshop (see p.111). Another useful starting point is South American Explorers (SAE; see p.80), which has an online catalogue and mail-order system at Ⓦwww.sam-explo.org. Many of the titles listed below are also available from Ⓦwww.amazon.com, including some of the out-of-print books, which Amazon can source from secondhand bookstores. Publishers are listed UK/US, unless there is only one, in which case this is indicated. Entries tagged with the 🌟 symbol are particularly recommended.

History and society

Michael Anderson *A Numismatic History of Ecuador* (Greenlight). Much more than a study of Ecuadorian coinage, the history of a relatively young nation's struggle for its own currency, intimately bound up in its political and cultural past – and particularly interesting in light of dollarization.

David Corkill *Ecuador: Fragile Democracy* (o/p). A clear and thorough summary of Ecuador's history and economy from the Spanish Conquest to the neoliberalism of the late 1980s.

Felix Denegri Luna *Notes for the History of a Frontier* (Bolsa de Valores, Lima). Meticulously researched, accessible study of the relationship between Ecuador and Peru, from their days as neighbouring colonial divisions within Spanish America right up to 1995, written by a Peruvian academic in a spirit of promoting mutual understanding and *rapprochement*.

🌟 **John Hemming** *The Conquest of the Incas* (Papermac/Harcourt Brace). Marrying an academic atten-tion to detail with a gripping narra-tive style, Hemming's book is widely regarded as the best account of this devastating conquest. His earlier work, *The Search for El Dorado* (UK: Michael Joseph), covers the Spaniards' unquenchable desire for gold that fuelled the Conquest, and pinpoints the origin of the myth of El Dorado, the legendary Golden Man, to 1540s Quito, from where it quickly spread throughout the continent.

Mark Honigsbaum *The Fever Trail: in Search of the Cure for Malaria* (Macmillan/Farrar, Straus and Giroux). A riveting story centring on three British explorers' long nine-teenth-century search for the elusive cinchona tree – a native of Ecuador, first discovered in the Podocarpus area, and the only source of quinine – and their hapless task of bringing it to the colonies.

Anita Isaacs *Military Rule and Transition in Ecuador 1972–92* (University of Pittsburgh). Incisive examination of the political actions of the military, and the impact mili-tary intervention has had on subse-quent civilian governments.

Magnus Mörner *The Andean Past: Land, Societies, and Conflicts* (o/p). Academic but readable study on the historical development of Ecuador, Peru and Bolivia – the three modern-day countries that made up the bulk of the Inca Empire – since the pre-Columbian era.

Sarah Radcliffe and Sallie Westwood *Remaking the Nation: Place, Identity and Politics in Latin America* (Routledge). Thought-provoking analysis of the complex and often contradictory factors informing perceptions of national identity in Latin America, using Ecuador as a case study. A fascinating insight into the country's self-image, as influenced by gender, age, class and ethnicity.

Wilma Roos and Omer van Renterghem *Ecuador in Focus* (Latin America Bureau/Interlink). An easy-to-read and up-to-date introduction to Ecuador, with chapters on history, people, environment, economy and culture.

Mary Weismantel *Cholas and Pishtacos: Stories of Race and Sex in the Andes* (University of Chicago). Brilliantly explores the relationship and tensions between the races and sexes, set against the vivid backdrop of the Andes. The author underpins her analysis on two colourful figures of South American popular culture, the *chola* (a voluptuous highland *mestiza*) and the *pishtaco* (a mythical white ghoul that feeds on human fat), and draws on wide-ranging sources, from the reminiscences of potato sellers to highbrow novels.

Memoirs and travel

Ludwig Bemelmans *The Donkey Inside* (o/p). Classic narrative based on the author's travels through Ecuador in the 1940s. A little old-fashioned and conservative, but masterfully written and a lively read.

Joe Fisher *Cotopaxi Visions* (Quarry). Fast-paced, picaresque account of the author's quest for self-discovery and spiritual ecstasy in the Ecuadorian Andes in the 1970s. An entertaining read, even if you don't share Fisher's mysticism.

Albert Franklin *Ecuador* (o/p). An affectionate and perceptive portrait of Ecuador in the early 1940s, as it stood, in the author's words, "at the threshold between the feudal world and the modern world". Highly readable, and worth ordering from your library before you head out there.

Toby Green *Saddled with Darwin: A Journey through South America* (Phoenix). Elegantly written and loaded with wonderful anecdotes, an account of a madcap undertaking to follow Darwin's travels across South America on horseback. The author's total lack of riding experience was only one of the obstacles he found himself up against.

Grace Halsell *Los Viejos: Secrets of Long Life from the Sacred Valley* (o/p). In 1974 the author set off to live in Vilcabamba – in the supposed "valley of eternal youth" – for a year to try to find out what allowed its residents to live useful, meaningful and active lives well into old age. The result was an engaging glimpse of Vilcabamba before the arrival of the tourist boom.

Peter Lourie *Sweat of the Sun, Tears of the Moon* (Grafton/University of Nebraska). Gripping account of the modern-day treasure seekers intent on retrieving Atahualpa's ransom from the Llanganates mountains, written by a young American who became embroiled in their obsessions in the 1980s.

★ **Henri Michaux** *Ecuador* (o/p UK and US; Gallimard, France). Beautifully written – and sometimes ether-induced – impressions of Ecuador, based on the mystical Belgian author's travels through the country in 1977, and presented in a mixture of prose, poetry and diary notes.

Tom Miller *The Panama Hat Trail* (o/p). Blending lively travel narrative with investigative journalism, an engaging book tracking the historical and geographical course of the Panama hat, from the *toquilla* fields of the lowlands to the hat exporters and boutiques of the United States.

Karin Muller *Along the Inca Road: A Woman's Journey into an Ancient Empire* (National Geographic). With a research grant and a cameraman, Muller searches for the Royal Inca highway that once linked Ecuador to Chile and has dozens of adventures on the way, including a tear-gas riot and a land-mine removal exercise, and being beaten with a *cuy* by a shaman for a diagnosis.

Blair Niles *Casual Wanderings in Ecuador* (o/p). Light-hearted travel narrative from an affable author who toured the country in the 1920s, stumbling on many of today's favourite tourist spots, such as Baños and the Devil's Nose. The superior photos make this a real sociohistoric document.

Richard Poole *The Inca Smiled* (o/p). Sensitive and enjoyable account of the author's two-year stint as a Peace Corps volunteer in Riobamba in the late 1960s, raising thoughtful questions about aid, development and poverty.

Diane Terezakis *Maíz y Coca Cola: Adventures, Scrapes, and Shamanism in the Amazon and Andes* (Xlibris). American city-girl seeks out the shamans and medicine men of Ecuador in an amusing voyage of self-discovery and altered states of consciousness.

Paul Theroux *The Old Patagonian Express* (Penguin/Houghton Mifflin). A cranky but entertaining account of the author's railway odyssey through the Americas, including a chapter on the time he spent in Quito (which he liked) and Guayaquil (which he hated), and attempting, and failing, to take the famous train ride between the two.

★ **Moritz Thomsen** *Living Poor* (Eland/University of Washington). An American Peace Corps volunteer writes lucidly about his time in the fishing community of Río Verde in Esmeraldas during the 1960s, and his mostly futile – sometimes farcical – efforts to haul its people out of poverty. Thomsen never left Ecuador and followed this book with three other autobiographical works – *Farm on the River of Emeralds* (UK: Barrie & Jenkins), *The Saddest Pleasure* (US: Graywolf) and *My Two Wars* (US: Steerforth) – before dying in a squalid apartment in Guayaquil in 1991. He refused to help himself, even though he had a shoe box full of uncashed royalty cheques worth $40,000.

Celia Wakefield *Searching for Isabel Godin: An Ordeal on the Amazon, Tragedy and Survival* (Creative Arts Book Co). Fascinating account of the heartbreaking story of Isabel Godin, the Peruvian wife of Jean Godin, one of the key scientists on La Condamine's mission. Briefly left in Ecuador while her husband made further travel arrangements, she found herself separated from him for the next twenty years, kept apart by disaster, disease, treachery, sheer bad luck and the vagaries of international politics.

Richard Wingate *Lost Outpost of Atlantis* (o/p). Fast-paced chronicle of the author's attempts to prove that South America was colonized by the mythical civilization of Atlantis, based on the discovery of thousands of artefacts buried in caves in the Oriente. A good read, if slightly barking.

Mountaineering and hiking

Chris Bonington *The Next Horizon* (o/p). Britain's most famous mountaineer looks back over his climbing achievements, and devotes a chapter to his two slightly anticlimactic ascents of Volcán Sangay.

Yossi Brain *Ecuador: A Climbing Guide* (Mountaineers). Covers climbing routes up Ecuador's most popular mountains and its lesser-known peaks.

Robert and Daisy Kunstaetter *Trekking in Ecuador* (Mountaineers). The most up-to-date trekking guide for Ecuador, which includes almost thirty beautiful, well-chosen routes, and plenty of maps, photos and elevation profiles.

Rob Rachowiecki, Mark Thurber and Betsy Wagenhauser *Climbing and Hiking in Ecuador* (Bradt). Long-standing climbing and hiking guide to Ecuador, now in its fifth edition, which details more than seventy routes throughout the country, concentrating on the sierra.

Richard Snailham *Sangay Survived* (o/p). Brisk account of the attempt of six British-army climbers – the advance party of a geological survey – to climb Sangay in 1976, when an unexpected eruption left two of them dead and the rest of the team seriously injured and stranded on the volcano.

★ **Edward Whymper** *Travels Amongst the Great Andes of the Equator* (o/p). Exploits of the pioneering mountaineer at the end of the nineteenth century, who managed to rack up a number of first summits, including Chimborazo, Cayambe and Antisana. Climbing stories and engaging travelogue are mixed with observations on insects and pre-Columbian pottery. Best of all are the stunning illustrations of brooding peaks and highland life.

Wildlife and the environment

Enrique Aguilar *Awakening in the Andes* (Enrique Aguilar, Ecuador) Elegant coffee-table tome with a spread of 120 dramatic photos depicting the volcanoes and inhabitants of the Ecuadorian Andes.

Helen Collinson (ed.) *Green Guerrillas* (Latin America Bureau /Monthly Review). A collection of essays on Latin America's environmental situation, including discussions on indigenous groups and rainforest ecotourism.

John Eisenberg and Kent Redford *Mammals of the Neotropics: Ecuador, Peru, Bolivia, Brazil* (University of Chicago). Useful guide to more than 650 species, including distribution maps, colour and monochrome photographs and background information on ecological and behavioural characteristics.

Steven Hilty and William Brown *A Guide to the Birds of Colombia* (Princeton University). Exhaustive, highly regarded guide detailing all 1695 of Colombia's recorded bird species, of which a large portion are also found in Ecuador. Essential reading for serious birders, with some beautiful colour plates.

Victor Wolfgang von Hagen *South America: The Green World of the Naturalists* (o/p). Fascinating overviews of the great naturalist-explorers who uncovered a continent, from Peter Martyr of 1494 to Sanderson in the 1930s, including excerpts and vivid illustrations. For Ecuador, there are accounts from von Humboldt, Herman Melville, La Condamine and Edward Whymper. On a similar theme, his *South America Called Them* (UK: Robert Hale /AMS) is an enjoyable, if sometimes overwritten, volume dealing with four ground-breaking scientific explorers (La Condamine, Darwin, von Humboldt and Richard Spruce), all of whom spent time in Ecuador or the Galápagos Islands.

★ **Alexander von Humboldt** *Personal Narrative of Travels to the Equinoctial Regions of the New Continent during the Years 1799–1804* (o/p). Written by perhaps the greatest of all scientist-explorers, who composed 29 volumes on his travels across South America. The sixth volume of his *Personal Narrative* touches on Ecuador, and includes the ground-breaking botanical map of Chimborazo (which von Humboldt failed to top after several attempts), showing the changes in the volcano's flora at different elevations. A heavily edited version of *Personal Narrative* is available as well (Penguin).

Kevin Kling *Ecuador, Island of the Andes* (Thames & Hudson). A collection of stunning photographs of the peoples and landscapes of the Ecuadorian sierra, invested with a haunting, timeless quality that makes them linger in the mind.

John Kricher *A Neotropical Companion* (Princeton University). Excellent and thorough introduction to the flora, fauna and ecosystems of the tropics of Central and South America, aimed at the general reader. Highly recommended.

★ **Robert S. Ridgely and Paul J. Greenfield** *The Birds of Ecuador* (Cornell University). Long-awaited, monumental two-volume book (each available separately) including a field guide with glorious colour plates of Ecuador's 1600 bird species. The country's definitive bird guide, and an indispensable resource for anyone interested in South American avifauna.

Robert S. R. Williams *Guide to Bird-watching in Ecuador and the Galápagos Islands* (Biosphere). Not the best choice for identification purposes, but still a useful field guide that offers details of 120 birding sites and maps, a full checklist of Ecuadorian species and information on habitats and conservation.

The Oriente

Philippe Drescola *The Spears of Twilight: Life and Death in the Amazon Jungle* (Flamingo/New Press). Drescola, a French ethnologist, spent two years living among the Achuar of the Oriente in the 1970s, a time vividly and intelligently recounted in this memoir.

★ **Joe Kane** *Savages* (Pan/Vintage). An affecting and sensitive book on the protests of the Huaorani against "the Company", the monolithic multinational oil industry and its supporting agencies. It's sprinkled with a poignant humour generated from the gap in cultures between the author and his subjects.

José Toribio Medina (ed.) *The Discovery of the Amazon* (o/p). The most detailed account of Francisco de Orellana's voyage down the Amazon, with half the book given to the original source documents, translated into English.

Anthony Smith *Explorers of the Amazon* (University of Chicago). An entertaining introduction to the exploration of the Amazon, streaked with a wry sense of humour. Includes chapters on Francisco de Orellana, Charles Marie de la Condamine and Alexander von Humboldt.

Randy Smith *Crisis Under the Canopy* (Abya Yala, Ecuador). An in-depth look at tourism in the Oriente and its effect on the Huaorani people.

Rolf Wesche *The Ecotourist's Guide to the Ecuadorian Amazon* (CEPEIGE, Ecuador). Focuses on old Napo province (Baeza, Tena, Misahuallí and Coca), and although the town and hotel accounts are a little out of date, there are some good descriptions of petroglyph sites, caves and hikes, as well as a selection of excellent 1:50,000 - scale maps.

Rolf Wesche and Andy Drumm *Defending Our Rainforest* (Acción Amazonia, Ecuador). Full practical details and descriptions of many indigenous ecotourism projects in the Oriente, accompanied by spirited analysis of why they could be the salvation of the forests and its people.

Galápagos

Johanna Angermeyer *My Father's Island* (o/p). The author uncovers the hidden past of her relatives through lyrical reminiscences on the Angermeyer family's struggle to settle on Santa Cruz, Galápagos.

William Beebe *Galápagos: World's End* (Dover). This pleasing book, which combines eager prose with keen scientific observation, brought the Galápagos to the attention of a new generation of travellers in the 1920s, and its popularity sparked a number of ill-fated attempts to colonize the islands. Beebe was the director of the New York Zoological Society and went to the Galápagos as head of a two-and-a-half-month scientific expedition, but problems with the water supply meant that he spent only "six thousand minutes" there.

Peter J. Bowler *Charles Darwin: The Man and his Influence* (Cambridge University). Of the countless Darwin biographies, this does a better job than most of stripping away the myths from the Darwin legend, and

paints a realistic backdrop illustrating his place in contemporary scientific society.

Isabel Castro and Antonia Phillips *A Guide to the Birds of the Galápagos Islands* (A & C Black /Princeton University). Comprehensive, easy-to-use bird guide with colour illustrations and detailed descriptions to help identification.

Ainslie and Francis Conway *The Enchanted Islands* and *Return to the Island* (o/p). Humorous stories of an American couple's thwarted attempts to settle in the Galápagos in the 1930s and 1940s.

Charles Darwin *Voyage of the Beagle* (Penguin). A hugely enjoyable book with a chapter devoted to the Galápagos; original insights and flashes of genius pepper Darwin's wonderfully vivid descriptions of the islands' landscapes and wildlife. As revolutionary science texts go, *On the Origin of Species* (Penguin) is arguably one of the most accessible, though still much harder work than *Voyage of the Beagle*.

Adrian Desmond and James Moore *Darwin: The Life of a Tormented Evolutionist* (Penguin/W. W. Norton). The enormous, definitive and best-selling biography of Darwin, so thorough and wide-ranging that it also serves as a compelling study of Victorian Britain as a whole.

Jack S. Grove, et al *The Fishes of the Galápagos Islands* (Stanford University Press). By far the most comprehensive guide to marine life in the Galápagos, using documents and research dating back to Darwin's visit in 1835, with illustrations or photos of more than four hundred fish species found within a 100-kilometre radius of the islands. However, weighing in at almost a thousand pages and with a price tag of more than US$120, it's strictly for fanatics.

Herman Heinzell and Barnaby Hall *Galápagos Diary: A Complete Guide to the Archipelago's Birdlife* (University of California). Charming and idiosyncratic guide to the islands' birds, using photos, colour illustrations, and diary entries that highlight breeding habits and behavioural oddities.

Thor Heyerdahl *Archaeological Evidence of Pre-Spanish Visits to the Galápagos Islands* (UK: Norwegian University). On the back of his ground-breaking *Kon-Tiki* expedition, this is Heyerdahl's academic attempt to unravel the mysteries of early human settlement on the islands.

John Hickman *The Enchanted Isles* (UK: Anthony Nelson). A succinct, well-researched and entertaining history of human life on the islands, especially strong on the many colourful episodes concerning early pirates and castaways.

Paul Humann (ed.) *Reef Fish Identification: Galápagos* (New World Publications). Colourful photos and concise information on Galápagos reef fish in a slim and manageable field guide.

Michael H. Jackson *Galápagos* (Academic & University Publishers Group/University of Calgary). The most accurate and complete guide to the natural history of the Galápagos Islands, containing a broad and readable overview of geography, geology, flora and fauna, and conservation. Includes some colour plates and a wildlife checklist.

Colney K. McMullen *Flowering Plants of the Galápagos* (Cornell University). Galápagos flora has often played second fiddle to the islands' famous animals, but this excellent field guide helps to redress the balance with its succinct descriptions of more than four hundred plants and their locations, and plenty of colour photos.

Tui de Roy *Spectacular Galápagos: Exploring an Extraordinary World* (Hugh Lauter Levin Associates) and *Galápagos: Islands Born of Fire* (Warwick). Stupendous photos of Galápagos wildlife and landscapes.

Keith Stewart Thomson *HMS Beagle: The Story of Darwin's Ship* (o/p). One for ship enthusiasts rather than nature buffs, as it concentrates on the voyages of the famous brig, with Darwin only impressing himself on the story halfway through the book.

★ **Andy Swash and Robert Still** *Birds, Mammals and Reptiles of the Galápagos Islands* (Yale). Excellent compact field guide with colour photos and sketches, including a fin guide to aid the identification of dolphins and whales.

★ **John Treherne** *The Galápagos Affair* (Pimlico). Excellent overview of the extraordinary events on Floreana in the early 1930s that led to unexplained deaths and disappearances, including a large appendix detailing the author's own theories.

Jonathan Weiner *The Beak of the Finch* (Vintage). The fascinating work of two British scientists who have spent twenty years cataloguing Darwin's finches – in effect, witnessing the processes of evolution at first hand.

Margret Wittmer *Floreana* (Anthony Nelson/Moyer Bell). One of Floreana's original colonists describes how she conquered the privations of Galápagos life, and gives her version of events in the "Galápagos affair" (see box, p.499).

Arts and popular culture

★ **Dawn Ades** *Art in Latin America: The Modern Era 1820–1980* (Yale University). Excellent and lavishly illustrated general history of Latin American art from Independence, with discussions of a number of Ecuadorian artists, including Guayasamín, Viteri, Troya, Galecio, and Antonio and Ramón Salas.

Christy Buchanan and Cesar Franco *The Ecuador Cookbook: Traditional Vegetarian and Seafood Recipes* (Christy Buchanan). Paperback cookbook offering a series of delightfully illustrated and easy-to-follow vegetarian and seafood recipes from Ecuador in English and Spanish.

Pablo Cuvi *Crafts of Ecuador* (o/p; available by mail order from SAE). Sumptuously illustrated coffee-table book taking in the gamut of Ecuador's traditional artesanías, from textiles to woodcarvings, accompanied by solid background information on the history and development of these crafts.

Lynn Meisch (ed.) *Traditional Textiles of the Andes* (Thames and Hudson). Beautiful colour illustrations accompany six interesting essays on weaving in the Andes. Meisch also wrote *Otavalo: Weaving,*

Costume and the Market (Ediciones Libri Mundi, Ecuador), which covers the history, the methods and the modern-day situation of Otavalo's weavers, with plenty of black-and-white illustrations; and *Andean Entrepreneurs: Otavalo Merchants and Musicians in the Global Arena* (University of Texas), an insightful discussion about the ability of Otavalo's indigenous communities to use modern technology and participate in the global economy without surrendering their cultural identity.

Gabrielle Palmer *Sculpture in the Kingdom of Quito* (University of New Mexico). Meticulously and thoughtfully researched exposé of the development of colonial sculpture in Quito, illustrated by some gorgeous photographs.

Gustavo Ramírez *Football in Ecuador* (Soccer Books: UK). A tiny history of the game in Ecuador, uninspiring photos of the country's mostly rather dishevelled stadiums, and lists of league clubs make up the bulk of this thin manual, but the international results table at the end makes for some interesting reading: Ecuador didn't win a game between August 1938 and May 1949, and once suffered the humiliation of a 12-0 defeat by Argentina.

Fiction

⭐ **Demetrio Aguilera Malta** *Don Goyo* (Humana). A spellbinding novel, first published in 1933, dealing with the lives of a group of *cholos* who eke out a living by fishing from the mangrove swamps in the Gulf of Guayaquil, which are in danger of being cleared by white landowners.

Kelly Aitken *Love in a Warm Climate* (o/p). Collection of short stories by a Canadian writer, all set in Ecuador and told by a series of North American female narrators. Imaginatively and compellingly written, bristling with tensions and conveying a strong sense of place.

Susan Benner and Kathy Leonard (eds.) *Fire from the Andes* (University of New Mexico). Impressive anthology of short stories by contemporary women authors from Ecuador, Bolivia and Peru. The eight Ecuadorian stories touch on themes such as patriarchy, racial prejudice, poverty and ageing.

William Burroughs *Queer* (o/p). Autobiographical, Beat-generation novel about a morphine addict's travels through Ecuador in an abortive search for *yage*, a hallucinatory drug from the Oriente.

Jorge Icaza *Huasipungo; the Villagers* (European Schoolbooks/Southern Illinois University). Iconic *indigenista* novel written in 1934, portraying the hardships and degradation suffered by the Andean *indígena* in a world dominated by exploitive, upper-class landowners.

Adalberto Ortiz *Juyungo* (Lynne Rienner). A 1940s novel set in the tropical lowlands, about the life of a black labourer who kills two white men in self-defence. An atmospheric read, full of evocative detail.

Luis Sepulveda *The Old Man Who Read Love Stories* (Harvest). Captivating and deceptively simple story of an itinerant dentist's twice-yearly voyages into a Shuar community in the Oriente – vividly evoking the sensations of travelling in the rainforest, while unobtrusively raising environmental questions.

Kurt Vonnegut *Galápagos* (Flamingo/Delta). A darkly comic novel which, turning natural selection on its head, has a handful of passengers on a Galápagos cruise ship marooned on the islands as the only survivors of a war and global pandemic. "Big brains" had been the species' fallibility, and a million years' evolution takes humanity in a quite different direction.

Language

Language

Language

The official language of Ecuador is Spanish, though at least twenty other first languages are spoken by native Ecuadorians, including nine dialects of Quichua and a further eight indigenous languages of the Oriente. English and some other European languages are spoken in tourist centres and well-to-do hotels and agencies, but otherwise you'll need to know a bit of Spanish.

It's an easy language to pick up, especially in Ecuador – or rather in the Ecuadorian **sierra**, whose inhabitants are known for speaking fairly slowly and clearly, usually pronouncing all the consonants of a word. On the **coast**, however, the task is made harder by a difficult accent that drops the letter "s" and trims down whole word endings, so that "*arroz con pescado*", for example, becomes "*arro' con pe'ca'o*". Many beginners spend a week or longer getting to grips with the basics at one of Quito's numerous **language schools**, most of which offer great-value one-to-one lessons for about $5 per hour (for more details, see p.78). Popular alternatives to Quito include the small mountain town of Baños (see p.216) and the colonial city of Cuenca (see p.256), both home to a number of language schools.

Those who already speak Spanish will have no trouble adjusting to the way it's spoken in Ecuador, which conforms to standard textbook **Castilian**, spoken without the lisped "c" and "z". That said, it does have its own idiomatic peculiarities, one of which is the compulsive use of the word "*nomás*" ("just" or "only"), which crops up all over the place ("*siga nomás*" for "go ahead", or "*siéntate nomás*" for "sit down", to give just a few examples). Something else that sets Ecuadorian Spanish apart from Iberian Spanish are the many indigenous words that pepper its vocabulary, particularly **Quichua** words such as *guagua* (baby), *mate* (herbal infusion), *pampa* (plain), *soroche* (altitude sickness) and *minga* (communal labour). Ecuador also readily borrows from **English**, resulting in a slew of words regarded with horror by Spaniards, such as *chequear* (to check), *parquear* (to park), *rentar* (to rent), *sánduche* (sandwich) and *computador* (computer). This somewhat flexible approach to their own language makes Ecuadorians more than willing to accommodate a foreigner's attempts to speak Spanish, which are invariably rewarded with smiles and compliments no matter how clumsy or inaccurate.

Pronunciation

The rules of **pronunciation** are pretty straightforward and, once you get to know them, strictly observed. Unless there's an accent, words ending in d, l, r, and z are **stressed** on the last syllable, all others on the second last. All **vowels** are pure and short.

A somewhere between the "a" sound of back and that of father

E as in get

I as in police

O as in hot

U as in rule

C is soft before E and I, hard otherwise: cerca is pronounced "serka".

G works the same way, a guttural "h" sound (like the ch in loch) before E or I, a hard G elsewhere – gigante becomes "higante".

H is always silent

LL sounds like an English Y: *tortilla* is pronounced "torteeya".

N is as in English unless it has a tilde over it, as with *mañana*, when it's pronounced like the "n" in onion or menu.

QU is pronounced like an English K.

R is rolled, RR doubly so.

V sounds more like B, *vino* becoming "beano".

X is slightly softer than in English – sometimes almost SH – except between vowels in place names where it has an "H" sound – for example México (meh-hee-ko).

Z is the same as a soft "C", so *cerveza* becomes "servesa".

If you're using a **dictionary**, bear in mind that in Spanish CH, LL, and Ñ count as separate letters and are listed after the Cs, Ls, and Ns, respectively.

Words and phrases

We've listed a few essential **words** and **phrases** below, but if you're travelling for any length of time a dictionary or phrasebook, such as the *Rough Guide Dictionary Phrasebook: Spanish*, is obviously a worthwhile investment.

Basics

yes, no	**sí, no**	with, without	**con, sin**
please, thank you	**por favor, gracias**	good, bad	**buen(o)/a, mal(o)/a**
where, when	**dónde, cuándo**	big	**gran(de)**
what, how much	**qué, cuánto**	small	**pequeño/a, chico**
here, there	**aquí, allí**	more, less	**más, menos**
this, that	**este, eso**	today, tomorrow	**hoy, mañana**
now, later	**ahora, más tarde**	yesterday	**ayer**
open, closed	**abierto/a, cerrado/a**		

Greetings and responses

Hello, Goodbye	**Hola, Adiós**	I don't speak Spanish	**(No) Hablo español**
Good morning	**Buenos días**	My name is . . .	**Me llamo . . .**
Good afternoon/night	**Buenas tardes/noches**	What's your name?	**¿Cómo se llama usted?**
See you later	**Hasta luego**	I am English	**Soy inglés (a)**
Sorry	**Lo siento/discúlpeme**	. . . American	**norteamericano (a)**
Excuse me	**Con permiso/perdón**	. . . Australian	**australiano (a)**
How are you?	**¿Cómo está (usted)?**	. . . Canadian	**canadiense (a)**
I (don't) understand	**(No) Entiendo**	. . . Irish	**irlandés (a)**
Not at all/You're welcome	**De nada**	. . . Scottish	**escosés (a)**
		. . . Welsh	**galés (a)**
Do you speak English?	**¿Habla (usted) inglés?**	. . . New Zealander	**neozelandés (a)**

Accommodation

Twin room	Una habitación doble	...with two beds/ double bed	...con dos camas/cama matrimonial
Room with double bed	Una habitación matrimonial	It's for one person/ two people	Es para una persona/dos personas
Single room	Una habitación sencilla	...for one night/ one week	...para una noche/ una semana
Private bathroom	Baño privado	It's fine, how much is it?	¿Está bien, cuánto es?
Shared bathroom	Baño compartido		
Hot water (all day)	Agua caliente (todo el día)	It's too expensive	Es demasiado caro
Cold water	Agua fría	Don't you have anything cheaper?	¿No tiene algo más barato?
Fan	Ventilador	Can one...?	¿Se puede..?
Air-conditioned	Aire-acondicionado	...camp (near) here?	¿...acampar aquí (cerca)?
Tax	Impuesto		
Mosquito net	Tolda/mosquitero	Is there a hotel nearby?	¿Hay un hotel aquí cerca?
Key	Llave		
Check-out time	Hora de salida	I want	Quiero
Do you know...?	¿Sabe...?	I'd like	Querría
I don't know	No sé	What is there to eat?	¿Qué hay para comer?
There is (is there)?	(¿) Hay (?)	What's that?	¿Qué es eso?
Give me... (one like that)	Deme... (uno así)	What's this called in Spanish?	¿Cómo se llama este en español?
Do you have...?	¿Tiene ...?		
...a room	...una habitación		

Directions and transport

Bus terminal	Terminal terrestre	...the post office	...el correo
Ticket	Pasaje	...the toilet	...el baño
Seat	Asiento	Where does the bus to... leave from?	¿De dónde sale el camión para...?
Aisle	Pasillo		
Window	Ventana	What time does the bus leave?	¿A qué hora sale el bus?
Luggage	Equipaje		
How do I get to...?	¿Por dónde se va a..?	What time does the bus arrive?	¿A qué hora llega el bus?
Left, right, straight on	Izquierda, derecha, derecho		
		How long does the journey take?	¿Cuánto tiempo demora el viaje?
Where is...?	¿Dónde está...?		
...the bus station	...el terminal de buses	Is this the train for...?	¿Es éste el tren para...?
...the train station	...la estación de fer rocarriles	I'd like a (return) ticket to...	Querría pasaje (de ida y vuelta) para...
...the nearest bank	...el banco más cer cano	What time does it leave (arrive in...)?	¿A qué hora sale (llega en...)?

Numbers

1	un/uno/una	16	dieciséis	200	doscientos
2	dos	17	diecisiete	201	doscientos uno
3	tres	18	dieciocho	500	quinientos
4	cuatro	19	diecinueve	1000	mil
5	cinco	20	veinte	2000	dos mil
6	seis	21	veitiuno	first	primero/a
7	siete	30	treinta	second	segundo/a
8	ocho	40	cuarenta	third	tercero/a
9	nueve	50	cincuenta	fourth	cuarto/a
10	diez	60	sesenta	fifth	quinto/a
11	once	70	setenta	sixth	sixto/a
12	doce	80	ochenta	seventh	séptimo/a
13	trece	90	noventa	eighth	octavo/a
14	catorce	100	cien(to)	ninth	noveno/a
15	quince	101	ciento uno	tenth	décimo/a

Days

Monday	lunes	Friday	viernes
Tuesday	martes	Saturday	sábado
Wednesday	miércoles	Sunday	domingo
Thursday	jueves		

Food and drink terms

The following should more than suffice as a basic menu reader for navigating restaurants, food stalls and markets throughout the country.

Basics

Aceite	Oil	La cuenta	The bill
Ají	Chilli	Desayuno	Breakfast
Ajo	Garlic	Galletas	Biscuits
Almuerzo	Lunch, set-menu lunch	Hielo	Ice
Arroz	Rice	Huevos	Eggs
Azúcar	Sugar	Mantequilla	Butter
La carta	The menu	Merienda	Set-menu dinner
Cena	Dinner	Mermelada	Jam
Comidas típicas	Traditional food	Miel	Honey
Cuchara	Spoon	Mixto	Mixed seafood or meats
Cuchillo	Knife	Mostaza	Mustard

Pan (integral)	(Wholemeal) bread	Queso	Cheese
Pimienta	Pepper	Sal	Salt
Plato fuerte	Main course	Salsa de tomate	Tomato sauce
Plato vegetariano	Vegetarian dish	Tenedor	Fork

Cooking terms

A la parrilla	Barbecued	Duro	Hard-boiled
A la plancha	Lightly fried	Encebollado	Cooked with onions
Ahumado	Smoked	Encocado	In coconut sauce
Al ajillo	In garlic sauce	Frito	Fried
Al horno	Oven-baked	Picante	Spicy hot
Al vapor	Steamed	Puré	Mashed
Apanado	Breaded	Relleno	Filled or stuffed
Asado	Roast	Revuelto	Scrambled
Asado al palo	Spit roasted, barbecued	Saltado	Sautéed
Crudo	Raw	Seco	Stew (also means dry)

Soups

Caldo	Broth	Sopa	Soup
Caldo de Gallina	Chicken broth	Sopa de bolas de verde	Plantain dumpling soup
Caldo de Patas	Cattle-hoof broth		
Crema de Espárragos	Cream of asparagus	Sopa del día	Soup of the day
		Yaguarlocro	Blood-sausage soup
Locro	Cheese and potato soup		

Meat and poultry

Aves	Poultry	Cuero/cueritos	Pork crackling (literally, skin)
Bistec	Beef steak		
Carne	Beef	Cuy	Guinea pig
Cerdo, or carne de chancho	Pork	Jamón	Ham
		Lechón	Suckling pig
Chicharrones	Pork scratchings, cracklings	Lomo	Steak of indiscriminate cut
		Pato	Duck
Chuleta	Cutlet, chop (usually pork)	Pavo	Turkey
		Pollo	Chicken
Churrasco	Beef steak with fried egg, rice and potatoes	Res	Beef
		Ternera	Veal
Conejo	Rabbit	Tocino	Bacon
Cordero	Lamb	Venado	Venison

Offal

Chunchules	Intestines	**Menudos**	Offal
Guatita	Tripe	**Patas**	Feet, trotters
Hígado	Liver	**Riñones**	Kidneys
Lengua	Tongue		

Seafood and fish

Anchoa	Anchovy	**Corvina**	Sea bass
Atún	Tuna	**Erizo**	Sea urchin
Bonito	Pacific bonito, similar to tuna	**Langosta**	Lobster
		Langostino	King prawn
Calamares	Squid	**Lenguado**	Sole
Camarón	Prawn	**Mariscos**	Seafood
Cangrejo	Crab	**Mejillón**	Mussel
Ceviche	Seafood marinated in lime juice with onions	**Ostra**	Oyster
		Pescado	Fish
Concha	Clam, scallop	**Trucha**	Trout

Snacks

Bocadillos	Snacks	**Salchipapas**	Chips, sausage and sauces
Bolón de verde	Baked cheese and plantain dumpling	**Sanduche**	Sandwich
Canguil	Popcorn	**Tamales**	Ground maize with meat or cheese wrapped in leaf
Chifles	Banana chips/crisps		
Empanada	Cheese or meat pasty	**Tortilla de huevos**	Omelette (also called omelet)
Hamburguesa	Hamburger		
Humitas	Ground corn and cheese wrapped in leaf and steamed	**Tortilla de maíz**	Corn tortilla
		Tostada	Toast
		Tostado	Toasted maize
Patacones	Thick-cut fried banana/plantain		

Fruit

Cereza	Cherry	**Maracuyá**	Passion fruit
Chirimoya	Custard apple; cherimoya	**Mora**	Blackberry
Ciruela	Plum	**Naranja**	Orange
Durazno	Peach	**Pera**	Pear
Frutas	Fruit	**Piña**	Pineapple
Frutilla	Strawberry	**Plátano**	Plantain
Guayaba	Guava	**Tomate de arbol**	Tree tomato
Higo	Fig	**Toronja**	Grapefruit
Manzana	Apple		

Vegetables

Aceitunas	Olives	Legumbres	Vegetables
Aguacate	Avocado	Lentejas	Lentils
Alcachofa	Artichoke	Menestra	Stew, typically beans and lentils
Arvejas	Peas		
Cebolla	Onion	Palmito	Palm heart
Champiñón	Mushroom	Papa	Potato
Choclo	Maize, sweetcorn	Papas fritas	Chips (French fries)
Coliflor	Cauliflower	Pepinillo	Gherkin
Espinaca	Spinach	Pepino	Cucumber
Frijoles	Beans	Tomate	Tomato
Hongo	Mushroom	Verduras	Vegetables
Lechuga	Lettuce	Zanahoria	Carrot

Desserts

Cocados	Coconut sweets	Pastas	Pastries
Ensalada de frutas	Fruit salad	Pastel	Cake
Flan	Crème caramel	Postres	Desserts
Helado	Ice cream	Torta	Tart
Manjar de leche	Very sweet caramel, made from condensed milk		

Drinks

Agua (mineral)	(Mineral) water	Caipiriña	Cocktail of rum, lime, ice and sugar
con gas	sparkling		
sin gas	still	Cerveza	Beer
sin hielo	without ice	Chicha	Fermented corn drink
Aguardiente	Sugarcane spirit	Cola, or gaseosa	Fizzy drink
Aromática	Herbal tea	Jugo	Juice
hierba luisa	Lemon verbena	Leche	Milk
manzanilla	Camomile	Limonada	Fresh lemonade
menta	Mint	Mate de coca	Coca leaf tea
Batido	Milkshake	Ron	Rum
Bebidas	Drinks	Té	Tea
Café	Coffee	Vino (blanco/tinto)	(White/red) wine
Café con leche	Milky coffee		

Glossary

adobe sun-dried mud brick

aguas termales hot springs

artesanía traditional handicraft

balneario thermal baths resort

bargueño colonial wooden chest, inlaid with bone, ivory and other decorative materials in geometric patterns

barrio district, quarter or suburb

cabaña cabin

calle street

camioneta pick-up truck

campesino literally from the countryside, used to describe *mestizo* rural farmers

canoa dugout canoe

CC abbreviation of *Centro Comercial*, or shopping centre

chicha fermented maize drink

chiva open-sided wooden bus mostly found in rural areas

cholo coastal fisherman, but also used in the sierra to refer to *mestizo* artisans and traders in the Cuenca region, most commonly applied to women ("*la chola cuencana*")

choza a rough-thatched hut or shack

cocha lake or lagoon in Quichua

colectivo collective taxi

cordillera mountain range

criollo "Creole": used historically to refer to a person of Spanish blood born in the American colonies, but nowadays as an adjective to describe something (such as food or music) as "typical" or "local"

curandero healer

encomendero possessor of an *encomienda*

encomienda a grant of indigenous labourers to landowners during colonial times

fibra open fibreglass boat used as transport between islands in the Galápagos

finca small farm

flete small boat for hire

gringo slightly (but not always) pejorative term for an American specifically, but also used generally for any foreigner from a non-Spanish speaking country

guardaparque park warden

hacienda farm or large estate

indígena used adjectivally to mean "indigenous", or as a noun to refer to an indigenous person

junta a ruling council; usually used to describe small groups who have staged a coup d'état

lancha launch, small boat

lek bird courtship display area

local "unit" or "shop" in a shopping centre

malecón coastal or riverside avenue

mestizo person of mixed Spanish and indigenous blood

minga Quichua term for collective community work

mirador viewpoint

montuvio *mestizo* farm worker in the coastal interior

municipio town hall or town council

nevado snowcapped mountain

pampa plain

panga dinghy, usually with a motor

páramo high-altitude grassland, found above 3000m.

peña nightclub where live music is performed, often folk music

petrolero oil-worker

plata silver; slang for money

pucará fort

quebrada ravine, dried-out stream

sacha forest or jungle in Quichua

sala room or hall

selva jungle or tropical forest

serrano from the sierra, or highlands

shigra a bag made of tightly woven straw, often dyed in bright colours

S/N used in addresses to indicate "*sin número*", or without a number.

soroche altitude sickness

SS HH abbreviation for *servicios higiénicos*, toilets.

tambo rest-house on Inca roads

termas thermal baths, hot springs

triciclero tricycle-taxi driver

yacu water or river in Quichua

Index

and small print

Index

Map entries are in colour

INDEX

INDEX

I

INDEX

INDEX

A Rough Guide to Rough Guides

In the summer of 1981, Mark Ellingham, a recent graduate from Bristol University, was travelling round Greece and couldn't find a guidebook that really met his needs. On the one hand there were the student guides, insistent on saving every last cent, and on the other the heavyweight cultural tomes whose authors seemed to have spent more time in a research library than lounging away the afternoon at a taverna or on the beach.

In a bid to avoid getting a job, Mark and a small group of writers set about creating their own guidebook. It was a guide to Greece that aimed to combine a journalistic approach to description with a thoroughly practical approach to travellers' needs – a guide that would incorporate culture, history and contemporary insights with a critical edge, together with up-to-date, value-for-money listings. Back in London, Mark and the team finished their Rough Guide, as they called it, and talked Routledge into publishing the book.

That first *Rough Guide to Greece*, published in 1982, was a student scheme that became a publishing phenomenon. The immediate success of the book – with numerous reprints and a Thomas Cook prize shortlisting – spawned a series that rapidly covered dozens of destinations. Rough Guides had a ready market among low-budget backpackers, but soon also acquired a much broader and older readership that relished Rough Guides' wit and inquisitiveness as much as their enthusiastic, critical approach. Everyone wants value for money, but not at any price.

Rough Guides soon began supplementing the "rougher" information about hostels and low-budget listings with the kind of detail on restaurants and quality hotels that independent-minded visitors on any budget might expect, whether on business in New York or trekking in Thailand.

These days the guides – distributed worldwide by the Penguin group – offer recommendations from shoestring to luxury and cover more than 200 destinations around the globe, including almost every country in the Americas and Europe, more than half of Africa and most of Asia and Australasia. Our ever-growing team of authors and photographers is spread all over the world, particularly in Europe, the USA and Australia.

In 1994, we published the *Rough Guide to World Music* and *Rough Guide to Classical Music*; and a year later the *Rough Guide to the Internet*. All three books have become benchmark titles in their fields – which encouraged us to expand into other areas of publishing, mainly around popular culture. Rough Guides now publish:

- Travel guides to more than 200 worldwide destinations
- Dictionary phrasebooks to 22 major languages
- History guides ranging from Ireland to Islam
- Maps printed on rip-proof and waterproof Polyart™ paper
- Music guides running the gamut from Opera to Elvis
- Restaurant guides to London, New York and San Francisco
- Reference books on topics as diverse as the Weather and Shakespeare
- Sports guides from Formula 1 to Man Utd
- Pop culture books from Lord of the Rings to Cult TV
- World Music CDs in association with World Music Network.

Visit **www.roughguides.com** to see our latest publications.

Rough Guide credits

Text editors: Jeff Dickey and Stephen Timblin
Managing director: Kevin Fitzgerald
Series editor: Mark Ellingham
Editorial: Martin Dunford, Jonathan Buckley,
Kate Berens, Ann-Marie Shaw, Helena Smith,
Olivia Swift, Ruth Blackmore, Geoff Howard,
Claire Saunders, Gavin Thomas, Alexander
Mark Rogers, Polly Thomas, Joe Staines,
Richard Lim, Duncan Clark, Peter Buckley,
Lucy Ratcliffe, Clifton Wilkinson, Alison
Murchie, Matthew Teller, Andrew Dickson,
Fran Sandham, Sally Schafer, Andy Turner,
Matthew Milton, Karoline Densley (UK);
Andrew Rosenberg, Yuki Takagaki, Richard
Koss, Hunter Slaton, Thomas Kohnstamm,
Steven Horak (US)
Design & layout: Helen Prior, Julia Bovis,
Dan May, John McKay, Sophie Hewat,
Diana Jarvis (UK); Madhulita Mohapatra,
Umesh Aggarwal, Sunil Sharma (India)
Cartography: Maxine Repath, Ed Wright,
Katie Lloyd-Jones (UK); Manish Chandra,
Rajesh Chhibber, Jai Prakash Mishra (India)
Cover art direction: Louise Boulton
Picture research: Sharon Martins, Mark
Thomas, Jj Luck
Online: Jennifer Gold, Suzanne Welles, Cree
Lawson (US); Manik Chauhan, Amarjyoti
Dutta, Narender Kumar (India)
Finance: Gary Singh
Marketing & publicity: Richard Trillo, Niki
Smith, David Wearn, Chloë Roberts, Demelza
Dallow, (UK); Geoff Colquitt, David Wechsler,
Megan Kennedy (US)
Administration: Julie Sanderson
RG India: Punita Singh

Publishing information

This 2nd edition published November 2003 by
Rough Guides Ltd,
80 Strand, London WC2R 0RL
345 Hudson St, 4th Floor,
New York, NY 10014, USA.
Distributed by the Penguin Group
Penguin Books Ltd,
80 Strand, London WC2R 0RL
Penguin Putnam, Inc.
375 Hudson Street, NY 10014, USA
Penguin Books Australia Ltd,
487 Maroondah Highway, PO Box 257,
Ringwood, Victoria 3134, Australia
Penguin Books Canada Ltd,
10 Alcorn Avenue, Toronto, Ontario,
Canada M4V 1E4
Penguin Books (NZ) Ltd,
182–190 Wairau Road, Auckland 10,
New Zealand
Typeset in Bembo and Helvetica to an original
design by Henry Iles.
Printed in Italy by LegoPrint S.p.A

592pp includes index
A catalogue record for this book is available from
the British Library

ISBN 1-84353-109-7

The publishers and authors have done their best
to ensure the accuracy and currency of all the
information in **The Rough Guide to Ecuador**,
however, they can accept no responsibility for
any loss, injury, or inconvenience sustained by
any traveller as a result of information or advice
contained in the guide.

1   3   5   7   9   8   6   4   2

Help us update

We've gone to a lot of effort to ensure that the
2nd edition of **The Rough Guide to Ecuador**
is accurate and up to date. However, things
change – places get "discovered", opening
hours are notoriously fickle, restaurants and
rooms raise prices or lower standards. If you
feel we've got it wrong or left something out,
we'd like to know, and if you can remember
the address, the price, the time, the phone
number, so much the better.

We'll credit all contributions, and send a
copy of the next edition (or any other Rough
Guide if you prefer) for the best letters.
Everyone who writes to us and isn't already a
subscriber will receive a copy of our full-
colour thrice-yearly newsletter. Please mark
letters: **"Rough Guide Ecuador Update"** and
send to: Rough Guides, 80 Strand, London
WC2R 0RL, or Rough Guides, 4th Floor, 345
Hudson St, New York, NY 10014. Or send an
email to **mail@roughguides.com**

Have your questions answered and tell
others about your trip at
www.roughguides.atinfopop.com

Acknowledgements

Harry Adès: First of all, many thanks to Christopher Sacco and Dominique Allen for their invaluable and very thorough additional research; to Melissa for her great support, advice and encouragement; and Fernando Luque of the Ecuadorian Embassy in London for his interest, help and friendship over the years – best of luck to him on his next placement. I would also like to thank Frank Kiefer and Margaret Goodhart for their kindness and generosity; Pancho Molina, Mary Finn and all at Santa Lucía; Patricia Cajas and colleagues; Carlos Donoso; Judith Barett; Piet Sabbe; Nicola Mears; Pepe Dávila, father and son; Isabelle Laroche; Popkje van der Ploeg; Diego Bonifaz; Douglas Dillon; Fabián Amores; Víctor Chiluiza; Manuela Omari Ima; Pablo of Tigua Chimbacucho; Miff and Humbs; Robert and Daisy Kuntstaetter; Betti Sachs; Andres Hammerman and Michelle Kirby; Jane Lyons; and Ricardo Falconi-Puig. Thanks too to the knowledgeable and helpful staff of Ecuador's tourist offices and municipios, in particular, Luigi Jarra in Salinas; Roberth Ríos in Baños; Elena de la Torre Andrade and Paola Cobo in Quito; Pilar Chiriboga in Riobamba; Ana Lucía Abad in Cuenca; Tania Cevallos in Puyo; Carlos Rodríguez in San Lorenzo; and Magdalena Reinoso Castillo in Loja. At Rough Guides, thanks are due to Andrew Rosenberg, Stephen Timblin, Jeff Dickey and Julie Feiner for their superb editorial work; Lisa Pusey and Sharon Martins for fine picture research; Katie Lloyd-Jones for pellucid cartography; and Mark Rogers and Karoline Densley for kind assistance. Finally a special thank-you to my friends and family for everything, and most importantly, to Shahla who kept me going throughout, and without whom the whole process would have been so much harder.

The editors would like to thank Rachel Holmes and Katie Pringle for tireless production work; Katie Lloyd-Jones and Ed Wright for adroit mapmaking; Lisa Pusey and Sharon Martins for their extensive photo research; and Jan Wiltshire for eagle-eyed proofreading.

Readers' letters

Many thanks to all the readers of the first edition who took the time and trouble to write in with their comments and suggestions:
Sarah Anthony, Cedric Bellanger, Iko Bavelaar, Víctor Chiluiza, Simón Corral Cordero, Alexandra Craigen, Tal Dehtiar, Darell & Ely Gibb, Stefan Giger, Olivier Girard, Steven Gleave, Brian Gormley, Monica Guerra, Christian Hänggi, Ward Hardeman, Tina Knipping, Sue Lasslett, Alejandro Lecaro, Ali McClure, Bianca Mergenthaler, Alan Michell, Fritha Mills, Jo Moore, Andreas Nilsson, Bernard Ouellet, Bridget Oppenheim, Gregory Papazian, Jon Parks, Andrea Plötz, Nina Rooke, Thomas Savage, James Spencer, Kevin Spencer, Gitte Stevnhoved, Andrea Strein, Ilse Tangerding, Jorge Tasiguano, Monika Tüscher, Brian & Lynne Utter, Teresa White, Børre Wickstrøm, Ulrike Wiedenfels, Allison Wright, Karen Wood, Esteban Yepez, Jon Zigmond. Sincere apologies to anyone whose name has been omitted or misspelt.

Photo Credits

Cover Credits
Front (main) Iguana © Getty
Front (small top) Textiles © Jamie Marshall
Front (small lower) Cotopaxi © Jamie Marshall
Back (top) Near Guamote © Getty
Back (lower) © Jamie Marshall

Colour introduction
Sheep, Andes © Morton Beebe/CORBIS
Sunset in Cotacachi © Pablo Corral V/CORBIS
Guamote © Melissa Graham
Hog Roast, Latacunga © Harry Adès
Ash exiting from Guagua © Pablo Corral Vega/CORBIS
Golden Beach, Bartholome Island, Galápagos Islands © TRIP/J.Sweeney
Tricycles, Atacames © Harry Adès
Carved wooden parrots for sale in Otavalo market © Jamie Marshall
Nuns visit the Angel of Quito monument, Quito © Jamie Marshall
Cock of the Rock © Gerard Mornie
Panama hats, made with local "toquilla" straw © South American Pictures/Tony Morrison
Aerial of Amazon River and rainforest, Oriente © TRIP/Viesti Collection

Things not to miss
22. Mama Negra festival, Latacunga © Harry Adès
23. La Tolita Sun-god gold mask c.3000BC, Banco Central Ecuador © South American Pictures/Tony Morrison
3. Ingapirca © Melissa Graham
4. Termas de Papallacta © Harry Adès
5. Devils Nose train © Melissa Graham
22. Climbers on Volcán Cotopaxi © South American Pictures/Kimball Morrison
23. Orchids, Amazon Mountain Forest © South American Pictures/Tony Morrison
8. Giant tortoise © South American Pictures/Peter Ryley;
Hammerhead shark © Stephen Frink/CORBIS;
Nesting magnificent frigate birds, South Seymour Island © TRIP/J.Sweeney;
Brown pelican, Rábida © Steven Coyne/Travel Ink;
Masked booby © Harry Adès;
Whale at sunset © Steven Frink/CORBIS;
Sally lightfoot crab © Harry Adès;
Sea lion © Harry Adès;
Marine iguanas © Harry Adès
9. Jungle canopy, Oriente © Harry Adès

10. Textiles at Otavalo market © Jamie Marshall
22. Pichincha Mountain and Quito at sunrise © Travel Ink/Stephen Coyne
12. Viteri's Studio, Quito © Harry Adès
13. Blue Footed Booby © Harry Adès
14. Ropey Pahoehoe Lava, Ferdinand Island, Galápagos Islands © TRIP / B.Gadsby
15. Cerro Santa Ana, Guayaquil © Harry Adès
16. Cuenca © Harry Adès
17. Melcocha maker, Banos © Harry Adès
22. Paramo, Reserva el Angel © Harry Adès
19. Jesuit Church of La Compania, Quito © South American Pictures/Tony Morrison
20. Good Friday procession © Pablo Corral Vega/CORBIS
21. Laguna Quilotoa © Melissa Graham
22. Zumbahua © Eric Lawrie/Hutchinson
23. Atacames Beach © Harry Adès

Black and white photos
La Condamine, Mitad del Mundo © South American Pictures/Tony Morrison (p.70)
Upper facade of Church of San Francisco, Quito © South American Pictures/Kathy Jarvis (p.119)
Ice cream vendor © Pablo Corral V/CORBIS (p.130)
Sign discouraging hunting, Cayambe-Coca Reserve © Kevin Schafer/CORBIS (p.155)
Shepherds and flock of sheep, Quilotoa © TRIP/R.Powers (p.182)
Volcán Cotopaxi © South American Pictures/Tony Morrison (p.201)
Guamote © Melissa Graham (p.240)
Close-up of door of colonial house, Cuenca © Travel Ink/Grazyna Bonati (p.277)
Lago Cuyabeno, northern Oriente © South American Pictures/Kimball Morrison (p.282)
San Rafael Falls © Patricia Fogden/CORBIS (p.287)
Tonchigue © Harry Adès (p.348)
Farmer harvesting palm fronds © Pablo Corral Vega/CORBIS (p.403)
Bamboo thatch housing, banana plantation © South American Pictures/Tony Morrison (p.410)
Malecon 2000, Guayaquil © Harry Adès (p.417)
Beach on Bartholome Island, Galápagos Islands © TRIP/J.Sweeney (p.454)
Waved albatross, Isla Española, Galápagos Islands © South American Pictures/Peter Ryley (p.477)
Mocking bird on camera, Hood Island, Galapagos © Wolfgang Kaehler/CORBIS (p.549)

stay in touch

roughnews

Rough Guides' FREE full-colour newsletter

News, travel issues, music reviews, readers' letters and the latest dispatches from authors on the road

If you would like to receive **rough**news, please send us your name and address:

Rough Guides, 80 Strand, London WC2R 0RL, UK

Rough Guides, 4th Floor, 345 Hudson St, New York NY10014, USA

newslettersubs@roughguides.co.uk

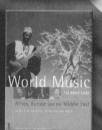

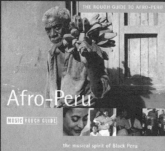
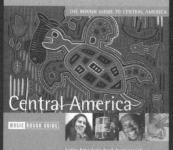

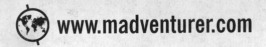